MANAGERIAL ACCOUNTING

Concepts for Planning, Control,
Decision Making

The Irwin Series in Undergraduate Accounting

Bernstein
Financial Statement Analysis: Theory, Application and Interpretation
Fifth Edition

Bernstein and Maksy
Cases in Financial Statement Reporting and Analysis
Second Edition

Boatsman, Griffin, Vickrey, and Williams
Advanced Accounting
Seventh Edition

Boockholdt
Accounting Information Systems
Third Edition

Danos and Imhoff
Introduction to Financial Accounting
Second Edition

Dyckman, Dukes, and Davis
Intermediate Accounting
Revised Edition

Dyckman, Dukes, and Davis
Intermediate Accounting
Standard Edition

Edwards, Hermanson, and Maher
Principles of Financial and Managerial Accounting
Revised Edition

Engler
Managerial Accounting
Third Edition

Engler and Bernstein
Advanced Accounting
Second Edition

Epstein and Spalding
The Accountant's Guide to Legal Liability and Ethics

FASB 1993–94 Editions
  Current Text: General Standards
  Current Text: Industry Standards
  Original Pronouncements, Volume I
  Original Pronouncements, Volume II
  Statements of Financial Accounting Concepts

Ferris
Financial Accounting and Corporate Reporting: A Casebook
Third Edition

Garrison and Noreen
Managerial Accounting
Seventh Edition

Hay and Engstrom
Essentials of Accounting for Governmental and Not-for-Profit Organizations
Third Edition

Hay and Wilson
Accounting for Governmental and NonProfit Entities
Ninth Edition

Hendriksen and Van Breda
Accounting Theory
Fifth Edition

Hermanson and Edwards
Financial Accounting
Fifth Edition

Hermanson, Edwards, and Maher
Accounting Principles
Fifth Edition

Hermanson, Walker, Plunkett, and Turner
Computerized Accounting with Peachtree, Version 60

Hermanson, Strawser, and Strawser
Auditing Theory and Practice
Sixth Edition

Hopson, Spradling, and Meyer
Income Tax Fundamentals for 1993 Tax Returns, 1994 Edition

Hoyle
Advanced Accounting
Fourth Edition

Hutton and Dalton
1993 Tax Return Practice Problems for Corporations, S Corporations, and Partnerships

Hutton and Dalton
Two 1993 Individual Tax Return Practice Problems

Jesser
Integrated Accounting Computer Applications

Koerber
College Accounting
Revised Edition

Larson and Miller
Financial Accounting
Fifth Edition

Larson and Miller
Fundamental Accounting Principles
Thirteenth Edition

Larson, Spoede, and Miller
Fundamentals of Financial and Managerial Accounting

Maher and Deakin
Cost Accounting
Fourth Edition

Marshall
A Survey of Accounting: What the Numbers Mean
Second Edition

Miller, Redding, and Bahnson
The FASB: The People, The Process, and the Politics
Third Edition

Mueller, Gernon, and Meek
Accounting: An International Perspective
Third Edition

Pany and Whittington
Auditing

Pratt and Kulsrud
Corporate Partnership, Estate and Gift Taxation, 1994 Edition

Pratt and Kulsrud
Federal Taxation, 1994 Edition

Pratt and Kulsrud
Individual Taxation, 1994 Edition

Rayburn
Cost Accounting: Using a Cost Management Approach
Fifth Edition

Robertson
Auditing
Seventh Edition

Schroeder and Zlatkovich
Survey of Accounting

Short
Fundamentals of Financial Accounting
Seventh Edition

Smith and Wiggins
Readings and Problems in Accounting Information Systems

Whittington, Pany, Meigs, and Meigs
Principles of Auditing
Tenth Edition

Seventh Edition

MANAGERIAL ACCOUNTING

Concepts for Planning, Control, Decision Making

Ray H. Garrison, D.B.A., CPA
School of Accountancy
Brigham Young University

•

Eric W. Noreen, Ph.D., CMA
School of Business Administration
University of Washington

IRWIN

Burr Ridge, Illinois
Boston, Massachusetts
Sydney, Australia

PHOTO CREDITS

Chapter 1: Courtesy KFC; Chapter 2: © Guyon/Photo Researchers, Inc.; Chapter 3: © Ted Horowitz/The Stock Market; Chapter 4: © Phil Moughner/Third Coast Stock; Chapter 5: Courtesy Hewlett-Packard; Chapter 6: © James Rudnick/The Stock Market; Chapter 7: Courtesy Elgin Sweeper Company; Chapter 8: © Shambroom/Photo Researchers, Inc.; Chapter 9: Wide World Photos, Inc.; Chapter 10: Courtesy AT&T; Chapter 11: Courtesy Caterpillar, Inc.; Chapter 12: © Albano Guatti/The Stock Market; Chapter 13: © Bob Coyle; Chapter 14: Vanessa Vick/Photo Researchers, Inc.; Chapter 15: © Gabe Palmer/The Stock Market; Chapter 16: © Tom Stewart/The Stock Market; Chapter 17: © Bob Coyle; Chapter 18: © David Pollack/The Stock Market; Appendix K: © John Madere/The Stock Market; Appendix L: © Marshall Harrington Photography.

Material from Uniform CPA Examination Questions and Unofficial Answers, copyright © 1971, 1972, 1974, 1975, 1980, 1981, 1990, 1991, and 1992 by the American Institute of Certified Public Accountants, Inc., is reprinted (or adapted) with permission.

Material from the Certificate in Management Accounting Examination, copyright © 1976 through 1992 by the Institute of Certified Management Accountants (formerly the National Association of Accountants), is reprinted (or adapted) with permission.

Material from the SMA Examination copyright © 1974 by the Society of Management Accountants of Canada, is reprinted (or adapted) with permission.

© RICHARD D. IRWIN, INC., 1976, 1979, 1982, 1985, 1988, 1991, and 1994

Cover photograph: Bernard Van Berg/The Image Bank

Senior sponsoring editor: *Ron Regis*
Senior developmental editor: *Diane M. Van Bakel*
Special editing: *Loretta Scholten*
Marketing manager: *John E. Biernat*
Project editor: *Karen M. Smith*
Production manager: *Bette K. Ittersagen*
Designer: *Heidi J. Baughman*
Art manager: *Kim Meriwether*
Art studio: *Precision Graphics*
Photo research coordinator: *Michelle Oberhoffer*
Logo researcher: *Randall Nicholas*
Photo research coordinator: *Patricia A. Seefelt*
Compositor: *Bi-Comp, Inc.*
Typeface: *10/12 Times Roman*
Printer: *Von Hoffmann Press*

Library of Congress Cataloging-in-Publication Data

Garrison, Ray H.
   Managerial accounting : concepts for planning, control, decision
making / Ray H. Garrison, Eric W. Noreen. — 7th ed.
      p.   cm.
   Includes index.
   ISBN 0-256-11010-7. — ISBN 0-256-13369-7
   1. Managerial accounting. I. Noreen, Eric W. II. Title.
HF5657.4.G37   1994
658.15′11—dc20   93–21847

Printed in the United States of America
   4 5 6 7 8 9 0 VH 0 9 8 7 6 5 4

*To the many colleagues who have
used prior editions of this book*

About the Authors

RAY H. GARRISON

Ray H. Garrison is Professor of Accounting at Brigham Young University, Provo, Utah. He received his B.S. and M.S. degrees from Brigham Young University and his D.B.A. degree from Indiana University. A certified public accountant, he has been involved in management consulting work with both national and regional accounting firms.

Professor Garrison has published articles in *The Accounting Review, Management Accounting*, and other professional journals. A popular teacher, he has received numerous teaching awards from students and the Karl G. Maeser Distinguished Teaching Award from Brigham Young University for innovation in the classroom.

ERIC W. NOREEN

Eric W. Noreen is Professor of Accounting at the University of Washington, Seattle, and frequently is a visiting professor at INSEAD, a graduate school of business in Fontainebleau, France. He received his B.A. degree from the University of Washington and his M.B.A. and Ph.D. degrees from Stanford University. A certified management accountant, he was awarded a Certificate of Distinguished Performance by the Institute of Certified Management Accountants.

Professor Noreen has served as associate editor of *The Accounting Review* and the *Journal of Accounting and Economics*. He has published numerous articles in academic journals including the *Journal of Accounting Research, The Accounting Review, Journal of Accounting and Economics, Accounting Horizons, Accounting Organizations and Society*, and the *Journal of Management Accounting Research*.

Active within the accounting profession and the academic community, he is a frequent presenter at workshops and conferences throughout the world. He teaches management accounting at the undergraduate, masters, and doctoral levels and has won a number of awards from students for his teaching.

Preface

This text is designed for a one-term course in managerial accounting after students have already completed one or two terms of basic financial accounting. The emphasis of *Managerial Accounting* is on uses of accounting data within an organization by its managers.

As suggested by the subtitle to the book, managers need information to carry out three essential functions in an organization: (1) planning operations, (2) controlling activities, and (3) making decisions. The purpose of *Managerial Accounting* is to show what kind of information is needed, where this information can be obtained, and how this information can be used by managers as they carry out their planning, control, and decision-making responsibilities.

A paramount objective of *Managerial Accounting* has always been to make a clear and balanced presentation of relevant subject matter. This focus on relevance continues in this seventh edition with extended coverage of current topics such as just-in-time systems, activity-based costing, flexible manufacturing systems, performance measures used in the new manufacturing environment, theory of constraints, ethical issues, and the cost of quality. As in the prior edition, these topics are integrated into the text and problem material *throughout the book*. Also, in recognition of the widespread application of management accounting concepts, many examples and problems in the book deal with not-for-profit, service, retail, and wholesale organizations as well as with manufacturing organizations. In short, the watchwords for this edition of *Managerial Accounting* have again been *relevance* of subject matter, *balance* of topics, and a continued tradition of *clarity* in presentation.

ORGANIZATION AND CONTENT

As in the prior editions, flexibility in meeting the needs of courses varying in length, content, and student composition continues to be a prime concern in the organization and content of the book. Sufficient text material is available to permit the instructor to choose topics and depth of coverage as desired. Appendixes, parts of chapters, or even (in some cases) whole chapters can be omitted without adversely affecting the continuity of the course. The Solutions Manual gives a number of alternatives for organizing the course.

New in This Edition

The seventh edition has a number of new features that are explained in greater detail elsewhere in this preface. These new features include "Focus on Current Practice" boxes throughout the book, new problem material dealing with ethical issues, and problems and cases requiring writing skills and analytical and critical thinking.

In addition to these new features, there are several general changes in this edition that enhance the relevance and "user-friendliness" of the book. Every chapter now contains one or more review problems that highlight the concepts covered in the chapter, along with a fully worked-out solution. Also, in addition to being listed at the beginning of each chapter, learning objectives are now placed in the margin next to the sections to which they relate. And there is an increased emphasis on international aspects of managerial accounting in this edition, including examples of how various management accounting concepts are applied throughout the world.

As in prior editions, special attention has been given to bringing new exercise, problem, and case material into the book. Users will again find a wide range of assignment material in terms of level of difficulty. Specific changes to the book are described in the following table.

Seventh Edition	Sixth Edition	Changes in the Seventh Edition
Chapter 1	Chapter 1	A section on professional ethics has been added.
Chapter 2	Chapter 2	The material on just-in-time systems in Chapter 2 in the prior edition has been moved to Chapter 5.
Chapter 3	Chapter 3	The material on activity-based costing in Chapter 3 in the prior edition has been moved to Chapter 5. A discussion of bar code technology in controlling manufacturing processes has been added to Chapter 3. In addition, a four-page acetate overlay has been added to enhance understanding of manufacturing cost flows.
Chapter 4	Chapter 4	The FIFO approach to the production report has been moved to an appendix, although the FIFO method of computing equivalent units has been retained in the chapter. Thus, students can still learn the essential difference between the FIFO and weighted-average methods even if the appendix is not covered.
Chapter 5	—	This new chapter, "Systems Design: JIT and Activity-Based Costing," greatly expands the coverage of JIT, activity-based costing, and related issues. Placing this material in a separate chapter allows more flexibility in its use. Instructors have the option of covering it in depth, assigning it as additional reading material in conjunction with either Chapter 3 or Chapter 4, or omitting it entirely.
Chapter 6	Chapter 5	The material relating to hand computation of the least-squares method has been placed in an appendix. Many calculators now perform least-squares computations, so

Seventh Edition	Sixth Edition	Changes in the Seventh Edition
		these procedural steps are receiving less emphasis at many schools.
Chapter 7	Chapter 6	The material in this chapter has been reorganized. The sections on cost structure and operating leverage have been combined with the section on automation and CVP analysis and placed near the end of the chapter. This reorganization allows the discussion of cost structure and operating leverage to come later in the chapter after students have a basic understanding of CVP concepts.
Chapter 8	Chapter 7	The contribution approach to costing has been expanded and now stands alone as a retitled chapter, "Variable Costing: A Tool for Management."
Chapter 9	Chapter 8	—
Chapter 10	Chapter 9	—
Chapter 11	Chapter 10	Material has been added to this chapter on how flexible budgets can be prepared and used when a company employs activity-based costing.
Chapter 12	Chapter 11	This new chapter, "Segment Reporting, Profitability Analysis, and Decentralization," blends material on segmented reporting from Chapter 7 with Chapter 11. Material has also been added on the value chain, customer profitability analysis, and the use of activity-based costing in assigning selling, general, and administrative expenses to segments.
Chatper 13	Chapter 13	Material has been added on the theory of constraints and on the use of activity-based costing data in decisions.
Chapter 14	Chapter 14	—
Chapter 15	Chapter 15	A discussion of the investment tax credit has been added.
Chapter 16	Chapter 16	Parts of this chapter have been rewritten to mesh with the activity-based costing material in Chapter 5, and the chapter has been retitled "Service Department Costing: An Activity Approach," which more accurately reflects the thrust of the chapter. Also, a general discussion of the reciprocal method of handling interdepartmental service costs has been added.
Chapter 17	Chapter 17	—
Chapter 18	Chapter 18	—
Appendix K	—	A new self-standing appendix titled "Quality Costs and Reports" has been added to the book. This appendix is not attached to any specific chapter so that instructors have flexibility in using the material it contains. The authors recommend that this appendix be assigned in conjunction with either Chapter 5 or Chapter 12. However, it can be assigned in conjunction with any chapter, or it can be omitted entirely. In addition to a discussion of quality costs and reports, this appendix contains a discussion of the new ISO 9000 standards that have become so important in international commerce.
Appendix L	Chapter 12	This self-standing appendix is a condensation of the chapter on "Pricing of Products and Services" from the prior

Seventh Edition	Sixth Edition	Changes in the Seventh Edition
		edition. Condensing the pricing material into a self-standing appendix allows instructors the flexibility to cover it in depth, assign it as additional reading material in conjunction with any chapter (Chapter 12 or Chapter 13 are probably best), or omit it entirely.

Many small "polishing" changes have been made throughout the book to improve flow, comprehension, and readability. However, change has not been made simply for the sake of change (other than in the assignment material). Rather, the revision has been completed with a single thought in mind—to make the seventh edition of *Managerial Accounting* the most up-to-date and teachable book available in its field.

NEW FEATURES

Focus On Current Practice

One of the strengths of *Managerial Accounting* has always been its "real world" orientation. This orientation is further strengthened in the current edition by "Focus on Current Practice" boxes throughout the book. These boxes contain glimpses of how actual companies use or are affected by the concepts discussed in the various chapters.

International Aspects of Managerial Accounting

International aspects of management have become increasingly important in recent years due to the emergence of regional and global markets. Discussions and examples that have an important international dimension are identified in the margin of the text by the logo shown here.

Assignments Requiring Writing Skills

Employers place great emphasis on the communication skills of their professional employees. This book contains over 100 exercises, problems, and cases that require written solutions and provide an opportunity for students to hone their communications skills. These exercises, problems, and cases are identified in the margin of the text by this logo.

Ethical Issues

Problems involving ethical issues are included in the assignment materials at the end of many of the chapters. These problems highlight an important and interesting dimension of management and help to bring the subject alive. These problems are identified in the margin of the text by this logo.

SUPPLEMENTS FOR THE INSTRUCTOR

A number of supplementary materials are available to adopters.

Solutions Manual
This manual provides completely worked-out solutions to all questions, exercises, problems, and cases in the text. In addition, the manual contains suggested course outlines, a listing of exercises, problems and case mate-

rial scaled as to difficulty, and a listing of suggested exercise, problem, and case assignments for each chapter.

Instructor's Resource Guide   This manual contains lecture notes and masters of the teaching transparencies (see below) for each chapter. A new feature in this edition is an "assignment map" for each chapter that indicates the topics covered by each exercise, problem, and case. Lecture notes are also available on both 5.25″ and 3.5″ diskettes for IBM® compatible microcomputers.

Solutions Transparencies   These transparencies feature completely worked-out solutions to all exercises, problems, and cases in the text. Masters of these transparencies are available in the Solutions Manual.

Teaching Transparencies   This comprehensive set of over 260 teaching transparencies covering every chapter can be used as the basis for classroom lectures and discussions.

Test Bank   The newly revised Test Bank, prepared by Professor Larry Deppe of Westminister College, contains over 1,200 true-false and multiple-choice questions, computational problems, and essay questions organized by chapter. Both a printed version and a microcomputer version of the Test Bank are available. The microcomputer version is available on both 5.25″ and 3.5″ diskettes for IBM® compatible microcomputers.

Computerized Testing Software   This microcomputer test generator program allows the instructor to select and edit exam questions from the Test Bank database. Questions can be selected using several criteria, such as chapter, type of question (e.g., multiple-choice, true-false, problem solving), and level of difficulty. The software is menudriven, requiring little computer knowledge. It comes with a program disk, data disks containing the Test Bank database, and clearly written documentation. It provides password protection, can be used on a network, and is available on both 5.25″ and 3.5″ diskettes for IBM® compatible microcomputers.

Check Figures   A list of check figures gives key amounts for selected problems and cases. These check figures are available in bulk.

Richard D. Irwin Managerial/Cost Accounting Video Library   Topical videos are available to adopters that cover special topics such as Computer-Integrated Manufacturing, where the subject matter lends itself particularly well to a visual approach. A separate Video Guide provides details about the content and length of the videos and discussions of how they can be used in the classroom.

SUPPLEMENTS FOR THE STUDENT

Workbook/Study Guide   This study aid provides suggestions for studying chapter material, summarizes the essential points in each chapter, and tests students' knowledge using self-test questions and exercises.

Working Papers   This study aid contains forms that help students organize their solutions to homework problems.

Ready Notes   Ready Notes are copies of the teaching transparencies that come with the book. These Ready Notes simplify taking notes in class.

Manual Practice Set   Prepared by Keith Weidkamp of Sierra College, *Shel-*

bourne Manufacturing, Inc., illustrates the accounting system used by a manufacturing company.

The Irwin Business Communication Handbook   Prepared by Kitty O. Locker of Ohio State University, this handbook is designed to give students the tools to improve written and verbal skills for business.

Computer Supplements   The following computer supplements are available:

- *Spreadsheet Applications Template Software (SPATS)*   This software was developed by Minta Berry of Berry Publication Services and contains innovatively designed Lotus® 1-2-3® templates that can be used to help solve selected problems and cases in the text. These selected problems and cases are identified in the margin of the text with the logo shown here. SPATS includes an effective tutorial for Lotus® 1-2-3®. SPATS is available on both 5.25″ and 3.5″ diskettes for IBM® compatible microcomputers.
- *Tutorial Software*   This microcomputer software was prepared by Professor Leland Mansuetti of Sierra College. It includes true-false, multiple-choice questions, and a glossary of key terms with explanations for both correct and incorrect answers by students. The tutorial is available on both 5.25″ and 3.5″ diskettes for IBM® compatible microcomputers.
- *Electronic Spreadsheet Problem (ESP)*   Prepared by Professor John Wanlass of DeAnza College, this spreadsheet package can be used to solve many of the problems in the text. ESP is available on both 5.25″ and 3.5″ diskettes for IBM® compatible microcomputers.
- *Ramblewood Manufacturing, Inc.*   This software, which was prepared by Leland Mansuetti and Keith Weidkamp, simulates the operations of a company that manufactures customized fencing. It can be used to illustrate job-order costing systems in a realistic setting and the entire simulation requires 10 to 14 hours to complete. It is available on both 5.25″ and 3.5″ diskettes for IBM® compatible microcomputers.

ACKNOWLEDGMENTS

Suggestions have been received from many of our colleagues throughout the world who have used the prior edition of *Managerial Accounting*. This is vital feedback that we rely on in revising each edition. Each of those who have offered comments and suggestions has our thanks.

The efforts of many people are needed to develop a book and improve it from edition to edition. Among these people are the reviewers who point out areas of concern, cite areas of strength, and make recommendations for change. In this regard, the following professors provided in-depth reviews that were enormously helpful in preparing the seventh edition of *Managerial Accounting:* Carol E. Brown, Oregon State University; Rosalie C. Hallbauer, Florida International University; Ilene K. Kleinsorge, Oregon State University; David J. Marcinko, State University of New York at Albany; Barbara K. Parrish, Colorado State University; Kenneth R. Pelfrey, Ohio State University; Rebecca L. Phillips, University of Louisville; Roxanne M. Spindle, Virginia Commonwealth University.

Special thanks goes to Loretta Scholten, who has always done a superb job of finetuning the readability of the text. We are also grateful to all of the people at Irwin for their outstanding support. In particular we would like to thank Lew Gossage, publisher; Ron Regis, senior sponsoring editor; Diane Van Bakel, senior developmental editor; Karen Smith, project editor; Bette Ittersagen, production manager; Heidi Baughman, designer; and Kim Meriwether, art manager. Finally, a special thanks goes to the Seventh Edition Task Force made up of John Biernat, Marketing Manager, and Michael Antonucci, David Fosnough, Sam Hussey, Kimberly Mack, Brian Murray, and Elizabeth Storey, who provided many valuable suggestions.

Finally, we would like to thank family members Mary Jean Garrison, Linnea Noreen, Sandee Noreen, Annika Noreen, and Arta Fowlds, who have provided invaluable assistance in everything from proofreading to computerizing text files for editing.

We are grateful to the Institute of Certified Management Accountants for permission to use questions and/or unofficial answers from past Certificate in Management Accounting (CMA) examinations. Likewise, we are grateful to the American Institute of Certified Public Accountants and to the Society of Management Accountants of Canada for permission to use (or to adapt) selected problems from their examinations. These problems bear the notations CMA, CPA, and SMA, respectively.

Ray H. Garrison
Eric W. Noreen

Contents in Brief

Contents

4   Systems Design: Process Costing   129

8   Variable Costing: A Tool for Management   325

9   Profit Planning   359

10 Standard Costs and JIT/FMS Performance Measures   419

PART III   THE CAPSTONE:
Using Cost Data in Decision Making 591

13 Relevant Costs for Decision Making   593

15 Further Aspects of Investment Decisions   713

PART IV   SELECTED TOPICS FOR FURTHER STUDY 747

16 Service Department Costing: An Activity Approach   749

17 "How Well Am I Doing?" Statement of Cash Flows   785

MANAGERIAL ACCOUNTING

Concepts for Planning, Control,
Decision Making

Product differentiation is often the key to a successful business strategy. The late Colonel Harland Sanders parlayed an investment of $105 into a $2 million fortune in nine years by successfully differentiating Kentucky Fried Chicken from other chicken products.

Managerial Accounting– A Perspective

LEARNING OBJECTIVES

After studying Chapter 1, you should be able to:

1 Explain what an organization is, and describe the work done by management in organizations.

2 Explain what is meant by decentralization, and prepare an organization chart.

3 Distinguish between line and staff responsibilities in an organization.

4 Name the three groups into which organizations can be classified, and identify the ways in which nearly all organizations are similar.

5 Describe the purposes for which the manager needs accounting information.

6 Identify the major differences and similarities between financial and managerial accounting.

7 Identify the events or forces that have spurred the development of managerial accounting.

8 Identify the organizational levels at which ethical conflicts can arise, and explain the purpose of a code of ethical conduct.

9 Define or explain the key terms listed at the end of the chapter.

Managerial accounting is concerned with providing information to *managers*—that is, to those who are *inside* an organization and who are charged with directing and controlling its operations. Managerial accounting can be contrasted with **financial accounting,** which is concerned with providing information to stockholders, creditors, and others who are *outside* an organization.

Because it is manager oriented, any study of managerial accounting must be preceded by some understanding of the management process and the organizations in which managers work. Accordingly, the purpose of this chapter is to examine briefly the work of the manager and to look at the characteristics, structure, and operation of the organizations in which this work is carried out. The chapter concludes by examining the major differences and similarities between financial and managerial accounting.

ORGANIZATIONS AND THEIR OBJECTIVES

Objective 1
Explain what an organization is, and describe the work done by management in organizations.

An **organization** can be defined as a group of people united for some common purpose. A bank providing financial services is an organization, as is a university providing educational services and a manufacturing firm providing appliances or other products for consumers. An organization consists of *people,* not physical assets. Thus, a bank building is not an organization; rather, the organization consists of the people who work for the bank and who are bound together for the common purpose of providing financial services to a community.

The common purpose toward which an organization works is called its *objective*. Not all organizations have the same objective. For some organizations the objective is to produce a product and earn a profit. For other organizations the objective may be to render humanitarian service (the Red Cross), to provide aesthetic enrichment (a symphony orchestra), or to provide government services (a water department). To assist in our discussion, we will focus on a single organization, Bestway Furniture Company, and look closely at this organization's objectives, structure, and management, and at how these factors influence its need for managerial accounting data.

Setting Objectives

Bestway Furniture Company is a corporation, and its owners have placed their money in the organization with the thought in mind of earning a return, or profit, on their investment. Thus, the first objective of the company is to earn a profit on the funds committed to it. The profit objective is tempered by other objectives, however. The company is anxious to acquire and maintain a reputation of integrity, fairness, and dependability. It also wants to be a positive force in the social and ecological environment in which it carries out its activities.

The owners (stockholders) of Bestway Furniture Company are not involved in the day-to-day operation of the company. Instead, they have outlined the broad objectives of the organization and have selected a president and other officers to oversee the implementation of these objectives. Although these officers are charged with the central objective of earning a profit on the owners' investment, they must do so with a sensitivity for the other objectives that the organization desires to achieve.

Strategic Planning

The implementation of an organization's long-term objectives is known as *strategic planning*. In any organization, **strategic planning** occurs in two phases:

1. Deciding on the products to produce and/or the services to render.
2. Deciding on the marketing and/or manufacturing strategy to employ in getting the intended products or services to the proper audience.

overall design way to achieve objectives.

The set of strategies emerging from strategic planning is often referred to as an organization's *policies,* and strategic planning itself is often referred to as *setting policy.*[1]

Phase 1: Product Strategy

In deciding on the products to produce or the services to render, there are several strategies that Bestway Furniture Company's management could follow. The company could specialize in office furniture, it could specialize in appliances, it could be a broad "supermarket" type of furniture outlet, or it could employ any one of a number of other product and/or service strategies.

After careful consideration of the various strategies available, Bestway's management has decided to sell only home furnishings, including appliances. For one reason or another, several other possible strategies were rejected. Management has decided, for example, not to service appliances, sell office furniture, or deal in institutional-type furnishings.

Phase 2: Marketing Strategy

Having decided to concentrate on home furnishings, Bestway's management is now faced with a second strategy decision. Some furniture dealers handle only the highest quality home furnishings, thereby striving to maintain the image of a "quality" dealer. The markups of these dealers are usually quite high, their volume is quite low, and their promotional efforts are directed toward a relatively small segment of the public. Other furniture dealers operate volume outlets. They try to keep markups relatively low, with the thought that overall profits will be augmented by a larger number of units sold. Still other dealers may follow different strategies. The selection of a particular strategy is simply a matter of managerial judgment; some companies make a profit by following one strategy, while other companies are equally profitable following another. Bestway's management has decided to operate volume outlets and to focus on maintaining a discount image.

Every organization must make similar strategy decisions. The set of strategies resulting from these decisions may not be written down, but they exist nonetheless and they are a central guiding force in the organization's activities and in its need for accounting information.

The Work of Management

The work of management centers on what is to be managed—the organization itself. Essentially, the manager carries out four broad functions in an organization:

1. Planning.
2. Organizing and directing.
3. Controlling.
4. Decision making.

---

[1] For an expanded discussion of strategic planning and particularly of its relationship to cost management, see Barry J. Brinker, ed., *Emerging Practices in Cost Management* (Boston, Mass.: Warren, Gorham & LaMont, 1990), pp. 451–99.

FOCUS ON CURRENT PRACTICE

Product differentiation is often the key to a successful marketing strategy. One 65-year-old man became bored with retirement and decided to start a fried chicken business. His initial investment was a single $105 Social Security check that he used to open his first outlet. Nine years later, this man—the late Colonel Harland Sanders—sold his Kentucky Fried Chicken business for $2 million. During those nine years, he successfully differentiated "Kentucky" fried chicken from all other chicken products.[2]

These functions are carried on more or less simultaneously and often under considerable stress, urgency, and pressure. Rarely (if ever) will managers stop to examine which function they are engaged in at a particular moment. Perhaps they couldn't tell even if they tried, since a specific action might touch on all four.

Planning   In **planning,** managers outline the steps to be taken in moving the organization toward its objectives. These plans will be both long and short term in nature. We saw the planning function in operation in Bestway Furniture Company, as the company's management decided on a set of strategies to be followed. Management's next step will be to develop further, more specific plans, such as store locations, methods of financing customer purchases, hours of operation, and discount policies. As these plans are made, they will be communicated throughout the organization. When implemented, the plans will serve to coordinate, or meld together, the efforts of all parts of the organization toward the company's objectives.

Organizing and Directing   In **organizing,** managers decide how to put together the organization's human and other resources so that the organization's plans can be carried out. As a customer enters one of Bestway Furniture Company's stores, the results of the managers' organizational efforts should be obvious in several ways. Certain persons will be performing specific functions, some directly with the customer and some not. Some persons will be overseeing the efforts of other persons. The store's physical assets will be arranged in particular ways, and certain procedures will be followed if a sale is made. These and a host of other things, seen and unseen, will all exist to ensure that the customer is assisted in the best way possible and to ensure that the company moves toward its profit objectives. In short, the organization that is apparent in most companies doesn't simply happen; it is a result of the efforts of managers who must visualize and fit together the structure that is needed to get the job done, whatever the job may be.

In **directing,** managers oversee day-to-day activities and keep the organization functioning smoothly. They assign tasks to employees, arbitrate disputes between departments or employees, answer questions, solve on-the-spot problems, and make many small routine and nonroutine decisions involving customers and/or procedures. In effect, directing is that part of the managers' work that deals largely with the routine and with the here and now.

---

[2] *The Wall Street Journal,* July 18, 1991, p. B1.

Controlling   In carrying out the **control** function, managers take those steps necessary to ensure that each part of the organization is following the plan that was outlined for it at the planning stage. To do this, managers study the accounting and other reports coming to them and compare these reports against the plans set earlier. These comparisons may show where operations are not proceeding effectively or where certain persons need help in carrying out their assigned duties. The accounting and other reports coming to management are called **feedback.** The feedback that management receives may suggest the need to revise existing plans, to set new strategies, or to reshape the organizational structure. Feedback is a key to the effective management of any organization. As we shall see in chapters following, the generation of feedback to the manager is one of the central purposes of internal accounting.

Decision Making   In **decision making,** managers attempt to make rational choices among alternatives. Decision making isn't a separate management function, per se; rather, it is an inseparable part of the *other* functions already discussed. Planning, organizing and directing, and controlling all require that decisions be made. For example, when establishing its organizational strategies, Bestway Furniture Company had to decide which of several available strategies it would follow. Such a decision is often called a *strategic decision* because of its long-term impact on the organization. In organizing and in directing day-to-day operations, as well as in controlling, managers must make scores of lesser decisions, all of which are important to the organization's overall well-being.

All decisions are based on *information.* In large part, the quality of management's decisions will be a reflection of the quality of the accounting and other information that it receives. Simply put, bad information will generally lead to bad decisions—thus the need for a course in managerial accounting in which we deal directly with the informational needs of management in carrying out decision-making responsibilities.

The Planning and Control Cycle

The work of management can be summarized very nicely in a model such as that shown in Exhibit 1–1. This model, which depicts the **planning and control cycle,** illustrates the smooth flow of management activities from planning through organizing, directing, and controlling, and then back to planning again. All of these activities turn on the hub of decision making.

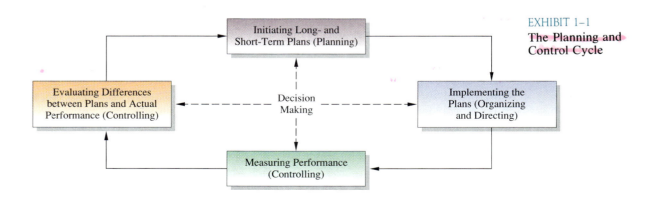

EXHIBIT 1–1
The Planning and Control Cycle

...NAL STRUCTURE

Just as organizations are made up of people, management accomplishes its objectives by working *through* people. The president of Bestway Furniture Company could not possibly execute all of the company's strategies alone. He or she must rely on other people to carry a large share of the management load. This is done by the creation of an organizational structure that permits a *decentralization* of management responsibilities.

Centralized: one person making decisions

Decentralization

Decentralization means the delegation of decision-making authority throughout an organization by allowing managers at various operating levels to make key decisions relating to their area of responsibility. In effect, decentralization moves the decision-making point to the lowest managerial level possible for each decision that must be made.

All organizations are decentralized to some extent out of economic necessity. It would be impossible for top management to have the time or to be well-enough informed to make every one of the myriad decisions that arise daily. Thus, top management in virtually all organizations must delegate some decision-making authority to managers at lower levels. The greater the degree of this delegation, the greater is the amount of decentralization that exists. In some companies, top management delegates virtually all decisions to managers at lower levels; these companies are viewed as being strongly decentralized. In other companies, top management delegates only minor or routine decisions to managers at lower levels; these companies are viewed as being strongly centralized. Most companies fall somewhere between these extremes.

Under the presumption that the manager closest to a problem is the one best qualified to solve the problem, Bestway's president has delegated broad decision-making authority to the various operating levels within the organization. These levels are as follows: The company has three stores, each of which has a furnishings department and an appliances department. Each store has a store manager, as well as a separate manager over each department. In addition, the company has a purchasing department, a treasurer's office, a personnel department, and an accounting department. As stated above, the managers of these stores and departments have broad decision-making authority over matters relating to their areas of responsibility. The organizational structure of the company is depicted in Exhibit 1–2.

The arrangement of boxes shown in Exhibit 1–2 is commonly called an **organization chart.** Each box depicts an area of management responsibility, and the lines between the boxes show the lines of authority between managers. The chart tells us, for example, that the managers of the stores are responsible to the vice president in charge of sales. In turn, the latter is responsible to the company president, who in turn is responsible to the board of directors. The purpose of an organization chart, then, is to show how responsibility has been divided between managers and to show formal lines of reporting and communication. If the manager of store 3 has a problem, she should not go directly to the company president but should take the problem to the sales manager, who is her immediate superior.

In very large organizations, *informal* relationships and channels of communication often develop. These informal lines of communication are spontaneous and come about through the personal and social contacts between managers. The informal structure that may exist in an organization is never depicted on a formal

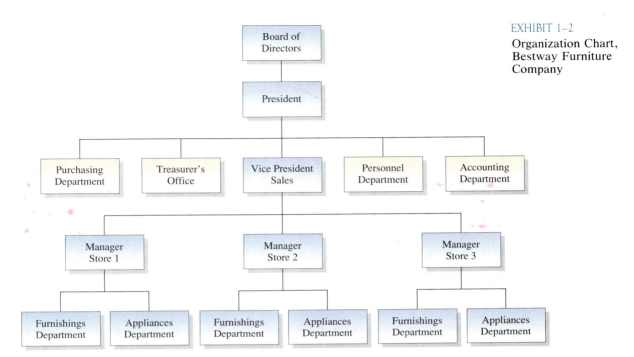

EXHIBIT 1–2
Organization Chart,
Bestway Furniture
Company

organization chart, but its existence is often very helpful in maintaining a smooth flow of activity. Generally, these informal channels are unstable and subject to frequent change.

directly related to production to the achievement of objective

Line and Staff Relationships

An organization chart also depicts *line* and *staff* positions in an organization. A **line** position is one that is *directly related* to the achievement of the basic objectives of an organization. A **staff** position, by contrast, is one that is only *indirectly related* to the achievement of these basic objectives. Staff positions are *supportive* in nature in that they provide service or assistance to line positions or to other parts of the organization. Refer again to the organization chart in Exhibit 1–2. Since the basic objective of Bestway Furniture Company is to sell furnishings and appliances to the public, those managers whose areas of responsibility are directly related to the sales effort occupy line positions. These positions, which are shown in darker color in the exhibit, would include the managers of the separate departments in each store, the store managers, the vice president in charge of sales, and members of top management.

By contrast, the manager of the purchasing department occupies a staff position, since the only function of the purchasing department is to support and serve the line (sales) departments by doing their purchasing for them. The company has found that better buys can be obtained by having one central unit purchase for the entire organization. Therefore, the purchasing department has been organized as a staff department to perform this service function. It cannot be called a line department, since it is involved only indirectly with the sales effort and since its role is *supportive* in nature. By this line of reasoning, the accounting department is also a staff department, since its purpose is to provide specialized accounting services to other departments.

Objective 3
Distinguish between line and staff responsibilities in an organization.

Bestway Furniture Company's organization chart shows only four staff departments. In a larger organization, there would be many more staff departments, including perhaps engineering, medical services, cafeteria, advertising, and research and development.

The distinction we have drawn between line and staff is important since the role of staff persons is basically advisory in nature, and therefore they have no authority over line units. Because their role is advisory, in most organizations persons occupying staff positions do not formulate policy. Rather, policy setting and the making of key operating decisions are done by line managers, with staff persons either providing input or carrying out other duties as directed by top management.

Since accounting is in a staff position, where does it get the authority to set policy in accounting and financial reporting matters? The answer is simple. Top management *delegates* to the accounting department the right to prescribe uniform accounting procedures and the right to require reports and other information from line units. In carrying out these duties, the accounting department is not exercising line authority over other departments; it is simply acting for top management as its delegated voice.

The Controller

The manager in charge of the accounting department is known as the controller. The controller is a member of the top-management team and an active participant in the planning, control, and decision-making processes. Although the controller does not control in terms of line authority (remember, accounting is a staff function), as chief information officer he or she is in a position to exercise control in a very special way. This is through the reporting and interpreting of data needed in decision making. By supplying and interpreting relevant and timely data, the controller has a significant influence on decisions and thus plays a key part in directing an organization toward its objectives.

Because of the controller's position as a member of the top-management team, his or her time is generally kept free of technical and detailed activities. The controller oversees the work of others, directs the preparation of special reports and studies, and advises top management in special problem situations. The organization of a modern controller's office is shown in Exhibit 1–3.

Since the focus of this book is on managerial accounting, we are particularly interested in the work of the controller and the department he or she manages. The information that the accounting department generates is used throughout an organization in many different ways, as we shall see in following chapters.

FOCUS ON CURRENT PRACTICE

The broad experience and companywide view gained in the controller's office often result in the controller being selected as one of the presiding officers in an organization. Many of the presidents of Fortune 500 companies are former accountants, as are the presidents of numerous smaller companies and many of the high-level officers in both federal and state government. Indeed, some business observers believe that one of the fastest ways to the top in an organization is through the accounting department.

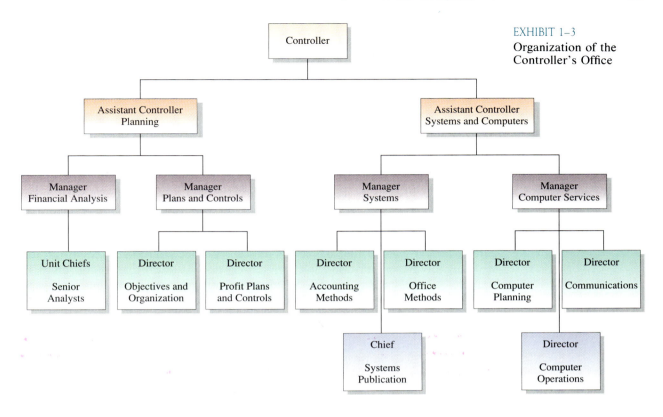

EXHIBIT 1–3
Organization of the
Controller's Office

Basic Similarities among Organizations

Organizations can be classified into three basic groups:

1. Profit-oriented business enterprises that are privately owned and operated as corporations, partnerships, and proprietorships.
2. Service-oriented agencies and associations that are privately controlled and usually operated as nonprofit corporations. Examples include the Red Cross, the Salvation Army, the American Medical Association, and private schools such as Stanford University.
3. Service-oriented agencies such as the Department of Defense, a state university, and a city water department that are created and controlled by government bodies.

Objective 4
Name the three groups into which organizations can be classified, and identify the ways in which nearly all organizations are similar.

Each of these groups contains thousands of organizations. These organizations may each be unique in some way, but nearly all will share certain basic similarities with other organizations in that they will have:

1. An *objective or group of objectives* toward which they are working.
2. A *set of strategies* designed to assist in achieving their basic objective or objectives.
3. A *manager or managers* who plan, organize, direct, and control their activities, and who make decisions of both a long- and a short-term nature.
4. An *organizational structure* that shows responsibility relationships between various managers and that shows line and staff relationships.

5.   An *insatiable need for information* to assist in the execution of their strategies.

Because of these basic similarities, much of what we say in this book about managerial accounting and its uses will have almost universal application among organizations. To the extent that organizations differ, some of our topics will of necessity be narrower in their focus. It is our intent, however, to be concerned with the nature and uses of managerial accounting data in *all* types of organizations; for this reason, the reader will find chapter examples and problems that relate to both profit-oriented *and* service-oriented organizations.

THE MANAGER'S NEED FOR INFORMATION

Information is the "fuel" that makes management go. In the absence of a steady flow of information, management would be powerless to do anything. Fortunately, a large part of management's information needs are satisfied within the structure of the organization itself. As suggested by the organization chart in Exhibit 1–2, there are channels of communication extending throughout an organization through which the various levels of management can communicate. Through these channels, policies and instructions are submitted to subordinates, problems are discussed, formal and informal contacts are made, reports and memos are transmitted, and so on. Without these channels of communication, it would be impossible for management to function effectively.

The management of an organization also depends on specialists to provide a large part of its information needs. Economists, marketing specialists, organizational behavior specialists, accountants, and others all provide information to management, and they advise on various phases of the organization's activities. Economists, for example, provide information on contemplated economic conditions; marketing specialists provide information essential to the effective promotion and distribution of goods and services; and organizational behavior specialists assist in the structure and functioning of the organization itself.

Accounting Information

Objective 5
Describe the purposes for which the manager needs accounting information.

The information provided by accounting is essentially financial in nature, helping the manager carry out the planning, controlling, organizing and directing, and decision-making functions discussed earlier. Brief examples of the use of accounting information in carrying out these functions are given below.

Planning   The plans of management are expressed formally as **budgets,** and the term *budgeting* is often applied to management planning generally. Budgets are usually prepared under the direction of the controller and with the assistance of the accounting department. They are typically prepared on an annual basis and express the desires and goals of management in specific, quantitative terms. For example, Bestway's management plans sales by month a full year in advance. These plans are expressed as departmental budgets, which are communicated throughout the organization.

Controlling   But planning is not enough. Once a company's budgets have been set, management will need information inflows that indicate how well the plans are working out. Accounting assists in meeting this information need by supplying *performance reports* that help focus a manager's attention on problems or opportunities that might otherwise go unnoticed. A **performance report** is a detailed report to management comparing budgeted data against actual data for a specific time period. If the performance report on a particular department indicates that problems exist, then the manager will need to find the cause of the problems and take corrective action. If the performance report indicates that things are going well, then the manager is free to do other work. In sum, performance reports are a form of feedback to managers, directing their attention toward those parts of the organization where managerial time can be used most effectively.

Organizing and Directing
Managers have a constant need for accounting information in the routine conduct of day-to-day operations. For example, as departmental managers in Bestway Furniture Company price new items going onto the display floor, they will rely on information provided by accounting to ensure that cost-price relationships are in harmony with the marketing strategies adopted by the firm. The company's store managers will rely on other accounting information such as sales volumes and inventory levels as they attempt to prepare advertising programs. And the purchasing department manager will rely on still other accounting information in evaluating the costs of storage and handling. In these and a score of other ways, the work of the accountant and the manager is inextricably connected in the conduct of day-to-day operations.

Decision Making
Accounting information is often a key factor in analyzing alternative methods of solving a problem. The reason is that various alternatives usually have specific costs and benefits that can be measured and used as an input in deciding which alternative is best. Accounting is generally responsible for gathering available cost and benefit data and for communicating it in a usable form to the appropriate manager. For example, Bestway Furniture Company may discover that competitors are making inroads on the company's business. In deciding among the alternatives of reducing prices, increasing advertising, or doing both in an attempt to maintain its market share, the company will rely heavily on cost-benefit data provided by accounting. It is important to note here that the needed information may not be in readily available form; in fact, accounting may find it necessary to do a large amount of special analytical work, including some forecasting, in order to prepare the needed data.

Information Must Be in Summary Form

An essential element of managerial accounting information is that it be in summary form. In your study of financial accounting, you learned that an accounting system handles an enormous amount of detail in recording the results of day-to-day transactions. The availability of this detail is vital to the effective management of an organization. However, a manager's *initial* need is not for detail but rather for *summaries* of detailed information that have been drawn from the accounting records. Using these summaries, the manager can see where problems exist and where time must be spent to improve the effectiveness of the organization.

Because of the great value of summarized data to the manager, the bulk of our time in this book is spent on learning the *kinds* of summarized data that the manager needs and on learning how these data are used in directing the affairs of an enterprise. Information can be summarized in many ways. As we shall see in chapters ahead, the appropriate way to summarize information in a given situation will depend on the purpose for which it is to be used.

COMPARISON OF FINANCIAL AND MANAGERIAL ACCOUNTING

In our discussion of managerial accounting, we have noted that it differs in several ways from financial accounting. To help the reader make a transition from the study of financial accounting to the study of managerial accounting, we have summarized these differences below. Following this summary, we also note certain similarities between the two fields of study.

Differences between Financial and Managerial Accounting

Objective 6
Identify the major differences and similarities between financial and managerial accounting.

We can identify eight major differences between financial and managerial accounting. In contrast to financial accounting, managerial accounting:

1. Focuses on providing data for internal uses by the manager.
2. Places more emphasis on the future.
3. Emphasizes the relevance and flexibility of data.
4. Places less emphasis on precision and more emphasis on nonmonetary data.
5. Emphasizes the segments of an organization, rather than just looking at the organization as a whole.
6. Draws heavily from other disciplines.
7. Is not governed by generally accepted accounting principles.
8. Is not mandatory.

Internal Uses by the Manager   For internal purposes, the manager does not need the same kinds of information as are needed externally by stockholders and others. The manager must direct day-to-day operations, plan for the future, solve problems, and make numerous routine and nonroutine decisions, all of which require their own special information inputs. Much of the information needed by the manager for these purposes would be either confusing or valueless to stockholders and others because of the form in which the information is prepared and used.

Emphasis on the Future   Since a large part of the overall responsibilities of the manager have to do with *planning,* the manager's information needs have a strong future orientation. Summaries of past costs and other historical data are useful in planning, but only to a point. The difficulty with summaries of the past is that the manager can't assume that the future will simply be a reflection of what has happened in the past. Changes are constantly taking place in economic conditions, customer needs and desires, competitive conditions, and so on. All of these changes demand that the manager's planning framework be built in large part on estimated data that may or may not be reflective of past experience.

By contrast, financial accounting records the *financial history* of an organization. Financial accounting has little to do with estimates and projections of the future. Rather, entries are made in the accounting records only after transactions have already occurred.

Relevance and Flexibility of Data   Financial accounting data are expected to be objectively determined and to be verifiable. For internal uses, the manager is often more concerned about receiving information that is relevant and flexible than about receiving information that is completely objective or even verifiable. By relevant, we mean *pertinent to the problem at hand.* So long as information inflows are relevant to problems that must be solved, the manager may view objectivity and verification as matters of secondary importance. The manager must also have information that is flexible enough to be used in a variety of decision-making situations. For example, the cost information needed for pricing transfers of goods between sister divisions may be far different from the cost information needed for pricing sales to outside customers.

Less Emphasis on Precision   When managers need information, speed is often more important than precision. The more rapidly managers receive information, the more rapidly they can attend to and resolve problems. For this reason, a manager is often willing to trade off some accuracy for information that is immediately available. If a decision must be made, waiting a week for information that will be slightly more accurate may be considered less desirable than simply acting on the information that is already available. This means that the manager's need is often for good estimates and good approximations rather than for numbers that are accurate to the last penny. Managerial accounting recognizes this need and therefore tends to place less emphasis on precision than does financial accounting. In addition, managerial accounting places considerable weight on nonmonetary data. For example, factors such as sales representatives' impressions concerning a new product, information on weather conditions, and even rumors could be helpful to the manager, even though some of this information might be difficult to quantify or express in a monetary form.

Segments of an Organization   Financial accounting is primarily concerned with the reporting of business activities for a company as a whole. By contrast, managerial accounting focuses less on the whole and more on the parts, or **segments,** of a company. These segments may be the product lines, the sales territories, the divisions, the departments, or any other way that a company can be broken down. In financial accounting, it is true that some companies do report some breakdown of revenues and costs, but this tends to be a secondary emphasis. In managerial accounting, segment reporting is the primary emphasis.

Draws from Other Disciplines   Managerial accounting extends beyond the boundaries of the traditional accounting system and draws heavily from other disciplines, including economics, finance, statistics, operations research, and organizational behavior. These outside sources give managerial accounting a strong interdisciplinary flavor as well as a decidedly pragmatic orientation.

Generally Accepted Accounting Principles   Financial accounting statements must be prepared in accordance with generally accepted accounting principles. The reason is that these statements are relied on by persons outside the organization. These outside persons must have some assurance that the information they are receiving has been prepared in accordance with some common set of ground rules; otherwise, great opportunity could exist for fraud or misrepresentation, and confidence in financial statements would be destroyed. The managers of a company, by contrast, are not governed by generally accepted accounting principles in the information that they receive. Managers can set their own ground rules on the form and content of information that is to be used internally. Whether these ground rules conform to generally accepted accounting principles is immaterial. For example, management might direct that for internal uses, financial statements be expressed on a cash basis or that depreciation of plant and equipment be based on appraised value, even though both of these procedures would be in violation of generally accepted accounting principles. In sum, when information is to be used internally, managers are free to reshape data as they desire in order to obtain information in its most useful form.

Not Mandatory   Financial accounting is mandatory; that is, it must be done. Financial records must be kept so that sufficient information will be available to satisfy the requirements of various outside parties. Often the financial records that are to be kept are specified by regulatory bodies, such as the Securities and Exchange Commission (SEC). Even if a company is not covered by SEC or other regulations, it must meet certain financial accounting requirements if it is to have its statements examined by professional outside accountants. In addition, *all* companies must keep adequate records to meet the requirements of taxing authorities. Managerial accounting, on the other hand, is not mandatory. A company is completely free to do as much or as little as it wishes. There are no regulatory bodies or other outside agencies that specify what is to be done, or for that matter, whether anything is to be done at all. Since managerial accounting is completely optional, the important question is always, ''Is the information useful?'' rather than, ''Is the information required?''

Similarities between Financial and Managerial Accounting

Although many differences exist between financial and managerial accounting, they are similar in at least three ways. First, both rely on the accounting information system. It would be a total waste of money to have two *different* data-collecting systems existing side by side. For this reason, managerial accounting makes extensive use of routinely generated financial accounting data, although it both expands on and adds to these data, as discussed earlier.

Second, both financial and managerial accounting rely heavily on the concept of *responsibility,* or *stewardship.* Financial accounting is concerned with stewardship over the company *as a whole;* managerial accounting is concerned with stewardship over its *parts,* and this concern extends to the last person in the organization who has any responsibility over cost. In effect, from a responsibility accounting point of view, financial accounting can be viewed as being the apex, with managerial accounting filling in the bulk of the pyramid underneath.

Third, both financial and managerial accounting focus on providing information for decision making. The decision makers who receive this information are different—some being external to the firm and some being internal—but the need for information to make wise and timely decisions is the same.

EXPANDING ROLE OF MANAGERIAL ACCOUNTING

Objective 7
Identify the events or forces that have spurred the development of managerial accounting.

Managerial accounting has its roots in the 19th century when cost information was sought by management in the production of textiles, steel, and other products on a mass basis. In those early years, the focus was on material and labor costs, with less attention being paid to other costs such as power, depreciation, and factory facilities.[3] After the turn of the century, as companies sought to expand their productive capacity through issue of capital stock to the investing public, auditors insisted that power, depreciation, and other factory costs be allocated to products. The purpose of these allocations was to properly value inventory so that accurate financial statements could be issued to the investing public. One pair of authors explain this early development as follows:

---

[3] A. D. Chandler, *The Visible Hand: The Managerial Revolution in American Business* (Cambridge, Mass.: Harvard University Press, 1977).

. . . the demand for financial reporting after 1900 burgeoned because of new pressures placed on corporate enterprises by capital markets, regulatory bodies, and federal taxation of income. But of all the new demands for corporate financial disclosure after 1900, the demand for financial reports audited by independent public accountants probably had the most profound and lasting influence on managerial cost accounting.

. . . many firms needed to raise funds from increasingly widespread and detached suppliers of capital. To tap these vast reservoirs of outside capital, firms' managers had to supply audited financial reports. And because outside suppliers of capital relied on audited financial statements, independent accountants had a keen interest in establishing well-defined procedures for corporate financial reporting.

The inventory costing procedures adopted by public accountants after the turn of the century had a profound effect on management accounting.[4]

As a result of the "profound effect" mentioned above, for a period of time managerial accounting became closely tied to financial accounting. Even today, some companies still use managerial accounting only for inventory valuation and financial statement preparation.

Fortunately, as product lines expanded and operations became more complex, forward-looking companies such as Du Pont saw a need for management-oriented data that was separate from financial-oriented data. In the early 1900s, these companies became innovators in developing information that was designed solely for management's use internally.[5] Events and forces of the last few decades have spurred the development of managerial accounting, and it has now become widely recognized as a field of expertise separate from financial accounting.

Increased Needs for Information

Among the forces that have spurred the development of managerial accounting, we can note increased business competition that has become worldwide in scope, a severe cost-price squeeze, rapidly developing technology, and a move toward deregulation of service-type industries. The changes brought about by these forces have intensified the manager's need for information, and particularly for information relating to internal operations that can't be obtained from the traditional income statement and balance sheet. Consider the following:

Dramatic changes have taken place in production methods over the last three decades. The term *automation* was coined in the early 1950s to describe a process that was new at the time. Today, through computer-integrated manufacturing (CIM), many products are produced virtually untouched by human hands. Oil refinery operations are controlled by massive computers; machine tools are electronically controlled; and entire manufacturing plants exist where workers do little more than monitor instrument panels. In many settings, robots are becoming the new steel collar workers of industry. These robots can be programmed to see and feel small objects and can work in virtually any environment.

---

[4] H. Thomas Johnson and Robert S. Kaplan, *Relevance Lost: The Rise and Fall of Management Accounting* (Boston, Mass.: Harvard Business School Press, 1987), pp. 129–30.

[5] H. Thomas Johnson, "Management Accounting in an Early Integrated Industrial: E. I. du Pont de Nemours Powder Company, 1903–1912," *Business History Review*, Summer 1975, pp. 186–87.

The widespread use of computers has brought about a dramatic reduction in the cost to record, store, and analyze information. Activities such as item-by-item tracking of high-volume products are now handled routinely by the computer, whereas such tracking would have been too costly to even consider a few years ago. IBM estimates that the cost of computing is being cut *in half* every four to five years.

In many industries, overall costs are increasing and at the same time are changing in form. For example, the move toward automation is causing a shift away from labor costs, with the result that labor costs are becoming less of a factor in total costs in both manufacturing and service activities. These labor costs are being replaced with less flexible costs such as depreciation.

Service industries are being deregulated with surprising speed. As companies in the transportation, financial services, and telecommunications industries break away from a highly regulated environment, managers are being forced to struggle with costing and pricing problems that did not previously exist.

Worldwide competition is fueling many changes, including a move toward flexible manufacturing systems that enhance a company's ability to respond quickly to customers' needs; the introduction of *total quality control* that reduces defects in output; the development of innovative inventory control methods that allow lower (or even zero) inventory levels; and greater use of the computer to generate on-line reports so that activities can be monitored on a continuous basis.

So great has been the impact of the changes above that many observers view them as constituting a second industrial revolution. As managers have grappled with the effects of this "revolution," the role of managerial accounting has expanded manyfold from what was common in earlier years. Rather than just employing *cost accounting* to direct the affairs of their firms, managers are now focusing on *cost management*. **Cost management** is different from cost accounting in that it goes beyond the mere accumulation and reporting of costs. It requires that managers consider how effectively resources are being used to create, market, and distribute products and services to customers. In these times of rising costs and fierce competition, if resources are not consumed effectively through careful cost management, a company's long-term strategic goals will not be met.

Looking to the future, we can expect the role of managerial accounting in organizational affairs to continue to expand. As various business writers have observed, the ability of an organization to survive in this time of rocketing change will be directly related to how quickly and how well it responds to new challenges. Certainly the role of managerial accounting in meeting these challenges will be very significant.[6]

INTERNATIONAL COMPETITION AND MANAGERIAL ACCOUNTING

We mentioned above that business competition has become worldwide in scope in many industries. Over the last 30 years the general tendency has been for countries to reduce tariffs, quotas, and other barriers to trade by creating free-trade zones and trade negotiations. At the same time, international markets have become more sophisticated, making it easier to conduct international trade. This

[6] For an expanded discussion of the points covered in this section, see Robert S. Kaplan, "The Evolution of Management Accounting," *Accounting Review* 59, no. 3 (July 1984), pp. 390–418.

tendency has been most dramatic in the European Community (EC). The EC has grown from a very small free-trade zone involving a few basic commodities such as coal and steel in the late 1950s to a free-trade zone of a dozen European nations involving almost unlimited movement of goods and services across national borders. This vast, largely unified market has a population of 345 million, as compared with 243 million in the United States and 122 million in Japan.

Such reductions in trade barriers have made it easier for agile and aggressive firms to expand outside of their home markets. Among the major economic powers in the world, the Japanese and Germans have clearly been more adept than others in taking advantage of these new opportunities. The implications of these developments are clear. Very few firms can afford to be complacent. A firm may be very successful today in its local market relative to its local competitors, but tomorrow the competition may come from halfway round the globe. As a matter of survival, even firms that are presently doing very well in their home markets must become world-class competitors. On the bright side, the freer international movement of goods and services presents tremendous export opportunities for those firms that can transform themselves into world-class competitors. And, from the standpoint of consumers, the heightened competition promises an even greater variety of goods, at higher quality and lower prices.

Hyster-Yale
Materials Handling, Inc.

FOCUS ON CURRENT PRACTICE

The most common barriers to trade are tariffs and quotas. Tariffs are taxes that are imposed on imports. Quotas are limits on the total amount of a particular good that can be imported in a year. In addition to tariffs and quotas, most nations have regulations that act as trade barriers. For example, Hyster-Yale Materials Handling, Inc., a U.S. manufacturer of forklift trucks, must divert all of its shipments from the United States to EC customers through its Scottish plant since EC rules specify that any forklifts sold in the EC must be certified on EC soil. This effectively makes it more expensive for Hyster-Yale to sell its forklift trucks in the EC.[7]

What are the implications of increased global competition for managerial accounting? It would be very difficult for a firm to become world class if it plans, directs, and controls its operations and makes decisions using a second-class management accounting system. An excellent management accounting system will not by itself turn a firm into a world-class competitor, but a poor management accounting system can stymie the best efforts of people in an organization to make the firm truly competitive. Unfortunately, the management accounting systems in many firms have not kept pace with changes in technology, competition, and the marketplace. Consequently, they are obsolete and may even impede real progress.

Throughout the book we will highlight the differences between obsolete management accounting systems that get in the way of success and well-designed

---

[7] Walter S. Mossberg, "Obstacle Course: As EC Markets Unite, U.S. Exporters Face New Trade Barriers," *The Wall Street Journal,* January 19, 1989, pp. 1, 4.

management accounting systems that can enhance a firm's performance. It is noteworthy that elements of well-designed management accounting systems have originated in countries throughout the world. More and more, managerial accounting has become a discipline that is worldwide in scope.

PROFESSIONAL ETHICS

Objective 8
Identify the organizational levels at which ethical conflicts can arise, and explain the purpose of a code of ethical conduct.

Webster's Dictionary defines ethics as ''the study of standards of conduct and moral judgment.'' In recent years, many concerns have been raised regarding ethical behavior in business. These concerns have resulted from reports of numerous unethical practices including insider trading scandals, violations of environmental standards by manufacturers, fraudulent billing by defense contractors, attempts by dealers in treasury bonds and other securities to illegally control markets, scandal in the Department of Housing and Urban Development, and management fraud in the savings and loan industry. Indeed, allegations of unethical conduct have been directed toward leaders in virtually all segments of society, including government, business, and even religion.

Although these violations of ethical standards have received much attention in the press, it is doubtful that they represent a wholesale breakdown in the moral fiber of the nation. The violations do suggest, however, that a need exists for *all* organizations to make a clear and forthright statement regarding ethical conduct and to provide ongoing education in ethical matters for employees.

Organizational Levels and Ethics

In discussing the topic of ethics, it is helpful to recognize that ethical considerations occur at several organizational levels, including the corporate, the intercorporate, the intracorporate, the professional, and the personal.[8] The types of ethical problems that may be encountered at each of these levels are discussed below.

Corporate Level
All organizations have interactions with society. These interactions give rise to ethical considerations in matters of human rights, environmental and safety concerns, plant closures, and compliance to government regulatory and collection agencies.

Intercorporate Level
In addition to interacting with society, organizations also interact with each other. Ethical considerations arise at the intercorporate level in matters dealing with mergers and acquisitions, the manipulation of security prices, antitrust laws, kickbacks from suppliers, bribes of corporate officials, and insider information.

Intracorporate Level
Ethical considerations also exist within the organization itself. Such considerations focus on conflicts of interest on the part of employees, personal use of corporate assets or supplies, testing of products, and accurate financial reporting to stockholders and others. Ethical conduct on the part of management in preparing accurate financial reports is particularly important, since investor confidence in these reports is crucial to the health of financial markets around the world.

---

[8] These classifications are taken from Fred Koehler, ''How You Play the Game Does Matter: Ethics in the Workplace,'' *Hilton Business Ethics Day* 7, Loyola Marymount University College of Business Administration (Los Angeles: October 22, 1987), pp. 10–11. Also see C. William Thomas, ''Are Younger Managers Less Ethical?'' *New Accountant* 6, no. 7 (March 1991), p. 4.

Professional Level Professional groups, such as certified public accountants and attorneys, perform services as independent contractors for various organizations. In addition, certified management accountants are employed directly by organizations in their accounting, finance, and internal audit departments. Ethical considerations can arise when the codes of ethical conduct that govern the actions of these professionals run counter to the policies and procedures of the organizations involved. For example, an accountant or attorney may be asked to do or say something that would be unethical according to his or her professional code of conduct.

Personal Level Underlying all of the levels discussed above we have ethics at the individual or personal level. In speaking of ethics at the personal level, one writer has noted that:

> First and foremost there are matters of honesty, integrity and fairness. The most simple of these is honesty; it is simply telling the truth. Integrity has a broader meaning, because integrity has a connotation of wholeness and soundness above and beyond that of honesty. Finally, there is fairness, which really moves to an entire other realm, [which is] to assure that both the process and the end result [are] proper for all parties.[9]

Personal ethical standards can be viewed as the "bedrock" underlying ethical conduct in *all* organizations, since, of course, all organizations are made up of people. No organization can rise above the standards of the people in its ranks—particularly in the ranks of its top management.

Codes of Ethical Conduct

Many companies have developed codes of ethical conduct to guide their employees in dealing with matters involving ethical judgments. These codes are generally broad-based statements of a company's responsibilities to its employees, its customers, its suppliers, and the communities in which the company operates. Codes rarely spell out specific do's and don'ts or suggest proper behavior in a specific situation. Instead, they give broad guidelines of responsibility and expect employees, managers, and others to direct their behavior accordingly. If developed and used properly, such codes can be effective organizational tools. As one writer has observed:

> When a code of ethics has been developed with the involvement of all concerned and when ethical considerations are integrated into the decision-making process (rather than treated as after-the-fact considerations), the organization is much better equipped to cope with ethical dilemmas that would otherwise seem insurmountable.[10]

Education is a key part of an effective code. Indeed, a code is not likely to be effective unless it is accompanied by a carefully planned and ongoing educational program in ethical matters for management at all levels of an organization.

Code of Conduct for Management Accountants We stated earlier that professional groups frequently have their own codes of ethical conduct. A code titled *Standards of Ethical Conduct for Management Accountants* has been developed

---

[9] Koehler, "How You Play the Game Does Matter," p. 11.
[10] Larry L. Axline, "The Bottom Line on Ethics," *Journal of Accountancy* 170, no. 6 (December 1990), p. 88.

by the Institute of Management Accountants (IMA) as a guide for management accountants in the performance of their duties. This code, which is presented in full in Exhibit 1–4, outlines the management accountant's responsibilities in four broad areas: first, to maintain a high level of professional competence; second, to treat sensitive matters with confidentiality; third, to maintain personal integrity; and fourth, to be objective in all disclosures.

The code of ethics provides sound practical advice for the managerial accountant (or manager for that matter). Most of the rules in the managerial code of ethics are motivated by a very practical consideration—if these rules were *not* generally followed in business, then the economy would come to a screeching halt. For example, if employees could not be trusted with confidential information, then that information would not be distributed and operations would deteriorate, since decisions would be based on incomplete information. Or, if employees did accept bribes from suppliers, contracts would likely go to the suppliers who give the biggest bribes rather than to the suppliers who can offer the best quality at the best price. Would you like to fly in an aircraft whose wings were made by the subcontractor who paid the highest bribe to a purchasing agent? What would happen to the airline industry if its safety record deteriorated due to shoddy workmanship on subcontracted parts? What would happen in the securities markets if we could not trust firms to honestly report the results of operations in financial statements? If the basic integrity of a company's financial statements could not be relied on, investors and creditors would have little basis for making an informed decision. Prices of securities offered by firms would fall, resulting in fewer funds for productive investments, and many firms would be unable to raise any capital.

Following ethical rules such as those in the Standards of Ethical Conduct for Management Accountants is not just a matter of being "nice"; it is absolutely essential for the smooth functioning of advanced market economies.

Codes of Conduct on the International Level

Managers of multinational companies (MNCs) should be aware that codes of ethical conduct also exist on the international level. A code titled, *Guideline on Ethics for Professional Accountants,* issued in July 1990 by the International Federation of Accountants (IFAC),[11] governs the activities of *all* professional accountants, regardless of whether they are practicing as independent CPAs, employed in government service, or employed as internal accountants for MNCs. In addition to outlining ethical requirements in matters dealing with competence, objectivity, independence, and confidentiality, the IFAC's code also outlines the accountant's ethical responsibilities in matters relating to taxes, fees and commissions, advertising and solicitation, the handling of monies, and cross-border activities. Where cross-border activities are involved, the IFAC ethical requirements must be followed if these requirements are stricter than the ethical requirements of the country in which the work is being performed.[12]

In addition to codes of ethical conduct, accountants and managers in the United States are subject to the legal requirements of *The Foreign Corrupt Practices Act of 1977.* The Act requires that companies devise and maintain a system

---

[11] A copy of this code can be obtained by writing to: International Federation of Accountants, 540 Madison Avenue, New York, New York 10022.

[12] *Guideline on Ethics for Professional Accountants,* International Federation of Accountants (New York: July 1990), p. 23.

EXHIBIT 1–4

Standards of Ethical Conduct for Management Accountants

Management accountants have an obligation to the organizations they serve, their profession, the public, and themselves to maintain the highest standards of ethical conduct. In recognition of this obligation, the Institute of Management Accountants, formerly the National Association of Accountants, has promulgated the following standards of ethical conduct for management accountants. Adherence to these standards is integral to achieving the *Objectives of Management Accounting.** Management accountants shall not commit acts contrary to these standards nor shall they condone the commission of such acts by others within their organizations.

Competence

Management accountants have a responsibility to:

- Maintain an appropriate level of professional competence by ongoing development of their knowledge and skills.
- Perform their professional duties in accordance with relevant laws, regulations, and technical standards.
- Prepare complete and clear reports and recommendations after appropriate analyses of relevant and reliable information.

Confidentiality

Management accountants have a responsibility to:

- Refrain from disclosing confidential information acquired in the course of their work except when authorized, unless legally obligated to do so.
- Inform subordinates as appropriate regarding the confidentiality of information acquired in the course of their work and monitor their activities to assure the maintenance of that confidentiality.
- Refrain from using or appearing to use confidential information acquired in the course of their work for unethical or illegal advantage either personally or through third parties.

Integrity

Management accountants have a responsibility to:

- Avoid actual or apparent conflicts of interest and advise all appropriate parties of any potential conflict.
- Refrain from engaging in any activity that would prejudice their ability to carry out their duties ethically.
- Refuse any gift, favor, or hospitality that would influence or would appear to influence their actions.
- Refrain from either actively or passively subverting the attainment of the organization's legitimate and ethical objectives.
- Recognize and communicate professional limitations or other constraints that would preclude responsible judgment or successful performance of an activity.
- Communicate unfavorable as well as favorable information and professional judgments or opinions.
- Refrain from engaging in or supporting any activity that would discredit the profession.

Objectivity

Management accountants have a responsibility to:

- Communicate information fairly and objectively.
- Disclose fully all relevant information that could reasonably be expected to influence an intended user's understanding of the reports, comments, and recommendations presented.

RESOLUTION OF ETHICAL CONFLICT

In applying the standards of ethical conduct, management accountants may encounter problems in identifying unethical behavior or in resolving an ethical conflict. When faced with significant ethical issues, management accountants should follow the established policies of the organization bearing on the resolution of such conflict. If these policies do not resolve the ethical conflict, management accountants should consider the following course of action:

- Discuss such problems with the immediate superior except when it appears that the superior is involved, in which case the problem should be presented initially to the next higher managerial level. If satisfactory resolution cannot be achieved when the problem is initially presented, submit the issues to the next higher managerial level.

    If the immediate superior is the chief executive officer, or equivalent, the acceptable reviewing authority may be a group such as the audit committee, executive committee, board of directors, board of trustees, or owners. Contact with levels above the immediate superior should be initiated only with the superior's knowledge, assuming the superior is not involved.
- Clarify relevant concepts by confidential discussion with an objective advisor to obtain an understanding of possible courses of action.
- If the ethical conflict still exists after exhausting all levels of internal review, the management accountant may have no other recourse on significant matters than to resign from the organization and to submit an informative memorandum to an appropriate representative of the organization.

    Except where legally prescribed, communication of such problems to authorities or individuals not employed or engaged by the organization is not considered appropriate.

* Institute of Management Accountants, formerly National Association of Accountants, *Statements on Management Accounting: Objectives of Management Accounting,* Statement No. 1B, New York, N.Y., June 17, 1982.

of internal controls sufficient to ensure that all transactions are executed and recorded properly. The Act specifically prohibits giving bribes, even if giving bribes is common practice in the country in which the company is doing business. However, the Act does not prohibit giving nominal tips where such tips are common practice for the service performed.

Resolving Ethical Dilemmas

When faced with an ethical dilemma, how should the manager proceed in seeking a resolution? Perhaps the most useful approach is to follow a step-by-step format such as the following:

1. Identify the ethical issues involved.
2. Identify the stakeholders involved. By *stakeholders* we mean the persons or organizations affected by the outcome of the dilemma.
3. Identify the alternative courses of action that can be taken.
4. Decide on the best course of action consistent with the principles of honesty, integrity, and fairness, and also consistent with any existing code of ethical conduct.

Throughout this book a number of "Ethics and the Manager" vignettes are presented as part of the end-of-chapter assignment material. Also, ethical considerations are woven into other problem material to heighten the reader's awareness of day-to-day ethical dilemmas faced by the manager.

THE CERTIFIED MANAGEMENT ACCOUNTANT (CMA)

Specific recognition is given to the management accountant as a trained professional in the Institute of Certified Management Accountants' (ICMA) *Certified Management Accountant (CMA)* program. The purpose and operation of the program are described in the following excerpts from a brochure issued by the ICMA:

> The Certified Management Accountant is prepared to be successful in today's complex and competitive business world. Possessing specialized skills and professional expertise, the CMA looks to the future as an influential member of the management team, employing effective decision-making skills to solve problems, confront challenges, and contribute to the overall success of an organization.
>
> The CMA program centers on the dynamic role the management accountant plays in the world of contemporary business. The program stresses all aspects of business, focusing on the key principle of effective decision making. . . .
>
> More and more, executives throughout the United States look for the CMA designation when filling key management accounting and financial management positions in organizations. The reason is simple. The Certified Management Accountant is a highly-qualified, skilled professional.

To earn the CMA and become a Certified Management Accountant, the following four steps must be completed:

1. File an Application for Admission with the ICMA and register for the CMA examination.
2. Pass all four parts of the CMA examination within a three-year period.

3. Meet the accounting experience requirement prior to or within seven years of passing the CMA examination.
4. Comply with the Standards of Ethical Conduct for Management Accountants.

SUMMARY

Understanding organizations and the work of those who manage organizations helps us to understand managerial accounting and its functions. All organizations have basic objectives and a set of strategies for achieving those objectives. Both the setting of strategy, sometimes called strategic planning, and planning of a more short-term nature are basic functions of the manager. In addition to planning, the work of the manager centers on organizing and directing day-to-day operations, controlling, and decision making.

The managers of an organization choose an organizational structure that will permit a decentralization of responsibility by placing managers over specific departments and other units. The responsibility relationships between managers are shown by the organization chart. The organization chart also shows which organizational units are performing line functions and which are performing staff functions. Line functions relate to the specific objectives of the organization, whereas staff functions are supportive in nature, their purpose being to provide specialized services of some type.

A large part of the information needs of management is provided within the structure of the organization itself. Channels of communication exist between various levels of management through which information flows. Management also calls on various specialists to provide information, including the economist, the engineer, the operations research specialist, and the accountant.

Since managerial accounting is geared to the needs of the manager rather than to the needs of stockholders and others, it differs substantially from financial accounting. Among other things, managerial accounting is oriented more toward the future, it places less emphasis on precision, it emphasizes segments of an organization (rather than the organization as a whole), it draws heavily on other disciplines, it is not governed by generally accepted accounting principles, and it is not mandatory. The role of managerial accounting is expanding rapidly, and managerial accounting has become recognized as a field of professional study through which professional certification can be obtained.

Ethical considerations can occur at several organizational levels, including the corporate, the intercorporate, the intracorporate, the professional, and the personal. Personal ethical standards can be viewed as the bedrock underlying ethical conduct at all organizational levels. Many companies have developed codes of ethical conduct to guide their employees in dealing with matters involving ethical judgments. Codes rarely spell out specific do's and don'ts or suggest proper behavior in a specific situation. Instead, they give broad guidelines of responsibility and expect employees to direct their behavior accordingly. Professional organizations also have codes of ethical conduct, and codes exist on the international level that outline ethical requirements in cross-border activities and other matters. The code developed by the IMA is somewhat more specific than the codes developed by many organizations in that it outlines steps for managers and accountants to follow in resolving ethical dilemmas.

KEY TERMS FOR REVIEW

Objective 9
Define or explain the key terms listed at the end of the chapter.

At the end of each chapter, a list of key terms for review is given, along with the definition of each term. (These terms are printed in boldface color where they are defined in the chapter.) Carefully study each term to be sure you understand its meaning, since these terms are used repeatedly in the chapters that follow. The list for Chapter 1 is:

Budget   A detailed plan for the future, usually expressed in formal quantitative terms. (p. 12)

Control   The process of instituting procedures and then obtaining feedback as needed to ensure that all parts of the organization are functioning effectively and moving toward overall company goals. (p. 7)

Controller   The manager in charge of the accounting department in an organization. (p. 10)

Cost management   The effective use of resources to create, market, and distribute products and services to customers. (p. 18)

Decentralization   The delegation of decision-making authority throughout an organization by allowing managers at various operating levels to make key decisions relating to their area of responsibility. (p. 8)

Decision making   The process of making rational choices among alternatives. (p. 7)

Directing   The overseeing of day-to-day activities in order to keep an organization functioning smoothly. (p. 6)

Feedback   Accounting and other reports that help managers monitor performance and focus on problems and/or opportunities that might otherwise go unnoticed. (p. 7)

Financial accounting   The phase of accounting concerned with providing information to stockholders and others outside the organization for use in evaluating operations and current financial condition. (p. 4)

Line   A position in an organization that is directly related to the achievement of the organization's basic objectives. (p. 9)

Managerial accounting   The phase of accounting concerned with providing information to managers for use in planning and controlling operations and for use in decision making. (p. 4)

Organization   A group of people united for some common purpose. (p. 4)

Organization chart   A visual diagram of a firm's organizational structure that depicts formal lines of reporting, communication, and responsibility between managers. (p. 8)

Organizing   The process of putting together an organization's human and other resources in such a way as to most effectively carry out established plans. (p. 6)

Performance report   A detailed report to management comparing budgeted data against actual data for a specific time period. (p. 13)

Planning   The development of objectives in an organization and the preparation of various budgets to achieve these objectives. (p. 6)

Planning and control cycle   The flow of management activities through the steps (in sequence) of planning, organizing and directing, controlling, and then back to planning again. (p. 7)

Segment   Any part of an organization that can be evaluated independently of other parts and about which the manager seeks cost data. Examples would include a product line, a sales territory, a division, or a department. (p. 15)

Staff   A position in an organization that is only indirectly related to the achievement of the organization's basic objectives. Such positions are supportive in nature in that they provide service or assistance to line positions or to other staff positions. (p. 9)

Strategic planning   The planning that leads to the implementation of an organization's objectives. Such planning occurs in two phases: (1) deciding on the products to produce and/or the services to render, and (2) deciding on the marketing and/or manufacturing methods to employ in getting the intended products or services to the proper audience. (p. 5)

QUESTIONS

1-1   Contrast financial and managerial accounting.

1-2   What objectives, other than earning a profit, might be important to the managers of a profit-oriented organization?

1-3   Assume that you are about to go into the retail grocery business. Describe some of the operating strategies that you might follow.

1-4   A labor union is an organization. Describe a labor union in terms of what might be its objectives, its strategies, its organizational structure, the work of its managers, and its need for information.

1-5   Some persons consider strategic planning to be the most important work that a manager does. In what ways might this be true? In what ways might this be false?

1-6   Assume that the central objective of a college basketball team is to win games. What strategies might the team follow to achieve this objective?

1-7   Managerial accounting isn't as important in the government as it is in private industry, since the government doesn't have to worry about earning a profit. Do you agree? Explain.

1-8   What function does *feedback* play in the work of the manager?

1-9   "Essentially, the job of a manager is to make decisions." Do you agree? Explain.

1-10   What is the relationship, if any, between information and decision making?

1-11   Choose an organization with which you are familiar. Prepare an organization chart depicting the structure of the organization you have chosen. (The organization you choose should be sufficiently complex to have at least one staff function.)

1-12   One of the key responsibilities of an accounting department is to keep records for the entire organization. Why don't line managers keep their own records?

1-13   Managerial accounting information is sometimes described as a means to an end, whereas financial accounting information is described as an end in itself. In what sense is this true?

1-14   A student planning a career in management commented, "Look, I'm going to be a manager, so why don't we just leave the accounting to the accountants?" Do you agree? Explain.

1-15   Accountants are sometimes compared to journalists in that accountants don't just report information to the manager; they editorialize the information. What implications does this hold for the accountant "managing the news," so to speak?

1-16   Distinguish between line and staff positions in an organization.

1-17   "The term *controller* is a misnomer because the controller doesn't 'control' anything." Do you agree? Explain.

1-18   A production superintendent once complained, "Accounting is a staff function. Those people have no right to come down here and tell us what to do." Do you agree? Why or why not?

1-19   What are the major differences between financial and managerial accounting? In what ways are the two fields of study similar?

1-20   "If an organization's managerial accounting system functions properly, it will provide management with all the information needed to operate with maximum effectiveness." Do you agree? Explain.

1-21 At what organizational levels can ethical conflicts arise? Many companies have developed codes of ethical conduct; do these codes explain how a manager is to act in a specific situation? Explain.

PROBLEMS

Ethics and the Manager

P1-1 Paul Sarver is the controller of a corporation whose stock is not listed on a national stock exchange. The company has just received a patent on a product that is expected to yield substantial profits in a year or two. At the moment, however, the company is experiencing financial difficulties, and because of inadequate working capital it is on the verge of defaulting on a note held by its bank.

At the end of the most recent fiscal year, the company's president instructed Sarver to not record several invoices as accounts payable. Sarver objected since the invoices represented bona fide liabilities. However, the president insisted that the invoices not be recorded until after year-end, at which time it was expected that additional financing could be obtained. After several very strenuous objections—expressed to both the president and other members of senior management—Sarver finally complied with the president's instructions.

Required

1. Did Sarver act in an ethical manner? Explain fully.
2. If the new product fails to yield substantial profits and the company becomes insolvent, can Sarver's actions be justified by the fact that he was following orders from a superior? Explain.

P1-2 Strategic Planning One element necessary to the life of an organization is strategic planning. Strategic planning establishes an organization's long-range goals or objectives and the means to achieve them. Even before a company can begin operations, its managers must develop the plan or plans necessary to determine its future. Among the questions that must be answered are the following: What products or services will the company provide? How will the company be financed and structured? Where will the company and its distributors be located? How will the company's products or services be marketed?

Line and staff management play specific roles in strategic planning. They have different responsibilities and functions in an organization. In addition, the activities of these two management groups must be coordinated.

Required

1. In the *formulation* of an organization's strategic plans, describe the contribution to be made by:
   a. The line managers.
   b. The staff groups or departments.

   In your answer, identify the types of decisions that these two groups of managers would probably make as they participate in the formulation of strategic plans.

2. In the *implementation* of an organization's strategic plans:
   a. State how the responsibilities of line management differ from those of staff management.
   b. Describe how line and staff responsibilities interrelate in the implementation of strategic planning.

(CMA, adapted)

P1-3 Line and Staff Positions Special Alloys Corporation is a specialized production firm that manufactures a variety of metal products for industrial use. Most of the revenues are generated by large contracts with companies that have government defense contracts. The company also develops and markets parts to the major automobile companies. It employs many metallurgists and skilled technicians because most of its products are made from highly sophisticated alloys.

The company recently signed two large contracts; as a result, the workload of Wayne Washburn, the general manager, has become overwhelming. To relieve some of this overload, Mark Johnson was transferred from the research planning department to the general manager's office. Johnson, who has been a senior metallurgist and supervisor in the planning department, was given the title "assistant to the general manager."

Washburn assigned several responsibilities to Johnson in their first meeting. Johnson will oversee the testing of new alloys in the product planning department and be given the authority to make decisions as to the use of these alloys in product development; he will also be responsible for maintaining the production schedules for one of the new contracts. In addition to these duties, he will be required to meet with the supervisors of the production departments regularly to consult with them about production problems they may be experiencing. Washburn is expecting that he will be able to manage the company much more efficiently with Johnson's help.

Required

1. Positions within organizations are often described as having (a) line authority or (b) staff authority. Describe what is meant by these two terms.
2. Of the responsibilities assigned to Mark Johnson as assistant to the general manager, which ones have line authority and which have staff authority?
3. Identify and discuss the conflicts Mark Johnson may experience in the production departments as a result of his new responsibilities.

(CMA, adapted)

Preparing an Organization Chart   Bristow University is a large private school located in the Midwest. The university is headed by a president who has five vice presidents reporting to him. These vice presidents are responsible for, respectively, auxiliary services, admissions and records, academics, financial services (controller), and physical plant.

P1–4

In addition, the university has managers over several areas who report to these vice presidents. These include managers over central purchasing, the university press, and the university bookstore, all of whom report to the vice president for auxiliary services; managers over computer services and over accounting and finance, who report to the vice president for financial services; and managers over grounds and custodial services and over plant and maintenance, who report to the vice president for physical plant.

The university has four colleges—business, humanities, fine arts, and engineering and quantitative methods—and a law school. Each of these units has a dean who is responsible to the academic vice president. There are several departments in each college.

Required

1. Prepare an organization chart for Bristow University.
2. Which of the positions on your chart would be line positions? Why would they be line positions? Which would be staff positions? Why?
3. Which of the positions on your chart would have need for accounting information? Explain.

THE FOUNDATION:
COST TERMS, COST BEHAVIOR, AND SYSTEMS DESIGN

Part

I

Unit costs in the steel industry, with its very large fixed costs, are very sensitive to fluctuations in volume. One of the greatest threats to the large established steel companies in the U.S. is loss of market share to new, small, highly automated "mini-mills" that focus on special market niches. Because of high fixed costs, loss of market share drives per ton costs upward.

Cost Terms, Concepts, and Classifications

LEARNING OBJECTIVES

After studying Chapter 2, you should be able to:

1 Identify and give examples of each of the three basic cost elements involved in the manufacture of a product.

2 Distinguish between product costs and period costs and give examples of each.

3 Explain the difference between the financial statements of a manufacturing company and those of a merchandising company.

4 Prepare a schedule of cost of goods manufactured in good form.

5 Explain the flow of direct materials cost, direct labor cost, and manufacturing overhead cost from the point of incurrence to sale of the completed product.

6 Identify and give examples of variable costs and fixed costs, and explain the difference in their behavior.

7 Identify and give examples of direct and indirect costs, controllable and noncontrollable costs, differential costs, opportunity costs, and sunk costs.

8 Define or explain the key terms listed at the end of the chapter.

9 (Appendix A) Properly classify costs associated with idle time, overtime, and labor fringe benefits in an organization.

As explained in Chapter 1, the work of management centers on (1) planning, which includes setting objectives and outlining the means of attaining those objectives; and (2) control, which includes the steps taken to ensure that objectives are realized. To carry out planning and control responsibilities, the manager needs *information* about the organization. From an accounting point of view, the manager's information needs most often relate to the *costs* of the organization.

In financial accounting, the term *cost* is defined as the sacrifice made to obtain some good or service. The sacrifice may be measured in cash expended, property transferred, service performed, and so on. This definition is easily stated and widely accepted in financial accounting.

In managerial accounting, the term *cost* is used in many different ways. The reason is that there are many different types of costs, and these costs are classified differently according to the immediate needs of management. In this chapter, we look at some of these different types of costs and at some of the ways in which managers classify them for their own use internally.

GENERAL COST CLASSIFICATIONS

Objective 1
Identify and give examples of each of the three basic cost elements involved in the manufacture of a product.

Costs are associated with all types of organizations—business, nonbusiness, service, retail, and manufacturing. Generally, the kinds of costs that are incurred and the way in which these costs are classified will depend on the type of organization involved. Managerial accounting is as applicable to one type of organization as to another; for this reason, we shall consider the cost characteristics of a variety of organizations—manufacturing, merchandising, and service—in our discussion.

Our initial focus will be on a manufacturing company, but in our discussion the reader should be aware that, in a conceptual sense, *manufacturing* encompasses much more than just firms in the industrial sector of our economy. It also encompasses many organizations that are typically viewed as being service in nature, such as movie studios and fast-food outlets. Organizations such as these are involved in manufacturing in the sense that they create a distinct product for their customers or patrons. As we proceed with our discussion, therefore, the reader should keep in mind that manufacturing is a broad term, and that the costs included under the manufacturing heading apply to a wide range of organizations—many of which may be involved in service-type activities.

Manufacturing Costs

A company involved in manufacturing is more complex than most other types of organizations. The reason is that such a company is broader in its activities, being involved in production as well as in marketing and administration. An understanding of the cost structure of a manufacturing company therefore provides a broad, general understanding of costing that can be very helpful in understanding the cost structures of other types of organizations.

Manufacturing involves the conversion of raw materials into finished products through the efforts of workers and the use of production equipment. By contrast, **merchandising** is the marketing of products that are in a finished form and that have been acquired from a manufacturer or other outside source. The cost of a manufactured product is made up of three basic elements:

1. Direct materials.
2. Direct labor.
3. Manufacturing overhead.

Direct Materials   A wide variety of materials can go into the manufacture of a product. These are generally termed **raw materials.** The term is somewhat misleading in that raw materials seems to imply basic, natural resources. Actually, raw materials are inclusive of any materials input into a product; and the finished product of one company can become the raw materials of another company. For example, the finished lumber products of a sawmill become the raw materials of a construction company.

Direct materials are those materials that become an integral part of a company's finished product and that can be conveniently traced into it. This would include, for example, the sheet steel in a file cabinet or the wood in a table. Some items of materials may become an integral part of the finished product but may be traceable into the product only at great cost and inconvenience. Such items might include the glue used to put a table together or the welding materials used to bond the sheet metal in a file cabinet. Glue and welding materials would be called indirect materials and would be included as part of manufacturing overhead. Other examples of indirect materials would be lubricants, sandpaper, and various cleaning supplies.

Direct Labor   The term **direct labor** is reserved for those labor costs that can be physically traced to the creation of products in a "hands on" sense, and that can be so traced without undue cost or inconvenience. The labor costs of assembly-line workers, for example, would be direct labor costs, as would the labor costs of carpenters, bricklayers, and machine operators.

Labor costs that cannot be physically traced to the creation of products, or that can be traced only at great cost and inconvenience, are termed **indirect labor** and are treated as part of manufacturing overhead, along with indirect materials. Indirect labor includes the labor costs of janitors, supervisors, materials handlers, engineers, and night security guards. Although the efforts of these workers are essential to production, it would be either impractical or impossible to accurately relate their costs to specific units of product. Hence, such labor costs are treated as indirect labor.

Due to automation, major shifts are taking place in the structure of labor costs in some industries. Direct labor is decreasing in importance as companies replace workers with equipment, and it has even disappeared as a separate cost element in a few highly automated situations. More is said in later chapters about this trend and about the impact it is having on cost systems. For the sake of completeness of coverage, in this book we continue to recognize direct labor as a separate cost element, since the majority of companies throughout the world are still highly dependent on direct labor inputs.

Manufacturing Overhead   **Manufacturing overhead,** the third element of product cost, includes all costs of manufacturing except direct materials and direct labor. Included in this classification one would expect to find such costs as indirect materials, indirect labor, heat and light, property taxes, insurance, depreciation on factory facilities, repairs, maintenance, and all other costs of operating the manufacturing division of a company. A company also incurs costs for heat and light, property taxes, insurance, depreciation, and so forth associated with its selling and administrative functions, but these costs are not included as part of manufacturing overhead. Only those costs that are associated with *operating the factory* are included in the manufacturing overhead category.

Manufacturing overhead is known by various names. Sometimes it is called manufacturing expense, factory expense, overhead, factory overhead, or factory burden. All of these terms are synonymous with *manufacturing overhead.*

Manufacturing overhead combined with direct labor is known as **conversion cost.** This term stems from the fact that direct labor costs and overhead costs are incurred in the *conversion* of materials into finished products. Direct labor combined with direct materials is known as **prime cost.**

FOCUS ON CURRENT PRACTICE

Material, labor, and overhead costs occur in varying amounts from company to company. Heavily automated companies tend to have high overhead costs, whereas companies that depend on hand work in the manufacture of their products tend to have high labor costs. Studies of current practice reveal the following *average* content of material, labor, and overhead in products manufactured in the United States: material, 55%; labor, 10%; and overhead, 35%.[1]

Nonmanufacturing Costs

Traditionally, the central focus of managerial accounting has been on manufacturing costs and activities. The reason is probably traceable to the complexity of manufacturing operations and to the need for carefully developed costs for pricing and other decisions. However, costing techniques are now coming into use in many nonmanufacturing areas, as firms attempt to get better control over their costs and to provide management with more usable cost data.

Generally, nonmanufacturing costs are subclassified into two categories:

1. Marketing or selling costs.
2. Administrative costs.

Marketing or selling costs include all costs necessary to secure customer orders and get the finished product or service into the hands of the customer. Since marketing costs relate to contacting customers and providing for their needs, these costs are often referred to as **order-getting and order-filling costs.** Examples of marketing costs include advertising, shipping, sales travel, sales commissions, sales salaries, and costs associated with finished goods warehouses. *All* organizations have marketing costs, regardless of whether the organizations are manufacturing, merchandising, or service in nature.

Administrative costs include all executive, organizational, and clerical costs that cannot logically be included under either production or marketing. Examples

---

[1] John P. Campi, "Corporate Mindset: Strategic Advantage or Fatal Vision," *Journal of Cost Management* 5, no. 1 (Spring 1991), p. 56.

of such costs include executive compensation, general accounting, secretarial, public relations, and similar costs having to do with the overall, general administration of the organization *as a whole*. As with marketing costs, *all* organizations have administrative costs.

As stated earlier, managerial accounting concepts and techniques apply just as much to nonmanufacturing activities as they do to manufacturing activities, although in the past the central focus has been on the manufacturing environment. Service organizations in particular are making increased use of cost concepts in analyzing and costing their services. For example, banks now use cost analysis in determining the cost of offering such services as checking accounts, consumer loans, and credit cards; and insurance companies determine costs of servicing customers by geographic location, age, marital status, and occupation. Cost breakdowns of these types provide data for control over selling and administrative functions in the same way that manufacturing cost breakdowns provide data for control over manufacturing functions.

Period Costs

In addition to being placed in manufacturing and nonmanufacturing categories, costs can also be classified as either *period* costs or *product* costs.

Period costs are those costs that are matched against revenues on a time period basis. As such, period costs are not included as part of the cost of either purchased or manufactured goods. Sales commissions and office rent are good examples of the kind of costs we are talking about. Neither commissions nor office rent is included as part of the cost of purchased or manufactured goods. Rather, both items are treated as expenses and deducted from revenues in the time period in which they are incurred. Thus, they are said to be period costs.

As suggested above, *all selling and administrative expenses are considered to be period costs*. Therefore, advertising, executive salaries, sales commissions, public relations, and other nonmanufacturing costs discussed earlier would all be period costs, and they will appear on the income statement as expenses in the time period in which they are incurred.

Product Costs

Some costs are better matched against products than they are against periods of time. Costs of this type—called **product costs**—consist of the costs involved in the purchase or manufacture of goods. In the case of manufactured goods, these costs consist of direct materials, direct labor, and manufacturing overhead. Product costs are viewed as "attaching" to units of product as the goods are purchased or manufactured, and they remain attached as the goods go into inventory awaiting sale. At the point of sale, the costs are released from inventory as expenses (typically called cost of goods sold) and matched against sales revenue.

We must emphasize that unlike period costs, product costs are not necessarily treated as expenses in the time period in which they are incurred. Rather, as explained above, they are treated as expenses in the time period in which the related products *are sold*. This means that a product cost such as direct materials or direct labor might be incurred during one time period but not treated as an expense until a following period when sale of the completed product takes place.

Exhibit 2–1 contains a summary of the cost terms that we have introduced so far in our discussion.

Objective 2
Distinguish between product costs and period costs and give examples of each.

*Direct Materials
Direct Labor
Overhead*

*Selling
General
Administrable*

EXHIBIT 2–1
Summary of Cost Terms

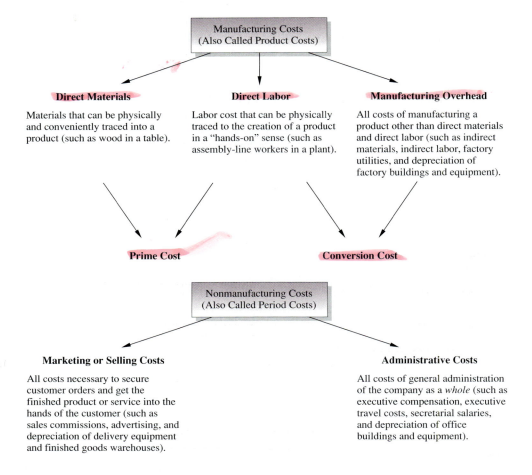

COST CLASSIFICATIONS ON FINANCIAL STATEMENTS

Objective 3
Explain the difference between the financial statements of a manufacturing company and those of a merchandising company.

In your prior accounting training, you learned that firms prepare periodic reports for creditors, stockholders, and others to show the financial condition of the firm and the firm's earnings performance over some specified interval. The reports you studied were probably those of merchandising companies, such as retail stores, which simply purchase goods from suppliers for resale to customers.

The financial statements prepared by a *manufacturing* company are more complex than the statements prepared by a merchandising company. As stated earlier, manufacturing companies are more complex organizations than merchandising companies because the manufacturing company must produce its goods as well as market them. The production process gives rise to many costs that do not exist in a merchandising company, and somehow these costs must be accounted for on the manufacturing company's financial statements. In this section, we focus our attention on how this accounting is carried out from a cost classification point of view.

The Income Statement

Exhibit 2–2 compares the income statement of a merchandising company with the income statement of a manufacturing company.

EXHIBIT 2–2

Comparative Income Statements: Merchandising and Manufacturing Companies

MERCHANDISING COMPANY

The cost of goods sold to customers comes from the purchased cost of these goods from an outside supplier.

Sales			$1,000,000
Cost of goods sold:			
Beginning inventory	$100,000		
Add purchases	650,000		
Goods available for sale	750,000		
Ending inventory	150,000	600,000	
Gross margin			400,000
Less operating expenses:			
Selling expense	100,000		
Administrative expense	200,000	300,000	
Net income			$ 100,000

MANUFACTURING COMPANY

The cost of goods sold to customers comes from the manufacturing costs that have been incurred in the manufacture of the goods. These costs consist of direct materials, direct labor, and manufacturing overhead (see Exhibit 2–3).

Sales			$1,500,000
Cost of goods sold:			
Beginning finished goods inventory	$125,000		
Add cost of goods manufactured	850,000		
Goods available for sale	975,000		
Ending finished goods inventory	175,000	800,000	
Gross margin			700,000
Less operating expenses:			
Selling expense	250,000		
Administrative expense	300,000	550,000	
Net income			$ 150,000

Notice in the case of a merchandising company that the cost of goods sold simply consists of the purchase cost of the goods from a supplier. By contrast, the cost of goods sold in a manufacturing company consists of many different costs that have been incurred in the manufacturing process.

The income statement of a manufacturing company is supported by a schedule of **cost of goods manufactured,** as illustrated in Exhibit 2–3. This schedule shows the specific costs that have gone into the goods that have been manufactured during the period. Notice that it contains the three elements of cost—direct materials, direct labor, and manufacturing overhead—that we discussed earlier as being the costs that go into any produced item. Also notice at the bottom of the schedule that one must add the beginning work in process inventory to the production costs of a period and then deduct the ending work in process inventory in order to determine the cost of goods manufactured. **Work in process** means goods that are only partially completed at the beginning or at the end of a period.

Objective 4
Prepare a schedule of cost of goods manufactured in good form.

The Balance Sheet

The preparation of the balance sheet, or statement of financial position, is also more complex in a manufacturing company than in a merchandising company. A merchandising company has only one class of inventory—goods purchased from suppliers that are awaiting resale to customers. By contrast, manufacturing companies have three classes of inventory—goods purchased as raw materials to go into manufactured products (known as *raw materials*), goods only partially completed as to manufacturing at the end of a period (known as *work in process*), and

EXHIBIT 2–3

Schedule of Cost of
Goods Manufactured

MANUFACTURING COMPANY

Schedule of Cost of Goods Manufactured
For the Year Ended May 31, 19xx

Direct materials:		
Beginning raw materials inventory*	$ 70,000	
Add: Purchases of raw materials	390,000	
Raw materials available for use	460,000	
Deduct: Ending raw materials inventory	50,000	
Raw materials used in production		$410,000
Direct labor		60,000
Manufacturing overhead:		
Insurance, factory	6,000	
Indirect labor	100,000	
Machine rental	50,000	
Utilities, factory	75,000	
Supplies	21,000	
Depreciation, factory	90,000	
Property taxes, factory	8,000	
Total overhead costs		350,000
Total manufacturing costs		820,000
Add: Beginning work in process inventory		90,000
		910,000
Deduct: Ending work in process inventory		60,000
Cost of goods manufactured (see Exhibit 2–2)		$850,000

* We assume in this example that the Raw Materials inventory account contains only direct
materials and that indirect materials are carried in a separate Supplies account. Using a
Supplies account for indirect materials is a common practice among companies. In Chapter 3,
we discuss the procedure to be followed if *both* direct and indirect materials are carried in a
single account.

goods completed as to manufacturing but not yet sold to customers (known as
finished goods).

The current asset section of a manufacturing company's balance sheet is compared to the current asset section of a merchandising company's balance sheet in
Exhibit 2–4. The inventory accounts shown in these current asset sections constitute the *only difference* between the balance sheets of the two types of companies.

EXHIBIT 2–4

Current Asset Data: Merchandising versus Manufacturing Companies

MERCHANDISING COMPANY

Current assets:		
Cash		$ 10,000
Accounts receivable		60,000
Merchandise inventory		150,000
Prepaid expenses		5,000
Total current assets		$225,000

A single inventory account
consisting of goods purchased
from suppliers.

MANUFACTURING COMPANY

Current assets:		
Cash		$ 15,000
Accounts receivable		100,000
Inventories:		
Raw materials	$ 15,000	
Work in process	60,000	
Finished goods	175,000	250,000
Prepaid expenses		10,000
Total current assets		$375,000

Three inventory accounts
consisting of materials to be
used in production, goods
partially manufactured, and
goods completely manufac-
tured.

PRODUCT COSTS—A CLOSER LOOK

Earlier in the chapter, we defined product costs as consisting of those costs that are involved in either the purchase or the manufacture of goods. For manufactured goods, we stated that these costs consist of direct materials, direct labor, and manufacturing overhead. To understand product costs more fully, it will be helpful at this point to look briefly at the flow of costs in a manufacturing company. By doing so, we will be able to see how product costs move through the various accounts and affect the balance sheet and the income statement in the course of the manufacture and sale of goods.

Exhibit 2–5 illustrates the flow of costs in a manufacturing company. Notice that direct materials cost, direct labor cost, and manufacturing overhead cost are all added into Work in Process. Work in Process can be viewed most simply as the assembly line in a manufacturing plant, where workers are stationed and where products slowly take shape as they move from one end of the assembly line to the other. The direct materials, direct labor, and manufacturing overhead costs shown in Exhibit 2–5 as being added into Work in Process are the costs needed to complete these products as they move along this assembly line.

As goods are completed, notice from the exhibit that their cost is transferred from Work in Process into Finished Goods. Here the goods await sale to a customer. As goods are sold, their cost is then transferred from Finished Goods into Cost of Goods Sold. It is at this point that the various material, labor, and overhead costs that have been involved in the manufacture of the units being sold are treated as expenses in determining the net income or loss for the period.

Objective 5
Explain the flow of direct materials cost, direct labor cost, and manufacturing overhead cost from the point of incurrence to sale of the completed product.

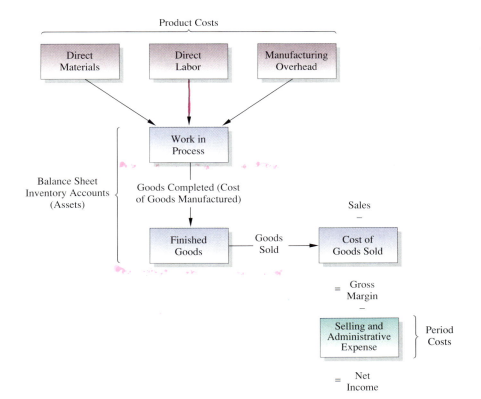

EXHIBIT 2–5

Cost Flows and Classifications

Inventoriable Costs

Product costs are often called **inventoriable costs.** The reason, of course, is that these costs go directly into inventory accounts as they are incurred (first into Work in Process and then into Finished Goods), rather than going into expense accounts. Thus, they are termed *inventoriable costs. This is a key concept in managerial accounting, since such costs can end up on the balance sheet as assets if goods are only partially completed or are unsold at the end of a period.* To illustrate this point, refer again to the data in Exhibit 2–5. The materials, labor, and overhead costs that are associated with the units in the Work in Process and Finished Goods inventory accounts at the end of a period will appear on the balance sheet at that time as part of the company's assets. As explained earlier, these costs will not become expenses until later when the goods are completed and sold.

As shown in Exhibit 2–5, selling and administrative expenses are not involved in the manufacture of a product. For this reason, they are not treated as product costs but rather as period costs that go directly into expense accounts as they are incurred.

An Example of Cost Flows

To provide a numerical example of cost flows in a manufacturing company, assume that a company's cost outlay for insurance is $2,000 annually. Three fourths of this amount ($1,500) applies to factory operations, and one fourth ($500) applies

EXHIBIT 2–6

An Example of Cost Flows in a Manufacturing Company

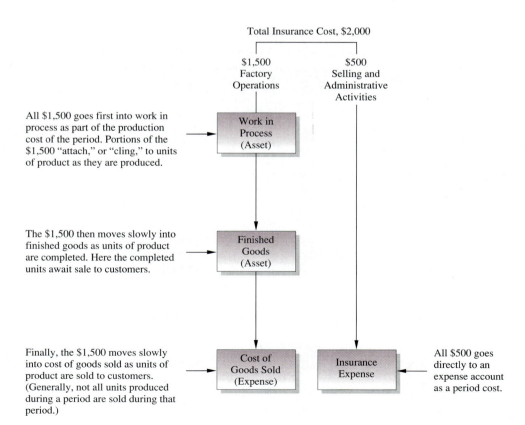

EXHIBIT 2–7
A Summary of Product and Period Costs

Type of Company	Product Costs (also called inventoriable costs)	Period Costs (also called noninventoriable costs)	Treatment
Merchandising company	Costs associated with purchased inventory from suppliers		These costs are placed in an inventory account until the goods are sold. When sale takes place, the costs are then taken to expense as cost of goods sold.
Manufacturing company	Direct materials Direct labor Manufacturing overhead (consists of all costs of production other than direct materials and direct labor)		These costs are placed in inventory accounts until the associated goods are completed and sold. When sale takes place, the costs are then taken (released) to expense as cost of goods sold.

Merchandising, manufacturing, and service companies		Selling expenses:
		  Salespeople's salaries
		  Depreciation on sales equipment
		  Insurance on sales equipment
		Administration expenses:
		  Secretarial salaries
		  Depreciation on office equipment
		  Insurance on office equipment
			These costs are taken directly to expense accounts. They are classified as operating expenses and deducted from gross margin.

to selling and administrative activities. Therefore, $1,500 of the $2,000 insurance cost would be a product (inventoriable) cost and would be added to the cost of the goods produced during the year. This concept is illustrated in Exhibit 2–6, where $1,500 of insurance cost is added into Work in Process. As shown in the exhibit, this portion of the year's insurance cost will not become an expense until the goods that are produced during the year are sold (sale may not take place until the following year). Until the goods are sold, the $1,500 will remain as part of the asset inventory (either as part of Work in Process or as part of Finished Goods), along with the other costs of producing the goods.

By contrast, the $500 of insurance cost that applies to the company's selling and administrative activities will go into an expense account immediately as a charge against the period.

The chart in Exhibit 2–7 contains a summary of product and period costs in both manufacturing and merchandising companies. The reader should carefully study this exhibit, noting particularly the treatment of each type of cost as shown in the extreme right column.

COSTS FOR PLANNING, CONTROL, AND DECISION MAKING

The classifications that a manager uses to cost products and services may not be the same classifications that are used to control operations, to make decisions, and to plan for the future. For control and other purposes, costs are often classified as being variable and fixed, direct and indirect, and in a variety of other ways. Some of these classifications are discussed in this section.

Variable and Fixed Costs

Objective 6
Identify and give examples of variable costs and fixed costs, and explain the difference in their behavior.

From a planning and control standpoint, perhaps the most useful way to classify costs is by behavior. **Cost behavior** means how a cost will react or respond to changes in the level of business activity. As the activity level rises and falls, a particular cost may rise and fall as well—or it may remain constant. For planning purposes, the manager must be able to anticipate which of these will happen, and if a cost can be expected to change, he or she must know by how much. To provide this information, costs are classified into two categories—variable and fixed.

Variable Costs   **Variable costs** are costs that vary, in total, in direct proportion to changes in the level of activity. The activity can be expressed in many ways, such as units produced, units sold, miles driven, beds occupied, lines of print, hours worked, and so forth. A good example of a variable cost is direct materials. The cost of direct materials used during a period will vary, in total, in direct proportion to the number of units that are produced. To illustrate this idea, assume that a company produces automobiles and that each auto requires one battery. As the output of autos increases and decreases, the number of batteries used will increase and decrease proportionately. If auto production goes up 10 percent, then the number of batteries used will also go up 10 percent. The concept of a variable cost is shown in graphic form in Exhibit 2–8.

It is important to note that when we speak of a cost as being variable, we do so in terms of its *total dollar amount*—the total cost rises and falls as the activity level rises and falls. This idea is presented below, assuming that batteries cost $12 each:

Number of Autos Produced	Cost per Battery	Total Variable Cost— Batteries
1	$12	$ 12
500	12	6,000
1,000	12	12,000

One interesting aspect of variable cost behavior is that a variable cost is constant if expressed on a *per unit* basis. Observe from the tabulation above that the per unit cost of batteries remains constant at $12 even though the total amount of cost involved increases and decreases with activity. The reader may be inclined to say, "Wait a minute, how can a variable cost be constant per unit, when quantity

EXHIBIT 2–8

Variable and Fixed Cost Behavior

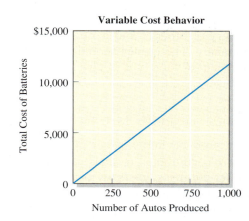

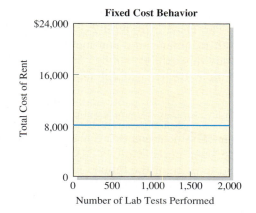

discounts are available for bulk purchases? The more I buy, the less I pay per unit.'' Although quantity discounts do exist for many items, managers typically focus on the price that must be paid within a ''normal'' range of operating activity. If, for example, an airline normally uses between 50,000 and 80,000 gallons of fuel a day, then it would focus on the price to be paid within that *relevant range* of activity. A **relevant range** can be defined as the range of activity within which assumptions relative to variable and fixed cost behavior are valid. More is said about the relevant range in Chapter 6.

There are many examples of variable costs. In a manufacturing company, they would usually include direct materials, direct labor, and some items of manufacturing overhead (such as utilities, supplies, and lubricants). In a merchandising company, they would include cost of goods sold, commissions to salespersons, and billing costs.

Fixed Costs   **Fixed costs** are costs that remain constant in total, regardless of changes in the level of activity within the relevant range. That is, unlike variable costs, fixed costs are not affected by changes in activity during a period. Consequently, as the activity level rises and falls, the fixed costs remain constant in total amount unless influenced by some outside force, such as price changes. Rent is a good example of a fixed cost. If the monthly rental cost of a piece of equipment in a hospital lab is $8,000, then that amount of cost will be sustained regardless of the number of tests that may be performed using the equipment during the month. The concept of a fixed cost is shown in graphic form in Exhibit 2–8.

The presence of fixed costs in an organization can create difficulties if it becomes necessary to express the costs on a per unit basis. This is because if fixed costs are expressed on a per unit basis, they will react *inversely* with changes in activity. In the hospital lab mentioned above, for example, the average cost per lab test will fall as the number of tests performed in the lab increases. This is because the $8,000 rental cost will be spread over more tests. Conversely, as the number of tests performed in the lab declines, the average cost per test will rise as the $8,000 rental cost is spread over fewer tests. This concept is illustrated in the table below:

Monthly Rental Cost	Number of Lab Tests Performed	Average Cost per Lab Test
$8,000	10	$800
8,000	500	16
8,000	2,000	4

Note that if the hospital performs only 10 tests each month, the rental cost of the equipment will average $800 per test. But if 2,000 tests are performed each month, the average cost will drop to only $4 per test. More will be said later about the problems created for both the accountant and the manager by this variation in unit costs.

Examples of fixed costs include depreciation, insurance, property taxes, rent, supervisory salaries, and advertising.

Summary of Variable and Fixed Costs   Understanding the behavior of variable and fixed costs is one of the most difficult parts of this chapter. To assist in this understanding, a summary of both variable and fixed cost behavior is presented in Exhibit 2–9. Study this exhibit carefully, along with the material in the preceding paragraphs, until you thoroughly understand the concepts involved.

EXHIBIT 2–9

Summary of Variable
and Fixed Cost
Behavior

	Behavior of the Cost	
Cost	**In Total**	**Per Unit**
Variable cost	Total variable cost increases and decreases in proportion to changes in the activity level.	Variable costs remain constant per unit.
Fixed cost	Total fixed cost is not affected by changes in the activity level (i.e., total fixed cost remains constant even if the activity level changes).	Fixed costs decrease per unit as the activity level rises and increase per unit as the activity level falls.

FOCUS ON CURRENT PRACTICE

During the 1980s, steel companies operating in the United States lost a substantial portion of their business to foreign producers. Since steel production involves a large amount of fixed cost, the loss of business drove per ton manufacturing costs upward for U.S. companies, resulting in huge operating losses. But by modernizing plants and focusing on regaining lost market share, U.S. companies have now driven per ton manufacturing costs back downward to the point where only South Korea and Britain produce for less.

The greatest threat now to U.S. steel companies is a loss of market share to new "minimills" that focus on various market niches. Such a loss of market share would again drive per ton manufacturing costs upward. The reason is that the level of fixed costs in major steel companies is even higher today than it was 15 years ago due to the large-scale modernization that has taken place.[2]

Direct and Indirect Costs

Objective 7
Identify and give
examples of direct and
indirect costs, controllable
and noncontrollable costs,
differential costs,
opportunity costs, and
sunk costs.

Costs are often classified as being either direct or indirect. However, these terms have no meaning unless one first identifies some organizational segment to which the costs are to be related. The organizational segment might be a product line, a sales territory, a division, or some other subpart of a company. A **direct cost** is a cost that can be obviously and physically traced to the particular segment under consideration. For example, if the segment under consideration is a product line, then the materials and labor involved in the manufacture of the line would both be direct costs.

An **indirect cost** is a cost that must be allocated in order to be assigned to the segment under consideration. Manufacturing overhead, for example, would be an indirect cost of a product line. The reason is that manufacturing overhead is not directly identifiable with any particular product line but rather is incurred as a consequence of general, overall operating activities. Indirect costs are also known as **common costs.**

In sum, the following guidelines prevail in distinguishing between direct and indirect (common) costs:

---

[2] "The Big Threat to Big Steel's Future," *Fortune* 124, no. 2 (July 15, 1991), pp. 106–8.

1. If a cost can be obviously and physically traced to a unit of product or some other organizational segment, then it is a direct cost with respect to that segment.
2. If a cost must be allocated in order to be assigned to a unit of product or some other organizational segment, then it is an indirect (common) cost with respect to that segment.

Controllable and Noncontrollable Costs

As with direct and indirect costs, whether a cost is controllable or noncontrollable depends on the point of reference. *All* costs are controllable at some level or another in a company. Only at the lower levels of management can some costs be considered noncontrollable. Top management has the power to expand or contract facilities, hire, fire, set expenditure policies, and generally exercise control over any cost as it desires. At lower levels of management, however, authority may not exist to control the incurrence of some costs, and these costs will therefore be considered noncontrollable *so far as that level of management is concerned.*

A cost is considered to be a **controllable cost** at a particular level of management if that level has power to *authorize* the cost. For example, entertainment expense would be controllable by a sales manager if he or she had power to authorize the amount and type of entertainment for customers. On the other hand, depreciation of warehouse facilities would not be controllable by the sales manager, since he or she would have no power to authorize warehouse construction.

In some situations, there is a time dimension to controllability. Costs that are controllable over the long run may not be controllable over the short run. A good example is advertising. Once an advertising program has been set and a contract signed, management has no power to change the amount of spending. But when the contract expires, advertising costs can be renegotiated, and thus management can exercise control over the long run. Another example is plant acquisition. Management is free to build any size plant it desires, but once a plant has been built, management is largely powerless to change the attendant costs over the short run.

Differential Costs

In making decisions, managers compare the alternatives before them. Each alternative will have certain costs associated with it that must be compared to the costs associated with the other alternatives available. Any cost that is present under one alternative but is absent in whole or in part under another alternative is known as a **differential cost.** Differential costs are also known as **incremental costs,** although technically an incremental cost should refer only to an increase in cost from one alternative to another; decreases in cost should be referred to as *decremental costs.* Differential cost is a broader term, encompassing both cost increases (incremental costs) and cost decreases (decremental costs) between alternatives.

The accountant's differential cost concept can be compared to the economist's marginal cost concept. In speaking of changes in cost and revenue, the economist employs the terms *marginal cost* and *marginal revenue.* The revenue that can be obtained from selling one more unit of product is called marginal revenue, and the cost involved in producing one more unit of product is called marginal cost. The economist's marginal concept is basically the same as the accountant's differential concept.

Differential costs can be either fixed or variable. To illustrate, assume that Cosmetics, Inc., is thinking about changing its marketing method from distribution through retailers to distribution by direct sale. Present costs and revenues are compared to projected costs and revenues in the following table:

	Retailer Distribution (present)	Direct Sale Distribution (proposed)	Differential Costs and Revenues
Revenues (V)	$700,000	$800,000	$100,000
Cost of goods sold (V)	350,000	400,000	50,000
Advertising (F)	80,000	45,000	(35,000)
Commissions (V).	–0–	40,000	40,000
Warehouse depreciation (F)	50,000	80,000	30,000
Other expenses (F).	60,000	60,000	–0–
Total	540,000	625,000	85,000
Net income	$160,000	$175,000	$ 15,000

V = Variable; F = Fixed.

The differential revenue is $100,000, and the differential costs total $85,000, leaving a positive differential net income of $15,000 under the proposed marketing plan. As noted earlier, those differential costs representing cost increases could have been referred to more specifically as incremental costs, and those representing cost decreases could have been referred to more specifically as decremental costs. The reader should be acquainted with all of these terms, since they are widely used in day-to-day business practice.

Opportunity Costs

An **opportunity cost** can be defined as the potential benefit that is lost or sacrificed when the selection of one course of action makes it necessary to give up a competing course of action. To illustrate, consider the following:

Example 1

Vicki has a part-time job that pays her $100 per week. She would like to spend a week at the beach during spring vacation from school, but she has no vacation time available. If she takes the trip anyway, the $100 in lost wages will be an opportunity cost of doing so.

Example 2

A firm is considering the investment of a large sum of money in land that is to be held for future expansion. Rather than being invested in land, the funds could be invested in high-grade securities. If the land is acquired, the opportunity cost will be the investment income that could have been realized if the securities had been purchased instead.

Example 3

Steve is employed with a company that pays him a salary of $20,000 per year. He is thinking about leaving the company and returning to school. Since returning to school would require that he give up his $20,000 salary, the forgone salary would be an opportunity cost of seeking further education.

Opportunity cost is not usually entered on the books of an organization, but it is a cost that must be explicitly considered in every decision a manager makes. Virtually every alternative has some opportunity cost attached to it. In example 3 above, for instance, if Steve decides to stay at his job there still is an opportunity cost involved: it is the greater income that could be realized in future years as a result of returning to school.

In short, every alternative course of action facing a manager has a mixture of good and bad features. In rejecting a course of action, the good features must be given up along with the bad. The net good features of a rejected alternative become the opportunity costs of the alternative that is selected.

Sunk Costs

A **sunk cost** is a cost *that has already been incurred* and that cannot be changed by any decision made now or in the future. Since sunk costs cannot be changed by any present or future decision, they are not differential costs, and therefore they should not be used in analyzing future courses of action.

To illustrate the notion of a sunk cost, assume that a firm has just paid $50,000 for a special-purpose machine. Since the cost outlay *has been made,* the $50,000 investment in the machine is a sunk cost. Even though by hindsight the purchase may have been unwise, no amount of regret can relieve the company of its decision, nor can any future decision cause the cost to be avoided. In short, the $50,000 is "out the window" from a decision point of view and will have to be reckoned with regardless of what future course of action the company may take. For this reason, such costs are said to be sunk.

SUMMARY

Although the term *cost* has a fairly distinctive meaning in financial accounting, it can be used in many different ways in managerial accounting. In this chapter, we have looked at some of the ways in which it is used by the manager in organizing and classifying data.

We have learned that costs can be classified as either period costs or product costs. Period costs are incurred as a function of time rather than as a function of the purchase or the manufacture of goods. Product costs, by contrast, are those costs involved in the purchase of goods in a merchandising company or the manufacture of goods in a manufacturing company.

In a manufacturing situation, product costs consist of all costs associated with operating the factory; these would include direct materials, direct labor, and manufacturing overhead. These costs go first into Work in Process. As goods are completed, the costs come out of Work in Process and go into Finished Goods. As goods are shipped to customers, the costs come out of Finished Goods and go into Cost of Goods Sold. The costs of partially completed or unsold goods appear on the balance sheet of a manufacturing company as assets in the form of work in process inventory or in the form of finished goods inventory.

We have found that costs can also be classified as being either variable or fixed, direct or indirect, and controllable or noncontrollable. In addition, we defined differential costs, opportunity costs, and sunk costs. A differential cost is the difference in cost between two alternatives. An opportunity cost is the benefit that is forgone in rejecting some course of action, and a sunk cost is a cost that has already been incurred.

All of these cost terms and classifications are basic to managerial accounting. We shall use them repeatedly, as well as refine them further, in chapters ahead.

REVIEW PROBLEM 1: COST TERMS

Many new cost terms have been introduced in this chapter. It will take you some time to learn what each term means and how to properly classify costs in an organization. To assist in this learning process, consider the following example: Porter Company manufactures a number of furniture products, including tables. Selected costs associated with the manufacture of the tables and the general operation of the company are given below:

1. Wood is used in the manufacture of the tables, at a cost of $100 per table.
2. The tables are assembled by workers, at a cost of $40 per table.
3. Workers assembling the tables are supervised by a factory supervisor who is paid $25,000 per year.
4. Electrical costs of $2 per machine-hour are incurred in the factory in the manufacture of the tables. (Four machine-hours are required to produce a table.)
5. The depreciation cost of the machines used in the manufacture of the tables totals $10,000 per year.
6. The salary of the president of Porter Company is $100,000 per year.
7. Porter Company spends $250,000 per year to advertise its products.
8. Salespersons are paid a commission of $30 for each table sold.
9. Instead of producing the tables, Porter Company could rent its factory space out at a rental income of $50,000 per year.

In the tabulation below, these costs are classified according to various cost terms used in the chapter. *Carefully study the classification of each cost.* If you don't understand why a particular cost is classified the way it is, turn back and read the section of the chapter dealing with the cost term involved.

Solution to Review Problem 1

	Variable Cost	Fixed Cost	Period (selling and administrative) Cost	Product Cost Direct Materials	Product Cost Direct Labor	Product Cost Manufacturing Overhead	To Units of Product Direct	To Units of Product Indirect	Sunk Cost	Opportunity Cost
1. Wood used in a table (at $100 per table)	X			X			X			
2. Labor cost to assemble a table (at $40 per table)	X				X		X			
3. Salary of the factory supervisor (at $25,000 per year)		X				X		X		
4. Cost of electricity to produce tables (at $2 per machine-hour)	X					X		X		
5. Depreciation of machines used to produce tables (at $10,000 per year)		X				X		X	X*	
6. Salary of the company president (at $100,000 per year)		X	X							
7. Advertising expense (at $250,000 per year)		X	X							
8. Commissions paid to salespersons (at $30 per table sold)	X		X							
9. Rental income forgone on factory space										X†

* This is a sunk cost, since the outlay for the equipment was made in some previous period.

† This is an opportunity cost, since it represents the potential benefit that is lost or sacrificed as a result of using the factory space to produce tables. Notice that the cost is not classified as a fixed cost or in any other way. Such classifications are of no significance, since opportunity costs are not recorded on the books of an organization.

REVIEW PROBLEM 2: SCHEDULE OF COST OF GOODS MANUFACTURED AND INCOME STATEMENT

The following information has been taken from the ledger accounts of Klear-Seal Company for the year ended December 31, 19x5:

Selling expenses	$ 140,000
Raw materials inventory, January 1	90,000
Raw materials inventory, December 31	60,000
Utilities, factory	36,000
Direct labor cost	150,000
Depreciation, factory	162,000
Purchases of raw materials	750,000
Sales	2,500,000
Insurance, factory	40,000
Supplies, factory	15,000
Administrative expenses	270,000
Indirect labor	300,000
Maintenance, factory	87,000
Work in process inventory, January 1	180,000
Work in process inventory, December 31	100,000
Finished goods inventory, January 1	260,000
Finished goods inventory, December 31	210,000

Management wants to organize these data into a better format so that statements can be prepared for the year.

1. Prepare a schedule of cost of goods manufactured for 19x5.   *Required*
2. Compute the cost of goods sold for 19x5.
3. Using data as needed from parts (1) and (2), prepare an income statement for 19x5.

1.

Solution to Review Problem 2

KLEAR-SEAL COMPANY

Schedule of Cost of Goods Manufactured
For the Year Ended December 31, 19x5

Direct materials:		
Raw materials inventory, January 1	$ 90,000	
Add: Purchases of raw materials	750,000	
Raw materials available for use	840,000	
Deduct: Raw materials inventory, December 31	60,000	
Raw materials used in production		$ 780,000
Direct labor		150,000
Manufacturing overhead:		
Utilities, factory	36,000	
Depreciation, factory	162,000	
Insurance, factory	40,000	
Supplies, factory	15,000	
Indirect labor	300,000	
Maintenance, factory	87,000	
Total overhead costs		640,000
Total manufacturing costs		1,570,000
Add: Work in process inventory, January 1		180,000
		1,750,000
Deduct: Work in process inventory, December 31		100,000
Cost of goods manufactured		$1,650,000

2. The cost of goods sold would be computed as follows:

Finished goods inventory, January 1	$ 260,000
Add: Cost of goods manufactured	1,650,000
Goods available for sale	1,910,000
Deduct: Finished goods inventory, December 31	210,000
Cost of goods sold	$1,700,000

3.

KLEAR-SEAL COMPANY
Income Statement
For the Year Ended December 31, 19x5

Sales		$2,500,000
Less cost of goods sold (above)		1,700,000
Gross margin		800,000
Less selling and administrative expenses:		
Selling expenses	$140,000	
Administrative expenses	270,000	
Total expenses		410,000
Net income		$ 390,000

KEY TERMS FOR REVIEW

Objective 8
Define or explain the key terms listed at the end of the chapter.

Administrative costs All executive, organizational, and clerical costs associated with the general management of an organization. (p. 36)

Common costs See *Indirect cost*. (p. 46)

Controllable costs A cost is controllable at a particular level of management if that level has power to authorize the cost. (p. 47)

Conversion cost The term used to describe direct labor cost combined with manufacturing overhead cost. (p. 36)

Cost behavior The way in which a cost will react or respond to changes in the level of business activity. (p. 44)

Cost of goods manufactured The materials, labor, and overhead costs that have gone into the products that have been produced during a period. (p. 39)

Differential cost Any cost that is present under one alternative but is absent in whole or in part under another alternative in a decision-making situation. Also see *Incremental cost*. (p. 47)

Direct cost A cost that can be obviously and physically traced to a unit of product or other organizational segment. (p. 46)

Direct labor Those factory labor costs that can be physically traced to the creation of products in a "hands on" sense. (p. 35)

Direct materials Those materials that become an integral part of a finished product and that can be conveniently traced into it. (p. 35)

Finished goods Goods that are completed as to manufacturing but not yet sold to customers. (p. 40)

Fixed cost A cost that remains constant, in total, regardless of changes in the level of activity within the relevant range. If a fixed cost is expressed on a per unit basis, it varies inversely with the level of activity. (p. 45)

Incremental cost An increase in cost between two alternatives. Also see *Differential cost*. (p. 47)

Indirect cost A cost that must be allocated in order to be assigned to a unit of product or some other organizational segment. An indirect cost is also known as a *common cost*. (p. 46)

Indirect labor The factory labor costs of janitors, supervisors, engineers, and others that cannot be traced directly to the creation of products in a "hands on" sense. (p. 35)

Indirect materials Small items of material such as glue and nails that may become an integral part of a finished product but that are traceable into the product only at great cost or inconvenience. (p. 35)

Inventoriable costs All costs that are involved in the purchase or manufacture of goods. In the case of manufactured goods, these costs consist of direct materials, direct labor, and manufacturing overhead costs used in the production process. Also see *Product costs*. (p. 42)

Manufacturing   The conversion of raw materials into finished products through the efforts of workers and the use of production equipment. (p. 34)

Manufacturing overhead   All costs associated with the manufacturing process except direct materials and direct labor. (p. 35)

Marketing or selling costs   All costs necessary to secure customer orders and get the finished product or service into the hands of the customer. This term is synonymous with *order-getting and order-filling costs*. (p. 36)

Merchandising   The sale of products that are in finished form and that have been acquired from a manufacturer or other outside source. (p. 34)

Opportunity cost   The potential benefit that is lost or sacrificed when the selection of one course of action makes it necessary to give up a competing course of action. (p. 48)

Order-getting and order-filling costs   All costs necessary to secure customer orders and get the finished product or service into the hands of the customer. This term is synonymous with *marketing or selling costs*. (p. 36)

Period costs   All costs that are matched against revenues on a time period basis; such costs consist of selling (marketing) and administrative expenses. (p. 37)

Prime cost   The term used to describe direct materials cost combined with direct labor cost. (p. 36)

Product costs   All costs that are involved in the purchase or manufacture of goods. In the case of manufactured goods, these costs consist of direct materials, direct labor, and manufacturing overhead. Also see *Inventoriable costs*. (p. 37)

Raw materials   Any materials going into a manufactured product. (p. 35)

Relevant range   The range of activity within which assumptions relative to variable and fixed cost behavior are valid. (p. 45)

Sunk cost   Any cost that has already been incurred and that can't be changed by any decision made now or in the future. (p. 49)

Variable cost   A cost that varies, in total, in direct proportion to changes in the level of activity. A variable cost is constant per unit. (p. 44)

Work in process   Goods that are only partially completed as to manufacturing at the beginning or end of a period and that will need further work before being ready for sale to a customer. (p. 39)

APPENDIX A: FURTHER CLASSIFICATION OF LABOR COSTS

Of all the costs of an organization, labor costs often present the most difficult problems of segregation and classification. Although companies vary considerably in their breakdown of labor costs, the following subdivisions represent the most common approach:

Objective 9
Properly classify costs associated with idle time, overtime, and labor fringe benefits in an organization.

Direct Labor	Indirect Labor (part of manufacturing overhead)	Other Labor Costs
(Discussed earlier)	Janitors Supervisors Materials handlers Engineers Night security guards Maintenance workers	Idle time Overtime premium Labor fringe benefits

The costs listed in the Indirect Labor and Other Labor Costs columns should not be viewed as being inclusive but rather as being representative of the kinds of costs that one might expect to find under these classifications. The costs in the Other Labor Costs column require further comment.

Idle Time

Idle time represents the costs of direct labor workers who are unable to perform their assignments due to machine breakdowns, materials shortages, power failures, and the like. Although direct labor workers are involved, the costs of idle time are treated as part of manufacturing overhead cost rather than as part of direct labor cost. The reason is that managers feel that such costs should be spread over *all* the production of a period rather than just over the jobs that happen to be in process when breakdowns and the like occur.

To give an example of how the cost of idle time is computed, assume that a press operator earns $12 per hour. If the press operator is paid for a normal 40-hour workweek but is idle for 3 hours during a given week due to breakdowns, labor cost would be allocated as follows:

Direct labor ($12 × 37 hours)	$444
Manufacturing overhead (idle time: $12 × 3 hours) . . .	36
Total cost for the week	$480

Overtime Premium

The overtime premium paid to *all* factory workers (direct labor as well as indirect labor) is usually considered to be part of manufacturing overhead and not assignable to any particular order or batch of production. At first glance this may seem strange, since overtime is always spent working on some particular order. Why not charge that order for the overtime cost? The reason is that production is usually scheduled on a random basis. If production is randomly scheduled, then it would be unfair to charge an overtime premium against a particular batch of goods simply because the batch *happened* to fall on the tail end of the daily scheduling sheet.

To illustrate, assume that two batches of goods, order A and order B, each take three hours to complete. The production run on order A is scheduled early in the day, but the production run on order B isn't scheduled until late in the afternoon. By the time the run on order B is completed, two hours of overtime have been logged in. The necessity to work overtime was a result of the fact that *total* production exceeded the regular time available. Order B was no more responsible for the overtime than was order A. Therefore, all production should share in the premium charge that resulted. This is a much more equitable way of handling overtime premium in that it doesn't penalize one run simply because it happens to fall late in the day.

Let us again assume that a press operator in a plant earns $12 per hour. He is paid time and a half for overtime (time in excess of 40 hours a week). During a given week, he works 45 hours and has no idle time. His labor cost for the week would be allocated as follows:

Direct labor ($12 × 45 hours)	$540
Manufacturing overhead (overtime premium: $6 × 5 hours). . .	30
Total cost for the week	$570

Observe from this computation that only the overtime premium of $6 per hour is charged to the overhead account—*not* the entire $18 earned for each hour of overtime work ($12 regular rate × 1.5 = $18).

Labor Fringe Benefits

The proper classification of labor fringe benefits is not so clearly defined in practice as is idle time or overtime premium. Labor fringe benefits are made up of employment-related costs paid by the employer and include the costs of insurance programs, retirement plans, various supplemental unemployment benefits, and hospitalization plans. Many firms treat all such costs as indirect labor by adding them in total to manufacturing overhead. Other firms treat that portion of fringe benefits that relates to direct labor as additional direct labor cost. This approach is conceptually superior since the fringe benefits provided to direct labor workers clearly represent an added cost of their services.

The cost to the employer for fringe benefits is substantial. A recent nationwide survey by the Chamber of Commerce shows that fringe benefits, on the average, cost 37 cents for every dollar of gross wages.

QUESTIONS

2-1 Distinguish between merchandising and manufacturing.

2-2 What are the three major elements in the cost of a manufactured product?

2-3 Distinguish between the following: (a) direct materials, (b) indirect materials, (c) direct labor, (d) indirect labor, and (e) manufacturing overhead.

2-4 Explain the difference between a product cost and a period cost.

2-5 Describe how the income statement of a manufacturing company differs from the income statement of a merchandising company.

2-6 Of what value is the schedule and cost of goods manufactured? How does it tie into the income statement?

2-7 Distinguish between prime cost and conversion cost. What is meant by conversion cost?

2-8 Describe how the balance sheet of a manufacturing company differs from the balance sheet of a merchandising company so far as current assets are concerned.

2-9 Why are product costs sometimes called inventoriable costs? Describe the flow of such costs in a manufacturing company from the point of incurrence until they finally become expenses on the income statement.

2-10 Is it possible for costs such as salaries or depreciation to end up as assets on the balance sheet? Explain.

2-11 Give at least three terms that may be substituted for the term *manufacturing overhead*.

2-12 What is meant by the term *cost behavior?*

2-13 "A variable cost is a cost that varies per unit of product, whereas a fixed cost is constant per unit of product." Do you agree? Explain.

2-14 How do fixed costs create difficulties in costing units of product?

2-15 Why is manufacturing overhead considered an indirect cost of a unit of product?

2-16 Under what conditions is a cost controllable at a particular level of management?

2-17 Define the following terms: differential cost, opportunity cost, and sunk cost.

2–18   Only variable costs can be differential costs. Do you agree? Explain.

2–19   (Appendix A)   Mary Adams is employed by Acme Company. Last week she worked 34 hours assembling one of the company's products and was idle 6 hours due to material shortages. Acme's employees are engaged at their workstations for a normal 40-hour week. Ms. Adams is paid $8 per hour. Allocate her earnings between direct labor cost and manufacturing overhead cost.

2–20   (Appendix A)   John Olsen operates a stamping machine on the assembly line of Drake Manufacturing Company. Last week Mr. Olsen worked 45 hours. His basic wage rate is $5 per hour, with time and a half for overtime (time worked in excess of 40 hours per week). How should last week's wage cost be allocated between direct labor cost and manufacturing overhead cost?

EXERCISES

E2–1   Below are a number of costs that might be incurred in a service, merchandising, or manufacturing company. Copy the list of costs onto your answer sheet, and then place an X in the appropriate column for each cost to indicate whether the cost involved would be variable or fixed.

	Cost Behavior	
Cost	**Variable**	**Fixed**
1. X-ray film used in a hospital.		
2. Advertising of products and services.		
3. Straight-line depreciation of a building.		
4. Electrical costs of running machines.		
5. Property taxes on a factory building.		
6. Commissions to salespersons.		
7. Insurance on an attorney's office.		
8. Leather used in manufacturing basketballs.		
9. Shipping costs of a TV manufacturer.		
10. Rent on a medical center.		

E2–2   The following cost and inventory data are taken from the books of Mason Company for the year 19x8:

Costs incurred:

Direct labor cost	$ 70,000
Purchases of raw materials	118,000
Indirect labor	30,000
Maintenance, factory equipment	6,000
Advertising expense	90,000
Insurance, factory equipment	800
Sales salaries	50,000
Rent, factory facilities	20,000
Supplies	4,200
Depreciation, office equipment	3,000
Depreciation, factory equipment	19,000

	January 1, 19x8	December 31, 19x8
Inventories:		
Raw materials . . .	$ 7,000	$15,000
Work in process . .	10,000	5,000
Finished goods . . .	20,000	35,000

Required   1.   Prepare a schedule of cost of goods manufactured in good form.

2.   Prepare the cost of goods sold section of Mason Company's income statement for the year.

Following are a number of cost terms introduced in the chapter:

Variable cost	Product cost
Fixed cost	Sunk cost
Prime cost	Conversion cost
Opportunity cost	Period cost

Choose the term or terms above that most appropriately describe the cost identified in each of the following situations. A cost term can be used more than once.

1. Lake Company produces a tote bag that is very popular with college students. The cloth going into the manufacture of the tote bag would be called direct materials and classified as a _____ cost. In terms of cost behavior, the cloth could also be described as a _____ cost.
2. The direct labor cost required to produce the tote bags, combined with the manufacturing overhead cost involved, would be known as _____ cost.
3. The company could have taken the funds that it has invested in production equipment and invested them in interest-bearing securities instead. The interest forgone on the securities would be called _____ cost.
4. Taken together, the direct materials cost and the direct labor cost required to produce tote bags would be called _____ cost.
5. The company used to produce a smaller tote bag that was not very popular. Some three hundred of these smaller bags are stored in one of the company's warehouses. The amount invested in these bags would be called a _____ cost.
6. The tote bags are sold through agents who are paid a commission on each bag sold. These commissions would be classified by Lake Company as a _____ cost. In terms of cost behavior, commissions would be classified as a _____ cost.
7. Depreciation on the equipment used to produce tote bags would be classified by Lake Company as a _____ cost. However, depreciation on any equipment used by the company in selling and administrative activities would be classified as a _____ cost. In terms of cost behavior, depreciation would probably be classified as a _____ cost.
8. A _____ cost is also known as an inventoriable cost, since such costs go into the Work in Process inventory account and then into the Finished Goods inventory account before appearing on the income statement as part of cost of goods sold.
9. The salary of Lake Company's president would be classified as a _____ cost, since the salary will appear on the income statement as an expense in the time period in which it is incurred.
10. Costs can often be classified in several ways. For example, Lake Company pays $5,000 rent each month on its factory building. The rent would be part of manufacturing overhead. In terms of cost behavior, it would be classified as a _____ cost. The rent can also be classified as a _____ cost and as part of _____ cost.

The Devon Motor Company produces automobiles. During April 19x5, the company purchased 8,000 batteries at a cost of $10 per battery. Devon withdrew 7,600 batteries from the storeroom during the month. Of these, 100 were used to replace batteries in autos being used by the company's traveling sales staff. The remaining 7,500 batteries withdrawn from the storeroom were placed in autos being produced by the company. Of the autos in production during April, 90 percent were completed and transferred from work in process to finished goods. Of the cars completed during the month, 30 percent were unsold at April 30.

There were no inventories of any type on April 1, 19x5.

Required   1.   Determine the cost of batteries that would appear in each of the following accounts at April 30, 19x5:
- a.   Raw Materials.
- b.   Work in Process.
- c.   Finished Goods.
- d.   Cost of Goods Sold.
- e.   Selling Expense.

2.   Specify whether each of the above accounts would appear on the balance sheet or on the income statement at April 30.

E2-5   A product cost is also known as an inventoriable cost. Classify the following costs as being either product (inventoriable) costs or period (noninventoriable) costs in a manufacturing company:

1.   Depreciation on salespersons' cars.
2.   Rent on equipment used in the factory.
3.   Lubricants used for maintenance of machines.
4.   Salaries of finished goods warehouse personnel.
5.   Soap and paper towels used by workers at the end of a shift.
6.   Factory supervisors' salaries.
7.   Heat, water, and power consumed in the factory.
8.   Materials used in boxing units of finished product for shipment overseas. (Units are not normally boxed.)
9.   Advertising outlays.
10.   Workers' compensation insurance on factory employees.
11.   Depreciation on chairs and tables in the factory lunchroom.
12.   The salary of the switchboard operator for the company.
13.   Depreciation on a Lear Jet used by the company's executives.
14.   Rent on rooms at a Florida resort for holding of the annual sales conference.
15.   Attractively designed box for packaging breakfast cereal.

E2-6   Below are listed various costs that might be found in a service, merchandising, or manufacturing company.

1.   Buns used to make hamburgers in a McDonald's outlet.
2.   Advertising by a dental office.
3.   Apples processed and canned by Del Monte Corporation.
4.   Shipping of canned apples from Del Monte's plant to customers.
5.   Insurance on a factory producing contact lenses.
6.   Insurance on IBM's corporate headquarters.
7.   Salary of a supervisor overseeing production of computer boards.
8.   Commissions paid to persons selling encyclopedias.
9.   Depreciation of factory lunchroom facilities at a General Electric plant.
10.   Steering wheels used by Ford Motor Company in auto production.

Required   Classify each cost as being either variable or fixed with respect to volume or level of activity. Also classify each cost as being either a selling and administrative cost or a product cost. Prepare your answer sheet as shown below:

| | Cost Behavior | | Selling and | |
Cost Item	Variable	Fixed	Administrative Cost	Product Cost

Place an *X* in the appropriate columns to show the proper classification of each cost.

E2-7   (Appendix A) Paul Clark is employed by Aerotech Products and assembles a component part for one of the company's product lines. He is paid $10 per hour for regular time and time and a half for all work in excess of 40 hours per week.

1. Assume that during a given week Paul is idle for five hours due to machine breakdowns and that he is idle for four more hours due to material shortages. No overtime is recorded for the week. Allocate Paul's wages for the week between direct labor cost and manufacturing overhead cost.

2. Assume that during the following week Paul works a total of 48 hours. He has no idle time for the week. Allocate Paul's wages for the week between direct labor cost and manufacturing overhead cost.

3. Paul's company provides an attractive package of fringe benefits for its employees. This package includes a retirement program and a health insurance program. So far as direct labor workers are concerned, explain two ways that the company could handle the costs of fringe benefits in its cost records.

Required

E2–8

(Appendix A) Several days ago you took your TV set into a shop to have some repair work done. When you later picked up the set, the bill showed a $75 charge for labor. This charge represented two hours of service time—$30 for the first hour and $45 for the second.

When questioned about the difference in hourly rates, the shop manager explained that work on your set was started at 4 o'clock in the afternoon. By the time work was completed two hours later at 6 o'clock, an hour of overtime had been put in by the repair technician. The second hour therefore contained a charge for an "overtime premium," since the company had to pay the repair technician time and a half for any work in excess of eight hours per day. The shop manager further explained that the shop was working overtime to "catch up a little" on its backlog of repairs, but it still needed to maintain a "decent" profit margin on the technicians' time.

1. Do you agree with the shop's computation of the service charge on your job?

2. Assume that the shop pays its technicians $14 per hour. Prepare computations to show how the cost of the repair technician's time for the day (nine hours) should be allocated between direct labor cost and general overhead cost on the shop's books.

3. Under what circumstances might the shop be justified in charging an overtime premium for repair work on your set?

Required

PROBLEMS

Marie Gallant is president of a company whose stock is widely held by the public. The company is struggling to meet its budgeted profit target, so Ms. Gallant has ordered the following two actions:

P2–9 Ethics and the Manager

a. All discretionary expenditures—such as advertising, travel, and maintenance—are to be deferred to the next period. By this process, it is expected that the company can avoid $250,000 in expenses for the current period.

b. Expenditures that can't be avoided are to be carefully scrutinized and as many as possible are to be treated as product costs rather than as period costs. By this process, it is expected that at least $100,000 that would have been treated as a current expense will be added to products that will be carried over and sold in the next period.

1. Assume that the company is struggling to meet its first quarter profit target. Thus, the postponed expenditures and the unsold inventory will be carried from March (the end of the first quarter) to April (the beginning of the second quarter). Identify the stakeholders involved, and explain why Ms. Gallant's actions are or are not ethical.

2. Assume that the company is struggling to meet its profit target for the year. Thus, the postponed expenditures and the unsold inventory will be carried from December of this year to January of next year (the company follows a calendar year reporting period). Are Ms. Gallant's actions ethical? Explain why they are or are not.

Required

Supply Missing Production and Cost Data   Supply the missing data in the following cases. Each case is independent of the others.

P2–10

	Case			
	1	2	3	4
Direct materials	$ 4,500	$ 6,000	$ 5,000	$ 3,000
Direct labor	?	3,000	7,000	4,000
Manufacturing overhead	5,000	4,000	?	9,000
Total manufacturing costs	18,500	?	20,000	?
Beginning work in process inventory	2,500	?	3,000	?
Ending work in process inventory	?	1,000	4,000	3,000
Cost of goods manufactured	$18,000	$14,000	$?	$?
Sales	$30,000	$21,000	$36,000	$40,000
Beginning finished goods inventory	1,000	2,500	?	2,000
Cost of goods manufactured	?	?	?	17,500
Goods available for sale	?	?	?	?
Ending finished goods inventory	?	1,500	4,000	3,500
Cost of goods sold	17,000	?	18,500	?
Gross margin	13,000	?	17,500	?
Operating expenses	?	3,500	?	?
Net income	$ 4,000	$?	$ 5,000	$ 9,000

P2–11 **Cost Classification** Various costs associated with the operation of a factory are given below:

1. Electricity used in operating machines.
2. Rent on a factory building.
3. Cloth used in drapery production.
4. Production superintendent's salary.
5. Cost of laborers assembling a product.
6. Glue used in furniture production.
7. Janitorial salaries.
8. Peaches used in canning fruit.
9. Lubricants needed for machines.
10. Sugar used in soft-drink production.
11. Property taxes on the factory.
12. Cost of workers painting a product.
13. Depreciation of cafeteria equipment.
14. Solder used in producing TV sets.
15. Cabinets used in producing TV sets.

Required Classify each cost as being either variable or fixed with respect to volume or level of activity. Also classify each cost as being either direct or indirect with respect to units of product. Prepare your answer sheet as shown below:

	Cost Behavior		To Units of Product	
Cost Item	Variable	Fixed	Direct	Indirect
Example: Factory insurance		X		X

If you are unsure whether a cost would be variable or fixed, consider how it would behave over fairly wide ranges of activity.

P2–12 **Schedule of Cost of Goods Manufactured; Cost Behavior** Various cost and sales data for Meriwell Company for 19x6 follow:

Finished goods inventory, January 1 . . . . . . $ 20,000
Finished goods inventory, December 31 40,000
Depreciation, factory 27,000
Administrative expenses 110,000
Utilities, factory 8,000
Maintenance, factory 40,000
Supplies, factory 11,000
Insurance, factory 4,000
Purchases of raw materials 125,000
Raw materials inventory, January 1 9,000
Raw materials inventory, December 31 6,000
Direct labor 70,000
Indirect labor 15,000
Work in process inventory, January 1 17,000
Work in process inventory, December 31 30,000
Sales 500,000
Selling expenses 80,000

Required

1. Prepare a schedule of cost of goods manufactured for 19x6.
2. Prepare an income statement for 19x6.
3. Assume that the company produced the equivalent of 10,000 units of product during 19x6. What was the unit cost for direct materials? What was the unit cost for factory depreciation?
4. Assume that the company expects to produce 15,000 units of product during the coming year. What per unit cost and what total cost would you expect the company to incur for direct materials at this level of activity? For factory depreciation? (In preparing your answer, assume that direct materials is a variable cost and that depreciation is a fixed cost; also assume that depreciation is computed on a straight-line basis.)
5. As the manager responsible for production costs, explain to the president any difference in unit costs between (3) and (4) above.

Cost Identification   Ridge Company acquired its factory building about 10 years ago. For several years the company has rented out a small annex attached to the rear of the building. Ridge Company has received a rental income of $30,000 per year on this space. The renter's lease will expire soon, and rather than renewing the lease, Ridge Company has decided to use the space itself to manufacture a new product.

P2–13

   Direct materials cost for the new product will total $80 per unit. To have a place to store finished units of product, the company will rent a small warehouse nearby. The rental cost will be $500 per month. In addition, the company must rent equipment for use in producing the new product; the rental cost will be $4,000 per month. Workers will be hired to manufacture the new product, with direct labor cost amounting to $60 per unit. The space in the annex will continue to be depreciated on a straight-line basis, as in prior years. This depreciation is $8,000 per year.

   Advertising costs for the new product will total $50,000 per year. A supervisor will be hired to oversee production; her salary will be $1,500 per month. Electricity for operating machines will be $1.20 per unit. Costs of shipping the new product to customers will be $9 per unit.

   To provide funds to purchase materials, meet payrolls, and so forth, the company will have to liquidate some temporary investments. These investments are presently yielding a return of about $3,000 per year.

Prepare an answer sheet with the following column headings:

Required

Name of the Cost	Variable Cost	Fixed Cost	Product Cost			Period (selling and administrative) Cost	Opportunity Cost	Sunk Cost
			Direct Materials	Direct Labor	Manufacturing Overhead			

   List the different costs associated with the new product decision down the extreme left column (under "Name of the Cost"). Then place an X under each heading that helps to describe the type of cost involved. There may be X's under several column headings for a single cost. (For example, a cost may be a fixed cost, a period cost, and a sunk cost; you would place an *X* under each of these column headings opposite the cost.)

P2–14   Cost Identification   The Dorilane Company specializes in a set of wood patio furniture consisting of a table and four chairs. The set enjoys great popularity, and the company has ample orders to keep production going at its full capacity of 2,000 sets per year. Annual cost data at full capacity follow:

Factory labor, direct	$118,000
Advertising	50,000
Factory supervision	40,000
Property taxes, factory building	3,500
Sales commissions	80,000
Insurance, factory	2,500
Depreciation, office equipment	4,000
Lease cost, factory equipment.	12,000
Indirect materials, factory	6,000
Depreciation, factory building	10,000
General office supplies (billing)	3,000
General office salaries	60,000
Materials used (wood, bolts, etc.)	94,000
Utilities, factory	20,000

Required   1.   Prepare an answer sheet with the column headings shown below. Enter each cost item on your answer sheet, placing the dollar amount under the appropriate headings. As examples, this has been done already for the first two items in the list above. Note that each cost item is classified in two ways: first, as being either variable or fixed; and second, as being either a selling and administrative cost or a product cost. (If the item is a product cost, it should be classified as being either direct or indirect as shown.)

	Cost Behavior		Selling or Administrative	Product Cost	
Cost Item	Variable	Fixed	Cost	Direct	Indirect*
Factory labor, direct . . .	$118,000			$118,000	
Advertising.		$50,000	$50,000		

* To units of product.

If you are uncertain whether a cost would be variable or fixed, consider how you would expect it to behave over fairly wide ranges of activity.

2.   Total the dollar amounts in each of the columns in (1) above. Compute the cost to produce one patio set.

3.   Assume that production drops to only 1,000 sets annually. Would you expect the cost per set to increase, decrease, or remain unchanged? Explain. No computations are necessary.

4.   Refer to the original data. The president's brother-in-law has considered making himself a patio set and has priced the necessary materials at a building supply store. The brother-in-law has asked the president if he could purchase a patio set from the Dorilane Company "at cost," and the president has agreed to let him do so.

   a.   Would you expect any disagreement between the two men over the price the brother-in-law should pay? Explain. What price does the president probably have in mind? The brother-in-law?

   b.   Since the company is operating at full capacity, what cost term used in the chapter might be justification for the president to charge the full, regular price to the brother-in-law and still be selling "at cost"?

P2–15   Classification of Salary Cost   You have just been hired by Ogden Company, which was organized on January 2 of the current year. The company manufactures and sells a single product. It is your responsibility to coordinate shipments of the product from the factory to distribution warehouses located in various parts of the United States so that goods will be available as orders are received from customers.

The company is unsure how to classify your $30,000 annual salary in its cost records. The company's cost analyst says that your salary should be classified as a manufacturing (product) cost; the controller says that it should be classified as a selling expense; and the president says that it doesn't matter which way your salary cost is classified.

1. Which viewpoint is correct? Why?
2. From the point of view of the reported net income for the year, is the president correct in his statement that it doesn't matter which way your salary cost is classified? Explain, using the data from Exhibit 2–5 and/or Exhibit 2–6 as needed.

Required

Allocating Labor Costs   (Appendix A) Mark Hansen is employed by Eastern Products, Inc., and works on the company's assembly line. Mark's basic wage rate is $10 per hour. The company's union contract states that employees are to be paid time and a half for any work in excess of 40 hours per week.

P2–16

1. Suppose that in a given week Mark works 46 hours. Compute Mark's total wages for the week. How much of this amount would be allocated to direct labor cost? To manufacturing overhead cost?
2. Suppose in another week that Mark works 48 hours but is idle for 3 hours during the week due to machine breakdowns. Compute Mark's total wages for the week. How much of this amount would be allocated to direct labor cost? To manufacturing overhead cost?
3. Eastern Products, Inc., has an attractive package of fringe benefits that costs the company $3 for each hour of employee time (either regular time or overtime). During a particular week, Mark works 50 hours but is idle for 2 hours due to material shortages. Compute Mark's total wages and fringe benefits for the week. If the company treats all fringe benefits as part of manufacturing overhead cost, how much of Mark's wages and fringe benefits for the week would be allocated to direct labor cost? To manufacturing overhead cost?
4. Refer to the data in (3) above. If the company treats that part of fringe benefits relating to direct labor as added direct labor cost, how much of Mark's wages and fringe benefits for the week will be allocated to direct labor cost? To manufacturing overhead cost?

Required

Preparing Manufacturing Statements   Swift Company was organized on March 1 of the current year. After five months of "start-up" losses, management had expected to earn a profit during August, the most recent month. Management was disappointed, however, when the income statement for August showed that losses were still being realized by the company. August's income statement follows:

P2–17

SWIFT COMPANY
Income Statement
For the Month Ended August 31, 19x5

Sales		$450,000
Less operating expenses:		
Indirect labor cost	$ 12,000	
Utilities	15,000	
Direct labor cost	70,000	
Depreciation, factory equipment	21,000	
Raw materials purchased	165,000	
Depreciation, sales equipment	18,000	
Insurance expired during the month. . .	4,000	
Rent on facilities	50,000	
Selling and administrative salaries . . .	32,000	
Advertising.	75,000	462,000
Net loss		$(12,000)

After seeing the $12,000 loss for August, Swift's president stated, "I was sure we'd be profitable within six months, but our six months are up and this loss for August is even worse than July's. I think it's time to start looking for someone to buy out the company's assets—if we don't, within a few months there won't be any assets to sell. By the way, I don't see any reason to look for a new controller. We'll just limp along with Sam for the time being.''

The company's controller resigned a month ago. Sam, a new assistant in the controller's office, prepared the income statement above. Sam has had little experience in manufacturing operations. Additional information about the company follows:

a. Some 60 percent of the utilities cost and 75 percent of the expired insurance apply to factory operations. The remaining amounts apply to selling and administrative activities.

b. Inventory balances at the beginning and end of August were:

	August 1	August 31
Raw materials.	$ 8,000	$13,000
Work in process.	16,000	21,000
Finished goods	40,000	60,000

c. Only 80 percent of the rent on facilities applies to factory operations; the remainder applies to selling and administrative activities.

The president has asked you to check over the income statement and make a recommendation as to whether the company should look for a buyer for its assets.

Required
1. As one step in gathering data for a recommendation to the president, prepare a schedule of cost of goods manufactured in good form for August 19x5.
2. As a second step, prepare a new income statement for August.
3. Based on your statements prepared in (1) and (2) above, would you recommend that the company look for a buyer?

P2–18 **Cost Classification** Listed below are a number of costs that might typically be found in a service, merchandising, or manufacturing company.

1. Property taxes, factory.
2. Boxes used for packaging detergent.
3. Salespersons' commissions.
4. Supervisor's salary, factory.
5. Depreciation, executive automobiles.
6. Workers assembling computers.
7. Packing supplies for out-of-state shipments.
8. Insurance, finished goods warehouses.
9. Lubricants for machines.
10. Advertising costs.
11. "Chips" used in producing calculators.
12. Shipping costs on merchandise sold.
13. Magazine subscriptions, factory lunchroom.
14. Thread in a garment factory.
15. Billing costs.
16. Executive life insurance.
17. Ink used in textbook production.
18. Fringe benefits, assembly-line workers.
19. Yarn used in sweater production.
20. Receptionist, executive offices.

Required
Prepare an answer sheet with column headings as shown below. For each cost item, indicate whether it would be variable or fixed in behavior, and then whether it would be a selling cost, an administrative cost, or a manufacturing cost. If it is a manufacturing cost, indicate whether it would be direct or indirect to units of product. Three sample answers are provided for illustration. If you are unsure about whether a cost would be variable or fixed, consider whether it would fluctuate substantially over a fairly wide range of volume.

Cost Item	Variable or Fixed	Selling Cost	Administrative Cost	Manufacturing (product) Cost	
				Direct	Indirect
Direct labor	V			X	
Executive salaries. . .	F		X		
Factory rent	F				X

P2-19

Staci Valek began dabbling in pottery several years ago as a hobby. Her work is quite creative, and it has been so popular with friends and others that she has decided to quit her job with an aerospace firm and manufacture pottery full time. The salary from Staci's aerospace job is $1,500 per month.

Staci will rent a small building near her home to use as a place for manufacturing the pottery. The rent will be $500 per month. She estimates that the cost of clay and glaze will be $2 for each finished piece of pottery. She will hire workers to produce the pottery at a labor rate of $8 per pot. To sell her pots, Staci feels that she must advertise heavily in the local area. An advertising agency states that it will handle all advertising for a fee of $600 per month. Staci's brother will sell the pots; he will be paid a commission of $4 for each pot sold.

Staci owns some pottery wheels and other items of equipment that were purchased several years ago. This equipment will be depreciated at a rate of $100 per month and used in the manufacturing operation. In addition, other equipment needed to manufacture the pots will be rented at a cost of $300 per month.

A small room has been located in a tourist area that Staci will use as a sales office. The rent will be $250 per month. A phone installed in the room for taking orders will cost $40 per month. In addition, a recording device will be attached to the phone for taking after-hours messages. The phone company will charge Staci $0.60 for each message recorded.

Staci has some money in savings that is earning interest of $1,200 per year. These savings will be withdrawn and used to get the business going. For the time being, Staci does not intend to draw any salary from the new company.

1. Prepare an answer sheet with the following column headings: *Required*

Name of the Cost	Variable Cost	Fixed Cost	Product Cost			Period (selling and administrative) Cost	Opportunity Cost	Sunk Cost
			Direct Materials	Direct Labor	Manufacturing Overhead			

List the different costs associated with the new company down the extreme left column (under "Name of the Cost"). Then place an *X* under each heading that helps to describe the type of cost involved. There may be *X*'s under several column headings for a single cost. (That is, a cost may be a fixed cost, a period cost, and a sunk cost; you would place an *X* under each of these column headings opposite the cost.)

2. All of the costs you have listed above, except one, would be differential costs between the alternatives of Staci producing pottery or staying with the aerospace firm. Which cost is *not* differential? Explain.

Schedule of Cost of Goods Manufactured; Cost Behavior   Selected account balances P2-20
for the year ended December 31, 19x4, are provided below for Superior Company:

Selling and administrative salaries. . .	$110,000
Insurance, factory.	8,000
Utilities, factory	45,000
Purchases of raw materials	290,000
Indirect labor	60,000
Direct labor	?
Advertising expense	80,000
Cleaning supplies, factory	7,000
Sales commissions	50,000
Rent, factory building	120,000
Maintenance, factory	30,000

Inventory balances at the beginning and end of the year were as follows:

	January 1, 19x4	December 31, 19x4
Raw materials . . .	$40,000	$10,000
Work in process . .	?	35,000
Finished goods. . .	50,000	?

The total manufacturing costs for the year were $683,000; the goods available for sale totaled $740,000; and the cost of goods sold totaled $660,000.

Required
1. Prepare a schedule of cost of goods manufactured in the form illustrated in Exhibit 2–3, and prepare the cost of goods sold section of the company's income statement for the year.
2. Assume that the dollar amounts given above are for the equivalent of 40,000 units produced during the year. Compute the unit cost for direct materials used, and compute the unit cost for rent on the factory building.
3. Assume that in 19x5 (the following year) the company expects to produce 50,000 units. What per unit and total cost would you expect to be incurred for direct materials? For rent on the factory building? (In preparing your answer, you may assume that direct materials is a variable cost and that rent is a fixed cost.)
4. As the manager in charge of production costs, explain to the president the reason for any difference in unit costs between (2) and (3) above.

P2–21   Cost Behavior; Manufacturing Statement; Unit Costs   Visic Company, a manufacturing firm, produces a single product. The following information has been taken from the company's production, sales, and cost records for the year ended December 31, 19x2:

Production in units	29,000
Sales in units	?
Ending finished goods inventory in units	?
Sales in dollars	$1,300,000
Costs:	
Advertising	105,000
Entertainment and travel	40,000
Direct labor	90,000
Indirect labor	85,000
Raw materials purchased	480,000
Building rent (production uses 80% of the space; administrative and sales offices use the rest)	40,000
Utilities, factory	108,000
Royalty paid for use of production patent, $1.50 per unit produced	?
Maintenance, factory	9,000
Rent for special production equipment, $7,000 per year plus $0.30 per unit produced	?
Selling and administrative salaries	210,000
Other factory overhead costs	6,800
Other selling and administrative expenses	17,000

	January 1, 19x2	December 31, 19x2
Inventories:		
Raw materials	$20,000	$30,000
Work in process	50,000	40,000
Finished goods	–0–	?

The finished goods inventory is being carried at the average unit production cost for the year. The selling price of the product is $50 per unit.

Required
1. Prepare a schedule of cost of goods manufactured for the year.

2. Compute the following:
   a. The number of units in the finished goods inventory at December 31, 19x2.
   b. The cost of the units in the finished goods inventory at December 31, 19x2.
3. Prepare an income statement for the year.

CASES

Missing Data; Statements; Inventory Computation   "I was sure that when our battery   **C2-22**
hit the market it would be an instant success," said Roger Strong, founder and president of
Solar Technology, Inc. "But just look at the gusher of red ink for the first quarter. It's
obvious that we're better scientists than we are businesspeople." The data to which Roger
was referring are shown below:

SOLAR TECHNOLOGY, INC.
Income Statement
For the Quarter Ended March 31, 19x7

Sales (32,000 batteries)		$ 960,000
Less operating expenses:		
Selling and administrative salaries	$110,000	
Advertising	90,000	
Maintenance, production	43,000	
Indirect labor cost	120,000	
Cleaning supplies, production	7,000	
Purchases of raw materials	360,000	
Rental cost, facilities	75,000	
Insurance, production	8,000	
Depreciation, office equipment	27,000	
Utilities	80,000	
Depreciation, production equipment . . .	100,000	
Direct labor cost	70,000	
Travel, salespersons	40,000	
Total operating expenses		1,130,000
Net loss		$ (170,000)

"At this rate we'll be out of business within a year," said Cindy Zhang, the company's
accountant. "But I've double-checked these figures, so I know they're right."

Solar Technology was organized at the beginning of the current year to produce and
market a revolutionary new solar battery. The company's accounting system was set up by
Margie Wallace, an experienced accountant who recently left the company to do independent consulting work. The statement above was prepared by Zhang, her assistant.

"We may not last a year if the insurance company doesn't pay the $226,000 it owes us
for the 8,000 batteries lost in the warehouse fire last week," said Roger. "The insurance
adjuster says our claim is inflated, but he's just trying to pressure us into a lower figure. We
have the data to back up our claim, and it will stand up in any court."

On April 3, just after the end of the first quarter, the company's finished goods storage
area was swept by fire and all 8,000 unsold batteries were destroyed. (These batteries were
part of the 40,000 units completed during the first quarter.) The company's insurance
policy states that the company will be reimbursed for the "cost" of any finished batteries
destroyed or stolen. Zhang has determined this cost as follows:

$$\frac{\text{Total costs for the quarter, } \$1,130,000}{\text{Batteries produced during the quarter, } 40,000} = \$28.25 \text{ per unit}$$

$$8,000 \text{ batteries} \times \$28.25 = \$226,000$$

The following additional information is available on the company's activities during the
quarter ended March 31:
a. Inventories at the beginning and end of the quarter were as follows:

	January 1, 19x7	March 31, 19x7
Raw materials	–0–	$10,000
Work in process	–0–	50,000
Finished goods	–0–	?

b. Eighty percent of the rental cost for facilities and 90 percent of the utilities cost relate to manufacturing operations. The remaining amounts relate to selling and administrative activities.

Required   1. What conceptual errors, if any, were made in preparing the income statement above?
2. Prepare a schedule of cost of goods manufactured for the first quarter.
3. Prepare a corrected income statement for the first quarter. Your statement should show in detail how the cost of goods sold is computed.
4. Do you agree that the insurance company owes Solar Technology, Inc., $226,000? Explain your answer.

C2–23   **Inventory Computations from Incomplete Data**   Hector P. Wastrel, a careless employee, left some combustible materials near an open flame in Salter Company's plant. The resulting explosion and fire destroyed the entire plant and administrative offices. Justin Quick, the company's controller, and Constance Trueheart, the operations manager, were able to save only a few bits of information as they escaped from the roaring blaze.

"What a disaster," cried Justin. "And the worse part is that we have no records to use in filing an insurance claim."

"I know," replied Constance. "I was in the plant when the explosion occurred, and I managed to grab only this brief summary sheet that contains information on one or two of our costs. It says that our direct labor cost this year has totaled $180,000 and that we have purchased $290,000 in raw materials. But I'm afraid that doesn't help much; the rest of our records are just ashes."

"Well, not completely," said Justin. "I was working on the year-to-date income statement when the explosion knocked me out of my chair. I instinctively held onto the page I was working on, and from what I can make out our sales to date this year have totaled $1,200,000 and our gross margin rate has been 40 percent of sales. Also, I can see that our goods available for sale to customers has totaled $810,000 at cost."

"Maybe we're not so bad off after all," exclaimed Constance. "My sheet says that prime cost has totaled $410,000 so far this year and that manufacturing overhead is 70 percent of conversion cost. Now if we just had some information on our beginning inventories."

"Hey, look at this," cried Justin. "It's a copy of last year's annual report, and it shows what our inventories were when this year started (January 1, 19x3). Let's see, Raw Materials was $18,000, Work in Process was $65,000, and Finished Goods was $45,000."

"Super," yelled Constance. "Let's go to work."

In order to file an insurance claim, the company must determine the amount of cost in its inventories as of August 20, 19x3, the date of the fire. You may assume that all materials used in production during the year were direct materials.

Required   Determine the amount of cost in the Raw Materials, Work in Process, and Finished Goods inventory accounts as of the date of the fire. (Hint: One way to proceed would be to reconstruct the various schedules and statements that would have been affected by the company's inventory accounts during the period.)

Aircraft manufacturers use job-order costing to track the costs of individual aircraft. Each airline orders special seating arrangements, interior trim, audio and video equipment, and exterior painting schemes. Consequently, the cost of each aircraft is unique and a job-order costing system is required.

Systems Design:

Job-Order Costing

LEARNING OBJECTIVES

After studying Chapter 3, you should be able to:

1 Distinguish between process costing and job-order costing, and identify companies that would use each costing method.

2 Identify the documents used to control the flow of costs in a job-order costing system.

3 Compute predetermined overhead rates, and explain why estimated overhead costs (rather than actual overhead costs) are used in the costing process.

4 Prepare journal entries to record the flow of direct materials cost, direct labor cost, and manufacturing overhead cost in a job-order costing system.

5 Apply overhead cost to Work in Process by use of a predetermined overhead rate.

6 Prepare T-accounts to show the flow of costs in a job-order costing system, and prepare schedules of cost of goods manufactured and cost of goods sold.

7 Compute any balance of under- or overapplied overhead cost for a period, and prepare the journal entry needed to close the balance into the appropriate accounts.

8 Explain why multiple overhead rates are needed in many organizations.

9 Define or explain the key terms listed at the end of the chapter.

A s discussed in Chapter 2, product costing is the process of assigning manufacturing costs to manufactured goods. An understanding of this process is vital to any manager, since the way in which a product is costed can have a substantial impact on reported net income, as well as on key decisions made by management in day-to-day operations.

In this chapter and in Chapter 4, we look at product costing from the **absorption cost** approach. The approach is so named because it provides for the absorption of all manufacturing costs, fixed and variable, into units of product. It is also known as the **full cost** approach. Later, in Chapter 8, we will look at product costing from another point of view (called *variable costing*) and then discuss the strengths and weaknesses of the two approaches.

As we study product costing, we must keep clearly in mind that *the essential purpose of any costing system is to accumulate costs for managerial use.* A costing system is not an end in itself. Rather, it is a managerial tool in that it exists to provide the manager with the cost data needed to direct the affairs of an organization.

THE NEED FOR UNIT COST DATA

In studying product costing, we will focus initially on *unit cost of production,* an item of cost data that is generally regarded as being highly useful to managers.

Managers need unit cost data for a variety of reasons. First, unit costs are needed to cost inventories on financial statements and to determine a period's net income. If unit costs are incorrectly computed, then both assets and net income will be equally incorrect, as well as the reported profitability of individual product lines.

Second, unit costs are needed to assist management in planning and control of operations. Budgets must be prepared on expected costs at various operating levels, and reports must be generated to provide feedback on where operations can be improved. The usefulness of these budgets and reports will depend in large part on the accuracy of unit cost data.

Finally, unit costs are needed to assist management in a broad range of decision-making situations. Without unit cost data, managers would find it very difficult to set selling prices for products and services.[1] A knowledge of unit costs is also vital in a number of special decision areas, such as whether to add or drop product lines, whether to make or buy production components, whether to expand or contract operations, and whether to accept special orders at special prices. The particular unit costs that are relevant in this variety of decision-making situations will differ, so we need to learn not only how to derive unit costs but also how to differentiate between those costs that are relevant in a particular situation and those that are not. The matter of relevant costs is reserved until later chapters. For the moment, we are concerned with gaining an understanding of the concept of unit cost in its broadest sense.

TYPES OF COSTING SYSTEMS

Objective 1
Distinguish between process costing and job-order costing, and identify companies that would use each costing method.

In computing unit costs, managers are faced with a difficult problem. Many costs (such as rent) are incurred uniformly from month to month whereas production may change frequently, with production going up in one month and then down in another. In addition to variations in the level of production, several different *types*

---

[1] We should note here that unit cost represents only one of many factors involved in pricing decisions. Pricing is discussed in depth in Appendix L at the end of the book.

of goods may be produced in a given period in the same facility. Under these conditions, how is it possible to determine accurate unit costs? The answer is that the computation of unit costs must involve an *averaging* of some type across time periods and across products. The way in which this averaging is carried out will depend heavily on the type of manufacturing process involved. Two costing systems have emerged in response to variations in the manufacturing process; these two systems are commonly known as *process costing* and *job-order costing*. Each has its own unique way of averaging costs and thus providing management with unit cost data.

Process Costing

A **process costing system** is employed in those situations where manufacturing involves a single, homogeneous product that is produced for long periods at a time. Examples of industries that use process costing include cement, flour, brick, and various utilities (e.g., natural gas, electricity). All of these industries are characterized by a basically homogeneous product that flows evenly through the production process on a continuous basis.

The basic approach in process costing is to accumulate costs in a particular operation or department for an entire period (month, quarter, year) and then to divide this total by the number of units produced during the period. The basic formula for process costing would be:

$$\frac{\text{Total costs of manufacturing}}{\text{Total units produced (gallons, pounds, bottles)}} = \text{Unit cost (per gallon, pound, bottle)}$$

Since one unit of product (gallon, pound, bottle) is completely indistinguishable from any other unit of product, each unit bears the same average cost as any other unit produced during the period. This costing technique results in a broad, average unit cost figure that applies to many thousands of like units flowing in an almost endless stream off the assembly or processing line.

Job-Order Costing

A **job-order costing system** is used in those situations where many *different* products, jobs, or batches of production are being produced each period. Examples of industries that would typically use job-order costing include special-order printing, furniture manufacturing, shipbuilding, and equipment manufacturing.

Job-order costing is also used extensively in the service industries. Hospitals, law firms, movie studios, accounting firms, advertising agencies, and repair shops, for example, all use job-order costing to accumulate costs for accounting and billing purposes. Although the detailed example of job-order costing provided in the following section deals with a manufacturing firm, the reader should keep in mind that the same basic concepts and procedures are used by many service organizations. More is said on this point later in the chapter.

Because the output of firms involved in the industries mentioned above tends to be heterogeneous, managers need a costing system in which costs can be accumulated *by job (or by client or by customer)* and in which distinct unit costs can be determined for each job completed. Job-order costing provides such a system. However, it is a more complex system than that required by process costing. Under job-order costing, rather than dividing total costs by many thousands of like units, one must somehow divide total costs by a few, basically unlike units.

Thus, job-order costing involves certain problems of record keeping and cost assignment that are not found in a process costing system.

Summary of Costing Methods

To summarize this brief introduction to process and job-order costing, regardless of which system one is dealing with, the problem of determining unit costs involves a need for averaging of some type. The essential difference between the process and job-order methods is the way in which this averaging is carried out. In this chapter, we focus on the design of a job-order costing system. In the following chapter, we focus on process costing and also look more closely at the similarities and differences between the two costing methods.

JOB-ORDER COSTING—AN OVERVIEW

Objective 2
Identify the documents used to control the flow of costs in a job-order costing system.

In Chapter 2, the point was made that companies generally classify manufacturing costs into three broad categories:

1. Direct materials.
2. Direct labor.
3. Manufacturing overhead.

As we study the design and operation of a job-order costing system, we will look at each of these costs to see how it is involved in the costing of a unit of product. In doing this, we will also look at the various documents involved in job-order costing and give special emphasis to a key document known as a job cost sheet.

Measuring Direct Materials Cost

The production process begins with the transfer of raw materials from the storeroom to the production line. The bulk of these raw materials will be traceable directly to the goods being produced and will therefore be termed *direct materials*. Other materials, generally termed *indirect materials,* will not be charged to a specific job but rather will be included within the general category of manufacturing overhead. As discussed in Chapter 2, indirect materials would include costs such as glue, nails, and miscellaneous supplies.

Raw materials are drawn from the storeroom on presentation of a **materials requisition form** similar to the form in Exhibit 3–1 for Rand Company.

This form shows that Rand's milling department has requisitioned 150 M46 Housings and 300 G7 Connectors to be used in completing job 2B47. Thus, the requisition form is a detailed source document that (1) specifies the type and quantity of materials to be drawn from the storeroom and (2) identifies the job to which the materials are to be charged. It therefore serves as a means for controlling the flow of materials into production and also for making entries in the accounting records.

If the job being worked on involves a product that is frequently manufactured by a company, then any requisition of materials will typically be based on a **bill of materials** that has been prepared for the product. A bill of materials is simply a control sheet that shows the type and quantity of each item of material needed to complete a unit of product.

EXHIBIT 3–1

Materials Requisition Form

Materials Requisition Number	14873	Date	March 2, 19x2

Job Number to Be Charged   2B47

Department   Milling

Description	Quantity	Unit Cost	Total Cost
M46 Housing	150	$1.64	$246
G7 Connector	300	1.38	414
			$660

Authorized
Signature   *Bill White*

Job Cost Sheet

The cost of direct materials is entered on a *job cost sheet* similar to the one presented in Exhibit 3–2. A **job cost sheet** is a form prepared for each separate job initiated into production. It serves (1) as a means for accumulating materials,

EXHIBIT 3–2

Job Cost Sheet

JOB COST SHEET

Job Number   2B47   Date Initiated   March 2, 19x2

                                             Date Completed _____

Department   Milling   Units Completed _____

Item   Special order coupling

For Stock _____

Direct Materials		Direct Labor			Manufacturing Overhead		
Req. No.	Amount	Ticket	Hours	Amount	Hours	Rate	Amount
14873	$660	843	5	$45			

Cost Summary		Units Shipped		
Direct Materials	$	Date	Number	Balance
Direct Labor	$			
Manufacturing Overhead	$			
Total Cost	$			
Unit Cost	$			

labor, and overhead costs chargeable to a job; and (2) as a means for computing unit costs. Normally, the job cost sheet is not prepared until the accounting department has received notification from the production department that a production order has been issued for a particular job. In turn, a production order is not issued until a definite agreement has been reached with the customer in terms of quantities, prices, and shipment dates.

As direct materials are issued, the accounting department makes entries directly on the job cost sheet, thereby charging the specific job noted on the sheet with the cost of materials used in production. Note from Exhibit 3–2, for example, that the $660 cost for direct materials shown earlier on the materials requisition form is charged to job 2B47 on its job cost sheet. The requisition number 14873 is also recorded on the job cost sheet to make it easier to identify the source document for the direct materials charge. When a job is completed, the cost of materials used can be summarized in the cost summary section as one element involved in determining the total unit cost of the order.

In addition to serving as a means for charging costs to jobs, the job cost sheet also serves as a key part of a firm's accounting records. The job cost sheets relating to all jobs in process at a given point in time form a *subsidiary ledger* to the Work in Process account. Thus, to determine the dollar amount of Work in Process at any point, the manager simply totals the costs appearing on the job cost sheets for all jobs still in production at that moment in time.

Measuring Direct Labor Cost

Direct labor cost is accumulated and measured in much the same way as direct materials cost. Direct labor includes those labor charges that are directly traceable to the particular job in process. By contrast, those labor charges that cannot be traced directly to a particular job, or that can be traced only with the expenditure of great effort, are treated as part of manufacturing overhead. As discussed in Chapter 2, this latter category of labor costs is termed *indirect labor* and would include such tasks as maintenance, supervision, and cleanup.

Labor costs are generally accumulated by means of some type of work record prepared each day by each employee. These work records, often termed **time tickets,** constitute an hour-by-hour summary of the activities completed during the day by the employee. An example of an employee time ticket is shown in Exhibit 3–3. When working on a specific job, the employee enters the job number on the

EXHIBIT 3–3
Employee Time Ticket

Time Ticket No. 843   Date   March 3, 19x2

Employee   Mary Holden   Station   4

Started	Ended	Time Completed	Rate	Amount	Job Number
7:00	12:00	5.0	$9	$45	2B47
12:30	2:30	2.0	9	18	2B50
2:30	3:30	1.0	9	9	Maintenance
Totals		8.0		$72	

Supervisor   R. W. Pace

time ticket and notes the number of hours spent on the particular task involved. When not assigned to a particular job, the employee enters the type of indirect labor tasks to which he or she was assigned (such as cleanup and maintenance) and the number of hours spent on each separate task.

At the end of the day, the time tickets are gathered and the accounting department carefully analyzes each in terms of the number of hours assignable as direct labor to specific jobs and the number of hours assignable to manufacturing overhead as indirect labor. Those hours assignable as direct labor are entered on individual job cost sheets, along with the appropriate charges involved. (See Exhibit 3–2 on page 75 for an example of how direct labor costs are entered on the job cost sheet.) When all direct labor charges associated with a particular job have been accumulated on the job cost sheet, the total can be summarized in the cost summary section. The daily time tickets, in essence, constitute basic source documents used as a basis for labor cost entries into the accounting records.

$$\frac{MOH}{Direct\ Lab\ Hrs} = \$\ DLH\ am$$

The system we have just described is a manual system for recording and posting labor costs. Many companies no longer record labor time manually; rather, they do this recording automatically with the aid of technology such as bar coding. Each employee and each job has a unique bar code. When an employee begins work on a job, he or she scans three bar codes—the bar code on his or her identity badge, another bar code signaling that work is beginning on a job, and the bar code attached to the job itself. This information is fed automatically by means of an electronic network to a computer where it is recorded. When the employee's work on the job is completed, he or she again scans three bar codes—the bar code on his or her identity badge, another bar code indicating that work is finished on the job, and the bar code attached to the job. This information is again relayed to the computer, and a time ticket is automatically prepared. Since all of the source data is already in computer files, the labor costs are automatically posted to job cost sheets (or their electronic equivalents). Computers, coupled with technology such as bar codes, can eliminate much of the drudgery involved in routine bookkeeping activities while at the same time increasing timeliness and accuracy.

Application of Manufacturing Overhead

Manufacturing overhead must be considered along with direct materials and direct labor in determining unit costs of production. However, the assignment of manufacturing overhead to units of product is often a difficult task. There are several reasons why this is so.

Objective 3
Compute predetermined overhead rates, and explain why estimated overhead costs (rather than actual overhead costs) are used in the costing process.

First, as explained in Chapter 2, manufacturing overhead is an *indirect* cost to units of product and therefore can't be traced directly to a particular product or job. Second, manufacturing overhead consists of many unlike items, involving both variable and fixed costs. It ranges from the grease used in machines to the annual salary of the production superintendent. Finally, firms with large seasonal variations in production often find that even though output is fluctuating, manufacturing overhead costs tend to remain relatively constant. The reason is that fixed costs generally constitute a large part of manufacturing overhead.

Given these problems, about the only way to assign overhead costs to products is to do so through an allocation process. This allocation of overhead costs to products is accomplished by selecting an *activity base* that is common to all products that the company manufactures or to all services that it renders. Then by means of this base, an appropriate amount of overhead cost is assigned to each product or service. The trick, of course, is to choose the right base so that the overhead application will be equitable between jobs.

Historically, the most widely used activity bases have been direct labor-hours (DLH) and direct labor cost, with machine-hours (MH) and even units of product (where a company has only a single product) also used to some extent.

Once an activity base has been chosen, it is divided into the estimated total manufacturing overhead cost of the period in order to obtain a **predetermined overhead rate.** The rate is called predetermined because it is computed *before* the period begins and because it is based entirely on estimated data. After the predetermined overhead rate has been computed, it is then used to apply overhead cost to jobs. In sum, the formula for computing the predetermined overhead rate is:

$$\frac{\text{Estimated total manufacturing overhead costs}}{\text{Estimated total units in the base (MH, DLH, etc.)}} = \text{Predetermined overhead rate}$$

Instead of using the term *estimated* in this formula, some companies prefer to use the terms *forecasted* or *budgeted*.

The Need for Estimated Data

Actual overhead costs are rarely used in overhead costing because they are not available until *after* a period is over. This is too late so far as computing unit costs is concerned, since the manager must have unit cost data available at once in order to set prices on products and make other key marketing and operating decisions. The postponing of such decisions until year-end (when actual overhead cost data are available) would destroy an organization's ability to compete effectively. Therefore, in order to have timely data for decision making, most firms *estimate* total overhead costs at the beginning of a year, *estimate* the level of activity for the year, and develop a predetermined overhead rate based on these estimates. Such rates are widely used by both manufacturing and service organizations for costing purposes.

Using the Predetermined Overhead Rate

The assigning of overhead cost to jobs (and thereby to units of product) is called **overhead application.** To illustrate the steps involved, assume that a firm has estimated its total manufacturing overhead costs for the year to be $320,000 and has estimated 40,000 total direct labor-hours for the year. Its predetermined overhead rate for the year would be $8 per direct labor-hour, as shown below:

$$\frac{\$320,000}{40,000 \text{ direct labor-hours}} = \$8 \text{ per direct labor-hour}$$

If a particular job required 27 direct labor-hours to complete, then $216 of overhead cost (27 hours × $8 = $216) would be applied to that job. This overhead application is shown on the job cost sheet in Exhibit 3–4. When a company applies overhead cost to jobs as we have done—that is, by multiplying actual activity times the predetermined overhead rate—it is using a **normal cost system.**

Whether the overhead application in Exhibit 3–4 is made slowly as the job is worked on during the period, or in a single application at the time of completion, is a matter of choice and convenience to the company involved. If a job is not completed at year-end, however, overhead should be applied to the extent needed to properly value the work in process inventory.

Although estimates are involved in computing predetermined overhead rates, managers typically become very skilled at making these estimates. As a result, predetermined overhead rates are generally quite accurate, and any difference between the amount of overhead cost that is actually incurred during a period and the amount that is applied to products is usually quite small. This point is discussed in more detail later in the chapter.

EXHIBIT 3–4

A Completed Job Cost Sheet

JOB COST SHEET

Job Number   2B47

Date Initiated   March 2, 19x2

Date Completed   March 8, 19x2

Department   Milling

Item   Special order coupling

Units Completed   150

For Stock _____

Direct Materials		Direct Labor			Manufacturing Overhead		
Req. No.	Amount	Ticket	Hours	Amount	Hours	Rate	Amount
14873	$ 660	843	5	$ 45	27	$8/DLH	$216
14875	506	846	8	60			
14912	238	850	4	21			
	$1,404	851	10	54			
			27	$180			

Cost Summary		Units Shipped		
Direct Materials	$1,404	Date	Number	Balance
Direct Labor	$ 180	3/8/x2	—	150
Manufacturing Overhead	$ 216			
Total Cost	$1,800			
Unit Cost	$ 12*			

* $1,800 ÷ 150 units = $12 per unit.

What Drives Overhead Cost?

We stated in Chapter 2 that major shifts are taking place in the structure of costs in some industries. In the past, direct labor has typically accounted for up to 60 percent of the cost of many products with overhead cost making up only a portion of the remainder. With the advent of automation, however, sophisticated new machines are now taking over various functions that used to be performed by direct labor workers. Robots are appearing on the assembly line, and computer-integrated manufacturing (CIM), which requires almost no direct labor input, is being used to control the entire manufacturing process in some companies. As a result of these shifts toward automation, direct labor is becoming less of a factor in the cost of a number of products.

This decrease in the importance of direct labor is accompanied by an increase in the importance of manufacturing overhead, since costly equipment must be depreciated, expensive software must be developed to control manufacturing operations, and so forth. Where processes are largely automated (sometimes referred to as *capital intensive*), direct labor probably has little to do with the incurrence of overhead cost and therefore may not be appropriate as a base for computing overhead rates. Instead, a base should be used that acts as a *cost driver* in the incurrence of overhead cost. A **cost driver** is a measure of activity, such as machine-hours, beds occupied, computer time, flight-hours, or miles driven that is a *causal factor* in the incurrence of cost in an organization. If a base is used to compute overhead rates that does not ''drive'' overhead costs, then the result will be inaccurate rates and distorted product costs.

We must hasten to add that although direct labor is decreasing in importance in some industries, in other industries it continues to be a significant part of total product cost. In these latter industries, therefore, it remains a viable base for computing overhead rates and for applying overhead cost to products. The key point managers must recognize is that direct labor is not an appropriate allocation base in *every* situation and indeed has become completely irrelevant in some settings. This point is discussed further in Chapter 5 where we deal with product costing in the new manufacturing environment.

FOCUS ON CURRENT PRACTICE

Despite the decreasing importance of direct labor in many industries, it is still widely used as a base in assigning overhead cost to products and services. A recent survey of 244 companies found that direct labor is used more often than any other base, and that this holds true regardless of the size of the company or the type of operation involved. (The survey covered companies in traditional manufacturing, high-tech operations, and service activities.) Results of the survey were (in terms of the *primary* base used):[2]

	Percent of Companies Using the Base
Direct labor (either hours or cost)	62%
Machine-hours.	12
Production volume.	5
Direct material (either weight or cost)	8
Revenue	3
Other (primarily combinations of more than one base)	10
Total	100%

Although direct labor is still widely used as an allocation base, evidence from other studies suggests that the trend is downward and that over time its use may be slowly decreasing.[3]

Computation of Unit Costs

With the application of manufacturing overhead to the job cost sheet, total costs of the job can be summarized in the cost summary section. (See Exhibit 3–4 for an example of a completed job cost sheet.) The cost of the individual units in the job

---

[2] Jeffrey R. Cohen and Laurence Paquette, ''Management Accounting Practices: Perceptions of Controllers,'' *Journal of Cost Management* 5, no. 3 (Fall 1991), p. 75.

[3] See Henry R. Schwarzbach, ''The Impact of Automation on Accounting for Indirect Costs,'' *Management Accounting* 67, no. 3 (December 1985); and James R. Emore and Joseph A. Ness, ''The Slow Pace of Meaningful Change in Cost Systems,'' *Journal of Cost Management* 4, no. 4 (Winter 1991). In his 1985 study, Schwarzbach surveyed 112 companies and found that nearly 94 percent used direct labor to some extent (either as the primary or secondary base) in overhead costing. In their 1991 study, Emore and Ness surveyed 70 midwestern manufacturers and found that only 74 percent used direct labor (either as the primary or secondary base) in overhead costing.

can then be obtained by dividing the total costs by the number of units produced. The completed job cost sheet is then ready to be transferred to the finished goods inventory file, where it will serve as a basis for either costing unsold units in the ending inventory or charging expense for units sold.

Summary of Document Flows

The sequence of events just discussed is summarized in Exhibit 3–5. A careful study of the flow of documents in this exhibit will provide a visual overview of the overall operation of a job-order costing system.

JOB-ORDER COSTING—THE FLOW OF COSTS

Having obtained a broad, conceptual perspective of the operation of a job-order costing system, we are now prepared to take a look at the flow of actual costs through the system itself. We shall consider a single month's activity for a hypothetical company, presenting all data in summary form. As a basis for discussion, let us assume that Rand Company had two jobs in process during April, the first month of its fiscal year. Job A was started during March and had $30,000 in manufacturing costs (materials, labor, and overhead) already accumulated on April 1. Job B was started during April.

Objective 4
Prepare journal entries to record the flow of direct materials cost, direct labor cost, and manufacturing overhead cost in a job-order costing system.

The Purchase and Issue of Materials

On April 1, Rand Company had $7,000 in raw materials on hand. During the month, the company purchased an additional $60,000 in raw materials. The purchase is recorded in entry (1) below:

(1)

Raw Materials.	60,000	
Accounts Payable		60,000

As explained in Chapter 2, Raw Materials is an asset account. Thus, when raw materials are purchased, they are initially recorded as an asset—not as an expense.

Issue of Direct and Indirect Materials During April, $52,000 in raw materials were requisitioned from the storeroom for use in production. Entry (2) records the issue of the materials to the production departments.

(2)

Work in Process.	50,000	
Manufacturing Overhead	2,000	
Raw Materials.		52,000

The materials charged to Work in Process represent direct materials assignable to specific jobs on the production line. As these materials are entered into the Work in Process account, they are also recorded on the separate job cost sheets to which they relate. This point is illustrated in Exhibit 3–6, where $28,000 of the $50,000 in direct materials is charged to job A's cost sheet and the remaining $22,000 is charged to job B's cost sheet.

The $2,000 charged to Manufacturing Overhead in entry (2) represents indirect materials used in production during April. Observe that the Manufacturing Overhead account is separate from the Work in Process account. The purpose of the

EXHIBIT 3–5

The Flow of Documents in a Job-Order Costing System

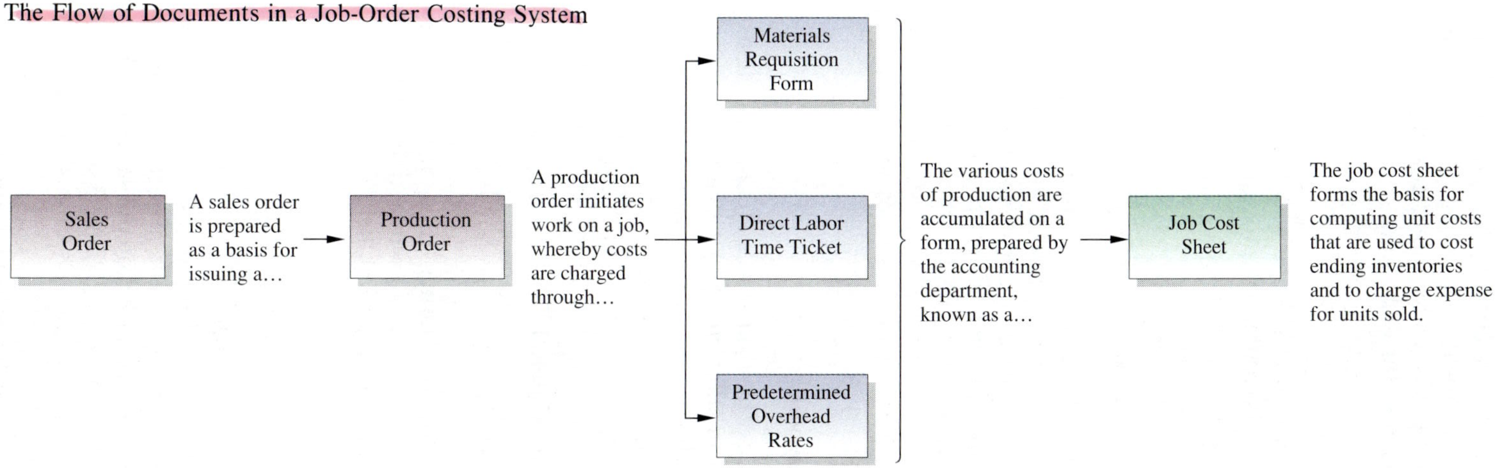

Sales Order

A sales order is prepared as a basis for issuing a...

Production Order

A production order initiates work on a job, whereby costs are charged through...

Materials Requisition Form

Direct Labor Time Ticket

Predetermined Overhead Rates

The various costs of production are accumulated on a form, prepared by the accounting department, known as a...

Job Cost Sheet

The job cost sheet forms the basis for computing unit costs that are used to cost ending inventories and to charge expense for units sold.

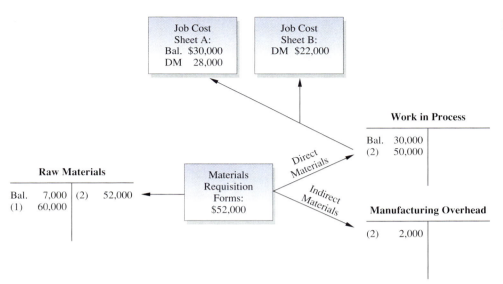

EXHIBIT 3–6
Raw Materials Cost Flows

DM = Direct materials.

Manufacturing Overhead account is to accumulate all manufacturing overhead costs as they are incurred during a period.

Before leaving Exhibit 3–6 we need to point out one additional thing. Notice from the exhibit that the job cost sheet for job A contains a beginning balance of $30,000. We stated earlier that this balance represents the cost of work done during March that has been carried forward to April. Also note that the Work in Process account contains the same $30,000 balance. *The reason the $30,000 appears in both places is that the Work in Process account is a control account and the job cost sheets form a subsidiary ledger. Thus, the Work in Process account contains a summarized total of all costs appearing on the individual job cost sheets for all jobs in process at any given point in time.* (Since Rand Company had only job A in process at the beginning of April, job A's $30,000 balance on that date is equal to the balance in the Work in Process account.)

Issue of Direct Materials Only   Sometimes the materials drawn from the Raw Materials inventory account are all direct materials. In this case, the entry to record the issue of the materials into production would be:

Work in Process. XXX
    Raw Materials.   XXX

Labor Cost

As work is performed in various departments of Rand Company from day to day, employee time tickets are generated, collected, and forwarded to the accounting department. There the tickets are costed according to the various rates paid to the employees, and the resulting costs are classified as being either direct or indirect labor. This costing and classification for April resulted in the following entry:

(3)

Work in Process. 60,000
Manufacturing Overhead 15,000
    Salaries and Wages Payable   75,000

EXHIBIT 3–7
Labor Cost Flows

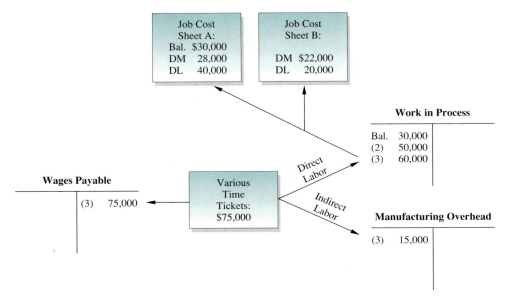

DM = Direct materials; DL = Direct labor.

Only that portion of labor cost that represents direct labor is added to the Work in Process account. For Rand Company, this amounted to $60,000 for April.

At the same time that direct labor costs are added to Work in Process they are also added to the individual job cost sheets, as shown in Exhibit 3–7. During April, $40,000 of direct labor cost was chargeable to job A and the remaining $20,000 was chargeable to job B.

The labor costs charged to Manufacturing Overhead represent the indirect labor costs of the period, such as supervision, janitorial work, and maintenance.

Manufacturing Overhead Costs

As we learned in Chapter 2, all costs of operating the factory other than direct materials and direct labor are classified as manufacturing overhead costs. These costs are entered directly into the Manufacturing Overhead account as they are incurred. To illustrate, assume that Rand Company incurred the following general factory costs during April:

Utilities (heat, water, and power)	$21,000
Rent on equipment	16,000
Miscellaneous factory costs	3,000
Total	$40,000

The entry to record the incurrence of these costs would be:

(4)

Manufacturing Overhead	40,000	
Accounts Payable		40,000

In addition, let us assume that during April, Rand Company recognized $13,000 in accrued property taxes and $7,000 in insurance expired on factory buildings and equipment. The entry to record these items would be:

(5)

Manufacturing Overhead	20,000	
Property Taxes Payable		13,000
Prepaid Insurance		7,000

Finally, let us assume that the company recognized $18,000 in depreciation on factory equipment during April. The entry to record the accrual of depreciation would be:

(6)

Manufacturing Overhead	18,000	
Accumulated Depreciation		18,000

In short, *all* manufacturing overhead costs are recorded directly into the Manufacturing Overhead account as they are incurred day by day throughout a period. It is important for the reader to understand that Manufacturing Overhead is a control account consisting of many—perhaps thousands—of subsidiary accounts such as Indirect Materials, Indirect Labor, Factory Utilities, and so forth. *As the Manufacturing Overhead account is debited for costs during a period, the various subsidiary accounts are also debited.* In the example above and also in the assignment material for this chapter, we omit the entries to the subsidiary accounts for the sake of brevity.

The Application of Manufacturing Overhead

How is the Work in Process account charged for manufacturing overhead cost? The answer is, by means of the predetermined overhead rate. Recall from our discussion earlier in the chapter that for costing purposes a predetermined overhead rate is established at the beginning of each year. The rate is calculated by dividing the estimated manufacturing overhead cost for the year by the estimated activity (measured in machine-hours, direct labor-hours, or some other base). As the year progresses, overhead cost is then applied to each job by multiplying the number of hours required to complete the job by the predetermined overhead rate that has been set.

To illustrate the cost flows involved, assume that Rand Company has used machine-hours in computing its predetermined overhead rate and that this rate is $6 per machine-hour. Also assume that during April, 10,000 machine-hours were worked on job A and 5,000 machine-hours were worked on job B (a total of 15,000 machine-hours). Thus, $90,000 in overhead cost (15,000 machine-hours × $6 = $90,000) would be applied to Work in Process. The entry to record the application would be:

Objective 5
Apply overhead cost to Work in Process by means of the predetermined overhead rate.

(7)

Work in Process.	90,000	
Manufacturing Overhead		90,000

The flow of costs through the Manufacturing Overhead account is shown in T-account format in Exhibit 3–8.

The "actual overhead costs" in the Manufacturing Overhead account in Exhibit 3–8 are the costs that were added to the account in entries (2)–(6). Observe that the incurrence of these actual overhead costs [entries (2)–(6)] and the application of overhead to Work in Process [entry (7)] represent two separate and distinct processes.

EXHIBIT 3–8
The Flow of Costs in Overhead Application

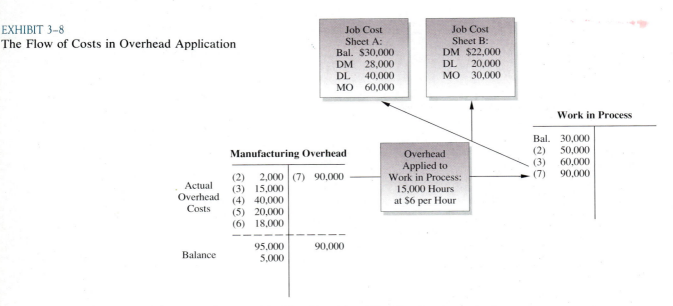

DM = Direct materials; DL = Direct labor; MO = Manufacturing overhead.

The Concept of a Clearing Account   The Manufacturing Overhead account operates as a clearing account. As we have noted, actual factory overhead costs are charged to it as they are incurred day by day throughout the year. At certain intervals during the year, usually when a job is completed, overhead cost is released from the Manufacturing Overhead account and is applied to the Work in Process account by means of the predetermined overhead rate. This sequence of events is illustrated below:

Manufacturing Overhead (a clearing account)	
Actual overhead costs are charged to the account as these costs are incurred day by day throughout the period. →	→ Overhead is applied to Work in Process on a periodic basis by means of the predetermined overhead rate.

As we emphasized earlier, the predetermined overhead rate is based entirely on estimates of what overhead costs are *expected* to be, and it is established before the year begins. As a result, the overhead cost applied during a year may turn out to be more or less than the overhead cost that is actually incurred. For example, notice from Exhibit 3–8 that Rand Company's actual overhead costs for the period are $5,000 greater than the overhead cost that has been applied to Work in Process, resulting in a $5,000 debit balance in the Manufacturing Overhead account. We will reserve discussion of what to do with this $5,000 balance until the next section, Problems of Overhead Application.

For the moment, we can conclude by noting from Exhibit 3–8 that the cost of a completed job consists of the actual materials cost of the job, the actual labor cost of the job, and an *applied* amount of overhead cost to the job. The fact that it is applied overhead cost (not actual overhead cost) that goes into the Work in Process account and onto the job cost sheets is a subtle point that is easy to miss. Thus, this portion of the chapter requires special study and consideration.

Nonmanufacturing Costs

In addition to incurring costs such as salaries, utilities, and insurance as part of the operation of the factory, manufacturing companies will also incur these same kinds of costs in relation to other parts of their operations. For example, there will be these types of costs arising from activities in the "front office" where secretaries, top management, and others work. There will be identical kinds of costs arising from the operation of the sales staff. *The costs of these nonfactory operations should not go into the Manufacturing Overhead account because the incurrence of these costs is not related to the manufacture of products.* Rather, these costs should be treated as expenses of the period, as explained in Chapter 2, and charged directly to the income statement. To illustrate, assume that Rand Company incurred selling and administrative costs as follows during April:

Top-management salaries	$21,000
Other office salaries.	9,000
Total salaries.	$30,000

The entry to record these salaries would be:

(8)

Salaries Expense	30,000	
Salaries and Wages Payable		30,000

Assume that depreciation on office equipment during April was $7,000. The entry would be:

(9)

Depreciation Expense	7,000	
Accumulated Depreciation		7,000

Pay particular attention to the difference between this entry and entry (6) on page 85, where we recorded depreciation on factory equipment.

Finally, assume that advertising was $42,000 and that other selling and administrative expenses in April totaled $8,000. The entry to record these items would be:

(10)

Advertising Expense.	42,000	
Other Selling and Administrative Expense	8,000	
Accounts Payable		50,000

Since the amounts in entries (8) through (10) all go directly into expense accounts, they will have no effect on the costing of Rand Company's production for April. The same will be true of all other selling and administrative expenses incurred during April, including sales commissions, depreciation on sales equipment, rent on office facilities, insurance on office facilities, and related costs.

Cost of Goods Manufactured

When a job has been completed, the finished output is transferred from the production departments to the finished goods warehouse. By this time, the accounting department will have charged the job with direct materials and direct labor cost, and the job will have absorbed a portion of manufacturing overhead through the application process discussed earlier. A transfer of these costs must be made within the costing system that *parallels* the physical transfer of the goods to the finished goods warehouse. The transfer within the costing system will be to move the costs of the completed job out of the Work in Process account and into the Finished Goods account. The sum of all amounts transferred between these two accounts represents the cost of goods manufactured for the period. (This point was illustrated earlier in Exhibit 2–5 in Chapter 2. The reader may wish to go back to Exhibit 2–5 and refresh this point before reading on.)

In the case of Rand Company, let us assume that job A was completed during April. The entry to transfer the cost of job A from Work in Process to Finished Goods would be:

(11)

Finished Goods	158,000	
Work in Process.		158,000

The $158,000 represents the completed cost of job A, as shown on the job cost sheet in Exhibit 3–8. Since job A was the only job completed during April, the $158,000 also represents the cost of goods manufactured for the month.

Job B was not completed by month-end, so its cost will remain in the Work in Process account and carry over to the next month. If a balance sheet is prepared at the end of April, the cost accumulated thus far on job B will appear under the caption "Work in process inventory" in the assets section.

Cost of Goods Sold

As units in finished goods are shipped to fill customers' orders, the unit cost appearing on the job cost sheets is used as a basis for transferring the cost of the items sold from the Finished Goods account into the Cost of Goods Sold account. If a complete job is shipped, as in the case where a job has been done to a customer's specifications, then it is a simple matter to transfer the entire cost appearing on the job cost sheet into the Cost of Goods Sold account. In most cases, however, only a portion of the units involved in a particular job will be sold. In these situations, the unit cost is particularly important in knowing how much product cost should be removed from Finished Goods and charged into Cost of Goods Sold.

For Rand Company, we will assume that three fourths of the units in job A were shipped to customers by month-end. The total selling price of these units was $225,000. The entries needed to record the sale would be (all sales are on account):

(12)

Accounts Receivable.	225,000	
Sales		225,000

(13)

Cost of Goods Sold	118,500	
Finished Goods		118,500
($158,000 total cost × ¾ = $118,500)		

With entry (13), the flow of costs through our job-order costing system is completed.

Summary of Cost Flows

To pull the entire Rand Company example together, a summary of cost flows is presented in T-account form in Exhibit 3–9 (page 90). The flows of costs through the exhibit are keyed to the numbers (1) through (13). These numbers relate to the numbers of the transactions appearing on the preceding pages.

Objective 6
Prepare T-accounts to show the flow of costs in a job-order costing system, and prepare schedules of cost of goods manufactured and cost of goods sold.

Exhibit 3–10 (page 91) presents a schedule of cost of goods manufactured and a schedule of cost of goods sold for Rand Company. Note particularly from Exhibit 3–10 that the cost of goods manufactured for the month ($158,000) agrees with the amount transferred from Work in Process to Finished Goods for the month as recorded earlier in entry (11). Also note that this $158,000 figure is used in computing the cost of goods sold for the month.

An income statement for April is presented in Exhibit 3–11 (page 91). Observe that the cost of goods sold figure on this statement ($123,500) is carried down from Exhibit 3–10.

PROBLEMS OF OVERHEAD APPLICATION

Before concluding our discussion of job-order costing, we need to briefly consider three potential problem areas relating to overhead application. These are: (1) the computation of underapplied and overapplied overhead, (2) the disposition of any balance remaining in the Manufacturing Overhead account at the end of a period, and (3) the use of multiple predetermined overhead rates by some companies.

Objective 7
Compute any balance of under- or overapplied overhead cost for a period, and prepare the journal entry needed to close the balance into the appropriate accounts.

Underapplied and Overapplied Overhead

Since the predetermined overhead rate is established before a period begins and is based entirely on estimated data, there generally will be a difference between the amount of overhead cost applied to Work in Process and the amount of overhead cost actually incurred during a period. In the case of Rand Company, for example, the predetermined overhead rate of $6 per hour resulted in $90,000 of overhead cost being applied to Work in Process, whereas actual overhead costs for April proved to be $95,000 (see Exhibit 3–8). The difference between the overhead cost applied to Work in Process and the actual overhead costs of a period is termed either **underapplied** or **overapplied overhead.** For Rand Company, overhead was underapplied because the applied cost ($90,000) was $5,000 less than the actual cost ($95,000). If the tables had been reversed and the company had applied $95,000 in overhead cost to Work in Process while incurring actual overhead costs of only $90,000, then a situation of overapplied overhead would have existed.

What is the cause of underapplied or overapplied overhead? Generally, the cause can be traced to one of two factors. First, the cost of inputs (lubricants, utilities, and so forth) may change from what was estimated at the beginning of the period because of external market forces. Second, the actual level of activity may be different from what was estimated at the beginning of the period because of either greater or less demand for the company's goods and services. To illustrate, refer again to the formula used in computing the predetermined overhead rate:

$$\frac{\text{Estimated total manufacturing overhead costs}}{\text{Estimated total units in the base (machine-hours, etc.)}} = \text{Predetermined overhead rate}$$

If either the estimated cost or the estimated level of activity used in this formula differs from the actual cost or the actual level of activity for a period, then the predetermined overhead rate will prove to be inaccurate. The result will be either under- or overapplied overhead for the period. Assume, for example, that two companies have prepared the following estimated data for the year 19x1:

EXHIBIT 3–9
Summary of Cost Flows—Rand Company

Accounts Receivable			Accounts Payable			Capital Stock	
XX*				XX			XX

Prepaid Insurance						Retained Earnings	
XX							XX

Raw Materials			Salaries and Wages Payable			Sales	
Bal.	7,000			XX			

Work in Process			Property Taxes Payable			Cost of Goods Sold	
Bal.	30,000			XX			

Salaries Expense

Finished Goods						Depreciation Expense	
Bal.	10,000						

Advertising Expense

Accumulated Depreciation						Other Selling and Administrative Expense	
	XX						

Manufacturing Overhead

* XX = Normal balance in the account (for example, Accounts Receivable normally carries a debit balance).

Cost of Goods Manufactured

Direct materials:

Raw materials inventory, April 1	$ 7,000	
Add: Purchases of raw materials	60,000	
Total raw materials available	67,000	
Deduct: Raw materials inventory, April 30.	15,000	
Raw materials used in production	$52,000	
Less indirect materials (below)	2,000	$ 50,000
Direct labor		60,000

Manufacturing overhead:

Indirect materials	2,000	
Indirect labor	15,000	
Utilities	21,000	
Rent	16,000	
Miscellaneous factory costs	3,000	
Property taxes	13,000	
Insurance	7,000	
Depreciation	18,000	
Actual overhead costs	95,000	
Less underapplied overhead	5,000*	
Overhead applied to work in process		90,000
Total manufacturing costs		200,000
Add: Beginning work in process inventory		30,000
		230,000
Deduct: Ending work in process inventory		72,000
Cost of goods manufactured		$158,000

Cost of Goods Sold

Opening finished goods inventory		$ 10,000
Add: Cost of goods manufactured		158,000
Goods available for sale		168,000
Ending finished goods inventory		49,500
Cost of goods sold		118,500
Add: Underapplied overhead		5,000
Adjusted cost of goods sold		$123,500

EXHIBIT 3–10

Schedules of Cost of Goods Manufactured and Cost of Goods Sold

* Note that underapplied overhead must be deducted from actual overhead costs and only the difference ($90,000) is added to direct materials and direct labor. The reason only $90,000 is added to materials and labor is that the schedule of cost of goods manufactured represents a summary of costs flowing through the Work in Process account during a period and therefore must exclude any overhead costs that were incurred but never applied to production. If a reverse situation had existed and overhead had been overapplied during the period, then the amount of overapplied overhead would have been added to actual overhead costs on the schedule. This would have brought the actual overhead costs up to the amount that had been applied to production.

Also note that the underapplied overhead deducted on the schedule of cost of goods manufactured is added to cost of goods sold. The reverse would be true if overhead had been overapplied.

EXHIBIT 3–11

RAND COMPANY

Income Statement
For the Month Ending April 30, 19xx

Sales		$225,000
Less cost of goods sold ($118,500 + $5,000)		123,500
Gross margin		101,500

Less selling and administrative expenses:

Salaries expense	$30,000	
Depreciation expense	7,000	
Advertising expense	42,000	
Other expense	8,000	87,000
Net income		$ 14,500

	Company	
	A	**B**
Predetermined overhead rate based on	Machine-hours	Direct materials cost
Estimated manufacturing overhead for 19x1.	$300,000 (a)	$120,000 (a)
Estimated machine-hours for 19x1	75,000 (b)	—
Estimated direct materials cost for 19x1	—	$ 80,000 (b)
Predetermined overhead rate, (a) ÷ (b).	$4 per machine-hour	150% of direct materials cost

Now assume that because of changes in the cost of inputs and changes in demand for the companies' products, the *actual* overhead cost and the *actual* activity recorded during the year in each company are as follows:

	Company	
	A	**B**
Actual manufacturing overhead costs	$290,000	$130,000
Actual machine-hours	68,000	—
Actual direct materials cost.	—	$ 90,000

For each company, note that the actual data for both cost and activity differ from the estimates used in computing the predetermined overhead rate. Therefore, the predetermined overhead rates used by the companies will be somewhat inaccurate, and either too much or too little overhead cost will be applied to products, as shown below:

	Company	
	A	**B**
Actual manufacturing overhead costs	$290,000	$130,000
Manufacturing overhead cost applied to Work in Process during 19x1:		
68,000 *actual* machine-hours × $4	272,000	
$90,000 *actual* direct materials cost × 150%		135,000
Underapplied (overapplied) overhead	$ 18,000	$ (5,000)

For Company A, notice that the amount of overhead cost that has been applied to Work in Process ($272,000) is less than the actual overhead cost for the year ($290,000). Therefore, overhead is underapplied. Also notice that the original estimate of overhead in Company A ($300,000) is not directly involved in this computation. Its impact is felt only through the $4 predetermined overhead rate that is used.

For Company B, the amount of overhead cost that has been applied to Work in Process ($135,000) is greater than the actual overhead cost for the year ($130,000), and so a situation of overapplied overhead exists.

A summary of the concepts discussed above is presented in Exhibit 3–12.

Disposition of Under- or Overapplied Overhead Balances

What disposition should be made of any under- or overapplied balance remaining in the Manufacturing Overhead account at the end of a period? Generally, any balance in the account is treated in one of two ways:

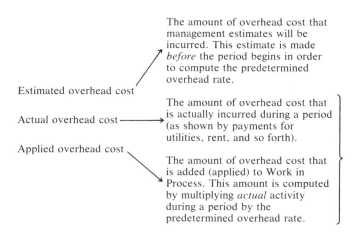

EXHIBIT 3-12
Summary of Overhead
Concepts

Estimated overhead cost — The amount of overhead cost that management estimates will be incurred. This estimate is made *before* the period begins in order to compute the predetermined overhead rate.

Actual overhead cost — The amount of overhead cost that is actually incurred during a period (as shown by payments for utilities, rent, and so forth).

Applied overhead cost — The amount of overhead cost that is added (applied) to Work in Process. This amount is computed by multiplying *actual* activity during a period by the predetermined overhead rate.

The difference between these two amounts represents under- or overapplied overhead.

1. Closed out to Cost of Goods Sold.
2. Allocated between Work in Process, Finished Goods, and Cost of Goods Sold in proportion to the ending balances in these accounts.[4]

The choice between these two approaches depends in large part on the amount of under- or overapplied overhead involved. The greater the amount, the more likely a company is to choose the second alternative.

Closed Out to Cost of Goods Sold   If the balance in the Manufacturing Overhead account is small, most companies will close it out directly to Cost of Goods Sold, since this approach is simpler than allocation. Returning to the example of Rand Company, the entry to close the underapplied overhead to Cost of Goods sold would be (see Exhibit 3–9 for the $5,000 cost figure):

(14)

Cost of Goods Sold	5,000	
Manufacturing Overhead		5,000

With this entry, the cost of goods sold for April increases to $123,500, as shown earlier:

Cost of goods sold (from Exhibit 3–9)	$118,500
Add underapplied overhead [entry (14) above] . . .	5,000
Adjusted cost of goods sold	$123,500

After this adjustment has been made, Rand Company's income statement for April will appear as was shown earlier in Exhibit 3–11.

Allocated between Accounts   Allocation of under- or overapplied overhead between Work in Process, Finished Goods, and Cost of Goods Sold is more accurate than closing the entire balance into Cost of Goods Sold. The reason is that allocation assigns overhead costs to where they would have gone in the first place had it not been for the errors in the estimates going into the predetermined overhead

[4] Some firms prefer to make the allocation on a basis of the amount of *overhead cost* in the above accounts at the end of a period. This approach to allocation will yield more accurate results in those situations where the amount of overhead cost differs substantially between jobs. For purposes of consistency, when we allocate in this book it will always be on a basis of the ending balances in the above accounts.

rate. Although allocation is more accurate than direct write-off, it is used less often in actual practice because of the time and difficulty involved in the allocation process. Most managers believe that the greater accuracy simply isn't worth the extra effort that allocation requires, particularly when the dollar amounts are small.

Had we chosen to allocate the underapplied overhead in the Rand Company example, the computations and entry would have been:

Work in process inventory, April 30	$ 72,000	30.0%
Finished goods inventory, April 30	49,500	20.6
Cost of goods sold	118,500	49.4
Total cost.	$240,000	100.0%
Work in Process (30.0% × $5,000).	1,500	
Finished Goods (20.6% × $5,000)	1,030	
Cost of Goods Sold (49.4% × $5,000)	2,470	
Manufacturing Overhead		5,000

If overhead had been overapplied, the entry above would have been just the reverse, since a credit balance would have existed in the Manufacturing Overhead account.

Multiple Predetermined Overhead Rates

Objective 8
Explain why multiple overhead rates are needed in many organizations.

Our discussion in this chapter has assumed that a single overhead rate was being used throughout an entire factory operation. In small companies, and even in some medium-sized companies, a single overhead rate (called a **plantwide overhead rate**) is used and is entirely adequate as a means of allocating overhead costs to production jobs. But in larger companies, **multiple predetermined overhead rates** are common for the reason that a single rate may not be capable of equitably handling the overhead costs of all departments. One department may be labor intensive, for example, and rely almost solely on the efforts of workers in performing needed functions. Allocation of overhead costs in such a department could, perhaps, be done most equitably on a basis of labor-hours or labor cost. Another department in the same factory may be machine intensive, requiring little in the way of worker effort. Allocation of overhead costs in this department could, perhaps, be done most equitably on a basis of machine-hours.

In short, larger organizations often have many predetermined overhead rates—perhaps a different one for each department. As a unit of product moves along the production line, overhead is applied in each department, according to the various overhead rates that have been set. The accumulation of all of these overhead applications represents the total overhead cost of the job.

A General Model of Product Cost Flows

The flow of costs in a product costing system can be presented in general model form, as shown in Exhibit 3–13. This model applies as much to a process costing system as it does to a job-order costing system. Visual inspection of the model can be very helpful in gaining a perspective as to how costs enter a system, flow through it, and finally end up as cost of goods sold on the income statement.

EXHIBIT 3–13

A General Model of Cost Flows

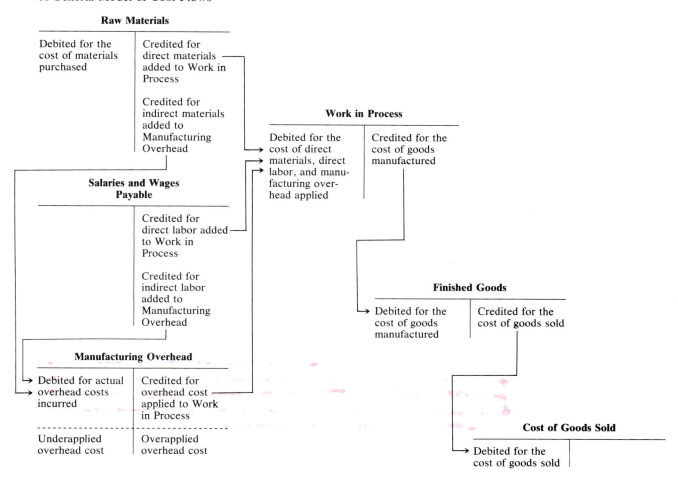

JOB-ORDER COSTING IN SERVICE COMPANIES

We stated earlier in the chapter that job-order costing is used extensively in service organizations such as law firms, movie studios, hospitals, and repair shops, as well as in manufacturing companies. In a law firm, for example, each client represents a "job," and the costs of that job are accumulated day by day on a job cost sheet as the client's case is handled by the firm. Legal forms and similar inputs represent the direct materials for the job; the time expended by attorneys represents the direct labor; and the costs of secretaries, clerks, rent, depreciation, and so forth, represent the overhead.

In a movie studio, each picture produced by the studio is a "job," and costs for direct materials (costumes, props, film, etc.) and direct labor (actors, directors, and extras) are carefully accounted for and charged to each picture's job cost sheet. A proportionate share of the studio's overhead costs, such as utilities, depreciation of equipment, salaries of maintenance workers, and so forth, is also charged to each picture. In a movie studio, overhead would typically be applied to jobs on a basis of camera time, or space and time occupied in a studio, rather than applied on a basis of actors' time or cost. On the other hand, in a law firm, an attorney's time would typically be used as the basis for recognizing overhead cost when determining the cost of a case and billing a client.

In sum, the reader should be aware that job-order costing is a versatile and widely used costing method, and that he or she can expect to encounter it in virtually any organization where the output differs between products, patients, clients, or customers.

USE OF BAR CODE TECHNOLOGY

Earlier in the chapter we discussed the use of bar code technology in recording labor time. Some companies are going beyond just labor in the use of bar codes and are extending bar code technology to include all steps in the manufacturing process. Since bar code languages (called symbologies) are typically numeric in nature, they allow people who speak different human languages to identify items, amounts, locations, work steps, and so forth, and also to communicate this information to others throughout the world. Thus, bar codes are becoming an international link that allows direct communication between a company, its customers, and its suppliers regardless of where they may be located.

Bar codes are often used in conjunction with electronic data interchange (EDI), which involves a networking of computers between organizations. The EDI network allows an electronic exchange of business documents and other information that extends into all areas of business activity from the order of raw materials to the shipment of completed goods.

In a company with a well-developed bar code system, the manufacturing cycle begins with the receipt of a customer's order via EDI. The raw materials to produce the goods come from suppliers who have bar coded the materials according to the company's preset specifications. When materials arrive at the company's plant, the bar codes are scanned to update inventory records. The bar codes are scanned again when the materials are requisitioned for use in production to relieve inventory of the amount and type of goods involved, and to charge the Work in Process account.

When materials are put into process, bar codes are attached that are scanned as the goods move along the production line. These bar codes indicate the manufacturing steps to be performed, and they also update Work in Process records for labor and other costs incurred in the manufacturing process. When goods are completed, another scan is performed that transfers both the cost and quantity of goods from the Work in Process inventory account to the Finished Goods inventory account, or charges Cost of Goods Sold for goods ready to be shipped.

Goods ready to be shipped are packed into containers, which are bar coded with information that includes the customer number, the type and quantity of goods being shipped, and the order number being filled. This bar code is then used for preparing billing information and for tracking the packed goods until placed on a carrier for shipment to the customer. Some customers require that the packed goods be bar coded with point-of-sale labels that can be scanned at retail checkout counters. These scans allow the retailer to update inventory records, verify price, and generate a customer receipt.

In short, bar code technology is being integrated into all areas of business activity. Use of this technology undoubtedly will continue to spread until it has penetrated all levels of manufacturing, distribution, and retail sales worldwide.

 FOCUS ON CURRENT PRACTICE

In an effort to be more responsive to customer needs, Pillowtex Corporation has combined bar code technology and EDI to shorten the time involved in the manufacturing process. (Pillowtex is one of the largest manufacturers of bed pillows.) The company has discarded its manual costing and tracking procedures and now has a fully integrated bar code system in operation. By use of bar code technology and EDI, "Pillowtex can track orders through every stage of the manufacturing process, from picking raw materials through shipment of the finished product to the customer. The implementation of this technology has enabled the company to move to a . . . manufacturing system which effectively allows it to meet unique retailer requirements with minimal disruption to [normal manufacturing] processes."[5]

In observing the growth of bar code technology, one pair of business consultants have aptly observed that "companies are taking the first steps toward that futuristic environment where all manufacturing takes place without human intervention."[6]

SUMMARY

Unit cost of production is one of the most useful items of cost data to a manager. There are two methods in widespread use for determining unit costs; these two methods are known as job-order costing and process costing, respectively. Job-order costing is used in those manufacturing situations where products differ from each other, such as in furniture manufacture and shipbuilding. Process costing is used in those situations where units of product are homogeneous, such as in the manufacture of flour or cement. We have also noted that job-order costing is used extensively in the service industries.

Materials requisition forms and labor time tickets control the assignment of direct materials and direct labor cost to production. Indirect manufacturing costs are assigned to production through use of a predetermined overhead rate, which is developed by estimating the level of manufacturing overhead to be incurred during a period and by dividing this estimate by a base common to all the jobs to be worked on during the period. The most frequently used bases are machine-hours and direct labor-hours.

Since the predetermined overhead rate is based on estimates, the actual overhead cost incurred during a period may be somewhat more or somewhat less than the amount of overhead cost applied to production. Such a difference is referred to as under- or overapplied overhead. The under- or overapplied overhead of a

---

[5] Lawrence Klein and Randy M. Jacques, " 'Pillow Talk' for Productivity," *Management Accounting* 72, no. 8 (February 1991), p. 49.

[6] Ibid.

period can be either (1) closed out to Cost of Goods Sold or (2) allocated between Work in Process, Finished Goods, and Cost of Goods Sold.

Bar code technology is now being used in all steps of the manufacturing process. Bar codes are attached to materials to control their purchase and use, and bar codes are attached to goods in process to control the steps in their manufacture. When goods are completed, they are packed into containers that are bar coded with information that includes the customer number, the quantity of goods being shipped, and the order number being filled. In addition, bar codes can be used to bill customers and prepare point-of-sale labels that can be scanned at retail check-out counters.

REVIEW PROBLEM: JOB-ORDER COSTING

Hogle Company is a manufacturing firm that uses job-order costing. On January 1, 19x5, the company's inventory balances were as follows:

Raw materials	$20,000
Work in process	15,000
Finished goods	30,000

The company applies overhead cost to jobs on the basis of machine-hours worked. For 19x5, the company estimated that it would work 75,000 machine-hours and incur $450,000 in manufacturing overhead cost. The following transactions were recorded for the year:

a.   Raw materials were purchased on account, $410,000.
b.   Raw materials were requisitioned for use in production, $380,000 ($360,000 direct and $20,000 indirect).
c.   The following costs were incurred for employee services: direct labor, $75,000; indirect labor, $110,000; sales commissions, $90,000; and administrative salaries, $200,000.
d.   Sales travel costs were incurred, $17,000.
e.   Utility costs were incurred in the factory, $43,000.
f.   Advertising costs were incurred, $180,000.
g.   Depreciation was recorded for the year, $350,000 (80 percent relates to factory operations, and 20 percent relates to selling and administrative activities).
h.   Insurance expired during the year, $10,000 (70 percent relates to factory operations, and the remaining 30 percent relates to selling and administrative activities).
i.   Manufacturing overhead was applied to production. Due to greater than expected demand for its products, the company worked 80,000 machine-hours during the year.
j.   Goods costing $900,000 to manufacture were completed during the year.
k.   Goods were sold on account to customers during the year at a total selling price of $1,500,000. The goods cost $870,000 to manufacture.

Required   1.   Prepare journal entries to record the transactions above.
2.   Post the entries in (1) to T-accounts (don't forget to enter the opening balances in the inventory accounts).
3.   Is Manufacturing Overhead underapplied or overapplied for the year? Prepare a journal entry to close any balance in the Manufacturing Overhead account to Cost of Goods Sold.
4.   Prepare an income statement for the year.

Solution to Review Problem

1.   a.   Raw Materials   410,000
                Accounts Payable   410,000
     b.   Work in Process   360,000
                Manufacturing Overhead   20,000
                Raw Materials   380,000

c. Work in Process   75,000
    Manufacturing Overhead   110,000
    Sales Commissions Expense   90,000
    Administrative Salaries Expense   200,000
        Salaries and Wages Payable   475,000

d. Sales Travel Expense   17,000
        Accounts Payable   17,000

e. Manufacturing Overhead   43,000
        Accounts Payable   43,000

f. Advertising Expense   180,000
        Accounts Payable   180,000

g. Manufacturing Overhead   280,000
    Depreciation Expense   70,000
        Accumulated Depreciation   350,000

h. Manufacturing Overhead   7,000
    Insurance Expense   3,000
        Prepaid Insurance   10,000

i. The predetermined overhead rate for the year would be computed as follows:

$$\frac{\text{Estimated manufacturing overhead, \$450,000}}{\text{Estimated machine-hours, 75,000}} = \$6/\text{MH}$$

Based on the 80,000 machine-hours actually worked during the year, the company would have applied $480,000 in overhead cost to production: 80,000 machine-hours × $6 = $480,000. The entry to record this application of overhead cost would be:

Work in Process   480,000
    Manufacturing Overhead   480,000

j. Finished Goods   900,000
        Work in Process   900,000

k. Accounts Receivable   1,500,000
        Sales   1,500,000

    Cost of Goods Sold   870,000
        Finished Goods   870,000

2.

Accounts Receivable		
(k)	1,500,000	

Manufacturing Overhead			
(b)	20,000	(i)	480,000
(c)	110,000		
(e)	43,000		
(g)	280,000		
(h)	7,000		
	460,000		480,000
		Bal.	20,000

Sales		
		(k)	1,500,000

Cost of Goods Sold		
(k)	870,000	

Prepaid Insurance		
	(h)	10,000

Accumulated Depreciation		
	(g)	350,000

Commissions Expense		
(c)	90,000	

Administrative Salary Expense		
(c)	200,000	

Raw Materials				Accounts Payable				Sales Travel Expense	
Bal.	20,000	(b)	380,000			(a)	410,000	(d)	17,000
(a)	410,000					(d)	17,000		
						(e)	43,000	**Advertising Expense**	
Bal.	50,000					(f)	180,000		
								(f)	180,000

Work in Process				Salaries and Wages Payable				Depreciation Expense	
Bal.	15,000	(j)	900,000			(c)	475,000	(g)	70,000
(b)	360,000								
(c)	75,000							**Insurance Expense**	
(i)	480,000								
Bal.	30,000							(h)	3,000

Finished Goods			
Bal.	30,000	(k)	870,000
(j)	900,000		
Bal.	60,000		

3. Manufacturing overhead is overapplied for the year. The entry to close it out to Cost of Goods Sold would be:

Manufacturing Overhead	20,000	
Cost of Goods Sold		20,000

4.

HOGLE COMPANY
Income Statement
For the Year Ended December 31, 19x5

Sales.		$1,500,000
Less cost of goods sold ($870,000 − $20,000).		850,000
Gross margin		650,000
Less selling and administrative expenses:		
Commissions expense	$ 90,000	
Administrative salaries expense.	200,000	
Sales travel expense	17,000	
Advertising expense	180,000	
Depreciation expense	70,000	
Insurance expense.	3,000	560,000
Net income		$ 90,000

KEY TERMS FOR REVIEW

Objective 9
Define or explain the key terms listed at the end of the chapter.

Absorption cost   A costing method that includes all manufacturing costs—direct materials, direct labor, and both variable and fixed overhead—as part of the cost of a finished unit of product. This term is synonymous with *full cost*. (p. 72)

Bill of materials   A control sheet that shows the type and quantity of each item of material going into a completed unit of product. (p. 74)

Cost driver   Machine-hours, direct labor-hours, or a similar base that is a causal factor in the incurrence of overhead cost, or is closely correlated with its incurrence. (p. 79)

Full cost   See *Absorption cost*. (p. 72)

Job cost sheet   A form prepared for each job initiated into production that serves as a means for accumulating the materials, labor, and overhead costs chargeable to the job and as a means for computing unit costs. (p. 75)

Job-order costing system   A costing system used in those situations where many different products, jobs, or batches of production are being produced each period. (p. 73)

Materials requisition form   A detailed source document that specifies the type and quantity of materials that are to be drawn from the storeroom and identifies the job to which the materials are to be charged. (p. 74)

Multiple predetermined overhead rates   Setting a different predetermined overhead rate for each department, rather than having a single predetermined overhead rate for the entire company. (p. 94)

Normal cost system   Applying overhead cost to jobs by multiplying actual activity times the predetermined overhead rate. (p. 78)

Overapplied overhead   A credit balance in the Manufacturing Overhead account that arises when the amount of overhead cost applied to Work in Process is greater than the amount of overhead cost actually incurred during a period. (p. 89)

Overhead application   The charging of manufacturing overhead cost to the job cost sheets and to the Work in Process account. (p. 78)

Plantwide overhead rate   A single predetermined overhead rate that is used in all departments of a company, rather than each department having its own separate predetermined overhead rate. (p. 94)

Predetermined overhead rate   A rate used to charge overhead cost to jobs in production; the rate is established in advance for each period by use of estimates of manufacturing overhead cost and production activity for the period. (p. 78)

Process costing system   A costing system used in those manufacturing situations where a single, homogeneous product (such as cement or flour) is produced for long periods of time. (p. 73)

Time ticket   A detailed source document that is used to record an employee's hour-by-hour activities during a day. (p. 76)

Underapplied overhead   A debit balance in the Manufacturing Overhead account that arises when the amount of overhead cost actually incurred is greater than the amount of overhead cost applied to Work in Process during a period. (p. 89)

QUESTIONS

3–1   State the purposes for which it is necessary or desirable to compute unit costs.

3–2   Distinguish between job-order costing and process costing.

3–3   What is the essential purpose of any costing system?

3–4   What is the purpose of the job cost sheet in a job-order costing system?

3–5   What is a predetermined overhead rate, and how is it computed?

3–6   Explain how a sales order, a production order, a materials requisition form, and a labor time ticket are involved in the production and costing of products.

3–7   Explain why some production costs must be assigned to products through an allocation process. Name several such costs. Would such costs be classified as *direct* or as *indirect* costs?

3–8   Why do firms use predetermined overhead rates rather than actual manufacturing overhead costs in applying overhead to units of product?

3–9   What factors should be considered in selecting a base to be used in computing the predetermined overhead rate?

3–10 What is meant by the statement that overhead is "absorbed" into units of product? If a company fully absorbs its overhead costs, does this guarantee that a profit will be earned for the period?

3–11 What account is credited when overhead cost is applied to Work in Process? Would you expect the amount applied for a period to equal the actual overhead costs of the period? Why or why not?

3–12 What is underapplied overhead? Overapplied overhead? What disposition is made of these amounts at period end?

3–13 Enumerate two reasons why overhead might be underapplied in a given year.

3–14 What adjustment is made for underapplied overhead on the schedule of cost of goods manufactured, and why is this adjustment necessary? What adjustment is made on the schedule of cost of goods sold?

3–15 What adjustment is made for overapplied overhead on the schedule of cost of goods manufactured, and why is this adjustment necessary? What adjustment is made on the schedule of cost of goods sold?

3–16 Sigma Company applies overhead cost to jobs on a basis of direct labor cost. Job A, which was started and completed during the current period, shows charges of $5,000 for direct materials, $8,000 for direct labor, and $6,000 for overhead on its job cost sheet. Job B, which is still in process at year-end, shows charges of $2,500 for direct materials and $4,000 for direct labor. Should any overhead cost be added to job B at year-end? Explain.

3–17 A company assigns overhead cost to completed jobs on a basis of 125 percent of direct labor cost. The job cost sheet for job 313 shows that $10,000 in direct material has been used on the job and that $12,000 in direct labor cost has been incurred. If 1,000 units were produced in job 313, what is the cost per unit?

3–18 What is a "plantwide" overhead rate? Why are multiple overhead rates, rather than a plantwide rate, used in some companies?

EXERCISES

E3–1 Which method of accumulating product costs, job-order costing or process costing, would be more appropriate in each of the following situations?

a. A manufacturer of glue.
b. A textbook publisher.
c. An oil refinery.
d. A manufacturer of powdered milk.
e. A manufacturer of ready-mix cement.
f. A custom home builder.
g. A shop for customizing vans.
h. A chemical manufacturer.
i. An auto repair shop.
j. A tire manufacturing plant.
k. An advertising agency.
l. A law office.

E3–2 Kingsport Manufacturing Company experiences a wide variation in demand for its product. Unit costs are computed on a quarterly basis by dividing each quarter's manufacturing costs (materials, labor, and overhead) by the quarter's production in units. The company's estimated costs, by quarter, for the coming year are given below:

	Quarter			
	First	**Second**	**Third**	**Fourth**
Direct materials	$240,000	$120,000	$ 60,000	$180,000
Direct labor	128,000	64,000	32,000	96,000
Manufacturing overhead	300,000	220,000	180,000	260,000
Total manufacturing costs.	$668,000	$404,000	$272,000	$536,000
Number of units to be produced	80,000	40,000	20,000	60,000
Estimated cost per unit	$8.35	$10.10	$13.60	$8.93
	3.75	*5.50*	*9.00*	*4.73*

Management finds the variation in unit costs to be confusing and difficult to work with. It has been suggested that the problem lies with manufacturing overhead, since it is the largest element of cost. Accordingly, you have been asked to find a more equitable way of assigning manufacturing overhead cost to units of product. After some analysis, you have determined that the company's overhead costs are mostly fixed and therefore show little sensitivity to changes in the level of production.

1. The company uses a job-order costing system. How would you recommend that manufacturing overhead cost be assigned to production? Be specific, and show computations. *Required*

2. Recompute the company's unit costs in accordance with your recommendations in (1) above.

E3–3 Harwood Company is a manufacturing firm that operates a job-order costing system. Overhead costs are charged to production on a basis of machine-hours. At the beginning of 19x6, management estimated that the company would incur $192,000 in manufacturing overhead costs for the year and work 80,000 machine-hours.

1. Compute the company's predetermined overhead rate for 19x6. *Required*

2. Assume that during the year the company works only 75,000 machine-hours and incurs the following costs in the Manufacturing Overhead and Work in Process accounts:

Manufacturing Overhead			Work in Process	
(Maintenance)	21,000	?	(Direct materials)	710,000
(Indirect materials)	8,000		(Direct labor)	90,000
(Indirect labor)	60,000		(Overhead)	?
(Utilities)	32,000			
(Insurance)	7,000			
(Depreciation)	56,000			

Copy the data in the T-accounts above onto your answer sheet. Compute the amount of overhead cost that should be applied to Work in Process for the year, and make the entry in your T-accounts.

3. Compute the amount of under- or overapplied overhead for the year, and show the balance in your Manufacturing Overhead T-account. Show the general journal entry that most companies would make to close out the balance in this account.

E3–4 The Polaris Company uses a job-order costing system. The following data relate to October 19x8, the first month of the company's fiscal year:

a. Raw materials purchased on account, $210,000.
b. Raw materials issued to production, $190,000 ($178,000 direct materials and $12,000 indirect materials).
c. Direct labor cost incurred, $90,000; indirect labor cost incurred, $110,000.
d. Depreciation recorded on factory equipment, $40,000.
e. Other manufacturing overhead costs incurred during October, $70,000 (credit Accounts Payable).

f. The company applies manufacturing overhead cost to production on a basis of $8 per machine-hour. There were 30,000 machine-hours recorded for October.

g. Production orders costing $520,000 were completed during October and transferred to Finished Goods.

h. Production orders that had cost $480,000 to complete were shipped to customers during the month. These goods were invoiced at 25 percent above cost. The goods were sold on account.

Required 1. Prepare journal entries to record the information given above.

2. Prepare T-accounts for Manufacturing Overhead and Work in Process. Post the relevant information above to each account. Compute the ending balance in each account, assuming that Work in Process has a beginning balance of $42,000.

E3–5 Estimated cost and operating data for three companies for 19x1 are given below:

	Company		
	X	**Y**	**Z**
Direct labor-hours.	80,000	45,000	60,000
Machine-hours	30,000	70,000	21,000
Direct materials cost	$400,000	$290,000	$300,000
Manufacturing overhead cost.	536,000	315,000	480,000

Predetermined overhead rates are computed on the following bases in the three companies:

Company	Overhead Rate Based on—
X	Direct labor-hours
Y	Machine-hours
Z	Direct materials cost

Required 1. Compute the predetermined overhead rate to be used in each company during 19x1.

2. Assume that three jobs are worked on during 19x1 in Company X. Direct labor-hours recorded by job are: job 418, 12,000 hours; job 419, 36,000 hours; job 420, 30,000 hours. How much overhead cost will the company apply to Work in Process for the year? If actual overhead costs total $530,000 for the year, will overhead be underapplied or overapplied? By how much?

E3–6 White Company has two departments, cutting and finishing. The company uses a job-order cost system and computes a predetermined overhead rate in each department. The cutting department bases its rate on machine-hours, and the finishing department bases its rate on direct labor cost. At the beginning of 19x3, the company made the following estimates:

	Department	
	Cutting	**Finishing**
Direct labor-hours	6,000	30,000
Machine-hours	48,000	5,000
Manufacturing overhead cost. . .	$360,000	$486,000
Direct labor cost	50,000	270,000

Required 1. Compute the predetermined overhead rate to be used in each department during 19x3.

2. Assume that the overhead rates that you computed in (1) are in effect. The job cost sheet for job 203, which was started and completed during the year, showed the following:

	Department	
	Cutting	**Finishing**
Direct labor-hours	6	20
Machine-hours	80	4
Materials requisitioned . . .	$500	$310
Direct labor cost.	70	150

Compute the total overhead cost of job 203.

3. Would you expect substantially different amounts of overhead cost to be assigned to some jobs if the company used a plantwide overhead rate based on direct labor cost, rather than using departmental rates? Explain. No computations are necessary.

The following cost data relate to the manufacturing activities of Black Company during 19x5: **E3–7**

Manufacturing overhead costs incurred:

Indirect materials	$ 15,000
Indirect labor.	130,000
Property taxes	8,000
Utilities	70,000
Depreciation	240,000
Insurance	10,000
Total actual costs incurred	$473,000

Other costs incurred:

Purchases of raw materials (both direct and indirect)	$400,000
Direct labor cost	60,000

Inventories:

Raw materials, January 1	20,000
Raw materials, December 31	30,000
Work in process, January 1	40,000
Work in process, December 31	70,000

The company uses a predetermined overhead rate to charge overhead cost to production. The rate for 19x5 was $25 per machine-hour. A total of 19,400 machine-hours was recorded for the year.

1. Compute the amount of under- or overapplied overhead cost for 19x5. *Required*
2. Prepare a schedule of cost of goods manufactured for 19x5.

Dillon Products manufactures various machine parts to customer specifications. The company uses a job-order costing system and applies overhead cost to jobs on a basis of machine-hours. For the year 19x1, it was estimated that the company would work 240,000 machine-hours and incur $4,800,000 in manufacturing overhead costs. **E3–8**

The company spent the entire month of January working on a large order, which called for 16,000 custom-made machine parts. The company had no work in process at the beginning of January. Cost data relating to January follow:

a. Raw materials purchased on account, $325,000.
b. Raw materials requisitioned for production, $290,000 (80 percent direct materials and 20 percent indirect materials).
c. Labor cost incurred in the factory, $180,000 (one-third direct labor and two-thirds indirect labor).
d. Depreciation recorded on factory equipment, $75,000.
e. Other manufacturing overhead costs incurred, $62,000 (credit Accounts Payable).
f. Manufacturing overhead cost was applied to production on a basis of 15,000 machine-hours worked during the month.
g. The completed job was moved into the finished goods warehouse on January 31 to await delivery to the customer. (In computing the dollar amount for this entry, remem-

ber that the cost of a completed job consists of direct materials, direct labor, and *applied* overhead.)

Required
1. Prepare journal entries to record items (a) through (f) above [ignore item (g) for the moment].
2. Prepare T-accounts for Manufacturing Overhead and Work in Process. Post the relevant items from your journal entries to these T-accounts.
3. Prepare a journal entry for item (g) above, and then compute the unit cost that will appear on the job cost sheet.

E3–9 The following information is taken from the end-of-year account balances of Latta Company:

Manufacturing Overhead			
(a)	460,000	(b)	390,000
Bal.	70,000		

Work in Process			
Bal.	5,000	(c)	710,000
	260,000		
	85,000		
(b)	390,000		
Bal.	40,000		

Finished Goods			
Bal.	50,000	(d)	640,000
(c)	710,000		
Bal.	120,000		

Cost of Goods Sold		
(d)	640,000	

Required
1. Identify the dollar figures appearing by the letters (a), (b), and so forth.
2. Assume that the company closes any balance in the Manufacturing Overhead account directly to Cost of Goods Sold. Prepare the necessary journal entry.
3. Assume instead that the company allocates any balance in the Manufacturing Overhead account to the other accounts. Prepare the necessary journal entry, with supporting computations.

E3–10 Leeds Company began operations on January 2, 19x1. The following activity was recorded in the company's Work in Process account for the first month of operations:

Work in Process			
Direct materials	230,000	To finished goods	390,000
Direct labor	75,000		
Manufacturing overhead	120,000		

Leeds Company uses a job-order costing system and applies manufacturing overhead to Work in Process on a basis of direct labor cost. At the end of January, only one job was still in process. This job (job 12) had been charged with $6,500 in direct labor cost.

Required
1. Compute the predetermined overhead rate that was in use during January.
2. Complete the following job cost sheet for the partially completed job 12:

Job Cost Sheet—Job 12
As of January 31, 19x1

Direct materials	$	?
Direct labor		?
Manufacturing overhead		?
Total cost to January 31	$	?

Tyler Company uses a job-order costing system. The table below provides selected data on **E3–11**
the three jobs worked on during the company's first month of operations:

	Job Number		
	101	**102**	**103**
Units of product in the job. . . .	2,000	1,800	1,500
Machine-hours worked	1,200	1,000	900
Direct materials cost	$4,500	$3,700	$1,400
Direct labor cost	9,600	8,000	7,200

Actual overhead costs totaling $30,000 were incurred during the month. Manufacturing overhead cost is applied to production on a basis of machine-hours at a predetermined rate of $9 per hour. Jobs 101 and 102 were completed during the month; job 103 was not completed.

1. Compute the amount of manufacturing overhead cost that would have been charged to *Required*
   each job during the month.
2. Compute the unit cost of jobs 101 and 102.
3. Prepare a journal entry showing the transfer of the completed jobs into the finished goods warehouse.
4. What is the balance in the Work in Process account at the end of the month?
5. What is the balance in the Manufacturing Overhead account at the end of the month?

PROBLEMS

Kazunas Industries is a manufacturer of auto parts with 70 percent of its sales to the large **P3–12 Ethics and the**
domestic auto companies and 30 percent to auto part retailers. Kazunas' sales to retailers **Manager**
are increasing at a 20 percent annual rate, largely due to the increasing average age of U.S.
automobiles. However, sales to domestic auto companies are decreasing because many of
the parts are not compatible with new auto technology.

Domestic auto companies currently are decreasing the number of their suppliers as they seek better inventory management and quality control, and Kazunas Industries is a prime candidate for deletion. Also, the sales to retailers have a built-in decline as old technology automobiles reach the end of their life cycles.

Kazunas has decided to build new production facilities and has applied for a $20 million loan from Commerce Bank to finance the modernization. Loan conditions were agreed to in a meeting between Peter Lisko, Kazunas' vice president of finance, and David Pearson, a loan officer for the bank. The loan conditions limit Kazunas' cash dividend payments to 50 percent of net income and provide for Commerce Bank's approval of several types of transactions should the current ratio fall below 1.5 to 1. The terms of the agreement were approved by Commerce Bank's Loan Committee and Kazunas Industries received the cash on August 15, 1993.

Joan Miraldi, Kazunas' controller, received instructions from Peter Lisko concerning the preparation of financial statements for the year ended May 31, 1994. After reviewing the preliminary statements, Lisko instructed Miraldi to capitalize some ordinary repairs and to charge some unrelated maintenance labor cost to the installation of new equipment. Lisko also directed Miraldi not to record a May 30 purchase and to omit it from the inventory.

Miraldi met with Lisko to tell him that she believes these actions are contrary to proper accounting practice and may materially misstate the financial statements. Lisko told Miraldi that he did not think these actions violated generally accepted accounting principles and that these principles were just guidelines anyway. He explained the loan conditions to her and said, "The loan conditions were sweeteners suggested by the bank's loan officer to get the loan application by the bank's loan committee. We are bound by the loan conditions but not by generally accepted accounting principles. Therefore, I want you to do as I told you so that these loan conditions are met!''

Required
1. Discuss the ethical considerations that Joan Miraldi should recognize in this situation.
2. Identify possible courses of actions that are open to Joan Miraldi.
3. Recommend the course of action you would follow. Also do the following:
   a. Explain the reasons for recommending the course of action you would follow.
   b. Discuss the consequences, if any, of this course of action.

(CMA, adapted)

P3–13   Entries Directly into T-Accounts; Income Statement   Hudson Company's trial balance as of January 1, 19x8, is given below:

Cash	$ 7,000	
Accounts Receivable	18,000	
Raw Materials	9,000	
Work in Process	20,000	
Finished Goods	32,000	
Prepaid Insurance	4,000	
Plant and Equipment	210,000	
Accumulated Depreciation		$ 53,000
Accounts Payable		38,000
Capital Stock		160,000
Retained Earnings		49,000
Totals	$300,000	$300,000

Hudson Company is a manufacturing firm and employs a job-order costing system. During 19x8, the following transactions took place:

a. Raw materials purchased on account, $40,000.
b. Raw materials were requisitioned for use in production, $38,000 (85 percent direct and 15 percent indirect).
c. Factory utility costs incurred, $19,100.
d. Depreciation was recorded on plant and equipment, $36,000. Three fourths of the depreciation related to factory equipment, and the remainder related to selling and administrative equipment.
e. Advertising expense incurred, $48,000.
f. Costs for salaries and wages were incurred as follows:

Direct labor	$45,000
Indirect labor	10,000
Administrative salaries	30,000

g. Insurance expired during the year, $3,000 (80 percent related to factory operations, and 20 percent related to selling and administrative activities).
h. Miscellaneous selling and administrative expenses incurred, $9,500.
i. Manufacturing overhead was applied to production. The company applies overhead on a basis of $8 per machine-hour; 7,500 machine-hours were recorded for the year.
j. Goods costing $140,000 to manufacture were transferred to the finished goods warehouse.
k. Goods that had cost $130,000 to manufacture were sold on account for $250,000.
l. Collections from customers during the year totaled $245,000.
m. Payments to suppliers on account during the year, $150,000; payments to employees for salaries and wages, $84,000.

Required
1. Prepare a T-account for each account in the company's trial balance, and enter the opening balances shown above.
2. Record the transactions above directly into the T-accounts. Prepare new T-accounts as needed. Key your entries to the letters (a) through (m) above. Find the ending balance in each account.

3. Is manufacturing overhead underapplied or overapplied for the year? Make an entry in the T-accounts to close any balance in the Manufacturing Overhead account to Cost of Goods Sold.
4. Prepare an income statement for the year. (Do not prepare a schedule of cost of goods manufactured; all of the information needed for the income statement is available in the T-accounts.)

Straightforward Journal Entries; Partial T-Accounts; Income Statement   Almeda   **P3–14**
Products, Inc., uses a job-order cost system to accumulate costs in its manufacturing plant. The company's inventory balances on April 1, 19x2 (the start of its fiscal year), were as follows:

Raw materials. $32,000
Work in process. 20,000
Finished goods 48,000

During the year, the following transactions were completed:

a. Raw materials were purchased on account, $170,000.
b. Raw materials were issued from the storeroom for use in production, $180,000 (80 percent direct and 20 percent indirect).
c. Employee salaries and wages were accrued as follows: direct labor, $200,000; indirect labor, $82,000; and selling and administrative salaries, $90,000.
d. Utility costs were incurred in the factory, $65,000.
e. Advertising costs were incurred, $100,000.
f. Prepaid insurance expired during the year, $20,000 (90 percent related to factory operations, and 10 percent related to selling and administrative activities).
g. Depreciation was recorded, $180,000 (85 percent related to factory assets, and 15 percent related to selling and administrative assets).
h. Overhead cost was applied to production at a rate of 175 percent of direct labor cost.
i. Goods costing $700,000 to complete were transferred to the finished goods warehouse.
j. Sales for the year (all on account) totaled $1,000,000. These goods had cost $720,000 to manufacture.

1. Prepare journal entries to record the transactions for the year.   *Required*
2. Prepare T-accounts for Raw Materials, Work in Process, Finished Goods, Manufacturing Overhead, and Cost of Goods Sold. Post the appropriate parts of your journal entries to these T-accounts. Compute the ending balance in each account. (Don't forget to enter the opening balances in the inventory accounts.)
3. Is Manufacturing Overhead underapplied or overapplied for the year? Prepare a journal entry to close this balance to Cost of Goods Sold.
4. Prepare an income statement for the year. (Do not prepare a schedule of cost of goods manufactured; all of the information needed for the income statement is available in the journal entries and T-accounts you have prepared.)

Video Producer; Entries Directly into T-Accounts; Income Statement   Supreme Vid-   **P3–15**
eos, Inc., produces short musical videos for sale to retail outlets. The company's balance sheet accounts as of January 1, 19x3, are given below:

SUPREME VIDEOS, INC.
Balance Sheet
January 1, 19x3

Assets

Current assets:

Cash		$ 63,000
Accounts receivable		102,000
Inventories:		
Raw materials (film, costumes).	$ 30,000	
Videos in process.	45,000	
Finished videos awaiting sale	81,000	156,000
Prepaid insurance.		9,000
Total current assets.		330,000
Studio and equipment.	730,000	
Less accumulated depreciation.	210,000	520,000
Total assets		$850,000

Liabilities and Stockholders' Equity

Accounts payable.		$160,000
Capital stock.	$420,000	
Retained earnings.	270,000	690,000
Total liabilities and stockholders' equity		$850,000

Since the videos differ in length and in complexity of production, the company uses a job-order costing system to determine the cost of each video produced. Studio (manufacturing) overhead is charged to videos on a basis of camera-hours of activity. For 19x3, the company estimated that it would work 7,000 camera-hours and incur $280,000 in studio overhead cost. The following transactions were recorded for the year:

a. Film, costumes, and similar raw materials purchased on account, $185,000.
b. Film, costumes, and other raw materials issued to production, $200,000 (85 percent of this material was considered direct to the videos in production, and the other 15 percent was considered indirect).
c. Utility costs incurred in the production studio, $72,000.
d. Depreciation recorded on the studio, cameras, and other equipment, $84,000. Three fourths of this depreciation related to actual production of the videos, and the remainder related to equipment used in marketing and administration.
e. Advertising expense incurred, $130,000.
f. Costs for salaries and wages were incurred as follows:

> Direct labor (actors and directors) . . . $ 82,000
> Indirect labor (carpenters to build sets,
>   costume designers, and so forth) . . .   110,000
> Administrative salaries   95,000

g. Insurance expired during the year, $7,000 (80 percent related to production of videos, and 20 percent related to marketing and administrative activities).
h. Miscellaneous marketing and administrative expenses incurred, $8,600.
i. Studio (manufacturing) overhead was applied to videos in production. The company recorded 7,250 camera-hours of activity during the year.
j. Videos costing $550,000 to produce were transferred to the Finished Videos storeroom to await sale and shipment.
k. Videos that had cost $600,000 to produce were sold on account for $925,000.
l. Collections from customers during the year totaled $850,000.
m. Payments to suppliers on account during the year, $500,000; payments to employees for salaries and wages, $285,000.

1. Prepare a T-account for each account on the company's balance sheet, and enter the   *Required*
    opening balances given above.
2. Record the transactions above directly into the T-accounts. Prepare new T-accounts
    as needed. Key your entries to the letters (a) through (m) above. Find the ending
    balance in each account.
3. Is the Studio (manufacturing) Overhead account underapplied or overapplied for the
    year? Make an entry in the T-accounts to close any balance in the Studio Overhead
    account to Cost of Goods Sold.
4. Prepare an income statement for the year. (Do not prepare a schedule of cost of goods
    manufactured; all of the information needed for the income statement is available in
    the T-accounts.)

Multiple Departments; Overhead Rates; Costing Units of Product   Morris Company   **P3–16**
manufactures products to customer specifications and employs a job-order costing system.
Predetermined overhead rates are used to apply manufacturing overhead cost to jobs. The
predetermined overhead rate in department A is based on machine-hours, and the rate in
department B is based on direct labor cost. At the beginning of 19x5, the company's
management made the following estimates:

	Department	
	A	**B**
Direct labor-hours	12,000	60,000
Machine-hours	70,000	8,000
Direct materials cost.	$510,000	$650,000
Direct labor cost	130,000	420,000
Manufacturing overhead cost . . .	602,000	735,000

Job 205 was initiated into production on August 1 and completed on August 10. The
company's cost records show the following information on the job:

	Department	
	A	**B**
Direct labor-hours	30	85
Machine-hours.	110	20
Materials placed into production.	$470	$332
Direct labor cost	290	680

1. Compute the predetermined overhead rate that should be used during the year in   *Required*
    department A. Compute the rate that should be used in department B.
2. Compute the total overhead cost applied to job 205.
3. What would be the total cost of job 205? If the job contained 50 units, what would be
    the cost per unit?
4. At the end of 19x5, the records of Morris Company revealed the following *actual* cost
    and operating data for all jobs worked on during the year:

	Department	
	A	**B**
Direct labor-hours	10,000	62,000
Machine-hours	65,000	9,000
Direct materials cost.	$430,000	$680,000
Direct labor cost	108,000	436,000
Manufacturing overhead cost . . .	570,000	750,000

What was the amount of under- or overapplied overhead in each department at the end
of 19x5?

P3–17 **Law Firm: Multiple Departments; Overhead Rates**   Hobart, Evans, and Nix is a small law firm that contains 10 partners and 12 support persons. The firm employs a job-order costing system to accumulate costs chargeable to each client, and it is organized into two departments—the research and documents department and the litigation department. The firm uses predetermined overhead rates to charge the costs of these departments to its clients. At the beginning of 19x1, the firm's management made the following estimates for the year:

	Department	
	Research and Documents	Litigation
Research-hours.	24,000	—
Direct attorney-hours	9,000	18,000
Legal forms and supplies	$ 16,000	$ 5,000
Direct attorney cost	450,000	900,000
Departmental overhead cost . . .	840,000	360,000

The predetermined overhead rate in the research and documents department is based on research-hours, and the rate in the litigation department is based on direct attorney cost.

The costs chargeable to each client are made up of three elements: legal forms and supplies used, direct attorney costs incurred, and an applied amount of overhead from each department in which work is performed on the case.

Case 418-3 was initiated on February 23 and completed on May 16. During this period, the following costs and time were recorded on the case:

	Department	
	Research and Documents	Litigation
Research-hours	26	—
Direct attorney-hours	7	114
Legal forms and supplies . .	$ 80	$ 40
Direct attorney cost	350	5,700

Required 1. Compute the predetermined overhead rate that should be used during the year in the research and documents department. Compute the rate that should be used in the litigation department.

2. Using the rates you computed in (1) above, compute the total overhead cost applied to case 418-3.

3. What would be the total cost charged to case 418-3? Show computations by department and in total for the case.

4. At the end of 19x1, the firm's records revealed the following *actual* cost and operating data for all cases handled during the year:

	Department	
	Research and Documents	Litigation
Research-hours	26,000	—
Direct attorney-hours	8,000	15,000
Legal forms and supplies	$ 19,000	$ 6,000
Direct attorney cost	400,000	750,000
Departmental overhead cost . . .	870,000	315,000

Determine the amount of underapplied or overapplied overhead cost in each department for 19x1.

P3–18 **Straightforward Journal Entries; Partial T-Accounts; Income Statement**   Slater Company manufactures products to customer specifications; a job-order cost system is used to accumulate costs in the company's plant. On July 1, 19x5, the start of Slater Company's fiscal year, inventory balances were as follows:

Raw materials.	$25,000
Work in process.	10,000
Finished goods	40,000

The company applies overhead cost to jobs on a basis of machine-hours of operating time. For the fiscal year starting July 1, 19x5, it was estimated that the plant would operate 45,000 machine-hours and incur $270,000 in manufacturing overhead cost. During the year, the following transactions were completed:

a. Raw materials purchased on account, $275,000.
b. Raw materials requisitioned for use in production, $280,000 (materials costing $220,000 were chargeable directly to jobs; the remaining materials were indirect).
c. Costs for employee services were incurred as follows:

Direct labor	$180,000
Indirect labor	72,000
Sales commissions	63,000
Administrative salaries. . .	90,000

d. Prepaid insurance expired during the year, $18,000 ($13,000 of this amount related to factory operations, and the remainder related to selling and administrative activities).
e. Utility costs incurred in the factory, $57,000.
f. Advertising costs incurred, $140,000.
g. Depreciation recorded on equipment, $100,000. (Some $88,000 of this amount was on equipment used in factory operations; the remaining $12,000 was on equipment used in selling and administrative activities.)
h. Manufacturing overhead cost was applied to production, $__?__. (The company recorded 50,000 machine-hours of operating time during the year.)
i. Goods costing $675,000 to manufacture were transferred into the finished goods warehouse.
j. Sales (all on account) to customers during the year totaled $1,250,000. These goods had cost $700,000 to manufacture.

1. Prepare journal entries to record the transactions for the year.
2. Prepare T-accounts for inventories, Manufacturing Overhead, and Cost of Goods Sold. Post relevant data from your journal entries to these T-accounts (don't forget to enter the opening balances in your inventory accounts). Compute an ending balance in each account.
3. Is Manufacturing Overhead underapplied or overapplied for the year? Prepare a journal entry to close any balance in the Manufacturing Overhead account to Cost of Goods Sold.
4. Prepare an income statement for the year. (Do not prepare a schedule of cost of goods manufactured; all of the information needed for the income statement is available in the journal entries and T-accounts you have prepared.)

Required

Schedule of Cost of Goods Manufactured; Pricing; Work in Process Analysis   Gitano   **P3-19**
Products operates a job-order cost system and applies overhead cost to jobs on a basis of direct materials *used in production* (*not* on a basis of raw materials purchased). In computing a predetermined overhead rate for 19x2, the company's estimates were: manufacturing overhead cost, $800,000; and direct materials to be used in production, $500,000. The company's inventory accounts at the beginning and end of the year were:

	January 1, 19x2	December 31, 19x2
Raw materials	$ 20,000	$ 80,000
Work in process . . .	150,000	70,000
Finished goods . . .	260,000	400,000

The following actual costs were incurred during 19x2:

Purchase of raw materials (all direct)	$510,000
Direct labor cost	90,000
Manufacturing overhead costs:	
Indirect labor	170,000
Property taxes	48,000
Depreciation of equipment	260,000
Maintenance.	95,000
Insurance	7,000
Rent, building	180,000

Required

1. a. Compute the predetermined overhead rate for 19x2.
   b. Compute the amount of under- or overapplied overhead for the year.
2. Prepare a schedule of cost of goods manufactured for the year.
3. Compute the cost of goods sold for the year. (Do not include any under- or overapplied overhead in your cost of goods sold figure.) What options are available for disposing of under- or overapplied overhead?
4. Job 215 was started and completed during the year. What price would have been charged to the customer if the job required $8,500 in direct materials and $2,700 in direct labor cost, and the company priced its jobs at 25 percent above cost to manufacture?
5. Direct materials made up $24,000 of the $70,000 ending Work in Process inventory balance. Supply the information missing below:

Direct materials.	$24,000
Direct labor	?
Manufacturing overhead	?
Work in process inventory . . .	$70,000

P3–20   **Job Cost Sheets; Overhead Rates; Journal Entries**   Madsen Company employs a job-order costing system. Only three jobs—job 208, job 209, and job 210—were worked on during May and June 19x1. Job 208 was completed on June 20; the other two jobs were uncompleted on June 30. Job cost sheets on the three jobs are given below:

	Job Cost Sheet		
	Job 208	**Job 209**	**Job 210**
May costs incurred:*			
Direct materials	$ 9,500	$5,100	$ —
Direct labor.	8,000	3,000	—
Manufacturing overhead	11,200	4,200	—
June costs incurred:			
Direct materials	—	6,000	7,200
Direct labor.	4,000	7,500	8,500
Manufacturing overhead	?	?	?

* Jobs 208 and 209 were started during May.

The following additional information is available:

a. Manufacturing overhead is assigned to jobs on a basis of direct labor cost.
b. Balances in the inventory accounts at May 31 were:

Raw materials	$30,000
Work in process	?
Finished goods	50,000

Required

1. Prepare T-accounts for Raw Materials, Work in Process, Finished Goods, and Manufacturing Overhead. Enter the May 31 balances given above; in the case of Work in Process, compute the May 31 balance and enter it into the Work in Process T-account.

2. Prepare journal entries for *June* as follows:
   a. Prepare an entry to record the issue of materials into production, and post the entry to appropriate T-accounts. (In the case of direct materials, it is not necessary to make a separate entry for each job.) Indirect materials used during June totaled $3,600.
   b. Prepare an entry to record the incurrence of labor cost, and post the entry to appropriate T-accounts. (In the case of direct labor cost, it is not necessary to make a separate entry for each job.) Indirect labor cost totaled $7,000 for June.
   c. Prepare an entry to record the incurrence of $19,400 in various actual manufacturing overhead costs for June. (Credit Accounts Payable.)
3. What apparent predetermined overhead rate does the company use to assign overhead cost to jobs? Using this rate, prepare a journal entry to record the application of overhead cost to jobs for June (it is not necessary to make a separate entry for each job). Post this entry to appropriate T-accounts.
4. As stated earlier, job 208 was completed during June. Prepare a journal entry to show the transfer of this job off of the production line and into the finished goods warehouse. Post the entry to appropriate T-accounts.
5. Determine the balance at June 30 in the Work in Process inventory account. How much of this balance consists of costs traceable to job 209? To job 210?

Entries into T-Accounts; Periodic Inventory Method; Overhead Balance Allocation; Income Statement   Wire Products, Inc., employs a job-order costing system. At the beginning of 19x1, the company's records showed inventory balances as follows: **P3–21**

Raw materials	$ 40,000
Work in process	90,000
Finished goods	120,000

During the year, the following transactions were completed:

a. Raw materials acquired from suppliers on account, $360,000.
b. Raw materials requisitioned for use in production, $350,000 ($320,000 direct materials and $30,000 indirect materials).
c. Costs for employee services were incurred as follows:

Direct labor	$ 70,000
Indirect labor	85,000
Administrative salaries . . .	160,000

d. Depreciation was recorded on equipment, of which $125,000 related to equipment used in the factory and $45,000 related to equipment used in selling and administrative activities.
e. Advertising expense accrued, $200,000.
f. Utility costs accrued, $90,000 (80 percent related to factory operations, and the remainder related to selling and administrative activities).
g. Rent accrued on facilities, $120,000 (90 percent related to factory operations, and the remainder related to selling and administrative activities).
h. Overhead was applied to jobs on a basis of 125 percent of direct materials cost.
i. The ending balance for the year in the Work in Process inventory account was determined to be $70,000.
j. Sales for the year (all on account) were $1,350,000. The ending balance for the year in the Finished Goods inventory account was determined to be $100,000.

1. Enter the above transactions directly into T-accounts. (Don't forget to enter the opening balances into the inventory accounts.)   *Required*
2. As stated in (1) above, the ending balance in Work in Process was $70,000. Direct materials constituted $28,000 of this balance. Given this information, complete the following schedule:

Direct materials.	$28,000
Direct labor	?
Manufacturing overhead . . .	?
Total work in process . . .	$70,000

3. Was manufacturing overhead underapplied or overapplied for the year? By how much?
4. What two options does the company have for disposing of its under- or overapplied overhead? Prepare a journal entry for *each* of these options showing disposition of the under- or overapplied overhead balance for the year.
5. Prepare an income statement for the year. Take your figures directly from the T-accounts you have prepared. (In determining the Cost of Goods Sold, assume that the company follows the practice of closing any under- or overapplied overhead directly to the Cost of Goods Sold account.)

P3–22 Job-Order Cost Journal Entries; Complete T-Accounts; Income Statement Warner Company's trial balance as of January 1, 19x3, is given below:

Cash	$ 8,000	
Accounts Receivable	35,000	
Raw Materials	20,000	
Work in Process	19,000	
Finished Goods	40,000	
Prepaid Insurance	6,000	
Plant and Equipment	280,000	
Accumulated Depreciation.		$ 86,000
Accounts Payable		70,000
Salaries and Wages Payable		4,000
Capital Stock		150,000
Retained Earnings		98,000
Totals	$408,000	$408,000

Warner Company manufactures custom-made products. A job-order costing system is used to accumulate and record costs in the company's plant. Manufacturing overhead costs are charged to production on a basis of machine-hours of activity. For 19x3, management estimated that the company would incur $315,000 in manufacturing overhead costs and operate at an activity level of 21,000 machine-hours.

The following transactions occurred during 19x3:

a. Raw materials were purchased on account, $225,000.
b. Raw materials were issued to production, $230,000 (80 percent direct and 20 percent indirect).
c. Factory payrolls were accrued, $300,000 (70 percent direct labor and 30 percent indirect labor).
d. Sales and administrative salaries were accrued, $85,000.
e. Insurance expired during the year, $4,000 (75 percent related to factory operations, and 25 percent related to selling and administrative activities).
f. Factory utility costs were incurred, $72,000.
g. Advertising costs were incurred, $130,000.
h. Depreciation was recorded for the year, $60,000 (90 percent related to factory operations, and the remainder related to selling and administrative activities).
i. Rental costs were incurred on factory equipment, $48,000.
j. Shipping costs were incurred in transporting goods to customers, $20,000.
k. Manufacturing overhead cost was applied to production, $___?___. (The company operated at an activity level of 20,000 machine-hours for the year.)
l. Goods costing $690,000 to manufacture were transferred into the finished goods warehouse.

m. Sales for the year (all on account) totaled $1,000,000; these goods cost $700,000 to manufacture.

n. Collections on account from customers during the year, $950,000.

o. Cash payments made during the year: to creditors on account, $550,000; to employees for salaries and wages, $380,000.

1. Prepare journal entries to record the year's transactions.   *Required*

2. Prepare a T-account for each account in the company's trial balance, and enter the opening balances given above. Post your journal entries to the T-accounts. Prepare new T-accounts as needed. Compute the ending balance in each account.

3. Is manufacturing overhead underapplied or overapplied for the year? Prepare the necessary journal entry to close the balance in Manufacturing Overhead to Cost of Goods Sold.

4. Prepare an income statement for the year. (Do not prepare a schedule of cost of goods manufactured; all of the information needed for the income statement is available in the T-accounts.)

Film Production Studio; Job-Order Cost Journal Entries; Complete T-Accounts; In- **P3–23**
come Statement   Film Specialties, Inc., operates a small production studio in which advertising films are made for TV and other uses. The company uses a job-order costing system to accumulate costs for each film produced. The company's trial balance as of May 1, 19x5 (the start of its fiscal year), is given below:

Cash	$ 60,000	
Accounts Receivable	210,000	
Materials, Costumes, and Supplies . . .	130,000	
Films in Process	75,000	
Finished Films	860,000	
Prepaid Insurance	90,000	
Studio and Equipment	5,200,000	
Accumulated Depreciation		$1,990,000
Accounts Payable		700,000
Salaries and Wages Payable		35,000
Capital Stock		2,500,000
Retained Earnings		1,400,000
Totals	$6,625,000	$6,625,000

Film Specialties, Inc., uses a Production Overhead account to record all activities relating to overhead costs and applies these costs to jobs on a basis of camera-hours of activity. For the current year, the company estimated that it would incur $1,350,000 in production overhead cost and film 15,000 camera-hours. During the year, the following transactions were completed in the production of films for customers:

a. Materials, costumes, and supplies purchased on account, $690,000.

b. Materials, costumes, and supplies issued from the storeroom for use in production of various films, $700,000 (80 percent direct to the films and 20 percent indirect).

c. Utility costs incurred in the production studio, $90,000.

d. Costs for employee salaries and wages were incurred as follows:

Actors, directors, and extras	$1,300,000
Indirect labor costs of support workers . . .	230,000
Marketing and administrative salaries	650,000

e. Advertising costs incurred, $800,000.

f. Prepaid insurance expired during the year, $70,000. Of this amount, $60,000 related to the operation of the production studio, and the remaining $10,000 related to the company's marketing and administrative activities.

g. Depreciation recorded for the year, $650,000 (80 percent represented depreciation of the production studio, cameras, and other production equipment; the remaining 20 percent represented depreciation on facilities and equipment used in marketing and administrative activities).

h. Rental costs incurred on various facilities and equipment used in production of films, $360,000; and rental costs incurred on equipment used in marketing and administrative activities, $40,000.

i. Production overhead was applied to jobs filmed during the year. The company recorded 16,500 camera-hours of activity.

j. Films costing $3,400,000 to complete were transferred to the Finished Films storeroom to await delivery to customers.

k. Sales of films for the year (all on account) totaled $6,000,000; these films cost $4,000,000 to produce.

l. Collections on account from customers during the year, $5,400,000.

m. Cash payments made during the year: to creditors on account, $2,500,000; and to employees for salaries and wages, $2,200,000.

Required 1. Prepare journal entries to record the year's transactions.

2. Prepare a T-account for each account in the company's trial balance, and enter the opening balances given above. Post your journal entries to the T-accounts. Prepare new T-accounts as needed. Compute the ending balance in each account.

3. Is production overhead underapplied or overapplied for the year? Prepare the necessary journal entry to close the balance in Production Overhead to Cost of Films Sold.

4. Prepare an income statement for the year. (Do not prepare a schedule of cost of goods manufactured; all of the information needed for the income statement is available in the T-accounts.)

P3–24 Disposition of Under- or Overapplied Overhead   Whitney Furniture Company uses a job-order costing system and applies manufacturing overhead cost to products on a basis of machine-hours of activity. The following estimates were used in preparing a predetermined overhead rate for 19x3:

Machine-hours	75,000
Manufacturing overhead cost . . .	$900,000

During 19x3, a glut of furniture on the market resulted in a curtailment of production and a buildup of furniture in Whitney Furniture Company's warehouses. The company's cost records revealed the following actual cost and operating data for the year:

Machine-hours	60,000
Manufacturing overhead cost . . .	$ 850,000
Inventories at year-end:	
Raw materials.	30,000
Work in process.	100,000
Finished goods	500,000
Cost of goods sold.	1,400,000

Required 1. Compute the company's predetermined overhead rate for 19x3.

2. Compute the under- or overapplied overhead for 19x3.

3. Assume that the company closes any under- or overapplied overhead directly to Cost of Goods Sold. Prepare the appropriate journal entry.

4. Assume that the company allocates any under- or overapplied overhead to the appropriate accounts. Prepare the journal entry to show the allocation for 19x3.

5. How much higher or lower will net income be for 19x3 if the under- or overapplied overhead is allocated rather than closed directly to Cost of Goods Sold?

P3–25 T-Account Analysis of Cost Flows   Selected ledger accounts of Moore Company are given below for the year 19x8:

Raw Materials			
Bal. 1/1	15,000	19x8 credits	?
19x8 debits	120,000		
Bal. 12/31	25,000		

Manufacturing Overhead			
19x8 debits	230,000	19x8 credits	?

Work in Process			
Bal. 1/1	20,000	19x8 credits	470,000
Direct materials	90,000		
Direct labor	150,000		
Overhead	240,000		
Bal. 12/31	?		

Factory Wages Payable			
19x8 debits	185,000	Bal. 1/1	9,000
		19x8 credits	180,000
		Bal. 12/31	4,000

Finished Goods			
Bal. 1/1	40,000	19x8 credits	?
19x8 debits	?		
Bal. 12/31	60,000		

Cost of Goods Sold		
19x8 debits	?	

Required

1. What was the cost of raw materials put into production during the year?
2. How much of the materials in (1) consisted of indirect materials?
3. How much of the factory labor cost for the year consisted of indirect labor?
4. What was the cost of goods manufactured for the year?
5. What was the cost of goods sold for the year (before considering under- or overapplied overhead)?
6. If overhead is applied to production on a basis of direct labor cost, what rate was in effect for 19x8?
7. Was manufacturing overhead under- or overapplied for 19x8? By how much?
8. Compute the ending balance in the Work in Process inventory account. Assume that this balance consists entirely of goods started during the year. If $8,000 of this balance is direct labor cost, how much of it is direct materials cost? Manufacturing overhead cost?

Plantwide and Departmental Overhead Rates   "Blast it!" said David Wilson, president   **P3–26**
of Teledex Company. "We've just lost the bid on the Koopers job. It seems we're either too high to get the job or too low to make any money on half the jobs we bid."

Teledex Company manufactures products to customers' specifications and operates a job-order cost system. Manufacturing overhead cost is applied to jobs on a basis of direct labor cost. The following estimates were made at the beginning of 19x7, the current year:

	Department			Total
	Fabricating	Machining	Assembly	Plant
Direct labor.	$200,000	$100,000	$300,000	$600,000
Manufacturing overhead . . .	350,000	400,000	90,000	840,000

Jobs require varying amounts of work in the three departments. The Koopers job, for example, would have required manufacturing costs in the three departments as follows:

	Department			Total
	Fabricating	Machining	Assembly	Plant
Direct materials	$3,000	$200	$1,400	$4,600
Direct labor.	2,800	500	6,200	9,500
Manufacturing overhead . . .	?	?	?	?

The company uses a plantwide overhead rate to apply manufacturing overhead cost to jobs.

Required 1. Assuming use of a plantwide overhead rate:
   a. Compute the rate for the current year.
   b. Determine the amount of manufacturing overhead cost that would have been applied to the Koopers job.

2. Suppose that instead of using a plantwide overhead rate, the company had used a separate predetermined overhead rate in each department. Under these conditions:
   a. Compute the rate for each department for the current year.
   b. Determine the amount of manufacturing overhead cost that would have been applied to the Koopers job.

3. Assume that it is customary in the industry to bid jobs at 150 percent of total manufacturing cost (direct materials, direct labor, and applied overhead). What was the company's bid price on the Koopers job? What would the bid price have been if departmental overhead rates had been used to apply overhead cost?

4. At the end of the current year, the company assembled the following *actual* cost data relating to all jobs worked on during the year:

	Department			Total Plant
	Fabricating	Machining	Assembly	
Direct materials	$190,000	$ 16,000	$114,000	$320,000
Direct labor.	210,000	108,000	262,000	580,000
Manufacturing overhead . . .	360,000	420,000	84,000	864,000

Compute the under- or overapplied overhead for the year (a) assuming that a plantwide overhead rate is used and (b) assuming that departmental overhead rates are used.

P3–27
Comprehensive Problem

Journal Entries; T-Accounts; Statements; Pricing   Rockwood Company is a manufacturer of custom-made equipment and relies heavily on direct labor in the completion of its jobs. The company uses a job-order costing system and applies manufacturing overhead cost to jobs on a basis of direct labor-hours. At the beginning of 19x5, the following estimates were made as a basis for computing a predetermined overhead rate for the year: manufacturing overhead cost, $360,000; and direct labor-hours, 18,000.

The following transactions took place during the year (all purchases and services were acquired on account):

a. Raw materials were purchased for use in production, $200,000.
b. Raw materials were requisitioned for use in production (all direct materials), $185,000.
c. Utility bills were incurred, $70,000 (90 percent related to factory operations, and the remainder related to selling and administrative activities).
d. Salary and wage costs were incurred:

Direct labor (19,500 hours)	$230,000
Indirect labor	90,000
Selling and administrative salaries . . .	110,000

e. Maintenance costs were incurred in the factory, $54,000.
f. Advertising costs were incurred, $136,000.
g. Depreciation was recorded for the year, $95,000 (80 percent related to factory equipment, and the remainder related to selling and administrative equipment).
h. Rental cost incurred on buildings, $120,000 (85 percent related to factory operations, and the remainder related to selling and administrative facilities).
i. Manufacturing overhead cost was applied to jobs, $_____?_____ .
j. Cost of goods manufactured for the year, $770,000.
k. Sales for the year (all on account) totaled $1,200,000. These goods cost $800,000 to manufacture.

The balances in the inventory accounts at the beginning of the year were:

Raw Materials	$30,000
Work in Process	21,000
Finished Goods	60,000

Required

1. Prepare journal entries to record the above data.
2. Post your entries to T-accounts. (Don't forget to enter the opening inventory balances above.) Determine the ending balances in the inventory accounts and in the Manufacturing Overhead account.
3. Prepare a schedule of cost of goods manufactured.
4. Prepare a journal entry to close any balance in the Manufacturing Overhead account to Cost of Goods Sold. Prepare a schedule of cost of goods sold.
5. Prepare an income statement for the year. Ignore income taxes.
6. Job 412 was one of the many jobs started and completed during the year. The job required $3,800 in materials and 350 hours of direct labor time at $12 per hour. If the job contained 640 units and the company billed at 60 percent above the cost to manufacture, what price per unit would have been charged to the customer?

T-Accounts; Job-Order Cost Flows; Statements; Pricing Chenko Products, Inc., manufactures goods to customers' orders and uses a job-order costing system. A trial balance for the company as of January 1, 19x4, is given below:

P3–28
Comprehensive Problem

Cash	$ 35,000	
Accounts Receivable	127,000	
Raw Materials	10,000	
Work in Process	44,000	
Finished Goods	75,000	
Prepaid Insurance	9,000	
Plant and Equipment	400,000	
Accumulated Depreciation		$110,000
Accounts Payable		86,000
Salaries and Wages Payable		9,000
Capital Stock		375,000
Retained Earnings		120,000
Totals	$700,000	$700,000

The company applies manufacturing overhead cost to jobs on a basis of direct materials cost. The following estimates were made at the beginning of 19x4 for purposes of computing a predetermined overhead rate for the year: manufacturing overhead cost, $510,000; and direct materials cost, $340,000. Summarized transactions of the company for 19x4 are given below:

a. Raw materials purchased on account, $400,000.
b. Raw materials requisitioned for use in production, $370,000 ($320,000 direct materials and $50,000 indirect materials).
c. Salary and wage costs were incurred as follows:

Direct labor	$ 76,000
Indirect labor	130,000
Selling and administrative salaries	110,000

d. Maintenance costs incurred in the factory, $81,000.
e. Travel costs incurred by salespeople, $43,000.
f. Insurance expired during the year on the factory, $7,000.
g. Utility costs incurred, $70,000 (90 percent related to factory operations, and 10 percent related to selling and administrative activities).
h. Property taxes incurred on the factory building, $9,000.
i. Advertising costs incurred, $200,000.

j. Rental cost incurred on special factory equipment, $120,000.
k. Depreciation recorded for the year, $50,000 (80 percent related to factory assets, and 20 percent related to selling and administrative assets).
l. Manufacturing overhead cost applied to jobs, $_____?_____ .
m. Cost of goods manufactured for the year, $890,000.
n. Sales for the year totaled $1,400,000 (all on account); the cost of goods sold totaled $930,000.
o. Cash collections from customers during the year totaled $1,350,000.
p. Cash payments during the year: to employees, $300,000; on accounts payable, $970,000.

Required   1. Enter the company's transactions directly into T-accounts. (Don't forget to enter the opening balances into the T-accounts.) Key your entries to the letters (a) through (p) above. Create new T-accounts as needed. Find the ending balance in each account.
2. Prepare a schedule of cost of goods manufactured.
3. Prepare a journal entry to close any balance in the Manufacturing Overhead account to Cost of Goods Sold. Prepare a schedule of cost of goods sold.
4. Prepare an income statement for 19x4. Ignore income taxes.
5. Job 412 was one of the many jobs started and completed during the year. The job required $8,000 in direct materials and $1,600 in direct labor cost. If the job contained 400 units and the company billed the job at 175 percent of the cost to manufacture, what price per unit would have been charged to the customer?

CASES

C3–29   Incomplete Data; Review of Cost Flows   In an attempt to conceal a theft of funds, Snake N. Grass, controller of Bucolic Products, Inc., placed a bomb in the company's record vault. The ensuing explosion left only fragments of the company's factory ledger, as shown below:

Raw Materials		Manufacturing Overhead	
Bal. 6/1 8,000		Actual costs for June 79,000	Overapplied overhead 6,100

Work in Process		Accounts Payable	
Bal. 6/1 7,200			Bal. 6/30 16,000

Finished Goods		Cost of Goods Sold	
Bal. 6/30 21,000			

To bring Mr. Grass to justice, the company must reconstruct its activities for June. You have been assigned to perform the task of reconstruction. After interviewing selected employees and sifting through charred fragments, you have determined the following additional information:

a. According to the company's treasurer, the accounts payable are for purchases of raw materials only. The company's balance sheet, dated May 31, shows that Accounts Payable had a $20,000 balance at the beginning of June. The company's bank has provided photocopies of all checks that cleared the bank during June. These photocopies show that payments to suppliers during June totaled $119,000. (All materials used during the month were direct materials.)

b. The production superintendent states that manufacturing overhead cost is applied to jobs on a basis of direct labor-hours. However, he does not remember the rate currently being used by the company.

c. Cost sheets kept in the production superintendent's office show that only one job was in process on June 30, at the time of the explosion. The job had been charged with $6,600 in materials, and 500 direct labor-hours at $8 per hour had been worked on the job.

d. A log is kept in the finished goods warehouse showing all goods transferred in from the factory. This log shows that the cost of goods transferred into the finished goods warehouse from the factory during June totaled $280,000.

e. The company's May 31 balance sheet indicates that the finished goods inventory totaled $36,000 at the beginning of June.

f. A charred piece of the payroll ledger, found after sifting through piles of smoking debris, indicates that 11,500 direct labor-hours were recorded for June. The company's employment department has verified that as a result of a firm union contract, there are no variations in pay rates among factory employees.

g. The production superintendent states that there was no under- or overapplied overhead in the Manufacturing Overhead account at May 31.

Determine the following amounts: *Required*

1. Predetermined overhead rate being used by the company.
2. Raw materials purchased during June.
3. Work in process inventory, June 30.
4. Overhead applied to work in process during June.
5. Raw materials usage during June.
6. Raw materials inventory, June 30.
7. Cost of goods sold for June.

(Hint: A good way to proceed is to bring the fragmented T-accounts up to date through June 30 by posting whatever entries can be developed from the information given.)

Overhead Cost Assignment   Rose Bach has recently been hired as controller of Empco Inc., a sheet metal manufacturer. Empco has been in the sheet metal business for many years and is currently investigating ways to modernize its manufacturing process. At the first staff meeting Bach attended, Bob Kelley, chief engineer, presented a proposal for automating the drilling department. Kelley recommended that Empco purchase two robots that would have the capability of replacing the eight direct labor workers in the department. The cost savings outlined in Kelley's proposal included the elimination of direct labor cost in the drilling department plus a reduction of manufacturing overhead cost in the department to zero because Empco charges manufacturing overhead on the basis of direct labor dollars using a plantwide rate.

C3-30
Critical Thought Case

The president of Empco was puzzled by Kelley's explanation of cost savings, believing it made no sense. Bach agreed, explaining that as firms become more automated, they should rethink their manufacturing overhead systems. The president then asked Bach to look into the matter and prepare a report for the next staff meeting.

To refresh her knowledge, Bach reviewed articles on manufacturing overhead allocation for an automated factory and discussed the matter with some of her peers. Bach also gathered the historical data presented below on the manufacturing overhead rates experienced by Empco over the years. Bach also wanted to have some departmental data to present at the meeting and, using Empco's accounting records, was able to estimate the annual averages presented below for each manufacturing department in the 1990s.

HISTORICAL DATA

Date	Average Annual Direct Labor Cost	Average Annual Manufacturing Overhead Cost	Average Manufacturing Overhead Application Rate
1950s	$1,000,000	$ 1,000,000	100%
1960s	1,200,000	3,000,000	250
1970s	2,000,000	7,000,000	350
1980s	3,000,000	12,000,000	400
1990s	4,000,000	20,000,000	500

ANNUAL AVERAGES

	Cutting Department	Grinding Department	Drilling Department
Direct labor	$ 2,000,000	$1,750,000	$ 250,000
Manufacturing overhead	11,000,000	7,000,000	2,000,000

Required   1. Disregarding the proposed use of robots in the drilling department, describe the short-comings of the system for applying overhead that is currently used by Empco Inc.

2. Explain the misconceptions underlying Bob Kelley's statement that the manufacturing overhead cost in the drilling department would be reduced to zero if the automation proposal was implemented.

3. Recommend ways to improve Empco Inc.'s method for applying overhead by describing how it should revise its overhead accounting system:
    a. in the cutting and grinding departments.
    b. to accommodate the automation of the drilling department.

(CMA, adapted)

C3-31 **Analysis of Cost Flows and Inventories under Job-Order Costing**   Targon, Inc., manufactures lawn equipment. A job-order costing system is used, since the products are manufactured in batches rather than on a continuous basis. The company started operations on January 2, 19x1. Operating activities during the first 11 months of the year (through November 30) resulted in the following balances in selected accounts:

Raw Materials		**Manufacturing Overhead**	
Bal. 36,000		2,260,000*	?
		Bal. ?	

Work in Process		**Cost of Goods Sold**	
Bal 1,200,000		Bal. 14,200,000	

Finished Goods	
Bal. 2,785,000	

* This figure represents actual manufacturing overhead costs incurred through November 30, 19x1.

The following additional information is available on the company:

a. The work in process inventory at November 30 consisted of two jobs:

Job No.	Units	Items	Total Cost as of November 30
1105.	50,000	Estate sprinklers	$ 700,000
1106.	40,000	Economy sprinklers	500,000
			$1,200,000

b. The finished goods inventory at November 30 consisted of five separate items in stock:

Items	Quantity and Unit Cost	Total Cost
Estate sprinklers.	5,000 units at $22 each	$ 110,000
Deluxe sprinklers	115,000 units at $17 each	1,955,000
Brass nozzles	10,000 gross at $14 per gross	140,000
Rainmaker nozzles. . . .	5,000 gross at $16 per gross	80,000
Connectors	100,000 gross at $5 per gross	500,000
		$2,785,000

c. Manufacturing overhead cost is applied to jobs on a basis of direct labor-hours. For 19x1, management estimated that the company would work 400,000 direct labor-hours and incur $2,400,000 in manufacturing overhead cost.

d. A total of 367,000 direct labor-hours were worked during the first 11 months of the year (through November 30).

Items (e) through (j) below summarize the activity that took place in the company during December 19x1.

e. A total of $708,000 in raw materials was purchased during the month.

f. Raw materials were drawn from inventory and charged as follows:

Job No.	Quantity and Items	Material Charged
1105.	See above	$210,000
1106.	See above	6,000
1201.	30,000 gross rainmaker nozzles	181,000
1202.	10,000 deluxe sprinklers	92,000
1203.	50,000 ring sprinklers	163,000
—	Indirect materials	20,000
		$672,000

g. The payroll during December was as follows:

Job No.	Hours	Total Cost
1105	6,000	$ 62,000
1106	2,500	26,000
1201	18,000	182,000
1202	500	5,000
1203	5,000	52,000
Indirect labor.	8,000	84,000
Sales and administration	—	120,000
		$531,000

h. Other costs incurred in the factory during December were:

Depreciation.	$62,500
Utilities	15,000
Insurance	1,000
Property taxes	3,500
Maintenance.	5,000
	$87,000

i. Jobs completed during December and the number of good units transferred to the finished goods warehouse were:

Job No.	Quantity	Items
1105.	48,000 units	Estate sprinklers
1106.	39,000 units	Economy sprinklers
1201.	29,500 gross	Rainmaker nozzles
1203.	49,000 units	Ring sprinklers

j. Finished products were shipped to customers during December as follows:

Items	Quantity
Estate sprinklers.	16,000 units
Deluxe sprinklers	32,000 units
Economy sprinklers	20,000 units
Ring sprinklers	22,000 units
Brass nozzles	5,000 gross
Rainmaker nozzles.	10,000 gross
Connectors	26,000 gross

Required 1. Determine the amount of under- or overapplied overhead for the year 19x1.
2. What is the appropriate accounting treatment for this under- or overapplied overhead balance? Explain your answer.
3. Determine the dollar balance in the Work in Process inventory account as of December 31, 19x1. Show all computations in good form.
4. For the estate sprinklers only, determine the dollar balance in the Finished Goods inventory account as of December 31, 19x1. Assume a FIFO flow of units. Show all computations in good form.

(CMA, heavily adapted)

Oil refineries use process costing, rather than job-order costing, to determine the costs of their outputs. Because every barrel of gasoline produced by a refinery is essentially the same, there is no reason to keep track of the costs of each individual barrel. Instead, costs are averaged across all the barrels produced during a period.

Systems Design:

Process Costing

LEARNING OBJECTIVES

After studying Chapter 4, you should be able to:

1 Enumerate the major similarities and differences between job-order and process costing.

2 Prepare journal entries to record the flow of materials, labor, and overhead through a process costing system.

3 Compute the equivalent units of production for a period by the weighted-average method.

4 Compute the equivalent units of production for a period by the FIFO method.

5 Prepare a quantity schedule for a period by the weighted-average method.

6 Compute the total and unit costs for a period by the weighted-average method.

7 Prepare a cost reconciliation for a period by the weighted-average method.

8 Combine the quantity schedule and equivalent units, the total and unit costs, and the cost reconciliation into a production report.

9 State the conditions under which operation costing is useful to management.

10 Define or explain the key terms listed at the end of the chapter.

11 (Appendix B) Prepare a quantity schedule for a period by the FIFO method.

12 (Appendix B) Compute the total and unit costs for a period by the FIFO method.

13 (Appendix B) Prepare a cost reconciliation for a period by the FIFO method.

A s explained in the preceding chapter, there are two basic costing systems in use: job-order costing and process costing. We have found that a job-order costing system is used in those situations where many different jobs or batches of production are worked on each period. Examples of industries that would typically use job-order costing include furniture manufacture, special-order printing, shipbuilding, and many types of service organizations.

By contrast, **process costing** is used in those industries that produce basically homogeneous products such as bricks, flour, cement, screws, bolts, and pharmaceutical items. In addition, process costing is employed in assembly-type operations that manufacture personal computers, automobiles, and small appliances, as well as in utilities producing gas, water, and electricity. As suggested by the length of this list, process costing is in widespread use and warrants study by anyone involved in accounting, management, or systems work.

Our purpose in this chapter is to extend the discussion of product costing that was started in the preceding chapter to include a process costing system.

COMPARISON OF JOB-ORDER AND PROCESS COSTING

In some ways process costing is very similar to job-order costing, and in some ways it is very different. In this section, we focus on these similarities and differences in order to provide a foundation for the detailed discussion of process costing that follows.

Similarities between Job-Order and Process Costing

Objective 1
Enumerate the major similarities and differences between job-order and process costing.

It is important to recognize that much of what was learned in the preceding chapter about costing and about cost flows applies equally well to process costing in this chapter. That is, we are not throwing out all that we have learned about costing and starting from "scratch" with a whole new system. The similarities that exist between job-order and process costing can be summarized as follows:

1. The same basic purposes exist in both systems, which are: (a) to assign material, labor, and overhead costs to products; (b) to provide a mechanism for computing unit costs; and (c) to provide data essential for planning, control, and decision making.
2. Both systems maintain and use the same basic manufacturing accounts, including Manufacturing Overhead, Raw Materials, Work in Process, and Finished Goods.
3. The flow of costs through the manufacturing accounts is basically the same in both systems.

As can be seen from this comparison, much of the knowledge that we have already acquired about costing is applicable to a process costing system. Our task now is simply to refine and extend this knowledge to meet special process costing needs.

Differences between Job-Order and Process Costing

The differences between job-order and process costing arise from two factors. The first is that the flow of units in a process costing system is more or less continuous, and the second is that these units are indistinguishable from one another. Under process costing, it makes no sense to try to identify materials, labor, and overhead costs with a particular order from a customer (as we did with

Job-Order Costing	Process Costing
1. Many different jobs are worked on during each period, with each job having different production requirements.	1. A single product is produced either on a continuous basis or for long periods of time. All units of product are identical.
2. Costs are accumulated by individual job.	2. Costs are accumulated by department.
3. The *job cost sheet* is the key document controlling the accumulation of costs by a job.	3. The *department production report* is the key document showing the accumulation and disposition of costs by a department.
4. Unit costs are computed *by job* on the job cost sheet.	4. Unit costs are computed *by department* on the department production report.

EXHIBIT 4–1

Differences between Job-Order and Process Costing

job-order costing), since each order is just one of many that are filled from a continuous flow of virtually identical units from the production line. Under process costing, we accumulate costs *by department,* rather than by order, and assign these costs equally to all units that pass through the department during a period.

A further difference between the two costing systems is that the job cost sheet has no use in process costing, since the focal point of that method is on departments. Instead of using job cost sheets, a document known as a **production report** is prepared for each department in which work is done on products. The production report serves several functions. It provides a summary of the number of units moving through a department during a period, and it also provides a computation of unit costs. In addition, it shows what costs were charged to a department during a period and what disposition was made of these costs. As these comments suggest, the department production report is a key document in a process costing system.

The major differences between job-order and process costing are summarized in Exhibit 4–1.

A PERSPECTIVE OF PROCESS COST FLOWS

Before presenting a detailed example of process costing, it will be helpful to gain a visual perspective of how manufacturing costs flow through a process costing system.

Processing Departments

A **processing department** is any location in the factory where work is performed on a product and where materials, labor, or overhead costs are added to the product. For example, a brick factory might have two processing departments—one for mixing and molding clay into brick form and one for firing the molded brick. There can be as many or as few processing departments as are needed to complete the manufacture of a product. Some products may go through several processing departments, while others may go through only one or two. Regardless of the number of departments involved, all processing departments have two essential features. First, the activity performed in the processing department must be performed uniformly on all of the units passing through it. Second, the output of the processing department must be homogeneous.

The processing departments involved in the manufacture of a product such as bricks would probably be organized in a *sequential* pattern. By **sequential processing,** we mean that units flow in sequence from one department to another. An example of processing departments arranged in a sequential pattern is given in Exhibit 4–2.

EXHIBIT 4–2
Sequential Processing
Departments

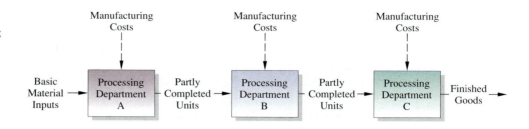

A different type of processing pattern, known as *parallel processing,* is required in the manufacture of some products. **Parallel processing is used in those situations where, after a certain point, some units may go through different processing departments than others.** For example, the petroleum industry may input crude oil into one processing department and then use the refined output for further processing into several end products. Each end product may undergo several steps of further processing after the initial refining, some of which may be shared with other end products and some of which may not. Exhibit 4–3 illustrates one type of parallel processing. The number of possible variations in parallel processing patterns is virtually limitless. The example given in Exhibit 4–3 is intended as just one sample of the many parallel patterns in use today.

The Flow of Materials, Labor, and Overhead Costs

Cost accumulation is simpler in a process costing system than in a job-order costing system. The reason is that costs need to be identified only by processing department—not by separate job. Thus, in a process costing system, instead of having to trace costs to hundreds of different jobs, costs are traced to only a few processing departments. This means that costs can be accumulated for longer periods of time and that just one allocation is needed at the end of a period (week, month, and so forth) in order to assign the accumulated costs to the period's output.

A T-account model of materials, labor, and overhead cost flows in a process costing system is given in Exhibit 4–4. Several key points should be noted from

EXHIBIT 4–3
Parallel Processing
Departments

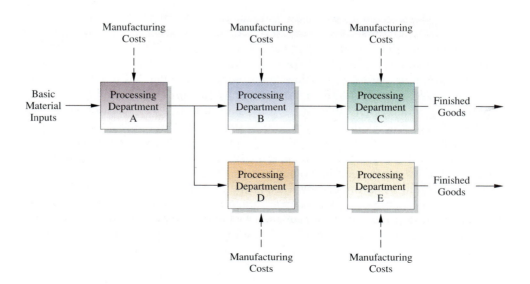

EXHIBIT 4–4
T-Account Model of Process Costing Flows

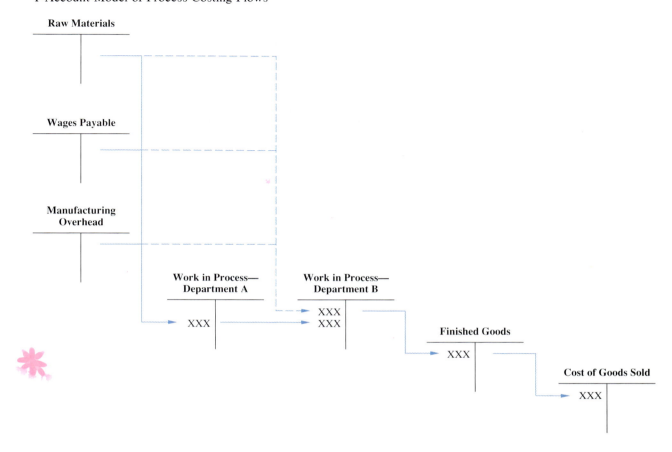

this exhibit. First, note that a separate Work in Process account is maintained for *each processing department,* rather than having only a single Work in Process account for the entire company. Second, note that the completed production of the first processing department (department A in the exhibit) is transferred into the Work in Process account of the second processing department (department B), where it undergoes further work. After this further work, the completed units are then transferred into Finished Goods. (In Exhibit 4–4, we show only two processing departments; there may be several such departments in some companies.)

Finally, note that materials, labor, and overhead costs can be entered directly into *any* processing department—not just the first. Costs in department B's Work in Process account would therefore consist of the materials, labor, and overhead costs entered directly into the account plus the costs attached to partially completed units transferred in from department A (called **transferred-in costs).**

Materials, Labor, and Overhead Cost Entries

To complete our discussion of cost flows in a process costing system, in the following paragraphs we show journal entries relating to materials, labor, and overhead costs and also make brief, further comments relating to each of these cost categories.

Objective 2
Prepare journal entries to record the flow of materials, labor, and overhead through a process costing system.

Materials Costs   As in job-order costing, materials are drawn from the storeroom by use of a materials requisition form. Charging these materials to departments, rather than to jobs, generally reduces the amount of requisitioning needed, since large amounts of materials can be drawn and put into production at a time. As stated earlier, materials can be added in any processing department, although it is not unusual for materials to be added only in the first processing department, with subsequent departments adding only labor and overhead costs as the partially completed units move along toward completion.

Assuming that the first processing department in a company is department A, the journal entry for placing materials into process would be:

Work in Process—Department A	XXX	
Raw Materials.		XXX

If other materials are subsequently added in another processing department, the entry would be:

Work in Process—Department B	XXX	
Raw Materials.		XXX

Labor Costs   Since it is not necessary to identify costs with specific jobs, a time clock is generally adequate for accumulating labor costs and for allocating them to the proper department in a process costing system. Assuming again that a company has two processing departments, A and B, the journal entry to record labor costs for a period would be:

Work in Process—Department A	XXX	
Work in Process—Department B	XXX	
Salaries and Wages Payable		XXX

Overhead Costs   The simplest method of handling overhead costs in a process costing system is to charge products with the actual overhead costs of the period rather than with applied overhead costs. Under this approach, no predetermined overhead rate is computed; overhead costs in each department are simply added directly to that department's Work in Process account either as the costs are incurred or at specified intervals. Since there is no "applied" overhead cost in the sense we talked about in Chapter 3, there is no under- or overapplied overhead balance remaining at the end of a period when this approach is used.

Why is it possible to use actual overhead costs in a process costing system when it is not possible under job-order costing? The answer lies in the nature of the work flowing through the two systems. Under job-order costing, jobs tend to be heterogeneous, requiring different inputs and different times to complete. Also, several jobs will be in process at a given time, each having different output requirements. Thus, the overhead cost chargeable to a job has to be estimated. Under process costing, homogeneous units flow continuously through a department, thus making it possible to charge units with the department's actual overhead costs as the costs are incurred. This approach works well, however, only if production is quite stable from period to period and only if overhead costs are incurred uniformly over the year.

If production levels fluctuate or if overhead costs are not incurred uniformly, then predetermined overhead rates should be used to charge overhead cost to products, the same as in job-order costing. When predetermined overhead rates are used, each department has its own separate rate with the rates being computed in the same way as was discussed in Chapter 3. Overhead cost is then applied to units of product as the units move through the various departments. Since predetermined overhead rates are widely used even in process costing situations, we will assume their use throughout the remainder of this chapter.

If a company has two processing departments, A and B, the journal entry to apply overhead cost to products would be:

```
Work in Process—Department A . . . . . . . . . . . . . . . . . . . . XXX
Work in Process—Department B . . . . . . . . . . . . . . . . . . . . XXX
    Manufacturing Overhead . . . . . . . . . . . . . . . . . . . . .        XXX
```

Completing the Cost Flows   Once processing has been completed in a department, the units are transferred to the next department for further processing, as illustrated earlier in the T-accounts in Exhibit 4–4. The entry to transfer partially completed units from department A into department B would be:

```
Work in Process—Department B . . . . . . . . . . . . . . . . . . . XXX
    Work in Process—Department A . . . . . . . . . . . . . . . . . .        XXX
```

After processing has been completed in department B, the completed units are then transferred into the Finished Goods inventory account:

```
Finished Goods . . . . . . . . . . . . . . . . . . . . . . . . . . . XXX
    Work in Process—Department B . . . . . . . . . . . . . . . . . .        XXX
```

Finally, when a customer's order is filled and units are sold, the cost of the units is transferred into Cost of Goods Sold:

```
Cost of Goods Sold . . . . . . . . . . . . . . . . . . . . . . . . . XXX
    Finished Goods . . . . . . . . . . . . . . . . . . . . . . . . .        XXX
```

To summarize, we stated earlier that the cost flows between accounts are basically the same in a process costing system as they are in a job-order costing system. As shown by the entries above, the reader can see that this is indeed correct. The only differences are that in a process costing system (a) a separate Work in Process account is maintained for each department, and (b) each department can be charged directly for manufacturing costs in addition to those transferred in from the preceding department.

EQUIVALENT UNITS OF PRODUCTION

After materials, labor, and overhead costs have been accumulated in a department, the department's output must be determined so that unit costs can be computed. A department's output is always stated in terms of **equivalent units of production.** Equivalent units can be defined as the number of units that would have been produced during a period if all of a department's efforts had resulted in completed units of product. Equivalent units are computed by taking completed units and adjusting them for partially completed units in the work in process inventory.

The reasoning behind the computation of equivalent units is as follows: Completed units alone will not accurately measure output in a department, since part of the department's efforts during a period will have been expended on units that are only partially complete. To accurately measure output, these partially completed units must also be considered in the output computation. This is done by mathematically converting the partially completed units into fully completed *equivalent units* and then adjusting the output figure accordingly.

To illustrate, assume that a company has 500 units in its ending work in process inventory that are 60 percent complete. Five hundred units 60 percent complete would be equivalent to 300 fully completed units (500 × 60% = 300). Therefore, the ending inventory would be said to contain 300 *equivalent units*. These equivalent units would be added to the fully completed units in determining the period's output.

There are two ways of computing a department's equivalent units, depending on whether the company is accounting for its cost flows by the *weighted-average method* or by the *first-in, first-out (FIFO) method*.

Weighted-Average Method

Objective 3
Compute the equivalent units of production for a period by the weighted-average method.

Under the **weighted-average method,** a department's equivalent units are computed just as described above: Equivalent units of production = Completed units + Equivalent units in the ending work in process inventory.

To provide an extended example, assume the following data:

Regal Company manufactures a product that goes through two departments—mixing and firing. During 19x1, the following activity took place in the mixing department:

		Percent Completed	
	Units	Materials	Conversion
Work in process, beginning	10,000	100	70
Units started into production during the year	150,000		
Units completed during the year and transferred to the firing department	140,000		
Work in process, ending	20,000	60	25

Recall from our discussion in Chapter 2 that **conversion cost** consists of direct labor combined with manufacturing overhead. Labor and overhead are frequently added together in process costing systems.

Since Regal Company's work in process inventories are at different stages of completion in terms of the amounts of materials cost and conversion cost that have been added, two equivalent unit figures will have to be computed—one for equivalent units in terms of materials and the other for equivalent units in terms of conversion. The equivalent units computations are given in Exhibit 4–5.

Note from the computations in Exhibit 4–5 that units in the beginning inventory are ignored and that an adjustment is made only for partially completed units in the ending inventory. This is a key point in the computation of equivalent units under the weighted-average method: *Units in the beginning inventory are always treated as if they were started and completed during the current period.* Thus, no adjustment is made for these units, regardless of how much work was done on them before the period started. Although this procedure may seem illogical and inconsistent, it greatly simplifies the preparation of a department production report, as we shall see shortly.

EXHIBIT 4–5
Equivalent Units of Production: Weighted-Average Method

	Materials	Conversion
Units transferred to firing	140,000	140,000
Work in process, ending:		
20,000 units × 60%	12,000	
20,000 units × 25%		5,000
Equivalent units of production	152,000	145,000

FIFO Method

The computation of equivalent units under the **FIFO method** differs from the computation under the weighted-average method in two ways.

Objective 4
Compute the equivalent units of production for a period by the FIFO method.

First, the "units transferred out" figure is divided into two parts. One part consists of the units from the beginning inventory that were completed and transferred out, and the other part consists of the units that were both *started* and *completed* during the current period.

Second, full consideration is given to the amount of work expended during the current period on units in the *beginning* work in process inventory as well as on units in the ending inventory. Thus, under the FIFO method, it is necessary to convert both inventories to an equivalent units basis. For the beginning inventory, the equivalent units represent the work done *to complete* the units; for the ending inventory, the equivalent units represent the work done to bring the units to a stage of partial completion at the end of the period (the same as with the weighted-average method).

In sum, the equivalent units figure under the FIFO method consists of three amounts:

1. The work needed *to complete* the units in the beginning inventory.
2. The work expended on the units *started and completed* during the period.
3. The work expended on partially completed units in the ending inventory.

To illustrate, refer again to the Regal Company data. The mixing department completed and transferred 140,000 units to the firing department during the year. Since 10,000 of these units came from the beginning inventory, the mixing department must have started and completed 130,000 units during the year. The 10,000 units in the beginning inventory had all materials added in the prior year and were 70 percent complete as to conversion costs when the current year started. Thus, during the current year, the mixing department would have added the other 30 percent of conversion cost (100% − 70% = 30%). Given these data, the equivalent units for the mixing department for the year would be computed as shown in Exhibit 4–6.

Comparison of the Weighted-Average and FIFO Methods

The reader should stop at this point and compare the data in Exhibit 4–6 with the data in Exhibit 4–5. Note that the major difference between the two exhibits is that the FIFO method separates the units in the beginning inventory from other

	Materials	Conversion
Work in process, beginning:		
10,000 units × 0%	—	
10,000 units × 30%*		3,000
Units started and completed this year . . .	130,000†	130,000†
Work in process, ending:		
20,000 units × 60%‡	12,000	
20,000 units × 25%‡		5,000
Equivalent units of production	142,000	138,000

EXHIBIT 4–6
Equivalent Units of Production: FIFO Method

* Work needed *to complete* the units in the beginning inventory.
† 140,000 units transferred out − 10,000 units in the beginning inventory = 130,000 units started and completed during the year.
‡ Work *completed* on the units in the ending inventory.

EXHIBIT 4–7
Visual Perspective of Equivalent Units

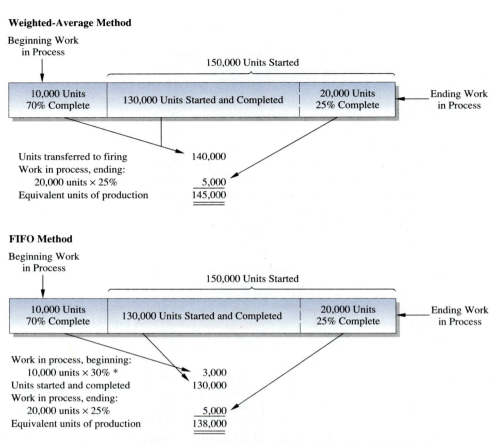

Weighted-Average Method

Beginning Work in Process

150,000 Units Started

| 10,000 Units 70% Complete | 130,000 Units Started and Completed | 20,000 Units 25% Complete |

Ending Work in Process

Units transferred to firing   140,000
Work in process, ending:
    20,000 units × 25%   5,000
Equivalent units of production   145,000

FIFO Method

Beginning Work in Process

150,000 Units Started

| 10,000 Units 70% Complete | 130,000 Units Started and Completed | 20,000 Units 25% Complete |

Ending Work in Process

Work in process, beginning:
    10,000 units × 30% *   3,000
Units started and completed   130,000
Work in process, ending:
    20,000 units × 25%   5,000
Equivalent units of production   138,000

* 100% − 70% = 30%. This 30% represents the work needed to complete the units in the beginning inventory.

units transferred out and converts the units in the beginning inventory to an equivalent units basis. A logical question to ask is, why the difference in the handling of the beginning inventory? The answer lies in what the two methods are trying to accomplish.

The purpose of the weighted-average method is to *simplify the computation of unit costs.* This is accomplished by treating units in the beginning inventory as if they were started and completed during the current period. By treating units in the beginning inventory in this way, the manager is relieved from having to distinguish between which units were on hand at the start of the year and which were not. Thus, he or she is able to treat all units equally when unit costs are computed. This greatly simplifies the costing process.

By contrast, the purpose of the FIFO method is to distinguish between (a) units in the beginning inventory and (b) units that were started during the period, so that separate unit costs can be computed for each. Under the FIFO method, units in the beginning inventory are assumed to be completed and transferred out first (thus, a "first-in, first-out" flow) and to carry their own unit costs. Units started during the year are assumed to be completed next and to carry their own unit costs. This is a more complex costing approach than the weighted-average method, although it can be argued that it is also more accurate.

Visual Perspective of Equivalent Units

To assist in your understanding of equivalent units, Exhibit 4–7 contains a visual perspective of the computation of equivalent units (the data are for Regal Company's conversion costs). The exhibit also shows the relationship between equivalent units as computed by the weighted-average method and equivalent units as computed by the FIFO method. Study Exhibit 4–7 carefully before going on.

PRODUCTION REPORT—WEIGHTED-AVERAGE METHOD

The purpose of the production report is to summarize for the manager all of the activity that takes place in a department's Work in Process account for a period. This activity includes the units that flow through the Work in Process account as well as the costs that flow through it. A separate production report is prepared for each department, as illustrated in Exhibit 4–8.

Earlier, when we outlined the differences between job-order costing and process costing, we stated that the production report takes the place of a job cost sheet in a process costing system. Thus, the production report is a key document for the manager and is vital to the proper operation of the system. The production report has three separate (though highly interrelated) parts:

1. A quantity schedule, which shows the flow of units through the department, and a computation of equivalent units.

EXHIBIT 4–8
The Position of the Production Report in the Flow of Costs

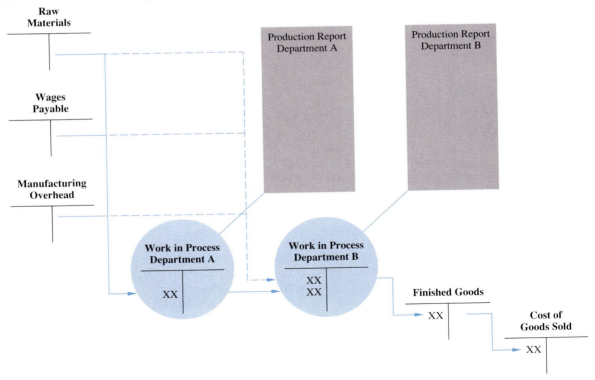

2. A computation of total and unit costs.
3. A reconciliation of all cost flows into and out of the department during the period.

We will use the data below for Stabler Chemical Company to show a numerical example of a production report.

Stabler Chemical Company has two departments—mixing and cooking. Production activity begins in the mixing department; after mixing, the units are transferred to the cooking department. From cooking, the units are transferred to finished goods.

All of the materials involved in mixing are added at the beginning of work in the mixing department. Labor and overhead costs in that department are incurred uniformly as work progresses. Overhead cost is applied at the rate of 150 percent of direct labor cost.

Cost and other data for May 19x1 include the following for the mixing department:

Work in process, beginning:
Units in process	20,000
Stage of completion*	30%
Cost in the beginning inventory:	
Materials cost	$ 8,000
Labor cost	3,600
Overhead cost	5,400
Total cost in process	$ 17,000

Units started into production during May	180,000
Units completed and transferred to cooking	170,000

Costs added to production during May:
Materials cost	$ 63,000
Labor cost	88,000
Overhead cost applied	132,000

Work in process, ending:
Units in process	30,000
Stage of completion*	40%

* This refers to labor and overhead costs only, since all materials are added at the beginning of work in the mixing department.

In this section, we show how a production report is prepared when the weighted-average method is used to compute equivalent units and unit costs. The preparation of a production report under the FIFO method is illustrated in Appendix B at the end of this chapter.

Step 1: Prepare a Quantity Schedule and Compute the Equivalent Units

Objective 5
Prepare a quantity schedule for a period by the weighted-average method.

The first part of a production report consists of a **quantity schedule,** which accounts for the physical flow of units through a department, and a computation of the equivalent units for the period. The equivalent units are computed in this part of the production report since the quantity schedule provides the data from which these figures are derived. To illustrate, a quantity schedule combined with a computation of equivalent units is given below for Stabler Chemical Company. (The quantity schedule is printed in color.)

	Quantity Schedule	Equivalent Units		
		Materials	**Labor**	**Overhead**
Units to be accounted for:				
Work in process, May 1 (all materials, 30% labor and overhead added last month)	20,000	(Work done last month)		
Started into production	180,000			
Total units	200,000			
Units accounted for as follows:				
Transferred to cooking.	170,000	170,000	170,000	170,000
Work in process, May 31 (all materials, 40% labor and overhead added this month)	30,000	30,000	12,000*	12,000*
Total units	200,000	200,000	182,000	182,000

* 30,000 units × 40% = 12,000 equivalent units.

   The quantity schedule permits the manager to see at a glance how many units moved through the department during a period as well as to see the stage of completion of any in-process units. In addition to providing this information, the quantity schedule serves as an essential guide in preparing and tying together the remaining parts of a production report. The equivalent units, for example, are easily computed by simply following the data provided in the quantity schedule, as shown above.

Step 2: Compute the Total and Unit Costs

As stated earlier, the weighted-average method treats units in the beginning work in process inventory as if they were started and completed during the current period. Thus, the cost in the beginning work in process inventory is added to the current period costs in determining both the total and unit costs for the period involved. These computations are shown below for Stabler Chemical Company:

Objective 6
Compute the total and unit costs for a period by the weighted-average method.

	Total Cost	Materials	Labor	Overhead	Whole Unit
Cost to be accounted for:					
Work in process, May 1	$ 17,000	$ 8,000	$ 3,600	$ 5,400	
Cost added by the department	283,000	63,000	88,000	132,000	
Total cost (a)	$300,000	$ 71,000	$ 91,600	$137,400	
Equivalent units (above) (b)	—	200,000	182,000	182,000	
Unit cost, (a) ÷ (b)	—	$0.355 +	$0.503 +	$0.755	= $1.613

   The unit costs that we have computed will be used to apply cost to units that are transferred to the next department and will also be used to compute the cost in the ending work in process inventory. A total of all unit costs from both the mixing and cooking departments will represent the final manufactured cost of a unit of product.

Step 3: Prepare a Cost Reconciliation

The purpose of **a cost reconciliation** is to show how the costs that have been charged to a department during a period are accounted for. Typically, the costs charged to a department will consist of:

Objective 7
Prepare a cost reconciliation for a period by the weighted-average method.

EXHIBIT 4–9

Graphic Illustration of the Cost Reconciliation Part of a Production Report

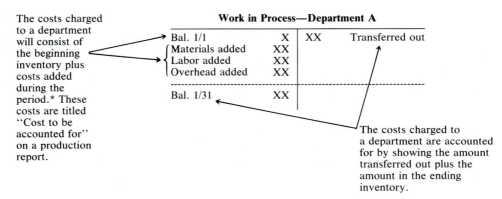

The costs charged to a department will consist of the beginning inventory plus costs added during the period.* These costs are titled "Cost to be accounted for" on a production report.

Work in Process—Department A

Bal. 1/1	X	XX	Transferred out
Materials added	XX		
Labor added	XX		
Overhead added	XX		
Bal. 1/31	XX		

The costs charged to a department are accounted for by showing the amount transferred out plus the amount in the ending inventory.

* Departments that follow department A (department B and so forth) will also need to show the amount of cost transferred in from the preceding department.

1. Cost in the beginning work in process inventory.
2. Materials, labor, and overhead cost added during the period.
3. Cost (if any) transferred in from the preceding department.

In a production report, these costs are generally titled "Cost to be accounted for." They are so titled in step 2 above where we summarized the costs chargeable to Stabler Chemical Company. These costs are accounted for in a production report by computing the following amounts:

1. Cost transferred out to the next department (or to Finished Goods).
2. Cost remaining in the ending work in process inventory.

In short, when a cost reconciliation is prepared, the "Cost to be accounted for" from step 2 is reconciled with the sum of the cost transferred out during the period plus the cost in the ending work in process inventory. This concept is shown graphically in Exhibit 4–9. Study this exhibit carefully before going on to the cost reconciliation below for Stabler Chemical Company.

Example of a Cost Reconciliation   The cost reconciliation depends heavily on the quantity schedule that was developed earlier. In fact, *the simplest way to prepare a cost reconciliation is to follow the quantity schedule line for line and show the cost associated with each group of units.* This is done in Exhibit 4–10, where we present a completed production report for Stabler Chemical Company.

The quantity schedule in the exhibit shows that 20,000 units were in process on May 1 and that an additional 180,000 units were started into production during the month. Looking at the "Cost to be accounted for" in the middle part of the exhibit, notice that the units in process on May 1 had $17,000 in cost attached to them and that the mixing department added another $283,000 in cost to production during the month. Thus, the department has $300,000 ($17,000 + $283,000) in cost to be accounted for.

This cost is accounted for in two ways. As shown on the quantity schedule, 170,000 units were transferred to the cooking department during May and another 30,000 units were still in process at the end of the month. Thus, part of the $300,000 "Cost to be accounted for" goes with the 170,000 units to the cooking department, and part of it remains with the 30,000 units in the ending work in process inventory.

Objective 8
Combine the quantity schedule and equivalent units, the total and unit costs, and the cost reconciliation into a production report.

EXHIBIT 4–10

Production Report—Weighted-Average Method

Quantity Schedule and Equivalent Units

		Equivalent Units		
	Quantity Schedule	Materials	Labor	Overhead
Units to be accounted for:				
Work in process, May 1 (all materials, 30% labor and overhead added last month)	20,000	(Work done last month)		
Started into production	180,000			
Total units	200,000			
Units accounted for as follows:				
Transferred to cooking	170,000	170,000	170,000	170,000
Work in process, May 31 (all materials, 40% labor and overhead added this month).	30,000	30,000	12,000*	12,000*
Total units	200,000	200,000	182,000	182,000

Total and Unit Costs

	Total Cost	Materials	Labor	Overhead	Whole Unit
Cost to be accounted for:					
Work in process, May 1	$ 17,000	$ 8,000	$ 3,600	$ 5,400	
Cost added by the department	283,000	63,000	88,000	132,000	
Total cost (a).	$300,000	$ 71,000	$ 91,600	$137,400	
Equivalent units (b).	—	200,000	182,000	182,000	
Unit cost, (a) ÷ (b)	—	$0.355 +	$0.503 +	$0.755 =	$1.613

Cost Reconciliation

		Equivalent Units (above)		
	Total Cost	Materials	Labor	Overhead
Cost accounted for as follows:				
Transferred to cooking: 170,000 units × $1.613 each	$274,254[†]	170,000	170,000	170,000
Work in process, May 31:				
Materials, at $0.355 per EU	10,650	30,000		
Labor, at $0.503 per EU.	6,036		12,000	
Overhead, at $0.755 per EU	9,060			12.000
Total work in process, May 31	25,746			
Total cost	$300,000			

* 40% × 30,000 units = 12,000 equivalent units.

[†] 170,000 units × $1.613 = $274,210; $44 in cost has been added to the $274,210 figure ($44 + $274,210 = $274,254) to compensate for a decimal discrepancy in the unit cost figures and to allow the company to account for all $300,000 in cost charged to the department for the month.

EU = Equivalent unit.

Each of the 170,000 units transferred to the cooking department is assigned $1.613 in cost, for a total of $274,254. The 30,000 units still in process at the end of the month are assigned cost according to their stage of completion. To determine the stage of completion, we refer to the equivalent units computation and bring the equivalent units figures down to the cost reconciliation part of the report. We then assign cost to these units, using the unit cost figures already computed.

After cost has been assigned to the ending work in process inventory, the total cost that we have accounted for ($300,000) agrees with the amount that we had to account for ($300,000). Thus, the cost reconciliation is complete.

A Comment about Rounding Errors

Since the computation of unit costs frequently results in uneven decimals, it is hard to obtain exact numbers in the cost reconciliation part of the production report. Note, for example, that in obtaining the exact $300,000 total cost figure that is accounted for in Exhibit 4–10 we had to show $274,254 in cost transferred to the cooking department. However, using the unit cost figure of $1.613, the *actual* amount of cost transferred would have been only $274,210 (170,000 units × $1.613). The $44 difference ($274,254 − $274,210) between the amount of cost appearing on the cost reconciliation and the amount of cost actually transferred to the cooking department is due to rounding errors in the unit cost figures.

To compensate for such rounding errors, the reader should do two things in completing homework assignments. First, carry all unit cost computations to *three* decimal places as we have done. Second, for purposes of consistency, any adjustment needed to complete the cost reconciliation should be made to the cost "transferred" amount rather than to the ending inventory figure, as we have done in Exhibit 4–10.

OPERATION COSTING

Objective 9
State the conditions under which operation costing is useful to management.

The costing systems discussed in Chapters 3 and 4 represent the two ends of a continuum. On one end we have job-order costing, which is used by companies that produce many different items—generally to customers' specifications. On the other end we have process costing, which is used by companies that produce basically homogeneous products in large quantities. Between these two extremes there are many hybrid systems that include characteristics of both job-order and process costing. One of these hybrids—called *operation costing*—is widely used in actual practice.

Operation costing is used in those situations where products have some common characteristics and also some individual characteristics. Shoes, for example, have certain common characteristics in that all styles involve cutting and sewing that can be done on a repetitive basis, using the same equipment and following the same basic procedures. These same shoes, however, can also have some individual characteristics in that some may be made of expensive leather and others may be made of inexpensive vinyl. In situations such as this, where products have some common characteristics but also must be handled individually to some extent, operation costing is typically used to determine unit costs.

As mentioned above, operation costing is a hybrid system in that it employs certain aspects of both job-order and process costing. Products are typically handled in batches when operation costing is in use, with each batch charged for the specific materials used in its production. In this sense, operation costing is similar to job-order costing. Labor and overhead costs are accumulated by operation or by department, however, and these costs are assigned to batches on an average per unit basis, as done in process costing. If shoes are being produced, for example, each style is charged the same per unit conversion cost, regardless of the style involved, but charged with its specific materials cost. Thus, the company is able to distinguish between batches in terms of materials, but it is able to employ the simplicity of a process costing system for labor and overhead costs.

Examples of other products for which operation costing is frequently used include electronic equipment (such as semiconductors), textiles, clothing, and jewelry (such as rings, bracelets, and medallions). Products of this type are typically produced in batches, but they can vary considerably from model to model or from style to style in terms of the cost of raw material inputs. Therefore, an operation costing system is well suited for providing necessary cost information for management.

SUMMARY

Process costing is used in those manufacturing situations where homogeneous products are produced on a continuous basis. A process costing system is similar to a job-order costing system in that (1) both systems have the same basic purpose of providing data for the manager, (2) both systems use the same manufacturing accounts, and (3) costs flow through the manufacturing accounts in basically the same way in both systems. A process costing system differs from a job-order system in that (1) a single product is involved, (2) costs are accumulated by department (rather than by job), (3) the department production report replaces the job cost sheet, and (4) unit costs are computed by department (rather than by job).

To compute unit costs in a department, the department's equivalent units must be determined. Equivalent units can be computed in two ways—by the weighted-average method and by the FIFO method. The weighted-average method treats partially completed units in the beginning work in process inventory as if they were started and completed during the current period. The FIFO method distinguishes between work completed in the prior period and work completed currently, so that equivalent units represent only work completed during the current period.

The activity in a department is summarized on a production report. There are three separate (though highly interrelated) parts to a production report. The first part is a quantity schedule, which includes a computation of equivalent units and shows the flow of units through a department during a period. The second part consists of a computation of total and unit costs, with unit costs being provided individually for materials, labor, and overhead as well as in total for the period. The third part consists of a cost reconciliation, which summarizes all cost flows through a department for a period.

Operation costing is a hybrid system in that it employs aspects of both job-order and process costing. Products are handled in batches when operation costing is in use, and each batch is charged with its specific materials, the same as in a job-order costing system. However, conversion costs are accumulated by operation or department, and each product is charged with the same per unit conversion cost, the same as in a process costing system.

REVIEW PROBLEM: PROCESS COST FLOWS AND REPORTS

Wicker Company manufactures a single product and uses a process costing system. The product goes through two sequential departments, A and B. Information relating to the company's operations for April 19x1 is given below.

a. Raw materials were issued for use in production: department A, $851,000; and department B, $629,000.
b. Direct labor costs were incurred: department A, $330,000; and department B, $270,000.
c. Manufacturing overhead cost was applied to products: department A, $665,000; and department B, $405,000.

d. Products that were complete as to processing in department A were transferred to department B, $1,850,000.

e. Products that were complete as to processing in department B were transferred to Finished Goods, $3,200,000.

Required   1. Prepare journal entries to record items (a) through (e) above.

2. Post the journal entries from (1) to T-accounts. The balance in department A's Work in Process account on April 1 was $150,000; the balance in department B's Work in Process account was $70,000. After posting entries to the T-accounts, find the ending balance in each department's Work in Process account.

3. Prepare a production report for department A for April. The following additional information is available regarding production in department A during the month:

Production data:

Units in process, April 1: 100% complete as to materials, 60% complete as to labor and overhead.	30,000
Units started into production during April	420,000
Units completed and transferred to department B	370,000
Units in process, April 30: 50% complete as to materials, 25% complete as to labor and overhead.	80,000

Cost data:

Work in process inventory, April 1:

Materials	$ 92,000
Labor	21,000
Overhead	37,000
Total cost.	$150,000

Cost added during April [see the entries in (1)]:

Materials	$851,000
Labor	330,000
Overhead	665,000

Solution to Review Problem

1. a.
Work in Process—Department A.	851,000	
Work in Process—Department B.	629,000	
Raw Materials		1,480,000

b.
Work in Process—Department A.	330,000	
Work in Process—Department B.	270,000	
Salaries and Wages Payable		600,000

c.
Work in Process—Department A.	665,000	
Manufacturing Overhead—Department A		665,000
Work in Process—Department B.	405,000	
Manufacturing Overhead—Department B		405,000

d.
Work in Process—Department B.	1,850,000	
Work in Process—Department A.		1,850,000

e.
Finished Goods	3,200,000	
Work in Process—Department B.		3,200,000

2.

Raw Materials

Bal.	XXX	(a)	1,480,000

Salaries and Wages Payable

	(b)	600,000

Work in Process— Department A

Bal.	150,000	(d)	1,850,000
(a)	851,000		
(b)	330,000		
(c)	665,000		
Bal.	146,000		

Manufacturing Overhead— Department A

(Various actual costs)	(c)	665,000

Manufacturing Overhead— Department B

(Various actual costs)	(c)	405,000

Work in Process—Department B			Finished Goods		
Bal.	70,000	(e) 3,200,000	Bal.	XXX	
(a)	629,000		(e)	3,200,000	
(b)	270,000				
(c)	405,000				
(d)	1,850,000				
Bal.	24,000				

3.

WICKER COMPANY

Production Report—Department A
For the Month Ended April 30, 19x1

Quantity Schedule and Equivalent Units

	Quantity Schedule	Equivalent Units		
		Materials	Labor	Overhead
Units to be accounted for:				
Work in process, April 1 (all materials, 60% labor and overhead added last month)	30,000	(Work done last month)		
Started into production	420,000			
Total units	450,000			
Units accounted for as follows:				
Transferred to department B	370,000	370,000	370,000	370,000
Work in process, April 30 (50% materials, 25% labor and overhead added this month)	80,000	40,000*	20,000*	20,000*
Total units	450,000	410,000	390,000	390,000

Total and Unit Costs

	Total Cost	Materials	Labor	Overhead	Whole Unit
Cost to be accounted for:					
Work in process, April 1	$ 150,000	$ 92,000	$ 21,000	$ 37,000	
Cost added by the department	1,846,000	851,000	330,000	665,000	
Total cost (a)	$1,996,000	$943,000	$351,000	$702,000	
Equivalent units (b)	—	410,000	390,000	390,000	
Unit cost, (a) ÷ (b)	—	$2.30 +	$0.90 +	$1.80 =	$5.00

Cost Reconciliation

	Total Cost	Equivalent Units (above)		
		Materials	Labor	Overhead
Cost accounted for as follows:				
Transferred to department B:				
370,000 units × $5.00	$1,850,000	370,000	370,000	370,000
Work in process, April 30:				
Materials, at $2.30 per EU	92,000	40,000		
Labor, at $0.90 per EU	18,000		20,000	
Overhead, at $1.80 per EU	36,000			20,000
Total work in process	146,000			
Total cost	$1,996,000			

* Materials: 80,000 units × 50% = 40,000 equivalent units; labor and overhead: 80,000 units × 25% = 20,000 equivalent units.

EU = Equivalent unit.

KEY TERMS FOR REVIEW

Objective 10
Define or explain the key
terms listed at the end of
the chapter.

Conversion cost   Direct labor cost combined with manufacturing overhead cost. (p. 136)

Cost reconciliation   The part of a production report that shows what costs a department has to account for during a period and how those costs are accounted for. (p. 141)

Equivalent units of production   The number of units that would have been produced during a period if all of a department's efforts had resulted in completed units of product. (p. 135)

FIFO method   A method of accounting for cost flows in a process costing system in which equivalent units and unit costs relate only to work done during the current period. (p. 137)

Operation costing   A costing system used when products are manufactured in batches and when the products have some common characteristics and some individual characteristics. This system handles materials the same as in job-order costing and labor and overhead the same as in process costing. (p. 144)

Parallel processing   A method of arranging processing departments in which, after a certain point, some units may go through different processing departments than others. (p. 132)

Process costing   A costing method used in those industries that produce homogeneous products on a continuous basis. (p. 130)

Processing department   Any location in a factory where work is performed on a product and where materials, labor, or overhead costs are added to the product. (p. 131)

Production report   A report that summarizes all activity in a department's Work in Process account during a period and that contains three parts: a quantity schedule and a computation of equivalent units, a computation of total and unit costs, and a cost reconciliation. (p. 131)

Quantity schedule   The part of a production report that shows the flow of units through a department during a period. (p. 140)

Sequential processing   A method of arranging processing departments in which all units flow in sequence from one department to another. (p. 131)

Transferred-in cost   The amount of cost attached to units of product that have been received from a prior processing department. (p. 133)

Weighted-average method   A method of accounting for cost flows in a process costing system in which units in the beginning work in process inventory are treated as if they were started and completed during the current period. (p. 136)

APPENDIX B: PRODUCTION REPORT—FIFO METHOD

When the FIFO method is used to account for cost flows in a process costing system, the steps followed in preparing a production report are the same as those discussed earlier for the weighted-average method. However, since the FIFO method makes a distinction between units in the opening inventory and units started during the year, the cost reconciliation portion of the report is more complex under the FIFO method than it is under the weighted-average method. To illustrate the FIFO method, we will again use the data for Stabler Chemical Company found on page 140.

Step 1: Prepare a Quantity Schedule and Compute the Equivalent Units

Objective 11
Prepare a quantity
schedule for a period by
the FIFO method.

There is only one difference between a quantity schedule prepared under the FIFO method and one prepared under the weighted-average method. This difference relates to units transferred out. As explained earlier in our discussion of equivalent units, the FIFO method divides units transferred out into two parts. One part consists of the units in the opening inventory, and the other part consists of the units started and completed during the current period. A quantity schedule showing this format for units transferred out is presented below for Stabler Chemical Company, along with a computation of equivalent units for the month. (The quantity schedule is printed in color.)

		Equivalent Units		
	Quantity Schedule	Materials	Labor	Overhead
Units to be accounted for:				
Work in process, May 1 (all materials, 30% labor and overhead added last month).	20,000	(Work done last month)		
Started into production.	180,000			
Total units	200,000			
Units accounted for as follows:				
Transferred to cooking:				
From the beginning inventory.	20,000	—	14,000*	14,000*
Started and completed this month	150,000†	150,000	150,000	150,000
Work in process, May 31 (all materials, 40% labor and overhead added this month)	30,000	30,000	12,000‡	12,000‡
Total units	200,000	180,000	176,000	176,000

* 100% − 30% = 70%; 70% × 20,000 units = 14,000 EU.

† 170,000 units transferred − 20,000 units from the beginning inventory = 150,000 units.

‡ 40% × 30,000 units = 12,000 EU.

We explained earlier that in computing equivalent units under the FIFO method, we must first show the amount of work required *to complete* the units in the beginning inventory. We then show the number of units started and completed during the period, and finally we show the amount of work *completed* on the units still in process at the end of the period. The reader should carefully trace through these computations for Stabler Chemical Company above.

Step 2: Compute the Total and Unit Costs

In computing unit costs under the FIFO method, we use only those costs that were incurred during the current period, and we ignore any costs in the beginning work in process inventory. The reason we ignore costs in the beginning inventory is that under the FIFO method, *unit costs are intended to relate only to work done during the current period.*

Objective 12
Compute the total and unit costs for a period by the FIFO method.

	Total Cost	Materials	Labor	Overhead	Whole Unit
Cost to be accounted for:					
Work in process, May 1	$ 17,000	—	—	—	
Cost added by the department (a) . . .	283,000	$ 63,000	$ 88,000	$132,000	
Total cost	$300,000	—	—	—	
Equivalent units (above) (b)	—	180,000	176,000	176,000	
Unit cost, (a) ÷ (b).	—	$0.35 +	$0.50 +	$0.75 =	$1.60

The unit costs we have computed are used to add cost to units of product as they are transferred to the next department; in addition, they are used to show the amount of cost attached to partially completed units in the ending work in process inventory.

EXHIBIT B–1
Production Report—FIFO Method

Quantity Schedule and Equivalent Units

	Quantity Schedule	Equivalent Units		
		Materials	Labor	Overhead
Units to be accounted for:				
Work in process, May 1 (all materials, 30% labor and overhead added last month)	20,000	(Work done last month)		
Started into production	180,000			
Total units	200,000			
Units accounted for as follows:				
Transferred to cooking:				
From the beginning inventory	20,000	—	14,000*	14,000*
Started and completed this month	150,000†	150,000	150,000	150,000
Work in process, May 31 (all materials, 40% labor and overhead added this month)	30,000	30,000	12,000‡	12,000‡
Total units	200,000	180,000	176,000	176,000

Total and Unit Costs

	Total Cost	Materials	Labor	Overhead	Whole Unit
Cost to be accounted for:					
Work in process, May 1	$ 17,000	—	—	—	
Cost added by the department (a)	283,000	$ 63,000	$ 88,000	$132,000	
Total cost	$300,000	—	—	—	
Equivalent units (b)	—	180,000	176,000	176,000	
Unit cost, (a) ÷ (b)	—	$0.35 +	$0.50 +	$0.75 =	$1.60

Cost Reconciliation

	Total Cost	Equivalent Units (above)		
		Materials	Labor	Overhead
Cost accounted for as follows:				
Transferred to cooking:				
From the beginning inventory:				
Cost in the beginning inventory	$ 17,000			
Cost to complete these units:				
Materials, at $0.35 per EU	—	—		
Labor, at $0.50 per EU	7,000		14,000	
Overhead, at $0.75 per EU	10,500			14,000
Total cost	34,500			
Units started and completed this month: 150,000				
units × $1.60	240,000	150,000	150,000	150,000
Total cost transferred	274,500			
Work in process, May 31:				
Materials, at $0.35 per EU	10,500	30,000		
Labor, at $0.50 per EU	6,000		12,000	
Overhead, at $0.75 per EU	9,000			12,000
Total work in process, May 31	25,500			
Total cost	$300,000			

* 100% − 30% = 70%; 70% × 20,000 units = 14,000 equivalent units.

† 170,000 units transferred − 20,000 units in the beginning inventory = 150,000 units.

‡ 40% × 30,000 units = 12,000 equivalent units.

EU = Equivalent unit.

Step 3: Prepare a Cost Reconciliation

In the main body of the chapter we learned that the purpose of a cost reconciliation is to show how the costs charged to a department during a period are accounted for. We also learned that the best way to prepare a cost reconciliation is to follow the quantity schedule line for line and show the costs associated with each group of units.

Objective 13
Prepare a cost reconciliation for a period by the FIFO method.

When the FIFO method is being used, two cost elements are associated with the units in the beginning work in process inventory. The first element is the cost carried over from the prior period. The second element is the cost needed *to complete* these units. For Stabler Chemical Company, $17,000 in cost was carried over from last month. In the cost reconciliation in Exhibit B–1, we add to this figure $7,000 in labor cost and $10,500 in overhead cost needed to complete these units. Note from the exhibit that these labor and overhead cost figures are computed by multiplying the unit costs for labor and overhead times the equivalent units of work needed *to complete* the items in the beginning inventory. (The equivalent units figures used in this computation are brought down from the "equivalent units" portion of the production report.)

For units started and completed during the month, we simply multiply the number of units started and completed by the total cost per unit to determine the amount transferred out. This would be $240,000 (150,000 units × $1.60 = $240,000) for Stabler Chemical Company.

Finally, the amount of cost attached to the ending work in process inventory is computed by multiplying the unit cost figures for the month times the equivalent units for materials, labor, and overhead in the ending inventory. Once again, the equivalent units needed for this computation are brought down from the "equivalent units" portion of the production report.

A Comparison of Production Report Content

The production report is the most difficult part of this chapter, and it will require some effort on the reader's part to master its content and structure. To assist in this study, Exhibit B–2 summarizes the major similarities and differences between production reports prepared under the weighted-average and FIFO methods.

A Comparison of Costing Methods

Although the weighted-average and FIFO methods seem to be very different, in most process costing situations they will produce unit costs that are nearly the same. Any major difference in unit costs between the two methods is likely to be traceable to erratic movements in raw materials prices. The reason is that conversion costs (labor and overhead) usually will not fluctuate widely from month to month due to the continuous nature of the flow of goods in process costing situations. In addition, inventory levels in most companies tend to remain quite stable, thereby adding to the general stability of unit costs. Raw materials prices can fluctuate considerably from period to period, however, which can result in a difference in unit costs between the two methods. This is because the weighted-average method will always be averaging the costs of one period with those of the following period.

From the standpoint of cost control, the FIFO method is clearly superior to the weighted-average method. The reason is that current performance should be measured in relation to costs of the current period only, and the weighted-average

EXHIBIT B–2
A Comparison of
Production Report
Content

Weighted-Average Method	FIFO Method
Quantity Schedule and Equivalent Units	
1. The quantity schedule includes all units transferred out in a single figure.	1. The quantity schedule divides the units transferred out into two parts. One part consists of units in the beginning inventory, and the other part consists of units started and completed during the current period.
2. In computing equivalent units, the units in the beginning inventory are treated as if they were started and completed during the current period.	2. Only work needed to *complete* units in the beginning inventory is included in the computation of equivalent units. Units started and completed during the current period are shown as a separate figure.
Total and Unit Costs	
1. The "Cost to be accounted for" part of the report is the same for both methods.	1. The "Cost to be accounted for" part of the report is the same for both methods.
2. Costs in the beginning inventory are added in with current period costs in unit cost computations.	2. Only current period costs are included in unit cost computations.
3. Unit costs will contain some element of cost from the prior period.	3. Unit costs will contain only elements of cost from the current period.
Cost Reconciliation	
1. All units transferred out are treated the same, regardless of whether they were part of the beginning inventory or started and completed during the period.	1. Units transferred out are divided into two groups: (a) units in the beginning inventory and (b) units started and completed during the period.
2. Units in the ending inventory have cost applied to them in the same way under both methods.	2. Units in the ending inventory have cost applied to them in the same way under both methods.

method inherently mixes these costs with costs of the prior period. Thus, under the weighted-average method, the manager's performance is influenced to some extent by what happened in a prior period. This problem does not arise under the FIFO method, since it makes a clear distinction between costs in the beginning inventory and costs incurred during the current period.

On the other hand, some managers feel that the weighted-average method is simpler to apply than the FIFO method. Although this may have been true in the past when much accounting work was done by hand, due to the advent of the computer it is doubtful whether it is still true today. The computer can handle either method with ease. The FIFO method would require a more complex programming effort when a process costing system is first set up, but after that there should be little difference between the two methods so far as difficulty in operating the system is concerned.

QUESTIONS

4–1 Under what conditions would it be appropriate to use a process costing system?

4–2 What similarities exist between job-order and process costing?

4–3 Costs are accumulated by job in a job-order costing system; how are costs accumulated in a process costing system?

4–4 What two essential features must characterize any processing department?

4–5 Distinguish between departments arranged in a sequential pattern and departments arranged in a parallel pattern.

4–6 Why is cost accumulation easier under a process costing system than it is under a job-order costing system?

4-7 How many Work in Process accounts are maintained in a company using process costing?

4-8 Assume that a company has two processing departments, mixing and firing. Prepare a journal entry to show a transfer of partially completed units from the mixing department to the firing department.

4-9 Assume again that a company has two processing departments, mixing and firing. Explain what costs might be added to the firing department's Work in Process account during a period.

4-10 What is meant by the term *equivalent units of production?*

4-11 Under the weighted-average method, what assumption is made relative to units in the beginning work in process inventory when equivalent units and unit costs are computed?

4-12 How does the computation of equivalent units under the FIFO method differ from the computation of equivalent units under the weighted-average method?

4-13 What is a quantity schedule, and what purpose does it serve?

4-14 Under process costing, it is often suggested that a product is like a rolling snowball as it moves from department to department. Why is this an apt comparison?

4-15 Watkins Trophies, Inc., produces thousands of medallions made of bronze, silver, and gold. The medallions are identical except for the materials used in their manufacture. What costing system would you advise the company to use?

4-16 Give examples of companies that might use operation costing.

4-17 (Appendix B) On the cost reconciliation part of the production report, the weighted-average method treats all units transferred out in the same way. How does this differ from the FIFO method of handling units transferred out?

4-18 (Appendix B) From the standpoint of cost control, why is the FIFO method superior to the weighted-average method?

EXERCISES

Clonex Labs, Inc., uses a process costing system. The following data are available for one department for October 19x6: **E4-1**

| | Units | Percent Completed | |
		Materials	Conversion
Work in process, October 1	30,000	65	30
Work in process, October 31	15,000	80	40

The department started 175,000 units into production during the month and transferred 190,000 completed units to the next department.

Compute the equivalent units of production for October, assuming that the company uses the weighted-average method of accounting for units and costs. *Required*

Refer to the data for Clonex Labs, Inc., in E4–1. **E4-2**

Compute the equivalent units of production for October, assuming that the company uses the FIFO method of accounting for units and costs. *Required*

The Superior Pulp Company processes wood pulp for various manufacturers of paper products. Data relating to tons of pulp processed during June 19x5 are provided below: **E4-3**

| | Tons of Pulp | Percent Completed | |
		Materials	Labor and Overhead
Work in process, June 1	20,000	90	80
Work in process, June 30	30,000	60	40
Started into processing during June	190,000	—	—

Required 1. Compute the number of tons completed and transferred out during June.
2. Prepare a quantity schedule for June, assuming that the company uses the weighted-average method.

E4-4 (Appendix B) Refer to the data in E4-3.

Required 1. Compute the number of tons completed and transferred out during June.
2. Prepare a quantity schedule for June, assuming that the company uses the FIFO method.

E4-5 The Alaskan Fisheries, Inc., processes salmon for various distributors. Two departments are involved—department 1 and department 2. Data relating to pounds of salmon processed in department 1 during July 19x3 are presented below:

	Pounds of Salmon	Percent Completed*
Work in process, July 1.	20,000	30
Started into processing during July	380,000	—
Work in process, July 31	25,000	60

* Labor and overhead only.

All materials are added at the beginning of processing in department 1. Labor and overhead (conversion) costs are incurred uniformly throughout processing.

Required Prepare a quantity schedule and a computation of equivalent units for July, assuming that the company uses the weighted-average method of accounting for units.

E4-6 (Appendix B) Refer to the data for The Alaskan Fisheries, Inc., in E4-5.

Required Prepare a quantity schedule and a computation of equivalent units for July, assuming that the company uses the FIFO method of accounting for units.

E4-7 Malex Company uses a process costing system. The company's single product passes through two processes, cooking and molding. T-accounts showing the flow of costs through the two processes for a recent month follow:

Work in Process—Cooking

Bal. 4/1	8,000	Transferred out	160,000
Direct materials	42,000		
Direct labor	50,000		
Overhead	75,000		

Work in Process—Molding

Bal. 4/1	4,000	Transferred out	240,000
Transferred in	160,000		
Direct labor	36,000		
Overhead	45,000		

Required Prepare journal entries showing the flow of costs through the two processes during April.

E4-8 Pureform, Inc., manufactures a product that passes through two departments. Data for a recent month for department A follow:

	Units	Materials	Labor	Overhead
Work in process, beginning	5,000	$ 4,500	$ 1,250	$ 1,875
Units started in process	45,000			
Units transferred out	42,000			
Work in process, ending	8,000			
Cost added during the month	—	52,800	21,500	32,250

The beginning work in process inventory was 80 percent complete as to materials and 60 percent complete as to processing. The ending work in process inventory was 75 percent complete as to materials and 50 percent complete as to processing.

1. Assume that the company uses the weighted-average method of accounting for units and costs. Prepare a quantity schedule and a computation of equivalent units for the month.
2. Determine the total and unit costs for the month.

Required

(Appendix B) Refer to the data for Pureform, Inc., in E4–8.

E4–9

1. Assume that the company uses the FIFO method of accounting for units and costs. Prepare a quantity schedule and a computation of equivalent units for the month.
2. Determine the total and unit costs for the month.

Required

Helox, Inc., manufactures a product that passes through two production processes. A quantity schedule for a recent month for process A follows:

E4–10

	Quantity Schedule	Equivalent Units	
		Materials	Conversion
Units to be accounted for:			
Work in process, May 1 (all materials, 40% conversion cost added last month)	5,000	(Work done last month)	
Started into production.	180,000		
Total units	185,000		
Units accounted for as follows:			
Transferred to process B	175,000	?	?
Work in process, May 31 (all materials, 30% conversion cost added this month)	10,000	?	?
Total units	185,000	?	?

Costs in the beginning work in process inventory were: materials, $1,200; and conversion cost, $3,800. Costs added during the month were: materials, $54,000; and conversion cost, $352,000.

1. Assume that the company uses the weighted-average method of accounting for units and costs. Determine the equivalent units for the month.
2. Compute the total and unit costs for the month.

Required

(This exercise should be assigned only if E4–10 is also assigned.) Refer to the data for Helox, Inc., in E4–10 and to the equivalent units and unit costs you have computed there.

E4–11

Complete the following cost reconciliation for process A:

Required

Cost Reconciliation

	Total Cost	Equivalent Units	
		Materials	Conversion
Cost accounted for as follows:			
Transferred to process B: (? units × $?).	$?		
Work in process, May 31:			
Materials, at _____ per EU	?	?	
Conversion, at _____ per EU	?		?
Total work in process	?		
Total cost.	$?		

(Appendix B) Refer to the data for Helox, Inc., in E4–10. Assume that the company uses the FIFO cost method.

E4–12

Required   1. Prepare a quantity schedule and a computation of equivalent units for the month.
2. Compute the total and unit costs for the month.

E4–13   (Appendix B) (This exercise should be assigned only if E4–12 is also assigned.) Refer to the data for Helox, Inc., in E4–10 and to the equivalent units and unit costs that you computed in E4–12.

Required   Complete the following cost reconciliation for process A:

Cost Reconciliation

	Total Cost	Equivalent Units Materials	Equivalent Units Conversion
Cost accounted for as follows:			
Transferred to process B:			
From the beginning inventory:			
Cost in the beginning inventory.	$?		
Cost to complete these units:			
Materials, at _____ per EU	?	?	
Conversion, at _____ per EU	?		?
Total cost	?		
Units started and completed this			
month: _____ units × _____ each	?	?	?
Total cost transferred	?		
Work in process, May 31:			
Materials, at _____ per EU	?	?	
Conversion, at _____ per EU	?		?
Total work in process	?		
Total cost	$?		

E4–14   Silvac Company manufactures a single product and uses a process costing system. Information relating to production during the most recent year in process A follows:

	Units	Percent Completed Materials	Percent Completed Conversion
Work in process, January 1.	50,000	70	40
Started into production.	790,000		
Completed and transferred out . . .	800,000		
Work in process, December 31 . . .	40,000	50	25

Required   1. Assume that the company uses the weighted-average method to account for units. Compute the equivalent units for the year for both materials and conversion.
2. Assume that the company uses the FIFO method to account for units. Compute the equivalent units for the year for both materials and conversion.

PROBLEMS ——————————————————————————————

P4–15   **Partial Production Report; Weighted-Average Method**   Martin Company uses a process costing system and manufactures a single product. Activity for June 19x6 has just been completed. An incomplete production report for department X for the month follows:

Quantity Schedule and Equivalent Units

	Quantity Schedule	Equivalent Units		
		Materials	Labor	Overhead
Units to be accounted for:				
Work in process, June 1 (all materials, 75% labor and overhead added last month)	8,000	(Work done last month)		
Started into production.	45,000			
Total units	53,000			
Units accounted for as follows:				
Transferred to department Y	48,000	?	?	?
Work in process, June 30 (all materials, 40% labor and overhead added this month)	5,000	?	?	?
Total units	53,000	?	?	?

Total and Unit Costs

	Total Cost	Materials	Labor	Overhead	Whole Unit
Cost to be accounted for:					
Work in process, June 1	$ 7,130	$ 5,150	$ 660	$ 1,320	
Cost added by the department	58,820	29,300	9,840	19,680	
Total cost (a)	$65,950	$34,450	$10,500	$21,000	
Equivalent units (b)	—	53,000	50,000	50,000	
Unit cost, (a) ÷ (b).	—	$0.65 +	$0.21 +	$0.42 =	$1.28

Cost Reconciliation

	Total Cost
Cost accounted for as follows:	
?	?

Required

1. By looking at the data used in the quantity schedule, explain how you can tell that the company is using the weighted-average method to account for the flow of units and costs.
2. Prepare a schedule showing how the equivalent units were computed.
3. Complete the "cost reconciliation" part of the production report.

Step-by-Step Production Report; Weighted-Average Method Builder Products, Inc., **P4–16** manufactures a caulking compound that goes through three processing stages prior to completion. Information on work in the first department, cooking, is given below for May 19x2:

Production data:	
Units in process, May 1; 80% complete as to labor and overhead	10,000
Units started into production during May	100,000
Units completed and transferred out	95,000
Units in process, May 31; 60% complete as to materials and 20% complete as to labor and overhead.	?
Cost data:	
Work in process inventory, May 1:	
Materials cost	$ 1,500
Labor cost	1,800
Overhead cost	5,400
Cost added during May:	
Materials cost	154,500
Labor cost	22,700
Overhead cost	68,100

Materials are added at several stages during the cooking process, whereas labor and overhead costs are incurred uniformly. The company uses the weighted-average method.

Required   Prepare a production report for the cooking department for May. Use the following three steps in preparing your report:

1. Prepare a quantity schedule and a computation of equivalent units.
2. Compute the total and unit costs for the month.
3. Using the data from (1) and (2), prepare a cost reconciliation.

P4–17   **Partial Production Report; FIFO Method**   (Appendix B) Tumwater, Inc., manufactures a single product that moves through two departments, A and B. A partially completed production report for a recent month in department A follows:

Department A—Production Report
For the Month Ended March 31, 19x5

Quantity Schedule and Equivalent Units

	Quantity Schedule	Equivalent Units		
		Materials	Labor	Overhead
Units to be accounted for:				
Work in process, March 1 (all materials, ⅔ labor and overhead added last month)	6,000	(Work done last month)		
Started into production	40,000			
Total units	46,000			
Units accounted for as follows:				
Transferred to department B:				
From the beginning inventory	6,000	?	?	?
Started and completed this month . .	36,000	?	?	?
Work in process, March 31 (all materials, ¼ labor and overhead added this month)	4,000	?	?	?
Total units	46,000	?	?	?

Total and Unit Costs

	Total Cost	Materials	Labor	Overhead	Whole Unit
Cost to be accounted for:					
Work in process, March 1	$ 27,000	—	—	—	
Cost added during March (a)	138,000	$60,000	$29,250	$48,750	
Total cost.	$165,000	—	—	—	
Equivalent units (b)	—	40,000	39,000	39,000	
Unit cost, (a) ÷ (b)	—	$1.50 +	$0.75 +	$1.25	= $3.50

Cost Reconciliation

	Total Cost
Cost accounted for as follows:	
?	?

Required
1. By scrutinizing the incomplete production report, identify two ways in which you can tell that the company is using the FIFO method to account for the flow of units and costs.
2. Prepare a schedule showing how the equivalent units were computed.
3. Complete the "cost reconciliation" part of the production report.

P4–18   **Step-by-Step Production Report; FIFO Method**   (Appendix B) Selzik Company manufactures a single product that goes through two processes, blending and packaging. The following activity was recorded in the blending department during July 19x4:

Production data:
  Units in process, July 1; 30% complete
    as to conversion costs   10,000
  Units started into production   170,000
  Units completed and transferred to packaging . . . . .   ?
  Units in process, July 31; 40% complete
    as to conversion costs   20,000

Cost data:
  Work in process inventory, July 1:
    Materials cost . . . . $ 8,500
    Conversion cost . . . . ?   4,900 $ 13,400
  Cost added during the month:
    Materials cost   139,400
    Conversion cost   244,200   383,600
        Total cost $397,000

All materials are added at the beginning of work in the blending department. Conversion costs are added uniformly during processing. The company uses the FIFO cost method.

Prepare a production report for the blending department for July. Use the following three   *Required*
steps as a guide in preparing your report:

1. Prepare a quantity schedule and compute the equivalent units.
2. Compute the total and unit costs for the month.
3. Using the data from (1) and (2) above, prepare a cost reconciliation.

Equivalent Units; Missing Data; Both Weighted-Average and FIFO Methods   P4–19
Hackey Company uses a process costing system with three departments: mixing, molding, and firing. The information below relates to activity in the mixing department for 19x1.

Production Data

	Units	Percent Completed Materials	Percent Completed Conversion
Work in process, January 1	?	?	75
Started into production	?		
Completed and transferred out	?		
Work in process, December 31	?	60	?

Equivalent Units—Weighted-Average Method

	Materials	Conversion
Units transferred to molding	?	?
Work in process, December 31:		
? units × ? %	?	
? units × ? %		8,000
Equivalent units of production	?	?

Equivalent Units—FIFO Method

	Materials	Conversion
Work in process, January 1:		
? units × 10%	?	
? units × ? %		15,000
Units started and completed this year	?	?
Work in process, December 31:		
? units × ? %	?	
? units × 40%		?
Equivalent units of production	868,000	?

Compute the missing amounts in the various schedules above.   *Required*

P4-20   **Basic Production Report; Weighted-Average Method**   (P4–21 uses these same data with the FIFO method.) Suncrest, Inc., manufactures a product that goes through several departments prior to completion. The following information is available on work in the mixing department during June 19x1:

| | Units | Percent Completed | |
		Materials	Conversion
Work in process, beginning.	20,000	100	75
Started into production.	180,000		
Completed and transferred out . . .	160,000		
Work in process, ending	40,000	100	25

Cost in the beginning work in process inventory and cost added during June were as follows:

	Materials	Conversion
Work in process, beginning	$ 25,200	$ 24,800
Cost added during June	334,800	238,700

The company uses the weighted-average method to compute unit costs. The mixing department is the first department in the production process; after mixing has been completed, the units are transferred to the molding department.

Required   Prepare a production report for the mixing department for June 19x1.

P4-21   **Basic Production Report; FIFO Method**   (Appendix B) Refer to the data in P4–20. Assume that the company uses the FIFO method to compute unit costs rather than the weighted-average method.

Required   Prepare a production report for the mixing department for June 19x1.

P4-22   **Interpreting a Production Report**   Dolce Company manufactures a product that goes through several departments. A hastily prepared production report for department A for April is given below:

Quantity Schedule

Units to be accounted for:	
Work in process, April 1 (90% materials,	
80% conversion cost added last month)	30,000
Started into production	200,000
Total units	230,000

Units accounted for as follows:	
Transferred to department B	190,000
Work in process, April 30 (75% materials,	
60% conversion cost added this month)	40,000
Total units	230,000

Total Cost

Cost to be accounted for:	
Work in process, April 1	$ 98,000
Cost added during the month.	827,000
Total cost	$925,000

Cost Reconciliation

Cost accounted for as follows:	
Transferred to department B	$805,600
Work in process, April 30	119,400
Total cost	$925,000

Dolce Company has just been acquired by another organization, and the management of the acquiring company wants some additional information about Dolce's operations.

Required

1. Is Dolce Company using the weighted-average method or the FIFO method to account for units and costs? How can you tell?
2. What were the equivalent units for the month?
3. What were the unit costs for the month? The beginning inventory consisted of the following costs: materials, $67,800; and conversion cost, $30,200. The costs added during the month consisted of: materials, $579,000; and conversion cost, $248,000.
4. How many of the units transferred to department B were started and completed during the month?
5. The manager of department A, anxious to make a good impression on Dolce's new owners, stated, "Materials prices jumped from about $2.50 per unit in March to $3 per unit in April, but due to good cost control I was able to hold our materials cost to less than $3 per unit for the month." Should this manager be rewarded for a sterling effort at cost control? Explain.

Analysis of Work in Process T-Account; Weighted-Average Method   Weston Products manufactures an industrial cleaning compound that goes through three processing departments—grinding, mixing, and cooking. Raw materials are introduced at the start of work in the grinding department, with conversion costs being incurred evenly throughout the grinding process. The Work in Process T-account for the grinding department for a recent month is given below:

P4-23

Work in Process—Grinding Department

Inventory, May 1 (18,000 lbs., ⅓ processed)	21,800	Completed and transferred to mixing (? lbs.)	?
May costs added: Raw materials (167,000 lbs.)	133,400		
Labor and overhead	226,800		
Inventory, May 31 (15,000 lbs., ⅔ processed)	?		

The May 1 work in process inventory consists of $14,600 in materials cost and $7,200 in labor and overhead cost. The company uses the weighted-average method to account for units and costs.

Required

1. Prepare a production report for the grinding department for the month.
2. What criticism can be made of the unit costs that you have computed on your production report?

Analysis of Work in Process T-Account; FIFO Method   (Appendix B) Superior Brands, Inc., manufactures paint. The paint goes through three processes—cracking, mixing, and cooking. Activity in the cracking department during a recent month is summarized in the department's Work in Process account below:

P4-24

Work in Process—Cracking Department

Inventory, April 1 (10,000 gals., 80% processed)	39,000	Completed and transferred to mixing (? gals.)	?
April costs added: Materials (140,000 gals.)	259,000		
Labor and overhead	312,000		
Inventory, April 30 (30,000 gals., 60% processed)	?		

The materials are entered into production at the beginning of work in the cracking department. Labor and overhead costs are incurred uniformly throughout the cracking process. The company uses the FIFO cost method.

Required   1.   Prepare a production report for the cracking department for the month.
2.   In a process costing system, would you expect per unit materials cost or per unit labor and overhead cost to show the greater fluctuation from period to period? Why?

P4-25

Comprehensive Problem

Journal Entries; T-Accounts; Production Report: Weighted-Average Method   Quality Adhesives, Inc., manufactures a high-quality rubber cement product. Two departments are involved—grinding and cooking. During June 19x8, the following activity was recorded in the company:

a.   Raw materials were issued for use in production: grinding department, $110,775; and cooking department, $93,225.

b.   Direct labor cost was incurred: grinding department, $10,380; and cooking department, $4,620.

c.   Manufacturing overhead cost was incurred: grinding department, $70,000; and cooking department, $40,000. (Credit Accounts Payable.) A separate manufacturing overhead account is maintained for each department.

d.   Manufacturing overhead cost was applied to production: grinding department, $68,000; and cooking department, $41,000.

e.   Products that were completed as to processing in the grinding department were transferred to the cooking department, $198,000.

f.   Products that were complete as to processing in the cooking department were transferred to Finished Goods, $325,000.

g.   Completed goods were sold on account, $500,000. These goods had cost $350,000 to manufacture.

Required   1.   Prepare journal entries to record transactions (a) through (g) above.
2.   Post the journal entries from (1) to T-accounts. The following account balances existed at the beginning of the month:

Raw Materials Inventory.	$240,000
Work in Process—Grinding Department.	21,445
Work in Process—Cooking Department	16,715
Finished Goods Inventory	68,000

After posting the entries to the T-accounts, find the ending balance in each of the inventory accounts and the manufacturing overhead accounts.

3.   Prepare a production report for the grinding department for June. The following additional information is available regarding production in the grinding department during the month:

	Pounds
Work in process, June 1: 100% complete as to materials, 60% complete as to labor and overhead.	15,000
Pounds started into production during June	105,000
Pounds completed and transferred to cooking	110,000
Work in process, June 30: 100% complete as to materials, 28% complete as to labor and overhead.	10,000

The grinding department's $21,445 beginning work in process inventory consists of the following amounts: materials, $15,225; labor, $900; and overhead, $5,320. The costs added during June in the grinding department are available in entries (a), (b), and (d) from (1) above.

P4-26

Comprehensive Problem

Journal Entries; T-Accounts; Production Report: FIFO Method   (Appendix B) Home Products, Inc., manufactures a plastering compound that goes through two processes, mixing and cooking. Information relating to the company's operations for July 19x2 is given below:

a.   Raw materials were issued for use in production: mixing department, $462,000; and cooking department, $138,000.

b.   Direct labor costs were incurred: mixing department, $117,000; and cooking department, $53,000.

c.   Manufacturing overhead cost was incurred: mixing department, $345,000; and cooking department, $165,000. (Credit Accounts Payable.) A separate Manufacturing Overhead account is maintained for each department.

d.   Manufacturing overhead cost was applied to products: mixing department, $351,000; and cooking department, $160,000.

e.   Products that were complete as to processing in the mixing department were transferred to the cooking department, $885,200.

f.   Products that were complete as to processing in the cooking department were transferred to Finished Goods, $1,250,000.

g.   Completed goods were sold on account, $2,000,000. These goods had cost $1,300,000 to manufacture.

1.   Prepare journal entries to record transactions (a) through (g) above.   *Required*

2.   Post the journal entries from (1) to T-accounts. The following account balances existed at the beginning of the month:

> Raw Materials $625,000
> Work in Process—Mixing Department   20,000
> Work in Process—Cooking Department.   17,000
> Finished Goods.   90,000

After posting the entries to the T-accounts, find the ending balance in each of the inventory accounts and the manufacturing overhead accounts.

3.   Prepare a production report for the mixing department for July. The following additional information is available regarding production in the mixing department during the month:

	Units
Work in process, July 1: 75% complete as to materials,	
20% complete as to labor and overhead	20,000
Started into production	380,000
Completed and transferred to the cooking department	370,000
Work in process, July 31: 100% complete as to materials,	
80% complete as to labor and overhead	30,000

The costs added during July in the mixing department are given in journal entries (a), (b), and (d) in (1) above.

Journal Entries; T-Accounts; Production Report: Weighted-Average Method   Lubricants, Inc., produces a special kind of grease that is widely used by race car drivers. The grease is produced in two processes: refining and blending.

P4-27
Comprehensive Problem

Raw oil products are introduced at various points in the refining department; labor and overhead costs are incurred evenly throughout the refining operation. The refined output is then transferred to the blending department.

The following incomplete Work in Process account is available for the refining department for March 19x3:

Work in Process—Refining Department

March 1 inventory (20,000 gal., all materials, 90% processed)	38,000	Completed and transferred to blending (? gal.)	?
March costs added: Raw oil materials (390,000 gal.)	495,000		
Direct labor	72,000		
Overhead	181,000		
March 31 inventory (40,000 gal., 75% materials, 25% processed)	?		

The March 1 work in process inventory in the refining department consists of the following cost elements: raw materials, $25,000; direct labor, $4,000; and overhead, $9,000.

Costs incurred during March in the blending department were: materials used, $115,000; direct labor, $18,000; and overhead cost applied to production, $42,000. The company accounts for units and costs by the weighted-average method.

Required

1. Prepare journal entries to record the costs incurred in both the refining and blending departments during March. Key your entries to the items (a) through (g) below.
    a. Raw materials were issued for use in production.
    b. Direct labor costs were incurred.
    c. Manufacturing overhead costs were incurred: refining department, $185,000; blending department, $40,000. (Credit Accounts Payable.)
    d. Manufacturing overhead cost was applied to production.
    e. Products that were complete as to processing in the refining department were transferred to the blending department, $740,000.
    f. Products that were complete as to processing in the blending department were transferred to Finished Goods, $950,000.
    g. Completed products were sold on account, $1,500,000. These goods had cost $900,000 to manufacture.

2. Post the journal entries from (1) to T-accounts. The following account balances existed at the beginning of March. (The beginning balance in the refining department's Work in Process account is given above.)

Raw Materials	$618,000
Work in Process—Blending Department	65,000
Finished Goods	20,000

After posting the entries to the T-accounts, find the ending balance in the inventory accounts and the manufacturing overhead accounts.

3. Prepare a production report for the refining department for March.

P4–28
Comprehensive Problem

Journal Entries; T-Accounts; Production Report: FIFO Method (Appendix B) ZAB, Inc., produces a popular low-calorie soft drink. The drink is produced in two processes—blending and bottling.

All materials are added at the start of work in the blending department; labor and overhead costs are incurred evenly during the blending operation. The blended liquid is then transferred to the bottling department, where it is put into bottles for distribution.

The following incomplete Work in Process account for the blending department is available for June 19x8:

Work in Process—Blending Department

June 1 inventory (10,000 gal., 10% processed)	6,500	Completed and transferred to bottling (70,000 gal.)	?
June costs added:			
Materials (? gal.)	32,500		
Direct labor	64,800		
Overhead	97,200		
June 30 inventory (5,000 gal., 60% processed)	?		

Costs incurred during June in the bottling department were: materials used, $16,000; direct labor, $25,200; and overhead cost applied to production, $32,800. The company accounts for units and costs by the FIFO method.

Required

1. Prepare journal entries to record the costs incurred in both the blending and bottling departments during June. Key your entries to the items (a) through (g) below.
   a. Raw materials were issued for use in production.
   b. Direct labor costs were incurred.
   c. Manufacturing overhead costs were incurred: blending department, $100,000; bottling department, $34,000. (Credit Accounts Payable.)
   d. Manufacturing overhead cost was applied to production.
   e. Products that were complete as to processing in the blending department were transferred to the bottling department, $191,750.
   f. Products that were complete as to processing in the bottling department were transferred to Finished Goods, $260,000.
   g. Completed products were sold on account, $500,000. These goods had cost $300,000 to manufacture.
2. Post the journal entries from (1) to T-accounts. The following account balances existed at the beginning of June. (The beginning balance in the blending department's Work in Process account is given above.)

Raw Materials	$61,500
Work in Process—Bottling Department	8,250
Finished Goods	50,000

After posting the entries to the T-accounts, find the ending balance in the inventory accounts and the manufacturing overhead accounts.
3. Prepare a production report for the blending department for June.

Equivalent Units; Costing of Inventories; Weighted-Average Method   You are employed by Spirit Company, a manufacturer of digital watches. The company's chief financial officer is trying to verify the accuracy of the December 31, 19x6, work in process and finished goods inventories prior to closing the books for the year. You have been asked to assist in this verification. The year-end balances shown on Spirit Company's books are as follows:

P4–29

	Units	Costs
Work in process (50% complete as to labor and overhead)	300,000	$ 660,960
Finished goods	200,000	1,009,800

Materials are added to production at the beginning of the manufacturing process, and overhead is applied to each product at the rate of 60% of direct labor cost. There was no finished goods inventory on January 1, 19x6. A review of Spirit Company's inventory and cost records has disclosed the following information:

		Costs	
	Units	Materials	Labor
Work in process, January 1, 19x6 (80% complete as to labor and overhead)	200,000	$ 200,000	$ 315,000
Units started into production	1,000,000		
Cost added during 19x6:			
Materials cost		1,300,000	
Labor cost			1,995,000
Units completed during 19x6	900,000		

The company uses the weighted-average cost method.

Required

1. Prepare a computation showing the equivalent units for 19x6 and unit costs for materials, labor, and overhead.
2. Determine the amount of cost that should be assigned to the ending work in process and finished goods inventories.
3. Prepare the necessary correcting journal entry to adjust the work in process and finished goods inventories to the correct balances as of December 31, 19x6.
4. Determine the cost of goods sold for the year.

(CPA, adapted)

CASES

C4-30   **Production Report: Second Department; Weighted-Average Method**   "I think we goofed when we hired that new assistant controller," said Ruth Scarpino, president of Provost Industries. "Just look at this production report that he prepared for last month for the finishing department. I can't make heads or tails out of it."

Finishing department costs:	
Work in process inventory, April 1, 450 units, 60% complete as to conversion costs	$ 8,208*
Costs transferred in during the month from the preceding department on 1,950 units	17,940
Materials cost added during the month (materials are added when processing is 50% complete in the finishing department)	6,210
Conversion costs incurred during the month	13,920
Total departmental costs	$46,278

Finishing department costs assigned to:	
Units completed and transferred to finished goods, 1,800 units at $25.71 per unit.	$46,278
Work in process inventory, April 30, 600 units, 35% complete as to processing	–0–
Total departmental costs assigned.	$46,278

* Consists of: cost transferred in, $4,068; materials cost, $1,980; and conversion cost, $2,160.

"He's struggling to learn our system," replied Frank Harrop, the operations manager. "The problem is that he's been away from process costing for a long time, and it's coming back slowly."

"It's not just the format of his report that I'm concerned about. Look at that $25.71 unit cost that he's come up with for April. Doesn't that seem high to you?" said Ms. Scarpino.

"Yes, it does seem high; but on the other hand, I know we had an increase in materials prices during April, and that may be the explanation," replied Mr. Harrop. "I'll get someone else to redo this report and then we may be able to see what's going on."

Provost Industries manufactures a ceramic product that goes through two processing departments—molding and finishing. The company uses the weighted-average method to account for units and costs.

Required

1. Prepare a revised production report for the finishing department.
2. As stated above, the company experienced an increase in materials prices during April. Would you expect unit costs for April to be lower under the weighted-average method or under the FIFO method? Why?

Production Report: Second Department; FIFO Method   (Appendix B) Refer to the data for Provost Industries in the preceding case. Assume that the company uses the FIFO method to account for units and costs.   C4–31

Required

1. Prepare a production report for the finishing department for April.
2. As stated in the case, the company experienced an increase in materials prices during April. Would the effects of this price increase tend to show up more under the weighted-average method or under the FIFO method? Why?

Journal Entries; T-Accounts; Production Report: Weighted-Average Method   Hilox,   C4–32
Inc., produces an antacid product that goes through two departments—cooking and bottling. The company has recently hired a new assistant accountant, who has prepared the following summary of production and costs for the cooking department for May 19x5:

Cooking department costs:
Work in process inventory, May 1: 70,000
    quarts, 60% complete as to materials
    and 30% complete as to labor and overhead . . . . . . $ 61,000*
Materials added during May   570,000
Labor added during May.   100,000
Overhead applied during May   235,000
    Total departmental costs. $966,000

Cooking department costs assigned to:
Quarts completed and transferred to the bottling
    department: 400,000 quarts at ___?___ per quart . . . . . $?
Work in process inventory, May 31: 50,000
    quarts, 70% complete as to materials and
    40% complete as to labor and overhead . . . .   ?
    Total departmental costs assigned. . . . . $?

* Consists of materials, $39,000; labor, $5,000; and overhead, $17,000.

The assistant accountant has determined the cost per quart transferred to be $2.415, as follows:

$$\frac{\text{Total departmental costs, \$966,000}}{\text{Quarts completed and transferred, 400,000}} = \$2.415$$

However, the assistant accountant is unsure how to use this unit cost figure in assigning cost to the ending work in process inventory. In addition, the company's general ledger shows only $900,000 in cost transferred from the cooking department to the bottling department, which does not agree with the $966,000 figure above.

The general ledger also shows the following costs incurred in the bottling department during May: materials used, $130,000; direct labor cost incurred, $80,000; and overhead cost applied to products, $158,000.

Required

1. Prepare journal entries as follows to record activity in the company during May 19x5. Key your entries to the letters (a) through (g) below.
   a. Raw materials were issued to the two departments for use in production.
   b. Direct labor costs were incurred in the two departments.
   c. Manufacturing overhead costs were incurred: cooking department, $240,000; and

bottling department, $160,000. (Credit Accounts Payable.) The company maintains a separate Manufacturing Overhead account for each department.

d. Manufacturing overhead cost was applied to production in each department.

e. Products completed as to processing in the cooking department were transferred to the bottling department, $900,000.

f. Products completed as to processing in the bottling department were transferred to finished goods, $1,300,000.

g. Products were sold on account, $2,000,000. These products had cost $1,250,000 to manufacture.

2. Post the entries from (1) to T-accounts. Balances in selected accounts on May 1 are given below:

Raw Materials $710,000
Work in Process—Bottling Department   85,000
Finished Goods   45,000

After posting the entries to the T-accounts, find the ending balance in the inventory accounts and the Manufacturing Overhead accounts.

3. Prepare a production report for the cooking department for May.

By adopting continuous improvement programs, some companies have achieved impressive and consistent improvements period after period. In the electronics industry, defect rates are often cut in half every six to twelve months by relentlessly pushing toward the goal of zero defects. For example, the Yokogawa Hewlett-Packard plant slashed dip soldering failures from 1 percent to less than .001 percent—a thousand-fold improvement—in under three years.

Systems Design:

JIT and Activity-Based Costing

LEARNING OBJECTIVES

After studying Chapter 5, you should be able to:

1 Explain what is meant by the term *just in time (JIT)* as it relates to products and services.

2 Identify the five key elements involved in the successful operation of a JIT system.

3 Explain how the plant layout in a JIT system differs from that used in a conventional manufacturing setting.

4 Articulate the JIT philosophy, and identify the ideas underlying this philosophy.

5 Explain how JIT reduces or eliminates the difference in unit costs between the FIFO and weighted-average methods of process costing.

6 Explain why overhead costing methods based on volume measures such as direct labor-hours are no longer adequate for costing products and services in some companies.

7 Describe activity-based costing and explain how it differs from more conventional costing methods.

8 Identify the four steps involved in the design of an activity-based costing system.

9 Compute the cost of a unit of product using activity-based costing.

10 Define or explain the key terms listed at the end of the chapter.

11 (Appendix C) Record the flow of costs in an activity-based costing system.

I n response to increased costs, reduced profits, and intensifying worldwide competition, companies have searched for ways to streamline their operations and gather more accurate data for decision-making purposes. The result of this search has been the development of two powerful new management tools—*just-in-time (JIT) inventory systems* and *activity-based costing*. JIT inventory systems help the manager to reduce costs, increase efficiency, and expand output. Activity-based costing helps the manager to focus directly on the cost to manufacture a particular product, and thereby provides him or her with more accurate unit cost information on which to base pricing and other decisions.

JUST-IN-TIME (JIT) INVENTORY SYSTEMS

Objective 1
Explain what is meant by the term *just in time (JIT)* as it relates to products and services.

In preceding chapters, we stated that manufacturing companies maintain three classes of inventories—raw materials, work in process, and finished goods. These inventories are designed to act as *buffers* so that operations can proceed smoothly even if suppliers are late with deliveries or if a department is unable to operate for a brief period due to breakdowns or for other reasons. But it is costly to carry inventories, and some managers argue that the presence of inventories actually encourages inefficient and sloppy work. These managers argue further that with careful planning, inventories can be kept to a nominal level and in some cases even eliminated. As a result of efforts to reduce or eliminate inventories (and thereby to reduce costs), JIT inventory systems are coming into use.

The JIT Concept

Under ideal conditions, a company operating a **just-in-time (JIT) inventory system** would purchase *only* enough materials each day to meet that day's needs. Moreover, the company would have no goods still in process at the end of the day, and all goods completed during the day would be shipped immediately to customers so that nothing would have to be placed in finished goods warehouses. As this sequence suggests, "just in time" means that raw materials are received *just in time* to go into production, manufactured parts are completed *just in time* to be assembled into products, and products are completed *just in time* to be shipped to customers.

Although few companies have been able to reach this ideal and therefore completely eliminate their inventories, JIT has made it possible for many companies to reduce inventories to only a fraction of their previous levels. The result has been a substantial reduction in ordering and warehousing costs, and a streamlining of operations that has permitted these companies to meet competition that has become global in nature.

How does a company avoid a buildup of parts and materials at various workstations and still ensure a smooth flow of goods when JIT is in use? In a JIT environment, the flow of goods is controlled by what is described as a *pull* approach to the manufacture of products. The pull approach can be explained as follows: At the final assembly stage, a signal is sent to the preceding workstation as to the exact amount of parts and materials that will be needed *over the next few hours* for the assembly of products, and *only* that amount of parts and materials is provided. The same signal is sent back through each preceding workstation so that a smooth flow of parts and materials is maintained with no inventory buildup at any point. Thus, all workstations respond to the pull exerted by the final assembly stage,

EXHIBIT 5–1

JIT Pull Approach to the Flow of Goods

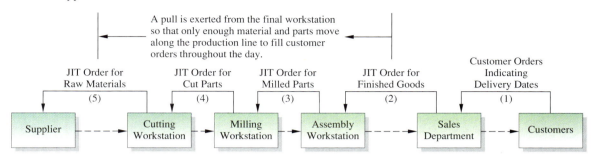

A pull is exerted from the final workstation so that only enough material and parts move along the production line to fill customer orders throughout the day.

| | JIT Order for Raw Materials (5) | JIT Order for Cut Parts (4) | JIT Order for Milled Parts (3) | JIT Order for Finished Goods (2) | Customer Orders Indicating Delivery Dates (1) |

Supplier → Cutting Workstation → Milling Workstation → Assembly Workstation → Sales Department → Customers

which in turn responds to customer orders. As one worker explained, "Under a JIT system you don't produce anything, anywhere, for anybody unless they *ask* for it somewhere *down*stream. Inventories are an evil that we're taught to avoid." The pull approach to the manufacture of products is illustrated in Exhibit 5–1.

The pull approach described above can be contrasted to the *push* approach used in conventional manufacturing systems. In conventional systems, when a workstation completes its processing on a batch of units, the partially completed goods are "pushed" forward to the next workstation regardless of whether that workstation is ready to receive them. The result is an unintentional stockpiling of partially completed goods that may not be completed for days or even weeks. This ties up funds and also results in operating inefficiencies. For one thing, it becomes very difficult to keep track of where everything is when so much is scattered all over the factory floor.

The Causes of Excessive Inventory

When a company has excessive stocks of inventory on hand, the reasons are usually traceable to one of five factors. First, the company may believe that it needs large inventories to guard against being out of stock. Second, errors may be made in production, resulting in stockpiles of raw materials or finished units. Such errors are frequent if a company's purchasing department is not coordinated with production or if a company's sales department fails to maintain timely communications with production. Third, workstations may be uncoordinated, thereby requiring that goods in process be held in storage areas for long periods awaiting the next production step. Fourth, the company's production department may insist on large batch sizes for parts, subassemblies, and finished goods in the belief that large batches are more economical to produce than small batches. And fifth, workstations may be directed to produce parts that are not needed just to "keep everyone busy."

Through use of the JIT approach, all five of these reasons for holding inventory can be eliminated with the result that inventories will no longer be a major factor in a company's operations. Although initially conceived as a method of inventory control, JIT has since evolved into a much broader concept that impacts all aspects of a company's operating activities. This point is discussed further in a later section titled Expansion of the JIT Concept.

KEY ELEMENTS IN A JIT SYSTEM

Objective 2
Identify the five key
elements involved in the
successful operation of a
JIT system.

Five key elements are involved in the successful operation of a JIT system. These elements include maintaining a limited number of suppliers, improving the plant layout, reducing the setup time needed for production runs, achieving total quality control, and developing a flexible work force.

Limited Number of Suppliers

To successfully operate a JIT system, a company must learn to rely on a few suppliers who are willing to make frequent deliveries in small lots. Rather than deliver a week's (or a month's) parts and materials at one time, suppliers must be willing to make deliveries as often as *several times a day,* and in the exact quantities specified by the buyer.

Both the company and its suppliers benefit when JIT is in operation. The company benefits because receiving materials just in time makes it unnecessary for the company to carry large inventories of materials on hand. This can translate into huge savings in storage, handling, and interest costs. The company's suppliers benefit because they are given long-term contracts that guarantee business so long as they meet the delivery terms stipulated by the company. For JIT to be successful, undependable or marginal suppliers must be weeded out and all purchasing concentrated in those suppliers who have proven records of dependability. Companies adopting JIT often eliminate up to 90 percent of their suppliers so they can focus all of their business on the remaining 10 percent. Thus, the suppliers chosen are relieved of the necessity of constantly bidding for work and can focus their time and attention on meeting short- and long-term delivery schedules provided by the company. Moreover, suppliers often find that the JIT discipline improves the efficiency of their own operations. We should note that the suppliers chosen are not necessarily the ones with the lowest prices. Rather, they are the suppliers who are willing to revamp their operating procedures and who show, by actual performance, that they can meet the delivery terms and conditions specified in a long-term contract. Typically, these suppliers are required to complete a *supplier certification program* that prepares them to operate in a JIT environment.

In sum, companies using JIT must cultivate a close working relationship with a few suppliers who can guarantee prompt and dependable service. Dependability is vital, since companies are highly vulnerable to any interruption in supply when JIT is in use.

Improving the Plant Layout

Objective 3
Explain how the plant
layout in a JIT system
differs from that used
in a conventional
manufacturing setting.

To properly implement JIT, a company must improve the manufacturing flow lines in its plant. A **flow line** can be defined as the physical path taken by a product as it moves through the manufacturing process from receipt of raw materials to shipment of the completed good.

Traditionally, companies have designed their plant floors so that similar machines are grouped together. Such a functional layout results in all drill presses in one place, all lathes in one place, and so forth. This approach to plant layout requires that products be moved from one group of machines to another—frequently across the plant or even to another building—in the process of manufacture. The result is extensive material-handling costs and the necessity to carry large work in process inventories as partially completed goods are moved from station to station.

In a JIT system, all machines needed in the production of a particular product are brought together, thereby splitting up large groups of similar equipment. The result is *multiple* product flow lines in which all tasks such as milling, cutting, and assembly are performed consecutively as a product moves from machine to machine. This approach to plant layout creates an individual "mini" factory for each separate product, frequently referred to as a **focused factory** or as a "factory within a factory." The flow line for a product can be straight, as shown earlier in Exhibit 5–1, or it can be in a U-shaped configuration as shown in Exhibit 5–2. The key point is that all machines in a product flow line are tightly grouped together so that partially completed units are not shifted from place to place all over the factory. This allows workers to focus all of their efforts on a product from start to finish.

Benefits Realized   A plant layout containing multiple flow lines provides cost savings in two ways. First, it minimizes material-handling costs. Forklift trucks are no longer needed to move materials from place to place in the factory since goods move only a few feet between machines. Workers can move materials by hand or conveyor systems can be used to move goods between workstations.

Second, multiple flow lines make it unnecessary to store partially completed units as they await the next step in the production process. Since each product flow line operates under JIT concepts, only enough goods are completed by one machine or workstation to supply the needs of the following machine or workstation. Thus, work in process inventories are minimized as partially completed goods move smoothly from machine to machine along the flow line. Work in process inventories are so small in a JIT environment that they can be visually controlled by the line supervisor. That is, the line supervisor can simply walk along the product flow line and visually determine whether partially completed goods are excessive at any particular workstation. This type of instant feedback and control is impossible in a plant with a functional layout since it is normal in that type of environment to have large amounts of goods piled about the factory floor as they await movement to another part of the factory.

In addition to inventory reduction, an improved plant layout can dramatically increase **throughput,** which is the total volume of production through a facility

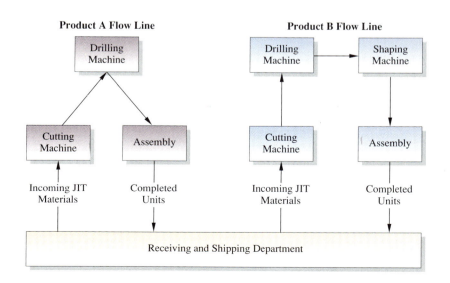

EXHIBIT 5–2
Plant Layout in a JIT System

during a period, and it can dramatically reduce **throughput time,** which is the length of time required to turn materials into products. Throughput time is also known as **cycle time.**

FOCUS ON CURRENT PRACTICE

After one large manufacturing company rearranged its plant layout and organized its products into individual flow lines, the company determined that the dis- tance traveled by one product had been decreased from three miles to just 300 feet.

Machines Grouped into Cells   Look again at the product flow lines in Exhibit 5–2. Instead of having a single piece of equipment (such as a cutting machine) on which a worker operates, a workstation on the flow line may consist of two or more different machines clustered together that are needed to complete one part or one component of the finished product. Such a clustering of machines at a single workstation is called a **cell.** The concept of a cell is illustrated in Exhibit 5–3. A single product flow line in a JIT system may consist of several cells in addition to several stand-alone machines.

Reduced Setup Time

We mentioned earlier that companies often manufacture products in large batches in the belief that large-batch production is more economical. The reason it is perceived as being more economical is traceable to the costly setup time involved with starting a production run of a product. By **setup time** we mean the time involved with changing equipment, moving material about, and getting forms and jigs in place to accommodate the production of a different item, such as the production of tables after having produced chairs for several days. Setup time is often so lengthy (and so costly) that once it is completed, companies believe they must make long production runs before stopping and getting ready to produce a different item. The problem with long production runs (large batches of produc-

EXHIBIT 5–3

Example of a
Manufacturing Cell

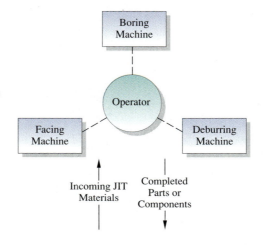

tion) is that they create inventory that must wait for days, weeks, or even months before sale or before further processing at the next workstation.

One way to avoid large-batch production is to reduce setup time. If a company is able to reduce the setup time for a product from one day to only one hour, for example, then it will be able to economically manufacture products in smaller batches. In turn, the smaller batches will reduce the level of the company's work in process and finished goods inventories. Savings will be realized in the form of lower inventory carrying costs, and greater revenues will be generated as a result of spending most of the day producing goods rather than simply getting ready to produce. Also, the company will be able to move from production of one product to another more quickly and thereby achieve a faster market response to customer needs.

But how does a company reduce its setup time? One approach is to simply employ the kind of dedicated flow lines illustrated in Exhibit 5–2. If equipment is dedicated to a single product, then setups are largely eliminated and products can be produced in any batch size desired. Another approach is to focus on employee training, thereby increasing employees' awareness of the need to complete setups quickly. The greatest reduction in setup time, however, is achieved through automation of production processes.

Automated Flow Lines   Many companies are replacing the conventional machines on their product flow lines with automated equipment. A common piece of automated equipment is known as a **numerical control (NC) machine;** it is so named because its functions are controlled by a computer that has been programmed to guide the equipment through all the steps necessary to complete some portion of the final product. When all of the equipment in a manufacturing cell consists of NC machines, then an **island of automation** is created. Frequently, these islands of automation are assisted by pick-and-place robots that control movements of material into and out of the cell and that perform certain tasks in the manufacture of the product. An island of automation is illustrated in Exhibit 5–4.

When equipment and cells are automated, dramatic reductions in setup time are possible. Instead of requiring hours to shift between production runs, setups can often be done in minutes because the setup consists mostly of just changing computer programs. Thus, a company can move from production of one product

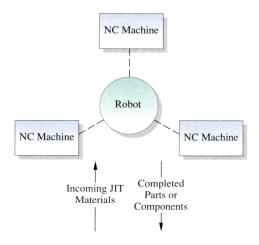

EXHIBIT 5–4

A Cell Organized as an Island of Automation

to another quickly and avoid the necessity of large production runs. The setup for one product in a General Electric plant used to take 40 hours to complete. After the product line was automated, the setup time was reduced to just *eight minutes*.[1]

Even greater efficiency in manufacturing is achieved when the cells on a product flow line are linked together with an automated material-handling system and the flows between cells are controlled by a central computer. Such an arrangement, which is illustrated in Exhibit 5–5, is called a **flexible manufacturing system**

EXHIBIT 5–5
Illustration of a Flexible Manufacturing System (FMS)

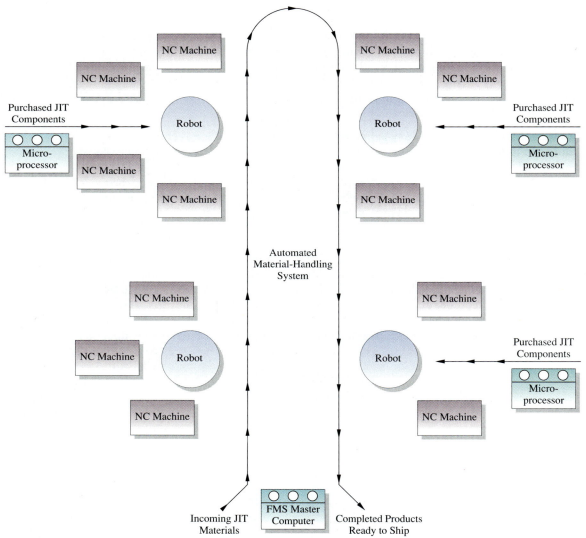

NC = Numerical control.

---
[1] David M. Dilts and Grant M. Russell, "Accounting for the Factory of the Future," *Management Accounting* 66, no. 10 (April 1985), p. 39.

(FMS). An FMS gives a company the power to manufacture a whole family of similar products on a single flow line because the system is *flexible*. That is, the FMS master computer can be programmed to command rapid setups in the various cells as changes are made from production of one product to another. Thus, a single flow line becomes capable of producing *dozens* of different products so long as they are somewhat similar in size, type of material required, design, and type of operations performed. With an FMS, therefore, changeovers between products are so rapid and setup costs are so nominal that a batch size of *one unit* becomes possible for a *whole family* of products, thereby giving a company the ability to respond almost instantly to customer needs.

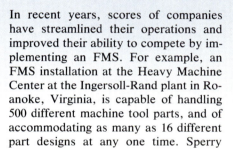

INGERSOLL-RAND FOCUS ON CURRENT PRACTICE

In recent years, scores of companies have streamlined their operations and improved their ability to compete by implementing an FMS. For example, an FMS installation at the Heavy Machine Center at the Ingersoll-Rand plant in Roanoke, Virginia, is capable of handling 500 different machine tool parts, and of accommodating as many as 16 different part designs at any one time. Sperry Vicker has been using an FMS to produce hydraulic pump cover castings in 25 different sizes and shapes. Sunstrand Corporation eliminated 100 conventional metal working machines, replacing them with 10 computer-linked numerical control machines. The new system can now process five times as many part designs at twice the volume.[2]

Computer-Integrated Manufacturing An FMS is just one part of the overall concept of **computer-integrated manufacturing (CIM).** The purpose of CIM is to integrate an organization's business functions (that is, functions outside the factory) with its manufacturing functions. One set of authors describe it as follows:

> CIM is the logical organization of individual engineering, production, sales and support functions into a single, computer-coordinated system. Functional areas outside the factory (e.g., design, analysis, planning, purchasing) are integrated with the functions within the factory (e.g., materials handling, process monitoring) through the use of computers.[3]

Although frequently referred to as a *system*, CIM is actually a *methodology*, or a way of operating, that encompasses the following computer-related components:

Management (business) information system (MIS)

Computer-aided design (CAD)

Computer-aided manufacturing (CAM)

Flexible manufacturing system (FMS)

---

[2] David M. Dilts and Grant W. Russell, "Accounting for the Factory of the Future," *Management Accounting* 66, no. 10 (April 1985), p. 35.

[3] William J. Ainsworth and York P. Freund, "Managing the Transition to the Factory of the Future," in Barry J. Brinker, ed., *Emerging Practices in Cost Management* (Boston, Mass.: Warren, Gorham & LaMont, 1990), p. 272.

The relationships between these computer-related components can be diagrammed as shown in Exhibit 5–6. For CIM to operate successfully, a company must have a hierarchy of computers that provide interface and linkages as shown in the exhibit. Typically, the central corporate computer interfaces with computers at the manufacturing level to exchange information relating to sales orders, shipment dates, material needs, and so forth. Computers at the manufacturing level are linked together and collect a wide array of data on products being manufactured. These data include processing time in the cells, wait time, cycle time, scrap, design changes, setup time, and so forth. All of this information is needed to cost products and to monitor performance. The hierarchy of computers needed in a CIM environment is shown in Exhibit 5–7.

EXHIBIT 5–6

Interface and Elements of CIM Components

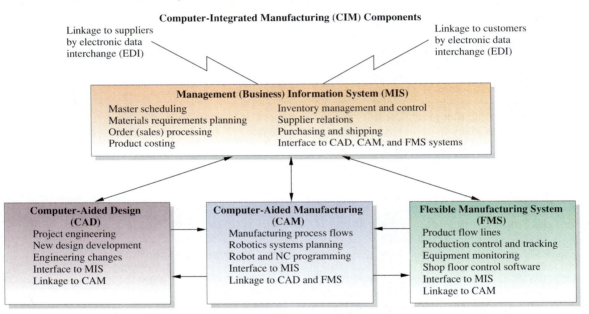

Source: Adapted from Leland Blank, "Planning and Evaluating CIM Systems," in Barry J. Brinker, ed., *Emerging Practices in Cost Management* (Boston, Mass.: Warren, Gorham & LaMont, 1990), p. 277.

EXHIBIT 5–7

Hierarchy of Computers in CIM

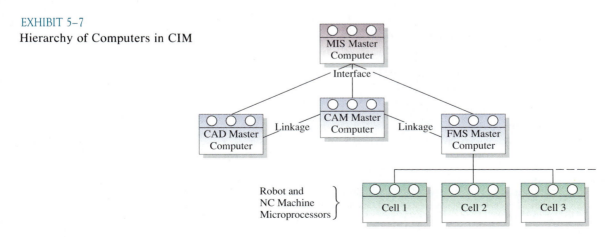

A manufacturing facility employing the CIM concept is sometimes referred to as a *lights out* factory. This term derives from the fact that very little direct labor is needed in an automated facility. So little direct labor is needed, the term implies, that management could just turn out the lights and the factory would go on running by itself. Although this is an obvious exaggeration, it does emphasize the high level of automation present in a CIM environment.

Mazak   FOCUS ON CURRENT PRACTICE

By employing CIM, Yamazaki Machinery Company in Japan was able to reduce the number of pieces of equipment on its processing lines from 68 to 18, the number of employees from 215 to 12, floor space for production from 103,000 square feet to just 30,000 square feet, and the average processing time from 35 days to only 1.5 days.[4]

Total Quality Control

For JIT to operate successfully, a company must develop a system of **total quality control (TQC)** over its parts and materials. TQC means that no defects can be allowed in parts and materials received from suppliers, in work in process, or in finished goods. The need for TQC is obvious; since one workstation provides only the parts and materials being requested (pulled) by the next workstation, one or two defective parts could close down the entire assembly line. To avoid this happening, a company must maintain an ongoing TQC program.

TQC starts with a company's suppliers. We noted earlier that undependable suppliers are culled out and all purchasing is focused on a few suppliers who show that they can be dependable in meeting JIT delivery schedules. This dependability extends to quality as well as to promptness, since as a part of their certification program, suppliers must demonstrate that they will inspect goods *before* they are shipped and thereby deliver material free of any defects. Thus, responsibility for inspection of incoming goods and responsibility for quality control is shifted from the company back onto its suppliers. A supplier who fails to deliver defect-free goods is quickly eliminated and replaced by a vendor who will meet quality standards.

A company's production workers also have direct responsibilities relating to TQC. Rather than having inspectors check materials and units as they move along the product flow line, all inspections are performed by the workers themselves. This is sometimes referred to as **continuous monitoring.** If materials or parts moving between workstations are found to be defective, an early warning system is activated. Quite literally, this sets off alarms and red lights. Typically, the warning system will stop the entire flow line until the cause of the defect is identified and the defect is corrected. This procedure lays a heavy responsibility on workers to ensure that parts and components sent on to the next workstation are free of any defects.

In an FMS where processes are automated, inspections on goods are per-

---

[4] Robert A. Howell and Stephen R. Soucy, "Major Trends for Management," *Management Accounting* 69, no. 1 (July 1987), p. 25.

formed by NC machines and by robots as the goods move from cell to cell. That is, the equipment is programmed to do tolerance checks as a routine part of the manufacturing process. Since automated equipment is more dependable and consistent than workers, defects largely disappear in an automated environment, and TQC is fairly easy to maintain.

Flexible Work Force

Since the plant layout in a JIT environment is different from that of a conventional factory, workers must be multiskilled. Recall that each of the cells in a JIT layout contains several different machines needed to complete some portion of the finished product. Workers assigned to a particular cell are expected to operate all of the equipment it contains. This means that workers will be assigned to different machines from day to day as needed, rather than working on a single piece of equipment. Moreover, since JIT requires that workers produce only what is requested (pulled) by the next workstation, when these requests have been filled, the workers in a cell are expected to perform minor repairs and do maintenance work on the equipment the cell contains. This approach can be contrasted to a conventional assembly line where a worker performs a single task, and where all maintenance work is done by a specialized maintenance crew.

Frequently, the work performed in a cell is so complex that a team of workers must be involved. Workers are expected to be cross-trained and therefore capable of performing whatever tasks they may be assigned as a member of the team. When a company adopts the JIT approach, it means that workers accustomed to working independently must reorient their thinking and develop teamwork skills.

In addition to flexibility in the production tasks they perform, workers in a JIT environment are also responsible for performing the inspections needed on their own output, as we noted in the above discussion on total quality control. Building this type of broad flexibility into the work force can result in more interesting jobs and greatly reduces the number of job descriptions that a company must carry.

 FOCUS ON CURRENT PRACTICE

An industrial machine manufacturer was able to reduce the number of labor classifications at one of its plants from 26 to just 5 when it adopted JIT production methods. When Borg-Warner adopted JIT, it was able to reduce the number of its labor classifications by 70 percent.[5]

Benefits of a JIT System

Although the requirements for a JIT system may seem unduly stringent, many companies have employed JIT with great success. Following are some of the benefits cited as coming from a JIT system:

---

[5] George Foster and Charles T. Horngren, "Cost Accounting and Cost Management in a JIT Environment," in Brinker, *Emerging Practices in Cost Management*, p. 205.

1. Worker productivity is increased through teams working in a cellular plant layout organized in product flow lines.
2. Setup time is decreased, resulting in smaller batch sizes and a smoother flow of goods between workstations.
3. Total production time is decreased, resulting in greater output and quicker response to customer needs.
4. Through TQC, waste is reduced with zero defects resulting in some cases.
5. Inventories of all types are reduced through better control of suppliers, less wait time between workstations, smaller production runs, and producing goods to customer orders.
6. Working capital is bolstered as investment funds that were previously tied up in inventories are released for use elsewhere in the company.
7. Usable space in the plant is increased as areas previously used to store inventory are made available for other, more productive uses.

As a result of benefits such as those cited above, more companies are employing JIT systems each year. In time, this approach probably will become the dominant method of inventory control in most industries.

FOCUS ON CURRENT PRACTICE

Among the major companies using JIT are Goodyear, Westinghouse, General Motors, Hughes Aircraft, Ford Motor Company, Black and Decker, Dynatork, Chrysler Corporation, Borg-Warner Corp., John Deere, Motorola, Harley-Davidson, Xerox, Tektronix, and Intel Corporation.

EXPANSION OF THE JIT CONCEPT

The JIT concept was pioneered in Japan about two decades ago. Since that time, it has expanded from simple inventory control into what is termed the **JIT philosophy.** This philosophy says that wherever possible in an organization, management should focus its efforts on *simplification* and on *elimination of waste*. Three ideas are pivotal to this philosophy, as presented below. The reader should note that these ideas summarize most of what we have said concerning JIT on the preceding pages.

Objective 4
Articulate the JIT philosophy, and identify the ideas underlying this philosophy.

1. *All activities should be eliminated that do not add value to a product or service.* Activities that do not add value to a product or service are known as **non-value-added activities.** For example, the manufacturing time for a product can be expressed as follows:

$$\frac{\text{Manufacturing}}{\text{time}} = \frac{\text{Process}}{\text{time}} + \frac{\text{Inspection}}{\text{time}} + \frac{\text{Move}}{\text{time}} + \frac{\text{Queue}}{\text{time}}$$

Process time is the amount of time in which work is actually done on the product. *Inspection time* is the amount of time spent ensuring that the product is of high quality. *Move time* is the time required to move materials or partially completed products from workstation to workstation. *Queue time* is the amount of time a product spends waiting to be worked on, to be moved, or in storage waiting shipment. The only one of these activities that adds value to a product is process time. Therefore, under the JIT philosophy, inspection time, move time, and queue time are all eliminated to the extent possible. These items represent non-value-added activities, which means that they add to a product's cost, but they do not add to its market value. Similar activities in any service, retail, or manufacturing organization are eliminated in a JIT setting if they do not add value to the organization's products or services.

2. *A commitment must be made to achieve and maintain high levels of quality in all aspects of a company's activities.* Under JIT, the emphasis is on doing things right the first time and avoiding rework or waste of any kind. We have already noted that companies strive for total quality control in a JIT environment through both worker training and automation. This emphasis on quality extends beyond the factory, however, to include the nonmanufacturing functions of marketing, engineering, and accounting.

3. *A commitment must be made to continuous improvement in all of a company's activities and in the usefulness of data generated for its management.* **Continuous improvement** can be defined as the constant pursuit of ever-greater value being provided for the customer. Inherent in the idea of continuous improvement is the notion that the major functions of a business—accounting, engineering, production, and marketing—deliver greater value only as a result of ongoing attention and effort. Thus, continuous improvement is not just a slogan. Companies that are committed to continuous improvement adopt formal procedures for identifying problems and their causes and for working on the elimination of these problems. A key element in a continuous improvement program is that when the causes of the most important problems have been eliminated, the process continues. The next most important problems are then identified and their causes eliminated. The cycle keeps repeating without end.

HEWLETT PACKARD   FOCUS ON CURRENT PRACTICE ◆

By adopting continuous improvement programs, some firms have been able to achieve impressive and consistent improvements period after period. In the electronics industry, defect rates are typically cut in half every 6 to 12 months by firms that have formal continuous improvement programs that relentlessly push toward zero defects. One example is the Yokogawa Hewlett Packard plant where dip soldering failures were reduced from nearly 1 percent to less than .001 percent in under three years. Moreover, this reduction in failures was steady and consistent throughout the three years.[6]

The thrust toward continuous improvement has led to a widespread restructuring of cost systems and to the development of new methods of costing products and services. These new methods are discussed in later sections of this chapter.

The impact of the JIT philosophy is pervasive in that it touches on many

---

[6] Robert S. Kaplan, ''Analog Devices: The Half-Life System,'' Harvard Business School Case 190-061, 1990.

aspects of the manager's work. As we move through the remaining chapters of the book, we will return to the JIT concept frequently as we discuss its impact on cost systems, product costs, income measurement, performance evaluation, investment decisions, and related topics. In short, the material on the preceding pages does not exhaust the idea of JIT; it just introduces the concept.

The JIT Wheel

If the key elements of JIT are installed and function properly, a wheel will be formed such as that illustrated in Exhibit 5–8. As shown in the exhibit, JIT is the hub from which many concepts emerge, each forming the spoke of a wheel that propels the company forward. This wheel can be visualized as resting on a road-bed consisting of the JIT philosophy. If nothing is allowed to impede the progress of the wheel, it will lead to the following levels of achievement in a company:

Lot size of production runs = 1
Wait time between workstations = 0
Setup time = 0
Level of inventories = 0
Defects in output = 0
Errors in customer service =0

Although to date no company has reported these levels of JIT achievement, the figures above stand as the ultimate goals toward which companies work through the process of continuous improvement.

JIT and Service Organizations

When JIT is viewed as a philosophy rather than as a set of operating procedures, the ideas behind it become equally as applicable to service companies as they are to manufacturing companies. That is, to improve profits, managers of service

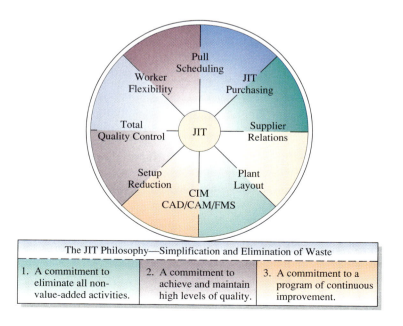

EXHIBIT 5–8
The JIT Management System

operations must also focus their efforts on *simplification* and *elimination of waste*. This is accomplished by eliminating all non-value-added activities, by achieving and maintaining high levels of quality in the service provided, and by a commitment to continuous improvement in all aspects of the company's operations.

Waste doesn't just apply to raw materials or to labor time; it applies to "any activity undertaken to provide a product or service that can be eliminated with no deterioration in the product or service attributes."[7] Thus, the key to improved profits in service organizations, the same as in manufacturing companies, is to simplify operations and to eliminate any activity that does not add value to the service being provided. This can be accomplished by applying the JIT philosophy to the activities involved. Many activities in service organizations are repetitive in nature and can be eliminated or modified to improve both the quality and the level of service being provided.

FOCUS ON CURRENT PRACTICE

A lending institution on the West Coast required 12 business days to approve a loan. By applying the JIT philosophy and eliminating non-value-added activities in the loan approval process, the company was able to reduce the approval time from 12 to just 4 or 5 business days.[8] On a broader scale, insurance companies that sell policies to individuals have programmed laptop computers with up-to-date actuarial data. When agents meet with a customer, they can enter specific data relating to the customer's status and needs directly into the computer and immediately print out a policy that is uniquely tailored to that customer. Moreover, by eliminating the non-value-added activities of multiple reviews and approvals at the home office, the cost of providing the policy is less than if traditional underwriting procedures had been followed.

JIT and Process Costing

Objective 5
Explain how JIT reduces or eliminates the difference in unit costs between the FIFO and weighted-average methods of process costing.

JIT impacts on process costing in two ways. First, it largely eliminates the differences in unit costs between the FIFO and weighted-average methods; and second, it allows companies that previously used job-order costing to use process costing instead.

JIT Impact on Unit Costs

The use of JIT has resulted in a significant narrowing of the difference in unit costs between the FIFO and weighted-average methods, and in some cases this difference has disappeared entirely. The reason is as follows: Recall that under the JIT concept, raw materials are received *just in time* to go into production and parts are completed *just in time* to be assembled into products. As a result, under JIT the raw materials and work in process inventories are either eliminated or reduced to nominal levels. Since the difference between the FIFO and weighted-average methods centers on how costs are handled in work in process inventories, *the elimination of these inventories through JIT automatically eliminates the distinction between the two costing methods.*

---

[7] Bill Steeves, "Trends in Management Accounting," *CMA Magazine* 64, no. 2 (March 1990), p. 18.

[8] John Y. Lee, "JIT Works for Services, Too," *CMA Magazine* 64, no. 6 (July/August 1990), pp. 21–22.

This point can be seen in Exhibit 5–9. Note that by year 3, when the JIT approach is fully operational, the equivalent units are the same for both the FIFO and weighted-average methods. Unit costs for year 3 will *also* be the same for either method since, with no beginning work in process inventory, both methods will be computing unit costs simply on a basis of costs incurred during the current period.

In short, when JIT is in use, the production reports under the two methods become virtually identical and also become greatly simplified. Note from Exhibit 5–9 that in year 3 the units started into production, the units completed and transferred out, and the equivalent units are all the same. The remainder of the production report will also be simplified since, with no inventories to account for, the part titled "Cost of units transferred out" will be assigned *all* costs appearing on the report under both the FIFO and weighted-average methods. Small wonder that companies find the JIT approach so appealing.

Expanded Use of Process Costing   JIT, through its focus on an improved plant layout combined with FMS, is allowing companies to switch their costing systems from the more costly job-order approach to the less costly process or operation approaches. This switch is possible because FMS is so effective in reducing the setup time required between products and jobs. With setup time only a fraction of previous levels, companies are able to move between products and jobs with about the same speed as if they were working in a continuous, process-type environment. The result is that these companies are able to employ process costing techniques in situations that previously required job-order costing. As the use of FMS grows, some managers predict that job-order costing will slowly disappear except in a few industries.

OVERHEAD COSTING IN THE NEW MANUFACTURING ENVIRONMENT

The most difficult task in computing accurate unit costs lies in determining the proper amount of overhead cost to assign to each job or to each unit of product. Three different approaches are available to help the manager in the task of overhead assignment. These approaches differ in terms of level of complexity, ranging from what we term Level One, the least complex, to Level Three, the most complex. Level Three, which deals with *activity-based costing,* is widely viewed as the most accurate of the three approaches to overhead cost assignment.

Objective 6
Explain why overhead costing methods based on volume measures such as direct labor-hours are no longer adequate for costing products and services in some companies.

Level One: Plantwide Overhead Rate

Our discussion in the two preceding chapters assumed that a single overhead rate was being used throughout an entire factory operation. We explained in Chapter 3 that such a rate is called a *plantwide overhead rate,* since it encompasses all parts of a company. Historically, such rates have dominated industry practice, but their accuracy is now being called into question because they tend to rely solely on direct labor as an allocation base, which in turn can lead to distorted unit costs.

Direct Labor as a Base   In the early part of the 20th century, when cost systems first began to be developed, direct labor constituted a major part of total product cost. Consequently, direct labor was typically chosen as the base for assigning overhead cost to products. Data relating to direct labor were readily available and highly convenient to use, and there was a high correlation in most companies between direct labor and the incurrence of overhead cost. Therefore, direct labor made an excellent allocation base.

EXHIBIT 5-9

JIT Impact on Process Costing

Basic Data

During year 1, the company operated a traditional process costing system in which there was both a beginning and an ending work in process inventory. During year 2, the company implemented a JIT inventory approach, so note that there was no ending work in process inventory for that year. By year 3, the company had the JIT approach fully operational, so in that year the work in process inventories were completely eliminated.

| | Year 1 | | | Year 2 | | | Year 3 | | |
| | | Percent Completed | | | Percent Completed | | | Percent Completed | |
	Units	Material	Conversion	Units	Material	Conversion	Units	Material	Conversion
Work in process, beginning	50,000	70	60	90,000	80	50	—	—	—
Units started into production	700,000			700,000			700,000		
Units completed and transferred out	660,000			790,000			700,000		
Work in process, ending	90,000	80	50	—	—	—	—	—	—

Equivalent Units Computations

| | Year 1 | | Year 2 | | Year 3 | |
	Material	Conversion	Material	Conversion	Material	Conversion
Weighted-average method:						
Units completed and transferred	660,000	660,000	790,000	790,000	700,000	700,000
Work in process, ending*	72,000	45,000	—	—	—	—
Equivalent units of production	732,000	705,000	790,000	790,000	700,000	700,000
FIFO method:						
Work in process, beginning†	15,000	20,000	18,000	45,000	—	—
Units started and completed	610,000‡	610,000‡	700,000	700,000	700,000	700,000
Work in process, ending*	72,000	45,000	—	—	—	—
Equivalent units of production	697,000	675,000	718,000	745,000	700,000	700,000

* Work completed on the units in the ending inventory.

† Work required to complete the units in the beginning inventory.

‡ 660,000 units − 50,000 units = 610,000 units.

Even today, direct labor remains a viable base for applying overhead cost in some companies, both in this country and abroad. In Japan, for example, which has become a world leader in manufacturing technology, direct labor-hours are still widely used as a base in overhead application.[9] Recent studies also reveal high correlations between direct labor and the incurrence of overhead costs in some industries.[10] The circumstances under which direct labor may be appropriate as a base for assigning overhead cost to products include the following:

1. Direct labor is a significant element of total product cost.
2. The amount of direct labor input and the amount of machine input do not differ greatly between products.
3. Products do not differ greatly in terms of volume, individual lot size, or complexity of manufacturing.
4. A high statistical correlation can be established between direct labor and the incurrence of overhead costs (i.e., direct labor acts as a cost driver for overhead).

Changing Manufacturing Environment   So long as the above circumstances exist, accurate unit costs can be obtained using direct labor as an allocation base. However, events of the past two decades have made drastic changes in these circumstances in some industries. Automation has greatly decreased the amount of direct labor required; **product diversity** has increased in that companies are manufacturing a wider range of products, and these products differ substantially in volume, lot size, and complexity of design; and total overhead cost has increased to the point in some companies that a correlation no longer exists between it and direct labor.

Where these changes have prevailed, companies that have continued to use plantwide overhead rates and direct labor as a basis for overhead assignment have experienced major distortions in unit costs. To overcome these distortions and to get better traceability of overhead costs to products, managers have turned to other overhead assignment methods.

Level Two: Departmental Overhead Rates

Rather than use a plantwide overhead rate, some companies use a "two-stage" allocation process. In the first stage, overhead costs are assigned to cost pools, such as individual departments or operations. In the second stage, costs are applied from the cost pools (departments) to individual jobs. These second-stage applications are made on various bases according to the nature of the work performed in the department, as explained in Chapter 3. The two-stage allocation process is illustrated in Exhibit 5–10.

Unfortunately, even departmental overhead rates will not correctly assign overhead costs in situations where a company has a range of products that differ in volume, lot size, or complexity of production. The reason is that the departmental approach relies solely on *volume* as the key factor in allocating overhead cost to products. Studies have shown that where diversity exists between products (that is, where products differ in terms of number of units produced, lot size,

---

[9] Callie Berliner and James A. Brimson, eds., *Cost Management for Today's Advanced Manufacturing* (Boston, Mass.: Harvard Business School Press, 1988), p. 232.

[10] George Foster and Mahendra Gupta, "Manufacturing Overhead Cost Driver Analysis," *Journal of Accounting and Economics* 12 (1990), pp. 309–37.

EXHIBIT 5–10
Two-Stage Overhead Costing

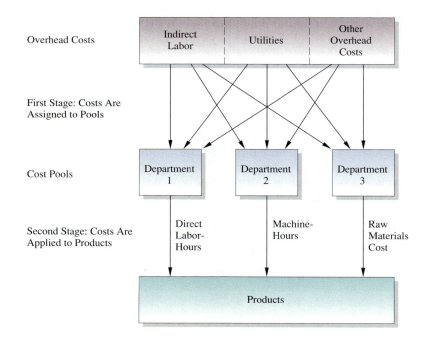

or complexity of production), volume alone is not adequate for overhead costing. These studies show that overhead costing based on volume will systematically overcost high-volume products and undercost low-volume products. Moreover, these studies show that this will be true regardless of whether volume is stated in terms of direct labor, machine time, or quantity of materials used.[11] In situations where product diversity exists, to obtain more accurate unit costs, *activity-based costing* should be used.

Level Three: Activity-Based Costing

Objective 7
Describe activity-based costing and explain how it differs from more conventional costing methods.

Activity-based costing involves a two-stage allocation process, as described earlier, with the first stage again assigning overhead costs to cost pools. However, more pools are used under this approach, and they are defined differently. Rather than being defined as departments, the pools represent *activities,* such as setups required, purchase orders issued, and number of inspections completed. In the second stage, costs are assigned to jobs according to the number of these activities required in their completion.

An **activity** is any event or transaction that is a cost driver—that is, acts as a causal factor in the incurrence of cost in an organization. Examples of activities that act as cost drivers include the following:

1. Machine setups.
2. Purchase orders.
3. Quality inspections.
4. Production orders (scheduling).
5. Engineering change orders.

6. Shipments.
7. Material receipts.
8. Inventory movements.
9. Maintenance requests.
10. Scrap/rework orders.

---

[11] See Robin Cooper and Robert S. Kaplan, "How Cost Accounting Distorts Product Costs," *Management Accounting* 69, no. 10 (April 1988), pp. 20–27. An example of the cost distortion caused by a volume base is contained on pages 199–203 following.

11. Machine time.
12. Power consumed.
13. Miles driven.
14. Computer-hours logged.
15. Beds occupied.
16. Flight-hours logged.

The number of these activities in an organization is a function of the complexity of operations. The more complex a company's operations, the more cost-driving activities it is likely to have. As companies have moved from the simple, direct labor-based operations of 30 years ago to the complex, highly automated operations of today, the number of cost-driving activities has increased manyfold. Managers have discovered, however, that not all products and services share equally in these activities.

One product in a company, for example, may be a low-volume item that requires frequent machine setups, has many intricate parts requiring numerous purchase orders, and requires constant inspections to maintain quality. Another product in the same company may be a high-volume item that requires few machine setups, few purchase orders, and no quality inspections at all. If this company ignores the impact of these two products on its cost-driving activities and simply assigns overhead costs to the products on a basis of volume (such as labor-hours, machine-hours, or quantity of materials used), the high-volume product will bear the lion's share of the overhead cost pool. The result will be a serious distortion in unit costs for *both* products.

As stated earlier, activity-based costing reduces the problem of cost distortion by creating a cost pool for *each* activity or transaction that can be identified as a cost driver, and by assigning overhead cost to products or jobs on a basis of the number of separate activities they require in their completion. Thus, in the situation above, the low-volume product would be assigned the bulk of the costs for machine setups, purchase orders, and quality inspections, thereby showing it to have high unit costs as compared to the other product.

Activity-based costing is sometimes referred to as **transactions costing.** Its major advantage over other costing methods is that *it improves the traceability of overhead costs* and thus results in more accurate unit cost data for management.

Activity-Based Costing Model   Exhibit 5–11 provides a model depicting the flow of information in an activity-based costing system.[12] Note that information in such a system can be viewed from two perspectives. The *cost view* in the model shows the flow of costs. This flow is from resources to activities, and from activities to products and services. For example, assume that one of the activities in a company is material handling. The resources consumed by moving materials around the plant will be traced to particular products based on some observed activity, such as the number of times an item is moved. This cost view in the model summarizes the key concept underlying activity-based costing: *resources are consumed by activities, and activities are consumed by products and services*.

The *process view* in the model shows the flow of input information, which would be the observed transactions associated with an activity. In the case of material handling, information is gathered on the number of times an item of material is moved to determine the extent of activity during a period. This gathering of information provides the "activity" data needed to complete the costing of products, and it also provides the data needed for performance evaluation, as depicted by the horizontal flow in the model.

---

[12] Adapted from Norm Raffish, "How Much Does that Product Really Cost?" *Management Accounting* 72, no. 9 (March 1991), p. 38. Used by permission.

EXHIBIT 5–11
Activity-Based Costing
Model

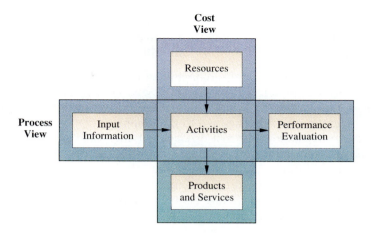

EXHIBIT 5–11
Activity-Based Costing
Model

In this chapter, we focus our attention on the product costing portion of the model. Discussion of performance evaluation is reserved until Chapter 10, where both the traditional and activity-based approaches to performance evaluation are discussed.

DESIGN OF AN ACTIVITY-BASED COSTING SYSTEM

Objective 8
Identify the four steps involved in the design of an activity-based costing system.

Four steps are involved in the design of an activity-based costing system. These steps include process value analysis (PVA), identifying activity centers, tracing costs to activity centers, and selecting cost drivers. After discussing these steps in this section, we then provide a numerical example of activity-based costing.

Process Value Analysis (PVA)

A well-designed activity-based costing system starts with *process value analysis*. **Process value analysis (PVA)** consists of systematically analyzing the activities required to make a product or perform a service. It identifies all resource-consuming activities involved in manufacturing a product or serving a customer and labels these activities as being either value-added or non-value-added in nature. As stated earlier, only the actual processing of goods is a value-added activity; all other steps in the manufacturing process, including moving goods from station to station, inspection, and waiting for processing, are non-value-added activities in that they consume resources without adding value to the product. In completing a PVA, the manager should proceed as follows:

1. Prepare a flowchart detailing each step in the manufacturing process from the receiving of materials to final inspection of the completed product. This requires walking through each operation and documenting *every* activity observed. The flowchart should consist of simple boxes, triangles, and circles that provide a clear, visual image of each product as it moves through the plant. Every step observed in the manufacturing process should be documented, including material handling, wait time, movement of goods between stations, storage, reworking of goods, inspection, and so forth. The time involved in each activity should be recorded on the flowchart, since time can be a good indicator of the amount of resources being consumed by a product.

EXHIBIT 5–12

Process Value Analysis: Value-Added and Non-Value-Added Activities

Present—20 Days

Receiving	Store Raw Materials	Move and Wait	Operation No. 1	Move and Wait	Operation No. 2	Store Finished Goods	Pack and Ship
NVA	NVA	NVA	VA	NVA	VA	NVA	VA
1	5	1	1	2	1	8	1

Total Time Required: VA   3
                      NVA   17
                      Total 20

Goal—10 Days

Receiving	Store Raw Materials	Operation No. 1	Move and Wait	Operation No. 2	Store Finished Goods	Pack and Ship
NVA	NVA	VA	NVA	VA	NVA	VA
1	2	1	1	1	3	1

Total Time Required: VA   3
                      NVA   7
                      Total 10

VA = Value-added activity; NVA = Non-value-added activity.

2. Analyze each activity documented on the flowchart and determine whether it is value-added or non-value-added in nature. In performing this analysis, the manager should ask, "Would the elimination of this step or activity detract in any way from our customers' satisfaction with the final product?" If the answer is no, then the step or activity is non-value-added in nature. For example, the elimination of excessive material handling, needless setups, or lengthy storage would not detract from customer satisfaction but perhaps would increase satisfaction since goods could be delivered more quickly. On the other hand, the elimination of essential processes such as drilling, painting, or packaging would clearly detract from customer satisfaction. Exhibit 5–12 contains the results of an actual PVA performed on a product manufactured by a large company. The PVA showed that 20 days of time were required from receipt of materials to shipment of goods to the customer, and that most of this time was non-value-added in nature.[13]

3. Identify ways to either reduce or eliminate the non-value-added activities documented on the flowchart. This will typically involve the adoption of JIT practices, such as pull scheduling, improved plant layout, reduced setup time, and so forth as discussed earlier in the chapter. The company in Exhibit 5–12, for example, was able to cut its manufacturing time in half through elimination of various non-value-added activities, resulting in a more efficient product flow and an annual savings of a half million dollars in manufacturing costs.

---

[13] Adapted from Mark E. Beischel, "Improving Production with Process Value Analysis," *Journal of Accountancy* 170, no. 3 (September 1990), p. 55.

Identifying Activity Centers

After a PVA has been completed, the activities involved with the production of each product will be clearly documented on a process flowchart. Since there may be dozens of activities identified, a decision must be made at this point as to how many of these activities to treat as separate *activity centers*. An **activity center** can be defined as a part of the production process for which management wants a separate reporting of the cost of the activity involved.

For most companies, it would not be economically feasible to treat every single activity as a separate activity center. Rather, companies frequently combine several related activities into one center to reduce the amount of detail and record-keeping cost involved. For example, several actions may be involved in the handling and movement of raw materials, but these are typically combined into a single activity center titled *material handling*.

Perhaps the greatest accuracy in costing is achieved by recognizing four general levels of activities, with various of these levels then subdivided into specific activity centers. These four general levels can be described as follows:[14]

1. *Unit-level activities,* which are performed each time a unit is produced;
2. *Batch-level activities,* which are performed each time a batch of goods is handled or processed;
3. *Product-level activities,* which are performed as needed to support the production of each different type of product; and
4. *Facility-level activities,* which simply sustain a facility's general manufacturing process.

Unit-level activities are those that arise as a result of the total volume of production going through a facility. The consumption of power, for example, is a function of the number of hours of machine time required to complete *all* units of product and would therefore be considered a unit-level activity. In like manner, maintenance performed, indirect labor support required, and factory supplies consumed are typically regarded as unit-level activities, since they are dependent on the volume of output. Some companies combine activities at the unit level into a single activity center, while others recognize at least two unit-level activity centers—one related to machine activity and the other related to labor activity.

Batch-level activities would include tasks such as the placement of purchase orders, setups of equipment, shipments to customers, and receipts of material. Costs at the batch level are generated *according to the number of batches processed* rather than according to the number of units produced, the number of units sold, or other measures of volume. In addition, costs at the batch level are generally independent of the size of the batch. The cost of placing a purchase order, for example, is the same regardless of whether one item is ordered or 5,000 items are ordered. Thus, the total cost generated by a batch-level activity such as purchasing would be a function of the *number* of orders placed and not a function of the size of these orders. The batch concept is recognized under activity-based costing by the creation of a separate activity center for each batch-level activity that can be identified.

Product-level activities are those that relate to specific products manufactured by a company. These activities are performed as needed to support production of each different type of product; thus, product-level activities will relate to some

[14] Robin Cooper, "Cost Classification in Unit-Based and Activity-Based Manufacturing Cost Systems," *Journal of Cost Management* 4, no. 3 (Fall 1990), p. 6.

products but not to others. For example, doing quality inspections is a product-level activity, since some products require inspections while others do not. In addition to quality inspections, product-level activities include maintaining parts inventories, issuing engineering change notices (the modifying of a product to meet a customer's specifications), and developing special test routines. Typically, a separate activity center is needed for each product-level activity that can be identified.

Facility-level activities are typically combined into a single activity center, since they relate to overall production and not to any specific batches handled or to any specific products manufactured. Facility-level costs include such items as factory management, insurance, property taxes, and worker recreational facilities. Theoretically, facility-level costs should not be added to products since doing so involves the use of arbitrary, volume-based measures such as direct labor-hours or machine-hours. However, virtually all companies *do* add facility-level costs to products. Some of these companies use activity-based costing as their primary costing system and therefore must generate full product costs for external reporting purposes (to be in compliance with generally accepted accounting principles). Other companies, which do not use activity-based costing as their primary costing system, probably allocate facility-level costs to products simply because they have always done so under their old, volume-based systems. If a company uses activity-based costing only as a secondary costing system—that is, only to provide data internally for management—*then facility-level costs should not be added to products*. Adding such costs to products can result in misleading data and unwise decisions on the part of management. This point is considered further in Chapter 13, where we deal with relevant costs in decision making. In the present chapter, to be comprehensive in our coverage, we assume that activity-based costing is being used as the primary costing system unless the data indicate otherwise.

Exhibit 5–13 contains examples of activity centers found at each of the four levels discussed above. The exhibit also contains examples of cost drivers used at each of these levels and examples of the costs involved.

The extent to which activities can be combined is affected by the amount of diversity that exists between a company's products. If the level of product diversity is low—that is, if products consume activities in about the same proportion as a result of being equal in lot size, in total volume, and in complexity of production—then activities can be combined more easily without substantial loss in accuracy of costing. As product diversity increases, however, less and less combining of activities is possible, and a greater number of separate activity centers will be needed to ensure accurate costing of products.

FOCUS ON CURRENT PRACTICE ◆

Product diversity is low enough for one manufacturer of electronic products that the company is able to combine all overhead costs into just two activity centers. On the other hand, product diversity is so great in a manufacturer of screws, bolts, and similar items that the company must recognize 16 separate activity centers in order to ensure accuracy in costing.

EXHIBIT 5–13

Examples of Activity Centers, Cost Drivers, and Traceable Costs

Unit-Level Activities

Examples of activity centers:
    Machine-related activities, such as milling, cutting, and maintenance
    Labor-related activities, including fringe benefits

Examples of cost drivers:
    Machine-hours
    Labor-hours
    Number of units of output

Examples of traceable costs:
    Power costs
    Maintenance costs
    Labor costs
    Factory supplies
    Depreciation of general-use machines and equipment
    Depreciation of maintenance equipment

Product-Level Activities

Examples of activity centers:
    Quality inspection
    Product testing
    Parts inventory management
    Product design
    Specialized processing (labor and machine)

Examples of cost drivers:
    Number of inspections
    Hours of inspection time
    Number of tests
    Hours of testing time
    Number of part types
    Hours of specialized processing time
    Hours of design time
    Number of engineering change orders

Examples of traceable costs:
    Quality control costs
    Testing facility costs
    Parts administration costs
    Parts carrying costs
    Product engineering costs
    Design costs
    Depreciation of specialized machines and equipment

Batch-Level Activities

Examples of activity centers:
    Purchase order processing
    Production order processing
    Equipment setups
    Material handling

Examples of cost drivers:
    Number of orders processed
    Number of material receipts
    Pounds of material handled
    Number of setups
    Hours of setup time

Examples of traceable costs:
    Clerical costs
    Supplies consumed
    Labor setup costs
    Labor cost to handle material
    Depreciation of office, setup, and material-handling equipment

Facility-Level Activities

Examples of activity centers:
    General factory
    Plant occupancy
    Personnel administration and training*

Examples of cost drivers:
    Machine-hours
    Labor-hours
    Number of employees (head count)
    Hours of training time

Examples of traceable costs:
    Plant management salaries
    Plant depreciation
    Property taxes and insurance
    Personnel administration costs
    Employee training costs
    Worker recreational facilities

* The costs of some activities may be traceable in part to the facility level and in part to *other* activity centers at the unit level, product level, and batch level. Personnel administration and training may be such an activity. Activities of this type, which provide essential, companywide services, are discussed in depth in Chapter 16.

Tracing Costs to Activity Centers

We stated earlier that activity-based costing utilizes a two-stage costing process. In the first stage, costs are assigned to the activity centers where they are accumulated while waiting to be applied to products. Costs can either be assigned *directly* to activity centers in this first stage or they can be assigned by use of first-stage cost drivers.

Where possible, companies prefer to assign costs directly to activity centers in order to avoid any distortion in costing. If a company has an activity center titled *material handling,* for example, then it would identify all costs directly associated with material handling and assign the costs to that center as they are incurred. Such costs may include salaries, depreciation, and the use of various supplies.

Other costs associated with material handling might arise from some resource that is shared by two or more activity centers; these costs would need to be assigned to the centers according to some first-stage cost driver that controls utilization of the costs involved. Plant space, for example, might be shared by several activity centers, including material handling. The costs associated with plant space would be assigned to the centers according to the amount of space occupied by each. The identification and use of first-stage cost drivers is discussed in detail in Chapter 16.

Selecting Cost Drivers

The second stage of the two-stage costing process involves assigning costs from the activity centers to products. This is accomplished through the selection and use of second-stage cost drivers. Two factors must be considered when selecting a cost driver for use in this second stage:[15]

1. The ease of obtaining data relating to the cost driver.
2. The degree to which the cost driver measures actual consumption by products of the activity involved.

The ease of obtaining data strikes at the very heart of activity-based costing, since detailed information relating to a particular cost driver may be difficult to find. Assume again that a company wants to establish an activity center titled *material handling*. After careful analysis, management has determined that *number of times handled* would be the appropriate cost driver to use in assigning material-handling cost to products. But then management discovers that no cost-effective means is available for recording how many times a particular item of material is handled during a period, thereby making use of the new activity center economically unfeasible. The matter of economic feasibility is a major barrier to the use of activity-based costing, and it is the factor most often mentioned by companies that have decided *not* to adopt the activity approach. To make activity-based costing workable, managers have found that they must either devise new methods of gathering data relating to cost drivers or they must use drivers for which data are readily available.

High-tech companies have a distinct edge in the matter of gathering data relating to cost drivers, since the computers controlling their systems routinely gather a wide range of information relating to each step in the manufacturing process. This fact probably explains in part why highly automated companies have been the leaders in adopting the activity-based approach.

In choosing a cost driver for an activity center, managers must be sure that it accurately measures the actual consumption of the activity by the company's various products. If a high degree of correlation does not exist between the cost driver and actual consumption, then inaccurate costing will result.

Graphic Example of Activity-Based Costing

Once the design decisions relating to PVA, identifying activity centers, tracing costs to activity centers, and selecting cost drivers have been made, the structure of a company's activity-based costing system will be evident. This structure will differ from company to company depending on the number and type of activity centers maintained. For some companies, the structure will be simple with only

---

[15] For a more detailed discussion, see Robin Cooper, ''Elements of Activity-Based Costing'' in Brinker, *Emerging Practices in Cost Management,* p. 16.

EXHIBIT 5–14
Graphic Example of Activity-Based Costing

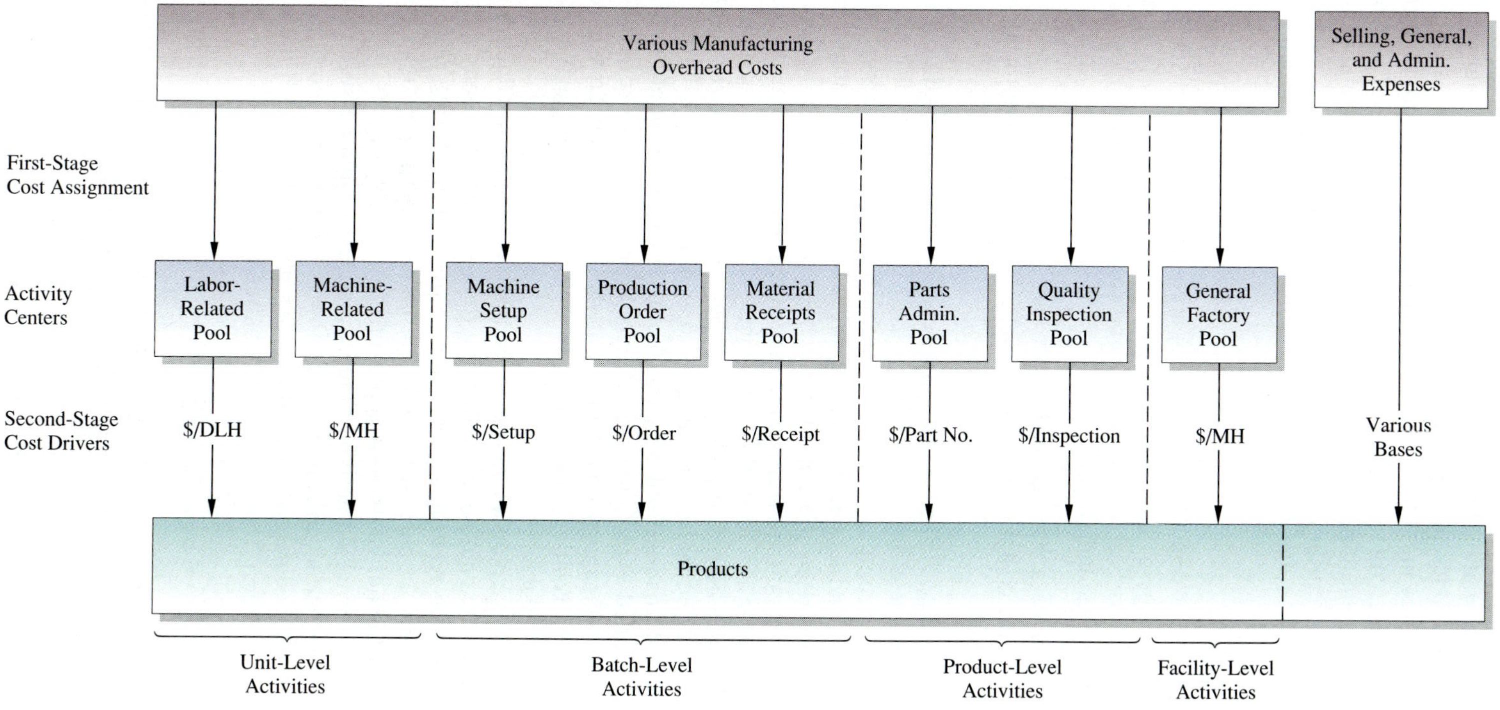

First-Stage Cost Assignment

Activity Centers

Second-Stage Cost Drivers

Various Manufacturing Overhead Costs

Selling, General, and Admin. Expenses

Various Bases

Labor-Related Pool — $/DLH

Machine-Related Pool — $/MH

Machine Setup Pool — $/Setup

Production Order Pool — $/Order

Material Receipts Pool — $/Receipt

Parts Admin. Pool — $/Part No.

Quality Inspection Pool — $/Inspection

General Factory Pool — $/MH

Products

Unit-Level Activities

Batch-Level Activities

Product-Level Activities

Facility-Level Activities

one or two activity centers at the unit, batch, or product level. For other companies, the structure will be complex with many such centers.

Exhibit 5–14 provides a graphic example of an activity-based costing system of medium complexity. The purpose of this exhibit is to tie together the concepts discussed on preceding pages and also to present a bird's-eye view of what an activity-based costing system looks like. In addition to manufacturing overhead costs, the exhibit shows that selling, general, and administrative expenses are also charged to products in an activity-based costing system. Our focus in this chapter, however, is only on the manufacturing overhead cost portion of the exhibit. Later, in Chapter 12, we broaden our focus and show how selling, general, and administrative expenses can be charged to products and services when activity-based costing is used.

NUMERICAL EXAMPLE OF ACTIVITY-BASED COSTING

To provide a numerical example of activity-based costing, assume the following situation:

Objective 9
Compute the cost of a
unit of product using
activity-based costing.

> Dillon Company manufactures two products known as product A and product B. Product A is a low-volume item, on which sales are only 5,000 units each year, and product B is a high-volume item, on which sales are 20,000 units each year. Both products require two direct labor-hours for completion. Therefore, the company works 50,000 direct labor-hours each year, computed as follows:

	Hours
Product A: 5,000 units × 2 hours	10,000
Product B: 20,000 units × 2 hours	40,000
Total hours	50,000

> Costs for materials and labor for one unit of each product are given below:

	Product	
	A	B
Direct materials	$35	$25
Direct labor (at $7.50 per hour)	15	15

> The company's manufacturing overhead costs total $1,000,000 each year. Although the same amount of direct labor time is used in each product, product A requires more machine setups and more quality inspections than B because of the complexity of its design. Also, it is necessary to manufacture product A in small lots, so it requires a relatively large number of production orders as compared to product B.
>
> The company has always used direct labor-hours as a basis for assigning overhead cost to its products.

Below we show allocations of Dillon Company's overhead costs to the products, first using direct labor-hours as a base, then using activities as a base.

Direct Labor-Hours as a Base

The company's overhead rate will be $20 per hour if direct labor-hours are used as a base for assigning overhead costs. This rate is computed as follows:

$$\frac{\text{Manufacturing overhead costs, \$1,000,000}}{\text{Direct labor-hours, 50,000}} = \$20/\text{DLH}$$

Using this rate, the cost to manufacture one unit of each of the products is given below:

	Product	
	A	**B**
Direct materials (above)	$35	$25
Direct labor (above)	15	15
Manufacturing overhead (2 hours × $20)	40	40
Total cost to manufacture	$90	$80

As stated earlier, the problem with this costing approach is that it looks only at labor time and does not consider the impact of other factors—such as setups required or inspections performed—on the overhead costs of the company. Therefore, since other factors are being ignored, and since the two products require equal amounts of labor time, they are assigned equal amounts of overhead cost.

While this method of computing costs is fast and simple, it is accurate only in those situations where other factors affecting overhead are not significant. In the case at hand, these other factors *are* significant, as we shall see in the following discussion.

Activities as a Base

Let us next assume that Dillon Company has analyzed its operations and has identified eight activity centers in the factory along with their associated cost drivers. (For simplicity in discussion, we will assume that these eight centers are identical to the ones illustrated earlier in Exhibit 5–14.) Cost and other data relating to the activity centers are presented in Exhibit 5–15.

As shown in the "Basic Data" at the top of the exhibit, the company has determined the amount of overhead cost traceable to each activity center, along with the expected number of events or transactions for each center's cost driver. The machine setups activity center, for example, has $160,000 in traceable cost, and it is expected to complete 2,000 setups during the year, of which 1,500 will be traceable to product A and 500 will be traceable to product B. Data for the other centers are as shown in the exhibit.

Using the appropriate cost drivers as a base, Dillon Company has computed a predetermined overhead rate for *each activity center*. These rates in turn have been used to assign the costs of the activity centers to the products.

Note from the exhibit that the use of an activity approach has resulted in $93.20 in overhead cost being assigned to each unit of product A and $26.70 in overhead cost being assigned to each unit of product B. These amounts are used in the table below to determine the cost to manufacture a unit of each product under activity-based costing. For comparison, we also present the unit costs derived earlier when direct labor was used to assign overhead cost to the products.

	Activity-Based Costing		Direct-Labor-Based Costing	
	Product A	**Product B**	**Product A**	**Product B**
Direct materials	$ 35.00	$25.00	$35.00	$25.00
Direct labor	15.00	15.00	15.00	15.00
Manufacturing overhead	93.20	26.70	40.00	40.00
Total cost to manufacture	$143.20	$66.70	$90.00	$80.00

Basic Data

EXHIBIT 5–15

Overhead Costing by
an Activity Approach

Activity Center and Cost Driver	Traceable Costs	Expected Number of Events or Transactions		
		Total	Product A	Product B
Labor related (labor-hours)	$ 80,000	50,000	10,000	40,000
Machine related (machine-hours).	210,000	100,000	30,000	70,000
Machine setups (setups).	160,000	2,000	1,500	500
Production orders (orders).	45,000	600	200	400
Material receipts (receipts)	100,000	2,500	900	1,600
Parts administration (part types)	35,000	175	100	75
Quality inspections (inspections)	170,000	5,000	4,000	1,000
General factory (machine-hours)	200,000	100,000	30,000	70,000
	$1,000,000			

Overhead Rates by Activity Center

Activity Center	(a) Traceable Costs	(b) Total Events or Transactions	(a) ÷ (b) Rate per Event or Transaction
Labor related.	$ 80,000	50,000	$1.60/DLH
Machine related	210,000	100,000	$2.10/MH
Machine setups.	160,000	2,000	$80/setup
Production orders.	45,000	600	$75/order
Material receipts	100,000	2,500	$40/receipt
Parts administration.	35,000	175	$200/part type
Quality inspections	170,000	5,000	$34/inspection
General factory.	200,000	100,000	$2/MH

Overhead Cost per Unit of Product

	Product A		Product B	
	Events or Transactions	Amount	Events or Transactions	Amount
Labor related, at $1.60/DLH	10,000	$ 16,000	40,000	$ 64,000
Machine related, at $2.10/MH.	30,000	63,000	70,000	147,000
Machine setups, at $80/setup	1,500	120,000	500	40,000
Production orders, at $75/order	200	15,000	400	30,000
Material receipts, at $40/receipt	900	36,000	1,600	64,000
Parts administration, at $200/part type	100	20,000	75	15,000
Quality inspections, at $34/inspection	4,000	136,000	1,000	34,000
General factory, at $2/MH	30,000	60,000	70,000	140,000
Total overhead cost assigned (a).		$466,000		$534,000
Number of units produced (b).		5,000		20,000
Overhead cost per unit, (a) ÷ (b)		$93.20		$26.70

In the past, Dillon Company has been charging $40 in overhead cost to a unit of either product, whereas it should have been charging $93.20 in overhead cost to each unit of product A and only $26.70 to each unit of product B. Thus, as a result of using direct labor as a base for overhead costing, in the past too little overhead cost has been charged to product A and too much has been charged to product B. Consequently, unit costs have been badly distorted. Depending on selling prices, the company may even have been suffering a loss on product A without knowing it (because A's unit cost has been understated). Through activity-based costing, we have been able to identify the overhead costs that are traceable to each product and thus derive more accurate cost data. The pattern of cost distortion shown in our example is quite common. Such distortion can happen in any company that relies solely on direct labor in assigning overhead cost to products and ignores other significant factors affecting overhead cost incurrence.

Shifting of Overhead Cost   When a company installs an activity-based costing system, overhead cost is often shifted from the high-volume products to the low-volume products, with a higher unit cost resulting from the low-volume products. We saw this happen in our example above, where overhead cost was shifted to product A—the low-volume product—and its unit cost increased from $90 to $143.20 per unit. Why does this shifting of cost take place? It is the result of two related factors.

First, rather than treating overhead cost as a lump amount and spreading it uniformly over all products, activity-based costing attempts to trace costs to specific products. Since low-volume products often require special equipment, special handling, and so forth, they typically are responsible for the incurrence of a disproportionately large amount of overhead cost. As this cost is traced to the low-volume products, it drives their unit costs upward.

Second, many overhead costs are incurred at the batch level. Since low-volume products typically have fewer units processed per batch than high-volume products, their average processing cost per unit is higher. For example, consider the cost of issuing production orders—a batch activity—in Exhibit 5–15. The cost to the company to issue a single production order is $75 (see the middle portion of Exhibit 5–15). For product A—the low-volume product—only 25 units are processed per production order:

Number of units produced (a)	5,000
Number of production orders issued (b).	200
Number of units processed per	
production order (a) ÷ (b)	25

Since the cost to the company to issue a production order is $75, and since only 25 units of product A are processed per order, the average cost for production orders for product A is $3 per unit ($75 order cost ÷ 25 units = $3 per unit).

However, for product B—the high-volume product—50 units are processed per production order:

Number of units produced (a)	20,000
Number of production orders issued (b).	400
Number of units processed per	
production order (a) ÷ (b)	50

Thus, the average cost for production orders for product B is only $1.50 per unit ($75 order cost ÷ 50 units = $1.50 per unit), which is just *half* the unit cost of product A. This subtle (but real) difference in cost to the company is ignored when direct labor is used to assign overhead cost to products, since the direct labor approach spreads the cost of *all* production orders evenly over the two products. As a result, product B—the high-volume product—is forced to subsidize the low-volume product. When this subsidy is taken away through activity-based costing, the unit cost of the low-volume product is driven upward.

Armed with more accurate cost data for the products, Dillon Company's management should now employ the JIT philosophy to find ways to reduce costs. Rather than continuing to use conventional production methods, for example, the company might use JIT purchasing to reduce the number of purchase orders and to control the quality of its incoming materials. It might also use product flow lines to reduce the number of production orders, machine setups, and the need for separate inspections.

Cost Flows under Activity-Based Costing   The flow of costs through Raw Materials, Work in Process, Finished Goods, and other accounts is the same under activity-based costing as was illustrated in Chapter 3. Since the flow of costs is the same, the journal entries to record this flow are also the same. The only difference is that a company will have *several* predetermined overhead rates—as we saw in Exhibit 5–15—rather than just one. A specific example to show the flow of costs in an activity-based costing system is provided in Appendix C at the end of this chapter.

BENEFITS AND LIMITATIONS OF ACTIVITY-BASED COSTING

At first glance, activity-based costing might seem to be the answer to all of a manager's costing problems. Although certain benefits can be identified, activity-based costing also has several limitations that severely restrict its use in some companies. These benefits and limitations are discussed in this section.

Benefits of Activity-Based Costing

Activity-based costing improves the costing systems of organizations in the following ways, thereby leading to more accurate product costs:

First, activity-based costing *increases the number of cost pools used to accumulate overhead costs*. Rather than accumulating all overhead costs in a single, companywide pool, or accumulating them in departmental pools, costs are accumulated by activity. As a result, many pools are created according to the number of cost-driving activities that can be identified.

Second, activity-based costing *changes the base used to assign overhead costs to products*. Rather than assigning costs on a basis of direct labor or some other measure of volume, costs are assigned on a basis of the portion of cost-driving activities that can be traced to the product or job involved.

Third, activity-based costing *changes a manager's perception of many overhead costs* in that costs that were formerly thought to be indirect (such as power, inspection, and machine setup) are identified with specific activities and thereby are recognized as being traceable to individual products.

As a result of having more accurate product costs, managers are in a position to make better decisions relating to product retention, marketing strategy, product profitability, and so forth. Moreover, activity-based costing leads to better cost control, since managers can see that the best way to control costs is to control the activities that generate the costs in the first place.

Limitations of Activity-Based Costing

The benefits above are offset somewhat by two limitations that surround activity-based costing. These limitations are (1) the necessity to still make some arbitrary allocations based on volume and (2) the high measurement costs associated with multiple activity centers and cost drivers.

The Need for Arbitrary Allocations   Critics of activity-based costing point out that even though some overhead costs can be traced directly to products through the use of activity centers, the portion that relates to facility-level activities must still be allocated to products by means of some arbitrary base such as machine-hours or labor-hours. It is argued that facility-level activities account for the bulk of overhead cost in many companies, thereby rendering any attempt to gain more accurate product costs through the use of activity-based costing largely meaningless.

Proponents of activity-based costing reply that it is not necessary to have the majority of overhead cost traceable to unit-level, batch-level, or product-level activity centers in order to have activity-based costing yield more accurate unit cost data. For some companies, only a small amount of overhead cost traceable to activity centers at these levels is adequate to improve the costing process.

SIEMENS   FOCUS ON CURRENT PRACTICE

Siemens Electric Motor Works has found that by adding only two batch-level activity centers to its costing system, it has been able to achieve significantly more accurate unit costs. The amount of overhead cost traceable to these two activity centers represents only *9 percent* of the total overhead cost of the company. The remaining 91 percent continues to be allocated to products on a volume basis (principally machine-hours, direct labor-hours, and material cost.)[16]

Moreover, proponents of activity-based costing state that *any* amount of overhead cost traceable directly to products through activity centers is preferable to just assigning all costs arbitrarily by some volume measure. In short, proponents say that it is better to have product costs approximately right than precisely wrong.

High Measurement Costs   Perhaps the most significant limitation of activity-based costing is the high measurement costs that are required for its operation. As shown earlier in Exhibit 5–15, even a moderately complex system requires a great amount of detail and many separate computations in order to determine the cost of a unit of product. In Exhibit 5–15, we had only two products; the complexities involved are multiplied manyfold for companies that have hundreds or thousands of products. In short, the implementation of activity-based costing can present a formidable challenge, and management may decide that the measurement costs involved are too great to justify the expected benefits. Companies that have some of the following characteristics are most likely to benefit from activity-based costing:

1. Products differ substantially in volume, lot size, or complexity of manufacture.
2. Products differ substantially in their need for various activities such as setups, inspections, and so forth, involved in the manufacturing process.
3. The variety of products being manufactured has increased significantly since the existing cost system was established.
4. Overhead costs are high and increasing.

---

[16] Robin Cooper, "Cost Classifications in Unit-Based and Activity-Based Manufacturing Cost Systems," *Journal of Cost Management* 4, no. 3 (Fall 1990), p. 11.

5. Top management and marketing people largely ignore the cost data provided by the existing system when setting prices or making other product decisions.
6. Manufacturing technology has changed significantly since the existing cost system was established. For example, the factory has been automated or product flow lines have been redesigned.

Because of the difficulty of gathering data relating to activities and cost drivers, activity-based costing has found its greatest applications to date in companies that have a fairly high degree of automation. The computers in such companies can be programmed to routinely gather data relating to setups performed, inspections made, and so forth, and to have such data immediately available for product costing purposes. Nonautomated companies that have used activity-based costing have tended to limit their systems to one or two activity centers because of the measurement problems involved. When a company has only one or two activity centers, it is said to have a *partial* activity-based costing system. As such a company grows and acquires more automated equipment, it can expand its costing system step by step until activity-based costing is in full use.

Activity-Based Costing and Service Industries

Although initially conceived as a tool for manufacturing companies, activity-based costing is also being used in some service industries. Successful implementation of an activity-based costing system depends on identifying the key activities that generate costs and being able to keep track of how many of those activities are performed for each service that is provided.

Two common problems exist in service firms that sometimes make implementation of activity-based costing relatively difficult. One problem is that a larger proportion of costs in service industries tend to be facility-level costs that cannot be traced to any particular billable service provided by the firm. Another problem is that it is more difficult to capture activity data in service companies, since so many of the activities tend to involve nonrepetitive human tasks that cannot be automatically recorded.[17] In a factory, a bar code reader can automatically record every job that passes through a testing center. No such facility exists for automatically recording each time a nurse takes someone's blood pressure. Nevertheless, activity-based costing systems have been implemented in a number of service firms, including railroads, hospitals, banks, and data services companies.

Our discussion in this chapter has focused on the use of activity-based costing in manufacturing companies. We will defer further discussion of its use in service-type operations to Chapter 16, where we discuss its specific application in greater depth.

INTERNATIONAL USE OF JIT AND ACTIVITY-BASED COSTING

JIT was conceived about two decades ago by managers at the Toyota Motor Company. The concept quickly spread throughout Japanese industry and now dominates manufacturing practices in that country. From Japan, JIT has spread into other industrialized nations, including England, Germany, and Canada. Managers in England were among the first to recognize the benefits of JIT, and some of the first articles describing the approach appeared in English journals. JIT is now

---

[17] William Rotch, "Activity-Based Costing in Service Industries," *Journal of Cost Management* 4, no. 2 (Summer 1990), p. 8.

so widespread that a manager can expect to encounter it in any progressive company, regardless of geographic location.

Activity-based costing was pioneered in the United States, although several of the early field studies were performed by American researchers on German companies. The concept is relatively new, with the term *activity-based costing* having been coined by the management of John Deere Company within the last 15 years. To date, activity-based costing has not spread as rapidly throughout the world as has JIT. Perhaps the reason is traceable to the costs of implementation and to the fact that it is sometimes difficult to collect the data needed to operate the system. Even in Japan, which has become a leader in automation technology, activity-based costing is rarely used. Instead, Japanese managers seem to prefer volume measures such as direct labor-hours to assign overhead cost to products. This preference, according to Japanese researchers, can be explained by the fact that Japanese managers are ". . . convinced that reducing direct labor is essential for ongoing cost improvement."[18] It is argued that by using direct labor as an overhead allocation base, managers are forced to watch direct labor more closely and to seek for ways to reduce it through increased automation. In short, Japanese managers as a group tend to be more concerned about cost reduction and working toward specific long-term company goals than they are about obtaining more accurate product costs.

To date, the most extensive application of activity-based costing has been in the United States, with some applications having been made in Europe, particularly in Germany.

SUMMARY

In an effort to reduce or eliminate inventories (and thereby to reduce costs), companies are adopting JIT inventory systems. Five key elements are involved in the successful operation of JIT. These include maintaining a limited number of suppliers who go through a certification program to ensure that they will meet stringent delivery terms; an improved plant layout that focuses on individual product flow lines; reducing the setup time needed for production runs through both training and automation; achieving total quality control through weeding out undependable suppliers and through employee training; and developing a flexible work force through cross-training of employees. Although initially conceived as a method of inventory control, JIT has expanded into what is termed the *JIT philosophy*. This philosophy is that wherever possible in an organization, management should focus its efforts on simplification and on elimination of waste.

Activity-based costing has been developed in response to the manager's need for more accurate product costs. Four steps are involved in the design of an activity-based costing system. These include PVA (process value analysis), which helps the manager to identify and eliminate non-value-added activities in the company; identifying activity centers, which are the "pools" used to accumulate overhead costs; tracing costs to the activity centers; and selecting cost drivers, which are the tools used to charge costs from the activity centers to the products. Activity-based costing provides several benefits to the manager, including more accurate product costs, better data for decision making, and tighter cost control. Activity-based costing also has several limitations, the chief of which is the difficulty involved with gathering data relating to activity centers and cost drivers.

---

[18] Toshiro Hiromoto, "Another Hidden Edge—Japanese Management Accounting," *Harvard Business Review* 66, no. 4 (July–August 1988), p. 23.

REVIEW PROBLEM: ACTIVITY-BASED COSTING

Aerodec, Inc., manufactures and sells two products, X and Y. Annual sales in units, labor time per unit, and total manufacturing time per year are provided below:

	Total Hours
Product X: 2,000 units × 5 hours.	10,000
Product Y: 10,000 units × 4 hours.	40,000
Total hours	50,000

Costs for materials and labor for one unit of each product are given below:

	Product	
	X	Y
Direct materials	$25	$17
Direct labor (at $6 per hour).	30	24

Manufacturing overhead costs total $800,000 each year. The breakdown of these costs between the company's six activity centers is given below. The cost driver for each activity center is shown in parentheses.

Activity Center and Cost Driver	Traceable Costs	Expected Number of Events or Transactions		
		Total	Product X	Product Y
Labor related (direct labor-hours)	$ 80,000	50,000	10,000	40,000
Machine setups (number of setups).	150,000	5,000	3,000	2,000
Quality inspections (number of inspections)	160,000	8,000	5,000	3,000
Production orders (number of orders).	70,000	400	100	300
Material receipts (number of receipts)	90,000	750	150	600
General factory (machine-hours)	250,000	40,000	12,000	28,000
	$800,000			

Required

1. Aerodec, Inc., has six activity centers. Refer to the data in Exhibit 5–13, page 196, and classify the activity in each of Aerodec's activity centers as either a unit-level, batch-level, product-level, or facility-level activity.
2. Assume that the company applies overhead cost to products on a basis of direct labor-hours.
   a. Compute the predetermined overhead rate that would be used.
   b. Determine the cost to manufacture a unit of each product, using the predetermined overhead rate computed in (2)(a).
3. Assume that the company uses activity-based costing to compute overhead rates.
   a. Compute the predetermined overhead rate per event or transaction for each of the six activity centers listed above.
   b. Using the rates developed in (3)(a), determine the amount of overhead cost that should be assigned to a unit of each product.
   c. Determine the cost to manufacture a unit of each product and compare this cost to the cost computed in (2)(b) above.

Solution to Review Problem

1.

Activity Center	Type of Activity
Labor related	Unit level
Machine setups	Batch level
Quality inspections.	Product level
Production orders	Batch level
Material receipts	Batch level
General factory	Facility level

2. a. $\dfrac{\text{Manufacturing overhead costs, \$800,000}}{\text{Direct labor-hours, 50,000}} = \$16/\text{DLH}$

b.

	Product	
	X	**Y**
Direct materials	$ 25	$ 17
Direct labor	30	24
Manufacturing overhead applied:		
Product X: 5 hours × $16	80	
Product Y: 4 hours × $16		64
Total cost per unit	$135	$105

3. a.

Activity Center	(a) Traceable Costs	(b) Total Events or Transactions	(a) ÷ (b) Rate per Event or Transaction
Labor related	$ 80,000	50,000	$1.60/DLH
Machine setups	150,000	5,000	$30/setup
Quality inspections	160,000	8,000	$20/inspection
Production orders	70,000	400	$175/order
Material receipts	90,000	750	$120/receipt
General factory	250,000	40,000	$6.25/MH

b.

	Product X		Product Y	
	Events or Transactions	Amount	Events or Transactions	Amount
Labor related, at $1.60/DLH	10,000	$ 16,000	40,000	$ 64,000
Machine setups, at $30/setup	3,000	90,000	2,000	60,000
Quality inspections, at $20/inspection . . .	5,000	100,000	3,000	60,000
Production orders, at $175/order	100	17,500	300	52,500
Material receipts, at $120/receipt	150	18,000	600	72,000
General factory, at $6.25/MH.	12,000	75,000	28,000	175,000
Total overhead cost assigned (a)		$316,500		$483,500
Number of units produced (b)		2,000		10,000
Overhead cost per unit, (a) ÷ (b)		$158.25		$48.35

c.

	Product	
	X	**Y**
Direct materials	$ 25.00	$17.00
Direct labor	30.00	24.00
Manufacturing overhead (see above)	158.25	48.35
Total cost per unit	$213.25	$89.35

Note that the cost to produce product X is much greater than the cost computed in (2)(b), and the cost to produce product Y is much less. Using volume (direct labor-hours) in (2)(b) as a basis for applying overhead cost to products has resulted in too little overhead cost being applied to product X (the low-volume product) and too much overhead cost being applied to product Y (the high-volume product).

KEY TERMS FOR REVIEW

Activity   Any event or transaction that is a cost driver—that is, acts as a causal factor in the incurrence of cost in an organization. (p. 190)

Activity-based costing   A two-stage costing method that creates a cost pool for each major activity in an organization (such as setups required, purchase orders issued, or number of inspections completed). Overhead costs are assigned to products and services on the basis of the number of these activities involved in manufacturing the product or providing the service. (p. 190)

Activity center   A part of the production process for which management wants a separate reporting of the cost of the activity involved. (p. 194)

Batch-level activities   Activities that are performed each time a batch of goods is handled or processed. Such activities would include purchase orders, setups of equipment, and shipments to customers (p. 194)

Cell   A clustering of two or more machines at a single workstation. (p. 176)

Computer-integrated manufacturing (CIM)   The integration of an organization's business functions (functions outside the factory) with its manufacturing functions, through the use of computers. (p. 179)

Continuous improvement   The constant pursuit of ever-greater value being provided for the customer. (p. 184)

Continuous monitoring   Workers performing their own inspections as units move along the product flow line. (p. 181)

Cycle time   The length of time required to turn materials into products. See *Throughput time*. (p. 176)

Facility-level activities   Activities that relate to overall production and therefore can't be traced to specific products. Cost associated with these activities pertain to a plant's general manufacturing process. (p. 195)

Flexible manufacturing system (FMS)   The use of an automated material-handling system to link together the cells on a product flow line, with the flows between cells being controlled by a central computer. Such a system gives a company the power to manufacture a whole family of similar products on a single flow line. (p. 178)

Flow line   The physical path taken by a product as it moves through the manufacturing process from receipt of raw materials to shipment of the completed good. (p. 174)

Focused factory   The use of multiple product flow lines, one for each product. All machines needed to make a product are brought together into one flow line so that tasks such as milling, cutting, and assembly are performed consecutively as a product moves from machine to machine. (p. 175)

Island of automation   A manufacturing cell that consists entirely of automated equipment. Frequently, these islands are assisted by pick-and-place robots that control movements of material into and out of the cell and that perform certain tasks in the manufacture of the product. (p. 177)

JIT philosophy   The belief that management should focus its efforts on simplification and on elimination of waste, wherever possible in an organization. (p. 183)

Just-in-time (JIT) inventory system   A method of inventory control designed to reduce or even eliminate inventories in a company. (p. 172)

Non-value-added activities   Any activities that add to the cost of a product or service but do not add to its market value. (p. 183)

Numerical control (NC) machine   A piece of automated equipment. The functions of an NC machine are controlled by a computer that has been programmed to guide the machine through all the steps necessary to complete some portion of the final product. (p. 177)

Process value analysis (PVA)   A systematic approach to gaining an understanding of the activities required to make a product or perform a service. PVA identifies all resource-

Objective 10
Define or explain the key terms listed at the end of the chapter.

consuming activities involved in the manufacturing or service process and labels these activities as being either value-added or non-value-added in nature. (p. 192)

Product diversity   A range of products that differ substantially in volume, lot size, or complexity of design. (p. 189)

Product-level activities   Activities that relate to specific products; such activities, which include quality inspections and maintaining parts inventories, are performed in behalf of specific products as needed to support production. (p. 194)

Setup time   The time involved in changing equipment, moving material about, and getting forms and jigs in place to accommodate the production of a different item. (p. 176)

Throughput   The total volume of production through a facility during a period. (p. 175)

Throughput time   The length of time required to turn materials into products. See *Cycle time*. (p. 176)

Total quality control (TQC)   A monitoring and early warning system used under JIT that is designed to detect defective parts and materials and to correct the problems that caused those defects. (p. 181)

Transactions costing   See *Activity-based costing*. (p. 191)

Unit-level activities   Activities that arise as a result of the total volume of production going through a facility, and which are performed each time a unit is produced. (p. 194)

APPENDIX C: COST FLOWS IN AN ACTIVITY-BASED COSTING SYSTEM

Objective 11
Record the flow of costs in an activity-based costing system.

As stated in the main body of the chapter, the flow of costs through Raw Materials, Work in Process, and other accounts is the same under activity-based costing as was illustrated in Chapter 3. Although the flow of costs is the same, a company must compute several predetermined overhead rates when activity-based costing is being used and that complicates the journal entries and T-accounts somewhat. Our purpose in this appendix is to provide a detailed example of cost flows in an activity-based costing system. After presenting this example, we make brief comments about how a costing system can be simplified if JIT is in use.

An Example of Cost Flows

Note that the company in the following example has five activity centers and therefore must compute five predetermined overhead rates. Also note from the example how underapplied and overapplied overhead cost is computed when activity-based costing is being used.

Basic Data   Sarvik Company installed an activity-based costing system several years ago. The company has five activity centers for costing purposes. These activity centers are listed below, along with the estimated overhead cost and the expected level of activity in each center for 19x3, the coming year.

Activity Center	Cost Driver	Estimated Overhead Cost—19x3	Expected Activity
Machine related	CPU hours	$175,000	5,000 CPU hours
Purchase orders	Number of orders	63,000	700 orders
Machine setups	Number of setups	92,000	460 setups
Product testing	Number of tests	160,000	200 tests
General factory	Machine-hours	300,000	25,000 machine-hours

On January 1, 19x3, the company had inventory balances as follows:

Raw materials	$3,000
Work in process	4,000
Finished goods	–0–

Selected transactions recorded by the company during the year are given below:

a. Raw materials were purchased on account, $915,000.

b. Raw materials were requisitioned for use in production, $900,000 ($810,000 direct and $90,000 indirect). The indirect materials were traceable to the activity centers as follows:

Machine related	$16,000
Purchase orders	3,000
Machine setups	8,000
Product testing	21,000
General factory	42,000
Total	$90,000

c. Labor costs were incurred in the factory, $370,000 ($95,000 direct labor and $275,000 indirect labor). The indirect labor costs were traceable to the activity centers as follows:

Machine related	$ 30,000
Purchase orders	40,000
Machine setups	25,000
Product testing	60,000
General factory	120,000
Total	$275,000

d. Depreciation was recorded on factory assets, $180,000. This depreciation was traceable to the activity centers as follows:

Machine related	$ 72,000
Purchase orders	9,000
Machine setups	16,000
Product testing	48,000
General factory	35,000
Total	$180,000

e. Miscellaneous manufacturing overhead costs were incurred, $230,000. These overhead costs were traceable to the activity centers as follows:

Machine related	$ 50,000
Purchase orders	18,000
Machine setups	45,000
Product testing	27,000
General factory	90,000
Total	$230,000

f. Manufacturing overhead cost was applied to production. *Actual* activity in the various activity centers during 19x3 was as follows:

Machine related	4,600 CPU hours
Purchase orders	800 orders issued
Machine setups	500 setups completed
Product testing	190 tests completed
General factory	23,000 machine-hours worked

g. Goods costing $1,650,000 to manufacture were completed during the year.

Required 1. Compute the predetermined overhead rate for each activity center for 19x3.
2. Prepare journal entries to record transactions (a) through (g) above. When applying overhead cost to production in entry (f), note that you have five predetermined overhead rates, rather than just one.
3. Post the entries in (2) to T-accounts. As part of this posting, *create a T-account for each activity center and treat these accounts as subsidiary accounts to Manufacturing Overhead.*
4. Compute the underapplied or overapplied overhead cost in the Manufacturing Overhead account and in each activity center.

Solution 1. Predetermined overhead rates for the activity centers:

Activity Center	(1) Estimated Overhead Cost—19x3	(2) Expected Activity	(1) ÷ (2) Predetermined Overhead Rate
Machine related	$175,000	5,000 CPU hours	$35/CPU hour
Purchase orders	63,000	700 orders	$90/order
Machine setups	92,000	460 setups	$200/setup
Product testing	160,000	200 tests	$800/test
General factory	300,000	25,000 machine-hours	$12/machine-hour

2. a.

Raw Materials	915,000	
Accounts Payable		915,000

b.

Work in Process	810,000	
Manufacturing Overhead	90,000	
Raw Materials		900,000

c.

Work in Process	95,000	
Manufacturing Overhead	275,000	
Salaries and Wages Payable		370,000

d.

Manufacturing Overhead	180,000	
Accumulated Depreciation		180,000

e.

Manufacturing Overhead	230,000	
Accounts Payable		230,000

f. Recall from Chapter 3 that the formula for computing applied overhead cost is:

Predetermined overhead rate × Actual activity = Applied overhead cost

Since we have *five* activity centers and *five* predetermined overhead rates, we must determine the amount of applied overhead cost for *each* activity center. The computations are:

Activity Center	(1) Predetermined Overhead Rate	(2) Actual Activity	(1) × (2) Applied Overhead Cost
Machine related . . .	$35/CPU hour	4,600 CPU hours	$161,000
Purchase orders . . .	$90/order	800 orders issued	72,000
Machine setups . . .	$200/setup	500 setups completed	100,000
Product testing. . . .	$800/test	190 tests completed	152,000
General factory . . .	$12/machine-hour	23,000 machine-hours	276,000
Total.			$761,000

By totaling these five applied overhead cost figures, we find that the company applied $761,000 in overhead cost to products during the year. The entry to record this application of overhead cost would be:

Work in Process	761,000	
Manufacturing Overhead		761,000
g. Finished Goods	1,650,000	
Work in Process		1,650,000

3. See the T-accounts in Exhibit C–1. Note from these T-accounts that when amounts are posted to Manufacturing Overhead, the amounts must also be posted to the activity center accounts to which they relate.

4. The underapplied or overapplied overhead cost is computed in the T-accounts in Exhibit C–1 for Manufacturing Overhead and for each of the activity center accounts. These computations can be summarized as follows:

		Activity Center				
	Total	Machine Related	Purchase Orders	Machine Setups	Product Testing	General Factory
Actual overhead cost	$775,000	$168,000	$70,000	$ 94,000	$156,000	$287,000
Applied overhead cost.	761,000	161,000	72,000	100,000	152,000	276,000
Underapplied or (overapplied) overhead cost.	$ 14,000	$ 7,000	$ (2,000)	$ (6,000)	$ 4,000	$ 11,000

Note from the computations above that the $14,000 total underapplied overhead cost is equal to the sum of the underapplied and overapplied amounts from the five activity centers.

The Impact of JIT on Cost Flows

When a company uses JIT, its cost system can be simplified from what was illustrated in Chapter 3 and illustrated above. In a *true* JIT setting, no separate stocks of raw materials are maintained. Therefore, the Raw Materials inventory account is merged with the Work in Process inventory account and a new account called **Raw and In-Process Inventory** is created. All purchases of raw materials are charged directly to this account. This simplifies the record-keeping process, since there are no Raw Materials inventory records to maintain, no requisition forms, no issue slips, and so forth.

To further simplify the record-keeping process, some companies using JIT make no effort to "track" costs through the system and therefore eliminate job cost sheets and other detailed cost records. Rather than tracking costs, these companies use a technique called *backflush costing* to charge costs to products. Under **backflush costing,** no detailed cost records are maintained. Instead, costs in the Raw and In-Process Inventory account and the Manufacturing Overhead account are "flushed" out of the system and charged to products *after* the products have been completed. These costs are charged to products according to some preset standard rate.

The reader should be aware that the simplified costing approaches described above are appropriate *only* in those situations where a *true* JIT system is in use. If either raw materials or work in process inventories exist at the end of a period, then backflush costing is not appropriate and will be costly to operate. The reason is that when inventories are present, frequent and expensive physical counts of inventory will be necessary to determine the amount of raw materials and partially completed goods still on hand. Moreover, with no requisition slips, job cost sheets, or other records available, it will be difficult to identify how much cost should be applied to inventories and how much should be applied to completed output. Thus, in the absence of a *true* JIT system, backflush costing may result in

EXHIBIT C–1
T-Accounts Showing Activity Centers

Raw Materials			
Bal.	3,000	(b)	900,000
(a)	915,000		
Bal.	18,000		

Finished Goods			
Bal.	–0–		
(g)	1,650,000		

Accounts Payable			
		(a)	915,000
		(e)	230,00

Work in Process			
Bal.	4,000	(g)	1,650,000
(b)	810,000		
(c)	95,000		
(f)	761,000		
Bal.	20,000		

Accumulated Depreciation		
(d)	180,000

Salaries and Wages Payable		
(c)	370,000

Manufacturing Overhead			
(b)	90,000	(f)	761,000
(c)	275,000		
(d)	180,000		
(e)	230,000		
	775,000		761,000
Bal.	14,000		

Manufacturing overhead cost flows are detailed in the individual activity center accounts, which form a subsidiary overhead ledger. For example, the $90,000 posted to Manufacturing Overhead in entry (b) above is detailed in the individual activity center accounts under entry (b).

Machine-Related Activity Center			
(b)	16,000	(f)	161,000
(c)	30,000		
(d)	72,000		
(e)	50,000		
	168,000		161,000
Bal.	7,000		

Purchase Orders Activity Center			
(b)	3,000	(f)	72,000
(c)	40,000		
(d)	9,000		
(e)	18,000		
	70,000		72,000
		Bal.	2,000

Machine Setups Activity Center			
(b)	8,000	(f)	100,000
(c)	25,000		
(d)	16,000		
(e)	45,000		
	94,000		100,000
		Bal.	6,000

Product Testing Activity Center			
(b)	21,000	(f)	152,000
(c)	60,000		
(d)	48,000		
(e)	27,000		
	156,000		152,000
Bal.	4,000		

General Factory Activity Center			
(b)	42,000	(f)	276,000
(c)	120,000		
(d)	35,000		
(e)	90,000		
	287,000		276,000
Bal.	11,000		

less timely, less accurate, and more expensive data than a conventional costing system. Due to these problems, the simplified costing procedures described above have not gained widespread acceptance and will not be illustrated here.

KEY TERMS FOR REVIEW (APPENDIX C)

Backflush costing   A term used under JIT that refers to "flushing" costs out of the system after goods are completed and without the use of detailed cost records. (p. 213)

Raw and In-Process Inventory   An account used in a JIT system that is a combination of the Raw Materials and Work in Process inventory accounts found in a job-order costing system. (p. 213)

QUESTIONS

5-1 In a JIT system, what is meant by the pull approach to the flow of goods, as compared to the push approach used in conventional systems?

5-2 What are the causes of excessive inventory in an organization?

5-3 People sometimes feel that JIT is unfair to suppliers, since the suppliers must make daily deliveries of parts and materials. How do suppliers benefit from a JIT system?

5-4 How does the plant layout differ in a company using JIT as compared to a company that uses a more conventional approach to manufacturing? What benefits accrue from the JIT layout?

5-5 Identify the benefits that can result from reducing the setup time for a product.

5-6 What is meant by the term *lights out factory?*

5-7 Identify the persons responsible for maintaining total quality control.

5-8 How does a work force in a JIT facility differ from the work force in a conventional facility?

5-9 What is meant by the term *JIT philosophy?* What three ideas are pivotal to this philosophy?

5-10 How does the use of JIT reduce or eliminate the difference in unit costs between the FIFO and weighted-average methods?

5-11 Why are new approaches to overhead application, such as activity-based costing, needed in many companies today?

5-12 Why are departmental overhead rates sometimes not accurate in assigning overhead cost to products?

5-13 When designing an activity-based costing system, why should PVA (process value analysis) always be the starting point?

5-14 What four general levels of activities can be identified in a company?

5-15 Why is activity-based costing described as a "two-stage" costing method?

5-16 In what three ways does activity-based costing improve the costing system of an organization?

5-17 What are the two chief limitations of activity-based costing?

5-18 What type of companies have found activity-based costing to be most useful? Why are these companies able to use activity-based costing while other companies are not?

EXERCISES

The steps listed below are followed in the manufacture of one of Eagle Company's products: **E5-1**

a. Materials are received from suppliers and checked to ensure that orders are complete and goods are free of defects.

b. Materials are transferred to a warehouse pending use in production.
c. A materials requisition is issued, and materials are transferred to the production line.
d. Materials are placed on pallets pending use in production.
e. Materials are milled to proper size.
f. Fabricated materials are checked for defects.
g. Fabricated materials are transferred to the assembly department.
h. Units of product are assembled by workers.
i. Completed units are inspected in a separate inspection department to ensure that they are free of defects.
j. Units of product are placed in a finished goods warehouse to wait for shipment to customers.

Required
1. Classify each step above as process time, inspection time, move time, or queue time.
2. In a PVA (process value analysis), which of these steps would probably be labeled as a non-value-added activity?

E5–2 Listed below are a number of activities that you have observed in Greenwich Company. The company manufactures a variety of products.

a. Receipts of material in the company's receiving department.
b. Management of parts inventories.
c. Rough milling work which is done on all products.
d. Hiring of new employees through a personnel office.
e. Design work for new products and to modify existing products.
f. Maintenance of general-use equipment by maintenance workers.
g. Occupancy of the general plant building.
h. Issue of purchase orders.

Required
1. Classify each of the activities above as either a unit-level, batch-level, product-level, or facility-level activity.
2. For each activity above, name one or more cost drivers that might be used to assign costs generated by the activity to products.

E5–3 Listed below are various activities observed in Ming Company. Each activity has been classified as unit level, batch level, product level, or facility level in nature.

Activity	Activity Classification	Examples of Traceable Costs	Examples of Cost Drivers
a. Direct labor workers assemble a product. . .	Unit level		
b. Products are designed by a specialized team.	Product level		
c. Equipment setups are performed on a regular basis.	Batch level		
d. Numerical control (NC) machines are used to cut and shape materials..	Unit level		
e. Ongoing training is provided for all employees..	Facility level		
f. Materials are moved from the receiving dock to product flow lines by a material-handling crew.	Batch level		
g. Goods requiring direct labor processing are in-spected by an inspection team.	Product level		

Required Complete the table above by listing examples of traceable costs and examples of cost drivers for each activity.

E5–4 Ellix Company manufactures two products, A and B. Data regarding the two products follow:

Product	Direct Labor-Hours per Unit	Annual Production	Total Direct Labor-Hours
A.	1.8	5,000 units	9,000
B.	0.9	30,000 units	27,000
			36,000

Additional information about the company follows:

a. Product A requires $72 in direct materials per unit, and product B requires $50.
b. The direct labor rate is $10 per hour.
c. The company has always used direct labor-hours as the base for applying manufacturing overhead cost to products. Manufacturing overhead totals $1,800,000 per year.
d. Product A is more complex to manufacture than product B, and it requires the use of special equipment and machining time.
e. Because of the special work required in (d), the company is considering the use of activity-based costing to apply overhead cost to products. Three activity centers have been identified as follows:

Activity Center	Cost Driver	Traceable Costs	Annual Events or Transactions		
			Total	Product A	Product B
Machine setups	Number of setups	$ 360,000	150	50	100
Special processing	CPU minutes	180,000	12,000	12,000	—
General factory	Direct labor-hours	1,260,000	36,000	9,000	27,000
		$1,800,000			

Required

1. Assume that the company continues to use direct labor-hours as the base for applying overhead cost to products.
    a. Compute the predetermined overhead rate.
    b. Determine the cost to produce one unit of each product.
2. Assume that the company decides to use activity-based costing to apply overhead cost to products.
    a. Classify the activity centers as being unit-level activities, batch-level activities, product-level activities, or facility-level activities.
    b. Compute the overhead rate for each activity center. Also compute the amount of overhead cost that would be applied to each product.
    c. Determine the cost to produce one unit of each product.
3. Explain why overhead cost shifted from the high-volume product to the low-volume product under activity-based costing.

(Appendix C) Sylvan Company manufactures four products and employs activity-based costing. The company has five activity centers, as shown below.

E5–5

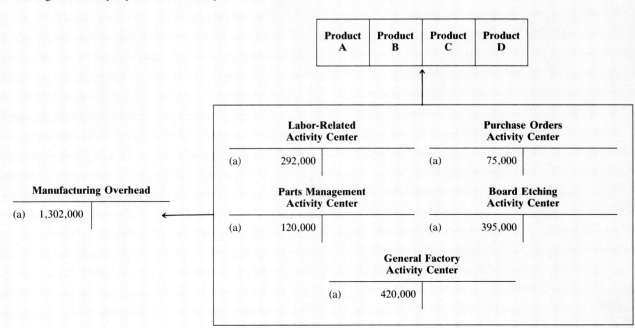

The company has completed part of its entries to the Manufacturing Overhead account for 19x2, the current year, as shown by entry (a) above.

Required   1.   In a general sense, what cost would be represented by entry (a)?

2.   At the beginning of the year, the company made the following estimates of cost and activity in the five activity centers in order to compute predetermined overhead rates:

Activity Center	Cost Driver	Estimated Overhead Cost—19x2	Expected Activity
Labor related	Direct labor-hours	$280,000	40,000 direct labor-hours
Purchase orders	Number of orders	90,000	1,500 orders
Parts management	Number of part types	120,000	400 part types
Board etching	Number of boards	360,000	2,000 boards
General factory	Machine-hours	400,000	80,000 machine-hours

Compute the predetermined overhead rate for each activity center.

3.   During 19x2, activity was recorded in the various activity centers as follows:

Activity Center	Actual Activity
Labor related	41,000 direct labor-hours
Purchase orders	1,300 orders
Parts management	420 part types
Board etching	2,150 boards
General factory	82,000 machine-hours

Determine the amount of manufacturing overhead cost applied to production for the year, and determine the amount of underapplied or overapplied overhead cost for each activity center and for Manufacturing Overhead.

E5–6   (Appendix C) Refer to the data in E5–5. During 19x2, the activities in the five activity centers were traceable to Sylvan Company's products as follows:

Activity Center	Actual Activity	Events or Transactions Relating to Products			
		Product A	Product B	Product C	Product D
Labor related	41,000 DLH	8,000	12,000	15,000	6,000
Purchase orders	1,300 orders	100	300	400	500
Parts management	420 part types	20	90	200	110
Board etching	2,150 boards	—	1,500	650	—
General factory	82,000 MH	16,000	24,000	30,000	12,000

Required   1.   Compute the amount of overhead cost charged to each product during 19x2.

2.   How do the dollar amounts charged to products in (1) above relate to the activity center accounts and to the Manufacturing Overhead account in E5–5?

E5–7   Listed below are activity centers that might be found in a company using activity-based costing.

a.   Product testing.
b.   Equipment setups.
c.   General factory.
d.   Machine related.
e.   Parts inventory management.
f.   Personnel administration.
g.   Material handling.
h.   Purchase orders.
i.   Product design.
j.   Labor related.

k.   Specialized processing.
l.   Quality inspections.
m.   Production orders.

Prepare an answer sheet with column headings as follows: *Required*

Activity Center	Cost Driver	Unit-Level Activities	Batch-Level Activities	Product-Level Activities	Facility-Level Activities
a.					
b.					
c.					

For each activity center, identify a cost driver that might be appropriate for applying overhead cost to products. Then place an *X* under the proper heading to indicate whether the activity center would be unit level, batch level, and so forth.

Listed below are a number of terms relating to JIT that are introduced in the chapter: **E5–8**

Simplification	Throughput time
Value-added	Product flow line
Cell	Elimination of waste
Multiskilled	Daily or frequent
Setup time	Non-value-added
Throughput	Certification program
Flexible manufacturing system	Pull
Continuous improvement	Total quality control
Team	

Choose the term or terms above that most appropriately complete the following statements.

1.   In a JIT environment, the flow of goods is controlled by what is described as a _____ approach to manufacturing.
2.   To successfully operate a JIT system, a company must learn to rely on a few suppliers who are willing to complete a _____ and make _____ deliveries.
3.   When JIT is in use, all machines on a _____ are tightly grouped to minimize the distance that goods must travel during the manufacturing process.
4.   An improved plant layout under JIT can dramatically increase _____, which is the total volume of production through a facility during a period, and it can dramatically reduce _____, which is the length of time required to turn materials into products.
5.   A clustering of machines to form a JIT workstation is called a _____.
6.   The time involved with getting equipment ready to produce a different product is called _____.
7.   When the cells on a product flow are linked together with an automated material-handling system and the flows between cells are controlled by a central computer, a _____ is in operation.
8.   It would be impossible to operate a JIT system in the absence of _____.
9.   Since the plant layout in a JIT environment is different from that of a conventional factory, workers must be _____ and operate as a _____.
10.   The JIT philosophy states that management must focus its efforts on _____ and _____.
11.   In a JIT environment, move time, inspection time, and queue time are all considered to be _____ activities.
12.   After a JIT system is in operation, further increases in efficiency and reductions in cost are achieved through a formal program of _____.

E5–9   Savic Company manufactures a single product and uses process costing. As of the beginning of June, the most recent month, the company switched to JIT for control of inventories. Therefore, no work in process inventories were on hand at the end of June, as shown by the summary of activity below:

	Units	Amount Completed	
		Materials	Conversion
Work in process, June 1	60,000	2/3	1/3
Started into production	850,000		
Completed and transferred out	910,000		
Work in process, June 30	—		

Required   1.   Assume that the company uses the weighted-average method to account for units. Prepare a quantity schedule and a computation of equivalent units for June.

2.   Assume that the company uses the FIFO method to account for units. Prepare a quantity schedule and a computation of equivalent units for June.

3.   If the company continues to employ the JIT concept and starts 900,000 units into production during the following month (July), what would be the equivalent units under the weighted-average method? The FIFO method?

PROBLEMS

Ethics and the   **P5–10**   **JIT Purchasing**   (The situation described below was written by the Institute of Manage-
Manager   ment Accountants' Committee on Ethics.[19])

WIW is a publicly owned corporation that makes various control devices used in the manufacture of mechanical equipment. J.B. is the president of WIW, Tony is the purchasing agent, and Diane is J.B.'s executive assistant. All three have been with WIW for about five years. Charlie is WIW's controller and has been with the company for two years.

J.B.:   Hi, Charlie, come on in. Diane said you had a confidential matter to discuss. What's on your mind?

Charlie: J.B., I was reviewing our increased purchases from A-1 Warehouse Sales last week and wondered why our volume has tripled in the past year. When I discussed this with Tony he seemed a bit evasive and tried to dismiss the issue by stating that A-1 can give us one-day delivery on our orders.

J.B.:   Well, Tony is right. You know we have been trying to install the new just-in-time philosophy of manufacturing and trying to get our inventory investment down.

Charlie: We still have to look at the overall cost. A-1 is more of a jobber than a warehouse. After investigating orders placed with them, I found that only 10 percent are delivered from their warehouse and the other 90 percent are drop-shipped from the manufacturers. The average markup by A-1 is 30 percent, which amounted to about $600,000 on our orders for the past year. If we had ordered directly from the manufacturers when A-1 didn't have an item in stock, we could have saved about $540,000 ($600,000 × 90%). In addition, some of the orders were late and not complete.

J.B.:   Now look, Charlie, we get quick delivery on most items, and who knows how much we are saving by not having to stock this stuff in advance or worry about it becoming obsolete. Is there anything else on your mind?

Charlie: Well, J.B., as a matter of fact, there is. I ordered a Dun & Bradstreet credit report on A-1 and discovered that Mike Bell is the principal owner. Isn't he your brother-in-law?

---

[19] Neil Holmes, ed., "Ethics," *Management Accounting* 73, no. 8 (February 1992), p. 16. Used (and adapted) by permission.

J.B.:   Sure he is. But don't worry about Mike. He has a Harvard MBA and he understands this just-in-time philosophy. Besides, he's looking out for our interests.

Charlie (to himself):   This conversation has been enlightening, but it doesn't really respond to my concerns. Can I legally or ethically ignore this apparent conflict of interests?

1. Would Charlie be justified in ignoring this situation, particularly since he is not the purchasing agent? In preparing your answer, consider the IMA's Standards of Ethical Conduct for Management Accountants found in Chapter 1, as well as concepts learned in this chapter.   *Required*
2. State the specific steps Charlie should follow to resolve this matter.

Classifying Activities under Activity-Based Costing   Juneau Company manufactures a   **P5–11**
variety of products in a single facility. You have just completed a PVA on the company, and as a result you have identified activities performed as follows:

a. Machine setups are performed for various products.
b. Worker recreational facilities are available and used by all employees.
c. Quality inspections are completed on some products.
d. Equipment is used for milling work on all products.
e. Parts inventories are maintained for various products.
f. Employees are trained in the company's personnel training center.
g. Purchase orders are issued for all materials.
h. General-purpose equipment is maintained by a maintenance crew.
i. Occupancy for all company operations is provided in the plant building.
j. Material is received on a receiving dock and moved about the plant.
k. Products are tested in a testing center.
l. Personnel administration hires all employees.
m. Production orders are issued for work on all products.
n. Specialized equipment is used to manufacture some products.

1. Classify each of the activities above as either a unit-level, batch-level, product-level, or facility-level activity.   *Required*
2. Identify one or more traceable costs for each activity listed above.
3. For each activity above, name one or more cost drivers that might be used to trace the costs of the activity to products.

JIT: Analysis of Cost Flows; Process Value Analysis   Snedden Products manufactures   **P5–12**
athletic equipment, including footballs. The footballs are manufactured in a number of steps, which are listed below.

a. Leather and other materials are received at a centrally located dock where the materials are checked to be sure they conform to exacting company standards. Rejected materials are returned to the supplier.
b. Acceptable materials are transported to a stores warehouse pending use in production.
c. A materials requisition form is issued, and materials are transferred from the stores warehouse to the cutting department where all cutting equipment is located.
d. Since the cutting department cuts materials for a variety of products, the leather is placed on large pallets and stationed by the appropriate machines.
e. The leather and other materials are cut to proper shape, with the operator taking care to cut all sections of a football from a single piece of leather. Waste materials are placed in a bin, and at the end of each day the materials are sorted to reclaim the items that can be used in manufacturing other products.
f. Each cut item of material is examined by one of three checkers to ensure uniformity of cut, thickness of the leather, and direction of the grain. Rejected pieces are tossed in the scrap bin.
g. Cut materials are placed on pallets and transferred to the centralized sewing department, where the pallets are placed in a staging area.

h. Materials are taken from the pallets, the company's name and logo are stamped into one section of each set of cut pieces, and the pieces are then sewn together.

i. The sewn pieces are placed in bins, which are then transferred to the staging area of the assembly department.

j. An operator in the assembly department installs a lining in the football, stitches the ball closed with a stitching machine, and then inflates it.

k. The completed footballs are placed on a conveyor belt that passes by another set of checkers. Each ball is checked for uniformity of shape and for other potential defects.

l. Completed footballs are boxed and transferred to the finished goods warehouse.

Required 1. Classify each step in (a) through (l) above as process time, inspection time, move time, or queue time. Use the following format in preparing your answer:

Step	Process Time	Inspection Time	Move Time	Queue Time
a.				

Place an X under the appropriate heading to classify each step. A step might involve more than one activity such as, for example, both move time and queue time.

2. In a PVA, which of these steps would probably be labeled as a non-value-added activity?

3. Assume that the company adopts JIT inventory practices and establishes individual product flow lines. Explain what changes would have to be made in manufacturing procedures and prepare a sketch of how the football product flow line would be arranged.

P5–13 Activity-Based Costing Siegel Company manufactures a product that is available in both a deluxe model and a regular model. The company has manufactured the regular model for years; the deluxe model was introduced several years ago to tap a new segment of the market. Since introduction of the deluxe model, the company's profits have steadily declined, and management has become concerned about the accuracy of its costing system. Sales of the deluxe model have been increasing rapidly.

Overhead is assigned to the products on a basis of direct labor-hours. For 19x1, the current year, the company has estimated that it will incur $2,000,000 in overhead cost and produce 5,000 units of the deluxe model and 40,000 units of the regular model. The deluxe model requires 1.6 hours of direct labor time per unit, and the regular model requires 0.8 hours. Materials and labor costs per unit are as follows:

	Model	
	Deluxe	**Regular**
Direct materials	$150	$112
Direct labor	16	8

Required 1. Using direct labor-hours as the base for assigning overhead cost to products, compute the predetermined overhead rate for 19x1. Using this rate and other data from the problem, determine the cost to manufacture one unit of each model.

2. Assume that the company's overhead costs can be traced to four activity centers. These activity centers, their cost drivers, and estimated cost and activity data for each center for 19x1 are given below:

Activity Center and Cost Driver	Traceable Costs	Expected Number of Events or Transactions		
		Total	**Deluxe**	**Regular**
Purchase orders (number of orders)	$ 84,000	1,200	400	800
Scrap/rework orders (number of orders)	216,000	900	300	600
Product testing (number of tests).	450,000	15,000	4,000	11,000
Machine related (machine-hours)	1,250,000	50,000	20,000	30,000
Total overhead cost	$2,000,000			

Determine the amount of overhead cost per event or transaction for each of the four activity centers.

3. Using activity-based costing and the data from (2) above, do the following:

 a. Determine the total amount of overhead cost assignable to each model for 19x1. After these totals have been computed, determine the amount of overhead cost per unit for each model.

 b. Compute the total cost to manufacture one unit of each model (materials, labor, and overhead).

4. From the data you have developed in (1) through (3) above, identify factors that may account for the company's declining profits.

Cost Flows under Activity-Based Costing; Partial T-Accounts   (Appendix C) Hendrix   P5–14
Company manufactures four products and uses activity-based costing. The company has five activity centers, as shown in the boxed T-accounts below. Direct materials and direct labor costs for 19x2, the current year, have been added to Work in Process and to the products, as shown by entires (a) and (b). However, no entries have been made for either actual or applied manufacturing overhead cost.

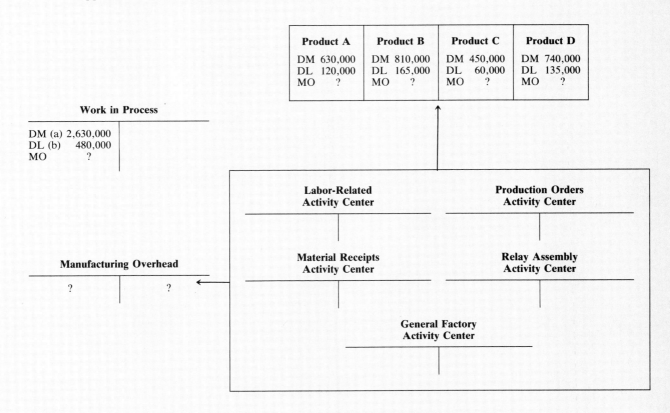

At the beginning of the year, the company made the following estimates of cost and activity in the five activity centers in order to compute predetermined overhead rates:

Activity Center	Cost Driver	Estimated Overhead Cost—19x2	Expected Activity
Labor related	Direct labor-hours	$270,000	30,000 direct labor-hours
Production orders	Number of orders	60,000	750 orders
Material receipts	Number of receipts	180,000	1,200 receipts
Relay assembly	Number of relays	320,000	8,000 relays
General factory	Machine-hours	840,000	60,000 machine-hours

Required
1. Compute the predetermined overhead rate for each activity center for 19x2.
2. During 19x2, actual manufacturing overhead cost and actual activity were recorded in the various activity centers as follows:

Activity Center	Actual Overhead Cost—19x2	Actual Activity
Labor related	$ 279,000	32,000 direct labor-hours
Production orders	58,000	700 orders
Material receipts.	190,000	1,300 receipts
Relay assembly	320,000	7,900 relays
General factory	847,000	61,000 machine-hours
Total overhead cost	$1,694,000	

Prepare a journal entry to record the incurrence of actual manufacturing overhead cost for the year (credit Accounts Payable). Label this as entry (c), and post the entry to the activity center T-accounts and to the Manufacturing Overhead T-account.

3. Refer to the "actual activity" data in (2) above.
   a. Determine the amount of overhead cost applied to production for the year. In determining this amount, remember that you have five predetermined overhead rates, rather than just one.
   b. Prepare a journal entry to record the amount of applied overhead cost for the year. Label this as entry (d), and post the entry to the appropriate T-accounts.
   c. Determine the amount of underapplied or overapplied manufacturing overhead cost for 19x2 for each activity center and for Manufacturing Overhead.
4. Refer to the "actual activity" data in (2) above. Assume that these activities were traceable to the company's four products as follows:

Activity Center	Actual Activity	Events or Transactions Relating to Products			
		Product A	Product B	Product C	Product D
Labor related	32,000 DLH	8,000	11,000	4,000	9,000
Production orders	700 orders	160	200	130	210
Material receipts.	1,300 receipts	100	460	240	500
Relay assembly	7,900 relays	2,700	—	5,200	—
General factory	61,000 MH	13,000	18,000	14,000	16,000

   a. Determine the amount of overhead cost for the year chargeable to each product.
   b. Does the total amount of cost charged to the products in (a) above "tie in" to the T-accounts in any way? Explain.

P5–15 Activity-Based Costing For many years, Zapro Company manufactured a single product called a mono-relay. Then three years ago, the company automated a portion of its plant and at the same time introduced a second product called a bi-relay. The bi-relay has become increasingly popular, and the company is now producing 10,000 units of it each year as compared to 40,000 units of the mono-relay. The bi-relay is a more complex product, requiring one hour of direct labor time per unit to manufacture and extensive machining in the automated portion of the plant. The mono-relay requires only 0.75 hour of direct labor time per unit and only a small amount of machining. Overhead costs are assigned to products on a basis of direct labor-hours.

Despite the popularity of the company's new bi-relay, profits have declined steadily since a portion of the plant was automated. Management is beginning to believe that a problem may exist with the company's costing system. Unit costs for materials and labor for the two products follow:

	Mono-Relay	Bi-Relay
Direct materials	$35	$48
Direct labor: $12 × 0.75 and 1.0 hours	9	12

For 19x4, the current year, the company estimates that it will incur $1,000,000 in manufacturing overhead costs and produce units of the two relays as stated above.

1. Compute the predetermined overhead rate for 19x4, assuming that the company continues to apply overhead cost to products on a basis of direct labor-hours. Using this rate and other data from the problem, determine the cost to manufacture one unit of each product. *Required*

2. Assume that the company's overhead costs can be traced to four activity centers. These activity centers, their cost drivers, and estimated data relating to each center for 19x4 are given below:

Activity Center and Cost Driver	Traceable Costs	Expected Number of Events or Transactions		
		Total	Mono-Relay	Bi-Relay
Parts inventory (number of part types) . . .	$ 180,000	225	75	150
Purchase orders (number of orders).	90,000	1,000	800	200
Quality control (number of tests)	230,000	5,750	2,500	3,250
Machine related (machine-hours).	500,000	10,000	4,000	6,000
Total overhead cost.	$1,000,000			

Determine the amount of overhead cost per event or transaction for each of the four activity centers.

3. Using activity-based costing and the data from (2) above, do the following:
   a. Determine the total amount of overhead cost assignable to each product for 19x4. After these totals have been computed, determine the amount of overhead cost per unit for each product.
   b. Compute the total cost to manufacture one unit of each product.

4. Look at the data you have computed in (3) above. In terms of overhead cost, what factors make the bi-relay more costly to produce than the mono-relay? Is the bi-relay as profitable as the company thinks it is? Explain.

Implementing a JIT System   The management at Megafilters, Inc., has been discussing **P5–16** the possible implementation of a JIT production system at its Illinois plant, where oil and air filters are manufactured. The metal stamping department at the Illinois plant has already instituted a JIT system for controlling raw materials inventory, but the remainder of the plant is still discussing how to proceed with the implementation of this concept. The metal stamping department implemented JIT with no advance planning, and some of the other department managers have become uneasy about adopting JIT after hearing about the problems that have arisen.

Robert Goertz, manager of the Illinois plant, is a strong proponent of the JIT production system. He recently made the following statement at a meeting of all departmental managers:

"Just in time is often referred to as a management philosophy of doing business rather than a technique for improving efficiency on the plant floor. We will all have to make many changes in the way we think about our employees, our suppliers, and our customers if we are going to be successful in using JIT procedures. Rather than dwelling on some of the negative things you have heard from the metal stamping department, I want each of you to prepare a list of things we can do to make a smooth transition to the JIT philosophy of management for the rest of the plant."

1. The JIT approach has several characteristics that distinguish it from conventional *Required* production systems. Describe these characteristics.

2. As Mr. Goertz stated, JIT is often referred to as a management philosophy. Identify the key ideas underlying this philosophy.

3. Discuss several steps that Megafilters, Inc., can take to ease the transition to a JIT production system.

4. For the JIT production system to be successful, Megafilters, Inc., must establish appropriate relationships with its suppliers, employees, and customers. Describe each of these relationships under JIT.

(CMA, adapted)

P5-17 Cost Flows under Activity-Based Costing; Partial T-Accounts   (Appendix C) Munoz Company installed an activity-based costing system several years ago. The company manufactures four products in a single facility and has identified five major activity centers, as listed below. Direct materials and direct labor costs for 19x3, the current year, have been added to Work in Process and to the products. These costs are shown by entries (a) and (b) in the Work in Process account. However, no entries have been made for either actual or applied manufacturing overhead cost.

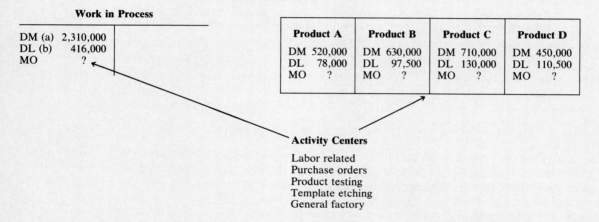

Work in Process

DM (a)	2,310,000
DL (b)	416,000
MO	?

Product A	**Product B**	**Product C**	**Product D**
DM 520,000	DM 630,000	DM 710,000	DM 450,000
DL 78,000	DL 97,500	DL 130,000	DL 110,500
MO ?	MO ?	MO ?	MO ?

Activity Centers

Labor related
Purchase orders
Product testing
Template etching
General factory

At the beginning of the year, the company made the following estimates of cost and activity in the five activity centers for the purpose of computing predetermined overhead rates:

Activity Center	Cost Driver	Estimated Overhead Cost—19x3	Expected Activity
Labor related	Direct labor-hours	$210,000	35,000 direct labor-hours
Purchase orders	Number of orders	72,000	900 orders
Product testing.	Number of tests	168,000	1,400 tests
Template etching.	Number of templates	315,000	10,500 templates
General factory	Machine-hours	840,000	70,000 machine-hours

Required   1. Compute the predetermined overhead rate for each activity center for 19x3.

2. During 19x3, actual manufacturing overhead cost and actual activity were recorded in the various activity centers as follows:

Activity Center	Actual Overhead Cost—19x3	Actual Activity
Labor related	$ 205,000	32,000 direct labor-hours
Purchase orders	74,000	950 orders
Product testing	160,000	1,300 tests
Template etching	338,000	11,500 templates
General factory	825,000	68,000 machine-hours
Total overhead cost	$1,602,000	

Prepare a journal entry to record the incurrence of actual manufacturing overhead cost for the year (credit Accounts Payable). Label this as entry (c). Prepare T-accounts for Manufacturing Overhead and for each of the activity centers, and post entry (c) to these accounts.

3. Refer to the "actual activity" data in (2) above.

    a. Determine the amount of overhead cost applied to production for the year. In determining this amount, remember that you have five predetermined overhead rates, rather than just one.

    b. Prepare a journal entry to record the amount of applied overhead cost for the year. Label this as entry (d), and post the entry to the appropriate T-accounts.

    c. Determine the amount of underapplied or overapplied manufacturing overhead cost for 19x3 for each activity center and for Manufacturing Overhead.

4. Refer again to the "actual activity" data in (2) above. Assume that these activities were traceable to the company's four products as follows:

| Activity Center | Actual Activity | Events or Transactions Relating to Products | | | |
		Product A	Product B	Product C	Product D
Labor related	32,000 DLH	6,000	7,500	10,000	8,500
Purchase orders . . .	950 orders	150	300	100	400
Product testing . . .	1,300 tests	400	175	225	500
Template etching . .	11,500 templates	—	4,500	—	7,000
General factory . . .	68,000 MH	10,000	20,000	17,000	21,000

    a. Determine the amount of overhead cost for the year chargeable to each product.

    b. Does the total amount of cost charged to the products in (a) above "tie in" to the T-accounts in any way? Explain.

Cost Savings from a JIT System

P5–18

AgriCorp is a manufacturer of farm equipment that is sold by a network of distributors throughout the United States. Most of the distributors are also repair centers for the AgriCorp equipment. These repair centers depend on AgriCorp's Service Division to provide a timely supply of spare parts.

The Service Division manufactures the spare parts and carries them in stock while waiting for orders from the various repair centers. In an effort to reduce the inventory costs incurred by the Service Division, Janice Grady, the division manager, implemented a JIT inventory program on June 1, 19x1, the beginning of the company's fiscal year. Since the JIT program has now been in place for a year, Grady has asked Richard Bachman, the division controller, to determine the effect the program has had on the Service Division's financial performance. Bachman has been able to document the following results of JIT implementation:

a. The Service Division's average inventory declined from $700,000 to $100,000.

b. Projected annual insurance costs of $130,000 declined 60 percent due to the lower average inventory.

c. A leased, 16,000 square foot warehouse, previously used for inventory storage, was not used at all during the year. The division paid $24,000 annual rent for the warehouse and was able to sublet three quarters of the building to several tenants at $2.50 per square foot. The balance of the space remained idle.

d. Two warehouse employees whose services were no longer needed were transferred on June 1, 19x1, to the purchasing department to assist in coordination of the JIT program. The annual salary expense for these two employees totaled $38,000 and continued to be charged to the indirect labor portion of fixed overhead.

e. In past years, the Service Division has carried a large inventory of parts as a protection against stockouts. Because of this large inventory, and because AgriCorp is continually improving the farm equipment it sells, obsolete inventory has been a problem for many years in the Service Division. It is estimated that the costs associated with obsolete inventory in an average year have totaled about $45,000. Since production over the past year under the JIT program has been geared closely to current orders, the Service Division expects no obsolete inventory to result from the current year's activities.

f.   In the absence of a large inventory of spare parts, the Service Division lost sales of 2,900 parts as a result of inability to make immediate delivery. Also, the Division was required to work overtime to manufacture 7,500 parts that were needed on a rush basis. The overtime premium incurred amounted to $5.60 per part manufactured. The use of overtime to fill spare parts orders was immaterial prior to June 1, 19x1.

Prior to the decision to implement the JIT inventory program, AgriCorp's Service Division had completed its current year budget. The Division's budgeted income statement for the current year (starting June 1, 19x1), without any adjustments for the JIT inventory program, is presented below. AgriCorp's incremental borrowing rate for inventory is 15 percent before income taxes.

AGRICORP SERVICE DIVISION
Budgeted Income Statement
For the Year Ended May 31, 19x2

Sales (280,000 spare parts)		$6,160,000
Cost of goods sold:		
Variable	$2,660,000	
Fixed.	1,310,000	3,970,000
Gross margin		2,190,000
Selling and administrative expense:		
Variable	700,000	
Fixed.	530,000	1,230,000
Net operating income		960,000
Other income		40,000
Income before interest and taxes		1,000,000
Interest expense.		150,000
Income before taxes		850,000
Income taxes (40%)		340,000
Net income		$ 510,000

Required   1.   Compute the before-tax savings (loss) for AgriCorp's Service Division that has resulted during the current year from adoption of the JIT inventory program.

2.   Identify and explain the factors, other than financial, that a company such as AgriCorp should consider before adopting a JIT inventory program.

(CMA, heavily adapted)

P5–19   **Activity-Based Costing: Journal Entries; Complete T-Accounts; Income Statement** (Appendix C) Austin Company is a manufacturing firm that has just installed an activity-based costing system. After completing a PVA, the company has identified five activity centers. The activity centers are listed below, along with the estimated overhead cost and expected level of activity in each center for the coming year.

Activity Center	Cost Driver	Estimated Overhead Cost—19x5	Expected Activity
Machining	CPU hours	$180,000	1,000 CPU hours
Purchase orders.	Number of orders	90,000	600 orders
Parts management.	Number of part types	60,000	300 part types
Testing.	Number of tests	150,000	250 tests
General factory	Machine-hours	280,000	20,000 machine-hours

On January 1, 19x5, the company had inventory balances as follows:

Raw materials.	$ 7,000
Work in process.	6,000
Finished goods	10,000

The following transactions were recorded for the year 19x5:

a. Raw materials were purchased on account, $595,000.
b. Raw materials were requisitioned for use in production, $600,000 ($560,000 direct and $40,000 indirect). The indirect materials were traceable to activity centers as follows:

Machining	$21,000
Purchase orders	4,000
Testing	15,000
Total	$40,000

c. The following costs were incurred for employee services: direct labor, $90,000; indirect labor, $300,000; sales commissions, $85,000; and administrative salaries, $245,000. The indirect labor costs were traceable to the activity centers as follows:

Purchase orders	$ 60,000
Parts management	50,000
Testing	80,000
General factory	110,000
Total	$300,000

d. Sales travel costs were incurred, $38,000.
e. Miscellaneous manufacturing overhead costs were incurred, $72,000. These overhead costs were traceable to activity centers as follows:

Machining	$16,000
Purchase orders	8,000
Parts management	3,000
Testing	12,000
General factory	33,000
Total	$72,000

f. Advertising costs were incurred, $190,000.
g. Depreciation was recorded for the year, $270,000 ($210,000 related to factory operations and $60,000 related to selling and administrative activities). The depreciation related to factory operations was traceable to activity centers as follows:

Machining	$105,000
Parts management	8,000
Testing	32,000
General factory	65,000
Total	$210,000

h. Miscellaneous manufacturing overhead costs were incurred, $165,000. These overhead costs were traceable to activity centers as follows:

Machining	$ 42,000
Purchase orders	13,000
Parts management	9,000
Testing	21,000
General factory	80,000
Total	$165,000

i. Manufacturing overhead cost was applied to production. *Actual* activity in the various activity centers during 19x5 was as follows:

Machining	1,050 CPU hours
Purchase orders	580 orders issued
Parts management	330 part types held in stock
Testing	265 tests completed
General factory	21,000 machine-hours worked

j. Goods costing $1,450,000 to manufacture were completed during the year.

k. Goods were sold on account to customers during the year at a total selling price of $2,100,000. The goods cost $1,400,000 to manufacture.

Required   1. Compute the predetermined overhead rate for each activity center for 19x5.

2. Prepare journal entries to record transactions (a) through (k) above. When applying overhead cost to production in entry (i), note that you have five predetermined overhead rates, rather than just one.

3. Post the entries in (2) to T-accounts. As part of this posting, *create a T-account for each activity center and treat these accounts as subsidiary accounts to Manufacturing Overhead*.

4. Compute the underapplied or overapplied overhead cost in Manufacturing Overhead and in each activity center for the year. Prepare a journal entry to close any balance in the Manufacturing Overhead account to Cost of Goods Sold.

5. Prepare an income statement for the year.

P5–20   JIT/FMS; Process Costing Production Report; Weighted-Average Method   Lovata Company uses process costing. Over the last year, the company has installed a flexible manufacturing system in its plant. The company has made extensive changes to the flow of its single product through the various cells, and as of the beginning of last month (May) the company initiated a JIT inventory system. In the past, the company was required to carry a large work in process inventory because of a poor flow of materials between workstations. But JIT, in conjunction with FMS, has allowed the company to control this flow and to avoid any buildup of materials within the cells. Production data for May follow:

	Units	Materials	Conversion
Work in process, May 1	40,000	$ 53,000	$ 10,000
Started into production	280,000		
Completed and transferred out	320,000	?	?
Work in process, May 31	—		
Cost added during the month		491,000	278,000

The May 1 work in process inventory was 75 percent complete as to materials and 25 percent complete as to conversion costs. The company uses the weighted-average method to account for cost flows.

Required   1. Prepare a production report for May.

2. Assume that in June the company begins to experience greater efficiency in its operations so that it is able to introduce 350,000 units into production and operate strictly in accordance with JIT concepts. (That is, work in process is maintained at a zero level.) The company incurs $560,000 in material costs during the month and $280,000 in conversion costs.

a. Prepare a production report for June.

b. Examine the report you have just prepared. How (if at all) would the report differ if the company were using the FIFO method to account for cost flows?

P5–21   JIT/FMS; Process Costing Production Report; FIFO Method   Walton Company uses process costing. After three months of intensive effort, the company has converted its Midvale plant to an FMS layout and has installed necessary automated equipment in the various cells. As of the first of last month (March) the company also initiated a JIT system of inventory control. In the past, work in process inventories have been a problem in that partially completed materials have accumulated in work areas and impeded the efficiency of operations. But during the last month, the company's new JIT system, in conjunction with the FMS layout, has allowed the company to clear out its in-process items and maintain a smooth flow of goods to meet current demand. Production data for March follow:

	Units	Materials	Conversion
Work in process, March 1.	80,000	$ 45,000	$ 21,000
Started into production	530,000		
Completed and transferred out.	610,000	?	?
Work in process, March 31	—		
Cost added during the month		385,000	649,000

The March 1 work in process inventory was 75 percent complete as to materials and 25 percent complete as to conversion costs. The company uses the FIFO method to account for cost flows.

Required

1. Prepare a production report for March.
2. During the following month (April), the company is able to increase its efficiency in the Midvale plant so that 630,000 units are started into production. Also, through JIT the company is able to keep work in process inventories from accumulating in the plant. The company incurs $378,000 in cost for materials and $567,000 in conversion cost for the month.
   a. Prepare a production report for April.
   b. Examine the report you have just prepared. How (if at all) would the report differ if the company were using the weighted-average method to account for cost flows?

CASES

Activity-Based Costing; Product Retention Decision   (Adapted from a case written by Professors Harold P. Roth and Imogene Posey for the Institute of Management Accountants.[20])

C5–22

"A dollar of gross margin per briefcase? That's ridiculous!" roared Art Dejans, president of CarryAll Company. "Why do we go on producing those standard briefcases when we're able to make $15 per unit on our specialty items? Maybe it's time to get out of the standard line and focus the whole plant on specialty work."

Mr. Dejans is referring to a summary of unit costs and revenues that he has just received from CarryAll's accounting department:

	Standard Briefcases	Specialty Briefcases
Selling price per unit.	$36	$40
Manufacturing cost per unit	35	25
Gross margin per unit	$ 1	$15

CarryAll Company produces briefcases from leather, fabric, and synthetic materials in a single plant. The basic product is a standard briefcase that is made from leather, lined with fabric. CarryAll has a good reputation in the market because the standard briefcase is a high-quality item and has been well produced for many years.

Last year, the company decided to expand its product line and produce specialty briefcases for special orders. These briefcases differ from the standard in that they vary in size, they contain both leather and synthetic materials, and they are imprinted with the buyer's logo, whereas the standard briefcase is simply imprinted with the CarryAll name in small letters. The use of some synthetic materials in the specialty briefcases is designed to hold down the materials cost. To reduce the labor costs on the specialty briefcases, most of the

[20] Harold P. Roth and Imogene Posey, "Management Accounting Case Study: CarryAll Company," *Management Accounting Campus Report,* Institute of Management Accountants (Fall 1991), p. 9. Used by permission.

cutting and stitching is done by automated machines. These machines are used to a much lesser degree in the production of standard briefcases. With the lower cost of materials and labor, CarryAll's accounting department has determined that the specialty briefcases are less costly to manufacture as shown by the summary data above. However, because the specialty briefcases are special-order items, they are priced slightly higher than the standard briefcases.

"I agree that the specialty business is looking better and better," replied Sally Henrie, the company's marketing manager. "And there seems to be plenty of specialty work out there, particularly since the competition hasn't been able to touch our price. Did you know that Armor Company, our biggest competitor, charges over $50 a unit for its specialty items? Now that's what I call gouging the customer!"

A breakdown of the manufacturing cost for each of CarryAll's product lines is given below:

		Standard Briefcases		Specialty Briefcases
Units produced each month		10,000		2,500
Direct materials:				
Leather	1.0 sq. yd.	$15.00	0.5 sq. yd.	$ 7.50
Fabric	1.0 sq. yd.	5.00	1.0 sq. yd.	5.00
Synthetic		—		5.00
Total materials.		20.00		17.50
Direct labor	0.5 hr. @ $12	6.00	0.25 hr. @ $12	3.00
Manufacturing overhead	0.5 hr. @ $18	9.00	0.25 hr. @ $18	4.50
Total cost per unit		$35.00		$25.00

Manufacturing overhead is applied to products on the basis of direct labor-hours. The rate of $18 per hour is determined by dividing the total manufacturing overhead cost for a month by the direct labor-hours:

$$\frac{\text{Manufacturing overhead cost, \$101,250}}{\text{Direct labor-hours, 5,625}} = \$18/\text{DLH}$$

The following additional information is available about the company and its products:

a. Standard briefcases are produced in batches of 200 units, and specialty briefcases are produced in batches of 25 units. Thus, the company makes 50 setups for the standard items each month and 100 setups for the specialty items. A setup for the standard items requires one hour of time, whereas a setup for the specialty items requires two hours of time.

b. All briefcases are inspected to ensure that quality standards are met. However, the final inspection of standard briefcases takes very little time because the employees identify and correct quality problems as they do the hand-cutting and stitching. A total of 300 hours of inspection time is spent on the standard briefcases and 500 hours of inspection time is spent on the specialty briefcases each month.

c. A standard briefcase requires 0.5 hours of machine time, and a specialty briefcase requires 2 hours of machine time.

Required 1. Assume that the company's $101,250 in monthly overhead cost is traceable to six activities, as follows:

Activity and Cost Driver	Traceable Costs	Number of Events or Transactions		
		Total	Standard Briefcases	Specialty Briefcases
Purchasing (number of orders)	$ 12,000			
Leather		40	34	6
Fabric.		60	48	12
Synthetic material		100	—	100
Material handling (number of receipts)	15,000			
Leather		60	52	8
Fabric.		80	64	16
Synthetic material		160	—	160
Production orders and equipment setup (setup hours)	20,250	?	?	?
Inspection (inspection hours).	16,000	?	?	?
Frame assembly (assembly-hours)	8,000	1,600	800	800
Machine related (machine-hours)	30,000	?	?	?
	$101,250			

Using activity-based costing, determine the amount of manufacturing overhead cost that should be applied to each standard briefcase and each specialty briefcase. Show all computations in good form.

2. Using the data computed in (1) and other data from the case as needed, determine the cost to manufacture one unit of each product line from the perspective of activity-based costing.

3. Evaluate the president's concern about the profitability of the two product lines. From the data you have computed, would you recommend that the company shift its resources entirely to the production of specialty briefcases? Explain.

4. Sally Henrie stated that "the competition hasn't been able to touch our price" on specialty business. Why do you suppose the competition hasn't been able to touch CarryAll's price?

5. Examine the costs in (1) above. Which of these costs might be reduced (or even eliminated) if the company adopted the JIT philosophy?

JIT/FMS; Activity-Based Costing   "I say it's time we cut back on the X-20 model and shift our resources toward the new Y-30 model," said Cheri Warnick, executive vice president of Cutler Products, Inc. "Just look at this statement I've received from accounting. The Y-30 is generating twice as much in profits as the X-20, and it has only about one fifth as much in sales. I've become convinced that our future depends on the Y-30." The statement to which Cheri was referring follows:

C5–23

CUTLER PRODUCTS, INC.

Income Statement
For the Year Ended December 31, 19x6

	Total	X-20	Y-30
Sales	$7,250,000	$6,000,000	$1,250,000
Cost of goods sold	4,500,000	3,600,000	900,000
Gross margin	2,750,000	2,400,000	350,000
Less selling and administrative expenses . . .	2,450,000	2,300,000	150,000
Net income	$ 300,000	$ 100,000	$ 200,000
Number of units produced and sold	—	30,000	5,000
Net income per unit sold	—	$3.33	$40.00

"The numbers sure look that way," replied Pete Zayas, the company's sales vice president. "But why aren't our competitors more excited about the Y-30? I know we've only been producing the model for three years, but it seems like more of them would recognize what a money maker it is."

"I think it's our new automated plant," said Cheri. "Now it takes only two direct labor-hours to produce a unit of the X-20 and three hours to produce a unit of the Y-30. That's half of what it used to take us."

"Automation is marvelous," replied Pete. "I suppose that's how we're able to hold down the price on the Y-30. Why, Saki Company in Japan started to bring out a Y-30 but discovered they couldn't touch our price. But Saki is killing us on the X-20; I suppose they'll pick up our X-20 customers as we move out of that market. But who cares? We don't even have to advertise the Y-30; it just seems to sell itself."

"My only concern about automation is how our overhead rate has shot up," said Cheri. "Our total overhead cost was $1,800,000 for 19x6. That comes out to a hefty amount per direct labor-hour, but old Fred down in accounting has been using labor-hours as a base for computing overhead rates for years and doesn't want to change. I don't suppose it matters so long as costs get assigned to products."

"That bookkeeping bores me," replied Pete. "But I think you've got a problem in production. I had lunch with Sally yesterday, and she was complaining about how complex the Y-30 is to produce. Apparently they have to do a lot of machine setups and other work just to keep production moving on the Y-30. And they have to inspect every single unit."

"It'll have to wait," said Cheri. "I'm writing a proposal to the board to phase out the X-20 as rapidly as possible. We've got to bring those profits up or we'll all be looking for jobs."

Required

1. Compute the predetermined overhead rate that the company would have used during 19x6. (You may assume that there was no under- or overapplied overhead for the year.)

2. Materials and labor costs per unit for the two products follow:

	X-20	Y-30
Direct materials.	$60	$90
Direct labor	12	18

Using these data and the rate computed in (1) above, determine the cost to produce one unit of each product.

3. Assume that the company's $1,800,000 in overhead cost is traceable to six activities, as follows:

Activity Center and Cost Driver	Traceable Costs	Number of Events or Transactions		
		Total	X-20	Y-30
Machine setups (number of setups)	$ 208,000	1,600	1,000	600
Quality inspections (number of inspections)	360,000	9,000	4,000	5,000
Purchase orders (number of orders).	90,000	1,200	840	360
Soldering (number of solder joints)	450,000	200,000	60,000	140,000
Shipments (number of shipments)	132,000	600	400	200
Machine related (machine-hours)	560,000	70,000	30,000	40,000
	$1,800,000			

Given these data, would you support a recommendation to expand sales of the Y-30? Explain your position, and show unit costs, an income statement, and other data to help the board make a decision.

4. From the data you have prepared in (3) above, why do you suppose the Y-30 "just seems to sell itself"?

5. If you were president of Cutler Products, Inc., what strategy would you follow from this point forward to improve the company's overall profits?

6. Examine the costs in (3) above. Which of these costs might be reduced (or even eliminated) if the company adopted the JIT philosophy?

Many processes in manufacturing and service companies now require highly skilled workers who must be carefully trained to operate sophisticated equipment. Firms are reluctant to lay off such skilled workers when there is a downturn in volume. In such companies, large portions of direct labor may be considered a fixed cost.

Cost Behavior:

Analysis and Use

1 Identify examples of variable costs, and explain the effect of a change in activity on both total variable costs and per unit variable costs.

2 Define the relevant range, and explain its significance in cost behavior analysis.

3 Identify examples of fixed costs, and explain the effect of a change in activity on both total fixed costs and fixed costs expressed on a per unit basis.

4 Distinguish between committed and discretionary fixed costs.

5 Analyze a mixed cost by the high-low method, the scattergraph method, and the least-squares method, and enumerate the strengths and weaknesses of each of these analytical approaches.

6 Prepare an income statement using the contribution format.

7 Define or explain the key terms listed at the end of the chapter.

I n our discussion of cost terms and concepts in Chapter 2, we stated that one way in which costs can be classified is by behavior. We defined cost behavior as meaning how a cost will react or change as changes take place in the level of business activity. An understanding of cost behavior is the key to many decisions in an organization. Managers who understand how costs behave are better able to predict what costs will be under various operating circumstances. Experience has shown that attempts at decision making without a thorough understanding of the costs involved—and how these costs may change with the activity level—can lead to disaster. A decision to double production of a particular product line, for example, might result in the incurrence of far greater costs than could be generated in additional revenues. To avoid such problems, a manager must be able to accurately predict what costs will be at various activity levels. In this chapter, we shall find that the key to effective cost prediction lies in an understanding of cost behavior patterns.

We briefly review in this chapter the definitions of variable costs and fixed costs and then discuss the behavior of these costs in greater depth than we were able to do in Chapter 2. After this review and discussion, we turn our attention to the identification and analysis of mixed costs. We conclude the chapter by introducing a new income statement format—called the contribution format—in which costs are organized by behavior rather than by the traditional functions of production, sales, and administration.

TYPES OF COST BEHAVIOR PATTERNS

In our brief discussion of cost behavior in Chapter 2, we mentioned only variable and fixed costs. There is a third behavior pattern, generally known as a *mixed* or *semivariable* cost. All three cost behavior patterns—variable, fixed, and mixed—are found in most organizations. The relative proportion of each type of cost present in a firm is known as the firm's **cost structure.** For example, a firm might have many fixed costs but few variable costs or mixed costs. Alternatively, it might have many variable costs but few fixed or mixed costs. A firm's cost structure is very significant in that the decision-making process can be affected by the relative amount of fixed or variable cost that is present in the firm. We must reserve a detailed discussion of cost structure until the next chapter, however, and concentrate for the moment on gaining a fuller understanding of the behavior of each type of cost.

Variable Costs

Objective 1
Identify examples of variable costs, and explain the effect of a change in activity on both total variable costs and per unit variable costs.

We found in Chapter 2 that a variable cost is so named because its total dollar amount varies in direct proportion to changes in the activity level. If the activity level doubles, then one would expect the total dollar amount of the variable costs to also double. If the activity level increases by only 10 percent, then one would expect the total dollar amount of the variable costs to increase by 10 percent as well.

We also found in Chapter 2 that a variable cost remains constant if expressed on a *per unit* basis. To provide an example, assume that Premier Motor Company produces trucks. Each truck has one radiator, and the radiators cost $30 each. Thus, if we look at the cost of radiators on a *per truck* basis, the cost remains constant at $30 per truck. The $30 figure will not change, regardless of how many trucks are produced during a period, unless influenced by some outside factor.[1] The behavior of a variable cost, on both a per unit and a total basis, is illustrated in the following tabulation:

Number of Trucks Produced	Radiator Cost per Truck	Total Radiator Cost
250	$30	$ 7,500
500	30	15,000
750	30	22,500
1,000	30	30,000

The idea that a variable cost is constant per unit but varies in total with the activity level is crucial to an understanding of cost behavior patterns. We shall rely on this concept again and again in this chapter and in chapters ahead.

Exhibit 6–1 provides a graphic illustration of variable cost behavior. The exhibit contains three cost lines—one at $30 per radiator, and then two others showing what would happen to the slope of the line if the cost of radiators increased to $40 each or dropped to $20 each. Note that as the variable cost per unit increases, the cost line becomes steeper.

The Activity Base   For a cost to be variable, it must be variable *with respect to something*. That "something" is its *activity base*. An **activity base** is a measure of whatever causes the incurrence of variable cost. In Chapter 5, we mentioned that an activity base is sometimes referred to as a *cost driver*. Some of the most common activity bases are machine-hours, units produced, and units sold. Other activity bases (cost drivers) might include the number of miles driven by salespersons, the number of pounds of laundry processed by a hotel, the number of letters

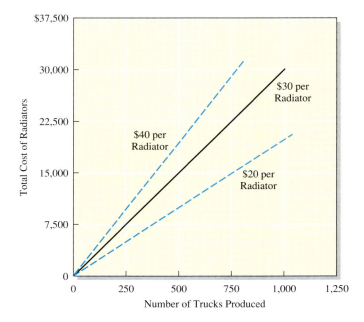

EXHIBIT 6–1
Variable Cost Behavior

---

[1] Frequently, discounts are allowed on quantity purchases. The handling of such discounts in the cost records of a firm is discussed in Chapter 10.

typed by a secretary, the number of hours of labor time logged, and the number of occupied beds in a hospital.

To plan and control variable costs, a manager must be well acquainted with the various activity bases within the firm. People sometimes get the notion that if a cost doesn't vary with production or with sales, then it is not really a variable cost. This is not correct. As suggested by the range of bases listed above, costs are caused by many different activities within an organization. Whether a cost is variable depends on whether it is caused by the activity under consideration. For example, if a manager is analyzing the cost of service calls under a product warranty, the relevant activity measure will be the number of service calls made. Those costs that vary in total with the number of service calls made are the variable costs of making service calls.

Extent of Variable Costs   The number and type of variable costs present in an organization will depend in large part on the organization's structure and purpose. An organization such as a public utility with large investments in equipment will tend to have few variable costs. The bulk of its costs will be associated with its plant, and these costs will tend to be quite insensitive to changes in levels of service provided. A manufacturing company, by contrast, will often have many variable costs; these costs will be associated with both the manufacture and distribution of its products to customers.

A merchandising company such as a grocery store will usually have a high proportion of variable costs in its cost structure. In most merchandising companies, the cost of merchandise purchased for resale, a variable cost, constitutes a very large component of total cost. Service companies, by contrast, have diverse cost structures. For example, fast-food outlets, with their food costs and hourly employees, have high variable cost components. On the other hand, service companies involved in consulting, auditing, engineering, dental, medical, and architectural activities have very large fixed costs in the form of expensive facilities and highly trained salaried employees.

Some of the more frequently encountered variable costs are listed in Exhibit 6–2. This exhibit is not a complete listing of all costs that can be considered variable. Moreover, some of the costs listed in the exhibit may behave more like fixed than variable costs in some firms. We will see some examples of this later in the chapter. Nevertheless, Exhibit 6–2 provides a useful listing of many of the costs that normally would be considered variable with respect to the volume of output.

EXHIBIT 6–2

Examples of Costs that Are Normally Variable with Respect to Volume

Type of Organization	Variable Costs
Merchandising company	Cost of goods (merchandise) sold
Manufacturing company	Manufacturing costs: 　Prime costs: 　　Direct materials 　　Direct labor 　Variable portion of manufacturing overhead: 　　Indirect materials 　　Lubricants 　　Supplies 　　Power 　　Setup 　　Indirect labor
Both merchandising and manufacturing companies	Selling, general, and administrative costs: 　Commissions 　Clerical costs, such as invoicing 　Shipping costs
Service organizations	Supplies, travel, clerical

True Variable versus Step-Variable Costs

Not all variable costs have exactly the same behavior pattern. Some variable costs behave in a *true variable* or *proportionately variable* pattern. Other variable costs behave in a *step-variable* pattern.

True Variable Costs   Direct materials would be a true or proportionately variable cost because the amount used during a period will vary in direct proportion to the level of production activity. Moreover, any amounts purchased but not used can be stored and carried forward to the next period as inventory.

Step-Variable Costs   Indirect labor is also considered to be a variable cost, but it doesn't behave in quite the same way as direct materials. As an example, let us consider the labor cost of maintenance workers, which would be part of indirect labor.

Unlike direct materials, the time of maintenance workers is obtainable only in large chunks, rather than in exact quantities. Moreover, any maintenance time not utilized cannot be stored as inventory and carried forward to the next period. Either the time is used effectively as it expires hour by hour, or it is gone forever. Furthermore, the utilization of indirect labor time can be quite flexible, whereas the utilization of direct materials is usually quite set. A maintenance crew, for example, can work at a fairly leisurely pace if pressures are light, but then the crew can intensify its efforts if pressures build up. For this reason, somewhat small changes in the level of production may have no effect on the number of maintenance people needed to properly carry on maintenance work.

A cost that is obtainable only in large chunks (such as the labor cost of maintenance workers) and that increases or decreases only in response to fairly wide changes in the activity level is known as a **step-variable cost.** The behavior of a step-variable cost, contrasted with the behavior of a true variable cost, is illustrated in Exhibit 6–3.

Notice that the need for maintenance help changes only with fairly wide changes in volume and that when additional maintenance time is obtained, it comes in large, indivisible pieces. The strategy of management in dealing with step-variable costs must be to obtain the fullest use of services possible for each separate step. Great care must be taken in working with these kinds of costs to prevent "fat" from building up in an organization. There is a tendency to employ additional help more quickly than might be needed, and there is generally a reluctance to lay people off when volume declines.

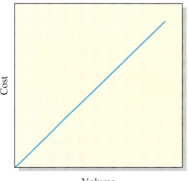

Volume
Direct Materials (True Variable)

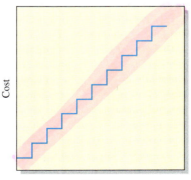

Volume
Maintenance Help (Step Variable)

EXHIBIT 6–3

True Variable versus Step-Variable Costs

The Linearity Assumption and the Relevant Range

Objective 2
Define the relevant range, and explain its significance in cost behavior analysis.

In dealing with variable costs, we have assumed a strictly linear relationship between cost and volume, except in the case of step-variable costs. Economists correctly point out that many costs that the accountant classifies as variable actually behave in a *curvilinear* fashion. The behavior of a **curvilinear cost** is shown in Exhibit 6–4. Notice that a strictly linear relationship between cost and volume does not exist either at very high or very low levels of activity.

Although accountants recognize that many costs are not strictly linear in their relationship to volume, they concentrate on cost behavior within a narrow band of activity known as the *relevant range*. The **relevant range** can be defined as that range of activity within which assumptions made about cost behavior are valid. Generally, the relationship between variable cost and activity is stable enough within this range that an assumption of strict linearity can be used with insignificant loss of accuracy. The concept of the relevant range is illustrated in Exhibit 6–4. Note that the accountant's straight-line approximation is reasonably accurate within this relevant range.

Fixed Costs

Objective 3
Identify examples of fixed costs, and explain the effect of a change in activity on both total fixed costs and fixed costs expressed on a per unit basis.

In our discussion of cost behavior patterns in Chapter 2, we stated that fixed costs remain constant in total dollar amount regardless of changes in the level of activity. To continue the Premier Motor Company example, if the company rents a factory building for $50,000 per year, the *total* amount of rent paid will be the same regardless of the number of trucks produced in a year within that building. This concept is shown graphically in Exhibit 6–5.

Since fixed costs remain constant in total, the amount of cost computed on a *per unit* basis will become progressively smaller as the number of units produced becomes greater. If Premier Motor Company produces only 250 trucks in a year, the $50,000 fixed rental cost would amount to $200 per truck. If 1,000 trucks are produced, the fixed rental cost would amount to only $50 per truck. As we noted in Chapter 2, this aspect of fixed costs can be confusing, although it is necessary in

EXHIBIT 6–4

Curvilinear Costs and the Relevant Range

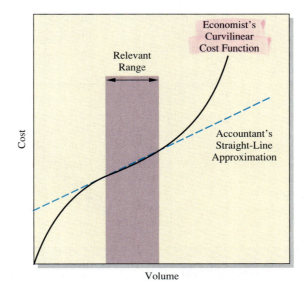

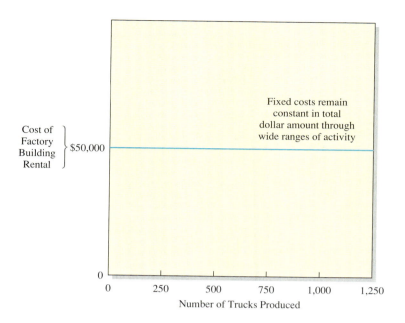

EXHIBIT 6–5
Fixed Cost Behavior

Fixed costs remain constant in total dollar amount through wide ranges of activity

Cost of Factory Building Rental } $50,000

Number of Trucks Produced

some contexts to express fixed costs on an average per unit basis. We found in Chapter 3, for example, that for purposes of preparing financial statements, the manager needs a broad unit cost figure containing both variable and fixed cost elements. For *internal* uses, however, fixed costs should not be expressed on a per unit basis because of the potential confusion involved. Experience has shown that for internal uses, fixed costs are most easily (and most safely) dealt with on a total basis rather than on a per unit basis.

The Trend toward Fixed Costs

The trend in many companies is toward greater fixed costs relative to variable costs. At least two factors are responsible for this trend. First, automation is becoming increasingly important in all types of organizations. Although automation has played a significant role in factory operations for well over a century, its role continues to increase. In addition, automation is rapidly becoming a significant factor in some traditionally service-oriented industries as well. Increased automation means increased investment in machinery and equipment, with the attendant fixed depreciation or lease charges.

Second, labor unions have been increasingly successful in stabilizing employment through labor contracts. Labor leaders have set guaranteed annual salaries or guaranteed minimum weeks of work high on their list of goals for the future. Although most people would agree that stabilization of employment is desirable from a social point of view, guaranteed salaries and workweeks do reduce the response of labor costs to changes in activity.

This shift away from variable costs toward fixed costs has been so significant in some firms that they have become largely ''fixed cost'' organizations. The textile industry, for example, can be cited as one in which most firms have moved heavily toward automation, with basically inflexible fixed costs replacing flexible, more responsive variable costs. These shifts are very significant in that planning in many ways becomes much more crucial when one is dealing with large amounts of fixed costs. The reason is that when dealing with fixed costs, the manager is much more "locked in" and generally has fewer options available in day-to-day decisions.

Types of Fixed Costs

Objective 4
Distinguish between committed and discretionary fixed costs.

Fixed costs are sometimes referred to as capacity costs, since they result from outlays made for plant facilities, equipment, and other items needed to provide the basic capacity for sustained operations. For planning purposes, fixed costs can be viewed as being either *committed* or *discretionary*.

Committed Fixed Costs

Committed fixed costs relate to the investment in plant, equipment, and the basic organizational structure of a firm. Examples of such costs include depreciation of plant facilities (buildings and equipment), taxes on real estate, insurance, and salaries of top management and operating personnel.

The two key factors about committed fixed costs are that (1) they are long term in nature and (2) they can't be reduced to zero even for short periods of time without seriously impairing either the profitability or the long-run goals of a firm. Even if operations are interrupted or cut back, the committed fixed costs will still continue largely unchanged. During a period of economic recession, for example, a firm won't usually discharge key executives or sell off part of the plant. Facilities and the basic organizational structure ordinarily must be kept intact. In terms of long-run goals, the costs of any other course of action are likely to be far greater than any short-run savings that might be realized.

Since committed fixed costs are basic to the long-run goals of a firm, their planning horizon usually encompasses many years. The commitments involved in these costs should be made only after careful analysis of long-run sales forecasts and after relating these forecasts to future capacity needs. Careful control must be exercised by management in the planning stage to ensure that a firm's long-run needs are properly evaluated. Once a decision is made to build a certain size plant, a firm becomes locked into that decision for many years to come.

After a firm becomes committed to a basic plant and organization, how are the associated costs controlled from year to year? Control of committed fixed costs comes through *utilization*. The strategy of management must be to utilize the plant and organization as effectively as possible in bringing about desired goals.

Discretionary Fixed Costs

Discretionary fixed costs (often referred to as *managed* fixed costs) arise from *annual* decisions by management to spend in certain fixed cost areas. Examples of discretionary fixed costs would include advertising, research, public relations, management development programs, and internships for students.

Basically, two key differences exist between discretionary fixed costs and committed fixed costs. First, the planning horizon for a discretionary fixed cost is fairly short term—usually a single year. By contrast, as we indicated earlier, committed fixed costs have a planning horizon that encompasses many years. Second, under dire circumstances it may be possible to cut certain discretionary fixed costs back for short periods of time with minimal damage to the long-run goals of the organization. For example, a firm that has been spending $50,000 annually on management development programs may be forced because of poor economic conditions to reduce its spending in that area during a given year. Although some unfavorable consequences might result from the cutback, it is doubtful that these consequences would be as great as those that would result if the company decided to economize during the year by disposing of a portion of its plant.

The key factor about discretionary fixed costs is that management is not locked into a decision regarding such costs for any more than a single budget period. Each year a fresh look can be taken at the expenditure level in the various discretionary fixed cost areas. A decision can then be made on whether to continue a particular expenditure, increase it, reduce it, or discontinue it altogether.

Top-Management Philosophy   In our discussion of fixed costs, we have drawn a sharp line between committed fixed costs and discretionary fixed costs. As a practical matter, the line between these two classes of costs is somewhat flexible. Whether a cost is committed or discretionary will depend in large part on the philosophy of top management.

Some management groups prefer to exercise discretion as often as possible on as many costs as possible. They prefer to review and adjust costs frequently as conditions warrant. Managers who are inclined in this direction tend to view fixed costs as being largely discretionary. Other management groups are slow to make adjustments in costs (especially adjustments downward) as conditions change. They prefer to maintain the status quo and to leave programs and personnel largely undisturbed, even though changing conditions might suggest the desirability of adjustments. Managers who are inclined in this direction tend to view virtually all fixed costs as being committed.

To cite an example, during recessionary periods when the level of home building is down, many construction companies lay off their workers and virtually disband operations for a period of time. Other construction companies continue large numbers of employees on the payroll, even though the workers have little or no work to do. In the first instance, management views its fixed costs as largely discretionary in nature. In the second instance, management views its fixed costs as largely committed. The philosophy of most management groups will fall somewhere between these two extremes.

Fixed Costs and the Relevant Range

The concept of the relevant range, which was introduced in our discussion of variable costs, also has application in dealing with fixed costs, particularly those of a discretionary nature. At the beginning of a period, programs are set and budgets established. The level of discretionary fixed costs will depend on the support needs of the programs that have been planned, which in turn will depend at least in part on the level of activity envisioned in the overall organization. At very high levels of activity, programs are usually broadened or expanded to include many things that might not be pursued at lower levels of activity. For example, the advertising needs of a company striving to increase sales by 25 percent would probably be much greater than if no sales increase was planned. Thus, fixed costs often move upward in steps as the activity level increases. This concept is illustrated in Exhibit 6–6, which depicts fixed costs and the relevant range.

Although discretionary fixed costs are more susceptible to adjustment than committed fixed costs, the step pattern depicted in Exhibit 6–6 also has application to committed fixed costs. As a company expands its level of activity, it may outgrow its present plant, or the key management core may need to be expanded. The result, of course, will be increased committed fixed costs as a larger plant is built and as new key management positions are created.

EXHIBIT 6–6
Fixed Costs and the
Relevant Range

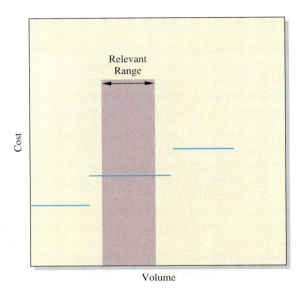

One reaction to the step pattern depicted in Exhibit 6–6 is to say that discretionary and committed fixed costs are really just step-variable costs. To some extent this is true, since *all* costs vary in the long-run. There are two major differences, however, between the step-variable costs depicted earlier in Exhibit 6–3 and the fixed costs depicted in Exhibit 6–6.

The first difference is that the step-variable costs can often be adjusted quickly as conditions change, whereas once fixed costs have been set, they often can't be changed easily. A step-variable cost such as maintenance labor, for example, can be adjusted upward or downward by hiring and laying off maintenance workers. By contrast, once a company has committed itself to a particular program, it becomes locked into the attendant fixed costs, at least for the budget period under consideration. Once an advertising contract has been signed, for example, the company is locked into that level of advertising costs for the contract period.

The second difference is that the *width of the steps* depicted for step-variable costs is much narrower than the width of the steps depicted for the fixed costs in Exhibit 6–6. The width of the steps relates to volume or level of activity. For step-variable costs, the width of a step may be 40 hours of activity or less if one is dealing, for example, with maintenance labor cost. For fixed costs, however, the width of a step may be *thousands* or even *tens of thousands* of hours of activity. In essence, the width of the steps for step-variable costs is generally so narrow that these costs can be treated essentially as variable costs for most purposes. The width of the steps for fixed costs, on the other hand, is so wide that these costs must generally be treated as being entirely fixed within the relevant range.

Mixed Costs

A **mixed cost** is one that contains both variable and fixed cost elements. Mixed costs are also known as **semivariable costs.** To continue the Premier Motor Company example, assume that the company leases machinery used in its operations. The lease agreement calls for a flat annual lease payment of $25,000, plus 10 cents

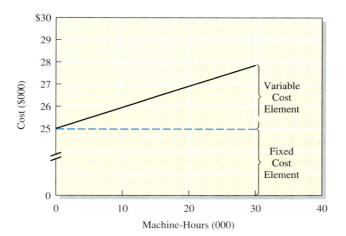

EXHIBIT 6–7
Mixed Cost Behavior

for each hour that the machines are operated during the year. If during a particular year the machines are operated a total of 30,000 hours, then the lease cost of the machines will be $28,000, made up of $25,000 in fixed cost plus $3,000 in variable cost. The behavior of this mixed cost is shown graphically in Exhibit 6–7.

Even if the machines leased by Premier Motor Company aren't used a single hour during the year, the company will still have to pay the minimum $25,000 charge. This is why the cost line in Exhibit 6–7 intersects the vertical cost axis at the $25,000 point. For each hour that the machines are used, the *total* cost of leasing will increase by 10 cents. Therefore, the total cost line slopes upward as the variable cost element is added onto the fixed cost element.

FOCUS ON CURRENT PRACTICE

A total of 257 American and 40 Japanese manufacturing firms responded to a questionnaire concerning their management accounting practices.[2] Among other things, the firms were asked whether they classified certain costs as variable, semivariable, or fixed. Some of the results are summarized in Exhibit 6–8. Note that firms do not all classify costs in the same way. For example, roughly 45 percent of the U.S. firms classify material-handling labor costs as variable, 35 percent as semivariable, and 20 percent as fixed. Also note that the Japanese firms are much more likely than U.S. firms to classify labor costs as fixed. This is a consequence of the lifetime employment policies followed by many Japanese firms. These policies make it very difficult and expensive for Japanese firms to adjust their labor force in response to changes in activity.

[2] NAA Tokyo Affiliate, "Management Accounting in the Advanced Management Surrounding—Comparative Study on Survey in Japan and U.S.A.," October 1988.

EXHIBIT 6–8
Percentages of Firms Classifying Specific Costs as Variable, Semivariable, or Fixed

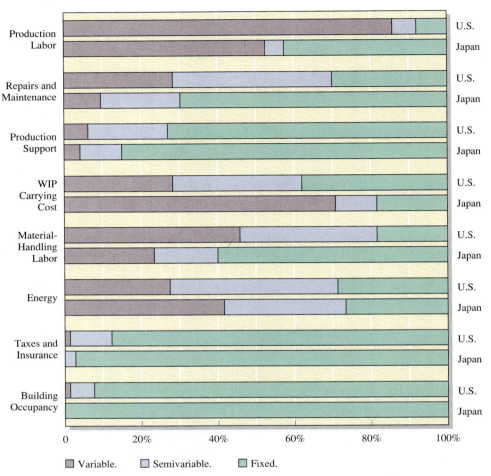

THE ANALYSIS OF MIXED COSTS

Objective 5
Analyze a mixed cost by the high-low method, the scattergraph method, and the least-squares method, and enumerate the strengths and weaknesses of each of these analytical approaches.

The concept of a mixed cost is important, since mixed costs are common to a wide range of firms. Examples of mixed costs include electricity, heat, repairs, telephone, and maintenance.

The fixed portion of a mixed cost represents the basic, minimum charge for just having a service *ready and available* for use. The variable portion represents the charge made for *actual consumption* of the service. As one would expect, the variable element varies in proportion to the amount of the service that is consumed.

For planning purposes, how does management handle mixed costs? The ideal approach would be to take each invoice as it comes in and break it down into its fixed and variable elements. As a practical matter, even if it were possible to make this type of minute breakdown, the cost of doing so would probably be prohibitive. Instead, analysis of mixed costs can be done on an aggregate basis, concentrating on the past behavior of a cost at various levels of activity. If this analysis is done carefully, good approximations of the fixed and variable elements of a cost can be obtained with a minimum of effort.

We will examine three methods of breaking mixed costs down into their fixed and variable elements—the *high-low method,* the *scattergraph method,* and the *least-squares method.*

The High-Low Method

most inaccurate method.

The **high-low method** of analyzing mixed costs is based on costs observed at both the high and low levels of activity within the relevant range. The difference in cost observed at the two extremes is divided by the change in activity between the extremes in order to determine the amount of variable cost involved.

To illustrate, assume that maintenance costs for Arnoldson Company have been observed as follows within the relevant range of 5,000 to 8,000 machine-hours:

Month	Cost Driver: Machine-Hours	Maintenance Cost Incurred
January	5.600	$7,900
February	7.100	8,500
March	5,000	7,400
April	6,500	8,200
May	7,300	9,100
June	8,000	9,800
July.	6,200	7,800

Since total maintenance cost increases as the activity level increases, it seems obvious that some variable cost element is present. To separate the variable cost element from the fixed cost element using the high-low method, we relate the change in machine-hours between the high and low activity levels to the change that we observe in cost:

	Machine-Hours	Maintenance Cost Incurred
High activity level (June).	8,000	$9,800
Low activity level (March)	5,000	7,400
Change observed	3,000	$2,400

$$\text{Variable cost} = \frac{\text{Change in cost}}{\text{Change in activity}} = \frac{\$2,400}{3,000} = \$0.80 \text{ per machine-hour}$$

Having determined that the variable rate for maintenance cost is 80 cents per machine-hour, we can now determine the amount of fixed cost. This is done by taking total cost at *either* the high or the low activity level and deducting the variable cost element. In the computation below, total cost at the high activity level is used in computing the fixed cost element:

Fixed cost element = Total cost − Variable cost element
= $9,800 − ($0.80 × 8,000 machine-hours)
= $3,400

Both the variable and fixed cost elements have now been isolated. The cost of maintenance within the relevant range analyzed can be expressed as $3,400 plus 80 cents per machine-hour. This is sometimes referred to as a **cost formula.**

$$\left.\begin{array}{c}\text{Cost formula for maintenance cost}\\ \text{over the relevant range of 5,000}\\ \text{to 8,000 machine-hours}\end{array}\right\} = \begin{array}{l}\text{\$3,400 fixed cost +}\\ \text{\$0.80 per machine-hour}\end{array}$$

The data used in this illustration are shown graphically in Exhibit 6–9. Three things should be noted in relation to this exhibit:

1. Notice that cost is plotted on the vertical axis and that it is represented by the letter Y. Cost is known as the **dependent variable,** since the amount of cost incurred during a period will be dependent on the level of activity for the period. (That is, as the level of activity increases, total cost will also increase.)
2. Notice that activity (machine-hours in this case) is plotted on the horizontal axis and that it is represented by the letter X. Activity is known as the **independent variable,** since it controls the amount of cost that will be incurred during a period.
3. Notice that the relevant range is highlighted on the exhibit. In using a cost formula, the manager must remember that the formula may not be valid outside the relevant range from which the underlying data have been drawn.

In completing a high-low analysis, what does the analyst do if the high and low levels of activity don't coincide with the high and low amounts in cost? For example, the period that has the highest level of activity may not have the highest amount of cost, or the period that has the lowest level of activity may not have the lowest amount of cost. In such cases, the analyst should always use the high and low levels of *activity* in analyzing the mixed cost involved. This is because it is

EXHIBIT 6–9
High-Low Method of Cost Analysis

Activity Level	Machine-Hours	Maintenance Cost
High	8,000	$9,800
Low	5,000	7,400

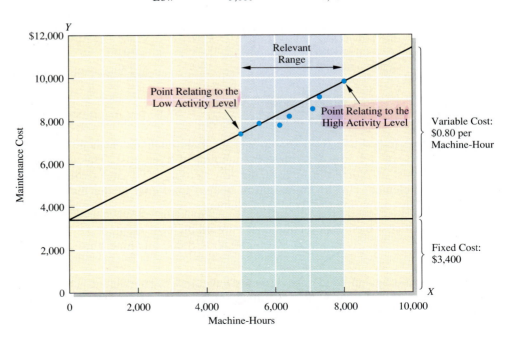

activity (the independent variable) that functions as a cost driver in an organization.

The high-low method is very simple to apply, but it suffers from a major (and sometimes critical) defect in that it utilizes only two points in determining a cost formula. Generally, two points are not enough to produce accurate results in cost analysis work. In particular, periods in which the activity level is unusually low or unusually high will tend to produce inaccurate results. A cost formula that is estimated solely using data from these unusual periods may seriously misrepresent the true cost relationship that holds during normal periods. Such a distortion is evident in Exhibit 6–9. The straight line should probably be shifted down somewhat so that it is closer to more of the data points. For these reasons, other methods of cost analysis that utilize a greater number of points will generally be more accurate than the high-low method in deriving a cost formula. If a manager chooses to use the high-low method, he or she should do so with a full awareness of the method's limitations.

The Scattergraph Method

In mixed cost analysis, the manager tries to find the *average* rate of variability in a mixed cost. A more accurate way of doing this than the high-low method is to use the **scattergraph method,** which takes into account all of the cost data through use of a graph. A graph like the one that we used in Exhibit 6–9 is constructed, in which cost is shown on the vertical axis and the volume or rate of activity is shown on the horizontal axis. Costs observed at various levels of activity are then plotted on the graph, and a line is fitted to the plotted points. However, rather than just fitting the line to the high and low points, *all points* are considered in the placement of the line. This is done through simple visual inspection of the data, with the analyst taking care that the placement of the line is representative of all points, not just the high and low ones. Typically, the line is placed so that approximately equal numbers of points fall above and below it.

A graph of this type is known as a *scattergraph,* and the line fitted to the plotted points is known as a **regression line.** The regression line, in effect, is a line of averages, with the average variable cost per unit of activity represented by the slope of the line and the average total fixed cost represented by the point where the regression line intersects the cost axis.

The scattergraph approach using the Arnoldson Company data is illustrated in Exhibit 6–10. Note that the regression line has been placed in such a way that approximately equal numbers of points fall above and below it. Also note that the line has been drawn so that it goes through one of the points. This is not absolutely necessary, but it makes subsequent calculations a little easier.

Since the regression line strikes the vertical cost axis at $3,300, that amount represents the fixed cost element. The variable cost element can be computed by subtracting the fixed cost of $3,300 from the total cost for any point lying on the regression line. Since the point representing 7,300 machine-hours lies on the regression line, we can use it. The variable cost (to the nearest tenth of a cent) would be 79.5 cents per machine-hour, computed as follows:

Total cost for 7,300 machine-hours
   (a point falling on the regression line) $9,100
Less fixed cost element   3,300
Variable cost element $5,800

$5,800 ÷ 7,300 machine-hours = $0.795 per machine-hour

EXHIBIT 6–10
**Scattergraph Method
of Cost Analysis**

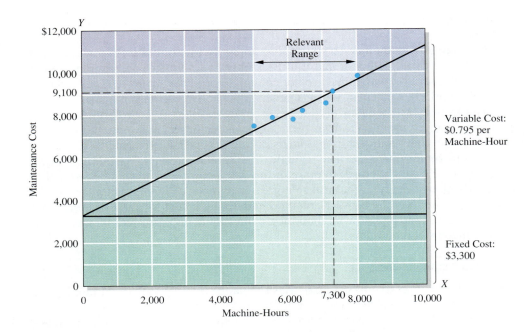

Thus, the cost formula using the regression line in Exhibit 6–10 would be $3,300 per month plus 79.5 cents per machine-hour.

For the Arnoldson example, there is not a great deal of difference between the cost formula derived using the high-low method and the cost formula derived using the scattergraph method. However, sometimes there *will* be a big difference. In those situations, more reliance should ordinarily be placed on the results of the scattergraph approach.

A scattergraph can be an extremely useful tool in the hands of an experienced analyst. Quirks in cost behavior due to strikes, bad weather, breakdowns, and so on, become immediately apparent to the trained observer, who can make appropriate adjustment to the data when fitting the regression line. Many cost analysts would argue that a scattergraph should be the beginning point in all cost analyses, due to the benefits to be gained from having the data visually available in graph form.

The scattergraph method is sometimes criticized because it is subjective. No two analysts who look at the same scattergraph are likely to draw exactly the same regression line. Also, the estimates of fixed costs are not as precise as they are with other methods since it is difficult to precisely measure the dollar amount where the regression line intersects the vertical cost axis. Some managers are uncomfortable with these elements of subjectivity and imprecision and desire a method that will yield a precise answer that will be the same no matter who does the analysis.

The Least-Squares Method

The **least-squares method** is a more objective and precise approach to estimating the regression line than the scattergraph method. Rather than fitting a regression line through the scattergraph data by visual inspection, the least-squares method uses mathematical formulas to fit the regression line. Also, unlike the high-low method, the least-squares method takes all of the data into account when estimating the cost formula.

The least-squares method is based on the equation for a straight line:

$$Y = a + bX$$

In this equation,

Y = Dependent variable (the total mixed cost observed)
a = Vertical intercept of the line (the total fixed cost)
b = Slope of the line (the variable rate)
X = Independent variable (the activity level observed)

This equation is illustrated in Exhibit 6–11, along with a number of hypothetical data points.

Notice from the exhibit that the deviations from the plotted points to the regression line are measured vertically on the graph. These vertical deviations are called the regression errors and are the key to understanding what least-squares regression does. There is nothing mysterious about the least-squares method. It simply computes the regression line that minimizes the sum of these squared errors. The formulas that accomplish this are fairly complex and involve numerous calculations, but the principle is very simple.

Fortunately, computers are adept at carrying out the computations required by the least-squares formulas. The data—the observed values of X and Y—are entered into the computer, and software does the rest. In the case of the Arnoldson maintenance cost data, we used a statistical software package on a personal computer to calculate the following least-squares estimates of the total fixed cost (a) and the variable cost rate (b):

$$a = \$3,431$$
$$b = \$0.759$$

Therefore, using the least-squares method, the fixed element of the maintenance cost is $3,431 per month and the variable portion is 75.9 cents per machine-hour.

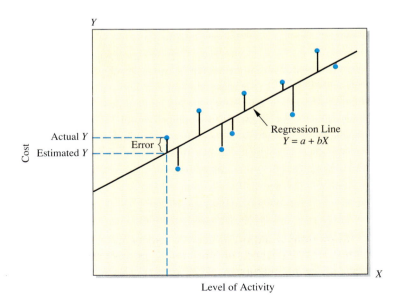

EXHIBIT 6–11
The Concept of Least Squares

The cost formula using this method is:

$$\left.\begin{array}{c}\text{Cost formula for maintenance cost} \\ \text{over the relevant range of 5,000} \\ \text{to 8,000 machine-hours}\end{array}\right\} = \begin{array}{l}\text{\$3,431 fixed cost} + \\ \text{\$0.759 per machine-hour}\end{array}$$

In terms of the linear equation $Y = a + bX$, the cost formula can be written as:

$$Y = \$3,431 + \$0.759X$$

where activity (X) is expressed in machine-hours.

We can see how the cost formula is used for planning purposes by assuming that 7,800 machine-hours will be required during the coming month. At this level of activity, the expected maintenance costs will be:

Fixed costs	$ 3,431
Variable costs: 7,800 machine-hours × $0.759.	5,920
Total expected maintenance costs	$ 9,351

While we used a personal computer to calculate the values of a and b in this example, they can also be calculated by hand. In Appendix D to this chapter, we show how this is done.

The Use of Judgment in Cost Analysis

Although a cost formula has the appearance of exactness, the breakdown of a mixed cost by any of the three techniques that we have discussed involves a substantial amount of estimating. The breakdowns represent *approximations* of the fixed and variable cost elements involved; they should not be construed as being precisely accurate. Managers must be ready to step in at any point in their analysis of a cost and adjust their computations for judgment factors that in their view are critical to a proper understanding of the mixed cost involved. However, the fact that computations are not exact and involve estimates and judgment does not prevent data from being useful and meaningful in decision making. Managers who wait to make a decision until they have perfect data will rarely have an opportunity to demonstrate their decision-making ability.

Multiple Regression Analysis

In all of our computations involving mixed costs, we have assumed a single causal factor as the basis for the behavior of the variable element. That causal factor has been the volume or rate of some activity, such as direct labor-hours, machine-hours, production, or sales. This assumption is acceptable for many mixed costs, but in some situations there may be more than one causal factor driving the variable cost element. For example, shipping costs might depend on both the number of units shipped *and* the weight of the units as dual causal factors. In a situation such as this, the regression equation would have to be expanded to include an additional variable:

$$Y = a + bX + cW$$

where c = the factor of variability and W = the weight of a unit. When dealing with an expanded equation such as this one, the simple regression analysis that we have been doing is no longer adequate. A **multiple regression analysis** is necessary. Although the added variable or variables will make the computations more complex, the principles involved are the same as in a simple regression such as we have been doing. Because of the complexity of the computations involved, multiple regression is generally done with the aid of a computer.

Engineering Approach to Cost Study

Some firms use the engineering approach to analyze cost behavior. Essentially, this approach involves a quantitative analysis of what cost behavior should be, based on an industrial engineer's evaluation of the production methods to be used, the materials specifications, labor requirements, equipment usage, efficiency of production, power consumption, and so on. The engineering approach must be used in those situations where no past experience is available concerning activity and costs. In addition, it is often used in tandem with the methods we have discussed above in order to sharpen the accuracy of cost analysis.

THE CONTRIBUTION FORMAT

Once the manager has separated costs into fixed and variable elements, what does he or she do with the data? To answer this question will require most of the remainder of this book, since much of what the manager does rests in some way on an understanding of cost behavior. One immediate and very significant application of the ideas we have developed, however, is found in a new income statement format known as the **contribution approach.** The unique thing about the contribution approach is that it provides the manager with an income statement geared directly to cost behavior.

Objective 6
Prepare an income statement using the contribution format.

Why a New Income Statement Format?

The **traditional approach** to the income statement, as illustrated in Chapter 2, is not organized in terms of cost behavior. Rather, it is organized in a "functional" format—emphasizing the functions of production, administration, and sales in the classification and presentation of cost data. No attempt is made to distinguish between the behavior of costs included under each functional heading. Under the heading "Administrative expense," for example, one can expect to find both variable and fixed costs lumped together.

Although an income statement prepared in the functional format may be useful for external reporting purposes, it has serious limitations when used for internal purposes. Internally, the manager needs cost data organized in a format that will facilitate carrying out planning, control, and decision-making responsibilities. As we shall see in chapters ahead, these responsibilities are discharged most effectively when cost data are available in a fixed and variable format. The contribution approach to the income statement has been developed in response to this need.

The Contribution Approach

Exhibit 6–12 illustrates the contribution approach to the income statement, along with the traditional approach discussed in Chapter 2.

Notice that the contribution approach separates costs into fixed and variable categories, first deducting variable expenses from sales to obtain what is known as the *contribution margin*. The **contribution margin** is the amount remaining from sales revenues after variable expenses have been deducted. This amount *contributes* toward the covering of fixed expenses and then toward profits for the period.

EXHIBIT 6–12

Comparison of the Contribution Income Statement with the Traditional Income Statement

Traditional Approach (costs organized by function)			**Contribution Approach** (costs organized by behavior)			
Sales		$12,000	Sales			$12,000
Less cost of goods sold		6,000*	Less variable expenses:			
Gross margin		6,000	Variable production	$2,000		
Less operating expenses:			Variable selling	600		
Selling	$3,100*		Variable administrative	400	3,000	
Administrative	1,900*	5,000	Contribution margin			9,000
Net income.		$ 1,000	Less fixed expenses:			
			Fixed production.	4,000		
			Fixed selling.	2,500		
			Fixed administrative	1,500	8,000	
			Net income			$ 1,000

* Contains both variable and fixed expenses. This is the income statement for a *manufacturing* company; thus, when the income statement is placed in the contribution format, the "cost of goods sold" figure is divided between variable production costs and fixed production costs. If this were the income statement for a *merchandising* company (which simply purchases completed goods from a supplier), then the "cost of goods sold" would *all* be variable.

The contribution approach to the income statement is used as an internal planning and decision-making tool. Its emphasis on costs by behavior facilitates cost-volume-profit analysis, such as we shall be doing in the following chapter. The approach is also very useful in appraising management performance, in segmented reporting of profit data, and in budgeting. Moreover, the contribution approach helps managers to organize data pertinent to all kinds of special decisions such as product line analysis, pricing, use of scarce resources, and make or buy analysis. All of these topics are covered in later chapters.

SUMMARY

Managers analyze cost behavior to have a basis for predicting how costs will respond to changes in activity levels. We have looked at three types of cost behavior—variable, fixed, and mixed. In the case of mixed costs, we have studied three methods of breaking a mixed cost into its basic variable and fixed elements. The high-low method is the simplest of the three, having as its underlying assumption that the variable element of a mixed cost can be determined by analyzing the change in cost between two extreme points. In most situations, however, two points are not enough to produce accurate results, and the manager should therefore use either the scattergraph method or the least-squares method to derive a cost formula. Both of these methods require the construction of a regression line, the slope of which represents the average rate of variability in the mixed cost being analyzed. The least-squares method is the more precise and objective of the two in that it uses mathematical formulas to fit a regression line to an array of data.

Managers use costs organized by behavior as a basis for many decisions. To facilitate this use, the income statement can be prepared in a contribution format. The contribution format classifies costs on the income statement by cost behavior rather than by the functions of production, administration, and sales.

REVIEW PROBLEM 1: COST BEHAVIOR

Neptune Rentals offers a boat rental service. Consider the following costs of the company over a relevant range of 5,000 to 20,000 hours of operating time for its boats:

	Hours of Operating Time			
	5,000	**10,000**	**15,000**	**20,000**
Total costs:				
Variable costs.	$ 20,000	$?	$?	$?
Fixed costs	180,000			?
Total costs	$200,000	$?	$?	$?
Cost per hour:				
Variable cost	$?	$?	$?	$?
Fixed cost		?	?	?
Total cost per hour . . .	$?	$?	$?	$?

Required

Compute the missing amounts, assuming that implied cost behavior patterns remain unchanged over the relevant range of 5,000 to 20,000 hours.

Solution to Review Problem 1

The variable cost per hour of operating time can be computed as follows:

$$\$20,000 \div 5,000 \text{ hours} = \$4 \text{ per hour}$$

Therefore, in accordance with the behavior of variable and fixed costs, the missing amounts are:

	Hours of Operating Time			
	5,000	**10,000**	**15,000**	**20,000**
Total costs:				
Variable costs.	$ 20,000	$ 40,000	$ 60,000	$ 80,000
Fixed costs	180,000	180,000	180,000	180,000
Total costs	$200,000	$220,000	$240,000	$260,000
Cost per hour:				
Variable cost	$ 4	$ 4	$ 4	$ 4
Fixed cost	36	18	12	9
Total cost per hour . . .	$ 40	$ 22	$ 16	$ 13

Observe that the variable costs increase, in total, proportionately with increases in the number of hours of operating time, but that these costs remain constant at $4 if expressed on a per hour basis.

In contrast, the fixed costs by definition do not change in total with changes in the level of activity. They remain constant at $180,000. With increases in activity, however, the fixed costs decrease on a per hour basis, dropping from $36 per hour when the boats are operated 5,000 hours a period to only $9 per hour when the boats are operated 20,000 hours a period. *Because of this troublesome aspect of fixed costs, they are most easily (and most safely) dealt with on a total basis, rather than on a unit basis, in cost analysis work.*

REVIEW PROBLEM 2: HIGH-LOW METHOD

The administrator of Azalea Hills Hospital would like a cost formula linking the costs involved in admitting patients to the number of patients admitted during a month. The admitting department's costs and the number of patients admitted during the immediately preceding eight months are given in the following table:

Month	Number of Patients Admitted	Admitting Department Costs
May	1,800	$14,700
June	1,900	15,200
July	1,700	13,700
August	1,600	14,000
September	1,500	14,300
October.	1,300	13,100
November	1,100	12,800
December.	1,500	14,600

Required
1. Use the high-low method to estimate a cost formula for admitting costs.
2. Express the cost formula as a linear equation in the form $Y = a + bX$.

Solution to Review Problem 2
1. The first step in the high-low method is to identify the periods of the lowest and highest activity. Those periods are November (1,100 patients admitted) and June (1,900 patients admitted).

The second step is to compute the variable cost per unit using those two points:

Month	Number of Patients Admitted	Admitting Department Costs
High activity level (June)	1,900	$15,200
Low activity level (November)	1,100	12,800
Change observed.	800	$ 2,400

$$\text{Variable cost} = \frac{\text{Change in cost}}{\text{Change in activity}} = \frac{\$2,400}{800} = \$3 \text{ per patient admitted}$$

The third step is to compute the fixed cost element by deducting the variable cost element from the total cost at either the high or low activity. In the computation below, the high point of activity is used:

Fixed cost element = Total cost − Variable cost element
= $15,200 − ($3 × 1,900 patients admitted)
= $9,500

The fourth and final step is to combine the variable and fixed elements into a single cost formula:

Cost formula for admitting costs over the relevant range of 1,100 to 1,900 patients admitted } = $9,500 fixed cost + $3 per patient admitted

2. The cost formula expressed in the linear equation form is $Y = \$9,500 + \$3X$.

KEY TERMS FOR REVIEW

Activity base   A measure of whatever causes the incurrence of a variable cost. For example, the total cost of X-ray film in a hospital will increase as the number of X rays taken increases. Therefore, the number of X rays is an activity base for explaining the total cost of X-ray film. (p. 239)

Committed fixed costs   Those fixed costs that are difficult to adjust and that relate to the investment in plant, equipment, and the basic organizational structure of a firm. (p. 244)

Contribution approach   An income statement format that is geared to cost behavior in that costs are separated into variable and fixed categories rather than being separated according to the functions of production, sales, and administration. (p. 255)

Contribution margin   The amount remaining from sales revenues after all variable expenses have been deducted. (p. 255)

Cost formula   A formula relating cost to activity. This expression is generally in the form of the linear equation $Y = a + bX$, where Y is the total cost, a is the total fixed cost, b is the variable cost rate, and X is the activity. (p. 249)

Cost structure   The relative proportion of fixed, variable, and mixed costs found within an organization. (p. 238)

Curvilinear costs   A relationship between cost and activity that is a curve rather than a straight line. (p. 242)

Dependent variable   A variable that reacts or responds to some controlling factor; total cost is the dependent variable, as represented by the letter Y, in the equation $Y = a + bX$. (p. 250)

Discretionary fixed costs   Those fixed costs that arise from annual decisions by management to spend in certain fixed cost areas, such as advertising and research. (p. 244)

High-low method   A method of separating a mixed cost into its fixed and variable elements by analyzing the change in cost between the high and low levels of activity. (p. 249)

Independent variable   A variable that acts as the controlling factor; activity is the independent variable, as represented by the letter X, in the equation $Y = a + bX$. (p. 250)

Least-squares method   A method of separating a mixed cost into its fixed and variable elements by fitting a regression line that minimizes the sum of the squared errors. (p. 252)

Mixed cost   A cost that contains both variable and fixed cost elements. Also see *Semivariable cost*. (p. 246)

Multiple regression analysis   An analytical method required in those situations where more than one causal factor is involved in the behavior of the variable element of a mixed cost. (p. 254)

Regression line   A line fitted to an array of plotted points. The slope of the line, denoted by the letter b in the linear equation $Y = a + bX$, represents the average variable cost per unit of activity. The point where the line intersects the cost axis, denoted by the letter a in the above equation, represents the average total fixed cost. (p. 251)

Relevant range   The range of activity within which assumptions relative to variable and fixed cost behavior are valid. (p. 242)

Scattergraph method   A method of separating a mixed cost into its fixed and variable elements. Under this method, a regression line is fitted to an array of plotted points by simple, visual inspection. (p. 251)

Semivariable cost   A cost that contains both variable and fixed cost elements. Also see *Mixed cost*. (p. 246)

Step-variable cost   A cost (such as the cost of a maintenance worker) that is obtainable only in large pieces and that increases and decreases only in response to fairly wide changes in the activity level. (p. 241)

Traditional approach   An income statement format in which costs are organized and presented according to the functions of production, administration, and sales. (p. 255)

APPENDIX D: THE LEAST-SQUARES METHOD

The least-squares method for estimating a linear relationship is based on the equation for a straight line:

$$Y = a + bX$$

The estimates of the vertical intercept *(a)* and slope *(b)* that minimize the sum of the squared errors are obtained by solving the following two simultaneous equations:[3]

$$\Sigma XY = a\Sigma X + b\Sigma X^2$$
$$\Sigma Y = na + b\Sigma X$$

where

X = Independent variable (the activity level observed)
Y = Dependent variable (the total mixed cost observed)
a = Vertical intercept of the line (the total fixed cost)
b = Slope of the line (the variable rate)
n = Number of observations
Σ = Sum across all n observations

The solution involves four steps:

Step 1.   Compute ΣX, ΣY, ΣXY, ΣX^2, and n.
Step 2.   Insert the values computed in step 1 into the simultaneous equations.
Step 3.   Solve the simultaneous equations for the variable cost rate (b).
Step 4.   Solve one of the equations for the total fixed cost (a).

Below we show an example of the least-squares method using the Arnoldson Company data found on page 249.

Step 1.   Compute ΣX, ΣY, ΣXY, ΣX^2, and n

Month	Machine-Hours X	Maintenance Costs Y	XY	X²
January	5,600	$ 7,900	$ 44,240,000	31,360,000
February.	7,100	8,500	60,350,000	50,410,000
March	5,000	7,400	37,000,000	25,000,000
April	6,500	8,200	53,300,000	42,250,000
May	7,300	9,100	66,430,000	53,290,000
June	8,000	9,800	78,400,000	64,000,000
July	6,200	7,800	48,360,000	38,440,000
Totals Σ	45,700	$58,700	$388,080,000	304,750,000

From this table:

$$\Sigma X = 45,700$$
$$\Sigma Y = \$58,700$$
$$\Sigma XY = \$388,080,000$$
$$\Sigma X^2 = 304,750,000$$
$$n = 7$$

Step 2.   Insert the values computed in step 1 into the simultaneous equations.

Substituting these amounts into the two simultaneous equations given earlier, we have:

$$\Sigma XY = a\Sigma X + b\Sigma X^2 \tag{1}$$
$$\Sigma Y = na + b\Sigma X \tag{2}$$
$$\$388,080,000 = 45,700a + 304,750,000b \tag{1}$$
$$\$58,700 = 7a + 45,700b \tag{2}$$

---

[3] See a calculus or statistics book for the details of how these simultaneous equations are derived.

Step 3.   Solve the simultaneous equations for the variable cost rate (b).

To solve the equations for *a* and *b*, it will be necessary to eliminate one of the terms. The *a* term can be eliminated by multiplying equation (1) by 7, multiplying equation (2) by 45,700, and then subtracting equation (2) from equation (1). These steps are shown below:

Multiply equation (1) by 7: $2,716,560,000 = 319,900a + 2,133,250,000b
Multiply equation (2) by 45,700: $2,682,590,000 = 319,900a + 2,088,490,000b

Subtract (2) from (1): $33,970,000 = 44,760,000b
                                                     $0.759 = b

Therefore, the variable maintenance cost is 75.9 cents per machine-hour.

Step 4.   Solve one of the equations for the total fixed cost (a).

The fixed cost can be computed by substituting the variable cost rate *(b)* we just obtained into either equation (1) or (2). We will use equation (2) since the numbers are smaller and easier to deal with.

$$\$58,700 = 7a + 45,700b \qquad (2)$$
$$\$58,700 = 7a + 45,700 \times \$0.759$$
$$\$58,700 = 7a + \$34,686$$
$$\$24,014 = 7a$$
$$\$3,431 = a$$

Therefore the fixed maintenance cost is $3,431 per month. The cost formula for maintenance cost is:

$$Y = a + bX$$
$$Y = \$3,431 + \$0.759X$$

QUESTIONS

6–1 Distinguish between (a) a variable cost, (b) a fixed cost, and (c) a mixed cost.

6–2 What effect does an increase in volume have on—
a.   Unit fixed costs?
b.   Unit variable costs?
c.   Total fixed costs?
d.   Total variable costs?

6–3 Define the following terms: (a) cost behavior and (b) relevant range.

6–4 What is meant by an *activity base* when dealing with variable costs? Give several examples of activity bases.

6–5 Distinguish between (a) a variable cost, (b) a mixed cost, and (c) a step-variable cost. Chart the three costs on a graph, with activity plotted horizontally and cost plotted vertically.

6–6 The accountant often assumes a strictly linear relationship between cost and volume. How can this practice be defended in light of the fact that many variable costs are curvilinear in form?

6–7 Distinguish between discretionary fixed costs and committed fixed costs.

6–8 Classify the following fixed costs as normally being either committed (C) or discretionary (D):
a.   Depreciation on buildings.
b.   Advertising.
c.   Research.

    d.   Long-term equipment leases.

    e.   Pension payments to the firm's retirees.

    f.   Management development and training.

6–9   What factors are contributing to the trend toward increasing fixed costs, and why is this trend significant from a managerial accounting point of view?

6–10   Does the concept of the relevant range have application to fixed costs? Explain.

6–11   What is the major disadvantage of the high-low method? Under what conditions would this analytical method provide an accurate cost formula?

6–12   What methods are available for separating a mixed cost into its fixed and variable elements? Which method is most accurate? Why?

6–13   What is meant by a regression line? Give the general formula for a regression line. Which term represents the variable cost? The fixed cost?

6–14   Once a regression line has been drawn, how does one determine the fixed cost element? The variable cost element?

6–15   What is meant by the term *least squares?*

6–16   What is the difference between single regression analysis and multiple regression analysis?

6–17   What is the difference between the contribution approach to the income statement and the traditional approach to the income statement?

6–18   What is meant by contribution margin? How is it computed?

EXERCISES

E6–1   The Lakeshore Hotel's guest-days of occupancy and custodial supplies expense over the last seven months were:

Month	Guest-Days of Occupancy	Custodial Supplies Expense
March	4,000	$ 7,500
April	6,500	8,250
May	8,000	10,500
June	10,500	12,000
July	12,000	13,500
August	9,000	10,750
September	7,500	9,750

Required 1. Using the high-low method, determine the cost formula for custodial supplies expense.

          2. Using the cost formula you derived above, what amount of custodial supplies expense would you expect to be incurred at an occupancy level of 11,000 guest-days?

E6–2   Refer to the data in E6–1.

Required 1. Prepare a scattergraph using the data from E6–1. Plot cost on the vertical axis and activity on the horizontal axis. Fit a regression line to your plotted points by visual inspection.

          2. What is the approximate monthly fixed cost? The approximate variable cost per guest-day?

          3. Scrutinize the points on your graph and explain why the high-low method would or would not yield an accurate cost formula in this situation.

E6–3   The following data relating to units shipped and total shipping expense have been assembled by Archer Company:

Month	Units Shipped	Total Shipping Expense
January	3	$18
February	6	23
March	4	17
April.	5	20
May	7	23
June	8	27
July	2	12

1. Using the high-low method, determine the cost formula for shipping expense.
2. For the scattergraph method, do the following:
   a. Prepare a scattergraph, using the data given above. Plot cost on the vertical axis and activity on the horizontal axis. Fit a regression line to your plotted points by visual inspection.
   b. Using your scattergraph, determine the approximate variable cost per unit shipped and the approximate fixed cost per month.

Required

(Appendix D) Refer to the data in E6–3.

E6–4

1. Using the least-squares method, determine the cost formula for shipping expense.
2. If you also completed E6–3, prepare a simple table comparing the variable and fixed cost elements of shipping expense as computed under the high-low method, the scattergraph method, and the least-squares method.

Required

St. Mark's Hospital contains 450 beds. The average occupancy rate is 80 percent per month. At this level of occupancy, the hospital's operating costs are $32 per occupied bed per day, assuming a 30-day month. This $32 figure contains both variable and fixed cost elements.

E6–5

During June, the hospital's occupancy rate was only 60 percent. A total of $326,700 in operating cost was incurred during the month.

1. Using the high-low method, determine:
   a. The variable cost per occupied bed on a daily basis.
   b. The total fixed operating costs per month.
2. Assume an occupancy rate of 70 percent. What amount of total operating cost would you expect the hospital to incur?

Required

Harris Company manufactures and sells a single product. The company typically operates within a relevant range of 30,000 to 50,000 units produced and sold annually. A partially completed schedule of the company's total and per unit costs over this range is given below:

E6–6

	Units Produced and Sold		
	30,000	40,000	50,000
Total costs:			
Variable costs	$180,000	?	?
Fixed costs	300,000	?	?
Total costs	$480,000	?	?
Cost per unit:			
Variable cost	?	?	?
Fixed cost.	?	?	?
Total cost per unit . . .	?	?	?

1. Complete the schedule of the company's total and unit costs above.
2. Assume that the company produces and sells 45,000 units during a year at a selling

Required

price of $16 per unit. Prepare an income statement in the contribution format for the year.

E6–7 Oki Products, Ltd., has observed the following processing costs at various levels of activity over the last 15 months:

Month	Units Produced	Processing Cost
1	4,500	$38,000
2	11,000	52,000
3	12,000	56,000
4	5,500	40,000
5	9,000	47,000
6	10,500	52,000
7	7,500	44,000
8	5,000	41,000
9	11,500	52,000
10	6,000	43,000
11	8,500	48,000
12	10,000	50,000
13	6,500	44,000
14	9,500	48,000
15	8,000	46,000

Required
1. Prepare a scattergraph by plotting the above data on a graph. Plot cost on the vertical axis and activity on the horizontal axis. Fit a line to your plotted points by visual inspection.
2. What is the approximate monthly fixed cost? The approximate variable cost per unit processed? Show computations.

E6–8 (Appendix D) One of Fenwick Company's products goes through an etching process. The company has observed etching costs as follows over the last six quarters:

Quarter	Units	Total Etching Cost
1	4	$ 18
2	3	17
3	8	25
4	6	20
5	7	24
6	2	16
	30	$120

For planning purposes, Fenwick Company's management would like to know the amount of variable etching cost per unit and the total fixed etching cost per quarter.

Required
1. Using the least-squares method, determine the variable and fixed elements of etching cost as desired by management.
2. Express the cost data in (1) above in the form $Y = a + bX$.
3. If the company processes five units next quarter, what would be the expected total etching cost?

E6–9 Mercury Transit, Inc., operates a fleet of delivery trucks in a large city. The company has determined that if a truck is driven 105,000 miles during a year, the operating cost is 11.4 cents per mile. If a truck is driven only 70,000 miles during a year, the operating cost increases to 13.4 cents per mile.

Required
1. Using the high-low method, determine the variable and fixed cost elements of the annual cost of truck operation.
2. Express the variable and fixed costs in the form $Y = a + bX$.
3. If a truck were driven 80,000 miles during a year, what total cost would you expect to be incurred?

The Alpine House, Inc., is a large retailer of winter sports equipment. An income statement for the company's Ski Department for the most recent quarter is presented below.

E6–10

THE ALPINE HOUSE, INC.
Income Statement—Ski Department
For the Quarter Ended March 31, 19x5

Sales		$150,000
Less cost of goods sold.		90,000
Gross margin		60,000
Less operating expenses:		
Selling expenses	$30,000	
Administrative expenses	10,000	40,000
Net income		$ 20,000

Skis sell, on the average, for $150 per pair. Variable selling expenses are $10 per pair of skis sold. The remaining selling expenses are fixed. The administrative expenses are 20 percent variable and 80 percent fixed. The company does not manufacture its own skis; it purchases them from a supplier for $90 per pair.

Required

1. Prepare an income statement for the quarter, using the contribution approach.
2. For every pair of skis sold during the quarter, what was the contribution toward covering fixed expenses and toward earning profits?

PROBLEMS

High-Low Method; Contribution Income Statement   Vencil Company, a merchandising firm, is the sole distributor of a product that is increasing in popularity among consumers. The company's income statements for the three most recent months are given below:

P6–11

VENCIL COMPANY
Income Statements
For the Three Months Ending September 30, 19x1

	July	August	September
Sales in units	4,000	4,500	5,000
Sales revenue	$400,000	$450,000	$500,000
Less cost of goods sold	240,000	270,000	300,000
Gross margin	160,000	180,000	200,000
Less operating expenses:			
Advertising expense	21,000	21,000	21,000
Shipping expense.	34,000	36,000	38,000
Salaries and commissions	78,000	84,000	90,000
Insurance expense	6,000	6,000	6,000
Depreciation expense	15,000	15,000	15,000
Total operating expenses . . .	154,000	162,000	170,000
Net income	$ 6,000	$ 18,000	$ 30,000

Required

1. Identify each of the company's expenses (including cost of goods sold) as being either variable, fixed, or mixed.
2. By use of the high-low method, separate each mixed expense into variable and fixed elements. State the cost formula for each mixed expense.
3. Redo the company's income statement at the 5,000-unit level of activity using the contribution format.

High-Low Method of Cost Analysis   Sawaya Company's management has noted that total factory overhead costs fluctuate considerably from year to year according to in-

P6–12

creases and decreases in the number of direct labor-hours worked in the factory. Total factory overhead costs at high and low levels of activity for recent years are given below:

	Level of Activity	
	Low	High
Direct labor-hours	50,000	75,000
Total factory overhead costs . . .	$142,500	$176,250

The factory overhead costs above consist of indirect materials, rent, and maintenance. The company has analyzed these costs at the 50,000-hour level of activity and has determined that at this activity level these costs exist in the following proportions:

Indirect materials (V)	$ 50,000
Rent (F)	60,000
Maintenance (M)	32,500
Total factory overhead costs . . .	$142,500

V = variable; F = fixed; M = mixed.

To have data available for planning, the company wants to break down the maintenance cost into its variable and fixed cost elements.

Required   1.   Determine how much of the $176,250 factory overhead cost at the high level of activity above consists of maintenance cost. (Hint: To do this, it may be helpful to first determine how much of the $176,250 consists of indirect materials and rent. Think about the behavior of variable and fixed costs within the relevant range!)
2.   By means of the high-low method of cost analysis, determine the cost formula for maintenance.
3.   Express the company's maintenance costs in the linear equation form $Y = a + bX$.
4.   What *total* factory overhead costs would you expect the company to incur at an operating level of 70,000 direct labor-hours? Show computations.

P6–13   **Least-Squares Method of Cost Analysis; Graphing**   (Appendix D) Professor John Morton has just been appointed chairperson of the finance department at Westland University. In reviewing the department's cost records, Professor Morton has found the following total cost associated with Finance 101 over the last several terms:

Term	Number of Sections Offered	Total Cost
Fall 19x1.	4	$10,000
Winter 19x2	6	14,000
Summer 19x2.	2	7,000
Fall 19x2.	5	13,000
Winter 19x3	3	9,500

Professor Morton knows that there are some variable costs, such as amounts paid to graduate assistants, associated with the course. He would like to have the variable and fixed costs separated for planning purposes.

Required   1.   Using the least-squares method, compute the variable cost per section and the total fixed cost per term for Finance 101.
2.   Express the cost data derived in (1) above in the linear equation form $Y = a + bX$.
3.   Assume that because of the small number of sections offered during the Winter Term 19x3, Professor Morton will have to offer eight sections of Finance 101 during the Fall Term. Compute the expected total cost for Finance 101. Can you see any problem with using the cost formula from (2) to derive this total cost figure?
4.   Prepare a scattergraph, and fit a regression line to the plotted points using the cost formula expressed in (2) above.

Least-Squares Analysis; Contribution Income Statement   (Appendix D) "Our managers need better information in order to plan more effectively and to get better control over costs," said Alfredo Ruiz, president of Comptex, Inc., a merchandising firm. "One way to get better information is to use a contribution-type income statement internally. We need to have our costs separated into fixed and variable categories." Accordingly, the accounting department has made the following analysis:

P6–14

Cost	Cost Formula
Cost of goods sold	$40 per unit
Advertising.	$70,000 per year
Sales commissions	8.5% of sales
Administrative salaries.	$160,000 per year
Clerical expense	?
Depreciation	$24,500 per year
Insurance	$18,000 per year

The accounting department believes that clerical expense is a mixed cost, containing both fixed and variable cost elements. A tabulation has been made of clerical expense and unit sales over the last several years, as follows:

Year	Units Sold (000)	Clerical Expense
19x1	10	$125,000
19x2	7	100,000
19x3	8	105,000
19x4	11	140,000
19x5	9	120,000
19x6	15	160,000

Mr. Ruiz would like a cost formula developed for clerical expenses so that a contribution-type income statement can be prepared for management's use.

Required

1. Using the least-squares method, derive a cost formula for clerical expense. (Since the "Units Sold" above are in thousands of units, the variable rate you compute will also be in thousands of units. It can be left in this form, or you can convert your variable rate to a per unit basis by dividing it by 1,000.)
2. The company plans to sell 12,000 units during 19x7 at a selling price of $100 per unit. Prepare a budgeted income statement for the year, using the contribution format.

High-Low Method of Cost Analysis   Nova Company's total overhead costs at various levels of activity are presented below:

P6–15

Month	Machine-Hours	Total Overhead Costs
April.	70,000	$198,000
May	60,000	174,000
June	80,000	222,000
July	90,000	246,000

Assume that the total overhead costs above consist of utilities, supervisory salaries, and maintenance. The proportion of these costs at the 60,000 machine-hour level of activity is:

Utilities (V)	$ 48,000
Supervisory salaries (F)	21,000
Maintenance (M)	105,000
Total overhead costs	$174,000

Nova Company's management wants to break down the maintenance cost into its basic variable and fixed cost elements.

Required   1. As shown above, overhead costs in July amounted to $246,000. Determine how much of this consisted of maintenance cost. (Hint: To do this, it may be helpful to first determine how much of the $246,000 consisted of utilities and supervisory salaries. Think about the behavior of variable and fixed costs within the relevant range!)

2. By means of the high-low method, determine the cost formula for maintenance.

3. Express the company's *total* overhead costs in the linear equation form $Y = a + bX$.

4. What *total* overhead costs would you expect to be incurred at an operating activity level of 75,000 machine-hours? Show computations.

P6–16 **Contribution versus Traditional Income Statement**   Marwick's Pianos, Inc., purchases pianos from a large manufacturer and sells them at the retail level. The pianos cost, on the average, $2,450 each from the manufacturer. Marwick's Pianos, Inc., sells the pianos at an average price of $3,125 each to its customers. The selling and administrative costs that the company incurs in a typical month are presented below:

Costs	Cost Formula
Selling:	
Advertising	$700 per month
Sales salaries and commissions	$950 per month, plus 8% of sales
Delivery of pianos to customers	$30 per piano sold
Utilities	$350 per month
Depreciation of sales facilities	$800 per month
Administrative:	
Executive salaries	$2,500 per month
Insurance	$400 per month
Clerical	$1,000 per month, plus $20 per piano sold
Depreciation of office equipment	$300 per month

During August 19x2, Marwick's Pianos, Inc., sold and delivered 40 pianos.

Required   1. Prepare an income statement for Marwick's Pianos, Inc., for August 19x2. Use the traditional format, with costs organized by function.

2. Redo (1), this time using the contribution format, with costs organized by behavior. Show costs and revenues on both a total and a per unit basis down through contribution margin.

3. Refer to the income statement you prepared in (2) above. Why might it be misleading to show the fixed costs on a per unit basis?

P6–17 **Identifying Cost Behavior Patterns**   Below are a number of cost behavior patterns that might be found in a company's cost structure. The vertical axis on each graph represents total cost, and the horizontal axis on each graph represents level of activity (volume).

Required   1. For each of the following situations, identify the graph that illustrates the cost pattern involved. Any graph may be used more than once.

a. Cost of raw materials, where the cost decreases by 5 cents per unit for each of the first 100 units purchased, after which it remains constant at $2.50 per unit.

b. Electricity bill—a flat fixed charge, plus a variable cost after a certain number of kilowatt-hours are used.

c. City water bill, which is computed as follows:

First 1,000,000 gallons or less . . .	$1,000 flat fee
Next 10,000 gallons	0.003 per gallon used
Next 10,000 gallons	0.006 per gallon used
Next 10,000 gallons	0.009 per gallon used
Etc.	Etc.

d. Depreciation of equipment, where the amount is computed by the straight-line method. When the depreciation rate was established, it was anticipated that the obsolescence factor would be greater than the wear and tear factor.

e. Rent on a factory building donated by the city, where the agreement calls for a fixed fee payment unless 200,000 labor-hours are worked, in which case no rent need be paid.

f. Salaries of maintenance workers, where one maintenance worker is needed for every 1,000 hours of machine-hours or less (that is, 0 to 1,000 hours requires one maintenance worker, 1,001 to 2,000 hours requires two maintenance workers, etc.)

g. Cost of raw material used.

h. Rent on a factory building donated by the county, where the agreement calls for rent of $100,000 less $1 for each direct labor-hour worked in excess of 200,000 hours, but a minimum rental payment of $20,000 must be paid.

i. Use of a machine under a lease, where a minimum charge of $1,000 is paid for up to 400 hours of machine time. After 400 hours of machine time, an additional charge of $2 per hour is paid up to a maximum charge of $2,000 per period.

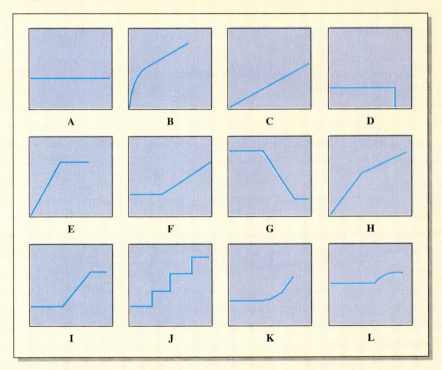

2. How would a knowledge of cost behavior patterns such as those above be of help to a manager in analyzing the cost structure of his or her firm?

(CPA, adapted)

Scattergraph Method of Cost Analysis   Molina Company has several autos that have   **P6–18** been purchased for use by the sales staff. All expenses of operating these autos have been entered into an "Automobile Expense" account on the company's books. Along with this record of expenses, the company has also kept a careful record of the number of miles the autos have been driven each month.

The company's records of miles driven and total auto expenses over the past 10 months are given below:

Month	Total Mileage (000)	Total Cost
January	4	$3,000
February	8	3,700
March	7	3,300
April	12	4,000
May	6	3,300
June	11	3,900
July	14	4,200
August	10	3,600
September	13	4,100
October	15	4,400

Molina Company's president wants to know the cost of operating the fleet of cars in terms of the fixed monthly cost and the variable cost per mile driven.

Required 1. Prepare a scattergraph using the data given above. Place cost on the vertical axis and activity (miles driven) on the horizontal axis. Fit a regression line to the plotted points by simple visual inspection.

2. By analyzing your scattergraph, compute the approximate fixed cost per month and the approximate variable cost per mile driven.

P6–19 **Least-Squares Method of Cost Analysis** (Appendix D) Refer to the data for Molina Company in P6–18.

Required 1. By use of the least-squares method, determine the variable and fixed cost elements associated with the company's fleet of autos. (Since the "Total mileage" is in thousands of miles, the variable rate you compute will also be in thousands of miles. The rate can be left in this form, or you can convert it to a per mile basis by dividing the rate you get by 1,000.)

2. From the data in (3) above, express the cost formula for auto use in the linear equation form $Y = a + bX$.

P6–20 **Manufacturing Statements; High-Low Method of Cost Analysis** Amfac Company manufactures a single product. The company keeps careful records of manufacturing activities from which the following information has been extracted:

	Level of Activity	
	March—Low	June—High
Equivalent number of units produced	6,000	9,000
Cost of goods manufactured	$168,000	$257,000
Work in process inventory, beginning	9,000	32,000
Work in process inventory, ending	15,000	21,000
Direct materials cost per unit	6	6
Direct labor cost per unit	10	10
Manufacturing overhead cost, total	?	?

The company's manufacturing overhead cost consists of both variable and fixed cost elements. To have data available for planning, management wants to determine how much of the overhead cost is variable with units produced and how much of it is fixed per month.

Required 1. For both March and June, determine the amount of manufacturing overhead cost added to production. The company had no under- or overapplied overhead in either month. (Hint: A useful way to proceed might be to construct a schedule of cost of goods manufactured.)

2. By means of the high-low method of cost analysis, determine the cost formula for manufacturing overhead. Express the variable portion of the formula in terms of a variable rate per unit of product.

3. If 7,000 units are produced during a month, what would be the cost of goods manufactured? (Assume that work in process inventories do not change and that there is no under- or overapplied overhead cost for the month.)

Least-Squares Analysis; Contribution Income Statement   (Appendix D) Milden Com-   **P6–21**
pany has an exclusive franchise to purchase a product from the manufacturer and distribute
it on the retail level. As an aid in planning, the company has decided to start using the
contribution approach to the income statement internally. To have data to prepare such a
statement, the company has analyzed its expenses and developed the following cost formulas:

Costs	Cost Formula
Cost of goods sold.	$35 per unit sold
Advertising expense	$210,000 per quarter
Sales commissions.	6% of sales
Shipping expense	?
Administrative salaries.	$145,000 per quarter
Insurance expense.	$9,000 per quarter
Depreciation expense	$76,000 per quarter

Management has concluded that shipping expense is a mixed cost, containing both
variable and fixed cost elements. Units sold and the related shipping expense over the last
eight quarters are given below:

Quarter	Units Sold (000)	Shipping Expense
19x1:		
First.	10	$119,000
Second	16	175,000
Third	18	190,000
Fourth.	15	164,000
19x2:		
First.	11	130,000
Second	17	185,000
Third	20	210,000
Fourth.	13	147,000

Milden Company's president would like a cost formula derived for shipping expense so
that a budgeted income statement using the contribution approach can be prepared for the
next quarter.

1. Using the least-squares method, derive a cost formula for shipping expense. (Since the   *Required*
   "Units Sold" above are in thousands of units, the variable rate you compute will also
   be in thousands of units. It can be left in this form, or you can convert your variable
   rate to a per unit basis by dividing it by 1,000.)
2. In the first quarter, 19x3, the company plans to sell 12,000 units at a selling price of
   $100 per unit. Prepare an income statement for the quarter, using the contribution
   format.

Mixed Cost Analysis; High-Low and Scattergraph Methods   Pleasant View Hospital   **P6–22**
has just hired a new chief administrator who is anxious to employ sound management and
planning techniques in the business affairs of the hospital. Accordingly, she has directed
her assistant to summarize the cost structure existing in the various departments so that
data will be available for planning purposes.
   The assistant is unsure how to classify the utilities costs in the radiology department
since these costs do not exhibit either strictly variable or fixed cost behavior. Utilities costs
are very high in the department due to a CAT scanner that draws a large amount of power
and is kept running at all times. The scanner can't be turned off due to the long warm-up
period required for its use. When the scanner is used to scan a patient, it consumes an
additional burst of power. The assistant has accumulated the following data on utilities
costs and use of the scanner since the first of the year.

Month	Number of Scans	Utilities Cost
January	60	$2,200
February	70	2,600
March	90	2,900
April	120	3,300
May	100	3,000
June	130	3,600
July	150	4,000
August	140	3,600
September	110	3,100
October	80	2,500

The chief administrator has informed her assistant that the utilities cost is probably a mixed cost that will have to be broken down into its variable and fixed cost elements by use of a scattergraph. The assistant feels, however, that if an analysis of this type is necessary, then the high-low method should be used, since it is easier and quicker. The controller has suggested that there may be a better approach. (See Problem 6–23 for further use of these data.)

Required
1. Using the high-low method, determine the cost formula for utilities. Express the formula in the form $Y = a + bX$. (The variable rate should be stated in terms of cost per scan.)
2. Prepare a scattergraph by plotting the above data on a graph. (The number of scans should be placed on the horizontal axis, and utilities cost should be placed on the vertical axis.) Fit a regression line to the plotted points by visual inspection, and determine the cost formula for utilities.

P6–23 Least-Squares Method of Cost Analysis   (Appendix D) Refer to the data for Pleasant View Hospital in P6–22.

Required
1. Using the least-squares method, calculate the cost formula for utilities. Express the formula in the form $Y = a + bX$. (Round the variable rate to two decimal places.)
2. Refer to the graph prepared in (2) of P6–22. Explain why in this case the high-low method would be the least accurate of the three methods in deriving a cost formula.

CASES

C6–24 Missing Data; Mixed Cost Analysis by Three Methods   (Appendix D) While arm wrestling at the office Christmas party, you accidently spilled the contents of a drink onto some papers on your desk. One of the papers contained an analysis of a mixed cost that the president had asked you to complete before leaving for the holidays. Unfortunately, the liquid from the drink obliterated much of your analysis, as shown below (the question marks indicate obliterated data):

Month	Units Sold (X)	Total Cost (Y)	?	?
January	3	$1,600	$ 4,800	9
February	5	?	?	?
March	?	3,200	25,600	?
April	9	3,700	33,300	81
May	7	?	?	?
June	?	?	18,000	36
July	?	?	9,600	?
Totals	?	$?	$126,000	?

(1) $\Sigma XY = a\Sigma X + b\Sigma?$
(2) $\Sigma Y = ?a + b\Sigma X$

(1) $\$126,000 = ?a + ?b$
(2) $\$\quad? \quad = ?a + ?b$

(1) $\qquad\qquad\qquad\qquad \$126,000 = ?a + ?b$
(2) Multiply by 6: $\qquad \$\quad? \quad = ?a + ?b$
$\qquad$ Subtract (2) from (1): $\$\quad? \quad = \qquad ?b$
$\qquad\qquad\qquad\qquad\qquad\quad \$\quad? \quad = b$

Therefore, the variable rate is **???** per unit sold. To compute the monthly fixed cost, substitute in equation (2):

$$\$\quad? \quad = ?a + ?b$$
$$\$\quad? \quad = ?a + \$12,600$$
$$\$\quad? \quad = ?a$$
$$\$1,000 = a$$

The fixed cost is therefore $1,000 per month.

Horrified at the accident, you realize that you will have to figure out the missing data before your commuter train leaves in 90 minutes. Working is particularly difficult with all of the merriment going on around you, but you are spurred on by the realization that the president is not an understanding person.

Before starting the reconstruction of the data, you remember that the total cost for May can be obtained by applying the cost formula (as derived by the least-squares method) to the month's activity. (That is, fixed cost plus variable rate times units sold.)

1. Copy all of the information above onto a clean, dry piece of paper. Complete the least-squares analysis by finding *all* items of missing data. (The president detests incomplete work.) *Required*

2. Since (1) above took only 45 minutes to complete and you still have another 45 minutes before your train leaves, you decide to "check out" your work by doing a high-low analysis of the data. Complete the high-low analysis, and state the cost formula derived by this analytical method.

3. Surprised that the cost formula by the high-low method is so different from that derived by the least-squares method, and still having 30 minutes before your train leaves, you decide to prepare a scattergraph as a final check on your work.
   a. Prepare a scattergraph, and fit a regression line to the plotted points by simple visual inspection.
   b. By analyzing the data on your scattergraph, compute the approximate fixed cost per month and the approximate variable rate per unit sold.

4. Look again at the graph prepared in (3). Explain why the cost formula derived by the high-low method is so different from the cost formula derived by the least-squares method.

Mixed Cost Analysis by Three Methods (Appendix D) The Ramon Company manufactures a wide range of products at several plant locations. The Franklin plant, which manufactures electrical components, has been experiencing difficulties with fluctuating monthly overhead costs. The fluctuations have made it difficult to estimate the level of overhead that will be incurred for any one month. **C6–25**

Management wants to be able to estimate overhead costs accurately in order to better plan its operational and financial needs. A trade association publication to which Ramon Company subscribes indicates that for companies manufacturing electrical components, overhead tends to vary with direct labor-hours.

One member of the accounting staff has proposed that the cost behavior pattern of the overhead costs be determined. Then overhead costs could be predicted from the budgeted direct labor-hours.

Another member of the accounting staff has suggested that a good starting place for determining the cost behavior pattern of overhead costs would be an analysis of historical data. The historical cost behavior pattern would provide a basis for estimating future overhead costs. The methods that have been proposed for determining the cost behavior pattern include the high-low method, the scattergraph method, simple linear regression, multiple regression, and exponential smoothing. Of these methods, Ramon Company has decided to employ the high-low method, the scattergraph method, and simple linear regression. Data on direct labor-hours and the respective overhead costs incurred have been collected for the past two years. The raw data are as follows:

	19x1		19x2	
Month	Direct Labor-Hours	Overhead Costs	Direct Labor-Hours	Overhead Costs
January	20,000	$84,000	21,000	$86,000
February	25,000	99,000	24,000	93,000
March	22,000	89,500	23,000	93,000
April	23,000	90,000	22,000	87,000
May	20,000	81,500	20,000	80,000
June	19,000	75,500	18,000	76,500
July	14,000	70,500	12,000	67,500
August	10,000	64,500	13,000	71,000
September	12,000	69,000	15,000	73,500
October	17,000	75,000	17,000	72,500
November	16,000	71,500	15,000	71,000
December	19,000	78,000	18,000	75,000

All equipment in the Franklin plant is leased under an arrangement calling for a flat fee up to 19,500 direct labor-hours of activity in the plant, after which lease charges are assessed on a hourly basis. Lease expense is a major item of overhead cost.

Required
1. Using the high-low method, determine the cost formula for overhead in the Franklin plant.
2. Repeat (1) above, this time using the least-squares method. Your assistant has computed the following amounts, which may be helpful in your analysis:

$$\Sigma X = 435,000$$
$$\Sigma Y = \$1,894,000$$
$$\Sigma XY = \$35,170,500,000$$
$$\Sigma X^2 = 8,275,000,000$$

3. Prepare a scattergraph, including on it all data for the two-year period. Fit a regression line to the plotted points by visual inspection. (Take care in how you fit your regression line; remember that it must reflect appropriate fixed and variable costs throughout the *entire* relevant range. In this part, however, it is not necessary to compute the fixed and variable cost elements.)
4. Assume that the Franklin plant works 22,500 direct labor-hours during a month. Compute the expected overhead cost for the month, using the cost formulas developed above with:
   a. The high-low method.
   b. The least-squares method.
   c. The scattergraph method [read the expected costs directly off the graph prepared in (3) above].
5. Of the three proposed methods, which one should the Ramon Company use to estimate monthly overhead costs in the Franklin plant? Explain fully, indicating the reasons why the other methods are less desirable.
6. Would the relevant range concept probably be more or less important in the Franklin plant than in most companies?

(CMA, adapted)

THE CENTRAL THEME:
PLANNING AND CONTROL

Part II

The management of Elgin Sweeper Company uses contribution format income statements for internal decision making. The company abandoned using income statements in the traditional format when it found that key financial relationships among products were being obscured.

Cost-Volume-Profit Relationships

LEARNING OBJECTIVES

After studying Chapter 7, you should be able to:

1 Explain how changes in activity affect contribution margin and net income.

2 Compute the contribution margin ratio (CM ratio) and use it to compute changes in contribution margin and net income.

3 Show the effects on contribution margin of changes in variable costs, fixed costs, selling price, and volume.

4 Compute the break-even point by both the equation method and the unit contribution method.

5 Prepare a cost-volume-profit (CVP) graph, and explain the significance of each of its components.

6 Use the CVP formulas to determine the activity level needed to achieve a desired target net profit figure.

7 Compute the margin of safety (MS), and explain its significance.

8 Compute the degree of operating leverage at a particular level of sales, and explain how the degree of operating leverage can be used to predict changes in net income.

9 Compute the break-even point for a multiple product company, and explain the effects of shifts in the sales mix on contribution margin and the break-even point.

10 Define or explain the key terms listed at the end of the chapter.

Chapter 7

C ost-volume-profit (CVP) analysis is one of the most powerful tools that managers have at their command. It helps them understand the interrelationship between cost, volume, and profit in an organization by focusing on interactions between the following five elements:

1. Prices of products.
2. Volume or level of activity.
3. Per unit variable costs.
4. Total fixed costs.
5. Mix of products sold.

Because CVP analysis helps managers understand the interrelationship between cost, volume, and profit, it is a key factor in many business decisions. These decisions include, for example, what products to manufacture or sell, what pricing policy to follow, what marketing strategy to employ, and what type of productive facilities to acquire. The CVP concept is so pervasive in managerial accounting that it touches on virtually everything a manager does. Because of its wide range of usefulness, CVP analysis is undoubtedly the best tool the manager has for discovering the untapped profit potential that may exist in an organization.

THE BASICS OF COST-VOLUME-PROFIT (CVP) ANALYSIS

Our study of CVP analysis begins where our study of cost behavior in the preceding chapter left off—with the contribution income statement. The contribution income statement has a number of interesting characteristics that can be helpful to the manager in trying to judge the impact on profits of changes in selling price, cost, or volume. To demonstrate these characteristics, we shall use the following income statement of Norton Company, a small manufacturer of microwave ovens:

NORTON COMPANY
Contribution Income Statement
For the Month of June 19x1

	Total	Per Unit
Sales (400 ovens)	$100,000	$250
Less variable expenses. . . .	60,000	150
Contribution margin	40,000	$100
Less fixed expenses	35,000	
Net income	$ 5,000	

For purposes of discussion, we shall assume that Norton Company produces only one model of oven.

Notice that the company expresses its sales, variable expenses, and contribution margin on a per unit basis as well as in total. This is commonly done on those income statements prepared for management's use internally, since, as we shall see, it facilitates profitability analysis.

Contribution Margin

Objective 1
Explain how changes in activity affect contribution margin and net income.

As explained in Chapter 6, contribution margin is the amount remaining from sales revenue after variable expenses have been deducted. Thus, it is the amount available to cover fixed expenses and then to provide profits for the period. Notice the sequence here—contribution margin is used *first* to cover the fixed expenses, and then whatever remains goes toward profits. If the contribution margin is not sufficient to cover the fixed expenses, then a loss occurs for the period. To illustrate, assume that by the middle of a particular month Norton Company has been able to sell only one oven. At that point, the company's income statement will appear as follows:

	Total	Per Unit
Sales (1 oven)	$ 250	$250
Less variable expenses	150	150
Contribution margin	100	$100
Less fixed expenses	35,000	
Net loss	$(34,900)	

For each additional oven that the company is able to sell during the month, $100 more in contribution margin will become available to help cover the fixed expenses. If a second oven is sold, for example, then the total contribution margin will increase by $100 (to a total of $200) and the company's loss will decrease by $100, to $34,800:

	Total	Per Unit
Sales (2 ovens)	$ 500	$250
Less variable expenses	300	150
Contribution margin	200	$100
Less fixed expenses	35,000	
Net loss	$(34,800)	

If enough ovens can be sold to generate $35,000 in contribution margin, then all of the fixed costs will be covered and the company will have managed to at least *break even* for the month—that is, to show neither profit nor loss but just cover all of its costs. To reach this **break-even point,** the company will have to sell 350 ovens in a month, since each oven sold yields $100 in contribution margin:

	Total	Per Unit
Sales (350 ovens)	$87,500	$250
Less variable expenses	52,500	150
Contribution margin	35,000	$100
Less fixed expenses	35,000	
Net income	$ 0	

Computation of the break-even point is discussed in detail later in the chapter; for the moment, we can note that it can be defined either as the point where total sales revenue equals total expenses, variable and fixed, or as the point where total contribution margin equals total fixed expenses.

Once the break-even point has been reached, net income will increase by the unit contribution margin for each additional unit sold. If 351 ovens are sold in a month, for example, then we can expect that the net income for the month will be $100, since the company will have sold 1 oven more than the number needed to break even:

	Total	Per Unit
Sales (351 ovens)	$87,750	$250
Less variable expenses	52,650	150
Contribution margin	35,100	$100
Less fixed expenses	35,000	
Net income	$ 100	

If 352 ovens are sold (2 ovens above the break-even point), then we can expect that the net income for the month will be $200, and so forth. To know what the profits will be at various levels of activity, therefore, it is not necessary for a manager to prepare a whole series of income statements. The manager can simply take the number of units to be sold over the break-even point and multiply that number by the unit contribution margin. The result will represent the anticipated profits for the period. Or, if an increase in sales is planned and the manager wants to know what the impact of that increase will be on profits, he or she can simply multiply the increase in units sold by the unit contribution margin. The result will be the expected increase in profits. To illustrate, if Norton Company is selling 400 ovens per month and plans to increase sales to 425 ovens per month, the impact on profits will be:

Increased number of ovens to be sold	25
Contribution margin per oven	×$100
Increase in net income	$2,500

As proof:

	Sales Volume		Difference	
	400 Ovens	425 Ovens	25 Ovens	Per Unit
Sales	$100,000	$106,250	$6,250	$250
Less variable expenses	60,000	63,750	3,750	150
Contribution margin	40,000	42,500	2,500	$100
Less fixed expenses	35,000	35,000	–0–	
Net income	$ 5,000	$ 7,500	$2,500	

To summarize the series of examples given above, we can say that the contribution margin first covers an organization's fixed expenses. We can further say that as sales are made, the potential loss represented by these fixed expenses is reduced successively by the unit contribution margin for each incremental unit sold up to the break-even point. Once the break-even point has been reached, then overall net income is increased by the unit contribution margin for each incremental unit sold from that point forward.

Objective 2
Compute the contribution margin ratio (CM ratio) and use it to compute changes in contribution margin and net income.

Contribution Margin Ratio (CM Ratio)

In addition to being expressed on a per unit basis, revenues, variable expenses, and contribution margin for Norton Company can also be expressed on a percentage basis:

	Total	Per Unit	Percent
Sales (400 ovens)	$100,000	$250	100
Less variable expenses	60,000	150	60
Contribution margin	40,000	$100	40
Less fixed expenses	35,000		
Net income	$ 5,000		

The percentage of contribution margin to total sales is referred to either as the **contribution margin ratio (CM ratio)** or as the **profit-volume ratio (P/V ratio).** This ratio is computed as follows:

$$\frac{\text{Contribution margin}}{\text{Sales}} = \text{CM ratio}$$

For Norton Company the computations are:

$$\frac{\text{Total contribution margin, \$40,000}}{\text{Total sales, \$100,000}} = 40\% \text{ or } \frac{\text{Per unit contribution margin, \$100}}{\text{Per unit sales, \$250}} = 40\%$$

The CM ratio is extremely useful in that it shows how the contribution margin will be affected by a given dollar change in total sales. To illustrate, notice that Norton Company has a CM ratio of 40 percent. This means that for each dollar increase in sales, total contribution margin will increase by 40 cents ($1 sales × CM ratio of 40 percent). Net income will also increase by 40 cents, assuming that there are no changes in fixed costs.

As this illustration suggests, *the impact on net income of any given dollar change in total sales can be computed in seconds by simply applying the CM ratio to the dollar change.* If Norton Company plans a $30,000 increase in sales during the coming month, for example, management can expect contribution margin to increase by $12,000 ($30,000 increased sales × CM ratio of 40 percent). As we noted above, net income will increase by a like amount if the fixed costs do not change. As proof:

	Sales Volume			
	Present	**Expected**	**Increase**	**Percent**
Sales	$100,000	$130,000	$30,000	100
Less variable expenses	60,000	78,000*	18,000	60
Contribution margin	40,000	52,000	12,000	40
Less fixed expenses	35,000	35,000	–0–	
Net income	$ 5,000	$ 17,000	$12,000	

* $130,000 × 60% = $78,000.

Many managers find the CM ratio easier to work with than the unit contribution margin figure, particularly where a company has multiple product lines. This is because an item in ratio form facilitates comparisons between products. Other things being equal, the manager will search out those product lines that have the highest CM ratios. The reason, of course, is that for a given dollar increase in sales these product lines will yield the greatest amount of contribution margin toward the covering of fixed costs and toward profits.

 FOCUS ON CURRENT PRACTICE

Elgin Sweeper Company, the leading manufacturer of street sweepers in North America, manufactures five distinct sweeper models in a single facility. Historically, the company has used the traditional format for the income statement, which shows cost of goods sold, gross margin, and so forth. In 1986, the company abandoned this format for internal use and adopted the contribution approach. By using the contribution approach, management has discovered that key differences exist between the five sweeper models. CM ratios differ by model due to differences in variable inputs. Also, due to differences in volume, the five models differ substantially in terms of the total amount of contribution margin generated each year. Income statements in the contribution format—with breakdowns of sales, contribution margin, and CM ratios by sweeper model—now serve as the basis for internal decision making by management.[1]

Some Applications of CVP Concepts

Objective 3
Show the effects on contribution margin of changes in variable costs, fixed costs, selling price, and volume.

The concepts that we have developed on the preceding pages have many applications in planning and decision making. We will now continue with the example of Norton Company (a manufacturer of microwave ovens) to illustrate some of these applications. Norton Company's basic cost and revenue data are:

	Per Unit	Percent
Sales price	$250	100
Less variable expenses	150	60
Contribution margin	$100	40

Recall that fixed expenses are $35,000 per month. We will use these data to show the effects of changes in variable costs, fixed costs, sales price, and sales volume on a company's profitability.

Change in Fixed Costs and Sales Volume   Assume that Norton Company is currently selling 400 ovens per month (monthly sales of $100,000). The sales manager feels that a $10,000 increase in the monthly advertising budget would increase monthly sales by $30,000. Should the advertising budget be increased?

Solution

Expected total contribution margin:	
$130,000 × 40% CM ratio	$52,000
Present total contribution margin:	
$100,000 × 40% CM ratio	40,000
Incremental contribution margin	12,000
Change in fixed costs:	
Less incremental advertising expense	10,000
Increased net income	$ 2,000

Yes, based on the information above and assuming that other factors in the company don't change, the advertising budget should be increased.

---

[1] John P. Callan, Wesley N. Tredup, and Randy S. Wissinger, "Elgin Sweeper Company's Journey toward Cost Management," *Management Accounting* 73, no. 1 (July 1991), p. 27; and telephone interviews with management.

Since in this case only the fixed costs and the sales volume change, the solution can be presented in an even shorter format, as follows:

Incremental contribution margin:	
$30,000 × 40% CM ratio	$12,000
Less incremental advertising expense	10,000
Increased net income	$ 2,000

Notice that this approach does not depend on a knowledge of what sales were previously. Also notice that it is unnecessary under either approach to prepare an income statement. Both of the solutions above involve an **incremental analysis** in that they consider only those items of revenue, cost, and volume that will change if the new program is implemented. Although in each case a new income statement could have been prepared, most managers would prefer the incremental approach. The reason is that it is simpler and more direct, and it permits the decision maker to focus attention on the specific items involved in the decision.

Change in Variable Costs and Sales Volume

Refer to the original data. Assume again that Norton Company is currently selling 400 ovens per month. Management is contemplating the use of higher-quality components in the manufacture of the ovens, which would increase variable costs (and thereby reduce the contribution margin) by $10 per oven. However, the sales manager predicts that the higher overall quality would increase sales to 480 ovens per month. Should the higher-quality components be used?

The $10 increase in variable costs will cause the unit contribution margin to decrease from $100 to $90.

Expected total contribution margin:	
480 ovens × $90	$43,200
Present total contribution margin:	
400 ovens × $100	40,000
Increase in total contribution margin	$ 3,200

Yes, based on the information above, the higher quality components should be used in the manufacture of the ovens. Since the fixed costs will not change, net income will increase by the $3,200 increase in contribution margin shown above.

Change in Fixed Cost, Sales Price, and Sales Volume

Refer to the original data. Assume again that Norton Company is currently selling 400 ovens per month. To increase sales, management would like to cut the selling price by $20 per oven and increase the advertising budget by $15,000 per month. Management feels that if these two steps are taken, unit sales will increase by 50 percent. Should the changes be made?

A decrease of $20 per oven in the selling price will cause the unit contribution margin to decrease from $100 to $80.

Expected total contribution margin:	
400 ovens × 150% × $80	$48,000
Present total contribution margin:	
400 ovens × $100	40,000
Incremental contribution margin	8,000
Change in fixed costs:	
Less incremental advertising expense	15,000
Reduction in net income	$ (7,000)

No, based on the information above, the changes should not be made. The same solution can be obtained by preparing comparative income statements:

| | Present 400 Ovens per Month | | Expected 600 Ovens per Month | | Difference |
	Total	Per Unit	Total	Per Unit	
Sales	$100,000	$250	$138,000	$230	$38,000
Less variable expenses	60,000	150	90,000	150	30,000
Contribution margin	40,000	$100	48,000	$ 80	8,000
Less fixed expenses	35,000		50,000*		15,000
Net income (loss)	$ 5,000		$ (2,000)		$(7,000)

* $35,000 + $15,000 = $50,000.

Notice that the answer is the same as that obtained by the incremental analysis above.

Change in Variable Cost, Fixed Cost, and Sales Volume

Refer to the original data. Assume again that Norton Company is currently selling 400 ovens per month. The sales manager would like to place the sales staff on a commission basis of $15 per oven sold, rather than on flat salaries that now total $6,000 per month. The sales manager is confident that the change will increase monthly sales by 15 percent. Should the change be made?

Solution   Changing the sales staff from a salaried basis to a commission basis will affect both fixed and variable costs. Fixed costs will decrease by $6,000, from $35,000 to $29,000. Variable costs will increase by $15, from $150 to $165, and the unit contribution margin will decrease from $100 to $85.

Expected total contribution margin:	
400 ovens × 115% × $85	$39,100
Present total contribution margin:	
400 ovens × $100	40,000
Decrease in total contribution margin	(900)
Change in fixed costs:	
Add salaries avoided if a commission is paid	6,000
Increase in net income.	$ 5,100

Yes, based on the information above, the changes should be made. Again, the same answer can be obtained by preparing comparative income statements:

| | Present 400 Ovens per Month | | Expected 460 Ovens per Month | | Difference: Increase or (Decrease) in Net Income |
	Total	Per Unit	Total	Per Unit	
Sales	$100,000	$250	$115,000*	$250	$ 15,000
Less variable expenses	60,000	150	75,900	165	(15,900)
Contribution margin	40,000	$100	39,100	$ 85	(900)
Less fixed expenses	35,000		29,000		6,000
Net income	$ 5,000		$ 10,100		$ 5,100

* 400 ovens × 115% = 460 ovens.
  460 ovens × $250 = $115,000.

Change in Regular Sales Price

Refer to the original data. Assume again that Norton Company is currently selling 400 ovens per month. The company has an opportunity to make a bulk sale of 150 ovens to a wholesaler if an acceptable price can be worked out. This sale would not disturb regular sales currently being made. What price per oven should be quoted to the wholesaler if Norton Company wants to increase its monthly profits by $3,000?

Solution

Variable cost per oven	$150
Desired profit per oven:	
$3,000 ÷ 150 ovens	20
Quoted price per oven	$170

Notice that no element of fixed cost is included in the computation. This is because Norton Company's regular business puts it beyond the break-even point, and the fixed costs are therefore covered. Thus, the quoted price on the special order only needs to be large enough to cover the variable costs involved with the order and to provide the desired $3,000 contribution margin. As shown above, this is $170 per unit, consisting of $150 in variable costs and $20 per unit in contribution margin.

If Norton Company had been operating at a loss rather than at a profit, how would the price on the new ovens have been computed? A loss would have meant that a portion of the fixed costs was not being covered by regular sales. Therefore, it would have been necessary to quote a price on the 150 new ovens that was high enough to include part or all of these unrecovered fixed costs (as represented by the loss), in addition to the variable costs and the desired profit on the sale.

To illustrate this point, assume that Norton Company is reporting a loss of $6,000 per month and that the company wants to turn this loss into a profit of $3,000 per month. Under these circumstances, the quoted price on the 150 new ovens would be computed as shown below:

Solution

Variable cost per oven	$150
Present net loss:	
$6,000 ÷ 150 ovens	40
Desired profit:	
$3,000 ÷ 150 ovens	20
Quoted price per oven	$210

The $210 price we have computed represents a substantial discount from the $250 regular selling price per oven. Thus, both the wholesaler and the company would benefit from the bulk order.

Importance of the Contribution Margin

As stated in the introduction to the chapter, CVP analysis seeks the most profitable combination of variable costs, fixed costs, selling price, and sales volume. The examples that we have just provided show that the effect on the contribution margin is a major consideration in deciding on the most profitable combination of these factors. We have seen that profits can sometimes be improved by reducing the contribution margin if fixed costs can be reduced by a greater amount. More commonly, however, we have seen that the way to improve profits is to increase the total contribution margin figure. Sometimes this can be done by reducing the selling price and thereby increasing volume; sometimes it can be done by increasing the fixed costs (such as advertising) and thereby increasing volume; and sometimes it can be done by trading off variable and fixed costs with appropriate changes in volume. Many other combinations of factors are possible.

The size of the unit contribution margin figure (and the size of the CM ratio) will have a heavy influence on what steps a company is willing to take to improve profits. For example, the greater the unit contribution margin for a product, the greater is the amount that a company will be willing to spend in order to increase sales of the product by a given percentage. This explains in part why companies with high unit contribution margins (such as auto manufacturers) advertise so heavily, while companies with low unit contribution margins (such as dishware manufacturers) tend to spend much less for advertising.

In short, the effect on the contribution margin holds the key to most cost-revenue decisions in a company.

BREAK-EVEN ANALYSIS

CVP analysis is sometimes referred to simply as break-even analysis. This is unfortunate because break-even analysis is just one part of the entire CVP concept. However, it is often a key part, and it can give the manager many insights into the data with which he or she is working.

As a basis for discussion, we will continue with the example of Norton Company. Recall that the selling price is $250 per oven, the variable expenses are $150 per oven, and the fixed costs total $35,000 per month.

Break-Even Computations

Objective 4
Compute the break-even point by both the equation method and the unit contribution method.

Earlier in the chapter, we stated that the break-even point can be defined equally well as the point where total sales revenue equals total expenses, variable and fixed, or as the point where total contribution margin equals total fixed expenses. As suggested by these two definitions of the break-even point, break-even analysis can be approached in two ways—first, by the *equation method;* and second, by the *unit contribution method.*

The Equation Method

The **equation method** centers on the contribution approach to the income statement illustrated earlier in the chapter. The format of this statement can be expressed in equation form as:

$$\text{Sales} - (\text{Variable expenses} + \text{Fixed expenses}) = \text{Profits}$$

Rearranging this equation slightly yields the following equation, which is widely used in CVP analysis:

$$\text{Sales} = \text{Variable expenses} + \text{Fixed expenses} + \text{Profits}$$

At the break-even point, profits will be zero. Therefore, the break-even point can be computed by finding that point where sales just equal the total of the variable expenses plus the fixed expenses. For Norton Company, this would be:

$$\text{Sales} = \text{Variable expenses} + \text{Fixed expenses} + \text{Profits}$$

$$\$250X = \$150X + \$35,000 + \$0$$
$$\$100X = \$35,000$$
$$X = 350 \text{ ovens}$$

where:

$$X = \text{Break-even point in ovens}$$
$$\$250 = \text{Unit sales price}$$
$$\$150 = \text{Unit variable expenses}$$
$$\$35,000 = \text{Total fixed expenses}$$

After the break-even point in units sold has been computed, the break-even point in sales dollars can be computed by multiplying the break-even level of units by the sales price per unit:

$$350 \text{ ovens} \times \$250 = \$87,500$$

At times, the *dollar* relationship between variable expenses and sales may not be known. In these cases, if one knows the *percentage* relationship between variable expenses and sales, then the break-even point can still be computed, as follows:

$$\text{Sales} = \text{Variable expenses} + \text{Fixed expenses} + \text{Profits}$$

$$X = 0.60X + \$35,000 + \$0$$
$$0.40X = \$35,000$$
$$X = \$87,500$$

where:

X = Break-even point in sales dollars
0.60 = Variable expenses as a percentage of sales
$\$35,000$ = Total fixed expenses

Firms often have data available only in percentage form, and the approach we have just illustrated must then be used to find the break-even point. Notice that use of percentages in the equation yields a break-even point in sales dollars rather than in units sold. The break-even point in units sold would be:

$$\$87,500 \div \$250 = 350 \text{ ovens}$$

The Unit Contribution Method   The **unit contribution method** is actually just a variation of the equation method already described. The approach centers on the idea discussed earlier that each unit sold provides a certain amount of contribution margin that goes toward the covering of fixed costs. To find how many units must be sold to break even, one must divide the total fixed costs by the contribution margin being generated by each unit sold:

$$\frac{\text{Fixed expenses}}{\text{Unit contribution margin}} = \text{Break-even point}$$

Each oven that Norton Company sells generates a contribution margin of $100 ($250 selling price, less $150 variable expenses). Since the total fixed expenses are $35,000, the break-even point is:

$$\frac{\text{Fixed expenses}}{\text{Unit contribution margin}} = \frac{\$35,000}{\$100} = 350 \text{ ovens}$$

If only the percentage relationship between variable expenses, contribution margin, and sales is known, the computation becomes:

$$\frac{\text{Fixed expenses}}{\text{CM ratio}} = \frac{\$35,000}{40\%} = \$87,500$$

This approach to break-even analysis is particularly useful in those situations where a company has multiple product lines and wishes to compute a single break-even point for the company as a whole. More is said on this point in a later section titled The Concept of Sales Mix.

CVP Relationships in Graphic Form

Objective 5
Prepare a
cost-volume-profit (CVP)
graph, and explain the
significance of each of its
components.

The cost data relating to Norton Company's microwave ovens can be expressed in graphic form by preparing a **cost-volume-profit (CVP) graph.** A CVP graph can be very helpful in that it highlights CVP relationships over wide ranges of activity and gives managers a perspective that can be obtained in no other way. Such graphing is sometimes referred to as preparing a **break-even chart.** This is correct to the extent that the break-even point is clearly shown on the graph. The reader should be aware, however, that a graphing of CVP data highlights CVP relationships throughout the *entire* relevant range—not just at the break-even point.

Preparing the CVP Graph   Preparing a CVP graph (sometimes called a *break-even chart*) involves three steps. These steps are keyed to the graph in Exhibit 7–1.

1.   Draw a line parallel to the volume axis to represent total fixed expenses. For Norton Company, total fixed expenses are $35,000.
2.   Choose some volume of sales, and plot the point representing total expenses (fixed and variable) at the activity level you have selected. In Exhibit 7–1, we have chosen a volume of 600 ovens. Total expenses at that activity level would be:

Fixed expenses	$ 35,000
Variable expenses (600 ovens × $150)	90,000
Total expenses	$125,000

After the point has been plotted, draw a line through it back to the point where the fixed expenses line intersects the dollars axis.
3.   Again choose some volume of sales, and plot the point representing total sales dollars at the activity level you have selected. In Exhibit 7–1, we have again chosen a volume of 600 ovens. Sales at that activity level total $150,000 (600 ovens × $250). Draw a line through this point back to the origin.

EXHIBIT 7–1

Preparing the CVP Graph

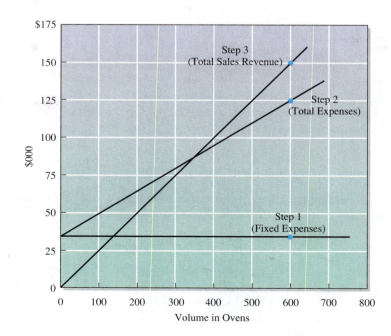

The interpretation of the completed CVP graph is given in Exhibit 7–2. The anticipated profit or loss at any given level of sales is measured by the vertical distance between the total revenue line (sales) and the total expenses line (variable expenses plus fixed expenses).

The break-even point is where the total revenue and total expenses lines cross. The break-even point of 350 ovens in Exhibit 7–2 agrees with the break-even point obtained for Norton Company in earlier computations.

An Alternative Format   Some managers prefer an alternative format to the CVP graph, as illustrated in Exhibit 7–3.

Note that the total revenue and total expenses lines are the same as in Exhibit 7–2. However, the new format in Exhibit 7–3 places the fixed expenses above the variable expenses, thereby allowing the contribution margin to be depicted on the graph. Otherwise, the graphs in the two exhibits are the same.

The Profitgraph   Another approach to the CVP graph is presented in Exhibit 7–4. This approach, called a **profitgraph,** is preferred by some managers because it focuses more directly on how profits change with changes in volume. It has the added advantage of being easier to interpret than the more traditional approaches illustrated in Exhibits 7–2 and 7–3. It has the disadvantage, however, of not showing as clearly how costs are affected by changes in the level of sales.

The profitgraph is constructed in two steps. These steps are illustrated in Exhibit 7–4.

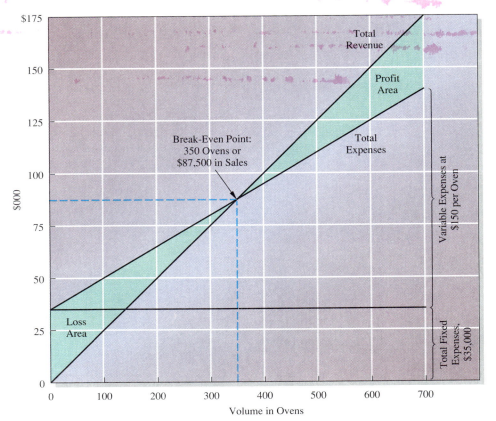

EXHIBIT 7–2
The Completed CVP Graph

EXHIBIT 7–3
Alternative Format to the CVP Graph

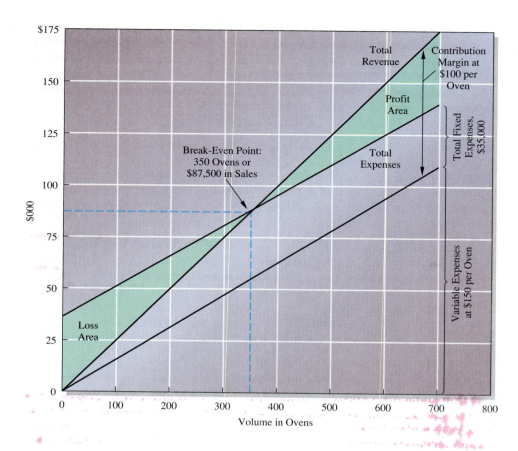

EXHIBIT 7–4
Preparing the Profitgraph

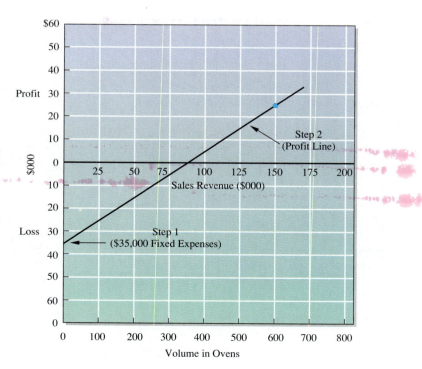

EXHIBIT 7–5
The Completed
Profitgraph

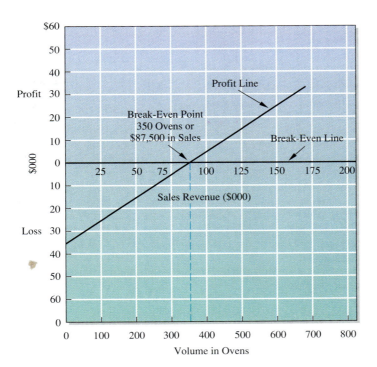

1. Locate total fixed expenses on the vertical axis, assuming zero level of activity. This point will be in the "loss area," equal to the total fixed expenses expected for the period.
2. Plot a point representing expected profit or loss at any chosen level of sales. In Exhibit 7–4, we have chosen to plot the point representing expected profits at a sales volume of 600 ovens. At this activity level, expected profits are:

Sales (600 ovens × $250)	$150,000
Less variable expenses (600 ovens × $150)	90,000
Contribution margin	60,000
Less fixed expenses	35,000
Net income	$ 25,000

After this point is plotted, draw a line through it back to the point on the vertical axis representing total fixed expenses. The interpretation of the completed profitgraph is given in Exhibit 7–5. The break-even point is where the profit line crosses the break-even line.

The vertical distance between the two lines represents the expected profit or loss at any given level of sales volume. This vertical distance can be translated directly into dollars by referring to the profit and loss figures on the vertical axis.

Target Net Profit Analysis

CVP formulas can be used to determine the sales volume needed to achieve a target net profit figure. Suppose that Norton Company would like to earn a target net profit of $40,000 per month. How many ovens would have to be sold?

Objective 6
Use the CVP formulas to determine the activity level needed to achieve a desired target net profit figure.

FOCUS ON CURRENT PRACTICE ◆

In 1986, USX Corporation closed its Geneva Steel facility, which consisted of an antiquated plant located in Utah that was losing millions each year. A year later the Geneva Steel facility was purchased by two attorneys who managed to negotiate a purchase price of $40 million for a plant that had cost $47 million to build in the 1940s. The attorneys, along with a newly assembled staff of managers and accountants, immediately set about to slash operating costs. Lower cost contracts were negotiated for *all* of the plant's variable costs, including iron ore, electricity, labor, and transportation. In addition, fixed costs were driven sharply downward through a reduction in the number of white-collar and other support workers.

With lower variable costs, the contribution margin per ton of steel rose sharply. This factor, combined with lower fixed costs, drove the plant's break-even point downward to a level where the company made a profit in the first year of its operation. Moreover, this profit was achieved in a year in which the steel industry was in a slump and competitors were struggling. By continuing to pay careful attention to CVP factors, the company has been earning as much as $53 per ton for steel shipped, which is three times as much as its "big steel" competitors.[2]

The CVP Equation   One approach to the solution would be to use the CVP equation. The target net profit requirement can be added into the basic equation data, and the solution will then show what level of sales is necessary to cover all expenses and yield the target net profit.

$$\text{Sales} = \text{Variable expenses} + \text{Fixed expenses} + \text{Profits}$$

$$\$250X = \$150X + \$35,000 + \$40,000$$
$$\$100X = \$75,000$$
$$X = 750 \text{ ovens}$$

where:

$$X = \text{Number of ovens sold}$$
$$\$250 = \text{Unit sales price}$$
$$\$150 = \text{Unit variable expenses}$$
$$\$35,000 = \text{Total fixed expenses}$$
$$\$40,000 = \text{Target net profit}$$

Thus, the target net profit can be achieved by selling 750 ovens per month, which represents $187,500 in total sales ($250 × 750 ovens).

The Unit Contribution Approach   A second approach would be to expand the unit contribution formula to include the target net profit requirement:

$$\frac{\$35,000 \text{ fixed expenses} + \$40,000 \text{ target net profit}}{\$100 \text{ contribution margin per oven}} = 750 \text{ ovens}$$

---

[2] "Miracle Mill: Utah's Geneva Steel, Once Called Hopeless, Is Racking Up Profits," *The Wall Street Journal*, November 20, 1991, p. 1.

This approach is simpler and more direct than using the CVP equation. In addition, it shows clearly that once the fixed costs are covered, the unit contribution margin is fully available for meeting profit requirements.

The Margin of Safety (MS)

The **margin of safety (MS)** can be defined as the excess of budgeted (or actual) sales over the break-even volume of sales. It states the amount by which sales can drop before losses begin to be incurred. The formula for its calculation is:

Objective 7
Compute the margin of safety (MS), and explain its significance.

$$\text{Total sales} - \text{Break-even sales} = \text{Margin of safety (MS)}$$

Computations involving the MS are presented in Exhibit 7–6. Notice that the two companies in the exhibit have equal sales and net income figures but that Alpha Company has an MS of $40,000, whereas Beta Company has an MS of only $20,000. The difference in the MS can be traced to the fact that the two companies have very different cost structures. Beta Company has higher fixed costs and thus will incur losses more quickly than Alpha Company if sales drop off. As indicated by the MS, if sales drop by only $20,000, Beta Company will be at its break-even point, whereas sales can drop by $40,000 before Alpha Company will be at its break-even point.

The MS can also be expressed in percentage form. This percentage is obtained by dividing the MS in dollar terms by total sales:

$$\frac{\text{MS in dollars}}{\text{Total sales}} = \text{MS percentage}$$

Exhibit 7–6 contains the MS expressed in percentage form for both Alpha Company and Beta Company. The MS can also be expressed in terms of units of product (if a company is a single-product firm) by dividing the MS in dollars by the unit selling price.

If the MS is low, as in Beta Company, what does management do to correct the problem? There is no universal answer to this question, other than to point out that management's efforts must be directed toward either reducing the break-even

	Alpha Company		Beta Company	
	Amount	Percent	Amount	Percent
Sales	$200,000	100	$200,000	100
Less variable expenses	150,000	75	100,000	50
Contribution margin.	50,000	25	100,000	50
Less fixed expenses	40,000		90,000	
Net income	$ 10,000		$ 10,000	
Break-even point:				
$40,000 ÷ 25%	$160,000			
$90,000 ÷ 50%			$180,000	
MS in dollars (total sales less break-even sales):				
$200,000 − $160,000	40,000			
$200,000 − $180,000			20,000	
MS in percentage form (MS in dollars divided by total sales):				
$40,000 ÷ $200,000	20%			
$20,000 ÷ $200,000			10%	

EXHIBIT 7–6
Margin of Safety (MS)

point or increasing the overall level of sales in the company. In short, the MS is a tool designed to point out a problem (or the lack of one), the solution to which must be found by analyzing the company's cost structure and by applying the general CVP techniques that have been illustrated in this chapter.

CVP CONSIDERATIONS IN CHOOSING A COST STRUCTURE

We stated in the preceding chapter that *cost structure* refers to the relative proportion of fixed and variable costs in an organization. We also stated that an organization often has some latitude in trading off between fixed and variable costs. Such a trade-off is possible, for example, by automating facilities rather than using direct labor workers.

In this section, we discuss various considerations involved in choosing a cost structure. We look first at the matter of cost structure and profit stability, and then we discuss the effect of cost structure on an important concept known as *operating leverage*. Finally, we conclude the section by comparing capital-intensive (automated) and labor-intensive companies in terms of the potential risks and rewards that are inherent in the cost structures these companies have chosen.

Cost Structure and Profit Stability

When a manager has some latitude in trading off between fixed and variable costs, which cost structure is better—high variable costs and low fixed costs, or the opposite? No categorical answer to this question is possible; we can simply note that there may be advantages either way, depending on the specific circumstances involved. To show what we mean by this statement, refer to the income statements given below for Company X and Company Y. Notice that the two companies have very different cost structures—Company X has high variable costs and low fixed costs, with the opposite true for Company Y.

	Company X		Company Y	
	Amount	Percent	Amount	Percent
Sales	$100,000	100	$100,000	100
Less variable expenses	60,000	60	30,000	30
Contribution margin	40,000	40	70,000	70
Less fixed expenses	30,000		60,000	
Net income	$ 10,000		$ 10,000	

The question as to which company has the better cost structure depends on many factors, including the long-run trend in sales, year-to-year fluctuations in the level of sales, and the attitude of the managers toward risk. If sales are expected to trend above $100,000 in the future, then Company Y probably has the better cost structure. The reason is that its CM ratio is higher, and its profits will therefore increase more rapidly as sales increase. To illustrate, assume that each company experiences a 10 percent increase in sales. The new income statements will be:

	Company X		Company Y	
	Amount	Percent	Amount	Percent
Sales	$110,000	100	$110,000	100
Less variable expenses	66,000	60	33,000	30
Contribution margin	44,000	40	77,000	70
Less fixed expenses	30,000		60,000	
Net income	$ 14,000		$ 17,000	

As we would expect, for the same dollar increase in sales, Company Y has experienced a greater increase in net income due to its higher CM ratio.

But what if $100,000 represents maximum sales for the two companies, and what if sales can be expected to drop well below $100,000 from time to time? Under these circumstances, Company X probably has the better cost structure. There are two reasons why this is so. First, due to its lower CM ratio, Company X will not lose contribution margin as rapidly as Company Y when sales fall off. Thus, Company X's income will tend to show more stability. Second, Company X has lower fixed costs, which suggests that it will not incur losses as quickly as Company Y in periods of sharply declining sales.

If sales fluctuate above and below $100,000, it becomes more difficult to tell which company is in a better position.

To summarize, Company Y will experience wider movements in net income as changes take place in sales, with greater profits in good years and greater losses in bad years. Company X will enjoy somewhat greater stability in net income, but it will do so at the risk of losing substantial profits if sales trend upward in the long run.

Operating Leverage

To the scientist, leverage explains how one is able to move a large object with a small force. To the manager, leverage explains how one is able to achieve a large increase in profits with only a small increase in sales and/or assets. One type of leverage that the manager uses to do this is known as *operating leverage*.[3]

Operating leverage is a measure of the extent to which fixed costs are being used in an organization. It is greatest in companies that have a high proportion of fixed costs in relation to variable costs. Conversely, operating leverage is lowest in companies that have a low proportion of fixed costs in relation to variable costs. If a company has high operating leverage (that is, a high proportion of fixed costs in relation to variable costs), then profits will be very sensitive to changes in sales. Just a small percentage increase (or decrease) in sales can yield a large percentage increase (or decrease) in profits.

Operating leverage can be illustrated by returning to the data given above for Company X and Company Y. Company Y has a higher proportion of fixed costs in relation to its variable costs than does Company X, although *total* costs are the same in the two companies at a $100,000 sales level. Observe that with a 10 percent increase in sales (from $100,000 to $110,000 in each company), net income in Company Y increases by 70 percent (from $10,000 to $17,000), whereas net

Objective 8
Compute the degree of operating leverage at a particular level of sales, and explain how the degree of operating leverage can be used to predict changes in net income.

---

[3] There are two types of leverage—operating and financial. Financial leverage is discussed in Chapter 18.

income in Company X increases by only 40 percent (from $10,000 to $14,000). Thus, for a 10 percent increase in sales, Company Y experiences a much greater percentage increase in profits than does Company X. The reason is that Company Y has greater operating leverage as a result of the greater amount of fixed cost used in the production and sale of its product.

The **degree of operating leverage** existing in a company at a given level of sales can be measured by the following formula:

$$\frac{\text{Contribution margin}}{\text{Net income}} = \text{Degree of operating leverage}$$

The degree of operating leverage is a measure, at a given level of sales, of how a percentage change in sales volume will affect profits. To illustrate, the degree of operating leverage existing in Company X and Company Y at a $100,000 sales level would be:

$$\text{Company X:} \quad \frac{\$40,000}{\$10,000} = 4$$

$$\text{Company Y:} \quad \frac{\$70,000}{\$10,000} = 7$$

By interpretation, these figures tell us that *for a given percentage change in sales* we can expect a change four times as great in the net income of Company X and a change seven times as great in the net income of Company Y. Thus, if sales increase by 10 percent, then we can expect the net income in Company X to increase by four times this amount, or by 40 percent, and the net income in Company Y to increase by seven times this amount, or by 70 percent.

	(1) Percent Increase in Sales	(2) Degree of Operating Leverage	(3) Percent Increase in Net Income (1) × (2)
Company X.	10	4	40
Company Y.	10	7	70

These computations explain why the 10 percent increase in sales mentioned earlier caused the net income of Company X to increase from $10,000 to $14,000 (an increase of 40 percent) and the net income of Company Y to increase from $10,000 to $17,000 (an increase of 70 percent).

The degree of operating leverage in a company is greatest at sales levels near the break-even point and decreases as sales and profits rise. This can be seen from the tabulation below, which shows the degree of operating leverage for Company X at various sales levels. (Data used earlier for Company X are shown in color.)

Sales	$75,000	$80,000	$100,000	$150,000	$225,000
Less variable expenses . . .	45,000	48,000	60,000	90,000	135,000
Contribution margin (a) . . .	30,000	32,000	40,000	60,000	90,000
Less fixed expenses.	30,000	30,000	30,000	30,000	30,000
Net income (b)	$ –0–	$ 2,000	$ 10,000	$ 30,000	$ 60,000
Degree of operating leverage, (a) ÷ (b)	∞	16	4	2	1.5

Thus, a 10 percent increase in sales would increase profits by only 15 percent (10% × 1.5) if the company were operating at a $225,000 sales level, as compared to the 40 percent increase we computed earlier at the $100,000 sales level. The degree of operating leverage will continue to decrease the farther the company moves from its break-even point. At the break-even point, the degree of operating leverage will be infinitely large ($30,000 contribution margin ÷ $0 net income = ∞).

The operating leverage concept provides the manager with a tool that can signify quickly what impact various percentage changes in sales will have on profits, without the necessity of preparing detailed income statements. As shown by our examples, the effects of operating leverage can be dramatic. If a company is fairly near its break-even point, then even small increases in sales can yield large increases in profits. *This explains why management will often work very hard for only a small increase in sales volume.* If the degree of operating leverage is 5, then a 6 percent increase in sales would translate into a 30 percent increase in profits.

EXHIBIT 7–7

CVP Comparison of Capital-Intensive (automated) and Labor-Intensive Companies

The comparison below is between two companies in the same industry that produce identical products for the same market. One of the companies has chosen to automate its facilities (capital intensive) and the other has chosen to rely heavily on direct labor inputs (labor intensive).

Item	Capital-Intensive (automated) Company	Labor-Intensive Company	Comments
The CM ratio for a given product will tend to be relatively. . .	High	Low	Variable costs in an automated company will tend to be lower than in a labor-intensive company, thereby causing the CM ratio for a given product to be higher.
Operating leverage will tend to be. . .	High	Low	Since operating leverage is a measure of the use of fixed costs in an organization, it will typically be higher in an automated company than in a company that relies on direct labor inputs.
In periods of increasing sales, net income will tend to increase. . .	Rapidly	Slowly	Since both operating leverage and product CM ratios tend to be high in automated companies, net income will increase rapidly after the break-even point has been reached.
In periods of decreasing sales, net income will tend to decrease. . .	Rapidly	Slowly	Just as net income increases rapidly in an automated company after the break-even point has been reached, so will net income decrease rapidly as sales decrease.
The volatility of net income with changes in sales will tend to be. . .	Greater	Less	Due to its higher operating leverage, the net income in an automated company will tend to be much more sensitive to changes in sales than in a labor-intensive company.
The break-even point will tend to be. . .	Higher	Lower	The break-even point in an automated company will tend to be higher because of its greater fixed costs.
The MS at a given level of sales will tend to be. . .	Lower	Higher	The MS in an automated company will tend to be lower because of its higher break-even point.
The latitude available to management in times of economic stress will tend to be. . .	Less	Greater	With high fixed costs in an automated company, management is more "locked in" and has fewer options when dealing with changing economic conditions.
The overall degree of risk associated with operating activities will tend to be. . .	Greater	Less	The risk factor is a summation of all the other factors listed above.

Automation: Risks and Rewards from a CVP Perspective

We have noted in preceding chapters that the move toward flexible manufacturing systems and other uses of automation has resulted in a shift toward greater fixed costs and less variable costs in organizations. In turn, this shift in cost structure has had an impact on product CM ratios, on the break-even point, and on other CVP factors in automated companies. Some of this impact has been favorable and some has not, as shown in Exhibit 7–7.

Many benefits can accrue from automation, but as shown in the exhibit, certain risks are introduced when a company moves toward greater amounts of fixed costs. These risks suggest that management must be careful as it automates to ensure that investment decisions are made in accordance with a carefully devised long-run operating strategy. This point is discussed further in Chapter 14 where we deal with investment decisions in an automated environment.

STRUCTURING SALES COMMISSIONS

Companies generally compensate salespeople by paying them either a commission based on sales or a salary plus a sales commission. Commissions based on sales dollars can lead to lower profits in a company. To illustrate, assume a company makes two products, model A and model B, as described below:

	Model	
	A	B
Selling price	$100	$150
Less variable expenses . . .	75	132
Contribution margin	$ 25	$ 18

Which model will salespeople push hardest if they are paid a commission of 10 percent of sales revenue? The answer is model B, since it has the higher selling price. On the other hand, from the standpoint of the company (assuming other factors are equal), will profits be greater if salespeople steer customers toward model A or model B? The answer this time is model A, since it has the higher contribution margin.

To eliminate such conflicts, some companies base salespersons' commissions on contribution margin generated rather than on sales generated. The reasoning goes like this: Since contribution margin represents the amount of sales revenue available to cover fixed expenses and profits, a firm's well-being will be maximized when contribution margin is maximized. By tying salespersons' commissions to contribution margin, the salespersons are automatically encouraged to concentrate on the element that is of most importance to the firm. There is no need to worry about what mix of products the salespersons sell because they will *automatically* sell the mix of products that will maximize the base on which their commissions are to be paid. That is, if salespersons are aware that their commissions will depend on the amount of contribution margin that they are able to generate, then they will use all of the experience, skill, and expertise at their command to sell the mix of products that will maximize the contribution margin base. In effect, by maximizing their own well-being, they automatically maximize the well-being of the firm.

As a further step, some firms deduct from the total contribution margin generated by salespersons the amount of the traveling, entertainment, and other expenses that are incurred. This encourages the salespersons to be sensitive to their own costs in the process of making sales.

THE CONCEPT OF SALES MIX

The preceding sections have given us some insights into the principles involved in CVP analysis, as well as some selected examples of how these principles are used by the manager. Before concluding our discussion, it will be helpful to consider one additional application of the ideas that we have developed—the use of CVP concepts in analyzing sales mix.

The Definition of Sales Mix

The term **sales mix** means the relative combination in which a company's products are sold. Managers try to achieve the combination, or mix, that will yield the greatest amount of profits. Most companies have several products, and often these products are not equally profitable. Where this is true, profits will depend to some extent on the sales mix that the company is able to achieve. Profits will be greater if high-margin items make up a relatively large proportion of total sales than if sales consist mostly of low-margin items.

Changes in the sales mix can cause interesting (and sometimes confusing) variations in a company's profits. A shift in the sales mix from high-margin items to low-margin items can cause total profits to decrease even though total sales may increase. Conversely, a shift in the sales mix from low-margin items to high-margin items can cause the reverse effect—total profits may increase even though total sales decrease. Given the possibility of these types of variations in profits, one measure of the effectiveness of a company's sales force is the sales mix that it is able to generate. It is one thing to achieve a particular sales volume; it is quite a different thing to sell the most profitable mix of products.

Sales Mix and Break-Even Analysis

If a company is selling more than one product, break-even analysis is somewhat more complex than discussed earlier in the chapter. The reason is that different products will have different selling prices, different costs, and different contribution margins. Consequently, the break-even point will depend on the mix in which the various products are sold. To illustrate, assume that a company has two product lines—line A and line B. For 19x1, the company's sales, costs, and break-even point were as shown in Exhibit 7–8.

Objective 9
Compute the break-even point for a multiple product company, and explain the effects of shifts in the sales mix on contribution margin and the break-even point.

	Line A		Line B		Total	
	Amount	**Percent**	**Amount**	**Percent**	**Amount**	**Percent**
Sales	$20,000	100	$80,000	100	$100,000	100
Less variable expenses	15,000	75	40,000	50	55,000	55
Contribution margin	$ 5,000	25	$40,000	50	45,000	45*
Less fixed expenses					27,000	
Net income					$ 18,000	

Computation of the break-even point:

$$\frac{\text{Fixed expenses, \$27,000}}{\text{Overall CM ratio, 45\%}} = \$60,000$$

* $45,000 ÷ $100,000 = 45%.

EXHIBIT 7–8
Multiple-Product Break-Even Analysis

	Line A		Line B		Total	
	Amount	Percent	Amount	Percent	Amount	Percent
Sales	$80,000	100	$20,000	100	$100,000	100
Less variable expenses	60,000	75	10,000	50	70,000	70
Contribution margin	$20,000	25	$10,000	50	30,000	30*
Less fixed expenses					27,000	
Net income					$ 3,000	

Computation of the break-even point:

$$\frac{\text{Fixed expenses, \$27,000}}{\text{Overall CM ratio, 30\%}} = \$90,000$$

* $30,000 ÷ $100,000 = 30%.

As shown in the exhibit, the break-even point is $60,000 in sales. This is computed by dividing the fixed costs by the company's *overall* CM ratio of 45 percent. But $60,000 in sales represents the break-even point for the company only so long as the sales mix does not change. *If the sales mix changes, then the break-even point will also change.* We can illustrate this by assuming that in 19x2, the following year, the sales mix shifts away from the more profitable line B (which has a 50 percent CM ratio) toward the less profitable line A (which has only a 25 percent CM ratio). Assume that sales in 19x2 are as shown in Exhibit 7–9.

Although sales have remained unchanged at $100,000, the sales mix is exactly the reverse of what it was in Exhibit 7–8, with the bulk of the sales now coming from line A rather than from line B. Notice that this shift in the sales mix has caused both the overall CM ratio and total profits to drop sharply from the prior year—the overall CM ratio has dropped from 45 percent in 19x1 to only 30 percent in 19x2, and net income has dropped from $18,000 to only $3,000. In addition, with the drop in the overall CM ratio, the company's break-even point is no longer $60,000 in sales. Since the company is now realizing less average contribution margin per dollar of sales, it takes more sales to cover the same amount of fixed costs. Thus, the break-even point has increased from $60,000 to $90,000 in sales per year.

In preparing a break-even analysis, some assumption must be made concerning the sales mix. Usually the assumption is that it will not change. However, if the manager knows that shifts in various factors (consumer tastes, market share, and so forth) are causing shifts in the sales mix, then these factors must be explicitly considered in any CVP computations. Otherwise, the manager may be making decisions on the basis of outmoded or faulty data.

Sales Mix and per Unit Contribution Margin

Sometimes the sales mix is measured in terms of the average per unit contribution margin. To illustrate, assume that a company has two products—X and Y. During 19x1 and 19x2, sales of products X and Y were as shown in Exhibit 7–10.

Two things should be noted about the data in this exhibit. First, note that the sales mix in 19x1 was 1,000 units of product X and 3,000 units of product Y. This sales mix yielded $7 in average per unit contribution margin.

Second, note that the sales mix in 19x2 shifted to 2,000 units for both products, although *total* sales remained unchanged at 4,000 units. This sales mix yielded $8 in average per unit contribution margin, an increase of $1 per unit over the prior year.

	Contribution Margin per Unit	Total Units Sold		Total Contribution Margin	
		19x1	19x2	19x1	19x2
Product X.	$10	1,000	2,000	$10,000	$20,000
Product Y.	6	3,000	2,000	18,000	12,000
		4,000	4,000	$28,000	$32,000
Average per unit contribution margin ($28,000 ÷ 4,000 units)				$7	
Average per unit contribution margin ($32,000 ÷ 4,000 units)					$8

EXHIBIT 7–10
Sales Mix and per Unit Contribution Margin Analysis

What caused the increase in average per unit contribution margin between the two years? The answer is the shift in sales mix toward the more profitable product X. Although total volume (in units) did not change, total and per unit contribution margin changed simply because of the change in sales mix.

LIMITING ASSUMPTIONS IN CVP ANALYSIS

Several limiting assumptions must be made when using data for CVP analysis. These assumptions are:

1. The behavior of both revenues and costs is linear throughout the entire relevant range. Economists would differ from this view. They would say that changes in volume will trigger changes in both revenues and costs in such a way that relationships will not remain linear.
2. Costs can be accurately divided into variable and fixed elements.
3. The sales mix is constant.
4. Inventories do not change; that is, the number of units produced equals the number of units sold (this assumption is considered further in Chapter 8).
5. Worker and machine productivity and efficiency do not change throughout the relevant range.
6. The value of a dollar received today is the same as the value of a dollar received in any future year (the time value of money is considered in Chapter 14).

SUMMARY

The analysis of CVP relationships is one of management's most significant responsibilities. Basically, it involves finding the most favorable combination of variable costs, fixed costs, selling price, sales volume, and mix of products sold. We have found that trade-offs are possible between types of costs, as well as between costs and selling price, and between selling price and sales volume. Sometimes these trade-offs are desirable, and sometimes they are not. CVP analysis provides the manager with a powerful tool for identifying those courses of action that will and will not improve profitability.

The concepts developed in this chapter represent a *way of thinking* rather than a mechanical set of procedures. That is, to put together the optimum combination of costs, selling price, and sales volume, the manager must be trained to think in terms of the unit contribution margin, the break-even point, the CM ratio, the sales mix, and the other concepts developed in this chapter. These concepts are dynamic in that a change in one will trigger changes in others—changes that may not be obvious on the surface. Only by learning to *think* in CVP terms can the manager move with assurance toward the firm's profit objectives.

REVIEW PROBLEM: CVP RELATIONSHIPS

Voltar Company manufactures and sells a telephone answering machine. The company's income statement for the most recent year is given below:

	Total	Per Unit	Percent
Sales (20,000 units)	$1,200,000	$60	100
Less variable expenses	900,000	45	?
Contribution margin	300,000	$15	?
Less fixed expenses	240,000		
Net income	$ 60,000		

Management is anxious to improve the company's profit performance and has asked for several items of information.

Required

1. Compute the company's CM ratio and variable expense ratio.
2. Compute the company's break-even point in both units and sales dollars. Use the equation method.
3. Assume that sales increase by $400,000 next year. If cost behavior patterns remain unchanged, by how much will the company's net income increase? Use the CM ratio to determine your answer.
4. Refer to the original data. Assume that next year management wants the company to earn a minimum profit of $90,000. How many units will have to be sold to meet this target profit figure?
5. Refer to the original data. Compute the company's MS (margin of safety) in both dollar and percentage form.
6. a. Compute the company's degree of operating leverage at the present level of sales.
   b. Assume that through a more intense effort by the sales staff the company's sales increase by 8 percent next year. By what percentage would you expect net income to increase? Use the operating leverage concept to obtain your answer.
   c. Prove your answer to (b) by preparing a new income statement showing an 8 percent increase in sales.
7. In an effort to increase sales and profits, management is considering the use of a higher-quality speaker in the answering machine. The higher-quality speaker would increase variable costs by $3 per unit, but management could eliminate one quality inspector who is paid a salary of $30,000 per year. The sales manager estimates that the higher-quality speaker would increase annual sales by at least 20 percent.
   a. Assuming that changes are made as described above, prepare a projected income statement for next year. Show data on a total, per unit, and percentage basis.
   b. Compute the company's new break-even point in both units and dollars of sales. Use the unit contribution method.
   c. Would you recommend that the changes be made?

Solution to Review Problem

1. CM ratio:

$$\frac{\text{Contribution margin, \$15}}{\text{Selling price, \$60}} = 25\%$$

Variable expense ratio:

$$\frac{\text{Variable expense, \$45}}{\text{Selling price, \$60}} = 75\%$$

2. Sales = Variable expenses + Fixed expenses + Profits

$60X = $45X + $240,000 + $0
$15X = $240,000
   X = 16,000 units; or at $60 per unit, $960,000

Alternative solution:

$$X = 0.75X + \$240,000 + \$0$$
$$0.25X = \$240,000$$
$$X = \$960,000; \text{ or at } \$60 \text{ per unit, } 16,000 \text{ units}$$

3. Increase in sales $400,000
    Multiply by the CM ratio . . . .   × 25%
    Expected increase in contribution margin . . . $100,000

Since the fixed expenses are not expected to change, net income will increase by the entire $100,000 increase in contribution margin computed above.

4. Equation method:

Sales = Variable expenses + Fixed expenses + Profits

$$\$60X = \$45X + \$240,000 + \$90,000$$
$$\$15X = \$330,000$$
$$X = 22,000 \text{ units}$$

Unit contribution method:

$$\frac{\text{Fixed expenses} + \text{Target profit}}{\text{Contribution margin per unit}} = \frac{\$240,000 + \$90,000}{\$15} = 22,000 \text{ units}$$

5. Total sales − Break-even sales = MS
    $1,200,000 − $960,000 = $240,000

$$\frac{\text{MS in dollars, \$240,000}}{\text{Total sales, \$1,200,000}} = 20\%$$

6. a. $\dfrac{\text{Contribution margin, \$300,000}}{\text{Net income, \$60,000}} = 5$ (degree of operating leverage)

    b. Expected increase in sales. 8%
        Degree of operating leverage. . . . .   × 5
        Expected increase in net income . . .   40%

    c. If sales increase by 8 percent, then 21,600 units (20,000 × 1.08 = 21,600) will be sold next year. The new income statement will be as follows:

	Total	Per Unit	Percent
Sales (21,600 units)	$1,296,000	$60	100
Less variable expenses	972,000	45	75
Contribution margin	324,000	$15	25
Less fixed expenses	240,000		
Net income.	$ 84,000		

Thus, the $84,000 expected net income for next year represents a 40 percent increase over the $60,000 net income earned during the current year:

$$\frac{\$84,000 - \$60,000 = \$24,000}{\$60,000} = 40\% \text{ increase}$$

Note from the income statement above that the increase in sales from 20,000 to 21,600 units has resulted in increases in *both* total sales and total variable expenses. It is a common error to overlook the increase in variable expenses when preparing a projected income statement such as this one!

7. a. A 20 percent increase in sales would result in 24,000 units being sold next year: 20,000 units × 1.20 = 24,000 units.

	Total	Per Unit	Percent
Sales (24,000 units)	$1,440,000	$60	100
Less variable expenses	1,152,000	48*	80*
Contribution margin	288,000	$12	20
Less fixed expenses	210,000†		
Net income	$ 78,000		

* $45 + $3 = $48; $48 ÷ $60 = 80%.
† $240,000 − $30,000 = $210,000.

Note that the change in per unit variable expenses results in a change in both the per unit contribution margin and the CM ratio.

b.
$$\frac{\text{Fixed expenses, } \$210,000}{\text{Contribution margin per unit, } \$12} = 17,500 \text{ units}$$

$$\frac{\text{Fixed expenses, } \$210,000}{\text{CM ratio, } 20\%} = \$1,050,000 \text{ break-even sales}$$

c. Yes, based on these data the changes should be made. The changes will increase the company's net income from the present $60,000 to $78,000 per year. Although the changes will also result in a higher break-even point (17,500 units as compared to the present 16,000 units), the company's MS will actually be wider than before:

Total sales − Break-even sales = MS
$1,440,000 − $1,050,000 = $390,000

As shown in (5) above, the company's present MS is only $240,000. Thus, several benefits will accrue from the proposed changes.

KEY TERMS FOR REVIEW

Objective 10
Define or explain the key terms listed at the end of the chapter.

Break-even chart   The relationship between revenues, costs, and level of activity in an organization presented in graphic form. Also see *Cost-volume-profit (CVP) graph*. (p. 288)

Break-even point   The level of activity at which an organization neither earns a profit nor incurs a loss. The break-even point can also be defined as the point where total revenue equals total costs and as the point where total contribution margin equals total fixed costs. (p. 279)

Contribution margin ratio (CM ratio)   The contribution margin per unit expressed as a percentage of the selling price per unit. This term is synonymous with *profit-volume ratio (P/V ratio)*. (p. 281)

Cost-volume-profit (CVP) graph   The relationship between revenues, costs, and level of activity in an organization, presented in graphic form. Also see *Break-even chart*. (p. 288)

Degree of operating leverage   A measure, at a given level of sales, of how a percentage change in sales volume will affect profits. The degree of operating leverage is computed by dividing contribution margin by net income. (p. 296)

Equation method   A method of computing the break-even point that relies on the equation: Sales = Variable expenses + Fixed expenses + Profits. (p. 286)

Incremental analysis   An analytical approach that focuses only on those items of revenue, cost, and volume that will change as a result of a decision in an organization. (p. 283)

Margin of safety (MS)   The excess of budgeted (or actual) sales over the break-even volume of sales. (p. 293)

Operating leverage   A measure of the extent to which fixed costs are being used in an organization. The greater the fixed costs, the greater is the operating leverage available and the greater is the sensitivity of net income to changes in sales. (p. 295)

Profitgraph   An alternative form of the CVP graph that focuses more directly on how profits change with changes in volume. (p. 289)

Profit-volume ratio (P/V ratio)   See *Contribution margin ratio (CM ratio)*. (p. 281)

Sales mix   The relative combination in which a company's products are sold. Sales mix is computed by expressing the sales of each product as a percentage of total sales. (p. 299)

Unit contribution method   A method of computing the break-even point in which the fixed costs are divided by the contribution margin per unit. (p. 287)

QUESTIONS

7-1 CVP analysis is a study of the interaction of a number of factors. Name the factors involved.

7-2 What is meant by a product's CM ratio? How is this ratio useful in the planning of business operations?

7-3 Able Company and Baker Company are competing firms. Each company sells a single product, widgets, in the same market at a price of $50 per widget. Variable costs are the same in each company—$35 per widget. Able Company has discovered a way to reduce its variable costs by $4 per unit and has decided to pass half of this cost savings on to its customers in the form of a lower price. Although Baker Company has not been able to reduce its variable costs, it must also lower its selling price to remain competitive with Able Company. If each company sells 10,000 units per year, what will be the effect of the changes on each company's profits?

7-4 Often the most direct route to a business decision is to make an incremental analysis based on the information available. What is meant by an *incremental analysis*?

7-5 Company A's cost structure includes costs that are mostly variable, whereas Company B's cost structure includes costs that are mostly fixed. In a time of increasing sales, which company will tend to realize the most rapid increase in profits? Explain.

7-6 What is meant by the term *operating leverage*?

7-7 A 10 percent decrease in the selling price of a product will have the same impact on net income as a 10 percent increase in the variable expenses. Do you agree? Why or why not?

7-8 "Changes in fixed costs are much more significant to a company than changes in variable costs." Do you agree? Explain.

7-9 What is meant by the term *break-even point?*

7-10 Name three approaches to break-even analysis. Briefly explain how each approach works.

7-11 Why is the term *break-even chart* a misnomer?

7-12 In response to a request from your immediate supervisor, you have prepared a CVP graph portraying the cost and revenue characteristics of your company's product and operations. Explain how the lines on the graph would change if (a) the selling price per unit decreased, (b) fixed costs increased throughout the entire range of activity portrayed on the graph, and (c) variable costs per unit increased.

7-13 Using the following notations, write out the correct formula for computing the break-even level of sales in units: S = sales in units, SP = selling price per unit, FC = total fixed costs, and VC = variable cost per unit. Is the formula you have derived the formula for the equation method or the formula for the unit contribution method?

7-14 Al's Auto Wash charges $4 to wash a car. The variable costs of washing a car are 15 percent of sales. Fixed costs total $1,700 monthly. How many cars must be washed each month for Al to break even?

7-15 What is meant by the MS (margin of safety)?

7-16 Companies X and Y are in the same industry. Company X is highly automated, whereas Company Y relies primarily on labor in the manufacture of its products. If sales in the two companies are about the same, which would you expect to have the lower MS? Why?

7-17 What is meant by the term *sales mix?* CVP analysis includes some inherent, simplifying assumptions. What assumption is usually made concerning sales mix?

7-18 Explain how a shift in the sales mix could result in both a higher break-even point and a lower net income.

EXERCISES

E7-1 Menlo Company manufactures and sells a single product. The company's sales and expenses for last quarter follow:

	Total	Per Unit
Sales	$450,000	$30
Less variable expenses	180,000	12
Contribution margin	270,000	$18
Less fixed expenses	216,000	
Net income	$ 54,000	

Required
1. What is the quarterly break-even point in units sold and in sales dollars?
2. Without resorting to computations, what is the total contribution margin at the break-even point?
3. How many units would have to be sold each quarter to earn a target net income of $90,000? Use the unit contribution method. Prove your answer by preparing a contribution income statement at the target level of sales.
4. Refer to the original data. Compute the company's MS (margin of safety) in both dollar and percentage terms.
5. What is the company's CM ratio? If sales increase by $50,000 per quarter, by how much would you expect quarterly net income to increase? (Do not prepare an income statement; use the CM ratio to compute your answer.)

E7-2 Lindon Company manufactures and sells a single product. The product sells for $40 per unit and has a CM ratio of 30 percent. The company's fixed expenses are $180,000 per year.

Required
1. What are the variable expenses per unit?
2. Using the equation method:
   a. What is the break-even point in units and in sales dollars?
   b. What sales level in units and in sales dollars is required to earn an annual profit of $60,000?
   c. Assume that by using less costly inputs, the company is able to reduce its variable expenses by $4 per unit. What is the company's new break-even point in units and in sales dollars?
3. Repeat (2) above, using the unit contribution method.

E7-3 Bestway Toys, Inc., has developed a new board game. The company sold 15,000 games last year at a selling price of $20 per game. Fixed costs associated with the game total $182,000 per year, and variable costs are $6 per game.

Required
1. Prepare an income statement for last year, and compute the degree of operating leverage.

2. Management is confident that the company can sell 18,000 games next year (an increase of 3,000 games, or 20 percent, over last year). Compute:
   a. The expected percentage increase in net income for next year.
   b. The expected total dollar net income for next year. (Do not prepare an income statement; use the operating leverage concept to compute your answer.)

E7–4

The Hartford Symphony Guild is planning its annual dinner-dance. The dinner-dance committee has assembled the following expected costs for the event:

Dinner (per person)	$ 18
Favors and program (per person)	2
Orchestra	2,800
Rental of ballroom	900
Professional entertainment during intermission	1,000
Tickets and advertising	1,300

6020

The committee members would like to charge $35 per person for the evening's activities.

Required

1. Compute the break-even point for the dinner-dance (in terms of the number of persons that must attend).
2. Assume that last year only 300 persons attended the dinner-dance. If the same number attend this year, what price per ticket must be charged in order to break even?
3. Refer to the original data ($35 ticket price per person). Prepare a CVP graph for the dinner-dance from a zero level of activity up to 900 tickets sold. Number of persons should be placed on the horizontal *(X)* axis, and dollars should be placed on the vertical *(Y)* axis. (Note: E7–5 has further requirements for the data in this exercise.)

(This exercise is a continuation of E7–4.) Refer to the data in E7–4.

E7–5

Required

1. Prepare a profitgraph for the dinner-dance. *boyet cheat it.*
2. If the dinner-dance committee charges $40 per person rather than $35, will this cause the slope of the profit line to be steeper or flatter? Explain. *boyet obel it*

Fill in the missing amounts in each of the eight case situations below. Each case is independent of the others. (Hint: One way to find the missing amounts would be to prepare a contribution income statement for each case, enter the known data, and then compute the missing items.)

E7–6

a. Assume that only one product is being sold in each of the four following case situations:

: by units

Case	Units Sold	Sales	Variable Expenses	Contribution Margin per Unit	Fixed Expenses	Net Income (Loss)
1	15,000	$180,000	$120,000	$?	$ 50,000	$?
2	?	100,000	?	10	32,000	8,000
3	10,000	?	70,000	13	?	12,000
4	6,000	300,000	?	?	100,000	(10,000)

b. Assume that more than one product is being sold in each of the four following case situations:

: by Sales

Case	Sales	Variable Expenses	Average Contribution Margin (percent)	Fixed Expenses	Net Income (Loss)
1	$500,000	$?	20	$?	$ 7,000
2	400,000	260,000	?	100,000	?
3	?	?	60	130,000	20,000
4	600,000	420,000	?	?	(5,000)

E7–7 Miller Company's most recent income statement is shown below:

	Total	Per Unit
Sales (20,000 units)	$300,000	$15.00
Less variable expenses.	180,000	9.00
Contribution margin	120,000	$ 6.00
Less fixed expenses	70,000	
Net income	$ 50,000	

Required   Prepare a new income statement under each of the following conditions (consider each case independently):

1. The sales volume increases by 15 percent.
2. The selling price decreases by $1.50 per unit, and the sales volume increases by 25 percent.
3. The selling price increases by $1.50 per unit, fixed expenses increase by $20,000, and the sales volume decreases by 5 percent.
4. The selling price increases by 12 percent, variable expenses increase by 60 cents per unit, and the sales volume decreases by 10 percent.

E7–8 Dixon Company manufactures and sells recreational equipment. One of the company's products, a small camp stove, sells for $50 per unit. Variable expenses are $32 per stove, and fixed expenses associated with the stove total $108,000 per month.

Required   1. Compute the break-even point in number of stoves and in total sales dollars.
2. If the variable expenses per stove increase as a percentage of the selling price, will it result in a higher or a lower break-even point? Why? (Assume that the fixed expenses remain unchanged.)
3. At present, the company is selling 8,000 stoves per month. The sales manager is convinced that a 10 percent reduction in the selling price would result in a 25 percent increase in monthly sales of stoves. Prepare two contribution income statements, one under present operating conditions, and one as operations would appear after the proposed changes. Show both total and per unit data on your statements.
4. Refer to the data in (3) above. How many stoves would have to be sold at the new selling price to yield a minimum net income of $35,000 per month?

E7–9 Wiley Company sells two products, X and Y. Monthly sales and the contribution margin ratios for the two products follow:

	Product		
	X	**Y**	**Total**
Sales	$150,000	$250,000	$400,000
CM ratio	80%	36%	?

Fixed expenses for Wiley Company total $183,750 per month.

Required   1. Prepare an income statement for the company as a whole. Use the format shown in Exhibit 7–8, and carry computations to one decimal place.
2. Compute the break-even point for the company, based on the current sales mix.

PROBLEMS

P7–10 **Basic CVP Analysis; Graphing**   The Fashion Headwear Company operates a chain of hat shops around the country. The shops carry many styles of hats that are all sold at the same price. Sales personnel in the shops are paid a substantial commission on each hat sold (in addition to a small basic salary) in order to encourage them to be aggressive in their sales efforts.

The following cost and revenue data relate to Shop 48 and are typical of one of the company's many outlets:

	Per Hat
Sales price	$ 30.00
Variable expenses:	
Invoice cost	$ 13.50
Sales commission	4.50
Total variable expenses	$ 18.00
	Annual
Fixed expenses:	
Advertising	$ 30,000
Rent	20,000
Salaries	100,000
Total fixed expenses	$150,000

Required

1. Calculate the annual break-even point in dollar sales and in unit sales for Shop 48.
2. Prepare a CVP graph showing cost and revenue data for Shop 48 from a zero level of activity up to 20,000 hats sold each year. Clearly indicate the break-even point on the graph.
3. If 12,000 hats are sold in a year, what would be Shop 48's net income or loss?
4. The company is considering paying the store manager of Shop 48 an incentive commission of 75 cents per hat (in addition to the salespersons' commission). If this change is made, what will be the new break-even point in dollar sales and in unit sales?
5. Refer to the original data. As an alternative to (4) above, the company is considering paying the store manager 50 cents commission on each hat sold in excess of the break-even point. If this change is made, what will be the shop's net income or loss if 15,000 hats are sold?
6. Refer to the original data. The company is considering eliminating sales commissions entirely in its shops and increasing fixed salaries by $31,500 annually. If this change is made, what will be the new break-even point in dollar sales and in unit sales for Shop 48? Would you recommend that the change be made? Explain.

Basics of CVP Analysis   Harwood Company manufactures a product that sells for $20 per unit. Variable costs are $8 per unit, and fixed costs total $180,000 per year.

P7–11

Answer the following independent questions:

Required

1. What is the product's CM ratio?
2. Use the CM ratio to determine the break-even point in sales dollars.
3. Due to an increase in demand, the company estimates that sales will increase by $75,000 during the next year. By how much should net income increase (or net loss decrease), assuming that fixed costs do not change?
4. Assume that the operating results for last year were:

Sales	$400,000
Less variable expenses	160,000
Contribution margin	240,000
Less fixed expenses	180,000
Net income	$ 60,000

   a. Compute the degree of operating leverage at the current level of sales.
   b. The president expects sales to increase by 20 percent next year. By what percentage should net income increase?
5. Refer to the original data. Assume that the company sold 18,000 units last year. The sales manager is convinced that a 10 percent reduction in the selling price, combined with a $30,000 increase in advertising, would cause annual sales in units to increase by

one third. Prepare two contribution income statements, one showing the results of last year's operations and one showing the results of operations if these changes are made. Would you recommend that the company do as the sales manager suggests?

6. Refer to the original data. Assume again that the company sold 18,000 units last year. The president does not want to change the selling price. Instead, he wants to increase the sales commission by $1 per unit. He thinks that this move, combined with some increase in advertising, would increase annual sales by 25 percent. By how much could advertising be increased with profits remaining unchanged? Do not prepare an income statement; use the incremental analysis approach.

7. Refer to the original data. Assume that due to a recession the company is selling only 14,000 units per year. An order has been received from a wholesale distributor who wants to purchase 4,000 units on a special price basis. What unit price would have to be quoted to the distributor if Harwood Company wants to earn an overall profit of $20,000 per year? (Present sales would not be disturbed by this special order.)

P7-12 Sales Mix Assumptions; Break-Even Analysis Valtek Company has recently acquired an exclusive franchise to sell three products—A, B, and C—in its area. The company is anxious to establish a budgeting and planning program as an aid to management. To this end, budgeted sales by product and in total for the coming month have been set as shown below:

	Product							
	A		**B**		**C**		**Total**	
Percentage of total sales . . .	20%		52%		28%		100%	
Sales.	$150,000	100%	$390,000	100%	$210,000	100%	$750,000	100%
Less variable expenses. . . .	108,000	72	78,000	20	84,000	40	270,000	36
Contribution margin	$ 42,000	28%	$312,000	80%	$126,000	60%	480,000	64%
Less fixed expenses							449,280	
Net income							$ 30,720	

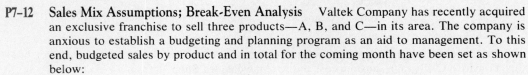

Break-even sales: $\dfrac{\text{Fixed expenses, } \$449,280}{\text{CM ratio, } 0.64} = \$702,000$

As shown by these data, net income is budgeted at $30,720 for the month, and break-even sales at $702,000.

Assume that actual sales for the month total $750,000 as planned. Actual sales by product are: A, $300,000; B, $180,000; and C, $270,000.

Required

1. Prepare a contribution income statement for the month based on actual sales data. Present the income statement in the format shown above.

2. Compute the break-even sales for the month, based on your actual data.

3. Considering the fact that the company met its $750,000 sales budget for the month, the president is shocked at the results shown on your income statement in (1). Prepare a brief memo for the president explaining why both the operating results and break-even sales are different from what was budgeted.

P7-13 Basics of CVP Analysis; Cost Structure Due to erratic sales, Mercer Company has been experiencing difficulty for some time. The company's income statement for the most recent month is given below:

Sales (19,500 units × $30)	$585,000
Less variable expenses	409,500
Contribution margin.	175,500
Less fixed expenses.	180,000
Net loss	$ (4,500)

1. Compute the company's CM ratio and its break-even point in both units and dollars. *Required*
2. The president is certain that a $16,000 increase in the monthly advertising budget, combined with an intensified effort by the sales staff, will result in an $80,000 increase in monthly sales. If the president is right, what will be the effect on the company's monthly net income or loss? (Use the incremental approach in preparing your answer.)
3. Refer to the original data. The sales manager is convinced that a 10 percent reduction in the selling price, combined with an increase of $60,000 in the monthly advertising budget, will cause unit sales to double. What will the new income statement look like if these changes are adopted?
4. Refer to the original data. The marketing department thinks that a fancy new package for Mercer Company's product would help sales. The new package would increase packaging costs by 75 cents per unit. Assuming no other changes in cost behavior, how many units would have to be sold each month to earn a profit of $9,750?
5. Refer to the original data. By automating certain operations, the company could reduce variable costs by $3 per unit. However, fixed costs would increase by $72,000 each month.
   a. Compute the new CM ratio and the new break-even point in both units and dollars.
   b. Assume that the company expects to sell 26,000 units next month. Prepare two income statements, one assuming that operations are not automated and one assuming that they are. (Show data on a per unit and percentage basis, as well as in total, for each alternative.)
   c. Would you recommend that the company automate its operations? Explain.
6. Refer to the original data. A large distributor has offered to make a bulk purchase of 5,000 units each month on a special price basis. Variable selling expenses of $1 per unit could be avoided on this sale. What price per unit should Mercer Company quote to this distributor if Mercer desires to make an overall net income of $18,000 each month for the company as a whole? (Present sales would not be disturbed by this order.)

Graphing; Incremental Analysis; Operating Leverage

P7–14

Angie Silva has recently opened The Sandal Shop, a store that specializes in fashionable sandals. Angie has just received a degree in business from state university, and she is anxious to apply principles she has learned to her business. In time, she hopes to open a chain of sandal shops. As a first step, she has prepared the following analysis for her new store:

Sales price per pair of sandals	$40
Variable expense per pair of sandals.	16
Contribution margin per pair of sandals . . .	$24
Fixed expenses per year:	
Building rental	$15,000
Equipment depreciation	7,000
Selling	20,000
Administrative	18,000
Total fixed expenses.	$60,000

1. How many pairs of sandals must be sold each year to break even? What does this represent in total dollar sales? *Required*
2. Prepare a CVP graph for the store from a zero level of activity up to 5,000 pairs of sandals sold each year. Indicate the break-even point on your graph.
3. Angie has decided that she must earn at least $18,000 the first year to justify her time and effort. How many pairs of sandals must be sold to reach this target net profit figure?
4. Angie now has two salespersons working in the store—one full time and one part time. It will cost her an additional $8,000 per year to convert the part-time position to a full-time position. Angie believes that the change would bring in an additional $25,000 in sales each year. Should she convert the position? Use the incremental approach (do not prepare an income statement).

5. Refer to the original data. During the first year, the store sold only 3,000 pairs of sandals and reported the following operating results:

Sales (3,000 pair)	$120,000
Less variable expenses	48,000
Contribution margin	72,000
Less fixed expenses	60,000
Net income	$ 12,000

a. What is the store's degree of operating leverage?
b. Angie is confident that with a more intense sales effort and with a more creative advertising program she can increase sales by 50 percent next year. What would be the expected percentage increase in net income? Use the operating leverage concept to compute your answer.

P7–15 Various CVP Questions: Break-Even Point; Cost Structure; Target Sales Northwood Company manufactures basketballs. The company has a standard ball that sells for $25. At present, the standard ball is manufactured in a small plant that relies heavily on direct labor workers. Thus, variable costs are high, totaling $15 per ball.
Last year, the company sold 30,000 standard balls, with the following results:

Sales (30,000 standard balls)	$750,000
Less variable expenses	450,000
Contribution margin	300,000
Less fixed expenses	210,000
Net income	$ 90,000

Required
1. Compute (a) the CM ratio and the break-even point in balls, and (b) the degree of operating leverage at last year's level of sales.
2. Due to an increase in labor rates, the company estimates that variable costs will increase by $3 per ball next year. If this change takes place and the selling price per ball remains constant at $25, what will be the new CM ratio and break-even point in balls?
3. Refer to the data in (2) above. If the expected change in variable costs takes place, how many balls will have to be sold next year to earn the same net income ($90,000) as last year?
4. Refer again to the data in (2) above. The president feels that the company must raise the selling price on the standard balls. If Norwood Company wants to maintain *the same CM ratio as last year,* what selling price per ball must it charge next year to cover the increased labor costs?
5. Refer to the original data. The company is discussing the construction of a new, automated plant to manufacture the standard balls. The new plant would slash variable costs per ball by 40 percent, but it would cause fixed costs to double in amount per year. If the new plant is built, what would be the company's new CM ratio and new break-even point in balls?
6. Refer to the data in (5) above.
    a. If the new plant is built, how many balls will have to be sold next year to earn the same net income ($90,000) as last year?
    b. Assume the new plant is built and that next year the company manufactures and sells 30,000 balls (the same number as sold last year). Prepare a contribution income statement, and compute the degree of operating leverage.
    c. Explain why the operating leverage figure you have just computed is so much higher than the operating leverage figure computed in (1) above. If you were a member of top management, would you have voted in favor of constructing the new plant? Explain.

The Case of the Elusive Contribution Margin   The Shirt Works sells a large variety of   **P7–16**
tee shirts and sweat shirts. Steve Hooper, the owner, is thinking of expanding his sales by
hiring local high school students, on a commission basis, to sell sweat shirts bearing the
name and mascot of the local high school.

These sweat shirts would have to be ordered from the manufacturer six weeks in
advance, and they could not be returned because of the unique printing required. The
sweat shirts would cost Mr. Hooper $8 each with a minimum order of 75 sweat shirts. Any
additional sweat shirts would have to be ordered in increments of 75.

Since Mr. Hooper's plan would not require any additional facilities, the only costs
associated with the project would be the costs of the sweat shirts and the costs of the sales
commissions. The selling price of the sweat shirts would be $13.50 each. Mr. Hooper
would pay the students a commission of $1.50 for each shirt sold.

1. To make the project worthwhile, Mr. Hooper would require a $1,200 profit for the first   *Required*
    three months of the venture. What level of sales in units and in dollars would be
    required to reach this target net income? Show all computations.
2. Assume that the venture is undertaken and an order is placed for 75 sweat shirts. What
    would be Mr. Hooper's break-even point in units and in sales dollars? Show computa-
    tions, and explain the reasoning behind your answer.

Sales Mix; Break-Even Analysis; Margin of Safety   Frutex, Inc., has two products,   **P7–17**
Hawaiian Fantasy and Tahitian Joy. Present revenue, cost, and sales data on the two
products follow:

	Hawaiian Fantasy	Tahitian Joy
Selling price per unit	$15	$100
Variable expenses per unit	9	20
Number of units sold annually . . .	20,000	5,000

Fixed expenses total $475,800 per year.

1. Assuming the sales mix given above, do the following: *Required*
    a. Prepare a contribution income statement showing both dollar and percent columns
        for each product and for the company as a whole.
    b. Compute the break-even point in dollars for the company as a whole and the MS
        (margin of safety) in both dollars and percent.
2. Another product, Samoan Delight, has just come onto the market. Assume that the
    company could sell 10,000 units at $45 each. The variable expenses would be $36 each.
    The company's fixed expenses would not change.
    a. Prepare another contribution income statement, including sales of the Samoan
        Delight (sales of the other two products would not change). Carry percentage
        computations to one decimal place.
    b. Compute the company's new break-even point in dollars and the new MS in both
        dollars and percent.
3. The president of the company examines your figures and says, "There's something
    strange here. Our fixed costs haven't changed and you show greater total contribution
    margin if we add the new product, but you also show our break-even point going up.
    With greater contribution margin, the break-even point should go down, not up.
    You've made a mistake somewhere." Explain to the president what has happened.

Interpretive Questions on the CVP Graph   A CVP graph such as the one shown on the   **P7–18**
next page is a useful technique for showing relationships between costs, volume, and
profits in an organization.

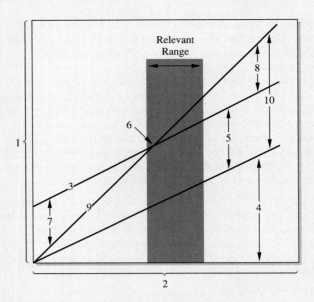

Required   1. Identify the numbered components in the CVP graph.
             2. State the effect of each of the following actions on line 3, line 9, and the break-even
                 point. For line 3 and line 9, state whether the action will cause the line to:

                 Remain unchanged.
                 Shift upward.
                 Shift downward.
                 Have a steeper slope (i.e., rotate upward).
                 Have a flatter slope (i.e., rotate downward).
                 Shift upward *and* have a steeper slope.
                 Shift upward *and* have a flatter slope.
                 Shift downward *and* have a steeper slope.
                 Shift downward *and* have a flatter slope.

             In the case of the break-even point, state whether the action will cause the break-even
             point to:

                 Remain unchanged.
                 Increase.
                 Decrease.
                 Probably change, but the direction is uncertain.

             Treat each case independently.

        x.   *Example.*   Fixed costs are reduced by $5,000 per period.
             Answer (see choices above):   Line 3:   Shift downward.
                                              Line 9:   Remain unchanged.
                                              Break-even point: Decrease.
        a.   The unit selling price is increased from $18 to $20.
        b.   Unit variable costs are decreased from $12 to $10.
        c.   Fixed costs are increased by $3,000 per period.
        d.   Two thousand more units are sold during the period than were budgeted.
        e.   Due to paying salespersons a commission rather than a flat salary, fixed costs are
             reduced by $8,000 per period and unit variable costs are increased by $3.
        f.   Due to an increase in the cost of materials, both unit variable costs and the selling
             price are increased by $2.
        g.   Advertising costs are increased by $10,000 per period, resulting in a 10 percent
             increase in the number of units sold.

h. Due to automating an operation previously done by workers, fixed costs are increased by $12,000 per period and unit variable costs are reduced by $4.

Sales Mix; Commission Structure; Break-Even Point   Larkin Shoes, Inc., manufactures several shoe lines, all of which are sold through the company's own retail outlets. Sales and expenses are accumulated by line for evaluation purposes.   **P7–19**

The company has a line of jogging shoes that includes two styles, the Regular and the Marathon. The Regular sells for $65 a pair, and the Marathon sells for $80 a pair. Variable expenses associated with each style are given below (in cost per pair of shoes):

	Regular	Marathon
Production expenses*	$18.20	$34.40
Sales commissions (12% of sales price) . . .	7.80	9.60

* Direct materials, direct labor, and variable overhead.

Monthly fixed expenses associated with the jogging shoes are:

Production	$215,000
Advertising	100,000
Insurance.	3,000
Administrative salaries	47,000

Salespersons are paid on a commission basis to encourage them to be aggressive in their sales efforts. Janet Rogers, the financial vice president, watches sales commissions carefully and has noted that they have risen steadily over the last year. For this reason, she was surprised to find that even though sales have increased, profits from the jogging shoes for the current month—July 19x2—are down substantially from July of the previous year. Sales of jogging shoes, in pairs, for July over the last two years are given below:

	Regular	Marathon	Total
July 19x1	9,000	3,000	12,000
July 19x2	4,000	8,000	12,000

1. Prepare an income statement for July 19x1 and an income statement for July 19x2. Use the contribution format, with the following headings: *Required*

	Regular		Marathon		Total	
	Amount	**Percent**	**Amount**	**Percent**	**Amount**	**Percent**
Sales . . .						
Etc..						

Place the fixed expenses only in the Total column. Carry all percentage computations to one decimal place. Do not show percentages for the fixed expenses.

2. Explain why net income is lower in July 19x2 than in July 19x1, even though the same *total* number of jogging shoes was sold in each month.

3. What can be done to the sales commissions to optimize the sales mix?

4. Using July 19x1's figures, what was the break-even point (in sales dollars) for jogging shoes for the month?

5. Has July 19x2's break-even point for jogging shoes gone up or down from that of July 19x1? Explain your answer without calculating the break-even point for July 19x2.

Sensitivity Analysis of Net Income; Changes in Volume   Minden Company introduced a new product last year for which it is trying to find an optimal selling price. Marketing studies suggest that the company can increase sales by 5,000 units for each $2 reduction in the selling price. The company's present selling price is $70 per unit, and variable expenses are $40 per unit. Fixed expenses are $540,000 per year. The present annual sales volume (at the $70 selling price) is 15,000 units.   **P7–20**

Required 1. What is the present yearly net income or loss?
2. What is the present break-even point in units and in dollar sales?
3. Assuming that the marketing studies are correct, what is the *maximum* profit that the company can earn yearly? At how many units and at what selling price per unit would the company generate this profit?
4. What would be the break-even point in units and in dollar sales using the selling price you determined in (3) above (e.g., the selling price at the level of maximum profits)? Why is this break-even point different from the break-even point you computed in (1) above?

P7-21 Sales Mix; Commission Structure; Break-Even Point   Carbex, Inc., produces cutlery sets out of high-quality wood and steel. The company makes a standard cutlery set and a deluxe set and sells them to retail department stores throughout the country. The standard set sells for $60, and the deluxe set sells for $75. The variable expenses associated with each set are given below (in cost per set):

	Standard	Deluxe
Production expenses	$15.00	$30.00
Sales commissions (15% of sales price)	9.00	11.25

The company's fixed expenses each month are:

Advertising	$105,000
Depreciation.	21,700
Administrative	63,000

Salespersons are paid on a commission basis to encourage them to be aggressive in their sales efforts. Mary Parsons, the financial vice president, watches sales commissions carefully and has noted that they have risen steadily over the last year. For this reason, she was shocked to find that even though sales have increased, profits for the current month—May 19x2—are down substantially from May of the previous year. Sales, in sets, for May over the last two years are given below:

	Standard	Deluxe	Total
May 19x1.	4,000	2,000	6,000
May 19x2.	1,000	5,000	6,000

Required 1. Prepare an income statement for May 19x1 and an income statement for May 19x2. Use the contribution format, with the following headings:

Standard		Deluxe		Total	
Amount	Percent	Amount	Percent	Amount	Percent

Sales . . .
Etc. . . . .

Place the fixed expenses only in the Total column. Carry percentage computations to one decimal place. Do not show percentages for the fixed expenses.
2. Explain why there is a difference in net income between the two months, even though the same *total* number of sets was sold in each month.
3. What can be done to the sales commissions to optimize the sales mix?
4. a. Using May 19x1's figures, what was the break-even point for the month in sales dollars?
   b. Has May 19x2's break-even point gone up or down from that of May 19x1? Explain your answer without calculating the break-even point for May 19x2.

P7-22 Changing Levels of Fixed and Variable Costs   Neptune Company produces toys and other items for use in beach and resort areas. A small, inflatable toy has come onto the market that the company is anxious to produce and sell. Enough capacity exists in the company's plant to produce 16,000 units of the toy each month. Variable costs to manufacture and sell one unit would be $1.25, and fixed costs associated with the toy would total $35,000 per month.

The company's marketing department predicts that demand for the new toy will exceed the 16,000 units that the company is able to produce. Additional manufacturing space can be rented from another company at a fixed cost of $1,000 per month. Variable costs in the rented facility would total $1.40 per unit, due to somewhat less efficient operations than in the main plant. The new toy will sell for $3 per unit.

Required

1. Compute the monthly break-even point for the new toy in units and in total dollar sales. Show all computations in good form.
2. How many units must be sold each month to make a monthly profit of $12,000?
3. If the sales manager receives a bonus of 10 cents for each unit sold in excess of the break-even point, how many units must be sold each month to earn a return of 25 percent on the monthly investment in fixed costs?

Changes in Cost Structure   Morton Company's income statement for last month is given below:

P7–23

Sales (15,000 units × $30)	$450,000
Less variable expenses	315,000
Contribution margin	135,000
Less fixed expenses	90,000
Net income.	$ 45,000

The industry in which Morton Company operates is quite sensitive to cyclical movements in the economy. Thus, profits vary considerably from year to year according to general economic conditions. The company has a large amount of unused capacity and is studying ways of improving profits.

Required

1. New equipment has come onto the market that would allow Morton Company to automate a portion of its operations. Variable costs would be reduced by $9 per unit. However, fixed costs would increase to a total of $225,000 each month. Prepare two contribution-type income statements, one showing present operations and one showing how operations would appear if the new equipment is purchased. Show an Amount column, a Per Unit column, and a Percent column on each statement. Do not show percentages for the fixed costs.
2. Refer to the income statements in (1) above. For both present operations and the proposed new operations, compute (a) the degree of operating leverage, (b) the break-even point in dollars, and (c) the margin of safety in both dollar and percentage terms.
3. Refer again to the data in (1) above. As a manager, what factor would be paramount in your mind in deciding whether to purchase the new equipment? (You may assume that ample funds are available to make the purchase.)
4. Refer to the original data. Rather than purchase new equipment, the president is thinking about changing the company's marketing method. Under the new method, sales would increase by 20 percent each month and net income would increase by one third. Fixed costs could be slashed to only $48,000 per month. Compute the break-even point for the company after the change in marketing method.

Break-Even Analysis with Step Fixed Costs   Wymont Hospital operates a general hospital that rents space and beds to separate departments such as pediatrics, maternity, and surgery. Wymont Hospital charges each separate department for common services to its patients such as meals and laundry and for administrative services such as billing and collections. Space and bed rentals are fixed for the year.

P7–24

For the year ended June 30, 19x7, the pediatrics department at Wymont Hospital charged its patients an average of $65 per day, had a capacity of 80 beds, operated 24 hours per day for 365 days, and had total revenue of $1,138,800.

Expenses charged by the hospital to the pediatrics department for the year were as follows:

	Basis for Allocation	
	Patient-Days (variable)	Bed Capacity (fixed)
Dietary	$ 42,952	
Janitorial		$ 12,800
Laundry	28,000	
Laboratory	47,800	
Pharmacy	33,800	
Repairs and maintenance	5,200	7,140
General administrative services . . .		131,760
Rent		275,320
Billings and collections	87,000	
Other	18,048	25,980
	$262,800	$453,000

The only personnel directly employed by the pediatrics department are supervising nurses, nurses, and aides. The hospital has minimum personnel requirements based on total annual patient-days. Hospital requirements, beginning at the minimum expected level of operation, follow:

Annual Patient-Days	Aides	Nurses	Supervising Nurses
10,000–14,000	21	11	4
14,001–17,000	22	12	4
17,001–23,725	22	13	4
23,726–25,550	25	14	5
25,551–27,375	26	14	5
27,376–29,200	29	16	6

These staffing levels represent full-time equivalents, and it should be assumed that the pediatrics department always employs only the minimum number of required full-time equivalent personnel.

Annual salaries for each class of employee are: supervising nurses, $18,000; nurses, $13,000; and aides, $5,000. Salary expense for the year ended June 30, 19x7, was $72,000, $169,000, and $110,000 for supervising nurses, nurses, and aides, respectively.

Required
1. Compute the following:
   a. The number of patient-days in the pediatrics department for the year ended June 30, 19x7. (Each day a patient is in the hospital is known as a *patient-day*.)
   b. The variable cost per patient-day for the year ended June 30, 19x7.
   c. The total fixed costs, including both allocated fixed costs and personnel costs, in the pediatrics department for each level of operation shown above (i.e., total fixed costs at the 10,000–14,000 patient-day level of operation, total fixed costs at the 14,001–17,000 patient-day level of operation, etc.).
2. Using the data computed in (1) above and any other data as needed, compute the *minimum* number of patient-days required for the pediatrics department to break even. You may assume that variable and fixed cost behavior and that revenue per patient-day will remain unchanged in the future.
3. Determine the minimum number of patient-days required for the pediatrics department to earn an annual profit of $200,000.

(CPA, heavily adapted)

P7-25 Missing Data; Integration of CVP Factors   You were employed just this morning by Pyrrhic Company, a prominent and rapidly growing organization. As your initial assignment, you were asked to complete an analysis of one of the company's products for the board of directors meeting later in the day. After completing the analysis, you left your office for a few moments only to discover on returning that a broken sprinkler in the ceiling had destroyed most of your work. Only the following bits remained:

PYRRHIC COMPANY
Actual Income Statement
For the Month Ended June 30, 19x1

	Total	Per Unit	Percent
Sales (? units)	$?	$?	100%
Less variable expenses	?	?	?
Contribution margin	?	$?	? %
Less fixed expenses	?		
Net income	$?		

Break-even point:
| In units | ? units |
| In dollars | $180,000 |

Margin of safety:
In dollars	$?
In percentage	20%
Degree of operating leverage	?

The computations above are all based on actual results for June 19x1. The company's *projected* income statement for this product for July 19x1 follows:

PYRRHIC COMPANY
Projected Income Statement
For the Month Ended July 31, 19x1

	Total	Per Unit	Percent
Sales (33,000 units)	$?	$?	? %
Less variable expenses	?	?	?
Contribution margin	?	$?	? %
Less fixed expenses	?		
Net income	$40,500		

To add to your woes, the computer is down so no data are available from that source. You do remember that sales for July are projected to increase by 10 percent over sales for June. You also remember that June's net income was $27,000—the same amount as your annual salary from the company. Finally, you remember that the degree of operating leverage is highly useful to the manager as a predictive tool.

Total fixed expenses, the unit selling price, and the unit variable expenses are planned to be the same in July as they were in June.

The board of directors meets in just one hour.

Required

1. For the June 19x1 data, do the following:
   a. Complete the June 19x1 income statement (all three columns).
   b. Compute the break-even point in units, and prove the break-even point in dollars. Use the unit contribution method.
   c. Compute the MS in dollars, and prove the MS percentage.
   d. Compute the degree of operating leverage as of June 30, 19x1.
2. For the July 19x1 data, do the following:
   a. Complete the July 19x1 projected income statement (all three columns).
   b. Compute the MS in dollars and percent, and compute the degree of operating leverage. Why has the MS gone up and the degree of operating leverage gone down?

3. Brimming with confidence after having completed (1) and (2) in less than one hour, you decide to give the board of directors some added data. You know that direct labor accounts for $1.80 of the company's per unit variable expenses. You have learned that direct labor costs may increase by one third next year. Assuming that this cost increase takes place and that selling price and other cost factors remain unchanged, how many units will the company have to sell in a month to earn a net income equal to 20 percent of sales?

Ethics and the

Manager*

P7–26 Serge Marovich is vice president of Brisco, Inc., a company that manufactures and sells products to customers throughout the world. In October 19x5, Mr. Marovich realized that the company had not yet reached a break-even level of sales for the year, and it appeared likely that the company would report the first loss in its history. Mr. Marovich was particularly concerned about incurring a loss for the year since the company had plans to borrow heavily in January 19x6 to obtain funds for plant modernization. He realized that even a small operating profit might reduce the interest rate the company would have to pay on the borrowed funds. Accordingly, Mr. Marovich did the following three things:

a. He approved a temporary sales program that offered liberal sales terms to customers. Those customers accepting delivery in the fourth quarter would have 120 days to pay their invoice, rather than the normal 30 days. This action allowed the company to pull some sales into the current year that normally would not have occurred until next year.

b. He ordered the company to work overtime during December so that the sales department's complete backlog of orders was completed and shipped by year-end.

c. He identified some idle assets that were sold during December at a profit of $150,000.

Required 1. Identify the stakeholders involved in this ethical situation.

2. Consider each of Mr. Marovich's actions separately and give reasons why you believe the action was or was not ethical.

CASES

C7–27 **Detailed Income Statement; CVP Sensitivity Analysis**   The most recent income statement for Whitney Company appears below:

WHITNEY COMPANY
Income Statement
For the Year Ended December 31, 19x8

Sales (45,000 units at $10)		$450,000
Less cost of goods sold:		
Direct materials	$ 90,000	
Direct labor	78,300	
Manufacturing overhead.	98,500	266,800
Gross margin.		183,200
Less operating expenses:		
Selling expenses:		
Variable:		
Sales commissions $27,000		
Shipping. 5,400	32,400	
Fixed (advertising, salaries) . . .	120,000	
Administrative:		
Variable (billing and other). . . .	1,800	
Fixed (salaries and other)	48,000	202,200
Net loss		$(19,000)

---

* Based on situations described by William J. Bruns, Jr., and Kenneth A. Merchant in "The Gray Area: Ethics Test for Everyday Managers," *Harvard Business Review* 67, no. 2 (March–April 1989), p. 220.

All variable expenses in the company vary in terms of units sold, except for sales commissions, which are based on sales dollars. Variable manufacturing overhead is 30 cents per unit. Whitney Company's plant has a capacity of 75,000 units per year.

The company has been operating at a loss for several years. Management is studying several possible courses of action to determine what should be done to make 19x9 profitable.

1. Redo Whitney Company's 19x8 income statement in the contribution format. Show both a Total column and a Per Unit column on your statement. Leave enough space to the right of your numbers to enter the solution to both parts of (2) below.   *Required*

2. The president is considering two proposals prepared by members of his staff:
   a. For next year, the vice president would like to reduce the unit selling price by 20 percent. She is certain that this would fill the plant to capacity.
   b. For next year, the sales manager would like to increase the unit selling price by 20 percent, increase the sales commission to 9 percent of sales, and increase advertising by $100,000. Based on marketing studies, he is confident this would increase unit sales by one third.

   Prepare two contribution income statements, one showing what profits would be under the vice president's proposal and one showing what profits would be under the sales manager's proposal. On each statement, include both Total and Per unit columns (do not show per unit data for the fixed costs).

3. Refer to the original data. The president believes it would be a mistake to change the unit selling price. Instead, he wants to use less costly materials in manufacturing units of product, thereby reducing unit costs by 70 cents. How many units would have to be sold next year to earn a target profit of $30,200?

4. Refer to the original data. Whitney Company's board of directors believes that the company's problem lies in inadequate promotion. By how much can advertising be increased and still allow the company to earn a target return of 4.5 percent on sales of 60,000 units?

5. Refer to the original data. The company has been approached by an overseas distributor who wants to purchase 9,500 units on a special price basis. There would be no sales commission on these units. However, shipping costs would be increased by 50 percent, and variable administrative costs would be reduced by 25 percent. In addition, a $5,700 special insurance fee would have to be paid by Whitney Company to protect the goods in transit. What unit price would have to be quoted on the 9,500 units by Whitney Company to allow the company to earn a profit of $14,250 on total operations? Regular business would not be disturbed by this special order.

Cost Structure; Break-Even; Target Profits   Pittman Company is a small but growing   C7–28
manufacturer of telecommunications equipment. The company has no sales force of its own; rather, it relies completely on independent sales agents to market its products. These agents are paid a commission of 15 percent of selling price for all items sold.

Barbara Cheney, Pittman's controller, has just prepared the company's budgeted income statement for next year. The statement follows:

PITTMAN COMPANY
Budgeted Income Statement
For the Year Ended December 31, 19x6

Sales		$16,000,000
Manufacturing costs:		
Variable	$7,200,000	
Fixed overhead	2,340,000	9,540,000
Gross margin		6,460,000
Selling and administrative costs:		
Commissions to agents	2,400,000	
Fixed marketing costs	120,000*	
Fixed administrative costs	1,800,000	4,320,000
Net operating income		2,140,000
Less fixed interest cost		540,000
Income before income taxes		1,600,000
Less income taxes (30%).		480,000
Net income.		$ 1,120,000

* Primarily depreciation on storage facilities

As Barbara handed the statement to Karl Vecci, Pittman's president, she commented, "I went ahead and used the agents' 15 percent commission rate in completing these statements, but we've just learned that they refuse to handle our products next year unless we increase the commission rate to 20 percent."

"That's the last straw," Frank replied angrily. "Those agents have been demanding more and more, and this time they've gone too far. How can they possibly defend a 20 percent commission rate?"

"They claim that after paying for advertising, travel, and the other costs of promotion, there's nothing left over for profit," replied Barbara.

"I say it's just plain robbery," retorted Karl. "And I also say it's time we dumped those guys and got our own sales force. Can you get your people to work up some cost figures for us to look at?"

"We've already worked them up," said Barbara. "Several companies we know about pay a 7.5 percent commission to their own salespeople, along with a small salary. Of course, we would have to handle all promotion costs, too. We figure our fixed costs would increase by $2,400,000 per year, but that would be more than offset by the $3,200,000 (20% × $16,000,000) that we would avoid on agents' commissions."

The breakdown of the $2,400,000 cost figure follows:

Salaries:		
Sales manager.	$	100,000
Salespersons		600,000
Travel and entertainment		400,000
Advertising		1,300,000
Total		$2,400,000

"Super," replied Karl. "And I note that the $2,400,000 is just what we're paying the agents under the old 15 percent commission rate."

"It's even better than that," explained Barbara. "We can actually save $75,000 a year, because that's what we're having to pay the auditing firm now to check out the agents' reports. So our overall administrative costs would be less."

"Pull all of these numbers together and we'll show them to the executive committee tomorrow," said Karl. "With the approval of the committee, we can move on the matter immediately."

Required 1. Compute Pittman Company's break-even point in sales dollars for 19x6, assuming:
    a. That the agents' commission rate remains unchanged at 15 percent.

    b.   That the agents' commission rate is increased to 20 percent.

    c.   That the company employs its own sales force.

2.   Assume that Pittman Company decides to continue selling through agents and pays the 20 percent commission rate. Determine the volume of sales that would be required to generate the same net income as contained in the budgeted income statement for 19x6.

3.   Determine the volume of sales at which net income would be equal regardless of whether Pittman Company sells through agents (at a 20 percent commission rate) or employs its own sales force.

4.   Compute the degree of operating leverage that the company would expect to have on December 31, 19x6, assuming:

    a.   That the agents' commission rate remains unchanged at 15 percent.

    b.   That the agents' commission rate is increased to 20 percent.

    c.   That the company employs its own sales force.

    Use income *before* income taxes in your operating leverage computation.

5.   Based on the data in (1) through (4) above, make a recommendation as to whether the company should continue to use sales agents (at a 20 percent commission rate) or employ its own sales force. Give reasons for your answer.

(CMA, heavily adapted)

Large amounts of work in process inventory, as in this Bell/Textron helicopter plant, can result in big differences between the net incomes and inventories reported under absorption costing and variable costing. However, when a company adopts a JIT production system, work in process inventories are largely eliminated. Consequently, JIT reduces the differences between absorption costing and variable costing financial statements.

Variable Costing:
A Tool for Management

LEARNING OBJECTIVES

After studying Chapter 8, you should be able to:

1 Explain how variable costing differs from absorption costing, and compute the cost of a unit of product under each method.

2 Describe how fixed overhead costs are deferred in inventory and released from inventory under absorption costing.

3 Prepare income statements using both variable and absorption costing, and reconcile the two net income figures.

4 Explain the effect of changes in production on the net income reported under both variable and absorption costing.

5 Explain the advantages and limitations of both the variable and absorption costing methods.

6 Explain how the use of JIT inventory methods decreases or eliminates the difference in net income reported under the variable and absorption costing methods.

7 Define or explain the key terms listed at the end of the chapter.

ne aspect of the accountant's work centers on the problem of assigning costs to various parts of an organization. Cost assignment is necessary to provide useful and relevant data for three purposes:

1. For product costing and for pricing.
2. For appraisal of managerial performance.
3. For making special decisions.

In assigning costs for these purposes, the accountant can use either of two approaches. One approach, known as *absorption costing,* was discussed at length in Chapter 3. The other approach, called *variable costing,* is preferred by some companies and must be used when an income statement is prepared in the contribution format. In this chapter, we learn how to compute the cost of products and services using variable costing. As we study variable costing, we will learn that a difference in net income can result from using it as compared to absorption costing, and we will learn the reasons for this difference. During our discussion, we consider the arguments for and against each costing method, and we show how management decisions can be affected by the costing method chosen.

OVERVIEW OF ABSORPTION AND VARIABLE COSTING

Objective 1
Explain how variable costing differs from absorption costing, and compute the cost of a unit of product under each method.

As discussed in Chapter 3, absorption costing allocates a portion of fixed manufacturing overhead to each unit produced during a period, along with variable manufacturing costs. Since absorption costing mingles variable and fixed costs together, units of product costed by that method are not well suited for inclusion in a contribution-type income statement. This has led to the development of variable costing, which focuses on *cost behavior* in computing unit costs. One of the strengths of variable costing is that it harmonizes fully with both the contribution approach and the CVP concepts discussed in the preceding chapter.

Absorption Costing

In Chapter 3, we learned that **absorption costing** treats *all* costs of production as product costs, regardless of whether they are variable or fixed in nature. Thus, absorption costing allocates a portion of fixed manufacturing overhead cost to each unit of product, along with the variable manufacturing costs. The cost of a unit of product under the absorption costing method therefore consists of direct materials, direct labor, and *both* variable and fixed overhead. Because absorption costing includes all costs of production as product costs, it is frequently referred to as the **full cost method.**

Variable Costing

Under **variable costing,** only those costs of production that vary with activity are treated as product costs. This would include direct materials, direct labor, and the variable portion of manufacturing overhead. Fixed manufacturing overhead is not treated as a product cost under this method. Rather, fixed manufacturing overhead is treated as a period cost and, like selling and administrative expenses, it is charged off in its entirety against revenue each period. Consequently, the inventory cost of a unit of product under the variable costing method contains no element of fixed overhead cost.

Variable costing is sometimes referred to as **direct costing** or **marginal costing.** The term *direct costing* was popular for many years, but it is slowly disappearing

EXHIBIT 8–1

Cost Classifications—Absorption versus Variable Costing

from day-to-day use. This is fortunate because the term *variable costing* is more descriptive of the way in which product costs are computed when a contribution income statement is prepared.

To complete this summary comparison of absorption and variable costing, we need to consider briefly the handling of selling and administrative expenses. These expenses are never treated as product costs, regardless of the costing method in use. Thus, under either absorption or variable costing, selling and administrative expenses are always treated as period costs and deducted from revenues as incurred.

The concepts discussed so far in this section are illustrated in Exhibit 8–1, which shows the classification of costs under both absorption and variable costing.

Unit Cost Computations

To illustrate the computation of unit costs under both absorption and variable costing, assume the following data:

Boley Company produces a single product. The cost characteristics of the product and of the manufacturing plant are given below:

Number of units produced each year.	6,000
Variable costs per unit:	
Direct materials	$ 2
Direct labor	4
Variable manufacturing overhead	1
Variable selling and administrative expenses . . .	3
Fixed costs per year:	
Manufacturing overhead	30,000
Selling and administrative expenses	10,000

1. Compute the cost of a unit of product under absorption costing.
2. Compute the cost of a unit of product under variable costing.

Required

Absorption Costing

Direct materials	$ 2
Direct labor	4
Variable overhead	1
Total variable production cost	7
Fixed overhead ($30,000 ÷ 6,000 units of product) . . .	5
Total cost per unit	$12

Variable Costing

Direct materials	$ 2
Direct labor	4
Variable overhead	1
Total cost per unit	$ 7

Solution

(The $30,000 fixed overhead will be charged off in total against income as a period expense along with the fixed selling and administrative expenses.)

Under the absorption costing method, notice that *all* production costs, variable and fixed, have been added when determining the cost of a unit of product. Thus, if the company sells a unit of product and absorption costing is being used, then $12 (consisting of $7 variable cost and $5 fixed cost) will be deducted on the income statement as cost of goods sold. Similarly, any unsold units will be carried as inventory on the balance sheet at $12 each.

Under the variable costing method, notice that only the variable production costs have been added when determining the cost of a unit of product. Thus, if the company sells a unit of product, only $7 will be deducted as cost of goods sold, and unsold units will be carried in the balance sheet inventory account at only $7 each.

The Controversy over Fixed Overhead Cost

Probably no subject in all of managerial accounting has created as much controversy among accountants as variable costing. The controversy isn't over whether costs should be separated as between variable and fixed in matters relating to planning and control. Rather, the controversy is over the theoretical justification for excluding fixed overhead costs from the cost of units produced and therefore from inventory.

Advocates of variable costing argue that fixed overhead costs relate to the *capacity* to produce rather than to the actual production of units of product in a given year. That is, they argue that costs for facilities and equipment, insurance, supervisory salaries, and the like, represent costs of being *ready* to produce and therefore will be incurred regardless of whether any actual production takes place during the year. For this reason, advocates of variable costing believe that such costs should be charged against the period rather than against the product.

Advocates of absorption costing argue, on the other hand, that so far as product costing is concerned, it makes no difference whether a manufacturing cost is variable or fixed. They argue that fixed overhead costs such as depreciation and insurance are just as essential to the production process as are the variable costs, and therefore cannot be ignored in costing units of product. They argue that to be fully costed, each unit of product must bear an equitable portion of *all* manufacturing costs.

Although this difference in the handling of fixed overhead might seem slight, it can have a substantial impact on both the clarity and the usefulness of statement data, as we shall see in this chapter.

INCOME COMPARISON OF ABSORPTION AND VARIABLE COSTING

Objective 2
Describe how fixed overhead costs are deferred in inventory and released from inventory under absorption costing.

Income statements prepared under the absorption and variable costing approaches are shown in Exhibit 8–2 (page 330). In preparing these statements, we use the data for Boley Company presented earlier, along with other information about the company as given below:

Beginning inventory in units	–0–
Units produced	6,000
Units sold	5,000
Ending inventory in units	1,000
Selling price per unit	$ 20
Selling and administrative expenses:	
Variable per unit	3
Fixed per year	10,000

	Absorption Costing	Variable Costing
Cost of a unit of product:		
Direct materials.	$ 2	$2
Direct labor	4	4
Variable overhead.	1	1
Fixed overhead ($30,000 ÷ 6,000 units) . . .	5	–
Total cost per unit.	$12	$7

Several points can be made from the statements in Exhibit 8–2:

1. Under the absorption costing method, it is possible to defer a portion of the fixed overhead costs of the current period to future periods through the inventory account. Such a deferral is known as **fixed overhead cost deferred in inventory.** The process involved can be explained by referring to the data for Boley Company. During the current period, Boley Company produced 6,000 units but sold only 5,000 units, thus leaving 1,000 units in the ending inventory. Under the absorption costing method, each unit produced was assigned $5 in fixed overhead cost (see the unit cost computations above). Therefore, each of the 1,000 units going into inventory at the end of the period has $5 in fixed overhead cost attached to it, or a total of $5,000 for the 1,000 units involved. *This amount of fixed overhead cost of the current period has thereby been deferred in inventory to the next period, when, hopefully, these units will be taken out of inventory and sold.* The deferral of fixed overhead cost we are talking about can be seen clearly by

---

FOCUS ON CURRENT PRACTICE

A survey of 219 companies found that 52 percent use variable costing as either the primary or supplementary format in reports prepared for top management. The study included companies listed on the New York and American stock exchanges, as well as smaller companies whose stock is sold over the counter.[1]

Although most of these companies use variable and absorption costing as we describe in this chapter, a few take a more extreme position as to what should and should not be included as product costs. For example, some managers advocate "super variable costing," in which only direct materials are added to the cost of products. All other costs— including labor and variable overhead— are viewed as being fixed costs and are expensed as incurred.[2] On the other hand, other managers advocate "super absorption costing," in which *all* costs— including research, product design, selling, administration, and distribution— are added to the cost of products.[3] The reader should be aware, however, that most companies operate between these extremes and employ variable and absorption costing in the more traditional way that we have described.

---

[1] William P. Cress and James B. Pettijohn, "A Survey of Budget-Related Planning and Control Policies and Procedures," *Journal of Accounting Education* 3, no. 2 (Fall 1985), p. 73.

[2] For a lively discussion of super variable costing, see Eliyahu M. Goldratt and Jeff Cox, *The Goal,* 2nd ed. (Croton-on-Hudson, N.Y.: North River Press, 1992).

[3] Robert S. Kaplan, "Management Accounting for Advanced Technological Environments," *Science* 245 (August 25, 1989), p. 822.

EXHIBIT 8–2
Comparison of Absorption and Variable Costing

Absorption Costing

Sales (5,000 units × $20)		$100,000
Cost of goods sold:		
Beginning inventory	$ –0–	
Cost of goods manufactured (6,000 units × $12)	72,000	
Goods available for sale	72,000	
Less ending inventory (1,000 units × $12)	12,000	
Cost of goods sold		60,000
Gross margin		40,000
Less selling and administrative expenses		
($15,000 total variable plus $10,000 fixed)		25,000
Net income		$ 15,000

> Note the difference in ending inventories. Fixed overhead cost at $5 per unit is included under the absorption approach. This explains the difference in ending inventory and in net income (1,000 units × $5 = $5,000).

Variable Costing

Sales (5,000 units × $20)		$100,000
Less variable expenses:		
Variable cost of goods sold:		
Beginning inventory	$ –0–	
Variable manufacturing costs (6,000 units × $7)	42,000	
Goods available for sale	42,000	
Less ending inventory (1,000 units × $7)	7,000	
Variable cost of goods sold	35,000	
Variable selling and administrative expenses (5,000 units × $3)	15,000	50,000
Contribution margin		50,000
Less fixed expenses:		
Fixed overhead costs.	30,000	
Fixed selling and administrative expenses.	10,000	40,000
Net income		$ 10,000

analyzing the $12,000 ending inventory figure under the absorption costing method:

Variable manufacturing costs: 1,000 units × $7	$ 7,000
Fixed overhead costs: 1,000 units × $5.	5,000
Total inventory value.	$12,000

In summary, of the $30,000 in fixed overhead cost incurred during the period, only $25,000 (5,000 units sold × $5) has been included in cost of goods sold. The remaining $5,000 (1,000 units *not* sold × $5) has been deferred in inventory to the next period.

2.   Under the variable costing method, the entire $30,000 in fixed overhead cost has been treated as an expense of the current period (see the bottom portion of the variable costing income statement).

3.   The ending inventory figure under the variable costing method is $5,000 lower than it is under the absorption costing method. The reason is that under variable costing, only the variable manufacturing costs have been added to units of product and therefore included in inventory:

Variable manufacturing costs: 1,000 units × $7	$7,000

The $5,000 difference in ending inventories explains the difference in net income reported between the two costing methods. Net income is $5,000 *higher* under absorption costing since, as explained above, $5,000 of fixed overhead cost has been deferred in inventory to the next period under that costing method.

4. The absorption costing income statement makes no distinction between fixed and variable costs; therefore, it is not well suited for CVP computations, which we have emphasized as being important to good planning and control. To generate data for CVP analysis, it would be necessary to spend considerable time reworking and reclassifying the absorption statement.

5. The variable costing approach to costing units of product blends very well with the contribution approach to the income statement, since both concepts are based on the idea of classifying costs by behavior. The variable costing data in Exhibit 8–2 could be used immediately in CVP computations.

The Definition of an Asset

Essentially, the difference between the absorption costing method and the variable costing method centers on the matter of timing. Advocates of variable costing say that fixed manufacturing costs should be released against revenues immediately in total, whereas advocates of absorption costing say that fixed manufacturing costs should be released against revenues bit by bit as units of product are sold. Any units of product not sold under absorption costing result in fixed costs being inventoried and carried forward *as assets* to the next period. The solution to the controversy as to which costing method is "right" should therefore rest in large part on whether fixed costs added to inventory fall within the definition of an asset as this concept is generally viewed in accounting theory.

What Is an Asset?
A cost is normally viewed as being an asset if it can be shown that it has revenue-producing powers, or if it can be shown that it will be beneficial in some way to operations in future periods. In short, a cost is an asset if it can be shown that it has *future service potential* that can be identified. For example, insurance prepayments are viewed as being assets, since they have future service potential. The prepayments acquire protection that can be used in future periods to guard against losses that might otherwise hinder operations. If fixed production costs added to inventory under absorption costing are indeed properly called assets, then they too must meet this test of service potential.

The Absorption Costing View
Advocates of absorption costing argue that fixed production costs added to inventory do, indeed, have future service potential. They take the position that if production exceeds sales, then a benefit to future periods is created in the form of an inventory that can be carried forward and sold, resulting in a future inflow of revenue. They argue that *all costs* involved in the creation of inventory should be carried forward as assets—not just the variable costs. The fixed costs of depreciation, taxes, insurance, supervisory salaries, and so on, are just as essential to the creation of units of product as are the variable costs. It would be just as impossible to create units of product in the absence of equipment as it would be to create them in the absence of raw materials or in the absence of workers to operate the machines.

In sum, proponents of absorption costing argue that until the fixed production costs have been recognized and attached, units of product have not been fully costed. Both variable and fixed costs become inseparably attached as units are produced and *remain* inseparably attached regardless of whether the units are sold immediately or carried forward as inventory to generate revenue in future periods.

The Variable Costing View   Advocates of variable costing argue that a cost has service potential and is therefore an asset *only if its incurrence now will make it unnecessary to incur the same cost again in the future*. Service potential is therefore said to hinge on the matter of *future cost avoidance*. If the incurrence of a cost now will have no effect on whether or not the same cost will be incurred again in the future, then that cost is viewed as having no relevance to future events. It is argued that such a cost can in no way represent a future benefit or service.

For example, the prepayment of insurance is viewed as being an asset because the cash outlays made when the insurance is acquired make it unnecessary to sustain the same outlays again in the future periods for which insurance protection has been purchased. In short, by making insurance payments now, a company *avoids* having to make payments in the future. Since prepayments of insurance result in *future cost avoidance,* the prepayments qualify as assets.

This type of cost avoidance does not exist in the case of fixed production costs. The incurrence of fixed production costs in one year in no way reduces the necessity to incur the same costs again in the following year. Since the incurrence of fixed production costs does not result in *future cost avoidance,* the costs of one year can have no relevance to future events and therefore cannot possibly represent a future benefit or service. Variable costing advocates argue, therefore, that no part of the fixed production costs of one year should ever be carried forward as an asset to the following year. Such costs do not result in future cost avoidance— the key test for any asset.

EXTENDED COMPARISON OF INCOME DATA

Objective 3
Prepare income statements using both variable and absorption costing, and reconcile the two net income figures.

Having gained some insights into the conceptual differences between absorption and variable costing, we are now prepared to take a more detailed look at the differences in the income data generated by these two approaches to the costing process. Exhibit 8–3 presents data covering a span of three years. In the first year, production and sales are equal. In the second year, production exceeds sales. In the third year, the tables are reversed, with sales exceeding production.

Certain generalizations can be drawn from the data in Exhibit 8–3.

1.   When production and sales are equal, the same net income will be realized regardless of whether absorption or variable costing is being used (see year 1 in Exhibit 8–3). The reason is that when production and sales are equal, there is no chance for fixed overhead costs to be deferred in inventory or released from inventory under absorption costing.

2.   When production exceeds sales, the net income reported under absorption costing will generally be greater than the net income reported under variable costing (see year 2 in Exhibit 8–3). The reason is that when more is produced than is sold, part of the fixed overhead costs of the current period are deferred in inventory to the next period under absorption costing, as discussed earlier. In year 2, for example, $30,000 of fixed overhead cost (5,000 units × $6 per unit) has been deferred in inventory to year 3 under the absorption approach. Only that portion of the fixed overhead costs of year 2 under absorption costing that is associated with *units sold* is charged against income for that year.

Under variable costing, however, *all* of the fixed overhead costs of year 2 have

EXHIBIT 8–3

Variable and Absorption Costing—Extended Income Data

Basic Data

Sales price per unit	$ 20
Variable manufacturing costs per unit (direct materials, direct labor, and variable overhead).	8
Fixed manufacturing overhead costs (total).	150,000

Cost of producing one unit of product:
Under variable costing:

Variable manufacturing costs	$ 8

Under absorption costing:

Variable manufacturing costs	$ 8
Fixed overhead costs (based on a normal production volume of 25,000 units per year—$150,000 ÷ 25,000 units).	6
Total absorption costs	$ 14

Selling and administrative expenses are assumed, for simplicity, to be all fixed at $90,000 per year.

	Year 1	Year 2	Year 3	Three Years Together
Beginning inventory in units	–0–	–0–	5,000	–0–
Number of units produced.	25,000	25,000	25,000	75,000
Number of units sold	25,000	20,000	30,000	75,000
Ending inventory in units	–0–	5,000	–0–	–0–

Variable Costing

	Year 1	Year 2	Year 3	Three Years Together
Sales	$500,000	$400,000	$600,000	$1,500,000
Less variable expenses:				
Variable cost of goods sold:				
Beginning inventory	–0–	–0–	40,000	–0–
Variable manufacturing costs (25,000 units × $8).	200,000	200,000	200,000	600,000
Goods available for sale.	200,000	200,000	240,000	600,000
Less ending inventory (5,000 units × $8)	–0–	40,000	–0–	–0–
Variable cost of goods sold	200,000*	160,000*	240,000*	600,000
Variable selling and administrative expenses.	–0–	–0–	–0–	–0–
Total variable expenses	200,000	160,000	240,000	600,000
Contribution margin	300,000	240,000	360,000	900,000
Less fixed expenses:				
Manufacturing overhead.	150,000	150,000	150,000	450,000
Selling and administrative expenses.	90,000	90,000	90,000	270,000
Total fixed expenses	240,000	240,000	240,000	720,000
Net income	$ 60,000	$ –0–	$120,000	$ 180,000

Absorption Costing

	Year 1	Year 2	Year 3	Three Years Together
Sales	$500,000	$400,000	$600,000	$1,500,000
Less cost of goods sold:				
Beginning inventory	–0–	–0–	70,000	–0–
Add cost of goods manufactured (25,000 units × $14).	350,000	350,000	350,000	1,050,000
Goods available for sale.	350,000	350,000	420,000	1,050,000
Less ending inventory (5,000 units × $14).	–0–	70,000	–0–	–0–
Cost of goods sold	350,000	280,000	420,000	1,050,000
Gross margin.	150,000	120,000	180,000	450,000
Less selling and administrative expenses	90,000	90,000	90,000	270,000
Net income	$ 60,000	$ 30,000	$ 90,000	$ 180,000

* The variable cost of goods sold could have been computed more simply as follows:
Year 1: 25,000 units sold × $8 = $200,000.
Year 2: 20,000 units sold × $8 = $160,000.
Year 3: 30,000 units sold × $8 = $240,000.

been charged immediately against income as a period cost. As a result, the net income for year 2 under variable costing is $30,000 *lower* than it is under absorption costing. Exhibit 8–4 contains a reconciliation of the variable costing and absorption costing net income figures.

3.   When production is less than sales, the net income reported under the absorption costing approach will generally be less than the net income reported under the variable costing approach (see year 3 in Exhibit 8–3). The reason is that when more is sold than is produced, inventories are drawn down and fixed overhead costs that were previously deferred in inventory under absorption costing are released and charged against income (known as **fixed overhead cost released from inventory**). In year 3, for example, the $30,000 in fixed overhead cost deferred in inventory under the absorption approach from year 2 to year 3 is released from inventory through the sales process and charged against income. As a result, the cost of goods sold for year 3 contains not only all of the fixed overhead costs for year 3 (since all that was produced in year 3 was sold in year 3) but $30,000 of fixed overhead cost from year 2 as well.

By contrast, under variable costing only the fixed overhead costs of year 3 have been charged against year 3. The result is that net income under variable costing is $30,000 *higher* than it is under absorption costing. Exhibit 8–4 contains a reconciliation of the variable costing and absorption costing net income figures.

4.   Over an *extended* period of time, the net income figures reported under absorption costing and variable costing will tend to be the same. The reason is that over the long run sales can't exceed production, nor can production much exceed sales. The shorter the time period, the more the net income figures will tend to differ.

EXHIBIT 8–4

Reconciliation of Variable Costing and Absorption Costing—Net Income Data from Exhibit 8–3

	Year 1	Year 2	Year 3
Variable costing net income	$60,000	$ –0–	$120,000
Add fixed overhead costs deferred in inventory under absorption costing (5,000 units × $6 per unit).	—	30,000	—
Deduct fixed overhead costs released from inventory under absorption costing (5,000 units × $6 per unit).	—	—	(30,000)
Absorption costing net income.	$60,000	$30,000	$ 90,000

EXHIBIT 8–5

Comparative Income Effects—Variable and Absorption Costing

Relationship between Production and Sales	Costing Method	
	Variable Costing	**Absorption Costing**
	As compared to the other costing method, net income will tend to be:	
Production is equal to sales	Same	Same
Production is greater than sales	Lower	Higher*
Production is less than sales	Higher	Lower†

* Net income will tend to be higher since fixed overhead cost will be *deferred* in inventory under absorption costing.

† Net income will tend to be lower since fixed overhead cost will be *released* from inventory under absorption costing.

The points that we have made above regarding variable and absorption costing are summarized in Exhibit 8–5.

EFFECT OF CHANGES IN PRODUCTION ON NET INCOME

Exhibit 8–6 presents a reverse situation from that depicted in Exhibit 8–3. In Exhibit 8–3, we made production constant and allowed sales to fluctuate from period to period. In Exhibit 8–6, sales are constant and production fluctuates. Our purpose in Exhibit 8–6 is to observe the effect of changes in production on net income under both variable and absorption costing.

Objective 4
Explain the effect of changes in production on the net income reported under both variable and absorption costing.

Variable Costing

Net income is *not* affected by changes in production under variable costing. Notice from Exhibit 8–6 that net income is the same for all three years under the variable costing approach, although production exceeds sales in one year and is less than sales in another year. In short, the only thing that can affect net income under variable costing is a change in sales—a change in production has no impact when variable costing is in use.

Absorption Costing

Net income *is* affected by changes in production when absorption costing is in use, however. As shown in Exhibit 8–6, net income under the absorption approach goes up in year 2, in response to the increase in production for that year, and then goes down in year 3, in response to the drop in production for that year. Note particularly that net income goes up and down between these two years *even though the same number of units is sold in each year*. The reason for this effect can be traced to the shifting of fixed overhead cost between periods under the absorption costing method.

Since this shifting of fixed overhead cost has already been discussed in preceding sections, at this point all we need to consider is how it affects the data in Exhibit 8–6. As shown in the exhibit, production exceeds sales in year 2, thereby causing 10,000 units to be carried forward as inventory to year 3. Each unit produced during year 2 has $6 in fixed overhead cost attached to it (see the unit cost computations at the top of Exhibit 8–6). Therefore, $60,000 (10,000 units × $6) of the fixed overhead costs of year 2 are not charged against that year but rather are added to the inventory account (along with the variable manufacturing costs). As a result, the net income of year 2 rises sharply, even though the same number of units is sold in year 2 as in the other years.

The reverse effect occurs in year 3. Since sales exceed production in year 3, that year is forced to cover all of its own fixed overhead costs as well as the fixed overhead costs carried forward in inventory from year 2. The result is a substantial drop in net income during year 3, although, as we have noted, the same number of units is sold in that year as in the other years.

The Impact on the Manager

Opponents of absorption costing argue that this shifting of fixed overhead cost between periods can be confusing to a manager and can cause him or her to misinterpret data or to make faulty decisions. Look again at the data in Exhibit 8–6; the manager might wonder why net income went up substantially in year 2

EXHIBIT 8–6

Sensitivity of Costing Methods to Changes in Production

Basic Data

Sales price per unit.	$ 25
Variable manufacturing costs per unit	10
Fixed manufacturing overhead costs (total)	300,000
Selling and administrative expenses (all assumed, for simplicity, to be fixed)	210,000

	Year 1	Year 2	Year 3
Number of units produced.	40,000	50,000	30,000
Number of units sold	40,000	40,000	40,000
Cost of producing one unit:			
Under variable costing (variable manufacturing costs only)	$10.00	$10.00	$10.00
Under absorption costing:			
Variable manufacturing costs.	$10.00	$10.00	$10.00
Fixed overhead costs ($300,000 total spread in each year over the number of units produced)	7.50	6.00	10.00
Total cost per unit	$17.50	$16.00	$20.00

Variable Costing

	Year 1	Year 2	Year 3
Sales (40,000 units)	$1,000,000	$1,000,000	$1,000,000
Less variable expenses:			
Variable cost of goods sold:			
Beginning inventory.	–0–	–0–	100,000
Variable manufacturing costs, at $10 per unit produced	400,000	500,000	300,000
Goods available for sale	400,000	500,000	400,000
Less ending inventory (10,000 units × $10)	–0–	100,000	–0–
Variable cost of goods sold	400,000	400,000	400,000
Variable selling and administrative expenses.	–0–	–0–	–0–
Total variable expenses	400,000	400,000	400,000
Contribution margin.	600,000	600,000	600,000
Less fixed expenses:			
Manufacturing overhead.	300,000	300,000	300,000
Selling and administrative expenses.	210,000	210,000	210,000
Total fixed expenses	510,000	510,000	510,000
Net income	$ 90,000	$ 90,000	$ 90,000

Absorption Costing

	Year 1	Year 2	Year 3
Sales (40,000 units)	$1,000,000	$1,000,000	$1,000,000
Less cost of goods sold:			
Beginning inventory.	–0–	–0–	160,000
Add cost of goods manufactured	700,000*	800,000*	600,000*
Goods available for sale	700,000	800,000	760,000
Less ending inventory.	–0–	160,000†	–0–
Cost of goods sold	700,000	640,000	760,000
Gross margin.	300,000	360,000	240,000
Less selling and administrative expenses	210,000	210,000	210,000
Net income	$ 90,000	$ 150,000	$ 30,000

* Cost of goods manufactured:
   Year 1: 40,000 units × $17.50 = $700,000.
   Year 2: 50,000 units × $16.00 = $800,000.
   Year 3: 30,000 units × $20.00 = $600,000.

† Observe that 50,000 units are produced in year 2, but only 40,000 units are sold. The 10,000 units going into the ending inventory have the following costs attached to them:

Variable manufacturing costs: 10,000 units × $10	$100,000
Fixed manufacturing overhead costs: 10,000 units × $6 . . .	60,000
Total inventory cost	$160,000

under absorption costing, when sales remained the same as in the prior year. Was it a result of lower selling costs, more efficient operations, or was some other factor involved? The manager is unable to tell, looking simply at the absorption costing income statement. Then in year 3, net income drops sharply, even though again the same number of units is sold as in the other two years. Why would income rise in one year and then drop in the next? The figures seem erratic and contradictory and can lead to confusion and a loss of confidence in the integrity of the statement data.

By contrast, the variable costing income statements in Exhibit 8–6 are clear and easy to read. Sales remain constant over the three-year period covered in the exhibit, so both contribution margin and net income also remain constant. The statements are consistent with what the manager would expect to happen under the circumstances, so they tend to generate confidence rather than confusion.

To avoid mistakes when absorption costing is used, the manager must be alert to any changes that may take place during a period in inventory levels or in unit costs. By this means, he or she should be able to properly interpret any erratic movement in net income that may occur under the absorption costing method.

One way to overcome problems such as those discussed above is to use normalized overhead rates. A **normalized overhead rate** is a rate based on the *average* activity of many periods—past and present—rather than based only on the expected activity of the current period. Thus, unit costs are stable from year to year. Even if normalized overhead rates are used, however, net income can still be erratic if the under- or overapplied overhead that results from an imbalance between production and sales is taken to cost of goods sold. The only way to avoid the problems entirely is to use normalized overhead rates and to place any under- or overapplied overhead in a balance sheet clearing account of some type. However, this is rarely done in practice.

OTHER FACTORS IN CHOOSING A COSTING METHOD

In choosing between variable and absorption costing, several additional factors should be considered by the manager. These factors are discussed in this section.

Objective 5
Explain the advantages and limitations of both the variable and absorption costing methods.

CVP Analysis and Absorption Costing

Absorption costing is widely regarded as a product costing method. Many firms use the absorption approach exclusively because of its focus on "full" costing of units of product. A weakness of the method, however, is its inability to dovetail well with CVP analysis.

To illustrate, refer again to Exhibit 8–3. Let us compute the break-even point for the firm represented by the data in this exhibit. To obtain the break-even point, we divide total fixed costs by the contribution margin per unit:

Sales price per unit	$20
Variable costs per unit	8
Contribution margin per unit	$12
Fixed overhead costs	$150,000
Fixed selling and administrative costs	90,000
Total fixed costs	$240,000

$$\frac{\text{Total fixed costs}}{\text{Contribution margin per unit}} = \frac{\$240,000}{\$12} = 20,000 \text{ units}$$

We have computed the break-even point to be 20,000 units sold. Notice from Exhibit 8–3 that in year 2 the firm sold exactly 20,000 units, the break-even volume. Under the contribution approach, using variable costing, the firm does break even in year 2, showing zero net income or loss. *Under absorption costing, however, the firm shows a positive net income of $30,000 for year 2.* How can this be so? How can absorption costing produce a positive net income when the firm sold exactly the break-even volume of units?

The answer lies in the fact that $30,000 in fixed overhead costs were deferred in inventory during year 2 under absorption costing and therefore did not appear as charges against income. By deferring these fixed overhead costs in inventory, the firm was able to show a profit even though it sold exactly the break-even volume of units. Absorption costing runs into similar kinds of difficulty in other areas of CVP analysis and often requires considerable manipulation of data before figures are available that are usable for decision-making purposes.

Pricing Decisions

In addition to the points mentioned above regarding CVP analysis, advocates of variable costing argue that it provides more useful cost information for pricing decisions than does absorption costing. Since variable costing focuses on cost behavior and permits the use of a contribution income statement, it is argued that management is able to see the effects of changes in price on volume and the effects of changes in volume on costs more readily than when absorption costing is in use. With better information available on the relationship between volume and cost, it is argued that management is in a better position to make effective pricing decisions.

Furthermore, it is argued that when absorption costing is in use, there is a tendency to reject any price that is less than full cost. We saw in the preceding chapter, however, that under some conditions a price less than full cost can be advantageous to a firm. It is believed that management is able to see such conditions more readily when variable costing is in use, and thereby management is able to price in such a way as to maximize profits for the firm. Pricing decisions are discussed more fully in Appendix L at the end of the book.

External Reporting and Income Taxes

For external reporting on financial statements, a company is required to cost units of product by the absorption costing method. In like manner, the absorption costing method must be used in preparing tax returns. In short, the contribution approach is limited to *internal* use by the managers of a company.

The majority of accountants would agree that absorption costing *should* be used in external reporting. That is, most accountants feel that for *external reporting purposes,* units of product *should* contain a portion of fixed manufacturing overhead, along with variable manufacturing costs. The absorption costing argument that a unit of product is not fully costed until it reflects a portion of the fixed costs of production is difficult to refute, particularly as it applies to the preparing of information to be reported to stockholders and others.

The contribution approach finds its greatest application internally as an assist to the manager. No particular problems are created by using *both* costing methods—the contribution method internally and the absorption method externally. As we demonstrated earlier in Exhibit 8–4, the adjustment from variable costing net income to absorption costing net income is a simple one and can be made in a few hours' time at year-end in order to produce an absorption costing net income figure for use on financial statements.

Advantages of the Contribution Approach

As stated above, many accountants feel that under the appropriate circumstances there are certain advantages to be gained from using the contribution approach (with variable costing) internally, even if the absorption approach is used externally for reporting purposes. These advantages can be summarized as follows:

1. CVP relationship data needed for profit planning purposes are readily obtained from the regular accounting statements. Hence, management does not have to work with two separate sets of data to relate one to the other.
2. The profit for a period is not affected by changes in absorption of fixed overhead costs resulting from building or reducing inventory. Other things remaining equal (for example, selling prices, costs, sales mix), profits move in the same direction as sales when variable costing is in use.
3. Manufacturing cost and income statements in the variable cost form follow management's thinking more closely than does the absorption cost form for these statements. For this reason, management finds it easier to understand and to use variable cost reports.
4. The impact of fixed costs on profits is emphasized because the total amount of such cost for the period appears in the income statement.
5. Marginal income figures facilitate relative appraisal of products, territories, classes of customers, and other segments of the business without having the results obscured by allocation of joint (common) fixed costs.
6. Variable costing ties in with cost control methods such as standard costs and flexible budgets.[4] In fact, the flexible budget is an aspect of variable costing, and many companies thus use variable costing methods for this purpose without recognizing them as such.
7. Variable cost constitutes a concept of inventory cost that corresponds closely with the current out-of-pocket expenditure necessary to manufacture the goods.

IMPACT OF JIT INVENTORY METHODS

We have learned in this chapter that variable and absorption costing will provide different net income figures whenever the number of units produced is different from the number of units sold. We have also learned that the absorption costing net income figure can be erratic, sometimes moving in a direction that is different from the movement in sales.

When companies employ JIT inventory methods, these problems with net income under absorption costing are either eliminated or reduced to insignificant proportions. The reason is as follows: The erratic movement of net income under absorption costing and the differences in net income between absorption and variable costing arise *because of changing levels of inventory.* Under JIT, goods are produced strictly to customers' orders. As a result, there are no goods in process at year-end, and no finished goods in warehouses waiting for orders from customers. Thus, with production geared strictly to sales, inventories are largely (or entirely) eliminated, thereby eliminating also any opportunity for fixed over-

Objective 6
Explain how the use of JIT inventory methods decreases or eliminates the difference in net income reported under the variable and absorption costing methods.

---

[4] Standard costs and flexible budgets are covered in Chapters 10 and 11.

head costs to be shifted between periods under absorption costing. When JIT is in operation, therefore, both variable and absorption costing will show the same net income figure, and the net income under absorption costing will move in the same direction as movements in sales.

Of course, the cost of a unit of product will still be different between variable and absorption costing, as explained earlier in the chapter. But the differences in net income will largely disappear when JIT is used, thereby making it easier for management to interpret the data produced on an absorption costing income statement. This is an important point, since we have already stated that absorption costing must be used for external reporting purposes. Thus, by employing the JIT concept, companies gain a major advantage in the form of an income statement that is clearer and easier to understand.

SUMMARY

In costing products and services, companies can use either variable or absorption costing. Under variable costing, only those production costs that vary with activity are treated as product costs. This includes direct materials, direct labor, and variable overhead. Fixed manufacturing overhead is treated as a period cost and charged off against revenue as it is incurred, the same as selling and administrative expenses. By contrast, absorption costing treats fixed manufacturing overhead as a product cost, along with direct materials, direct labor, and variable overhead.

Since absorption costing treats fixed manufacturing overhead as a product cost, a portion of fixed overhead is added to each unit as it is produced. If units of product are unsold at the end of a period, then the fixed overhead cost attached to the units is carried with them into the inventory account and deferred to the next period. When these units are sold during the next period, the fixed overhead cost attached to them is released from the inventory account and charged against revenues as part of cost of goods sold. Thus, under absorption costing, it is possible to defer a portion of the fixed overhead cost of one period to the next period through the inventory account.

Unfortunately, this shifting of fixed overhead cost between periods can cause net income to move in an erratic manner and can result in confusion and unwise decisions on the part of management. To guard against mistakes when they interpret income statement data, managers must be alert to any changes that may have taken place in inventory levels or in unit costs during the period.

Variable costing can't be used externally for either financial reporting or income tax purposes. However, it is often used internally for planning purposes. The popularity of the variable costing approach can be traced to the fact that it dovetails well with CVP concepts that are often indispensable in profit planning and decision making.

REVIEW PROBLEM

Dexter Company produces and sells a single product. Selected cost and operating data relating to the product for a recent year are given below:

Beginning inventory in units	–0–
Units produced during the year. . . .	10,000
Units sold during the year	8,000
Ending inventory in units	2,000
Selling price per unit	$ 50

Selling and administrative costs:
    Variable per unit . . . . $ 5
    Fixed per year   70,000

Manufacturing costs:
    Variable per unit:
        Direct materials.   11
        Direct labor   6
        Variable overhead.   3
    Fixed per year 100,000

Required

1. Assume that the company uses absorption costing.
   a. Compute the manufactured cost of one unit of product.
   b. Prepare an income statement for the year.
2. Assume that the company uses variable costing.
   a. Compute the manufactured cost of one unit of product.
   b. Prepare an income statement for the year.
3. Reconcile the variable costing and absorption costing net income figures.

1. a. Under absorption costing, all manufacturing costs, variable and fixed, are added *Solution to Review*
    to the cost of a unit of product: *Problem*

        Direct materials. $11
        Direct labor   6
        Variable overhead.   3
        Fixed overhead ($100,000 ÷ 10,000 units) . . . 10
        Total cost per unit. $30

   b. The absorption costing income statement follows:

Sales (8,000 units × $50)		$400,000
Cost of goods sold:		
Beginning inventory	$ –0–	
Add cost of goods manufactured		
(10,000 units × $30)	300,000	
Goods available for sale	300,000	
Less ending inventory (2,000 units × $30)	60,000	240,000
Gross margin		160,000
Less selling and administrative expenses		110,000*
Net income		$ 50,000

    * Variable (8,000 units × $5) . . . $ 40,000
      Fixed per year.   70,000
        Total $110,000

2. a. Under variable costing, only the variable manufacturing costs are added to the
    cost of a unit of product:

        Direct materials $11
        Direct labor 6
        Variable overhead 3
        Total cost per unit $20

   b. The variable costing income statement follows. Notice that the variable cost of
    goods sold is computed in a simpler, more direct manner than in the examples
    provided earlier. On a variable costing income statement, either approach is ac-
    ceptable.

Sales (8,000 units × $50)		$400,000
Less variable expenses:		
Variable cost of goods sold		
(8,000 units × $20)	$160,000	
Variable selling and administrative		
expenses (8,000 units × $5)	40,000	200,000
Contribution margin.		200,000
Less fixed expenses:		
Fixed overhead cost for the year	100,000	
Fixed selling and administrative expenses	70,000	170,000
Net income		$ 30,000

3.   The reconciliation of the variable and absorption costing net income figures follows:

Variable costing net income	$30,000
Add fixed overhead costs deferred in	
inventory under absorption costing	
(2,000 units × $10)	20,000
Absorption costing net income	$50,000

KEY TERMS FOR REVIEW

Objective 7
Define or explain the key
terms listed at the end of
the chapter.

Absorption costing   A costing method that includes all manufacturing costs—direct materials, direct labor, and both variable and fixed manufacturing overhead—in the cost of a unit of product. Absorption costing is also referred to as the *full cost* method. (p. 326)

Direct costing   Another term for variable costing. See *Variable costing*. (p. 326)

Fixed overhead cost deferred in inventory   The portion of the fixed overhead cost of a period that goes into inventory under the absorption costing method as a result of production exceeding sales. (p. 329)

Fixed overhead cost released from inventory   The portion of the fixed overhead cost of a *prior* period that becomes an expense of the current period under the absorption costing method as a result of sales exceeding production. (p. 334)

Full cost method   See *Absorption costing*. (p. 326)

Marginal costing   Another term for variable costing. See *Variable costing*. (p. 326)

Normalized overhead rate   A rate based on the average activity of many periods—past and present—rather than based only on the expected activity of the current period. (p. 337)

Variable costing   A costing method that includes only variable manufacturing costs—direct materials, direct labor, and variable overhead—in the cost of a unit of product. Also see *Marginal costing* or *Direct costing*. (p. 326)

QUESTIONS

8–1   What is the basic difference between absorption costing and variable costing?

8–2   Are selling and administrative expenses treated as product costs or as period costs under variable costing?

8–3   Explain how fixed overhead costs are shifted from one period to another under absorption costing.

8–4   What arguments can be advanced in favor of treating fixed overhead costs as product costs?

8–5   What arguments can be advanced in favor of treating fixed overhead costs as period costs?

8–6 If production and sales are equal, which method would you expect to show the higher net income, variable costing or absorption costing? Why?

8–7 If production exceeds sales, which method would you expect to show the higher net income, variable costing or absorption costing? Why?

8–8 If fixed overhead costs are released from inventory under absorption costing, what does this tell you about the level of production in relation to the level of sales?

8–9 During 19x3, Parker Company had $5,000,000 in sales and reported a $300,000 loss in its annual report to stockholders. According to a CVP analysis prepared for management's use, $5,000,000 in sales is the break-even point for the company. Did the company's inventory level for the year increase, decrease, or remain unchanged? Explain.

8–10 Under absorption costing, how is it possible to increase net income without increasing sales?

8–11 What limitations are there to the use of variable costing?

8–12 How does the use of JIT inventory methods reduce or eliminate the difference in reported net income between absorption and variable costing?

EXERCISES

Selected information on the operations of Diston Company for 19x8 follows: **E8–1**

Beginning inventory in units	–0–
Units produced during the year	25,000
Units sold during the year	20,000
Ending inventory in units	5,000
Variable costs per unit:	
Direct materials	$7
Direct labor	4
Variable overhead	1
Variable selling expenses	2
Fixed costs per year:	
Manufacturing overhead	$200,000
Selling and administrative expenses	90,000

The company produces and sells a single product. Work in process inventories are nominal and can be ignored.

1. Assume that the company uses absorption costing. Compute the cost of one unit of product.   *Required*
2. Assume that the company uses variable costing. Compute the cost of one unit of product.

Refer to the data in E8–1. An income statement prepared under the absorption costing method for 19x8 follows: **E8–2**

Sales (20,000 units × $30)		$600,000
Cost of goods sold:		
Beginning inventory	$ –0–	
Cost of goods manufactured (25,000 units × $?)	500,000	
Goods available for sale	500,000	
Less ending inventory (5,000 units × $?)	100,000	400,000
Gross margin		200,000
Less selling and administrative expenses:		
Variable selling	40,000	
Fixed selling and administrative expenses	90,000	130,000
Net income		$ 70,000

Required   1.   Determine how much of the $100,000 ending inventory above consists of fixed over-head cost deferred in inventory to the next period.

          2.   Prepare an income statement for 19x8, using the variable costing method. How do you explain the difference in net income between the two costing methods?

E8-3   Sierra Company produces and sells a single product. The following costs relate to its production and sale:

Variable costs per unit:	
Direct materials	$ 9
Direct labor	10
Manufacturing overhead	5
Selling and administrative expenses . . .	3
Fixed costs per year:	
Manufacturing overhead	$150,000
Selling and administrative expenses . . .	400,000

During the last year, 25,000 units were produced and 22,000 units were sold. The Finished Goods inventory account at the end of the year shows a balance of $72,000 for the 3,000 unsold units.

Required   1.   Is the company using absorption costing or variable costing to carry units in the Finished Goods inventory account? Show computations to support your answer.

          2.   Assume that the company wishes to prepare financial statements for the year to issue to its stockholders.

             a.   Is the $72,000 figure for finished goods inventory the correct amount to use on these statements for external reporting purposes? Explain.

             b.   At what dollar amount *should* the 3,000 units be carried in the inventory for external reporting purposes?

E8-4   Whitman Company has just completed its first year of operations. The company's accountant has prepared an income statement for the year, as follows (absorption costing basis):

WHITMAN COMPANY
Income Statement
For the Year 19x1

Sales (35,000 units at $25).		$875,000
Less cost of goods sold:		
Opening inventory	$ –0–	
Cost of goods manufactured (40,000 units at $16) . . .	640,000	
Goods available for sale	640,000	
Ending inventory (5,000 units at $16).	80,000	560,000
Gross margin		315,000
Less selling and administrative expenses		280,000
Net income		$ 35,000

The company's selling and administrative expenses consist of $210,000 per year in fixed expenses and $2 per unit sold in variable expenses. The $16 manufacturing cost per unit given above is computed as follows:

Direct materials	$ 5
Direct labor	6
Variable factory overhead.	1
Fixed factory overhead ($160,000 ÷ 40,000 units) . . .	4
Total cost per unit	$16

Required   1.   Redo the company's income statement in the contribution format, using variable cost-ing.

2. Reconcile any difference between the net income figure on your variable costing income statement and the net income figure on the absorption costing income statement above.

Lynch Company manufactures and sells a single product. The following costs were incurred during 19x1, the company's first year of operations:

E8-5

> Variable costs per unit:
>   Production:
>   Direct materials $6
>   Direct labor   9
>   Variable manufacturing overhead . . .   3   — *Never part of C/G/Sdz*
>   Selling and administrative   4
>   Fixed costs per year:
>   Manufacturing overhead $300,000
>   Selling and administrative   190,000

During 19x1, the company produced 25,000 units and sold 20,000 units. The selling price of the company's product is $50 per unit.

1. Assume that the company uses the absorption costing method:
   a. Compute the cost to produce one unit of product.
   b. Prepare an income statement for 19x1.
2. Assume that the company uses the variable costing method:
   a. Compute the cost to produce one unit of product.
   b. Prepare an income statement for 19x1.

Required

PROBLEMS

Production Schedule   The date is September 30, 19x5. Fred Cavalas, the manager of Echo Products' Eastern Division, is trying to decide what production schedule to set for the last quarter of the year. The Eastern Division had planned to sell 3,600 units during 19x5, its first year of operations, but by September 30 only the following activity had been reported:

P8-6 Ethics and the Manager

	Units
Inventory, January 1	–0–
Production	2,400
Sales	2,000
Inventory, September 30.	400

The division can rent warehouse space to store up to 1,000 units. The minimum inventory level that the division should carry is 50 units. Mr. Cavalas is aware that production must be at least 200 units per quarter in order to retain a nucleus of key employees. Maximum production is 1,500 units per quarter.

Demand has been soft during 19x5, and the sales forecast for the last quarter is only 600 units. Due to the nature of the division's operations, fixed manufacturing overhead is a major element of product cost.

1. Assume that the division is using variable costing. How many units should be scheduled for production during the last quarter of the year? (The basic formula for computing the required production for a period in a company is: Expected sales + Desired ending inventory − Beginning inventory = Required production.) Show computations and explain your answer. Will the number of units scheduled for production affect the division's reported income or loss for the year? Explain.
2. Assume that the division is using absorption costing and that the divisional manager is given an annual bonus based on divisional operating income. If Mr. Cavalas wants to maximize his division's operating income for 19x5, how many units should be sched-

Required

uled for production during the last quarter? [See the formula in (1) above.] Show computations and explain your answer.

3. Identify the ethical issues involved in the decision Mr. Cavalas must make.

P8–7 Straightforward Variable Costing Statements   Heaton Company was organized on January 1, 19x4. During its first two years of operations, the company reported net income as follows (absorption costing basis):

	19x4	19x5
Sales (@ $25).	$1,000,000	$1,250,000
Less cost of goods sold:		
Opening inventory	–0–	90,000
Add cost of goods manufactured (@ $18) . . .	810,000	810,000
Goods available for sale	810,000	900,000
Less ending inventory (@ $18)	90,000	–0–
Cost of goods sold	720,000	900,000
Gross margin.	280,000	350,000
Less selling and administrative expenses*	210,000	230,000
Net income	$ 70,000	$ 120,000

* $2 per unit variable; $130,000 fixed each year.

The company's $18 unit cost is computed as follows:

Direct materials	$ 4
Direct labor	7
Variable manufacturing overhead.	1
Fixed manufacturing overhead ($270,000 ÷ 45,000 units) . . .	6
Total cost per unit	$18

Production and cost data for the two years are:

	19x4	19x5
Units produced	45,000	45,000
Units sold	40,000	50,000

Required 1. Prepare an income statement for each year in the contribution format, using variable costing.

2. Reconcile the absorption costing and the variable costing net income figures for each year.

P8–8 Straightforward Comparison of Costing Methods   High Country, Inc., produces and sells many recreational products. The company has just opened a new plant to produce a folding camp cot that will be marketed throughout the United States. The following cost and revenue data relate to May 19x8, the first month of the plant's operation:

Opening inventory.	–0–
Units produced	10,000
Units sold	8,000
Sales price per unit	$ 75
Selling and administrative expenses:	
Variable per unit	6
Fixed (total)	200,000
Manufacturing costs:	
Direct materials cost per unit	20
Direct labor cost per unit.	8
Variable overhead cost per unit	2
Fixed overhead cost (total).	100,000

Management is anxious to see how profitable the new camp cot will be and has asked that an income statement be prepared for May.

1. Assume that the company uses absorption costing.   *Required*
   a. Determine the cost to produce one unit of product.
   b. Prepare an income statement for May.
2. Assume that the company uses the contribution approach with variable costing.
   a. Determine the cost to produce one unit of product.
   b. Prepare an income statement for May.
3. Explain the reason for any difference in the ending inventory under the two costing methods and the impact of this difference on reported net income.

A Comparison of Costing Methods   Audio Products, Inc., has organized a new division   **P8–9**
to manufacture and sell CB radios. Monthly costs associated with the radios and with the plant in which the radios are manufactured are shown below:

Manufacturing costs:
Variable costs per unit:
Direct materials.	$ 40
Direct labor	8
Variable overhead.	2
Fixed overhead costs (total) . . .	360,000

Selling and administrative costs:
Variable	12% of sales
Fixed (total)	470,000

The radios sell for $150 each. During September 19x6, the first month of operations, the following activity was recorded:

Units produced . . .	12,000
Units sold.	10,000

1. Compute the cost of a single unit of product under: *Required*
   a. Absorption costing.
   b. Variable costing.
2. Prepare an income statement for the month, using absorption costing.
3. Prepare an income statement for the month, using variable costing.
4. Assume that the company must obtain additional financing in order to continue operations. As a member of top management, would you prefer to take the statement in (2) above or in (3) above with you as you meet with a group of prospective investors?
5. Reconcile the absorption costing and variable costing net income figures in (2) and (3) above for September.

Prepare and Reconcile Variable Costing Statements   Denton Company was organized   **P8–10**
on July 1, 19x3. The company manufactures and sells a single product. Cost data for the product are given below:

Variable costs per unit:
Direct materials.	$ 7
Direct labor	10
Variable manufacturing overhead	5
Variable selling and administrative . . .	3
Total variable cost per unit.	$25

Fixed costs per month:
Manufacturing overhead	$315,000
Selling and administrative	245,000
Total fixed cost per month	$560,000

The product sells for $60 per unit. Production and sales data for July and August follow:

	Units Produced	Units Sold
July.	17,500	15,000
August . . .	17,500	20,000

The company's accounting department has prepared income statements for both July and August. These statements, which have been prepared using absorption costing, are presented below:

	July 19x3	August 19x3
Sales	$900,000	$1,200,000
Less cost of goods sold:		
Opening inventory	–0–	100,000
Add cost of goods manufactured	700,000	700,000
Goods available for sale	700,000	800,000
Less ending inventory	100,000	–0–
Cost of goods sold	600,000	800,000
Gross margin	300,000	400,000
Less selling and administrative expenses . .	290,000	305,000
Net income	$ 10,000	$ 95,000

Required   1. Determine the cost of a single unit of product under:
   a. Absorption costing.
   b. Variable costing.
2. Prepare income statements for July and August using the contribution approach, with variable costing.
3. Reconcile the variable costing and absorption costing net income figures.
4. The company's accounting department has determined the company's break-even point to be 16,000 units per month, computed as follows:

$$\frac{\text{Fixed cost per month,} \quad \$560,000}{\text{Unit contribution margin,} \quad \$35} = 16,000 \text{ units}$$

"I'm confused," said the president. "The accounting people say that our break-even point is 16,000 units per month, but we sold only 15,000 units in July, and the income statement they prepared shows a $10,000 profit for that month. Either the income statement is wrong or the break-even point is wrong." Prepare a brief memo for the president, explaining what happened on the July income statement.

P8–11   Absorption and Variable Costing; Production Constant, Sales Fluctuate   Tami Tyler opened Tami's Creations, Inc., a small manufacturing company, at the beginning of the year. To get the company through its first quarter of operations, it has been necessary for Ms. Tyler to place a considerable strain on her own personal finances. An income statement for the first quarter is shown below. The statement was prepared by a friend who has just completed a course in managerial accounting at State University.

TAMI'S CREATIONS, INC.
Income Statement
For the Quarter Ended March 31, 19x1

Sales (28,000 units)		$1,120,000
Less variable expenses:		
Variable cost of goods sold*	$462,000	
Selling and administrative	168,000	630,000
Contribution margin		490,000
Less fixed expenses:		
Fixed manufacturing overhead . . .	300,000	
Selling and administrative	200,000	500,000
Net loss		$ (10,000)

* Consists of direct materials, direct labor, and variable overhead.

Ms. Tyler is discouraged over the loss shown for the quarter, particularly since she had planned to use the statement as support for a bank loan. Another friend, a CPA, insists that the company should be using absorption costing rather than variable costing, and argues that if absorption costing had been used the company would probably have reported at least some profit for the quarter.

At this point, Ms. Tyler is manufacturing only one product, a swimming suit. Production and cost data relating to the suit for the first quarter follow:

Units produced	30,000
Units sold	28,000
Variable costs per unit:	
Direct materials.	$ 3.50
Direct labor	12.00
Variable overhead.	1.00
Variable selling and administrative . . .	6.00

Required

1. Complete the following:
   a. Compute the cost of a unit of product under absorption costing.
   b. Redo the company's income statement for the quarter, using absorption costing.
   c. Reconcile the variable and absorption costing net income (loss) figures.
2. Was the CPA correct in suggesting that the company really earned a "profit" for the quarter? Explain.
3. During the second quarter of operations, the company again produced 30,000 units but sold 32,000 units. (Assume no change in total fixed costs.)
   a. Prepare an income statement for the quarter, using variable costing.
   b. Prepare an income statement for the quarter, using absorption costing.
   c. Reconcile the variable costing and absorption costing net income figures.

Prepare Variable Costing Statements; Sales Constant, Production Varies; JIT Impact   P8–12

"This makes no sense at all," said Bill Sharp, president of Essex Company. "We sold the same number of units this year as we did last year, yet our profits have more than doubled. Who made the goof—the computer or the people who operate it?" The statements to which Mr. Sharp was referring are shown below (absorption costing basis):

	19x1	19x2
Sales (20,000 units each year)	$700,000	$700,000
Less cost of goods sold	460,000	400,000
Gross margin	240,000	300,000
Less selling and administrative expenses . . .	200,000	200,000
Net income	$ 40,000	$100,000

The company was organized on January 1, 19x1, so the statements above show the results of its first two years of operation. In the first year, the company produced and sold 20,000 units; in the second year, the company again sold 20,000 units, but it increased production in order to have a stock of units on hand, as shown below:

	19x1	19x2
Production in units.	20,000	25,000
Sales in units	20,000	20,000
Variable production cost per unit . . .	$8	$8
Fixed overhead costs (total)	$300,000	$300,000

Essex Company produces a single product; fixed overhead costs are applied to the product on the basis of *each year's production*. (Thus, a new fixed overhead rate is computed each year, as in Exhibit 8–6.) Variable selling and administrative expenses are $1 per unit sold.

Required

1. Compute the cost of a single unit of product for each year under:
   a. Absorption costing.
   b. Variable costing.
2. Prepare an income statement for each year, using the contribution approach with variable costing.
3. Reconcile the variable costing and absorption costing net income figures for each year.
4. Explain to the president why, under absorption costing, the net income for 19x2 was higher than the net income for 19x1, although the same number of units was sold in each year.
5. a. Explain how operations would have differed in 19x2 if the company had been using JIT inventory methods.
   b. If JIT had been in use during 19x2, what would the company's net income have been under absorption costing? Explain the reason for any difference between this income figure and the figure reported by the company in the statements above.

P8–13 **Prepare and Interpret Statements; Changes in Both Sales and Production; Automation; JIT**   Starfax, Inc., was organized on January 2, 19x1. The company manufactures a small part that is widely used in various electronic products such as home computers. Operating results for the first three years of activity were as follows (absorption costing basis):

	19x1	19x2	19x3
Sales	$800,000	$640,000	$800,000
Cost of goods sold:			
Beginning inventory.	–0–	–0–	200,000
Add cost of goods manufactured	580,000	600,000	560,000
Goods available for sale	580,000	600,000	760,000
Less ending inventory.	–0–	200,000	140,000
Cost of goods sold	580,000	400,000	620,000
Gross margin	220,000	240,000	180,000
Selling and administrative expenses	190,000	180,000	190,000
Net income (loss)	$ 30,000	$ 60,000	$(10,000)

In the latter part of 19x2, a competitor went out of business and in the process dumped a large number of units on the market. As a result, Starfax's sales dropped by 20 percent during 19x2 even though production increased during that year. Management had expected sales to remain constant at 50,000 units; the increased production was designed to provide the company with a buffer of protection against unexpected spurts in demand. By the start of 19x3, management could see that inventory was excessive and that spurts in demand were unlikely. To work off the excessive inventories, Starfax cut back production during 19x3, as shown below:

	19x1	19x2	19x3
Production in units . . .	50,000	60,000	40,000
Sales in units	50,000	40,000	50,000

Additional information about the company follows:

a.   The company's plant is highly automated. Variable manufacturing costs (direct materials, direct labor, and variable overhead) total only $2 per unit, and fixed manufacturing costs total $480,000 per year.

b.   Fixed manufacturing costs are applied to units of product on the basis of each year's production. (That is, a new fixed overhead rate is computed each year, as in Exhibit 8–6.)

c.   Variable selling and administrative expenses were $1 per unit sold in each year. Fixed selling and administrative expenses totaled $140,000 each year.

d.   The company uses a FIFO inventory flow.

Starfax's management can't understand why profits doubled during 19x2 when sales dropped by 20 percent, and why a loss was incurred during 19x3 when sales recovered to previous levels.

1.   Prepare a new income statement for each year using the contribution approach, with variable costing.   *Required*

2.   Refer to the absorption costing income statements above.

   a.   Compute the cost to produce one unit of product in each year under absorption costing. (Show how much of this cost is variable and how much is fixed.)

   b.   Reconcile the variable costing and absorption costing net income figures for each year.

3.   Refer again to the absorption costing income statements. Explain why net income was higher in 19x2 than it was in 19x1 under the absorption approach, in light of the fact that fewer units were sold in 19x2 than in 19x1.

4.   Refer again to the absorption costing income statements. Explain why the company suffered a loss in 19x3 but reported a profit in 19x1, although the same number of units was sold in each year.

5.   a.   Explain how operations would have differed in 19x2 and 19x3 if the company had been using JIT inventory methods.

   b.   If JIT had been in use during 19x2 and 19x3, what would the company's net income (or loss) have been in each year under absorption costing? Explain the reason for any differences between these income figures and the figures reported by the company in the statements above.

CASES

The Case of the Plummeting Profits; Automation; JIT Impact   "These statements   **C8–14**
can't be right," said Ben Yoder, president of Rayco, Inc. "Our sales in the second quarter were up by 25 percent over the first quarter, yet these income statements show a precipitous drop in net income for the second quarter. Those accounting people have fouled something up." Mr. Yoder was referring to the following statements.

RAYCO, INC.
Income Statements
For the First Two Quarters

	First Quarter		Second Quarter	
Sales		$480,000		$600,000
Cost of goods sold:				
Beginning inventory	$ 80,000		$140,000	
Cost of goods manufactured. . . .	300,000		180,000	
Goods available for sale	380,000		320,000	
Ending inventory	140,000		20,000	
Cost of goods sold	240,000		300,000	
Add underapplied overhead	—	240,000	72,000	372,000
Gross margin		240,000		228,000
Less selling and administrative				
expenses		200,000		215,000
Net income		$ 40,000		$ 13,000

After studying the statements briefly, Mr. Yoder called in the controller to see if the mistake in the second quarter could be located before the figures were released to the press. The controller stated, "I'm sorry to say that those figures are correct, Ben. I agree that sales went up during the second quarter, but the problem is in production. You see, we budgeted to produce 15,000 units each quarter, but a strike on the west coast among some of our suppliers forced us to cut production in the second quarter back to only 9,000 units. That's what caused the drop in net income."

Mr. Yoder was confused by the controller's explanation. He replied, "This doesn't make sense. I ask you to explain why net income dropped when sales went up and you talk about production! So what if we had to cut back production? We still were able to increase sales by 25 percent. If sales go up, then net income should go up. If your statements can't show a simple thing like that, then it's time for some changes in your area!"

Budgeted production and sales for the year, along with actual production and sales for the first two quarters, are given below:

	Quarter			
	First	Second	Third	Fourth
Budgeted sales (units)	12,000	15,000	15,000	18,000
Actual sales (units)	12,000	15,000	—	—
Budgeted production (units) . . .	15,000	15,000	15,000	15,000
Actual production (units)	15,000	9,000	—	—

The company's plant is heavily automated, and fixed manufacturing overhead amounts to $180,000 each quarter. Variable manufacturing costs are $8 per unit. The fixed overhead is applied to units of product at a rate of $12 per unit (based on the budgeted production shown above). Any under- or overapplied overhead is taken directly to cost of goods sold for the quarter. The company had 4,000 units in inventory to start the first quarter and uses the FIFO inventory method. Variable selling and administrative expenses are $5 per unit.

Required
1. What characteristic of absorption costing caused the drop in net income for the second quarter and what could the controller have said to explain the problem more fully?
2. Prepare income statements for each quarter using the contribution approach, with variable costing.
3. Reconcile the absorption costing and the variable costing net income figures for each quarter.
4. Identify and discuss the advantages and disadvantages of using the variable costing method for internal reporting purposes.
5. Assume that the company had introduced JIT inventory methods at the beginning of

the second quarter. (Sales and production during the first quarter were as shown above.)

a. How many units would have been produced during the second quarter under JIT?
b. Starting with the third quarter, would you expect any difference between the net income reported under absorption costing and under variable costing? Explain why there would or would not be any difference.

Absorption and Variable Costing; Uneven Production; Break-Even Analysis; JIT Impact "Now this doesn't make any sense at all," said Flora Fisher, financial vice president for Warner Company. "Our sales have been steadily rising over the last several months, but profits have been going in the opposite direction. In September we finally hit $2,000,000 in sales, but the bottom line for that month drops off to a $100,000 loss. Why aren't profits more closely correlated with sales?"

C8-15

The statements to which Ms. Fisher was referring are shown below:

WARNER COMPANY
Monthly Income Statements

	July	August	September
Sales (@ $25)	$1,750,000	$1,875,000	$2,000,000
Less cost of goods sold:			
Beginning inventory	80,000	320,000	400,000
Cost applied to production:			
Variable manufacturing costs (@ $9)	765,000	720,000	540,000
Fixed manufacturing overhead	595,000	560,000	420,000
Cost of goods manufactured	1,360,000	1,280,000	960,000
Goods available for sale	1,440,000	1,600,000	1,360,000
Less ending inventory	320,000	400,000	80,000
Cost of goods sold	1,120,000	1,200,000	1,280,000
Underapplied or (overapplied) fixed overhead cost	(35,000)	—	140,000
Adjusted cost of goods sold	1,085,000	1,200,000	1,420,000
Gross margin	665,000	675,000	580,000
Less selling and administrative expenses	620,000	650,000	680,000
Net income (loss)	$ 45,000	$ 25,000	$ (100,000)

Hal Taylor, a recent graduate from State University who has just been hired by Warner Company, has stated to Ms. Fisher that the contribution approach, with variable costing, is a much better way to report profit data to management. "The contribution approach is a particularly good method to use when production is not moving in the same direction as sales," said Taylor. Sales and production data for the last quarter follow:

	July	August	September
Production in units	85,000	80,000	60,000
Sales in units	70,000	75,000	80,000

Additional information about the company's operations is given below:

a. Five thousand units were in inventory on July 1.
b. Fixed manufacturing overhead costs total $1,680,000 per quarter and are incurred evenly throughout the quarter. This fixed overhead cost is applied to units of product on the basis of a budgeted production volume of 80,000 units per month.
c. Variable selling and administrative expenses are $6 per unit sold. The remainder of the selling and administrative expenses on the statements above are fixed.
d. The company uses a FIFO inventory flow. Work in process inventories are nominal and can be ignored.

"I know production is somewhat out of step with sales," said Carla Vorhees, the company's controller. "But we had to build inventory early in the quarter in anticipation of a strike in September. Since the union settled without a strike, we then had to cut back production in September in order to work off the excess inventories. The income statements you have are completely accurate."

Required

1. Prepare an income statement for each month, using the contribution approach with variable costing.
2. Compute the monthly break-even point under:
   a. Variable costing.
   b. Absorption costing.
3. Explain to Ms. Fisher why profits have moved erratically over the three-month period shown in the absorption costing statements above and why profits have not been more closely correlated with changes in sales volume.
4. Reconcile the variable costing and absorption costing net income (loss) figures for each month. Show all computations, and show how you derive each figure used in your reconciliation.
5. Assume that the company had decided to introduce JIT inventory methods at the beginning of September. (Sales and production during July and August were as shown above.)
   a. How many units would have been produced during September under JIT?
   b. Starting with the next quarter (October, November, and December), would you expect any difference between the income reported under absorption costing and under variable costing? Explain why there would or would not be any difference.
   c. Refer to your computations in (2) above. How would JIT help break-even analysis "make sense" under absorption costing?

C8–16 Multiple Inventories; Prepare and Reconcile Variable Costing Statement without Unit Cost Data

Portland Optics, Inc., specializes in manufacturing lenses for large telescopes and cameras used in space exploration. Since the specifications for the lenses are determined by the customer and vary considerably, the company uses a job-order costing system. Factory overhead is applied to jobs on the basis of direct labor-hours, utilizing the absorption costing method. Portland's predetermined overhead rates for 19x1 and 19x2 were based on the following estimated data:

	19x1	19x2
Direct labor-hours	32,500	44,000
Variable factory overhead	$162,500	$198,000
Fixed factory overhead	130,000	176,000

Jim Bradford, Portland's controller, would like to use variable costing for internal reporting purposes since he believes statements prepared using variable costing are more appropriate for making product decisions. To explain the benefits of variable costing to the other members of Portland's management team, Mr. Bradford plans to convert the company's 19x2 income statement to a variable costing basis. For this purpose, he has gathered the information below.

a. Portland's comparative income statement for 19x1–x2 follows:

	19x1	19x2
Sales	$1,140,000	$1,520,000
Cost of goods sold:		
Finished goods inventory, January 1	16,000	25,000
Add cost of goods manufactured	720,000	976,000
Goods available for sale	736,000	1,001,000
Finished goods inventory, December 31	25,000	14,000
Cost of goods sold	711,000	987,000
Add underapplied overhead	12,000	7,000
Adjusted cost of goods sold	723,000	994,000
Gross margin.	417,000	526,000
Less operating expenses:		
Selling expense	150,000	190,000
Administrative expense	160,000	187,000
Total operating expenses	310,000	377,000
Net income	$ 107,000	$ 149,000

b. The company's cost of goods manufactured for 19x2 is based on the following statement:

Direct materials used		$ 210,000
Direct labor cost		435,000
Manufacturing overhead cost:		
Actual manufacturing overhead cost	$364,000	
Less underapplied overhead	7,000	
Overhead applied to work in process		357,000
Total manufacturing costs		1,002,000
Add work in process, January 1		34,000
		1,036,000
Deduct work in process, December 31		60,000
Cost of goods manufactured		$ 976,000

The $364,000 actual fixed overhead cost above consists of $189,000 in actual variable overhead cost and $175,000 in actual fixed overhead cost incurred during 19x2.

c. The company's inventories at the beginning and end of the year 19x2 contained the following cost elements:

	January 1, 19x2		December 31, 19x2	
Work in process:				
Direct material		$ 7,500		$12,000
Direct labor		13,900		26,750
Manufacturing overhead:				
Variable overhead.	$?		$?	
Fixed overhead	?	12,600	?	21,250
Total cost in inventory		$34,000		$60,000
Direct labor-hours expended		1,400		2,500
Finished goods:				
Direct material		$ 5,000		$ 3,000
Direct labor		10,280		6,325
Manufacturing overhead:				
Variable overhead.	$?		$?	
Fixed overhead	?	9,720	?	4,675
Total cost in inventory		$25,000		$14,000
Direct labor-hours expended		1,080		550

d.   All administrative expenses in the company are fixed. The only variable selling expense is an 8 percent commission on sales.

e.   As shown on the statements above, the company closes any under- or overapplied overhead to cost of goods sold.

Required   1.   Prepare an income statement for the company for 19x2 using the contribution approach with variable costing. Show *all* supporting computations in good form.

2.   Prepare a reconciliation of the variable costing and absorption costing net income figures for 19x2.

(CMA, heavily adapted)

Firms with international operations must carefully plan in order to reduce the financial risks that accompany changes in exchange rates. For example, most of the Toronto Blue Jays' expenses are paid in U.S. dollars, whereas most of their revenue is earned in Canadian dollars. To protect the ball club from losses due to changes in exchange rates, the management of the Blue Jays makes forward purchases of U.S. dollars at the beginning of the year to cover their budgeted outlays in U.S. dollars.

Profit Planning

LEARNING OBJECTIVES

After studying Chapter 9, you should be able to:

1 Define budgeting and explain the difference between planning and control.
2 Enumerate the principal advantages of budgeting.
3 Diagram and explain the master budget interrelationships.
4 Prepare a sales budget, including a computation of expected cash receipts.
5 Prepare a production budget.
6 Prepare a direct materials budget, including a computation of expected cash disbursements for purchases of materials.

7 Prepare a manufacturing overhead budget and a selling and administrative expense budget.
8 Prepare a cash budget.
9 Prepare a budgeted income statement and a budgeted balance sheet.
10 Describe JIT purchasing and explain how it differs from JIT production.
11 Define or explain the key terms listed at the end of the chapter.
12 (Appendix E) Compute the economic order quantity (EOQ) and the reorder point.

I n this chapter, we focus our attention on those steps taken by business organizations to achieve certain desired levels of profits—a process that is generally called *profit planning*. In our study, we shall see that profit planning is accomplished through the preparation of a number of budgets, which, when brought together, form an integrated business plan known as the *master budget*. We shall find that the data going into the preparation of the master budget focus heavily on the future, rather than on the past.

THE BASIC FRAMEWORK OF BUDGETING

Definition of Budgeting

Objective 1
Define budgeting and explain the difference between planning and control.

A **budget** is a detailed plan outlining the acquisition and use of financial and other resources over some given time period. It represents a plan for the future expressed in formal quantitative terms. The act of preparing a budget is called *budgeting*. The use of budgets to control a firm's activities is known as *budgetary control*.

The **master budget** is a summary of all phases of a company's plans and goals for the future. It sets specific targets for sales, production, distribution, and financing activities, and it generally culminates in a projected statement of net income and a projected statement of cash flows. In short, it represents a comprehensive expression of management's plans for the future and how these plans are to be accomplished.

Personal Budgets

Nearly everyone budgets to some extent, even though many of the people who prepare and use budgets do not recognize what they are doing as budgeting. For example, most people make estimates of the income to be realized over some future time period and plan expenditures for food, clothing, housing, and so on, accordingly. As a result of this planning, spending will usually be restricted by limiting it to some predetermined, allowable amount. In taking these steps, the individual clearly goes through a budget process in that he or she (1) makes an estimate of income, (2) plans expenditures, and (3) restricts spending in accordance with the plan. In other situations, individuals use estimates of income and expenditures to predict what their financial condition will be in the future. The budgets involved here may exist only in the mind of the individual, but they are budgets nonetheless in that they involve plans of how resources will be acquired and used over some specific time period.

The budgets of a business firm serve much the same functions as the budgets prepared informally by individuals. Business budgets tend to be more detailed and to involve more work in preparation (mostly because they are formal rather than informal), but they are similar to the budgets prepared by individuals in most other respects. Like personal budgets, they assist in planning and controlling expenditures; they also assist in predicting operating results and financial condition in future periods.

Difference between Planning and Control

The terms *planning* and *control* are often confused, and occasionally these terms are used in such a way as to suggest that they mean the same thing. Actually, planning and control are two quite distinct concepts. **Planning** involves the development of future objectives and the preparation of various budgets to achieve these objectives. **Control** involves the steps taken by management to ensure that the objectives set down at the planning stage are attained, and to ensure that all parts of the organization function in a manner consistent with organizational policies. To be completely effective, a good budgeting system must provide for *both* planning and control. Good planning without effective control is time wasted. On the other hand, unless plans are laid down in advance, there are no objectives toward which control can be directed.

Advantages of Budgeting

There is an old saying to the effect that "a man is usually down on what he isn't up on." Managers who have never tried budgeting or attempted to find out what benefits might be available through the budget process are usually quick to state that budgeting is a waste of time. These managers may argue that even though budgeting may work well in *some* situations, it would never work well in their companies because operations are too complex or because there are too many uncertainties involved. In reality, however, managers who argue this way usually will be deeply involved in planning (albeit on an informal basis). These managers will have clearly defined thoughts about what they want to accomplish and when they want it accomplished. The difficulty is that unless they have some way of communicating their thoughts and plans to others, the only way their companies will ever attain the desired objectives will be through accident. In short, even though companies may attain a certain degree of success without budgets, they never attain the heights that could have been reached had a coordinated system of budgets been in operation.

Objective 2
Enumerate the principal advantages of budgeting.

One of the great values of budgeting is that it requires managers to give planning top priority among their duties. Moreover, budgeting provides managers with a vehicle for communicating their plans in an orderly way throughout an entire organization. When budgets are in use, no one has any doubt about what the managers want to accomplish or how they want it done. Other benefits of budgeting are:

1. It provides managers with a way to *formalize* their planning efforts.
2. It provides definite goals and objectives that serve as *benchmarks* for evaluating subsequent performance.
3. It uncovers potential *bottlenecks* before they occur.
4. It *coordinates* the activities of the entire organization by *integrating* the plans and objectives of the various parts. By so doing, budgeting ensures that the plans and objectives of the parts are consistent with the broad goals of the entire organization.

In the past, some managers have not initiated a budgeting program because of the time and cost involved in the budgeting process. It can be argued that budgeting is actually "free" in that the time and cost involved are more than offset by greater efficiency and profits. Moreover, with the advent of computer spreadsheet programs *any* company—large or small—can implement and maintain a budgeting program at minimal cost. Budgeting lends itself well to spreadsheet programs, and such programs are readily available for any microcomputer.

Responsibility Accounting

Most of what we say in the remainder of this chapter and in Chapters 10, 11, and 12 centers on the concept of *responsibility accounting*. The basic idea behind **responsibility accounting** is that each manager's performance should be judged by

FOCUS ON CURRENT PRACTICE

Consider the following situation encountered by one of the authors at a mortgage banking firm: For years, the company operated with virtually no system of budgets whatever. Management contended that budgeting wasn't well suited to the firm's type of operation. Moreover, management pointed out that the firm was already profitable. Indeed, outwardly the company gave every appearance of being a well-managed, smoothly operating organization. A careful look within, however, disclosed that day-to-day operations were far from smooth, and often approached chaos. The average day was nothing more than an exercise in putting out one brush fire after another. The Cash account was always at crisis levels. At the end of a day, no one ever knew whether enough cash would be available the next day to cover required loan closings. Departments were uncoordinated, and it was not uncommon to find that one department was pursuing a course that conflicted with the course pursued by another department. Employee morale was low, and turnover was high. Employees complained bitterly that when a job was well done, nobody ever knew about it.

The company was bought out by a new group of stockholders who required that an integrated budgeting system be established to control operations. Within one year's time, significant changes were evident. Brush fires were rare. Careful planning virtually eliminated the problems that had been experienced with cash, and departmental efforts were coordinated and directed toward predetermined overall company goals. Although the employees were wary of the new budgeting program initially, they became "converted" when they saw the positive effects that it brought about. The more efficient operations caused profits to jump dramatically. Communication increased throughout the organization. When a job was well done, everybody knew about it. As one employee stated, "For the first time, we know what the company expects of us."

how well he or she manages those items directly under his or her control. To judge a manager's performance in this way, the costs (and revenues) of an organization must be carefully scrutinized and classified according to the various levels of management under whose control the costs rest. Each level of management is then charged with those costs under its care, and the managers at each level are held responsible for variations between budgeted goals and actual results. In effect, responsibility accounting *personalizes* accounting information by looking at costs from a *personal control* standpoint, rather than from an *institutional* standpoint. This concept is central to any effective profit planning and control system.

We will look at responsibility accounting in more detail in Chapters 10, 11, and 12. For the moment, we can summarize the overall idea by noting that it rests on three basic premises. The first premise is that costs can be organized in terms of levels of management responsibility. The second premise is that the costs charged to a particular level are controllable at that level by its managers. And the third premise is that effective budget data can be generated as a basis for evaluating actual performance. This chapter on profit planning is concerned with the third of these premises, in that the purpose of the chapter is to show the steps involved in budget preparation.

Choosing a Budget Period

Budgets covering acquisition of land, buildings, and other items of capital equipment (often called **capital budgets**) generally have quite long time horizons and may extend 30 years or more into the future. The later years covered by such budgets may be quite indefinite, but the lengthy time horizon is needed to assist management in its planning and to ensure that funds will be available when purchases of equipment become necessary. As time passes, capital equipment plans that were once somewhat indefinite come more sharply into focus, and the capital budget is updated accordingly. Without such long-term planning, an organization can suddenly come to the realization that substantial purchases of capital equipment are needed, but find that no funds are available to make the purchases.

Operating budgets are ordinarily set to cover a one-year period. The one-year period should correspond to the company's fiscal year so that the budget figures can be compared with the actual results. Many companies divide their budget year into four quarters. The first quarter is then subdivided into months, and monthly budget figures are established. These near-term figures can usually be established with considerable accuracy. The last three quarters are carried in the budget at quarterly totals only. As the year progresses, the figures for the second quarter are broken down into monthly amounts, then the third quarter figures are broken down, and so forth. This approach has the advantage of requiring a constant review and reappraisal of budget data.

Continuous or perpetual budgets are becoming quite popular. A **continuous or perpetual budget** is one that covers a 12-month period but which is constantly adding a new month or quarter on the end as the current month or quarter is completed. Advocates of continuous budgets state that this approach to budgeting is superior to other approaches in that it keeps management thinking and planning a full 12 months ahead. Thus, it stabilizes the planning horizon. Under other budget approaches, the planning horizon becomes shorter as the year progresses.

FOCUS ON CURRENT PRACTICE

In a survey of 219 companies, 80.5 percent reported that they prepare their budgets on a periodic basis, such as annually. The remaining 19.5 percent reported that they prepare their budgets on a continuous basis. For those companies using continuous budgeting, the majority—76.7 percent—extend the budget horizon quarter by quarter as time progresses, rather than extending it month by month. This survey included companies listed on the New York and American stock exchanges, as well as companies whose stock is sold over the counter.[1]

The Self-Imposed Budget

The success of any budget program will be determined in large part by the way in which the budget itself is developed. Generally, the most successful budget programs are those that permit managers with responsibility over cost control to

---

[1] William P. Cress and James B. Pettijohn, "A Survey of Budget-Related Planning and Control Policies and Procedures," *Journal of Accounting Education* 3, no. 2 (Fall 1985), p. 72.

EXHIBIT 9–1

The Initial Flow of
Budget Data

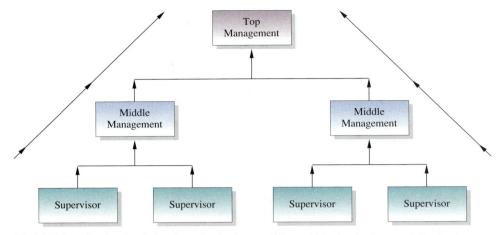

The initial flow of budget data is from lower levels of responsibility to higher levels of responsibility. Each person with responsibility for cost control will prepare his or her own budget estimates and submit them to the superior. These estimates are consolidated as they move upward in the organization.

prepare their own budget estimates, as illustrated in Exhibit 9–1. This approach to preparing budget data is particularly important if the budget is to be used in controlling a manager's activities after it has been developed. If a budget is forced on a manager from above, it will probably generate resentment and ill will rather than cooperation and increased productivity.

When managers prepare their own budget figures, the budgets that they prepare become *self-imposed* in nature. Certain distinct advantages arise from the **self-imposed budget** (also called a **participative budget**):

1. Individuals at all levels of the organization are recognized as members of the team, whose views and judgments are valued by top management.
2. The person in direct contact with an activity is in the best position to make budget estimates. Therefore, budget estimates prepared by such persons tend to be more accurate and reliable.
3. A person is more apt to work at fulfilling a budget that he has set himself than he is to work at fulfilling a budget imposed on him from above.
4. A self-imposed budget contains its own unique system of control in that if people are not able to meet budget specifications, they have only themselves to blame. On the other hand, if a budget is imposed on them from above, they can always say that the budget was unreasonable or unrealistic to start with, and therefore was impossible to meet.

Once self-imposed budgets are prepared, are they subject to any kind of review? The answer is yes. Even though individual preparation of budget estimates is critical to a successful budgeting program, such budget estimates cannot necessarily be accepted without question by higher levels of management. If no system of checks and balances is present, the danger exists that self-imposed budgets will be too loose and allow too much freedom in activities. The result will be inefficiency and waste. Therefore, before budgets are accepted, they must be carefully reviewed by immediate superiors. If changes from the original budget seem desirable, the items in question are discussed, and compromises are reached that are acceptable to all concerned.

In essence, all levels of an organization should work together to produce the budget. Since top management is generally unfamiliar with detailed, day-to-day cost matters, it should rely on subordinates to provide detailed budget information. On the other hand, top management has a perspective on the company as a whole that is vital in making broad policy decisions in budget preparation. Each level of responsibility in an organization contributes in the way that it best can in a *cooperative* effort to develop an integrated budget document.

The Matter of Human Relations

Whether or not a budget program is accepted by lower management personnel will be reflective of (1) the degree to which top management accepts the budget program as a vital part of the company's activities, and (2) the way in which top management uses budgeted data.

If a budget program is to be successful, it must have the complete acceptance and support of the persons who occupy key management positions. If lower or middle management personnel sense that top management is lukewarm about budgeting, or if they sense that top management simply tolerates budgeting as a necessary evil, then their own attitudes will reflect a similar lack of enthusiasm. Budgeting is hard work, and if top management is not enthusiastic about and committed to the budget program, then it is unlikely that anyone else in the organization will be either.

In administering the budget program, it is particularly important that top management not use the budget as a "club" to pressure employees or as a way to find someone to "blame" for a particular problem. This type of negative emphasis will simply breed hostility, tension, and mistrust rather than greater cooperation and productivity. Unfortunately, research suggests that the budget is often used as a pressure device and that great emphasis is placed on "meeting the budget" under all circumstances.[2]

Rather than being used as a pressure device, the budget should be used as a positive instrument to assist in establishing goals, in measuring operating results, and in isolating areas that are in need of extra effort or attention. Any misgivings that employees have about a budget program can be overcome by meaningful involvement at all levels and by proper use of the program over a period of time. Administration of a budget program requires a great deal of insight and sensitivity on the part of management. The ultimate objective must be to develop the realization that the budget is designed to be a positive aid in achieving both individual and company goals.

Management must keep clearly in mind that the human dimension in budgeting is of key importance. It is easy for the manager to become preoccupied with the technical aspects of the budget program to the exclusion of the human aspects. Accountants are particularly open to criticism in this regard. Indeed, the study cited earlier found that use of budget data in a rigid and inflexible manner was the greatest single complaint of persons whose performance was being evaluated through the budget process.[3] In light of these facts, management should remember that the purposes of the budget are to motivate employees and to coordinate efforts. Preoccupation with the dollars and cents in the budget, or being rigid and inflexible in budget administration, can only lead to frustration of these purposes.

---

[2] Paul J. Carruth, Thurrell O. McClendon, and Milton R. Ballard, "What Supervisors Don't Like about Budget Evaluations," *Management Accounting* 64, no. 8 (February 1983), p. 42.
[3] Ibid.

The Budget Committee

A standing **budget committee** will usually be responsible for overall policy matters relating to the budget program and for coordinating the preparation of the budget itself. This committee generally consists of the president; vice presidents in charge of various functions such as sales, production, and purchasing; and the controller. Difficulties and disputes between segments of the organization in matters relating to the budget are resolved by the budget committee. In addition, the budget committee approves the final budget and receives periodic reports on the progress of the company in attaining budgeted goals.

The Master Budget—A Network of Interrelationships

Objective 3
Diagram and explain the master budget interrelationships.

The master budget is a network consisting of many separate budgets that are interdependent. This network is illustrated in Exhibit 9–2.

The Sales Budget A **sales budget** is a detailed schedule showing the expected sales for coming periods; typically, it is expressed in both dollars and units of product. Much time and effort is put into preparing an accurate sales budget, since it is the key to the entire budgeting process. The reason it is the key is that all other parts of the master budget are dependent on the sales budget in some way, as illustrated in Exhibit 9–2. Thus, if the sales budget is sloppily done, then the rest of the budgeting process is largely a waste of time.

After the sales budget has been set, a decision can be made on the level of production that will be needed for the period to support sales, and the production budget can be set as well. The production budget then becomes a key factor in the determination of other budgets, including the direct materials budget, the direct

EXHIBIT 9–2

The Master Budget Interrelationships

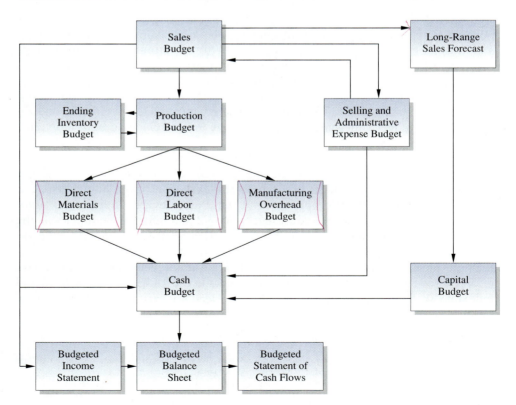

labor budget, and the manufacturing overhead budget. These budgets, in turn, are needed to assist in formulating a cash budget for the budget period. In essence, the sales budget triggers a chain reaction that leads to the development of many other budget figures in an organization.

As shown in Exhibit 9–2, the selling and administrative expense budget is both dependent on and a determinant of the sales budget. This reciprocal relationship arises from the fact that sales will in part be determined by the funds available for advertising and sales promotion.

FOCUS ON CURRENT PRACTICE

In establishing a budget, how challenging should budget targets be? In practice, companies typically set their budgets either at a "stretch" level or a "highly achievable" level. A stretch-level budget is one that has only a small chance of being met and in fact may be met less than half the time by even the most capable managers. A highly achievable budget is one that is challenging, but which can be met through hard work. Research shows that managers prefer highly achievable budgets.[4] Such budgets are generally coupled with bonuses that are given when budget targets are met, along with added bonuses when these targets are exceeded. Highly achievable budgets are believed to build a manager's confidence and to generate greater commitment to the budget program.

The Cash Budget   Once the operating budgets (sales, production, and so on) have been established, the cash budget and other financial budgets can be prepared. A **cash budget** is a detailed plan showing how cash resources will be acquired and used over some specified time period. Observe from Exhibit 9–2 that all of the operating budgets, including the sales budget, have an impact of some type on the cash budget. In the case of the sales budget, the impact comes from the planned cash receipts to be received on sales. In the case of the other budgets, the impact comes from the planned cash expenditures within the budgets themselves.

Sales Forecasting—A Critical Step

The sales budget is prepared from the *sales forecast*. A **sales forecast** is broader than a sales budget, generally encompassing potential sales for the entire industry, as well as potential sales for the firm preparing the forecast. Factors that are considered in making a sales forecast include the following:

1. Past experience in terms of sales volume.
2. Prospective pricing policy.
3. Unfilled order backlogs.
4. Market research studies.
5. General economic conditions.

---

[4] See Kenneth A. Merchant, *Rewarding Results: Motivating Profit Center Managers* (Boston, Mass.: Harvard Business School Press, 1989). For further discussion of budget targets, see Kenneth A. Merchant, "How Challenging Should Profit Budget Targets Be?" *Management Accounting* 72, no. 5 (November 1990), pp. 46–48.

6. Industry economic conditions.
7. Movements of economic indicators such as gross national product, employment, prices, and personal income.
8. Advertising and product promotion.
9. Industry competition.
10. Market share.

Sales results from prior years are used as a starting point in preparing a sales forecast. Forecasters examine sales data in relation to various factors, including prices, competitive conditions, availability of supplies, and general economic conditions. Projections are then made into the future, based on those factors that the forecasters feel will be significant over the budget period. In-depth discussions generally characterize the gathering and interpretation of all data going into the sales forecast. These discussions, held at all levels of the organization, develop perspective and assist in assessing the significance and usefulness of data.

Statistical tools such as regression analysis, trend and cycle projection, and correlation analysis are used in sales forecasting. In addition, some firms have found it useful to build econometric models of their industry or of the nation to assist in forecasting problems. Such models hold great promise for improving the overall quality of budget data.

PREPARING THE MASTER BUDGET

To show how the separate budgets making up the master budget are developed and integrated, we focus now on Meredith Company. Meredith Company produces and sells a single product that we will call product A. Each year the company prepares the following budget documents:

1. A sales budget, including a computation of expected cash receipts.
2. A production budget (or merchandise purchases budget for a merchandising company).
3. A direct materials budget, including a computation of expected cash payments for raw materials.
4. A direct labor budget.
5. A manufacturing overhead budget.
6. An ending finished goods inventory budget.
7. A selling and administrative expense budget.
8. A cash budget.
9. A budgeted income statement.
10. A budgeted balance sheet.

These budgets for the year 19x1 are illustrated in Schedules 1 through 10 that appear in this section.

The Sales Budget

Objective 4
Prepare a sales budget, including a computation of expected cash receipts.

The sales budget is the starting point in preparing the master budget. As shown earlier in Exhibit 9–2, nearly all other items in the master budget, including production, purchases, inventories, and expenses, depend on it in some way.

The sales budget is constructed by multiplying the expected sales in units by the selling price. Schedule 1 contains the sales budget for Meredith Company for 19x1, by quarters. Notice from the schedule that the company plans to sell 100,000 units during the year, with sales peaking in the third quarter.

SCHEDULE 1

MEREDITH COMPANY
Sales Budget
For the Year Ended December 31, 19x1

	Quarter				
	1	**2**	**3**	**4**	**Year**
Expected sales in units	10,000	30,000	40,000	20,000	100,000
Selling price per unit	× $20	× $20	× $20	× $20	× $20
Total sales	$200,000	$600,000	$800,000	$400,000	$2,000,000

Schedule of Expected Cash Collections

	1	2	3	4	Year
Accounts receivable, 12/31/x0	$ 90,000*				$ 90,000
First-quarter sales ($200,000 × 70%, 30%)†	140,000	$ 60,000			200,000
Second-quarter sales ($600,000 × 70%, 30%)		420,000	$180,000		600,000
Third-quarter sales ($800,000 × 70%, 30%)			560,000	$240,000	800,000
Fourth-quarter sales ($400,000 × 70%)‡				280,000	280,000
Total cash collections	$230,000	$480,000	$740,000	$520,000	$1,970,000

* Cash collections from last year's fourth-quarter sales. See the beginning-of-year balance sheet on page 378.

† Cash collections from sales are as follows: 70 percent collected in the quarter of sale, and the remaining 30 percent collected in the quarter following.

‡ Uncollected fourth-quarter sales appear as accounts receivable on the company's end-of-year balance sheet (see Schedule 10 on page 379).

Generally, the sales budget is accompanied by a "Schedule of Expected Cash Collections" for the forthcoming budget period. This schedule is needed to assist in preparing the cash budget for the year. Expected cash receipts are composed of collections on sales made to customers in prior periods, plus collections on sales made in the current budget period. Schedule 1 above contains a schedule of expected cash collections for Meredith Company.

The Production Budget

After the sales budget has been prepared, the production requirements for the forthcoming budget period can be determined and organized in the form of a **production budget.** Sufficient goods will have to be available to meet sales needs and provide for the desired ending inventory. A portion of these goods will already exist in the form of a beginning inventory. The remainder will have to be produced. Therefore, production needs can be determined by adding budgeted sales (in units or in dollars) to the desired ending inventory (in units or in dollars) and deducting the beginning inventory (in units or in dollars) from this total. Schedule 2 contains a production budget for Meredith Company.

Objective 5
Prepare a production budget.

Students are often surprised to learn that firms budget the level of their ending inventories. Budgeting of inventories is a common practice, however. If inventories are not carefully planned, the levels remaining at the end of a period may be excessive, causing an unnecessary tie-up of funds and an unneeded expense of carrying the unwanted goods. On the other hand, without proper planning, inventory levels may be too small, thereby requiring crash production efforts in following periods, and perhaps loss of sales due to inability to meet shipping schedules.

SCHEDULE 2

MEREDITH COMPANY
Production Budget
For the Year Ended December 31, 19x1
(in units)

| | Quarter | | | | |
	1	2	3	4	Year
Expected sales (Schedule 1)	10,000	30,000	40,000	20,000	100,000
Add desired ending inventory of finished goods*	6,000	8,000	4,000	3,000†	3,000
Total needs	16,000	38,000	44,000	23,000	103,000
Less beginning inventory of finished goods‡	2,000	6,000	8,000	4,000	2,000
Units to be produced	14,000	32,000	36,000	19,000	101,000

* Twenty percent of the next quarter's sales.

† Estimated.

‡ The same as the prior quarter's *ending* inventory.

Inventory Purchases—Merchandising Firm

Meredith Company prepares a production budget since it is a *manufacturing* firm. If it were a *merchandising* firm, then instead of a production budget it would prepare a **merchandise purchases budget** showing the amount of goods to be purchased from its suppliers during the period. The merchandise purchases budget is in the same basic format as the production budget, except that it shows goods to be purchased rather than goods to be produced, as shown below:

Budgeted cost of goods sold (in units or in dollars)	XXXXX
Add desired ending merchandise inventory	XXXXX
Total needs	XXXXX
Less beginning merchandise inventory	XXXXX
Required purchases (in units or in dollars)	XXXXX

The merchandising firm would prepare an inventory purchases budget such as this one for each item carried in stock. Some large retail organizations make such computations on a frequent basis (particularly at peak seasons) to ensure that adequate stocks are on hand to meet customer needs.

The Direct Materials Budget

Objective 6
Prepare a direct materials budget, including a computation of expected cash disbursements for purchases of materials.

Returning to the Meredith Company example, after production needs have been computed, a **direct materials budget** should be prepared to show the materials that will be required in the production process. Sufficient raw materials will have to be available to meet production needs, and to provide for the desired ending raw materials inventory for the budget period. Part of this raw materials requirement will already exist in the form of a beginning raw materials inventory. The remainder will have to be purchased from suppliers. In sum, the format for computing raw materials needs is:

Raw materials needed to meet the production schedule . . . XXXXX
Add desired ending inventory of raw materials XXXXX

    Total raw materials needs XXXXX
Less beginning inventory of raw materials XXXXX

Raw materials to be purchased XXXXX

Preparing a budget of this kind is one step in a company's overall **material requirements planning (MRP).** MRP is an operations research tool that employs the computer to assist the manager in overall materials and inventory planning. The objective of MRP is to ensure that the right materials are on hand, in the right quantities, and at the right time to support the production process. The detailed operation of MRP is covered in most operations research books; for this reason, it will not be considered further here, other than to point out that the concepts we are discussing are an important part of the overall MRP technique.

Schedule 3 contains a direct materials purchases budget for Meredith Company. Notice that materials requirements are first determined in units (pounds, gallons, and so on) and then translated into dollars by multiplying by the appropriate unit cost.

SCHEDULE 3

MEREDITH COMPANY
Direct Materials Budget
For the Year Ended December 31, 19x1

	Quarter				
	1	2	3	4	Year
Units to be produced (Schedule 2)	14,000	32,000	36,000	19,000	101,000
Raw materials needed per unit (pounds).	× 5	× 5	× 5	× 5	× 5
Production needs (pounds).	70,000	160,000	180,000	95,000	505,000
Add desired ending inventory of raw materials (pounds)*	16,000	18,000	9,500	7,500	7,500
Total needs (pounds)	86,000	178,000	189,500	102,500	512,500
Less beginning inventory of raw materials (pounds)	7,000	16,000	18,000	9,500	7,000
Raw materials to be purchased (pounds).	79,000	162,000	171,500	93,000	505,500
Cost of raw materials to be purchased at $0.60 per pound	$47,400	$ 97,200	$102,900	$ 55,800	$303,300

* Ten percent of the next quarter's production needs. For example, the second-quarter production needs are 160,000 pounds. Therefore, the desired ending inventory for the first quarter would be 10 percent × 160,000 pounds = 16,000 pounds. The ending inventory of 7,500 pounds for the fourth quarter is estimated.

Schedule of Expected Cash Disbursements

	1	2	3	4	Year
Accounts payable, 12/31/x0	$25,800*				$ 25,800
First-quarter purchases ($47,400 × 50%, 50%)†	23,700	$ 23,700			47,400
Second-quarter purchases ($97,200 × 50%, 50%).		48,600	$ 48,600		97,200
Third-quarter purchases ($102,900 × 50%, 50%)			51,450	$ 51,450	102,900
Fourth-quarter purchases ($55,800 × 50%)‡				27,900	27,900
Total cash disbursements	$49,500	$ 72,300	$100,050	$ 79,350	$301,200

* Cash payments for last year's fourth-quarter material purchases. See the beginning-of-year balance sheet on page 378.

† Cash payments for purchases are as follows: 50 percent paid for in the quarter of purchase, and the remaining 50 percent paid for in the quarter following.

‡ Unpaid fourth-quarter purchases appear as accounts payable on the company's end-of-year balance sheet (see Schedule 10 on page 379).

The direct materials budget is usually accompanied by a computation of expected cash disbursements for raw materials. This computation is needed to assist in developing a cash budget. Disbursements for raw materials will consist of payments for prior periods, plus payments for purchases for the current budget period. Schedule 3 contains a computation of expected cash disbursements for Meredith Company.

The Direct Labor Budget

The **direct labor budget** is also developed from the production budget. Direct labor requirements must be computed so that the company will know whether sufficient labor time is available to meet production needs. By knowing in advance just what will be needed in the way of labor time throughout the budget year, the company can develop plans to adjust the labor force as the situation may require. Firms that neglect to budget run the risk of facing labor shortages or having to hire and lay off at awkward times. Erratic labor policies lead to insecurity and inefficiency on the part of employees.

To compute direct labor requirements, the number of units of finished product to be produced each period (month, quarter, and so on) is multiplied by the number of direct labor-hours required to produce a single unit. Many different types of labor may be involved. If so, then computations should be by type of labor needed. The direct labor requirements can then be translated into expected direct labor costs. How this is done will depend on the labor policy of the firm. In Schedule 4, we assume that the direct labor force can be adjusted as the work requirements change from quarter to quarter. In that case, the total direct labor cost can be computed by simply multiplying the direct labor-hour requirements by the direct labor rate per hour as we have done in Schedule 4.

However, many companies have employment policies or contracts that prevent them from laying off and rehiring workers as needed. Suppose, for example, that Meredith Company has 50 workers who are classified as direct labor and each of them is guaranteed at least 480 hours of pay each quarter at a rate of $7.50 per hour. In that case, the minimum direct labor cost for a quarter would be:

$$50 \text{ workers} \times 480 \text{ hours} \times \$7.50 = \$180,000$$

Note that in Schedule 4 the direct labor costs for the first and fourth quarters would have to be increased to a $180,000 level if Meredith Company's labor policy did not allow it to adjust the work force at will. Such a "no layoff" policy

SCHEDULE 4

MEREDITH COMPANY
Direct Labor Budget
For the Year Ended December 31, 19x1

	Quarter				
	1	2	3	4	Year
Units to be produced (Schedule 2)	14,000	32,000	36,000	19,000	101,000
Direct labor time per unit (hours)	× 0.8	× 0.8	× 0.8	× 0.8	× 0.8
Total hours of direct labor time needed	11,200	25,600	28,800	15,200	80,800
Direct labor cost per hour	× $7.50	× $7.50	× $7.50	× $7.50	× $7.50
Total direct labor cost	$84,000	$192,000	$216,000	$114,000	$606,000

would have a dramatic impact on Meredith Company's cash flows and profitability.

The Manufacturing Overhead Budget

The **manufacturing overhead budget** should provide a schedule of all costs of production other than direct materials and direct labor. These costs should be broken down by cost behavior for budgeting purposes, and a predetermined overhead rate developed. This rate will be used to apply manufacturing overhead to units of product throughout the budget period.

Objective 7
Prepare a manufacturing overhead budget and a selling and administrative expense budget.

A computation showing budgeted cash disbursements for manufacturing overhead should be made for use in developing the cash budget. The critical thing to remember in making this computation is that *depreciation is a noncash charge.* Therefore, any depreciation charges included in manufacturing overhead must be deducted from the total in computing expected cash payments.

We will assume that the variable overhead rate is $2 per direct labor-hour and that fixed overhead costs are budgeted at $60,600 per quarter, of which $15,000 represents depreciation. All overhead costs involving cash disbursements are paid for in the quarter incurred. The manufacturing overhead budget, by quarters, and the expected cash disbursements, by quarters, are both shown in Schedule 5.

The Ending Finished Goods Inventory Budget

After completing Schedules 1–5, sufficient data will have been generated to compute the cost of a unit of finished product. This computation is needed for two reasons: first, to know how much to charge as cost of goods sold on the budgeted income statement; and second, to know what amount to place on the balance sheet for unsold units. The dollar value of the unsold units planned to be on hand is computed in the **ending finished goods inventory budget.** In this example, we use absorption costing to compute the value of inventory. Top managers often prefer that absorption costing be used in budgets, since managers are evaluated on this basis in the reports they make to stockholders and others outside of the firm.

For Meredith Company, the cost of a unit of finished product is $13—consisting of $3 of direct materials, $6 of direct labor, and $4 of manufacturing overhead— and the ending finished goods inventory is budgeted to be $39,000. The computations behind these figures are shown in Schedule 6.

SCHEDULE 5

MEREDITH COMPANY
Manufacturing Overhead Budget
For the Year Ended December 31, 19x1

	Quarter				
	1	2	3	4	Year
Budgeted direct labor-hours	11,200	25,600	28,800	15,200	80,800
Variable overhead rate	× $2	× $2	× $2	× $2	× $2
Budgeted variable overhead	$22,400	$ 51,200	$ 57,600	$30,400	$161,600
Budgeted fixed overhead	60,600	60,600	60,600	60,600	242,400
Total budgeted overhead	83,000	111,800	118,200	91,000	404,000
Less depreciation	15,000	15,000	15,000	15,000	60,000
Cash disbursements for overhead	$68,000	$ 96,800	$103,200	$76,000	$344,000

SCHEDULE 6

MEREDITH COMPANY
Ending Finished Goods Inventory Budget
For the Year Ended December 31, 19x1

Item	Quantity	Cost	Total
Production cost per unit:			
Direct materials	5.0 pounds	$0.60 per pound	$ 3
Direct labor	0.8 hours	7.50 per hour	6
Manufacturing overhead	0.8 hours	5.00 per hour*	4
			$13
Budgeted finished goods inventory:			
Ending finished goods inventory in units (Schedule 2)			3,000
Total production cost per unit (see above)			× $13
Ending finished goods inventory in dollars			$39,000

* $404,000 ÷ 80,800 hours = $5.

The Selling and Administrative Expense Budget

The **selling and administrative expense budget** contains a list of anticipated expenses for the budget period that will be incurred in areas other than manufacturing. The budget will be made up of many smaller, individual budgets submitted by various persons having responsibility for cost control in selling and administrative matters. If the number of expense items is very large, separate budgets may be needed for the selling and administrative functions.

Schedule 7 contains the selling and administrative expense budget for Meredith Company for 19x1.

SCHEDULE 7

MEREDITH COMPANY
Selling and Administrative Expense Budget
For the Year Ended December 31, 19x1

	Quarter 1	2	3	4	Year
Budgeted sales in units	10,000	30,000	40,000	20,000	100,000
Variable selling and administrative expense per unit*	× $1.80	× $1.80	× $1.80	× $1.80	× $1.80
Budgeted variable expense	$18,000	$ 54,000	$ 72,000	$ 36,000	$180,000
Budgeted fixed selling and administrative expenses:					
Advertising	40,000	40,000	40,000	40,000	160,000
Executive salaries	35,000	35,000	35,000	35,000	140,000
Insurance	—	1,900	37,750	—	39,650
Property taxes	—	—	—	18,150	18,150
Total	75,000	76,900	112,750	93,150	357,800
Total budgeted selling and administrative expenses	$93,000	$130,900	$184,750	$129,150	$537,800

* Commissions, clerical, and shipping.

The Cash Budget

The cash budget pulls together much of the data developed in the preceding steps, as illustrated earlier in Exhibit 9–2. The reader should restudy this exhibit before reading on.

Objective 8
Prepare a cash budget.

The cash budget is composed of four major sections:

1. The receipts section.
2. The disbursements section.
3. The cash excess or deficiency section.
4. The financing section.

The receipts section consists of the opening cash balance added to whatever is expected in the way of cash receipts during the budget period. Generally, the major source of receipts will be from sales, as discussed earlier.

The disbursements section consists of all cash payments that are planned for the budget period. These payments will include raw materials purchases, direct labor payments, manufacturing overhead costs, and so on, as contained in their respective budgets. In addition, other cash disbursements such as income taxes, capital equipment purchases, and dividend payments will also be included.

The cash excess or deficiency section consists of the difference between the cash receipts section totals and the cash disbursements section totals. If a deficiency exists, the company will need to arrange to borrow funds from its bank. If an excess exists, funds borrowed in previous periods can be repaid or the idle funds can be placed in short-term investments.

The financing section provides a detailed account of the borrowings and repayments projected to take place during the budget period. It also includes a detail of interest payments that will be due on money borrowed. Banks are becoming increasingly insistent that firms in need of borrowed money give long advance notice of the amounts and times that funds will be needed. This permits the banks to plan and helps to assure that funds will be ready when needed. Moreover, careful planning of cash needs via the budgeting process avoids unpleasant surprises for companies as well. Few things are more disquieting to an organization than to run into unexpected difficulties in the Cash account. A well-coordinated budgeting program eliminates uncertainty as to what the cash situation will be two months, six months, or a year from now.

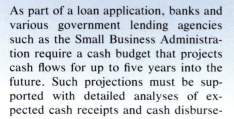

FOCUS ON CURRENT PRACTICE

As part of a loan application, banks and various government lending agencies such as the Small Business Administration require a cash budget that projects cash flows for up to five years into the future. Such projections must be supported with detailed analyses of expected cash receipts and cash disbursements. Companies receiving loans are then required to submit detailed annual cash budgets as part of the loan monitoring process. The same requirements are often imposed on companies seeking advisory or development support from governmental agencies.

SCHEDULE 8

MEREDITH COMPANY
Cash Budget
For the Year Ended December 31, 19x1

	Schedule	Quarter 1	Quarter 2	Quarter 3	Quarter 4	Year
Cash balance, beginning		$ 42,500	$ 40,000	$ 40,000	$ 40,500	$ 42,500
Add receipts:						
Collections from customers	1	230,000	480,000	740,000	520,000	1,970,000
Total cash available before current financing		272,500	520,000	780,000	560,500	2,012,500
Less disbursements:						
Direct materials	3	49,500	72,300	100,050	79,350	301,200
Direct labor	4	84,000	192,000	216,000	114,000	606,000
Manufacturing overhead	5	68,000	96,800	103,200	76,000	344,000
Selling and administrative	7	93,000	130,900	184,750	129,150	537,800
Income taxes	9	18,000	18,000	18,000	18,000	72,000
Equipment purchases		30,000	20,000	—	—	50,000
Dividends		10,000	10,000	10,000	10,000	40,000
Total disbursements		352,500	540,000	632,000	426,500	1,951,000
Excess (deficiency) of cash available over disbursements		(80,000)	(20,000)	148,000	134,000	61,500
Financing:						
Borrowings (at beginning)		120,000*	60,000	—	—	180,000
Repayments (at ending)		—	—	(100,000)	(80,000)	(180,000)
Interest (at 10% per annum)		—	—	(7,500)†	(6,500)†	(14,000)
Total financing		120,000	60,000	(107,500)	(86,500)	(14,000)
Cash balance, ending		$ 40,000	$ 40,000	$ 40,500	$ 47,500	$ 47,500

* The company requires a minimum cash balance of $40,000. Therefore, borrowing must be sufficient to cover the cash deficiency of $80,000 and to provide for the minimum cash balance of $40,000. All borrowings and all repayments of principal are in round $1,000 amounts.

† The interest payments relate only to the principal being repaid at the time it is repaid. For example, the interest in quarter 3 relates only to the interest due on the $100,000 principal being repaid from quarter 1 borrowing, as follows: $100,000 × 10% × ¾ = $7,500. The interest paid in quarter 4 is computed as follows:

$20,000 × 10% × 1 year $2,000
$60,000 × 10% × ¾ 4,500

Total interest paid $6,500

376

The cash budget should be broken down into time periods that are as short as feasible. Many firms budget cash on a weekly basis, and some larger firms go so far as to plan daily cash needs. The more common planning horizons are geared to monthly or quarterly figures. The cash budget for Meredith Company for 19x1 is shown on a quarterly basis in Schedule 8. In preparing this budget, we have assumed that Meredith Company has an open line of credit with its bank that can be used as needed to bolster the cash position. Interest on loans is 10 percent per annum. *For purposes of simplicity in computations,* we assume that all borrowings and repayments must be in round $1,000 amounts. *Also for purposes of simplicity,* we assume that all borrowings take place at the beginning of a quarter and that all repayments are made at the end of a quarter.

In the case of Meredith Company, all loans have been repaid by year-end. If all loans are not repaid and a budgeted income statement or balance sheet is being prepared, then interest must be accrued on the unpaid loans. This interest will *not* appear on the cash budget (since it has not yet been paid), but it will appear as part of interest expense on the budgeted income statement and as a liability on the budgeted balance sheet.

The Budgeted Income Statement

A budgeted income statement can be prepared from the data developed in Schedules 1–8. *The budgeted income statement is one of the key schedules in the budget process.* It is the document that tells how profitable operations are anticipated to be in the forthcoming period. After it has been developed, it stands as a benchmark against which subsequent company performance can be measured.

Schedule 9 contains a budgeted income statement for Meredith Company for 19x1.

Objective 9
Prepare a budgeted income statement and a budgeted balance sheet.

The Budgeted Balance Sheet

The budgeted balance sheet is developed by beginning with the current balance sheet and adjusting it for the data contained in the other budgets. A Meredith Company budgeted balance sheet for 19x1 is presented in Schedule 10 (p. 379).

SCHEDULE 9

MEREDITH COMPANY
Budgeted Income Statement
For the Year Ended December 31, 19x1

	Schedule	
Sales (100,000 units at $20)	1	$2,000,000
Less cost of goods sold (100,000 units at $13). . . .	6	1,300,000
Gross margin		700,000
Less selling and administrative expenses	7	537,800
Net operating income		162,200
Less interest expense	8	14,000
Income before taxes		148,200
Less income taxes	*	72,000
Net income		$ 76,200

* Estimated.

The company's beginning-of-year balance sheet, from which the budgeted balance sheet in Schedule 10 has been derived in part, is presented below:

MEREDITH COMPANY
Balance Sheet
December 31, 19x0

Assets

Current assets:		
Cash	$ 42,500	
Accounts receivable	90,000	
Raw materials inventory (7,000 pounds)	4,200	
Finished goods inventory (2,000 units)	26,000	
Total current assets		$162,700
Plant and equipment:		
Land	80,000	
Buildings and equipment	700,000	
Accumulated depreciation	(292,000)	
Plant and equipment, net		488,000
Total assets		$650,700

Liabilities and Stockholders' Equity

Current liabilities:		
Accounts payable (raw materials)		$ 25,800
Stockholders' equity:		
Common stock, no par	$175,000	
Retained earnings	449,900	
Total stockholders' equity		624,900
Total liabilities and stockholders' equity		$650,700

Expanding the Budgeted Income Statement

The master budget income statement in Schedule 9 focuses on a single level of activity and has been prepared using absorption costing. Some managers prefer an alternate format that focuses on a *range* of activity and that is prepared using the

EXHIBIT 9–3

EXAMPLE COMPANY
Master Budget Income Statement

	Budget Formula (per unit)	Sales in Units			
		800	1,400	2,000	2,800
Sales	$75.00	$ 60,000	$105,000	$150,000	$210,000
Less variable expenses:					
Direct materials	12.00	9,600	16,800	24,000	33,600
Direct labor	31.00	24,800	43,400	62,000	86,800
Variable overhead	7.50	6,000	10,500	15,000	21,000
Variable selling and other	4.00	3,200	5,600	8,000	11,200
Total variable expenses	54.50	43,600	76,300	109,000	152,600
Contribution margin	$20.50	16,400	28,700	41,000	57,400
Less fixed expenses:					
Manufacturing overhead		18,000	18,000	18,000	18,000
Selling and administrative		9,000	9,000	9,000	9,000
Total fixed expenses		27,000	27,000	27,000	27,000
Net income (loss)		$(10,600)	$ 1,700	$ 14,000	$ 30,400

SCHEDULE 10

MEREDITH COMPANY
Budgeted Balance Sheet
December 31, 19x1

Assets

Current assets:

Cash	$ 47,500	(a)
Accounts receivable	120,000	(b)
Raw materials inventory	4,500	(c)
Finished goods inventory	39,000	(d)

Total current assets $211,000

Plant and equipment:

Land	80,000	(e)
Buildings and equipment	750,000	(f)
Accumulated depreciation	(352,000)	(g)

Plant and equipment, net   478,000

Total assets $689,000

Liabilities and Stockholders' Equity

Current liabilities:

Accounts payable (raw materials)	$ 27,900	(h)

Stockholders' equity:

Common stock, no par	$175,000	(i)
Retained earnings	486,100	(j)

Total stockholders' equity   661,100

Total liabilities and stockholders' equity $689,000

Explanation of December 31, 19x1, balance sheet figures:

a. The ending cash balance, as projected by the cash budget in Schedule 8.
b. Thirty percent of fourth-quarter sales, from Schedule 1 ($400,000 × 30% = $120,000).
c. From Schedule 3, the ending raw materials inventory will be 7,500 pounds. This material costs $0.60 per pound. Therefore, the ending inventory in dollars will be 7,500 pounds × $0.60 = $4,500.
d. From Schedule 6.
e. From the December 31, 19x0, balance sheet (no change).
f. The December 31, 19x0, balance sheet indicated a balance of $700,000. During 19x1, $50,000 additional equipment will be purchased (see Schedule 8), bringing the December 31, 19x1, balance to $750,000.
g. The December 31, 19x0, balance sheet indicated a balance of $292,000. During 19x1, $60,000 of depreciation will be taken (see Schedule 5), bringing the December 31, 19x1, balance to $352,000.
h. One half of the fourth-quarter raw materials purchases, from Schedule 3.
i. From the December 31, 19x0, balance sheet (no change).
j. December 31, 19x0, balance $449,900
    Add net income, from Schedule 9   76,200

                                   526,100
    Deduct dividends paid, from Schedule 8 . .   40,000

    December 31, 19x1, balance $486,100

contribution approach. An example of a master budget income statement using this alternative format is presented in Exhibit 9–3.

A statement such as that in Exhibit 9–3 is *flexible* in its use since it is geared to more than one level of activity. If, for example, the company planned to sell 2,000 units during a period but actually sold only 1,400 units, then the budget figures at the 1,400-unit level would be used to compare against actual costs and revenues. Other columns could be added to the budget as needed by simply applying the budget formulas provided.

In short, a master budget income statement in this expanded format can be very useful to the manager in the planning and control of operations. The concepts underlying a flexible approach to budgeting are covered in the following two chapters.

JIT PURCHASING

Objective 10
Describe JIT purchasing and explain how it differs from JIT production.

It is important that we distinguish between JIT production and JIT purchasing. JIT *production* can only be used by manufacturing companies, since it focuses on the manufacture of goods. We have learned that it is based on a demand-pull concept, where inventories are largely (or entirely) eliminated and where all production activities respond to the "pull" exerted by the final assembly stage. JIT *purchasing,* on the other hand, can be used by *any* organization—retail, wholesale, distribution, service, or manufacturing. It focuses on the *acquisition* of goods. These goods might either be resold to customers (such as in a retail store) or be used as raw materials in the production process.

In Chapter 5, we stated that the central thrust of the JIT philosophy was toward simplification and elimination of waste. This philosophy is just as applicable to JIT purchasing as it is to JIT production. Below we outline the key features relating to JIT purchasing in an organization. (Some of these features were discussed briefly in Chapter 5.)

Under JIT purchasing:

1. *Goods are delivered immediately before demand or use*. Companies that have adopted JIT purchasing require an increase in the number of deliveries, accompanied by a decrease in the number of items per delivery. We have already stated that a manufacturing company might receive several deliveries of a particular raw material each day. This concept of daily (or at least frequent) delivery also has application at the retail level. For many years, retail food stores have received daily deliveries of milk and bread. Various other retail organizations are now moving toward this concept for their goods as well. Food outlets are guaranteeing that baked goods are no more than a few *hours* old, which means that output must be geared to anticipated demand at various times of the day. Even in those manufacturing or retailing situations where some inventories must be maintained, the level of these inventories under JIT purchasing can be reduced to only a fraction of previous amounts.

2. *The number of suppliers is greatly decreased*. All purchases are concentrated on a few, highly dependable suppliers who can meet stringent delivery requirements. IBM, for example, eliminated *95 percent* of the suppliers from one of its plants, reducing the number from 640 to only 32.[5] With this decrease in suppliers comes a corresponding decrease in the amount of resources needed for purchase negotiations and for processing of purchasing data.

3. *Long-term agreements are signed with suppliers; these agreements stipulate the delivery schedule, the quality of the goods, and the price to be paid*. Long-term agreements make it unnecessary to have separate negotiations for each purchase. Thus, minimal paperwork is involved with individual purchase transactions. Delivery schedules are set far in advance, and these schedules must be strictly adhered to by suppliers. Although adhering to a preset delivery schedule is important, the real key to the successful operation of JIT is *quality*. In the absence of an absolute standard for high quality, JIT would be impossible to use.

---

[5] George Foster and Charles T. Horngren, "JIT: Cost Accounting and Cost Management Issues," *Management Accounting* 68 (June 1987), p. 20.

4. *Little or no inspection is made as to the quantity of goods received in a shipment, nor is the shipment inspected for defects.* Through the long-term agreements that have been signed, suppliers are fully aware of the importance of exact quantities and "zero defect" quality. This eliminates the need for inspection, which JIT views as being a non-value-added activity. Many companies require that suppliers deliver goods in "shop-ready" containers. A shop-ready container is one that contains exactly the number and type of items needed for a particular cell. Such containers eliminate the need for packing and unpacking of materials, which JIT views as being another non-value-added activity.

5. *Payments are not made for each individual shipment; rather, payments are "batched" for each supplier.* Since a supplier may be making several shipments each day to a manufacturer or several shipments each week to a retailer, it would be costly to make payments for these shipments individually. Typically, invoices are "batched" into a single monthly payment for each supplier. The computer is used to track the shipments, to match the ensuing invoices to the goods received, and to determine the amount due.

Companies that have adopted JIT purchasing have realized substantial savings in the cost of placing purchase orders and administering the purchasing function. Note particularly that the adoption of purchasing practices such as those outlined above does not require that a company eliminate *all* inventories. Indeed, retail organizations must maintain *some* inventories or they couldn't operate. But the amount of time a good spends on the shelf or in the warehouse can be greatly reduced even in a retail organization through the JIT approach.

ZERO-BASE BUDGETING

Zero-base budgeting has received considerable attention recently as a new approach to preparing budget data, particularly for use in not-for-profit, governmental, and service-type organizations. The type of budget prepared under this approach—called a **zero-base budget**—is so named because managers are required to start at zero budget levels every year and justify all costs as if the programs involved were being initiated for the first time. By "justify," we mean that no costs are viewed as being ongoing in nature; the manager must start at the ground level each year and present justification for all costs in the proposed budget, regardless of the type of cost involved. This is done in a series of "decision packages" in which the manager ranks all of the activities in the department according to relative importance, going from those that he or she considers essential to those that he or she considers of least importance. Presumably, this allows top management to evaluate each decision package independently and to pare back in those areas that appear less critical or that do not appear to be justified in terms of the cost involved.

This process differs from traditional budgeting, in which budgets are generally initiated on an incremental basis; that is, the manager starts with last year's budget and simply adds to it (or subtracts from it) according to anticipated needs. The manager doesn't have to start at the ground each year and justify ongoing costs (such as salaries) for existing programs.

In a broader sense, zero-base budgeting isn't really a new concept at all. Managers have always advocated in-depth reviews of departmental costs. The only difference is the frequency with which this review is carried out. Zero-base budgeting says that it should be done annually; critics of the zero-base idea say that this is too often and that such reviews should be made only every five years or so. These critics say that annual in-depth reviews are too time-consuming and too costly to be really feasible, and that in the long run such reviews probably cannot be justified in terms of the cost savings involved. In addition, it is argued that annual reviews soon become mechanical and that the whole purpose of the zero-base idea is then lost.

The question of frequency of zero-base reviews must be left to the judgment of the individual manager. In some situations, annual zero-base reviews may be justified; in other situations, they may not because of the time and cost involved. Whatever the time period chosen, however, most managers would agree that zero-base reviews can be helpful and should be an integral part of the overall budgeting process.

INTERNATIONAL ASPECTS OF BUDGETING

A multinational company (MNC) faces special problems in preparing a budget. These problems arise because of two major factors that can impact a company operating in international markets. These factors are foreign currency exchange rates and inflation.

Foreign currency exchange rates are important in the budgeting process because such rates control the exchange of monetary units between countries, and these rates fluctuate on a daily basis. A common approach to the exchange rate problem is to use a single exchange rate throughout the budget period and then attempt to compensate for rate changes through hedging operations.

FOCUS ON CURRENT PRACTICE

"[In] 1985 the Toronto Blue Jays budgeted a loss for the season despite the fact that the team had the best win-loss record in the major leagues. The majority of team expenses were paid in U.S. dollars in contrast to their revenue, which was earned in Canadian dollars. To protect themselves against adverse changes in the exchange rate, the Blue Jays made forward purchases of U.S. dollars in late 1984 at 75 cents per Canadian dollar to cover a large portion of their budgeted 1985 U.S. dollar denominated expenses. In 1985, the Blue Jays profited on their hedged position when the Canadian dollar depreciated, which helped to offset losses on unhedged U.S. dollar denominated expenses during the same period."[6]

When an MNC uses hedging operations, the costs of the hedging activities must be budgeted along with other expense items.

Sometimes an MNC will have operations in a country with a high inflation rate and this creates additional difficulties in the budgeting process. The inflation rate in some countries may exceed 100 percent annually. Such high inflation rates—called *hyperinflation*—require that the lead time for preparing a budget be reduced to minimize inflationary effects. Even when budget lead times are reduced, it is

---

[6] Paul V. Mannino and Ken Milani, "Budgeting for an International Business," *Management Accounting* 73, no. 8 (February 1992), p. 37. Used by permission.

generally necessary to revise the budget just before implementation to adjust for the inflation that has taken place since the budget process started. Then, at the end of the budget period, it is necessary to adjust data for the actual inflation experienced during the year. Only after such inflation adjustments have been made can the manager determine the variations between budgeted and actual revenues and expenses.

In addition to problems with exchange rates and inflation, MNCs must be sensitive to government policies in the countries in which they operate that might affect labor costs, equipment purchases, cash management, or other budget items.

THE NEED FOR FURTHER BUDGETING MATERIAL

The material covered in this chapter represents no more than an introduction into the vast area of budgeting and profit planning. Our purpose has been to present an overview of the budgeting process and to show how the various operating budgets build on each other in guiding a firm toward its profit objectives. However, the matter of budgeting and profit planning is so critical to the intelligent management of a firm in today's business environment that we can't stop with simply an overview of the budgeting process. We need to look more closely at budgeting to see how it helps managers in the day-to-day conduct of business affairs. We will do this by studying standard costs and flexible budgets in the following two chapters and by introducing the concept of performance reporting. In Chapter 12, we will expand on these ideas by looking at budgeting and profit planning as tools for control of decentralized operations and as facilitating factors in judging managerial performance.

In sum, the materials in the following three chapters build on the budgeting and profit planning foundation that has been laid in this chapter by expanding on certain concepts that have been introduced and by refining others. The essential thing to keep in mind at this point is that the material covered in this chapter does not conclude our study of budgeting and profit planning, but rather just introduces the ideas.

REVIEW PROBLEM: BUDGET SCHEDULES

Mylar Company manufactures and sells a product that has a highly seasonal variation in demand, with peak sales coming in the third quarter. The following information is available concerning expected sales and other operating data for 19x2—the coming year—and for the first two quarters of 19x3:

a. The company's single product sells for $8 per unit. Budgeted sales in units for the next six quarters are as follows:

	19x2 Quarter				19x3 Quarter	
	1	2	3	4	1	2
Budgeted sales in units.	40,000	60,000	100,000	50,000	70,000	80,000

b. Sales are collected in the following pattern: 75 percent in the quarter the sales are made, and the remaining 25 percent in the following quarter. On January 1, 19x2, the company's balance sheet showed $65,000 in accounts receivable, all of which will be collected in the first quarter of the year. Bad debts are negligible and can be ignored.

c. The company requires an ending inventory of finished units on hand at the end of each quarter equal to 30 percent of the budgeted sales for the next quarter. This requirement was met on December 31, 19x1, in that the company had 12,000 units on hand to start the new year.

d. Five pounds of raw materials are required to complete one unit of product. The company requires an ending inventory of raw materials on hand at the end of each quarter equal to 10 percent of the production needs of the following quarter. This requirement was met on December 31, 19x1, in that the company had 23,000 pounds of raw materials on hand to start the new year.

e. The raw material costs $0.80 per pound. Purchases of raw material are paid for in the following pattern: 60 percent paid in the quarter the purchases are made, and the remaining 40 percent paid in the following quarter. On January 1, 19x2, the company's balance sheet showed $81,500 in accounts payable for raw material purchases, all of which will be paid for in the first quarter of the year.

Required   Prepare the following budgets and schedules for the year, showing both quarterly and total figures:

1. A sales budget and a schedule of expected cash collections.
2. A production budget.
3. A direct materials purchases budget and a schedule of expected cash payments for material purchases.

Solution to Review 1. The sales budget would be prepared as follows:
Problem

| | 19x2 Quarter | | | | |
	1	2	3	4	Year
Budgeted sales in units	40,000	60,000	100,000	50,000	250,000
Selling price per unit	× $8	× $8	× $8	× $8	× $8
Budgeted sales	$320,000	$480,000	$800,000	$400,000	$2,000,000

Based on the budgeted sales above, the schedule of expected cash collections would be prepared as follows:

| | 19x2 Quarter | | | | |
	1	2	3	4	Year
Accounts receivable, 12/31/x1	$ 65,000				$ 65,000
First-quarter sales: $320,000 × 75%, 25%	240,000	$ 80,000			320,000
Second-quarter sales: $480,000 × 75%, 25% . . .		360,000	$120,000		480,000
Third-quarter sales: $800,000 × 75%, 25%			600,000	$200,000	800,000
Fourth-quarter sales: $400,000 × 75%				300,000	300,000
Total cash collections	$305,000	$440,000	$720,000	$500,000	$1,965,000

2. Based on the sales budget in units, the production budget would be prepared as follows:

| | 19x2 Quarter | | | | | 19x3 Quarter | |
	1	2	3	4	Year	1	2
Budgeted sales in units	40,000	60,000	100,000	50,000	250,000	70,000	80,000
Add desired ending inventory*	18,000	30,000	15,000	21,000†	21,000	24,000	
Total needs.	58,000	90,000	115,000	71,000	271,000	94,000	
Less beginning inventory	12,000	18,000	30,000	15,000	12,000	21,000	
Units to be produced	46,000	72,000	85,000	56,000	259,000	73,000	

* 30% of the following quarter's budgeted sales in units.

† 30% of the budgeted 19x3 first-quarter sales.

3. Based on the production budget figures, raw materials will need to be purchased as follows during the year:

| | 19x2 Quarter | | | | | 19x3 Quarter |
	1	2	3	4	Year	1
Units to be produced	46,000	72,000	85,000	56,000	259,000	73,000
Raw materials needed per unit (pounds)	× 5	× 5	× 5	× 5	× 5	× 5
Production needs (pounds).	230,000	360,000	425,000	280,000	1,295,000	365,000
Add desired ending inventory (pounds)*	36,000	42,500	28,000	36,500†	36,500	
Total needs (pounds)	266,000	402,500	453,000	316,500	1,331,500	
Less beginning inventory (pounds)	23,000	36,000	42,500	28,000	23,000	
Raw materials to be purchased (pounds).	243,000	366,500	410,500	288,500	1,308,500	

* 10% of the following quarter's production needs in pounds.

† 10% of the 19x3 first-quarter production needs in pounds.

Based on the raw material purchases above, expected cash payments would be computed as follows:

| | 19x2 Quarter | | | | |
	1	2	3	4	Year
Cost of raw materials to be purchased at $0.80 per pound	$194,400	$293,200	$328,400	$230,800	$1,046,800
Accounts payable, 12/31/x1	$ 81,500				$ 81,500
First-quarter purchases:					
$194,400 × 60%, 40%	116,640	$ 77,760			194,400
Second-quarter purchases:					
$293,200 × 60%, 40%		175,920	$117,280		293,200
Third-quarter purchases:					
$328,400 × 60%, 40%			197,040	$131,360	328,400
Fourth-quarter purchases:					
$230,800 × 60%.				138,480	138,480
Total cash payments	$198,140	$253,680	$314,320	$269,840	$1,035,980

KEY TERMS FOR REVIEW

Budget   A detailed plan outlining the acquisition and use of financial and other resources over some given time period. (p. 360)

Budget committee   A group of key management persons who are responsible for overall policy matters relating to the budget program and for coordinating the preparation of the budget itself. (p. 366)

Capital budget   A budget covering the acquisition of land, buildings, and items of capital equipment; such a budget may have a time horizon extending 30 years or more into the future. (p. 363)

Cash budget   A detailed plan showing how cash resources will be acquired and used over some specific time period. (p. 367)

Continuous or perpetual budget   A budget that covers a 12-month period but is constantly adding a new month on the end as the current month is completed. (p. 363)

Control   Those steps taken by management to ensure that the objectives set down at the planning stage are attained and to ensure that all parts of the organization function in a manner consistent with organizational policies. (p. 361)

Objective 11
Define or explain the key terms listed at the end of the chapter.

Direct labor budget   A detailed plan showing labor requirements over some specific time period. (p. 372)

Direct materials budget   A detailed plan showing the amount of raw materials that must be purchased during a period to meet both production and inventory needs. (p. 370)

Ending finished goods inventory budget   A budget showing the dollar amount of cost expected to appear on the balance sheet for unsold units at the end of a period. (p. 373)

Manufacturing overhead budget   A detailed plan showing the production costs, other than direct materials and direct labor, that will be incurred in attaining the output budgeted for a period. (p. 373)

Master budget   A summary of all phases of a company's plans and goals for the future in which specific targets are set for sales, production, and financing activities and that generally culminates in a projected statement of net income and a projected statement of cash position. (p. 360)

Material requirements planning (MRP)   An operations research tool that employs the computer to assist the manager in overall materials and inventory planning. (p. 371)

Merchandise purchases budget   A budget used by a merchandising company that shows the amount of goods that must be purchased from suppliers during the period. (p. 370)

Participative budget   See *Self-imposed budget.* (p. 364)

Planning   The development of objectives in an organization and the preparation of various budgets to achieve these objectives. (p. 360)

Production budget   A detailed plan showing the number of units that must be produced during a period in order to meet both sales and inventory needs. (p. 369)

Responsibility accounting   A system of accounting in which costs are assigned to various managerial levels according to where control of the costs is deemed to rest, with the managers then held responsible for differences between budgeted and actual results. (p. 361)

Sales budget   A detailed schedule showing the expected sales for coming periods; these sales are typically expressed in both dollars and units. (p. 366)

Sales forecast   A schedule of expected sales for an entire industry. (p. 367)

Self-imposed budget   A method of budget preparation in which managers with responsibility over cost control prepare their own budget figures; these budget figures are reviewed by the managers' supervisors, and any questions are then resolved in face-to-face meetings. (p. 364)

Selling and administrative expense budget   A detailed schedule of planned expenses that will be incurred in areas other than manufacturing during a budget period. (p. 374)

Zero-base budget   A method of budgeting in which managers are required to start at zero budget levels every year and to justify all costs as if the programs involved were being initiated for the first time. (p. 381)

APPENDIX E: ECONOMIC ORDER QUANTITY (EOQ) AND THE REORDER POINT

Objective 12
Compute the economic order quantity (EOQ) and the reorder point.

As stated in the main body of the chapter, inventory planning and control are an essential part of a budgeting system. We have seen that inventory levels are not left to chance but rather are carefully planned for, in terms of both opening and closing balances. Major questions that we have left unanswered are, "How does the manager know what inventory level is 'right' for the firm?" and "Won't the level that is 'right' vary from organization to organization?" The purpose of this section is to examine the inventory control methods available to the manager for answering these questions.

Costs Associated with Inventory

Three groups of costs are associated with inventory. The first group is known as **inventory ordering costs.** These costs are driven by the number of orders placed, but not by the size of the orders. Examples include the clerical costs associated with ordering inventory and some handling and transportation costs.

The second group of costs are known as **inventory carrying costs.** These costs are driven by the amount of inventory that is held. Common examples include storage costs, handling costs, property taxes, insurance, and the interest on the capital invested in inventories. Experts now maintain that these commonly cited inventory carrying costs understate the real costs of building and holding inventory—particularly work in process inventory. Inventories physically get in the way, cluttering workspaces and making it difficult to keep track of operations. Moreover, they hide problems that often are not discovered until it is too late to take corrective action. This results in erratic production, inefficient operations, "lost" orders, high defect rates, and substantial risks of obsolescence. These intangible costs are largely responsible for the movement to JIT.

The third group of costs, known as the **costs of not carrying sufficient inventory,** consists of costs that result from not having enough inventory in stock to meet customers' needs. Costs in this group tend to be intangible and include lost sales and customer ill will. Also included are costs of expediting orders for goods not held in stock and costs associated with quantity discounts forgone.

In a broad conceptual sense, the "right" level of inventory to carry is the level that will minimize the total of these three groups of costs. Such a minimization is difficult to achieve, however, since certain of the costs involved are in direct conflict with one another. Notice, for example, that as inventory levels increase, the costs of carrying inventory will also increase, but the costs of not carrying sufficient inventory will decrease. In working toward total cost minimization, therefore, the manager must balance off the three groups of costs against one another. The problem really has two dimensions—how much to order (or how much to produce in a production run) and how often to do it.

Computing the Economic Order Quantity (EOQ)

The "how much to order" is commonly referred to as the **economic order quantity (EOQ).** It is the order size that will result in a minimization of the first two groups of costs above. We will consider two approaches to computing the EOQ—the tabular approach and the formula approach.

The Tabular Approach
Given a certain annual consumption of an item, a firm might place a few orders each year of a large quantity each, or it might place many orders of a small quantity each. Placing only a few orders would result in low inventory ordering costs but in high inventory carrying costs, since the average inventory level would be very large. On the other hand, placing many orders would result in high inventory ordering costs but in low inventory carrying costs, since in this case the average inventory level would be quite small. As stated above, the EOQ seeks the order size that will balance off these two groups of costs. To show how it is computed, assume that a manufacturer uses 3,000 subassemblies in the manufacturing process each year. The subassemblies are purchased from a supplier at a cost of $20 each. Other cost data are given below:

Inventory carrying costs, per unit, per year . . . $ 0.80
Cost of placing a purchase order 10.00

EXHIBIT E–1
Tabulation of Costs Associated with Various Order Sizes

Symbol*		Order Size in Units (O)								
		25	50	100	200	250	300	400	1,000	3,000
$O/2$	Average inventory in units	12.5	25	50	100	125	150	200	500	1,500
Q/O	Number of purchase orders	120	60	30	15	12	10	7.5	3	1
$C(O/2)$	Annual carrying cost at $0.80 per unit	$ 10	$ 20	$ 40	$ 80	$100	$120	$160	$400	$1,200
$P(Q/O)$	Annual purchase order cost at $10 per order	1,200	600	300	150	120	100	75	30	10
T	Total annual cost.	$1,210	$620	$340	$230	$220	$220	$235	$430	$1,210

* Symbols:

O = Order size in units (see headings above).
Q = Annual quantity used in units (3,000 in this example).
C = Annual cost of carrying one unit in stock.
P = Cost of placing one order.
T = Total annual cost.

Exhibit E–1 contains a tabulation of the total costs associated with various order sizes for the subassemblies. Notice that total annual cost is lowest (and is equal) at the 250- and 300-unit order sizes. The EOQ will lie somewhere between these two points. We could locate it precisely by adding more columns to the tabulation, and we would in time zero in on 274 units as being the exact EOQ.

The cost relationships from this tabulation are shown graphically in Exhibit E–2. Notice from the graph that total annual cost is minimized at that point where annual carrying costs and annual purchase order costs are equal. The same point identifies the EOQ, since the purpose of the computation is to find the point of exact trade-off between these two classes of costs.

EXHIBIT E–2
Graphic Solution to Economic Order Quantity (EOQ)

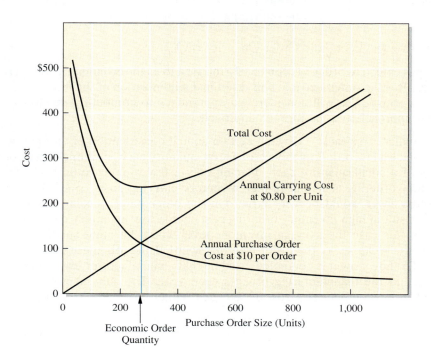

Observe from the graph that total cost shows a tendency to flatten out between 200 and 400 units. Most firms look for this minimum cost range and choose an order size that falls within it, rather than choosing the exact EOQ. The primary reason is that suppliers will often ship goods only in round-lot sizes.

The Formula Approach   The EOQ can also be found by means of a formula. The formula is (derived by calculus):

$$E = \sqrt{\frac{2\,QP}{C}}$$

where:

E = Economic order quantity (EOQ)
Q = Annual quantity used in units
P = Cost of placing one order
C = Annual cost of carrying one unit in stock

Substituting with the data used in our preceding example, we have:

Q = 3,000 subassemblies used per year
P = $10 cost to place one order
C = $0.80 cost to carry one subassembly in stock for one year

$$E = \sqrt{\frac{2\,QP}{C}} = \sqrt{\frac{2(3,000)(\$10)}{\$0.80}} = \sqrt{\frac{\$60,000}{\$0.80}} = \sqrt{75,000}$$

$$E = 274 \text{ units (the EOQ)}$$

Although data can be obtained very quickly using the formula approach, it has the drawback of not providing as great a range of information as the tabular method discussed above.

JIT and the Economic Order Quantity (EOQ)

The EOQ will decrease if:

1. The cost of placing an order decreases, or
2. The cost of carrying inventory in stock increases.

Managers who advocate JIT purchasing argue that the cost of carrying inventory in stock is much greater than generally realized because of the waste and inefficiency that inventories create, as we mentioned earlier. These managers argue that this fact, combined with the fact that JIT purchasing dramatically reduces the cost of placing an order, is solid evidence that companies should purchase more frequently in smaller amounts. Assume, for example, that a company has used the following data to compute its EOQ:

Q = 4,800 units needed each year
P = $75 cost to place one order
C = $4.50 cost to carry one unit in stock for one year

Given these data, the EOQ would be:

$$E = \sqrt{\frac{2\,QP}{C}} = \sqrt{\frac{2(4,800)(\$75)}{\$4.50}} = \sqrt{160,000}$$

$$E = 400 \text{ units}$$

Now assume that as a result of JIT purchasing the company is able to decrease the cost of placing an order to only $3. Also assume that due to the waste and inefficiency caused by inventories, the true cost of carrying a unit in stock is $8 per year. The revised EOQ would be:

$$E = \sqrt{\frac{2\,QP}{C}} = \sqrt{\frac{2(4{,}800)(\$3)}{\$8}} = \sqrt{3{,}600}$$

$$E = 60 \text{ units}$$

Under JIT purchasing, the company would *not* necessarily order in 60-unit lots since purchases would be geared to current demand. This example shows quite dramatically, however, the economics behind the JIT concept so far as the purchasing of goods is concerned.

FOCUS ON CURRENT PRACTICE

Research suggests that companies do, indeed, understate the cost of carrying a unit in stock. The reason for the understatement is that companies tend to consider only the variable costs of carrying goods and to ignore other costs such as depreciation (or rent) on facilities, material handling, accounting, and administration.[7] Yet these other costs can be more significant in the EOQ computation than the variable costs. Indeed, one factor that has propelled the Japanese toward JIT has been the extremely high cost of storage space in Japan. Real estate is so costly that companies can't afford to use valuable space to store inventory. In effect, the high inventory carrying costs in Japan have pushed the EOQ downward to the point where JIT is the only feasible alternative.

Production Runs

The EOQ concept can also be applied to the problem of determining the **economic production-run size.** Deciding when to start and when to stop production runs is a problem that has plagued manufacturers for years. The problem can be solved quite easily by inserting the **setup cost** for a new production run into the EOQ formula in place of the purchase order cost. The setup cost includes the labor and other costs involved in getting facilities ready for a run of a different production item.

To illustrate, assume that Chittenden Company has determined that the following costs are associated with one of its product lines:

Q = 15,000 units produced each year
P = $150 setup costs to change a production run
C = $2 to carry one unit in stock for one year

What is the optimal production-run size for this product line? It can be determined by using the same formula as is used to compute the EOQ:

$$E = \sqrt{\frac{2\,QP}{C}} = \sqrt{\frac{2(15{,}000)(\$150)}{\$2}} = \sqrt{2{,}250{,}000}$$

$$E = 1{,}500 \text{ (economic production-run size in units)}$$

---

[7] Daniel J. Jones, "JIT and the EOQ Model," *Management Accounting* 72, no. 8 (February 1991), p. 57.

Chittenden Company will minimize its overall costs by producing in runs of 1,500 units each.

In computing the economic production-run size, note again the impact of JIT concepts. We learned in Chapter 5 that through the JIT concept of continuous improvement, companies are reducing the setup time from days or hours to just minutes. As the setup time (and therefore the setup cost) is reduced, it becomes economically feasible to produce in smaller production-run sizes. Consider the Chittenden Company data. Assume that through the process of continuous improvement the company is able to reduce the cost of a setup to only $3. Also assume that due to high storage costs the true cost of carrying a unit in stock is $36 per year. The new economic production-run size would be:

$$E = \sqrt{\frac{2\ QP}{C}} = \sqrt{\frac{2(15{,}000)(\$3)}{\$36}} = \sqrt{2{,}500}$$

$$E = 50 \text{ units}$$

Thus, the company's economic production-run size has gone from 1,500 units to only 50 units—a 96.7 percent reduction.

Reorder Point and Safety Stock

We stated earlier that the inventory problem has two dimensions—how much to order and how often to do it. The "how often to do it" involves what are commonly termed the *reorder point* and the *safety stock,* and seeks to find the optimal trade-off between the second two groups of inventory costs outlined earlier (the costs of carrying inventory and the costs of not carrying sufficient inventory). First, we will discuss the reorder point and the factors involved in its computation. Then, we will discuss the circumstances under which a safety stock must be maintained.

The **reorder point** tells the manager when to place an order or when to initiate production to replenish depleted stocks. It is dependent on three factors—the EOQ (or economic production-run size), the *lead time,* and the rate of usage during the lead time. The **lead time** can be defined as the interval between the time that an order is placed and the time that the order is finally received from the supplier or from the production line.

Constant Usage during the Lead Time   If the rate of usage during the lead time is known with certainty, the reorder point can be determined by the following formula:

Reorder point = Lead time × Average daily or weekly usage

To illustrate the formula's use, assume that a company's EOQ is 500 units, that the lead time is three weeks, and that the average weekly usage is 50 units.

Reorder point = 3 weeks × 50 units per week = 150 units

The reorder point would be 150 units. That is, the company will automatically place a new order for 500 units when inventory stocks drop to a level of 150 units, or three weeks' supply, left on hand.

Variable Usage during the Lead Time   The previous example assumed that the 50 units per week usage rate was constant and was known with certainty. Although some firms enjoy the luxury of certainty, the more common situation is to find considerable variation in the rate of usage of inventory items from period to

EXHIBIT E–3

Determining the
Reorder Point—
Variable Usage

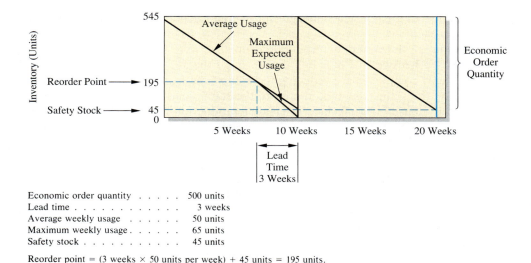

EXHIBIT E–3

Determining the
Reorder Point—
Variable Usage

Economic order quantity	500 units
Lead time	3 weeks
Average weekly usage	50 units
Maximum weekly usage	65 units
Safety stock	45 units

Reorder point = (3 weeks × 50 units per week) + 45 units = 195 units.

period. If usage varies from period to period, the firm that reorders in the way computed above may soon find itself out of stock. A sudden spurt in demand, a delay in delivery, or a snag in processing an order may cause inventory levels to be depleted before a new shipment arrives.

Companies that experience problems in demand, delivery, or processing of orders have found that they need some type of buffer to guard against stockouts. Such a buffer is usually called a **safety stock**. A safety stock serves as a kind of insurance against greater than usual demand and against problems in the ordering and delivery of goods. Its size is determined by deducting *average usage* from the *maximum usage* that can reasonably be expected during a period. For example, if the firm in the preceding example was faced with variable demand for its product, it would compute a safety stock as follows:

Maximum expected usage per week . . .	65 units
Average usage per week	50 units
Excess	15 units
Lead time	× 3 weeks
Safety stock	45 units

The reorder point is then determined by *adding the safety stock to the average usage during the lead time*. In formula form, the reorder point would be:

Reorder point = (Lead time × Average daily or weekly usage) + Safety stock

Computation of the reorder point by this approach is shown both numerically and graphically in Exhibit E–3. As shown in the exhibit, the company will place a new order for 500 units when inventory stocks drop to a level of 195 units left on hand.

KEY TERMS FOR REVIEW (APPENDIX E)

Costs of not carrying sufficient inventory   Those costs that result from not having enough inventory in stock to meet customers' needs; such costs would include customer ill will, quantity discounts forgone, and costs of expediting orders for items not in stock. (p. 387)

Economic order quantity (EOQ)   The order size for materials that will result in a minimization of the costs of ordering inventory and carrying inventory. (p. 387)

Economic production-run size   The number of units produced in a production run that will result in a minimization of setup costs and the costs of carrying inventory. (p. 390)

Inventory carrying costs   Those costs that result from having inventory in stock, such as rental of storage space, handling costs, property taxes, insurance, and interest on funds. These costs also should include costs of excess work in process inventories such as inefficient production, excess lead times, high defect rates, and risks of obsolescence. (p. 387)

Inventory ordering costs   Those costs associated with the acquisition of inventory, such as clerical costs and transportation costs. (p. 387)

Lead time   The interval between the time that an order is placed and the time that the order is finally received from the supplier. (p. 391)

Reorder point   The point in time when an order must be placed to replenish depleted stocks; it is determined by multiplying the lead time by the average daily or weekly usage. (p. 391)

Safety stock   The difference between average usage of materials and maximum usage of materials that can reasonably be expected during the lead time. (p. 392)

Setup costs   Labor and other costs involved in getting facilities ready for a run of a different production item. (p. 390)

QUESTIONS

9–1 What is a budget? What is budgetary control?

9–2 Discuss some of the major benefits to be gained from budgeting.

9–3 What is meant by the term *responsibility accounting?*

9–4 "Budgeting is designed primarily for organizations that have few complexities and uncertainties in their day-to-day operations." Do you agree? Why or why not?

9–5 What is a master budget? Briefly describe its contents.

9–6 Which is a better basis for judging actual results, budgeted performance or past performance? Why?

9–7 Why is the sales forecast always the starting point in budgeting?

9–8 Is there any difference between a sales forecast and a sales budget? Explain.

9–9 "As a practical matter, planning and control mean exactly the same thing." Do you agree? Explain.

9–10 Describe the flow of budget data in an organization. Who are the participants in the budgeting process, and how do they participate?

9–11 "To a large extent, the success of a budget program hinges on education and good salesmanship." Do you agree? Explain.

9–12 What is a self-imposed budget? What are the major advantages of self-imposed budgets? What caution must be exercised in their use?

9–13 How can budgeting assist a firm in its employment policies?

9–14 "The principal purpose of the cash budget is to see how much cash the company will have in the bank at the end of the year." Do you agree? Explain.

9–15 How does JIT purchasing differ from JIT production?

9–16 What are the five key ideas associated with JIT purchasing?

9–17 Does a company have to eliminate all inventories in order to adopt JIT purchasing?

9–18 How does zero-base budgeting differ from traditional budgeting?

9–19 (Appendix E) What three classes of costs are associated with a company's inventory policy? Which of these classes of costs is the most difficult to quantify?

9–20   (Appendix E) List at least three costs associated with a company's inventory policy that do not appear as an expense on the income statement.

9–21   (Appendix E) What trade-offs in costs are involved in computing the EOQ (economic order quantity)?

9–22   (Appendix E) "Managers are more interested in a minimum cost *range* than they are in a minimum cost point." Explain.

9–23   (Appendix E) Define *lead time* and *safety stock*.

EXERCISES

E9–1   Silver Company makes a product that is very popular as a Mother's Day gift. Thus, peak sales occur in May of each year. The company's sales budget for the second quarter of 19x1, showing these peak sales, is given below:

	April	May	June	Total
Budgeted sales	$300,000	$500,000	$200,000	$1,000,000

From past experience, the company has learned that 20 percent of a month's sales are collected in the month of sale, that another 70 percent is collected in the month following sale, and that the remaining 10 percent is collected in the second month following sale. Bad debts are negligible and can be ignored. February sales totaled $230,000, and March sales totaled $260,000.

Required   1.   Prepare a schedule of budgeted cash collections from sales, by month and in total, for the second quarter.

2.   Assume that the company will prepare a budgeted balance sheet as of June 30. Compute the accounts receivable as of that date.

E9–2   Atwood Products, Ltd., has budgeted sales for the next four months as follows:

	Sales in Units
April	50,000
May	75,000
June	90,000
July	80,000

The company is now in the process of preparing a production budget for the second quarter. Past experience has shown that end-of-month inventory levels must equal 10 percent of the following month's sales. The inventory at the end of March was 5,000 units.

Required   Prepare a production budget for the second quarter; in your budget, show the number of units to be produced each month and for the quarter in total.

E9–3   Three ounces of musk oil are required for each bottle of "Allure," a very popular perfume. The cost of the musk oil is $1.50 per ounce. Budgeted production of "Allure" is given below by quarters for 19x2 and for the first quarter of 19x3:

	19x2 Quarter				19x3 Quarter
	First	Second	Third	Fourth	First
Budgeted production, in bottles . . .	60,000	90,000	150,000	100,000	70,000

Musk oil has become so popular as a perfume base that it has become necessary to carry large inventories as a precaution against stock-outs. For this reason, the inventory of musk oil at the end of a quarter must be equal to 20 percent of the following quarter's production needs. Some 36,000 ounces of musk oil will be on hand to start the first quarter of 19x2.

Prepare a materials purchases budget for musk oil, by quarter and in total, for 19x2. At the bottom of your budget, show the dollar amount of purchases for each quarter and for the year in total.   *Required*

A cash budget, by quarters, is given below. Fill in the missing amounts (000 omitted). The company requires a minimum cash balance of at least $5,000 to start each quarter.   **E9–4**

	1	2	3	4	Year
Cash balance, beginning	$ 6	$?	$?	$?	$?
Add collections from customers.	?	?	96	?	323
Total cash available	71	?	?	?	?
Less disbursements:					
Purchase of inventory	35	45	?	35	?
Operating expenses	?	30	30	?	113
Equipment purchases	8	8	10	?	36
Dividends	2	2	2	2	?
Total disbursements	?	85	?	?	?
Excess (deficiency) of cash available					
over disbursements	(2)	?	11	?	?
Financing:					
Borrowings	?	15	—	—	?
Repayments (including interest)* . . .	—	—	(?)	(17)	(?)
Total financing	?	?	?	?	?
Cash balance, ending	$?	$?	$?	$?	$?

* Interest will total $1,000 for the year.

You have been asked to prepare a cash budget for December 19x8 for Ashton Company. The following information is available about the company's operations: **E9–5**

a. The cash balance on December 1 will be $40,000.
b. Actual sales for October and November and expected sales for December are as follows:

	October	November	December
Cash sales	$ 65,000	$ 70,000	$ 83,000
Sales on account . . .	400,000	525,000	600,000

Sales on account are collected over a three-month period in the following ratio: 20 percent collected in the month of sale, 60 percent collected in the month following sale, and 18 percent collected in the second month following sale. The remaining 2 percent is uncollectible.

c. Purchases of inventory will total $280,000 for December. Thirty percent of a month's inventory purchases are paid during the month of purchase. The accounts payable remaining from November's inventory purchases total $161,000, all of which will be paid in December.
d. Selling and administrative expenses are budgeted at $430,000 for December. Of this amount, $50,000 is for depreciation.
e. Equipment costing $76,000 will be purchased for cash during December, and dividends totaling $9,000 will be paid during the month.
f. The company must maintain a minimum cash balance of $20,000. An open line of credit is available from the company's bank to bolster the cash position as needed.

1. Prepare a schedule of expected cash collections for December.   *Required*
2. Prepare a schedule of expected cash payments during December to suppliers for inventory purchases.
3. Prepare a cash budget for December. Indicate in the financing section any borrowing that will be needed during the month.

E9–6 Greatday, Inc., makes a product that has peak sales in June of each year. The company has prepared a sales budget for the second quarter of 19x5, as shown below:

	April	May	June	Total
Budgeted sales . . .	$600,000	$750,000	$900,000	$2,250,000

The company is in the process of preparing a cash budget for the second quarter and must determine the expected cash collections by month. To this end, the following information has been assembled:

Collections on sales
$\begin{cases} \text{70\% in month of sale} \\ \text{20\% in month following sale} \\ \text{8\% in second month following sale} \\ \text{2\% uncollectible} \end{cases}$

The company gives a 2 percent cash discount for payments made by customers during the month of sale. The accounts receivable balance to start the quarter is $195,000, of which $45,000 represents uncollected February sales and $150,000 represents uncollected March sales.

Required   1. What were the total sales for February? For March?
2. Prepare a schedule showing the budgeted cash collections from sales, by month and in total, for the second quarter.

E9–7 (Appendix E) Classify the following as either (a) costs of carrying inventory or (b) costs of not carrying sufficient inventory:

1. Airfreight on a rush order of a critical part needed in production.
2. Interest paid on investment funds.
3. State and local taxes on personal property.
4. Spoilage of perishable goods.
5. Excessive setup costs.
6. Customers lost through inability of the company to make prompt delivery.
7. Quantity discounts lost as a result of purchasing in small lots.
8. Fire insurance on inventory.
9. Loss sustained when a competitor comes out with a less expensive, more efficient product.
10. A general feeling of ill will among customers, due to broken delivery promises.

E9–8 (Appendix E) Bedford Motor Company uses 4,500 units of Part S-10 each year. The cost of placing one order for Part S-10 is estimated to be about $20. Other costs associated with Part S-10 are:

	Annual Cost per Part
Insurance	$0.20
Property taxes	0.09
Interest on funds invested	0.15
Other	0.06
Total cost	$0.50

Required   1. Compute the EOQ for Part S-10.
2. Assume that the company has adopted JIT purchasing policies and has been able to reduce the cost of placing an order to only $1. Also assume that when the waste and inefficiency caused by inventories is considered, the cost to carry a part in inventory jumps to $1.60 per unit. Under these conditions, what would be the EOQ?

E9–9 (Appendix E) Selected information relating to an inventory item carried by the Santos Company is given below:

```
EOQ . . . . . . . . . . . . .    700 units
Maximum weekly usage  . . . . .   60 units
Lead time. . . . . . . . . . .     4 weeks
Average weekly usage  . . . . .   50 units
```

Santos Company is trying to determine the proper safety stock to carry on this inventory item, and to determine the proper reorder point.

1. Assume that no safety stock is to be carried. What is the reorder point?   *Required*
2. Assume that a full safety stock is to be carried.
   a. What would be the size of the safety stock in units?
   b. What would be the reorder point?

(Appendix E) Flint Company uses 9,000 units of part AK-4 each year. To get better control   **E9–10**
over its inventories, the company is anxious to determine the economic order quantity (EOQ) for this part.

1. The company has determined that the cost to place an order for the part is $30, and it   *Required*
   has determined that the cost to carry one part in inventory for one year is $1.50.
   Compute the EOQ for the part.
2. Assume that the cost to place an order increases from $30 to $40 per order. What will
   be the effect on the EOQ? Show computations.
3. Assume that the cost to carry a part in inventory increases from $1.50 to $2.00 per
   part. (Ordering costs remain unchanged at $30 per order.) What will be the effect on
   the EOQ? Show computations.
4. In (2) and (3) above, why does an increase in cost cause the EOQ to go up in one case
   and to go down in the other?

PROBLEMS

Behavioral Impact of Budgeting Methods   An effective budget converts the objectives   **P9–11**
and goals of management into data. Once completed, the budget serves as a blueprint that
represents management's plan for operating the organization. Moreover, the budget frequently is a basis for control in that management performance can be evaluated by comparing actual results with the budget.

   Given the importance of budgeting, the creation of an effective budget is essential for
the successful operation of an organization. There are several ways in which budget data
can be generated, and all of these ways involve extensive contacts with people at various
operating levels. The manner in which the people involved perceive their roles in the
budget process is important to the successful use of the budget as a management tool.

1. Discuss the behavioral implications associated with preparing the budget and with   *Required*
   using the budget as a method to control activities when a company employs:
   a. A budgetary approach in which budget data are imposed from above.
   b. A budgetary approach in which budget data are prepared at various levels in a self-
      imposed (participative) manner.
2. Communication plays an important part in the budget process regardless of whether
   the budget is imposed from above or a participative budget approach is used. Describe
   the differences in communication flows between these two approaches to budget preparation.

(CMA, heavily adapted)

Norton Company, a manufacturer of infant furniture and carriages, is in the initial stages of   **P9–12 Ethics and the**
preparing the annual budget for 1996. Scott Ford has recently joined Norton's accounting   **Manager**
staff and is interested to learn as much as possible about the company's budgeting process.
During a recent lunch with Marge Atkins, sales manager, and Pete Granger, production
manager, Ford initiated the following conversation.

Ford: Since I'm new around here and am going to be involved with the preparation of the annual budget, I'd be interested to learn how the two of you estimate sales and production numbers.

Atkins: We start out very methodically by looking at recent history, discussing what we know about current accounts, potential customers, and the general state of consumer spending. Then, we add that usual dose of intuition to come up with the best forecast we can.

Granger: I usually take the sales projections as the basis for my projections. Of course, we have to make an estimate of what this year's closing inventories will be, which is sometimes difficult.

Ford: Why does that present a problem? There must have been an estimate of closing inventories in the budget for the current year.

Granger: Those numbers aren't always reliable since Marge makes some adjustments to the sales numbers before passing them on to me.

Ford: What kind of adjustments?

Atkins: Well, we don't want to fall short of the sales projections so we generally give ourselves a little breathing room by lowering the initial sales projection anywhere from 5–10 percent.

Granger: So, you can see why this year's budget is not a very reliable starting point. We always have to adjust the projected production rates as the year progresses and, of course, this changes the ending inventory estimates. By the way, we make similar adjustments to expenses by adding at least 10 percent to the estimates; I think everyone around here does the same thing.

Required 1. Marge Atkins and Pete Granger have described the use of what is sometimes called *budgetary slack*.
   a. Explain why Atkins and Granger behave in this manner, and describe the benefits they expect to realize from the use of budgetary slack.
   b. Explain how the use of budgetary slack can adversely affect Atkins and Granger.
2. As a management accountant, Scott Ford believes that the behavior described by Marge Atkins and Pete Granger may be unethical. By referring to the Standards of Ethical Conduct for Management Accountants on page 23 of this textbook, explain why the use of budgetary slack may be unethical.

(CMA, adapted)

P9-13   **Production and Purchases Budgets**   Regal Products manufactures and distributes toys to retail outlets. One of the company's products, Supermix, requires 3 pounds of material A in the manufacture of each unit. The company is now planning raw materials needs for the third quarter of 19x1, the quarter in which peak sales of Supermix occur. To keep production and sales moving smoothly, the company has the following inventory requirements:

a. The finished goods inventory on hand at the end of each month must be equal to 3,000 units plus 20 percent of the next month's sales. The finished goods inventory on June 30 is budgeted to be 10,000 units.
b. The raw materials inventory on hand at the end of each month must be equal to one half of the following month's production needs for raw materials. The raw materials inventory on June 30 is budgeted to be 54,000 pounds.
c. The company maintains no work in process inventories.

A sales budget for Supermix for the last six months of 19x1 follows.

**Budgeted Sales
in Units**

July	35,000
August	40,000
September	50,000
October.	30,000
November	20,000
December.	10,000

Required

1. Prepare a production budget for Supermix for the months July–October.
2. Examine the production budget that you prepared in (1) above. Why will the company produce more units than it sells in July and August, and less units than it sells in September and October?
3. Prepare a budget showing the quantity of material A to be purchased for July, August, and September 19x1, and for the quarter in total.

Cash Budget   Atlas Company is ready to begin its third quarter, in which peak sales occur. The company has requested a $40,000, 90-day loan from its bank to help meet cash requirements during the quarter. Since Atlas Company has experienced difficulty in paying off its loans in the past, the loan officer at the bank has asked the company to prepare a cash budget for the quarter. In response to this request, the following data have been assembled:

P9–14

a. On July 1, the beginning of the third quarter, the company will have a cash balance of $44,500.
b. Actual sales for the last two months and budgeted sales for the third quarter follow:

May (actual)	$250,000
June (actual)	300,000
July (budgeted).	400,000
August (budgeted)	600,000
September (budgeted).	320,000

Past experience shows that 25 percent of a month's sales are collected in the month of sale, 70 percent in the month following sale, and 3 percent in the second month following sale. The remainder is uncollectible.

c. Budgeted merchandise purchases and budgeted expenses for the third quarter are given below:

	July	August	September
Merchandise purchases . . .	$240,000	$350,000	$175,000
Salaries and wages	45,000	50,000	40,000
Advertising.	130,000	145,000	80,000
Rent payments	9,000	9,000	9,000
Depreciation	10,000	10,000	10,000

Merchandise purchases are paid in full during the month following purchase. Accounts payable for merchandise purchases on June 30, which will be paid during July, total $180,000.

d. Equipment costing $10,000 will be purchased for cash during July.
e. In preparing the cash budget, assume that the $40,000 loan will be made in July and repaid in September. Interest on the loan will total $1,200.

Required

1. Prepare a schedule of budgeted cash collections for July, August, and September and for the quarter in total.
2. Prepare a cash budget, by month and in total, for the third quarter.
3. If the company needs a minimum cash balance of $20,000 to start each month, can the loan be repaid as planned? Explain.

P9–15   Production and Direct Materials Budgets   A sales budget for the first six months of 19x3 is given below for a product manufactured by Bloor, Ltd.

Month	Budgeted Sales (units)
January	6,000
February	10,000
March	15,000
April	9,000
May	7,000
June	6,500

The inventory of finished goods on hand at the end of each month must be equal to 30 percent of the budgeted sales for the next month. On January 1, there were 1,800 units of product on hand. Work in process inventories are nominal and can be ignored.

Each unit of product requires 5 yards of a material called Silven. The material is extremely expensive; therefore, Bloor has a policy of carrying only enough Silven in stock at the end of each month to meet 10 percent of the following month's production needs. You may assume that this requirement will be met on January 1 of the current year.

Required   Prepare a budget showing the quantity of Silven to be purchased each month for January, February, and March and in total for the three-month period. (Hint: Remember that a production budget must be prepared before a materials purchases budget can be prepared.)

P9–16   Master Budget Preparation   Minden Company's balance sheet as of April 30, 19x2, is given below:

MINDEN COMPANY

Balance Sheet
April 30, 19x2

Assets

Cash	$ 9,000
Accounts receivable, customers	54,000
Inventory	30,000
Plant and equipment, net of depreciation	207,000
Total assets	$300,000

Liabilities and Stockholders' Equity

Accounts payable, suppliers	$ 63,000
Note payable	14,500
Capital stock, no par	180,000
Retained earnings	42,500
Total liabilities and stockholders' equity	$300,000

The company is in the process of preparing budget data for May 19x2. A number of budget items have already been prepared, as stated below:

a.   Sales are budgeted at $200,000 for May. Of these sales, $60,000 will be for cash; the remainder will be credit sales. One half of a month's credit sales are collected in the month the sales are made, and the remainder is collected in the month following. All of the April 30 receivables will be collected in May.

b.   Purchases of inventory are expected to total $120,000 during May. These purchases will all be on account. Forty percent of all purchases are paid for in the month of purchase; the remainder is paid in the following month. All of the April 30 accounts payable to suppliers will be paid during May.

c.   The May 31 inventory balance is budgeted at $40,000.

d.   Operating expenses for May are budgeted at $72,000, exclusive of depreciation. These expenses will be paid in cash. Depreciation is budgeted at $2,000 for the month.

e. The note payable on the April 30 balance sheet will be paid during May, with $100 in interest. (All of the interest relates to May.)
f. New equipment costing $6,500 will be purchased for cash during May.
g. During May, the company will borrow $20,000 from its bank by giving a new note payable to the bank for that amount. The new note will be due in one year.

Required

1. Prepare a cash budget for May 19x2. Support your budget with schedules showing budgeted cash receipts from sales and budgeted cash payments for inventory purchases.
2. Prepare a budgeted income statement for May 19x2. Use the traditional income statement format. Ignore income taxes.
3. Prepare a budgeted balance sheet as of May 31, 19x2.

Integration of the Sales, Production, and Purchases Budgets   Milo Company manufactures a single product for which peak sales occur in August of each year. The company is now preparing detailed budgets for the third quarter and has assembled the following information to assist in the budget preparation:

P9–17

a. The marketing department has estimated sales as follows for the remainder of the year (in units):

July	30,000	October	20,000
August.	70,000	November	10,000
September	50,000	December	10,000

The selling price of the company's product is $12 per unit.
b. All sales are on account. Based on past experience, sales are collected in the following pattern:

30 percent in the month of sale
65 percent in the month following sale
5 percent uncollectible

Sales for June 19x6 totaled $300,000.
c. The company maintains finished goods inventories equal to 15 percent of the following month's sales. This requirement will be met at the end of June.
d. Each finished unit of product requires 4 feet of Gilden, a material that is sometimes hard to get. Therefore, the company requires that the inventory of Gilden on hand at the end of each month be equal to 50 percent of the following month's production needs. The inventory of Gilden on hand at the beginning and end of the quarter will be:

June 30 . . . . . . 72,000 feet
September 30 . . .   ?   feet

e. The Gilden costs $0.80 per foot. One half of a month's purchases of Gilden is paid for in the month of purchase; the remainder is paid for in the following month. The accounts payable on July 1 for purchases of Gilden during June will be $76,000.

Required

1. Prepare a sales budget, by month and in total, for the third quarter. (Show your budget in both units and dollars.) Also prepare a schedule of expected cash collections, by month and in total, for the third quarter.
2. Prepare a production budget for each of the months July–October.
3. Prepare a materials purchases budget for Gilden, by month and in total, for the third quarter. Also prepare a schedule of expected cash payments for Gilden, by month and in total, for the third quarter.

Planning Bank Financing by Means of a Cash Budget   When the treasurer of Westex Products, Inc., approached the company's bank in late 19x1 seeking short-term financing, he was told that money was very tight and that any borrowing over the next year would

P9–18

have to be supported by a detailed statement of cash receipts and disbursements. The treasurer also was told that it would be very helpful to the bank if borrowers would indicate the quarters in which they would be needing funds, as well as the amounts that would be needed, and the quarters in which repayments could be made.

Since the treasurer is unsure as to the particular quarters in which the bank financing will be needed, he has assembled the following information to assist in preparing a detailed cash budget:

a. Budgeted sales and merchandise purchases for 19x2, as well as actual sales and purchases for the last quarter of 19x1, are:

	Sales	Merchandise Purchases
19x1:		
Fourth quarter actual.	$200,000	$126,000
19x2:		
First quarter estimated	300,000	186,000
Second quarter estimated	400,000	246,000
Third quarter estimated.	500,000	305,000
Fourth quarter estimated	200,000	126,000

b. The company normally collects 65 percent of a quarter's sales before the quarter ends and another 33 percent in the following quarter. The remainder is uncollectible. This pattern of collections is now being experienced in the 19x1 fourth-quarter actual data.

c. Eighty percent of a quarter's merchandise purchases are paid for within the quarter. The remainder is paid in the quarter following.

d. Operating expenses for 19x2 are budgeted quarterly at $50,000 plus 15 percent of sales. Of the fixed amount, $20,000 each quarter is depreciation.

e. The company will pay $10,000 in dividends each quarter.

f. Equipment purchases of $75,000 will be made in the second quarter, and purchases of $48,000 will be made in the third quarter. These purchases will be for cash.

g. The Cash account contained $10,000 at the end of 19x1. The treasurer feels that this represents a minimum balance that must be maintained.

h. Any borrowing will take place at the beginning of a quarter, and any repayments will be made at the end of a quarter at an annual interest rate of 10 percent. Interest is paid only when principal is repaid. All borrowings and all repayments of principal must be in round $1,000 amounts. Interest payments can be in any amount. (Compute interest on whole months, e.g., $1/12$, $2/12$.)

i. At present, the company has no loans outstanding.

Required
1. Prepare the following by quarter and in total for 19x2:
   a. A schedule of budgeted cash collections on sales.
   b. A schedule of budgeted cash payments for merchandise purchases.
2. Compute the expected cash payments for operating expenses, by quarter and in total, for the year 19x2.
3. Prepare a cash budget, by quarter and in total, for the year 19x2. Show clearly in your budget the quarter(s) in which borrowing will be necessary and the quarter(s) in which repayments can be made, as requested by the company's bank.

P9–19 **Master Budget Preparation** 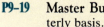 Hillyard Company prepares its master budget on a quarterly basis. The following data have been assembled to assist in preparation of the master budget for the first quarter of 19x5:

a. As of December 31, 19x4 (the end of the prior quarter), the company's general ledger showed the following account balances:

	Debits	Credits
Cash	$ 48,000	
Accounts Receivable.	224,000	
Inventory.	60,000	
Plant and Equipment (net) . . .	370,000	
Accounts Payable		$ 93,000
Capital Stock		500,000
Retained Earnings		109,000
	$702,000	$702,000

b. Actual sales for December and budgeted sales for the next four months are as follows:

December (actual) . . .	$280,000
January	400,000
February	600,000
March	300,000
April	200,000

c. Sales are 20 percent for cash and 80 percent on credit. All credit sale terms are n/30; therefore, accounts are collected in the month following sale. The accounts receivable at December 31 are a result of December credit sales.

d. The company's gross profit rate is 40 percent of sales.

e. Monthly expenses are budgeted as follows: salaries and wages, $27,000 per month; advertising, $70,000 per month; freight-out, 5 percent of sales; depreciation, $14,000 per month; other expense, 3 percent of sales.

f. At the end of each month, inventory is to be on hand equal to 25 percent of the following month's sales needs, stated at cost.

g. One half of a month's inventory purchases is paid for in the month of purchase; the other half is paid for in the following month.

h. During February, the company will purchase a new copy machine for $1,700 cash. During March, other equipment will be purchased for cash at a cost of $84,500.

i. During January, the company will declare and pay $45,000 in cash dividends.

j. The company must maintain a minimum cash balance of $30,000. An open line of credit is available at a local bank for any borrowing that may be needed during the quarter. All borrowing is done at the beginning of a month, and all repayments are made at the end of a month. Borrowings and repayments of principal must be in multiples of $1,000. Interest is paid only at the time of payment of principal. The interest rate is 12 percent per annum. (Figure interest on whole months, e.g., $1/12$, $2/12$.)

Using the data above, complete the following statements and schedules for the first quar- *Required*
ter:

1. Schedule of expected cash collections:

	January	February	March	Quarter
Cash sales	$ 80,000			
Credit sales	224,000			
Total cash collections	$304,000			

2. a. Inventory purchases budget:

	January	February	March	Quarter
Budgeted cost of goods sold	$240,000*	$360,000		
Add: Desired ending inventory . . .	90,000†			
Total needs	330,000			
Deduct: Beginning inventory	60,000			
Required purchases	$270,000			

* For January sales: $400,000 sales × 60% cost ratio = $240,000.

† $360,000 × 25% = $90,000.

b. Schedule of cash disbursements for purchases:

	January	February	March	Quarter
December purchases	$ 93,000			$ 93,000
January purchases ($270,000)	135,000	$135,000		270,000
February purchases				
March purchases				
Total cash disbursements	$228,000			

3. Schedule of cash disbursements for expenses:

	January	February	March	Quarter
Salaries and wages	$ 27,000			
Advertising	70,000			
Freight-out	20,000			
Other expenses	12,000			
Total cash disbursements	$129,000			

4. Cash budget:

	January	February	March	Quarter
Cash balance, beginning	$ 48,000			
Add cash collections	304,000			
Total cash available	352,000			
Less disbursements:				
Purchases of inventory	228,000			
Operating expenses	129,000			
Purchases of equipment	—			
Cash dividends	45,000			
Total disbursements	402,000			
Excess (deficiency) of cash	(50,000)			
Financing:				
Etc.				

5. Prepare an income statement for the quarter ending March 31. (Use the functional format in preparing your income statement, as shown in Schedule 9. Ignore income taxes.)
6. Prepare a balance sheet as of March 31.

P9–20 **Cash Budget with Supporting Schedules**   Garden Sales, Inc., is planning its cash needs for the second quarter of 19x2. The company usually has to borrow money during this quarter to support peak sales of lawn care equipment, which occur during May. The following information has been assembled to assist in preparing a cash budget for the quarter:

a. Budgeted monthly income statements for April–July 19x2 are:

	April	May	June	July
Sales	$600,000	$900,000	$500,000	$400,000
Cost of goods sold	420,000	630,000	350,000	280,000
Gross margin	180,000	270,000	150,000	120,000
Less operating expenses:				
Selling expense	79,000	120,000	62,000	51,000
Administrative expense* . . .	45,000	52,000	41,000	38,000
Total expenses	124,000	172,000	103,000	89,000
Net income	$ 56,000	$ 98,000	$ 47,000	$ 31,000

* Includes $20,000 depreciation each month.

b.   Sales are 20 percent for cash and 80 percent on account.

c.   Sales on account are collected over a three-month period in the following ratio: 10 percent collected in the month of sale; 70 percent collected in the first month following the month of sale; and the remaining 20 percent collected in the second month following the month of sale. February's sales totaled $200,000, and March's sales totaled $300,000.

d.   Inventory purchases are paid for within 15 days. Therefore, 50 percent of a month's inventory purchases are paid for in the month of purchase. The remaining 50 percent is paid in the following month. Accounts payable at March 31 for inventory purchases during March total $126,000.

e.   At the end of each month, inventory must be on hand equal to 20 percent of the cost of the merchandise to be sold in the following month. The merchandise inventory at March 31 is $84,000.

f.   Dividends of $49,000 will be declared and paid in April.

g.   Equipment costing $16,000 will be purchased for cash in May.

h.   The cash balance at March 31 is $52,000; the company must maintain a cash balance of at least $40,000 at all times.

i.   The company can borrow from its bank as needed to bolster the Cash account. Borrowings must be in multiples of $1,000. All borrowings take place at the beginning of a month, and all repayments are made at the end of a month. The interest rate is 12 percent per annum. Compute interest on whole months ($1/12$, $2/12$, and so forth).

1.   Prepare a schedule of budgeted cash collections from sales for each of the months April, May, and June, and for the quarter in total.   *Required*

2.   Prepare the following for merchandise inventory:
   a.   An inventory purchases budget for each of the months April, May, and June.
   b.   A schedule of expected cash disbursements for inventory for each of the months April, May, and June, and for the quarter in total.

3.   Prepare a cash budget for the third quarter of 19x2. Show figures by month as well as in total for the quarter. Show borrowings from the company's bank and repayments to the bank as needed to maintain the minimum cash balance.

Production Budget; Purchases Budget; Income Statement   Marvel Glue Company   **P9–21**
sells a number of products including a very popular adhesive called Formula 7. The company is in the process of preparing budgeted data on Formula 7 for the third quarter of 19x2. The following data are available on manufacture and sale of the product:

a.   The selling price of Formula 7 is $5 per bottle. The company plans to sell 250,000 bottles during the third quarter.

b.   Each bottle of Formula 7 contains 4 ounces of a material called Lactex and 2 ounces of a material called Mural.

c.   The finished goods inventory of Formula 7 is planned to be reduced by 40 percent by the end of the third quarter. The inventory at the beginning of the quarter will be 90,000 bottles. Other inventory levels are planned as follows:

	Beginning of Quarter	End of Quarter
Lactex—ounces	60,000	74,000
Mural—ounces	115,000	82,000
Empty bottles	62,000	56,000

The inventory of Lactex is budgeted to increase during the quarter, since the material is sometimes hard to find.

d.   Lactex costs $0.12 per ounce; Mural costs $0.65 per ounce; and empty bottles cost $0.10 each.

e.   Only six minutes of labor time are required to process and fill one bottle of Formula 7. Direct labor cost is $9.50 per hour. Assume the work force is adjusted as work requirements change.

f. Variable manufacturing overhead costs are $0.07 per bottle. Fixed manufacturing overhead costs total $216,000 per quarter.

g. Variable selling and administrative expenses are 6 percent of sales. Fixed selling and administrative expenses total $140,000 per quarter.

Required
1. Prepare a production budget for Formula 7 for the third quarter.
2. Prepare a raw materials purchases budget for Lactex, Mural, and empty bottles for the third quarter. Show the budgeted purchases in dollars as well as in ounces or bottles.
3. Compute the budgeted cost to manufacture one bottle of Formula 7. (Include only the variable manufacturing costs in your computations.)
4. Prepare a budgeted income statement for Formula 7 for the third quarter. Use the contribution approach, and show both per unit and total cost data.

P9-22 Master Budget Completion Following is selected information relating to the operations of Shilow Company:

Current assets as of March 31, 19x4:

Cash.	$ 8,000
Accounts receivable.	20,000
Inventory	36,000
Plant and equipment, net	120,000
Accounts payable.	21,750
Capital stock .	150,000
Retained earnings .	12,250

a. Gross profit is 25 percent of sales.

b. Actual and budgeted sales data:

March (actual)	$50,000
April.	60,000
May .	72,000
June .	90,000
July .	48,000

c. Sales are 60 percent for cash and 40 percent on credit. Credit sale terms are n/30, and therefore accounts are collected in the month following sale. The accounts receivable at March 31 are a result of March credit sales.

d. At the end of each month, inventory is to be on hand equal to 80 percent of the following month's sales needs, stated at cost.

e. One half of a month's inventory purchases is paid for in the month of purchase; the other half is paid for in the following month. The accounts payable at March 31 are a result of March purchases of inventory.

f. Monthly expenses are as follows: salaries and wages, 12 percent of sales; rent, $2,500 per month; other expenses (excluding depreciation), 6 percent of sales. Assume that these expenses are paid monthly. Depreciation is $900 per month (includes depreciation on new assets).

g. Equipment costing $1,500 will be purchased for cash in April.

h. The company must maintain a minimum cash balance of $4,000. An open line of credit is available at a local bank. All borrowing is done at the beginning of a month, and all repayments are made at the end of a month; borrowing must be in multiples of $1,000. The interest rate is 12 percent per annum. Interest is paid only at the time of repayment of principal; figure interest on whole months ($1/12$, $2/12$, and so forth).

Required Using the data above:

1. Complete the following schedule:

Schedule of Expected Cash Collections

	April	May	June	Total
Cash sales	$36,000			
Credit sales	20,000			
Total collections	$56,000			

2. Complete the following:

Inventory Purchases Budget

	April	May	June	Total
Budgeted cost of goods sold	$45,000*	$54,000		
Add: Desired ending inventory . . .	43,200†			
Total needs	88,200			
Deduct: Beginning inventory	36,000			
Required purchases	$52,200			

* For April sales: $60,000 sales × 75% cost ratio = $45,000.

† $54,000 × 80% = $43,200.

Schedule of Expected Cash Disbursements—Purchases

	April	May	June	Total
March purchases	$21,750			$21,750
April purchases	26,100	$26,100		52,200
May purchases				
June purchases				
Total disbursements	47,850			

3. Complete the following:

Schedule of Expected Cash Disbursements—Expenses

	April	May	June	Total
Salaries and wages	$ 7,200			
Rent	2,500			
Other expenses	3,600			
Total disbursements	$13,300			

4. Complete the following cash budget:

Cash Budget

	April	May	June	Quarter
Cash balance, beginning	$ 8,000			
Add cash collections	56,000			
Total cash available	64,000			
Less cash disbursements:				
For inventory	47,850			
For expenses	13,300			
For equipment	1,500			
Total cash disbursements	62,650			
Excess (deficiency) of cash	1,350			
Financing:				
Etc.				

5. Prepare an income statement for the quarter ended June 30. (Use the functional format in preparing your income statement, as shown in Schedule 9. Ignore income taxes.)
6. Prepare a balance sheet as of June 30.

P9–23 **Cash Budget for One Month** Wallace Products, Ltd., is planning its cash needs for July 19x5. Since the company will be buying some new equipment during the month, the treasurer is sure that some borrowing will be needed, but he is uncertain how much. The following data have been assembled to assist the treasurer in preparing a cash budget for the month:

a. Equipment will be purchased during July for cash at a cost of $45,000.

b. Selling and administrative expenses will be:

Advertising	$110,000
Sales salaries	50,000
Administrative salaries	35,000
Freight-out	2,100

c. Sales are budgeted at $800,000 for July. Customers are allowed a 2½ percent cash discount on accounts paid within 10 days after the end of the month of sale. Only 50 percent of the payments made in the month following sale fall within the discount period. (All of the company's sales are on account.)

d. On June 30, the company will have the following accounts receivable outstanding:

Month	Sales	Accounts Receivable at June 30	Percentage of Sales Uncollected at June 30	Percentage to Be Collected in July
March	$430,000	$ 6,450	1½%	?
April	590,000	35,400	6	?
May	640,000	128,000	20	?
June	720,000	720,000	100	?

Bad debts are negligible. All March receivables shown above will have been collected by the end of July, and the collection pattern implicit in the schedule above will be the same in July as in previous months.

e. Production costs are budgeted as follows for July:

Prime costs:		
Raw materials to be used in production		$342,000
Direct labor		95,000
Overhead costs:		
Indirect labor	$36,000	
Utilities	1,900	
Payroll benefits	14,800	
Depreciation	28,000	
Property taxes	1,100	
Fire insurance	1,700	
Amortization of patents	3,500	
Scrapping of obsolete goods	2,600	89,600
Total production costs		$526,600

f. The raw materials inventory is budgeted to increase by $18,000 during July; other inventories will not change.

g. Half of the raw materials purchased each month is paid for in the month of purchase; the other half is paid for in the following month. Accounts payable at June 30 for raw materials purchases will be $172,000.

h. All July payroll amounts will be paid for within the month of July.

i. Utilities costs are paid for within the month.

j. The $14,800 monthly charge above for "Payroll benefits" includes the following items:

Company pension plan, including ¹⁄₁₂ of a $9,600 special adjustment made in April	$7,000

Group insurance (payable semiannually, with the
last payment having been made in January). . . . . . $ 900
Unemployment insurance (payable monthly) 1,300
Vacation pay, which represents ¹⁄₁₂ of the annual
cost (July's vacations will require $14,100) 5,600

k. Property taxes are paid in June of each year.
l. Fire insurance premiums are payable in January, in advance.
m. The company has an open line of credit with the Royal Calgary Bank. All borrowing from the bank must be in round $1,000 amounts.
n. The cash balance on June 30 will be $78,000; the company must maintain a cash balance of at least $75,000 at all times.

1. Prepare a schedule showing expected cash collections for July 19x5.   *Required*
2. Compute (a) budgeted cash disbursements for raw materials purchases and (b) budgeted cash disbursements for overhead for July 19x5.
3. Prepare a cash budget for July 19x5 in good form. Ignore income taxes.

Integrated Operating Budgets The West Division of Vader Corporation produces an   **P9–24**
intricate component part used in Vader's major product line. The divisional manager has recently been concerned about a lack of coordination between purchasing and production personnel and believes that a monthly budgeting system would be better than the present system.

   The manager of West Division has decided to develop budget information for the third quarter of the current year as a trial before the budget system is implemented for an entire fiscal year. In response to the manager's request for data that could be used to develop budget information, the controller of West Division accumulated the following data:

Sales Sales through June 30, 19x7, the first six months of the current year, were 24,000 units. Actual sales in units for May and June and estimated unit sales for the next five months are detailed as follows:

> May (actual). 4,000
> June (actual) 4,000
> July (estimated) 5,000
> August (estimated) 6,000
> September (estimated) 7,000
> October (estimated) 7,500
> November (estimated) 8,000

West Division expects to sell 65,000 units during the year ending December 31, 19x7.

Direct Material Data regarding the materials used in the component are shown in the following schedule. The desired monthly ending inventory for all direct materials is to have sufficient materials on hand to provide for 50 percent of the next month's production needs.

Direct Material	Units of Direct Materials per Finished Component	Cost per Unit	Inventory Level 6/30/x7
No. 101	6 ounces	$2.40	35,000 ounces
No. 211	4 pounds	5.00	30,000 pounds

Direct Labor Each component must pass through three processes to be completed. Data regarding the direct labor are as follows:

Process	Direct Labor-Hours per Finished Component	Cost per Direct Labor-Hour
Forming.	0.80	$8.00
Assembly	2.00	5.50
Finishing	0.25	6.00

Factory Overhead   West Division produced 27,000 components during the six-month period through June 30, 19x7. The actual variable overhead costs incurred during this six-month period are shown below. The controller of West Division believes that the variable overhead costs will be incurred at the same rate during the last six months of 19x7.

Supplies	$ 59,400
Electricity	27,000
Indirect labor	54,000
Other	8,100
Total variable overhead . . .	$148,500

The fixed-overhead costs incurred during the first six months of 19x7 amounted to $93,500. Fixed-overhead costs are budgeted for the full year as follows:

Supervision	$ 60,000
Taxes	7,200
Depreciation	86,400
Other	32,400
Total fixed overhead . . .	$186,000

Finished Goods Inventory   The desired monthly ending inventory in units of completed components is 80 percent of the next month's estimated sales. There are 4,000 finished units in inventory on June 30, 19x7.

Required

1. Prepare a production budget for the West Division for the third quarter ending September 30, 19x7. Show computations by month and in total for the quarter.

2. Prepare a direct materials purchases budget in units and in dollars for each type of material for the third quarter ending September 30, 19x7. Again show computations by month and in total for the quarter.

3. Prepare a direct labor budget in hours and in dollars for the third quarter ending September 30, 19x7. This time it is *not* necessary to show monthly figures; show quarterly totals only. Assume that the work force is adjusted as work requirements change.

4. Assume that the company plans to produce a total of 65,000 units for the year. Prepare a factory overhead budget for the six-month period ending December 31, 19x7. Again, it is *not* necessary to show monthly figures.

(CMA, adapted)

P9–25   Tabulation Approach to Economic Order Quantity   (Appendix E)   The Tolby Manufacturing Company uses 15,000 ingots of Klypton each year. The Klypton is purchased from a supplier in another state, according to the following price schedule:

Ingots	Per Ingot
500	$30.00
1,000	29.90
1,500	29.85
2,000	29.80
2,500	29.75

The Tolby Manufacturing Company sends its own truck to the supplier's plant to pick up the ingots. The truck's capacity is 2,500 ingots per trip. The company has been getting a full load of ingots each trip, making six trips each year. The cost of making one round trip to the supplier's plant is $500. The paperwork associated with each trip is $30.

The supplier requires that all purchases be made in round 500-ingot lots. The company's cost analyst estimates that the cost of storing one ingot for one year is $10.

1. By use of the tabulation approach to EOQ, compute the volume in which the company *Required* should be purchasing its ingots. Treat the savings arising from quantity discounts as a reduction in total annual trucking and storing costs.
2. Compute the annual cost savings that will be realized if the company purchases in the volume which you have determined in (1) above, as compared to its present purchase policy.

Economic Order Quantity, Safety Stock, JIT Purchasing Impact (Appendix E)   **P9–26**
Myron Metal Works, Inc., uses a small casting in one of its finished products. The castings are purchased from a foundry located in another state. In total, Myron Metal Works, Inc., purchases 54,000 castings per year at a cost of $8 per casting.

The castings are used evenly throughout the year in the production process on a 360-day-per-year basis. The company estimates that it costs $90 to place a single purchase order and about $3 to carry one casting in inventory for a year. The high carrying costs result from the need to keep the castings in carefully controlled temperature and humidity conditions, and from the high cost of insurance.

Delivery from the foundry generally takes 6 days, but it can take as much as 10 days. The days of delivery time and the percentage of their occurrence are shown in the following tabulation:

Delivery Time (days)	Percentage of Occurrence
6	75
7	10
8	5
9	5
10	5
	100

1. Compute the EOQ. *Required*
2. Assume that the company is willing to assume a 15 percent risk of being out of stock. What would be the safety stock? The reorder point?
3. Assume that the company is willing to assume only a 5 percent risk of being out of stock. What would be the safety stock? The reorder point?
4. Assume a 5 percent stock-out risk as stated in (3) above. What would be the total cost of ordering and carrying inventory for one year?
5. Refer to the original data. Assume that the company decides to adopt JIT purchasing policies, as stated in the chapter. This change allows the company to reduce its cost of placing a purchase order to only $6. Also, the company estimates that when the waste and inefficiency caused by inventories are considered, the true cost of carrying a unit in stock is $7.20 per year.
   a. Compute the new EOQ.
   b. How frequently would the company be placing an order, as compared to the old purchasing policy?

Economic Order Quantity; Safety Stock; JIT Purchasing Impact (Appendix E)   **P9–27**
Pearl Company uses 10,800 units of material A each year. The material is used evenly throughout the year in the company's production process. A recent cost study indicates that it costs $6 to carry one unit of material A in stock for a year. The company estimates that the cost of placing an order for material A is $81.

On the average, it takes 10 days to receive an order from the supplier of material A. Sometimes, orders do not arrive for 13 days, and at rare intervals (about 1 percent of the time) they do not arrive for 15 days. Each unit of material A costs the company $45. Pearl Company works an average of 360 days per year.

Required 1. Compute the EOQ for material A.

2. What size safety stock would you recommend for material A? Why?

3. What is the reorder point for material A in units?

4. Compute the total cost associated with ordering and carrying material A in stock for a year. (Do *not* include the $45 purchase cost in this computation.)

5. Refer to the original data. Assume that as a result of adopting JIT purchasing policies, the company is able to reduce the cost of placing a purchase order to only $3. Also assume that after considering the waste and inefficiency caused by inventories, the actual cost of carrying one unit of material A in stock for a year is $18.

    a. Compute the new EOQ for material A.

    b. How frequently would the company be placing a purchase order, as compared to the old purchasing policy?

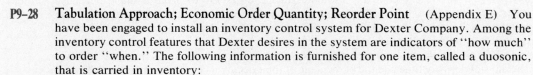

P9–28   Tabulation Approach; Economic Order Quantity; Reorder Point   (Appendix E) You have been engaged to install an inventory control system for Dexter Company. Among the inventory control features that Dexter desires in the system are indicators of "how much" to order "when." The following information is furnished for one item, called a duosonic, that is carried in inventory:

a. Duosonics are sold by the gross (12 dozen) at a list price of $800 per gross, FOB shipper. Dexter receives a 40 percent trade discount off list price on purchases in gross lots.

b. Freight cost is $20 per gross from the shipping point to Dexter's plant.

c. Dexter uses about 5,000 duosonics during a 259-day production year but must purchase a total of 36 gross per year to allow for normal breakage. Minimum and maximum usages are 12 and 28 duosonics per day, respectively.

d. Normal delivery time to receive an order is 20 working days from the date that a purchase request is initiated. A stock-out (complete exhaustion of the inventory) of duosonics would stop production, and Dexter would purchase duosonics locally at list price rather than shut down.

e. The cost of placing an order is $30.

f. Space storage cost is $24 per year per average gross in storage.

g. Insurance and taxes are approximately 12 percent of the net delivered cost of average inventory, and Dexter expects a return of at least 8 percent on its average investment. (Ignore ordering costs and carrying costs in making these computations.)

Required 1. Prepare a schedule computing the total annual cost of duosonics based on uniform order lot sizes of one, two, three, four, five, and six gross of duosonics. (The schedule should show the total annual cost according to each lot size.) Indicate the EOQ.

2. Prepare a schedule computing the minimum stock reorder point for duosonics. This is the point below which reordering is necessary to guard against a stock-out. Factors to be considered include average lead period usage and safety stock requirements.

(CPA, adapted)

CASES

C9–29   Cash Budget for a Growing Company CrossMan Corporation, a rapidly expanding crossbow distributor to retail outlets, is in the process of formulating plans for 19x2. Joan Caldwell, director of marketing, has completed her 19x2 sales budget and is confident that sales estimates will be met or exceeded. The following budgeted sales figures show the growth expected and will provide the planning basis for other corporate departments.

	Budgeted Sales		Budgeted Sales
January	$1,800,000	July.	$3,000,000
February.	2,000,000	August	3,000,000
March	1,800,000	September.	3,200,000
April	2,200,000	October	3,200,000
May	2,500,000	November	3,000,000
June.	2,800,000	December	3,400,000

George Brownell, assistant controller, has been given the responsibility for formulating the cash budget, a critical element during a period of rapid expansion. The following information will be used in preparing the cash budget.

a. CrossMan has experienced an excellent record in accounts receivable collection and expects this trend to continue. Sixty percent of billings are collected in the month after the sale and 40 percent in the second month after the sale. Uncollectible accounts are nominal and will not be considered in this analysis.

b. The purchase of the crossbows is CrossMan's largest expenditure; the cost of these items equals 50 percent of sales. Sixty percent of the crossbows are received one month prior to sale and 40 percent are received during the month of sale.

c. Prior experience shows that 80 percent of accounts payable are paid by CrossMan one month after receipt of the purchased crossbows, and the remaining 20 percent are paid the second month after receipt.

d. Hourly wages, including fringe benefits, are a factor of sales volume and are equal to 20 percent of the current month's sales. These wages are paid in the month incurred.

e. General and administrative expenses are budgeted to be $2,640,000 for 19x2. The composition of these expenses is given below. All of these expenses are incurred evenly throughout the year except the property taxes. Property taxes are paid in four equal installments in the last month of each quarter.

Salaries	$ 480,000
Promotion.	660,000
Property taxes	240,000
Insurance	360,000
Utilities	300,000
Depreciation.	600,000
Total	$2,640,000

f. Income tax payments are made by CrossMan in the first month of each quarter based on the income for the prior quarter. CrossMan's income tax rate is 40 percent. Cross-Man's net income for the first quarter of 19x2 is projected to be $612,000.

g. Equipment and warehouse facilities are being acquired to support the company's rapidly growing sales. Purchases of equipment and facilities are budgeted at $28,000 for April and $324,000 for May 19x2.

h. CrossMan has a corporate policy of maintaining an end-of-month cash balance of $100,000. Cash is borrowed or invested monthly, as needed, to maintain this balance. Interest expense on borrowed funds is budgeted at $8,000 for the second quarter, all of which will be paid during June.

i. CrossMan uses a calendar year reporting period.

1. Prepare a cash budget for CrossMan Corporation by month and in total for the second quarter of 19x2. Be sure that all receipts, disbursements, and borrowing/investing amounts are shown for each month. Ignore any interest income associated with amounts invested. *Required*

2. Discuss why cash budgeting is particularly important for a rapidly expanding company such as CrossMan Corporation.

(CMA, adapted)

C9-30 Evaluating a Company's Budget Procedures   Springfield Corporation operates on a calendar-year basis. It begins the annual budgeting process in late August, when the president establishes targets for the total dollar sales and net income before taxes for the next year.

The sales target is given to the marketing department, where the marketing manager formulates a sales budget by product line in both units and dollars. From this budget, sales quotas by product line in units and dollars are established for each of the corporation's sales districts.

The marketing manager also estimates the cost of the marketing activities required to support the target sales volume and prepares a tentative marketing expense budget.

The executive vice president uses the sales and profit targets, the sales budget by product line, and the tentative marketing expense budget to determine the dollar amounts that can be devoted to manufacturing and corporate office expense. The executive vice president prepares the budget for corporate expenses, and then forwards to the production department the product-line sales budget in units and the total dollar amount that can be devoted to manufacturing.

The production manager meets with the factory managers to develop a manufacturing plan that will produce the required units when needed within the cost constraints set by the executive vice president. The budgeting process usually comes to a halt at this point because the production department does not consider the financial resources allocated to be adequate.

When this standstill occurs, the vice president of finance, the executive vice president, the marketing manager, and the production manager meet to determine the final budgets for each of the areas. This normally results in a modest increase in the total amount available for manufacturing costs, while the marketing expense and corporate office expense budgets are cut. The total sales and net income figures proposed by the president are seldom changed. Although the participants are seldom pleased with the compromise, these budgets are final. Each executive then develops a new detailed budget for the operations in his or her area.

None of the areas has achieved its budget in recent years. Sales often run below the target. When budgeted sales are not achieved, each area is expected to cut costs so that the president's profit target can still be met. However, the profit target is seldom met because costs are not cut enough. In fact, costs often run above the original budget in all functional areas. The president is disturbed that Springfield has not been able to meet the sales and profit targets. He hired a consultant with considerable experience with companies in Springfield's industry. The consultant reviewed the budgets for the past four years. He concluded that the product-line sales budgets were reasonable and that the cost and expense budgets were adequate for the budgeted sales and production levels.

Required   1. Discuss how the budgeting process as employed by Springfield Corporation contributes to the failure to achieve the president's sales and profit targets.
2. Suggest how Springfield Corporation's budgeting process could be revised to correct the problems.
3. Should the functional areas be expected to cut their costs when sales volume falls below budget? Explain your answer.

(CMA, adapted)

C9-31 Master Budget with Supporting Schedules   You have just been hired as a new management trainee by Earrings Unlimited, a distributor of earrings to various retail outlets located in shopping malls across the country. In the past, the company has done very little in the way of budgeting and at certain times of the year has experienced a shortage of cash.

Since you are well trained in budgeting, you have decided to prepare comprehensive budgets for the upcoming second quarter in order to show management the benefits that can be gained from an integrated budgeting program. To this end, you have worked with accounting and other areas to gather the information assembled below.

The company sells many styles of earrings, but all are sold for the same price—$10 per pair. Actual sales of earrings for the last three months and budgeted sales for the next six months follow (in pairs of earrings):

January (actual)	20,000	June	50,000
February (actual) . . .	26,000	July	30,000
March (actual)	40,000	August	28,000
April	65,000	September . . .	25,000
May	100,000		

The concentration of sales before and during May is due to Mother's Day. Sufficient inventory should be on hand at the end of each month to supply 40 percent of the earrings sold in the following month.

Suppliers are paid $4 for a pair of earrings. One half of a month's purchases is paid for in the month of purchase; the other half is paid for in the following month. All sales are on credit, with no discount, and payable within 15 days. The company has found, however, that only 20 percent of a month's sales are collected in the month of sale. An additional 70 percent is collected in the following month, and the remaining 10 percent is collected in the second month following sale. Bad debts have been negligible.

Monthly operating expenses for the company are given below:

Variable:	
Sales commissions	4% of sales
Fixed:	
Advertising	$200,000
Rent	18,000
Salaries	106,000
Utilities	7,000
Insurance expired	3,000
Depreciation	14,000

Insurance is paid on an annual basis, in November of each year.

The company plans to purchase $16,000 in new equipment during May and $40,000 in new equipment during June; both purchases will be for cash. The company declares dividends of $15,000 each quarter, payable in the first month of the following quarter.

A listing of the company's ledger accounts as of March 31 is given below:

Assets

Cash	$ 74,000
Accounts receivable ($26,000 February sales;	
$320,000 March sales)	346,000
Inventory	104,000
Prepaid insurance	21,000
Property and equipment (net)	950,000
Total assets	$1,495,000

Liabilities and Stockholders' Equity

Accounts payable	$ 100,000
Dividends payable	15,000
Capital stock	800,000
Retained earnings	580,000
Total liabilities and stockholders' equity	$1,495,000

Part of the use of the budgeting program will be to establish an ongoing line of credit at a local bank. Therefore, determine the borrowing that will be needed to maintain a minimum cash balance of $50,000. All borrowing will be done at the beginning of a month; any repayments will be made at the end of a month.

The interest rate will be 12 percent per annum. Interest will be computed and paid at the end of each quarter on all loans outstanding during the quarter. Compute interest on whole months ($1/12$, $2/12$, and so forth).

Required Prepare a master budget for the three-month period ending June 30. Include the following detailed budgets:

1. a. A sales budget, by month and in total.
   b. A schedule of expected cash collections from sales, by month and in total.
   c. A merchandise purchases budget in units and in dollars. Show the budget by month and in total.
   d. A schedule of expected cash payments for merchandise purchases, by month and in total.
2. A cash budget. Show the budget by month and in total.
3. A budgeted income statement for the three-month period ending June 30. Use the contribution approach.
4. A budgeted balance sheet as of June 30.

C9–32 **Evaluating a Company's Budget Procedures** Tom Emory and Jim Morris strolled back to their plant from the administrative offices of Ferguson & Son Mfg. Company. Tom was manager of the machine shop in the company's factory; Jim was manager of the equipment maintenance department.

The men had just attended the monthly performance evaluation meeting for plant department heads. These meetings had been held on the third Tuesday of each month since Robert Ferguson, Jr., the president's son, had become plant manager a year earlier.

As they were walking, Tom Emory spoke. "Boy, I hate those meetings! I never know whether my department's accounting reports will show good or bad performance. I'm beginning to expect the worst. If the accountants say I saved the company a dollar, I'm called 'Sir,' but if I spend even a little too much—boy, do I get in trouble. I don't know if I can hold on until I retire."

Tom had just been given the worst evaluation he had ever received in his long career with Ferguson & Son. He was the most respected of the experienced machinists in the company. He had been with Ferguson & Son for many years and was promoted to supervisor of the machine shop when the company expanded and moved to its present location. The president (Robert Ferguson, Sr.) had often stated that the company's success was due to the high quality of the work of machinists like Tom. As supervisor, Tom stressed the importance of craftsmanship and told his workers that he wanted no sloppy work coming from his department.

When Robert Ferguson, Jr., became the plant manager, he directed that monthly performance comparisons be made between actual and budgeted costs for each department. The departmental budgets were intended to encourage the supervisors to reduce inefficiencies and to seek cost reduction opportunities. The company controller was instructed to have his staff "tighten" the budget slightly whenever a department attained its budget in a given month; this was done to reinforce the plant supervisor's desire to reduce costs. The young plant manager often stressed the importance of continued progress toward attaining the budget; he also made it known that he kept a file of these performance reports for future reference when he succeeded his father.

Tom Emory's conversation with Jim Morris continued as follows:

Emory: I really don't understand. We've worked so hard to get up to budget, and the minute we make it they tighten the budget on us. We can't work any faster and still maintain quality. I think my men are ready to quit trying. Besides, those reports don't tell the whole story. We always seem to be interrupting the big jobs for all those small rush orders. All that setup and machine adjustment time is killing us. And quite frankly, Jim, you were no help. When our hydraulic press broke down last month, your people were nowhere to be found. We had to take it apart ourselves and got stuck with all that idle time.

Morris: I'm sorry about that, Tom, but you know my department has had trouble making budget, too. We were running well behind at the time of that problem, and if we'd spent a day on that old machine, we would never have made it up. Instead we made the scheduled inspections of the forklift trucks because we knew we could do those in less than the budgeted time.

Emory: Well, Jim, at least you have some options. I'm locked into what the scheduling department assigns to me and you know they're being harrassed by sales for those special orders. Incidentally, why didn't your report show all the supplies you guys wasted last month when you were working in Bill's department?

Morris: We're not out of the woods on that deal yet. We charged the maximum we could to our other work and haven't even reported some of it yet.

Emory: Well, I'm glad you have a way of getting out of the pressure. The accountants seem to know everything that's happening in my department, sometimes even before I do. I thought all that budget and accounting stuff was supposed to help, but it just gets me into trouble. Its all a big pain. I'm trying to put out quality work; they're trying to save pennies.

1.   Identify the problems which appear to exist in Ferguson & Son Mfg. Company's budgetary control system and explain how the problems are likely to reduce the effectiveness of the system.   *Required*

2.   Explain how Ferguson & Son Mfg. Company's budgetary control system could be revised to improve its effectiveness.

(CMA, adapted)

*There is a "manufacturing excellence" board posted in each
production cell on the shop floor at this AT&T transformer factory.
The board measures performance against goals on a monthly basis
for a variety of performance measures including the number of
defective units, the first pass quality percent yield, the percent of
orders shipped on-time, turnover, cost of scrap, and the percent of
workers who have been cross-trained.*

Standard Costs and JIT/FMS Performance Measures

LEARNING OBJECTIVES

After studying Chapter 10, you should be able to:

1 Distinguish between ideal standards and practical standards.

2 Explain how direct materials standards and direct labor standards are set.

3 Enumerate the advantages and disadvantages of using standard costs.

4 Compute the direct materials price and quantity variances and explain their significance.

5 Compute the direct labor rate and efficiency variances and explain their significance.

6 Compute the variable overhead spending and efficiency variances.

7 Explain how the manager would determine whether a variance constituted an "exception" that would require his or her attention.

8 Explain why traditional standards may be inappropriate for companies operating in an automated environment.

9 Enumerate the JIT/FMS performance measures and explain how they are used.

10 Compute the delivery cycle time, the throughput time, and the manufacturing cycle efficiency (MCE) as these measures relate to JIT/FMS.

11 Define or explain the key terms listed at the end of the chapter.

12 (Appendix F) Prepare journal entries to record standard costs and variances.

I n attempting to control costs and to optimize output, managers have many decisions to make. Some of these decisions relate to the inputs of the firm in terms of prices paid and quantities used. As managers acquire inputs, they are expected to pay the lowest possible prices that are consistent with the quality of output desired. They are also expected to consume the minimum quantity of whatever inputs they have at their command, again consistent with the quality of output desired. Breakdowns in control over either price or quantity will lead to excessive costs and to deteriorating profit margins.

How do managers control prices paid and quantities used? They could examine every transaction that takes place, but this obviously would be an inefficient use of management time. For many companies, the answer to the control problem lies in *standard costs*. For other companies, particularly for those operating in a JIT/FMS environment, standard costs are supplemented by various other methods of control, many of which are nonfinancial in nature. In this chapter, we focus our attention first on the development and use of standard costs. We then turn our attention to the other methods of control that are gaining in popularity—particularly with companies that operate in an automated environment.

STANDARD COSTS—MANAGEMENT BY EXCEPTION

A *standard* can be defined as a benchmark or "norm" for measuring performance. Standards are found in many facets of day-to-day life. Students who wish to enter a college or university are often required to perform at a certain level on a standard achievement exam as a condition for admittance; the autos we drive are built under exacting engineering standards; and the food we eat is prepared under standards of both cleanliness and nutritional content. Standards are also widely used in managerial accounting. Here the standards relate to the *quantity* and *cost* of inputs used in manufacturing goods or providing services.

Quantity and cost standards are set by managers for the three elements of cost input—materials, labor, and overhead—that we have discussed in preceding chapters. *Quantity standards* indicate how much of a cost element, such as labor time or raw materials, should be used in manufacturing a unit of product or in providing a unit of service. *Cost standards* indicate what the cost of the time or the materials should be. Actual quantities and actual costs of inputs are measured against these standards to see whether operations are proceeding within the limits that management has set. If either the quantity or the cost of inputs exceeds the bounds that management has set, attention is directed to the difference, thereby permitting the manager to focus his or her efforts where they will do the most good. This process is called **management by exception.**

Who Uses Standard Costs?

Manufacturing, service, food, and not-for-profit organizations all make use of standards (in terms of either costs or quantities) to some extent. Auto service centers, for example, often set specific labor time standards for the completion of certain work tasks, such as installing a carburetor or doing a valve job, and then measure actual performance against these standards. Fast-food outlets such as McDonald's have exacting standards as to the quantity of meat going into a sandwich, as well as standards for the cost of the meat. Hospitals have standard costs (for food, laundry, and other items) for each occupied bed per day, as well as standard time allowances for the performing of certain routine activities, such as laboratory tests. In short, the business student is likely to run into standard cost concepts in virtually any line of business that she or he may enter.

FOCUS ON CURRENT PRACTICE

A survey of manufacturing companies with annual sales in excess of $500 million found that 87 percent use standard costing. The survey also found that the use of standard cost systems is increasing and that standards are being applied to smaller and smaller units within the firms.[1]

Another study of 244 companies involved in traditional manufacturing, high-tech operations, and service activities found that 67 percent use standard cost systems. No statistically significant difference was found between companies in the use of standard costs based on either type of operation or size of company.[2]

The broadest application of the standard cost idea is probably found in manufacturing companies, where standards relating to materials, labor, and overhead are developed in detail for each separate product line. These standards are then organized into a **standard cost card** that tells the manager what the final, manufactured cost should be for a single unit of product. In the following section, we provide a detailed example of the setting of standard costs and the preparation of a standard cost card.

SETTING STANDARD COSTS

The setting of standard costs is more an art than a science. It requires the combined thinking and expertise of all persons who have responsibility over prices and quantities of inputs. In a manufacturing setting, this would include the managerial accountant, the purchasing agent, the industrial engineer, production supervisors, line managers, and the production workers themselves.

The beginning point in setting standard costs is a rigorous look at past experience. The managerial accountant can be of great help in this task by preparing data on the cost characteristics of prior years' activities at various levels of operations. A standard for the future must be more than simply a projection of the past, however. Data must be adjusted for changing economic patterns, changing demand and supply characteristics, and changing technology. Past experience in certain costs may be distorted due to inefficiencies. To the extent that such inefficiencies can be identified, the data must be appropriately adjusted. The manager must realize that the past is of value only insofar as it helps to predict the future. In short, standards must be reflective of efficient *future* operations, not inefficient *past* operations.

---

[1] Bruce R. Gaumnitz and Felix P. Kollaritsch, "Manufacturing Cost Variances: Current Practice and Trends," *Journal of Cost Management* 5, no. 1 (Spring 1991), pp. 58–64.

[2] Jeffrey R. Cohen and Laurence Paquette, "Management Accounting Practices: Perceptions of Controllers," *Journal of Cost Management* 5, no. 3 (Fall 1991), pp. 73–83.

Ideal versus Practical Standards

Should standards be attainable all of the time, should they be attainable only part of the time, or should they be so tight that they become, in effect, "the impossible dream"? Opinions among managers vary, but standards tend to fall into one of two categories—either ideal or practical.

Ideal standards are those that can be attained only under the best circumstances. They allow for no machine breakdowns or other work interruptions, and they call for a level of effort that can be attained only by the most skilled and efficient employees working at peak effort 100 percent of the time. Some managers feel that such standards have a motivational value. These managers argue that even though employees know they will never stay within the standard set, it is a constant reminder of the need for ever-increasing efficiency and effort. Few firms use ideal standards. Most managers are of the opinion that ideal standards tend to discourage even the most diligent workers. Moreover, when ideal standards are used, variances from standards have little meaning. The reason is that the variances contain elements of "normal" inefficiencies, not just the abnormal inefficiencies that managers would like to have isolated and brought to their attention.

Practical standards can be defined as standards that are "tight but attainable." They allow for normal machine downtime and employee rest periods, and are such that they can be attained through reasonable, though highly efficient, efforts by the average worker at a task. Variances from such a standard are very useful to management in that they represent deviations that fall outside of normal, recurring inefficiencies and signal a need for management attention. Furthermore, practical standards can serve multiple purposes. In addition to signaling abnormal deviations in costs, they can also be used in forecasting cash flows and in planning inventory. By contrast, ideal standards cannot be used in forecasting and planning; they do not allow for normal inefficiencies, and therefore they result in unrealistic planning and forecasting figures.

Throughout the remainder of this chapter, we will assume the use of practical rather than ideal standards.

Setting Direct Materials Standards

As stated earlier, managers prepare separate standards for the price and quantity of inputs. The **standard price per unit** for direct materials should reflect the final, delivered cost of the materials, net of any discounts taken. For example, the standard price of a pound of material A might be determined as follows:

Purchase price, top grade, in 500-pound quantities . . .	$3.60
Freight, by truck, from the supplier's plant	0.44
Receiving and handling	0.05
Less purchase discount	(0.09)
Standard price per pound	$4.00

Notice that the standard price reflects a particular grade of material (top grade), purchased in particular lot sizes (500 pounds), and delivered by a particular type of carrier (truck). Allowances have also been made for handling and discounts. If all proceeds according to plans, the net standard price of a pound of material A should therefore be $4.

The **standard quantity per unit** for direct materials should reflect the amount of material going into each unit of finished product, as well as an allowance for unavoidable waste, spoilage, and other normal inefficiencies. To illustrate, the standard quantity of material A going into a unit of product might be determined as follows:

Per bill of materials, in pounds	2.7
Allowance for waste and spoilage, in pounds	0.2
Allowance for rejects, in pounds	0.1
Standard quantity per unit of product, in pounds . . .	3.0

A **bill of materials** is simply a list that shows the type and quantity of each item of material going into a unit of finished product. It is a handy source for determining the basic material input per unit, but it must be adjusted for waste and other factors, as shown above, in determining the full standard quantity per unit of product. Although it is common to recognize a waste factor in setting standard costs, this practice is now coming into question due to the JIT emphasis on continuous improvement. If a waste factor is built into a standard cost, it must be carefully monitored to ensure that it is eliminated over time through improved processes, modernized equipment, and so forth.

FOCUS ON CURRENT PRACTICE

After many years of operating a standard cost system, a major wood products company reviewed the materials standards for its products by breaking each standard down into its basic elements. In doing so, the company discovered that there was a 20 percent waste factor built into the standard cost for every product. This discovery completely surprised management, and they were dismayed to learn that the dollar amount of "allowable" waste was very large. Since the quantity standards had not been scrutinized for many years, management was unaware of the existence of this significant cost improvement potential in the company.[3]

"Rejects" represent the direct material contained in units of product that are rejected at final inspection. The cost of this material must be added back to good units. As in the case of waste, rejects must be carefully monitored to ensure that there is a constant improvement in the integrity of production. These ideas are discussed further in Appendix K titled Quality Costs and Reports, located at the end of the book.

Once the price and quantity standards have been set, the standard cost of material A per unit of finished product can be computed as follows:

$$3.0 \text{ pounds} \times \$4 = \$12 \text{ per unit}$$

This $12 cost figure will appear as one item on the standard cost card of the product under consideration.

---

[3] James M. Reeve, "The Impact of Variation on Operating System Performance," *Performance Excellence* (Sarasota, Fla: American Accounting Association, 1990), p. 77.

Setting Direct Labor Standards

Direct labor price and quantity standards are usually expressed in terms of labor rate and labor-hours. The **standard rate per hour** for direct labor would include not only wages earned but also an allowance for fringe benefits and other labor-related costs. The computation might be as follows:

Basic wage rate per hour	$10
Employment taxes at 10% of the basic rate . . .	1
Fringe benefits at 30% of the basic rate	3
Standard rate per direct labor-hour	$14

Many companies prepare a single standard rate for all employees in a department that reflects an expected "mix" of workers, even though the actual wage rates may vary somewhat due to skills or seniority. This simplifies the use of standard costs and also permits the manager to monitor the use of employees within departments. More is said on this point a little later. If all proceeds according to plans, the direct labor rate for our mythical company should average $14 per hour.

The standard direct labor time required to complete a unit of product (generally called the **standard hours per unit**) is perhaps the single most difficult standard to determine. One approach is to divide each operation performed on the product into elemental body movements (such as reaching, pushing, and turning over). Published tables of standard times for such movements are available. These times can be applied to the movements and then added together to determine the total standard time allowed per operation. Another approach is for an industrial engineer to do a time and motion study, actually clocking the time required for certain tasks. As stated earlier, the standard time developed must include allowances for coffee breaks, personal needs of employees, cleanup, and machine downtime. The resulting standard time might appear as follows:

Basic labor time per unit, in hours.	1.9
Allowance for breaks and personal needs	0.1
Allowance for cleanup and machine downtime . . .	0.3
Allowance for rejects	0.2
Standard hours per unit of product	2.5

Once the rate and time standards have been set, the standard labor cost per unit of product can be computed as follows:

$$2.5 \text{ hours} \times \$14 = \$35 \text{ per unit}$$

This $35 cost figure will appear along with direct materials as one item on the standard cost card of the product under consideration.

Setting Variable Overhead Standards

As with direct labor, the price and quantity standards for variable overhead are generally expressed in terms of rate and hours. The rate represents *the variable portion of the predetermined overhead rate* discussed in Chapter 3; the hours represent whatever hours base is used to apply overhead to units of product (often machine-hours, computer time, or direct labor-hours, as we learned in Chapter 3). To illustrate, if the variable portion of the predetermined overhead rate was $3 and if overhead was applied to units of product on a basis of direct labor-hours, the standard variable overhead cost per unit of product in our example would be:

EXHIBIT 10–1

Standard Cost
Card—Variable
Production Cost

Inputs	(1) Standard Quantity or Hours	(2) Standard Price or Rate	(3) Standard Cost (1) × (2)
Direct materials	3.0 pounds	$ 4.00	$12.00
Direct labor.	2.5 hours	14.00	35.00
Variable overhead	2.5 hours	3.00	7.50
Total standard cost per unit . .			$54.50

2.5 hours × $3.00 = $7.50 per unit

A more detailed look at the setting of overhead standards is reserved until Chapter 11.

To summarize our example on the setting of standard costs, the completed standard cost card for one unit of product in our mythical company is presented in Exhibit 10–1. Observe that the **standard cost per unit** is computed by multiplying the standard quantity or hours by the standard price or rate.

Are Standards the Same as Budgets?

Essentially, standards and budgets are the same thing. The only distinction between the two terms is that a standard is a *unit* amount, whereas a budget is a *total* amount. That is, the standard cost for materials in a unit of product may be $5. If 1,000 units of the product are to be produced during a period, then the budgeted cost of materials is $5,000. In effect, a standard may be viewed as being the *budgeted cost for one unit of product*.

Advantages of Standard Costs

A number of distinct advantages can be cited in favor of using standard costs in an organization.

Objective 3
Enumerate the advantages and disadvantages of using standard costs.

1. As stated earlier, the use of standard costs makes possible the concept of management by exception. So long as costs remain within the standards set, no attention by management is needed. When costs fall outside the standards set, then the matter is brought to the attention of management at once as an "exception." Management by exception makes possible more productive use of management time.
2. Standard costs facilitate cash planning and inventory planning.
3. So long as standards are set on a "practical" basis, they promote economy and efficiency in that employees normally become very cost and time conscious. In addition, wage incentive systems can be tied to a system of standard costs once the standards have been set.
4. In income determination, a system of standard costs may be more economical and simpler to operate than a historical cost system. Standard cost cards can be kept for each product or operation, and costs for material, labor, and manufacturing overhead charged out according to the standards set. This greatly simplifies the bookkeeping process.
5. Standard costs can assist in the implementation of "responsibility accounting," in which responsibility over cost control is assigned, and the extent to which that responsibility has been discharged can be evaluated through performance reports.

Disadvantages of Standard Costs

Although the advantages of using standard costs are significant, we must recognize that certain difficulties can be encountered by the manager in applying the standard cost idea. Moreover, improper use of standard costs and the management by exception principle can lead to adverse behavioral problems in an organization. Managers cite the following as being either problems or potential problems in using standard costs:

1. Difficulty may be experienced in determining which variances are "material" or significant in amount. (Ways to overcome this problem are discussed later in the chapter.)
2. By focusing only on variances above a certain level (that is, on variances that are considered to be material in amount), other useful information, such as trends, may not be noticed at an early stage.
3. If management performance evaluation is tied to the exception principle, subordinates may be tempted to cover up negative exceptions or not report them at all. In addition, subordinates may not receive reinforcement for the positive things they do, such as controlling or reducing costs charged to their area of responsibility, but may only receive reprimands for those items that exceed the acceptable cost standards. Thus, subordinate morale may suffer because of the lack of positive reinforcement for work well done.
4. The management by exception technique may also affect supervisory employees in an unsatisfactory manner. Supervisors may feel that they are not getting a complete review of operations because they are always just keying in on problems. In addition, supervisors may feel that they are constantly being critical of their subordinates, that is, always "running them down." This may have a negative impact on supervisory morale.

These potential problems suggest that considerable care must be exercised by the manager in organizing and administering a standard cost system. It is particularly important that the manager focus on the positive, rather than on the negative, and that work that is well done be appropriately recognized.

A GENERAL MODEL FOR VARIANCE ANALYSIS

One reason for separating standards into two categories—price and quantity—is that control decisions relating to price paid and quantity used will generally fall at different points in time. In the case of raw materials, for example, control over price paid comes at the time of purchase. By contrast, control over quantity used does not come until the raw materials are used in production, which may be many weeks or months after the purchase date. In addition, control over price paid and quantity used will generally be the responsibility of two different managers and will therefore need to be assessed independently. As we have stressed earlier, no manager should be held responsible for a cost over which he or she has no control. It is important, therefore, that we separate price considerations from quantity considerations in our approach to the control of costs.

Price and Quantity Variances

The manager separates price considerations from quantity considerations in the control of costs through the use of a general model that distinguishes between

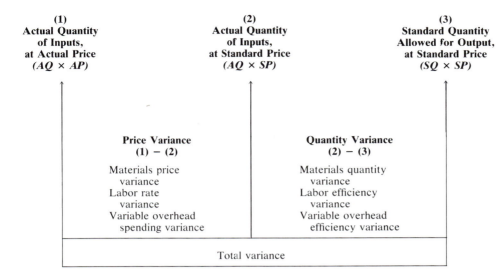

these two cost elements and that provides a base for *variance* analysis. A **variance** is the difference between *standard* prices and quantities and *actual* prices and quantities. This model, which deals with variable costs, isolates price variances from quantity variances and shows how each of these variances is computed.[4] The model is presented in Exhibit 10–2.

Three things should be noted from Exhibit 10–2. First, note that a price variance and a quantity variance can be computed for all three variable cost elements—direct materials, direct labor, and variable manufacturing overhead—even though the variance is not called by the same name in all cases. For example, a price variance is called a *materials price variance* in the case of direct materials but a *labor rate variance* in the case of direct labor and an *overhead spending variance* in the case of variable manufacturing overhead.

Second, note that even though a price variance may be called by different names, it is computed in exactly the same way regardless of whether one is dealing with direct materials, direct labor, or variable manufacturing overhead. The same is true with the quantity variance.

Third, note that variance analysis is actually a matter of input-output analysis. The inputs represent the actual quantity of direct materials, direct labor, and variable manufacturing overhead used; the output represents the good production of the period, expressed in terms of the *standard quantity (or the standard hours) allowed* in its manufacture (see column 3 in Exhibit 10–2). By **standard quantity allowed** or **standard hours allowed,** we mean the amount of direct materials, direct labor, or variable manufacturing overhead *that should have been used* to produce what was produced during the period. This might be more or less than what was *actually* used, depending on the efficiency or inefficiency of operations. The standard quantity allowed is computed by multiplying the actual output in units by the standard input allowed per unit.

With this general model as a foundation, we will now examine the price and quantity variances in more detail.

---

[4] Variance analysis of fixed costs is reserved until Chapter 11.

USING STANDARD COSTS—DIRECT MATERIAL VARIANCES

To illustrate the computation and use of direct material variances, we will return to the standard cost data for direct materials contained in Exhibit 10–1. This exhibit shows the standard cost of direct materials per unit of product in our mythical company to be:

$$3.0 \text{ pounds} \times \$4 = \$12 \text{ per unit}$$

We will assume that during June the company purchased 6,500 pounds of material at a cost of \$3.80 per pound, including freight and handling costs, and net of the quantity discount. All of the material was used in the manufacture of 2,000 units of product. The computation of the price and quantity variances for the month is shown in Exhibit 10–3.

A variance is unfavorable (commonly denoted by U) if the actual price or quantity exceeds the standard price or quantity; a variance is favorable (commonly denoted by F) if the actual price or quantity is less than the standard.

The data in Exhibit 10–3 assumes that all of the material purchased was used in production during the period. How are the variances computed if a different amount of material is purchased than is used? To illustrate, assume that during June the company purchased 6,500 pounds of material, as before, but that it used only 5,000 pounds of material during the month and produced only 1,600 units. In this case, the variances would be as shown in Exhibit 10–4.

Note from the exhibit that the price variance is computed on the entire amount of material purchased (6,500 pounds), as before, whereas the quantity variance is computed only on the portion of this material used in production during the month (5,000 pounds). A quantity variance on the 1,500 pounds of material that was purchased during the month but *not* used in production (6,500 pounds purchased − 5,000 pounds used = 1,500 pounds unused) will be computed in a future period when these materials are drawn out of inventory and used in production. The situation illustrated in Exhibit 10–4 is common for companies that purchase materials several weeks (or months) in advance of use and store the materials in warehouses while awaiting the production process.

EXHIBIT 10–3
Variance
Analysis—Direct
Materials

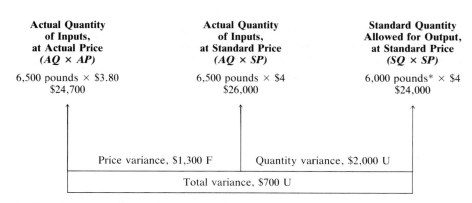

Actual Quantity of Inputs, at Actual Price (AQ × AP)	Actual Quantity of Inputs, at Standard Price (AQ × SP)	Standard Quantity Allowed for Output, at Standard Price (SQ × SP)
6,500 pounds × $3.80	6,500 pounds × $4	6,000 pounds* × $4
$24,700	$26,000	$24,000

Price variance, $1,300 F   Quantity variance, $2,000 U

Total variance, $700 U

* 2,000 units × 3.0 pounds per unit = 6,000 pounds.
F = Favorable; U = Unfavorable.

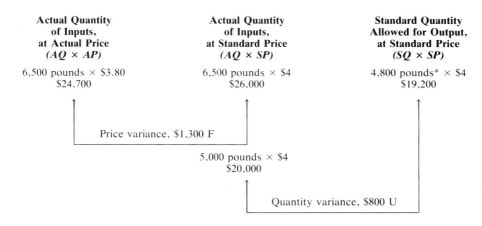

Actual Quantity of Inputs, at Actual Price $(AQ \times AP)$	Actual Quantity of Inputs, at Standard Price $(AQ \times SP)$	Standard Quantity Allowed for Output, at Standard Price $(SQ \times SP)$
6,500 pounds × $3.80 $24,700	6,500 pounds × $4 $26,000	4,800 pounds* × $4 $19,200

Price variance, $1,300 F

5,000 pounds × $4
$20,000

Quantity variance, $800 U

EXHIBIT 10–4
Variance Analysis—Direct Materials, When the Amount Purchased Differs from the Amount Used

A total variance can't be computed in this situation, since the amount of materials purchased (6,500 pounds) differs from the amount used in production (5,000 pounds).

* 1,600 units × 3.0 pounds per unit = 4,800 pounds.

Materials Price Variance—A Closer Look

A **materials price variance** measures the difference between what is paid for a given quantity of materials and what should have been paid according to the standard that has been set. From Exhibit 10–3, this difference can be expressed by the following formula:

$$(AQ \times AP) - (AQ \times SP) = \text{Materials price variance}$$

The formula can be factored into simpler form as:

$$AQ(AP - SP) = \text{Materials price variance}$$

Some managers prefer this simpler formula, since it permits variance computations to be made very quickly. Using the data from Exhibit 10–3 in this formula, we have:

$$6,500 \text{ pounds } (\$3.80 - \$4.00) = \$1,300 \text{ F}$$

Notice that the answer is the same as that yielded in Exhibit 10–3. If the company wanted to put these data into a performance report, the data would appear as follows:

MYTHICAL COMPANY
Performance Report—Purchasing Department

Item Purchased	(1) Quantity Purchased	(2) Actual Price	(3) Standard Price	(4) Difference in Price (2) − (3)	(5) Total Price Variance (1) × (4)	Explanation
Material A	6,500 pounds	$3.80	$4.00	$0.20	$1,300 F	Second-grade materials purchased, rather than top grade

F = Favorable; U = Unfavorable.

Isolation of Variances

At what point should variances be isolated and brought to the attention of management? The answer is, the earlier the better. One of the basic reasons for utilizing standard costs is to facilitate cost control. Therefore, the sooner deviations from standard are brought to the attention of management, the sooner problems can be evaluated and corrected. If long periods are allowed to elapse before variances are computed, costs that could otherwise have been controlled may accumulate to the point of doing significant damage to profits. Most firms compute the materials price variance, for example, when materials *are purchased* rather than when the materials are placed into production. This permits earlier isolation of the variance, since materials may remain in the warehouse for many months before being used in production. Isolating the price variance when materials are purchased also permits the company to carry its raw materials in the inventory accounts at standard cost. This greatly simplifies the selection of the proper cost figure to use when raw materials are later placed into production.[5]

FOCUS ON CURRENT PRACTICE

The Gaumnitz and Kollaritsch study of large manufacturing companies cited earlier found that about 60 percent prepare variance reports on a monthly basis, another 13 percent prepare reports on a weekly basis, and nearly 22 percent prepare reports on a daily basis. The number of companies preparing daily reports has more than doubled over the past five years.[6] The Cohen and Paquette study cited earlier reported essentially the same results, with only slightly fewer companies preparing monthly reports and only slightly more preparing weekly or daily reports.[7]

Another study of 104 large industrial companies found that 88 percent compute the materials price variance at the time the materials are purchased.[8]

Once a performance report has been prepared, what does management do with the price variance data? The variances should be viewed as "red flags," calling attention to the fact that an exception has occurred that will require some follow-up effort. Normally, the performance report itself will contain some explanation of the reason for the variance, as shown above.

Responsibility for the Variance   Who is responsible for the materials price variance? Generally speaking, the purchasing agent has control over the price to be paid for goods and is therefore responsible for any price variances. Many factors influence the price paid for goods, including size of lots purchased, delivery method used, quantity discounts available, rush orders, and the quality of materials purchased. To the extent that the purchasing agent can control these factors, he or she is responsible for seeing that they are kept in agreement with the factors anticipated when the standard costs were initially set. A deviation in any factor from what was intended in the initial setting of a standard cost can result in a price variance. For example, purchase of second-grade materials rather than top-grade materials would result in a favorable price variance, since the lower-grade materials would generally be less costly (but perhaps less suitable for production).

---

[5] See Appendix F at the end of the chapter for an illustration of journal entries in a standard cost system.

[6] See Gaumnitz and Kollaritsch, "Manufacturing Cost Variances: Current Practice and Trends," p. 60.

[7] See Cohen and Paquette, "Management Accounting Practices: Perceptions of Controllers," p. 77.

[8] Max Laudeman and F. W. Schaeberle, "The Cost Accounting Practices of Firms Using Standard Costs," *Cost and Management* 57, no. 4 (July–August 1983), p. 24.

There may be times, however, when someone other than the purchasing agent is responsible for a materials price variance. Production may be scheduled in such a way, for example, that the purchasing agent is required to obtain delivery by airfreight, rather than by truck, or he or she may be forced to buy in uneconomical quantities. In these cases, the production manager would bear responsibility for the variances that develop.

A word of caution is in order. Variance analysis should not be used as an excuse to conduct witch hunts or as a means of beating line managers over the head. The emphasis must be on the control function in the sense of *supporting* the line managers and *assisting* them in meeting the goals that they have participated in setting for the company. In short, the emphasis should be positive rather than negative. Excessive dwelling on what has already happened, particularly in terms of trying to find someone to "blame," can often be destructive to the functioning of an organization.

Materials Quantity Variance—A Closer Look

The **materials quantity variance** measures the difference between the quantity of materials used in production and the quantity that should have been used according to the standard that has been set. Although the variance is concerned with the physical usage of materials, it is generally stated in dollar terms, as shown in Exhibit 10–3. The formula for the materials quantity variance is:

$$(AQ \times SP) - (SQ \times SP) = \text{Materials quantity variance}$$

Again, the formula can be factored into simpler terms:

$$SP(AQ - SQ) = \text{Materials quantity variance}$$

Using the data from Exhibit 10–3 in the formula, we have:

$$\$4(6{,}500 \text{ pounds} - 6{,}000 \text{ pounds*}) = \$2{,}000 \text{ U}$$

  * 2,000 units × 3.0 pounds per unit = 6,000 pounds.

The answer, of course, is the same as that yielded in Exhibit 10–3. The data would appear as follows if a formal performance report were prepared:

MYTHICAL COMPANY
Performance Report—Production Department

	(1)	(2)	(3)	(4)	(5)	
					Total	
			Standard	Difference	Quantity	
Type of	Standard	Actual	Quantity	in Quantity	Variance	
Materials	Price	Quantity	Allowed	(2) − (3)	(1) × (4)	Explanation
Material A . . .	$4	6,500 pounds	6,000 pounds	500 pounds	$2,000 U	Second-grade materials, unsuitable for production

F = Favorable; U = Unfavorable.

The materials quantity variance is best isolated at the time that materials are placed into production.[9] Materials are drawn for the number of units to be pro-

---

[9] If a company uses process costing, then it may be necessary in some situations to compute the materials quantity variance on a periodic basis as production is *completed*. This is because under process costing it is sometimes difficult to know in advance what the output will be for a period. We assume the use of a job-order costing system throughout this chapter (including all assignment materials).

duced, according to the standard bill of materials for each unit. Any additional materials are usually drawn on an excess materials requisition slip, which is different in color from the normal requisition slips. This procedure calls attention to the excessive usage of materials *while production is still in process* and provides an opportunity for early control of any developing problem.

Excessive usage of materials can result from many factors, including faulty machines, inferior quality of materials, untrained workers, and poor supervision. Generally speaking, it is the responsibility of the production department to see that material usage is kept in line with standards. There may be times, however, when the *purchasing* department may be responsible for an unfavorable materials quantity variance. If the purchasing department obtains materials of inferior quality in an effort to economize on price, the materials may prove to be unsuitable for use on the production line and may result in excessive waste. Thus, purchasing rather than production would be responsible for the quantity variance.

USING STANDARD COSTS—DIRECT LABOR VARIANCES

Objective 5
Compute the direct labor rate and efficiency variances and explain their significance.

To illustrate the computation and use of direct labor variances, we will use the standard cost data for direct labor contained in Exhibit 10–1. This exhibit shows the standard cost of direct labor per unit of product in our mythical company to be:

$$2.5 \text{ hours} \times \$14 = \$35 \text{ per unit}$$

We will assume that during June the company recorded 4,500 hours of direct labor time. The actual cost of this labor time was $64,350 (including employment taxes and fringe benefits), or an average of $14.30 per hour. Recall that the company produced 2,000 units of product during June. The computation of the labor rate and efficiency variances for the month is shown in Exhibit 10–5.

Notice that the column headings in Exhibit 10–5 are the same as those used in the prior two exhibits, except that in Exhibit 10–5 the terms *hours* and *rate* are used in place of the terms *quantity* and *price*.

Labor Rate Variance—A Closer Look

As explained earlier, the price variance for direct labor is commonly termed a **labor rate variance**. This variance measures any deviation from standard in the average hourly rate paid to direct labor workers. From Exhibit 10–5, the formula for the labor rate variance would be expressed as follows:

EXHIBIT 10–5

Variance Analysis—Direct Labor

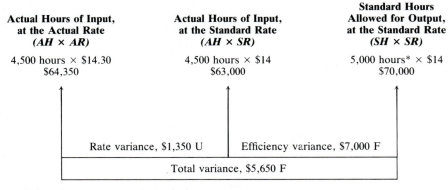

Actual Hours of Input, at the Actual Rate (AH × AR)	Actual Hours of Input, at the Standard Rate (AH × SR)	Standard Hours Allowed for Output, at the Standard Rate (SH × SR)
4,500 hours × $14.30 $64,350	4,500 hours × $14 $63,000	5,000 hours* × $14 $70,000

Rate variance, $1,350 U   Efficiency variance, $7,000 F

Total variance, $5,650 F

* 2,000 units × 2.5 hours per unit = 5,000 hours.
F = Favorable; U = Unfavorable.

$$(AH \times AR) - (AH \times SR) = \text{Labor rate variance}$$

The formula can be factored into simpler form as:

$$AH(AR - SR) = \text{Labor rate variance}$$

Using the data from Exhibit 10–5 in the formula, we have:

$$4{,}500 \text{ hours } (\$14.30 - \$14.00) = \$1{,}350 \text{ U}$$

In most firms, the rates paid to workers are set by union contract; therefore, rate variances, in terms of amounts paid to workers, tend to be almost nonexistent. Rate variances can arise, though, through the way labor is used. Skilled workers with high hourly rates of pay can be given duties that require little skill and call for low hourly rates of pay. This type of misallocation of the work force will result in unfavorable labor rate variances, since the actual hourly rate of pay will exceed the standard rate authorized for the particular task being performed. A reverse situation exists when unskilled or untrained workers are assigned to jobs that require some skill or training. The lower pay scale for these workers will result in favorable rate variances, although the workers may be highly inefficient in terms of output. Finally, unfavorable rate variances can arise from overtime work at premium rates if any portion of the overtime premium is added to the direct labor account.

Who is responsible for controlling the labor rate variance? Since rate variances generally arise as a result of how labor is used, those supervisors in charge of effective utilization of labor time bear responsibility for seeing that labor rate variances are kept under control.

Labor Efficiency Variance—A Closer Look

The quantity variance for direct labor, more commonly called the **labor efficiency variance,** measures the productivity of labor time. No variance is more closely watched by management, since increasing productivity of labor time is a vital key to reducing unit costs of production. From Exhibit 10–5, the formula for the labor efficiency variance would be expressed as follows:

$$(AH \times SR) - (SH \times SR) = \text{Labor efficiency variance}$$

Factored into simpler terms, the formula is:

$$SR(AH - SH) = \text{Labor efficiency variance}$$

Using the data from Exhibit 10–5 in the formula, we have:

$$\$14(4{,}500 \text{ hours} - 5{,}000 \text{ hours*}) = \$7{,}000 \text{ F}$$

* 2,000 units × 2.5 hours per unit = 5,000 hours.

Causes of the labor efficiency variance include poorly trained workers; poor quality materials, requiring more labor time in processing; faulty equipment, causing breakdowns and work interruptions; and poor supervision of workers. The managers in charge of production would generally be responsible for control of the labor efficiency variance. However, the variance might be chargeable to purchasing if the acquisition of poor materials resulted in excessive labor processing time.

When the labor force is essentially fixed in the short term, another important cause of an unfavorable labor efficiency variance is insufficient demand for the output of the factory. In some firms, the actual labor-hours worked is basically fixed—particularly in the short term. Managers in these firms argue that it is difficult, and perhaps even unwise, to constantly adjust the work force in response to changes in the workload. Therefore, the only way a work center manager can avoid an unfavorable labor efficiency variance in such firms is by keeping everyone busy all of the time. The option of reducing the number of workers on hand is not available.

Thus, if there are insufficient orders from customers to keep the workers busy, the work center manager has two options—either accept an unfavorable labor efficiency variance or build inventory.[10] A central lesson of JIT is that building inventory is a bad idea. Inventory—particularly work in process inventory— leads to high defect rates, obsolete goods, and generally inefficient operations. As a consequence, when the work force is basically fixed in the short term, managers must be cautious about how labor efficiency variances are used. Some managers advocate dispensing with labor efficiency variances entirely in such situations—at least for the purposes of motivating and controlling workers on the shop floor.

USING STANDARD COSTS—VARIABLE OVERHEAD VARIANCES

Objective 6
Compute the variable overhead spending and efficiency variances.

The variable portion of manufacturing overhead can be analyzed and controlled using the same basic variance formulas that are used in analyzing direct materials and direct labor. To lay a foundation for the following chapter, where we discuss overhead control at length, it will be helpful at this time to illustrate the analysis of variable overhead using these basic formulas. As a basis for discussion, we will again use the cost data found in Exhibit 10–1. The exhibit shows the standard variable overhead cost per unit of product in our mythical company to be:

$$2.5 \text{ hours} \times \$3.00 = \$7.50 \text{ per unit}$$

We will assume that the total actual variable overhead cost for June was $13,950. Recall from our earlier discussion that 4,500 hours of direct labor time were recorded during the month and that the company produced 2,000 units of product. Exhibit 10–6 contains an analysis of the variable overhead variances.

Notice the similarities between Exhibits 10–5 and 10–6. These similarities arise from the fact that direct labor-hours are being used as a base for allocating overhead cost to units of product; thus, the same hourly figures appear in Exhibit 10–6

EXHIBIT 10–6
Variance Analysis—Variable Overhead

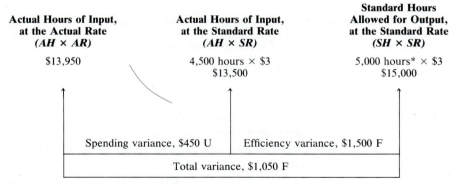

Actual Hours of Input, at the Actual Rate (AH × AR)	Actual Hours of Input, at the Standard Rate (AH × SR)	Standard Hours Allowed for Output, at the Standard Rate (SH × SR)
$13,950	4,500 hours × $3 $13,500	5,000 hours* × $3 $15,000

Spending variance, $450 U   Efficiency variance, $1,500 F

Total variance, $1,050 F

* 2,000 units × 2.5 hours per unit = 5,000 hours.
F = Favorable; U = Unfavorable.

[10] For further discussion, see Eliyahu M. Goldratt and Jeff Cox, *The Goal*, 2nd rev. ed. (Croton-on-Hudson, N.Y.: North River Press, 1992).

for variable overhead as in Exhibit 10–5 for direct labor. The main difference between the two exhibits is in the standard hourly rate being used, which is much lower for variable overhead.

Overhead Variances—A Closer Look

As its name implies, the **variable overhead spending variance** measures deviations in amounts spent for overhead inputs such as lubricants and utilities. The formula for the variance can be expressed as:

$$(AH \times AR) - (AH \times SR) = \text{Variable overhead spending variance}$$

Or, factored into simpler terms:

$$AH(AR - SR) = \text{Variable overhead spending variance}$$

Using the data from Exhibit 10–6 in the formula, we have:

$$4,500 \text{ hours}(\$3.10^* - \$3.00) = \$450 \text{ U}$$

$$* \$13,950 \div 4,500 \text{ hours} = \$3.10.$$

The **variable overhead efficiency variance** is a measure of the difference between the actual activity of a period and the standard activity allowed, multiplied by the variable part of the predetermined overhead rate. The formula for the variance can be expressed as:

$$(AH \times SR) - (SH \times SR) = \text{Variable overhead efficiency variance}$$

Or, factored into simpler terms:

$$SR(AH - SH) = \text{Variable overhead efficiency variance}$$

Again using the data from Exhibit 10–6, the computation of the variance would be:

$$\$3(4,500 \text{ hours} - 5,000 \text{ hours}^*) = \$1,500 \text{ F}$$

$$* 2,000 \text{ units} \times 2.5 \text{ hours per unit} = 5,000 \text{ hours.}$$

We will reserve further discussion of the variable overhead spending and efficiency variances until Chapter 11, where overhead analysis is discussed in depth.

Before proceeding further, it will be helpful for the reader to pause at this point and go back and review the data contained in Exhibits 10–1 through 10–6. These exhibits and the accompanying text discussion represent a comprehensive, integrated illustration of standard setting and variance analysis.

STRUCTURE OF PERFORMANCE REPORTS

On preceding pages we have learned that performance reports are used in a standard cost system to communicate variance data to management. Exhibit 10–7 provides an overview of how these reports can be integrated to form a responsibility reporting system.

Note from the exhibit that the performance reports *start at the bottom and build upward,* with managers at each level receiving information on their own performance as well as information on the performance of each manager under them in the chain of responsibility. This variance information flows upward from level to level in a pyramid fashion, with the president finally receiving a summary of all activities in the organization. If the manager at a particular level (such as the

EXHIBIT 10–7
Upward Flow of Performance Reports

President's Report

The president's performance report summarizes all company data. Since variances are given, the president can trace the variances downward through the company as needed to determine where top management time should be spent.

Responsibility center:	Budget	Actual	Variance
Sales manager.	X	X	X
Production superintendent	$26.000	$29,000	$3,000 U
Engineering head	X	X	X
Personnel supervisor.	X	X	X
Controller	X	X	X
	$54,000	$61,000	$7,000 U

Production Superintendent

The performance of each department head is summarized for the production superintendent. The totals on the superintendent's performance report are then passed upward to the next level of responsibility.

Responsibility center:	Budget	Actual	Variance
Cutting department	X	X	X
Machining department	X	X	X
Finishing department.	$11,000	$12,500	$1,500 U
Packaging department	X	X	X
	$26,000	$29,000	$3,000 U

Finishing Department Head

The performance report of each supervisor is summarized on the performance report of the department head. The department totals are then summarized upward to the production superintendent.

Responsibility center:	Budget	Actual	Variance
Sanding operation	$ 5,000	$ 5,800	$ 800 U
Wiring operation	X	X	X
Assembly operation	X	X	X
	$11,000	$12,500	$1,500 U

Wiring Operation Supervisor

The supervisor of each operation receives a performance report on his or her center of responsibility. The totals on these reports are then communicated upward to the next higher level of responsibility.

Variable costs:	Budget	Actual	Variance
Direct materials	X	X	X
Direct labor.	X	X	X
Manufacturing overhead	X	X	X
	$ 5,000	$ 5,800	$ 800 U

production superintendent) wants to know the reasons behind a variance, he or she can ask for the detailed performance reports prepared by the various operations or departments.

In the following section, we turn our attention to the question of how a manager can determine which variances on these reports are significant enough to warrant further attention.

VARIANCE ANALYSIS AND MANAGEMENT BY EXCEPTION

Objective 7
Explain how the manager would determine whether a variance constituted an "exception" that would require his or her attention.

Variance analysis and performance reports provide a vehicle for implementing the concept of *management by exception*. Simply put, management by exception means that the manager's attention must be directed toward those parts of the organization where things are not proceeding according to plans. Since a manager's time is limited, every hour must be used as effectively as possible, and time and effort must not be wasted looking after those parts of the organization where things are going smoothly.

The budgets and standards discussed in this chapter and in the preceding chapter represent the "plans" of management. If all goes smoothly, then costs would be expected to fall within the budgets and standards that have been set. To the extent that this happens, the manager is free to spend time elsewhere, with the assurance that at least in the budgeted areas all is proceeding according to expectations. To the extent that actual costs and revenues do not conform to the budget, however, a signal comes to the manager that an "exception" has occurred. This exception comes in the form of a variance from the budget or standard that was originally set.

The major question at this point is, "Are *all* variances to be considered exceptions that will require the attention of management?" The answer is no. If every variance was considered an exception, then management would get little else done other than chasing down nickel-and-dime differences. It is probably safe to say that only by the rarest of coincidences will actual costs and revenues ever conform exactly to the budgeted pattern. The reason is that actual costs are subject to large numbers of random and unpredictable influences. Workers seldom work at exactly the pace set in the standard, and their efficiency may be influenced by random factors such as the weather. Prices of some raw materials can change suddenly and without warning. Because of these unpredictable random factors, one can expect that in every period virtually every cost category will produce a variance of some kind.

How then should managers decide which variances are worth investigating? One clue is the size of the variance. A variance of $5 is probably not big enough to warrant attention, whereas a variance of $5,000 might well be worth tracking down. Another clue is the size of the variance relative to the amount of spending involved. A variance that is only 0.1 percent of spending on an item is likely to be well within the bounds one would normally expect due to random factors. On the other hand, a variance of 10 percent of spending is much more likely to be a signal that something is basically wrong.

A more dependable approach is to plot variance data on a statistical control chart, such as illustrated in Exhibit 10–8. The basic idea underlying a statistical control chart is that some random fluctuations in variances from period to period are normal and to be expected even when costs are well under control. A variance should only be investigated when it is unusual relative to that normal level of

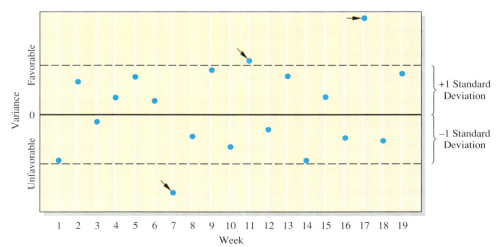

EXHIBIT 10–8
A Statistical Control Chart

random fluctuation. Typically the standard deviation of the variances is used as a measure of the normal level of fluctuations. A rule of thumb is adopted such as "investigate all variances that are more than X standard deviations from zero." In the control chart in Exhibit 10–8, X is 1.0. That is, the rule of thumb in this company is to investigate all variances that are more than one standard deviation in either direction (favorable or unfavorable) from zero. This means that the variances in weeks 7, 11, and 17 would have been investigated, but none of the others.

What value of X should be chosen? The bigger the value of X, the wider the band of acceptable variances that would not be investigated. Thus, the bigger the value of X, the less time will be spent tracking down variances, but the more likely it is that a real out-of-control situation would be overlooked. Ordinarily, if X is selected to be 1.0, roughly 30 percent of all variances will trigger an investigation even when there is no real problem. If X is set at 1.5, the figure drops to about 13 percent. If X is set at 2.0, the figure drops all the way to about 5 percent. Don't forget, however, that selecting a big value of X will result not only in fewer investigations but also a higher probability that a real problem will be overlooked.

PERFORMANCE MEASURES IN AN AUTOMATED ENVIRONMENT

Objective 8
Explain why traditional standards may be inappropriate for companies operating in an automated environment.

As stated earlier, standard costs are widely used in manufacturing, service, food, and not-for-profit organizations. Indeed, the list of companies that employ standards as a method for controlling costs and for measuring performance continues to grow. In an automated environment, however, the traditional standards discussed on preceding pages are being used less frequently and in some cases may be inappropriate for management's needs. In place of these standards, a wide range of new performance measures is emerging.

Standard Costs and Automation

There are several reasons why traditional standards may be inappropriate for companies operating in an automated environment. First, in this new environment, labor is less significant and tends to be more fixed. Thus, the traditional labor variances are of little value to management, and a focus on items such as the labor efficiency variance may even prompt companies to overproduce and create needless inventories. Second, a key objective in the new manufacturing environment is to increase quality rather than to just minimize cost. Managers argue that a preoccupation with items such as the materials price variance often results in the purchase of low-quality materials or in the stockpiling of materials in order to take advantage of quantity discounts. Finally, the manufacturing process is more reliable and consistent in an automated environment, and as a result the traditional variances are either minimal or cease to exist.

New Performance Measures

Objective 9
Enumerate the JIT/FMS performance measures and explain how they are used.

Many new performance measures are emerging as managers seek to streamline their operations, to improve quality and service, and to employ sophisticated new concepts such as JIT and FMS. These new measures can be classified into five general groupings consisting of quality control, material control, inventory control, machine performance, and delivery performance. These groupings, along with the specific measures that they encompass, are provided in Exhibit 10–9.

The new performance measures listed in the exhibit tend to be nonfinancial in nature and some are more subjective than traditional standard costs. Also, their computation and use differ in several ways from standard costs. First, these new measures are often computed on an *on-line* basis so that management is able to monitor activities continually. On-line access to data allows problems to be identified and corrected "on the factory floor" as the problems occur, rather than waiting several days for a report to be generated. This approach to the control process is easy when managers routinely use personal computers in their work, as is true in many companies today. Second, many of the measures are computed at the *plant* level in order to emphasize the concept of an integrated, interdependent operation. Although performance is also measured at the cell level, plantwide performance is especially important in an automated setting. And third, in using the measures, managers focus more directly on *trends* over time than on any particular change during the current period. The key objectives are *progress* and *improvement*, rather than meeting any specific standards.

In the discussion that follows, we look at each of these groupings in more detail. The reader should be aware that the measures included in these groupings are representative and not exhaustive of the possibilities. Many other measures are possible, depending on individual company needs.

Measures	Desired Change
Quality Control Measures	
Number of warranty claims	Decrease
Number of customer complaints	Decrease
Number of defects	Decrease
First-time pass rate	Increase
Field failure rate	Decrease
Total quality cost	Decrease
Material Control Measures	
Material as a percentage of total cost	Decrease
Lead time	Decrease
Scrap as a percentage of good pieces	Decrease
Scrap as a percentage of total cost	Decrease
Actual scrap loss	Decrease
Inventory Control Measures	
Inventory turnover:	
Raw materials (by type)	Increase
Finished goods (by product)	Increase
Number of inventoried items	Decrease
Machine Performance Measures	
Percentage of machine availability	Increase
Percentage of machine downtime	Decrease
Setup time	
Machine stops (breakdowns)	
Preventative maintenance	
Use as a percentage of availability	Increase
Setup time	Decrease
Delivery Performance Measures	
Percentage of on-time deliveries	Increase
Delivery cycle time	Decrease
Throughput time, or velocity*	Decrease
Manufacturing cycle efficiency (MCE)	Increase
Order backlog	Decrease
Total throughput, or output rate	Increase

* Sometimes referred to as *manufacturing cycle time*.

EXHIBIT 10-9

Operating Measures in a JIT/FMS Setting

FOCUS ON CURRENT PRACTICE

An AT&T facility located in Dallas, Texas, that manufactures electronic transformers has devised the following measures to monitor performance on its production line:[11]

Measurement	Typical Monthly Results*	Goal
Number of defective items	300 PPM†	0
First pass quality percent yield	97%	100%
On-time percent shipped	94%	100%
Manufacturing cycle time	8 hours	5 hours
Shop WIP inventory	$19,000	$8,000
WIP turnover	87 turns/yr.	160 turns/yr.
Finished goods inventory	$16,000	0
WIP & FG turnover	47.1 turns/yr.	100 turns/yr.
Cost of scrap	$2,400	$1,500
Scrap as a percent of output	2.2%	1%
Number of line disruptions	29	0
Percent of workers cross trained	70%	100%
Percent completion JIT/TQC checklist	65%	100%

* Hypothetical figures are used (actual figures proprietary).

† PPM = Parts per million.

Quality Control Measures

We have stated several times in preceding chapters that high quality is a major objective in the new manufacturing environment. To monitor quality, managers look at measures such as warranty claims, customer complaints, and defects in units. Although such items have always been watched by management, the difference today is *speed*. Immediate steps are taken to correct design defects that may result in claims, and immediate steps are taken to resolve complaints. Managers have learned that insensitivity to such matters can be disastrous in markets that have become worldwide in scope.

Managers also pay close attention to the first-time pass rate in each process and in the company as a whole, which indicates whether products are being built to specifications. In addition to being a measure of quality, a high first-time pass rate means less rework and less output going into the scrap bin. To get a full picture of the costs associated with quality assurance, some companies prepare a **quality cost report.** Such a report crosses the lines between departments and accumulates all costs traceable to the quality program. By means of this report, management can monitor both the magnitude and trend of total quality cost in a company. Discussion relating to the preparation and use of a quality cost report is provided in Appendix K at the end of this book.

---

[11] F. B. Green, Felix Amenkhienan, and George Johnson, "Performance Measures and JIT," *Management Accounting* 72, no. 8 (February 1991), p. 53.

Material Control Measures

We stated earlier that traditional standard costing seeks to control material cost through the materials price variance. In an automated setting, the focus is in a different direction—it is toward higher quality, shorter lead time, and greater control over scrap.

In Chapter 9, we defined the lead time as the interval between when an order is placed and when the order is finally received from the supplier. Where JIT is in use, the goal is to reduce the lead time to only a few hours so that materials are available immediately as needed on the production line. Lead time is computed by supplier as well as by type of material so that undependable suppliers can be identified and eliminated.

A major difference between traditional standard costing and the new performance measures is the focus of the latter on the cost of scrap. Under standard costing, the cost of scrap is included as part of the materials quantity variance. But this variance doesn't include *all* the cost of scrap, since some "acceptable" level is built right into the standard itself. Under the new performance measures, scrap is treated as a separate item and there is no "acceptable" level. *Any* amount of scrap is viewed as a loss that must be eliminated. As shown in Exhibit 10–9, managers monitor progress toward achieving zero scrap by computing the dollar amount and the ratio of scrapped parts to good parts.

Inventory Control Measures

Historically, companies have operated under the assumption that some level of inventory was needed to act as a buffer against stock-outs. Now managers are recognizing that the cost of carrying inventory is much greater than was previously supposed. As a result, orders are placed more frequently and in smaller amounts. To monitor progress toward the goal of zero inventories, companies compute inventory turnover by type of material and also by individual product. Broadly defined, **inventory turnover** means how many times the average inventory balance has been used (and thereby replaced) during the period. The smaller the inventory balance, the greater the number of times that turnover will occur. Therefore, an increase in the turnover rate is a positive indicator of progress toward reducing the amount of inventory on hand.

Machine Performance Measures

The most significant trend in the new manufacturing environment is toward greater use of automation. With greater automation comes a massive, fixed investment in equipment that requires considerably more attention from management than is needed in a nonautomated setting. Several measures have been developed to determine the availability and use of equipment, as shown in Exhibit 10–9.

The first two of these measures, which focus on machine availability and machine downtime, are the inverse of each other. That is, if a machine isn't available, then it's down for some reason; the reasons for being down are given in the exhibit. The goal, of course, is to minimize the amount of downtime so that machines are available as much as possible.

The third measure, "Use as a percentage of available capacity," is designed primarily for control of bottleneck operations, which hinder throughput. The goal in a bottleneck operation is to keep machine use at 100 percent of available capacity so that maximum output can be achieved. This measure has less significance in a *non*bottleneck operation since the goal there should be to use the equipment *only* as needed to support JIT production. Trying to achieve 100 percent use in a nonbottleneck operation might result in producing more than is required to maintain a smooth JIT flow, and thereby precipitate a needless buildup of inventory.

Setup time is a key element relating to all equipment. We learned in Chapter 5 that one of the central benefits of a flexible manufacturing system is the reduction in time required to change from one production run to another or to change from one job to another. Through FMS, companies have been able to reduce setup time in many cases from several hours to only a few minutes. Since setup time constitutes part of non-value-added time, throughput is increased in a cell or plant as it is reduced. Thus, setup time is carefully monitored to allow maximum machine availability.

Delivery Performance Measures

Objective 10

Compute the delivery cycle time, the throughput time, and the manufacturing cycle efficiency (MCE) as these measures relate to JIT/FMS.

The purpose of production is to get a high-quality product into the hands of a customer as quickly as possible. If a customer has to wait months for a delivery and a competitor can provide the needed item in a few weeks, then the competitor probably will get the business. Thus, in the new manufacturing environment with its worldwide competition, speed has become as important as quality in gaining (or retaining) customers. Moreover, an automated plant has high operating leverage (due to its high fixed costs), and therefore it must obtain a large number of orders and fill them quickly if it expects to generate a satisfactory profit margin.

There are several key measures of delivery performance. As shown in Exhibit 10–9, the first of these is the percentage of on-time deliveries. Companies strive for 100 percent on-time deliveries, but whether or not this goal is achieved depends on several other factors. One of these is the **delivery cycle time,** which represents the amount of time required from receipt of an order from a customer to shipment of the completed goods.[12] Another factor is the **throughput time,** which measures the amount of time required to turn raw materials into completed products. Throughput time is also known as the **manufacturing cycle time** or **velocity** of production. The relationship between the delivery cycle time and the throughput (manufacturing cycle) time is illustrated in Exhibit 10–10.

Through concerted efforts to eliminate waste and improve efficiency, some companies have reduced the delivery cycle time from five or six months to only a few weeks, and they have cut the throughput time to only a fraction of previous levels. Throughput time, which is considered to be a key measure in delivery performance, can be put into better perspective by computing the **manufacturing cycle efficiency (MCE).** The MCE is computed by relating the value-added time to the throughput time. The formula is:

$$MCE = \frac{\text{Value-added time}}{\text{Throughput (manufacturing cycle) time}}$$

If the MCE is less than 1, then non-value-added time is present in the production process. An MCE of 0.5, for example, would mean that half of the total

---

[12] Sometimes the delivery cycle time is improperly referred to as the lead time. The term *lead time* should be used only in conjunction with the purchase of raw materials.

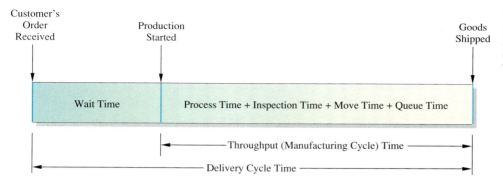

EXHIBIT 10–10

Delivery Cycle Time and Throughput (Manufacturing Cycle) Time

Value-Added Time	Non-Value-Added Time
Process Time	Wait Time
	Inspection Time
	Move Time
	Queue Time

production time consisted of inspection, moving, and similar non-value-added activities. In many manufacturing companies today, the MCE is less than 0.1 (10 percent), which means that 90 percent of the time a unit is in process is spent on activities that do not add value to the product.[13] By monitoring the MCE, companies are able to pare away non-value-added activities and thus get products into the hands of customers more quickly.

To provide a numeric example of these measures, assume the following data for Novex Company:

> Novex Company keeps careful track of the time relating to orders and to the production of goods. During the most recent quarter, the following average times were recorded for each unit or order:
>
> | | Days |
> |---|---|
> | Wait time . . . . | 17.0 |
> | Inspection time . . . . | 0.4 |
> | Process time . . . . | 2.0 |
> | Move time . . . . | 0.6 |
> | Queue time . . . . | 5.0 |

Goods are shipped as soon as production is completed.

1. Compute the throughput time, or velocity of production.   *Required*
2. Compute the manufacturing cycle efficiency (MCE).
3. What percentage of the production time is spent in non-value-added activities?
4. Compute the delivery cycle time.

1. Throughput time = Process time + Inspection time + Move time   *Solution*
                              + Queue time
       = 2.0 days + 0.4 days + 0.6 days + 5.0 days
       = 8.0 days

[13] Callie Berlinger and James A. Brimson, eds., *Cost Management for Today's Advanced Manufacturing* (Boston, Mass.: Harvard Business School Press, 1988), p. 4.

2. Only process time represents value-added time; therefore, the computation of the MCE would be:

$$\text{MCE} = \frac{\text{Value-added time, 2.0 days}}{\text{Throughput time, 8.0 days}}$$
$$= 0.25$$

As stated earlier in the chapter, the MCE puts the throughput time into perspective by showing how efficiently units are being produced. Thus, the MCE is 0.25, or 25%.

3. Since the MCE is 25%, the complement of this figure, or 75% of the total production time, is spent in non-value-added activities.

4. Delivery cycle time = Wait time + Throughput time
$$= 17.0 \text{ days} + 8.0 \text{ days}$$
$$= 25.0 \text{ days}$$

FOCUS ON CURRENT PRACTICE

One of the most effective ways for companies to reduce their costs is to decrease the throughput time (and thus increase the MCE) of their plants. For example, by paring out non-value-added activities, a manufacturer of metal products in Canada was able to reduce the throughput time from 22 days to just 7 days, thus dramatically increasing its MCE and slashing its total costs. Moreover, since part of the reduction in throughput time was in the form of more rapid processing, the company effectively increased its manufacturing capacity. These results were achieved in just one year's time.[14]

Use in a Nonautomated Environment

Although the new performance measures discussed on the preceding pages were developed specifically for use in the new manufacturing environment, many nonautomated companies are also beginning to use them. The reader should refer again to the list of performance measures given in Exhibit 10–9 and note that most of these measures would benefit nearly any organization. Moreover, these measures can be (and are) used side by side in some companies along with the standard costs developed earlier in the chapter.[15] In a nonautomated environment, such measures actually complement the use of standard costs since they focus on many key areas (such as warranty claims, on-time deliveries, and delivery cycle time) that traditional standards do not cover. In sum, there is nothing exclusive about the new performance measures; they simply represent added tools available to managers in the planning and control of operations.

---

[14] Patrick Northey, "Cut Total Costs with Cycle Time Reduction," *CMA Magazine* 65, no. 1 (February 1991), p. 22.

[15] James A. Hendricks, "Applying Cost Accounting to Factory Automation," *Management Accounting* 70, no. 6 (December 1988), p. 28. This is an excellent study that provides many insights into current practice.

ARE STANDARD COSTS OBSOLETE?

Given the increasing popularity of the new performance measures, a legitimate question can be asked, "Are standard costs obsolete?" The answer is an emphatic, "No, they are not obsolete!" However, companies report that as operations become more automated and as JIT methods are introduced, important changes take place in the way that standard costs are used.

First, in JIT/FMS settings, standard costs generally are not used to measure performance. Their use shifts more toward the financial purposes of valuing inventory and determining cost of goods sold.

Second, in JIT/FMS settings, engineered standards are often replaced either by a rolling average of actual costs or by target costs. The reason for this change is that engineered standards are static, whereas companies in an automated environment need a dynamic standard that shows decreasing costs brought about through the JIT concept of continuous improvement.

Third, in JIT/FMS settings, variances are computed on a more frequent basis. With the short production runs possible through FMS, monthly variance reports are virtually useless. In some companies, variances are now computed on a daily basis as noted earlier in the chapter. Moreover, it is the *trend* of these variances—not their magnitude—that is of interest to management. Variances tend to be positive more often than negative due to the concept of continuous improvement.

Fourth, in JIT/FMS settings, standard costs are generally used only for materials and overhead, since labor often is not accounted for as a separate element of cost. In addition, the only variance computed for materials is the quantity variance. Price variances for materials tend to be small or nonexistant due to long-term contracts with a selected group of suppliers.

In sum, standard costs are still found in all types of companies, but in heavily automated settings their use is more limited and focuses on dynamic standards, long-term trends in variances, inventory valuation, and efficiency in record keeping.

INTERNATIONAL USES OF STANDARD COSTS

Standard costs are used by companies worldwide. A comparative study of cost accounting practices in four countries—the United States, the United Kingdom, Canada, and Japan—found that three fourths of the companies surveyed in the United Kingdom, two thirds of the companies surveyed in Canada, and 40 percent of the companies surveyed in Japan used standard cost systems.[16]

Standard costs were first introduced in Japan after World War II, with Nippon Electronics Company (NEC) being one of the first Japanese companies to adopt standard costs for all of its products. Many other Japanese companies followed NEC's lead after the war and developed standard cost systems. The ways in which these standard costs are used in Japan—and also in the other three countries cited above—are shown in Exhibit 10–11.

[16] Shin'ichi Inoue, "Comparative Studies of Recent Development of Cost Management Problems in U.S.A., U.K., Canada, and Japan," Research Paper No. 29, Kagawa University (March 1988), p. 17. The study included 95 United States companies, 52 United Kingdom companies, 82 Canadian companies, and 646 Japanese companies.

EXHIBIT 10–11
Uses of Standard Costs
in Four Countries

	United States	United Kingdom	Canada	Japan
Cost management	1*	2	2	1
Budgetary planning and control†	2	3	1	3
Pricing decisions	3	1	3	2
Financial statement preparation	4	4	4	4

* The numbers 1 through 4 denote importance of use, from greatest to least.

† Includes management planning.

Source: Compiled from data in a study by Shin'ichi Inoue, "Comparative Studies of Recent Development of Cost Management Problems in U.S.A., U.K., Canada, and Japan," Research Paper No. 29, Kagawa University (March 1988), p. 20.

Over time the pattern of use shown in Exhibit 10–11 may change, but at present managers can expect to encounter standard costs in most industrialized nations, and unless a company is automated, these standards are likely to be used primarily for either cost management or budgetary planning purposes.

SUMMARY

A standard is a benchmark or "norm" for measuring performance. Standards are found in many facets of life, including in the business community. In business organizations, standards are set for both the cost and the quantity of inputs needed to manufacture goods or to provide services. Quantity standards indicate how much of a cost element, such as labor time or raw materials, should be used in manufacturing a unit of product or in providing a unit of service. Cost standards indicate what the cost of the time or the materials should be.

Generally, standards are set by the cooperative effort of many people in an organization, including the accountant, the industrial engineer, and various levels of management. Standards are normally "practical" in nature, meaning that they can be attained by reasonable, though highly efficient, efforts. Such standards are generally felt to have a favorable motivational impact on employees.

When standards are compared against actual performance, the difference is referred to as a *variance*. Variances are computed and reported to management on a regular basis for both the price and the quantity elements of materials, labor, and overhead. Specific formulas are available to assist in these computations.

Not all variances are considered to be "exceptions" that require management time or attention. Rather, parameters or limits are set within which variances are considered to be due to chance causes. If a variance falls outside the limits set by management, it is then considered to be an exception toward which management time and attention must be directed.

In automated environments, the traditional standard costs are being used less frequently, and in some cases they are thought to be inappropriate for management's needs. In place of standard costs, managers have developed new performance measures that can be classified into five general groupings. These groupings consist of quality control measures, material control measures, inventory control measures, machine performance measures, and delivery performance measures. These new measures are generally computed on an on-line basis, with managers looking at the trend over time rather than toward the attainment of a specific standard.

Although standard costs continue to be used by some companies that have automated and that have introduced JIT methods, important changes have taken place in the way these standards are used. Instead of being used for performance evaluation, they are used primarily for inventory valuation, for determining long-term trends in variances, and for efficiency in record keeping.

Standard costs are used worldwide. Thus, managers can expect to encounter them in virtually any industralized country.

REVIEW PROBLEM: STANDARD COSTS

Xavier Company produces a single product. The standard costs for one unit of product are:

Direct material: 6 ounces at $0.50 per ounce . . .	$ 3
Direct labor: 1.8 hours at $10 per hour	18
Variable overhead: 1.8 hours at $5 per hour . . .	9
Total standard variable cost per unit	$30

During June, 2,000 units were produced. The costs associated with the month were:

Material purchased: 18,000 ounces at $0.60 . . .	$10,800
Material used in production: 14,000 ounces . . .	—
Direct labor: 4,000 hours at $9.75.	39,000
Variable overhead costs incurred	20,800

Materials Variances

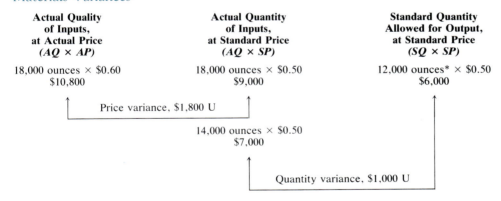

Actual Quality of Inputs, at Actual Price (AQ × AP)	Actual Quantity of Inputs, at Standard Price (AQ × SP)	Standard Quantity Allowed for Output, at Standard Price (SQ × SP)
18,000 ounces × $0.60 $10,800	18,000 ounces × $0.50 $9,000	12,000 ounces* × $0.50 $6,000

Price variance, $1,800 U

14,000 ounces × $0.50
$7,000

Quantity variance, $1,000 U

A total variance can't be computed in this situation, since the amount of materials purchased (18,000 ounces) differs from the amount of materials used in production (14,000 ounces).

* 2,000 units × 6 ounces = 12,000 ounces.

The same variances in shortcut format would be:

$AQ(AP - SP)$ = Materials price variance
18,000 ounces($0.60 - $0.50) = $1,800 U

$SP(AQ - SQ)$ = Materials quantity variance
$0.50(14,000 ounces - 12,000 ounces) = $1,000 U

Labor Variances

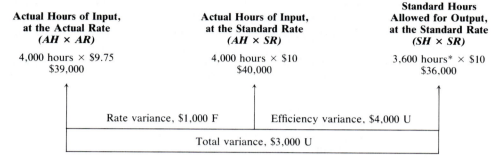

Actual Hours of Input, at the Actual Rate (AH × AR)	Actual Hours of Input, at the Standard Rate (AH × SR)	Standard Hours Allowed for Output, at the Standard Rate (SH × SR)
4,000 hours × $9.75 $39,000	4,000 hours × $10 $40,000	3,600 hours* × $10 $36,000

Rate variance, $1,000 F   Efficiency variance, $4,000 U

Total variance, $3,000 U

* 2,000 units × 1.8 hours = 3,600 hours.

The same variances in shortcut format would be:

$$AH(AR - SR) = \text{Labor rate variance}$$
$$4{,}000 \text{ hours}(\$9.75 - \$10) = \$1{,}000 \text{ F}$$
$$SR(AH - SH) = \text{Labor efficiency variance}$$
$$\$10(4{,}000 \text{ hours} - 3{,}600 \text{ hours}) = \$4{,}000 \text{ U}$$

Variable Overhead Variances

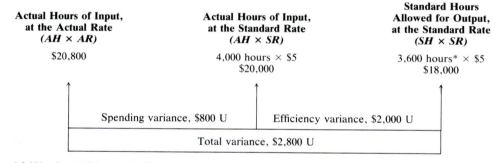

Actual Hours of Input, at the Actual Rate (AH × AR)	Actual Hours of Input, at the Standard Rate (AH × SR)	Standard Hours Allowed for Output, at the Standard Rate (SH × SR)
$20,800	4,000 hours × $5 $20,000	3,600 hours* × $5 $18,000

Spending variance, $800 U   Efficiency variance, $2,000 U

Total variance, $2,800 U

* 2,000 units × 1.8 hours = 3,600 hours.

The same variances in shortcut format would be:

$$AH(AR - SR) = \text{Variable overhead spending variance}$$
$$4{,}000 \text{ hours}(\$5.20^* - \$5.00) = \$800 \text{ U}$$

*$20,800 ÷ 4,000 hours = $5.20.

$$SR(AH - SH) = \text{Variable overhead efficiency variance}$$
$$\$5(4{,}000 \text{ hours} - 3{,}600 \text{ hours}) = \$2{,}000 \text{ U}$$

KEY TERMS FOR REVIEW

Objective 11
Define or explain the key terms listed at the end of the chapter.

Bill of materials   A listing of the type and quantity of each item of material required in the manufacture of a unit of product. (p. 423)

Delivery cycle time   The amount of time required from receipt of an order from a customer to shipment of the completed goods. (p. 442)

Ideal standards   Standards that allow for no machine breakdowns or other work interruptions and that require peak efficiency at all times. (p. 422)

Inventory turnover   The number of times the average inventory balance has been used (and thereby replaced) during the period. (p. 441)

Labor efficiency variance   A measure of the difference between the actual hours required to complete a task and the standard hours allowed, multiplied by the standard hourly rate. (p. 433)

Labor rate variance   A measure of the difference between the actual hourly labor rate and the standard rate allowed, multiplied by the number of hours worked during the period. (p. 432)

Management by exception   A system of management in which standards are set for various operating activities, with actual results then compared against these standards. Any differences that are deemed significant are brought to the attention of management as "exceptions." (p. 420)

Manufacturing cycle efficiency (MCE)   Process (value-added) time as a percentage of throughput time. (p. 442)

Manufacturing cycle time   See *Throughput time*. (p. 442)

Materials price variance   A measure of the difference between the actual unit price paid for an item and the standard price that should have been paid, multiplied by the quantity purchased. (p. 429)

Materials quantity variance   A measure of the difference between the actual quantity of materials used in production and the standard quantity allowed, multiplied by the standard price per unit of materials. (p. 431)

Practical standards   Standards that allow for normal machine downtime and other work interruptions and that can be attained through reasonable, though highly efficient, efforts by the average worker at a task. (p. 422)

Quality cost report   A report that crosses departmental lines and accumulates all costs traceable to the quality program. (p. 440)

Standard cost card   A detailed listing of the standard amounts of materials, labor, and overhead that should go into a unit of product, multiplied by the standard price or rate that has been set. (p. 421)

Standard cost per unit   The expected cost of a unit of product as shown on the standard cost card; it is computed by multiplying the standard quantity or hours by the standard price or rate. (p. 425)

Standard hours allowed   The time that should have been taken to complete the period's output as computed by multiplying the number of units produced by the standard hours per unit. (p. 427)

Standard hours per unit   The amount of labor time that should be required to complete a single unit of product, including allowances for breaks, machine downtime, cleanup, rejects, and other normal inefficiencies. (p. 424)

Standard price per unit   The price that should be paid for a single unit of materials, including allowances for quality, quantity purchased, freight-in, receiving, and other such costs, net of any discounts allowed. (p. 422)

Standard quantity allowed   The amount of materials that should have been used to complete the period's output as computed by multiplying the number of units produced by the standard quantity per unit. (p. 427)

Standard quantity per unit   The amount of materials that should be required to complete a single unit of product, including allowances for normal waste, spoilage, rejects, and similar inefficiencies. (p. 422)

Standard rate per hour   The labor rate that should be incurred per hour of labor time, including allowances for employment taxes, fringe benefits, and other such labor costs. (p. 424)

Throughput time   The amount of time required to turn raw materials into completed products. (p. 442)

Variable overhead efficiency variance   A measure of the difference between the actual activity (direct labor-hours, machine-hours, or some other base) of a period and the standard activity allowed, multiplied by the variable part of the predetermined overhead rate. (p. 435)

Variable overhead spending variance   A measure of the difference between the actual variable overhead cost incurred during a period and the standard cost that should have been incurred, based on the actual activity of the period. (p. 435)

Variance   The difference between standard prices and quantities and actual prices and quantities. (p. 427)

Velocity   A measure of the speed that goods move through the production process. See *Throughput time*. (p. 442)

APPENDIX F: GENERAL LEDGER ENTRIES TO RECORD VARIANCES

Objective 12
Prepare journal entries to record standard costs and variances.

Although standard costs and variances can be computed and used by management without being formally entered into the accounting records, most organizations prefer to make formal entries for three reasons. First, entry into the accounting records encourages early recognition of variances. As mentioned in the main body of the chapter, the earlier that variances can be recognized, the greater is their value to management in the control of costs. Second, formal entry tends to give variances a greater emphasis than is generally possible through informal, out-of-record computations. This emphasis gives a clear signal of management's desire to keep costs within the limits that have been set. Third, formal use of standard costs simplifies the bookkeeping process. By using standard costs within the accounting system itself, management eliminates the need to keep track of troublesome variations in actual costs and quantities, thereby providing for a flow of costs that is smoother, simpler, and more easily accounted for.

Direct Materials Variances

To illustrate the general ledger entries needed to record standard cost variances, we will return to the data contained in the review problem at the end of the chapter. The entry to record the purchase of direct materials would be:

```
Raw Materials (18,000 ounces at $0.50) . . . . . . . . . . . . . .    9,000
Materials Price Variance (18,000 ounces at $0.10 U). . . . . . . . . . .    1,800
    Accounts Payable (18,000 ounces at $0.60) . . . . . . . . . . . .              10,800
```

Notice that the price variance is recognized when purchases are made, rather than when materials are actually used in production. This permits the price variance to be isolated early, and it also permits the materials to be carried in the inventory account at standard cost. As direct materials are later drawn from inventory and used in production, the quantity variance is isolated as follows:

```
Work in Process (12,000 ounces at $0.50) . . . . . . . . . . . . .    6,000
Materials Quantity Variance (2,000 ounces U at $0.50). . . . . . . . . .    1,000
    Raw Materials (14,000 ounces at $0.50) . . . . . . . . . . . . . .             7,000
```

Thus, direct materials enter into the Work in Process account at standard cost, in terms of both price and quantity.

Notice that both the price variance and the quantity variance above are unfavorable, thereby showing up as debit (or additional cost) balances. If these variances had been favorable, they would have appeared as credit (or reduction in cost) balances, as in the case of the direct labor rate variance below.

Direct Labor Variances

Referring again to the cost data in the review problem at the end of the chapter, the general ledger entry to record the incurrence of direct labor cost would be:

Work in Process (3,600 hours at $10)	36,000	
Labor Efficiency Variance (400 hours U at $10)	4,000	
Labor Rate Variance (4,000 hours at $0.25 F)		1,000
Wages Payable (4,000 hours at $9.75)		39,000

Thus, as with direct materials, direct labor costs enter into the Work in Process account at standard, both in terms of the rate and in terms of the hours allowed for the production of the period.

Variable Overhead Variances

Variable overhead variances generally are not recorded in the accounts separately but rather are determined as part of the general analysis of overhead, which is discussed in Chapter 11.

QUESTIONS

10-1 What types of organizations make use of standard costs?

10-2 What is a quantity standard? What is a price standard?

10-3 What is the beginning point in setting a standard? Where should final responsibility for standard setting fall?

10-4 Why must a standard for the future be more than simply a projection of the past?

10-5 Distinguish between ideal and practical standards.

10-6 If employees are unable to meet a standard, what effect would you expect this to have on their productivity?

10-7 What is the difference between a standard and a budget?

10-8 What is meant by the term *variance?*

10-9 What is meant by the term *management by exception?*

10-10 Why are variances generally segregated in terms of a price variance and a quantity variance?

10-11 Who is generally responsible for the materials price variance? The materials quantity variance? The labor efficiency variance?

10-12 The materials price variance can be computed at what two different points in time? Which point is better? Why?

10-13 An examination of the cost records of the Chittenden Furniture Company reveals that the materials price variance is favorable but that the materials quantity variance is unfavorable by a substantial amount. What might this indicate?

10-14 What dangers lie in using standards as punitive tools?

10-15 "Our workers are all under labor contracts; therefore, our labor rate variance is bound to be zero." Discuss.

10-16 What effect, if any, would you expect poor quality materials to have on direct labor variances?

10-17 If variable manufacturing overhead is applied to production on a basis of direct labor-hours and the direct labor efficiency variance is unfavorable, will the variable overhead efficiency variance be favorable or unfavorable, or could it be either? Explain.

10-18 What is a statistical control chart, and how is it used?

10–19   How does the nature, computation, and use of performance measures in an auto-mated environment differ from the nature, computation, and use of standard costs?

10–20   Into what five general groupings can the JIT/FMS performance measures be placed?

10–21   What danger is there in trying to keep the use of equipment at 100 percent of available capacity in all operations?

10–22   What is the difference between the delivery cycle time and the throughput time? What four elements make up the throughput time? Into what two classes can these four elements be placed?

10–23   If a company has an MCE of less than 1, what does it mean? How would you interpret an MCE of 0.40?

10–24   (Appendix F)   What advantages can be cited in favor of making formal journal entries in the accounting records for variances?

EXERCISES

E10–1   Huron Company produces a commerical cleaning compound known as Zoom. The direct materials and direct labor standards for one unit of Zoom are given below:

	Standard Quantity or Hours	Standard Price or Rate	Standard Cost
Direct materials . . .	4.6 pounds	$ 2.50 per pound	$11.50
Direct labor	0.2 hours	12.00 per hour	2.40

During the most recent month, the following activity was recorded:

a.   Twenty thousand pounds of material were purchased at a cost of $2.35 per pound.
b.   All of the material purchased was used to produce 4,000 units of Zoom.
c.   A total of 750 hours of direct labor time were recorded at a total labor cost of $10,425.

Required   1.   Compute the direct materials price and quantity variances for the month.
2.   Compute the direct labor rate and efficiency variances for the month.

E10–2   Refer to the data in E10–1. Assume that instead of producing 4,000 units during the month, the company produced only 3,000 units, using 14,750 pounds of material in the production process. (The rest of the material purchased remained in inventory.)

Required   Compute the direct materials price and quantity variances for the month.

E10–3   Dawson Toys, Ltd., produces a toy called the Maze. The company has recently established a standard cost system to help control costs and has established the following standards for the Maze toy:

Direct materials: 6 pieces per toy at $0.50 per piece
Direct labor: 1.3 hours per toy at $8 per hour

During July 19x6, the company produced 3,000 Maze toys. Production data for the month on the toy follow:

Direct materials: 25,000 pieces were purchased for use in production at a cost of $0.48 per piece. Some 5,000 of these pieces were still in inventory at the end of the month.

Direct labor: 4,000 direct labor-hours were worked at a cost of $36,000.

Required   1.   Compute the following variances for July:
a.   Direct materials price and quantity variances.
b.   Direct labor rate and efficiency variances.
2.   Prepare a brief explanation of the significance and possible cause of each variance.

As business organizations grow in size and complexity, cost control becomes more difficult. A system to provide information and assist in cost control is imperative for effective management. Management by exception is one technique that is often used to foster cost control.

E10–4

Required

1. Describe how a standard cost system helps to make management by exception possible.
2. Discuss the potential benefits of management by exception to an organization.
3. Identify and discuss the behavioral problems that might occur in an organization using standard costs and management by exception.

(CMA, adapted)

E10–5

Bronson Equipment, Inc., manufactures sporting equipment. One of the company's products, a football helmet, requires a special plastic in its manufacture. During the quarter ending June 30, the company manufactured 35,000 helmets, using 22,500 pounds of plastic in the process. The plastic cost the company $171,000.

According to the standard cost card, each helmet should require 0.6 pounds of plastic, at a cost of $8 per pound.

Required

1. What cost for plastic should have been incurred in the manufacture of the 35,000 helmets? How much greater or less is this than the cost that was incurred?
2. Break down the difference computed in (1) in terms of a materials price variance and a materials quantity variance.

E10–6

Erie Company manufactures a small cassette player called the Jogging Mate. The company uses standards to control its costs. The labor standards that have been set for one Jogging Mate cassette player are as follows:

Standard Hours	Standard Rate per Hour	Standard Cost
18 minutes	$12	$3.60

During August, 5,750 hours of direct labor time were recorded in the manufacture of 20,000 units of the Jogging Mate. The direct labor cost totaled $73,600 for the month.

Required

1. What direct labor cost should have been incurred in the manufacture of the 20,000 units of the Jogging Mate? By how much does this differ from the cost that was incurred?
2. Break down the difference in cost from (1) above in terms of a labor rate variance and a labor efficiency variance.
3. The budgeted variable overhead rate is $4 per direct labor-hour. During August, the company incurred $21,850 in variable overhead cost. Compute the variable overhead spending and efficiency variances for the month.

E10–7

Martin Company manufactures a powerful cleaning solvent. The main ingredient in the solvent is a raw material called Echol. Information on the purchase and use of Echol follows:

Purchase of Echol   Echol is purchased in 15-gallon containers at a cost of $115 per container. Discount terms of 2/10, n/30 are offered by the supplier, and Martin Company takes all discounts. Shipping costs, which Martin Company must pay, amount to $130 for an average shipment of 100 15-gallon containers of Echol.

Use of Echol   The bill of materials calls for 7.6 quarts of Echol per bottle of cleaning solvent. About 5 percent of all Echol used is lost through spillage or evaporation (the 7.6 quarts above is the *actual* content per bottle). In addition, statistical analysis has shown that every 41st bottle is rejected at final inspection because of contamination.

Required

1. Compute the standard price for purchase of one quart of Echol.
2. Compute the standard quantity of echol (in quarts) per salable bottle of cleaning solvent.

3.   Using the data from (1) and (2), prepare a standard cost card showing the standard cost of Echol per bottle of cleaning solvent.

E10-8 The auto repair shop of Quality Motor Company uses standards to control labor time and labor cost in the shop. The standard labor cost for a motor tune-up is given below:

Job	Standard Hours	Standard Rate	Standard Cost
Motor tune-up	2.5	$9	$22.50

The record showing the time spent in the shop last week on motor tune-ups has been misplaced. However, the shop supervisor recalls that 50 tune-ups were completed during the week, and the controller recalls the following variance data relating to tune-ups:

Labor rate variance	$87 F
Total labor variance	93 U

Required   1.   Determine the number of actual labor-hours spent on tune-ups last week.
2.   Determine the actual hourly rate of pay for tune-ups last week.

(Hint: A useful way to proceed would be to work from known to unknown data either by using the variance formulas or by using the columnar format shown in Exhibit 10–5.)

E10-9 Zargon Industries has automated one of its plants and employs both JIT and FMS concepts. For the first quarter of operations during the current year the following data were reported for each unit processed:

	Days
Inspection time.	0.3
Wait time (from order to start of production) . . .	14.0
Process time	2.7
Move time	1.0
Queue time	5.0

Management is unsure how to use these data to measure performance and control operations.

Required   1.   Compute the throughput time, or velocity of operations.
2.   Compute the MCE (manufacturing cycle efficiency) for the quarter. How do you interpret the MCE?
3.   What percentage of the throughput time was spent in non-value-added activities?
4.   Compute the delivery cycle time.
5.   If by use of JIT all queue time during production is eliminated, what will be the new MCE?

E10-10 (Appendix F)   Genola Fashions began production of a new product on June 1, 19x4. The company uses a standard cost system and has established the following standards for one unit of the new product:

	Standard Quantity or Hours	Standard Price or Rate	Standard Cost
Direct materials . . .	2.5 yards	$14 per yard	$35.00
Direct labor	1.6 hours	8 per hour	12.80

During June, the following activity was recorded in relation to the new product:

a.   Purchasing acquired 10,000 yards of material at a cost of $13.80 per yard.
b.   Production used 8,000 yards of the material to manufacture 3,000 units of the new product.
c.   Production reported 5,000 hours of labor time worked directly on the new product; the cost of this labor time was $43,000.

1. For materials:
   a. Compute the direct materials price and quantity variances.
   b. Prepare journal entries to record the purchase of materials and the use of materials in production.
2. For direct labor:
   a. Compute the direct labor rate and efficiency variances.
   b. Prepare journal entries to record the incurrence of direct labor cost for the month.
3. Post the entries you have prepared to the T-accounts below:

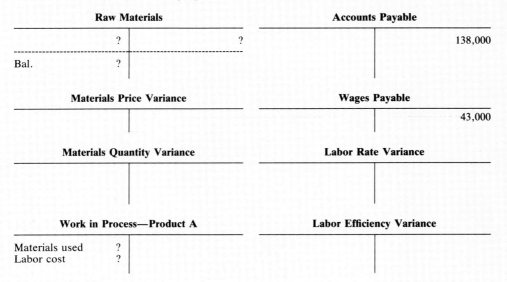

Raw Materials		Accounts Payable	
?	?		138,000
Bal. ?			

Materials Price Variance		Wages Payable	
			43,000

Materials Quantity Variance		Labor Rate Variance	

Work in Process—Product A		Labor Efficiency Variance	
Materials used ?			
Labor cost ?			

PROBLEMS

FulRange, Inc., produces complex printed circuits for stereo amplifiers. The circuits are sold primarily to major component manufacturers, and any production overruns are sold to small manufacturers at a substantial discount. The small manufacturer market segment appears very profitable because the basic operating budget assigns all fixed expenses to production for the major manufacturers, the only predictable market.

P10–11 Ethics and the Manager

A common product defect that occurs in production is a "drift" that is caused by failure to maintain precise heat levels during the production process. Rejects from the 100 percent testing program can be reworked to acceptable levels if the defect is drift. However, in a recent analysis of customer complaints, George Wilson, the cost accountant, and the quality control engineer have ascertained that normal rework does not bring all the circuits up to standard. Sampling shows that about one half of the reworked circuits will fail after extended, high-volume amplifier operation over a one- to five-year period of time.

Unfortunately, there is no way to determine which reworked circuits will fail because testing will not detect this problem. The rework process could be changed to correct the problem, but the cost-benefit analysis for the suggested change in the rework process indicates that it is not feasible. FulRange's marketing analyst has indicated that this problem will have a significant impact on the company's reputation and customer satisfaction if the problem is not corrected. Consequently, the board of directors would interpret this problem as having serious negative implications on the company's profitability.

Wilson has included the circuit failure and rework problem in his report that has been prepared for the upcoming quarterly meeting of the board of directors. Due to the potential adverse economic impact, Wilson has followed a long-standing practice of highlighting this information.

After reviewing the reports to be presented, the plant manager and his staff were upset and indicated to the controller that he should control his people better. "We can't upset the board of directors with this kind of material. Tell Wilson to tone that down. Maybe we can get it by this meeting and have some time to work on it. People that buy those cheap systems and play them that loud shouldn't expect them to last forever."

The controller called Wilson into his office and said, "George, you'll have to bury this one. The probable failure of reworks can be referred to briefly in the oral presentation, but it should not be mentioned or highlighted in the advance material mailed to the board."

Wilson feels strongly that the board will be misinformed on a potentially serious loss of income if he follows the controller's orders. Wilson discussed the problem with the quality control engineer who simply remarked, "That's your problem, George."

Required
1. Discuss the ethical considerations that George Wilson should recognize in deciding how to proceed in this matter.
2. Explain what ethical responsibilities should be accepted in this situation by the following persons:
   a. The controller.
   b. The quality control engineer.
   c. The plant manager and staff.
3. What should George Wilson do in this situation? Explain your answer.

(CMA, adapted)

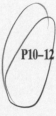

P10-12 **Straightforward Variance Analysis**   Becton Labs, Inc., produces various chemical compounds for industrial use. One compound, called Fludex, is prepared by means of an elaborate distilling process. The company has developed standard costs for one unit of Fludex, as follows:

	Standard Quantity	Standard Price or Rate	Standard Cost
Direct materials	2.5 ounces	$20.00 per ounce	$50.00
Direct labor	1.4 hours	12.50 per hour	17.50
Variable overhead . . .	1.4 hours	3.50 per hour	4.90
			$72.40

During November 19x5, the following activity was recorded by the company relative to production of Fludex:

a. Material purchased, 12,000 ounces at a cost of $225,000.
b. There was no beginning inventory of materials on hand to start the month; at the end of the month, 2,500 ounces of material remained in the warehouse unused.
c. The company employs 35 lab technicians to work on the production of Fludex. During November, each worked an average of 160 hours at an average rate of $12 per hour.
d. Variable overhead is assigned to Fludex on a basis of direct labor-hours. Variable overhead costs during November totaled $18,200.
e. During November, 3,750 good units of Fludex were produced.

The company's management is anxious to determine the efficiency of the activities surrounding the production of Fludex.

Required
1. For materials used in the production of Fludex:
   a. Compute the price and quantity variances.
   b. The materials were purchased from a new supplier who is anxious to enter into a long-term purchase contract. Would you recommend that the company sign the contract? Explain.
2. For direct labor employed in the production of Fludex:
   a. Compute the rate and efficiency variances.
   b. In the past, the 35 technicians employed in the production of Fludex consisted of 20 senior technicians and 15 assistants. During November, the company experimented with only 15 senior technicians and 20 assistants in order to save costs. Would you recommend that the new labor mix be continued? Explain.

3. Compute the variable overhead spending and efficiency variances. What relationship can you see between this efficiency variance and the labor efficiency variance?

Computations from Incomplete Data   Sharp Company manufactures a product for   **P10–13** which the following standards have been set:

	Standard Quantity or Hours	Standard Price or Rate	Standard Cost
Direct materials . . .	3 feet	$5 per foot	$15
Direct labor	? hours	? per hour	?

During March, the company purchased direct materials at a cost of $55,650, all of which were used in the production of 3,200 units of product. In addition, 4,900 hours of direct labor time were worked on the product during the month. The cost of this labor time was $36,750. The following variances have been computed for the month:

> Materials quantity variance . . . . . $4,500 U
> Total labor variance . . . . 1,650 F
> Labor efficiency variance . . . . . . 800 U

Required

1. For direct materials:
   a. Compute the actual cost per foot for materials for March.
   b. Compute the materials price variance and a total variance for materials.
2. For direct labor:
   a. Compute the standard direct labor rate per hour.
   b. Compute the standard hours allowed for the month's production.
   c. Compute the standard hours allowed per unit of product.

(Hint: In completing the problem, it may be helpful to move from known to unknown data either by using the columnar format shown in Exhibits 10–3 and 10–5 or by using the variance formulas.)

JIT/FMS Performance Measures   Tombro Industries is in the process of automating one   **P10–14** of its plants and developing a flexible manufacturing system. Since this plant previously relied heavily on direct labor workers, the company is finding it necessary to make many changes in operating procedures. Progress has been slow, particularly in trying to develop new performance measures for the factory.

In an effort to evaluate performance and determine where improvements can be made, management has gathered the following data relating to activities over the last four months:

	Month			
	1	2	3	4
Quality control measures:				
Number of defects	185	163	124	91
First-time pass rate	32%	41%	58%	64%
Number of warranty claims	46	39	30	27
Number of customer complaints	102	96	79	58
Material control measures:				
Purchase order lead time.	8 days	7 days	5 days	4 days
Scrap as a percent of total cost	1%	1%	2%	3%
Inventory control measures:				
Raw material turnover (times)	15	18	20	24
Finished goods turnover (times).	12	12	13	13
Machine performance measures:				
Percentage of machine downtime	3%	4%	4%	6%
Use as a percentage of availability	95%	92%	89%	85%
Setup time (hours).	8	10	11	12
Delivery performance measures:				
Throughput time, or velocity	?	?	?	?
Manufacturing cycle efficiency (MCE).	?	?	?	?
Delivery cycle time	?	?	?	?
Percentage of on-time deliveries	96%	95%	92%	89%

The president has read in industry journals that the throughput time, the MCE, and the delivery cycle time are important measures of performance, but no one is sure how they are computed. You have been asked to assist the company, and you have gathered the following data from the computer relating to these measures:

	Average per Month (in days)			
	1	2	3	4
Wait time per order before start of production	9.0	11.5	12.0	14.0
Inspection time per unit	0.8	0.7	0.7	0.7
Process time per unit	2.1	2.0	1.9	1.8
Queue time per unit	2.8	4.4	6.0	7.0
Move time per unit	0.3	0.4	0.4	0.5

As part of its modernization process, the company is also moving toward a JIT inventory system. Over the next year, the company hopes to have the bulk of its raw materials and parts on a JIT basis.

Required 1. For each month, compute the following performance measures:
  a. The throughput time, or velocity of production.
  b. The MCE.
  c. The delivery cycle time.
2. Using the performance measures given in the main body of the problem and the performance measures computed in (1) above, do the following:
  a. Identify the areas where the company seems to be improving.
  b. Identify the areas where performance seems to be deteriorating, and from scrutiny of the various measures, explain why this deterioration is taking place.
3. Refer to the inspection time, process time, and so forth given above for month 4.
  a. Assume in month 5 the inspection time, process time, and so forth are the same as for month 4, except that through the JIT concept of continuous improvement the company is able to completely eliminate the queue time during production. Compute the new throughput time and MCE.
  b. Assume in month 6 the inspection time, process time, and so forth are again the same as in month 4, except that the company is able to eliminate both the queue time during production and the inspection time. Compute the new throughput time and MCE.

P10–15 **Setting Labor Standards** Mason Company is going to expand its punch press department. The company is about to purchase several new punch presses from Equipment Manufacturers, Inc. Equipment Manufacturers' engineers report that their mechanical studies indicate that for Mason's intended use, the output rate for one press should be 1,000 pieces per hour. Mason Company has similar presses now in operation. At present, production from these presses averages 600 pieces per hour.

A detailed study of Mason Company's experience shows that the average is derived from the following individual outputs:

Worker	Output per Hour (pieces)
J. Smith	750
H. Brown	750
R. Jones	600
J. Hardy	550
P. Clark	500
B. Randall	450
Total	3,600
Average	600

Mason's management also plans to institute a standard cost accounting system in the near future. The company's engineers are supporting a standard based on 1,000 pieces per hour; the accounting department is arguing for a standard of 750 pieces per hour; and the department supervisor is arguing for a standard of 600 pieces per hour.

1. What arguments would each proponent be likely to use to support his or her case?   *Required*
2. Which alternative best reconciles the needs of cost control and motivation for improved performance? Explain the reasons for your choice.

(CMA, adapted)

Hospital; Basic Variance Analysis   John Fleming, chief administrator for Valley View   **P10–16**
Hospital, is concerned about costs for tests in the hospital's lab. Charges for lab tests are consistently higher at Valley View than at other hospitals and have resulted in many complaints. Also, because of strict regulations on amounts reimbursed for lab tests, payments received from insurance companies and governmental units have not been high enough to provide an acceptable level of profit for the lab.

Mr. Fleming has asked you to evaluate costs in the hospital's lab for the past month. The following information is available:

a. Basically, two types of tests are performed in the lab—blood tests and smears. During the past month, 1,800 blood tests and 2,400 smears were performed in the lab.
b. Small glass plates are used in both types of tests. During the past month, the hospital purchased 12,000 plates at a cost of $28,200 (net of a 6 percent quantity discount). Some 1,500 of these plates were still on hand unused at the end of the month; there were no plates on hand at the beginning of the month.
c. During the past month, 1,150 hours of labor time were recorded in the lab. The cost of this labor time was $13,800.
d. Variable overhead cost last month in the lab for utilities and supplies totaled $7,820.

Valley View Hospital has never used standard costs. By searching industry literature, however, you have determined the following nationwide averages for hospital labs:

Plates: Two plates are required per lab test. These plates cost $2.50 each and are disposed of after the test is completed.

Labor: Each blood test should require 0.3 hours to complete, and each smear should require 0.15 hours to complete. The average cost of this lab time is $14 per hour.

Overhead: Overhead cost is based on direct labor-hours. The average rate for variable overhead is $6 per hour.

Mr. Fleming would like a complete analysis of the cost of plates, labor, and overhead in the lab for last month so that he can get to the root of the lab's cost problem.

1. Compute a materials price variance for the plates purchased last month, and compute   *Required*
   a materials quantity variance for the plates used last month.
2. For labor cost in the lab:
   a. Compute a labor rate variance and a labor efficiency variance.
   b. In most hospitals, one half of the workers in the lab are senior technicians and one half are assistants. In an effort to reduce costs, Valley View Hospital employs only one fourth senior technicians and three fourths assistants. Would you recommend that this policy be continued? Explain.
3. Compute the variable overhead spending and efficiency variances. Is there any relationship between the variable overhead efficiency variance and the labor efficiency variance? Explain.

Basic Variance Analysis; the Impact of Variances on Unit Costs   Landers Company   **P10–17**
manufactures a number of products. The standards relating to one of these products is shown below, along with actual cost data for May 19x6 (per unit):

	Standard Cost	Actual Cost
Direct materials:		
Standard: 3.6 feet at $1.50 per foot	$ 5.40	
Actual: 3.5 feet at $1.60 per foot		$ 5.60
Direct labor:		
Standard: 1.8 hours at $9 per hour	16.20	
Actual: 1.9 hours at $8.70 per hour		16.53
Variable overhead:		
Standard: 1.8 hours at $2.50 per hour	4.50	
Actual: 1.9 hours at $2.30 per hour		4.37
Total cost per unit	$26.10	$26.50
Excess of actual cost over standard cost		$0.40

Sam Davis, the production superintendent, was pleased when he saw the report above and commented: "This $0.40 excess cost is well within the 2 percent parameter management has set for acceptable variances. It's obvious that there's not much to worry about with this product."

Actual production for the month was 6,000 units. Overhead is assigned to products on a basis of direct labor-hours.

Required

1. Compute the following variances for May:
   a. Materials price and quantity.
   b. Labor rate and efficiency.
   c. Variable overhead spending and efficiency.
2. Show how much of the $0.40 excessive unit cost is traceable to each of the variances computed in (1) above.
3. Scrutinize the data prepared in (1) and (2). Do you agree that there isn't "much to worry about" with the product? How much of the $0.40 excessive unit cost is traceable to the inefficient use of labor time?

P10–18   JIT/FMS Performance Measures   Devani Products, Inc., has automated its plant and set up a flexible manufacturing system. The company is also trying to move toward a JIT inventory system. This has been a dramatic move for the company after operating a traditional, labor-based facility for many years. Progress has been slow, particularly in trying to measure performance in the factory.

The company has gathered the following data relating to operating activities over the last four months:

	Month			
	1	2	3	4
Quality control measures:				
Number of warranty claims	27	24	19	16
Number of customer complaints	31	32	24	18
Material control measures:				
Purchase order lead time	6 days	6 days	5 days	4 days
Scrap as a percent of good pieces	3%	3%	4%	5%
Inventory control measures:				
Raw material turnover (times)	15	17	19	20
Finished goods turnover (times)	11	10	8	6
Machine performance measures:				
Percentage of machine availability	98%	96%	92%	90%
Use as a percentage of availability	95%	89%	88%	85%
Setup time (hours)	9	10	12	13
Delivery performance measures:				
Percentage of on-time deliveries	93%	91%	89%	84%
Delivery cycle time.	?	?	?	?
Throughput time, or velocity	?	?	?	?
Manufacturing cycle efficiency (MCE)	?	?	?	?

Management is uncertain how to compute the delivery cycle time, the throughput time, and the MCE, and has asked for your assistance. You have gathered the following data from the computer relating to these measures:

	Average per Month (in days)			
	1	**2**	**3**	**4**
Wait time per order before start of production	16.5	18.0	19.0	21.0
Inspection time per unit	0.9	0.8	0.9	0.9
Process time per unit	1.7	1.6	1.7	1.8
Queue time per unit	5.6	6.2	7.0	8.0
Move time per unit	0.3	0.4	0.4	0.3

Required

1. For each month, compute the following performance measures:
   a. The throughput time, or velocity of production.
   b. The MCE.
   c. The delivery cycle time.
2. Using the performance measures given in the main body of the problem and the performance measures computed in (1) above, do the following:
   a. Identify the areas where the company seems to be improving.
   b. Identify the areas where performance seems to be deteriorating and, from scrutiny of the various measures, explain why this deterioration is taking place.
3. Refer to the inspection time, process time, and so forth given above for month 4.
   a. Assume in month 5 the inspection time, process time, and so forth are the same as in month 4, except that through the use of JIT the company is able to completely eliminate the queue time during production. Compute the new throughput time and MCE.
   b. Assume in month 6 the inspection time, process time, and so forth are again the same as in month 4, except that the company is able to eliminate both the queue time during production and the inspection time. Compute the new throughput time and MCE.

Basic Variance Analysis   Miller Toy Company manufactures a plastic swimming pool at its Westwood Plant. The plant has been experiencing problems for some time as shown by its June 19x3 income statement below:

P10–19

	Budgeted	Actual
Sales (15,000 pools)	$450,000	$450,000
Less variable expenses:		
Variable cost of goods sold*	180,000	196,290
Variable selling expenses.	20,000	20,000
Total variable expenses	200,000	216,290
Contribution margin	250,000	233,710
Less fixed expenses:		
Manufacturing overhead	130,000	130,000
Selling and administrative	84,000	84,000
Total fixed expenses.	214,000	214,000
Net income	$ 36,000	$ 19,710

* Contains direct materials, direct labor, and variable overhead.

Janet Dunn, who has just been appointed general manager of the Westwood Plant, has been given instructions to "get things under control." Upon reviewing the plant's income statement, Ms. Dunn has concluded that the major problem lies in the variable cost of goods sold. She has been provided with the following standard cost per swimming pool:

	Standard Quantity or Hours	Standard Price or Rate	Standard Cost
Direct materials	3.0 pounds	$2.00 per pound	$ 6.00
Direct labor	0.8 hours	6.00 per hour	4.80
Variable overhead	0.4 hours*	3.00 per hour	1.20
Total standard cost . . .			$12.00

* Based on machine-hours.

Ms. Dunn has determined that during June the plant produced 15,000 pools and incurred the following costs:

a. Purchased 60,000 pounds of materials at a cost of $1.95 per pound.

b. Used 49,200 pounds of materials in production. (Finished goods and work in process inventories are nominal and can be ignored.)

c. Worked 11,800 direct labor-hours at a cost of $7 per hour.

d. Incurred variable overhead cost totaling $18,290 for the month. A total of 5,900 machine-hours was recorded.

It is the company's policy to close all variances to cost of goods sold on a monthly basis.

Required   1. Compute the following variances for June:
     a. Direct materials price and quantity variance.
     b. Direct labor rate and efficiency variances.
     c. Variable overhead spending and efficiency variances.

2. Summarize the variances that you computed in (1) above by showing the net overall favorable or unfavorable variance for the month. What impact did this figure have on the company's income statement? Show computations.

3. Pick out the two most significant variances that you computed in (1) above. Explain to Ms. Dunn the possible causes of these variances.

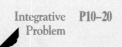

Integrative Problem   **P10–20**   **JIT/FMS Measures and Standard Costs**   "I've never seen such awful results," roared Ben Carrick, manufacturing vice president of Vorelli Industries. "I thought JIT and automation were supposed to make us more efficient, but just look at last month's efficiency report on Zets, our major product in this plant. The labor efficiency variance was $120,000 *unfavorable*. That's four times higher than its ever been before. If you add on the $102,000 unfavorable material price variance on Zets, that's over $220,000 down the drain in a single month on just one product. Have you people in purchasing and production lost control over everything?"

"Now take it easy, Ben," replied Sandi Shipp, the company's purchasing agent. "We knew when we adopted JIT that our material costs would go up somewhat. But we're locking onto the very best suppliers and they're making deliveries three times a day for our Zets product. In a few months, we'll be able to offset most of our higher purchasing costs by completely vacating three rented warehouses."

"And I know our labor efficiency variance looks bad," responded Raul Duvall, the company's production superintendent, "but it doesn't tell the whole story. With JIT flow lines and our new equipment, we've never been more efficient in the plant."

"How can you say you're efficient when you took 90,000 direct labor-hours to produce just 30,000 Zets last month?" asked Ben Carrick. "That works out to be 3 hours per unit, but according to the standard cost card you should be able to produce a Zet in just 2.5 hours. Do you call that efficient?"

"The problem is that the president wants us to use JIT on the finished goods side of the plant as well as on the raw materials side," explained Raul. "So we're trying to gear production to demand, but at the moment we have to cut production back somewhat in order to work off our finished goods inventory of Zets. This will go on for several more months before we'll be able to get production completely in balance with current demand. And don't forget that our line people aren't just standing around when their machines are idle. Under the new system, they're doing their own inspections and they do maintenance on their own equipment.''

"It had better *not* go on for several more months," roared Ben Carrick, "at least not if you people down in production want any bonuses this year. I've been looking at these reports for 30 years, and I know inefficiency when I see it. Let's get things back under control.''

After leaving Ben Carrick's office, Raul Duvall has approached you for help in developing some performance measures that will show the actual efficiency of the company's production process. Working with Raul, you have gathered the following information:

a. The company manufactures several products in this plant. A standard cost card for Zets is given below:

	Standard Quantity or Hours	Standard Price or Rate	Standard Cost
Direct materials.	18 feet	$3.00 per foot	$54.00
Direct labor	2.5 hours	8.00 per hour	20.00
Variable overhead.	2.5 hours	2.80 per hour	7.00
Total standard cost . . .			$81.00

b. During June, the most recent month, the company purchased 510,000 feet of material for production of Zets at a cost of $3.20 per foot. All of this material was used in the production of 30,000 units during the month. A large part of the production process is now automated, and the company is experiencing less waste each month.

c. The company maintains a stable work force to produce Zets. Persons who previously were inspectors and on the maintenance crew are being absorbed into this work force through natural attrition. During June, 90,000 hours were logged by direct labor workers on the Zets flow lines. The average pay rate was $7.85 per hour.

d. Variable overhead cost has always been assigned to products on a basis of direct labor-hours. During June, the company incurred $207,000 in variable overhead cost associated with the manufacture of Zets.

e. Demand for Zets is increasing over time, and top management is discussing the possibility of constructing additional production facilities.

f. The following information has been gathered from computers located on the production line. This information is expressed in hours per unit of the Zets product.

Processing: As workers have become more familiar with the new equipment, processing time per unit has declined over the past three months, from 2.6 hours in April, to 2.5 hours in May, to 2.4 hours in June.

Inspection: Workers are now directly responsible for quality control, which accounts for the following changes in inspection time per unit over the past three months: April, 1.3 hours; May, 0.9 hours; and June, 0.1 hours.

Movement of goods: With the change to JIT flow lines, goods now move shorter distances between machines. Move time per unit over the past three months has been: April, 1.9 hours; May, 1.4 hours; and June, 0.6 hours.

Queue time in cells: Better correlation of production with demand has resulted in less queue time per unit as goods move along the production line. The data for the last three months are: April, 8.2 hours; May, 5.2 hours; and June, 1.9 hours.

1. Compute the materials price and quantity variances, using traditional variance analysis. Is the decrease in waste apparent in this computation? Explain. If the company wants to continue to compute the materials price variance, what should be done to make this computation more appropriate?

2. Compute the direct labor rate and efficiency variances, using traditional variance analysis. Do you agree with Ben Carrick that the efficiency variance is still appropriate as a measure of performance for the company? Explain why you do or do not agree.

Required

3. Compute the variable overhead spending and efficiency variances, using traditional variance analysis. Would you expect that a correlation still exists between direct labor and the incurrence of variable overhead cost in the company? Explain, using data from your variance computations to support your position.
4. Compute the following for April, May, and June for Zets:
   a. The throughput time per unit.
   b. The MCE.
5. Are the results you have computed in (4) above consistent with the unfavorable labor efficiency variance computed in (2) above? Explain, giving reasons for any inconsistency and reasons as to which performance measure is more appropriate in this situation. What other performance measures might be useful to management in assessing performance in the production and sale of Zets?

P10–21   Standards and Variances from Incomplete Data   Highland Company produces a lightweight backpack that is popular with college students. Standard variable costs relating to a single backpack are given below:

	Standard Quantity or Hours	Standard Price or Rate	Standard Cost
Direct materials	?	$6 per yard	$?
Direct labor	?	?	?
Variable overhead	?	$3 per hour	?
Total standard cost . . .			$?

During March 19x1, 1,000 backpacks were manufactured and sold. Selected information relating to the month's production is given below:

	Materials Used	Direct Labor	Variable Overhead
Total standard cost allowed*	$16,800	$10,500	$4,200
Actual costs incurred	15,000	?	3,600
Materials price variance	?		
Materials quantity variance	1,200 U		
Labor rate variance		?	
Labor efficiency variance.		?	
Overhead spending variance			?
Overhead efficiency variance			?

* For the month's production.

The following additional information is available for March's production:

Actual direct labor-hours   1,500
Standard overhead rate per hour $3.00
Standard price of one yard of materials 6.00
Difference between standard and actual
    cost per backpack produced during March   . .   0.15F

Overhead is applied to production on a basis of direct labor-hours.

Required
1. What is the standard cost of a single backpack?
2. What was the actual cost per backpack produced during March?
3. How many yards of material are required at standard per backpack?
4. What was the materials price variance for March?
5. What is the standard direct labor rate per hour?
6. What was the labor rate variance for March? The labor efficiency variance?
7. What was the overhead spending variance for March? The overhead efficiency variance?
8. Prepare a standard cost card for one backpack.

JIT/FMS Performance Measures   After operating for many years as a labor-based facility, DataSpan, Inc., automated its plant at the start of the current year and installed a flexible manufacturing system. The company is also evaluating its suppliers and moving toward a JIT inventory system. Many adjustment problems have been encountered, among which are problems relating to performance measurement. After much study, the company has decided to use the performance measures below, and it has gathered data relating to these measures for the first four months of operations.

P10–22

	Month			
	1	2	3	4
Quality control measures:				
Number of customer complaints	75	68	59	45
Number of warranty claims	42	39	30	27
Cost of rework	$6,402	$6,910	$7,215	$8,130
Material control measures:				
Purchase order lead time (days)	8	6	5	3
Scrap as a percentage of total cost . . .	1.3%	1.7%	2.4%	2.8%
Inventory control measures:				
Raw material turnover (times)	27	20	18	14
Finished goods turnover (times)	16	13	11	10
Machine performance measures:				
Percentage of machine downtime	4.3%	5.1%	6.2%	7.0%
Use as a percentage of availability . . .	97%	92%	89%	86%
Setup time (hours)	1.3	1.8	2.5	3.0
Delivery performance measures:				
Throughput time (days)	?	?	?	?
Delivery cycle time (days)	?	?	?	?
Manufacturing cycle efficiency	?	?	?	?
Percentage of on-time deliveries	91%	86%	83%	79%
Total throughput (units)	3,210	3,072	2,915	2,806

Management has heard that throughput time, delivery cycle time, and MCE are important measures in an automated environment, but no one knows how to compute the figures. Fortunately, the company's computer logs time by element as a unit goes through the production process. The following average times have been logged over the last four months:

	Average per Month (in days)			
	1	2	3	4
Move time per unit	0.4	0.3	0.4	0.4
Process time per unit	2.1	2.0	1.9	1.8
Wait time per order before start				
of production.	16.0	17.5	19.0	20.5
Queue time per unit	4.3	5.0	5.8	6.7
Inspection time per unit	0.6	0.7	0.7	0.6

1. For each month, compute the following performance measures:
   a. The throughput time, or velocity of production.
   b. The MCE.
   c. The delivery cycle time.
2. Copy the performance measures above onto your answer sheet, and evaluate the company's performance over the last four months as follows:

Required

Measure	Trend	Probable Cause
Quality control measures:		
Number of customer complaints . . .	Favorable	Use of automated equipment; more care in production; better quality materials.
Cost of rework	Unfavorable	Poorly adjusted machines; poorly trained employees.
Number of warranty claims	?	?
Material control measures:		
Etc.		

3. Refer to the move time, process time, and so forth given above for month 4.
   a. Assume in month 5 that the move time, process time, and so forth are the same as in month 4, except that through the use of JIT inventory methods the company is able to completely eliminate the queue time during production. Compute the new throughput time and MCE.
   b. Assume in month 6 that the move time, process time, and so forth are again the same as in month 4, except that the company is able to eliminate both the queue time during production and the inspection time. Compute the new throughput time and MCE.

P10–23 **Variance Analysis with Multiple Lots**   Hillcrest Leisure Wear, Inc., manufactures men's clothing. The company has a single line of slacks that is produced in lots, with each lot representing an order from a customer. As a lot is completed, the customer's store label is attached to the slacks before shipment.

Hillcrest has a standard cost system and has established the following standards for a dozen slacks:

	Standard Quantity or Hours	Standard Price or Rate	Standard Cost
Direct materials . . .	32 yards	$2.40 per yard	$76.80
Direct labor	6 hours	7.50 per hour	45.00

During October, Hillcrest worked on three orders for slacks. The company's job cost records for the month reveal the following:

Lot	Units in Lot (dozens)	Materials Used (yards)	Hours Worked
48	1,500	48,300	8,900
49	950	30,140	6,130
50	2,100	67,250	10,270

The following additional information is available:

a. Hillcrest purchased 180,000 yards of material during October at a cost of $424,800.
b. Direct labor cost incurred during the month for production of slacks amounted to $192,280.
c. There was no work in process inventory on October 1. During October, lots 48 and 49 were completed, and lot 50 was 100 percent complete as to materials and 80 percent complete as to labor.

Required
1. Compute the materials price variance for the materials purchased during October.
2. Determine the materials quantity variance for October in both yards and dollars:
   a. For each lot worked on during the month.
   b. For the company as a whole.
3. Compute the labor rate variance for October.

4.   Determine the labor efficiency variance for the month in both hours and dollars:
     a.   For each lot worked on during the month.
     b.   For the company as a whole.
5.   In what situations might it be better to express variances in units (hours, yards, and so forth) rather than in dollars? In dollars rather than in units?

Developing Standard Costs   Danson Company is a chemical manufacturer which supplies various products to industrial users. The company plans to introduce a new chemical solution, called Nysap, for which it needs to develop a standard product cost. The following information is available on the production of Nysap: **P10–24**

a.   Nysap is made by combining a chemical compound (nyclyn) and a solution (salex), and boiling the mixture. A 20 percent loss in volume occurs for both the salex and the nyclyn during boiling. After boiling, the mixture consists of 9.6 liters of salex and 12 kilograms of nyclyn per 10-liter batch of Nysap.
b.   After the boiling process is complete, the solution is cooled slightly before 5 kilograms of protet are added per 10-liter batch of Nysap. The addition of the protet does not affect the total liquid volume. The resulting solution is then bottled in 10-liter containers.
c.   The finished product is highly unstable, and one 10-liter batch out of six is rejected at final inspection. Rejected batches have no commercial value and are thrown out.
d.   It takes a worker 35 minutes to process one 10-liter batch of Nysap. Employees work an eight-hour day, including one hour per day for rest breaks and cleanup.

1.   Determine the standard quantity for each of the raw materials needed to produce an acceptable 10-liter batch of Nysap.   *Required*
2.   Determine the standard labor time to produce an acceptable 10-liter batch of Nysap.
3.   Assuming the following purchase prices and costs, prepare a standard cost card for materials and labor for one acceptable 10-liter batch of Nysap:

Salex	$1.50 per liter
Nyclyn	2.80 per kilogram
Protet	3.00 per kilogram
Direct labor cost	9.00 per hour

(CMA, adapted)

Preparation of a Variance Report   Weaver Company produces and sells a single product. The company's most recent monthly income statement is given below: **P10–25**

WEAVER COMPANY
Income Statement
For the Month Ended June 30, 19x8

	Budget	Actual	Variance
Sales (500 units)	$30,000	$30,000	—
Less variable expenses:			
Variable production costs	10,500	11,710	$1,210 U
Other variable expenses	3,500	3,500	—
Total variable expenses	14,000	15,210	
Contribution margin	16,000	14,790	
Less fixed expenses:			
Production	8,000	8,000	—
Selling and administrative	4,250	4,290	40 U
Total fixed expenses	12,250	12,290	
Net income	$ 3,750	$ 2,500	$1,250 U

Weaver Company uses a standard cost system for planning and control purposes. Management is unhappy with the system because great difficulty has been experienced in trying to interpret the cost variance reports coming from the accounting department. A typical cost variance report is shown below. This report relates to the $1,210 variance above in variable production costs:

Cost Variance Report—Variable Production Costs
For the Month of June 19x8

	Total	Per Unit
Excess plastic used in production	$ 370	$0.74
Excess direct labor cost incurred	600	1.20
Excess variable overhead cost incurred . . .	240	0.48
Total excess cost incurred	$1,210	$2.42

During June, 500 units of this product were produced and sold. The per unit actual costs of production were:

Plastic: 3.8 pounds at $4.30 per pound	$16.34
Direct labor: 0.8 hours at $5.25 per hour.	4.20
Variable overhead: 0.8 hours at $3.60 per hour	2.88
Total actual cost per unit	$23.42

The standard cost of one unit of product is given below:

Plastic: 3.9 pounds at $4 per pound	$15.60
Direct labor: 0.6 hours at $5 per hour	3.00
Variable overhead: 0.6 hours at $4 per hour	2.40
Total standard cost per unit	$21.00

Weaver Company has hired you, as an expert in cost analysis, to help management clarify the reports coming from accounting.

Required
1. What criticisms can be made of the cost variance reports presently being prepared by accounting?
2. Compute the following variances for June 19x8:
   a. Materials price and quantity.
   b. Labor rate and efficiency.
   c. Variable overhead spending and efficiency.
3. Prepare a new cost variance report for management for the month of June. Show your variances on both a total and a per unit basis.

P10–26 **Standard Costs and Variance Analysis** Marvel Parts, Inc., manufactures auto accessories. One of the company's products is a set of seat covers that can be adjusted to fit nearly any small car. The company has a standard cost system in use for all of its products. According to the standards that have been set for the seat covers, the factory should work 2,850 hours each month in order to produce 1,900 sets of covers. The standard costs associated with this level of production activity are:

	Total	Per Set of Covers
Direct materials	$42,560	$22.40
Direct labor.	17,100	9.00
Variable overhead (based on direct labor-hours)	6,840	3.60
		$35.00

During August 19x7, the factory worked only 2,800 direct labor-hours and produced 2,000 sets of covers. The following actual costs were recorded during the month:

	Total	Per Set of Covers
Direct materials (12,000 yards)	$45,600	$22.80
Direct labor.	18,200	9.10
Variable overhead	7,000	3.50
		$35.40

At standard, each set of covers should require 5.6 yards of materials. All of the materials purchased during the month were used in production.

Compute the following variances for August 19x7:   *Required*

1. The materials price and quantity variances.
2. The labor rate and efficiency variances.
3. The variable overhead spending and efficiency variances.

Multiple Products; Standard Cost Card; Variance Analysis   Princeton Company pro- **P10–27**
duces two products, Lags and Vits, which pass through two operations. The company uses a standard cost system, with standard usage of materials and labor as follows for each product (on a per unit basis):

	Raw Material		Standard Labor Time	
Product	X	Y	Operation 1	Operation 2
Lags	1.8 pounds	2.0 gallons	0.4 hours	1.6 hours
Vits	3.0 pounds	4.5 gallons	0.7 hours	1.8 hours

Information relating to materials purchased and materials used in production during May 19x5 follows:

Material	Purchases	Purchase Cost	Standard Price	Used in Production*
X	14,000 pounds	$51,800	$3.50 per pound	8,500 pounds
Y	15,000 gallons	19,500	1.40 per gallon	13,000 gallons

* Materials purchased but not used in production remain in inventory and will be used in production in a following period.

The following additional information is available:

a. The company recognizes price variances at the time of purchase of material.
b. The standard labor rate is $10 per hour in operation 1 and $9.50 per hour in operation 2.
c. During May 19x5, 2,400 direct labor-hours were worked in operation 1 at a total labor cost of $27,000, and 5,700 direct labor-hours were worked in operation 2 at a total labor cost of $59,850.
d. Production during May 19x5 was: 1,500 Lags and 2,000 Vits.

1. Prepare a standard cost card for each product, showing the standard cost of direct   *Required*
   materials and direct labor.
2. For materials, compute the following variances for May 19x5:
   a. The price variance for each type of material.

b. The quantity variance for each type of material. Express the variance both in units (pounds or gallons) and in dollars.

3. For labor, compute the following variances for May 19x5:
a. The labor rate variance for each operation.
b. The labor efficiency variance for each operation. Express the variance both in hours and in dollars.

4. When might it be better to express variances in units (pounds, gallons, hours) rather than in dollars? In dollars rather than in units?

P10–28   Development of Standard Costs   ColdKing Company is a small producer of fruit-flavored frozen desserts. For many years, ColdKing's products have had strong regional sales on the basis of brand recognition; however, other companies have begun marketing similar products in the area, and price competition has become increasingly important. John Wakefield, the company's controller, is planning to implement a standard cost system for ColdKing and has gathered considerable information from his co-workers on production and material requirements for ColdKing's products. Wakefield believes that the use of standard costing will allow ColdKing to improve cost control and make better pricing decisions.

ColdKing's most popular product is raspberry sherbert. The sherbert is produced in 10-gallon batches, and each batch requires 6 quarts of good raspberries. The fresh raspberries are sorted by hand before they enter the production process. Because of imperfections in the raspberries and normal spoilage, 1 quart of berries is discarded for every 4 quarts of acceptable berries. Three minutes is the standard direct labor time for the sorting that is required to obtain 1 quart of acceptable raspberries. The acceptable raspberries are then blended with the other ingredients; blending requires 12 minutes of direct labor time per batch. After blending, the sherbert is packaged in quart containers. Wakefield has gathered the following pricing information.

a. ColdKing purchases raspberries at a cost of $0.80 per quart. All other ingredients cost a total of $0.45 per gallon.
b. Direct labor is paid at the rate of $9 per hour.
c. The total cost of material and labor required to package the sherbert is $0.38 per quart.

Required 1. Develop the standard cost for the direct cost components (materials, labor, and packaging) of a 10-gallon batch of raspberry sherbert. The standard cost should identify the standard quantity, standard rate, and standard cost per batch for each direct cost component of a batch of raspberry sherbert.

2. As part of the implementation of a standard cost system at ColdKing, John Wakefield plans to train those responsible for maintaining the standards on how to use variance analysis. Wakefield is particularly concerned with the causes of unfavorable variances.
a. Discuss the possible causes of unfavorable materials price variances, and identify the individual(s) who should be held responsible for these variances.
b. Discuss the possible causes of unfavorable labor efficiency variances, and identify the individual(s) who should be held responsible for these variances.

(CMA, adapted)

P10–29   Variances; Unit Costs; Journal Entries   (Appendix F)   Trueform Products, Inc., produces a broad line of sports equipment and uses a standard cost system for control purposes. Last year the company produced 8,000 of its varsity footballs. The standard costs associated with this football, along with the actual costs incurred last year, are given below (per football):

	Standard Cost	Actual Cost
Direct materials:		
Standard: 3.7 feet at $5 per foot.	$18.50	
Actual: 4.0 feet at $4.80 per foot		$19.20
Direct labor:		
Standard: 0.9 hours at $7.50 per hour	6.75	
Actual: 0.8 hours at $8 per hour.		6.40
Variable overhead:		
Standard: 0.9 hours at $2.50 per hour	2.25	
Actual: 0.8 hours at $2.75 per hour		2.20
Total cost per football	$27.50	$27.80

The president was elated when he saw that actual costs exceeded standard costs by only $0.30 per football. He stated, "I was afraid that our unit costs might get out of hand when we gave out those raises last year in order to stimulate output. But it's obvious our costs are well under control."

There was no inventory of materials on hand to start the year. During the year, 32,000 feet of materials were purchased and used in production.

Required

1. For direct materials:
   a. Compute the price and quantity variances for the year.
   b. Prepare journal entries to record all activity relating to direct materials for the year.
2. For direct labor:
   a. Compute the rate and efficiency variances.
   b. Prepare a journal entry to record the incurrence of direct labor cost for the year.
3. Compute the variable overhead spending and efficiency variances.
4. Was the president correct in his statement that "our costs are well under control"? Explain.
5. State the possible causes of each variance that you have computed.

Variance Analysis; Incomplete Data; Journal Entries (Appendix F) Maple Products, Ltd., manufactures a hockey stick that is used worldwide. The standard cost of one hockey stick is:

P10–30

	Standard Quantity or Hours	Standard Price or Rate	Standard Cost
Direct materials	? feet	$3.00 per foot	$?
Direct labor	2 hours	? per hour	?
Variable overhead	? hours	1.30 per hour	?
Total standard cost			$27.00

Last year, 8,000 hockey sticks were produced and sold. Selected cost data relating to last year's operations follow:

	Dr.	Cr.
Direct materials purchased (60,000 feet)	$174,000	
Wages payable (? hours)		$79,200*
Work in process—direct materials	115,200	
Direct labor rate variance		3,300
Variable overhead efficiency variance	650	

* Relates to the actual direct labor cost for the year.

The following additional information is available for last year's operations:

a. There were no materials on hand at the start of last year. Some of the materials purchased during the year were still on hand in the warehouse at the end of the year.

b. The variable overhead rate is based on direct labor-hours. Total actual variable overhead cost for last year was $19,800.

c. Actual direct materials usage for last year exceeded the standard by 0.2 feet per stick.

Required 1. For direct materials:

   a. Compute the price and quantity variances for last year.

   b. Prepare journal entries to record all activities relating to direct materials for last year.

2. For direct labor:

   a. Prove the rate variance given above, and compute the efficiency variance for last year.

   b. Prepare a journal entry to record activity relating to direct labor for last year.

3. Compute the variable overhead spending variance for last year, and prove the variable overhead efficiency variance given above.

4. State the possible causes of each variance that you have computed.

5. Prepare a completed standard cost card for one hockey stick.

CASES

C10-31 Unit Costs, Variances, and Journal Entries from Incomplete Data   (Appendix F)
You are employed by Olster Company, which manufactures products for the senior citizen market. As a rising young executive in the company, you are scheduled to make a presentation in a few hours to your superior. This presentation relates to last week's production of Maxitol, a popular health tonic that is manufactured by Olster Company. Unfortunately, while studying ledger sheets and variance summaries by poolside in the company's fitness area, you were bumped and dropped the papers into the pool. In desperation, you fished the papers from the water, but you have discovered that only the following fragments are readable:

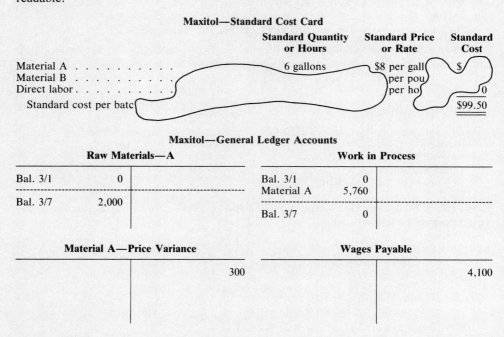

Maxitol—Standard Cost Card

	Standard Quantity or Hours	Standard Price or Rate	Standard Cost
Material A	6 gallons	$8 per gall	$
Material B		per pou	
Direct labor		per ho	0
Standard cost per batc			$99.50

Maxitol—General Ledger Accounts

Raw Materials—A			Work in Process		
Bal. 3/1	0		Bal. 3/1	0	
			Material A	5,760	
Bal. 3/7	2,000		Bal. 3/7	0	

Material A—Price Variance		Wages Payable	
	300		4,100

Raw Materials—B		
Bal. 3/1	700	2,500
Bal. 3/7	1,400	

Labor Rate Variance	
500	

Material B—Quantity Variance	
100	

Accounts Payable	
	11,460

You remember that the accounts payable are for purchases of both material A and material B. You also remember that only 10 direct labor workers are involved in the production of Maxitol and that each worked 40 hours last week. The wages payable above are for wages earned by these workers.

You realize that you must reconstruct all data relating to Maxitol very quickly in order to be ready for your presentation. As a start, you have called purchasing and found that 1,000 gallons of material A and 800 pounds of material B were purchased last week.

Required

1. How many batches of Maxitol were produced last week? (This is a key figure; be sure it's right before going on.)
2. For material A:
   a. What was the cost of material A purchased last week?
   b. How many gallons were used in production last week?
   c. What was the quantity variance?
   d. Prepare journal entries to record all activity relating to material A for last week.
3. For material B:
   a. What is the standard cost per pound for material B?
   b. How many pounds of material B were used in production last week? How many pounds should have been used at standard?
   c. What is the standard quantity of material B per batch?
   d. What was the price variance for material B last week?
   e. Prepare journal entries to record all activity relating to material B for last week.
4. For direct labor:
   a. What is the standard rate per direct labor-hour?
   b. What are the standard hours per batch?
   c. What were the standard hours allowed for last week's production?
   d. What was the labor efficiency variance for last week?
   e. Prepare a journal entry to record all activity relating to direct labor for last week.
5. Complete the standard cost card shown above for one batch of Maxitol.

JIT/FMS Performance Measures; Missing Data   "I'm having a really hard time with these new production measures," said Ruth Dancie, president of Kendrix Products. "I understood standard costs and variances, because we were always aiming for a specific figure. But with no standards to shoot for, what's good and what's bad? To make matters worse, the computer garbled some of the numbers in this report on the first four months of our fiscal year."

The report to which Ms. Dancie was referring is shown below:

C10-32

Production and Cycle Times
April–July 19x1

	April	May	June	July
Average time required per unit, in days:				
Inspection time	0.6	0.5	0.5	0.4
Process time.	1.3	?	?	?
Wait time from order to start of production	27.0	24.5	19.0	14.0
Queue time	6.4	5.9	4.2	2.7
Move time	0.9	0.8	0.8	?

General Performance Measures
April–July 19x1

	April	May	June	July
Quality control measures:				
Number of warranty claims	105	96	81	72
Number of customer complaints	76	61	53	39
Number of defects in parts	27	30	34	40
Material control measures:				
Purchase order lead time (days)	10	7	6	4
Scrap as a percentage of total cost	2.1%	2.8%	3.4%	3.9%
Inventory control measures:				
Raw material turnover (times)	35	29	21	18
Finished goods turnover (times)	9	10	13	16
Number of items of raw material carried in inventory	4,806	5,210	6,724	7,805
Machine performance measures:				
Percentage of machine availability	95%	91%	87%	84%
Use as a percentage of availability	86%	90%	94%	100%
Setup time (hours)	4.3	3.9	3.1	2.5
Delivery performance measures:				
Throughput time, or velocity (days) . . .	?	8.5	?	?
Manufacturing cycle efficiency (MCE) . .	?	?	?	22.0%
Delivery cycle time (days)	?	?	25.7	19.0
Percentage of on-time deliveries	?	?	?	?

Kendrix Products moved into a new, automated facility four months ago, at the start of its fiscal year. The company is now in the process of moving toward JIT purchasing and production. Management has been so busy with the new system that little time has been available to develop or interpret any new performance measures. Accordingly, you have been asked to supply the missing data in the report above, and to give a line-by-line critique to management as to how the company is doing.

Required 1. For each month, determine the following items:
    a. The throughput time (velocity) per unit, including all elements that make up the throughput time.
    b. The MCE (manufacturing cycle efficiency), including all elements from which the MCE is computed.
    c. The delivery cycle time, including all elements that make up the delivery cycle time.

    2. Refer to the "General Performance Measures" given above. Copy these measures down on your answer sheet, and for each measure indicate the trend (either favorable or unfavorable) and the probable cause of the trend that you observe. Use the following format:

Measure	Trend	Probable Cause
Quality control measures:		
Number of warranty claims	Favorable	Better quality equipment, materials, and construction.
Number of customer complaints . . .	?	?

3. Refer again to the "General Performance Measures" given above, and to the "Percentage of on-time deliveries." In view of your analysis in (2) above, would you expect the percentage of on-time deliveries to be increasing or decreasing? Explain.
4. Refer to the "Production and Cycle Times" given above for July.
   a. Assume in August that these times are the same as for July, except that through the use of JIT production the company is able to completely eliminate the queue time during production. Compute the new throughput time and MCE.
   b. Assume in September that the "Production and Cycle Times" again are the same as in July, except that the company is able to eliminate both the queue time during production and the move time. Compute the new throughput time and MCE.
   c. What do you think is the purpose of the computations in (a) and (b) above?

Behavioral Impact of Standard Costs and Variances   Terry Travers is the manufacturing supervisor of Aurora Manufacturing Company, which produces a variety of plastic products. Some of these products are standard items that are listed in the company's catalog, while others are made to customer specifications. Each month, Travers receives a performance report showing the budget for the month, the actual activity, and the variance between budget and actual. Part of Travers' annual performance evaluation is based on his department's performance against budget. Aurora's purchasing manager, Sally Christensen, also receives monthly performance reports and she, too, is evaluated in part on the basis of these reports.

C10–33

The monthly reports for June 19x5 had just been distributed when Travers met Christensen in the hallway outside their offices. Scowling, Travers began the conversation, "I see we have another set of monthly performance reports hand-delivered by that not very nice junior employee in the budget office. He seemed pleased to tell me that I'm in trouble with my performance again."

Christensen: I got the same treatment. All I ever hear about are the things I haven't done right. Now I'll have to spend a lot of time reviewing the report and preparing explanations. The worst part is that it's now the 21st of July so the information is almost a month old, and we have to spend all this time on history.

Travers: My biggest gripe is that our production activity varies a lot from month to month, but we're given an annual budget that's written in stone. Last month we were shut down for three days when a strike delayed delivery of the basic ingredient used in our plastic formulation, and we had already exhausted our inventory. You know about that problem, though, because we asked you to call all over the country to find an alternate source of supply. When we got what we needed on a rush basis, we had to pay more than we normally do.

Christensen: I expect problems like that to pop up from time to time—that's part of my job—but now we'll both have to take a careful look at our reports to see where the charges are reflected for that rush order. Every month I spend more time making sure I should be charged for each item reported than I do making plans for my department's daily work. It's really frustrating to see charges for things I have no control over.

Travers: The way we get information doesn't help, either. I don't get copies of the reports you get, yet a lot of what I do is affected by your department, and by most of the other departments we have. Why do the budget and accounting people assume that I should only be told about my operations even though the president regularly gives us pep talks about how we all need to work together, as a team?

Christensen: I seem to get more reports than I need, and I am never asked to comment on them until top management calls me on the carpet about my department's shortcomings. Do you ever hear comments when your department shines?

Travers: I guess they don't have time to review the good news. One of my problems is that all the reports are in dollars and cents. I work with people, machines, and materials. I need information to help me *this* month to solve *this* month's problems—not another report of the dollars expended *last* month or the month before.

Required   1.   Based on the conversation between Terry Travers and Sally Christensen, describe the likely motivation and behavior of these two employees resulting from Aurora Manufacturing Company's standard cost and variance reporting system.

2.   When properly implemented, both employees and companies should benefit from a system involving standard costs and variances.
    a.   Describe the benefits that can be realized from a standard cost system.
    b.   Based on the situation presented above, recommend ways for Aurora Manufacturing Company to improve its standard cost and variance reporting system so as to increase employee motivation.

(CMA, adapted)

Caterpillar, Inc., is a pioneer in the development of activity-based costing. The company divides its overhead costs into three cost pools—logistics, manufacturing, and general. Each of these three cost pools is further subdivided into scores of activity centers, and each of these centers has its own flexible budget with variable and fixed overhead rates.

Flexible Budgets and Overhead Analysis

LEARNING OBJECTIVES

After studying Chapter 11, you should be able to:

1 Prepare a flexible budget, and explain the advantages of the flexible budget approach over the static budget approach.

2 Use the flexible budget to prepare a variable overhead performance report containing only a spending variance

3 Use the flexible budget to prepare a variable overhead performance report containing both a spending and an efficiency variance.

4 Prepare a flexible budget that contains both variable and fixed costs.

5 Explain how flexible budgets are used in a company that employs activity-based costing.

6 Explain the significance of the denominator activity figure in determining the standard cost of a unit of product.

7 Properly apply overhead cost to units of product in a standard cost system.

8 Compute and properly interpret the fixed overhead budget and volume variances.

9 Show how variances can be presented on the income statement for management's use.

10 Define or explain the key terms listed at the end of the chapter.

F our problems are involved in overhead cost control. First, manufacturing overhead is usually made up of many separate costs. Second, these separate costs are often very small in dollar amount, making it impractical to control them in the same way that direct materials and direct labor costs are controlled. Third, these small, separate costs are often the responsibility of different managers. And fourth, manufacturing overhead costs vary in behavior, some being variable, some fixed, and some mixed in nature.

Most of these problems can be overcome by use of a *flexible budget*. Flexible budgets were touched on briefly in Chapter 9. In this chapter, we study flexible budgets in greater detail and learn how they are used to control costs. We also expand the study of overhead variances that we started in Chapter 10.

FLEXIBLE BUDGETS

Characteristics of a Flexible Budget

Objective 1
Prepare a flexible budget, and explain the advantages of the flexible budget approach over the static budget approach.

The budgets that we studied in Chapter 9 were essentially static budgets in nature. A **static budget** has two characteristics:

1. It is geared toward only one level of activity.
2. Actual results are always compared against budgeted costs at the *original* budget activity level.

A **flexible budget** differs from a static budget on both of these points. First, it does not confine itself to only one level of activity, but rather is geared toward a *range* of activity. Second, actual results do not have to be compared against budgeted costs at the original budget activity level. Since the flexible budget covers a *range* of activity, if actual costs are incurred at a different activity level from what was originally planned, then the manager is able to construct a new budget, as needed, to compare against actual results. Hence, the term *flexible budget*. In sum, the characteristics of a flexible budget are:

1. It is geared toward *all* levels of activity within the relevant range, rather than toward only one level of activity.
2. It is *dynamic* in nature rather than static. A budget can be tailored for any level of activity within the relevant range, even after the period is over. That is, a manager can look at what activity level *was attained* during a period and then turn to the flexible budget to determine what costs *should have been* at that activity level.

Deficiencies of the Static Budget

To illustrate the difference between a static budget and a flexible budget, let us assume that the assembly operation of Rocco Company has budgeted to produce 10,000 units during March. The variable overhead budget that has been set is shown in Exhibit 11–1.

Let us assume that the production goal of 10,000 units is not met. The company is able to produce only 9,400 units during the month. *If a static budget approach is used,* the performance report for the month will appear as shown in Exhibit 11–2.

What's wrong with this report? The deficiencies of the static budget can be explained as follows. A production manager has two prime responsibilities to discharge in the performance of his or her duties—*production control* and *cost control.* Production control is involved with seeing that production goals in terms

ROCCO COMPANY
Static Budget
Assembly Operation
For the Month Ended March 31, 19x1

EXHIBIT 11–1

Budgeted production in units   10,000

Budgeted variable overhead costs:
Indirect materials $4,000
Lubricants   1,000
Power   3,000
    Total $8,000

of output are met. Cost control is involved with seeing that output is produced at the least possible cost, consistent with quality standards. These are different responsibilities, and they must be kept separate in attempting to assess how well the production manager is doing his or her job. The main difficulty with the static budget is that it fails completely to distinguish between the production control and the cost control dimensions of a manager's performance.

Of the two, the static budget does a good job of measuring only whether production control is being maintained. Look again at the data in Exhibit 11–2. The data on the top line relate to the production superintendent's responsibility for production control. These data for Rocco Company properly reflect the fact that production control was not maintained during the month. The company failed to meet its production goal by 600 units.

The remainder of the data in the report deal with cost control. These data are useless in that they are comparing apples with oranges. Although the production manager may be very proud of the favorable cost variances, they tell nothing about how well costs were controlled during the month. The problem is that the budget costs are based on an activity level of 10,000 units, whereas the actual costs were incurred at an activity level substantially below this (only 9,400 units). From a cost control point of view, it is total nonsense to try to compare costs at one activity level with costs at a different activity level. Such comparisons will always make a production manager look good so long as the actual production is less than the budgeted production.

ROCCO COMPANY
Static Budget Performance Report
Assembly Operation
For the Month Ended March 31, 19x1

EXHIBIT 11–2

	Actual	Budget	Variance
Production in units.	9,400	10,000	600 U
Variable overhead costs:			
Indirect materials	$3,800	$4,000	$200 F*
Lubricants	950	1,000	50 F*
Power	2,900	3,000	100 F*
Total	$7,650	$8,000	$350 F*

* These cost variances are useless, since they have been derived by comparing actual costs at one level of activity against budgeted costs at a *different* level of activity.

How the Flexible Budget Works

The basic idea of the flexible budget approach is that through a study of cost behavior patterns, a budget can be prepared that is geared to a *range* of activity, rather than to a single level. The basic steps in preparing a flexible budget are:

1. Determine the relevant range over which activity is expected to fluctuate during the coming period.
2. Analyze costs that will be incurred over the relevant range in order to determine cost behavior patterns (variable, fixed, or mixed).
3. Separate costs by behavior, and determine the formula for variable and mixed costs, as discussed in Chapter 6.
4. Using the formula for the variable portion of the costs, prepare a budget showing what costs will be incurred at various points throughout the relevant range.

To illustrate, let us assume that Rocco Company's production normally fluctuates between 8,000 and 11,000 units each month. A study of cost behavior patterns over this relevant range has revealed the following formulas for the variable portion of overhead:

Overhead Costs	Variable Cost Formula (per unit)
Indirect materials	$0.40
Lubricants	0.10
Power	0.30

Based on these cost formulas, a flexible budget for Rocco Company would appear as shown in Exhibit 11–3.

Using the Flexible Budget   Once the flexible budget has been prepared, the manager is ready to compare actual results for a period against the comparable budget level anywhere within the relevant range. The manager isn't limited to a single budget level as with the static budget. To illustrate, let us again assume that Rocco Company is unable to meet its production goal of 10,000 units during March. As before, we will assume that only 9,400 units are produced. Under the flexible budget approach, the performance report would appear as shown in Exhibit 11–4.

EXHIBIT 11–3

ROCCO COMPANY

Flexible Budget
Assembly Operation
For the Month Ended March 31, 19x1

Budgeted production in units.   10,000

Overhead Costs	Cost Formula (per unit)	Range of Production in Units			
		8,000	9,000	10,000	11,000
Variable costs:					
Indirect materials	$0.40	$3,200	$3,600	$4,000	$4,400
Lubricants	0.10	800	900	1,000	1,100
Power	0.30	2,400	2,700	3,000	3,300
Total variable costs	$0.80	$6,400	$7,200	$8,000	$8,800

EXHIBIT 11–4

ROCCO COMPANY
Performance Report
Assembly Operation
For the Month Ended March 31, 19x1

Budgeted production in units   10,000
Actual production in units.   9,400

Overhead Costs	Cost Formula (per unit)	Actual Costs Incurred 9,400 Units	Budget Based on 9,400 Units	Variance
Variable costs:				
Indirect materials.	$0.40	$3,800	$3,760*	$ 40 U†
Lubricants	0.10	950	940	10 U†
Power.	0.30	2,900	2,820	80 U†
Total variable costs	$0.80	$7,650	$7,520	$130 U†

* 9,400 units × $0.40 = $3,760. Other budget allowances are computed in the same way.

† These cost variances are usable in evaluating cost control, since they have been derived by comparing actual costs and budgeted costs at the *same* level of activity.

In contrast to the performance report prepared earlier under the static budget approach (Exhibit 11–2), this performance report distinguishes clearly between production control and cost control. The production data at the top of the report indicate whether the production goal was met. The cost data at the bottom of the report tell how well costs were controlled for the 9,400 units that were actually produced.

Notice that all cost variances are *unfavorable,* as contrasted to the favorable cost variances on the performance report prepared earlier under the static budget approach. The reason for the change in variances is that by means of the flexible budget approach we are able to compare budgeted and actual costs at *the same activity level* (9,400 units produced), rather than being forced to compare budgeted costs at one activity level against actual costs at a different activity level. Herein lies the strength and dynamic nature of the flexible budget approach. By simply applying the cost formulas, it is possible to develop a budget *at any time* for *any* activity level within the relevant range. Thus, even if actual activity results in some odd figure that does not appear in the flexible budget, such as the 9,400 units above, budgeted costs can still be prepared to compare against actual costs. One simply develops a budget at the 9,400-unit level, as we have done, by using the cost formulas contained in the flexible budget. The result shows up in more usable variances.

The Measure of Activity—A Critical Choice

In the Rocco Company example, we chose to use units of production as the activity base for developing a flexible budget. Rather than use units, which are a measure of output, most companies find it more practical to use some *input* measure, such as machine-hours (MH) or direct labor-hours (DLH), to plan and control overhead costs. This is especially true when more than one product is manufactured. At least three factors are important in selecting an activity base for an overhead flexible budget:

1. There should be a causal relationship between the activity base and overhead costs.
2. The activity base should not be expressed in dollars.
3. The activity base should be simple and easily understood.

Causal Relationship   There should be a direct causal relationship between the activity base and the variable overhead costs in the flexible budget. That is, the variable overhead costs in the budget should vary as a result of changes in the activity base. In a machine shop, for example, one would expect power usage and attendant energy costs to vary in relationship to the number of machine-hours worked. Machine-hours would therefore be the proper base to use in a flexible budget relating to energy consumption. As explained in Chapter 3, an activity base is frequently referred to as a *cost driver,* since it is the controlling factor in the incurrence of cost.

Other common activity bases (cost drivers) include direct labor-hours, miles driven by salespersons, contacts made by salespersons, number of invoices processed, number of occupied beds in a hospital, and number of X rays given. Any one of these could be used as the base for preparing a flexible budget in the proper situation.

Do Not Use Dollars   Whenever possible, the activity base should be expressed in units rather than in dollars. If dollars are used, they should be standard dollars rather than actual dollars.

The problem with dollars is that they are subject to price-level changes, which can cause a distortion in the activity base if it is expressed in dollar terms. A similar problem arises when wage-rate changes take place if direct labor cost is being used as the activity base in a flexible budget. The change in wage rates will cause the activity base to change, even though a proportionate change may not take place in the overhead costs themselves. These types of fluctuations generally make dollars difficult to work with, and argue strongly for units rather than dollars in the activity base. The use of *standard* dollar costs rather than *actual* dollar costs overcomes the problem to some degree, but standard costs still have to be adjusted from time to time as changes in actual costs take place. On the other hand, *units* as a measure of activity (beds, hours, miles, and so on) are subject to few distorting influences and are less likely to cause problems in preparing and using a flexible budget.

Keep the Base Simple   The activity base should be simple and easily understood. A base that is not easily understood by the manager who works with it day by day will probably result in confusion and misunderstanding rather than serve as a positive means of cost control.

THE OVERHEAD PERFORMANCE REPORT—A CLOSER LOOK

A special problem arises in preparing overhead performance reports when the flexible budget is based on *hours* of activity (such as direct labor-hours) rather than on units of product. The problem relates to what hour base to use in constructing budget allowances on the performance report.

The Problem of Budget Allowances

The nature of the problem can best be seen through a specific example. Assume that Donner Company is budgeting its activities for the year 19x1. The flexible budget that has been prepared is shown in Exhibit 11–5.

As shown in Exhibit 11–5, the company uses machine-hours as an activity base in its flexible budget and has budgeted to operate at an activity level of 50,000 machine-hours for the year. Let us assume that two machine-hours are required to

EXHIBIT 11–5

DONNER COMPANY
Flexible Budget

Budgeted machine-hours   50,000

Overhead Costs	Cost Formula (per hour)	Machine-Hours 30,000	40,000	50,000	60,000
Variable costs:					
Indirect labor	$0.80	$24,000	$32,000	$40,000	$48,000
Lubricants	0.30	9,000	12,000	15,000	18,000
Power	0.40	12,000	16,000	20,000	24,000
Total variable costs	$1.50	$45,000	$60,000	$75,000	$90,000

produce one unit of output. Under this assumption, budgeted production for the year is 25,000 units (50,000 budgeted machine-hours ÷ 2 hours per unit = 25,000 units). After the year is over, suppose the company finds that actual production for the year was only 20,000 units and that 42,000 hours of machine time were required to produce these units. A summary of the year's activities follows:

Budgeted machine-hours	50,000
Actual machine-hours	42,000
Standard machine-hours allowed	40,000*
Actual variable overhead costs:	
Indirect labor	$36,000
Lubricants	11,000
Power	24,000
Total actual costs	$71,000

* 20,000 units produced × 2 hours per unit = 40,000 standard hours allowed for the year's output.

In preparing a performance report for the year, what hour base should Donner Company use in computing budget allowances to compare against actual results? There are two alternatives. The company could use:

1. The 42,000 hours *actually worked* during the year.
2. The 40,000 hours that *should have been worked* during the year to produce 20,000 units of output.

Which base the company chooses will depend on how much detailed variance information it wants. As we learned in the preceding chapter, variable overhead can be analyzed in terms of a *spending* variance and an *efficiency* variance. The two bases provide different variance output.

Spending Variance Alone

If Donner Company chooses alternative 1 and bases its performance report on the 42,000 machine-hours actually worked during the year, then the performance report will show only a spending variance for variable overhead. A performance report prepared in this way is shown in Exhibit 11–6.

The formula behind the spending variance was introduced in the preceding chapter. For review, that formula is:

$$(AH \times AR) - (AH \times SR) = \text{Variable overhead spending variance}$$

Or, in factored form:

$$AH(AR - SR) = \text{Variable overhead spending variance}$$

Objective 2
Use the flexible budget to prepare a variable overhead performance report containing only a spending variance.

EXHIBIT 11–6

DONNER COMPANY
Variable Overhead Performance Report
For the Year Ended March 31, 19x1

Budget allowances are based on 42,000 machine-hours actually worked.

Comparing the budget against actual overhead cost yields only a spending variance.

Budgeted machine-hours 50,000
Actual machine-hours 42,000
Standard machine-hours allowed . . . 40,000

Overhead Costs	Cost Formula (per hour)	Actual Costs Incurred 42,000 Hours	Budget Based on 42,000 Hours	Spending Variance
Variable costs:				
Indirect labor	$0.80	$36,000	$33,600*	$2,400 U
Lubricants	0.30	11,000	12,600	1,600 F
Power	0.40	24,000	16,800	7,200 U
Total variable costs	$1.50	$71,000	$63,000	$8,000 U

* 42,000 hours × $0.80 = $33,600. Other budget allowances are computed in the same way.

The report in Exhibit 11–6 is structured around the first, or unfactored, format.

Interpreting the Spending Variance   The overhead spending variance is affected by two things. First, a spending variance may occur simply because of price increases over what is shown in the flexible budget. For Donner Company, this means that prices paid for overhead items may have gone up during the year, resulting in unfavorable spending variances. This portion of the overhead spending variance is just like the price variance for raw materials.

Second, the overhead spending variance is affected by waste or excessive usage of overhead materials. A first reaction is to say that waste or excessive usage of materials ought to show up as part of the efficiency variance. But this isn't true so far as overhead is concerned. Waste or excessive usage will show up as part of the spending variance. The reason is that the Manufacturing Overhead account is charged with *all* overhead costs incurred during a period, including those costs that arise as a result of waste. Since the spending variance represents any difference between the standard rate per hour and the actual costs incurred, waste will automatically show up as part of this variance, along with any excessive prices paid for variable overhead items.

In sum, the overhead spending variance contains both price and quantity (waste) elements. These two elements could be broken out and shown separately on the performance report, but this is rarely done in actual practice.

Usefulness of the Spending Variance   Most firms consider the overhead spending variance to be highly useful. Generally, the price element in this variance will be small, so the variance permits a focusing of attention on that thing over which the supervisor probably has the greatest control—waste of supplies and similar items used in production. In many cases, firms will limit their overhead analysis to the spending variance alone, feeling that the information it yields is sufficient for overhead cost control.

Both Spending and Efficiency Variances

If Donner Company wants both a spending and an efficiency variance for overhead, then it should compute budget allowances for *both* the 40,000 machine-hour and the 42,000 machine-hour levels of activity. A performance report prepared in this way is shown in Exhibit 11–7.

Note from Exhibit 11–7 that the spending variance is the same as the spending variance shown in Exhibit 11–6. The performance report in Exhibit 11–7 has simply been expanded to include an efficiency variance as well. Together, the spending and efficiency variances make up the total variance, as explained in the preceding chapter.

Objective 3
Use the flexible budget to prepare a variable overhead performance report containing both a spending and an efficiency variance.

Interpreting the Efficiency Variance   The term *overhead efficiency variance* is a misnomer, since this variance has nothing to do with efficiency in the use of overhead. What the variance really measures is how efficiently the *base* underlying the flexible budget is being utilized in production. Recall from the preceding chapter that the variable overhead efficiency variance is a function of the difference between the actual hours utilized in production and the hours that should have been taken to produce the period's output:

$$(AH \times SR) - (SH \times SR) = \text{Variable overhead efficiency variance}$$

Or, in factored form:

$$SR(AH - SH) = \text{Variable overhead efficiency variance}$$

EXHIBIT 11–7

DONNER COMPANY
Variable Overhead Performance Report
For the Year Ended March 31, 19x1

> Budget allowances are based on 40,000 machine-hours—the time it *should have taken* to produce 20,000 units of output—as well as on the 42,000 *actual* machine-hours worked.

> This approach yields both a spending and an efficiency variance.

		Budgeted machine-hours	50,000
Actual machine-hours			42,000
Standard machine-hours allowed			40,000

Overhead Costs	Cost Formula (per hour)	(1) Actual Costs Incurred 42,000 Hours	(2) Budget Based on 42,000 Hours	(3) Budget Based on 40,000 Hours	(4) Total Variance (1) − (3)	Breakdown of the Total Variance Spending Variance (1) − (2)	Efficiency Variance (2) − (3)
Variable costs:							
Indirect labor	$0.80	$36,000	$33,600*	$32,000	$ 4,000 U	$2,400 U	$1,600 U
Lubricants	0.30	11,000	12,600	12,000	1,000 F	1,600 F	600 U
Power	0.40	24,000	16,800	16,000	8,000 U	7,200 U	800 U
Total variable costs	$1.50	$71,000	$63,000	$60,000	$11,000 U	$8,000 U	$3,000 U

* 42,000 hours × $0.80 = $33,600. Other budget allowances are computed in the same way.

If more hours are worked than are allowed at standard, then the overhead efficiency variance will be unfavorable to reflect this inefficiency. As a practical matter, however, the inefficiency is not in the use of overhead *but rather in the use of the base itself.*

This point can be illustrated by looking again at Exhibit 11–7. Two thousand more machine-hours were used during the period than should have been used to produce the period's output. Each of these hours required the incurrence of $1.50 of variable overhead cost, resulting in an unfavorable variance of $3,000 (2,000 hours × $1.50 = $3,000). Although this $3,000 variance is called an overhead efficiency variance, it could better be called a machine-hours efficiency variance, since it measures the efficiency of utilization of machine time. However, the term *overhead efficiency variance* is so firmly ingrained in day-to-day use that a change is unlikely. Even so, the user must be careful to interpret the variance with a clear understanding of what it really measures.

Control of the Efficiency Variance   Who is responsible for control of the overhead efficiency variance? Since the variance really measures efficiency in the utilization of the base underlying the flexible budget, whoever is responsible for control of this base is responsible for control of the variance. If the base is direct labor-hours, then the supervisor responsible for the use of labor time will be chargeable for any overhead efficiency variance.

EXPANDING THE FLEXIBLE BUDGET

Before concluding our discussion on the preparation of an overhead flexible budget, we need to consider two additional topics: first, we need to consider the inclusion of fixed costs on the flexible budget; and second, we need to consider the preparation of a flexible budget when activity-based costing is in use. These two topics are discussed in the following two sections.

Fixed Costs and the Flexible Budget

Objective 4
Prepare a flexible budget that contains both variable and fixed costs.

Should the flexible budget contain fixed costs as well as variable costs? The term *flexible budget* implies variable costs only. As a practical matter, however, most firms include fixed overhead costs in the budget as well.

EXHIBIT 11–8

DONNER COMPANY
Flexible Budget

Budgeted machine-hours   50,000

Overhead Costs	Cost Formula (per hour)	Machine-Hours 30,000	40,000	50,000	60,000
Variable costs:					
Indirect labor	$0.80	$ 24,000	$ 32,000	$ 40,000	$ 48,000
Lubricants	0.30	9,000	12,000	15,000	18,000
Power	0.40	12,000	16,000	20,000	24,000
Total variable costs	$1.50	45,000	60,000	75,000	90,000
Fixed costs:					
Depreciation		100,000	100,000	100,000	100,000
Supervisory salaries		160,000	160,000	160,000	160,000
Insurance.		40,000	40,000	40,000	40,000
Total fixed costs.		300,000	300,000	300,000	300,000
Total overhead costs.		$345,000	$360,000	$375,000	$390,000

Exhibit 11–8 illustrates the flexible budget of Donner Company, which has been expanded to include the company's fixed overhead costs as well as its variable overhead costs. Actually, the fixed portion of the budget is a *static budget* in that the amounts remain unchanged throughout the relevant range.

Fixed costs are often included in the flexible budget for at least two reasons. First, to the extent that a fixed cost is controllable by a manager, it should be included in the evaluation of his or her performance. Such costs should be placed on the manager's performance report, along with the variable costs for which he or she is responsible. And second, fixed costs are needed in the flexible budget for product costing purposes. Recall from Chapter 3 that overhead costs are added to units of product by means of the predetermined overhead rate. *The flexible budget provides the manager with the information needed to compute this rate, and thereby it assists in the costing of products.* Later in the chapter we illustrate the use of the flexible budget in computing overhead rates and in product costing.

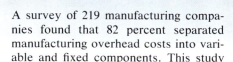

FOCUS ON CURRENT PRACTICE

A survey of 219 manufacturing companies found that 82 percent separated manufacturing overhead costs into variable and fixed components. This study included manufacturing companies listed on the New York and American Stock Exchanges, as well as smaller companies whose stock is sold over the counter.[1]

Activity-Based Costing and the Flexible Budget

If a company has an activity-based costing system in use, does it have any need for a flexible budget? The answer is an emphatic yes. In fact, the use of flexible budgeting actually enhances a company's ability to construct and operate an activity-based costing system. The key difference between a company that employs activity-based costing and one that employs a more traditional costing system lies in the *number* of flexible budgets that are used.

We learned in Chapter 5 that when a company employs activity-based costing, it identifies various activity centers associated with the manufacture of its products and then traces its overhead costs to these centers. In Exhibit 5–14 on page 198, for example, we identified eight activity centers for the company involved, and in Exhibit 5–15 on page 201 we showed the amount of overhead cost traceable to each. If the company in these exhibits uses flexible budgeting, it will construct a flexible budget *for each activity center*. Thus, rather than having a single flexible budget for the entire company, it will have *eight* flexible budgets. The flexible budget for each activity center will be geared to the activity measure (cost driver) that controls the incurrence of overhead cost in that center. The concept of multiple flexible budgets is illustrated in Exhibit 11–9.

Objective 5
Explain how flexible budgets are used in a company that employs activity-based costing.

---

[1] William P. Cress and James B. Pettijohn, "A Survey of Budget-Related Planning and Control Policies and Procedures," *Journal of Accounting Education* 3, no. 2 (Fall 1985), p. 73.

EXHIBIT 11–9
Multiple-Flexible
Budgets and
Activity-Based Costing

Flexible Budget
Activity Center—Machine Setups

Cost Driver: Setups Completed

Overhead Costs	Cost Formula (per setup)	Number of Setups			
		1,500	2,000	2,500	3,000
Variable costs: (detailed)	$80	$120,000	$160,000	$200,000	$240,000
Fixed costs: (detailed)		70,000	70,000	70,000	70,000
Total overhead costs		$190,000	$230,000	$270,000	$310,000

Flexible Budget
Activity Center—Production Orders

Cost Driver: Orders Issued

Overhead Costs	Cost Formula (per order)	Number of Orders			
		400	500	600	700
Variable costs: (detailed)	$130	$ 52,000	$ 65,000	$ 78,000	$ 91,000
Fixed costs: (detailed)		9,000	9,000	9,000	9,000
Total overhead costs.		$ 61,000	$ 74,000	$ 87,000	$100,000

Flexible Budget
Activity Center—Material Receipts

Cost Driver: Deliveries Received

Overhead Costs	Cost Formula (per delivery)	Number of Deliveries			
		2,000	3,000	4,000	5,000
Variable costs: (detailed)	$40	$ 80,000	$120,000	$160,000	$200,000
Fixed costs: (detailed)		30,000	30,000	30,000	30,000
Total overhead costs		$110,000	$150,000	$190,000	$230,000

FOCUS ON CURRENT PRACTICE

Caterpillar, Inc., a manufacturer of heavy equipment and a pioneering company in the development and use of activity-based costing, divides its overhead costs into three large pools—the logistics cost pool, the manufacturing cost pool, and the general cost pool. In turn, these three cost pools are subdivided into scores of activity centers, with each center having its own flexible budget from which variable and fixed overhead rates are developed. In an article describing the company's cost system, the systems manager stated that "the many manufacturing cost center rates are the unique elements that set Caterpillar's system apart from simple cost systems."[2]

---

[2] Lou F. Jones, "Product Costing at Caterpillar," *Management Accounting* 72, no. 8 (February 1991), p. 39.

In sum, the concept of a flexible budget is not unique to a company that uses a single, plantwide overhead rate to cost its products. Flexible budgets can be (and are) used to develop multiple overhead rates in a company, with the company having as many flexible budgets and overhead rates as it has activity centers.

The use of multiple flexible budgets actually enhances the accuracy of a company's costing system. This is because multiple budgets provide a closer correlation between overhead costs and the base on which these costs are applied to products. In addition to more accurate costing, multiple budgets also result in more usable variance data, since the costs on which the variances are computed relate to a single activity center.[3]

OVERHEAD RATES AND FIXED OVERHEAD ANALYSIS

The analysis of fixed overhead differs considerably from the analysis of variable overhead, simply because of the difference in the nature of the costs involved. To provide a background for our discussion, we will first review briefly the need for, and computation of, predetermined overhead rates. This review will be helpful, since the predetermined overhead rate plays a role in fixed overhead analysis. We will then show how fixed overhead variances are computed and make some observations as to their usefulness to the manager.

Flexible Budgets and Overhead Rates

Fixed costs come in large, indivisible pieces that by definition do not change with changes in the level of activity. As we learned in Chapter 3, this creates a problem in product costing, since a given level of fixed overhead cost spread over a small number of units will result in a higher cost per unit than if the same amount of cost is spread over a large number of units. Consider the data in the table below:

Objective 6
Explain the significance of the denominator activity figure in determining the standard cost of a unit of product.

Month	(1) Fixed Overhead Cost	(2) Number of Units Produced	(3) Unit Cost (1) ÷ (2)
January.	$6,000	1,000	$6.00
February	6,000	1,500	4.00
March	6,000	800	7.50

Notice that the large number of units produced in February results in a low unit cost ($4), whereas the small number of units produced in March results in a high unit cost ($7.50). This problem arises only in connection with the fixed portion of overhead, since by definition the variable portion of overhead remains constant on a per unit basis, rising and falling in total proportionately with changes in the activity level. For product costing purposes, managers need to stabilize the fixed portion of unit cost so that a single unit cost figure can be used throughout the year without regard to month-by-month changes in activity levels. As we learned in Chapter 3, this stability can be accomplished through use of the predetermined overhead rate.

---

[3] For further discussion of these points, see Robert E. Malcom, "Overhead Control Implications of Activity Costing," *Accounting Horizons* 5, no. 4 (December 1991), pp. 69–77. This is an excellent paper that raises several stimulating questions regarding traditional variance analysis.

Denominator Activity   The formula that we used in Chapter 3 to compute the predetermined overhead rate is given below, with one added feature. We have titled the estimated activity portion of the formula as being the **denominator activity:**

$$\frac{\text{Estimated total manufacturing overhead costs}}{\substack{\text{Estimated total units in the base (MH, DLH, etc.)} \\ \text{(denominator activity)}}} = \substack{\text{Predetermined} \\ \text{overhead rate}}$$

Recall from our discussion in Chapter 3 that once an estimated activity level (denominator activity) has been chosen, it remains unchanged throughout the year, even if actual activity later proves the estimate (denominator) to be somewhat in error. The reason for not changing the denominator, of course, is to maintain stability in the amount of overhead applied to each unit of product regardless of when it is produced during the year.

Computing the Overhead Rate   When we discussed predetermined overhead rates in Chapter 3, we did so without elaboration as to the source of the estimated data going into the formula. These data are normally derived from the flexible budget. To illustrate, refer to Donner Company's flexible budget in Exhibit 11–8. Notice that the budgeted activity level for 19x1 is 50,000 machine-hours. These 50,000 hours *become the denominator activity in the formula,* with the overhead cost (variable and fixed) at this activity level becoming the estimated overhead cost in the formula ($375,000 from Exhibit 11–8). In sum, the 19x1 predetermined overhead rate for Donner Company will be:

$$\frac{\$375,000}{50,000 \text{ MH}} = \$7.50 \text{ per machine-hour}$$

Or the company can break its predetermined overhead rate down into variable and fixed elements rather than using a single combined figure:

$$\text{Variable element: } \frac{\$75,000}{50,000 \text{ MH}} = \$1.50 \text{ per machine-hour}$$

$$\text{Fixed element: } \frac{\$300,000}{50,000 \text{ MH}} = \$6 \text{ per machine-hour}$$

For every standard machine-hour of operation, work in process will be charged with $7.50 of overhead, of which $1.50 will be variable overhead and $6 will be fixed overhead. If a unit of product takes two machine-hours to complete, then its cost will include $3 variable overhead and $12 fixed overhead, as shown on the following standard cost card:

Standard Cost Card—Per Unit

Direct materials (assumed).	$14
Direct labor (assumed)	6
Variable overhead (2 machine-hours at $1.50) . . .	3
Fixed overhead (2 machine-hours at $6).	12
Total standard cost per unit	$35

In sum, the flexible budget provides the manager with both the overhead cost figure and the denominator activity figure needed to compute the predetermined overhead rate. Thus, the flexible budget plays a key role in determining the amount of fixed and variable overhead cost that will be charged to units of product.

Overhead Application in a Standard Cost System

To understand the fixed overhead variances, it is necessary first to understand how overhead is applied to work in process in a standard cost system. In Chapter 3, recall that we applied overhead to work in process on a basis of actual hours of activity (multiplied by the predetermined overhead rate). This procedure was correct, since at the time we were dealing with a normal cost system.[4] However, we are now dealing with a standard cost system; and when standards are in operation, overhead is applied to work in process on a basis of the *standard hours allowed for the output of the period* rather than on a basis of the actual number of hours worked. This point is illustrated in Exhibit 11–10.

The reason for using standard hours to apply overhead to production in a standard cost system is to assure that every unit of product moving along the production line bears the same amount of overhead cost, regardless of any variations in efficiency that may be involved in its manufacture.

Objective 7
Properly apply overhead cost to units of product in a standard cost system.

The Fixed Overhead Variances

To illustrate the computation of fixed overhead variances, we will refer again to the flexible budget data for Donner Company contained in Exhibit 11–8.

Objective 8
Compute and properly interpret the fixed overhead budget and volume variances.

Denominator activity in machine-hours	50,000
Budgeted fixed overhead costs	$300,000
Fixed portion of the predetermined overhead rate (computed earlier)	$6

Let us assume that the following actual operating results were recorded for the year:

Actual machine-hours	42,000
Standard machine-hours allowed*	40,000
Actual fixed overhead costs:	
Depreciation	$100,000
Supervisory salaries	172,000
Insurance	36,000
Total actual costs	$308,000

* For the actual production of the year.

From these data, two variances can be computed for fixed overhead—a *budget variance* and a *volume variance*. The variances are shown in Exhibit 11–11.

Normal Cost System		**Standard Cost System**	
Manufacturing Overhead		**Manufacturing Overhead**	
Actual overhead costs incurred.	Applied overhead costs: Actual hours × Predetermined overhead rate.	Actual overhead costs incurred.	Applied overhead costs: Standard hours allowed for output × Predetermined overhead rate.
Under- or overapplied overhead		Under- or overapplied overhead	

EXHIBIT 11–10
Applied Overhead Costs: Normal Cost System versus Standard Cost System

---

[4] Normal cost systems are discussed on page 78 in Chapter 3.

EXHIBIT 11–11
Computation of the
Fixed Overhead
Variances

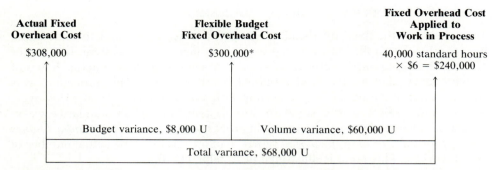

Actual Fixed Overhead Cost	Flexible Budget Fixed Overhead Cost	Fixed Overhead Cost Applied to Work in Process
$308,000	$300,000*	40,000 standard hours × $6 = $240,000

Budget variance, $8,000 U   Volume variance, $60,000 U

Total variance, $68,000 U

* As originally budgeted (see Exhibit 11–8). This figure can also be expressed as 50,000 denominator hours × $6 = $300,000.

Notice from the exhibit that overhead has been applied to work in process on a basis of 40,000 standard hours allowed for the output of the year rather than on a basis of 42,000 actual hours worked. As stated earlier, this keeps unit costs from being affected by any efficiency variations.

The Budget Variance—A Closer Look

The **budget variance** represents the difference between actual fixed overhead costs incurred during the period and budgeted fixed overhead costs as contained in the flexible budget. The variance can also be presented in the following format:

Actual fixed overhead costs	$308,000
Budgeted fixed overhead costs (from the flexible budget in Exhibit 11–8)	300,000
Budget variance	$ 8,000 U

Although the budget variance is somewhat similar to the variable overhead spending variance, care must be exercised in how it is used. One must keep in mind that fixed costs are often beyond immediate managerial control. Therefore, rather than serving as a measure of managerial performance, in many cases the budget variance will be computed simply for information purposes in order to call management's attention to changes in price factors.

Fixed overhead costs and variances are often presented on the overhead performance report, along with the variable overhead costs. To show how this is done, an overhead performance report for Donner Company containing the fixed overhead budget variance is found in Exhibit 11–12. (The variable overhead cost data in the exhibit are taken from Exhibit 11–6.)

The Volume Variance—A Closer Look

The **volume variance** is a measure of utilization of plant facilities. The variance arises whenever the standard hours allowed for the output of a period are different from the denominator activity level that was planned when the period began. It can be computed as shown in Exhibit 11–11 or by means of the formula below:

$$\begin{pmatrix} \text{Fixed portion of} \\ \text{the predetermined} \\ \text{overhead rate} \end{pmatrix} \times \left(\begin{array}{c} \text{Denominator} \\ \text{hours} \end{array} - \begin{array}{c} \text{Standard hours} \\ \text{allowed} \end{array} \right) = \begin{array}{c} \text{Volume} \\ \text{variance} \end{array}$$

EXHIBIT 11–12

Fixed Overhead Costs
on the Overhead
Performance Report

DONNER COMPANY
Overhead Performance Report
For the Year Ended March 31, 19x1

Budgeted machine-hours.   50,000
Actual machine-hours   42,000
Standard machine-hours allowed . . .   40,000

Overhead Costs	Cost Formula (per hour)	Actual Costs 42,000 Hours	Budget Based on 42,000 Hours	Spending or Budget Variance
Variable costs:				
Indirect labor	$0.80	$ 36,000	$ 33,600	$ 2,400 U
Lubricants.	0.30	11,000	12,600	1,600 F
Power.	0.40	24,000	16,800	7,200 U
Total variable costs.	$1.50	71,000	63,000	8,000 U
Fixed costs:				
Depreciation		100,000	100,000	—
Supervisory salaries		172,000	160,000	12,000 U
Insurance		36,000	40,000	4,000 F
Total fixed costs		308,000	300,000	8,000 U
Total overhead costs		$379,000	$363,000	$16,000 U

Applying this formula to Donner Company, the volume variance would be:

$$\$6 \ (50{,}000 \ MH - 40{,}000 \ MH) = \$60{,}000 \ \text{unfavorable}$$

Note that this computation agrees with the volume variance as shown in Exhibit 11–11. As stated earlier, the volume variance is a measure of utilization of available plant facilities. An unfavorable variance, as above, means that the company operated at an activity level *below* that planned for the period. A favorable variance would mean that the company operated at an activity level *greater* than that planned for the period.

It is important to note that the volume variance does not measure over- or underspending. A company normally would incur the same dollar amount of fixed overhead cost regardless of whether the period's activity was above or below the planned (denominator) level. In short, the volume variance is an activity-related variance in that it is explainable only by activity and is controllable only through activity.

To summarize:

1. If the denominator activity and the standard hours allowed for the output of the period are the same, then there is no volume variance.
2. If the denominator activity is greater than the standard hours allowed for the output of the period, then the volume variance is unfavorable, signifying an underutilization of available facilities.
3. If the denominator activity is less than the standard hours allowed for the output of the period, then the volume variance is favorable, signifying an overutilization of available facilities.

Graphic Analysis of Fixed Overhead Variances

Some insights into the budget and volume variances can be gained through graphic analysis. A graph containing these variances is presented in Exhibit 11–13.

EXHIBIT 11–13

**Graphic Analysis of
Fixed Overhead Variances**

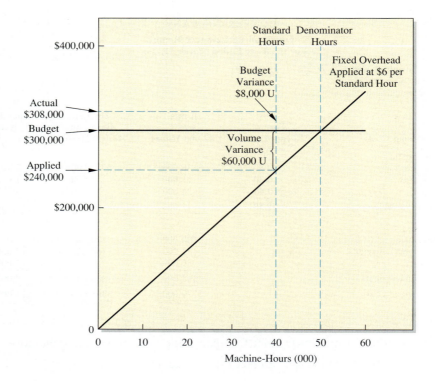

As shown in the graph, fixed overhead cost is applied to work in process at the predetermined rate of $6 for each standard hour of activity. (The applied-cost line is the upward-sloping line on the graph.) Since a denominator level of 50,000 machine-hours was used in computing the $6 rate, the applied-cost line crosses the budget-cost line at exactly the 50,000 machine-hour point. Thus, if the denominator hours and the standard hours allowed for output are the same, there can be no volume variance, since the applied-cost line and the budget-cost line will exactly meet on the graph. It is only when the standard hours differ from the denominator hours that a volume variance can arise.

In the case at hand, the standard hours allowed for output (40,000 hours) are less than the denominator hours (50,000 hours); the result is an unfavorable volume variance, since less cost was applied to production than was originally budgeted. If the tables had been reversed and the standard hours allowed for output had exceeded the denominator hours, then the volume variance on the graph would have been favorable.

Cautions in Fixed Overhead Analysis

There can be no volume variance for variable overhead, since applied costs and budgeted costs are both dependent on activity and thus will always be moving together. The reason we get a volume variance for fixed overhead is that the incurrence of the fixed costs does not depend on activity; yet when applying the costs to work in process, we do so *as if* the costs were variable and depended on activity. This point can be seen from the graph in Exhibit 11–13. Notice from the graph that the fixed overhead costs are applied to work in process at a rate of $6 per hour *as if* they were indeed variable. Treating these costs as if they were variable is necessary for product costing purposes, but there are some real dangers here. The manager can easily become misled and start thinking of the fixed costs as if they were *in fact* variable.

The manager must keep clearly in mind that fixed overhead costs come in large, indivisible pieces. Any breakdown of such costs on a unit basis, though necessary for product costing purposes, is artificial in nature and has no significance in matters relating either to actual cost behavior or to cost control. This is why the volume variance, which arises as a result of treating fixed costs as if they were variable, is not a controllable variance from a spending point of view. The fixed overhead rate used to compute the variance is simply a derived figure needed for product costing purposes, but it has no significance in terms of cost control.

Because of these factors, some companies present the volume variance in physical units (hours) rather than in dollars. These companies feel that stating the variance in physical units gives management a clearer signal as to the cause of the variance and how it can be controlled.

Overhead Variances and Under- or Overapplied Overhead Cost

Four variances relating to overhead cost have been computed for Donner Company in this chapter. These four variances are as follows:

Variable overhead spending variance (p. 487)	$ 8,000 U
Variable overhead efficiency variance (p. 487)	3,000 U
Fixed overhead budget variance (p. 494).	8,000 U
Fixed overhead volume variance (p. 494)	60,000 U
Total overhead variance	$79,000 U

The total of these four variances *will represent a company's under- or overapplied overhead cost for a period*. Thus, for Donner Company, overhead cost was underapplied by $79,000 for the year (unfavorable variances denote underapplied overhead and favorable variances denote overapplied overhead). To solidify this point in your mind, *carefully study the review problem at the end of the chapter!* This review problem provides a comprehensive summary of all aspects of overhead analysis, including the computation of under- or overapplied overhead cost in a standard cost system.

PRESENTATION OF VARIANCES ON THE INCOME STATEMENT

To complete our discussion of standard costs and variance analysis, we will show how variances can be presented on the income statement. Even though the variances may have already been presented on individual managers' performance reports and fully analyzed as to causes, many companies find it helpful to present them on the income statement as well, so that top management can see the cumulative effect on profits.

Objective 9
Show how variances can be presented on the income statement for management's use.

To illustrate, assume that Donner Company had the following variances for the most recent month. (The variances for materials and labor are assumed; the variances for variable and fixed overhead are the ones computed for Donner Company on preceding pages.)

EXHIBIT 11–14
Variances on the
Income Statement

DONNER COMPANY
Income Statement
For the Year Ended March 31, 19x1

20,000 Units

	Actual	Budgeted	Variance
Sales ($50 per unit)	$1,000,000	$1,000,000	$ —
Less cost of goods sold (standard cost, $35 per unit*).	790,000	700,000	90,000 U
Gross margin	210,000	300,000	90,000 U
Less operating expenses:			
Selling expense	105,000	105,000	—
Administrative expense	65,000	65,000	—
Total operating expenses.	170,000	170,000	—
Net income.	$ 40,000	$ 130,000	$90,000 U

* The $35 standard cost is taken from Donner Company's standard cost card found on page 492.

Direct materials price variance	$ 5,000 F
Direct materials quantity variance.	19,000 U
Direct labor rate variance	7,000 U
Direct labor efficiency variance	10,000 F
Variable overhead spending variance (p. 487). . . .	8,000 U
Variable overhead efficiency variance (p. 487) . . .	3,000 U
Fixed overhead budget variance (p. 494)	8,000 U
Fixed overhead volume variance (p. 494)	60,000 U
Total variances	$90,000 U

An income statement for Donner Company containing the total of these variances is presented in Exhibit 11–14. Note that the actual cost of goods sold on the statement exceeds the budgeted amount by $90,000, which agrees with the total of the variances summarized above. This type of presentation provides management with a clear picture of the impact of the variances on profits—a picture that could not be obtained by looking at performance reports alone. In the case at hand, Donner Company's profits have been dramatically reduced by the variances that developed during the period.

We should note that separate presentation of variances on the income statement is generally done only on those income statements that are prepared for management's own internal use. Income statements prepared for external use (for stockholders and others) typically show only actual cost figures.

REVIEW PROBLEM: OVERHEAD ANALYSIS

(This problem provides a comprehensive review of all parts of Chapter 11, including the computation of under- or overapplied overhead and its breakdown into the four overhead variances.)

A flexible budget for Aspen Company is given below:

	Cost Formula (per hour)	Machine-Hours		
Overhead Costs		4,000	6,000	8,000
Variable costs:				
Supplies	$0.20	$ 800	$ 1,200	$ 1,600
Indirect labor	0.30	1,200	1,800	2,400
Total variable costs	$0.50	2,000	3,000	4,000

Overhead Costs	Cost Formula (per hour)	Machine-Hours		
		4,000	6,000	8,000
Fixed costs:				
Depreciation		4,000	4,000	4,000
Supervision.		5,000	5,000	5,000
Total fixed costs		9,000	9,000	9,000
Total overhead costs		$11,000	$12,000	$13,000

Five hours of machine time are required per unit of product. The company has set denominator activity for the coming period at 6,000 hours (or 1,200 units). The computation of the predetermined overhead rate would be:

$$\text{Total: } \frac{\$12,000}{6,000 \text{ MH}} = \$2 \text{ per MH}$$

$$\text{Variable element: } \frac{\$3,000}{6,000 \text{ MH}} = \$0.50 \text{ per MH}$$

$$\text{Fixed element: } \frac{\$9,000}{6,000 \text{ MH}} = \$1.50 \text{ per MH}$$

Assume the following *actual* results for the period:

Number of units produced	1,300
Actual machine-hours.	6,800
Standard machine-hours allowed* . . .	6,500
Actual variable overhead cost	$4,200
Actual fixed overhead cost	9,400

* For 1,300 units of product.

Therefore, the company's Manufacturing Overhead account would appear as follows at the end of the period:

Manufacturing Overhead

Actual overhead costs	13,600*	13,000†	Applied overhead costs
Underapplied overhead	600		

* $4,200 variable + $9,400 fixed = $13,600.
† 6,500 standard hours × $2 = $13,000.

Analyze the $600 underapplied overhead in terms of: *Required*

1. A variable overhead spending variance.
2. A variable overhead efficiency variance.
3. A fixed overhead budget variance.
4. A fixed overhead volume variance.

Variable Overhead Variances

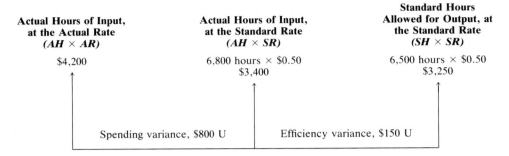

Actual Hours of Input, at the Actual Rate $(AH \times AR)$	Actual Hours of Input, at the Standard Rate $(AH \times SR)$	Standard Hours Allowed for Output, at the Standard Rate $(SH \times SR)$
$4,200	6,800 hours × $0.50 $3,400	6,500 hours × $0.50 $3,250

Spending variance, $800 U   Efficiency variance, $150 U

These same variances in the alternative format would be:

Variable overhead spending variance:

```
Actual variable overhead cost  . . . . .   $4,200
Actual inputs at the standard rate:
    6,800 hours × $0.50. . . . . . . .      3,400
Spending variance  . . . . . . . . .     $  800 U
```

Variable overhead efficiency variance:

$$SR(AH - SH) = \text{Efficiency variance}$$

$$\$0.50(6,800 \text{ hours} - 6,500 \text{ hours}) = \$150 \text{ U}$$

Fixed Overhead Variances

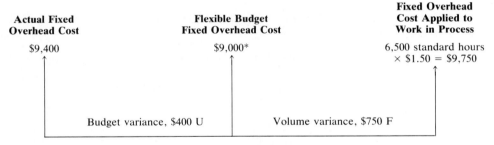

Actual Fixed Overhead Cost	Flexible Budget Fixed Overhead Cost	Fixed Overhead Cost Applied to Work in Process
$9,400	$9,000*	6,500 standard hours × $1.50 = $9,750

Budget variance, $400 U   Volume variance, $750 F

* Can be expressed as: 6,000 denominator hours × $1.50 = $9,000.

These same variances in the alternative format would be:

Fixed overhead budget variance:

```
Actual fixed overhead  . . . . .   $9,400
Budgeted fixed overhead  . . . .    9,000
Budget variance . . . . . . .    $  400 U
```

Fixed overhead volume variance:

$$\text{Fixed portion of the predetermined overhead rate} \times \left(\text{Denominator hours} - \text{Standard hours} \right) = \text{Volume variance}$$

$$\$1.50 \ (6,000 \text{ hours} - 6,500 \text{ hours}) = \$750 \text{ F}$$

Summary of Variances

A summary of the four overhead variances is given below:

Variable overhead:	
Spending variance	$800 U
Efficiency variance	150 U
Fixed overhead:	
Budget variance	400 U
Volume variance	750 F
Underapplied overhead	$600

Notice that the $600 summary variance figure agrees with the underapplied balance in the company's Manufacturing Overhead account. This agreement verifies the accuracy of our variance analysis. *Each period* the under- or overapplied overhead balance should be analyzed as we have done above. These variances will help the manager to see where his or her time and the time of subordinates should be directed for better control of costs and operations.

KEY TERMS FOR REVIEW

Budget variance   A measure of the difference between the actual fixed overhead costs incurred during the period and budgeted fixed overhead costs as contained in the flexible budget. (p. 494)

Denominator activity   The estimated activity figure used to compute the predetermined overhead rate. (p. 492)

Flexible budget   A budget that is designed to cover a range of activity and that can be used to develop budgeted costs at any point within that range to compare against actual costs incurred. (p. 480)

Static budget   A budget designed to cover only one level of activity and in which actual costs are always compared against budgeted costs at this one activity level. (p. 480)

Volume variance   A measure of utilization of plant facilities. The variance arises whenever the standard hours allowed for the output of a period are different from the denominator activity level that was planned when the period began. (p. 494)

Objective 10
Define or explain the key terms listed at the end of the chapter.

QUESTIONS

11–1   What is a static budget?

11–2   What is a flexible budget, and how does it differ from a static budget? What is the main deficiency of the static budget?

11–3   What are the two prime responsibilities of the production manager? How do these two responsibilities differ?

11–4   Name three criteria that should be considered in choosing an activity base on which to construct a flexible budget.

11–5   In comparing budgeted data with actual data in a performance report for variable manufacturing overhead, what variance(s) will be produced if the budgeted data are based on actual hours worked? On both actual hours worked and standard hours allowed?

11–6   What is meant by the term *standard hours allowed?*

11–7   How does the variable manufacturing overhead spending variance differ from the materials price variance?

11–8   Why is the term *overhead efficiency variance* a misnomer?

11-9   "Fixed costs have no place in a flexible budget." Discuss.

11-10   In what way is the flexible budget involved in product costing?

11-11   What costing problem is created by the fact that fixed overhead costs come in large, indivisible chunks?

11-12   What is meant by the term *denominator level of activity?*

11-13   Why do we apply overhead to work in process on a basis of standard hours allowed in Chapter 11, when we applied it on a basis of actual hours in Chapter 3? What is the difference in costing systems between the two chapters?

11-14   In a standard cost system, what two variances can be computed for fixed overhead?

11-15   What does the fixed overhead budget variance measure? Is the variance controllable by management? Explain.

11-16   Under what circumstances would you expect the volume variance to be favorable? Unfavorable? Does the variance measure deviations in spending for fixed overhead items? Explain.

11-17   How might the volume variance be measured, other than in dollars?

11-18   What dangers are there in expressing fixed costs on a per unit basis?

11-19   In Chapter 3, you became acquainted with the concept of under- or overapplied overhead. What four variances can be computed from the under- or overapplied overhead total?

11-20   If factory overhead is overapplied for August, would you expect the total of the overhead variances to be favorable or unfavorable? Why?

EXERCISES

E11-1   An incomplete flexible budget is given below:

Overhead Costs	Cost Formula (per hour)	Machine-Hours 10,000	15,000	20,000	25,000
Variable costs:					
Indirect materials			$ 9,000			
Maintenance			36,000			
Utilities			15,000			
Total variable costs						
Fixed costs:					
Supervisory salaries			180,000			
Rent			30,000			
Insurance.			20,000			
Total fixed costs.						
Total overhead costs.						

Required   Provide the missing information in the budget.

E11-2   The cost formulas for Emory Company's overhead costs are given below. These cost formulas cover a relevant range of 15,000 to 25,000 machine-hours each year.

Cost	Cost Formula
Utilities	$0.30 per machine-hour
Indirect labor	$52,000 plus $1.40 per machine-hour
Supplies	$0.20 per machine-hour
Maintenance.	$18,000 plus $0.10 per machine-hour
Depreciation.	$90,000

Required   Prepare a flexible budget in increments of 5,000 machine-hours. Include all costs in your budget.

The variable portion of Murray Company's flexible budget is given below:

Variable Overhead Costs	Cost Formula (per hour)	Machine-Hours 10,000	Machine-Hours 12,000	Machine-Hours 14,000
Supplies	$0.20	$ 2,000	$ 2,400	$ 2,800
Maintenance.	0.80	8,000	9,600	11,200
Utilities	0.10	1,000	1,200	1,400
Rework time	0.40	4,000	4,800	5,600
Total variable costs	$1.50	$15,000	$18,000	$21,000

During a recent period, the company recorded 11,500 machine-hours of activity. The variable overhead costs incurred were:

Supplies	$2,400
Maintenance	8,000
Utilities	1,100
Rework time	5,300

The budgeted activity for the period had been 12,000 machine-hours.

1. Prepare a variable overhead performance report for the period. Indicate whether variances are favorable (F) or unfavorable (U). Show only a spending variance on your report.
2. Discuss the significance of the variances. Might some variances be the result of others? Explain.

Required

Operating at a normal level of 30,000 direct labor-hours, Lasser Company produces 10,000 units of product each period. The direct labor wage rate is $6 per hour. Two and one-half yards of direct materials go into each unit of product; the material costs $8.60 per yard. The flexible budget used to plan and control overhead costs is given below (in condensed form):

Flexible Budget Data

	Cost Formula (per hour)	Direct Labor-Hours 20,000	Direct Labor-Hours 30,000	Direct Labor-Hours 40,000
Variable costs	$1.90	$ 38,000	$ 57,000	$ 76,000
Fixed costs.		168,000	168,000	168,000
Total overhead costs		$206,000	$225,000	$244,000

1. Using 30,000 direct labor-hours as the denominator activity, compute the predetermined overhead rate and break it down into variable and fixed elements.
2. Complete the standard cost card below for one unit of product:

Required

Direct materials, 2.5 yards at $8.60 . . .	$21.50
Direct labor,	?	?
Variable overhead, ?	. . . .	?
Fixed overhead,	?	?
Total standard cost per unit	$?

Marchant Company's flexible budget (in condensed form) is given below:

Overhead Costs	Cost Formula (per hour)	Machine-Hours 10,000	Machine-Hours 15,000	Machine-Hours 20,000
Variable costs	$2.40	$ 24,000	$ 36,000	$ 48,000
Fixed costs.		90,000	90,000	90,000
Total overhead costs		$114,000	$126,000	$138,000

The following information is available for 19x5:

a. For 19x5, the company chose 15,000 machine-hours as the denominator activity level for computing the predetermined overhead rate.

b. During 19x5, the company produced 7,250 units of product and worked 14,600 actual hours. The standard machine time is two hours per unit.

c. Actual overhead costs incurred during 19x5 were: variable overhead, $34,800; and fixed overhead, $90,650.

Required

1. Compute the predetermined overhead rate used during 19x5. Divide it into fixed and variable elements.

2. Compute the standard hours allowed for the output of 19x5.

3. Compute the fixed overhead budget and volume variances for 19x5.

E11–6 Selected operating information on four different companies for the year 19x6 is given below:

	Company			
	A	**B**	**C**	**D**
Full-capacity machine-hours	10,000	18,000	20,000	15,000
Budgeted machine-hours*	9,000	17,000	20,000	14,000
Actual machine-hours	9,000	17,800	19,000	14,500
Standard machine-hours allowed for actual production	9,500	16,000	20,000	13,000

* Denominator activity.

Required In each case, state whether the company would have:

1. No volume variance.

2. A favorable volume variance.

3. An unfavorable volume variance.

Also state in each case why you chose (1), (2), or (3).

E11–7 Norwall Company's flexible budget (in condensed form) is given below:

	Cost Formula	Machine-Hours		
Overhead Costs	**(per hour)**	**50,000**	**60,000**	**70,000**
Variable costs	$3	$150,000	$180,000	$210,000
Fixed costs		300,000	300,000	300,000
Total overhead costs		$450,000	$480,000	$510,000

The following information is available:

a. For 19x3, a denominator activity figure of 60,000 machine-hours was chosen to compute the predetermined overhead rate.

b. At the 60,000 standard machine-hours level of activity, the company should produce 40,000 units of product.

c. During 19x3, the company's actual operating results were:

Number of units produced	42,000
Actual machine-hours	64,000
Actual variable overhead costs	$185,600
Actual fixed overhead costs.	302,400

Required

1. Compute the predetermined overhead rate for 19x3, and break it down into variable and fixed cost elements.

2. Compute the standard hours allowed for 19x3's production.

3. Compute the variable overhead spending and efficiency variances and the fixed overhead budget and volume variances for 19x3.

Selected information relating to Yost Company's operations for 19x6 is given below: **E11–8**

Activity:
Denominator activity (machine-hours). . .   45,000
Standard hours allowed per unit   3
Number of units produced   14,000

Costs:
Actual fixed overhead costs incurred . . . $267,000
Fixed overhead budget variance . . . . .   3,000 F

The company applies overhead cost to products on a basis of machine-hours.

1. What were the standard hours allowed for 19x6 production? *Required*
2. What was the fixed portion of the predetermined overhead rate for 19x6?
3. What was the volume variance for 19x6?

The standard cost card for the single product manufactured by Cutter, Inc., is given below: **E11–9**

Standard Cost Card—per Unit

Direct materials, 3 yards at $6 . . . . $18
Direct labor, 4 hours at $7.75   31
Variable overhead, 4 hours at $1.50   6
Fixed overhead, 4 hours at $5.   20
Total standard cost per unit. $75

Overhead is applied to production on a basis of direct labor-hours. During 19x4, the company worked 37,000 hours and manufactured 9,500 units of product. Selected data relating to the company's operations for the year are shown below:

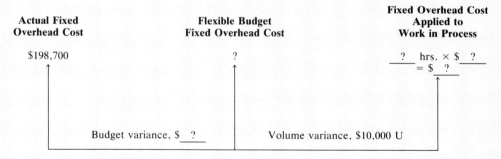

Actual Fixed Overhead Cost	Flexible Budget Fixed Overhead Cost	Fixed Overhead Cost Applied to Work in Process
$198,700	?	? hrs. × $? = $?

Budget variance, $?   Volume variance, $10,000 U

1. What were the standard hours allowed for 19x4 production? *Required*
2. What was the amount of fixed overhead cost contained in the flexible budget for the year?
3. What was the fixed overhead budget variance for the year?
4. What denominator activity level did the company use in setting the predetermined overhead rate for the year?

PROBLEMS

Tom Savin has recently been hired as a cost accountant by the Offset Press Company, a privately held company that produces a line of offset printing presses and lithograph machines. During his first few months on the job, Savin discovered that Offset has been underapplying factory overhead to the Work in Process account, while overstating expense through the General and Administrative account. This practice has been going on since the **P11–10 Ethics and the Manager**

start of the company, which is in its sixth year of operation. The effect in each year has been favorable in that the company's taxable income has been reduced, thus significantly decreasing its income tax liability. No internal audit function exists at Offset, and the external auditors have not yet discovered the underapplied factory overhead.

Prior to the sixth year audit, Savin had pointed out the practice and its effect to Mary Brown, the corporate controller, and had asked her to let him make the necessary adjustments. Brown directed him not to make the adjustments but to wait until the external auditors had completed their work and see what they uncovered.

The sixth year audit has now been completed, and the external auditors have once more failed to discover the underapplication of factory overhead. Savin again asked Brown if he could make the required adjustments and was again told not to make them. Savin, however, believes that the adjustments should be made and that the external auditors should be informed of the situation.

Since there are no established policies at Offset Press Company for resolving ethical conflicts, Savin is considering following one of the three alternative courses of action listed below.

1. Follow Brown's directive and do nothing further.
2. Attempt to convince Brown to make the proper adjustments and to advise the external auditors of her actions.
3. Tell the audit committee of the board of directors about the problem and give them the appropriate accounting data.

Required
1. For each of the three alternative courses of action that Tom Savin is considering, explain whether or not the action is appropriate. In preparing your answer, refer to specific standards contained in the Standards of Ethical Conduct for Management Accountants found on page 23.
2. Without prejudice to your answer in (1) above, assume that Tom Savin again approaches Mary Brown to make the necessary adjustments and that she again refuses to do so. Describe the steps that Tom Savin should take in proceeding to resolve this situation. Again use the Standards document on page 23 to prepare your answer.

(CMA, adapted)

P11-11   Standard Cost Card; Materials, Labor, and All Overhead Variances   Flandro Company uses a standard cost system and sets predetermined overhead rates on a basis of direct labor-hours. The following data are taken from the company's flexible budget for 19x1:

Denominator activity (direct labor-hours) . . .	10,000
Variable overhead cost	$25,000
Fixed overhead cost	59,000

A standard cost card showing the standard cost to produce one unit of the company's product is given below:

Direct materials, 3 yards at $4.40	$13.20
Direct labor, 2 hours at $6	12.00
Overhead, 140% of direct labor cost	16.80
Standard cost per unit	$42.00

During 19x1, the company produced 6,000 units of product and incurred the following costs:

Materials purchased, 24,000 yards at $4.80.	$115,200
Materials used in production (in yards)	18,500
Direct labor cost incurred, 11,600 hours at $6.50	$ 75,400
Variable overhead cost incurred	29,580
Fixed overhead cost incurred	60,400

1. Redo the standard cost card in a clearer, more usable format by detailing the variable
   and fixed overhead cost elements.
2. Prepare an analysis of the variances for materials and labor for the year.
3. Prepare an analysis of the variances for variable and fixed overhead for the year.
4. What effect, if any, does the choice of a denominator activity level have on unit costs?
   Is the volume variance a controllable variance from a spending point of view? Explain.

Basic Overhead Analysis   Baxter Company manufactures a single product and uses a
standard cost system to help in the control of costs. Overhead is applied to production on a
basis of machine-hours. According to the company's flexible budget, the following overhead costs should be incurred at an activity level of 35,000 machine-hours (the denominator activity level chosen for 19x3):

P11–12

Variable overhead costs	$ 87,500
Fixed overhead costs	210,000
Total overhead costs	$297,500

During 19x3, the following operating results were recorded:

Activity:
Actual machine-hours worked	30,000
Standard machine-hours allowed for output	32,000

Cost:
Actual variable overhead cost incurred	$ 78,000
Actual fixed overhead cost incurred	209,400

At the end of the year, the company's Manufacturing Overhead account contained the
following data:

Manufacturing Overhead

Actual	287,400	Applied	272,000
	15,400		

Management would like to determine the cause of the $15,400 underapplied overhead
before closing the amount to cost of goods sold.

1. Compute the predetermined overhead rate that would have been used during 19x3.
   Break the rate down into variable and fixed cost elements.
2. Show how the $272,000 "Applied" figure in the Manufacturing Overhead account was
   computed.
3. Analyze the $15,400 underapplied overhead figure in terms of the variable overhead
   spending and efficiency variances and the fixed overhead budget and volume variances.
4. Explain the meaning of each variance that you computed in (3) above, and indicate
   how each variance is controlled.

Required

**Absorption Costing Statement; Integration of Materials, Labor, and Overhead Vari-
ances**   "Wonderful! Not only did our salespeople do a good job in meeting the sales
budget this year, but our production people did a good job in controlling costs as well,"
said Kim Clark, president of Martell Company. "Our $18,000 cost variance is only 1.5
percent of the $1,200,000 standard cost of products sold during the year. That's well within
the 3 percent parameter set by management for acceptable variances. It looks like everyone will be in line for a bonus this year." The company's income statement for the year is
presented below:

P11–13 Integrative
Problem

	30,000 Units		
	Actual	**Budgeted**	**Variance**
Sales.	$1,680,000	$1,680,000	$ —
Less cost of goods sold (standard cost, $40 per unit)	1,218,000	1,200,000	18,000 U
Gross margin	462,000	480,000	18,000 U
Less operating expenses:			
Selling expenses.	250,000	250,000	—
Administrative expenses	60,000	60,000	—
Total operating expenses	310,000	310,000	—
Net income	$ 152,000	$ 170,000	$18,000 U

The company produces and sells a single product. A standard cost card for the product follows:

Standard Cost Card—per Unit of Product

Direct materials, 2 feet at $8.45	$16.90
Direct labor, 1.4 hours at $8	11.20
Variable overhead, 1.4 hours at $2.50	3.50
Fixed overhead, 1.4 hours at $6	8.40
Standard cost per unit	$40.00

The following additional information is available for the year just completed:

a. The company manufactured and sold 30,000 units of product during the year.
b. A total of 64,000 feet of material were purchased during the year at a cost of $8.55 per foot. All of this material was used to manufacture the 30,000 units. There were no beginning or ending inventories for the year.
c. The company worked 45,000 direct labor-hours during the year at a cost of $7.80 per hour.
d. Overhead is applied to products on a basis of direct labor-hours. Data relating to overhead costs follow:

Denominator activity level (direct labor-hours)	35,000
Budgeted fixed overhead costs (from the overhead flexible budget)	$210,000
Actual variable overhead costs incurred	108,000
Actual fixed overhead costs incurred	211,800

e. All variances are closed to cost of goods sold at the end of each year.

Required 1. Compute the direct materials price and quantity variances for the year.
2. Compute the direct labor rate and efficiency variances for the year.
3. For overhead compute:
    a. The variable overhead spending and efficiency variances for the year.
    b. The fixed overhead budget and volume variances for the year.
4. Total the variances you have computed, and compare the net amount with the $18,000 variance on the income statement. Do you agree that bonuses should be given to everyone for good cost control during the year? Explain.

P11–14 **Overhead Flexible Budget and Overhead Analysis** Harper Company assembles all of its products in the assembly department. Budgeted costs for the operation of this department during 19x2 have been set as follows:

Variable costs:	
Direct materials.	$ 900,000
Direct labor	675,000
Utilities	45,000
Indirect labor.	67,500
Supplies	22,500
Total variable costs	1,710,000
Fixed costs:	
Insurance	8,000
Supervisory salaries.	90,000
Depreciation	160,000
Equipment rental	42,000
Total fixed costs	300,000
Total budgeted costs	$2,010,000
Budgeted direct labor-hours	75,000

Since the assembly work is done mostly by hand, operating activity in this department is best measured by direct labor-hours. The cost formulas used to develop the budgeted costs above are valid over a relevant range of 60,000 to 90,000 direct labor-hours per year.

Required

1. Prepare an overhead flexible budget in good form for the assembly department. Make your budget in increments of 15,000 direct labor-hours. (The company does not include direct materials and direct labor costs in the flexible budget.)
2. Assume that the company computes predetermined overhead rates by department. Compute the rates that will be used by the assembly department during 19x2 to apply overhead costs to production. Break this rate down into variable and fixed cost elements.
3. Suppose that during 19x2 the following actual activity and costs are recorded by the assembly department:

Actual direct labor-hours worked	73,000
Standard direct labor-hours allowed	
for the output of the year	70,000
Actual variable overhead cost incurred	$124,100
Actual fixed overhead cost incurred.	301,600

Complete the following:

a. A T-account for manufacturing overhead costs in the assembly department for 19x2 is given below. Determine the amount of applied overhead cost for the year, and compute the under- or overapplied overhead.

Manufacturing Overhead

Actual costs 425,700	

b. Analyze the under- or overapplied overhead figure in terms of the variable overhead spending and efficiency variances and the fixed overhead budget and volume variances.

Standard Cost Card and Overhead Analysis   Lane Company manufactures a single product that requires a large amount of labor time. Therefore, overhead cost is applied on a basis of direct labor-hours. The company's condensed flexible budget is given below:

P11–15

Overhead Costs	Cost Formula (per hour)	Direct Labor-Hours		
		45,000	60,000	75,000
Variable costs	$2	$ 90,000	$120,000	$150,000
Fixed costs.		480,000	480,000	480,000
Total overhead costs		$570,000	$600,000	$630,000

The company's product requires 3 pounds of material that has a standard cost of $7 per pound and 1.5 hours of direct labor time that has a standard rate of $6 per hour.

During 19x1, the company planned to operate at a denominator activity level of 60,000 direct labor-hours and to produce 40,000 units of product. Actual activity and costs for the year were as follows:

Number of units produced.	42,000
Actual direct labor-hours worked	65,000
Actual variable overhead cost incurred	$123,500
Actual fixed overhead cost incurred	483,000

Required

1. Compute the predetermined overhead rate that would have been used during 19x1. Break the rate down into variable and fixed elements.

2. Prepare a standard cost card for the company's product; show the details for all manufacturing costs on your standard cost card.

3. Do the following:
   a. Compute the standard hours allowed for 19x1 production.
   b. Complete the following Manufacturing Overhead T-account for the year:

Manufacturing Overhead

?	?
?	?

4. Determine the reason for any under- or overapplied overhead for the year by computing the variable overhead spending and efficiency variances and the fixed overhead budget and volume variances.

5. Suppose the company had chosen 65,000 direct labor-hours as the denominator activity rather than 60,000 hours. State which, if any, of the variances computed in (4) would have changed, and explain how the variance(s) would have changed. No computations are necessary.

Integrative Problem **P11–16**

Absorption Costing Statement; Integration of Materials, Labor, and Overhead Variances "Wow! Just look at the size of that variance," said John Baker, president of Marvel, Inc. "We've got to do something to get costs back under control." The variance to which Mr. Baker was referring is shown in the company's most recent income statement below:

| | 12,500 Units | | |
	Budgeted	Actual	Variance
Sales	$1,000,000	$1,000,000	$ —
Less cost of goods sold (standard cost, $60 per unit)	750,000	802,000	52,000*
Gross margin	250,000	198,000	(52,000)
Less operating expenses:			
Selling expenses	120,000	120,000	—
Administrative expenses	70,000	70,000	—
Total operating expenses	190,000	190,000	—
Net income	$ 60,000	$ 8,000	$(52,000)

* Consists of the following variances:

Direct materials	$ 8,000 U
Direct labor	5,000 F
Manufacturing overhead . . .	49,000 U
Total variance	$52,000 U

The company produces and sells a single product. A standard cost card for the product follows:

Standard Cost Card—per Unit of Product

Direct materials: 3 pounds at $4 per pound	$12
Direct labor: 2.5 hours at $10 per hour	25
Variable manufacturing overhead: 2.5 hours at $2 per hour.	5
Fixed manufacturing overhead: 2.5 hours at $7.20 per hour*	18
Total standard cost per unit	$60

* Based on a denominator activity of 37,500 hours.

The following additional information is available for the period:

a. The company purchased 40,000 pounds of materials during the period, at a cost of $3.95 per pound. All of the material was used to produce 12,500 units. There were no beginning or ending inventories.
b. The company worked 30,000 actual direct labor-hours during the period, at an average cost of $10.25 per hour.
c. The company incurred $63,000 in variable overhead cost during the period. Overhead is applied to products on a basis of direct labor-hours.
d. The company incurred $273,500 in fixed overhead costs during the period; according to the flexible budget, the company had planned to incur $270,000 in fixed overhead cost. A denominator activity of 37,500 hours is used to set overhead rates.
e. The company closes all variances to cost of goods sold each period, as shown in the income statement above.

1. Compute the direct materials price and quantity variances for the period.   *Required*
2. Compute the direct labor rate and efficiency variances for the period.
3. Compute the variable overhead spending and efficiency variances and the fixed overhead budget and volume variances for the period.
4. Is the company's problem primarily one of poor control over costs? Explain.

Standard Cost Card; Fixed Overhead Analysis; Graphing In planning operations for   P11–17
19x2, Southbrook Company chose a denominator activity figure of 40,000 direct labor-hours. According to the company's flexible budget, the following overhead costs should be incurred at this activity level:

Variable overhead costs . . . $ 72,000
Fixed overhead costs   360,000

The company produces a single product that requires 2.5 hours to complete. The direct labor rate is $6 per hour. Eight yards of material are needed to complete one unit of product; the material has a standard cost of $4.50 per yard. Overhead is applied to production on a basis of direct labor-hours.

Required   1. Compute the predetermined overhead rate that the company will use during 19x2. Break the rate down into variable and fixed cost elements.
2. Prepare a standard cost card for one unit of product, using the following format:

Direct materials, 8 yards at $4.50 . . . $36
Direct labor,   ? . . . .   ?
Variable overhead, ? . . . .   ?
Fixed overhead,   ? . . . .   ?
Standard cost per unit . . . . $?

3. Prepare a graph with cost on the vertical *(Y)* axis and direct labor-hours on the horizontal *(X)* axis. Plot a line on your graph from a zero level of activity to 60,000 direct labor-hours for each of the following costs:
a. Budgeted fixed overhead (in total).
b. Applied fixed overhead [applied at the hourly rate computed in (1) above].
4. Assume that during 19x2 actual activity is as follows:

Number of units produced   14,000
Actual direct labor-hours worked   33,000
Actual fixed overhead cost incurred . . . $361,800

a. Compute the fixed overhead budget and volume variances for the year.
b. Show the volume variance on the graph you prepared in (3) above.
5. Disregard the data in (4). Assume instead that actual activity during 19x2 is as follows:

Number of units produced   20,000
Actual direct labor-hours worked 52,000
Actual fixed overhead costs incurred . . . $361,800

a. Compute the fixed overhead budget and volume variances for the year.
b. Show the volume variance on the graph you prepared in (3) above.

P11–18   Selection of a Denominator; Overhead Analysis   Morton Company's condensed flexible budget is given below:

Overhead Costs	Cost Formula (per hour)	Direct Labor-Hours		
		20,000	**30,000**	**40,000**
Variable costs	$4.50	$ 90,000	$135,000	$180,000
Fixed costs		270,000	270,000	270,000
Total overhead costs		$360,000	$405,000	$450,000

The company manufactures a single product that requires two direct labor-hours to complete. The direct labor wage rate is $5 per hour. Four feet of raw material are required for each unit of product; the standard cost of the material is $8.75 per foot.

Although long-run normal activity is 30,000 direct labor-hours each year, for the coming year (19x9) the company expects to operate at a 40,000-hour level of activity.

1. Assume that the company chooses 30,000 direct labor-hours as the denominator level   *Required*
    of activity. Compute the predetermined overhead rate, breaking it down into variable
    and fixed cost elements.
2. Assume that the company chooses 40,000 direct labor-hours as the denominator level
    of activity. Repeat the computations in (1).
3. Complete two standard cost cards as outlined below. Each card should relate to a
    single unit of product.

Denominator Activity: 30,000 DLH

Direct materials, 4 feet at $8.75	$35.00
Direct labor, ?	?
Variable overhead, ?	?
Fixed overhead, ?	?
Standard cost per unit	$?

Denominator Activity: 40,000 DLH

Direct materials, 4 feet at $8.75	$35.00
Direct labor, ?	?
Variable overhead, ?	?
Fixed overhead, ?	?
Standard cost per unit	$?

4. Assume that the company produces 18,000 units and works 38,000 actual direct labor-
    hours during 19x6. Actual overhead costs for the year are:

Variable costs	$174,800
Fixed costs	271,600
Total overhead costs . . .	$446,400

Do the following:

a. Compute the standard hours allowed for 19x6 production.
b. Complete the Manufacturing Overhead account below. Assume that the company
    uses 30,000 direct labor-hours (long-run normal activity) as the denominator activ-
    ity figure in computing predetermined overhead rates, as you have done in (1)
    above.

Manufacturing Overhead

Actual costs	446,400	?
	?	?

c. Determine the cause of the under- or overapplied overhead for the year by com-
    puting the variable overhead spending and efficiency variances and the fixed
    overhead budget and volume variances.
5. Looking at the variances you have computed, what appears to be the major disadvan-
    tage of using long-run normal activity rather than expected actual activity as a denomi-
    nator in computing the predetermined overhead rate? What advantages can you see to
    offset this disadvantage?

Standard Cost Card; Overhead Analysis; Graphing   A condensed flexible budget for   **P11–19**
Eaton Company is given below:

Overhead Costs	Cost Formula (per hour)	Direct Labor-Hours 8,000	10,000	12,000
Variable costs	$1.50	$ 12,000	$ 15,000	$ 18,000
Fixed costs		90,000	90,000	90,000
Total overhead costs		$102,000	$105,000	$108,000

The company produces a single product, which requires two hours of direct labor time to complete, at a rate of $5 per hour. Each unit of product requires 3 yards of material at $5.60 per yard. Overhead is applied to units of product on a basis of direct labor-hours. During the most recent period, the following actual costs and output were recorded:

Number of units produced	4,250
Actual direct labor-hours	9,000
Actual fixed overhead cost	$88,500

Required

1. Assume that the company computes predetermined overhead rates by using a denominator activity of 8,000 direct labor-hours.
   a. Compute the predetermined overhead rate, and break it down into variable and fixed cost elements.
   b. Prepare a standard cost card, showing the cost to produce one unit of product.
2. Refer to the original data. Assume that the company computes predetermined overhead rates by using a denominator activity of 12,000 direct labor-hours.
   a. Compute the predetermined overhead rate under this assumption, and break it down into variable and fixed cost elements.
   b. Prepare a standard cost card, showing the cost to produce one unit of product.
3. Refer to your computations in (1) above.
   a. Using these data, compute the budget and volume variances for the most recent period.
   b. Prepare a graph showing budgeted fixed costs throughout the relevant range and showing an applied overhead line for fixed costs from a zero level of activity through the denominator level of activity. Indicate on your graph the volume variance that you have just computed. In your own words, explain why a volume variance arises.
4. Refer to your computations in (2) above.
   a. Using these data, compute the budget and volume variances for the most recent period.
   b. Prepare another graph showing budgeted fixed overhead and applied fixed overhead, as well as the volume variance that you have just computed.
5. What are the implications of this problem regarding the setting of fixed overhead rates for product costing purposes? Are such rates useful control tools? Explain.

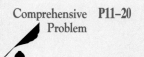

Comprehensive Problem P11–20

Comprehensive Overhead Analysis   Pallas Company manufactures and sells a single product. Each unit requires 6 pounds of raw material, which has a standard cost of $3.75 per pound, and 1.25 hours of direct labor time, which has a standard rate of $8 per hour. Overhead costs are planned and controlled through a flexible budget, which is shown in condensed form below:

Overhead Costs	Cost Formula (per hour)	Machine-Hours 15,000	30,000	45,000
Variable costs	$3	$ 45,000	$ 90,000	$135,000
Fixed costs		360,000	360,000	360,000
Total overhead costs		$405,000	$450,000	$495,000

The company applies overhead cost to the product on a basis of machine-hours, as shown in the flexible budget above. At standard, each unit should require 2.5 machine-hours to complete. Actual operating results for the most recent period are shown below:

Activity:
Number of units produced.	14,000
Standard machine-hours allowed for output	?
Actual machine-hours worked	36,000

Cost:
Actual variable overhead cost	$107,100
Actual fixed overhead cost	362,500

Required

1. Assume that the company normally operates at an activity level of 30,000 standard machine-hours each period and that this figure is used as the denominator activity in computing predetermined overhead rates.

    a. Compute the predetermined overhead rate, and break it down into fixed and variable cost elements.

    b. Prepare a standard cost card, showing the standard cost to produce one unit of product.

2. Refer to the original data. Assume that the company decides to use 45,000 standard machine-hours as the denominator activity in computing predetermined overhead rates.

    a. Under this assumption, compute the predetermined overhead rate and break it down into fixed and variable cost elements.

    b. Prepare another standard cost card, showing the standard cost to produce one unit of product.

3. Refer to the computations you made in (1) above.

    a. Prepare a T-account for manufacturing overhead, and enter the actual overhead costs for the most recent period as shown in the original data to the problem. Determine the amount of overhead that would have been applied to production during the period, and enter this amount into the T-account.

    b. Compute the amount of under- or overapplied overhead for the period, and then analyze it in terms of the variable overhead spending and efficiency variances and the fixed overhead budget and volume variances.

4. Refer to the computations you made in (2) above.

    a. Prepare another T-account for manufacturing overhead, and again enter the actual overhead costs for the most recent period. Determine the amount of overhead that would have been applied to production during the period, and enter this amount into the T-account.

    b. Compute the amount of under- or overapplied overhead for the period, and then analyze it in terms of the variable overhead spending and efficiency variances and the fixed overhead budget and volume variances.

5. Firms are sometimes accused by competitors and others of selling products "below cost." What implications does this problem have for the "cost" of a unit of product so far as the setting of fixed overhead rates is concerned?

Preparing a Revised Performance Report   Several years ago, Westmont Company developed a comprehensive budgeting system for profit planning and control purposes. The line supervisors have been very happy with the system and with the reports being prepared on their performance, but both middle and upper management have expressed considerable dissatisfaction with the information being generated by the system. A typical overhead performance report for a recent period is shown below:

P11–21

WESTMONT COMPANY
Overhead Performance Report—Assembly Department
For the Quarter Ended March 31, 19x5

	Actual	Budget	Variance
Machine-hours	35,000	40,000	
Variable overhead:			
Indirect materials	$ 29,700	$ 32,000	$2,300 F
Rework time	7,900	8,000	100 F
Utilities	51,800	56,000	4,200 F
Machine setup	11,600	12,000	400 F
Total variable costs	101,000	108,000	7,000 F
Fixed overhead:			
Maintenance	79,200	80,000	800 F
Inspection	60,000	60,000	—
Total fixed costs	139,200	140,000	800 F
Total overhead costs	$240,200	$248,000	$7,800 F

After receiving a copy of this overhead performance report, the supervisor of the assembly department stated, "These reports are super. It makes me feel really good to see how well things are going in my department. I can't understand why those people upstairs complain so much."

The "budget" data above are taken from the department's overhead flexible budget and represent the original planned level of activity for the quarter.

Required

1. The company's vice president is uneasy about the performance reports being prepared and would like you to evaluate their usefulness to the company.
2. What changes, if any, would you recommend be made in the overhead performance report above in order to give better insight into how well the supervisor is doing his job?
3. Prepare a new overhead performance report for the quarter, incorporating any changes you suggested in (2). (Include both the variable and the fixed costs in your report.)

P11–22   Flexible Budget and Performance Report   You have just been hired by FAB Company, the manufacturer of a revolutionary new garage door opening device. John Foster, the president, has asked that you review the company's costing system and "do what you can to help us get better control of our overhead costs." You find that the company has never used a flexible budget, and you suggest that preparing such a budget would be an excellent first step in overhead planning and control.

After much effort and cost analysis, you are able to determine the following overhead cost formulas for the company's normal operating range of 20,000 to 30,000 machine-hours each month:

Cost	Cost Formula
Utilities	$0.90 per machine-hour
Maintenance	$1.60 per machine-hour plus $40,000 per month
Machine setup	$0.30 per machine-hour
Indirect labor	$0.70 per machine-hour plus $130,000 per month
Depreciation	$70,000 per month

To show the president how the flexible budget concept works, you have gathered the following actual cost data for the most recent month (March 19x1), in which the company worked 26,000 machine-hours and produced 15,000 units:

Utilities	$ 24,200
Maintenance	78,100
Machine setup	8,400
Indirect labor.	149,600
Depreciation	71,500
Total costs	$331,800

The only variance in the fixed costs for the month was with depreciation, which was increased as a result of a purchase of new equipment.

The company had originally planned to work 30,000 machine-hours during March.

1. Prepare a flexible budget for the company in increments of 5,000 hours.
2. Prepare an overhead performance report for the company for March 19x1. (Use the format illustrated in Exhibit 11–12.)
3. What additional information would you need to have in order to compute an overhead efficiency variance for the company?
4. Explain to the president how the flexible budget can be used for product costing purposes as well as for cost control purposes.

Required

Spending and Efficiency Variances; Evaluating a Performance Report   Frank Western, supervisor of the machining department for Freemont Company, was visibly upset after being reprimanded for his department's poor performance over the prior month. The department's performance report is given below:

P11-23

FREEMONT COMPANY
Overhead Performance Report—Machining Department

	Cost Formula (per hour)	Actual	Budget	Variance
Machine-hours		38,000	35,000	
Variable overhead:				
Utilities	$0.40	$ 15,700	$ 14,000	$ 1,700 U
Indirect labor	2.30	86,500	80,500	6,000 U
Supplies	0.60	26,000	21,000	5,000 U
Maintenance	1.20	44,900	42,000	2,900 U
Total variable costs	$4.50	173,100	157,500	15,600 U
Fixed overhead:				
Supervision		38,000	38,000	—
Maintenance		92,400	92,000	400 U
Depreciation		80,000	80,000	—
Total fixed costs		210,400	210,000	400 U
Total overhead costs		$383,500	$367,500	$16,000 U

"I just can't understand all the red ink," said Western to Sarah Mason, supervisor of another department. "When the boss called me in, I thought he was going to give me a pat on the back, because I know for a fact that my department worked more efficiently last month than it has ever worked before. Instead, he tore me apart. I thought for a minute that it might be over the supplies that were stolen out of our warehouse last month. But they only amounted to a couple of thousand dollars, and just look at this report. *Everything* is unfavorable, and I don't even know why."

The master budget for the machining department had called for production of 14,000 units last month, which is equal to a budgeted activity level of 35,000 machine-hours (at a standard time of 2.5 hours per unit). Actual production in the machining department for the month was 16,000 units.

1. Evaluate the overhead performance report given above, and explain why the variances are all unfavorable.

Required

2. Prepare a new overhead performance report that will help Mr. Western's superiors assess efficiency and cost control in the machining department. (Hint: Exhibit 11–6 may be helpful in structuring your report; the report you prepare should include both variable and fixed costs.)

3. Would the supplies stolen out of the warehouse be included as part of the variable overhead spending variance or as part of the variable overhead efficiency variance for the month? Explain.

P11–24 Detailed Performance Report   The cost formulas for variable overhead costs in a machining operation are given below:

Variable Overhead Cost	Cost Formula (per Machine-Hour)
Power	$0.30
Setup time	0.20
Polishing wheels	0.16
Maintenance	0.18
Total	$0.84

During August, the machining operation was scheduled to work 11,250 machine-hours and to produce 4,500 units of product. The standard machine time per unit of product is 2.5 hours. A strike near the end of the month forced a curtailment of production. Actual results for the month were:

Actual machine-hours worked 9,250
Actual number of units produced 3,600

Actual costs for the month were:

	Total Actual Costs	Per Machine-Hour
Power	$2,405	$0.26
Setup time	2,035	0.22
Polishing wheels	1,110	0.12
Maintenance	925	0.10
Total cost	$6,475	$0.70

Required   Prepare an overhead performance report for the machining operation for August. Use column headings in your report as shown below:

Overhead Item	Cost Formula	Actual Costs Incurred 9,250 Hours	Budget Based on ? Hours	Budget Based on ? Hours	Total Variance	Breakdown of the Total Variance	
						Spending Variance	Efficiency Variance

Comprehensive Problem

P11–25 Flexible Budget; Performance Report   Gant Products, Inc., has recently introduced budgeting as an integral part of its corporate planning process. The company's first effort at constructing a flexible budget is shown below.

Percentage of capacity	80%	100%
Machine-hours	4,800	6,000
Maintenance	$1,480	$ 1,600
Supplies	1,920	2,400
Utilities	1,940	2,300
Supervision	3,000	3,000
Machine setup	960	1,200
Total overhead cost	$9,300	$10,500

The budgets above are for costs over a relevant range of 80 percent to 100 percent of capacity on a monthly basis. The managers who will be working under these budgets have control over both fixed and variable costs.

Required

1. Redo the company's flexible budget, presenting it in better format. Show the budget at 80 percent, 90 percent, and 100 percent levels of capacity. (Use the high-low method to separate fixed and variable costs.)
2. Express the budget prepared in (1) above in cost formula form, using a single cost formula to express all overhead costs.
3. The company operated at 95 percent of capacity during April in terms of actual hours of machine time recorded in the factory. Five thousand six hundred standard machine-hours were allowed for the output of the month. Actual overhead costs incurred were:

Maintenance	$ 2,083
Supplies	3,420
Utilities	2,666
Supervision	3,000
Machine setup	855
Total costs	$12,024

There were no variances in the fixed costs. Prepare an overhead performance report for April. Structure your report so that it shows only a spending variance for overhead. You may assume that the master budget for April called for an activity level during the month of 6,000 machine-hours.

4. Upon receiving the performance report you have prepared, the production manager commented, "I have two observations to make. First, I think there's an error on your report. You show an unfavorable spending variance for supplies, yet I know that we paid exactly the budgeted price for all the supplies we used last month. Pat Stevens, the purchasing agent, made a comment to me that our supplies prices haven't changed in over a year. Second, I wish you would modify your report to include an efficiency variance for overhead. The reason is that waste has been a problem in the factory for years, and the efficiency variance would help us get overhead waste under control."
   a. Explain the probable cause of the unfavorable spending variance for supplies.
   b. Compute an efficiency variance for *total* variable overhead, and explain to the production manager why it would or would not contain elements of overhead waste.

CASES

Working Backwards from Variance Data   You have recently graduated from State University and have accepted a position with Vitex, Inc., the manufacturer of a popular consumer product. During your first week on the job, the vice president has been favorably impressed with your work. She has been so impressed, in fact, that yesterday she called you into her office and asked you to attend the executive committee meeting this morning for the purpose of leading a discussion on the variances reported for last period. Anxious to

C11–26
Integrative Case

favorably impress the executive committee, you took the variances and supporting data home last night to study.

On your way to work this morning, the papers were laying on the seat of your new, red convertible. As you were crossing a bridge on the highway, a sudden gust of wind caught the papers and blew them over the edge of the bridge and into the stream below. You managed to retrieve only one page, which contains the following information:

Standard Cost Card

Direct materials, 6 pounds at $3	$18.00
Direct labor, 0.8 hours at $5	4.00
Variable overhead, 0.8 hours at $3 . . .	2.40
Fixed overhead, 0.8 hours at $7	5.60
Standard cost per unit	$30.00

	Total Standard Cost*	Variances Reported			
		Price or Rate	Spending or Budget	Quantity or Efficiency	Volume
Direct materials	$405,000	$6,900 F		$9,000 U	
Direct labor	90,000	4,850 U		7,000 U	
Variable overhead . . .	54,000		$1,300 F	?† U	
Fixed overhead	126,000		500 F		$14,000 U

* Applied to Work in Process during the period.

† Figure obliterated.

You recall that overhead cost is applied to production on a basis of direct labor-hours, and that all of the materials purchased during the period were used in production. Since the company uses JIT to control work flows, work in process inventories are nominal and can be ignored.

It is now 8:30 A.M. The executive committee meeting starts in just one hour; you realize that to avoid looking like a bungling fool you must somehow generate the necessary "backup" data for the variances before the meeting begins. Without backup data it will be impossible to lead the discussion or answer any questions.

Required
1. How many units were produced last period? (Think hard about this one!)
2. How many pounds of direct material were purchased and used in production?
3. What was the actual cost per pound of material?
4. How many actual direct labor-hours were worked during the period?
5. What was the actual rate paid per direct labor-hour?
6. How much actual variable overhead cost was incurred during the period?
7. What is the total fixed cost in the company's flexible budget?
8. What were the denominator hours for last period?

C11–27 Incomplete Data   Each of the cases below is independent. You may assume that each company uses a standard cost system and that each company's flexible budget is based on standard machine-hours.

	Item	Company A	Company B
1.	Denominator activity in hours	?	40,000
2.	Standard hours allowed for units produced	32,000	?
3.	Actual hours worked	30,000	?
4.	Flexible budget variable overhead per machine-hour	$?	$ 2.80
5.	Flexible budget fixed overhead (total)	?	?
6.	Actual variable overhead cost incurred	54,000	117,000
7.	Actual fixed overhead cost incurred	209,400	302,100
8.	Variable overhead cost applied to production*	?	117,600

Item	Company A	Company B
9. Fixed overhead cost applied to production*	192,000	?
10. Variable overhead spending variance	?	?
11. Variable overhead efficiency variance	3,500 F	8,400 U
12. Fixed overhead budget variance	?	2,100 U
13. Fixed overhead volume variance	18,000 U	?
14. Variable portion of the predetermined overhead rate	?	?
15. Fixed portion of the predetermined overhead rate	?	?
16. Underapplied or (overapplied) overhead	?	?

* Based on standard hours allowed for units produced.

Compute the unknown amounts. (Hint: One way to proceed would be to use the columnar format for variance analysis found in Exhibit 10–6 for variable overhead and in Exhibit 11–11 for fixed overhead.)

Required

Service Organization; Preparing a Performance Report   Boyne University offers an extensive continuing education program in many cities throughout the state. For the convenience of its faculty and administrative staff and to save costs, the university employs a supervisor to operate a motor pool. The motor pool operated with 20 vehicles until February, when an additional automobile was acquired. The motor pool furnishes gasoline, oil, and other supplies for its automobiles. A mechanic does routine maintenance and minor repairs. Major repairs are done at a nearby commercial garage.

C11–28

Each year, the supervisor prepares an operating budget, which informs the university administration of the funds needed for operating the motor pool. Depreciation (straight line) on the automobiles is recorded in the budget in order to determine the cost per mile of operating the vehicles.

The schedule below presents the operating budget for the current year, which has been approved by the university. The schedule also shows actual operating costs for March of the current year, compared to one twelfth of the annual operating budget.

UNIVERSITY MOTOR POOL

Budget Report for March

	Annual Operating Budget	Monthly Budget*	March Actual	(Over) Under Budget
Gasoline	$ 42,000	$ 3,500	$ 4,300	$(800)
Oil, minor repairs, parts	3,600	300	380	(80)
Outside repairs	2,700	225	50	175
Insurance	6,000	500	525	(25)
Salaries and benefits	30,000	2,500	2,500	—
Depreciation of vehicles	26,400	2,200	2,310	(110)
Total costs	$110,700	$ 9,225	$10,065	$(840)
Total miles	600,000	50,000	63,000	
Cost per mile	$ 0.1845	$0.1845	$0.1598	
Number of automobiles in use	20	20	21	

* Annual operating budget ÷ 12 months.

The annual operating budget was constructed upon the following assumptions:

a. Twenty automobiles in the motor pool.
b. Thirty thousand miles driven per year per automobile.

    c.   Fifteen miles per gallon per automobile.

    d. $1.05 per gallon of gasoline.

    e. $0.006 cost per mile for oil, minor repairs, and parts.

    f. $135 cost per automobile per year for outside repairs.

    g. $300 cost per automobile per year for insurance.

    The supervisor of the motor pool is unhappy with the monthly report comparing budget and actual costs for March, claiming it presents an unfair picture of performance. A previous employer used flexible budgeting to compare actual costs to budgeted amounts.

Required   1.   Prepare a new performance report for March, showing budgeted costs, actual costs, and variances. In preparing your report, use flexible budgeting techniques to compute the "monthly budget" figures.

           2.   What are the deficiencies in the performance report presented above? How does the report which you prepared in (1) overcome these deficiencies?

(CMA, adapted)

The woolen goods product line in a sewing notions company showed substantial losses even though its sales were increasing steadily year by year. It was discovered that the woolen goods were being penalized by the company's practice of allocating selling, general, and administrative overhead costs on the basis of sales dollars. When sales dollars were abandoned in favor of other, more appropriate allocation bases, the woolen goods line immediately began to show a healthy profit.

Segment Reporting, Profitability Analysis, and Decentralization

LEARNING OBJECTIVES

After studying Chapter 12, you should be able to:

1 Identify three business practices that hinder proper cost assignment.

2 Prepare a segmented income statement using the contribution format, and explain the difference between traceable fixed costs and common fixed costs.

3 Explain how to determine customer profitability.

4 Explain the importance of decentralization in a responsibility accounting system.

5 Differentiate between cost centers, profit centers, and investment centers, and explain how performance is measured in each.

6 Compute the return on investment (ROI) by means of the ROI formula.

7 Show how changes in sales, expenses, and assets affect an organization's ROI.

8 Compute the residual income and enumerate the strengths and weaknesses of this method of measuring performance.

9 Identify three ways that transfer prices can be set.

10 Use the transfer pricing formula to compute an appropriate transfer price between segments, assuming the selling division (a) is operating at full capacity and (b) has idle capacity.

11 Define or explain the key terms listed at the end of the chapter.

T o operate effectively, managers need more information at their disposal than is available in a single, companywide income statement. A company-wide income statement provides only a summary of overall operations; as such, it typically does not contain enough detail to allow the manager to detect opportunities and problems that may exist in the organization. For example, some product lines may be profitable while others may be unprofitable; some sales offices may be more effective than others; or some factories may be ineffectively using their capacity and/or resources. To uncover problems such as these, the manager needs not just one but several income statements, and these statements must be designed to focus on various *segments* of the company. The preparation of income statements of this type is known as **segment reporting.**

A **segment** can be defined as any part or activity of an organization about which a manager seeks cost, revenue, or profit data. Examples of segments include sales territories, individual stores, service centers, manufacturing divisions or plants, sales departments, and product lines. In this chapter, we learn how to construct income statements that show the results of segment activities. We also learn how to analyze the profitability of segments and how to measure the performance of segment managers. In addition, as we study these topics, we will learn how to use segment data to extend the concept of responsibility accounting to the company as a whole.

HINDRANCES TO PROPER COST ASSIGNMENT

Objective 1
Identify three business practices that hinder proper cost assignment.

For segment reporting to accomplish its intended purposes, costs must be analyzed and properly assigned to the segments to which they relate. If the purpose of a segmented statement is to determine the profitability of a customer, then all of the costs attributable to that customer—and only those costs—should be assigned to the customer. If the purpose is to determine the rate of return being generated by a particular division, then all of the costs attributable to that division—and only those costs—should be assigned to it. Unfortunately, three business practices are in use that greatly hinder proper cost assignment. These three practices are (1) omission of some costs in the assignment process, (2) the use of inappropriate methods for allocating costs among segments of a company, and (3) assignment of costs to segments that are really common costs of the entire organization.

Omission of Costs

The costs assigned to a segment should include all costs attributable to that segment from the company's entire *value chain*. The **value chain,** which is illustrated in Exhibit 12–1, consists of the major business functions that add value to a company's products and services. All of these functions, from research and development, through product design, manufacturing, marketing, distribution, and customer service, are required to bring a product or service to the customer and generate revenues.

EXHIBIT 12–1

Business Functions Making Up the Value Chain

Research and Development	Product Design	Manufacturing	Marketing	Distribution	Customer Service

However, under generally accepted accounting principles, only manufacturing costs are included in product costs for financial reporting purposes.[1] Consequently, when trying to determine product profitability for internal decision-making purposes, some companies deduct only manufacturing costs from product revenues. As a result, such companies omit from their profitability analysis part or all of the "upstream" costs in the value chain, which consist of research and development and product design, or the "downstream" costs, which consist of marketing, distribution, and customer service. Yet these nonmanufacturing costs are just as essential in determining product profitability as are the manufacturing costs. These upstream and downstream costs, which are usually titled *Selling, general, and administrative (SG&A)* on the income statement, can represent half or more of the total costs of an organization. If either the upstream or downstream costs are omitted in profitability analysis, then the product is undercosted and management may unwittingly develop and maintain products that in the long run result in losses rather than profits for the company. For this and other reasons, it is important to properly assign these SG&A costs to the various products or other segments to which they relate.

Partly to avoid omitting costs that are an essential part of profitability analysis, some firms are turning to a concept known as *life cycle costing*. Essentially, **life cycle costing** focuses on all costs along the value chain that will be generated throughout the *entire* life of a product. This approach to costing helps to ensure that no costs are omitted in profitability analysis.

Inappropriate Methods for Allocating Costs among Segments

Cross-subsidization, or cost distortion, occurs when costs are improperly assigned among a company's segments. Cross-subsidization can occur in two ways: first, when companies fail to trace costs directly to segments in those situations where it is feasible to do so; and second, when companies use inappropriate bases to allocate costs.

Failure to Trace Costs Directly

Costs that can be traced directly to a specific segment of a company should not be charged against other segments through some averaging process. Rather, such costs should be charged directly to the responsible segment. For example, the rent for a branch office should be charged directly against the branch to which it relates rather than included in a company-wide overhead pool and then spread throughout the company.

Inappropriate Allocation Base

When costs cannot be easily traced to segments, some companies allocate these costs to segments using arbitrary bases such as sales dollars or cost of goods sold. For example, under the sales dollars approach, costs are allocated to the various segments according to the percentage of company sales generated by each segment. Thus, if a segment generates 20 percent of total company sales, it would be allocated 20 percent of the company's SG&A expenses as its "fair share." This same basic procedure is followed if cost of goods sold or some other such measure is used as the allocation base.

The problem with this approach is that frequently no real cause-and-effect relationship exists between the costs being assigned and the allocation base being

---

[1] AICPA, *Accounting Research Bulletin 43: Restatement and Revision of Accounting Research Bulletins* (June 1953), chap. 4, par. 5.

used. This approach assumes, in effect, that a dollar of sales for any product generates the same amount of SG&A expense. Such an assumption is rarely valid. Some products are much more costly to market and distribute than others, and some products require much greater customer service. Thus, use of an inappropriate assignment base such as sales dollars, *which ignores the actual consumption of resources,* will result in cross-subsidization of costs.

Arbitrarily Dividing Common Costs among Segments

The third business practice that results in distortion of segment costs is the practice of assigning costs to segments even when the costs are not in any way caused by the segments. For example, some companies allocate the costs of the corporate headquarters building to products, although these costs would be unaffected even if an entire product line was eliminated. Costs such as those associated with the corporate headquarters building are sometimes called **common costs,** since they relate to overall operating activities rather than to particular segments.

Common costs are necessary, of course, to have a functioning organization.

---

[2] Beth M. Chaffman and John Talbott, "Activity-Based Costing in a Service Organization," *CMA* 64, no. 10 (December/January 1991), p. 18.

[3] Thomas Dudick, "Why SG&A Doesn't Always Work," *Harvard Business Review* 65, no. 1 (January/February 1987), p. 4.

Although such costs cannot be significantly reduced even by eliminating whole segments such as product lines, some firms allocate them to segments anyway. This practice is often justified on the grounds that "someone" has to "cover the common costs." While it is undeniably true that the common costs must be covered, arbitrarily allocating common costs to segments does not ensure that this will happen. In fact, adding a share of common costs to the real costs of a segment may make an otherwise profitable segment appear to be unprofitable. If a manager then erroneously eliminates the segment, the net effect will be to *reduce* the profits of the company as a whole and make it even more difficult to "cover the common costs."

In sum, the way many companies handle segment reporting results in cost distortion. We have noted in our discussion that this distortion results from three practices—the failure to trace costs directly to a specific segment when it is feasible to do so, the use of inappropriate bases for allocating costs, and the allocation of common costs to segments. These practices are widespread. A recent study found that 60 percent of the companies surveyed made no attempt to assign SG&A costs to segments on a cause-and-effect basis.[4]

How *should* costs be assigned to segments? On the following pages we present an approach to segment reporting and cost assignment that provides useful data to managers in making a variety of decisions. This approach clearly segregates costs that are attributable to the segments from those that are not and also highlights the behavior of costs.

SEGMENT REPORTING AND PROFITABILITY ANALYSIS

The approach to segment reporting presented here uses the contribution format to the income statement discussed in earlier chapters. Recall that when the contribution format is used, (1) the cost of goods sold consists only of the variable manufacturing costs, (2) the variable and fixed costs are listed in separate sections, and (3) a contribution margin is computed. In this chapter, we will learn that when such a statement is segmented, a further breakdown is made of the fixed costs. This breakdown allows a *segment margin* to be computed for each segment of the company. In our study, we will find that the segment margin is a valuable tool for assessing the long-run profitability of a segment.

Objective 2
Prepare a segmented income statement using the contribution approach, and explain the difference between traceable fixed costs and common fixed costs.

Levels of Segmented Statements

Segmented income statements can be prepared for activities at many levels in a company. Exhibit 12–2 illustrates three possible levels. Observe from this exhibit that the total company is first segmented in terms of divisions. Then one of these divisions, Division 2, is further segmented in terms of the product lines sold within the division. In turn, one of these product lines, the regular model, is further segmented in terms of the territories in which it is sold. Notice that as we go from one segmented statement to another, we are looking at smaller and smaller pieces of the company. If management desired, Division 1 could also be segmented into smaller pieces in the same way as we have segmented Division 2, thereby providing an even more detailed look at the company's operations.

---

[4] James R. Emore and Joseph A. Ness, "The Slow Pace of Meaningful Change in Cost Systems," *Journal of Cost Management* 4, no. 4 (Winter 1991), p. 39.

EXHIBIT 12–2
Segmented Income
Statements in the
Contribution Format

Segments Defined as Divisions

	Total Company	Segment	
		Division 1	Division 2
Sales	$500,000	$300,000	$200,000
Less variable expenses:			
Variable cost of goods sold	180,000	120,000	60,000
Other variable expenses	50,000	30,000	20,000
Total variable expenses	230,000	150,000	80,000
Contribution margin	270,000	150,000	120,000
Less traceable fixed expenses	170,000	90,000	80,000*
Divisional segment margin	100,000	$ 60,000	$ 40,000
Less common fixed expenses	25,000		
Net income	$ 75,000		

**Segments Defined as Product Lines
of Division 2**

	Division 2	Segment	
		Deluxe Model	Regular Model
Sales	$200,000	$75,000	$125,000
Less variable expenses:			
Variable cost of goods sold	60,000	20,000	40,000
Other variable expenses	20,000	5,000	15,000
Total variable expenses	80,000	25,000	55,000
Contribution margin	120,000	50,000	70,000
Less traceable fixed expenses	70,000	30,000	40,000
Product-line segment margin	50,000	$20,000	$ 30,000
Less common fixed expenses	10,000		
Divisional segment margin	$ 40,000		

**Segments Defined as Sales Territories for
One Product Line of Division 2**

	Regular Model	Segment	
		Home Sales	Foreign Sales
Sales	$125,000	$100,000	$25,000
Less variable expenses:			
Variable cost of goods sold	40,000	32,000	8,000
Other variable expenses	15,000	5,000	10,000
Total variable expenses	55,000	37,000	18,000
Contribution margin	70,000	63,000	7,000
Less traceable fixed expenses	25,000	15,000	10,000
Territorial segment margin	45,000	$ 48,000	$(3,000)
Less common fixed expenses	15,000		
Product-line segment margin	$ 30,000		

* Notice that this $80,000 in traceable fixed expense is divided into two parts—$70,000 traceable and $10,000 common—when Division 2 is broken down into product lines. The reasons for this are discussed later under "Traceable Costs Can Become Common."

There are substantial benefits from a series of statements such as those contained in Exhibit 12–2. By carefully examining trends and results in each segment, a manager is able to gain considerable insight into the company's operations viewed from many different angles.

Assigning Costs to Segments

Note particularly how the fixed costs are handled in Exhibit 12–2. Fixed costs are divided into two parts. One part is labeled *traceable* and the other part is labeled *common*. Only those fixed costs labeled *traceable* are charged to the various segments. If a cost is not traceable to some segment, then it is treated as a common cost and kept separate from the segments themselves. Thus, under the approach illustrated here, a cost should never be averaged, allocated, or otherwise assigned to segments in an *arbitrary* manner.

Two guidelines are followed in assigning costs to the various segments of a company when the contribution format is used:

- First, according to cost behavior patterns (that is, variable and fixed).
- Second, according to whether the costs are *directly traceable* to the segments involved.

We will now consider various parts of Exhibit 12–2 in greater depth.

Sales and Contribution Margin

To prepare segmented statements, it is necessary to keep records of sales by individual segment, as well as in total for the organization. After deducting related variable expenses, a contribution margin figure can then be computed for each segment and for the total company as a whole, as illustrated in Exhibit 12–2.

It is important to keep in mind that the contribution margin tells us what happens to profits as volume changes—*holding a segment's capacity and fixed costs constant*. As such, the contribution margin is especially valuable in short-run decisions concerning temporary uses of capacity such as special orders. Decisions concerning the most effective uses of existing capacity often involve only variable costs and revenues, which of course are the very elements involved in contribution margin. By carefully monitoring segment contribution margins, the manager will be in a position to make those short-run decisions that will most effectively utilize each segment's capacity and thereby maximize profits. Such decisions will be discussed in greater detail in Chapter 13.

Traceable and Common Fixed Costs

Traceable fixed costs can be defined as those fixed costs that arise because of the existence of a particular segment and therefore can be identified with that segment. A **common fixed cost** is a fixed cost that cannot be identified with a particular segment but rather arises because of overall operations. To be assigned to segments, a common fixed cost would have to be allocated on some highly arbitrary basis having little to do with cause and effect, such as sales dollars.[5]

Examples of traceable fixed costs would include advertising outlays made on behalf of a particular segment, the salary of a segment manager (such as a product-

---

[5] It can be argued that *all* cost allocations are arbitrary. The use of the term *arbitrary* in this book is intended to convey the thought that a cost is being charged to a segment on something other than a cause-and-effect basis.

line supervisor), and depreciation of buildings and equipment devoted to the manufacture of a specific product. Examples of common fixed costs would include corporate image advertising (from which many segments benefit), salaries of top administrative officers, and depreciation of corporate administrative facilities.

Identifying Traceable Fixed Costs

The distinction between traceable and common fixed costs is crucial in segment reporting, since traceable fixed costs are charged to the segments, whereas common fixed costs are not. In an actual situation, it is sometimes hard to determine whether a cost should be classified as traceable or common. Two approaches are available to help make this classification. One approach is to use broad, general guidelines in deciding which costs are traceable, and the other approach is to use activity-based costing.

General Guidelines   A useful guideline or rule of thumb is to treat as traceable costs *only those costs that would disappear over time if the segment itself disappeared.* For example, if Division 1 in Exhibit 12–2 were discontinued, it would no longer be necessary to pay a salary for a division manager. Therefore the division manager's salary should be classified as a traceable fixed cost of the division. On the other hand, the president of the company undoubtedly would continue to be paid even if Division 1 were dropped. In fact, he or she might even be paid more if dropping the division was a good idea. Therefore, the president's salary is common to both divisions. The same idea can be expressed in another way: *treat as traceable costs only those costs that are added as a result of the creation of a segment.*

Activity-Based Costing   Some costs, such as advertising of a specific product, are easy to identify as traceable costs. A more difficult situation arises when a building or other resource is shared by two or more segments. For example, assume that a multiproduct company leases warehouse space that is used in the distribution of two of its products. Would the lease cost of the warehouse be a traceable or a common cost? Managers familiar with modern profitability analysis would argue that if a cost driver can be identified and consumption measured, then the lease cost is traceable and should be assigned to the two products according to their use of the resource involved. In like manner, these managers would argue that order processing costs, sales support costs, and other SG&A expenses should be charged to segments *according to the segments' use of the services involved,* as determined by an activity approach.

To illustrate, assume that Holt Company has three products—A, B, and C. Warehouse space is leased on a yearly basis as needed and used in the distribution of products A and B. The lease cost of this space is $4 per square foot per year. Product A occupies 3,000 square feet of space, and product B occupies 7,000 square feet. The company also has an order processing department that incurred $150,000 in order processing costs last year. In the judgment of management, order processing costs are driven by the number of orders placed. Last year 2,500 orders were placed, of which 1,200 were for product A, 800 were for product B, and 500 were for product C. Given these data, the following costs would be assigned to each product:

Warehouse space cost:
Product A: $4 × 3,000 square feet . . . . . $ 12,000
Product B: $4 × 7,000 square feet   28,000
Total cost assigned . . . . $ 40,000

Order processing costs:
$150,000 ÷ 2,500 orders = $60 per order

Product A: $60 × 1,200 orders	$ 72,000
Product B: $60 × 800 orders	48,000
Product C: $60 × 500 orders	30,000
Total cost assigned	$150,000

This method of assigning costs combines the strength of activity-based costing with the power of the contribution approach and greatly enhances the manager's ability to measure the profitability of segments.

FOCUS ON CURRENT PRACTICE

In the past, only the fixed costs that could be identified with a single segment (such as product advertising) were charged to that segment under the contribution approach. In today's business environment, managers are recognizing that true profitability can be measured only if *all* resources consumed by a segment are charged to it. This view has expanded the concept of a traceable cost to include the fixed costs assignable to a segment as a result of the *activities* in which it is involved.[6]

In assigning costs to segments, the key point is to resist the temptation to allocate costs (such as depreciation of corporate facilities) that are clearly common in nature. *Any allocation of common costs to segments will reduce the value of the segment margin as a guide to long-run segment profitability.*

Traceable Costs Can Become Common

Fixed costs that are traceable on one segmented statement can become common if the company is divided into smaller segments. This is because there are limits to how finely a cost can be separated without resorting to arbitrary allocation. The more finely segments are defined, the more costs there are that become common.

This concept can be seen from the diagram in Exhibit 12–3. Notice from the diagram that when segments are defined as divisions, Division 2 has $80,000 in traceable fixed expenses. Only $70,000 of this amount remains traceable, however, when we narrow our definition of a segment from divisions to that of the product lines of Division 2. Notice that the other $10,000 then becomes a common cost of these product lines.

Why would $10,000 of traceable fixed cost become a common cost when the division is divided into product lines? The $10,000 could be the monthly salary of the manager of Division 2. This salary would be a traceable cost when we are speaking of the division as a whole, but it would be *common* to the product lines manufactured and sold by the division. Any allocation of this salary cost between the two product lines would have to be on some arbitrary basis. To avoid this, the salary cost of the division's manager should be treated as a common cost when the division is segmented into product lines.

---

[6] See Peter R. Santori, "Measuring Product Profitability in Today's Manufacturing Environment," in Barry J. Brinker, ed., *Emerging Practices in Cost Management* (Boston, Mass.: Warren, Gorham & LaMont, 1990).

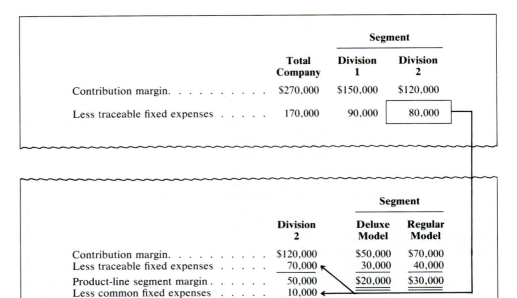

	Total Company	Segment	
		Division 1	Division 2
Contribution margin.	$270,000	$150,000	$120,000
Less traceable fixed expenses	170,000	90,000	80,000

	Division 2	Segment	
		Deluxe Model	Regular Model
Contribution margin.	$120,000	$50,000	$70,000
Less traceable fixed expenses	70,000	30,000	40,000
Product-line segment margin	50,000	$20,000	$30,000
Less common fixed expenses	10,000		
Divisional segment margin	$ 40,000		

The $70,000 that remains a traceable fixed cost even after Division 2 is segmented into product lines consists of costs that can be identified directly with the product lines on a nonarbitrary (that is, cause-and-effect) basis. This $70,000 might consist of advertising, for example, expended for product-line promotion, of which $30,000 was expended for promotion of the deluxe model and $40,000 was expended for promotion of the regular model. Product-line advertising would be a traceable fixed cost of the product lines, since it could be assigned to the lines without having to make an arbitrary allocation.

Segment Margin

Observe from Exhibit 12–2 that the **segment margin** is obtained by deducting the traceable fixed costs of a segment from the segment's contribution margin. It represents the margin available after a segment has covered all of its own costs. *The segment margin is the best gauge of the long-run profitability of a segment,* since only those costs that are caused by the segment are used in its computation. If in the long run a segment can't cover its own costs, then that segment probably should not be retained (unless it has important side effects on other segments). Notice from Exhibit 12–2, for example, that one sales territory (foreign) has a negative segment margin. This means that the segment is not covering its own costs; it is generating more costs than it collects in revenue.[7]

From a decision-making point of view, the segment margin is most useful in long-run decisions such as capacity changes, long-run pricing, and outsourcing of production. By contrast, as we noted earlier, the contribution margin is most useful in decisions relating to short-run changes in volume, such as pricing of special orders and utilization of existing capacity.

[7] Retention or elimination of product lines and other segments is covered in more depth in Chapter 13.

EXHIBIT 12–4
Graphic Presentation
of Segment
Reporting—Detroit
Motor Company

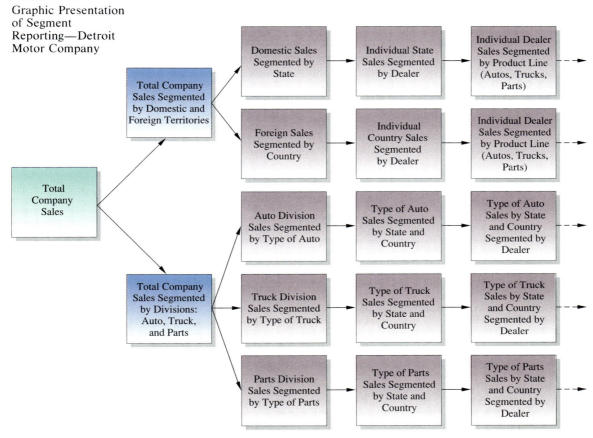

Varying Breakdowns of Total Sales

In order to obtain more detailed information, a company may show total sales broken down into several different segment arrangements. For example, a company may show total sales segmented in three different ways: (1) segmented according to divisions; (2) segmented according to product lines, without regard to the divisions in which the products are sold; and (3) segmented according to the sales territories in which the sales were made. In each case, the sum of sales by segments would add up to total company sales; the variation in segment breakdowns would simply give management the ability to look at the total company from several different directions.

After this type of segmentation of total sales has been made, many companies then break each segment down more finely, such as we illustrated earlier in Exhibit 12–2. Another breakdown by segments is illustrated graphically in Exhibit 12–4. Using personal computers, the kind of segmentation shown in these exhibits is well within the reach of most companies today.

CUSTOMER PROFITABILITY ANALYSIS

In prior sections, we have noted that companies analyze profitability in many ways, including by product, by market segment, and by channel of distribution. One frequently overlooked way to analyze profitability is by customer. Although

Objective 3
Explain how to determine customer profitability.

managers generally assume that a dollar of sales to one customer is just as profitable as a dollar of sales to any other customer, this assumption often is not correct. The reason is that customers have varying demands for resource-consuming activities, just as products, markets, or other segments of a company have varying demands. For example, some customers order in smaller lots and more frequently than other customers, requiring more paperwork and materials handling. Some customers order nonstandard parts that require special engineering work, special machinery setups, and perhaps special packaging and handling. Other customers always seem to be in a hurry and want special expediting and delivery services. Customers who demand high levels of these resource-consuming activities should not be cross-subsidized by customers who demand little in the way of customized services, special packaging, and so forth. However, unless the activities that are provided for customer support are traced to the company's various customers, cross-subsidization almost certainly will occur.

FOCUS ON CURRENT PRACTICE

"A small machine shop . . . was operating three shifts per day, seven days per week, but was making very little profit. The major customer—a Fortune 100 company that the machine shop considered its bread and butter—provided 50 percent of the machine shop's volume. But the reality was far different, as a careful examination of customer-driven activities revealed. The major customer ordered high-precision machined parts in low lot sizes. The jobs for this customer, therefore, required long setups, intense engineering support, intense NC [numerical control] programming support, intense sales support, high order activity, higher scrapped units, high inspection intensity, and high inventory for this firm. Rather than assigning these incremental costs to the products manufactured for the major customer, however, these costs were spread across the machine shop's complete product line. As a result, this major customer enjoyed subsidized pricing; the machine shop's number-one customer was actually its number-one loser."[8]

After the various customer-support activities in a company have been identified, the costs of providing these activities should be charged to the customers who require them. Thus, a customer who requires special accounts receivable terms, many small orders and deliveries, the packing of goods in shop-ready containers, and specialized field service should be quoted a price that reflects these costly activities. This is why we stated in Chapter 5 that suppliers who make deliveries to customers in a JIT environment frequently quote prices that are somewhat higher than prices charged by other suppliers. The higher prices are needed to compensate these suppliers for the special activities required on their part to support JIT customers.

Businesses that have analyzed customer profitability have been surprised to find that a fairly small number of customers are apparently responsible for most of their profits. It is also common to find that a small number of customers consume far more resources than are warranted by their revenues.

---

[8] Peter B. B. Turney and James M. Reeve, "The Impact of Continuous Improvement on the Design of Activity-Based Cost Systems," *Journal of Cost Management* 4, no. 2 (Summer 1990), p. 49.

RESPONSIBILITY ACCOUNTING

Segment reporting is just an extension of the responsibility accounting concept that was introduced in Chapter 9. By assigning costs and revenues to segments, top management is able to see where responsibility lies for control purposes and is able to measure the performance of segment managers.

In this section, we discuss the various levels of responsibility into which companies typically classify their segments. Before discussing these levels of responsibility, however, we must first explain why a *decentralized* approach to decision making is imperative if segment reporting is to achieve the purposes for which it is intended.

Decentralization and Segment Reporting

Managers have found that segment reporting is of greatest value in organizations that are decentralized. A **decentralized organization** is one in which decision making is not confined to a few top executives but rather is spread throughout the organization, with managers at various levels making key operating decisions relating to their sphere of responsibility. Decentralization must be viewed in terms of degree, since all organizations are decentralized to some extent out of economic necessity. At one extreme, a strongly decentralized organization is one in which there are few, if any, constraints on the freedom of a segment manager to make a decision, even at the lowest levels. At the other extreme, a strongly centralized organization is one in which little freedom exists to make a decision other than at top levels of management. Although most firms today fall somewhere between these two extremes, there is a pronounced tendency toward the decentralized end of the spectrum.

Many benefits are felt to accrue from decentralization. These benefits include the following:

1. By spreading the burden of decision making among many levels of management, top management is relieved of much day-to-day problem solving and is left free to concentrate on long-range planning and on coordination of efforts.
2. Allowing managers greater decision-making control over their segments provides excellent training as these managers rise in the organization. In the absence of such training, managers may be ill-prepared to function in a decision-making capacity as they are given greater responsibility.
3. Added responsibility and decision-making authority often result in increased job satisfaction and provide greater incentive for the segment manager to put forth his or her best efforts.
4. Decisions are best made at that level in an organization where problems and opportunities arise. Top management can't be intimately acquainted with local conditions in all of a company's segments.
5. Decentralization provides a more effective basis for measuring a manager's performance, since through decentralization he or she has power to control segment results.

Cost, Profit, and Investment Centers

Decentralized companies typically divide their segments into three levels of responsibility. These levels consist of cost centers, profit centers, and investment centers, such as illustrated in Exhibit 12–5. The level (or degree) of responsibility

Objective 4
Explain the importance of decentralization in a responsibility accounting system

Objective 5
Differentiate between cost centers, profit centers, and investment centers, and explain how performance is measured in each.

EXHIBIT 12–5
Segments Classified as Cost, Profit, and Investment Centers

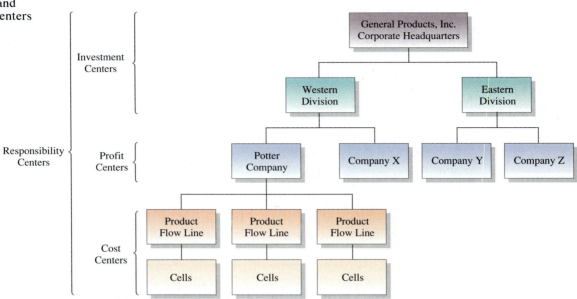

ranks from lowest in a cost center to highest in an investment center, as explained below.[9]

Cost Center   A segment that has control over the incurrence of cost is known as a *cost center*. A distinguishing feature of a **cost center** is that it has no control over either the generating of revenue or the use of investment funds.

Profit Center   By contrast to a cost center, a **profit center** is any segment that has control over both cost and revenue. Potter Company in Exhibit 12–5, for example, would be a profit center in the General Products, Inc., organization, since it would be concerned with marketing its goods as well as producing them. Like a cost center, however, a profit center generally does not have control over how investment funds are used.

Investment Center   An **investment center** is any segment of an organization that has control over cost and revenue and also over the use of investment funds. The corporate headquarters of General Products, Inc., would clearly be an example of an investment center. Corporate officers have ultimate responsibility for seeing that production and marketing goals are met. In addition, they have responsibility for seeing that adequate facilities are available to carry out the production and marketing functions, and for seeing that adequate working capital is available for operating needs. Whenever a segment of an organization has control over investment in such areas as physical plant and equipment, receivables, inventory, and entry into new markets, then it is termed an *investment center*. Potter Company in Exhibit 12–5 could be an investment center if it were given control over invest-

---

[9] Some organizations also identify *revenue centers,* which are responsible for sales activities only (products are shipped directly from the plant or from a warehouse as orders are submitted). An example of such a revenue center would be a Sears Surplus Store. Other companies would consider this to be just another type of profit center, since costs of some kind (salaries, rent, utilities) are usually present.

ment funds for some of these purposes. In the more usual situation, however, Potter Company would be a profit center within the larger organization, with most (or all) investment decisions being made at the divisional or central headquarters levels.

The reader should be cautioned that in everyday business practice the distinction between a profit center and an investment center is sometimes blurred, and the term *profit center* is often used to refer to either one. Thus, a company may refer to one of its segments as being a profit center when in fact the manager has full control over investment decisions in the segment. For purposes of our discussion, we will continue to maintain a distinction between the two, as made above.

Note from Exhibit 12–5 that cost centers, profit centers, and investment centers are *all* identified as responsibility centers. **Responsibility center** is a broad term, meaning any point in an organization that has control over the incurrence of cost, the generating of revenue, or the use of investment funds.

Measuring Management Performance

These concepts of responsibility accounting are very important, since they assist in defining a manager's sphere of responsibility and also in determining how performance will be evaluated.

Cost centers are evaluated by means of performance reports, either in terms of meeting cost standards that have been set or in terms of activity-based measures that focus on continuous improvement. Profit centers are evaluated by means of contribution income statements, in terms of meeting sales and cost objectives. Investment centers are also evaluated by means of contribution income statements, but normally in terms of the *rate of return* that they are able to generate on *invested funds*. In the following section, we discuss rate of return as a tool for measuring managerial performance in a segment that operates as an investment center.

RATE OF RETURN FOR MEASURING MANAGERIAL PERFORMANCE

When a company is decentralized, segment managers are given a great deal of autonomy in directing the affairs in their particular areas of responsibility. So great is this autonomy that the various profit and investment centers are often viewed as being virtually independent businesses, with their managers having about the same control over decisions as if they were in fact running their own independent firms. With this autonomy, fierce competition often develops among managers, with each striving to make his or her segment the "best" in the company.

Competition between investment centers is particularly keen when it comes to passing out funds for expansion of product lines, or for introduction of new product lines. How do top managers in corporate headquarters go about deciding who gets new investment funds as they become available, and how do these managers decide which investment centers are most profitably using the funds that have already been entrusted to their care? One of the most popular ways of making these judgments is to measure the rate of return that investment center managers are able to generate on their assets. This can be done through the *return on investment (ROI)* formula.

Objective 6
Compute the return on investment (ROI) by means of the ROI formula.

FOCUS ON CURRENT PRACTICE

The granting of autonomy to profit and investment center managers has been a hallmark of General Motors for many years. As explained by one of the company's presidents, "The most effective results and the maximum progress and stability of the business are achieved by placing its executives in the same relative position, so far as possible, that they would occupy if they were conducting a business on their own account. This provides opportunity for accomplishment through the exercise of individual initiative . . . ."[10]

The Return on Investment (ROI) Formula

To understand the elements behind the ROI formula, refer to Exhibit 12–6. As shown in the exhibit, **return on investment (ROI)** is the product of an investment center's *margin* multiplied by its *turnover*. The **margin** portion of the ROI formula is a measure of management's ability to control operating expenses in relation to

EXHIBIT 12–6

Elements of Return on Investment (ROI)

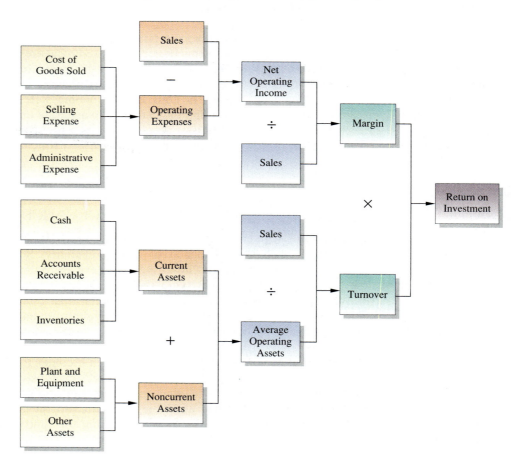

[10] Alfred P. Sloan, Jr., *My Years with General Motors* (New York: Doubleday, 1964), p. 407. Copyright © 1963 by Alfred P. Sloan, Jr. Reprinted by permission of Harold Matson Company, Inc.

sales. The lower the operating expenses per dollar of sales, the higher the margin earned. The **turnover** portion of the ROI formula is a measure of the amount of sales that can be generated in an investment center for each dollar invested in operating assets. In sum, the ROI formula can be expressed as follows:

$$\text{Margin} \times \text{Turnover} = \text{ROI}$$

$$\text{Margin} = \frac{\text{Net operating income}}{\text{Sales}} \qquad \text{Turnover} = \frac{\text{Sales}}{\text{Average operating assets}}$$

Therefore,

$$\frac{\text{Net operating income}}{\text{Sales}} \times \frac{\text{Sales}}{\text{Average operating assets}} = \text{ROI}$$

In the past, managers have tended to focus only on the margin earned and have ignored the turnover of assets. To some degree at least, the margin earned can be a valuable measure of a manager's performance. Standing alone, however, it overlooks one very crucial area of a manager's responsibility—the control of investment in operating assets. Excessive funds tied up in operating assets can be just as much of a drag on profitability as excessive operating expenses. One of the real advantages of the ROI formula is that it forces the manager to control his or her investment in operating assets as well as to control expenses and the margin earned.

Du Pont was the first major corporation to recognize the importance of looking at both margin *and* turnover in assessing the performance of a manager. To it must go the credit for pioneering the ROI concept. Monsanto Company and other major corporations have followed Du Pont's lead, and the ROI formula is now widely used as the key measure of a manager's performance when that manager has control of an investment center. The ROI formula blends together many aspects of the manager's responsibilities into a single figure that can be compared against the return of competing investment centers, as well as against that of other firms in the industry.

Net Operating Income and Operating Assets Defined

Note from Exhibit 12–6 that *net operating income,* rather than net income, is used in the ROI formula to compute the margin percentage. **Net operating income** is income before interest and taxes. In business jargon, it is sometimes referred to as EBIT (earnings before interest and taxes). The reader should become familiar with these terms. The reason for using net operating income in the formula is that the income figure used should be consistent with the base to which it is applied. Notice that the base in the turnover part of the formula consists of *operating assets.* Thus, to be consistent we use net operating income in computing the margin figure.

Operating assets would include cash, accounts receivable, inventory, plant and equipment, and all other assets held for productive use in the organization. Examples of assets that would not be included in the operating assets category (that is, examples of nonoperating assets) would include land being held for future use, or a factory building being rented to someone else. The operating assets base used in the formula is typically computed as the average between the beginning and the end of the year.

Plant and Equipment: Net Book Value or Gross Cost?

A major issue in ROI computations is the dollar amount of plant and equipment that should be included in the operating assets base. To illustrate the problem involved, assume that a company reports the following amounts for plant and equipment on its balance sheet:

Plant and equipment	$3,000,000
Less accumulated depreciation . . .	900,000
Net book value	$2,100,000

What dollar amount of plant and equipment should the company include with its operating assets in computing ROI? One widely used approach is to include only the plant and equipment's *net book value*—that is, the plant's original cost less accumulated depreciation ($2,100,000 in the example above). A second approach is to ignore depreciation and include the plant's entire *gross cost* in the operating assets base ($3,000,000 in the example above). Both of these approaches are used in actual practice, even though they will obviously yield very different operating asset and ROI figures.

The following arguments can be raised for and against including only a plant's net book value as part of operating assets:

Arguments for Net Book Value

1. It is consistent with how plant and equipment items are reported on the balance sheet (that is, cost less accumulated depreciation to date).
2. It is consistent with the computation of net operating income, which includes depreciation as an operating expense.

Arguments against Net Book Value

1. It allows ROI to increase over time as net book value declines through the depreciation process.
2. It discourages the replacement of old, worn-out equipment in that the purchase of new equipment can have a dramatic, adverse effect on ROI.

The following arguments can be raised for and against including a plant's entire gross cost as part of operating assets:

Arguments for Gross Cost

1. It eliminates both age of equipment and method of depreciation as factors in ROI computations.
2. It allows the manager to replace old, worn-out equipment with a minimum adverse impact on ROI.

Arguments against Gross Cost

1. It is not consistent with either the income statement or the balance sheet in that it ignores depreciation.
2. It involves double counting in that the original cost of an asset plus any recovery of that original cost (through the depreciation process) are both included in the operating assets base.

Managers generally view consistency as the most important of the considerations above. As a result, a majority of companies use the net book value approach in ROI computations. In this book, we will also use the net book value approach unless a specific exercise or problem directs otherwise.

CONTROLLING THE RATE OF RETURN

When being measured by the ROI formula, an investment center manager can improve profitability in three ways:

Objective 7
Show how changes in sales, expenses, and assets affect an organization's ROI.

1. By increasing sales.
2. By reducing expenses.
3. By reducing assets.

To illustrate how the rate of return can be improved by each of these three actions, let us assume the following data for an investment center:

$$\begin{array}{ll} \text{Net operating income.} & \$\ 10{,}000 \\ \text{Sales} & 100{,}000 \\ \text{Average operating assets} & 50{,}000 \end{array}$$

The rate of return generated by the investment center would be:

$$\frac{\text{Net operating income}}{\text{Sales}} \times \frac{\text{Sales}}{\text{Average operating assets}} = \text{ROI}$$

$$\frac{\$10{,}000}{\$100{,}000} \times \frac{\$100{,}000}{\$50{,}000} = \text{ROI}$$

$$10\% \quad \times \quad 2 \quad = 20\%$$

As we stated above, to improve the ROI figure the manager must either (1) increase sales, (2) reduce expenses, or (3) reduce the operating assets.

Approach 1: Increase Sales   Assume that the manager in our example is able to increase sales from $100,000 to $110,000. Assume further that either because of good cost control or because most costs in the company are fixed, the net operating income increases even more rapidly, going from $10,000 to $12,000 per period. The operating assets remain constant.

$$\frac{\$12{,}000}{\$110{,}000} \times \frac{\$110{,}000}{\$50{,}000} = \text{ROI}$$

$$10.91\% \ \times \ \ 2.2 \ \ = 24\% \text{ (as compared to 20\% above)}$$

Approach 2: Reduce Expenses   Assume that the manager is able to reduce expenses by $1,000, so that net operating income increases from $10,000 to $11,000. Both sales and operating assets remain constant.

$$\frac{\$11{,}000}{\$100{,}000} \times \frac{\$100{,}000}{\$50{,}000} = \text{ROI}$$

$$11\% \ \times \ \ 2 \ \ = 22\% \text{ (as compared to 20\% above)}$$

Approach 3: Reduce Assets   Assume that the manager is able to reduce operating assets from $50,000 to $40,000. Sales and net operating income remain unchanged.

$$\frac{\$10,000}{\$100,000} \times \frac{\$100,000}{\$40,000} = \text{ROI}$$

$$10\% \quad \times \quad 2.5 \quad = 25\% \text{ (as compared to 20\% above)}$$

A clear understanding of these three approaches to improving the ROI figure is critical to the effective management of an investment center. We will now look at each approach in more detail.

Increase Sales

In first looking at the ROI formula, one is inclined to think that the sales figure is neutral, since it appears as the denominator in the margin computation and as the numerator in the turnover computation. We *could* cancel out the sales figure, but we don't do so for two reasons. First, this would tend to draw attention away from the fact that the rate of return is a function of *two* variables, margin and turnover. And second, it would tend to conceal the fact that a change in sales can affect *either* the margin or the turnover in an organization. To explain, a change in sales can affect the *margin* if expenses increase or decrease at a different rate than sales. For example, a company may be able to keep a tight control on its costs as its sales go up, thereby allowing the net operating income to increase more rapidly than sales and thus allowing the margin percentage to rise. Or a company may have many fixed expenses that will remain constant as sales go up, thereby again allowing a rapid increase in the net operating income and causing the margin percentage to rise. Either (or both) of these factors could have been responsible for the increase in the margin percentage from 10 percent to 10.91 percent illustrated in approach 1 above.

Further, a change in sales can affect the *turnover* if sales either increase or decrease without a proportionate increase or decrease in the operating assets. In the first approach above, for example, sales increased from $100,000 to $110,000, but the operating assets remained unchanged. As a result, the turnover increased from 2 to 2.2 for the period.

In sum, because a change in sales can affect either the margin or the turnover in a company, such changes are particularly significant to the manager in his or her attempts to control the ROI figure.

Reduce Expenses

Often the easiest route to increased profitability and to a stronger ROI figure is to simply cut the "fat" out of an organization through a concerted effort to control expenses. When profit margins begin to be squeezed, this is generally the first line of attack by a manager. The discretionary fixed costs usually come under scrutiny first, and various programs are either curtailed or eliminated in an effort to cut costs. Managers must be careful, however, lest they cut out muscle and bone along with the fat. Also, they must remember that frequent cost-cutting binges can be destructive to the morale of an organization. Most managers now agree that it is best to stay "lean and mean" all of the time.

Reduce Operating Assets

Managers have always been sensitive to the need to control sales, operating expenses, and operating margins. They have not always been equally sensitive, however, to the need to control investment in operating assets. Firms that have adopted the ROI approach to measuring managerial performance report that one of the first reactions on the part of investment center managers is to trim down their investment in operating assets. The reason, of course, is that these managers soon realize that an excessive investment in operating assets will reduce the asset turnover and hurt the rate of return. As these managers pare down their investment in operating assets, funds are released that can be used elsewhere in the organization.

FOCUS ON CURRENT PRACTICE

X Company, a firm located in a western state, is a manufacturer of high-quality cast-iron pipe. A few years ago a large conglomerate acquired a controlling interest in the stock of X Company, and X Company became an investment center of the larger organization. The parent company measured the performance of the investment center managers by the ROI formula. X Company managers quickly found that their performance was below that of other investment centers within the organization. Because of their mediocre performance, X Company managers realized that they were in a poor position to compete for new investment funds. As one step in an effort to improve the rate of return, the company took a hard look at its investment in operating assets. As a result, it was able to reduce inventory alone by nearly 40 percent. This resulted in several million dollars becoming available for productive use elsewhere in the company. Within two years' time, the rate of return being generated by X Company improved dramatically. The controller of X Company, speaking at a management development conference, stated that the company had always been profitable in terms of net income to sales, so there really had been no incentive to watch the investment in operating assets prior to being put under the ROI microscope.

What approaches are open to an investment center manager in attempts to control the investment in operating assets? One approach is to pare out unneeded inventory. JIT purchasing and JIT manufacturing have been extremely helpful in reducing inventories of all types, with the result that ROI figures have improved dramatically in some companies. Another approach is to devise various methods of speeding up the collection of receivables. For example, many firms now employ the lockbox technique by which customers in distant states send their payments directly to local post office boxes. The funds are received and deposited by a local bank in behalf of the payee firm. This speeds up the collection process, thereby reducing the total investment required to carry accounts receivable. (The released funds are typically used to pay amounts due to short-term creditors.) As the accounts receivable balance is reduced, the asset turnover is increased.

The Problem of Allocated Expenses and Assets

In decentralized organizations such as General Products, Inc., it is common practice to allocate to the separate divisions the expenses incurred in operating corporate headquarters. When such allocations are made, a very thorny question arises as to whether these allocated expenses should be considered in the divisions' rate of return computations.

It can be argued on the one hand that allocated expenses should be included in rate of return computations, since they represent the value of services rendered to the divisions by central headquarters. On the other hand, it can be argued that they should not be included, since the divisional managers have no control over the incurrence of the expenses and since the "services" involved are often of questionable value, or are hard to pin down.

At the very least, *arbitrary* allocations should be avoided in rate of return computations. If arbitrary allocations are made, great danger exists of creating a bias for or against a particular division, as discussed earlier in the chapter. Expense allocations should be limited to the cost of those *actual* services provided by central headquarters that the divisions would *otherwise* have had to provide for themselves. The amount of expense allocated to a division should not exceed the cost that the division would have incurred if it had provided the service for itself.

These same guidelines apply to asset allocations from central corporate headquarters to the separate divisions. Assets relating to overall corporate operations should not be included as part of the divisional operating assets in divisional ROI computations, unless there are clear and traceable benefits to the divisions from the assets involved. As before, any type of arbitrary allocations (such as allocations on the basis of sales dollars) should be avoided.

Criticisms of ROI

Although ROI is widely used in evaluating performance, it is far from being a perfect tool. The method is subject to the following criticisms:

1. ROI tends to emphasize short-run performance rather than long-run profitability. In an attempt to protect the current ROI, a manager may be motivated to reject otherwise profitable investment opportunities. (This point is discussed further in the following section.)
2. ROI is not consistent with the cash flow models used for capital expenditure analysis. (Cash flow models are discussed in Chapters 14 and 15.)
3. ROI may not be fully controllable by the division manager due to the presence of committed costs. This inability to control the ROI can make it difficult to distinguish between the performance of the manager and the performance of the division as an investment.

In an effort to overcome these problems, some companies use multiple criteria in evaluating performance rather than relying on ROI as a single measure. Other criteria used include the following:

Growth in market share.

Increases in productivity.

Dollar profits.

Receivables turnover.

Inventory turnover.

Product innovation.

Ability to expand into new and profitable areas.

It is felt that the use of multiple performance measures such as those above provide a more comprehensive picture of a manager's performance than can be obtained by relying on ROI alone.

RESIDUAL INCOME—ANOTHER MEASURE OF PERFORMANCE

We have assumed in our discussion that the purpose of an investment center should be to maximize the rate of return that it is able to generate on operating assets. There is another approach to measuring performance in an investment center that focuses on a concept known as *residual income*. **Residual income** is the net operating income that an investment center is able to earn *above* some minimum rate of return on its operating assets. When residual income is used to measure performance, the purpose is to maximize the total amount of residual income, *not* to maximize the overall ROI figure.

Objective 8
Compute the residual income and enumerate the strengths and weaknesses of this method of measuring performance.

Consider the following data for two comparable divisions:

	Performance Measured by—	
	Rate of Return (Division A)	Residual Income (Division B)
Average operating assets	$100,000 (a)	$100,000
Net operating income	$ 20,000 (b)	$ 20,000
ROI, (b) ÷ (a).	20%	
Minimum required rate of return is assumed to be 15% (15% × $100,000) . . .		15,000
Residual income		$ 5,000

Notice that Division B has a positive residual income of $5,000. The performance of the manager of Division B is assessed according to how large or how small this residual income figure is from year to year. The larger the residual income figure, the better is the performance rating received by the division's manager.

Motivation and Residual Income

Many companies believe that residual income is a better measure of performance than rate of return. They argue that the residual income approach encourages managers to make profitable investments that would be rejected by managers who are being measured by the ROI formula. To illustrate, assume that each of the divisions above is presented with an opportunity to make an investment of $25,000 in a new project that would generate a return of 18 percent on invested assets. The manager of Division A would probably reject this opportunity. Note from the tabulation above that his division is already earning a return of 20 percent on its assets. If he takes on a new project that provides a return of only 18 percent, then his overall ROI will be reduced, as shown below:

	Present	New Project	Overall
Average operating assets (a) . . .	$100,000	$25,000	$125,000
Net operating income (b).	$ 20,000	$ 4,500*	$ 24,500
ROI, (b) ÷ (a)	20%	18%	19.6%

* $25,000 × 18% = $4,500.

Since the performance of the manager of this division is being measured according to the *maximum* rate of return that he is able to generate on invested assets, he will be unenthused about any investment opportunity that reduces his current ROI figure. He will tend to think and act along these lines, even though the opportunity he rejects might have benefited the company *as a whole*.

On the other hand, the manager of Division B will be very anxious to accept the new investment opportunity. The reason is that she isn't concerned about maximizing her rate of return. She is concerned about maximizing her residual income. Any project that provides a return greater than the minimum required 15 percent will be attractive, since it will add to the *total amount* of the residual income figure. Under these circumstances, the new investment opportunity with its 18 percent return will clearly be attractive, as shown below:

	Present	New Project	Overall
Average operating assets.	$100,000	$25,000	$125,000
Net operating income	$ 20,000	$ 4,500*	$ 24,500
Minimum required rate of return is again assumed to be 15%	15,000	3,750†	18,750
Residual income	$ 5,000	$ 750	$ 5,750

* $25,000 × 18% = $4,500.
† $25,000 × 15% = $3,750.

Thus, by accepting the new investment project, the manager of Division B will increase her division's overall residual income figure and thereby show an improved performance as a manager. The fact that her division's overall ROI might be lower as a result of accepting the project is immaterial, since performance is being evaluated by residual income, not ROI. The well-being of both the manager and the company as a whole will be maximized by accepting all investment opportunities down to the 15 percent cutoff rate.

Divisional Comparison and Residual Income

The residual income approach has one major disadvantage. It can't be used to compare the performance of divisions of different sizes, since by its very nature it creates a bias in favor of larger divisions. That is, one would expect larger divisions to have more residual income than smaller divisions, not necessarily because they are better managed but simply because of the bigger numbers involved.

As an example, consider the following residual income computations for Division X and Division Y:

	Division	
	X	Y
Average operating assets (a)	$1,000,000	$250,000
Net operating income	$ 120,000	$ 40,000
Minimum required return: 10% × (a) . . .	100,000	25,000
Residual income	$ 20,000	$ 15,000

Observe that Division X has slightly more residual income than Division Y, but that Division X has $1,000,000 in operating assets as compared to only $250,000 in operating assets for Division Y. Thus, Division X's greater residual income is probably more a result of its size than the quality of its management. In fact, it appears that the smaller division is better managed, since it has been able to generate nearly as much residual income with only one fourth as much in operating assets to work with.

TRANSFER PRICING

Special problems arise in evaluating segment performance when segments of a company do business with each other. The problems revolve around the question of what transfer price to charge between the segments. A **transfer price** is defined as the price charged when one segment of a company provides goods or services to another segment of the company.

Objective 9
Identify three ways that transfer prices can be set.

The Need for Transfer Prices

Assume that a vertically integrated firm has three divisions. The three divisions are:

Mining Division.
Processing Division.
Manufacturing Division.

The Mining Division mines raw materials that are transferred to the Processing Division. After processing, the Processing Division transfers the processed materials to the Manufacturing Division. The Manufacturing Division then includes the processed materials as part of its finished product.

In this example, we have two transfers of goods between divisions within the same company. What price should control these transfers? Should the price be set so as to include some "profit" element to the selling division? Should it be set so as to include only the accumulated costs to that point? Or should it be set at yet another figure? The choice of a transfer price can be complicated by the fact that each division may be supplying portions of its output to outside customers, as well as to sister divisions. Another complication is that the price charged by one division becomes a cost to the other division, and the higher this cost, the lower will be the purchasing division's rate of return. Thus, the purchasing division would like the transfer price to be low, whereas the selling division would like it to be high. The selling division may even want to charge the same "market" price internally as it charges to outside customers.

As the reader may guess, the problem of what transfer price to set between segments of a company has no easy solution and often leads to protracted and heated disputes between investment center managers. Yet some transfer price *must* be set if data are to be available for evaluating performance in the various parts or divisions of a company. In practice, three general approaches are used in setting transfer prices:

1. Set transfer prices at cost using:
   a. Variable cost.
   b. Full (absorption) cost.
2. Set transfer prices at the market price.
3. Set transfer prices at a negotiated price.

In the following discussion, we consider each of these approaches to the transfer pricing problem.

Transfer Prices at Cost

Many firms make transfers between divisions on a basis of the accumulated cost of the goods being transferred, thus ignoring any profit element to the selling division. A transfer price computed in this way might be based only on the variable costs involved, or fixed costs might also be considered and the transfer price thus based on full (absorption) costs accumulated to the point of transfer. Although the cost approach to setting transfer prices is relatively simple to apply, it has some major defects. These defects can be brought out by the following illustration:

> Assume that a multidivisional company has a Relay Division that manufactures an electrical relay widely used as a component part by various governmental contractors. The relay requires $12 in variable costs to manufacture and sells for $20. Each relay requires one direct labor-hour to complete, and the division has a capacity of 50,000 relays per year.
>
> The company also has a Motor Division. This division has developed a new motor requiring an electrical relay, but this relay is different from the one presently being manufactured by the Relay Division. To acquire the needed relay, the Motor Division has two alternatives:
>
> 1. The new relay can be purchased from an outside supplier at a price of $15 per relay, based on an order of 50,000 relays per year.
> 2. The new relay can be manufactured by the company's Relay Division. This would require that the Relay Division give up its present business, since manufacture of the new relay would require all of its capacity. One direct labor-hour would be required to produce each relay (the same time as that required by the old relay). Variable manufacturing costs would total $10 per relay.
>
> In addition to the relay, each motor would require $25 in other variable cost inputs. The motors would sell for $60 each.

Should the Relay Division give up its present relay business and start producing the new relays for the Motor Division, or should it continue its present business and let the Motor Division purchase the new relays from the outside supplier? Let us assume first that the Motor Division decides to purchase the new relays from the outside supplier at $15 each, thereby permitting the Relay Division to continue to produce and sell the old relay. Partial income statements are given at the top of Exhibit 12–7 to show the effects of this decision on each division and on the company as a whole. Notice from the exhibit (alternative 1) that each division will have a positive contribution margin, and that the company as a whole will have a contribution margin of $1,400,000 for the year if this alternative is accepted.

Let us assume second that the Motor Division purchases the new relays internally from the Relay Division at a transfer price of $10 per relay (the Relay Division's variable costs per unit). This would require that the Relay Division give up its present outside business. On the surface this would seem to be a good decision, since the variable costs to the Relay Division would be only $10 for the new relay as compared to $12 for the old relay, and since the Motor Division would otherwise have to purchase the new relays from the outside supplier at $15 each. But this illusion quickly vanishes when we look at the data at the bottom of Exhibit 12–7 (alternative 2). Notice that this alternative would reduce the contribution margin for the company as a whole by $150,000 per year.

Herein lies one of the defects of the cost approach to setting transfer prices: Cost-based transfer prices can lead to dysfunctional decisions in a company because this approach has no built-in mechanism for telling the manager when

Alternative 1: The Motor Division purchases the new relays from the outside supplier at $15 each; the Relay Division continues to produce and sell the old relays.

EXHIBIT 12–7

Effects of Pricing Transfers between Divisions at Cost

| | 50,000 Units per Year | | |
	Relay Division	Motor Division	Total Company
Sales (at $20 per old relay and $60 per motor, respectively)	$1,000,000	$3,000,000	$4,000,000
Less variable expenses (at $12 per old relay and $40* per motor, respectively)	600,000	2,000,000	2,600,000
Contribution margin	$ 400,000	$1,000,000	$1,400,000

Alternative 2: The Motor Division purchases the new relays from the Relay Division at an internal transfer price of $10 per relay (the Relay Division's variable cost of producing the new relay). This requires that the Relay Division give up its present outside business.

	Relay Division	Motor Division	Total Company
Sales (at $10 per new relay and $60 per motor, respectively)	$ 500,000	$3,000,000	$3,000,000‡
Less variable expenses (at $10 per new relay and $35† per motor, respectively)	500,000	1,750,000	1,750,000‡
Contribution margin	$ –0–	$1,250,000	$1,250,000
Decrease in contribution margin for the company as a whole if alternative 2 is accepted			$ 150,000

* $15 outside supplier's cost per new relay + Other variable costs of $25 per motor = $40 per motor.
† $10 internal transfer price per new relay + Other variable costs of $25 per motor = $35 per motor.
‡ The $500,000 in intracompany sales has been eliminated.

transfers should or should not be made between divisions. In the case at hand, transfers should *not* be made; the Relay Division should go on selling the old relay to the governmental contractors, and the Motor Division should buy the new relay from the outside supplier. Although this is obvious after seeing the income statement data in Exhibit 12–7, such matters can be obscured when dealing with multiproduct divisions. Thus, as a result of using cost as a transfer price, profits for the company as a whole may be adversely affected and the manager may never know about it.

Exhibit 12–7 also illustrates another defect associated with cost-based transfer prices: The only division that will show any profits is the one that makes the final sale to an outside party. Other divisions, such as the Relay Division in the bottom portion of Exhibit 12–7, will show no profits for their efforts; thus, evaluation by the ROI formula or by the residual income approach will not be possible.

Another serious criticism of cost-based transfer prices lies in their general inability to provide incentive for control of costs. If the costs of one division are simply passed on to the next, then there is little incentive for anyone to control costs. The final selling division is simply burdened with the accumulated waste and inefficiency of intermediate processors and will be penalized with a rate of return that is deficient in comparison to that of competitors. Experience has shown that unless costs are subject to some type of competitive pressures at transfer points, waste and inefficiency almost invariably develop.

Despite these shortcomings, cost-based transfer prices are in fairly common use. Advocates argue that they are easily understood and highly convenient to use. If transfer prices are to be based on cost, then the costs should be standard costs rather than actual costs. This will at least avoid passing inefficiency on from one division to another.

A General Formula for Computing Transfer Prices

Objective 10
Use the transfer pricing formula to compute an appropriate transfer price between segments, assuming the selling division (a) is operating at full capacity and (b) has idle capacity.

A general formula exists that can be used by the manager as a starting point in computing the appropriate transfer price between divisions or segments in a multidivisional company.[13] The formula is that *the transfer price should be equal to the unit variable costs of the good being transferred, plus the contribution margin per unit that is lost to the selling division as a result of giving up outside sales.* The formula can be expressed as:

$$\text{Transfer price} = \frac{\text{Variable costs}}{\text{per unit}} + \frac{\text{Lost contribution margin per}}{\text{unit on outside sales}}$$

Applying this formula to the preceding data for the Relay Division and the Motor Division, the proper transfer price for the Relay Division to charge for the new relay would be:

Transfer price = $10 (the variable costs of the new relay) + $8 (the contribution margin per unit lost to the Relay Division as a result of giving up outside relay sales: $20 selling price − $12 variable costs = $8 lost contribution margin on the old relays)

Transfer price = $18 per unit

Upon seeing this transfer price, it becomes immediately obvious to management that no transfers should be made between the two divisions, since the Motor Division can buy its relays from an outside supplier at only $15 each. Thus, the

---

[11] Roger Y. W. Tang, C. K. Walter, and Robert H. Raymond, "Transfer Pricing—Japanese vs. American Style," *Management Accounting* 60, no. 7 (January 1979), p. 14.

[12] Roger Y. W. Tang, "Transfer Pricing in the 1990s," *Management Accounting* 73, no. 8 (February 1992), p. 25.

[13] For background discussion, see Ralph L. Benke, Jr., and James Don Edwards, "Transfer Pricing: Techniques and Uses," *Management Accounting* 61, no. 12 (June 1980), pp. 44–46.

transfer price enables management to reach the correct decision and to avoid any adverse effect on profits.

Two additional points should be noted before going on. First, *the price set by the transfer pricing formula always represents a lower limit for a transfer price, since the selling division must receive at least the amount shown by the formula in order to be as well off as if it only sold to outside customers.* Under certain conditions (discussed later), the price can be more than the amount shown by the formula, but it can't be less or the selling division and the company as a whole will suffer. Second, the transfer price computed by using the formula is a price based on competitive market conditions. The remainder of our discussion will focus on the setting of market-based transfer prices.

Transfers at Market Price: General Considerations

Some form of competitive **market price** (that is, the price charged for an item on the open market) is generally regarded as the best approach to the transfer pricing problem. The reason is that the use of market prices dovetails well with the profit center concept and makes profit-based performance evaluation feasible at many levels of an organization. By using market prices to control transfers, *all* divisions or segments are able to show profits for their efforts—not just the final division in the chain of transfers. The market price approach also helps the manager to decide when transfers should be made, as we saw earlier, and tends to lead to the best decisions involving transfer questions that may arise on a day-to-day basis.

The market price approach is designed for use in highly decentralized organizations. By this we mean that it is used in those organizations where divisional managers have enough autonomy in decision making so that the various divisions can be viewed as being virtually independent businesses with independent profit responsibility. The idea in using market prices to control transfers is to create the competitive market conditions that would exist if the various divisions were *indeed* separate firms and engaged in arm's-length, open-market bargaining. To the extent that the resulting transfer prices reflect actual market conditions, divisional operating results provide an excellent basis for evaluating managerial performance.

The National Association of Accountants describes other advantages and the overall operation of the market price approach as follows:

> Internal procurement is expected where the company's products and services are superior or equal in design, quality, performance, and price, and when acceptable delivery schedules can be met. So long as these conditions are met, the receiving unit suffers no loss and the supplier unit's profit accrues to the company. Often the receiving division gains advantages such as better control over quality, assurance of continued supply, and prompt delivery.[14]

In addition to the formula given earlier, there are certain guidelines that should be followed when using market prices to control transfers between divisions. These guidelines are:

1. The buying division must purchase internally so long as the selling division meets all bona fide outside prices and wants to sell internally.

---

[14] National Association of Accountants, *Research Series No. 30,* ``Accounting for Intra-Company Transfers'' (New York: National Association of Accountants, June 1956), pp. 13–14.

2. If the selling division does not meet all bona fide outside prices, then the buying division is free to purchase outside.

3. The selling division must be free to reject internal business if it prefers to sell outside.[15]

4. An impartial board must be established to help settle disagreements between divisions over transfer prices.

Transfers at Market Price: Well-Defined Intermediate Market

Not all companies or divisions face the same market conditions. Sometimes the only customer a division has for its output is a sister division. In other situations, an **intermediate market** may exist for part or all of a division's output. By intermediate market, we mean that a market exists in which an item can be sold *immediately* and *in its present form* to outside customers, if desired, rather than being transferred to another division for use in its manufacturing process. Thus, if an intermediate market exists, a division will have a choice between selling its products to outside customers on the intermediate market or selling them to other divisions within the company. In the paragraphs that follow, we consider transfer pricing in those situations where intermediate markets are strong and well defined.

Let us assume that Division A of International Company has a product that can be sold either to Division B or to outside customers in an intermediate market. The cost and revenue structures of the two divisions are given below:

Division A		**Division B**	
Intermediate selling price if sold outside	$25	Final market price outside	$100
Variable costs	15	Transfer price from Division A (or outside purchase price)	25
		Variable costs added in Division B	40

What transfer price should control transfers between the two divisions? In this case, the answer is easy; the transfer price should be $25—the price that Division A can get by selling in the intermediate market and the price that Division B would otherwise have to pay to purchase the desired goods from an outside supplier in the intermediate market. This price can also be obtained by applying the formula developed earlier:

$$\text{Transfer price} = \frac{\text{Variable costs}}{\text{per unit}} + \frac{\text{Lost contribution margin per}}{\text{unit on outside sales}}$$

Transfer price = $15 + ($25 − $15 = $10)

Transfer price = $25

The choices facing the two divisions are shown graphically in Exhibit 12–8.

So long as Division A receives a transfer price of $25 per unit from Division B, it will be willing to sell all of its output internally. In selling to Division B, Division A will be just as well off as if it had sold its product outside at the $25 price. In like manner, so long as the price charged by outside suppliers is not less than $25 per unit, Division B will be willing to pay that price to Division A. The $25 per unit intermediate market price therefore serves as an acceptable transfer price between the two divisions. The result of transfers at this price is summarized in the next table.

---

[15] Ibid., p. 14. Outside sales may provide the selling division with a greater return (as in the case of the Relay Division in our earlier example).

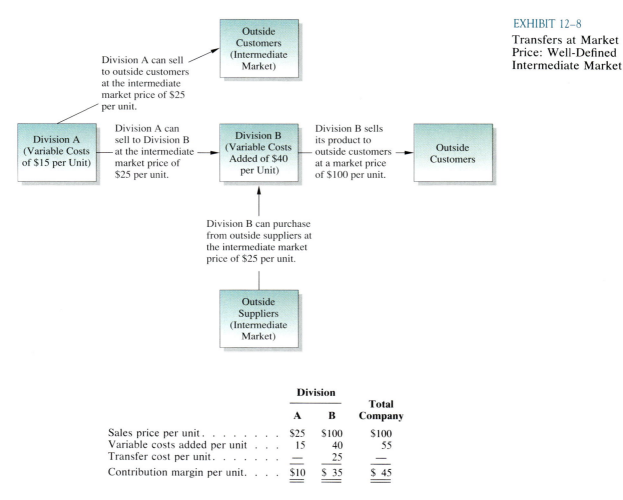

| | **Division** | | |
	A	**B**	**Total Company**
Sales price per unit.	$25	$100	$100
Variable costs added per unit . . .	15	40	55
Transfer cost per unit.	—	25	—
Contribution margin per unit. . . .	$10	$ 35	$ 45

The contribution margin realized for the entire company is $45 per unit. By using the $25 intermediate market price to control intracompany transfers, the firm is able to show that a portion of this margin accrues from the efforts of Division A and that a portion accrues from the efforts of Division B. These data will then serve as an excellent basis for evaluating managerial performance in the divisions, using the rate of return or residual income approaches.

Transfers at Market Price: Price Changes in the Intermediate Market

We have assumed in the above discussion that there was complete price agreement in the intermediate market, and therefore that Division B could purchase the needed goods from an outside supplier at the same $25 price as being charged by Division A. In reality, complete price agreement often doesn't exist, or it may be upset by some suppliers deciding to cut their prices for various reasons. Returning to the preceding example, let us assume that an outside supplier has offered to supply the goods to Division B for only $20 per unit, rather than at the normal $25 intermediate market price being charged by Division A. Should Division B accept this offer, or should Division A cut its price to $20 in order to get Division B's business? The answer will depend on whether Division A (the selling division) is operating at full or at partial capacity.

Selling Division at Full Capacity   If Division A (the selling division) is operating at capacity, then it will have to give up outside sales in order to sell to Division B. Under these circumstances, the transfer price will be computed in the same way as we computed it earlier:

$$\text{Transfer price} = \frac{\text{Variable costs}}{\text{per unit}} + \frac{\text{Lost contribution margin per}}{\text{unit on outside sales}}$$

$$\text{Transfer price} = \$15 + \left(\begin{array}{c} \$25 \text{ outside} \\ \text{selling price} \end{array} - \begin{array}{c} \$15 \text{ variable} \\ \text{costs} \end{array} = \begin{array}{c} \$10 \text{ lost contribution} \\ \text{margin per unit} \end{array} \right)$$

$$\text{Transfer price} = \$25$$

Recall that the price set by the formula always represents a *lower limit* for a transfer price, since the selling division must receive at least the amount shown by the formula in order to be as well off as if it sold only to outside customers. Therefore, Division A should not cut its price to $20 in order to sell to Division B. If Division A cuts its price, it will lose $5 per unit in contribution margin, and both it and the company as a whole will be worse off.

In short, whenever the selling division must give up outside sales in order to sell internally, it has an opportunity cost that must be considered in setting the transfer price. As shown by the formula, this opportunity cost is the contribution margin that will be lost as a result of giving up outside sales. Unless the transfer price can be set high enough to cover this opportunity cost, along with the variable costs associated with the sale, then no transfers should be made.

Selling Division with Idle Capacity   If the selling division has idle capacity, then a different situation exists. Under these conditions, the selling division's opportunity cost *may* be zero (depending on what alternative uses it has for its idle capacity). Even if the opportunity cost is zero, many managers would argue that the transfer price should still be based on prevailing market prices, to the extent that these prices can be determined accurately and fairly. Other managers would argue that idle capacity combined with an opportunity cost of zero, or near zero, calls for a negotiation of the transfer price downward from prevailing market rates, so that both the buyer and the seller can profit from the intracompany business.

Under idle capacity conditions, so long as the selling division receives a price greater than its variable costs (at least in the short run), all parties will benefit by keeping business inside the company rather than having the buying division go outside. The accuracy of this statement can be shown by returning to the example in the preceding section. Assume again that an outside supplier offers to sell the needed goods to Division B at $20 per unit. In this case, however, we will assume that Division A has enough idle capacity to supply all of Division B's needs, with no prospects for additional outside sales at the current $25 intermediate market price. Using our formula, the transfer price between Divisions A and B would be:

$$\text{Transfer price} = \frac{\text{Variable costs}}{\text{per unit}} + \frac{\text{Lost contribution margin per}}{\text{unit on outside sales}}$$

$$\text{Transfer price} = \$15 + \$0$$

$$\text{Transfer price} = \$15$$

As stated before, the $15 figure represents a lower limit for a transfer price. Actually, the transfer price can be anywhere between this figure and the $20 price being quoted to Division B from the outside. In this situation, therefore, we have a transfer price *range* in which to operate, as shown below:

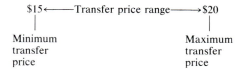

If Division A (the selling division) is hesitant to reduce its price, should it be required to at least meet the $20 figure to supply Division B's needs? The answer is no. The guidelines given earlier indicate that the selling division is not required to sell internally. Rather than accept a $20 price for its goods, Division A may prefer to let its capacity remain idle and search for other, more profitable products.

If Division A decides not to reduce its price to $20 to meet outside competition, should Division B be forced to continue to pay $25 and to buy internally? The answer again is no. The guidelines given earlier state that if the selling division is not willing to meet all bona fide outside prices, then the buying division is free to go outside to get the best price it can. However, if the selling division has idle capacity and the buying division purchases from an outside supplier, then *suboptimization* will result for the selling division, possibly for the buying division, and certainly for the company as a whole. By **suboptimization** we mean that the overall level of profitability will be less than the segment or the company is capable of earning. In our example, if Division A refuses to meet the $20 price, then *both it and the company as a whole will lose $5 per unit in potential contribution margin ($20 − $15 = $5).* In short, where idle capacity exists, every effort should be made to negotiate a price acceptable to both the buyer and the seller that will keep business within the company as a whole.

Negotiated Transfer Price

There are some situations where a transfer price below the intermediate market price can be justified. For example, selling and administrative expenses may be less when intracompany sales are involved, or the volume of units may be large enough to justify quantity discounts. In addition, we have already seen that a price below the prevailing market price may be justified when the selling division has idle capacity. Situations such as these can probably be served best by some type of **negotiated transfer price.** A negotiated transfer price is one agreed on between the buying and selling divisions that reflects unusual or mitigating circumstances.

Possibly the widest use of negotiated market prices is in those situations where no intermediate market prices are available. For example, one division may require an item that is not available from any outside source and therefore must be produced internally. Under these circumstances, the buying division must negotiate with another division in the company and agree to a transfer price that is attractive enough to the other division to cause it to take on the new business. To provide an example of how a transfer price would be set in such a situation, consider the following data:

> Division X has developed a new product that requires a custom-made fitting. Another division in the company, Division Y, has both the experience and the equipment necessary to produce the fitting. Division X has approached Division Y for a quoted unit price based on the production of 5,000 fittings per year.
> Division Y has determined that the fitting would require variable costs of $8 per unit. However, in order to have time to produce the fitting, Division Y would have to

reduce production of a different product, product A, by 3,500 units per year. Product A sells for $45 per unit and has variable costs of $25 per unit. What transfer price should Division Y quote to Division X for the new fittings? Employing our formula, we get:

$$\text{Transfer price} = \frac{\text{Variable costs}}{\text{per unit}} + \frac{\text{Lost contribution margin per}}{\text{unit on outside sales}}$$

The lost contribution margin per unit would be:

Selling price of product A	$ 45
Variable costs of product A	25
Contribution margin of product A . . .	20
Unit sales of product A given up. . . .	× 3,500
Total lost contribution margin	$70,000

$$\frac{\$70,000 \text{ lost contribution margin on product A}}{5,000 \text{ fittings to be manufactured for Division X}} = \frac{\$14 \text{ lost contribution}}{\text{margin per fitting}}$$

Transfer price = $8 variable costs + $14 lost contribution margin
Transfer price = $22 per fitting

Thus, the transfer price quoted by Division Y should not be less than $22 per fitting. Division Y might quote a higher price if it wants to increase its overall profits (at the expense of Division X), but it should not quote less than $22, or the profits of the company as a whole will suffer. If Division X is not happy with the $22 price, it can get a quote from an outside manufacturer for the fitting.

If Division Y in our example has idle capacity, then the appropriate transfer price is less clear. The lower limit for a transfer price would be the $8 variable costs, as discussed earlier. However, no division wants to simply recover its costs, so the actual transfer price would undoubtedly be greater than $8, according to what could be negotiated between the two divisional managers. In situations such as this, the selling division will often add some "target" markup figure to its costs in quoting a transfer price to the buying division.

Divisional Autonomy and Suboptimization

A question often arises as to how much autonomy should be granted to divisions in setting their own transfer prices and in making decisions concerning whether to sell internally or to sell outside. Should the divisional heads have complete authority to make these decisions, or should top corporate management step in if it appears that a decision is about to be made that would result in suboptimization? For example, if idle capacity exists in the selling division and divisional managers are unable to agree on a transfer price, should top corporate management step in and *force* settlement of the dispute?

Efforts should always be made, of course, to bring disputing managers together. But the almost unanimous feeling among top corporate executives is that divisional heads should not be forced into an agreement over a transfer price. That is, if a particular divisional head flatly refuses to change his or her position in a dispute, *then this decision should be respected* even if it results in suboptimization. This is simply the price that is paid for the concept of divisional autonomy. If top corporate management steps in and forces the decisions in difficult situations, then the purposes of decentralization are defeated and the company simply becomes a centralized operation with decentralization of only minor decisions and responsibilities. In short, if a division is to be viewed as an autonomous unit with independent profit responsibility, then it must have control over its own destiny— even to the extent of having the right to make bad decisions.

We should note, however, that if a division consistently makes bad decisions, the results will soon have an impact on its rate of return, and the divisional manager may find that he or she has to defend the division's performance. Even so, the manager's right to get into an embarrassing situation must be respected if decentralization is to operate successfully. The overwhelming experience of multidivisional companies is that divisional autonomy and independent profit responsibility lead to much greater success and profitability than do closely controlled, centrally administered operations. Part of the price of this success and profitability is an occasional situation of suboptimization due to pettiness, bickering, or just plain managerial stubbornness.

International Aspects of Transfer Pricing

Transfer pricing is used worldwide to control the flow of goods and services between segments of an organization. However, the objectives of transfer pricing change when a multinational corporation (MNC) is involved and the goods and services being transferred must cross international borders. The objectives of international transfer pricing, as compared to domestic transfer pricing, are summarized in Exhibit 12–9.[16]

As shown in the exhibit, the objectives of international transfer pricing focus on minimizing taxes, duties, and foreign exchange risks, along with enhancing a company's competitive position and improving its relations with foreign governments. Although domestic objectives such as managerial motivation and divisional autonomy are always desirable in an organization, they usually become secondary when international transfers are involved. Companies will focus instead on charging a transfer price that will slash its total tax bill or that will strengthen a foreign subsidiary.

For example, charging a low transfer price for parts shipped to a foreign subsidiary may reduce customs duty payments as the parts cross international borders, or it may help the subsidiary to compete in foreign markets by keeping the subsidiary's costs low. On the other hand, charging a high transfer price may help an MNC draw excess profits out of a country that has stringent controls on foreign remittances, or it may allow an MNC to shift income from a country that has high income tax rates to a country that has low rates.

EXHIBIT 12–9

Domestic and International Transfer Pricing Objectives

---

[16] Data in the exhibit are taken in part from Wagdy M. Abdallah, "Guidelines for CEOs in Transfer Pricing Policies," *Management Accounting* 70, no. 3 (September 1988), p. 61.

In sum, managers must be sensitive to the geographic, political, and economic circumstances in which they are operating, and set transfer prices in such a way as to optimize total company performance.

SUMMARY

The purpose of segment reporting is to provide information needed by the manager to determine the profitability of product lines, divisions, sales territories, and other segments of a company. Under the contribution approach to segment reporting, costs are classified as either traceable or common. Only those costs that are traceable are assigned to segments; common costs are not allocated to segments since doing so might result in misleading data.

Costs that are traceable to a segment are further classified as either variable or fixed. Deducting variable costs from sales yields a contribution margin, which is highly useful in short-run planning and decision making. The traceable fixed costs of a segment are then deducted from the contribution margin to obtain a segment margin. The segment margin is highly useful in long-run planning and decision making.

Segments are often divided into three levels of responsibility—cost centers, profit centers, and investment centers. The ROI formula is widely used as a method of evaluating performance in an investment center because it summarizes into one figure many aspects of an investment center manager's responsibilities. As an alternative to the ROI formula, some companies use residual income as a measure of investment center performance. These companies argue that the residual income approach encourages profitable investment in many situations where the ROI approach might discourage investment.

Transfer pricing relates to the price to be charged in a transfer of goods or an exchange of services between two segments (such as divisions) within an organization. A transfer price can be based on the cost of the goods being transferred, on the intermediate market price of the goods being transferred, or on a price negotiated between the buying and selling divisions. The predominant feeling is that the best transfer price is some version of market price—either intermediate or negotiated—to the extent that such a price exists or can be determined for the good or service involved. The use of either market price or a negotiated price to record transfers facilitates performance evaluation by permitting both the buyer and the seller to be treated as independent, autonomous units.

REVIEW PROBLEM: TRANSFER PRICING

Situation A

Collyer Products, Inc., has a Valve Division that manufactures and sells a standard valve as follows:

Capacity in units.	100,000
Selling price to outside customers on the intermediate market	$30
Variable costs per unit	16
Fixed costs per unit (based on capacity) . . .	9

The company has a Pump Division that could use this valve in the manufacture of one of its pumps. The Pump Division is currently purchasing 10,000 valves per year from an overseas supplier at a cost of $29 per valve.

Required

1. Assume that the Valve Division has ample idle capacity to handle all of the Pump Division's needs. What should be the transfer price between the two divisions?
2. Assume that the Valve Division is selling all that it can produce to outside customers on the intermediate market. What should be the transfer price between the two divisions? At this price, will any transfers be made?
3. Assume again that the Valve Division is selling all that it can produce to outside customers on the intermediate market. Also assume that $3 in variable expenses can be avoided on intracompany sales, due to reduced selling costs. What should be the transfer price between the two divisions?

Solution to Review Problem Situation A

1. Since the Valve Division has idle capacity, it does not have to give up any outside sales in order to take on the Pump Division's business. Therefore, applying the transfer pricing formula, we get:

$$\text{Transfer price} = \frac{\text{Variable costs}}{\text{per unit}} + \frac{\text{Lost contribution margin per}}{\text{unit on outside sales}}$$

Transfer price = $16 + $0
Transfer price = $16

However, a transfer price of $16 represents a minimum price to cover the Valve Division's variable costs. The actual transfer price would undoubtedly fall somewhere between this amount and the $29 that the Pump Division is currently paying for its valves. Thus, we have a transfer price range in this case of from $16 to $29 per unit, depending on negotiations between the two divisions.

2. Since the Valve Division is selling all that it can produce on the intermediate market, it would have to give up some of these outside sales in order to take on the Pump Division's business. Applying the transfer pricing formula, we get:

$$\text{Transfer price} = \frac{\text{Variable costs}}{\text{per unit}} + \frac{\text{Lost contribution margin per}}{\text{unit on outside sales}}$$

Transfer price = $16 + $14*
Transfer price = $30

* $30 selling price − $16 variable costs = $14 contribution margin per unit.

Since the Pump Division can purchase valves from an outside supplier at only $29 per unit, no transfers will be made between the two divisions.

3. Applying the transfer pricing formula, we get:

$$\text{Transfer price} = \frac{\text{Variable costs}}{\text{per unit}} + \frac{\text{Lost contribution margin per}}{\text{unit on outside sales}}$$

Transfer price = $13* + $14
Transfer price = $27

* $16 variable costs − $3 variable costs avoided = $13.

In this case, we again have a transfer price range; it is between $27 (the lower limit) and $29 (the Pump Division's outside price) per unit.

Situation B

Refer to the original data in situation A above. Assume that the Pump Division needs 20,000 special valves per year that are to be supplied by the Valve Division. The Valve Division's variable costs to manufacture and ship the special valve would be $20 per unit. To produce these special valves, the Valve Division would have to give up one half of its production of the regular valves (that is, cut its production of the regular valves from 100,000 units per year to 50,000 units per year). You can assume that the Valve Division is selling all of the regular valves that it can produce to outside customers on the intermediate market.

Required   If the Valve Division decides to produce the special valves for the Pump Division, what transfer price should it charge per valve?

Solution to Review Problem Situation B   To produce the 20,000 special valves, the Valve Division will have to give up sales of 50,000 regular valves to outside customers. The lost contribution margin on the 50,000 regular valves will be:

$$50,000 \text{ valves} \times \$14 \text{ per unit} = \$700,000$$

Spreading this lost contribution margin over the 20,000 special valves, we get:

$$\frac{\$700,000 \text{ lost contribution margin}}{20,000 \text{ special valves}} = \$35 \text{ per unit}$$

Using this amount in the transfer pricing formula, we get the following transfer price per unit on the special valves:

$$\text{Transfer price} = \frac{\text{Variable costs}}{\text{per unit}} + \frac{\text{Lost contribution margin per}}{\text{unit on outside sales}}$$
$$\text{Transfer price} = \$20 + \$35$$
$$\text{Transfer price} = \$55$$

Thus, the Valve Division must charge a transfer price of $55 per unit on the special valves in order to be as well off as if it just continued to manufacture and sell the regular valves on the intermediate market. If the Valve Division wishes to increase its profits, it could charge more than $55 per valve, but it must charge at least $55 in order to maintain its present level of profits.

KEY TERMS FOR REVIEW

Objective 11
Define or explain the key terms listed at the end of the chapter.

Common fixed cost   A cost that can't be identified with any particular segment of a company. Such costs, which are also known as *indirect costs*, exist to serve overall operating activities. (p. 531).

Cost center   A segment of a company that has control over the incurrence of cost but has no control over generating revenue or the use of investment funds. (p. 538)

Cross-subsidization   The result of improperly assigning costs between segments of an organization. (p. 527)

Decentralized organization   An organization in which decision making is not confined to a few top executives but rather is spread throughout the organization. (p. 537)

Intermediate market   A market in which an item can be sold immediately and in its present form to outside customers rather than just being transferred to another division for use in its manufacturing process. (p. 554)

Investment center   A segment that has control over the incurrence of cost and over the generating of revenue and that also has control over the use of investment funds. (p. 538)

Life cycle costing   A costing approach that focuses on all costs along the value chain that will be generated throughout the entire life of a product. (p. 527)

Margin   A measure of management's ability to control operating expenses in relation to sales. It is computed by dividing net operating income by the sales figure. (p. 540)

Market price   The price being charged for an item on the open (intermediate) market. (p. 553)

Negotiated transfer price   A transfer price agreed on between buying and selling divisions that reflects unusual or mitigating circumstances. (p. 557)

Net operating income   The income of an organization before interest and income taxes have been deducted. (p. 541)

Operating assets   Cash, accounts receivable, inventory, plant and equipment, and all other assets held for productive use in an organization. (p. 541)

Profit center   A segment that has control over the incurrence of cost and the generating of revenue but has no control over the use of investment funds. (p. 538)

Residual income   The net operating income that an investment center is able to earn above some minimum rate of return on its operating assets. (p. 547)

Responsibility center   Any point in an organization that has control over the incurrence of cost, the generating of revenue, or the use of investment funds. (p. 539)

Return on investment (ROI)   A measure of profitability in an organization that is computed by multiplying the margin by the turnover. (p. 540)

Segment   Any part or activity of an organization about which the manager seeks cost, revenue, or profit data. (p. 526)

Segment margin   The amount computed by deducting the traceable fixed costs of a segment from the segment's contribution margin. It represents the margin available after a segment has covered all of its own costs. (p. 534)

Segment reporting   An income statement or other report in an organization in which data are divided according to product lines, divisions, territories, or similar organizational segments. (p. 526)

Suboptimization   An overall level of profitability that is less than a segment or a company is capable of earning. (p. 557)

Traceable fixed cost   A cost that can be identified with a particular segment and that arises because of the existence of that segment. (p. 531)

Transfer price   The price charged when one division or segment provides goods or services to another division or segment of an organization. (p. 549)

Turnover   A measure of the amount of sales that can be generated in an investment center for each dollar invested in operating assets. It is computed by dividing sales by the average operating assets figure. (p. 541)

Value chain   The major business functions that add value to a company's products and services. These functions consist of research and development, product design, manufacturing, marketing, distribution, and customer service. (p. 526)

QUESTIONS

12-1   Identify three business practices that hinder proper cost assignment to segments of a company.

12-2   Define a segment of an organization. Give several examples of segments.

12-3   How does the contribution approach attempt to assign costs to segments of an organization?

12-4   Distinguish between a traceable cost and a common cost. Give several examples of each.

12-5   How does the manager benefit from having the income statement in a segmented format?

12-6   Explain how the segment margin differs from the contribution margin. Which concept is most useful to the manager? Why?

12-7   Why aren't common costs allocated to segments under the contribution approach?

12-8   How is it possible for a cost that is traceable under one segment arrangement to become a common cost under another segment arrangement?

12-9   What is meant by the term *decentralization*?

12–10   What benefits are felt to result from decentralization in an organization?

12–11   Distinguish between a cost center, a profit center, and an investment center.

12–12   How is performance in a cost center generally measured? Performance in a profit center? Performance in an investment center?

12–13   What is meant by the terms *margin* and *turnover?*

12–14   In what way is the ROI formula a more exacting measure of performance than the ratio of net income to sales?

12–15   When the ROI formula is being used to measure performance, what three approaches to improving the overall profitability are open to the manager?

12–16   The sales figure could be canceled out in the ROI formula, leaving simply net operating income over operating assets. Since this abbreviated formula would yield the same ROI figure, why leave sales in?

12–17   A student once commented to one of the authors, "It simply is not possible for a decrease in operating assets to result in an increase in profitability. The way to increase profits is to *increase* the operating assets." Discuss.

12–18   X Company has high fixed expenses and is currently operating somewhat above the break-even point. From this point on, will percentage increases in net income tend to be greater than, about equal to, or less than percentage increases in total sales? Why? (Ignore income taxes.)

12–19   What is meant by residual income?

12–20   In what way can ROI lead to dysfunctional decisions on the part of the investment center manager? How does the residual income approach overcome this problem?

12–21   Division A has operating assets of $100,000, and Division B has operating assets of $1,000,000. Can residual income be used to compare performance in the two divisions? Explain.

12–22   What is meant by the term *transfer price,* and why are transfer pricing systems needed?

12–23   Why are cost-based transfer prices in widespread use? What are the disadvantages of cost-based transfer prices?

12–24   If a market price for a product can be determined, why is it generally considered to be the best transfer price?

12–25   Under what circumstances might a negotiated price be a better approach to pricing transfers between divisions than the actual market price?

12–26   In what ways can suboptimization result if divisional managers are given full autonomy in setting, accepting, and rejecting transfer prices?

EXERCISES

E12–1   Royal Company produces and sells two products, X and Y. Revenue and cost information relating to the products follow:

	Product	
	X	**Y**
Selling price per unit	$ 6.00	$ 7.50
Variable expenses per unit.	2.40	5.25
Traceable fixed expenses per year . . .	45,000	21,000

Common fixed expenses in the company total $33,000 annually. During 19x2, the company produced and sold 15,000 units of product X and 28,000 units of product Y.

Required   Prepare an income statement for 19x2 segmented by product lines. Show both Amount and Percent columns for the company as a whole and for each of the product lines.

Raintree, Ltd., operates two divisions, A and B. A segmented income statement for the   **E12–2**
company's most recent year is given below:

	Total Company		Segment			
			Division A		Division B	
Sales	$450,000	100%	$150,000	100%	$300,000	100%
Less variable expenses	225,000	50	45,000	30	180,000	60
Contribution margin.	225,000	50	105,000	70	120,000	40
Less traceable fixed expenses . . .	126,000	28	78,000	52	48,000	16
Divisional segment margin.	99,000	22	$ 27,000	18%	$ 72,000	24%
Less common fixed expenses . . .	63,000	14				
Net income	$ 36,000	8%				

Required

1. By how much would the company's net income increase if Division B increased its
    sales by $75,000 per year? Assume no change in cost behavior patterns in the com-
    pany.
2. Refer to the original data. Assume that sales in Division A increase by $50,000 next
    year and that sales in Division B remain unchanged. Assume no change in fixed costs
    in the divisions or in the company.
    a. Prepare a new segmented income statement for the company, using the format
        above. Show both amounts and percentages.
    b. Observe from the income statement you have prepared that the contribution
        margin ratio for Division A has remained unchanged at 70 percent (the same as in
        the data above) but that the segment margin ratio has changed. How do you
        explain the change in the segment margin ratio?

Refer to the data in E12–2. Assume that Division B's sales by product line are: **E12–3**

	Division B		Segment			
			Product X		Product Y	
Sales	$300,000	100%	$200,000	100%	$100,000	100%
Less variable expenses	180,000	60	128,000	64	52,000	52
Contribution margin.	120,000	40	72,000	36	48,000	48
Less traceable fixed expenses . . .	33,000	11	12,000	6	21,000	21
Product-line segment margin	87,000	29	$ 60,000	30%	$ 27,000	27%
Less common fixed expenses . . .	15,000	5				
Divisional segment margin.	$ 72,000	24%				

The company would like to initiate an intensive advertising campaign on one of the two
products during the next month. The campaign would cost $5,000. Marketing studies
indicate that such a campaign would increase sales of product X by $40,000 or increase
sales of product Y by $35,000.

Required

1. On which of the products would you recommend that the company focus its advertis-
    ing campaign? Show computations to support your answer.
2. In E12–2, Division B shows $48,000 in traceable fixed expenses. What happened to the
    $48,000 in this exercise?

You have a client who operates a large retail self-service grocery store that has a full range   **E12–4**
of departments. The management has encountered difficulty in using accounting data as a
basis for decisions as to possible changes in departments operated, products, marketing
methods, and so forth. List several overhead costs, or costs not applicable to a particular
department, and explain how the existence of such costs (sometimes called *common costs*

or *joint costs*) complicates and limits the use of accounting data in making decisions in such a store.

(CPA, adapted)

E12–5   Wingate Company has been experiencing losses for some time, as shown by its most recent monthly income statement below:

Sales	$1,000,000
Less variable expenses	390,000
Contribution margin	610,000
Less fixed expenses	625,000
Net income (loss)	$ (15,000)

In an effort to isolate the problem, the president has asked for an income statement segmented by division. Accordingly, the accounting department has developed the following information:

	Division		
	East	**Central**	**West**
Sales	$250,000	$400,000	$350,000
Variable expenses as a percentage of sales	52%	30%	40%
Traceable fixed expenses	$160,000	$200,000	$175,000

Required
1. Prepare an income statement segmented by divisions, as desired by the president. Show both Amount and Percent columns for the company as a whole and for each division.
2. As a result of a marketing study, the president believes that sales in the West Division could be increased by 20 percent if advertising in that division were increased by $15,000 each month. Would you recommend the increased avertising? Show computations.

E12–6   Selected operating data for two divisions of Regal Company are given below:

	Division	
	Southern	**Northern**
Sales	$4,000,000	$7,000,000
Average operating assets	2,000,000	2,000,000
Net operating income	360,000	420,000
Property, plant, and equipment (net)	950,000	800,000

Required
1. Compute the rate of return for each division, using the ROI formula.
2. So far as you can tell from the data, which divisional manager seems to be doing the better job? Why?

E12–7   Provide the missing data in the following tabulation:

	Division		
	A	**B**	**C**
Sales	$?	$11,500,000	$?
Net operating income	?	920,000	210,000
Average operating assets	800,000	?	?
Margin	4%	?	7%
Turnover	5	?	?
ROI	?	20%	14%

Holiday Products, Inc., has two divisions, A and B. Selected data on the two divisions follow:

E12–8

	Division	
	A	**B**
Sales	$3,000,000	$9,000,000
Net operating income	210,000	720,000
Average operating assets	1,000,000	4,000,000

1. Compute the ROI for each division. Where necessary, carry computations to two decimal places.
2. Assume that the company evaluates performance by use of residual income and that the minimum required return for any division is 15 percent. Compute the residual income for each division.
3. Is Division B's greater amount of residual income an indication that it is better managed? Explain.

Required

Sako Company's Audio Division produces a speaker that is widely used by manufacturers of various audio products. Sales and cost data on the speaker follow:

E12–9

Selling price per unit on the intermediate market	$60
Variable costs per unit	42
Fixed costs per unit (based on capacity)	8
Capacity in units	25,000

Sako Company has just organized a Hi-Fi Division that could use this speaker in one of its products. The Hi-Fi Division will need 5,000 speakers per year. It has received a quote of $60 per speaker from another manufacturer, less a 5 percent quantity discount.

1. Assume that the Audio Division is now selling only 20,000 speakers per year to outside customers on the intermediate market. If it begins to sell to the Hi-Fi Division and if each division is to be treated as an independent investment center, what transfer price would you recommend? Why?
2. Assume that the Audio Division is selling all of the speakers it can produce to outside customers on the intermediate market. Would this change the recommended transfer price? Explain.

Required

Supply the missing data in the tabulation below:

E12–10

	Company		
	A	**B**	**C**
Sales	$9,000,000	$7,000,000	$4,500,000
Net operating income	?	280,000	?
Average operating assets	3,000,000	?	1,800,000
ROI	18%	14%	?
Minimum required rate of return:			
Percentage	16%	?	15%
Dollar amount	?	320,000	?
Residual income	?	?	90,000

Division A manufactures electronic circuit boards. The boards can be sold either to Division B or to outside customers. During 19x5, the following activity occurred in Division A:

E12–11

Selling price per circuit board	$125
Production cost per circuit board	90
Number of circuit boards:	
Produced during the year	20,000
Sold to outside customers	16,000
Sold to Division B	4,000

Sales to Division B were at the same price as sales to outside customers. The circuit boards purchased by Division B were used in an electronic calculator manufactured by that division (one board per calculator). Division B incurred $100 in additional cost per calculator and then sold the calculators for $300 each.

Required   1.   Prepare income statements for 19x5 for Division A, Division B, and the company as a whole.
2.   Assume that Division A's manufacturing capacity is 20,000 circuit boards. In 19x6, Division B wants to purchase 5,000 circuit boards from Division A, rather than only 4,000 as in 19x5. (Circuit boards of this type are not available from outside sources.) Should Division A sell the 1,000 additional circuit boards to Division B, or continue to sell them to outside customers? Explain why this would or would not make any difference from the point of view of the company as a whole.

E12-12   In each of the cases below, assume that Division X has a product that can be sold either to outside customers on an intermediate market or to Division Y for use in its production process.

	Case	
	A	B
Division X:		
Capacity in units.	200,000	200,000
Number of units being sold on the		
intermediate market	200,000	160,000
Selling price per unit on the		
intermediate market	$90	$75
Variable costs per unit	70	60
Fixed costs per unit (based on capacity)	13	8
Division Y:		
Number of units needed for production.	40,000	40,000
Purchase price per unit now being paid		
to an outside supplier	$86	$74

Required   1.   Refer to the data in case A above. Assume in this case that $3 per unit in variable costs can be avoided on intracompany sales.
a.   Using the transfer pricing formula, determine the transfer price that Division X should charge for any sales to Division Y.
b.   Will any transfers be made between the two divisions? Explain.
2.   Refer to the data in case B above. Within what range should the transfer price be set for any sales between the two divisions? (Use the transfer pricing formula as needed.)

E12-13   Selected sales and operating data for three companies are given below:

	Company		
	A	B	C
Sales.	$12,000,000	$14,000,000	$25,000,000
Average operating assets.	3,000,000	7,000,000	5,000,000
Net operating income	600,000	560,000	800,000
Stockholders' equity.	1,500,000	2,900,000	3,000,000
Minimum required rate of return	14%	10%	16%

Required   1.   Compute the ROI for each company.
2.   Compute the residual income for each company.
3.   Assume that each company is presented with an investment opportunity that would yield a 15 percent rate of return.
a.   If performance is being measured by ROI, which company or companies will probably accept the opportunity? Reject? Why?

b.   If performance is being measured by residual income, which company or companies will probably accept the opportunity? Reject? Why?

PROBLEMS

Problems 12–14 through 12–20 deal primarily with segment reporting issues; Problems 12–21 through 12–37 deal primarily with ROI and transfer pricing issues.

Segment Reporting   Vulcan Company's income statement for last month is given below: **P12–14**

VULCAN COMPANY
Income Statement
For the Month Ended June 30, 19x1

Sales	$750,000
Less variable expenses	336,000
Contribution margin.	414,000
Less fixed expenses.	378,000
Net income	$ 36,000

Management is disappointed with the company's performance and is wondering what can be done to improve profits. By examining sales and cost records, you have determined the following:

a.   The company is divided into two sales territories—Northern and Southern. The Northern territory recorded $300,000 in sales and $156,000 in variable expenses during June; the remaining sales and variable expenses were recorded in the Southern territory. Fixed expenses of $120,000 and $108,000 are traceable to the Northern and Southern territories, respectively. The rest of the fixed expenses are common to the two territories.

b.   The company sells two products—Paks and Tibs. Sales of Paks and Tibs totaled $50,000 and $250,000, respectively, in the Northern territory during June. Variable expenses are 22 percent of the selling price for Paks and 58 percent for Tibs. Cost records show that $30,000 of the Northern territory's fixed expenses are traceable to Paks and $40,000 to Tibs, with the remainder common to the two products.

1.   Prepare segmented income statements such as illustrated in Exhibit 12–2, first showing the total company broken down between sales territories and then showing the Northern territory broken down by product line. Show both Amount and Percent columns for the company in total and for each segment.   *Required*

2.   Look at the statement you have prepared showing the total company segmented by sales territory. What points revealed by this statement should be brought to the attention of management?

3.   Look at the statement you have prepared showing the Northern territory segmented by product lines. What points revealed by this statement should be brought to the attention of management?

Restructuring a Segmented Statement   Losses have been incurred in Millard Company   **P12–15**
for some time. In an effort to isolate the problem and thereby improve the company's performance, management has requested that the monthly income statement be segmented by sales region. The company's first effort at preparing a segmented statement is given below. This statement is for May 19x5, the most recent month of activity.

	Sales Region		
	A	**B**	**C**
Sales	$450,000	$800,000	$ 750,000
Less regional expenses:			
Cost of goods sold	162,900	280,000	376,500
Advertising	108,000	200,000	210,000
Salaries	90,000	88,000	135,000
Utilities	13,500	12,000	15,000
Depreciation	27,000	28,000	30,000
Shipping expense	17,100	32,000	28,500
Total regional expenses	418,500	640,000	795,000
Regional income (loss) before			
corporate expenses	31,500	160,000	(45,000)
Less corporate expenses:			
Advertising (general)	18,000	32,000	30,000
General administrative expense	50,000	50,000	50,000
Total corporate expenses	68,000	82,000	80,000
Net income (loss)	$ (36,500)	$ 78,000	$(125,000)

Cost of goods sold and shipping expense are both variable; other costs are all fixed.

Millard Company is a wholesale distributor of office products. It purchases various office products from the manufacturer and distributes them in the three regions given above. The three regions are about the same size, and each has its own manager and sales staff. The products that the company distributes vary widely in profitability.

Required

1. List any disadvantages or weaknesses that you see to the statement format illustrated above.

2. Explain the basis being used to allocate the corporate expenses to the regions. Do you agree with these allocations? Explain.

3. Prepare a new segmented income statement for May 19x5, using the contribution approach. Show a Total column as well as data for each region. Include percentages on your statement for all columns.

4. Analyze the statement that you prepared in (3) above. What points that might help to improve the company's performance would you be particularly anxious to bring to the attention of management?

P12–16 Segment Reporting; Activity-Based Cost Assignment Diversified Products, Inc., has recently acquired a small publishing company that Diversified Products intends to operate as one of its investment centers. The newly acquired company has three books that it offers for sale—a cookbook, a travel guide, and a handy speller. Each book sells for $10. The publishing company's most recent monthly income statement is given below:

	Total Company		Product Line		
			Cookbook	Travel Guide	Handy Speller
Sales	$300,000	100%	$90,000	$150,000	$60,000
Less expenses:					
Printing costs	102,000	34	27,000	63,000	12,000
Advertising	36,000	12	13,500	19,500	3,000
General sales	18,000	6	5,400	9,000	3,600
Salaries	33,000	11	18,000	9,000	6,000
Equipment depreciation	9,000	3	3,000	3,000	3,000
Sales commissions	30,000	10	9,000	15,000	6,000
General administration	42,000	14	14,000	14,000	14,000
Warehouse rent	12,000	4	3,600	6,000	2,400
Depreciation—office					
facilities	3,000	1	1,000	1,000	1,000
Total expenses	285,000	95	94,500	139,500	51,000
Net income (loss)	$ 15,000	5%	$ (4,500)	$ 10,500	$ 9,000

The following additional information is available about the company:

a. Only printing costs and sales commissions are variable; all other costs are fixed. The printing costs (which include materials, labor, and variable overhead) are traceable to the three product lines as shown in the statement above. Sales commissions are 10 percent of sales for any product.

b. The same equipment is used to produce all three books, so the equipment depreciation cost has been allocated equally among the three product lines. An analysis of the company's activities indicates that the equipment is used 30 percent of the time to produce cookbooks, 50 percent of the time to produce travel guides, and 20 percent of the time to produce handy spellers.

c. The warehouse is used to store finished units of product, so the rental cost has been allocated to the product lines on the basis of sales dollars. The warehouse rental cost is $3 per square foot per year. The warehouse contains 48,000 square feet of space, of which 7,200 square feet is used by the cookbook line, 24,000 square feet by the travel guide line, and 16,800 square feet by the handy speller line.

d. The general sales cost above includes the salary of the sales manager and other sales costs not traceable to any specific product line. This cost has been allocated to the product lines on the basis of sales dollars.

e. The general administration cost and depreciation of office facilities both relate to overall administration of the company as a whole. These costs have been allocated equally to the three product lines.

f. All other costs are traceable to the three product lines in the amounts shown on the statement above.

The management of Diversified Products, Inc., is anxious to improve the new investment center's 5 percent return on sales.

Required

1. Prepare a new segmented income statement for the month, using the contribution approach. Show both an Amount column and a Percent column for the company as a whole and for each product line.
2. After seeing the statement in the main body of the problem, management has decided to eliminate the cookbook, since it is not returning a profit, and to focus all available resources on promoting the travel guide.
    a. Based on the statement you have prepared, do you agree with the decision to eliminate the cookbook? Explain.
    b. Based on the statement you have prepared, do you agree with the decision to focus all available resources on promoting the travel guide? Explain. (You may assume that an ample market is available for all three product lines.)
3. What additional points would you bring to the attention of management that might help to improve profits?

Multiple Segmented Income Statements   Kelvin Products, Inc.'s income statement segmented by divisions for last year is given below: **P12–17**

	Total Company	Division	
		Plastics	Glass
Sales	$1,500,000	$900,000	$600,000
Less variable expenses	700,000	400,000	300,000
Contribution margin.	800,000	500,000	300,000
Less traceable fixed expenses:			
Advertising	300,000	180,000	120,000
Depreciation	140,000	92,000	48,000
Administration	220,000	118,000	102,000
Total	660,000	390,000	270,000
Divisional segment margin	140,000	$110,000	$ 30,000
Less common fixed expenses . . .	100,000		
Net income	$ 40,000		

Top management doesn't understand why the Glass Division has such a low segment margin when its sales are only one third less than sales in the Plastics Division. Accordingly, management has directed that the Glass Division be further segmented into product lines. The following information is available on the product lines in the Glass Division:

	Product Line		
	X	Y	Z
Sales	$200,000	$300,000	$100,000
Traceable fixed expenses:			
Advertising	30,000	42,000	48,000
Depreciation	10,000	24,000	14,000
Administration	14,000	21,000	7,000
Variable expenses as a percentage of sales	65%	40%	50%

Analysis shows that $60,000 of the Glass Division's administration expenses are common to the product lines.

Required
1. Prepare a segmented income statement for the Glass Division, with segments defined as product lines. Use the contribution approach and the format shown in Exhibit 12–2. Show both an Amount column and a Percent column for the division in total and for each product line.
2. Management is surprised by product line Z's poor showing and would like to have the product line segmented by market. The following information is available about the two markets in which product line Z is sold:

	Market	
	Domestic	Foreign
Sales	$60,000	$40,000
Traceable fixed expenses:		
Advertising	18,000	30,000
Variable expenses as a percentage of sales	50%	50%

All of product line Z's depreciation and administration expenses are common to the markets in which the product is sold. Prepare a segmented income statement for product line Z, with segments defined as markets. Again use the format in Exhibit 12–2 and show both Amount and Percent columns.
3. Refer to the statement prepared in (1) above. The sales manager wants to run a special promotional campaign on one of the products over the next month. A market study indicates that such a campaign would increase sales of product line X by $40,000 or sales of product line Y by $30,000. The campaign would cost $8,000. Show computations to determine which product line should be chosen.

P12–18   Activity-Based Segment Reporting   "That commercial market has been dragging us down for years," complained Shanna Reynolds, president of Morley Products. "Just look at that anemic income figure for the commercial market. That market had three million dollars more in sales than the home market, but only a few thousand dollars more in profits. What a loser it is!"

The income statement to which Ms. Reynolds was referring is shown below:

	Total Company		Commerical Market	Home Market	School Market
Sales	$20,000,000	100.0%	$8,000,000	$5,000,000	$7,000,000
Less expenses:					
Cost of goods sold	9,500,000	47.5	3,900,000	2,400,000	3,200,000
Sales support	3,600,000	18.0	1,440,000	900,000	1,260,000
Order processing	1,720,000	8.6	688,000	430,000	602,000
Warehousing	940,000	4.7	376,000	235,000	329,000
Packing and shipping	520,000	2.6	208,000	130,000	182,000
Advertising	1,690,000	8.5	676,000	422,500	591,500
General management	1,310,000	6.6	524,000	327,500	458,500
Total expenses	19,280,000	96.4	7,812,000	4,845,000	6,623,000
Net income	$ 720,000	3.6%	$ 188,000	$ 155,000	$ 377,000

"I agree," said Walt Divot, the company's vice president. "We need to focus more of our attention on the school market, since it's our best segment. Maybe that will bolster profits and get the stockholders off our backs."

The following additional information is available about the company:

a. Morley Products is a wholesale distributor of various goods; the cost of goods sold figures above are traceable to the markets in the amounts shown.

b. Sales support, order processing, and packing and shipping are considered by management to be variable costs. Warehousing, general management, and advertising are fixed costs. These costs have all been allocated to the markets on the basis of sales dollars—a practice that the company has followed for years.

c. After careful analysis, you have determined the following events or transactions relating to the company's major activities:

			Number of Events or Transactions		
Activity Center and Cost Driver	Traceable Expenses	Total	Commercial Market	Home Market	School Market
Sales support (number of calls)	$3,600,000	24,000	8,000	5,000	11,000
Order processing (number of orders) . .	1,720,000	8,600	1,750	5,200	1,650
Warehousing (square feet of space) . . .	940,000	117,500	35,000	65,000	17,500
Packing and shipping (pounds shipped) .	520,000	104,000	24,000	16,000	64,000

d. You have determined the following breakdown of the company's advertising expense and general management expense:

		Market		
	Total	Commercial	Home	School
Advertising:				
Traceable	$1,460,000	$700,000	$180,000	$580,000
Common	230,000			
General management:				
Traceable—salaries	410,000	150,000	120,000	140,000
Common	900,000			

The company is searching for ways to improve profits, and you have suggested that a segmented statement in which costs are assigned on the basis of activities might provide some useful insights for management.

1. Refer to the data in (c) above. Determine a rate per event or transaction for each *Required* activity center. Then, using this rate, compute the amount of activity center cost assignable to each market.

2.   Using the data from (1) above and other data from the problem, prepare a revised segmented statement for the company. Use the contribution format. Show an Amount column and a Percent column for the company as a whole and for each market segment. Carry percentage figures to one decimal place. (Remember to include warehousing among the fixed expenses.)

3.   Scrutinize the data in your statement and identify those factors that should be brought to the attention of management.

P12-19   Multiple Segmented Income Statements   Hopwood Company divided its products into two divisions about a year ago. Since that time, one of the divisions has done well but the other division has shown steadily declining profits. The company's most recent monthly income statement is presented below:

	Total Company	Division — Metal Products	Division — Wood Products
Sales	$2,800,000	$1,600,000	$1,200,000
Less variable expenses:			
Production	891,000	420,000	471,000
Selling and other	273,000	140,000	133,000
Total variable expenses	1,164,000	560,000	604,000
Contribution margin	1,636,000	1,040,000	596,000
Less traceable fixed expenses	1,302,000	710,000	592,000
Divisional segment margin	334,000	$ 330,000	$ 4,000
Less common fixed expenses	185,000		
Net income	$ 149,000		

In an attempt to isolate the problem in the Wood Products Division, management has decided to segment that division by product line. The following data are available on the three products that the division manufactures and sells:

	Total	Product Line A	Product Line B	Product Line C
Sales	$1,200,000	$300,000	$500,000	$400,000
Variable costs as a percentage of sales:				
Production	—	35%	30%	54%
Selling and other	—	13	10	11
Traceable fixed expenses	$ 502,000	$120,000	$170,000	$212,000

Required

1.   Prepare a segmented income statement for the Wood Products Division, with segments defined by product lines. Use the contribution approach and the format shown in Exhibit 12–2. Show both an Amount column and a Percent column for the division in total and for each product line.

2.   The president now wants more information about product line C. This product is sold in two sales markets—the East and the West. Sales and other data about the two markets follow:

	Total	Sales Market — East	Sales Market — West
Sales	$400,000	$150,000	$250,000
Variable expenses as a percentage of sales:			
Production	—	54%	54.0%
Selling and other	—	20	5.6
Traceable fixed expenses	$160,000	$108,000	$ 52,000

Prepare a segmented income statement for product line C, with segments defined as markets. Again use the format in Exhibit 12–2 and show both Amount and Percent columns.

3. Scrutinize the statements you have prepared in (1) and (2). What points should be brought to the attention of management?

4. Assume that the president wants more information about the East sales market. Suggest ways in which this market might be further segmented.

Segmented Statements; Product-Line Analysis "At last, I can see some light at the end **P12–20** of the tunnel," said Steve Adams, president of Jelco Products. "Our losses have shrunk from over $75,000 a month at the beginning of the year to only $26,000 for August. If we can just isolate the remaining problems with products A and C, we'll be in the black by the first of next year."

 The company's income statement for the latest month (August) is presented below (absorption costing basis):

JELCO PRODUCTS
Income Statement
For August 19x1

	Total Company	Product A	Product B	Product C
Sales	$1,500,000	$600,000	$400,000	$500,000
Less cost of goods sold	922,000	372,000	220,000	330,000
Gross margin	578,000	228,000	180,000	170,000
Less operating expenses:				
Selling	424,000	162,000	112,000	150,000
Administrative	180,000	72,000	48,000	60,000
Total operating expenses	604,000	234,000	160,000	210,000
Net income (loss)	$ (26,000)	$ (6,000)	$ 20,000	$(40,000)

"What recommendations did that business consultant make?" asked Mr. Adams. "We paid the guy $100 an hour; surely he found something wrong." "He says our problems are concealed by the way we make up our statements," replied Sally Warren, the executive vice president. "He left us some data on what he calls 'traceable' and 'common' costs that he says we should be isolating in our reports." The data to which Ms. Warren was referring are shown below:

	Total Company	Product A	Product B	Product C
Variable costs:*				
Production (materials, labor,				
and variable overhead)	—	18%	32%	20%
Selling	—	10	8	10
Traceable fixed costs:				
Production	$376,000	$180,000	$36,000	$160,000
Selling	282,000	102,000	80,000	100,000
Common fixed costs:				
Production	210,000	—	—	—
Administrative	180,000	—	—	—

* As a percentage of sales.

"I don't see anything wrong with our statements," said Mr. Adams. "Bill, our chief accountant, says that he has been using this format for over 30 years. He's also very careful to allocate all of our costs to the products."

"I'll admit that Bill always seems to be on top of things," replied Ms. Warren. "By the way, purchasing says that the X7 chips we use in products A and B are on back order and won't be available for several weeks. From the looks of August's income statement, we had better concentrate our remaining inventory of X7 chips on product B.'' (Two X7 chips are used in both product A and product B.)

The following additional information is available on the company:

a. Work in process and finished goods inventories are nominal and can be ignored.
b. Products A and B each sell for $250 per unit, and product C sells for $125 per unit. Strong market demand exists for all three products.

Required 1. Prepare a new income statement for August, segmented by product and using the contribution approach. Show both Amount and Percent columns for the company in total and for each product.
2. Assume that Mr. Adams is considering the elimination of product C, due to the losses it is incurring. Based on the statement you prepared in (1), what points would you make for or against elimination of product C?
3. Do you agree with the company's decision to concentrate the remaining inventory of X7 chips on product B? Why or why not?
4. Product C is sold in both a vending and a home market, with sales and cost data as follows:

		Market	
	Total	Vending	Home
Sales.	$500,000	$50,000	$450,000
Variable costs:*			
Production	—	20%	20%
Selling	—	28	8
Traceable fixed costs:			
Selling	$ 75,000	$45,000	$ 30,000

* As a percentage of sales.

The remainder of product C's fixed selling costs and all of product C's fixed production costs are common to the markets in which product C is sold.

a. Prepare an income statement showing product C segmented by market. Use the contribution approach, and show both Amount and Percent columns for the product in total and for each market.
b. What points revealed by this statement would you be particularly anxious to bring to the attention of management?

P12–21 **ROI; Comparison of Industry Performance**   Comparative data on three companies in the same industry are given below:

	Company		
	A	B	C
Sales	$600,000	$500,000	$?
Net operating income	84,000	70,000	?
Average operating assets	300,000	?	1,000,000
Margin	?	?	3.5%
Turnover	?	?	2
ROI.	?	7%	?

Required 1. What advantages can you see in breaking down the ROI computation into two separate elements, margin and turnover?

2. Fill in the missing information above, and comment on the relative performance of the three companies in as much detail as the data permit. Make *specific recommendations* on steps to be taken to improve the return on investment, where needed.

(Adapted from National Association of Accountants, *Research Report No. 35*, p. 34)

The Appropriate Transfer Price; Well-Defined Intermediate Market   Hrubec Products, Inc., operates a Pulp Division that manufactures wood pulp for use in the production of various paper goods. Revenue and costs associated with a ton of pulp follow: **P12–22**

Selling price		$70
Less expenses:		
Variable	$42	
Fixed (based on a capacity of 50,000 tons per year)	18	60
Net income		$10

Hrubec Products has just acquired a small company that manufactures paper cartons. This company will be treated as a division of Hrubec with full profit responsibility. The newly formed Carton Division is currently purchasing 5,000 tons of pulp per year from a supplier at a cost of $70 per ton, less a 10 percent quantity discount. Hrubec's president is anxious for the Carton Division to begin purchasing its pulp from the Pulp Division, if an acceptable transfer price can be worked out.

For (1)–(4) below, assume that the Pulp Division can sell all of its pulp to outside customers at the normal $70 price.   *Required*

1. If the Carton Division purchases 5,000 tons of pulp per year from the Pulp Division, what price should control the transfers? Why?
2. Refer to your computations in (1). What is the lower limit and the upper limit for a transfer price? Is an upper limit relevant in this situation?
3. If the Pulp Division meets the price that the Carton Division is currently paying to its supplier and sells 5,000 tons of pulp to the Carton Division each year, what will be the effect on the profits of the Pulp Division, the Carton Division, and the company as a whole?
4. If the intermediate market price for pulp is $70 per ton, is there any reason why the Pulp Division should sell to the Carton Division for less than $70? Explain.

For (5)–(8) below, assume that the Pulp Division is currently selling only 30,000 tons of pulp each year to outside customers at the stated $70 price.

5. If the Carton Division purchases 5,000 tons of pulp from the Pulp Division each year, what price should control the transfers? Why?
6. Suppose that the Carton Division's outside supplier drops its price (net of the quantity discount) to only $59 per ton. Should the Pulp Division meet this price? Explain. If the Pulp Division does *not* meet the $59 price, what will be the effect on the profits of the company as a whole?
7. Refer to (6) above. If the Pulp Division refuses to meet the $59 price, should the Carton Division be required to purchase from the Pulp Division at a higher price, for the good of the company as a whole?
8. Refer to (6) above. Assume that due to inflexible management policies, the Carton Division is required to purchase 5,000 tons of pulp each year from the Pulp Division at $70 per ton. What will be the effect on the profits of the company as a whole?

Basic Transfer Pricing Computations   Alpha and Beta are divisions within the same company. Assume the following information relative to the two divisions: **P12–23**

| | Case | | | |
	1	2	3	4
Alpha Division:				
Capacity in units	80,000	400,000	150,000	300,000
Number of units now being sold to outside customers on the intermediate market	80,000	400,000	100,000	300,000
Selling price per unit on the intermediate market	$30	$90	$75	$50
Variable costs per unit	18	65	40	26
Fixed costs per unit (based on capacity)	6	15	20	9
Beta Division:				
Number of units needed annually	5,000	30,000	20,000	120,000
Purchase price now being paid to an outside supplier	$27	$89	$75*	—

* Before any quantity discount.

In cases 1–3, assume that Alpha Division's product can be sold either to Beta Division or to outside customers on an intermediate market.

Required 1. Refer to case 1 above. Alpha Division can avoid $2 per unit in commissions on any sales to Beta Division. Use the transfer pricing formula to determine what transfer price should be charged on any sales between the two divisions. Will any sales be made?

2. Refer to case 2 above. A study indicates that Alpha Division can avoid $5 per unit in shipping costs on any sales to Beta Division.
   a. Again use the transfer pricing formula to compute an appropriate transfer price. Would you expect any disagreement between the two divisional managers over what the transfer price should be? Explain.
   b. Assume that Alpha Division offers to sell 30,000 units to Beta Division for $88 per unit and that Beta Division refuses this price. What will be the loss in potential profits for the company as a whole?

3. Refer to case 3 above. Assume that Beta Division is now receiving an 8 percent quantity discount from the outside supplier.
   a. Within what range should the transfer price be set for any sales between the two divisions?
   b. Assume that Beta Division offers to purchase 20,000 units from Alpha Division at $60 per unit. If Alpha Division accepts this price, would you expect its ROI to increase, decrease, or remain unchanged? Why?

4. Refer to case 4 above. Assume that Beta Division wants Alpha Division to provide it with 120,000 units of a *different* product from the one that Alpha Division is now producing. The new product would require $21 per unit in variable costs and would require that Alpha Division cut back production of its present product by 45,000 units annually. Use the transfer pricing formula to determine the minimum transfer price per unit that Alpha Division should charge Beta Division for the new product.

P12–24 ROI and Residual Income   "I know headquarters wants us to add on that new product line," said Dell Havasi, manager of Billings Company's Office Products Division. "But I want to see the numbers before I make any move. Our division has led the company for three years, and I don't want any letdown."

Billings Company is a decentralized organization with five autonomous divisions. The divisions are evaluated on a basis of the return that they are able to generate on invested assets, with year-end bonuses given to the divisional managers who have the highest ROI figures. Operating results for the company's Office Products Division for the most recent year are given below.

Sales	$10,000,000
Less variable expenses	6,000,000
Contribution margin	4,000,000
Less fixed expenses	3,200,000
Net operating income	$ 800,000
Divisional operating assets	$ 4,000,000

The company had an overall ROI of 15 percent last year (considering all divisions). The Office Products Division has an opportunity to add a new product line that would require an additional investment in operating assets of $1,000,000. The cost and revenue characteristics of the new product line per year would be:

Sales	$2,000,000
Variable expenses	60% of sales
Fixed expenses	$640,000

Required

1. Compute the Office Products Division's ROI for the most recent year; also compute the ROI as it will appear if the new product line is added.
2. If you were in Dell Havasi's position, would you be inclined to accept or reject the new product line? Explain.
3. Why do you suppose "headquarters" is anxious for the Office Products Division to add the new product line?
4. Suppose that the company views a return of 12 percent on invested assets as being the minimum that any division should earn, and that performance is evaluated by the residual income approach.
   a. Compute the Office Products Division's residual income for the most recent year; also compute the residual income as it will appear if the new product line is added.
   b. Under these circumstances, if you were in Dell Havasi's position, would you accept or reject the new product line? Explain.

Basic Transfer Pricing Computations   Unless indicated otherwise, assume that each of the following situations is independent: **P12–25**

1. Given the following data for a product manufactured by East Division:

Selling price on the intermediate market	$80
Variable costs per unit	60
Fixed costs per unit (based on capacity)	9
Capacity in units.	100,000

   East Division is selling all it can produce to outside customers on the intermediate market. Another division in the company, West Division, is currently purchasing 30,000 units of an identical product from an outside supplier at a price of $80 per unit, less a 6.25 percent quantity discount. If East Division begins selling to West Division, $12 per unit in sales commissions and shipping costs can be avoided. From the standpoint of the company as a whole, any sales made by East Division to West Division should be priced at what amount per unit?

2. Refer to the data in (1) above. Assume that East Division offers to sell 30,000 units to West Division each year at a price of $72 per unit. If West Division accepts this offer, what will be the effect on the profits of the company as a whole?

3. Petrovich Company has two divisions, A and B. Division A manufactures a product, called product X, which has the following cost and revenue characteristics:

Selling price on the intermediate market	$45
Variable costs per unit	27
Fixed costs per unit (based on capacity)	6
Capacity in units.	75,000

Division A is operating at capacity, producing 75,000 units of product X each period and selling the units to outside customers. Division B would like Division A to start producing 9,000 units of a new product—called product Y—for it each period. This would require that Division A cut back production of product X by 20 percent, to only 60,000 units each period. Division A has estimated the following cost per unit for the new product Y:

Selling price to Division B	$?
Variable costs per unit	50
Fixed costs per unit	10

Division A would use existing personnel and equipment to manufacture product Y. What transfer price per unit should Division A charge to Division B for product Y?

P12–26 ROI Analysis   The income statement for Huerra Company for last year is given below:

	Total	Unit
Sales	$4,000,000	$80.00
Less variable expenses	2,800,000	56.00
Contribution margin	1,200,000	24.00
Less fixed expenses	840,000	16.80
Net operating income	360,000	7.20
Less income taxes (30%)	108,000	2.16
Net income	$ 252,000	$ 5.04

The company had average operating assets of $2,000,000 during the year.

Required   1.   Compute the company's ROI for the period, using the ROI formula.

For each of the following questions, indicate whether the margin and turnover will increase, decrease, or remain unchanged as a result of the events described, and then compute the new ROI figure. Consider each question separately, starting in each case from the data used to compute the original ROI in (1) above.

2.   By use of JIT to control the purchase of some items of raw materials, the company is able to reduce the average level of inventory by $400,000. (The released funds are used to pay off short-term creditors.)

3.   The company is able to achieve a cost savings of $32,000 per year by using less costly labor inputs.

4.   The company issues bonds and uses the proceeds to purchase $500,000 in machinery and equipment. Interest on the bonds is $60,000 per year. Sales remain unchanged. The new, more efficient equipment reduces production costs by $20,000 per year.

5.   As a result of a more intense effort by salespeople, sales are increased by 20 percent; operating assets remain unchanged.

6.   Obsolete items of inventory carried on the records at a cost of $40,000 are scrapped and written off as a loss, since they are unsalable.

7.   The company uses $200,000 of cash (received on accounts receivable) to repurchase and retire some of its common stock.

P12–27   Choosing an Appropriate Transfer Price   Whirlwind Products, Inc., has just acquired a small company that produces condenser units for refrigerators and similar products. The company will operate as a division of Whirlwind under the name of the Condenser Division. Selected data regarding the condenser units are given below:

Selling price per unit	$50
Cost per unit:	
Direct materials	$18
Direct labor	10
Variable overhead	2
Fixed overhead	5*
Total cost per unit	$35

* Based on 60,000 units capacity.

Whirlwind Products, Inc., also has a Refrigerator Division that is currently purchasing 20,000 condenser units each year from an outside supplier. The Refrigerator Division is paying $48 per condenser, which represents the normal $50 price less a 4 percent quantity discount due to the large number of units being purchased. Whirlwind's president is anxious for the Refrigerator Division to begin purchasing its condenser units from the Condenser Division, but she is unsure what transfer price should control any sales.

1. Assume that the Condenser Division has enough idle capacity to supply all of the   *Required*
    Refrigerator Division's needs. Explain why each of the following transfer prices would
    or would not be an appropriate price to charge the Refrigerator Division on the intra-
    company sales:
    a. $50.
    b. $48.
    c. $39.
    d. $35.
    e. $30.
2. Assume that the Condenser Division is currently selling to outside customers all the
    condenser units that it can produce. Under these circumstances, explain why each of
    the transfer prices given in (1a) through (1e) above would or would not be an appropri-
    ate price to charge the Refrigerator Division on the intracompany sales.

ROI and Residual Income   Raddington Industries produces tool and die machinery for   **P12–28**
manufacturers. The company expanded vertically several years ago by acquiring Reigis
Steel Company, one of its suppliers of alloy steel plates. Raddington decided to maintain
Reigis' separate identity and therefore established the Reigis Steel Division as one of its
investment centers.

Raddington monitors its divisions on the basis of the ROI they are able to achieve, with
investment defined as average operating assets employed. Management bonuses are also
based on ROI. All investments in operating assets are expected to earn a minimum return
of 11 percent before income taxes.

Reigis' ROI has ranged from 14 to 17 percent since it was acquired by Raddington.
During the past year, Reigis had an investment opportunity that would yield an estimated
ROI of 13 percent. Reigis' management decided against the investment because it believed
the investment would decrease the division's overall ROI.

Last year's (19x5) income statement for Reigis Steel Division is given below. The
division's operating assets employed were $12,960,000 at the end of the year, which repre-
sents an 8 percent increase over the 19x4 year-end balance.

REIGIS STEEL DIVISION

Divisional Income Statement

For the Year Ended December 31, 19x5

Sales		$31,200,000
Cost of goods sold		16,500,000
Gross margin		14,700,000
Less operating expenses:		
Selling expenses	$5,620,000	
Administrative expenses	7,208,000	12,828,000
Net operating income		$ 1,872,000

1. Compute the following performance measures for 19x5 for the Reigis Steel Division: *Required*
    a. ROI. (Remember, ROI is based on the *average* operating assets, computed from
        the beginning-of-year and end-of-year balances.)
    b. Residual income.
2. Would the management of Reigis Steel Division have been more likely to accept the
    investment opportunity it had in 19x5 if residual income were used as a performance
    measure instead of ROI? Explain.

3. The Reigis Steel Division is a separate investment center within Raddington Industries. Identify the items Reigis must be free to control if it is to be evaluated fairly by either the ROI or residual income performance measures.

(CMA, heavily adapted)

P12–29 **Negotiated Transfer Price** Ditka Industries has several independent divisions. The company's Tube Division manufactures a picture tube used in television sets. The Tube Division's income statement for last year, in which 8,000 tubes were sold, is given below:

	Total	Unit
Sales	$1,360,000	$170.00
Less cost of goods sold	840,000	105.00
Gross margin	520,000	65.00
Less selling and administrative expenses	390,000	48.75
Divisional net income	$ 130,000	$ 16.25

As shown above, it costs the Tube Division $105 to produce a single tube. This figure consists of the following costs:

Direct materials	$ 38
Direct labor	27
Manufacturing overhead (75% fixed)	40
Total cost per tube	$105

The Tube Division has fixed selling and administrative expenses of $350,000 per year.

Ditka Industries has just formed a new division, called the TV Division, that will produce a television set that requires a high-resolution picture tube. The Tube Division has been asked to manufacture 2,500 of these tubes each year and sell them to the TV Division. As one step in determining the price that should be charged to the TV Division, the Tube Division has estimated the following cost for each of the new high-resolution tubes:

Direct materials	$ 60
Direct labor	49
Manufacturing overhead (⅔ fixed)	54
Total cost per tube	$163

To manufacture the new tubes, the Tube Division would have to reduce production of its regular tubes by 3,000 units per year. There would be no variable selling and administrative expenses on the intracompany business, and total fixed overhead costs would not change.

Required

1. Determine the price that the Tube Division should charge the TV Division for each of the new high-resolution tubes.
2. Assume that the TV Division has found an outside supplier that will provide the new tubes for only $200 each. If the Tube Division meets this price, what will be the effect on the profits of the company as a whole?

P12–30
Integrative Problem

Cost-Volume-Profit Analysis; ROI; Transfer Pricing The Valve Division of Bendix, Inc., produces a small valve that is used by various companies as a component part in the manufacture of their products. Bendix, Inc., operates its divisions as autonomous units, giving its divisional managers great discretion in pricing and other decisions. Each division is expected to generate a return of at least 14 percent on its assets. The Valve Division has average operating assets as follows:

Cash.	$ 9,000
Accounts receivable	81,000
Inventory	250,000
Plant and equipment (net)	360,000
Total assets	$700,000

The valves are sold for $5 each. Variable costs are $3 per valve, and fixed costs total $462,000 per year. The division has a capacity of 300,000 valves each year.

1. How many valves must the Valve Division sell each year in order to generate the desired rate of return on its assets? *Required*
   a. What is the margin earned at this level of sales?
   b. What is the turnover of assets at this level of sales?
2. Assume that the Valve Division's current ROI is just equal to the minimum required 14 percent. In order to increase the division's ROI, the divisional manager wants to increase the selling price per valve by 4 percent. Market studies indicate that an increase in the selling price would cause sales to drop by 20,000 units each year. However, operating assets could be reduced by $50,000 due to decreased needs for accounts receivable and inventory. Compute the margin, turnover, and ROI if these changes are made.
3. Refer to the original data. Assume again that the Valve Division's current ROI is just equal to the minimum required 14 percent. Rather than increase the selling price, the sales manager wants to reduce the selling price per valve by 4 percent. Market studies indicate that this would fill the plant to capacity. In order to carry the greater level of sales, however, operating assets would increase by $50,000. Compute the margin, turnover, and ROI if these changes are made.
4. Refer to the original data. Assume that the normal volume of sales is 280,000 valves each year at a price of $5 per valve. Another division of the company is currently purchasing 20,000 valves each year from an overseas supplier, at a price of $4.25 per valve. The manager of the Valve Division has adamantly refused to meet this price, pointing out that it would result in a loss for his division:

Selling price per valve.		$ 4.25
Cost per valve:		
Variable	$3.00	
Fixed ($462,000 ÷ 300,000 valves) . . . : .	1.54	4.54
Net loss per valve		$(0.29)

The manager of the Valve Division also points out that the normal $5 selling price barely allows his division the required 14 percent rate of return. "If we take on some business at only $4.25 per unit, then our ROI is obviously going to suffer," he reasons, "and maintaining that ROI figure is the key to my future. Besides, taking on these extra units would require us to increase our operating assets by at least $50,000 due to the larger inventories and receivables we would be carrying." Would you recommend that the Valve Division sell to the other division at $4.25? Show ROI computations to support your answer.

Impact of Transfer Price on Marketing Decisions   Stavos Company's Cabinet Division manufactures a standard cabinet for television sets. The cost per cabinet is: **P12–31**

Variable cost per cabinet	$ 70
Fixed cost per cabinet	30*
Total cost per cabinet.	$100

* Based on a capacity of 10,000 cabinets per year.

Part of the Cabinet Division's output is sold to outside manufacturers of television sets, and part is sold to Stavos Company's Quark Division, which produces a TV set under its own name. The Cabinet Division charges $140 per cabinet for all sales.

The costs, revenue, and net income associated with the Quark Division's TV set is given below:

Selling price per TV set		$480
Less variable cost per TV set:		
Cost of the cabinet	$140	
Variable cost of electronic parts	210	
Total variable cost		350
Contribution margin.		130
Less fixed costs per TV set		80*
Net income per TV set		$ 50

* Based on a capacity of 3,000 sets per year.

The Quark Division has an order from an overseas source for 1,000 TV sets. The overseas source wants to pay only $340 per set.

Required 1. Assume that the Quark Division has enough idle capacity to fill the 1,000-set order. Is the division likely to accept the $340 price, or to reject it? Explain.
2. Assume that both the Cabinet Division and the Quark Division have idle capacity. Under these conditions, would it be an advantage or a disadvantage to the company as a whole for the Quark Division to reject the $340 price? Show computations to support your answer.
3. Assume that the Quark Division has idle capacity, but that the Cabinet Division is operating at capacity and could sell all of its cabinets to outside manufacturers. Compute the dollar advantage or disadvantage of the Quark Division accepting the 1,000-set order at the $340 unit price.
4. What kind of transfer pricing information is needed by the Quark Division in making decisions such as these?

P12–32   Critique of a Performance Evaluation Program   The Motor Works Division of Roland Industries is located in Fort Wayne, Indiana. A major expansion of the division's only plant was completed in April 19x4. The expansion consisted of an addition to the existing building, additional new equipment, and the replacement of obsolete and fully depreciated equipment that was no longer efficient or cost effective.

Donald Futak became the Division Manager of the Motor Works Division effective May 1, 19x4. Futak had a brief meeting with John Poskey, vice president of operations for Roland Industries, when he assumed the division manager position. Poskey told Futak that the company employed ROI for measuring performance of divisions and division managers. Futak asked whether any other performance measures were ever used in place of or in conjunction with ROI. Poskey replied, "Roland's top management prefers to use a single performance measure. There is no conflict when there is only one measure. Motor Works should do well this year now that it has expanded and replaced all of that old equipment. You should have no problem exceeding the division's historical rate. I'll check back with you at the end of each quarter to see how you are doing."

Poskey called Futak after the first-quarter results were complete because the Motor Works' ROI was considerably below the historical rate for the division. Futak told Poskey at that time that he did not believe that ROI was a valid performance measure for the Motor Works Division. Poskey indicated that he would get back to Futak. Futak did receive perfunctory memorandums after the second and third quarters, but there was no further discussion on the use of ROI. Now Futak has received the memorandum reproduced below.

May 24, 19x5

To: Donald Futak, Manager—Motor Works Division
From: John Poskey, Vice President of Operations
Subject: Division Performance

The operating results for the fourth quarter and for our fiscal year ended on April 30 are now complete. Your fourth quarter return on investment was only 9 percent, resulting in a return for the year of slightly under 11 percent. I recall discussing your low return after the first quarter and reminding you after the second and third quarters that this level of return is not considered adequate for the Motor Works Division.

The return on investment at Motor Works has ranged from 15 percent to 18 percent for the past five years. An 11 percent return may be acceptable at some of Roland's other divisions, but not at a proven winner like Motor Works—especially in light of your recently improved facility.

I would like to meet with you at your office on Monday, June 3, to discuss ways to restore Motor Work's return on investment to its former level. Please let me know if this date is acceptable to you.

Futak is looking forward to meeting with Poskey. He knows the division's ROI is below the historical rate, but the dollar profits for the year are greater than prior years. He plans to explain to Poskey why he believes ROI is not an appropriate performance measure for the Motor Works Division. He also plans to recommend that ROI be replaced with three measures—dollar profit, receivables turnover, and inventory turnover. These three measures would constitute a set of multiple criteria that would be used to evaluate performance.

Required

1. On the basis of the relationship between John Poskey and Donald Futak as well as the memorandum from Poskey, identify apparent weaknesses in the performance evaluation process of Roland Industries. Do not include in your answer any discussion on the use of ROI as a performance measure.
2. From the information presented, identify a possible explanation of why Motor Works Division's ROI declined in the fiscal year ended April 30, 19x5.
3. Identify criteria that should be used in selecting performance measures to evaluate operating managers.

(CMA, adapted)

Transfer Pricing with and without Idle Capacity   Division A manufactures an electrical switching unit that can be sold either to outside customers or to Division B. Selected operating data on the two divisions are given below: P12–33

Division A:
Unit selling price to outside customers . . . . . . $ 80
Variable production cost per unit   52
Variable selling and administrative
expense per unit   9
Fixed production cost in total 300,000*
Division B:
Outside purchase price per unit (before
any quantity discount)   80

* Capacity 25,000 units per year.

Division B now purchases the electrical unit from an outside supplier at the regular $80 intermediate price less a 5 percent quantity discount. Since the relay manufactured by Division A is of the same quality and type used by Division B, consideration is being given to buying internally rather than from the outside supplier. As the company's president stated, "It's just plain smart to buy and sell within the corporate family."

A study has determined that the variable selling and administrative expenses of Division A would be cut by one third for any sales to Division B. Top management wants to treat each division as an autonomous unit with independent profit responsibility.

Required 1. Assume that Division A is currently selling only 20,000 units per year to outside customers and that Division B needs 5,000 units per year.
   a. What is the lowest transfer price that can be justified between the two divisions? Explain.
   b. What is the highest transfer price that can be justified between the two divisions? Explain.
   c. Assume that Division B finds an outside supplier that will sell the electrical unit for only $65 per unit. Should Division A be required to meet this price? Explain.
   d. Refer to the original data. Assume that Division A decides to raise its price to $85 per unit. If Division B is forced to pay this price and to start purchasing from Division A, will this result in greater or less total corporate profits? How much per unit?
   e. Under the circumstances posed in (d) above, should Division B be forced to purchase from Division A? Explain.
2. Assume that Division A can sell all that it produces to outside customers. Repeat (a) through (e) above.

CASES

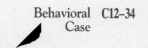

Behavioral Case   C12–34   **Transfer Pricing; Divisional Performance**   Weller Industries is a decentralized organization containing six divisions. The company's Electrical Division produces a variety of electrical items, including an X52 electrical fitting. The Electrical Division (which is operating at capacity) sells this fitting to its regular customers for $7.50 each; the fitting has a variable manufacturing cost of $4.25.

The company's Brake Division has asked the Electrical Division to supply it with a large quantity of X52 fittings for only $5 each. The Brake Division, which is operating at 50 percent of capacity, will put the fitting into a brake unit that it will produce and sell to a large commercial airplane manufacturer. The cost of the brake unit being built by the Brake Division follows:

Purchased parts (from outside vendors)	$22.50
Electrical fitting X52	5.00
Other variable costs	14.00
Fixed overhead and administration	8.00
Total cost per brake unit	$49.50

Although the $5 price for the X52 fitting represents a substantial discount from the regular $7.50 price, the manager of the Brake Division believes that the price concession is necessary if his division is to get the airplane manufacturer contract for the brake units. He has heard "through the grapevine" that the airplane manufacturer plans to reject his bid if it is more than $50 per brake unit. Thus, if the Brake Division is forced to pay the regular $7.50 price for the X52 fitting, it will either not get the contract or it will be forced to suffer a substantial loss at a time when it is already operating at only 50 percent of capacity. In addition, if the Brake Division doesn't get the contract it will have to discharge a large part of its core of highly trained people. The manager of the Brake Division argues, therefore, that the price concession is imperative to the well-being of both his division and the company as a whole.

Weller Industries uses ROI and dollar profits in measuring divisional performance.

Required

1. Assume that you are the manager of the Electrical Division. Would you recommend that your division supply the X52 fitting to the Brake Division for $5 each as requested? Why or why not? Show all computations. (Ignore income taxes.)
2. Would it be to the short-run economic advantage of the company as a whole for the Electrical Division to supply the fittings to the Brake Division for $5 each? Show all computations, and explain your answer.
3. Discuss the organizational and manager behavior problems, if any, inherent in this situation. As the Weller Industries controller, what would you advise the company's president to do in this situation?

(CMA, heavily adapted)

Negotiated Transfer Price   Flores Products, Inc., is made up of several autonomous divisions. Each division's performance is evaluated on the basis of total dollar profits and return on division investment. Bonuses are given to divisional managers on a basis of improvements in these performance measures from year to year.   C12–35

The company's Edger Division manufactures and sells a lawn edger. The division's budgeted income statement for the coming year, based on an expected sales volume of 18,000 edgers, is given below.

EDGER DIVISION
Budgeted Income Statement
For the Year 19x8

	Total	Per Unit
Sales revenue	$5,400,000	$300
Less cost of goods sold	3,312,000	184
Gross margin	2,088,000	116
Less operating expenses:		
Variable selling	216,000	12
Fixed selling	432,000	24
Fixed administrative	630,000	35
Total operating expenses	1,278,000	71
Net income	$ 810,000	$ 45

The division's $184 per unit cost of goods sold consists of the following items:

Motor	$ 60
Other material and parts	39
Direct labor	50
Variable overhead	7
Fixed overhead	28
Total cost per edger	$184

Edger Division's manager is searching for ways to improve the division's profits and ROI. A market research study just completed indicates that a 5 percent reduction in the selling price per edger would increase sales volume (in units) by 20 percent. The Edger Division has ample production capacity to manage this increased volume with no increase in fixed costs.

The manager of the Edger Division is also studying the possibility of purchasing the motors used in the edgers from the company's Motor Division. At present, the Edger Division is using a motor that it purchases from an outside supplier at a cost of $60. The Edger Division has offered to pay the Motor Division $54 per motor, which represents the current price less a 10 percent discount. The manager of the Edger Division believes that this discount is justified since the motor needed by the Edger Division is somewhat different in design from the motor normally produced by the Motor Division and would require $3 less per motor in raw materials. Also, there would be no variable selling expenses associated with the intracompany sales. The manager of the Edger Division has specified, however, that all motors must come from a single supplier.

The Motor Division has a capacity to produce 80,000 motors per year. The division's budgeted income statement for the coming year is shown below. This statement is based on an expected sales volume of 70,000 motors without considering the Edger Division's proposal.

MOTOR DIVISION
Budgeted Income Statement
For the Year 19x8

	Total	Per Unit
Sales revenue	$6,300,000	$90
Less cost of goods sold	3,570,000	51
Gross margin	2,730,000	39
Less operating expenses:		
Variable selling	420,000	6
Fixed selling	770,000	11
Fixed administrative	980,000	14
Total operating expenses	2,170,000	31
Net income	$ 560,000	$ 8

The division's $51 per unit cost of goods sold consists of the following items:

Direct materials	$21
Direct labor	10
Variable overhead	3
Fixed overhead	17
Total cost per motor	$51

Required
1. Should the Edger Division institute the 5 percent price reduction on its edgers even if it can't purchase the motors internally for $54 each? Support your answer with appropriate computations.

2. Assume that the Edger Division decides to institute the 5 percent price reduction and thus will need 21,600 motors next year. If you were the manager of the Motor Division, would you be willing to supply these motors for $54 each? Support your answer with appropriate computations.

3. As the manager of the Motor Division, what is the minimum transfer price per motor that you could charge the Edger Division? Show computations.

4. Assume again that the Edger Division will need 21,600 motors next year. Considering the company as a whole, would it be in the best interest of Flores Products, Inc., for the Motor Division to supply the motors to the Edger Division at $54 each? Support your answer with appropriate computations.

C12–36   **Service Organization; Segment Reporting**   Music Teachers, Inc., is an educational association for music teachers that had 20,000 members during 19x5. The association operates from a central headquarters but has local membership chapters throughout the United States. Monthly meetings are held by the local chapters to discuss recent developments on topics of interest to music teachers. The association's journal, *Teachers' Forum,* is issued monthly with features about recent developments in the field. The association publishes books and reports and also sponsors professional courses that qualify for continuing professional education credit. The association's statement of revenues and expenses for the current year is presented below.

MUSIC TEACHERS, INC.
Statement of Revenues and Expenses
For the Year Ended November 30, 19x5

Revenues	$3,275,000
Less expenses:	
Salaries	920,000
Personnel costs.	230,000
Occupancy costs	280,000
Reimbursement of member costs to local chapters	600,000
Other membership services	500,000
Printing and paper	320,000
Postage and shipping	176,000
Instructors fees.	80,000
General and administrative.	38,000
Total expenses	3,144,000
Excess of revenues over expenses	$ 131,000

The board of directors of Music Teachers, Inc., has requested that a segmented statement of operations be prepared showing the contribution of each profit center to the association. The association has four profit centers: Membership Division, Magazine Subscriptions Division, Books and Reports Division, and Continuing Education Division. Mike Doyle has been assigned responsibility for preparing the segmented statement, and he has gathered the following data prior to its preparation.

a. Membership dues are $100 per year, of which $20 is considered to cover a one-year subscription to the association's journal. Other benefits include membership in the association and chapter affiliation. The portion of the dues covering the magazine subscription ($20) should be assigned to the Magazine Subscription Division.

b. One-year subscriptions to *Teachers' Forum* were sold to nonmembers and libraries at $30 per subscription. A total of 2,500 of these subscriptions were sold for 19x5. In addition to subscriptions, the magazine generated $100,000 in advertising revenues. The costs per magazine subscription were $7 for printing and paper and $4 for postage and shipping.

c. A total of 28,000 technical reports and professional texts were sold by the Books and Reports Division at an average unit selling price of $25. Average costs per publication were $4 for printing and paper and $2 for postage and shipping.

d. The association offers a variety of continuing education courses to both members and nonmembers. The one-day courses had a tuition cost of $75 each and were attended by 2,400 students in 19x5. A total of 1,760 students took two-day courses at a tuition cost of $125 for each student. Outside instructors were paid to teach some courses.

e. Salary costs and space occupied by division follow:

	Salaries	Space Occupied (square feet)
Membership.	$210,000	2,000
Magazine Subscriptions.	150,000	2,000
Books and Reports	300,000	3,000
Continuing Education.	180,000	2,000
Corporate staff.	80,000	1,000
Total	$920,000	10,000

Personnel costs are 25 percent of salaries in the separate divisions as well as for the corporate staff. The $280,000 in occupancy costs incurred during 19x5 includes $50,000 in rental cost for a warehouse used by the Books and Reports Division for storage purposes.

f.   Printing and paper costs other than for magazine subscriptions and for books and reports relate to the Continuing Education Division.

g.   General and administrative expenses include costs relating to overall administration of the association as a whole. The company's corporate staff does some mailing of materials for general administrative purposes.

Mike Doyle has decided that he will assign all revenue and expenses to the profit centers that can be:

•   Traced directly to a profit center.
•   Assigned on a reasonable and logical basis to a profit center.

The expenses that can be traced or assigned to the corporate staff, as well as any other expenses that can't be assigned to the profit centers, will be treated as common costs. It is not necessary to distinguish between variable and fixed costs.

Required   1.   Prepare a segmented statement of revenues and expenses for Music Teachers, Inc., for 19x5. This statement should show the segment margin for each division as well as results for the association as a whole.

2.   If segment reporting is adopted by the association for continuing usage, discuss the ways the information provided by the report can be utilized by management.

3.   Give arguments for and against allocating *all* costs of the association to the four divisions.

(CMA, adapted)

THE CAPSTONE:
USING COST DATA IN DECISION MAKING

Part
III

Bakeries distribute their products through route salespersons who deliver a full range of products to customers on a daily basis. The management of one bakery asked its accountants to determine the profitability of each product. The accountants allocated all manufacturing and marketing costs to products—even those costs that would be unaffected if the products were eliminated. The resulting figures indicated that some of the products were being sold at a loss. Shortly after management discontinued these products, the company's overall profit declined. By dropping these products, the sales revenues were lost; but most of the costs had to be continued anyway to support sales of the remaining products.

Relevant Costs for Decision Making

LEARNING OBJECTIVES

After studying Chapter 13, you should be able to:

1 State a general rule for distinguishing between relevant and irrelevant costs in a decision-making situation.

2 Identify sunk costs and explain why they are not relevant in decision making, including decisions about whether to keep or replace old equipment.

3 Prepare an analysis showing whether a product line or other organizational segment should be dropped or retained.

4 Explain what is meant by a make or buy decision and prepare a well-organized make or buy analysis.

5 Make appropriate computations to determine the most profitable utilization of scarce resources in an organization.

6 Prepare an analysis showing whether joint products should be sold at the split-off point or processed further.

7 Explain why a manager should exercise caution in relevant cost analysis when activity-based costing is being used.

8 Define or explain the key terms listed at the end of the chapter.

9 (Appendix G) Construct a graph that shows the optimal solution to a linear programming problem.

Chapter 13

Decision making is one of the basic functions of a manager. Managers are constantly faced with problems of deciding what products to sell, what production methods to use, whether to make or buy component parts, what prices to charge, what channels of distribution to use, whether to accept special orders at special prices, and so forth. At best, decision making is a difficult and complex task. The difficulty of this task is usually increased by the existence of not just one or two but numerous courses of action that might be taken in any given situation facing a firm.

In decision making, *cost* is always a key factor. The costs of one alternative must be compared against the costs of other alternatives as one step in the decision-making process. The problem is that some costs associated with an alternative may not be *relevant* to the decision to be made. A **relevant cost** can be defined as a cost that is *applicable to a particular decision* in the sense that it will have a bearing on which alternative the manager selects.

To be successful in decision making, managers must have tools at their disposal to assist them in distinguishing between relevant and irrelevant costs so that the latter can be eliminated from the decision framework. The purpose of this chapter is to acquire these tools and to show their application in a wide range of decision-making situations.

COST CONCEPTS FOR DECISION MAKING

Three cost terms discussed in Chapter 2 are particularly applicable to this chapter. These terms are *differential costs, opportunity costs,* and *sunk costs.* You may find it helpful to turn back to Chapter 2 and refresh your memory concerning these terms before reading on.

Identifying Relevant Costs

Objective 1
State a general rule for distinguishing between relevant and irrelevant costs in a decision-making situation.

What costs are relevant in decision making? The answer is easy. Any cost that is *avoidable* is relevant for decision purposes. An **avoidable cost** can be defined as a cost that can be eliminated (in whole or in part) as a result of choosing one alternative over another in a decision-making situation. *All* costs are considered to be avoidable, *except:*

1. Sunk costs.
2. Future costs that *do not differ* between the alternatives at hand.

As we learned in Chapter 2, a **sunk cost** is a cost that has already been incurred and that cannot be avoided regardless of which course of action a manager may decide to take. As such, sunk costs have no relevance to future events and must be ignored in decision making. Similarly, if a cost will be incurred regardless of which course of action a manager may take, then the cost cannot possibly be of any help in deciding which course of action is best. Such a cost is not avoidable, and hence it is not relevant to the manager's decision.

The term *avoidable cost* is synonymous with the term **differential cost** that we introduced in Chapter 2, and the terms are frequently used interchangeably. To identify the costs that are avoidable (differential) in a particular decision situation, the manager's approach to cost analysis should include the following steps:

1. Assemble *all* of the costs associated with *each* alternative being considered.
2. Eliminate those costs that are sunk.
3. Eliminate those costs that do not differ between alternatives.

4. Make a decision based on the remaining costs. These costs will be the *differential costs* or *avoidable costs,* and hence the costs relevant to the decision to be made.

Different Costs for Different Purposes

We need to recognize from the outset of our discussion that costs that are relevant in one decision situation are not necessarily relevant in another. Simply put, this means (as we've stated before) that *the manager needs different costs for different purposes.* For one purpose, a particular group of costs may be relevant; for another purpose, an entirely different group of costs may be relevant. Thus, in *each* decision situation the manager must examine the data at hand and then take the steps necessary to isolate the relevant costs. Otherwise, he or she runs the risk of being misled by irrelevant data.

The concept of "different costs for different purposes" is basic to managerial accounting; we shall see its application frequently in the pages that follow.

SUNK COSTS ARE NOT RELEVANT COSTS

One of the most difficult conceptual lessons that managers have to learn is that sunk costs are never relevant in decisions. The tendency to want to include sunk costs within the decision framework is especially strong in the case of book value of old equipment. We focus on book value of old equipment below, and then we consider other kinds of sunk costs in other parts of the chapter. We shall see that regardless of the kind of sunk cost involved, the conclusion is always the same— sunk costs are not avoidable, and therefore they must be eliminated from the manager's decision framework.

Objective 2
Identify sunk costs and explain why they are not relevant in decision making, including decisions about whether to keep or replace old equipment

Book Value of Old Equipment

Assume the following data:

Old Machine		Proposed New Machine	
Original cost	$175,000	List price new	$200,000
Remaining book value	140,000	Expected life	4 years
Remaining life	4 years	Disposal value in four years	$ –0–
Disposal value now	$ 90,000	Annual variable expenses	
Disposal value in four years	–0–	to operate	300,000
Annual variable expenses		Annual revenue from sales	500,000
to operate	345,000		
Annual revenue from sales	500,000		

Should the old machine be disposed of and the new machine purchased? Some managers would say no, since disposal of the old machine would result in a "loss" of $50,000:

Old Machine	
Remaining book value	$140,000
Disposal value now	90,000
Loss if disposed of now	$ 50,000

Given this potential loss if the old machine is sold, there is a general inclination for the manager to reason, "We've already made an investment in the old machine, so now we have no choice but to use it until our investment has been fully recovered.'' The manager will tend to think this way even though the new machine is clearly more efficient than the old machine. Although it may be appealing to think that an error of the past can be corrected by simply *using* the item involved, this, unfortunately, is not correct. The investment that has been made in the old machine is a sunk cost. The portion of this investment that remains on the company's books (the book value of $140,000) should not be considered in a decision about whether to buy the new machine. We can prove this assertion by the following analysis:[1]

	Total Costs and Revenues— Four Years		
	Keep Old Machine	Differential Costs	Purchase New Machine
Sales	$ 2,000,000	–0–	$ 2,000,000
Variable expenses.	(1,380,000)	$ 180,000	(1,200,000)
Cost (depreciation) of the new machine	—	(200,000)	(200,000)
Depreciation of the old machine or book value write-off.	(140,000)	–0–	(140,000)*
Disposal value of the old machine	—	90,000	90,000*
Total net income over the four years . . .	$ 480,000	$ 70,000	$ 550,000

* For external reporting purposes, the $140,000 remaining book value of the old machine and the $90,000 disposal value would be netted together and deducted as a single $50,000 "loss" figure.

Looking at all four years together, notice that the firm will be $70,000 better off by purchasing the new machine. Also notice that the $140,000 book value of the old machine had *no effect* on the outcome of the analysis. Since this book value is a sunk cost, it must be absorbed by the firm regardless of whether the old machine is kept and used or whether it is sold. If the old machine is kept and used, then the $140,000 book value is deducted in the form of depreciation. If the old machine is sold, then the $140,000 book value is deducted in the form of a lump-sum write-off. Either way, the company bears the same $140,000 deduction.

Focusing on Relevant Costs   What costs in the example above are relevant in the decision concerning the new machine? Following the steps outlined earlier and looking at the original cost data, we should eliminate (1) the sunk costs and (2) the future costs that do not differ between the alternatives at hand.

1. The sunk costs:
    a.   The remaining book value of the old machine ($140,000).
2. The future costs that do not differ:
    a.   The sales revenue ($500,000 per year).
    b.   The variable expenses (to the extent of $300,000 per year).

The costs that remain will form the basis for a decision. The analysis is:

[1] The computations involved in this example are taken one step further in Chapters 14 and 15 where we discuss the time value of money and the use of present value in decision making.

	Differential Costs— Four Years
Reduction in variable expense promised by the new machine ($45,000* per year × 4 years)	$ 180,000
Cost of the new machine	(200,000)
Disposal value of the old machine	90,000
Net advantage of the new machine	$ 70,000

* $345,000 − $300,000 = $45,000.

Note that the items above are the same as those in the middle column of the earlier analysis and represent those costs and revenues that differ between the two alternatives.

FOCUS ON CURRENT PRACTICE

A failure to recognize the existence of sunk costs can lead to bad business decisions. As evidence, consider the following incident related by a business consultant after encountering a frustrated and angry fellow traveler ("Mr. Smith") whose flight home faced a lengthy delay:

Mr. Smith had recently flown into St. Louis on a commercial airline for a two-day business trip. While there, he learned that his company's private airplane had flown in the day before and would leave on the same day that he was scheduled to leave. Mr. Smith immediately cashed in his $200 commercial airline ticket and made arrangements to fly back on the company plane. He flew home feeling pretty good about saving his company the $200 fare and being able to depart on schedule.

About two weeks later, however, Mr. Smith's boss asked him why the department had been cross-charged $400 for his return trip when the commercial airfare was only $200. Mr. Smith explained that "the company plane was flying back regardless, and there were a number of empty seats."

How could Mr. Smith's attempt to save his company $200 end up "costing" his department $400? The problem is that Mr. Smith recognized something that his company's cost allocation system did not: namely, that the vast majority of the costs associated with flying the plane home were already sunk and, thus, unavoidable at the time he made the decision to fly home. By failing to distinguish between sunk (i.e., unavoidable) and avoidable cost, the cost allocation system was causing the firm and its managers to make uneconomic business decisions.

It is now clear why Mr. Smith was so frustrated the day I ran into him in St. Louis. His company's plane was sitting on the runway with a number of empty seats and ready to take off for the very same destination. Yet there was no way Mr. Smith was going to fly on that plane even though doing so was the "best business decision."[2]

Depreciation and Relevant Costs

Since the book value of old equipment is not a relevant cost in decision making, there is a tendency to assume that depreciation of *any* kind is irrelevant in the decision-making process. This is not a correct assumption. Depreciation is irrelevant in decisions only if it relates to a sunk cost. Notice from the comparative income statements in the preceding section that the $200,000 depreciation on the new machine appears in the middle column as a relevant item in trying to assess the desirability of the new machine's purchase. By contrast, depreciation on the old machine does not appear as a relevant cost. The difference is that the investment in the new machine has *not yet been made*, and therefore it does not represent depreciation of a sunk cost.

FUTURE COSTS THAT DO NOT DIFFER ARE NOT RELEVANT COSTS

Any future cost that does not differ between the alternatives in a decision situation is not a relevant cost so far as that decision is concerned. As stated earlier, if a company is going to sustain the same cost regardless of what decision it makes, then that cost can in no way tell the company which decision is best. The only way a future cost can help in the decision-making process is by being different as between the alternatives under consideration.

An Example of Irrelevant Future Costs

To illustrate the irrelevance of future costs that do not differ, let us assume that a firm is contemplating the purchase of a new laborsaving machine. The machine will cost $30,000 and have a 10-year useful life. The company's sales and cost structure on an annual basis with and without the new machine are shown below:

	Present Costs	Expected Costs with the New Machine
Units produced and sold	5,000	5,000
Sales price per unit	$ 40	$ 40
Direct materials cost per unit	14	14
Direct labor cost per unit	8	5
Variable overhead cost per unit	2	2
Fixed costs, other	62,000	62,000
Fixed costs, new machine	—	3,000

The new machine promises a saving of $3 per unit in direct labor costs ($8 − $5 = $3), but it will increase fixed costs by $3,000 per period. All other costs, as well as the total number of units produced and sold, will remain the same. Following the steps outlined earlier, the analysis is:

1. Eliminate the sunk costs. (No sunk costs are identified in this example.)
2. Eliminate the future costs (and revenues) that do not differ:
   a. The sales price per unit does not differ.
   b. The direct materials cost per unit does not differ.
   c. The variable overhead cost per unit does not differ.
   d. The total "fixed costs, other" do not differ.

This leaves just the per unit labor costs and the fixed costs associated with the new machine as being differential costs:

---

[2] Dennis L. Weisman, "How Cost Allocation Systems Can Lead Managers Astray," *Journal of Cost Management* 5, no. 1 (Spring 1991), p. 4. Used by permission.

Savings in direct labor costs (5,000 units at a cost saving of $3 per unit)	$15,000
Less increase in fixed costs	3,000
Net annual cost savings promised by the new machine . . .	$12,000

The accuracy of this solution can be proved by looking at *all* items of cost data (both those that are relevant and those that are not) under the two alternatives for a period and then comparing the net income results. This is done in Exhibit 13–1. Notice from the exhibit that we obtain the same $12,000 net advantage in favor of buying the new machine as we obtained above when we focused only on relevant costs. Thus, we can see that future costs that do not differ between alternatives are indeed irrelevant in the decision-making process and can be safely eliminated from the manager's decision framework.

Why Isolate Relevant Costs?

In the preceding example, we used two different approaches to show that the purchase of the new machine was desirable. First, we considered only the relevant costs; and second, we considered all costs, both those that were relevant and those that were not. We obtained the same answer under both approaches. When students see that the same answer can be obtained under either approach, they often ask, "Why bother to isolate relevant costs when total costs will do the job just as well?" The isolation of relevant costs is desirable for at least two reasons.

First, only rarely will enough information be available to prepare a detailed income statement such as we have done in the preceding examples. Since normally only limited data are available, the decision maker *must* know how to recognize which costs are relevant and which are not. Assume, for example, that you are called on to make a decision relating to a *single operation* of a multidepartmental, multiproduct firm. Under these circumstances, it would be virtually impossible to prepare an income statement of any type. You would have to rely on your ability to recognize which costs were relevant and which were not in order to assemble the data necessary to make a decision.

Second, the use of irrelevant costs mingled with relevant costs may confuse the picture and draw the decision maker's attention away from the matters that are really critical to the problem at hand. Furthermore, the danger always exists that

	5,000 Units Produced and Sold			
	Present Method	Differential Costs	New Machine	
Sales	$200,000	$ –0–	$200,000	EXHIBIT 13–1
				Differential Cost Analysis
Variable expenses:				
Direct materials.	70,000	–0–	70,000	
Direct labor	40,000	15,000	25,000	
Variable overhead.	10,000	–0–	10,000	
Total variable expenses	120,000		105,000	
Contribution margin	80,000		95,000	
Less fixed expenses:				
Other	62,000	–0–	62,000	
New machine.	–0–	(3,000)	3,000	
Total fixed expenses.	62,000		65,000	
Net income.	$ 18,000	$12,000	$ 30,000	

an irrelevant piece of data may be used improperly, resulting in an incorrect decision. The best approach is to isolate the relevant items and to focus all attention directly on them and on their impact on the decision to be made.

Relevant cost analysis, combined with the contribution approach to the income statement, provides a powerful tool for making decisions in special, nonroutine situations. We will investigate various uses of this tool in the remaining sections of this chapter.

ADDING AND DROPPING PRODUCT LINES AND OTHER SEGMENTS

Objective 3
Prepare an analysis showing whether a product line or other organizational segment should be dropped or retained.

Decisions relating to whether old product lines or other segments of a company should be dropped and new ones added are among the most difficult that a manager has to make. In such decisions, many factors must be considered that are both qualitative and quantitative in nature. Ultimately, however, any final decision to drop an old segment or to add a new one is going to hinge primarily on the impact the decision will have on net income. To assess this impact, it is necessary to make a careful analysis of the costs involved.

An Illustration of Cost Analysis

As a basis for discussion, let us consider the product lines of the Discount Drug Company. The company has three major product lines—drugs, cosmetics, and housewares. Sales and cost information for the preceding month for each separate product line and for the store in total is given in Exhibit 13–2.

What can be done to improve the company's overall performance? One product line—housewares—shows a net loss for the month. Perhaps dropping this line would cause profits in the company as a whole to improve. In deciding whether the line should be dropped, management will need to reason as follows:

If the housewares line is dropped, then the company will lose $20,000 per month in contribution margin that is now available to help cover the fixed costs. By dropping the line, however, it may be possible to avoid certain of these fixed costs. It may be possible, for example, to discharge certain employees, or it may be possible to reduce advertising costs. If by dropping the housewares line the company is able to avoid more in fixed costs than it loses in contribution margin, then it will be better off if the line is eliminated, since overall net income should improve. On the other hand, if the company is not able to avoid as much in fixed

EXHIBIT 13–2
Discount Drug Company Product Lines

	Total	Product Line Drugs	Cosmetics	Housewares
Sales	$250,000	$125,000	$75,000	$50,000
Less variable expenses	105,000	50,000	25,000	30,000
Contribution margin	145,000	75,000	50,000	20,000
Less fixed expenses:				
Salaries	50,000	29,500	12,500	8,000
Advertising	15,000	1,000	7,500	6,500
Utilities	2,000	500	500	1,000
Depreciation—fixtures . . .	5,000	1,000	2,000	2,000
Rent	20,000	10,000	6,000	4,000
Insurance	3,000	2,000	500	500
General administrative . . .	30,000	15,000	9,000	6,000
Total fixed expenses . . .	125,000	59,000	38,000	28,000
Net income (loss)	$ 20,000	$ 16,000	$12,000	$ (8,000)

costs as it loses in contribution margin, then the housewares line should be retained. In short, in order to identify the differential costs in decisions of this type, the manager must ask, "What costs can I avoid to offset my loss of revenue (or loss of contribution margin) if I drop this product line?"

As we have seen from our earlier discussion, not all costs are avoidable. For example, some of the costs associated with a product line may be sunk costs. Other costs may be allocated common costs that will not differ in total regardless of whether the product line is dropped or retained. To show how the manager should proceed in a product line analysis, suppose that the management of the Discount Drug Company has analyzed the costs being charged to the three product lines and has determined the following:

1. The salaries represent salaries paid to employees working directly in each product line area. All of the employees working in housewares can be discharged if the line is dropped.
2. The advertising represents direct advertising of each product line and is avoidable if the line is dropped.
3. The utilities represent utilities costs for the entire company. The amount charged to each product line represents an allocation based on space occupied.
4. The depreciation represents depreciation on fixtures used for display of the various product lines. Although the fixtures are nearly new, they are custombuilt and will have little resale value if the housewares line is dropped.
5. The rent represents rent on the entire building housing the company; it is allocated to the product lines on a basis of sales dollars. The monthly rent of $20,000 is fixed under a long-term lease agreement.
6. The insurance represents insurance carried on inventories maintained within each of the three product-line areas.
7. The general administrative expense represents the costs of accounting, purchasing, and general management, which are allocated to the product lines on a basis of sales dollars. Total administrative costs will not change if the housewares line is dropped.

With this information, management can identify those costs that are avoidable and those costs that are not avoidable if the product line is dropped:

	Total Cost	Not Avoidable*	Avoidable
Salaries	$ 8,000		$ 8,000
Advertising	6,500		6,500
Utilities	1,000	$ 1,000	
Depreciation—fixtures	2,000	2,000	
Rent	4,000	4,000	
Insurance	500		500
General administrative	6,000	6,000	
Total fixed expenses	$28,000	$13,000	$15,000

* These costs represent either (1) sunk costs or (2) costs that will not change regardless of whether the housewares line is retained or discontinued.

To determine how dropping the line will affect the overall profits of the company, we can compare the contribution margin that will be lost against the costs that can be avoided if the line is dropped:

Contribution margin lost if the housewares
  line is discontinued (see Exhibit 13–2). . . . . . . $(20,000)
Less fixed costs that can be avoided if the
  housewares line is discontinued (see above)   15,000
Decrease in overall company net income . . . . . $ (5,000)

In this case, the fixed costs that can be avoided by dropping the product line are less than the contribution margin that will be lost. Therefore, based on the data given, the housewares line should not be discontinued unless a more profitable use can be found for the floor and counter space that it is occupying.

A Comparative Format

Some managers prefer to approach decisions of this type by preparing comparative income statements showing the effects on the company as a whole of either keeping or dropping the product line in question. A comparative analysis of this type for the Discount Drug Company is shown in Exhibit 13–3.

As shown by column 3 in the exhibit, overall company net income will decrease by $5,000 each period if the housewares line is dropped. This is the same answer, of course, as we obtained in our earlier analysis.

Beware of Allocated Fixed Costs

Our conclusion that the housewares line should not be dropped seems to conflict with the data shown in Exhibit 13–2. Recall from the exhibit that the housewares line is showing a loss rather than a profit. Why keep a line that is showing a loss? The explanation for this apparent inconsistency lies at least in part with the common fixed costs that are being allocated to the product lines. As we observed in Chapter 12, one of the great dangers in allocating common fixed costs is that such allocations can make a product line (or other segment of a business) *look* less profitable than it really is. Consider the actual business situation described in the box on the following page.

The same thing has happened in the Discount Drug Company as happened in the bakery company. That is, by allocating the common fixed costs among all product lines, the Discount Drug Company has made the housewares line *look* as if it were unprofitable, whereas, in fact, dropping the line would result in a decrease in overall company net income. This point can be seen clearly if we recast

EXHIBIT 13–3

A Comparative Format
for Product-Line
Analysis

	Keep Housewares	Drop Housewares	Difference: Net Income Increase or (Decrease)
Sales	$50,000	$ –0–	$(50,000)
Less variable expenses	30,000	–0–	30,000
Contribution margin	20,000	–0–	(20,000)
Less fixed expenses:			
Salaries	8,000	–0–	8,000
Advertising	6,500	–0–	6,500
Utilities	1,000	1,000	–0–
Depreciation—fixtures	2,000	2,000	–0–
Rent	4,000	4,000	–0–
Insurance	500	–0–	500
General administrative	6,000	6,000	–0–
Total fixed expenses	28,000	13,000	15,000
Net income (loss)	$ (8,000)	$(13,000)	$ (5,000)

A bakery distributed its products through route salespersons, each of whom loaded a truck with an assortment of products in the morning and spent the day calling on customers in an assigned territory. Believing that some items were more profitable than others, management asked for an analysis of product costs and sales. The accountants to whom the task was assigned allocated all manufacturing and marketing costs to products to obtain a net profit for each product. The resulting figures indicated that some of the products were being sold at a loss, and management discontinued these products. However, when this change was put into effect, the company's overall profit declined. It was then seen that by dropping some products, sales revenues had been reduced without commensurate reduction in costs because the joint manufacturing costs and route sales costs had to be continued in order to make and sell remaining products.

the data in Exhibit 13–2 and eliminate the allocation of the common fixed costs. This recasting of data—using the segmented approach from Chapter 12—is shown in Exhibit 13–4.

Exhibit 13–4 gives us a much different perspective of the housewares line than does Exhibit 13–2. As shown in Exhibit 13–4, the housewares line is covering all of its own traceable fixed costs and is generating a $3,000 segment margin toward covering the common fixed costs of the company. Unless another product line can be found that will generate a greater segment margin than this, then, as we have noted, the company will be better off keeping the housewares line. By keeping the

| | Total | Product Line | | |
		Drugs	Cosmetics	Housewares
Sales	$250,000	$125,000	$75,000	$50,000
Less variable expenses	105,000	50,000	25,000	30,000
Contribution margin	145,000	75,000	50,000	20,000
Less traceable fixed expenses:				
Salaries	50,000	29,500	12,500	8,000
Advertising	15,000	1,000	7,500	6,500
Depreciation—fixtures. . . .	5,000	1,000	2,000	2,000
Insurance	3,000	2,000	500	500
Total	73,000	33,500	22,500	17,000
Product-line segment margin . .	72,000	$ 41,500	$27,500	$ 3,000*
Less common fixed expenses:				
Utilities	2,000			
Rent	20,000			
General administrative	30,000			
Total	52,000			
Net income	$ 20,000			

EXHIBIT 13–4

Discount Drug Company Product Lines—Recast in Contribution Format (from Exhibit 13–2)

* If the housewares line is dropped, this $3,000 in segment margin will be lost to the company. In addition, we have seen that the $2,000 depreciation on the fixtures is a sunk cost that cannot be avoided. The sum of these two figures ($3,000 + $2,000 = $5,000) represents another way of obtaining the $5,000 figure that we found earlier would be the decrease in the company's overall profits if the housewares line were discontinued.

line, the company will get at least some contribution toward the common fixed costs of the organization from the space it is occupying.

When we talk about another product to replace housewares, we are talking about the *opportunity cost* of space. As a next step, management should explore alternative uses for the space in the store, such as adding a new product, expanding the existing products, or even renting the space out that is now being occupied by housewares.

To conclude, we should note that even in those situations where the contribution of a particular product line is small in comparison with other products, managers will often retain the line instead of replacing it, if the line is necessary to the sale of other products or if it serves as a "magnet" to attract customers. Bread, for example, is not an especially profitable line in food stores, but customers expect it to be available, and many would undoubtedly shift their buying elsewhere if a particular store decided to stop carrying it.

THE MAKE OR BUY DECISION

Objective 4
Explain what is meant by a make or buy decision and prepare a well-organized make or buy analysis.

Many steps are involved in getting a finished product into the hands of a consumer. First, raw materials must be obtained through mining, drilling, growing crops, raising animals, and so forth. Second, these raw materials must be processed to remove impurities or to extract the desirable and usable materials from the bulk of materials available. Third, the usable materials must be fabricated into desired form to serve as basic inputs for manufactured products. Fourth, the actual manufacturing of the finished product must take place, with several products perhaps coming from the same basic raw materials input (as, for example, several different items of clothing coming from the same basic cloth input). And finally, the finished product must be distributed to the ultimate consumer.

When a company is involved in more than one of these steps, it is following a policy of **vertical integration.** Vertical integration is very common. Some firms go so far as to control *all* of the activities relating to their products, from the mining of raw materials or the raising of crops right up to the final distribution of finished goods. Other firms are content to integrate on a less grand scale and produce only certain fabricated parts that go into their finished products.

A decision to produce a fabricated part internally, rather than to buy the part externally from a supplier, is often called a **make or buy decision.** Actually, any decision relating to vertical integration is a make or buy decision, since the company is deciding whether to meet its own needs internally rather than to buy externally.

The Advantages of Integration

Certain advantages arise from integration. The integrated firm is less dependent on its suppliers and may be able to ensure a smoother flow of parts and materials for production than the nonintegrated firm. For example, a strike against a major parts supplier might cause the operations of a nonintegrated firm to be interrupted for many months, whereas the integrated firm that is producing its own parts might be able to continue operations. Also, many firms feel that they can control quality better by producing their own parts and materials, rather than by relying on the quality control standards of outside suppliers. In addition, the integrated firm realizes profits from the parts and materials that it is "making" rather than "buying," as well as profits from its regular operations.

The advantages of integration are counterbalanced by a number of hazards. A firm that produces all of its own parts runs the risk of destroying long-run relationships with suppliers, which may prove harmful and disruptive to the firm. Once relationships with suppliers have been severed, they are often difficult to reestablish. If product demand becomes heavy, a firm may not have sufficient capacity to continue producing all of its own parts internally, but then it may experience great difficulty in its efforts to secure assistance from a severed supplier. In addition, changing technology often makes continued production of one's own parts more costly than purchasing them from the outside, but this change in cost may not be obvious to the firm. In sum, these factors suggest that although certain advantages may accrue to the integrated firm, the make or buy decision should be weighed very carefully before any move is undertaken that may prove to be costly in the long run.

An Example of Make or Buy

How does a firm approach the make or buy decision? Basically, the matters that must be considered fall into two broad categories—qualitative and quantitative. Qualitative matters deal with issues such as those raised in the preceding section. Quantitative matters deal with cost—what is the cost of producing as compared to the cost of buying? Several kinds of costs may be involved here, including opportunity costs.

To provide an illustration, assume that Bonner Company is now producing a small subassembly that is used in the production of one of the company's main product lines. Bonner Company's accounting department reports the following "costs" of producing the subassembly internally:

	Per Unit	8,000 Units
Direct materials	$ 6	$ 48,000
Direct labor	4	32,000
Variable overhead	1	8,000
Supervisor's salary	3	24,000
Depreciation of special equipment	2	16,000
Allocated general overhead	5	40,000
Total cost	$21	$168,000

Bonner Company has just received an offer from an outside supplier who will provide 8,000 subassemblies a year at a price of only $19 each. Should Bonner Company stop producing the subassemblies internally and start purchasing them from the outside supplier? To approach the decision from a financial point of view, the manager must again focus on the differential costs. As we have seen, the differential costs can be obtained by eliminating from the cost data those costs that are not avoidable—that is, by eliminating (1) the sunk costs and (2) the future costs that will continue regardless of whether the subassemblies are produced internally or purchased outside. The costs that remain after making these eliminations will be the costs that are avoidable to the company by purchasing outside. If these costs are less than the outside purchase price, then the company should continue to manufacture its own subassemblies and reject the outside supplier's offer. That is, the company should purchase outside only if the outside purchase price is less than the costs that can be avoided internally as a result of stopping production of the subassemblies.

Looking at the data above, notice first that depreciation of special equipment is one of the "costs" of producing the subassemblies internally. Since the equipment has already been purchased, this depreciation represents a sunk cost. Also notice that the company is allocating a portion of its general overhead costs to the subassemblies. Since these costs are common to all items produced in the factory, they will continue unchanged even if the subassemblies are purchased from the outside. These allocated costs, therefore, are not differential costs (since they will not differ between the make or buy alternatives), and they must be eliminated from the manager's decision framework along with the sunk costs.

The variable costs of producing the subassemblies (materials, labor, and variable overhead) are differential costs, since they can be avoided by buying the subassemblies from the outside supplier. If the supervisor can be discharged and his or her salary avoided by buying the subassemblies, then it too will be a differential cost and relevant to the decision. Assuming that both the variable costs and the supervisor's salary can be avoided by buying from the outside supplier, then the analysis takes the form shown in Exhibit 13–5.

Since it costs $5 less per unit to continue to make the subassemblies, Bonner Company should reject the outside supplier's offer. There is one additional factor that the company may wish to consider before coming to a final decision, however. This factor is the opportunity cost of the space now being used to produce the subassemblies.

The Matter of Opportunity Cost

If the space now being used to produce the subassemblies *would otherwise be idle,* then Bonner Company should continue to produce its own subassemblies and the supplier's offer should be rejected, as we stated above. Idle space that has no alternative use has an opportunity cost of zero.

But what if the space now being used to produce subassemblies would not sit idle, but rather could be used for some other purpose? In that case, the space would have an opportunity cost that would have to be considered in assessing the desirability of the supplier's offer. What would this opportunity cost be? It would be the segment margin that could be derived from the best alternative use of the space.

To illustrate, assume that the space now being used to produce subassemblies

EXHIBIT 13–5
Make or Buy Analysis

	Production "Cost" per Unit	Per Unit Differential Costs Make	Buy	Total Differential Costs—8,000 Units Make	Buy
Direct materials	$ 6	$ 6		$ 48,000	
Direct labor	4	4		32,000	
Variable overhead	1	1		8,000	
Supervisor's salary	3	3		24,000	
Depreciation of special equipment	2	—		—	
Allocation of general overhead	5	—		—	
Outside purchase price			$19		$152,000
Total cost	$21	$14	$19	$112,000	$152,000
Difference in favor of continuing to make			$5		$40,000

could be used to produce a new product line that would generate a segment margin of $60,000 per year. Under these conditions, Bonner Company would be better off to accept the supplier's offer and to use the available space to produce the new product line:

	Make	Buy
Differential cost per unit (see prior example)	$ 14	$ 19
Number of units needed annually	× 8,000	× 8,000
Total annual cost	112,000	152,000
Opportunity cost—segment margin forgone on a potential new product line.	60,000	
Total cost.	$172,000	$152,000
Difference in favor of purchasing from the outside supplier		$20,000

Perhaps we should again emphasize that opportunity costs are not recorded in the accounts of an organization. They do not represent actual dollar outlays. Rather, they represent those economic benefits that are *forgone* as a result of pursuing some course of action. The opportunity costs of Bonner Company are sufficiently large in this case to make continued production of the subassemblies very costly from an economic point of view.

UTILIZATION OF SCARCE RESOURCES

Managers are routinely faced with the problem of deciding how scarce resources are going to be utilized. A department store, for example, has a limited amount of floor space and therefore cannot stock every product that may be available. A manufacturing firm has a limited number of machine-hours and a limited number of direct labor-hours at its disposal. When capacity becomes pressed because of a scarce resource, the firm is said to have a **constraint.** Because of the constrained scarce resource, the company cannot fully satisfy demand, so the manager must decide how the scarce resource should be used. Fixed costs are usually unaffected by such choices, so the manager should select the course of action that will maximize the firm's *total* contribution margin.

Objective 5
Make appropriate computations to determine the most profitable utilization of scarce resources in an organization.

Contribution in Relation to Scarce Resources

To maximize total contribution margin, a firm should not necessarily promote those products that have the highest *unit* contribution margins. Rather, total contribution margin will be maximized by promoting those products or accepting those orders that provide the highest unit contribution margin *in relation to the scarce resources of the firm*. This concept can be illustrated with a firm that has two products, A and B. Cost and revenue data for the two products are given below:

	Product	
	A	B
Sales price per unit	$25	$30
Variable cost per unit	10	18
Contribution margin per unit . . .	$15	$12
CM ratio	60%	40%

Product A appears to be much more profitable than product B. It has a $15 per unit contribution margin as compared to only $12 per unit for product B, and it has a 60 percent CM ratio as compared to only 40 percent for product B.

But now let us add one more piece of information—the plant is operating at capacity. Ordinarily this does not mean that every machine and every person in the plant is working at the maximum possible rate. Because machines have different capacities, some machines will be operating at less than 100 percent of capacity. However, if the plant as a whole cannot produce any more units, some machine or process must be operating at capacity. The machine or process that is limiting overall output is called the **bottleneck.**

Suppose that in our example the bottleneck is a particular milling machine on which each unit of product A requires 2 minutes of processing time and each unit of product B requires 1 minute of processing time. Since this milling machine already has more work than it can handle, something will have to be cut back. In this situation, which product is more profitable? To answer this question, the manager should look at the *contribution margin per unit of the scarce resource.* This figure is computed by dividing the contribution margin for a unit of product by the amount of the scarce resource it requires. These calculations are carried out below for products A and B.

	Product	
	A	**B**
Contribution margin per unit (above) (a). . . .	$15.00	$12.00
Time on the milling machine required to produce one unit (b)	2 min.	1 min.
Contribution margin per unit of the scarce resource, (a) ÷ (b)	$7.50/min.	$12.00/min.

With these data in hand, it is easy to decide which product is less profitable and should be de-emphasized. Each minute of processing time on the milling machine that is devoted to product B results in an increase of $12 in contribution margin and profits. The comparable figure for product A is only $7.50 per minute. Therefore, product B should be emphasized in this situation. Even though product A has the larger per unit contribution margin and the larger CM ratio, product B provides the larger contribution margin in relation to the scarce resource.

To verify that product B is indeed the more profitable product in this situation, suppose an hour of additional processing time is available at the bottleneck and that there are unfilled orders for both product A and product B. The additional hour on the milling machine could be used to make either 30 units of A (60 minutes ÷ 2 minutes) or 60 units of B (60 minutes ÷ 1 minute), with the following consequences:

	Product	
	A	**B**
Contribution margin per unit (above) (a).	$ 15	$ 12
Additional units that can be processed in one hour.	× 30	× 60
Additional contribution margin	$450	$720

This example clearly shows that looking at unit contribution margins alone is not enough; the contribution margin must be viewed in relation to whatever resource constraint a firm may be working under.

Managing Constraints

Profits can be increased by effectively managing the constraints an organization faces. One aspect of managing constraints is to decide how to best utilize them. As discussed above, if the constraint is a bottleneck in the production process, the manager should select the product mix that maximizes the total contribution margin. In addition, the manager should take an active role in managing the constraint itself. Management should focus efforts on increasing the efficiency of the bottleneck operation and on increasing its capacity. Such efforts directly increase the output of finished goods and will often pay off in an almost immediate increase in profits.

It is often possible for a manager to effectively increase the capacity of the bottleneck, which is called **relaxing (or elevating) the constraint.** The milling machine operator in the example could be asked to work overtime. This would result in more available processing time on the milling machine and hence more finished goods that can be sold. The benefits from relaxing the constraint in such a manner are often enormous and can be easily quantified. The manager should first ask ''What would I do with additional capacity at the bottleneck if it were available?'' In the example, if there are unfilled orders for both products A and B, the additional capacity would be used to process more product B since that would be a better use of the additional capacity. In that situation, the additional capacity would be worth $12 per minute or $720 per hour. This is because adding an hour of capacity would generate an additional $720 of contribution margin if it would be used solely to process more product B. Since overtime pay for the operator is likely to be much less than $720 per hour, running the milling machine on overtime would be an excellent way to increase the profits of the company while at the same time satisfying customers.

To reinforce this concept, suppose that product B has been given top priority and consequently there are only unfilled orders for product A. How much would it be worth to the company to run the milling machine overtime in this situation? Since the additional capacity would be used to process product A, the value of that additional capacity would drop to $7.50 per minute or $450 per hour. Nevertheless, the value of relaxing the constraint would still be quite high.

These calculations indicate that managers should pay great attention to bottleneck operations. If a bottleneck machine breaks down or is ineffectively utilized, the losses to the company can be quite large. In our example, for every minute the milling machine is out of commission due to breakdowns or setups, the company loses between $7.50 and $12.00. The losses on an hourly basis are between $450 and $720! In contrast, there is no such loss of contribution margin if time is lost on a machine that is not a bottleneck—such machines have excess capacity anyway.

The implications are clear. Managers should focus much of their attention on managing bottlenecks. As we have discussed, managers should emphasize products that most profitably utilize the scarce resource. They should also make sure that products are processed smoothly through the bottlenecks, with minimal lost time due to breakdowns and setups. And they should try to find ways to increase the capacity at the bottlenecks.

There are a number of ways of effectively increasing the capacity of a bottleneck including:

- Working overtime on the bottleneck.
- Subcontracting some of the processing that would be done at the bottleneck.
- Investing in additional machines at the bottleneck.

- Shifting workers from processes that are not bottlenecks to the process that *is* a bottleneck.
- Rethinking the way the bottleneck resource is used and eliminating waste—particularly nonproductive time.
- Reducing defective units. Each defective unit that is processed through the bottleneck and that is subsequently scrapped takes the place of a good unit that could be sold.

The last three methods of increasing the capacity of the bottleneck are particularly attractive, since they are essentially free and may even yield additional cost savings.

The Problem of Multiple Constraints

What does a firm do if it is operating under *several* scarce resource constraints? For example, a firm may have limited raw materials available, limited direct labor-hours available, limited floor space, and limited advertising dollars to spend on product promotion. How would it proceed to find the right combination of products to produce under such a variety of constraints? The proper combination or "mix" of products can be found by use of a quantitative method known as *linear programming*. Linear programming, a very powerful analytical tool, is illustrated in Appendix G at the end of this chapter.

JOINT PRODUCT COSTS AND THE CONTRIBUTION APPROACH

Objective 6
Prepare an analysis showing whether joint products should be sold at the split-off point or processed further.

The manufacturing processes of some firms are such that several end products are produced from a single raw material input. The meat-packing industry, for example, inputs a pig into the manufacturing process and comes out with a great variety of end products—bacon, ham, spare ribs, pork roasts, and so on. Firms that produce several end products from a common input (e.g., a pig) are faced with the problem of deciding how the cost of that input is going to be divided among the end products (bacon, ham, pork roasts, and so on) that result. Before we address this problem, it will be helpful to define three terms—joint products, joint product costs, and split-off point.

Two or more products that are produced from a common input are known as **joint products.** The term **joint product costs** is used to describe those manufacturing costs that are incurred in producing joint products up to the split-off point. The **split-off point** is that point in the manufacturing process at which the joint products (bacon, ham, spare ribs, and so on) can be recognized as individual units of output. At that point, some of the joint products will be in final form, ready to be marketed to the consumer. Others will still need further processing on their own before they are in marketable form. These concepts are presented graphically in Exhibit 13–6.

The Pitfalls of Allocation

Joint product costs are really common costs incurred to simultaneously produce a variety of end products. Traditional cost accounting books contain various approaches to allocating these common costs among the different products at the split-off point. The most usual approach is to allocate the joint product costs according to the relative sales value of the end products.

Although allocation of joint product costs is needed for some purposes, such as balance sheet inventory valuation, allocations of this kind should be used with

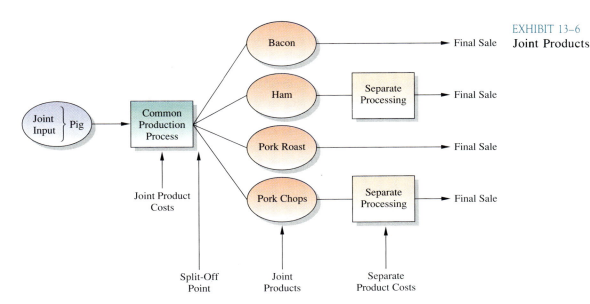

EXHIBIT 13–6
Joint Products

great caution *internally* in the decision-making process. Unless a manager proceeds with care, he or she may be led into incorrect decisions as a result of relying on allocated common costs. The box on the next page discusses an actual business situation showing an incorrect decision that resulted from using allocated costs.

Sell or Process Further Decisions

Joint product costs are irrelevant in decisions regarding what to do with a product from the split-off point forward. The reason is that by the time one arrives at the split-off point, the joint product costs have already been incurred and therefore are sunk costs. In the case of the soap company (see the next box), the $150,000 in allocated joint product costs should not have been permitted to influence what was done with the waste product from the split-off point forward. The analysis should have been:

	Dump in Gulf	Process Further
Sales value.	–0–	$300,000
Additional processing costs	–0–	175,000
Contribution margin.	–0–	$125,000
Advantage of processing further . . .	$125,000	

Decisions of this type are known as **sell or process further decisions.** As a general guide, it will always be profitable to continue processing a joint product after the split-off point *so long as the incremental revenue from such processing exceeds the incremental processing costs.* Joint product costs that have already been incurred up to the split-off point are sunk costs, and are always irrelevant in decisions concerning what to do from the split-off point forward.

To provide a detailed example of a sell or process further decision, assume that three products are derived from a single raw material input. Cost and revenue data relating to the products are presented in Exhibit 13–7 (page 613) along with an analysis of which products should be sold at the split-off point and which should

FOCUS ON CURRENT PRACTICE

A company located on the Gulf of Mexico is a producer of soap products. Its six main soap product lines are produced from common inputs. Joint product costs up to the split-off point constitute the bulk of the production costs for all six product lines. These joint product costs are allocated to the six product lines on the basis of the relative sales value of each line at the split-off point.

The company has a waste product that results from the production of the six main product lines. Until a few years ago, the company loaded the waste onto barges and dumped it into the Gulf of Mexico, since the waste was thought to have no commercial value. The dumping was stopped, however, when the company's research division discovered that with some further processing the waste could be made commercially salable as a fertilizer ingredient. The further processing was initiated at a cost of $175,000 per year. The waste was then sold to fertil- izer manufacturers at a total price of $300,000 per year.

The accountants responsible for allo- cating manufacturing costs included the sales value of the waste product along with the sales value of the six main prod- uct lines in their allocation of the joint product costs at the split-off point. This allocation resulted in the waste product being allocated $150,000 in joint product cost. This $150,000 allocation, when added to the further processing costs of $175,000 for the waste, caused the waste product to show the net loss computed in the table below.

When presented with this analysis, the company's management decided that further processing of the waste was not desirable after all. The company went back to dumping the waste in the Gulf. In addition to being unwise from an eco- nomic viewpoint, this dumping also raises questions regarding the compa- ny's social responsibility and the envi- ronmental impact of its actions.

Sales value of the waste product after further processing	$300,000
Less costs assignable to the waste product . . .	325,000
Net loss	$ (25,000)

be processed further. As shown in the exhibit, products B and C should both be processed further; product A should be sold at the split-off point.

ACTIVITY-BASED COSTING AND RELEVANT COSTS

Objective 7
Explain why a manager should exercise caution in relevant cost analysis when activity-based costing is being used.

In various places throughout this book, we have discussed the growing use of activity-based costing as a means for assigning costs to products or other seg- ments of a company. In our discussion, we have explained that the purpose of activity-based costing is to improve the traceability of costs through focusing on the activities in which a product or other segment is involved. Although improved traceability of costs does benefit a company in many ways, managers must exer- cise caution against reading more into this "traceability" than really exists. Why is caution needed? It is needed because there is a tendency to assume that if a cost is traceable to a segment through the activities in which it is involved, then the cost is automatically an avoidable cost in decision making.

Just because a cost is traceable to a product or other segment is no reason to

EXHIBIT 13–7

Sell or Process Further
Decision

| | **Product** | | |
	A	**B**	**C**
Sales value at the split-off point	$120,000	$150,000	$60,000
Sales value after further processing	160,000	240,000	90,000
Allocated joint product costs	80,000	100,000	40,000
Cost of further processing	50,000	60,000	10,000
Analysis of sell or process further:			
Sales value after further processing	$160,000	$240,000	$90,000
Sales value at the split-off point	120,000	150,000	60,000
Incremental revenue from further			
processing	40,000	90,000	30,000
Cost of further processing	50,000	60,000	10,000
Profit (loss) from further processing	$(10,000)	$ 30,000	$20,000

assume that the cost can be avoided if the segment is dropped or if some other special decision is made regarding the segment. As evidence, refer again to the data relating to the housewares line in Exhibit 13–4 on page 603. The $2,000 depreciation on fixtures is a traceable cost of the housewares line because it relates to activities in that department. We found, however, that the $2,000 is *not* avoidable if the housewares line is dropped. The key lesson here is that *the method used to assign a cost to a product or other segment does not change the basic nature of the cost.* A sunk cost such as depreciation of old equipment is still a sunk cost regardless of whether it is traced directly to a particular segment on an activity basis, allocated to all segments on a basis of labor-hours, or treated in some other way in the costing process.

Thus, managers must exercise care in relevant cost analysis when activity-based costing is in use, or they may be led into the trap of assuming that a traceable cost is automatically an avoidable cost. Regardless of the method used to assign costs to products or other segments, the manager still must apply the principles discussed in this chapter to determine the costs that are avoidable in each special-decision situation.[3]

SUMMARY

The accountant is responsible for seeing that relevant, timely data are available to guide management in all of its decisions, including those that relate to special, nonroutine situations. Reliance by management on irrelevant data can lead to incorrect decisions, reduced profitability, and inability to meet stated objectives. *All* costs are relevant in decision making, *except:*

1. Sunk costs.
2. Future costs that will not differ between the alternatives under consideration.

The concept of cost relevance has wide application. In this chapter, we have observed its use in equipment replacement decisions, in make or buy decisions, in

---

[3] For further discussion, see Douglas Sharp and Linda P. Christensen, "A New View of Activity-Based Costing," *Management Accounting* 73, no. 7 (September 1991), pp. 32–34; and Maurice L. Hirsch, Jr., and Michael C. Nibbelin, "Incremental, Separable, Sunk, and Common Costs in Activity-Based Costing," *Journal of Cost Management* 6, no. 1 (Spring 1992), pp. 39–47.

discontinuance of product-line decisions, in joint product decisions, and in decisions relating to the effective use of scarce resources. This list does not include all of the possible applications of the relevant cost concept. Indeed, *any* decision involving costs hinges on the proper identification and use of those costs that are relevant, if the decision is to be made properly. For this reason, we shall continue to focus on the concept of cost relevance in the following two chapters, where we consider long-run investment decisions.

REVIEW PROBLEM: RELEVANT COSTS

Charter Sports Equipment manufactures round, rectangular, and octagonal trampolines. Data on sales and expenses for the past month follow:

| | Total | Trampoline | | |
		Round	Rectangular	Octagonal
Sales.	$1,000,000	$140,000	$500,000	$360,000
Less variable expenses	410,000	60,000	200,000	150,000
Contribution margin	590,000	80,000	300,000	210,000
Less fixed expenses:				
Advertising—traceable.	216,000	41,000	110,000	65,000
Depreciation of special				
equipment	95,000	20,000	40,000	35,000
Salary of line supervisor	19,000	6,000	7,000	6,000
General factory overhead*	200,000	28,000	100,000	72,000
Total fixed expenses.	530,000	95,000	257,000	178,000
Net income (loss)	$ 60,000	$(15,000)	$ 43,000	$ 32,000

* Allocated on a basis of sales dollars.

The data above are representative of the long-run trend of sales and costs. Management is concerned about the continued losses shown by the round trampolines and wants a recommendation as to whether or not the line should be discontinued. The special equipment used to produce the trampolines has no resale value.

Required
1. Should production and sale of the round trampolines be discontinued? You may assume that the company has no other use for the capacity now being used to produce the round trampolines. Show computations to support your answer.
2. Recast the above data in a format that would be more usable to management in assessing the long-run profitability of the various product lines.

Solution to Review Problem
1. No, production and sale of the round trampolines should not be discontinued. Computations to support this answer follow:

Contribution margin lost if the round trampolines are discontinued . . .		$(80,000)
Less fixed costs that can be avoided:		
Advertising—traceable	$41,000	
Salary of the line supervisor	6,000	47,000
Decrease in net income for the company as a whole		$(33,000)

The depreciation of special equipment represents a sunk cost, and therefore it is not relevant to the decision. The general factory overhead is allocated and will continue regardless of whether or not the round trampolines are discontinued; thus, it also is not relevant to the decision.

*Alternative Solution to
Review Problem*

	Keep Round Tramps	Drop Round Tramps	Difference: Net Income Increase or (Decrease)
Sales.	$140,000	$ –0–	$(140,000)
Less variable expenses.	60,000	–0–	60,000
Contribution margin	80,000	–0–	(80,000)
Less fixed expenses:			
Advertising—traceable	41,000	–0–	41,000
Depreciation of special equipment.	20,000	20,000	–0–
Salary of the line supervisor	6,000	–0–	6,000
General factory overhead.	28,000	28,000	–0–
Total fixed expenses	95,000	48,000	47,000
Net income (loss)	$(15,000)	$(48,000)	$ (33,000)

2. If management wants a clear picture of the long-run profitability of the segments, the general factory overhead should not be allocated. It is a common cost and therefore should be deducted from the total product-line segment margin, as we learned in the preceding chapter. The proper income statement format would be as follows:

		Trampoline		
	Total	Round	Rectangular	Octagonal
Sales	$1,000,000	$140,000	$500,000	$360,000
Less variable expenses	410,000	60,000	200,000	150,000
Contribution margin	590,000	80,000	300,000	210,000
Less traceable fixed expenses:				
Advertising—traceable	216,000	41,000	110,000	65,000
Depreciation of special equipment.	95,000	20,000	40,000	35,000
Salary of line supervisor	19,000	6,000	7,000	6,000
Total traceable fixed expenses .	330,000	67,000	157,000	106,000
Product-line segment margin	260,000	$ 13,000	$143,000	$104,000
Less common fixed expenses	200,000			
Net income (loss)	$ 60,000			

KEY TERMS FOR REVIEW

Avoidable cost   Any cost that can be eliminated (in whole or in part) as a result of choosing one alternative over another in a decision-making situation. This term is synonymous with *relevant cost* and *differential cost*. (p. 594)

Objective 8
Define or explain the key terms listed at the end of the chapter.

Bottleneck   A machine or process that limits total output because it is operating at capacity. (p. 608)

Constraint   A limitation under which a company must operate, such as limited machine time available or limited raw materials available. (p. 607)

Differential cost   Any cost that is present under one alternative in a decision-making situation but is absent in whole or in part under another alternative. This term is synonymous with *avoidable cost* and *relevant cost*. (p. 594)

Joint product costs   Those manufacturing costs that are incurred up to the split-off point in producing joint products. (p. 610)

Joint products   Two or more items that are produced from a common input. (p. 610)

Make or buy decision   A decision as to whether an item should be produced internally or purchased from an outside supplier. (p. 604)

Relaxing (or elevating) the constraint   Some action that increases the capacity at a bottleneck. (p. 609)

Relevant cost   A cost that is applicable to a particular decision in the sense that it will have a bearing on which alternative the manager selects. This term is synonymous with *avoidable cost* and *differential cost*. (p. 594)

Sell or process further decision   A decision as to whether a joint product should be sold at the split-off point or processed further and sold at a later time in a different form. (p. 611)

Split-off point   That point in the manufacturing process where some or all of the joint products can be recognized as individual units of output. (p. 610)

Sunk cost   Any cost that has already been incurred and that cannot be changed by any decision made now or in the future. (p. 594)

Vertical integration   The involvement by a company in more than one of the steps from extracting or otherwise securing basic raw materials to the manufacture and distribution of a finished product. (p. 604)

APPENDIX G: LINEAR PROGRAMMING

Linear programming is a mathematical tool designed to assist management in making decisions in situations where constraining or limiting factors are present. The limiting factors might include, for example, a scarcity of raw materials needed in the production of a firm's products, or a plant with inadequate machine time to produce all of the products being demanded by a firm's customers. Linear programming is designed to assist the manager in putting together the right mix of products in situations such as these, so that the scarce resources of the firm (e.g., raw materials, machine time) can be utilized in a way that will maximize profits.

A Graphic Approach to Linear Programming

Objective 9
Construct a graph that shows the optimal solution to a linear programming problem.

To demonstrate a linear programming analysis, let us assume the following data:

A firm produces two products, X and Y. The contribution margin per unit of X is $8, and the contribution margin per unit of Y is $10. The firm has 36 hours of production time available each period. It takes 6 hours of production time to produce one unit of X and 9 hours of production time to produce one unit of Y.

The firm has only 24 pounds of raw materials available for use in production each period. It takes 6 pounds of raw materials to produce one unit of X and 3 pounds to produce one unit of Y.

Management estimates that no more than three units of Y can be sold each period. The firm is interested in maximizing contribution margin. What combination of X and Y should be produced and sold?

There are four basic steps in a linear programming analysis:

1. Determine the *objective function*, and express it in algebraic terms.
2. Determine the *constraints* under which the firm must operate, and express each constraint in algebraic terms.
3. Determine the *feasible production area* on a graph. This area will be bounded by the constraint equations derived in (2) above, after the constraint equations have been expressed on the graph in linear form.
4. Determine from the feasible production area the *product mix* that will maximize (or minimize) the objective function.

We will now examine each of these steps using the data in the above example.

1. Determine the objective function, and express it in algebraic terms.

The **objective function** represents the goal that management is trying to achieve. This goal might be to maximize total contribution margin, as in our example; alternatively, it might be to minimize total cost.

Looking at the data in our example, for each unit of X that is sold, $8 in contribution margin will be realized. For each unit of Y that is sold, $10 in contribution margin will be realized. Therefore, the total contribution margin for the firm can be expressed by the following **objective function equation:**

$$Z = \$8X + \$10Y \tag{1}$$

where Z = the total contribution margin that will be realized with an optimal mix of X and Y, X = the number of units of product X that should be produced and sold to yield the optimal mix, and Y = the number of units of product Y that should be produced and sold to yield the optimal mix.

2. Determine the constraints under which the firm must operate, and express each constraint in algebraic terms.

A constraint, as explained in the main body of the chapter, is simply some limitation under which the company must operate, such as limited production time available or a limited amount of raw materials on hand. From the data in our example, we can identify three constraints. First, only 36 hours of production time are available. Since it requires six hours to produce one unit of X and nine hours to produce one unit of Y, this constraint can be expressed in algebraic terms in the form of a **constraint equation,** as follows:

$$6X + 9Y \leq 36 \tag{2}$$

Notice the inequality sign ($\leq$) in the equation. This signifies that the total production of both products X and Y taken together cannot *exceed* the 36 hours available, but that this production *could* require *less* than the 36 hours available.

The second constraint deals with raw materials usage. Only 24 pounds are available each period. It takes 6 pounds of raw materials to produce one unit of X and 3 pounds to produce one unit of Y. This constraint can be expressed in the following algebraic terms:

$$6X + 3Y \leq 24 \tag{3}$$

The third constraint deals with market acceptance of product Y. The market can absorb only three units of Y each period. This constraint can be expressed as follows:

$$Y \leq 3 \tag{4}$$

Perhaps it goes without saying, but neither X nor Y can be negative. Equations showing a nonnegativity constraint for X and Y follow:

$$\begin{aligned} X &\geq 0 \\ Y &\geq 0 \end{aligned} \tag{5}$$

3. Determine the feasible production area on a graph.

A graph containing the constraint equations [equations (2) through (4) above] is presented in Exhibit G–1. In placing these three equations on the graph, we have asked the questions "How much product X could be produced if all resources were allocated to it and none were allocated to product Y?" and "How much product Y could be produced if all resources were allocated to it and none were allocated to product X?" For example, consider equation (2), dealing with production capacity. A total of 36 hours of production time is available. If all 36 hours are allocated to product X, six units can be produced each period (since it takes 6 hours to produce one unit of X, and 36 hours are available). On the other hand, if all 36 hours are allocated to product Y, then four units of Y can be produced each period (since it takes 9 hours to produce one unit of Y, and 36 hours are available).

If All Production Capacity Is Allocated to Product X	If All Production Capacity Is Allocated to Product Y
$6X + 0 \leq 36$	$0 + 9Y \leq 36$
$X = 6$	$Y = 4$

EXHIBIT G–1

A Linear Programming Graphic Solution

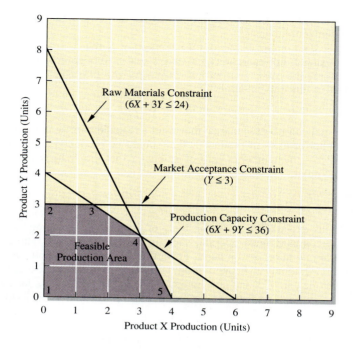

Therefore, the line on the graph in Exhibit G–1 expressing the production constraint equation [equation (2)] extends from the six-unit point on the *X* axis to the four-unit point on the *Y* axis. Of course, production could fall *anywhere* on this constraint line; the points on the axes (6, 4) simply represent the *extremes* that would be possible.

The equation associated with the raw materials constraint [equation (3)] has been placed on the graph through a similar line of reasoning. Since 24 pounds of raw materials are available, the firm could produce either four units of X or eight units of Y if all of the raw materials were allocated to one or the other (since it takes 6 pounds to produce a unit of X and 3 pounds to produce a unit of Y). Therefore, the line expressing the equation extends from the four-unit point on the *X* axis to the eight-unit point on the *Y* axis. Again, production could fall *anywhere* on this constraint line; the points on the axes (4, 8) simply represent the *extremes* that would be possible.

Since the third constraint equation [equation (4)] concerns only product Y, the line expressing the equation on the graph does not touch the *X* axis at all. It extends from the three-unit point on the *Y* axis and runs horizontal to the *X* axis, thereby signifying that regardless of the number of units of X that are produced, there can never be more than three units of Y produced.

The nonnegativity constraints in equation (5) confine our attention to the positive quadrant where both *X* and *Y* are positive.

Having now plotted on the graph the lines representing all of the constraint equations, we have isolated the **feasible production area.** This area has been shaded on the graph. Notice that the feasible production area is formed by the lines of the constraint equations. Each line has served to limit the size of the area to some extent. The reason, of course, is that these lines represent *constraints* under which the firm must operate, and thereby serve to *limit* the range of choices available. The firm could operate *anywhere* within the feasible production area. One point within this area, however, represents an optimal mix of products X and Y that will result in a maximization of the objective function (contribution margin). Our task now is to find precisely where that point lies.

4. Determine from the feasible production area the product mix that will maximize the objective function.

The **optimal product mix** will always fall on a *corner* of the feasible production area. If we scan the graph in Exhibit G–1, we can see that the feasible production area has five corners. The five corners will yield the following product mixes between X and Y (starting at the origin and going clockwise around the feasible production area):

	Units Produced	
Corner	X	Y
1	0	0
2	0	3
3	1½	3
4	3	2
5	4	0

Which production mix is optimal? To answer this question, we will need to calculate the total contribution margin promised at each corner. We can do this by referring to the unit contribution margin data given in the objective function equation:

$$Z = \$8X + \$10Y \tag{1}$$

This equation tells us that each unit of X promises \$8 of contribution margin and that each unit of Y promises \$10 of contribution margin. Relating these figures to the production mixes at the five corners, we find that the following total contribution margins are possible:

X		Y		Total Contribution Margin
\$8(0)	+	\$10(0)	=	\$ 0
8(0)	+	10(3)	=	30
8(1½)	+	10(3)	=	42
8(3)	+	10(2)	=	44
8(4)	+	10(0)	=	32

The firm should produce three units of X and two units of Y. This production mix will yield a maximum contribution margin of \$44. Given the constraints under which the firm must operate, it is not possible to obtain a greater total contribution margin than this amount. Any production mix different from three units of X and two units of Y will result in *less* total contribution margin.

Why Always on a Corner?

It was stated earlier that we will always find the optimal product mix on a *corner* of the feasible production area. Why does the optimal mix always fall on a corner? Look again at the objective function equation [equation (1)]. This equation expresses a straight line with a $-\frac{4}{5}$ slope. Place a ruler on the graph in Exhibit G–1 extending from the 8-unit point on the Y axis to the 10-unit point on the X axis (a $-\frac{4}{5}$ slope). Now bring your ruler down toward the origin of the graph, taking care to keep it parallel to the line from which you started. Note that the first point that your ruler touches is the corner of the feasible production area showing a production mix of three units of X and two units of Y. Your ruler touches this point first because it is the farthest point from the origin in relation to the objective function line. Therefore, that point must yield the greatest total contribution margin for the firm. Any point closer to the origin would result in less total contribution margin.[4]

---

[4] The objective function line could coincide with one of the lines bounding the feasible production area. A number of different product combinations would then be possible, each resulting in the same total contribution margin. However, our statement that the solution will always be found on a corner is still true even under these conditions, since the product mix at the corners of the line would yield the same total contribution margin as any point on the line.

Direction of the Constraint

Exhibit G–1 shows the direction of all the constraints to be *inward* toward the origin of the graph. The direction of the constraint will always be inward, so long as the constraint equation is stated in terms of less than or equal to ($\leq$).

The direction of the constraint will be *outward*, away from the origin of the graph, whenever the constraint equation is stated in terms of greater than or equal to ($\geq$). To illustrate, assume the following constraint:

X weighs 4 ounces, and Y weighs 9 ounces. X and Y must be mixed in such a way that their total weight is at least 72 ounces.

Constraint equation: $4X + 9Y \geq 72$ ounces

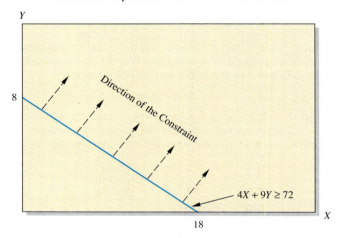

Since the direction of this constraint line is upward rather than downward, the feasible production area will be found *above* it rather than below it. Constraints expressed in terms of *greater than or equal to,* as illustrated above, can be found in any linear programming problem but are most common in *minimization* problems.

The Simplex Method

In our examples, we have dealt with only two products, X and Y. When more than two products are involved in a linear programming problem, the graphic method is no longer adequate to provide a solution. In these cases, a more powerful version of linear programming is needed. This more powerful version is commonly called the **simplex method.**

The simplex method is more complex than the graphic method; however, the principles underlying the two methods are the same. Special computer software is available for using the simplex method to solve linear programming problems. The mechanics of the simplex method are covered in detail in quantitative methods courses.

Applications of Linear Programming

Linear programming has been applied to an extremely wide range of problems in many different fields. Decision makers have found that it is by far the best tool available for combining labor, materials, and equipment to the best advantage of a firm. Although the use of linear programming has been most extensive in the industrial, agricultural, and military sectors, it has also been applied to problems in economics, engineering, and the sciences. Problems to which linear programming has been successfully applied include gasoline blending, production scheduling to optimize the use of total facilities, livestock feed blending to obtain a desired nutritional mix at the least cost, the routing of boxcars to desired points at the least cost, the selection of sites for electrical transformers, forestry maintenance, and the choice of flight paths for space satellites.

KEY TERMS FOR REVIEW (APPENDIX)

Constraint equation   An algebraic expression of one of the limitations (constraints) under which a company must operate. (p. 617)

Feasible production area   The area on a linear programming graph, bounded by the constraint equations, within which production can take place. (p. 618)

Linear programming   A mathematical tool designed to assist the manager in making decisions in situations where constraining or limiting factors are present. (p. 616)

Objective function   A statement of the goal that management is trying to achieve. This goal might be, for example, to maximize total contribution margin or to minimize total cost. (p. 616)

Objective function equation   An algebraic expression of the goal that management is trying to achieve in a linear programming analysis. (p. 617)

Optimal product mix   The product mix that allows the firm to achieve the objective expressed in the objective function equation. (p. 619)

Simplex method   A linear programming method that is particularly suited to handling three or more variables in the objective function equation (for example, the optimal production mix of three or more products). (p. 620)

QUESTIONS

13-1   What is a *relevant cost?*

13-2   Define the following terms: *incremental cost, opportunity cost,* and *sunk cost.*

13-3   Are variable costs always relevant costs? Explain.

13-4   The book value of a machine (as shown on the balance sheet) is an asset to a company, but this same book value is irrelevant in decision making. Explain why this is so.

13-5   "Sunk costs are easy to spot—they're simply the fixed costs associated with a decision." Do you agree? Explain.

13-6   "Sometimes depreciation on equipment is a relevant cost in a decision, and sometimes it isn't." Do you agree? Explain.

13-7   "My neighbor offered me $25 for the use of my boat over the weekend, but I decided that renting it out is just too risky." What cost term would you use to describe the $25? Explain.

13-8   "Variable costs and differential costs mean the same thing." Do you agree? Explain.

13-9   "All future costs are relevant in decision making." Do you agree? Why?

13-10   Prentice Company is considering dropping one of its product lines. What costs of the product line would be relevant to this decision? Irrelevant?

13-11   Why is the term *avoidable cost* used in connection with product line and make or buy decisions?

13-12   "If a product line is generating a loss, then that's pretty good evidence that the product line should be discontinued." Do you agree? Explain.

13-13   What is the danger in allocating common fixed costs among product lines or other segments of an organization?

13-14   What is meant by the term *make or buy?*

13-15   How does opportunity cost enter into the make or buy decision?

13-16   Give four examples of limiting or scarce factors that might be present in an organization.

13-17   How will the relating of product line contribution margins to scarce resources help a company ensure that profits will be maximized?

13-18   Define the following terms: *joint products, joint product costs,* and *split-off point.*

13–19   From a decision-making point of view, what pitfalls are there in allocating common costs among joint products?

13–20   What guideline can be used in determining whether a joint product should be sold at the split-off point or processed further?

13–21   Airlines sometimes offer reduced rates during certain times of the week to members of a businessperson's family if they accompany him or her on trips. How does the concept of relevant costs enter into the decision to offer reduced rates of this type?

13–22   Why must a manager exercise special caution in relevant cost analysis when activity-based costing is in use?

13–23   (Appendix G)   Schloss Company has decided to use linear programming as a planning tool. The company can't decide whether to use contribution margin per unit or gross profit per unit in its linear programming computations. Which would you suggest? Why?

13–24   (Appendix G)   Define *objective function* and *constraint* as these concepts relate to linear programming.

13–25   (Appendix G)   Sever Company produces two products. Product A has a contribution margin per unit of $10. Product B has a contribution margin per unit of $8. Explain why a linear programming analysis might suggest that the company produce more of product B than product A. (Ample market exists for either product.)

13–26   (Appendix G)   What is meant by the term *feasible production area?*

EXERCISES

E13–1   Listed below are a number of "costs" incurred by Rialdo Company:

	Case 1		Case 2	
Item	Relevant	Not Relevant	Relevant	Not Relevant
a. Sales revenue				
b. Direct materials				
c. Direct labor				
d. Variable production overhead				
e. Depreciation—machine A				
f. Depreciation—machine B				
g. Fixed production overhead (general)				
h. Variable selling expense				
i. Fixed selling expense				
j. General administrative salaries				
k. Book value—machine A				
l. Market value—machine A (current resale)				
m. Market value—machine B (cost)				
n. Rate of return available from outside investments				

Required   Copy the information above onto your answer sheet, and place an X in the appropriate column to indicate whether each item is relevant or not relevant in the following situations (requirement 1 relates to Case 1 above, and requirement 2 relates to Case 2):

1.   Rialdo Company wants to purchase machine B to replace machine A (machine A will be sold). Both machines have the same capacity and a remaining life of five years. Machine B will reduce direct materials costs by 20 percent, due to less waste. Other production costs will not change.

2.   Rialdo Company wants to purchase machine B to increase production and sales. Machine A will continue to be used.

The costs associated with the acquisition and annual operation of a truck are given below: **E13–2**

Insurance	$1,600
Licenses	250
Taxes (vehicle)	150
Garage rent for parking (per truck) . . .	1,200
Depreciation ($9,000 ÷ 5 years).	1,800*
Gasoline, oil, tires, and repairs	0.07 per mile

* Based on obsolescence rather than on wear and tear.

1. Assume that Hollings Company has purchased one truck, and that the truck has been driven 50,000 miles during the first year. Compute the average cost per mile of owning and operating the truck.   *Required*
2. At the beginning of the second year, Hollings Company is unsure whether to use the truck or leave it parked in the garage and have all hauling done commercially. (The state requires the payment of vehicle taxes even if the vehicle isn't used.) What costs above are relevant to this decision?
3. Assume that the company decides to use the truck during the second year. Near year-end an order is received from a customer over 1,000 miles away. What costs above are relevant in a decision between using the truck to make the delivery and having the delivery done commercially?
4. Occasionally, the company could use two trucks at the same time. For this reason, some thought is being given to purchasing a second truck. The total miles driven would be the same as if only one truck were owned. What costs above are relevant to a decision over whether to purchase the second truck?

Waukee Railroad is considering the purchase of a powerful, high-speed teletype machine to replace a standard teletype machine that is now in use. Selected information on the two machines is given below: **E13–3**

	Standard Teletype	High-Speed Teletype
Original cost new	$20,000	$30,000
Accumulated depreciation to date	6,000	—
Current salvage value	9,000	—
Estimated cost per year to operate . . .	15,000	7,000
Remaining years of useful life	5 years	5 years

Prepare a computation covering the five-year period that will show the net advantage or disadvantage of purchasing the high-speed teletype machine. Ignore income taxes, and use only relevant costs in your analysis.   *Required*

Swanson Company has been experiencing losses on product line 6 for several years. The most recent quarterly income statement on product line 6 is given below: **E13–4**

SWANSON COMPANY
Income Statement—Product Line 6
For the Quarter Ended March 31, 19x7

Sales.		$850,000
Less variable expenses:		
Variable manufacturing expenses	$330,000	
Sales commissions.	42,000	
Freight-out	18,000	
Total variable expenses		390,000
Contribution margin		460,000
Less fixed expenses:		
Advertising	270,000	
Depreciation of equipment (no resale value) . . .	80,000	
General factory overhead	105,000*	
Salary of line manager	32,000	
Insurance on inventories	8,000	
Purchasing department expenses	45,000†	
Total fixed expenses		540,000
Net loss		$ (80,000)

* Allocated on a basis of machine-hours.
† Allocated on a basis of sales dollars.

The discontinuance of product line 6 would not affect sales of other product lines.

Required   Would you recommend that product line 6 be discontinued? Support your answer with appropriate computations.

E13–5   Troy Engines, Ltd., manufactures a variety of engines for use in heavy equipment. The company has always produced all of the necessary parts for its engines, including all of the carburetors. An outside supplier has offered to produce and sell one type of carburetor to Troy Engines, Ltd., for a cost of $35 per unit. In order to evaluate this offer, Troy Engines, Ltd., has gathered the following information relating to its own cost of producing the carburetor internally:

	Per Unit	15,000 Units per Year
Direct materials	$14	$210,000
Direct labor	10	150,000
Variable manufacturing overhead	3	45,000
Fixed manufacturing overhead, traceable . . .	6*	90,000
Fixed manufacturing overhead, allocated . . .	9	135,000
Total cost	$42	$630,000

* One-third supervisory salaries; two-thirds depreciation of special equipment (no resale value).

Required 1. Assuming that the company has no alternative use for the facilities that are now being used to produce the carburetors, should the outside supplier's offer be accepted? Show all computations.

2. Assuming that a new product that will generate a segment margin of $150,000 per year could be produced if the carburetors were purchased, should the offer be accepted? Show all computations.

E13–6   Dorsey Company manufactures three products from a common input in a joint processing operation. Joint processing costs up to the split-off point total $350,000 per quarter. The company allocates these costs to the joint products on the basis of their total sales value at the split-off point. Unit selling prices and total output at the split-off point are as follows:

Product	Selling Price	Quarterly Output
A.	$16 per pound	15,000 pounds
B.	8 per pound	20,000 pounds
C.	25 per gallon	4,000 gallons

Each product can be processed further after the split-off point. Additional processing requires no special facilities. The additional processing costs (per quarter) and unit selling prices after further processing are given below:

Product	Additional Processing Costs	Selling Price
A	$63,000	$20 per pound
B	80,000	13 per pound
C	36,000	32 per gallon

Required

1. Which product or products should be sold at the split-off point, and which product or products should be processed further? Show computations.
2. What general statement can be made with respect to joint costs and the decision to process further?

E13–7

Barlow Company manufactures three products: A, B, and C. The selling price, variable costs, and contribution margin for one unit of each product follow:

	Product		
	A	B	C
Selling price	$180	$270	$240
Less variable expenses:			
Direct materials	24	72	32
Other variable expenses. . . .	102	90	148
Total variable expenses . . .	126	162	180
Contribution margin	$ 54	$108	$ 60
Contribution margin ratio	30%	40%	25%

The same raw material is used in all three products. Barlow Company has only 5,000 pounds of material on hand and will not be able to obtain any more material for several weeks due to a strike in its supplier's plant. Management is trying to decide which product(s) to concentrate on next week in filling its backlog of orders. The material costs $8 per pound.

Required

1. Compute the amount of contribution margin that will be obtained per pound of material used in each product.
2. Which orders would you recommend that the company work on next week— the orders for product A, product B, or product C? Show computations.
3. A foreign supplier could furnish Barlow with additional stocks of the raw material at a substantial premium over the usual price. If there is unfilled demand for all three products, what is the highest price that Barlow Company would be willing to pay for an additional pound of materials?

E13–8

Bill has just returned from a duck hunting trip. He has brought home eight ducks. Bill's friend, John, disapproves of duck hunting, and to discourage Bill from further hunting, John has presented him with the following cost estimate per duck:

Camper and equipment: Cost, $12,000; usable for eight seasons; 10 hunting trips per season	$150
Travel expense (pickup truck): 100 miles at $0.12 per mile (gas, oil, and tires—$0.07 per mile; depreciation and insurance—$0.05 per mile)	12
Shotgun shells (two boxes)	20
Boat: Cost, $320; usable for eight seasons; 10 hunting trips per season . . .	4
Fine paid for speeding on the way to the river	25
Hunting license: Cost, $30 for the season; 10 hunting trips per season	3
Money lost playing poker: Loss, $18 (Bill plays poker every weekend)	18
A fifth of Old Grandad: Cost, $8 (used to ward off the cold)	8
Total cost.	$240
Cost per duck ($240 ÷ 8 ducks)	$ 30

Required   1. Assuming that the duck hunting trip Bill has just completed is typical, what costs are relevant to a decision as to whether Bill should go duck hunting again this season?

            2. Discuss John's computation of the cost per duck.

E13–9   Hasbro Products manufactures 30,000 units of part S-6 each year for use on its production line. At this level of activity, the cost per unit for part S-6 is as follows:

Direct materials	$ 3.60
Direct labor	10.00
Variable overhead	2.40
Fixed overhead	9.00
Total cost per part	$25.00

An outside supplier has offered to sell 30,000 units of part S-6 each year to Hasbro Products for $21 per part. If Hasbro Products accepts this offer, the facilities now being used to manufacture part S-6 could be rented to another company at an annual rental of $80,000. However, Hasbro has determined that two thirds of the fixed overhead being applied to part S-6 would continue even if part S-6 were purchased from the outside supplier.

Required   Prepare computations to show the net dollar advantage or disadvantage of accepting the outside supplier's offer.

E13–10   The Regal Cycle Company manufactures three types of bicycles—a dirt bike, a mountain bike, and a racing bike. Data on sales and expenses for the past six months follow:

	Total	Dirt Bikes	Mountain Bikes	Racing Bikes
Sales.	$300,000	$90,000	$150,000	$60,000
Less variable manufacturing and selling expenses	120,000	27,000	60,000	33,000
Contribution margin	180,000	63,000	90,000	27,000
Less fixed expenses:				
Advertising, traceable	30,000	10,000	14,000	6,000
Depreciation of special equipment	23,000	6,000	9,000	8,000
Salary of line supervisor	35,000	12,000	13,000	10,000
Common, but allocated*	60,000	18,000	30,000	12,000
Total fixed expenses	148,000	46,000	66,000	36,000
Net income (loss)	$ 32,000	$17,000	$ 24,000	$(9,000)

* Allocated on a basis of sales dollars.

Management is concerned about the continued losses shown by the racing bikes and wants a recommendation as to whether or not the line should be discontinued. The special equipment used to produce racing bikes has no resale value.

1. Should production and sale of the racing bikes be discontinued? Show computations to support your answer. *Required*

2. Recast the above data in a format that would be more usable to management in assessing the long-run profitability of the various product lines.

E13–11

(Appendix G) Greenup Company produces two high-quality fertilizer products—Nitro-X and Nitro-Y. Each fertilizer product is produced in batches, with one batch of Nitro-X yielding a contribution margin of $70 and one batch of Nitro-Y yielding a contribution margin of $80. The company wants to maximize contribution margin. Either product can be sold in unlimited quantities.

Two raw materials go into the production of both Nitro-X and Nitro-Y, although not in the same proportions, as shown in the table below. In addition, Nitro-X uses a third raw material.

	Material A (pounds)	Material B (pounds)	Material C (gallons)
Nitro-X usage per batch	40	30	15
Nitro-Y usage per batch	30	60	—
Total raw material available each day	6,000	9,000	1,500

1. Prepare equations to express the objective function and the constraints under which the company must operate. *Required*

2. Determine how many batches of Nitro-X and Nitro-Y should be produced each day. Use the linear programming graphic method, with Nitro-X on the horizontal *(X)* axis and Nitro-Y on the vertical *(Y)* axis.

PROBLEMS

Sometimes it's hard for a manager to determine what costs are relevant when faced with an ethical dilemma. Consider the following situation that occurred some years ago at BankAmerica:

P13–12 Ethics and the Manager

"The bank discovered that it had inadvertently made a rounding error of a few pennies on several hundred consumer loans that it had taken over from other businesses. According to California's so-called Unruh law, any error in interest charges would exempt the consumer from the entire interest payment on that loan. The kicker, however, was that no statute of limitations had been established for this kind of mistake. BankAmerica's problem was uncovered during a standard internal audit and had not been noticed by any consumer. Depending on where it set the statute of limitations and how it counted the applicable loans, the bank would have to forfeit vastly different amounts of interest payments—the actual range was several million dollars. What should the bank do?"[5]

The lack of a statute of limitations was particularly important in this situation since some of the loans had been paid off for years.

1. Assume you are a member of the bank's board of directors and therefore responsible to stockholders for the bank's profitability. Identify at least three courses of action that the bank could reasonably have followed. *Required*

2. Which of the courses of action identified in (1) do *you* think the bank should have followed? Explain your answer.

---

[5] Laura L. Nash, *Good Intentions Aside* (Boston, Mass.: Harvard Business School Press, 1990), pp. 174–75. Used by permission.

P13-13   **Dropping a Flight; Analysis of Operating Policy**   Profits have been decreasing for several years at Pegasus Airlines. In an effort to improve the company's performance, consideration is being given to dropping several flights that appear to be unprofitable.

A typical income statement for one such flight (flight 482) is given below (per flight):

Ticket revenue (175 seats × 40% occupancy × $200 ticket price)	$14,000	100.0%
Less variable expenses ($15 per person) . . .	1,050	7.5
Contribution margin	12,950	92.5%
Less flight expenses:		
Salaries, flight crew.	1,800	
Flight promotion	750	
Depreciation of aircraft	1,400*	
Fuel for aircraft	6,800	
Liability insurance	4,200	
Salaries, flight assistants	500	
Hangar parking fee for aircraft at destination	150	
Baggage loading and flight preparation . . .	1,700	
Overnight costs for flight crew and assistants at destination	300	
Total flight costs	17,600	
Net loss.	$ (4,650)	

* Based on obsolescence.

The following additional information is available about flight 482:

a.   Members of the flight crew are paid fixed annual salaries, whereas the flight assistants are paid by the flight.

b.   One third of the liability insurance is a special charge assessed against flight 482 because in the opinion of the insurance company, the destination of the flight is in a "high-risk" area.

c.   The hangar parking fee is a standard fee charged for aircraft at all airports.

d.   The baggage loading and flight preparation expense is an allocation of ground crews' salaries and depreciation of ground equipment.

e.   If flight 482 is dropped, Pegasus Airlines has no authorization at present to replace it with another flight.

Required   1.   Using the data available, prepare an analysis showing what impact dropping flight 482 would have on the airline's profits.

2.   The airline's scheduling officer has been criticized because only about 50 percent of the seats on Pegasus' flights are being filled compared to an average of 60 percent for the industry. The scheduling officer has explained that Pegasus' average seat occupancy could be improved considerably by eliminating about 10 percent of the flights, but that doing so would reduce profits. Explain how this could happen.

P13-14   **Relevant Cost Analysis; Book Value**   Murl Plastics, Inc., purchased a new machine one year ago at a cost of $60,000. Although the machine operates well, the president of Murl Plastics is wondering if the company should replace it with a new electronically operated machine that has just come on the market. The new machine would slash annual operating costs by two thirds, as shown in the comparative data below:

	Present Machine	Proposed New Machine
Purchase cost new	$60,000	$90,000
Estimated useful life new	6 years	5 years
Annual cost to operate.	$42,000	$14,000
Annual straight-line depreciation . . .	10,000	18,000
Remaining book value	50,000	—
Salvage value now	10,000	—
Salvage value in 5 years	–0–	–0–

In trying to decide whether to purchase the new machine, the president has prepared the following analysis:

Book value of the old machine . . .	$50,000
Less salvage value.	10,000
Net loss from disposal	$40,000

"Even though the new machine looks good," said the president, "we can't get rid of that old machine if it means taking a huge loss on it. We'll have to use the old machine for at least a few more years."

Sales in the company are expected to be $200,000 per year, and selling and administrative expenses are expected to be $126,000 per year, regardless of which machine is used.

1. Prepare a summary income statement covering the next five years, assuming: *Required*
   a. That the new machine is not purchased.
   b. That the new machine is purchased.
2. Determine the desirability of purchasing the new machine, using only relevant costs in your analysis.

Sell or Process Further Decision   (Prepared from a situation suggested by Professor   **P13–15** John W. Hardy.) Lone Star Meat Packers is a major processor of beef and other meat products. The company has a large amount of T-bone steak on hand, and it is trying to decide whether to sell the T-bone steaks as they are initially cut or to process them further into filet mignon and the New York cut.

If the T-bone steaks are sold as initially cut, the company figures that a 1-pound T-bone steak would yield the following profit:

Selling price ($2.25 per pound) . . .	$2.25
Less joint product cost.	1.80
Profit per pound.	$0.45

Instead of being sold as initially cut, the T-bone steaks could be further processed into filet mignon and New York cut steaks. Cutting one side of a T-bone steak provides the filet mignon, and cutting the other side provides the New York cut. One 16-ounce T-bone steak thus cut will yield one 6-ounce filet mignon and one 8-ounce New York cut; the remaining ounces are waste. The cost of processing the T-bone steaks into these cuts is $0.25 per pound. The filet mignon can be sold for $4 per pound, and the New York cut can be sold for $2.80 per pound.

1. Determine the profit per pound from further processing the T-bone steaks.   *Required*
2. Would you recommend that the T-bone steaks be sold as initially cut or processed further? Why?

Make or Buy Analysis   "In my opinion, we ought to stop making our own drums and   **P13–16** accept that outside supplier's offer," said Frank Avaroni, president of Trent Oil Refinery. "At a price of $18 per drum, we would be paying $5 less than it costs us to manufacture the drums in our own plant. Since we use 60,000 drums a year, that would be an annual cost savings of $300,000.'' Trent Oil's present cost to manufacture one drum is given below (based on 60,000 drums per year):

Direct materials	$10.35
Direct labor	6.00
Variable overhead	1.50
Fixed overhead ($2.80 general company overhead, $1.60 depreciation, and $0.75 supervision)	5.15
Total cost per drum	$23.00

A decision about whether to make or buy the drums is especially important at this time since the equipment being used to make the drums is completely worn out and must be replaced. The choices facing the company are:

Alternative 1: Purchase new equipment and continue to make the drums. The equipment would cost $810,000; it would have a six-year useful life and no salvage value. The company uses straight-line depreciation.

Alternative 2: Purchase the drums from an outside supplier at $18 per drum under a six-year contract.

The new equipment would be more efficient than the equipment that Trent Oil has been using and, according to the manufacturer, would reduce direct labor and variable overhead costs by 30 percent. Supervision cost ($45,000 per year) and direct materials cost per drum would not be affected by the new equipment. The new equipment's capacity would be 90,000 drums per year. The company has no other use for the space now being used to produce the drums.

Required

1. To assist the president in making a decision, prepare an analysis showing what the total cost and the cost per drum would be under each of the two alternatives given above. Assume that 60,000 drums are needed each year. Which course of action would you recommend to the president?

2. Would your recommendation in (1) above be the same if the company's needs were: (a) 75,000 drums per year or (b) 90,000 drums per year? Show computations to support your answer, with costs presented on both a total and a per unit basis.

3. What other factors would you recommend that the company consider before making a decision?

P13–17
Comprehensive Problem

Relevant Cost Potpourri   Unless otherwise indicated, each of the following parts is independent. In all cases, show computations to support your answer.

1. A merchandising company has two departments, A and B. A recent monthly income statement for the company follows:

	Total	Department A	Department B
Sales	$4,000,000	$3,000,000	$1,000,000
Less variable expenses	1,300,000	900,000	400,000
Contribution margin	2,700,000	2,100,000	600,000
Less fixed expenses	2,200,000	1,400,000	800,000
Net income (loss)	$ 500,000	$ 700,000	$ (200,000)

A study indicates that $340,000 of the fixed expenses being charged to department B are sunk costs and allocated costs that will continue even if B is dropped. In addition, the elimination of department B will result in a 10 percent decrease in the sales of department A. If department B is dropped, what will be the effect on the income of the company as a whole?

2. For many years Futura Company has purchased the starters that it installs in its standard line of farm tractors. Due to a reduction in output of certain of its products, the company has idle capacity that could be used to produce the starters. The chief engineer has recommended against this move, however, pointing out that the cost to produce the starters would be greater than the current $8.40 per unit purchase price:

	Per Unit	Total
Direct materials.	$3.10	
Direct labor	2.70	
Supervision	1.50	$60,000
Depreciation	1.00	40,000
Variable overhead	0.60	
Rent.	0.30	12,000
Total cost	$9.20	

A supervisor would have to be hired to oversee production of the starters. However, the company has sufficient idle tools and machinery that no new equipment would have to be purchased. The rent charge above is based on space utilized in the plant. The total rent on the plant is $80,000 per period. Prepare computations to show the dollar advantage or disadvantage per period of making the starters.

3. Wexpro, Inc., produces several products from processing of 1 ton of clypton, a rare mineral. Material and processing costs total $60,000 per ton, one fourth of which is allocable to product X. Seven thousand units of product X are produced from each ton of clypton. The units can either be sold at the split-off point for $9 each, or processed further at a total cost of $9,500 and then sold for $12 each. Should product X be processed further or sold at the split-off point?

4. Benoit Company produces three products, A, B, and C. Cost and revenue characteristics of the three products follow (per unit):

	Product		
	A	B	C
Selling price	$80	$56	$70
Less variable expenses:			
Direct materials	24	15	9
Labor and overhead	24	27	40
Total variable expenses	48	42	49
Contribution margin	$32	$14	$21
Contribution margin ratio	40%	25%	30%

Demand for the company's products is very strong, with far more orders on hand each month than the company has raw materials available to produce. The same material is used in each product. The material costs $3 per pound, with a maximum of 5,000 pounds available each month. Which orders would you advise the company to accept first, those for A, for B, or for C? Which orders second? Third?

5. Delta Company produces a single product. The cost of producing and selling a single unit of this product at the company's normal activity level of 60,000 units per year is:

Direct materials	$5.10
Direct labor	3.80
Variable overhead	1.00
Fixed overhead.	4.20
Variable selling and administrative expense . . .	1.50
Fixed selling and administrative expense	2.40

The normal selling price is $21 per unit. The company's capacity is 75,000 units per year. An order has been received from a mail-order house for 15,000 units at a special price of $14 per unit. This order would not disturb regular sales. If the order is accepted, by how much will annual profits be increased or decreased? (The order will not change the company's total fixed costs.)

6. Refer to the data in (5) above. Assume the company has 1,000 units of this product left over from last year that are vastly inferior to the current model. The units must be sold through regular channels at reduced prices. What unit cost figure is relevant for establishing a minimum selling price for these units? Explain.

P13–18   Utilization of Scarce Resources; Product Mix   The Walton Toy Company manufactures a line of dolls and a doll dress sewing kit. Demand for the dolls is increasing, and management requests assistance from you in determining an economical sales and production mix for the coming year. The company's sales department provides the following information:

Product	Estimated Demand Next Year (units)	Selling Price per Unit
Debbie.	50,000	$13.50
Trish	42,000	5.50
Sarah	35,000	21.00
Mike	40,000	10.00
Sewing kit	325,000	8.00

The standard costs for direct materials and direct labor per unit are as follows:

Product	Direct Materials	Direct Labor
Debbie.	$4.30	$3.20
Trish	1.10	2.00
Sarah	6.44	5.60
Mike	2.00	4.00
Sewing kit	3.20	1.60

The following additional information is available:

a. The company's plant has a capacity of 130,000 direct labor-hours per year on a single-shift basis. The company's present employees and equipment can produce all five products.

b. The direct labor rate is $8 per hour; this rate is expected to remain unchanged during the coming year.

c. Fixed costs total $520,000 per year. Variable overhead costs are equal to 25 percent of direct labor costs.

d. All of the company's nonmanufacturing costs are fixed.

e. The company's present inventory of finished products is nominal and can be ignored.

Required
1. Determine the contribution margin for a unit of each product.
2. Determine the contribution margin that will be realized per direct labor-hour expended on each product.
3. Prepare a schedule showing the total direct labor-hours that will be required to produce the units estimated to be sold during the coming year.
4. Examine the data you have computed in (1)–(3). Indicate which product should be increased or decreased in production, and the amount of this increase or decrease, so that total production time is equal to the 130,000 hours available.
5. Assume that the company does not want to reduce production and sales of any product. What is the highest price, in terms of a rate per hour, that Walton Company would be willing to pay for additional capacity (that is, for added direct labor time available)?

6.   Assume again that the company does not want to reduce sales of any product. Identify ways in which the company could obtain the additional output.

(CPA, heavily adapted)

Discontinuance of a Department   Sales have never been good in department C of Stacey's Department Store. For this reason, management is considering the elimination of the department. A summarized income statement for the store, by departments, for the most recent month is given below: **P13–19**

STACEY'S DEPARTMENT STORE
Income Statement
For the Month Ended June 30, 19x6

		Department		
	Total	A	B	C
Sales.	$1,000,000	$500,000	$320,000	$180,000
Less variable expenses.	574,300	338,000	166,000	70,300
Contribution margin	425,700	162,000	154,000	109,700
Less fixed expenses:				
Salaries.	49,000	18,000	16,000	15,000
Utilities	6,200	2,600	2,000	1,600
Direct advertising	89,000	32,000	27,000	30,000
General advertising*	25,000	12,500	8,000	4,500
Rent on building†	38,000	16,000	12,000	10,000
Employment taxes‡	4,900	1,800	1,600	1,500
Depreciation of fixtures	36,000	12,000	15,000	9,000
Insurance and property taxes				
on inventory and fixtures. . . .	7,900	2,300	4,000	1,600
General office expenses	54,000	18,000	18,000	18,000
Service department expenses	81,000	27,000	27,000	27,000
Total fixed expenses	391,000	142,200	130,600	118,200
Net income (loss)	$ 34,700	$ 19,800	$ 23,400	$(8,500)

* Allocated on a basis of sales dollars.

† Allocated on a basis of space occupied.

‡ Based on salaries paid directly in each department.

The following additional information is available:

a.   If department C is eliminated, the utilities bill will be reduced by $700 per month.

b.   All departments are housed in the same building. The store leases the entire building at a fixed annual rental rate.

c.   One of the employees in department C is Fred Jones, who has been with the company for many years. Mr. Jones will be transferred to another department if department C is eliminated. His salary is $1,000 per month.

d.   The fixtures in department C would be transferred to the other departments if department C is eliminated. One fourth of the insurance and property taxes in department C relates to the fixtures in the department.

e.   The company has two service departments—purchasing and warehouse. If department C is eliminated, one employee in the warehouse can be discharged. This employee's combined salary and other employment costs is $900 per month. General office expenses will not change.

1.   Assume that the store has no alternative use for the space now being occupied by department C. Prepare computations to show whether or not the department should be eliminated. (You may assume that eliminating department C would have no effect on sales in the other departments.)   *Required*

2.   Assume that due to an extreme shortage of store facilities, the space being occupied by department C could be subleased at a rental rate of $48,000 per month. Would you

advise the company to eliminate department C and sublease the space? Show computations to support your answer.

P13–20
Comprehensive Problem

Selected Relevant Cost Questions   Andretti Company has a single product called a Dak. The company normally produces and sells 60,000 Daks each year at a selling price of $32 per unit. The company's unit costs at this level of activity are given below:

Direct materials.	$10.00	
Direct labor	4.50	
Variable overhead.	2.30	
Fixed overhead	5.00	($300,000)
Variable selling expenses . . .	1.20	
Fixed selling expenses.	3.50	($210,000)
Total cost per unit	$26.50	

A number of questions relating to the production and sale of Daks are given below. Each question is independent.

Required
1. Assume that Andretti Company has sufficient capacity to produce 90,000 Daks each year. The company could increase its sales by 25 percent above the present 60,000 units each year if it were willing to increase the fixed selling expenses by $80,000. Would the increased fixed expenses be justified?
2. Assume again that Andretti Company has sufficient capacity to produce 90,000 Daks each year. A customer in a foreign market wants to purchase 20,000 Daks. Import duties on the Daks would be $1.70 per unit, and costs for permits and licenses would be $9,000. The only selling costs that would be associated with the order would be $3.20 per unit shipping cost. You have been asked by the president to compute the per unit break-even price on this order.
3. The company has 1,000 Daks on hand that have some irregularities and are therefore considered to be "seconds." Due to the irregularities, it will be impossible to sell these units at the regular price. If the company wishes to sell them through regular distribution channels, what unit cost figure is relevant for setting a minimum selling price?
4. Due to a strike in its supplier's plant, Andretti Company is unable to purchase more material for the production of Daks. The strike is expected to last for two months. Andretti Company has enough material on hand to continue to operate at 30 percent of normal levels for the two-month period. As an alternative, Andretti could close its plant down entirely for the two months. If the plant were closed, fixed overhead costs would continue at 60 percent of their normal level during the two-month period; the fixed selling costs would be reduced by 20 percent while the plant was closed. What would be the dollar advantage or disadvantage of closing the plant for the two-month period?
5. An outside manufacturer has offered to produce Daks for Andretti Company and to ship them directly to Andretti's customers. If Andretti Company accepts this offer, the facilities that it uses to produce Daks would be idle; however, fixed overhead costs would be reduced by 75 percent of their present level. Since the outside manufacturer would pay for all the costs of shipping, the variable selling costs would be only two thirds of their present amount. Compute the unit cost figure that is relevant for comparison against whatever quoted price is received from the outside manufacturer.

P13–21   **Shutdown versus Continue-to-Operate Decision**   (Note to the student: This type of decision is similar to that of dropping a product line, and the portion of the book dealing with that topic should be referred to, if needed.)

Birch Company normally produces and sells 30,000 units of RG-6 each month. RG-6 is a small electrical relay used in the automotive industry as a component part in various products. The selling price is $22 per unit, variable expenses are $14 per unit, fixed overhead costs total $150,000 per month, and fixed selling costs total $30,000 per month.

Employment-contract strikes in the companies that purchase the bulk of the RG-6 units have caused Birch Company's sales to temporarily drop to only 8,000 units per month. Birch Company estimates that the strikes will last for about two months, after which time sales of RG-6 should return to normal. Due to the current low level of sales, however, Birch Company is thinking about closing down its own plant during the two months that the strikes are on. If Birch Company does close down its plant, it is estimated that fixed overhead costs can be reduced to only $105,000 per month and that fixed selling costs can be reduced by 10 percent. Start-up costs at the end of the shutdown period would total $8,000. Since Birch Company uses JIT production methods, no inventories are on hand.

1. Assuming that the strikes continue for two months, as estimated, would you recommend that Birch Company close its own plant? Show computations in good form.   *Required*
2. At what level of sales (in units) for the two-month period would Birch Company be indifferent as between closing the plant or keeping it open? Show computations. (Hint: This is a type of break-even analysis, except that the fixed cost portion of your break-even computation should include only those fixed costs that are relevant [i.e., avoidable] over the two-month period.)

Discontinuance of a Store   Superior Markets, Inc., operates three stores in a large   **P13–22**
metropolitan area. A segmented income statement for the company for the last quarter is given below:

SUPERIOR MARKETS, INC.
Income Statement
For the Quarter Ended September 30, 19x8

	Total	North Store	South Store	East Store
Sales	$3,000,000	$720,000	$1,200,000	$1,080,000
Cost of goods sold	1,657,200	403,200	660,000	594,000
Gross margin	1,342,800	316,800	540,000	486,000
Operating expenses:				
Selling expenses	817,000	231,400	315,000	270,600
Administrative expenses . . .	383,000	106,000	150,900	126,100
Total expenses	1,200,000	337,400	465,900	396,700
Net income (loss)	$ 142,800	$ (20,600)	$ 74,100	$ 89,300

The North Store has consistently shown losses over the past two years. For this reason, management is giving consideration to closing the store. The company has retained you to make a recommendation as to whether the store should be closed or kept open. The following additional information is available for your use:

a. The breakdown of the selling and administrative expenses is as follows:

	Total	North Store	South Store	East Store
Selling expenses:				
Sales salaries	$239,000	$ 70,000	$ 89,000	$ 80,000
Direct advertising	187,000	51,000	72,000	64,000
General advertising*	45,000	10,800	18,000	16,200
Store rent	300,000	85,000	120,000	95,000
Depreciation of store fixtures . . .	16,000	4,600	6,000	5,400
Delivery salaries	21,000	7,000	7,000	7,000
Depreciation of delivery equipment	9,000	3,000	3,000	3,000
Total selling expenses	$817,000	$231,400	$315,000	$270,600

* Allocated on a basis of sales dollars.

	Total	North Store	South Store	East Store
Administrative expenses:				
Store management salaries	$ 70,000	$ 21,000	$ 30,000	$ 19,000
General office salaries*	50,000	12,000	20,000	18,000
Insurance on fixtures and				
inventory	25,000	7,500	9,000	8,500
Utilities	106,000	31,000	40,000	35,000
Employment taxes	57,000	16,500	21,900	18,600
General office—other*	75,000	18,000	30,000	27,000
Total administrative				
expenses	$383,000	$106,000	$150,900	$126,100

* Allocated on a basis of sales dollars.

b. The lease on the building housing the North Store can be broken with no penalty.

c. The fixtures being used in the North Store would be transferred to the other two stores if the North Store were closed.

d. The general manager of the North Store would be retained and transferred to another position in the company if the North Store were closed. Her salary is $9,000 per quarter. All other employees in the store would be discharged.

e. The company has one delivery crew that serves all three stores. One delivery person could be discharged if the North Store were closed. This person's salary is $4,000 per quarter.

f. The company's employment taxes are 15 percent of salaries.

g. One third of the insurance in the North Store is on the store's fixtures.

h. The "General office salaries" and "General office—other" relate to the overall management of Superior Markets, Inc. If the North Store were closed, one person in the general office could be discharged because of the decrease in overall workload. This person's salary is $6,000 per quarter.

Required

1. Prepare a schedule showing the change in revenues and expenses and the impact on the company's overall net income that would result if the North Store were closed.

2. Assuming that the store space can't be subleased, what recommendation would you make to the management of Superior Markets, Inc.?

3. Assume that if the North Store were closed, at least one fourth of its sales would transfer to the East Store, due to strong customer loyalty to Superior Markets. The East Store has ample capacity to handle the increased sales. You may assume that the increased sales in the East Store would yield the same gross margin rate as present sales in that store. What effect would these factors have on your recommendation concerning the North Store? Show all computations to support your answer.

P13–23 Make or Buy Decision   Silven Industries, which manufactures and sells a highly successful line of summer lotions and insect repellants, has decided to diversify in order to stabilize sales throughout the year. A natural area for the company to consider is the production of winter lotions and creams to prevent dry and chapped skin.

After considerable research, a winter products line has been developed. However, because of the conservative nature of the company management, Silven's president has decided to introduce only one of the new products for this coming winter. If the product is a success, further expansion in future years will be initiated.

The product selected (called Chap-Off) is a lip balm that will be sold in a lipstick-type tube. The product will be sold to wholesalers in boxes of 24 tubes for $8 per box. Because of available capacity, no additional fixed overhead costs will be incurred to produce the product. However, a $90,000 charge for fixed overhead will be absorbed by the product to allocate a fair share of the company's present fixed overhead costs to the new product.

Using the estimated sales and production of 100,000 boxes of Chap-Off as the expected volume, the accounting department has developed the following costs per box:

Direct material $3.60
Direct labor 2.00
Manufacturing overhead . . .   1.40
    Total cost $7.00

The costs above include costs for producing both the lip balm and the tube into which the lip balm is to be placed. As an alternative to making the tubes, Silven has approached a cosmetics manufacturer to discuss the possibility of purchasing the tubes for Chap-Off. The purchase price of the empty tubes from the cosmetics manufacturer would be $1.35 per box of 24 tubes. If Silven Industries accepts the purchase proposal, it is predicted that direct labor and variable overhead costs per box of Chap-Off would be reduced by 10 percent, and that direct materials costs would be reduced by 25 percent.

Required

1. Should Silven Industries make or buy the tubes? Show calculations to support your answer.
2. What would be the maximum purchase price acceptable to Silven Industries? Support your answer with an appropriate explanation.
3. Instead of sales of 100,000 boxes, revised estimates show sales volume at 120,000 boxes. At this new volume, additional equipment at an annual rental of $40,000 must be acquired to manufacture the tubes. Assuming that the outside supplier will not accept an order for less than 100,000 boxes, should Silven Industries make or buy the tubes? Show computations to support your answer.
4. Refer to the data in (3). Assume that the outside supplier will accept an order of any size for the tubes at $1.35 per box. How, if at all, would this change your answer? Show computations.
5. What nonquantifiable factors should Silven Industries consider in determining whether they should make or buy the tubes?

(CMA, heavily adapted)

Sell or Process Further Decision Cum-Clean Corporation produces a variety of cleaning compounds and solutions for both industrial and household use. While most of its products are processed independently, a few are related, such as the company's Grit 337 and its Sparkle silver polish.   **P13–24**

Grit 337 is a coarse cleaning powder with many industrial uses. It costs $1.60 a pound to make, and it has a selling price of $2 a pound. A small portion of the annual production of Grit 337 is retained in the factory for further processing in the mixing department, where it is combined with several other ingredients to form a paste that is marketed as Sparkle silver polish. The silver polish sells for $4 per jar.

This further processing requires one-fourth pound of Grit 337 per jar of silver polish. Other ingredients added and labor costs involved in the processing of a jar of silver polish are:

Other ingredients . . . $0.65
Direct labor 1.48
    Total cost $2.13

Overhead costs associated with the processing of the silver polish are:

Variable overhead cost . . . . 25 percent of
                                            direct labor cost

Fixed overhead cost (per month):
    Production supervisor $1,600
    Depreciation of mixing equipment . . . 1,400

The production supervisor has no duties other than to oversee production of the silver polish. The mixing equipment is special-purpose equipment acquired specifically to produce the silver polish. It has only a nominal resale value.

Advertising costs for the silver polish total $4,000 per month. Variable selling costs associated with the silver polish are 7.5 percent of sales.

Due to a recent decline in the demand for silver polish, the company is wondering whether its continued production is advisable. The sales manager feels that it would be more profitable to just sell all of the Grit 337 as a cleaning powder.

Required   1.   What is the incremental contribution margin per jar from further processing of Grit 337 into silver polish?

2.   What is the minimum number of jars of silver polish that must be sold each month to justify the continued processing of Grit 337 into silver polish? Show all computations in good form.

(CMA, heavily adapted)

P13–25
Integrative
Problem

Break Even; Eliminating an Unprofitable Line   Kathy Woods, president of Eastern Company, wants guidance on the advisability of eliminating product C, one of the company's three similar products, in hope of improving the company's overall operating performance. The company's three products are manufactured in a single plant and occupy roughly equal amounts of floor space. Below is a condensed statement of operating income for the company and for product C for the quarter ended October 31, 19x6:

	All Three Products	Product C
Sales	$2,900,000	$315,000
Cost of sales:		
Raw materials	515,000	133,850
Direct labor	1,305,000	72,000
Fringe benefits (15% of labor)	195,750	10,800
Royalties (1% of product C sales)	3,500	3,150
Building rent and maintenance	6,000	4,000
Factory supplies	15,000	2,000
Depreciation (straight line)	75,200	19,100
Electrical power—machines	29,300	3,600
Total cost of sales	2,144,750	248,500
Gross margin	755,250	66,500
Selling and administrative expenses:		
Sales commissions	120,000	15,000
Officers' salaries	31,500	10,500
Product-line managers' salaries	14,000	5,300
Fringe benefits (15% of salaries and commissions)	24,825	4,620
Shipping	81,225	9,350
Advertising	227,000	37,300
Total selling and administrative expenses	498,550	82,070
Net operating income (loss)	$ 256,700	$(15,570)

Inventories carried by the company are small and can be ignored. Each element of cost is entirely fixed or variable within the relevant range. The dropping of product C would have little (if any) effect on sales of the other two product lines.

Required   1.   Before a decision is made on whether product C should be dropped, Ms. Woods would first like to know the overall break-even point for product C (in sales dollars), given the cost and revenue data shown above.

2.   Would you recommend to Ms. Woods that product C be dropped? Prepare appropriate computations to support your answer. You may assume that the plant space now being used to produce product C would otherwise be idle. The equipment being used to produce product C has no resale value.

(CPA, adapted)

Accept or Reject Special Orders; Make or Buy; Utilization of Scarce Resources   Parts
(1), (2), and (3) apply to one situation and parts (4) and (5) apply to a different situation.

1. Polaski Company manufactures and sells a single product called a Ret. Operating at
    capacity, the company can produce and sell 30,000 Rets per year. Costs associated
    with this level of production and sales are given below:

	Unit	Total
Direct materials	$15	$ 450,000
Direct labor	8	240,000
Variable overhead	3	90,000
Fixed overhead	9	270,000
Variable selling expense	4	120,000
Fixed selling expense	6	180,000
Total cost	$45	$1,350,000

The Rets sell for $50 each. Assume that due to a recession, Polaski Company expects
to sell only 25,000 Rets through regular channels next year. A large retail chain has
offered to purchase 5,000 Rets if Polaski is willing to accept a 16 percent discount off
the regular price. There would be no sales commissions on this order; thus, variable
selling expenses would be slashed by 75 percent. However, Polaski Company would
have to purchase a special machine in order to engrave the retail chain's name on the
5,000 units. This machine would cost $10,000. Polaski Company has no assurance that
the retail chain will purchase additional units any time in the future. Determine the
impact on profits next year if this special order is accepted.

2. Refer to the original data. Assume again that Polaski Company expects to sell only
    25,000 Rets through regular channels next year. The U.S. Army would like to make a
    one-time-only purchase of 5,000 Rets. The Army would pay a fixed fee of $1.80 per
    Ret, and in addition it would reimburse Polaski Company for all costs of production
    (variable and fixed) associated with the units. Since the Army would pick up the Rets
    with its own trucks, there would be no variable selling expenses of any type associated
    with this order. If Polaski Company accepts the order, by how much will profits be
    increased or decreased for the year?

3. Assume the same situation as that described in (2) above, except that the company
    expects to sell 30,000 Rets through regular channels next year. Thus, accepting the
    U.S. Army's order would require giving up regular sales of 5,000 Rets. If the Army's
    order is accepted, by how much will profits be increased or decreased from what they
    would be if the 5,000 Rets were sold through regular channels?

4. Fairmont Company has been producing two bearings, B30 and B50, for use on its
    assembly line. Data relating to these bearings are presented below:

	B30	B50
Machine-hours required per unit	2.5	4.0
Standard cost per unit:		
Direct materials	$ 7.00	$10.00
Direct labor	4.00	6.00
Manufacturing overhead:		
Variable*	2.00	3.00
Fixed†	5.00	8.00
Total cost per unit	$18.00	$27.00

* Variable overhead is applied on a basis of direct labor-hours.

† Fixed overhead is applied on a basis of machine-hours. One
fourth of the fixed overhead consists of supervisory salaries for
direct supervision of production of the bearings. The remainder
consists of general factory overhead.

Fairmont Company needs 8,000 units of the B30 bearing and 15,000 units of the B50 bearing each year. Fairmont's management is thinking about devoting additional machine time to other products. This additional machine time devoted to other products would generate $100,000 in added contribution margin each year. If the company does devote extra time to other products, only 60,000 machine-hours will be available each year for the production of bearings, which is not adequate to provide all of the company's bearing needs. An outside supplier has offered to sell Fairmont Company all the bearings it needs at a price of $17 for the B30 and $24 for the B50. The outside supplier will not accept an order for only part of Fairmont's needs, so the 60,000 available machine-hours will be idle if Fairmont purchases its bearings outside. What will be the net benefit or loss to the company if it accepts the outside supplier's offer for all of its bearing needs?

5. Refer to the data in (4) above. Assume that a decision has been made to devote additional machine time to other product lines, and assume that the outside supplier has agreed to accept an order for only part of Fairmont's bearing needs. Fairmont Company wants to schedule the 60,000 available machine-hours in such a way as to minimize its total costs. Previously, the company had two supervisors over the production of bearings. Since the company will be producing fewer bearings than before, one of these supervisors has been discharged; the remaining supervisor will be paid $24,000 per year. How many units of the B30 and the B50 bearings should be manufactured in the available facilities and how many units of each should be purchased from the outside supplier? Be prepared to show computations and to present reasoning in class to support your answer.

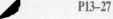

P13–27 Special Order; Relevant Costs   Sommers Valve Company, located in southern Wisconsin, manufactures a variety of industrial valves and pipe fittings that are sold to customers in nearby states. Currently, the company is operating at about 70 percent capacity and is earning a satisfactory return on investment.

Management has been approached by Glascow Industries Ltd. of Scotland with an offer to buy 120,000 units of a pressure valve. Glascow Industries manufactures a valve that is almost identical to Sommers' pressure valve; however, a fire in Glascow Industries' valve plant has shut down its manufacturing operations. Glascow needs the 120,000 valves over the next four months to meet commitments to its regular customers; the company is prepared to pay $19 each for the valves, FOB shipping point.

Sommers' product cost, based on current attainable standards, for the pressure valve is:

Direct materials	$ 5
Direct labor	6
Manufacturing overhead.	9
Total cost	$20

Manufacturing overhead is applied to production at the rate of $18 per standard direct labor-hour. This overhead rate is made up of the following components:

Variable factory overhead.	$ 6
Fixed factory overhead—direct	8
Fixed factory overhead—allocated	4
Applied manufacturing overhead rate.	$18

Additional costs normally incurred in connection with sales of the pressure valve include sales commissions of 5 percent and freight expense of $1 per unit. However, the company does not pay sales commissions on special orders that come directly to management.

In determining selling prices, Sommers Valve Company adds a 40 percent markup to product cost. This provides a $28 suggested selling price for the pressure valve. The marketing department, however, has set the current selling price at $27 in order to maintain market share.

Production management believes that it can handle the Glascow Industries order without disrupting its scheduled production. The order, however, would require the purchase of a stamping machine to stamp Glascow Industries' name and logo on the valves. The machine would cost $48,000.

If management accepts the order, 30,000 pressure valves will be manufactured and shipped to Glascow Industries each month for the next four months. Shipments will be made in weekly consignments, FOB shipping point.

Required

1. Determine how many additional direct labor-hours would be required each month to fill the Glascow Industries order.
2. Prepare an incremental analysis showing the impact of accepting the Glascow Industries order.
3. Calculate the minimum unit price that Sommers' management could accept for the Glascow Industries order without reducing net income.
4. Identify the factors, other than price, that Sommers Valve Company should consider before accepting the Glascow Industries order.

(CMA, adapted)

Optimum Production Mix to Maximize Profits   (Appendix G) Ron Green has just retired and is anxious to open a small pottery business to occupy his time. Mr. Green has decided to produce just two items initially—pots and bowls. The local pottery supply house has indicated that because of shortages in supplies, Mr. Green can be allowed only 80 pounds of high-quality clay and only 11¼ gallons of glazing material each week.   **P13–28**

Mr. Green has purchased a used kiln that he feels can be operated about 60 hours per week. His wife will package all finished products; she will have a maximum of 11 hours per week to work for the pottery business. Mr. Green has determined the following additional information:

		Per Batch	
Operation	Item Needed	Pots	Bowls
Molding	Clay	8 lbs.	5 lbs.
Glazing	Glaze	5 qts.	3 qts.
Firing.	—	4 hrs.	6 hrs.
Packaging	—	1 hr.	1 hr.

Mr. Green feels that no more than nine batches of bowls can be sold each week. The pots yield $50 in profits per batch, and the bowls yield $40 per batch. Mr. Green wishes to maximize his profits.

Required

1. Prepare linear programming equations to express the objective function and each of the constraints. Identify pots as X and bowls as Y.
2. Prepare a linear programming graph to determine how many batches of pots and how many batches of bowls should be produced each week. Place pots on the horizontal (X) axis and bowls on the vertical (Y) axis.

Product Mix to Exhaust Remaining Stock of Materials   (Appendix G) Elton Company manufactures a line of carpeting that includes a commercial carpeting and a residential carpeting. Two grades of fiber—heavy duty and regular—are used in manufacturing both types of carpeting. The mix of the two grades of fiber differs in each type of carpeting, with the commercial grade using a greater amount of heavy-duty fiber.   **P13–29**

In two months, Elton will introduce a new line of carpeting to replace the current line. The present fiber in stock will not be used in the new line. Management wants to exhaust the present stock of regular and heavy-duty fiber during the last month of production.

Data regarding the current line of commercial and residential carpeting are presented below:

	Commercial	Residential
Selling price per roll of carpet	$1,000	$800
Production specifications per roll of carpet:		
Heavy-duty fiber	80 pounds	40 pounds
Regular fiber	20 pounds	40 pounds
Direct labor-hours.	15 hours	15 hours
Standard cost per roll of carpet:		
Heavy-duty fiber ($3/pound)	$240	$120
Regular fiber ($2/pound)	40	80
Direct labor ($10/DLH)	150	150
Variable manufacturing overhead (60% of direct labor cost)	90	90
Fixed manufacturing overhead (120% of direct labor cost)	180	180
Total standard cost per roll of carpet	$700	$620

Elton has 42,000 pounds of heavy-duty fiber and 24,000 pounds of regular fiber in stock. A maximum of 10,500 direct labor-hours are available during the month. The labor force can work on either type of carpeting.

The demand for the present line of carpeting is such that all of the quantities produced can be sold.

Required

1. A member of Elton Company's cost accounting staff has stated that linear programming should be used to determine how many rolls of commercial and residential carpeting to manufacture during the last month of production. Explain why linear programming should be used in this situation.

2. Prepare the objective function equation and the constraint equations needed for a linear programming solution to the problem. Use the letter *C* to denote rolls of commercial carpeting and the letter *R* to denote rolls of residential carpeting.

3. Using the equations from (2) above, prepare a linear programming graphic solution to the problem, showing how many rolls of commercial carpeting and how many rolls of residential carpeting should be produced. (Place commercial carpeting on the horizontal axis and residential carpeting on the vertical axis.)

4. Assume that any scrap fiber can be sold for 25 cents per pound. How much revenue would be realized from sale of the scrap? Show computations.

(CMA, adapted)

P13–30   **Cost Minimization**   (Appendix G)   (Prepared from a situation described by Naylor and Byrne, *Linear Programming* [Wadsworth Publishing Company, p. 45].) Recycled Metals, Inc., has received an order from a customer who wants to purchase a minimum of 2,500 pounds of scrap metal. The customer requires that the scrap metal contain at least 1,200 pounds of high-quality aluminum that can be melted down and used in fabrication. The customer also requires that the scrap delivered to him contain no more than 480 pounds of unfit metal. By "unfit" the customer means metal that contains so many impurities that it can't be melted down and used at all.

Recycled Metals, Inc., can purchase aluminum scrap metal from either of two suppliers. The scrap being sold by the two suppliers contains the following proportions of high-quality aluminum and unfit scrap:

	Supplier	
	A	B
High-quality aluminum	80%	30%
Unfit scrap	20	15

Either supplier has unlimited quantities of scrap metal available. Supplier A charges 25 cents per pound, and supplier B charges 12 cents per pound. Recycled Metals, Inc., would like to minimize the total cost it will have to pay to acquire the needed scrap metal to fill the customer's order.

1. Prepare equations to express the objective function and the constraints under which Recycled Metals, Inc., must make its purchase.
2. Using the linear programming graphic method, determine the amount of scrap metal that should be purchased from each supplier.

CASES

Sell or Process Further Decision   The Scottie Sweater Company is a large producer of   C13–31 sweaters under the "Scottie" label. The company buys raw wool on the market and processes it into wool yarn from which the sweaters are woven. One spindle of wool yarn is required to produce one sweater. The costs and revenues associated with the sweaters are given below:

	Per Sweater
Selling price	$30.00
Cost to manufacture:	
Raw materials:	
Buttons, thread, lining. . . . . $ 2.00	
Wool yarn 16.00	
Total raw materials 18.00	
Direct labor 5.80	
Manufacturing overhead. 8.70	32.50
Manufacturing profit (loss).	$ (2.50)

Originally, all of the wool yarn was used to produce sweaters, but in recent years a market has developed for the wool yarn itself. The yarn is purchased by other companies for use in production of wool blankets and other wool products. Since the development of the market for the wool yarn, a continuing dispute has existed in the Scottie Sweater Company as to whether the yarn should be sold simply as yarn or processed into sweaters. Current cost and revenue data on the yarn are given below:

	Per Spindle of Yarn
Selling price	$20.00
Cost to manufacture:	
Raw materials (raw wool) $7.00	
Direct labor 3.60	
Manufacturing overhead. 5.40	16.00
Manufacturing profit	$ 4.00

The market for sweaters is temporarily depressed, due to unusually warm weather in the western states where the sweaters are sold. This has made it necessary for the company to discount the selling price of the sweaters to $30 from the normal $40 price. Since the market for wool yarn has remained strong, the dispute has again surfaced over whether the yarn should be sold outright rather than processed into sweaters. The sales manager thinks that the production of sweaters should be discontinued; she is upset about having to sell sweaters at a $2.50 loss, when the yarn could be sold for a $4 profit. However, the production superintendent is equally upset at the suggestion that he close down a large portion of the factory. He argues that the company is in the sweater business, not the yarn business, and that the company should focus on its area of strength.

Due to the nature of the production process, virtually all of the overhead costs are fixed. Overhead is assigned to products on a basis of 150 percent of direct labor cost.

Required
1. Would you recommend that the wool yarn be sold outright, or processed into sweaters? Show computations in good form to support your answer, and explain your reasoning.
2. What is the lowest price that the company should accept for a sweater? Show computations in good form to support your answer, and explain your reasoning.

C13–32 **Plant Closing Decision**   GianAuto Corporation manufactures automobiles, vans, and trucks. Among the various GianAuto plants around the United States is the Denver Cover Plant. Coverings made primarily of vinyl and upholstery fabric are sewn at the Denver Cover Plant and used to cover interior seating and other surfaces of GianAuto products.

Ted Vosilo is the plant manager for Denver Cover. The Denver Cover Plant was the first GianAuto plant in the region. As other area plants were opened, Vosilo, in recognition of his management ability, was given responsibility for managing them. Vosilo functions as a regional manager although the budget for him and his staff is charged to the Denver Cover Plant.

Vosilo has just received a report indicating that GianAuto could purchase the entire annual output of Denver Cover from outside suppliers for $30 million. Vosilo was astonished at the low outside price because the budget for Denver Cover's operating costs for the coming year was set at $52 million. Vosilo believes that GianAuto will have to close down operations at Denver Cover in order to realize the $22 million in annual cost savings.

The budget for Denver Cover's operating costs for the coming year is presented on the following page. Additional facts regarding the plant's operations are as follows.

a. Due to Denver Cover's commitment to use high-quality fabrics in all its products, the purchasing department was instructed to place blanket purchase orders with major suppliers to ensure the receipt of sufficient materials for the coming year. If these orders are canceled as a consequence of the plant closing, termination charges would amount to 20 percent of the cost of direct materials.

b. Approximately 800 plant employees will lose their jobs if the plant is closed. This includes all of the direct laborers and supervisors as well as the plumbers, electricians, and other skilled workers classified as indirect plant workers. Some would be able to find new jobs while many others would have difficulty. All employees would have difficulty matching Denver Cover's base pay of $9.40 per hour that is the highest in the area. A clause in Denver Cover's contract with the union may help some employees; the company must provide employment assistance to its former employees for 12 months after a plant closing. The estimated cost to administer this service would be $1.5 million for the year.

c. Some employees would probably elect early retirement because GianAuto has an excellent pension plan. In fact, $3 million of the 19x6 pension expense would continue whether Denver Cover is open or not.

d. Vosilo and his staff would not be affected by the closing of Denver Cover. They would still be responsible for administering three other area plants.

e. Denver Cover considers equipment depreciation to be a variable cost and uses the units-of-production method to depreciate its equipment; Denver Cover is the only GianAuto plant to use this depreciation method. However, Denver Cover uses the customary straight-line method to depreciate its building.

DENVER COVER PLANT
Budget for Operating Costs
For the Year Ending December 31, 19x6

Materials		$14,000,000
Labor:		
Direct.	$13,100,000	
Supervision	900,000	
Indirect plant	4,000,000	18,000,000
Overhead:		
Depreciation—equipment	3,200,000	
Depreciation—building	7,000,000	
Pension expense	5,000,000	
Plant manager and staff	800,000	
Corporate allocation	4,000,000	20,000,000
Total budgeted costs		$52,000,000

Required

1. Without regard to costs, identify the advantages to GianAuto Corporation of continuing to obtain covers from its own Denver Cover Plant.
2. GianAuto Corporation plans to prepare a dollar analysis that will be used in deciding whether or not to close the Denver Cover Plant. Management has asked you to identify:
    a. The recurring annual budgeted costs that are relevant to the decision regarding closing the plant (show the dollar amounts).
    b. The recurring annual budgeted costs that are *not* relevant to the decision regarding closing the plant, and explain why they are not relevant (again show the dollar amounts).
    c. Any nonrecurring costs that would arise due to the closing of the plant, and explain how they would affect the decision (again show any dollar amounts).
3. Looking at the data you have prepared in (2), should the plant be closed? Show computations, and explain your answer.
4. Identify any revenues or costs not specifically mentioned in the problem that GianAuto should consider before making a decision.

(CMA, adapted)

Make or Buy; Optimal Use of Scarce Resources   Sportway, Inc., is a wholesale distributor supplying a wide range of moderately priced sporting equipment to large chain stores. About 60 percent of Sportway's products are purchased from other companies while the remainder of the products are manufactured by Sportway. The company has a plastics department that is currently manufacturing molded fishing tackle boxes. Sportway is able to manufacture and sell 8,000 tackle boxes annually, making full use of its direct labor capacity at available work stations. Presented below are the selling price and costs associated with Sportway's tackle boxes.

C13–33

Selling price per box		$86.00
Costs per box:		
Molded plastic	$ 8.00	
Hinges, latches, handle	9.00	
Direct labor ($15.00/hr.)	18.75	
Manufacturing overhead	12.50	
Selling and administrative cost	17.00	65.25
Net income per box		$20.75

Because Sportway believes it could sell 12,000 tackle boxes if it had sufficient manufacturing capacity, the company has looked into the possibility of purchasing the tackle boxes for distribution. Maple Products, a steady supplier of quality products, would be able to provide up to 9,000 tackle boxes per year at a price of $68.00 per box delivered to Sportway's facility.

Traci Kader, Sportway's product manager, has suggested that the company could make better use of its plastics department by manufacturing skateboards. To support her position, Traci has a market study that indicates an expanding market for skateboards and a need for additional suppliers. Traci believes that Sportway could expect to sell 17,500 skateboards annually at a price of $45.00 per skateboard. Traci's estimate of the costs to manufacture the skateboards is presented below.

Selling price per skateboard		$45.00
Costs per skateboard:		
Molded plastic	$5.50	
Wheels, hardware	7.00	
Direct labor ($15.00/hr.).	7.50	
Manufacturing overhead.	5.00	
Selling and administrative cost	9.00	34.00
Net income per skateboard		$11.00

In the plastics department, Sportway uses direct labor-hours as the application base for manufacturing overhead. Included in the manufacturing overhead for the current year is $50,000 of fixed overhead cost, of which 40 percent is traceable to the plastics department and 60 percent is allocated, factorywide manufacturing overhead cost. The remaining amount of manufacturing overhead cost included in the computations above is variable. The skateboards could be produced with existing equipment and personnel in the plastics department.

For each unit of product that Sportway sells, regardless of whether the product has been purchased or is manufactured by Sportway, there is an allocated $6 fixed cost per unit for distribution. This $6 per unit is included in the selling and administrative cost figure for all products. The remaining amount of selling and administrative cost for all products— purchased or manufactured—is variable. The total selling and administrative cost figure for the purchased tackle boxes would be $10 per unit.

Required
1. Determine the number of labor-hours per year being used to manufacture tackle boxes.
2. Compute the contribution margin per unit for:
   a. Purchased tackle boxes.
   b. Manufactured tackle boxes.
   c. Manufactured skateboards.
3. Determine the number of tackle boxes (if any) that Sportway should purchase and the number of tackle boxes and/or skateboards that it should manufacture, and compute the improvement in net income that will result from this product mix over current operations.

(CMA, adapted)

Exxon was fined $1 billion as a consequence of the Exxon Valdez oil spill in Alaska's Prince William Sound in 1989. However, the government agreed to allow Exxon to pay most of the $1 billion over a 10-year period. This 10-year deferral of payments, along with its tax deductibility, reduced Exxon's actual cost to only $486 million.

Capital Budgeting Decisions

LEARNING OBJECTIVES

After studying Chapter 14, you should be able to:

1 Distinguish between capital budgeting screening and preference decisions and identify the key characteristics of business investments.

2 Determine the acceptability of an investment project, using the net present value method.

3 Enumerate the typical cash inflows and cash outflows that might be associated with an investment project and explain how they would be used in a present value analysis.

4 Determine the acceptability of an investment project, using the time-adjusted rate of return method (with interpolation, if needed).

5 Explain how the cost of capital is used as a screening tool.

6 Prepare a net present value analysis of two competing investment projects, using either the incremental-cost approach or the total-cost approach.

7 Make a capital budgeting analysis involving automated equipment.

8 Determine the payback period for an investment, using the payback formula.

9 Compute the simple rate of return for an investment, using the simple rate of return formula.

10 Define or explain the key terms listed at the end of the chapter.

11 (Appendix H) Explain the concept of present value and make present value computations with and without the present value tables.

Chapter 1

T he term **capital budgeting** is used to describe actions relating to the planning and financing of capital outlays for such purposes as the purchase of new equipment, the introduction of new product lines, and the modernization of plant facilities. As such, capital budgeting decisions are a key factor in the long-run profitability of a firm. This is particularly true in situations where a firm has only limited investment funds available but has almost unlimited investment opportunities to choose from. The long-run profitability of the firm will depend on the skill of the manager in choosing those uses for limited funds that will provide the greatest return. This selection process is complicated by the fact that most investment opportunities are long term in nature, and the future is often distant and hard to predict.

To make wise investment decisions, managers need tools that will guide them in comparing the relative advantages and disadvantages of various investment alternatives. We are concerned in this chapter with gaining understanding and skill in the use of such tools.

CAPITAL BUDGETING—AN INVESTMENT CONCEPT

Objective 1
Distinguish between capital budgeting screening and preference decisions and identify the key characteristics of business investments.

Capital budgeting is an *investment* concept, since it involves a commitment of funds now in order to receive some desired return in the future. When speaking of investments, one is inclined to think of a commitment of funds to corporate stocks and bonds. This is just one type of investment, however. The commitment of funds by a business to inventory, equipment, and related uses is *also* an investment in that the commitment is made with the expectation of receiving some return in the future from the funds committed.

Typical Capital Budgeting Decisions

What types of business decisions require capital budgeting analysis? Virtually any decision that involves an outlay now in order to obtain some return (increase in revenue or reduction in costs) in the future. Typical capital budgeting decisions encountered by the manager are:

1. Cost reduction decisions. Should new equipment be purchased in order to reduce costs?
2. Plant expansion decisions. Should a new plant, warehouse, or other facility be acquired in order to increase capacity and sales?
3. Equipment selection decisions. Would machine A, machine B, or machine C be the most cost-effective?
4. Lease or buy decisions. Should new plant facilities be leased or purchased?
5. Equipment replacement decisions. Should old equipment be replaced now or later?

Capital budgeting decisions tend to fall into two broad categories—*screening decisions* and *preference decisions*. **Screening decisions** are those relating to whether a proposed project meets some preset standard of acceptance. For example, a firm may have a policy of accepting cost reduction projects only if they promise a return of, say, 20 percent before taxes.

Preference decisions, by contrast, relate to selecting from among several *competing* courses of action. To illustrate, a firm may be considering five different machines to replace an existing machine on the assembly line. The choice as to which of the five machines to purchase is a *preference* decision.

In this chapter, we discuss ways of making screening decisions. The matter of preference decisions is reserved until the following chapter.

Characteristics of Business Investments

Business investments have two key characteristics that must be recognized as we begin our study of capital budgeting methods. These characteristics are (1) that most business investments involve *depreciable assets* and (2) that the returns on most business investments extend over long periods of time.

Depreciable Assets

An important feature of depreciable assets is that they generally have little or no resale value at the end of their useful lives. By contrast, the original sum invested in a *non*depreciable asset will still exist when the project terminates. For example, if a firm purchases land (a nondepreciable asset) for $5,000 and rents it out at $750 a year for 10 years, at the end of the 10-year term the land will still be intact and should be salable for at least its purchase price. The computation of the rate of return on such an investment is fairly simple. Since the asset (the land) will still be intact at the end of the 10-year period, each year's $750 inflow is a return *on* the original $5,000 investment. The rate of return is therefore a straight 15 percent ($750 ÷ $5,000).

Computation of the rate of return on *depreciable* assets is more difficult, since the assets are "used up," so to speak, over their useful lives. Thus, any returns provided by such assets must be sufficient to do two things:

1. Provide a return *on* the original investment.
2. Return the total amount *of* the original investment itself.

To illustrate, assume that the $5,000 investment above was made in equipment rather than in land. Also assume that the equipment will reduce the firm's operating costs by $750 each year for 10 years. Is the return on the equipment a straight 15 percent, the same as it was on the land? The answer is no. The return being promised by the equipment is much less than the return being promised by the land. The reason is that part of the yearly $750 inflow from the equipment *must go to recoup the original $5,000 investment itself, since the equipment will be worthless at the end of its 10-year life.* Only what remains *after* recovery of this investment can be viewed as a return *on* the investment over the 10-year period.

The Time Value of Money

As stated earlier, another characteristic of business investments is that they promise returns that are likely to extend over fairly long periods of time. Therefore, in approaching capital budgeting decisions, it is necessary to employ techniques that recognize *the time value of money*. Any business leader would rather receive a dollar today than a year from now. The same concept applies in choosing between investment projects. Those that promise returns earlier in time are preferable to those that promise returns later in time.

The capital budgeting techniques that recognize the above two characteristics of business investments most fully are those that involve *discounted cash flows*. We will spend most of this chapter illustrating the use of discounted cash flow methods in making capital budgeting decisions. Before starting this material, the reader should study Appendix H to this chapter, The Concept of Present Value, if he or she is not familiar with discounting and with the use of present value tables.

FOCUS ON CURRENT PRACTICE

To appreciate the time value of money, consider the case of Exxon Valdez, an oil tanker that spilled 11 million gallons of crude oil in Alaska's Prince William Sound in March 1989. Exxon Corporation, the owner of the tanker, agreed to pay $1 billion to cover damages and government fines, which was the largest single amount ever assessed as a result of an environmental violation. But the government agreed to allow Exxon to pay the bulk of the $1 billion over a 10-year period. The public was shocked to learn that this 10-year deferral of payments, along with the payments being tax deductible, reduced Exxon's actual cost to only $486 million—less than half of the reported $1 billion settlement figure.

DISCOUNTED CASH FLOWS—THE NET PRESENT VALUE METHOD

There are two approaches to making capital budgeting decisions by means of discounted cash flow. One is the *net present value method,* and the other is the *time-adjusted rate of return method* (sometimes called the *internal rate of return method*). The net present value method is discussed in this section; the time-adjusted rate of return method is discussed in the next section.

The Net Present Value Method Illustrated

Objective 2
Determine the acceptability of an investment project, using the net present value method.

Under the net present value method, the present value of all cash inflows is compared against the present value of all cash outflows that are associated with an investment project. The difference between the present value of these cash flows, called the **net present value,** determines whether or not the project is an acceptable investment. To illustrate, let us assume the following data:

Example A

Harper Company is contemplating the purchase of a machine capable of performing certain operations that are now performed manually. The machine will cost $5,000 new, and it will last for five years. At the end of the five-year period, the machine will have a zero scrap value. Use of the machine will reduce labor costs by $1,800 per year. Harper Company requires a minimum return of 20 percent before taxes on all investment projects.

Should the machine be purchased? To answer this question, it will be necessary first to isolate the cash inflows and cash outflows associated with the proposed project. In order to keep the example free of unnecessary complications, we have assumed only one cash inflow and one cash outflow. The cash inflow is the $1,800 annual reduction in labor costs. The cash outflow is the $5,000 initial investment in the machine.

The investment decision: Harper Company must determine whether a cash investment now of $5,000 can be justified if it will result in an $1,800 reduction in cost each year over the next five years, assuming that the company can get a 20 percent return on its money invested elsewhere.

To determine whether the investment is desirable, it will be necessary to discount the stream of annual $1,800 cost reductions to present value and to compare

		Initial cost	$5,000	
		Life of the project (years)	5	
		Annual cost savings	$1,800	
		Salvage value.	–0–	
		Required rate of return	20%	

EXHIBIT 14–1
Net Present Value
Analysis of a Proposed
Project

Item	Year(s)	Amount of Cash Flow	20 Percent Factor	Present Value of Cash Flows
Annual cost savings	1–5	$ 1,800	2.991*	$ 5,384
Initial investment	Now	(5,000)	1.000	(5,000)
Net present value				$ 384

* From Table J–4 in Appendix J at the end of this chapter.

this discounted present value with the cost of the new machine. Since Harper Company requires a minimum return of 20 percent on all investment projects, we will use this rate in the discounting process. Exhibit 14–1 gives a net present value analysis of the desirability of purchasing the machine.

According to the analysis, Harper Company should purchase the new machine. The present value of the cost savings is $5,384, as compared to a present value of only $5,000 for the investment required (cost of the machine). Deducting the present value of the investment required from the present value of the cost savings gives a *net present value* of $384. Whenever the net present value is zero or greater, as in our example, an investment project is acceptable. Whenever the net present value is negative (the present value of the cash outflows exceeds the present value of the cash inflows), an investment project is not acceptable. In sum,

If the Net Present Value Is . . .	Then the Project Is . . .
Positive.	Acceptable, since it promises a return greater than the required rate of return.
Zero	Acceptable, since it promises a return equal to the required rate of return.
Negative	Not acceptable, since it promises a return less than the required rate of return.

A full interpretation of the solution would be as follows: The new machine promises slightly more than the required 20 percent rate of return. This is evident from the positive net present value of $384. Harper Company could spend up to $5,384 for the new machine and still obtain the 20 percent rate of return it desires. The net present value of $384, therefore, shows the amount of "cushion" or "margin of error" that the company has in estimating the cost of the new machine. Alternatively, it also shows the amount of error that can exist in the present value of the cost savings, with the project remaining acceptable. That is, if the present value of the cost savings were only $5,000 rather than $5,384, the project would still promise the required 20 percent rate of return.

Emphasis on Cash Flows

In organizing data for making capital budgeting decisions, the reader may have noticed that our emphasis has been on cash flows and not on accounting net income. The reason is that accounting net income is based on accrual concepts that ignore the timing of cash flows into and out of an organization. As we stated earlier in the chapter, from a capital budgeting standpoint the timing of cash flows is important, since a dollar received today is more valuable than a dollar received

Objective 3
Enumerate the typical cash inflows and cash outflows that might be associated with an investment project and explain how they would be used in a present value analysis.

in the future. Therefore, even though the accounting net income figure is useful for many things, it must be ignored in those capital budgeting computations that involve discounted cash flow analysis. Instead of determining accounting net income, the manager must concentrate on identifying the specific cash flows associated with various investment projects and on determining when these cash flows will take place.

In considering an investment project, what kinds of cash flows should the manager look for? Although the specific cash flows will vary from project to project, certain types of cash flows tend to recur and should be looked for, as explained in the following paragraphs.

Typical Cash Outflows   Usually a cash outflow in the form of an initial investment in equipment or other assets will be present. This investment is often computed on an incremental basis, in that any salvage realized from the sale of old equipment is deducted from the cost of the new equipment, leaving only the net difference as a cash outflow for capital budgeting purposes. In addition to this type of investment, some projects require that a company expand its working capital to service the greater volume of business that will be generated. **Working capital** means the amount of current assets (cash, accounts receivable, and inventory) in excess of current liabilities that is available to meet day-to-day operating needs. When a company takes on a new project, the balances in the current asset accounts will often increase. For example, opening a new store would require additional cash to operate sales registers, increased accounts receivable to carry new customers, and more inventory to stock the shelves. Any such incremental working capital needs should be treated as part of the initial investment in a project. Also, many projects require periodic outlays for repairs and maintenance and for additional operating costs. These should all be treated as cash outflows for capital budgeting purposes.

Typical Cash Inflows   On the cash inflow side, a project will normally either increase revenues or reduce costs. Either way, the amount involved should be treated as a cash inflow for capital budgeting purposes. (In regard to this point, notice that so far as cash flows are concerned, a *reduction in costs is equivalent to an increase in revenues*.) Cash inflows are also frequently realized from salvage of equipment when a project is terminated. In addition, upon termination of a project, any working capital that is released for use elsewhere should be treated as a cash inflow. Working capital is released, for example, when a company sells off its inventory, collects its receivables, and uses the resulting funds elsewhere in another investment project. (If the released working capital is not shown as a cash inflow at the termination of a project, then the project will go on being charged for the use of the funds forever!)

In summary, the following types of cash flows are common in business investment projects:

Cash outflows:
  Initial investment (including installation costs).
  Increased working capital needs.
  Repairs and maintenance.
  Incremental operating costs.
Cash inflows:
  Incremental revenues.
  Reduction in costs.

Salvage value.

Release of working capital.

Recovery of the Original Investment

When first introduced to present value analysis, students are often surprised by the fact that depreciation is not deducted in computing the profitability of a project. There are two reasons for not deducting depreciation.

First, depreciation is an accounting concept not involving a current cash outflow.[1] As discussed above, discounted cash flow methods of making capital budgeting decisions focus on *flows of cash*. Although depreciation is a vital concept in computing accounting net income for financial statement purposes, it is not relevant in an analytical framework that focuses on flows of cash.

A second reason for not deducting depreciation is that discounted cash flow methods *automatically* provide for return of the original investment, thereby making a deduction for depreciation unnecessary. To demonstrate this point, let us assume the following data:

Example B

Carver Hospital is considering the purchase of an attachment for its X-ray machine that will cost $3,170. The attachment will be usable for four years, after which time it will have no salvage value. It is estimated that the attachment will increase net cash inflows by $1,000 per year in the X-ray department. The hospital's board of directors has instructed that no investments are to be made unless they promise an annual return of at least 10 percent.

A present value analysis of the desirability of purchasing the attachment is presented in Exhibit 14–2. Notice that the attachment promises exactly a 10 percent return on the original investment, since the net present value is zero at a 10 percent discount rate.

Each annual $1,000 cash inflow arising from use of the attachment is made up of two parts. One part represents a recovery of a portion of the original $3,170 paid for the attachment, and the other part represents a return *on* this investment. The breakdown of each year's $1,000 cash inflow between recovery *of* investment and return *on* investment is shown in Exhibit 14–3.

EXHIBIT 14–2

Net Present Value Analysis of X-Ray Attachment

Initial cost			$3,170
Life of the project (years)			4
Annual net cash inflow			$1,000
Salvage value			–0–
Required rate of return			10%

Item	Year(s)	Amount of Cash Flow	10 Percent Factor	Present Value of Cash Flows
Annual net cash inflow	1–4	$ 1,000	3.170*	$ 3,170
Initial investment	Now	(3,170)	1.000	(3,170)
Net present value				$ –0–

* From Table J–4 in Appendix J.

---

[1] Although depreciation itself does not involve a cash outflow, it does have an effect on cash outflows for income taxes. We shall take a look at this effect in the following chapter when we discuss the impact of income taxes on management planning.

EXHIBIT 14–3

The Carver
Hospital—Breakdown
of Annual Cash Inflows

Year	(1) Investment Outstanding during the Year	(2) Cash Inflow	(3) Return on Investment (1) × 10%	(4) Recovery of Investment during the Year (2) − (3)	(5) Unrecovered Investment at the End of the Year (1) − (4)
1.	$3,170	$1,000	$317	$ 683	$2,487
2.	2,487	1,000	249	751	1,736
3.	1,736	1,000	173	827	909
4.	909	1,000	91	909	–0–
Total investment recovered. . . .				$3,170	

The first year's $1,000 cash inflow consists of a $317 interest return (10 percent) *on* the $3,170 original investment, plus a $683 return *of* that investment. Since the amount of the unrecovered investment decreases over the four years, the dollar amount of the interest return also decreases. By the end of the fourth year, all $3,170 of the original investment has been recovered.

Limiting Assumptions

In working with discounted cash flows, at least two limiting assumptions are usually made. The first is that all cash flows occur at the end of a period. This is somewhat unrealistic in that cash flows typically occur somewhat uniformly *throughout* a period. The purpose of this assumption is just to simplify computations.

The second assumption is that all cash flows generated by an investment project are immediately reinvested in another project. It is further assumed that the second project will yield a rate of return at least as large as the discount rate used in the first project. Unless these conditions are met, the return computed for the first project will not be accurate. To illustrate, we used a discount rate of 10 percent for the Carver Hospital in Exhibit 14–2. Unless the funds released each period are immediately reinvested in another project yielding at least a 10 percent return, the net present value computed for the X-ray attachment will be overstated.

Choosing a Discount Rate

In using the net present value method, it is necessary to choose some rate of return for discounting cash flows to present value. In Example A we used a rate of return of 20 percent before taxes, and in Example B we used a rate of return of 10 percent. These rates were chosen somewhat arbitrarily simply for the sake of illustration.

As a practical matter, firms put much time and study into the choice of a discount rate. The rate generally viewed as being most appropriate is a firm's *cost of capital*. A firm's cost of capital is not simply the interest rate that it must pay for long-term debt. Rather, **cost of capital** is a broad concept, involving a blending of the costs of *all* sources of investment funds, both debt and equity. The mechanics involved in cost of capital computations are covered in finance texts and will not be considered here. The cost of capital is known by various names. It is sometimes called the **hurdle rate,** the **cutoff rate,** or the **required rate of return.**

Most finance people would agree that a before-tax cost of capital of 16 percent to 20 percent would be typical for an average industrial corporation. The appropriate after-tax figure would depend on the corporation's tax circumstances, but it would probably average around 10 to 12 percent.

An Extended Example of the Net Present Value Method

To conclude our discussion of the net present value method, we present below an extended example of how it is used in analyzing an investment proposal. This example will also help to tie together (and to reinforce) many of the ideas we have developed thus far.

Example C

Under a special licensing arrangement, Swinyard Company has an opportunity to market a new product in the western United States for a five-year period. The product would be purchased from the manufacturer, with Swinyard Company responsible for all costs of promotion and distribution. The licensing arrangement could be renewed at the end of the five-year period at the option of the manufacturer. After careful study, Swinyard Company has estimated that the following costs and revenues would be associated with the new product:

Cost of equipment needed	$ 60,000
Working capital needed.	100,000
Salvage value of the equipment in five years . . .	10,000
Overhaul of the equipment in four years	5,000
Annual revenues and costs:	
Sales revenues	200,000
Cost of goods sold	125,000
Out-of-pocket operating costs (for salaries,	
advertising, and other direct costs)	35,000

At the end of the five-year period, the working capital would be released for investment elsewhere if the manufacturer decided not to renew the licensing arrangement. Swinyard Company's cost of capital is 20 percent. Would you recommend that the new product be introduced? Ignore income taxes.

As shown by the data above, Example C involves a variety of cash inflows and cash outflows. The solution is given in Exhibit 14–4.

Sales revenues	$200,000
Less cost of goods sold	125,000
Gross margin	75,000
Less out-of-pocket costs for	
salaries, advertising, etc..	35,000
Annual net cash inflows	$ 40,000

EXHIBIT 14–4

The Net Present Value Method—An Extended Example

Item	Year(s)	Amount of Cash Flows	20 Percent Factor	Present Value of Cash Flows
Purchase of equipment	Now	$ (60,000)	1.000	$ (60,000)
Working capital needed	Now	(100,000)	1.000	(100,000)
Overhaul of equipment	4	(5,000)	0.482*	(2,410)
Annual net cash inflows from				
sales of the product line. . . .	1–5	40,000	2.991†	119,640
Salvage value of the				
equipment	5	10,000	0.402*	4,020
Working capital released	5	100,000	0.402*	40,200
Net present value				$ 1,450

* From Table J–3 in Appendix J.
† From Table J–4 in Appendix J.

Notice particularly how the working capital is handled in the exhibit. Also notice how the sales revenues, cost of goods sold, and out-of-pocket costs are handled. **Out-of-pocket costs** are actual cash outlays made during the period for salaries, advertising, and other operating expenses. Depreciation would not be an out-of-pocket cost, since it involves no current cash outlay.

Since the overall net present value is positive, the new product should be added, assuming that there is no better use for the investment funds involved.

DISCOUNTED CASH FLOWS—THE TIME-ADJUSTED RATE OF RETURN METHOD

Objective 4

Determine the acceptability of an investment project, using the time-adjusted rate of return method (with interpolation, if needed).

The **time-adjusted rate of return** (or **internal rate of return**) can be defined as the true interest yield promised by an investment project over its useful life. It is sometimes referred to simply as the **yield** on a project. The time-adjusted rate of return is computed by finding the discount rate that will equate the present value of the investment (cash outflows) required by a project with the present value of the returns (cash inflows) that the project promises. In other words, the time-adjusted rate of return is that discount rate that will cause the net present value of a project to be equal to zero.

The Time-Adjusted Rate of Return Method Illustrated

Finding a project's time-adjusted rate of return can be very helpful to a manager in making capital budgeting decisions. To illustrate, let us assume the following data:

Example D

Glendale School District is considering the purchase of a large tractor-pulled lawn mower. If the large mower is purchased, it will replace the hiring of persons to mow with small, individual gas mowers. The large mower will cost $16,950 and will have a life of 10 years. It will have only a negligible scrap value, which can be ignored, and it will provide a savings of $3,000 per year in mowing costs because of the labor it will replace.

To compute the time-adjusted rate of return promised by the new mower, it will be necessary to find the discount rate that will cause the net present value of the project to be zero. How do we proceed to do this? The simplest and most direct approach is to divide the investment in the project by the expected annual cash inflow. This computation will yield a factor from which the time-adjusted rate of return can be determined. The formula is:

$$\frac{\text{Investment required}}{\text{Net annual cash inflow}} = \text{Factor of the time-adjusted rate of return} \qquad (1)$$

The factor derived from formula (1) is then located in the present value tables to see what rate of return it represents. We will now perform these computations for Glendale School District's proposed project. Using formula (1), we get:

$$\frac{\$16,950}{\$3,000} = 5.650$$

Thus, the discount factor that will equate a series of $3,000 cash inflows with a present investment of $16,950 is 5.650. Now we need to find this factor in Table J–4 in Appendix J to see what rate of return it represents. If we refer to Table J–4 and scan along the 10-period line, we find that a factor of 5.650 represents a 12 percent rate of return. Therefore, the time-adjusted rate of return promised by the

Initial cost $16,950
Life of the project (years)   10
Annual cost savings . . . . $ 3,000
Salvage value. . . . .   –0–

Item	Year(s)	Amount of Cash Flow	12 Percent Factor	Present Value of Cash Flows
Annual cost savings	1–10	$ 3,000	5.650*	$ 16,950
Initial investment	Now	(16,950)	1.000	(16,950)
Net present value				$ –0–

* From Table J–4 in Appendix J.

mower project is 12 percent. We can verify this by computing the project's net present value, using a 12 percent discount rate. This computation is made in Exhibit 14–5.

Notice from Exhibit 14–5 that using a 12 percent discount rate equates the present value of the annual cash inflows with the present value of the investment required in the project, leaving a zero net present value. The 12 percent rate therefore represents the time-adjusted rate of return promised by the project.

Salvage Value and Other Cash Flows

The technique just demonstrated works very well if a project's cash flows are identical every year. But what if they are not? For example, what if a project will have some salvage value at the end of its life in addition to the annual cash inflows? Under these circumstances, a trial-and-error process is necessary to find the rate of return that will equate the cash inflows with the cash outflows. The trial-and-error process can be carried out by hand, or it can be carried out by means of computer software programs that perform the necessary computations in seconds. In short, simply because cash flows are erratic or uneven will not in any way prevent a manager from determining a project's time-adjusted rate of return.

The Process of Interpolation

Interpolation is the process of finding odd rates of return that do not appear in published interest tables. It is an important concept, since published interest tables are usually printed in terms of whole percentages (10 percent, 12 percent, and so forth), whereas projects often have rates of return that involve fractional amounts. To illustrate the process of interpolation, assume the following data:

Investment required $6,000
Annual cost savings 1,500
Life of the project . . . . 10 years

What is the time-adjusted rate of return promised by this project? We can proceed as before and find that the relevant factor is 4.000:

$$\frac{\text{Investment required}}{\text{Annual cost savings}} = \frac{\$6,000}{\$1,500} = 4.000$$

Looking at Table J–4 in Appendix J and scanning along the 10-period line, we find that a factor of 4.000 represents a rate of return somewhere between 20 and 22 percent. To find the rate we are after, we must interpolate, as follows:

	Present Value Factors	
20% factor	4.192	4.192
True factor	4.000	
22% factor		3.923
Difference.	0.192	0.269

$$\text{Time-adjusted rate of return} = 20\% + \left(\frac{0.192}{0.269} \times 2\%\right)$$

$$\text{Time-adjusted rate of return} = 21.4\%$$

Using the Time-Adjusted Rate of Return

Once the time-adjusted rate of return has been computed, what does the manager do with the information? The time-adjusted rate of return is compared against whatever rate of return (usually the cost of capital) the organization requires on its investment projects. If the time-adjusted rate of return is *equal* to or *greater* than the cost of capital, then the project is acceptable. If it is *less* than the cost of capital, then the project is rejected. A project is not a profitable undertaking if it can't provide a rate of return at least as great as the cost of the funds invested in it.

In the case of the Glendale School District example used earlier, let us assume that the district has set a minimum required rate of return of 10 percent on all projects. Since the large mower promises a rate of return of 12 percent, it clears this hurdle and would therefore be an acceptable investment.

FOCUS ON CURRENT PRACTICE

Over the years, discounted cash flow methods have become increasingly popular as a means for making capital budgeting decisions. Three surveys—all directed toward large industrial firms—reveal an increase in usage of dis-counted cash flow methods over the years (see the table below).

In addition, the 1988 survey disclosed that 96 percent of the reporting firms include lease decisions in the capital budgeting process.[2]

	Percent of Firms Using Discounted Cash Flow Methods by Year		
Type of Decision	1988	1975	1965
Replacement projects.	60%	45%	21%
Expansion projects—existing operations . . .	86	62	30
Expansion projects—new operations	87	58	31
Foreign investment projects	79	59	32

---

[2] Thomas Klammer, Bruce Koch, and Neil Wilner, "Capital Budgeting Practices—A Survey of Corporate Use," *Journal of Management Accounting Research* 3 (Fall 1991), pp. 118 and 127.

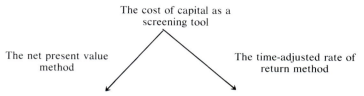

EXHIBIT 14–6
Capital Budgeting
Screening Decisions

The cost of capital as a screening tool

The net present value method

The time-adjusted rate of return method

The cost of capital is used as the *actual* discount rate in computing the net present value of a project. Any project with a negative net present value is rejected unless social, environmental, or other nonquantitative factors dictate its acceptance.

The cost of capital is used to *compare against* the time-adjusted rate of return promised by a project. To be acceptable, the project's rate of return cannot be less than the cost of capital unless social, environmental, or other nonquantitative factors dictate its acceptance.

THE COST OF CAPITAL AS A SCREENING TOOL

As we have seen in preceding examples, the cost of capital operates as a *screening* tool, helping the manager to screen out undesirable investment projects. This screening is accomplished in different ways, depending on whether the company is using the time-adjusted rate of return method or the net present value method in its capital budgeting analysis.

Objective 5
Explain how the cost of capital is used as a screening tool.

When the time-adjusted rate of return method is being used, the cost of capital takes the form of a *hurdle rate* that a project must clear for acceptance. If the time-adjusted rate of return on a project is not great enough to clear the cost of capital hurdle, then the project is rejected. We saw the application of this idea in the Glendale School District example, where the hurdle rate was set at 10 percent.

When the net present value method is used, the cost of capital becomes the *actual discount rate* used to compute the net present value of a proposed project. Any project yielding a negative net present value is screened out and rejected unless nonquantitative factors such as social responsibility, employee morale, or improvements in a company's ability to compete are significant enough to require its acceptance. (This point is discussed further in a following section, Investments in Automated Equipment.)

The operation of the cost of capital as a screening tool is summarized in Exhibit 14–6.

COMPARISON OF THE NET PRESENT VALUE AND THE TIME-ADJUSTED RATE OF RETURN METHODS

The net present value method has a number of advantages over the time-adjusted rate of return method of making capital budgeting decisions.

First, the net present value method is simpler to use. As explained earlier, the time-adjusted rate of return method often requires a trial-and-error process to find the exact rate of return that will equate a project's cash inflows and outflows. No such trial-and-error process is necessary when working with the net present value method.

Second, using the net present value method makes it easier to adjust for risk. The point was made earlier in the chapter that the longer one has to wait for a cash inflow, the greater is the risk that the cash inflow will never materialize. To show the greater risk connected with cash flows that are projected to occur many years in the future, firms often discount such amounts at higher discount rates than the discount rates used for flows that are projected to occur earlier in time. For example, a firm might anticipate that a project will provide cash inflows of $10,000 per year for 15 years. If the firm's cost of capital is 18 percent before taxes, then it might discount the first five years' inflows at this rate. The discount rate might then be raised to, say, 20 percent for the next five years and then to, say, 25 percent for the last five years. This successive raising of the discount rate is a way of adjusting for the greater risk connected with the cash flows that are projected to be received far into the future.

No such selective adjustment of discount rates is possible under the time-adjusted rate of return method. About the only way to adjust for risk is to raise the hurdle rate that the rate of return for a project must clear for acceptance. This is a somewhat crude approach to the risk problem in that it attaches the same degree of increased risk to *all* of the cash flows associated with a project—those that occur earlier in time as well as those that occur later in time.

Third, the net present value method provides more usable information than does the time-adjusted rate of return method. The dollar net present value figure generated by the net present value method is viewed as being particularly useful for decision-making purposes. This point is considered further in the following chapter.

EXPANDING THE NET PRESENT VALUE METHOD

Objective 6
Prepare a net present value analysis of two competing investment projects, using either the incremental-cost approach or the total-cost approach.

So far we have confined all of our examples to the consideration of a single investment alternative. We will now expand the net present value method to include two alternatives. In addition, we will integrate the concept of relevant costs into discounted cash flow analysis.

There are two ways that the net present value method can be used to compare competing investment projects. One is the *total-cost approach,* and the other is the *incremental-cost approach.* Each approach is illustrated below.

The Total-Cost Approach

The total-cost approach is the most flexible and the most widely used method of making a net present value analysis of competing projects. To illustrate the mechanics of the approach, let us assume the following data:

Example E

Harper Ferry Company provides a ferry service across the Mississippi River. One of its ferryboats is in poor condition. This ferry can be renovated at an immediate cost of $20,000. Further repairs and an overhaul of the motor will be needed five years from now at a cost of $8,000. In all, the ferry will be usable for 10 years if this work is done. At the end of 10 years, the ferry will have to be scrapped at a salvage value of approximately $6,000. The scrap value of the ferry right now is $7,000. It will cost $30,000 each year to operate the ferry, and revenues will total $40,000 annually.

As an alternative, Harper Ferry Company can purchase a new ferryboat at a cost of $36,000. The new ferry will have a life of 10 years, but it will require some repairs at the end of 5 years. It is estimated that these repairs will amount to $3,000. At the end of 10 years, it is estimated that the ferry will have a scrap value of $6,000. It will cost $21,000 each year to operate the ferry, and revenues will total $40,000 annually.

Harper Ferry Company requires a return of at least 18 percent before taxes on all investment projects.

Should the company purchase the new ferry or renovate the old ferry? The solution is given in Exhibit 14–7.

EXHIBIT 14–7
The Total-Cost
Approach to Project
Selection

	New Ferry	Old Ferry
Annual revenues	$40,000	$40,000
Annual cash operating costs . . .	21,000	30,000
Net annual cash inflows	$19,000	$10,000

Item	Year(s)	Amount of Cash Flows	18 Percent Factor*	Present Value of Cash Flows
Buy the new ferry:				
Initial investment	Now	$(36,000)	1.000	$(36,000)
Repairs in five years	5	(3,000)	0.437	(1,311)
Net annual cash inflows	1–10	19,000	4.494	85,386
Salvage of the old ferry	Now	7,000	1.000	7,000
Salvage of the new ferry	10	6,000	0.191	1,146
Net present value				56,221
Keep the old ferry:				
Initial repairs	Now	$(20,000)	1.000	(20,000)
Repairs in five years	5	(8,000)	0.437	(3,496)
Net annual cash inflows	1–10	10,000	4.494	44,940
Salvage of the old ferry	10	6,000	0.191	1,146
Net present value				22,590
Net present value in favor of buying the new ferry				$ 33,631

* All factors are from Tables J–3 and J–4 in Appendix J.

Two points should be noted from the exhibit. First, observe that *all* cash inflows and *all* cash outflows are included in the solution under each alternative. No effort has been made to isolate those cash flows that are relevant to the decision and those that are not relevant. The inclusion of all cash flows associated with each alternative gives the approach its name—the *total-cost* approach.

Second, notice that a net present value figure is computed for each of the two alternatives. This is a distinct advantage of the total-cost approach in that an unlimited number of alternatives can be compared side by side to determine the most profitable course of action. For example, another alternative for Harper Ferry Company would be to get out of the ferry business entirely. If management desired, the net present value of this alternative could be computed to compare with the alternatives shown in Exhibit 14–7. Still other alternatives might be open to the company. Once management has determined the net present value of each alternative that it wishes to consider, it can select the course of action that promises to be most profitable. In the case at hand, given only the two alternatives, the data indicate that the most profitable course is to purchase the new ferry.[3]

The Incremental-Cost Approach

When only two alternatives are being considered, the incremental-cost approach offers a simpler and more direct route to a decision. Unlike the total-cost approach, it focuses only on differential costs.[4] The procedure is to include in the

---

[3] The alternative with the highest net present value is not always the best choice, although it is the best choice in this case. For further discussion, see the section Preference Decisions—The Ranking of Investment Projects in Chapter 15.

[4] Technically, the incremental-cost approach is misnamed, since it focuses on differential costs (that is, on both cost increases and decreases) rather than just on incremental costs. As used here, the term *incremental costs* should be interpreted broadly to include both cost increases and cost decreases.

EXHIBIT 14–8
The Incremental-Cost
Approach to Project
Selection

Items	Year(s)	Amount of Cash Flows	18 Percent Factor*	Present Value of Cash Flows
Incremental investment required to purchase the new ferry	Now	$(16,000)	1.000	$(16,000)
Repairs in five years avoided	5	5,000	0.437	2,185
Increased net annual cash inflows	1–10	9,000	4.494	40,446
Salvage of the old ferry	Now	7,000	1.000	7,000
Difference in salvage value in 10 years	10	–0–	—	–0–
Net present value in favor of buying the new ferry				$ 33,631

* All factors are from Tables J–3 and J–4 in Appendix J.

discounted cash flow analysis only those costs and revenues that *differ* between the two alternatives being considered. To illustrate, refer again to the data in Example E relating to Harper Ferry Company. The solution using only differential costs is presented in Exhibit 14–8.

Two things should be noted from the data in this exhibit. First, notice that the net present value of $33,631 shown in Exhibit 14–8 agrees with the net present value shown under the total-cost approach in Exhibit 14–7. This agreement should be expected, since the two approaches are just different roads to the same destination.

Second, notice that the costs used in Exhibit 14–8 are just mathematical differences between the costs shown for the two alternatives in the prior exhibit. For example, the $16,000 incremental investment required to purchase the new ferry in Exhibit 14–8 is the difference between the $36,000 cost of the new ferry and the $20,000 cost required to renovate the old ferry from Exhibit 14–7. The other figures in Exhibit 14–8 have been computed in the same way.

Least-Cost Decisions

Revenues are not directly involved in some decisions. For example, a company that makes no charge for delivery service may need to replace an old delivery truck, or a company may be trying to decide whether to lease or to buy its fleet of executive cars. In situations such as these, where no revenues are involved, the most desirable alternative will be the one that promises the *least total cost* from a present value perspective. Hence, these are known as least-cost decisions. To illustrate a least-cost decision, assume the following data:

Example F
Val-Tek Company is considering the replacement of an old threading machine that is used in the manufacture of a number of products. A new threading machine is available on the market that could substantially reduce annual operating costs. Selected data relating to the old and the new machines are presented below:

	Old Machine	New Machine
Purchase cost new	$20,000	$25,000
Salvage value now	3,000	—
Annual cash operating costs	15,000	9,000
Overhaul needed immediately	4,000	—
Salvage value in six years	–0–	5,000
Remaining life	6 years	6 years

Val-Tek Company's cost of capital is 10 percent.

Items	Year(s)	Amount of Cash Flows	10 Percent Factor*	Present Value of Cash Flows	
Buy the new machine:					EXHIBIT 14–9
Initial investment	Now	$(25,000)	1.000	$(25,000)†	The Total-Cost
Salvage of the old machine	Now	3,000	1.000	3,000†	Approach (Least-Cost
Annual cash operating costs	1–6	(9,000)	4.355	(39,195)	Decision)
Salvage of the new machine	6	5,000	0.564	2,820	
Present value of net cash outflows . . .				(58,375)	
Keep the old machine:					
Overhaul needed now	Now	$ (4,000)	1.000	(4,000)	
Annual cash operating costs	1–6	(15,000)	4.355	(65,325)	
Present value of net cash outflows . . .				(69,325)	
Net present value in favor of buying the new machine				$ 10,950	

* All factors are from Tables J–3 and J–4 in Appendix J.

† These two items could be netted into a single $22,000 incremental-cost figure ($25,000 − $3,000 = $22,000).

An analysis of the alternatives, using the total-cost approach, is provided in Exhibit 14–9.

As shown in the exhibit, the new machine promises the lowest present value of total costs. An analysis of the two alternatives using the incremental-cost approach is presented in Exhibit 14–10. As before, the data going into this exhibit represent the differences between the alternatives as shown under the total-cost approach.

CAPITAL BUDGETING AND NONPROFIT ORGANIZATIONS

Capital budgeting concepts have equal application to all types of organizations, regardless of whether they are profit or nonprofit in nature. Note, for example, the different types of organizations used in the examples in this chapter. These organizations include a hospital, a company working under a licensing agreement, a school district, a company operating a ferryboat service, and a manufacturing company. The diversity of these examples shows the range and power of the capital budgeting model.

The only real problem in the use of capital budgeting by nonprofit organizations is determining the proper discount rate to use in the analysis of data. Some nonprofit organizations use the rate of interest paid on special bond issues (such as an issue for street improvements or an issue to build a school) as their discount rate; others use the rate of interest that could be earned by placing money in an

Items	Year(s)	Amount of Cash Flows	10 Percent Factor*	Present Value of Cash Flows	
					EXHIBIT 14–10
Incremental investment required to purchase					The Incremental-Cost
the new machine	Now	$(21,000)	1.000	$(21,000)†	Approach (Least-Cost
Salvage of the old machine	Now	3,000	1.000	3,000†	Decision)
Savings in annual cash					
operating costs	1–6	6,000	4.355	26,130	
Difference in salvage value					
in six years	6	5,000	0.564	2,820	
Net present value in favor of buying the new machine				$ 10,950	

* All factors are from Tables J–3 and J–4 in Appendix J.

† These two items could be netted into a single $18,000 incremental-cost figure ($21,000 − $3,000 = $18,000).

endowment fund rather than spending it on capital improvements; and still others use discount rates that are set somewhat arbitrarily by governing boards.

The greatest danger lies in using a discount rate that is too low. Most government agencies, for example, at one time used the interest rate on government bonds as their discount rate. It is now recognized that this rate is too low and has resulted in the acceptance of many projects that should not have been undertaken.[5] To resolve this problem, the Office of Management and Budget has specified that federal government units must use a discount rate of at least 10 percent on all projects.[6] For nonprofit units such as schools and hospitals, it is generally recommended that the discount rate should "approximate the average rate of return on private sector investments."[7] Since this rate would include the experience of thousands of companies, it undoubtedly would provide more satisfactory results as a discount rate than simply using the interest rate on a special bond issue or the interest return on an endowment fund.

INVESTMENTS IN AUTOMATED EQUIPMENT

Objective 7
Make a capital budgeting analysis involving automated equipment.

Investments in automated equipment differ in several ways from investments in other types of equipment. First, such investments tend to be very large in dollar amount, even when only a few items are purchased. Second, automation is sometimes improperly viewed as being a cure-all for competitive deficiencies, so any purchases of automated equipment must be carefully evaluated in terms of a company's long-term goals and objectives. And third, the benefits from automated equipment are often indirect and intangible, and therefore hard to quantify. Each of these factors is discussed in the following sections.

Cost of Automation

The cost involved in automating a process is much greater than the cost of purchasing conventional equipment. Single pieces of automated equipment, such as a robot or a computerized numerical control machine, can cost $1 million or more. A flexible manufacturing system, involving one or more cells, can cost up to $50 million, and the cost of even a small, fully automated factory can exceed $100 million.

Even more important, the front-end investment in robots and other hardware usually constitutes no more than half of the total cost to automate. Some companies have discovered to their surprise that the costs of engineering, software development, and implementation of the system can equal or exceed the cost of the equipment itself. This suggests that before any equipment is ordered, management must take more than just an ordinary amount of care in assessing the potential costs that may be involved with getting (and keeping) the equipment in an operational mode.

Long-Term Objectives and Automation

The first step in any move toward automation is for management to carefully evaluate the company's products, the needs of its customers, the nature of its

---

[5] See *Federal Capital Budgeting: A Collection of Haphazard Practices*, GAO, P.O. Box 6015, Gaithersburg, MD, PAD-81-19, February 26, 1981.

[6] Office of Management and Budget Circular No. A-94, March 1972. The U.S. Postal Service is exempted from the 10 percent rate as are all water resource projects and all lease or buy decisions.

[7] Robert N. Anthony and David W. Young, *Management Control in Nonprofit Organizations*, 5th ed. (Homewood, Ill: Richard D. Irwin, Inc., 1994), p. 445.

markets, and its position in relation to domestic and foreign competition. Goals and objectives should then be set, and a comprehensive long-term manufacturing strategy should be developed that will allow the company to meet these goals and objectives. Too often, automation is approached in a hodge-podge manner with no long-term manufacturing strategy in mind. The result in some cases has been a belated realization that automation was both unwise and unnecessary. One pair of management consultants has aptly observed:

> Although automation often is viewed as a "cure-all" for competitive deficiencies, this view is incorrect. The key to effective and successful automation is to first analyze, understand, and if necessary, redesign and simplify the manufacturing process. Many companies are achieving significant benefits, without significantly automating, by simply rearranging the plant floor, eliminating nonvalue activities such as inventory storage and material handling, and establishing more streamlined and flexible process flows.[8]

In short, automation isn't for everyone, or at the least it is often better if taken in small doses. Once a company has carefully studied, redesigned, and simplified its manufacturing process, then automated equipment can be added (if needed) to boost output, improve quality, or strengthen the company's competitive position. Because of its high cost and complexity of operation, automated equipment represents a much more risky investment than conventional equipment. Thus, it should be purchased only if it is compatible with a well-defined, long-term manufacturing strategy.

Benefits from Automation

Perhaps the most difficult task associated with a purchase of automated equipment lies in identifying the benefits that the equipment will provide. At least one of these benefits is obvious in that direct labor cost is generally reduced. But a reduction in direct labor cost is rarely sufficient in itself to justify the purchase of an expensive, automated machine.

 **Rockwell International**   FOCUS ON CURRENT PRACTICE

In 1982, Rockwell International Corp.'s Herman M. Reininga wanted to buy an $80,000 laser to etch contract numbers on communications systems sold to the Pentagon. But the division's financial staff laughed him out of the meeting [in which he recommended the purchase]. The laser would save only $4,000 in direct labor each year. At that rate, it would take 20 years to recover the cost.

Three years later, Reininga got his laser. He presented data showing that finished radios sat around for two weeks waiting for an antique etching operation to finish identity plates. The laser would do the job in 10 minutes, moving shipments out faster—and saving the company $200,000 a year in inventory-holding costs.[9]

---

[8] Robert A. Howell and Stephen R. Soucy, "Capital Investment in the New Manufacturing Environment," *Management Accounting* 69 (November 1987), p. 27.

[9] Reprinted from "The Productivity Paradox," *Business Week*, No. 3055 (June 6, 1988), p. 104, by special permission.

The literature contains many examples of companies refusing to purchase automated equipment because of inadequate savings in labor costs. Managers often fail to recognize that the most significant benefits from automation are indirect—as in the example above—or intangible in nature. Indeed, the intangible benefits can be the most significant benefits of all. These include improved product quality, reduced throughput time, and increased manufacturing flexibility. Unfortunately, these benefits are difficult to quantify and therefore tend to be ignored in capital budgeting analyses.

An annotated listing of benefits to look for in evaluating a purchase of automated equipment is given below.

Tangible benefits:

1.   *Reduced direct labor costs.* Direct labor cost is generally reduced when automated equipment is purchased. However, a reduction in labor cost is rarely sufficient to justify automation.

2.   *Reduced inventory costs.* Automated equipment is more reliable, more consistent, and faster than conventional equipment. Therefore, it can reduce inventory costs in two ways—first, by reducing the quantity of inventory needed to sustain production and sales; and second, by freeing the space in which inventory is stored. The reduced quantity of inventory means less money tied up in inventory and also reduced inventory carrying costs. The freed space means less rental cost to store inventory or, if the company owns its facilities, greater revenue from expanded output.

3.   *Reduced cost-of-quality problems.* Due to greater reliability and consistency of output, automation results in less defects and in less waste, scrap, and rework costs. In turn, reductions in defects and related problems lead to reductions in warranty expenses. General Electric reports, for example, that automating its dishwasher operation resulted in a 50 percent reduction in its service call rate. Moreover, greater product uniformity and reliability through automation means that fewer inspections are needed. We have already noted that some automated companies have virtually eliminated manual inspections of their materials and products.

Intangible benefits:

1.   *Faster throughput time.* The greater efficiency of an automated process will decrease the production throughput time and thereby increase the total output for a given period.

2.   *Increased manufacturing flexibility.* Setup time can be reduced through automation, thereby increasing manufacturing flexibility. Also, the flexibility of automated equipment generally translates into a longer service life than conventional equipment.

3.   *Faster response to market shifts.* Automated equipment allows a company to respond more quickly to shifts in customer tastes and needs, due to the flexibility of the equipment.

4.   *Increased learning effects.* Automating a facility or a process is difficult, both in a technical and an operational sense. Much learning is required, and these learning effects can be of great value as new technology unfolds and becomes available. Companies that hold back, fearing the complexities of automation, soon

fall behind their competitors in recognizing and in being able to utilize the newer technology as it comes onto the market.

5.   *Avoiding capital decay.* **Capital decay** can be defined as a loss in market share resulting from technologically obsolete products and operations. Retention of market share—or even an increase in market share—is perhaps the most significant intangible benefit that can be gained from automation. Companies sometimes reject automation by assuming that sales will remain unchanged even if they don't automate. However, if a more efficient process is available, a competitor undoubtedly will invest in it, thereby gaining a competitive advantage. The correct assumption, therefore, is that if a company fails to take advantage of new technology, it will *not* face the status quo in terms of sales; rather, it will face declining sales due to capital decay.

6.   *Higher quality of output.* Automation allows a higher quality of output that can greatly strengthen the image and competitive position of a company. High quality promotes confidence on the part of customers and creates an aura of reliability that can provide access to expanding, worldwide markets.

The reader should note that the tangible benefits above represent potential *cost savings,* whereas the intangible benefits represent potential *revenue enhancements.* Generally, it's easy to measure the amount of cost savings associated with an investment project, and that's why items such as reduced direct labor cost always show up in a capital budgeting analysis. But it's hard to measure the impact of a potential revenue enhancement such as greater flexibility or faster market response. As a result, managers tend to overlook such items when evaluating the benefits from automated equipment. The intangible benefits must be explicitly considered, however, or faulty decisions will follow.

Decision Framework for Automated Equipment

We now tie together the ideas developed on preceding pages by presenting a decision framework that can be used for purchases of automated equipment. This framework consists of five steps,[10] as follows:

1.   Determine the long-term strategic goals and objectives of the company, and determine a manufacturing strategy that will allow these goals and objectives to be achieved.
2.   List all the expected benefits and costs associated with the automated equipment under consideration.
3.   Quantify those items from step 2 that can be readily estimated.
4.   Determine the net present value or time-adjusted rate of return for those items quantified in step 3. These computations may justify acquisition of the equipment under study. If not, then proceed to step 5.
5.   Try to quantify the intangible benefits from step 2, and recompute the net present value or the time-adjusted rate of return. As an alternate step, determine the amount of additional cash flow per year that would be needed to make the project acceptable, and then ask the question, "Are the intangible benefits worth at least this much to the company?" If so, the project should be accepted; if not, it should be rejected.

---

[10] These steps are adapted from Robert E. Bennett and James A. Hendricks, "Justifying the Acquisition of Automated Equipment," *Management Accounting* 69 (July 1987), p. 46. This thoughtful and well-written article deserves careful study.

To illustrate step 5, assume that a company with a 16 percent cost of capital is considering a piece of automated equipment that would have a 15-year useful life. By applying steps 1–4, the equipment shows a negative net present value of $223,000. Given these data, the amount of additional cash flow per year that would be needed to make the project acceptable can be computed as follows:

Net present value (negative) . . . . . . $(223,000)
Factor for an annuity of 16%
  for 15 periods (from Table J–4
  in Appendix J) 5.575

$$\frac{\text{Net present value, \$(223,000)}}{\text{Factor, 5.575}} = \$40,000$$

Thus, if intangible benefits such as greater flexibility, higher quality of output, and avoidance of capital decay are worth at least $40,000 a year to the company, then the automated equipment should be purchased. If, in the judgment of management, these intangible benefits are *not* worth $40,000 a year, then no purchase should be made.

OTHER APPROACHES TO CAPITAL BUDGETING DECISIONS

The discounted cash flow methods of making capital budgeting decisions are relatively new. They were first introduced on a widespread basis in the 1950s, although their appearance in business literature predates this period by many years. Discounted cash flow methods have gained widespread acceptance as accurate and dependable decision-making tools. Other methods of making capital budgeting decisions are also available, however, and are preferred by some managers. In this section, we discuss two such methods, known as *payback* and *simple rate of return*. Both methods have been in use for a hundred years or more, but they are now declining in popularity as primary tools for project evaluation.

The Payback Method

Objective 8
Determine the payback period for an investment, using the payback formula.

The payback method centers on a span of time known as the *payback period*. The **payback period** can be defined as the length of time that it takes for an investment project to recoup its own initial cost out of the cash receipts that it generates. In business jargon, this period is sometimes spoken of as "the time that it takes for an investment to pay for itself." The basic premise of the payback method is that the more quickly the cost of an investment can be recovered, the more desirable is the investment.

The payback period is expressed in years. The formula used in computing the payback period is:

$$\text{Payback period} = \frac{\text{Investment required}}{\text{Net annual cash inflow*}} \qquad (2)$$

* If new equipment is replacing old equipment, this becomes incremental net annual cash inflow.

To illustrate the mechanics involved in payback computations, assume the following data:

Example G

York Company needs a new milling machine. The company is considering two machines, machine A and machine B. Machine A costs $15,000 and will reduce

FOCUS ON CURRENT PRACTICE

The surveys of capital budgeting practices cited earlier clearly document the decreasing use of the payback and simple rate of return methods. Consider the data in the table below, which relate to the use of payback and simple rate of return as the *primary* methods of project evaluation.

The surveys found, however, that these methods are often used as *secondary* methods of evaluation—that is, as backups to the discounted cash flow methods. Thus, although decreasing in *primary* use, payback and simple rate of return are still considered to be valuable tools in some companies.[11]

Type of Decision	Percent of Firms Using the Payback and Simple Rate of Return Methods by Year		
	1988	1975	1965
Replacement projects:			
Payback	5%	8%	12%
Simple rate of return	4	14	15
Expansion projects—existing operations:			
Payback	5	9	19
Simple rate of return	4	16	30
Expansion projects—new operations:			
Payback	4	12	19
Simple rate of return	4	17	33
Foreign investment projects:			
Payback	4	8	18
Simple rate of return	5	20	26

operating costs by $5,000 per year. Machine B costs only $12,000 but will also reduce operating costs by $5,000 per year.

Which machine should be purchased? Make your calculations by the payback method.   *Required*

$$\text{Machine A payback period} = \frac{\$15,000}{\$5,000} = 3.0 \text{ years}$$

$$\text{Machine B payback period} = \frac{\$12,000}{\$5,000} = 2.4 \text{ years}$$

According to the payback calculations, York Company should purchase machine B, since it has a shorter payback period than machine A.

Evaluation of the Payback Method

The payback method is not a measure of how profitable one investment project is as compared to another. Rather, it is a measure of *time* in the sense that it tells the manager how many years will be required to recover the investment in one project as compared to another. This is a major defect in the approach, since a shorter

---

[11] Klammer et al., "Capital Budgeting Practices—A Survey of Corporate Use," pp. 117–20.

payback period is not always an accurate guide as to whether one investment is more desirable than another.

To illustrate, consider again the two machines used in the example above. Since machine B has a shorter payback period than machine A, it *appears* that machine B is more desirable than machine A. But if we add one more piece of data, this illusion quickly disappears. Machine A has a projected 10-year life, and machine B has a projected 5-year life. It would take two purchases of machine B to provide the same length of service as would be provided by a single purchase of machine A. Under these circumstances, machine A would be a much better investment than machine B, even though machine B has a shorter payback period. Unfortunately, the payback method has no inherent mechanism for highlighting differences in useful life between investments for the decision maker. Such differences can be very important, and relying on payback alone can cause the manager to make incorrect decisions.

A further criticism of the payback method is that it does not consider the time value of money. A cash inflow to be received several years in the future is weighed equally with a cash inflow to be received right now. To illustrate, assume that for an investment of $8,000 you can purchase either of the two following streams of cash inflows:

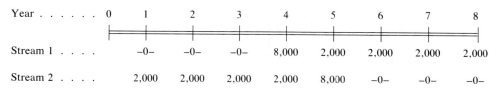

Year	0	1	2	3	4	5	6	7	8
Stream 1		–0–	–0–	–0–	8,000	2,000	2,000	2,000	2,000
Stream 2		2,000	2,000	2,000	2,000	8,000	–0–	–0–	–0–

Which stream of cash inflows would you prefer to receive in return for your $8,000 investment? Each stream has a payback period of 4.0 years. Therefore, if payback alone were relied on in making the decision, you would be forced to say that the streams are equally desirable. However, from the point of view of the time value of money, stream 2 is much more desirable than stream 1.

On the other hand, under certain conditions the payback method can be very useful to the manager. For one thing, it can help the manager to identify which investment proposals are in the "ballpark." That is, it can be used as a screening tool to help answer the question "Should I consider this proposal further?" If a proposal doesn't provide a payback within some specified period, then there may be no need to consider it further. In addition, the payback period is often of great importance to new firms that are "cash poor." When a firm is cash poor, a project with a short payback period but a low rate of return might be preferred over another project with a high rate of return but a long payback period. The reason is that the company may simply need a faster return of its cash investment. And finally, the payback method is sometimes used in industries where products become obsolete very rapidly—such as consumer electronics. Since products may last only a year or two, the payback period on investments must be very short.

An Extended Example of Payback

As shown by formula (2) given earlier, the payback period is computed by dividing the investment in a project by the net annual cash inflows that the project will generate. If new equipment is replacing old equipment, then any salvage to be received on disposal of the old equipment should be deducted from the cost of the new equipment, and only the *incremental* investment should be used in the payback computation. In addition, any depreciation deducted in arriving at the net income promised by an investment project must be added back to obtain the project's expected net annual cash inflow. To illustrate, assume the following data:

Example H

Goodtime Fun Centers, Inc., operates many outlets in the eastern states. Some of the vending machines in one of its outlets provide very little revenue, so the company is considering the removal of the machines and the installation of equipment to dispense soft ice cream. The equipment would cost $80,000 and have an eight-year useful life. Incremental annual revenues and costs associated with the sale of ice cream would be:

Sales	$150,000
Less cost of ingredients	90,000
Contribution margin	60,000
Less fixed expenses:	
Salaries	27,000
Maintenance	3,000
Depreciation	10,000
Total fixed expenses	40,000
Net income	$ 20,000

The vending machines can be sold for a $5,000 scrap value. The company will not purchase equipment unless it has a payback of three years or less. Should the equipment to dispense ice cream be purchased?

An analysis as to whether the proposed equipment meets the company's payback requirements is given in Exhibit 14–11. Several things should be noted from the data in this exhibit. First, notice that depreciation is added back to net income to obtain the net annual cash inflow promised by the new equipment. As stated earlier in the chapter, depreciation does not represent a present cash outlay; thus, it must be added back to net income in order to adjust net income to a cash basis. Second, notice in the payback computation that the salvage value from the old machines has been deducted from the cost of the new equipment, and that only the incremental investment has been used in computing the payback period.

Step 1: *Compute the net annual cash inflow.* Since the net annual cash inflow is not given, it must be computed before the payback period can be determined:

Net income (given above)	$20,000
Add: Noncash deduction for depreciation . . .	10,000
Net annual cash inflow	$30,000

Step 2: *Compute the payback period.* Using the net annual cash inflow figure from above, the payback period can be determined as follows:

$$\frac{\text{Cost of the new equipment} - \text{Salvage from the old machines}}{\text{Net annual cash inflow}} = \text{Payback period}$$

$$\frac{\$80,000 - \$5,000}{\$30,000} = 2.5 \text{ years}$$

EXHIBIT 14–11
Computation of the Payback Period

Since the proposed equipment has a payback period of less than three years, the company's payback requirement has been met and the new equipment should be purchased.

Payback and Uneven Cash Flows

When the cash flows associated with an investment project are erratic or uneven, the simple payback formula that we outlined earlier is no longer usable, and the computations involved in deriving the payback period can be fairly complex. Consider the following data:

Year	Investment	Cash Inflow
1	$4,000	$1,000
2		–0–
3		2,000
4	2,000	1,000
5		500
6		3,000
7		2,000
8		2,000

What is the payback period on this investment? The answer is 5.5 years, but to obtain this figure it is necessary to balance off the cash inflows against the investment outflows on a year-by-year basis. The steps involved in this process are shown in Exhibit 14–12. By the middle of the sixth year, sufficient cash inflows will have been realized to recover the entire investment of $6,000 ($4,000 + $2,000).

The Simple Rate of Return Method

Objective 9
Compute the simple rate of return for an investment, using the simple rate of return formula.

The **simple rate of return** method is another capital budgeting technique that does not involve discounted cash flows. The method is also known as the accounting rate of return, the unadjusted rate of return, and the financial statement method. It derives its popularity from the belief that it parallels conventional financial statements in its handling of investment data.

Unlike the other capital budgeting methods that we have discussed, the simple rate of return method does not focus on cash flows. Rather, it focuses on accounting net income. The approach is to estimate the revenues that will be generated by a proposed investment and then to deduct from these revenues all of the projected operating expenses associated with the project. This net income figure is then related to the initial investment in the project, as shown in the following formula:

EXHIBIT 14–12

Payback and Uneven Cash Flows

Year	(1) Beginning Unrecovered Investment	(2) Additional Investment	(3) Total Unrecovered Investment (1) + (2)	(4) Cash Inflow	(5) Ending Unrecovered Investment (3) – (4)
1	$4,000		$4,000	$1,000	$3,000
2	3,000		3,000	–0–	3,000
3	3,000		3,000	2,000	1,000
4	1,000	$2,000	3,000	1,000	2,000
5	2,000		2,000	500	1,500
6	1,500		1,500	3,000	–0–
7	–0–		–0–	2,000	–0–
8	–0–		–0–	2,000	–0–

$$\text{Simple rate of return} = \frac{\begin{array}{c}\text{Incremental} \\ \text{revenues}\end{array} - \begin{array}{c}\text{Incremental expenses,} \\ \text{including depreciation}\end{array} = \begin{array}{c}\text{Net} \\ \text{income}\end{array}}{\text{Initial investment*}} \quad (3)$$

* The investment should be reduced by any salvage from the sale of old equipment.

Or, if a cost reduction project is involved, formula (3) becomes:

$$\text{Simple rate of return} = \frac{\begin{array}{c}\text{Cost} \\ \text{savings}\end{array} - \begin{array}{c}\text{Depreciation on} \\ \text{new equipment}\end{array}}{\text{Initial investment*}} \quad (4)$$

* The investment should be reduced by any salvage from the sale of old equipment.

Example I

Brigham Tea, Inc., is a processor of a nontannic acid tea product. The company is contemplating the purchase of equipment for an additional processing line. The additional processing line would increase revenues by $90,000 per year. Incremental cash operating expenses would be $40,000 per year. The equipment would cost $180,000 and have a nine-year life. No salvage value is projected.

1. Compute the simple rate of return.   *Required*
2. Compute the time-adjusted rate of return, and compare it to the simple rate of return.

1. By applying the formula for the simple rate of return found in equation (3), we   *Solution* can compute the simple rate of return to be 16.7 percent:

Simple rate of return

$$= \frac{\left[\begin{array}{c}\$90,000 \\ \text{incremental} \\ \text{revenues}\end{array}\right] - \left[\begin{array}{c}\$40,000 \text{ cash operating expenses} \\ + \$20,000 \text{ depreciation}\end{array}\right] = \begin{array}{c}\$30,000 \\ \text{net income}\end{array}}{\$180,000 \text{ initial investment}}$$

Simple rate of return = 16.7%

2. The rate computed in (1) above, however, is far below the time-adjusted rate of return of approximately 24 percent:

$$\text{Time-adjusted rate of return} = \frac{\$180,000}{\$50,000*} = \text{Factor of 3.600}$$

Time-adjusted rate of return =   Approximately 24% from Table J–4 in Appendix J, scanning across the nine-year line

* $30,000 net income + $20,000 depreciation = $50,000; or the annual cash inflow can be computed as: $90,000 increased revenues − $40,000 cash expenses = $50,000.

Example J

Midwest Farms, Inc., hires people on a part-time basis to sort eggs. The cost of this hand sorting process is $30,000 per year. The company is investigating the purchase of an egg sorting machine that would cost $90,000 and have a 15-year useful life. The machine would have only a nominal salvage value, and it would cost $10,000 per year to operate and maintain. The egg sorting equipment currently being used could be sold now for a scrap value of $2,500.

Required   Compute the simple rate of return on the new egg sorting machine.

Solution   A cost reduction project is involved in this situation. By applying the formula for the simple rate of return found in equation (4), we can compute the simple rate of return as follows:

$$\text{Simple rate of return} = \frac{\begin{array}{cc}\$20{,}000^* \text{ cost} & \$6{,}000^\dagger \text{ depreciation} \\ \text{savings} & \text{on the new equipment}\end{array}}{\$90{,}000 - \$2{,}500}$$

$$= 16.0\%$$

* $30,000 - $10,000 = $20,000 cost savings.
† $90,000 ÷ 15 years = $6,000 depreciation.

Criticisms of the Simple Rate of Return

The most damaging criticism of the simple rate of return method is that it does not consider the time value of money. A dollar received 10 years from now is viewed as being just as valuable as a dollar received today. Thus, the manager can be misled in attempting to choose between competing courses of action if the alternatives being considered have different cash flow patterns. For example, assume that project A has a high simple rate of return but yields the bulk of its cash flows many years from now. Another project, B, has a somewhat lower simple rate of return but yields the bulk of its cash flows over the next few years. The manager would probably choose project A over project B because of its higher simple rate of return; however, project B might in fact be a much better investment if the time value of money were considered.

A further criticism of the simple rate of return method is that it often proves to be misleading in its basic approach. The method is supposed to parallel conventional financial statements in its handling of data. Yet studies show that this parallelism is rarely present.[12] The problem is that conventional accounting practice tends to write costs off to expense very quickly. As a result, the net income and asset structure actually reflected on financial statements may differ substantially from comparable items in rate of return computations, where costs tend to be expensed less quickly. This disparity in the handling of data is especially pronounced in those situations where rate of return computations are carried out by nonaccounting personnel.

The Choice of an Investment Base

In our examples, we have defined the investment base for simple rate of return computations to be the entire initial investment in the project under consideration [see formula (3)]. Actual practice varies between using the entire initial investment, as we have done, and using only the *average* investment over the life of a project. As a practical matter, which approach one chooses to follow is unimportant so long as consistency is maintained between projects and between years. If the average investment is used rather than the entire initial investment, then the resulting rate of return will be approximately doubled.

---

[12] See National Association of Accountants, *Research Report No. 35,* "Return on Capital as a Guide to Managerial Decisions" (New York: National Association of Accountants, December 1959), p. 64.

POSTAUDIT OF INVESTMENT PROJECTS

Postaudit of an investment project means a follow-up after the project has been approved to see whether or not expected results are actually realized. This is a key part of the capital budgeting process in that it provides management with an opportunity, over time, to see how realistic the proposals are that are being submitted and approved. It also provides an opportunity to reinforce successful projects as needed, to strengthen or perhaps salvage projects that are encountering difficulty, to terminate unsuccessful projects before losses become too great, and to improve the overall quality of future investment proposals.

In performing a postaudit, the same technique should be used as was used in the original approval process. That is, if a project was approved on a basis of a net present value analysis, then the same procedure should be used in performing the postaudit. However, the data going into the analysis should be *actual data* as observed in the actual operation of the project, rather than estimated data. This affords management with an opportunity to make a side-by-side comparison to see how well the project has worked out. It also helps assure that estimated data received on future proposals will be carefully prepared, since the persons submitting the data will know that their estimates will be given careful scrutiny in the postaudit process. Actual results that are far out of line with original estimates should be carefully reviewed by management, and corrective action taken as necessary. In accordance with the management by exception principle, those managers responsible for the original estimates should be required to provide a full explanation of any major differences between estimated and actual results.[13]

SUMMARY

Decisions relating to the planning and financing of capital outlays are known as capital budgeting decisions. Such decisions are of key importance to the long-run profitability of a firm, since large amounts of money are usually involved and since whatever decisions are made may "lock in" a firm for many years.

A decision to make a particular investment hinges basically on whether the future returns promised by the investment can be justified in terms of the present cost outlay that must be made. A valid comparison between the future returns and the present cost outlay is difficult because of the difference in timing involved. This timing problem is overcome through use of the concept of present value and through employment of the technique of discounting. The future sums are discounted to their present value so that they can be compared on a valid basis with current cost outlays. The discount rate used may be the firm's cost of capital, or it may be some arbitrary rate of return that the firm requires on all investment projects.

There are two ways of using discounted cash flow in making capital budgeting decisions. One is the net present value method, and the other is the time-adjusted rate of return method. The net present value method involves choosing a discount rate, then discounting all cash flows to present value, as described in the preceding paragraph. If the present value of the cash inflows exceeds the present value of the cash outflows, then the net present value is positive and the project is accept-

---

[13] For further discussion, see Lawrence A. Gordon and Mary D. Myers, "Postauditing Capital Projects," *Management Accounting* 72, no. 7 (January 1991), pp. 39–42. This study of 282 large U.S. companies states that "an increasing number of firms are recognizing the importance of the postaudit stage" (p. 41).

able. The opposite is true if the net present value is negative. The time-adjusted rate of return method finds the discount rate that equates the cash inflows and the cash outflows, leaving a zero net present value.

Instead of using discounted cash flow, some companies prefer to use either payback or the simple rate of return in evaluating investment proposals. Payback is determined by dividing a project's cost by the annual cash inflows that it will generate in order to find out how quickly the original investment can be recovered. The simple rate of return is determined by dividing a project's accounting net income either by the initial investment in the project or by the average investment over the life of the project. Both payback and the simple rate of return can be useful to the manager, so long as they are used with a full understanding of their limitations.

After an investment proposal has been approved, a postaudit should be performed to see whether expected results are actually being realized. This is a key part of the capital budgeting process, since it tends to strengthen the quality of the estimates going into investment proposals and affords management with an early opportunity to recognize any developing problems or opportunities.

REVIEW PROBLEM 1: BASIC PRESENT VALUE COMPUTATIONS

Each of the following situations is independent. Work out your own solution to each situation, and then check it against the solution provided.

1. John has just reached age 58. In 12 years, he plans to retire. Upon retiring, he would like to take an extended vacation, which he expects will cost at least $4,000. What lump-sum amount must he invest now in order to have the needed $4,000 at the end of 12 years if the desired rate of return is:
    a. Eight percent?
    b. Twelve percent?
2. The Morgans would like to send their daughter to an expensive music camp at the end of each of the next five years. The camp costs $1,000 each year. What lump-sum amount would have to be invested now in order to have the $1,000 at the end of each year if the desired rate of return is:
    a. Eight percent?
    b. Twelve percent?
3. You have just received an inheritance from your father's estate. You can invest the money and either receive a $20,000 lump-sum amount at the end of 10 years or receive $1,400 at the end of each year for the next 10 years. If the minimum desired rate of return is 12 percent, which alternative would you prefer?

Solution to Review Problem 1

1. a. The amount that must be invested now would be the present value of the $4,000, using a discount rate of 8 percent. From Table J–3 in Appendix J, the factor for a discount rate of 8 percent for 12 periods is 0.397. Multiplying this discount factor times the $4,000 needed in 12 years will give the amount of the present investment required: $4,000 × 0.397 = $1,588.
    b. We will proceed as we did in (*a*) above, but this time we will use a discount rate of 12 percent. From Table J–3 in Appendix J, the factor for a discount rate of 12 percent for 12 periods is 0.257. Multiplying this discount factor times the $4,000 needed in 12 years will give the amount of the present investment required: $4,000 × 0.257 = $1,028.

    Notice that as the discount rate (desired rate of return) increases, the present value decreases.

2. This part differs from (1) above in that we are now dealing with an annuity rather than

with a single future sum. The amount that must be invested now will be the present value of the $1,000 needed at the end of each year for five years. Since we are dealing with an annuity, or a series of cash flows, we must refer to Table J–4 in Appendix J for the appropriate discount factor.

a. From Table J–4 in Appendix J, the discount factor for 8 percent for five periods is 3.993. Therefore, the amount that must be invested now in order to have $1,000 available at the end of each year for five years is: $1,000 × 3.993 = $3,993.

b. From Table J–4 in Appendix J, the discount factor for 12 percent for five periods is 3.605. Therefore, the amount that must be invested now in order to have $1,000 available at the end of each year for five years is: $1,000 × 3.605 = $3,605.

Again notice that as the discount rate (desired rate of return) increases, the present value decreases. This is logical, since at a higher rate of return we would expect to have to invest less than would have to be invested if a lower rate of return were being earned.

3. For this part we will need to refer to both Tables J–3 and J–4 in Appendix J. From Table J–3, we will need to find the discount factor for 12 percent for 10 periods, then apply it to the $20,000 lump sum to be received in 10 years. From Table J–4, we will need to find the discount factor for 12 percent for 10 periods, then apply it to the series of $1,400 payments to be received over the 10-year period. Whichever alternative has the higher present value is the one that should be selected.

$$\$20,000 \times 0.322 = \$6,440$$
$$\$1,400 \times 5.650 = \$7,910$$

Thus, you would prefer to receive the $1,400 per year for 10 years, rather than the $20,000 lump sum.

REVIEW PROBLEM 2: COMPARISON OF CAPITAL BUDGETING METHODS

Lamar Company is studying a project that would have an eight-year life and require a $1,600,000 investment in equipment. At the end of eight years, the project would terminate and the equipment would have no salvage value. The project would provide net income each year as follows:

Sales.	$3,000,000
Less variable expenses.	1,800,000
Contribution margin	1,200,000
Less fixed expenses:	
Advertising, salaries, and other fixed out-of-pocket costs $700,000	
Depreciation 200,000	
Total fixed expenses.	900,000
Net income.	$ 300,000

The company's cost of capital is 18 percent.

Required

1. Compute the net annual cash inflow promised by the project.
2. Compute the project's net present value. Is the project acceptable? Explain.
3. Compute the project's time-adjusted rate of return. Interpolate to one decimal place.
4. Compute the project's payback period. If the company requires a maximum payback of three years, is the project acceptable?
5. Compute the project's simple rate of return. Is the project acceptable? Explain.

Solution to Review Problem 2

1. The net annual cash inflow can be computed by deducting the cash expenses from sales:

```
Sales  . . . . . . . . . . . . . . . .    $3,000,000
Less variable expenses  . . . . . . . . .   1,800,000
Contribution margin . . . . . . . . . . .   1,200,000
Less advertising, salaries, and
    other fixed out-of-pocket costs . . . . .    700,000
Net annual cash inflow  . . . . . . . . .   $  500,000
```

Or it can be computed by adding depreciation back to net income:

```
Net income . . . . . . . . . . . . . . . . . . .   $300,000
Add: Noncash deduction for depreciation . . . . .    200,000
Net annual cash inflow . . . . . . . . . . . . .   $500,000
```

2.   The net present value can be computed as follows:

Items	Year(s)	Amount	18 Percent Factor	Present Value of Cash Flows
Cost of new equipment	Now	$(1,600,000)	1.000	$(1,600,000)
Net annual cash inflow	1–8	500,000	4.078	2,039,000
Net present value				$ 439,000

Yes, the project is acceptable since it has a positive net present value when using the cost of capital as the discount rate.

3.   The formula for computing the factor of the time-adjusted rate of return is:

$$\frac{\text{Investment required}}{\text{Net annual cash inflow}} = \text{Factor of the time-adjusted rate of return}$$

$$\frac{\$1,600,000}{\$500,000} = 3.200$$

Looking in Table J–4 in Appendix J at the end of the chapter and scanning along the 8-period line, we find that a factor of 3.200 represents a rate of return somewhat between 26 and 28 percent. To find the rate we are after, we must interpolate as follows:

```
26% factor.  . . . .   3.241       3.241
True factor  . . . .   3.200
28% factor.  . . . .               3.076
Difference . . . . .   0.041       0.165
```

$$\text{Time-adjusted rate of return} = 26\% + \left(\frac{0.041}{0.165} \times 2\%\right)$$

$$= 26.5\%$$

4.   The formula for the payback period is:

$$\text{Payback period} = \frac{\text{Investment required}}{\text{Net annual cash inflow}}$$

$$= \frac{\$1,600,000}{\$500,000}$$

$$= 3.2 \text{ years}$$

No, the project is not acceptable when measured by the payback method. The 3.2 years payback period is greater than the maximum 3 years set by the company.

5.   The formula for the simple rate of return is:

$$\text{Simple rate of return} = \frac{\text{Incremental revenues} - \text{Incremental expenses, including depreciation}}{\text{Initial investment}} = \text{Net income}$$

$$= \frac{\$300,000}{\$1,600,000}$$

$$= 18.75\%$$

Yes, the project is acceptable when measured by the simple rate of return. The 18.75 percent return promised by the project is greater than the company's 18 percent cost of capital. Notice, however, that the simple rate of return greatly understates the true rate of return, which is 26.5 percent as shown in (3) above.

KEY TERMS FOR REVIEW

Capital budgeting   Actions relating to the planning and financing of capital outlays for such purposes as the purchase of new equipment, the introduction of new product lines, and the modernization of plant facilities. (p. 650)

Capital decay   A loss in market share resulting from technologically obsolete products and operations. (p. 669)

Cost of capital   The overall cost to an organization of obtaining investment funds, including the cost of both debt sources and equity sources. This term is synonymous with *cutoff rate*, *hurdle rate*, and *required rate of return*. (p. 656)

Cutoff rate   This term is synonymous with *cost of capital*, *hurdle rate*, and *required rate of return*. (p. 656)

Hurdle rate   This term is synonymous with *cost of capital*, *cutoff rate*, and *required rate of return*. (p. 656)

Internal rate of return   The discount rate that will cause the net present value of an investment project to be equal to zero; thus, the internal rate of return represents the true interest return promised by a project over its useful life. This term is synonymous with *time-adjusted rate of return*. (p. 658)

Interpolation   The process of finding odd rates of return (such as 12.6 percent or 9.4 percent) that do not appear in published interest tables. (p. 659)

Net present value   The difference between the present value of the cash inflows and the cash outflows associated with an investment project. (p. 652)

Out-of-pocket costs   The actual cash outlays made during a period for salaries, advertising, repairs, and similar costs. (p. 658)

Payback period   The length of time that it takes for an investment project to recoup its own initial cost out of the cash receipts that it generates. (p. 670)

Postaudit   The follow-up after a project has been approved and implemented to determine whether expected results are actually realized. (p. 677)

Preference decision   A decision as to which of several competing acceptable investment proposals is best. (p. 650)

Required rate of return   The minimum rate of return that an investment project must yield in order to be acceptable. This term is synonymous with *cost of capital, cutoff rate,* and *hurdle rate.* (p. 656)

Screening decision   A decision as to whether a proposed investment meets some preset standard of acceptance. (p. 650)

Simple rate of return   The rate of return promised by an investment project when the time value of money is not considered; it is computed by dividing a project's annual net income by the initial investment required. (p. 674)

Time-adjusted rate of return   The discount rate that will cause the net present value of an investment project to be equal to zero; thus, the time-adjusted rate of return represents

Objective 10
Define or explain the key terms listed at the end of the chapter.

the true interest return promised by a project over its useful life. This term is synonymous with *internal rate of return*. (p. 658)

Working capital   The excess of current assets over current liabilities. (p. 654)

   Yield   A term synonymous with *internal rate of return* and *time-adjusted rate of return*. (p. 658)

APPENDIX H: THE CONCEPT OF PRESENT VALUE

Objective 11
Explain the concept of present value and make present value computations with and without present value tables.

The point was made in the main body of the chapter that a business leader would rather receive a dollar today than a year from now. There are two reasons why this is true. First, a dollar received today is more valuable than a dollar received a year from now. The dollar received today can be invested immediately, and by the end of a year it will have earned some return, making the total amount in hand at the end of the year *greater* than the investment started with. The person receiving the dollar a year from now will simply have a dollar in hand at that time.

Second, the future involves uncertainty. The longer people have to wait to receive a dollar, the more uncertain it becomes that they will ever get the dollar that they seek. As time passes, conditions change. The changes may be such as to make future payments of the dollar impossible.

Since money has a time value, the manager needs a method of determining whether a cash outlay made now in an investment project can be justified in terms of expected receipts from the project in future years. That is, the manager must have a means of expressing future receipts in present dollar terms so that the future receipts can be compared *on an equivalent basis* with whatever investment is required in the project under consideration. The theory of interest provides managers with the means of making such a comparison.

The Theory of Interest

If a bank pays $105 one year from now in return for a deposit of $100 now, we would say that the bank is paying interest at an annual rate of 5 percent. The relationships involved in this notion can be expressed in mathematical terms by means of the following equation:

$$F_1 = P(1 + r) \tag{5}$$

where F_1 = the amount to be received in one year, P = the present outlay to be made, and r = the rate of interest involved.

If the present outlay is $100 deposited in a bank savings account that is to earn interest at 5 percent, then P = $100 and r = 0.05. Under these conditions, F_1 = $105, the amount to be received in one year.

The $100 present outlay can be called the **present value** of the $105 amount to be received in one year. It is also known as the *discounted value* of the future $105 receipt. The $100 figure represents the value in present terms of a receipt of $105 to be received a year from now by an investor who requires a return of 5 percent on his or her money.

Compound Interest   What if the investor wants to leave his or her money in the bank for a second year? In that case, by the end of the second year the original $100 deposit will have grown to $110.25:

Original deposit	$100.00
Interest for the first year:	
$100 × 0.05	5.00
Amount at the end of the first year.	105.00
Interest for the second year:	
$105 × 0.05	5.25
Amount at the end of the second year . . .	$110.25

Notice that the interest for the second year is $5.25, as compared to only $5 for the first year. The reason for the greater interest earned during the second year is that during the second year, interest is being paid *on interest*. That is, the $5 interest earned during the first year has been left in the account and has been added to the original $100 deposit in computing interest for the second year. This concept is known as **compound interest.** The compounding we have done is annual compounding. Interest can be compounded on a semiannual, quarterly, or even more frequent basis. Many savings institutions are now compounding interest on a daily basis. Of course, the more frequently compounding is done, the more rapidly the invested balance will grow.

How is the concept of compound interest expressed in equation form? It is expressed by taking equation (5) and adjusting it to state the number of years, n, that a sum is going to be left deposited in the bank:

$$F_n = P(1 + r)^n \tag{6}$$

where n = years.

If $n = 2$ years, then our computation of the value of F in two years will be:

$$F_2 = \$100(1 + 0.05)^2$$
$$F_2 = \$110.25$$

Present Value and Future Value   Exhibit H–1 shows the relationship between present value and future value as expressed in the theory of interest equations. As

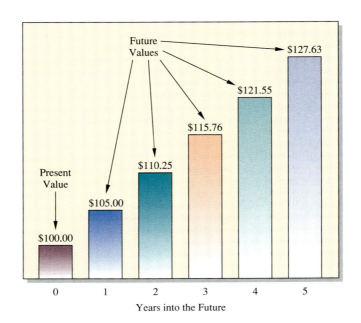

EXHIBIT H–1

The Relationship between Present Value and Future Value

shown in the exhibit, if $100 is deposited in a bank at 5 percent interest, it will grow to $127.63 by the end of five years if interest is compounded annually.

Computation of Present Value

An investment can be viewed in two ways. It can be viewed either in terms of its future value or in terms of its present value. We have seen from our computations above that if we know the present value of a sum (such as our $100 deposit), it is a relatively simple task to compute the sum's future value in n years by using equation (6). But what if the tables are reversed, and we know the *future* value of some amount but we do not know its present value?

For example, assume that you are to receive $200 two years from now. You know that the future value of this sum is $200, since this is the amount that you will be receiving in two years. But what is the sum's present value—what is it worth *right now?* The present value of any sum to be received in the future can be computed by turning equation (2) around and solving for P:

$$P = \frac{F_n}{(1 + r)^n} \tag{7}$$

In our example, F = $200 (the amount to be received in the future), r = 0.05 (the rate of interest), and n = 2 (the number of years in the future that the amount is to be received).

$$P = \frac{\$200}{(1 + 0.05)^2}$$

$$P = \frac{\$200}{1.1025}$$

$$P = \$181.40$$

As shown by the computation above, the present value of a $200 amount to be received two years from now is $181.40 if an interest return of 5 percent is required. In effect, we are saying that $181.40 received *right now* is equivalent to $200 received two years from now if the investor requires a 5 percent return on his or her money. The $181.40 and the $200 are just two ways of looking at the same item.

The process of finding the present value of a future cash flow, which we have just completed, is called **discounting.** We have *discounted* the $200 to its present value of $181.40. The 5 percent interest figure that we have used to find this present value is called the **discount rate.** Discounting of future sums to their present value is a common practice in business. A knowledge of the present value of a sum to be received in the future can be very useful to the manager, particularly in making capital budgeting decisions. However, we need to find a simpler way of computing present value than using equation (7) every time we need to discount a future sum. The computations involved in using this equation are complex and time-consuming.

Fortunately, tables are available in which most of the mathematical work involved in the discounting process has been done. Table J–3 in Appendix J shows the discounted present value of $1 to be received at various periods in the future at various interest rates. The table indicates that the present value of $1 to be received two periods from now at 5 percent is 0.907. Since in our example we want to know the present value of $200 rather than just $1, we need to multiply the factor in the table by $200:

$$\$200 \times 0.907 = \$181.40$$

The answer we obtain is the same answer as we obtained earlier using the formula in equation (7).

Present Value of a Series of Cash Flows

Although some investments involve a single sum to be received (or paid) at a single point in the future, other investments involve a *series* of cash flows. A series (or stream) of identical cash flows is known as an **annuity.** To provide an example, assume that a firm has just purchased some government bonds in order to temporarily invest funds that are being held for future plant expansion. The bonds will yield interest of $15,000 each year and will be held for five years. What is the present value of the stream of interest receipts from the bonds? As shown in Exhibit H–2, the present value of this stream is $54,075 if we assume a discount rate of 12 percent compounded annually. The discount factors used in this exhibit were taken from Table J–3 in Appendix J.

Two points are important in connection with Exhibit H–2. First, notice that the farther we go forward in time, the smaller is the present value of the $15,000 interest receipt. The present value of $15,000 received a year from now is $13,395, as compared to only $8,505 for the $15,000 interest payment to be received five years from now. This point simply underscores the fact that money has a time value.

The second point is that even though the computations involved in Exhibit H–2 are accurate, they have involved unnecessary work. The same present value of $54,075 could have been obtained more easily by referring to Table J–4 in Appendix J. Table J–4 contains the present value of $1 to be received each year over a *series* of years at various interest rates. Table J–4 has been derived by simply adding together the factors from Table J–3. To illustrate, we used the following factors from Table J–3 in the computations in Exhibit H–2.

	Table J–3 Factors at
Year	12 Percent
1	0.893
2	0.797
3	0.712
4	0.636
5	0.567
	3.605

The sum of the five factors above is 3.605. Notice from Table J–4 that the factor for $1 to be received each year for five years at 12 percent is also 3.605. If we use

Year	Factor at 12 Percent (Table J–3)	Interest Received	Present Value
1	0.893	$15,000	$13,395
2	0.797	15,000	11,955
3	0.712	15,000	10,680
4	0.636	15,000	9,540
5	0.567	15,000	8,505
			$54,075

EXHIBIT H–2
Present Value of a Series of Cash Receipts

this factor and multiply it by the $15,000 annual cash inflow, then we get the same $54,075 present value that we obtained earlier in Exhibit H–2.

$$\$15,000 \times 3.605 = \$54,075$$

Therefore, when computing the present value of a series (or stream) of cash flows, Table J–4 should be used.

To summarize, the present value tables in Appendix J should be used as follows:

Table J–3: This table should be used to find the present value of a single cash flow (such as a single payment or receipt) occurring in the future.

Table J–4: This table should be used to find the present value of a series (or stream) of identical cash flows beginning in the current year and continuing into the future.

The use of both of these tables is illustrated in various exhibits in the main body of the chapter. *When a present value factor appears in an exhibit, the reader should take the time to trace it back into either Table J–3 or Table J–4 in order to get acquainted with the tables and how they work.* (Review Problem 1 at the end of the chapter is designed for those readers who would like some practice in present value analysis before attempting the homework exercises and problems. A solution to Review Problem 1 is provided immediately following the problem.)

KEY TERMS FOR REVIEW (APPENDIX H)

Annuity   A series, or stream, of identical cash flows. (p. 685)

Compound interest   The process of paying interest on interest in an investment. (p. 683)

Discount rate   The rate of return that is used to find the present value of a future cash flow. (p. 684)

Discounting   The process of finding the present value of a future cash flow. (p. 684)

Present value   The estimated value now of an amount that will be received in some future period. (p. 682)

APPENDIX I: INFLATION AND CAPITAL BUDGETING

Students frequently raise the question "What about inflation—doesn't it have an impact in a capital budgeting analysis?" The answer is a qualified yes in that inflation does have an impact on the *numbers* that are used in a capital budgeting analysis, but it does not have an impact on the *results* that are obtained. To show what we mean by this statement, assume the following data:

Example K

Martin Company wants to purchase a new machine that costs $36,000. The machine would provide annual cost savings of $20,000, and it would have a three-year life with no salvage value. For each of the next three years, the company expects a 10 percent inflation rate in cost items associated with its activities. If the company's cost of capital is 16 percent, should the new machine be purchased?

Two solutions to this example are provided in Exhibit I–1. In the first solution (solution A), inflation is ignored and the net present value of the proposed investment is computed in the same way as we have been computing it throughout the chapter. In the second solution (solution B), inflation is given full consideration.

EXHIBIT I–1
Capital Budgeting and Inflation

Solution A: Inflation Not Considered

Items	Year(s)	Amount of Cash Flows	16 Percent Factor	Present Value of Cash Flows
Initial investment	Now	$(36,000)	1.000	$(36,000)
Annual cost savings	1–3	20,000	2.246	44,920
Net present value				$ 8,920

Solution B: Inflation Considered

Items	Year(s)	Amount of Cash Flows	Price Index Number	Price-Adjusted Cash Flows	27.6 Percent Factor†	Present Value of Cash Flows
Initial investment . . .	Now	$(36,000)	—	$(36,000)	1.0000	$(36,000)
Annual cost savings . .	1	20,000	1.10	22,000	0.7837‡	17,241
	2	20,000	1.21*	24,200	0.6142‡	14,864
	3	20,000	1.331*	26,620	0.4814‡	12,815
Net present value . . .						$ 8,920

* Computation of the price-index numbers, assuming a 10 percent inflation rate each year: year 2, $(1.10)^2 = 1.21$; year 3, $(1.10)^3 = 1.331$.
† The inflation-adjusted cost of capital consists of three elements:

The basic cost of capital	16.0%
The inflation factor	10.0
The combined effect (16% × 10% = 1.6%) . . .	1.6
Inflation-adjusted cost of capital	27.6%

‡ Discount factors are computed using the formula $1/(1 + r)^n$ where r = discount factor and n = number of years. For year 1, the computations are: $1/1.276 = 0.7837$; for year 2: $1/(1.276)^2 = 0.6142$; for year 3: $1/(1.276)^3 = 0.4814$. Computations have been carried to four decimal places to avoid a rounding error.

Adjustments for Inflation

Several points should be noted about solution B. First, note that the annual cost savings are adjusted for the effects of inflation by multiplying each year's savings by a price-index number that reflects a 10 percent inflation rate. (Observe from the footnotes to the exhibit how the index number is computed for each year.)

Second, note that the cost of capital must also be adjusted for the effects of inflation. This is done by adding together three cost elements: the cost of capital itself, the inflation rate, and a combined factor that allows for the reinvestment of inflation-generated earnings. A frequent error in adjusting data for inflation is to omit any adjustment at all to the cost of capital; or, if an adjustment is made, to simply add together the cost of capital and the inflation rate. Both of these procedures are incorrect and will yield erroneous results.[14]

Finally, note that the net present value obtained in solution B is *identical* to that obtained in solution A. It sometimes surprises students to learn that the same net present value will be obtained regardless of whether or not the data are adjusted for the effects of inflation. But if the reader will stop and reflect for a moment, this is a logical result. The reason is that in adjusting the data for the effects of inflation, we adjust *both* the cash flows and the discount rate, and thus the inflationary effects cancel themselves out. As a result, the net present value is the same as if no adjustments had been made.

---

[14] The proper way to adjust the discount rate for inflationary effects is widely misunderstood. If the manager omits any adjustment to the cost of capital, or just adds together the cost of capital and the inflation rate, then the result will be to overstate the net present value of an investment project.

How Practical Are Adjustments for Inflation?

In actual practice, not all companies make adjustments for inflation when doing a capital budgeting analysis. The reasons are obvious—the computations are very complex, and the same net present value can be obtained by using unadjusted data. The one advantage that is sometimes cited in favor of using inflation-adjusted data is that it may be of more value in the postaudit process. It is argued that using inflation-adjusted data in the original capital budgeting analysis allows the manager to later compare like items in the postaudit because *both* the estimated data and the actual data will contain the effects of inflation. If unadjusted data are used in the original capital budgeting analysis, then it is argued that the manager is forced to compare *unlike* items in the postaudit. Thus, the manager may be misled in his or her evaluation of how the investment turned out.

Unfortunately, this "advantage" is more illusory than real. For one thing, if inflation-adjusted data are used in the original capital budgeting analysis, then these data and the actual data will be comparable only if the *same rate* of inflation is present in both. The likelihood of having the same rate present in both is small, since inflation is very difficult to predict. Economists rarely agree on the expected rate for the next year, let alone several years into the future. In addition, the use of inflation-adjusted data may conceal sloppy estimates of cash flows by enabling the manager to hide behind the excuse that inflation rates turned out to be different than expected, thus throwing his or her estimates off.

To overcome these problems, a better approach is to use unadjusted data (because of its simplicity) in the original capital budgeting analysis, and then *in the postaudit* to adjust the actual data in order to remove the effects of any inflation that may have taken place. This approach will then allow for a comparison of like items, since neither the original data nor the actual data will contain any inflationary elements. It will also preclude the manager from hiding behind the excuse that his or her estimates were thrown off because the rate of inflation was different than expected.

Summary

Although it is possible to make adjustments for inflation in a capital budgeting analysis, it is a very difficult and complex process. Moreover, if the adjustments are properly done, the same net present value will be obtained as if no adjustments had been made. A simpler and more effective approach is to use unadjusted data in capital budgeting computations, as we have done in the chapter, and then to make adjustments to the actual data in the postaudit (when the actual rate of inflation is known), if it is thought that such adjustments are warranted.

APPENDIX J: FUTURE VALUE AND PRESENT VALUE TABLES

TABLE J–1

Future Value of $1;
$F_n = P(1 + r)^n$

Periods	4%	6%	8%	10%	12%	14%	20%
1	1.040	1.060	1.080	1.100	1.120	1.140	1.200
2	1.082	1.124	1.166	1.210	1.254	1.300	1.440
3	1.125	1.191	1.260	1.331	1.405	1.482	1.728
4	1.170	1.263	1.361	1.464	1.574	1.689	2.074
5	1.217	1.338	1.469	1.611	1.762	1.925	2.488
6	1.265	1.419	1.587	1.772	1.974	2.195	2.986
7	1.316	1.504	1.714	1.949	2.211	2.502	3.583
8	1.369	1.594	1.851	2.144	2.476	2.853	4.300
9	1.423	1.690	1.999	2.359	2.773	3.252	5.160
10	1.480	1.791	2.159	2.594	3.106	3.707	6.192
11	1.540	1.898	2.332	2.853	3.479	4.226	7.430
12	1.601	2.012	2.518	3.139	3.896	4.818	8.916
13	1.665	2.133	2.720	3.452	4.364	5.492	10.699
14	1.732	2.261	2.937	3.798	4.887	6.261	12.839
15	1.801	2.397	3.172	4.177	5.474	7.138	15.407
20	2.191	3.207	4.661	6.728	9.646	13.743	38.338
30	3.243	5.744	10.063	17.450	29.960	50.950	237.380
40	4.801	10.286	21.725	45.260	93.051	188.880	1469.800

TABLE J–2

Future Value of
an Annuity of $1
in Arrears;

$$F_n = \frac{(1 + r)^n - 1}{r}$$

Periods	4%	6%	8%	10%	12%	14%	20%
1	1.000	1.000	1.000	1.000	1.000	1.000	1.000
2	2.040	2.060	2.080	2.100	2.120	2.140	2.220
3	3.122	3.184	3.246	3.310	3.374	3.440	3.640
4	4.247	4.375	4.506	4.641	4.779	4.921	5.368
5	5.416	5.637	5.867	6.105	6.353	6.610	7.442
6	6.633	6.975	7.336	7.716	8.115	8.536	9.930
7	7.898	8.394	8.923	9.487	10.089	10.730	12.916
8	9.214	9.898	10.637	11.436	12.300	13.233	16.499
9	10.583	11.491	12.488	13.580	14.776	16.085	20.799
10	12.006	13.181	14.487	15.938	17.549	19.337	25.959
11	13.486	14.972	16.646	18.531	20.655	23.045	32.150
12	15.026	16.870	18.977	21.385	24.133	27.271	39.580
13	16.627	18.882	21.495	24.523	28.029	32.089	48.497
14	18.292	21.015	24.215	27.976	32.393	37.581	59.196
15	20.024	23.276	27.152	31.773	37.280	43.842	72.035
20	29.778	36.778	45.762	57.276	75.052	91.025	186.690
30	56.085	79.058	113.283	164.496	241.330	356.790	1181.900
40	95.026	154.762	259.057	442.597	767.090	1342.000	7343.900

TABLE J-3

Present Value of \$1; $P = \dfrac{F_n}{(1 + r)^n}$

Periods	4%	5%	6%	8%	10%	12%	14%	16%	18%	20%	22%	24%	26%	28%	30%	40%
1	0.962	0.952	0.943	0.926	0.909	0.893	0.877	0.862	0.847	0.833	0.820	0.806	0.794	0.781	0.769	0.714
2	0.925	0.907	0.890	0.857	0.826	0.797	0.769	0.743	0.718	0.694	0.672	0.650	0.630	0.610	0.592	0.510
3	0.889	0.864	0.840	0.794	0.751	0.712	0.675	0.641	0.609	0.579	0.551	0.524	0.500	0.477	0.455	0.364
4	0.855	0.823	0.792	0.735	0.683	0.636	0.592	0.552	0.516	0.482	0.451	0.423	0.397	0.373	0.350	0.260
5	0.822	0.784	0.747	0.681	0.621	0.567	0.519	0.476	0.437	0.402	0.370	0.341	0.315	0.291	0.269	0.186
6	0.790	0.746	0.705	0.630	0.564	0.507	0.456	0.410	0.370	0.335	0.303	0.275	0.250	0.227	0.207	0.133
7	0.760	0.711	0.665	0.583	0.513	0.452	0.400	0.354	0.314	0.279	0.249	0.222	0.198	0.178	0.159	0.095
8	0.731	0.677	0.627	0.540	0.467	0.404	0.351	0.305	0.266	0.233	0.204	0.179	0.157	0.139	0.123	0.068
9	0.703	0.645	0.592	0.500	0.424	0.361	0.308	0.263	0.225	0.194	0.167	0.144	0.125	0.108	0.094	0.048
10	0.676	0.614	0.558	0.463	0.386	0.322	0.270	0.227	0.191	0.162	0.137	0.116	0.099	0.085	0.073	0.035
11	0.650	0.585	0.527	0.429	0.350	0.287	0.237	0.195	0.162	0.135	0.112	0.094	0.079	0.066	0.056	0.025
12	0.625	0.557	0.497	0.397	0.319	0.257	0.208	0.168	0.137	0.112	0.092	0.076	0.062	0.052	0.043	0.018
13	0.601	0.530	0.469	0.368	0.290	0.229	0.182	0.145	0.116	0.093	0.075	0.061	0.050	0.040	0.033	0.013
14	0.577	0.505	0.442	0.340	0.263	0.205	0.160	0.125	0.099	0.078	0.062	0.049	0.039	0.032	0.025	0.009
15	0.555	0.481	0.417	0.315	0.239	0.183	0.140	0.108	0.084	0.065	0.051	0.040	0.031	0.025	0.020	0.006
16	0.534	0.458	0.394	0.292	0.218	0.163	0.123	0.093	0.071	0.054	0.042	0.032	0.025	0.019	0.015	0.005
17	0.513	0.436	0.371	0.270	0.198	0.146	0.108	0.080	0.060	0.045	0.034	0.026	0.020	0.015	0.012	0.003
18	0.494	0.416	0.350	0.250	0.180	0.130	0.095	0.069	0.051	0.038	0.028	0.021	0.016	0.012	0.009	0.002
19	0.475	0.396	0.331	0.232	0.164	0.116	0.083	0.060	0.043	0.031	0.023	0.017	0.012	0.009	0.007	0.002
20	0.456	0.377	0.312	0.215	0.149	0.104	0.073	0.051	0.037	0.026	0.019	0.014	0.010	0.007	0.005	0.001
21	0.439	0.359	0.294	0.199	0.135	0.093	0.064	0.044	0.031	0.022	0.015	0.011	0.008	0.006	0.004	0.001
22	0.422	0.342	0.278	0.184	0.123	0.083	0.056	0.038	0.026	0.018	0.013	0.009	0.006	0.004	0.003	0.001
23	0.406	0.326	0.262	0.170	0.112	0.074	0.049	0.033	0.022	0.015	0.010	0.007	0.005	0.003	0.002	
24	0.390	0.310	0.247	0.158	0.102	0.066	0.043	0.028	0.019	0.013	0.008	0.006	0.004	0.003	0.002	
25	0.375	0.295	0.233	0.146	0.092	0.059	0.038	0.024	0.016	0.010	0.007	0.005	0.003	0.002	0.001	
26	0.361	0.281	0.220	0.135	0.084	0.053	0.033	0.021	0.014	0.009	0.006	0.004	0.002	0.002	0.001	
27	0.347	0.268	0.207	0.125	0.076	0.047	0.029	0.018	0.011	0.007	0.005	0.003	0.002	0.001	0.001	
28	0.333	0.255	0.196	0.116	0.069	0.042	0.026	0.016	0.010	0.006	0.004	0.002	0.002	0.001	0.001	
29	0.321	0.243	0.185	0.107	0.063	0.037	0.022	0.014	0.008	0.005	0.003	0.002	0.001	0.001	0.001	
30	0.308	0.231	0.174	0.099	0.057	0.033	0.020	0.012	0.007	0.004	0.003	0.002	0.001	0.001	0.001	
40	0.208	0.142	0.097	0.046	0.022	0.011	0.005	0.003	0.001	0.001						

TABLE J-4

Present Value of an Annuity of $1 in Arrears; $P_n = \dfrac{1}{r}\left[1 - \dfrac{1}{(1+r)^n}\right]$

Periods	4%	5%	6%	8%	10%	12%	14%	16%	18%	20%	22%	24%	26%	28%	30%	40%
1	0.962	0.952	0.943	0.926	0.909	0.893	0.877	0.862	0.847	0.833	0.820	0.806	0.794	0.781	0.769	0.714
2	1.886	1.859	1.833	1.783	1.736	1.690	1.647	1.605	1.566	1.528	1.492	1.457	1.424	1.392	1.361	1.224
3	2.775	2.723	2.673	2.577	2.487	2.402	2.322	2.246	2.174	2.106	2.042	1.981	1.923	1.868	1.816	1.589
4	3.630	3.546	3.465	3.312	3.170	3.037	2.914	2.798	2.690	2.589	2.494	2.404	2.320	2.241	2.166	1.879
5	4.452	4.330	4.212	3.993	3.791	3.605	3.433	3.274	3.127	2.991	2.864	2.745	2.635	2.532	2.436	2.035
6	5.242	5.076	4.917	4.623	4.355	4.111	3.889	3.685	3.498	3.326	3.167	3.020	2.885	2.759	2.643	2.168
7	6.002	5.786	5.582	5.206	4.868	4.564	4.288	4.039	3.812	3.605	3.416	3.242	3.083	2.937	2.802	2.263
8	6.733	6.463	6.210	5.747	5.335	4.968	4.639	4.344	4.078	3.837	3.619	3.421	3.241	3.076	2.925	2.331
9	7.435	7.108	6.802	6.247	5.759	5.328	4.946	4.607	4.303	4.031	3.786	3.566	3.366	3.184	3.019	2.379
10	8.111	7.722	7.360	6.710	6.145	5.650	5.216	4.833	4.494	4.192	3.923	3.682	3.465	3.269	3.092	2.414
11	8.760	8.306	7.887	7.139	6.495	5.988	5.453	5.029	4.656	4.327	4.035	3.776	3.544	3.335	3.147	2.438
12	9.385	8.863	8.384	7.536	6.814	6.194	5.660	5.197	4.793	4.439	4.127	3.851	3.606	3.387	3.190	2.456
13	9.986	9.394	8.853	7.904	7.103	6.424	5.842	5.342	4.910	4.533	4.203	3.912	3.656	3.427	3.223	2.468
14	10.563	9.899	9.295	8.244	7.367	6.628	6.002	5.468	5.008	4.611	4.265	3.962	3.695	3.459	3.249	2.477
15	11.118	10.380	9.712	8.559	7.606	6.811	6.142	5.575	5.092	4.675	4.315	4.001	3.726	3.483	3.268	2.484
16	11.652	10.838	10.106	8.851	7.824	6.974	6.265	5.669	5.162	4.730	4.357	4.033	3.751	3.503	3.283	2.489
17	12.166	11.274	10.477	9.122	8.022	7.120	6.373	5.749	5.222	4.775	4.391	4.059	3.771	3.518	3.295	2.492
18	12.659	11.690	10.828	9.372	8.201	7.250	6.467	5.818	5.273	4.812	4.419	4.080	3.786	3.529	3.304	2.494
19	13.134	12.085	11.158	9.604	8.365	7.366	6.550	5.877	5.316	4.844	4.442	4.097	3.799	3.539	3.311	2.496
20	13.590	12.462	11.470	9.818	8.514	7.469	6.623	5.929	5.353	4.870	4.460	4.110	3.808	3.546	3.316	2.497
21	14.029	12.821	11.764	10.017	8.649	7.562	6.687	5.973	5.384	4.891	4.476	4.121	3.816	3.551	3.320	2.498
22	14.451	13.163	12.042	10.201	8.772	7.645	6.743	6.011	5.410	4.909	4.488	4.130	3.822	3.556	3.323	2.498
23	14.857	13.489	12.303	10.371	8.883	7.718	6.792	6.044	5.432	4.925	4.499	4.137	3.827	3.559	3.325	2.499
24	15.247	13.799	12.550	10.529	8.985	7.784	6.835	6.073	5.451	4.937	4.507	4.143	3.831	3.562	3.327	2.499
25	15.622	14.094	12.783	10.675	9.077	7.843	6.873	6.097	5.467	4.948	4.514	4.147	3.834	3.564	3.329	2.499
26	15.983	14.375	13.003	10.810	9.161	7.896	6.906	6.118	5.480	4.956	4.520	4.151	3.837	3.566	3.330	2.500
27	16.330	14.643	13.211	10.935	9.237	7.943	6.935	6.936	5.492	4.964	4.525	4.154	3.839	3.567	3.331	2.500
28	16.663	14.898	13.406	11.051	9.307	7.984	6.961	6.152	5.502	4.970	4.528	4.157	3.840	3.568	3.331	2.500
29	16.984	15.141	13.591	11.158	9.370	8.022	6.983	6.166	5.510	4.975	4.531	4.159	3.841	3.569	3.332	2.500
30	17.292	15.373	13.765	11.258	9.427	8.055	7.003	6.177	5.517	4.979	4.534	4.160	3.842	3.569	3.332	2.500
40	19.793	17.159	15.046	11.925	9.779	8.244	7.105	6.234	5.548	4.997	4.544	4.166	3.846	3.571	3.333	2.500

QUESTIONS

14–1 What is meant by the term *capital budgeting?*

14–2 Distinguish between capital budgeting screening decisions and capital budgeting preference decisions.

14–3 What is meant by the term *time value of money?*

14–4 What is meant by the term *discounting,* and why is it important to the business manager?

14–5 Why can't accounting net income figures be used in the net present value and time-adjusted rate of return methods of making capital budgeting decisions?

14–6 Why are discounted cash flow methods of making capital budgeting decisions superior to other methods?

14–7 What is net present value? Can it ever be negative? Explain.

14–8 One real shortcoming of discounted cash flow methods is that they ignore depreciation. Do you agree? Why or why not?

14–9 Identify two limiting assumptions associated with discounted cash flow methods of making capital budgeting decisions.

14–10 If a firm has to pay interest of 14 percent on long-term debt, then its cost of capital is 14 percent. Do you agree? Explain.

14–11 What is meant by an investment project's time-adjusted rate of return? How is the time-adjusted rate of return computed?

14–12 Explain how the cost of capital serves as a screening tool when dealing with (a) the net present value method and (b) the time-adjusted rate of return method.

14–13 Companies that invest in underdeveloped countries usually require a higher rate of return on their investment than when they invest in countries that are better developed and that have more stable political and economic conditions. Some people say that the higher rate of return required in the underdeveloped countries is evidence of exploitation. What other explanation can you offer?

14–14 Riskier investment proposals should be discounted at lower rates of return. Do you agree? Why or why not?

14–15 As the discount rate increases, the present value of a given future sum also increases. Do you agree? Explain.

14–16 Refer to Exhibit 14–4. Is the return promised by this investment proposal exactly 20 percent, slightly more than 20 percent, or slightly less than 20 percent? Explain.

14–17 If an investment project has a zero net present value, then it should be rejected since it will provide no return on funds invested. Do you agree? Why?

14–18 A machine costs $12,000. It will provide a cost savings of $3,000 per year. If the company requires a 16 percent rate of return, how many years will the machine have to be used to provide the desired 16 percent return?

14–19 Frontier Company is investigating the purchase of a piece of automated equipment, but after considering the savings in labor costs the machine has a negative net present value. If no other cost savings can be identified, should the company reject the equipment? Explain.

14–20 What is meant by the term *payback period?* How is the payback period determined?

14–21 Sharp Company is considering the purchase of certain new equipment in order to sell a new product line. Expected yearly net income from the new product line is given below. From these data, compute the net annual cash inflow that would be used to determine the payback period on the new equipment.

Sales	$150,000
Less cost of goods sold	45,000
Gross margin.	105,000

Less operating expenses:
Advertising	$35,000	
Salaries and wages	50,000	
Depreciation	12,000	97,000
Net income		$ 8,000

14-22 In what ways can the payback method be useful to the manager?

14-23 What is the formula for computing the simple rate of return?

14-24 What is the major criticism of the payback and simple rate of return methods of making capital budgeting decisions?

EXERCISES

(Ignore income taxes in all exercises.)

Consider each of the following situations independently.   **E14-1**

1. In three years, when he is discharged from the Air Force, Steve wants to buy a power boat that will cost $8,000. What lump-sum amount must he invest now in order to have the $8,000 at the end of three years if he can invest money at:
    a. Ten percent?
    b. Fourteen percent?
2. Annual cash inflows that will arise from two competing investment projects are given below.

	Investment	
Year	**A**	**B**
1	$ 3,000	$12,000
2	6,000	9,000
3	9,000	6,000
4	12,000	3,000
	$30,000	$30,000

Each investment project will require the same investment outlay. You can invest money at an 18 percent rate of return. Compute the present value of the cash inflows for each investment.

3. Julie has just retired. Her company's retirement program has two options as to how retirement benefits can be received. Under the first option, Julie would receive a lump sum of $150,000 immediately as her full retirement benefit. Under the second option, she would receive $14,000 each year for 20 years plus a lump-sum payment of $60,000 at the end of the 20-year period. If she can invest money at 12 percent, which option would you recommend that she accept? (Use present value analysis.)

Each of the following parts is independent.   **E14-2**

1. The Atlantic Medical Clinic can purchase a new computer system that will save $7,000 annually in billing costs. The computer system will last for eight years and have only a nominal salvage value, which can be ignored. What is the maximum purchase price that the Atlantic Medical Clinic would be willing to pay for the new computer system if the clinic's required rate of return is:
    a. Sixteen percent?
    b. Twenty percent?
2. The Caldwell Herald newspaper reported the following story:

    Frank Ormsby of Caldwell is the state's newest millionaire. By choosing the six winning numbers on last week's state lottery, Mr. Ormsby has won the week's grand prize totaling $1.6 million. The State Lottery Commission has indicated that Mr. Ormsby will receive his prize in 20 annual installments of $80,000 each.

    a.   If Mr. Ormsby can invest money at a 12 percent rate of return, what is the present value of his winnings?

    b.   Is it correct to say that Mr. Ormsby is the "state's newest millionaire"? Explain your answer.

3.   Fraser Company will need a new warehouse in five years. The warehouse will cost $500,000 to build. What lump-sum amount should the company invest now in order to have the $500,000 available at the end of the five-year period? Assume that the company can invest money at:

    a.   Ten percent.

    b.   Fourteen percent.

E14-3   Complete the following cases:

1.   Preston Company requires a minimum return of 14 percent on all investments. The company can purchase a new machine at a cost of $84,900. The new machine would generate cash inflows of $15,000 per year and have a 12-year useful life with no salvage value. Compute the machine's net present value. (Use the format shown in Exhibit 14–1.) Is the machine an acceptable investment? Explain.

2.   The Walton Daily News is investigating the purchase of a new auxiliary press that has a projected life of 18 years. It is estimated that the new press will save $30,000 per year in cash operating costs. If the new press costs $217,500, what is its time-adjusted rate of return? Is the press an acceptable investment if the company's cost of capital is 16 percent? Explain.

3.   Refer to the data above for the Walton Daily News. How much would the annual cash inflows (cost savings) have to be in order for the new press to provide the required 16 percent rate of return? (Round your answer to the nearest whole dollar.)

E14-4   Kathy Myers frequently purchases stocks and bonds, but she is uncertain how to determine the rate of return that she is earning. For example, on January 2, 19x1, she paid $13,000 for 200 shares of the common stock of Malti Company. She received a $420 cash dividend on the stock each year for three years. At the end of three years, she sold the stock for $16,000. Kathy would like to earn a return of at least 14 percent on all of her investments. She is not sure whether the Malti Company stock provided a 14 percent return and would like some help with the necessary computations.

Required   By use of the net present value method, determine whether or not the Malti Company stock provided a 14 percent return. Use the general format illustrated in Exhibit 14–4, and round all computations to the nearest whole dollar.

E14-5   Henrie's Drapery Service is investigating the purchase of a new machine for cleaning and blocking drapes. The machine would cost $130,400, including invoice cost, freight, and installation. Henrie's has estimated that the new machine would increase the company's cash inflows, net of expenses, by $25,000 per year. The machine would have a 10-year useful life and no salvage value.

Required   1.   Compute the machine's time-adjusted rate of return. (Do not round your computations.)

    2.   Compute the machine's net present value. Use a discount rate of 14 percent, and use the format shown in Exhibit 14–5. Why do you have a zero net present value? If the company's cost of capital is 10 percent, is this an acceptable investment? Explain.

    3.   Suppose that the new machine would increase the company's annual cash inflows, net of expenses, by only $22,500 per year. Under these conditions, compute the time-adjusted rate of return. Interpolate as needed, and round your final answer to the nearest tenth of a percent.

Wendell's Donut Shoppe is investigating the purchase of a new donut-making machine. **E14-6**
The new machine would permit the company to reduce the amount of part-time help
needed, at a cost savings of $3,800 per year. In addition, the new machine would allow the
company to produce one new style of donut, resulting in the sale of at least 1,000 dozen
more donuts each year. The company realizes a contribution margin of $1.20 per dozen
donuts sold. The new machine would cost $18,600 and have a six-year useful life.

1. What would be the total annual cash inflows associated with the new machine for *Required*
   capital budgeting purposes?
2. Compute the time-adjusted rate of return promised by the new machine. Interpolate,
   and round your final answer to the nearest tenth of a percent.
3. In addition to the data given above, assume that the machine will have a $9,125 salvage
   value at the end of six years. Under these conditions, compute the time-adjusted rate
   of return to the nearest *whole* percent. (Hint: You may find it helpful to use the net
   present value approach; find the discount rate that will cause the net present value to
   be closest to zero. Use the format shown in Exhibit 14–4.)

Labeau Products has $35,000 to invest. The company is trying to decide between two **E14-7**
alternative uses for the funds. The alternatives are:

	Invest in Project X	Invest in Project Y
Investment required	$35,000	$35,000
Annual cash inflows	9,000	—
Single cash inflow at the end of 10 years	—	150,000
Life of the project	10 years	10 years

The company's cost of capital is 18 percent.

Which alternative would you recommend that the company accept? (Use the net present *Required*
value method and the format shown in Exhibit 14–4. Prepare a separate computation for
each alternative.)

Perot Industries has $100,000 to invest. The company is trying to decide between two **E14-8**
alternative uses of the funds. The alternatives are:

	Project	
	A	B
Cost of equipment required	$100,000	—
Working capital investment required	—	$100,000
Annual cash inflows	21,000	16,000
Salvage value of equipment in six years	8,000	—
Life of the project	6 years	6 years

The working capital needed for project B will be released at the end of six years for
investment elsewhere. Perot Industries' cost of capital is 14 percent.

Which investment alternative (if either) would you recommend that the company accept? *Required*
Show all computations using the net present value format. (Prepare a separate computation
for each project.)

Solve the three following present value exercises: **E14-9**

1. The Cambro Foundation, a nonprofit organization, is planning to invest $104,950 in a
   project that will last for three years. The project will provide cash inflows as follows:

Year 1	$30,000
Year 2	40,000
Year 3	?

Assuming that the project will yield exactly a 12 percent rate of return, what is the expected cash inflow for year 3?

2. Lukow Products is investigating the purchase of a piece of automated equipment that will save $400,000 each year in direct labor and inventory carrying costs. This equipment costs $2,500,000 and is expected to have a 15-year useful life with no salvage value. The company requires a minimum 20 percent return on all equipment purchases. Management anticipates that this equipment will provide certain intangible benefits such as greater flexibility, higher quality of output, and a positive learning experience in automation. What dollar value per year would management have to attach to these intangible benefits in order to make the equipment an acceptable investment?

3. The Matchless Dating Service has made an investment in video and recording equipment that cost $106,700. The equipment is expected to generate cash inflows of $20,000 per year. How many years will the equipment have to be used in order to provide the company with a 10 percent rate of return on its investment?

E14–10   Nick's Novelties, Inc., is considering the purchase of electronic pinball machines to place in amusement houses. The machines would cost a total of $300,000, have an eight-year useful life, and have a total salvage value of $20,000. Based on experience with other equipment, the company estimates that annual revenues and expenses associated with the machines would be as follows:

Revenues from use		$200,000
Less operating expenses:		
Commissions to amusement houses	$100,000	
Insurance	7,000	
Depreciation	35,000	
Maintenance	18,000	160,000
Net income		$ 40,000

Required 1. Assume that Nick's Novelties, Inc., will not purchase new equipment unless it provides a payback period of four years or less. Would you recommend purchase of the pinball machines?

2. Compute the simple rate of return promised by the pinball machines (compute the investment at initial cost). If the company's before-tax cost of capital is 12 percent, would you recommend that the pinball machines be purchased?

E14–11   A piece of laborsaving equipment has just come onto the market that Meriweather Company could use to reduce costs in one of its plants. Relevant data relating to the equipment follow:

Purchase cost of the equipment	$432,000
Annual cost savings that will be	
provided by the equipment	90,000
Life of the equipment	12 years
Cost of capital	14%

Required 1. Compute the payback period for the equipment. If the company requires a payback period of four years or less, would you recommend purchase of the equipment? Explain.

2. Compute the simple rate of return on the equipment. Use straight-line depreciation based on the equipment's useful life. Would you recommend that the equipment be purchased? Explain.

PROBLEMS

P14–12   Basic Net Present Value Analysis   The Sweetwater Candy Company would like to buy a new machine that would automatically "dip" chocolates as they are formed in the production process. The "dipping" operation is currently done largely by hand. The machine the company is considering costs $120,000. The manufacturer estimates that the machine would be usable for 12 years but would require the replacement of several key parts at the end of the sixth year. These parts would cost $9,000, including installation. After 12 years, the machine could be sold for about $7,500.

The company estimates that the cost to operate the machine will be only $7,000 per year. The present method of dipping chocolates costs $30,000 per year. In addition to reducing costs, the new machine will increase production by 6,000 boxes of chocolates per year. The company realizes a contribution margin of $1.50 per box. A 20 percent rate of return is required on all investments.

1. What are the net annual cash inflows that will be provided by the new dipping machine?
2. Compute the new machine's net present value. Use the incremental cost approach, and round all dollar amounts to the nearest whole dollar.

Required (ignore income taxes)

Basic Net Present Value Analysis   Dayton Mines, Inc., is contemplating the purchase of equipment to exploit a mineral deposit that is located on land to which the company has mineral rights. An engineering and cost analysis has been made, and it is expected that the following cash flows would be associated with opening and operating a mine in the area:

P14–13

Cost of new equipment and timbers	$275,000
Working capital required	100,000
Net annual cash receipts	120,000*
Cost to construct new roads in three years	40,000
Salvage value of equipment in four years	65,000

* Receipts from sales of ore, less out-of-pocket costs for salaries, utilities, insurance, and so forth.

It is estimated that the mineral deposit would be exhausted after four years of mining. At that point, the working capital would be released for reinvestment elsewhere. The company's cost of capital is 20 percent.

Determine the net present value of the proposed mining project. Should the project be undertaken? Explain.

Required (ignore income taxes)

Time-Adjusted Rate of Return; Sensitivity Analysis   Big Piney Lumber Company is investigating the purchase of a new laser saw that has just come onto the market. It would cost $300,000 but would save $40,000 per year in operating costs (primarily through less waste and reduced labor costs). If the new saw were purchased, present equipment could be sold to another mill for $65,000. The manufacturer estimates that the laser saw would have a service life of 12 years.

P14–14

1. What would be the net initial (incremental) cost of the new saw for capital budgeting purposes?
2. Using the investment cost figure computed in (1) above, compute the time-adjusted rate of return on the new saw. Interpolate, and round your answer to the nearest tenth of a percent.
3. Since laser saws have just come onto the market, Big Piney's management is unsure about the estimated 12-year life. Compute what the time-adjusted rate of return would be if the useful life of the new saw were (a) 9 years and (b) 15 years, instead of 12 years. Again interpolate, and round your answer to the nearest tenth of a percent.
4. Refer to the original data. Technology in the laser saw industry is moving so rapidly that management may not want to keep the new saw for more than six years. If the new saw were disposed of at the end of six years, it would have a salvage value of $107,800.
   a. Again using the investment figure computed in (1) above, compute the time-adjusted rate of return to the nearest *whole* percent. (Hint: A useful way to

Required (ignore income taxes)

proceed is to find the discount rate that will cause the net present value to be equal to, or near, zero.)

b. If the company's cost of capital is 10 percent, would you recommend purchase? Explain.

P14–15   **Net Present Value Analysis; FMS/Automation Decision**   "I'm not sure we should lay out $500,000 for that automated welding machine," said Jim Alder, president of the Superior Equipment Company. "That's a lot of money, and it would cost us $80,000 for software and installation, and another $3,000 every month just to maintain the thing. In addition, the manufacturer admits that it would cost $45,000 more at the end of seven years to replace worn out parts."

"I admit it's a lot of money," said Franci Rogers, the controller. "But you know the turnover problem we've had with the welding crew. This machine would replace six welders at a cost savings of $108,000 per year. And we would save another $6,500 per year in reduced material waste. When you figure that the automated welder would last for 12 years, that adds up to a pile of savings. I'm sure the return would be greater than our 16 percent cost of capital."

"I'm still not convinced," countered Mr. Alder. "We can only get $12,000 scrap value out of our old welding equipment if we sell it now, and all that new machine will be worth in 12 years is $20,000 for parts. But have your people work up the figures and we'll talk about them at the executive committee meeting tomorrow."

Required (ignore income taxes)

1. Compute the net annual cost savings promised by the automated welding machine.
2. Using the data from (1) above and other data from the problem, compute the automated welding machine's net present value. (Use the incremental-cost approach.) Would you recommend purchase? Explain.
3. Assume that management can identify several intangible benefits associated with the automated welding machine, including greater flexibility in shifting from one type of product to another, improved quality of output, and faster delivery as a result of reduced throughput time. What dollar value per year would management have to attach to these intangible benefits in order to make the new welding machine an acceptable investment?

P14–16   **Simple Rate of Return; Payback**   Paul Swanson has an opportunity to acquire a franchise from The Yogurt Place, Inc., to dispense frozen yogurt products under The Yogurt Place name. Mr. Swanson has assembled the following information relating to the franchise:

a. A suitable location in a large shopping mall can be rented for $3,500 per month.
b. Remodeling and necessary equipment would cost $270,000. The equipment would have an estimated 15-year life and an estimated $18,000 salvage value. Straight-line depreciation would be used, and salvage value would be considered in computing depreciation deductions.
c. Based on similar outlets elsewhere, Mr. Swanson estimates that sales would total $300,000 per year. Ingredients would cost 20 percent of sales.
d. Operating costs would include $70,000 per year for salaries, $3,500 per year for insurance, and $27,000 per year for utilities. In addition, Mr. Swanson would have to pay a commission to The Yogurt Place, Inc., of 12.5 percent of sales.

Rather than obtain the franchise, Mr. Swanson could invest his funds in long-term corporate bonds that would yield a 12 percent annual return.

Required (ignore income taxes)

1. Prepare an income statement that shows the expected net income each year from the franchise outlet. Use the contribution format.
2. Compute the simple rate of return promised by the outlet. Based on this return, should it be opened?
3. Compute the payback period on the outlet. If Mr. Swanson wants a payback of four years or less, should the outlet be opened?

Opening a Small Business; Net Present Value   In eight years, Kent Duncan will retire. He has $150,000 to invest, and he is exploring the possibility of opening a self-service auto wash. The auto wash could be managed in the free time he has available from his regular occupation, and it could be closed easily when he retires. After careful study, Mr. Duncan has determined the following:

P14–17

a.   A building in which an auto wash could be installed is available under an eight-year lease at a cost of $1,700 per month.

b.   Purchase and installation costs of equipment would total $150,000. In eight years the equipment could be sold for about 10 percent of its original cost.

c.   An investment of an additional $2,000 would be required to cover working capital needs for cleaning supplies, change funds, and so forth. After eight years, this working capital would be released for investment elsewhere.

d.   Both an auto wash and a vacuum service would be offered, with a wash costing $1.50 and the vacuum costing 25 cents per use.

e.   The only variable costs associated with the operation would be 23 cents per wash for water and 10 cents per use of the vacuum for electricity.

f.   In addition to rent, monthly costs of operation would be: cleaning, $450; insurance, $75; and maintenance, $500.

g.   Gross receipts from the auto wash would be about $1,350 per week. According to the experience of other auto washes, 70 percent of the customers using the wash would also use the vacuum.

Mr. Duncan will not open the auto wash unless it provides at least a 10 percent return, since this is the amount that could be earned by simply placing the $150,000 in high-grade securities.

1.   Assuming that the auto wash will be open 52 weeks a year, compute the expected net annual cash receipts (gross cash receipts less cash disbursements) from its operation. (Do not include the cost of the equipment, the working capital, or the salvage value in these computations.)

2.   Would you advise Mr. Duncan to open the car wash? Show computations using the net present value method of investment analysis. Round all dollar figures to the nearest whole dollar.

Required (ignore income taxes)

Time-Adjusted Rate of Return; Sensitivity Analysis   "In my opinion, a tanning salon would be a natural addition to our spa and very popular with our customers," said Stacey Winder, manager of the Lifeline Spa. "Our figures show that we could remodel the building next door to our spa and install all of the necessary equipment for $330,000. I have contacted tanning salons in other areas, and I am told that the tanning beds will be usable for about nine years. I am also told that a four-bed salon such as we are planning would generate a cash inflow of about $80,000 per year after all expenses."

P14–18

"It does sound very appealing," replied Kevin Leblanc, the spa's accountant. "Let me push the numbers around a bit and see what kind of a return the salon would generate."

1.   Compute the time-adjusted rate of return promised by the tanning salon. Interpolate to the nearest tenth of a percent.

2.   Assume that Ms. Winder will not open the salon unless it promises a return of at least 14 percent. Compute the amount of annual cash inflow that would provide this return on the $330,000 investment.

3.   Although nine years is the average life of tanning salon equipment, Ms. Winder has found that this life can vary substantially. Compute the time-adjusted rate of return if the life were (a) 6 years, and (b) 12 years, rather than 9 years. Interpolate to the nearest tenth of a percent. Is there any information provided by these computations that you would be particularly anxious to show Ms. Winder?

4.   Ms. Winder has also found that although $80,000 is an average cash inflow from a four-bed salon, some salons vary as much as 20 percent from this figure. Compute the time-adjusted rate of return if the annual cash inflows were (a) 20 percent less, and (b) 20 percent greater, than $80,000. Interpolate to the nearest tenth of a percent.

Required (ignore income taxes)

5. Assume that the $330,000 investment is made and that the salon is opened as planned. Because of concerns about the effects of excessive tanning, however, the salon is not able to attract as many customers as planned. Cash inflows are only $50,000 per year, and after eight years the salon equipment is sold to a competitor for $135,440. Compute the time-adjusted rate of return (to the nearest *whole* percent) earned on the investment over the eight-year period. (Hint: A useful way to proceed is to find the discount rate that will cause the net present value to be equal to, or near, zero.)

P14–19 **Simple Rate of Return; Payback**   Sharkey's Fun Center contains a number of electronic games as well as a miniature golf course and various rides located outside the building. Paul Sharkey, the owner, would like to construct a water slide on one portion of his property. Mr. Sharkey has gathered the following information about the slide:

a. Water slide equipment could be purchased and installed at a cost of $330,000. According to the manufacturer, the slide would be usable for 12 years after which it would have little or no salvage value.
b. Mr. Sharkey would use straight-line depreciation on the slide equipment.
c. In order to make room for the water slide, several rides would be dismantled and sold. These rides are fully depreciated, but they could be sold for $60,000 to an amusement park in a nearby city.
d. Mr. Sharkey has concluded that about 50,000 more people would use the water slide each year than have been using the rides. The admission price would be $3.60 per person (the same price that the Fun Center has been charging for the rides).
e. Based on experience at other water slides, Mr. Sharkey estimates that incremental operating expenses each year for the slide would be: salaries, $85,000; insurance, $4,200; utilities, $13,000; and maintenance, $9,800.
f. The before-tax cost of capital for Sharkey's Fun Center is 14 percent.

Required (ignore income taxes)

1. Prepare an income statement showing the expected net income each year from the water slide.
2. Compute the simple rate of return expected from the water slide. Based on this computation, should the water slide be constructed?
3. Compute the payback period for the water slide. If Mr. Sharkey requires a payback period of five years or less, should the water slide be constructed?

P14–20 **Replacement Decision**   Redwing Freightlines, Inc., has a small truck that it uses for intracity deliveries. The truck is in bad repair and must be either overhauled or replaced with a new truck. The company has assembled the following information:

	Present Truck	New Truck
Purchase cost new.	$21,000	$30,000
Remaining book value	11,500	—
Overhaul needed now	7,000	—
Annual cash operating costs	10,000	6,500
Salvage value—now	9,000	—
Salvage value—eight years from now . . .	1,000	4,000

If the company keeps and overhauls its present delivery truck, then the truck will be usable for eight more years. If a new truck is purchased, it will be used for eight years, after which it will be traded in on another truck. The new truck would be diesel-operated, resulting in a substantial reduction in annual operating costs, as shown above.

The company computes depreciation on a straight-line basis. All investment projects are evaluated on a basis of a 16 percent before-tax rate of return.

Required (ignore income taxes)

1. Should Redwing Freightlines, Inc., keep the old truck or purchase the new one? Use the total-cost approach to net present value in making your decision. Round to the nearest whole dollar.
2. Redo (1) above, this time using the incremental-cost approach.

Net Present Value Analysis of Securities   In late 19x1, Linda Clark received $175,000   **P14–21**
from her mother's estate. She placed the funds into the hands of a broker, who purchased
the following securities on Linda's behalf:

a. Common stock was purchased at a cost of $95,000. The stock paid no dividends, but it
    was sold for $160,000 at the end of three years.
b. Preferred stock was purchased at its par value of $30,000. The stock paid a 6 percent
    dividend (based on par value) each year for three years. At the end of three years, the
    stock was sold for $27,000.
c. Bonds were purchased at a cost of $50,000. The bonds paid $3,000 in interest every six
    months. After three years, the bonds were sold for $52,700. (Note: In discounting a
    cash flow that occurs semiannually, the procedure is to halve the discount rate and
    double the number of periods. Use the same procedure in discounting the proceeds
    from the sale.)

The securities were all sold at the end of three years so that Linda would have funds
available to open a new business venture. The broker stated that the investments had
earned more than a 16 percent return, and he gave Linda the following computation to
support his statement:

Common stock:	
Gain on sale ($160,000 − $95,000)	$65,000
Preferred stock:	
Dividends paid (6% × $30,000 × 3 years).	5,400
Loss on sale ($27,000 − $30,000).	(3,000)
Bonds:	
Interest paid ($3,000 × 6 periods)	18,000
Gain on sale ($52,700 − $50,000).	2,700
Net gain on all investments	$88,100

$$\frac{\$88,100 \div 3 \text{ years}}{\$175,000} = 16.8\%$$

*Required (ignore income
taxes)*

1. Using a 16 percent discount rate, compute the net present value of *each* of the three
    investments. On which investment(s) did Linda earn a 16 percent rate of return?
    (Round computations to the nearest whole dollar.)
2. Considering all three investments together, did Linda earn a 16 percent rate of return?
    Explain.
3. Linda wants to use the $239,700 proceeds ($160,000 + $27,000 + $52,700 = $239,700)
    from sale of the securities to open a retail store under a 12-year franchise contract.
    What net annual cash inflow must the store generate in order for Linda to earn a 14
    percent return over the 12-year period? (Round computations to the nearest whole
    dollar.)

Simple Rate of Return; Payback; Time-Adjusted Rate of Return   Honest John's Used   **P14–22**
Cars, Inc., has always hired students from the local university to wash the cars on the lot.
Honest John is considering the purchase of an automatic car wash that would be used in
place of the students. The following information has been gathered by Honest John's
accountant in order to help Honest John make a decision on the purchase:

a. Payments to students for washing cars total $15,000 per year at present.
b. The car wash would cost $21,000 installed, and it would have a ten-year useful life.
    Honest John uses straight-line depreciation on all assets. The car wash would have a
    negligible salvage value in 10 years.
c. Annual out-of-pocket costs associated with the car wash would be: wages of students
    to operate the wash, keep the soap bin full, and so forth, $6,300; utilities, $1,800; and
    insurance and maintenance, $900.
d. Honest John now earns a return of 20 percent before taxes on the funds invested in his

inventory of used cars. He feels that he would have to earn an equivalent rate on the car wash in order for the purchase to be attractive.

Required (ignore income taxes)

1. Determine the annual savings that would be realized in cash operating costs if the car wash were purchased.
2. Compute the simple rate of return promised by the car wash. (Hint: Note that this is a cost reduction project.) Based on the simple rate of return, should the car wash be purchased?
3. Compute the payback period on the car wash. Honest John (who has a reputation for being somewhat of a nickel-nurser) will not purchase any equipment unless it has a payback of four years or less. Should the car wash be purchased?
4. Compute (to the nearest whole percent) the time-adjusted rate of return promised by the car wash. Based on this computation, does it appear that the simple rate of return would normally be an accurate guide in investment decisions?

P14–23 **Net Present Value; Automated Equipment; Postaudit**   Saxon Products, Inc., is investigating the purchase of a robot for use on the company's assembly line. Selected data relating to the robot are provided below:

Cost of the robot	$1,800,000
Installation and software.	900,000
Annual savings in labor costs.	?
Annual savings in inventory carrying costs.	210,000
Monthly increase in power and maintenance costs	2,500
Salvage value in 10 years	70,000
Useful life	10 years

Engineering studies suggest that use of the robot will result in a savings of 50,000 direct labor-hours each year. The labor rate is $8 per hour. Also, the smoother work flow made possible by the use of automation will allow the company to reduce the amount of inventory on hand by $400,000. This inventory reduction will take place in the first year of operation; the released funds will be available for use elsewhere in the company. Saxon Products requires a 20 percent return on all purchases of equipment.

Shelly Martins, the controller, has noted that all of Saxon's competitors are automating their plants. She is pessimistic, however, about whether Saxon's management will allow it to automate. In preparing the proposal for the robot, she stated to a colleague, "Let's just hope that reduced labor and inventory costs can justify the purchase of this automated equipment. Otherwise, we'll never get it. You know how the president feels about equipment paying for itself out of reduced costs."

Required (ignore income taxes)

1. Determine the net *annual* cost savings if the robot is purchased. (Do not include the $400,000 inventory reduction or the salvage value in this computation.)
2. Compute the net present value of the proposed investment in the robot. Based on these data, would you recommend that the robot be purchased? Explain.
3. Assume that the robot is purchased. At the end of the first year, Shelly Martins has found that some items didn't work out as planned. Software and installation costs were $75,000 more than estimated, due to unforeseen problems; and direct labor has been reduced by only 45,000 hours per year, rather than by 50,000 hours. Assuming that all other items of cost data were accurate, does it appear that the company made a wise investment? Show computations, using the net present value format as in (2) above. (Hint: It might be helpful to place yourself back at the beginning of the first year, with the new data.)
4. Upon seeing your analysis in (3) above, Saxon's president stated, "That robot is the worst investment we've ever made. And now we'll be stuck with it for years."
   a. Explain to the president what benefits other than cost savings might accrue from use of the new automated equipment.
   b. Compute for the president the dollar amount of cash inflow that would be needed each year from the benefits in (a) above in order for the automated equipment to yield a 20 percent rate of return.

Lease or Buy Decision   The Riteway Ad Agency provides cars for its sales staff. In the past, the company has always purchased its cars outright from a dealer and then sold the cars after three years' use. The company's present fleet of cars is three years old and will be sold very shortly. In order to provide a replacement fleet, the company is considering two alternatives:

> *Alternative 1.* The company can purchase the cars outright, as in the past, and sell the cars after three years' use. Twenty cars will be needed, which can be purchased at a discounted price of $8,500 each. If this alternative is accepted, the following costs will be incurred on the fleet as a whole:

Annual cost of servicing, taxes, and licensing.	$3,000
Repairs, first year	1,500
Repairs, second year	4,000
Repairs, third year	6,000

> At the end of three years, the fleet could be sold for about one half of the original purchase price.

> *Alternative 2.* The company can lease the cars under a three-year lease contract. The lease cost would be $55,000 per year (the first payment due in year 1). As part of this lease cost, the owner would provide all servicing and repairs, license the cars, and pay all taxes. Riteway would be required to make a $10,000 security deposit at the beginning of the lease period, which would be refunded when the cars were returned to the owner at the end of the lease contract.

1. Assume that the Riteway Ad Agency has an 18 percent cost of capital. Use the total-cost approach to determine the present value of the cash flows associated with each alternative. (Round all dollar amounts to the nearest whole dollar.) Which alternative should the company accept?
2. Using the data in (1) and other data as needed, explain why it is often less costly for a company to lease equipment and facilities rather than to buy them.

Required (ignore income taxes)

Simple Rate of Return; Payback; Time-Adjusted Rate of Return   The Elberta Fruit Farm has always hired transient workers to pick its annual cherry crop. Francie Wright, the farm manager, has just received information on a cherry picking machine that is being purchased by many fruit farms. The machine is a motorized device that shakes the cherry tree, causing the cherries to fall onto plastic tarps that funnel the cherries into bins. Ms. Wright has gathered the following information in order to decide whether a cherry picker would be a profitable investment for the Elberta Fruit Farm:

a. At present, the farm is paying an average of $40,000 per year to transient workers to pick the cherries.
b. The cherry picker would cost $94,500, and it would have an estimated 12-year useful life. The farm uses straight-line depreciation on all assets and considers salvage value in computing depreciation deductions. The estimated salvage value of the cherry picker is $4,500.
c. Annual out-of-pocket costs associated with the cherry picker would be: cost of an operator and an assistant, $14,000; insurance, $200; fuel, $1,800; and a maintenance contract, $3,000.
d. The Elberta Fruit Farm now earns a return of 16 percent before taxes on its investment in orchard properties. Ms. Wright feels that the farm would have to earn an equivalent return on the cherry picker in order to justify the purchase.

1. Determine the annual savings in cash operating costs that would be realized if the cherry picker were purchased.
2. Compute the simple rate of return expected from the cherry picker. (Hint: Note that this is a cost reduction project.) Based on the simple rate of return, should the cherry picker be purchased?

Required (ignore income taxes)

3. Compute the payback period on the cherry picker. The Elberta Fruit Farm will not purchase equipment unless it has a payback period of five years or less. Should the cherry picker be purchased?

4. Compute (to the nearest whole percent) the time-adjusted rate of return promised by the cherry picker. Based on this computation, does it appear that the simple rate of return would normally be an accurate guide in investment decisions?

P14–26 **Net Present Value; FMS/Automated Equipment; Postaudit**   "I know that $1.9 million sounds like a lot of money," said Jana Bywater, operations manager for Darrow Products. "But that new automated equipment would let us create three cells in the Ogden plant and turn its assembly line into a state-of-the-art flexible manufacturing system."

"It doesn't just *sound* like a lot of money," replied Dan Carmack, the company's president. "It *is* a lot of money. And you seem to be forgetting that software and installation will cost another $750,000. But the key question is whether or not this equipment will pay for itself in labor savings. If it doesn't, then I'm not interested."

"The people in engineering figure that we'll need 40 less people a year on the assembly line," replied Jana. "And insurance, storage, and other inventory carrying costs will be reduced by $80,000 per year, since we will have less inventory on hand. In fact, the controller's office estimates that with the smoother flow and greater dependability of the FMS our inventory will be reduced by a half of a million dollars by the end of the first year."

"You operations people are eternal optimists," said Dan. "The savings in inventory carrying costs will be more than eaten up by increased maintenance and by the extra power that those robots will gobble up. In fact, the manufacturer admits that these increased costs will come to at least $240,000 a year. By the way, how much would we get out of our old equipment?"

"Only about $20,000," replied Jana, "because it's so obsolete. But the new automated equipment won't do much better. Right now technology is moving so fast that in 15 years it will be worth only about $70,000."

"I figure that sales will grow by 20 percent a year from our present $10 million level regardless of whether or not we buy the equipment," asserted Dan. "So that means the key is cost savings. Let's see, our assembly-line people work 40 hours a week, 50 weeks a year, and they're paid $7 per hour. If the new equipment has a 15-year useful life, like the manufacturer says, see how it stacks up against our 16 percent cost of capital."

Required (ignore income taxes)

1. Compute the net annual cost savings that will be provided by the new equipment.
2. Use the incremental-cost approach to determine the net present value of the new equipment. Based on these data, should the equipment be purchased?
3. Assume that the new equipment is purchased. Due to unforeseen problems, installation costs are $130,000 greater than estimated. Also, at the end of the first year Dan Carmack is surprised to learn that only 35 people have been replaced on the assembly line, and he has requested that a postaudit be performed on the new equipment. Assuming that all other items of data were accurate, does it appear that the company made a wise investment? Show computations, using the net present value format, as in (2) above. (Hint: It might be helpful to place yourself back at the beginning of the first year, with the new data.)
4. Upon seeing your analysis in (3) above, Dan Carmack exclaims, "I said that labor savings was the key to this equipment, and I was right! We've never made a worse investment! I don't foresee a single benefit, and I'm amazed that our competitors are making the same mistake."
   a. Explain to the president what benefits other than cost savings might accrue from use of automated equipment.
   b. Compute for the president the dollar amount of cash inflow that would be needed each year from the benefits in (a) above in order for the equipment to yield a 16 percent rate of return.

Lease or Buy Decision   Flamingo Auto Parts, Inc., operates a chain of auto supply stores in the Midwest. The company plans to open a new store soon in a rapidly growing area, and an excellent site has been located for construction of a building. Flamingo Auto Parts has two alternatives as to how the desired site can be acquired, the building constructed, and needed fixtures obtained for use in the store.

P14–27

> *Purchase alternative.* The company could purchase the building site, construct the building, and purchase store fixtures at a total cost of $750,000. This alternative would require the immediate payment of $300,000 and then a payment of $150,000 each year for the next four years (including interest). Flamingo Auto Parts estimates that the annual costs associated with the property would be:

Property taxes	$ 9,000
Insurance	3,000
Repairs and maintenance . . .	6,000
Total annual costs	$18,000

> The company would occupy the property for 15 years. Based on prior experience, it is estimated that the property would have a resale value of about $400,000 at the end of the 15-year period.

> *Lease alternative.* The Worldwide Insurance Company has offered to purchase the site, construct the building, and install fixtures to Flamingo Auto Parts' specifications. The insurance company would then lease the property back to Flamingo Auto Parts under a 15-year lease at an annual lease cost of $100,000. (The first payment would be due now, and the remaining payments would be due in years 1–14.) The insurance company would require a $15,000 security deposit immediately; this would be returned at the termination of the lease. Under the lease agreement, the insurance company would pay for the property taxes and insurance; thus, Flamingo Auto Parts would be required to pay only the repair and maintenance costs associated with the property.

Flamingo Auto Parts' cost of capital is 16 percent.

Using discounted cash flow, determine whether Flamingo Auto Parts, Inc., should lease or buy the desired store facilities. Use the total-cost approach.

Required (ignore income taxes)

Simple Rate of Return; Payback   Westwood Furniture Company is considering the purchase of two different items of equipment, as described below:

P14–28
Comprehensive Problem

> *Machine A.* A compacting machine has just come onto the market that would permit Westwood Furniture Company to compress sawdust into various shelving products. At present the sawdust is disposed of as a waste product. The following information is available on the machine:

> a. The machine would cost $420,000 and would have a 10 percent salvage value at the end of its 12-year useful life. The company uses straight-line depreciation and considers salvage value in computing depreciation deductions.

> b. The shelving products manufactured from use of the machine would generate revenues of $300,000 per year. Variable manufacturing costs would be 20 percent of sales.

> c. Fixed expenses associated with the new shelving products would be (per year): advertising, $40,000; salaries, $110,000; utilities, $5,200; and insurance, $800.

> *Machine B.* A second machine has come onto the market that would allow Westwood Furniture Company to automate a sanding process that is now done largely by hand. The following information is available:

> a. The new sanding machine would cost $234,000 and would have little or no salvage value at the end of its 13-year useful life. The company would use straight-line depreciation on the new machine.

b. Several old pieces of sanding equipment that are fully depreciated would be disposed of at a scrap value of $9,000.

c. The new sanding machine would provide substantial annual savings in cash operating costs. It would require an operator at an annual salary of $16,350 and $5,400 in annual maintenance costs. The current, hand-operated sanding procedure costs the company $78,000 per year in total.

Westwood Furniture Company requires a return of 15 percent on all equipment purchases. Also, the company will not purchase equipment unless the equipment has a payback period of 4.0 years or less.

Required (ignore income taxes)

1. For machine A:
   a. Prepare an income statement showing the expected net income each year from the new shelving products. Use the contribution format.
   b. Compute the simple rate of return.
   c. Compute the payback period.
2. For machine B:
   a. Compute the simple rate of return.
   b. Compute the payback period.
3. Which machine, if either, should the company purchase?

P14–29 **Rental Property Decision**   Raul Martinas, professor of languages at Eastern University, owns a small office building adjacent to the university campus. He acquired the property 10 years ago at a total cost of $530,000—$50,000 for the land and $480,000 for the building. He has just received an offer from a realty company that wants to purchase the property; however, the property has been a good source of income over the years, so Professor Martinas is unsure whether he should keep it or sell it. His alternatives are:

Keep the property. Professor Martinas' accountant has kept careful records of the income realized from the property over the past 10 years. These records indicate the following annual revenues and expenses:

Rental receipts.		$140,000
Less building expenses:		
Utilities	$25,000	
Depreciation of building	16,000	
Property taxes and insurance . . .	18,000	
Repairs and maintenance	9,000	
Custodial help and supplies	40,000	108,000
Net income		$ 32,000

Professor Martinas makes a $12,000 mortgage payment each year on the property. The mortgage will be paid off in eight more years. He has been depreciating the building by the straight-line method, assuming a salvage value of $80,000 for the building which he still thinks is an appropriate figure. He feels sure that the building can be rented for another 15 years. He also feels sure that 15 years from now the land will be worth three times what he paid for it.

Sell the property. A realty company has offered to purchase the property by paying $175,000 immediately and $26,500 per year for the next 15 years. Control of the property would go to the realty company immediately. In order to sell the property, Professor Martinas would need to pay the mortgage off, which could be done by making a lump-sum payment of $90,000.

Required (ignore income taxes)

Assume that Professor Martinas requires a 12 percent rate of return. Would you recommend he keep or sell the property? Show computations using discounted cash flow and the total-cost approach.

P14–30 **Net Present Value Analysis of a New Product Line**   Matheson Electronics has just developed a new electronic device which, when mounted on an automobile, will tell the driver how many miles the automobile is traveling per gallon of gasoline. The device can be mounted on any model or make of automobile in a few minutes' time, and with negligible cost.

The company is anxious to begin production of the new device. To this end, marketing and cost studies have been made to determine probable costs and market potential. These studies have provided the following information.

a. New equipment would have to be acquired in order to produce the device. The equipment would cost $315,000 and have a 12-year useful life. After 12 years, it would have a salvage value of about $15,000.
b. Sales in units over the next 12 years are projected to be as follows:

Year	Sales in Units
1	6,000
2	12,000
3	15,000
4–12	18,000

c. Production and sales of the device would require working capital of $60,000 in order to finance accounts receivable, inventories, and day-to-day cash needs. This working capital would be released at the end of the project's life.
d. The devices would sell for $35 each; variable costs for production, administration, and sales would be $15 per unit.
e. Fixed costs for salaries, maintenance, property taxes, insurance, and straight-line depreciation on the equipment would total $135,000 per year. (Depreciation is based on cost less salvage value.)
f. In order to gain rapid entry into the market, the company would have to advertise heavily. The advertising program would be:

Year	Amount of Yearly Advertising
1–2	$180,000
3	150,000
4–12	120,000

g. Matheson Electronics' board of directors has specified that all new product lines must promise a return of at least 14 percent in order to be acceptable.

Required (ignore income taxes)

1. Compute the net cash inflow (cash receipts less yearly cash operating expenses) anticipated from sale of the device for each year over the next 12 years.
2. Using the data computed in (1) above and other data provided in the problem, determine the net present value of the proposed investment. Would you recommend that Matheson accept the device as a new product line?

CASES

Expansion Decision; Net Present Value; Postaudit of a Project   Romano's Pizzas, Inc., operates pizza shops in several states. One of the company's most profitable shops is located adjacent to the campus of a large university. A small bakery next to the shop has just gone out of business, and Romano's Pizzas has an opportunity to least the vacated space for $18,000 per year under a 15-year lease. Romano's management is considering two ways in which the available space might be used.

C14–31

Alternative 1. The pizza shop in this location is currently selling 40,000 pizzas per year. Management is confident that sales could be increased by 75 percent by taking out the wall between the pizza shop and the vacant space and expanding the pizza outlet. Costs for remodeling and for new equipment would be $550,000. Management estimates that 20 percent of the new sales would be small pizzas, 50 percent would be medium pizzas, and 30 percent would be large pizzas. Selling prices and costs for ingredients for the three sizes of pizzas follow (per pizza):

	Selling Price	Cost of Ingredients
Small	$ 6.70	$1.30
Medium	8.90	2.40
Large	11.00	3.10

An additional $7,500 of working capital would be needed to carry the larger volume of business. This working capital would be released at the end of the lease term. The equipment would have a salvage value of $30,000 in 15 years, when the lease ended.

Alternative 2. Romano's sales manager feels that the company needs to diversify its operations. He has suggested that an opening be cut in the wall between the pizza shop and the vacant space and that video games be placed in the space, along with a small snack bar. Costs for remodeling and for the snack bar facilities would be $290,000. The games would be leased from a large distributor of such equipment. The distributor has stated that based on the use of game centers elsewhere, Romano's could expect about 26,000 people to use the center each year and to spend an average of $5 each on the machines. In addition, it is estimated that the snack bar would provide a net cash inflow of $15,000 per year. An investment of $4,000 in working capital would be needed to provide change funds and to provide inventory for the snack bar. This working capital investment would be released at the end of the lease term. The snack bar equipment would have a salvage value of about $12,000 in 15 years.

Romano's management is unsure which alternative to select and has asked you to help in making the decision. You have gathered the following information relating to added costs that would be incurred each year under the two alternatives:

	Expand the Pizza Shop	Install the Game Center
Rent—building space	$18,000	$18,000
Rent—video games	—	30,000
Salaries	54,000	17,000
Utilities	13,200	5,400
Insurance and other	7,800	9,600

Required (ignore income taxes)

1. Compute the expected net *annual* cash inflow from each alternative (cash receipts from sales and games less related cash expenses). Do *not* include present sales from the pizza shop in the computation.

2. Assume that the company's cost of capital is 16 percent. Compute the net present value of each alternative. (Use the total-cost approach, and round all dollar amounts to the nearest whole dollar.) Which alternative would you recommend?

3. Assume that the company decides to accept alternative 2. At the end of the first year, the company finds that only 21,000 people used the game center during the year (each person spent $5 on games). Also the snack bar provided a net cash inflow of only $13,000. In light of this information, does it appear that the game center will provide the company's 16 percent required rate of return? Show computations to support your answer. (Hint: It might be useful to go back to the beginning of the first year under alternative 2, with the new information.)

4. The sales manager has suggested that an advertising program be initiated to draw another 5,000 people into the game center each year. Assuming that another 5,000 people can be attracted into the center and that the snack bar receipts increase to the

level originally estimated, how much can be spent on advertising each year and still allow the game center to provide a 16 percent rate of return?

Equipment Acquisition; Uneven Cash Flows   Kingsley Products, Ltd., is using a single model 400 shaping machine in the manufacture of one of its products. The company is expecting to have a large increase in demand for the product and is anxious to expand its productive capacity. Two possibilities are under consideration:

C14–32

> *Alternative 1.* Purchase another model 400 shaping machine to operate along with the currently owned model 400 machine.
>
> *Alternative 2.* Purchase a model 800 shaping machine and use the currently owned model 400 machine as standby equipment. The model 800 machine is a high-speed unit with double the capacity of the model 400 machine.

The following additional information is available on the two alternatives:

a. Both the model 400 machine and the model 800 machine have a 10-year life from the time they are first used in production. The scrap value of both machines is nominal and can be ignored. Straight-line depreciation is used.

b. The cost of a new model 800 machine is $300,000.

c. The model 400 machine now in use cost $160,000 three years ago. Its present book value is $112,000, and its present market value is $90,000.

d. A new model 400 machine costs $170,000 now. If the company decides not to buy the model 800 machine, then the currently owned model 400 machine will have to be replaced in seven years at a cost of $200,000. The replacement machine will have a market value of about $140,000 when it is three years old.

e. Production over the next 10 years is expected to be:

Year	Production in Units
1	40,000
2	60,000
3	80,000
4–10	90,000

f. The two models of machines are not equally efficient in output. Comparative variable costs per unit are:

	Model	
	400	**800**
Materials per unit	$0.25	$0.40
Direct labor per unit	0.49	0.16
Supplies and lubricants per unit	0.06	0.04
Total variable cost per unit	$0.80	$0.60

g. The model 400 machine is less costly to maintain than the model 800 machine. Annual repairs and maintenance costs on a single model 400 machine are $2,500.

h. Repairs and maintenance costs on a model 800 machine, with a model 400 machine used as standby, would total $3,800 per year.

i. No other factory costs will change as a result of the decision between the two machines.

j. Kingsley Products requires a before-tax rate of return of 20 percent on all investments.

1. Which alternative should the company choose? Show computations using discounted cash flow.

2. Suppose that the cost of labor increases by 10 percent. Would this make the model 800 machine more or less desirable? Explain. No computations are needed.

Required (ignore income taxes)

3. Suppose that the cost of materials doubles. Would this make the model 800 machine more or less desirable? Explain. No computations are needed.

C14–33   **Lease or Buy Decision**   Top-Quality Stores, Inc., owns a nationwide chain of supermarkets. The company is going to open another store soon, and a suitable building site has been located in an attractive and rapidly growing area. In discussing how the company can acquire the desired building and other facilities needed to open the new store, Sam Watkins, the company's vice president in charge of sales, stated, "I know most of our competitors are starting to lease facilities, rather than buy, but I just can't see the economics of it. Our development people tell me that we can buy the building site, put a building on it, and get all the store fixtures we need for just $850,000. They also say that property taxes, insurance, and repairs would run $20,000 a year. When you figure that we plan to keep a site for 18 years, that's a total cost of $1,210,000. But then when you realize that the property will be worth at least a half million in 18 years, that's a net cost to us of only $710,000. What would it cost to lease the property?"

"I understand that Beneficial Insurance Company is willing to purchase the building site, construct a building and install fixtures to our specifications, and then lease the facility to us for 18 years at an annual lease payment of $120,000," replied Lisa Coleman, the company's executive vice president.

"That's just my point," said Sam. "At $120,000 a year, it would cost us a cool $2,160,000 over the 18 years. That's three times what it would cost to buy, and what would we have left at the end? Nothing! The building would belong to the insurance company!"

"You're overlooking a few things," replied Lisa. "For one thing, the treasurer's office says that we could only afford to put $350,000 down if we buy the property, and then we would have to pay the other $500,000 off over four years at $175,000 a year. So there would be some interest involved on the purchase side that you haven't figured in."

"But that little bit of interest is nothing compared to over 2 million bucks for leasing," said Sam. "Also, if we lease I understand we would have to put up an $8,000 security deposit that we wouldn't get back until the end. And besides that, we would still have to pay all the yearly repairs and maintenance costs just like we owned the property. No wonder those insurance companies are so rich, if they can swing deals like this."

"Well, I'll admit that I don't have all the figures sorted out yet," replied Lisa. "But I do have the operating cost breakdown for the building, which includes $7,500 annually for property taxes, $8,000 for insurance, and $4,500 for repairs and maintenance. If we lease, Beneficial will handle its own insurance costs and of course the owner will have to pay the property taxes. I'll put all this together and see if leasing makes any sense with our 16 percent cost of capital. The president wants a presentation and recommendation in the executive committee meeting tomorrow. Let's see, development said the first lease payment would be due now and the remaining ones due in years 1–17. Development also said that this store should generate a net cash inflow that's well above the average for our stores."

Required (ignore income taxes)

1. By means of discounted cash flow, determine whether Top-Quality Stores, Inc., should lease or buy the new facility. Assume that you will be making your presentation before the company's executive committee, and remember that the president detests sloppy, disorganized reports.

2. What reply will you make in the meeting if Sam Watkins brings up the issue of the building's future sales value?

C14–34   **CVP Analysis; Discounted Cash Flow**   Mercury Transit, Inc., has decided to inaugurate express bus service between its headquarters city and a nearby suburb (one-way fare, 50 cents) and is considering the purchase of either 32- or 52-passenger buses, on which pertinent estimates are as follows:

	32-Passenger Bus	52-Passenger Bus
Number of each to be purchased	6	4
Useful life	8 years	8 years
Purchase price of each bus (paid on delivery) . . .	$80,000	$110,000
Mileage per gallon	10	7½
Salvage value per bus	$ 6,000	$ 7,000
Drivers' hourly wage	3.50	4.20
Price per gallon of gasoline	1.50	1.50
Other annual cash expenses	52,000	47,000

During the four daily rush hours, all buses will be in service and all are expected to operate at full capacity (state law prohibits standees) in both directions of the route, each bus covering the route 12 times (six round trips) during the four-hour period. During the remaining 12 hours of the 16-hour day, 500 passengers would be carried and Mercury Transit would operate only four buses on the route. Part-time drivers would be employed to drive the extra hours during the rush hours. A bus traveling the route all day would go 480 miles each day, and one traveling only during rush hours would go 120 miles each day, during the 260-day year.

Required (ignore income taxes)

1. Prepare a schedule showing the computation of the estimated annual gross revenues from the new route for each alternative.
2. Prepare a schedule showing the computation of the estimated annual drivers' wages for each alternative.
3. Prepare a schedule showing the computation of the estimated annual cost of gasoline for each alternative.
4. Assume that your computations in (1), (2), and (3) above are as follows:

	32-Passenger Bus	52-Passenger Bus
Estimated annual revenues	$365,000	$390,000
Estimated annual drivers' wages	67,000	68,000
Estimated annual cost of gasoline	85,000	100,000

Assuming that a minimum rate of return of 14 percent before income taxes is desired and that all annual cash flows occur at the end of the year, determine whether the 32-passenger buses or the 52-passenger buses should be purchased. Use discounted cash flow and the total-cost approach.

(CPA, adapted)

Income taxes complicate financial decisions. Alternatives should be compared on an after-tax basis for the simple reason that after-tax cash flows are what really count. For example, the true cost of a tax-deductible item is not the dollars paid out, since the payment reduces the income taxes that must be paid. A complete analysis must take this tax effect into account.

Further Aspects of Investment Decisions

LEARNING OBJECTIVES

After studying Chapter 15, you should be able to:

1 Compute the after-tax cost of a tax-deductible cash expense and the after-tax benefit from a taxable cash receipt.

2 Explain how depreciation deductions are computed under the Modified Accelerated Cost Recovery System (MACRS).

3 Compute the tax savings arising from the depreciation tax shield, using both the MACRS tables and the optional straight-line method.

4 Compute the after-tax net present value of an investment proposal.

5 Rank investment projects in order of preference using (1) the time-adjusted rate of return method, and (2) the net present value method with the profitability index.

6 Define or explain the key terms listed at the end of the chapter.

W e continue our discussion of capital budgeting in this chapter by focusing on two new topics. First, we focus on income taxes and their impact on the capital budgeting decision. And second, we focus on methods of ranking competing capital investment projects according to their relative desirability.

INCOME TAXES AND CAPITAL BUDGETING

Objective 1
Compute the after-tax cost of a tax-deductible cash expense and the after-tax benefit from a taxable cash receipt.

In our discussion of capital budgeting in the preceding chapter, the matter of income taxes was omitted for two reasons. First, many organizations have no taxes to pay. Such organizations include schools, hospitals, and governmental units on local, state, and national levels. These organizations will always use capital budgeting techniques on a before-tax basis, as illustrated in the preceding chapter. Second, the topic of capital budgeting is somewhat complex, and it is best absorbed in small doses. Now that we have laid a solid groundwork in the concepts of present value and discounting, we can explore the effects of income taxes on capital budgeting decisions with little difficulty.

The Concept of After-Tax Cost

If someone were to ask you how much the rent is on your apartment, you would probably answer with the dollar amount that you pay out each month. If someone were to ask a business executive how much the rent is on a factory building, he or she might answer by stating a lesser figure than the dollar amount being paid out each month. The reason is that rent is a tax-deductible expense to a business firm, and expenses such as rent are often looked at on an *after-tax* basis rather than on a before-tax basis. The true cost of a tax-deductible item is not the dollars paid out; rather, it is the amount of net cash outflow that results *after* taking into consideration any reduction in income taxes that the payment will bring about. An expenditure net of its tax effect is known as **after-tax cost.**

After-tax cost is not a difficult concept. To illustrate the ideas behind it, assume that two companies, A and B, have sales of $850,000 and cash expenses of $700,000 each month. Thus, the two companies are identical except that Company A is now considering an advertising program that will cost $60,000 each month. The tax rate is 30 percent.[1] What will be the after-tax cost to Company A of the contemplated $60,000 monthly advertising expenditure? The computations needed to compute the after-tax cost figure are shown in Exhibit 15–1.

As shown in the exhibit, the after-tax cost of the advertising program would be only $42,000 per month. This figure, which is computed by finding the difference in net income between the two otherwise identical companies, represents the true cost of the advertising program to Company A. In effect, a $60,000 monthly advertising expenditure would *really* cost Company A only $42,000 *after taxes.*

---

[1] Under current tax law, the first $50,000 of corporate income is taxed at a 15 percent rate, the next $25,000 is taxed at a 25 percent rate, and any amount over $75,000 is taxed at a 34 percent rate. An additional 5 percent tax is levied on taxable income between $100,000 and $335,000. As a result of this additional tax, corporations with taxable income in excess of $335,000 effectively pay tax at a flat rate of 34 percent. These rates are subject to change; at the time of this writing a proposal was before Congress to raise the top corporate rate from 34 to 36 percent on taxable income above $10 million. When state income taxes are included in tax computations, the total tax bill can exceed 40 percent in some companies. For ease of computations, in this book we use an average, overall corporate tax rate of either 30 percent or 40 percent.

EXHIBIT 15–1

The Computation of
After-Tax Cost

	Company	
	A	**B**
Sales	$850,000	$850,000
Less expenses:		
Salaries, insurance, and other	700,000	700,000
New advertising program	60,000	—
Total expenses	760,000	700,000
Income before taxes	90,000	150,000
Income taxes (30%).	27,000	45,000
Net income	$ 63,000	$105,000
After-tax cost of the new advertising program ($105,000 − $63,000)		$42,000

A formula can be developed from these data that will give the after-tax cost of *any* tax-deductible cash expense.[2] The formula is:

$$(1 - \text{Tax rate}) \times \text{Cash expense} = \text{After-tax cost (net cash outflow)} \quad (1)$$

We can prove the accuracy of this formula by applying it to Company A's $60,000 advertising expenditure:

$$(1 - 0.30) \times \$60,000 = \$42,000 \text{ after-tax cost of the advertising program}$$

The concept of after-tax cost is very useful to the manager, since it measures the *actual* amount of cash that will be leaving a company as a result of an expenditure decision. As we now integrate income taxes into capital budgeting decisions, it will be necessary to place all cash expense items on an after-tax basis by applying the formula above.

The same reasoning applies to revenues and other *taxable* cash receipts. When a cash receipt occurs, the amount of cash inflow realized by an organization will be the amount that remains after taxes have been paid. The **after-tax benefit,** or net cash inflow, realized from a particular cash receipt can be obtained by applying a simple variation of the cash expenditure formula used above:

$$(1 - \text{Tax rate}) \times \text{Cash receipt} = \text{After-tax benefit (net cash inflow)} \quad (2)$$

We emphasize the term *taxable cash receipts* in our discussion because not all cash inflows are taxable. For example, the release of working capital at the termination of an investment project would not be a taxable cash inflow since it simply represents a return of original investment.

The Concept of Depreciation Tax Shield

The point was made in the preceding chapter that depreciation deductions in and of themselves do not involve cash flows. For this reason, depreciation deductions were ignored in Chapter 14 in all discounted cash flow computations.

Even though depreciation deductions do not involve cash flows, they have an impact on the amount of income taxes that a firm will pay, and income taxes *do* involve cash flows. Therefore, as we now integrate income taxes into capital budgeting decisions, it will be necessary to consider depreciation deductions to the extent that they affect tax payments.

---

[2] This formula assumes that a company is operating at a profit; if it is operating at a loss, then the after-tax cost of an item is simply the amount paid, since no tax benefits will be realized.

EXHIBIT 15–2

The Impact of Depreciation Deductions on Tax Payments—A Comparison of Cash Flows

Income Statements

	Company	
	X	**Y**
Sales.	$500,000	$500,000
Expenses:		
Cash operating expenses	310,000	310,000
Depreciation expense	90,000	—
Total.	400,000	310,000
Net income before taxes	100,000	190,000
Income taxes (30%)	30,000	57,000
Net income	$ 70,000	$133,000

Cash Flow Comparison

Cash inflow from operations:		
Net income, as above	$ 70,000	$133,000
Add: Noncash deduction for depreciation	90,000	—
Net cash inflow	$160,000	$133,000
Greater amount of cash available to Company X	$27,000	

A Cash Flow Comparison

To illustrate the effect of depreciation deductions on tax payments, let us compare two companies, X and Y. Both companies have annual sales of $500,000 and cash operating expenses of $310,000. In addition, Company X has a depreciable asset on which the depreciation deduction is $90,000 per year. The tax rate is 30 percent. A cash flow comparison of the two companies is given at the bottom of Exhibit 15–2.

Notice from the exhibit that Company X's net cash inflow exceeds Company Y's by $27,000. Also notice that in order to obtain Company X's net cash inflow, it is necessary to add the $90,000 depreciation deduction back to the company's net income. This step is necessary since depreciation is a noncash deduction on the income statement.

Exhibit 15–2 presents an interesting paradox. Notice that even though Company X's net cash inflow is $27,000 *greater* than Company Y's, its net income is much *lower* than Company Y's (only $70,000, as compared to Company Y's $133,000). The explanation for this paradox lies in the concept of the *depreciation tax shield*.

The Depreciation Tax Shield

Company X's greater net cash inflow comes about as a result of the *shield* against tax payments that is provided by depreciation deductions. Although depreciation deductions involve no outflows of cash, they are fully deductible in arriving at taxable income. In effect, depreciation deductions *shield* revenues from taxation and thereby *lower* the amount of taxes that a company must pay.

In the case of Company X, the $90,000 depreciation deduction involved no outflow of cash to the company. Yet this depreciation was fully deductible on the company's income statement and thereby *shielded* $90,000 in revenues from taxation. If the company did not have this depreciation deduction, its income taxes would have been $27,000 higher, since the entire $90,000 in shielded revenues would have been taxable at the regular tax rate of 30 percent (30 percent × $90,000 = $27,000). In effect, the depreciation tax shield *has reduced Company X's taxes by $27,000*, permitting these funds to be retained within the company rather than going to the tax collector. Viewed another way, we can say that

Item	Treatment
Cash expense*	Multiply by (1 − Tax rate) to get after-tax cost.
Cash receipt*.	Multiply by (1 − Tax rate) to get after-tax cash inflow.
Depreciation deduction	Multiply by the tax rate to get the tax savings from the depreciation tax shield.

EXHIBIT 15–3
Tax Adjustments
Required in a Capital
Budgeting Analysis

* When cash receipts and cash expenses recur *each year*, the expenses should be deducted from the receipts and only the difference should be multiplied by (1 − Tax rate). See the example at the top of Exhibit 15–7.

Company X has realized a $27,000 *cash inflow* (through reduced tax payments) as a result of its $90,000 depreciation deduction.

Because depreciation deductions shield revenues from taxation, they are generally referred to as a **depreciation tax shield.** The reduction in tax payments made possible by the depreciation tax shield will always be equal to the amount of the depreciation deduction taken, multiplied by the tax rate. The formula is:

Tax rate × Depreciation deduction
$$= \text{Tax savings from the depreciation tax shield} \qquad (3)$$

We can prove this formula by applying it to the $90,000 depreciation deduction taken by Company X in our example:

0.30 × $90,000 = $27,000 reduction in tax payments (shown as "Greater amount of cash available to Company X" in Exhibit 15–2)

As we now integrate income taxes into capital budgeting computations, it will be necessary to consider the impact of depreciation deductions on tax payments by showing the tax savings provided by the depreciation tax shield.

The concepts that we have introduced so far in this section and in the preceding section are not complex and can be mastered fairly quickly. To assist you in your study, a summary of these concepts is given in Exhibit 15–3.

Modified Accelerated Cost Recovery System

Historically, depreciation has been closely tied to the useful life of an asset, with year-by-year depreciation deductions typically computed by the straight-line method, the sum-of-the-years'-digits method, or the double-declining-balance method. Also, in computing depreciation deductions, companies have generally given recognition to an asset's expected salvage value by deducting the salvage value from the asset's cost and depreciating only the remainder. Although these concepts can still be used for computing depreciation deductions on financial statements, sweeping changes were made by Congress in 1981, and then modified somewhat by Congress in 1986, in the way that depreciation deductions are computed for tax purposes.

The new approach was named the **Accelerated Cost Recovery System (ACRS)** and, after modification in 1986, is now known as the **Modified Accelerated Cost Recovery System (MACRS).** MACRS largely abandons the concept of useful life and accelerates depreciation by placing all depreciable assets into one of eight property classes. Under MACRS, the only function of an asset's useful life is to determine the property class into which the asset should be placed. The various property classes under the MACRS rules are presented in Exhibit 15–4.

Objective 2
Explain how depreciation deductions are computed under the Modified Accelerated Cost Recovery System (MACRS).

EXHIBIT 15–4

MACRS Property Classes

MACRS Property Class and Depreciation Method	Useful Life of Assets Included in This Class	Examples of Assets Included in This Class
3-year property 200% declining balance	4 years or less	Most small tools are included; the law specifically *excludes* autos and light trucks from this property class.
5-year property 200% declining balance	More than 4 years to less than 10 years	Autos and light trucks, computers, typewriters, copiers, duplicating equipment, heavy general-purpose trucks, and research and experimentation equipment are included.
7-year property 200% declining balance	10 years or more to less than 16 years	Office furniture and fixtures, and most items of machinery and equipment used in production are included.
10-year property 200% declining balance	16 years or more to less than 20 years	Various machinery and equipment, such as that used in petroleum distilling and refining and in the milling of grain, are included.
15-year property 150% declining balance	20 years or more to less than 25 years	Sewage treatment plants, telephone and electrical distribution facilities, and land improvements are included.
20-year property 150% declining balance	25 years or more	Service stations and other real property with a useful life of less than 27.5 years are included.
27.5-year property Straight line	Not applicable	All residential rental property is included.
31.5-year property Straight line	Not applicable	All nonresidential real property is included.

Two key points should be noted about the data in Exhibit 15–4. First, each MACRS property class has a prescribed life. This is the life that must be used to depreciate any asset within that property class, regardless of the asset's actual useful life. Thus, an asset with a useful life of, say, 12 years, would be in the 7-year property class and would therefore be depreciated over 7 years rather than over 12 years. (Remember, the only function of an asset's useful life is to place it in the correct MACRS property class.) These property classes make it possible to depreciate assets over quite short periods of time. Office equipment, for example, typically has a useful life of 10 years or more, but it is in the MACRS 7-year property class. Therefore, the MACRS rules permit office equipment to be depreciated over a period equal to about 70 percent of its actual useful life. Similarly, an office building generally has a useful life of about 40 years, but it is depreciated over a 31.5-year period under MACRS.

Second, note from Exhibit 15–4 that the MACRS property classes utilize various depreciation methods and rates. To simplify depreciation computations, preset tables are available that show allowable depreciation deductions by year for each of the MACRS property classes. These tables are presented in Exhibit 15–5.[3]

---

[3] For ease of computations, percentage figures in the tables have been rounded to three decimal places (e.g., 33.3 percent for three-year property would be 0.333 in decimal form). Tables prepared by the Internal Revenue Service carry these computations to either four or five decimal places, depending on the property class (no official tables were provided by Congress in the Tax Reform Act). In preparing tax returns and other data for the Internal Revenue Service, the IRS tables should be used.

EXHIBIT 15–5

MACRS Depreciation
Tables by Property
Class

Year		Property Class					
	3-Year	5-Year	7-Year	10-Year	15-Year	20-Year
1.	33.3%	20.0%	14.3%	10.0%	5.0%	3.8%
2.	44.5	32.0	24.5	18.0	9.5	7.2
3.	14.8*	19.2	17.5	14.4	8.6	6.7
4.	7.4	11.5*	12.5	11.5	7.7	6.2
5.		11.5	8.9*	9.2	6.9	5.7
6.		5.8	8.9	7.4	6.2	5.3
7.			8.9	6.6*	5.9*	4.9
8.			4.5	6.6	5.9	4.5*
9.				6.5	5.9	4.5
10.				6.5	5.9	4.5
11.				3.3	5.9	4.5
12.					5.9	4.5
13.					5.9	4.5
14.					5.9	4.5
15.					5.9	4.5
16.					3.0	4.4
17.						4.4
18.						4.4
19.						4.4
20.						4.4
21.						2.2
Total	100.0%	100.0%	100.0%	100.0%	100.0%	100.0%

* Denotes the year of changeover to straight-line depreciation.

The percentage figures used in the tables are based on the declining-balance method of depreciation. A 200 percent rate was used to develop the figures dealing with the 3-, 5-, 7-, and 10-year property classes; and a 150 percent rate was used to develop the figures dealing with the 15- and 20-year property classes. In all cases, the tables automatically switch to straight-line depreciation at the point where depreciation deductions would be greater under that method. The tables in Exhibit 15–5 apply to both new and used property.

Factors in the Implementation of MACRS   When computing depreciation deductions under the MACRS approach for the first six property classes (3-year property through 20-year property), taxpayers are permitted to take only a half year's depreciation in the first year and the last year of an asset's life. This is known as the **half-year convention.** In effect, the half-year convention adds a full year onto the recovery period for an asset, as shown in the tables in Exhibit 15–5. (The half-year convention is built right into the figures in the tables.) Note from the exhibit, for example, that assets in the three-year property class are depreciated over *four* years with only a half year's depreciation being allowed in the first and fourth years. In like manner, assets in the five-year property class are depreciated over *six* years, with the same pattern holding true for the other property classes. The half-year convention must be followed regardless of the time of year in which an asset is purchased or the time of year in which it is sold.

Another factor in the implementation of MACRS is that salvage value is not considered in computing depreciation deductions. Thus, depreciation deductions are computed on a basis of the full, original cost of an asset without any offset for the asset's expected salvage value. This is actually a benefit to an organization, since it allows the entire cost of an asset to be written off as depreciation expense. However, since the entire cost of an asset is written off, any salvage value realized from sale of the asset at the end of its useful life is fully taxable as income.

Using the MACRS Tables

To illustrate how the tables in Exhibit 15–5 are used to compute depreciation deductions, assume that Wendover Company purchased a piece of new equipment on January 2, 1990. Cost and other data relating to the equipment follow:

Cost of the equipment	$200,000
Salvage value	3,000
Useful life	14 years

Since the equipment has a useful life of 14 years, it will be in the MACRS 7-year property class (see Exhibit 15–4). Under MACRS, salvage value is ignored in computing depreciation deductions; therefore, Wendover Company's depreciation deductions for tax purposes will be computed on the equipment's full $200,000 original cost, as follows:

Year	Equipment Cost	MACRS Percentage*	Depreciation Deduction
1	$200,000	14.3%	$ 28,600
2	200,000	24.5	49,000
3	200,000	17.5	35,000
4	200,000	12.5	25,000
5	200,000	8.9	17,800
6	200,000	8.9	17,800
7	200,000	8.9	17,800
8	200,000	4.5	9,000
		100.0%	$200,000

* From the table for seven-year property in Exhibit 15–5.

Note that eight years are involved in the depreciation process, as discussed earlier, since the tables provide for only a half year's depreciation in the first and last years.

Optional Straight-Line Method

MACRS allows flexibility to the extent that a company can elect to compute depreciation deductions by the **optional straight-line method** if it desires. Under the optional straight-line method, a company is permitted to ignore the MACRS tables and to spread its depreciation deductions somewhat evenly over an asset's property class life.

To provide an example, assume that Emerson Company purchases duplicating equipment at a cost of $10,000 on April 1, 1991. The equipment has a $600 salvage value, and it has a useful life of eight years. Thus, according to the data in Exhibit 15–4, it is in the MACRS five-year property class. If the company elects to use the optional straight-line method, it can deduct $1,000 depreciation in 1991:

$$\$10,000 \div 5 \text{ years} = \$2,000 \text{ per year}; \$2,000 \times \tfrac{1}{2} = \$1,000$$

For 1992–95 (the next four years) the company can deduct $2,000 depreciation each year, and in 1996 it can deduct the final $1,000 amount, as shown below:

Year	Depreciation Deduction
1991 (half year's depreciation)	$1,000
1992	2,000
1993	2,000
1994	2,000
1995	2,000
1996 (half year's depreciation)	1,000

Note that the half-year convention must be observed when using the optional straight-line method, the same as with the MACRS tables. Also note that in accordance with the MACRS rules, the asset's salvage value was not considered in computing the depreciation deductions.

The option of being able to use the straight-line method in lieu of the percentages in the MACRS tables is of particular value to new firms and to firms experiencing economic difficulties. The reason, of course, is that such firms often have little or no income and thus may prefer to stretch out depreciation deductions rather than to accelerate them.

The Choice of a Depreciation Method

As stated earlier, companies can still use any depreciation method they want (including sum-of-the-years' digits) on financial statements, even though they must use the MACRS rules for tax purposes. If a company uses a different depreciation method on its financial statements than it does for tax purposes, which method should be used in a capital budgeting analysis? Since capital budgeting is concerned with *actual cash flows*, the answer is that the same depreciation method should be used for capital budgeting purposes as is being used for tax purposes. Under the new law, this will be either the MACRS tables or the MACRS optional straight-line method.

For tax purposes, most companies will choose the MACRS tables, since this highly accelerated approach to depreciation will be more advantageous than the optional straight-line method from a present value of tax savings point of view. To illustrate, refer to the data in Exhibit 15–6. This exhibit compares the two depreci-

Objective 3
Compute the tax savings arising from the depreciation tax shield, using both the MACRS tables and the optional straight-line method.

Cost of the asset	$300,000
Useful life	9 years
Property class life	5 years
Salvage value	–0–
Cost of capital	14% after taxes
Income tax rate	30%

EXHIBIT 15–6

Tax Shield Effects of Depreciation

Straight-Line Depreciation, with Half-Year Convention:

Year	Depreciation Deduction	Tax Shield: Income Tax Savings at 30 Percent	14 Percent Factor	Present Value of Tax Savings
1	$30,000	$ 9,000	0.877	$ 7,893
2	60,000	18,000	0.769	13,842
3	60,000	18,000	0.675	12,150
4	60,000	18,000	0.592	10,656
5	60,000	18,000	0.519	9,342
6	30,000	9,000	0.456	4,104
				$57,987

MACRS Tables, Five-Year Property Class:

Year	Cost	MACRS Percentage				
1	$300,000	20.0%	$60,000	$18,000	0.877	$15,786
2	300,000	32.0	96,000	28,800	0.769	22,147
3	300,000	19.2	57,600	17,280	0.675	11,664
4	300,000	11.5	34,500	10,350	0.592	6,127
5	300,000	11.5	34,500	10,350	0.519	5,372
6	300,000	5.8	17,400	5,220	0.456	2,380
						$63,476

ation methods in terms of the present value of the tax savings they provide on a hypothetical asset costing $300,000.

As shown by Exhibit 15–6, the MACRS table approach (which is based on declining-balance depreciation) provides a larger present value of tax savings than does the optional straight-line method. This example shows why companies often prefer the accelerated method of depreciation over the straight-line method for tax purposes. Since the accelerated method provides more of its tax shield early in the life of an asset, the present value of the resulting tax savings will always be greater than the present value of the tax savings under the straight-line method.

The Investment Tax Credit

From time to time Congress allows companies to take an **investment tax credit** for purchases of equipment used in a trade or business. The investment tax credit is computed by multiplying the cost of new equipment by a specified percentage figure. The resulting dollar amount of credit is a direct reduction of income taxes and is taken in the year that equipment is placed in service. This credit is generally in addition to the depreciation deductions allowed under MACRS.

The investment tax credit was first enacted by Congress in 1962 and at that time was set at 7 percent of the cost of qualifying equipment. A few years later—in 1969—the investment tax credit was repealed by Congress. But in 1971 the credit was reinstated, only to be repealed again a few years later. It has since been reinstated and repealed several times. When the credit has been in effect, it has ranged from 4 percent to 10 percent of the cost of qualifying property.

The purpose of the investment tax credit is to stimulate the economy by encouraging companies to purchase new, depreciable equipment. Assume, for example, that a 10 percent investment tax credit is in effect. Also assume that a company is uncertain whether it should purchase $1 million in new equipment now or wait for several years. If the equipment is purchased now, the 10 percent investment tax credit will reduce the company's tax bill by $100,000 (10% × $1 million), which will, in effect, reduce the net cost of the equipment to only $900,000. This reduction in cost may be enough to cause the company to make the purchase immediately rather than to delay it.

At the time of this writing, Congress was again considering the reinstatement of the investment tax credit. If such a reinstatement does take place, the effect will be to make equipment purchases more attractive by effectively reducing their cost. The reduction in cost will be equal to the invoice cost of the equipment purchased, multiplied by whatever percentage credit figure is mandated by Congress (which can change from year to year). Since the investment tax credit comes and goes at the discretion of Congress, it is not included in the assignment material at the end of this chapter. However, when a company contemplates equipment purchases, its managers should determine whether an investment tax credit is in effect so they can assess its impact on the investment decision. In a capital budgeting analysis, the dollar amount of investment tax credit relating to a purchase should be treated as a cash inflow in the first year of the life of the equipment being analyzed.

Example of Income Taxes and Capital Budgeting

Objective 4
Compute the after-tax net present value of an investment proposal.

Armed with an understanding of the MACRS depreciation rules, and with an understanding of the concepts of after-tax cost, after-tax revenue, and depreciation tax shield, we are now prepared to examine a comprehensive example of income taxes and capital budgeting. Assume the following data:

Holland Company owns the mineral rights to land on which there is a deposit of ore. The company is uncertain as to whether it should purchase equipment and open a mine on the property. After careful study, the following data have been assembled by the company:

Cost of equipment needed	$300,000
Working capital needed	75,000
Estimated annual cash receipts from sales of ore	250,000
Estimated annual cash expenses for salaries, insurance, utilities, and other cash expenses of mining the ore	170,000
Cost of road repairs needed in 6 years.	40,000
Salvage value of the equipment in 10 years	100,000
Useful life of the equipment	15 years

The ore in the mine would be exhausted after 10 years of mining activity, at which time the mine would be closed. The equipment would then be sold for its salvage value. Holland Company uses the MACRS tables in computing depreciation deductions. The company's after-tax cost of capital is 12 percent, and its tax rate is 30 percent.

Should Holland Company purchase the equipment and open a mine on the property? The solution to the problem is given in Exhibit 15–7. The reader should go through this solution item by item and note the following points:

Cost of new equipment.   The initial investment of $300,000 in the new equipment is included in full, with no reductions for taxes. The tax effects of this investment are considered in the depreciation deductions.

Working capital.   Observe that the working capital needed for the project is included in full, with no reductions for taxes. This represents an *investment,* not an expense, so no tax adjustment is needed. (Only revenues and expenses are adjusted for the effects of taxes.) Also observe that no tax adjustment is needed when the working capital is released at the end of the project's life. The release of working capital would not be a taxable cash inflow, since it merely represents a return of investment funds back to the company.

Net annual cash receipts.   The net annual cash receipts from sales of ore are adjusted for the effects of income taxes, as discussed earlier in the chapter. Note at the top of Exhibit 15–7 that the annual cash expenses are deducted from the annual cash receipts to obtain a net cash receipts figure. This just simplifies computations. (Many of the exercises and problems that follow already provide a net annual cash receipts figure, thereby eliminating the need to make this computation.)

Road repairs.   Since the road repairs occur just once (in the sixth year), they are treated separately from other expenses. Road repairs would be a tax-deductible cash expense, and therefore they are adjusted for the effects of income taxes, as discussed earlier in the chapter.

Depreciation deductions.   Since the equipment has a 15-year useful life, it is in the MACRS 7-year property class. The tax savings provided by depreciation deductions under the MACRS rules are included in the present value computations in the same way as was illustrated earlier in the chapter (see Exhibit 15–6). Note that depreciation deductions are kept separate from cash expenses. These are unlike items, and they should be treated separately in a capital budgeting analysis.

Salvage value of equipment.   Since under the MACRS rules a company does not consider salvage value in computing depreciation deductions, book

EXHIBIT 15–7
Example of Income Taxes and Capital Budgeting

Per Year

Cash receipts from sales of ore	$250,000
Less payments for salaries, insurance, utilities, and other cash expenses	170,000
Net cash receipts	$ 80,000

Items and Computations	Year(s)	(1) Amount	(2) Tax Effect*	After-Tax Cash Flows (1) × (2)	12 Percent Factor	Present Value of Cash Flows
Cost of new equipment	Now	$(300,000)	—	$(300,000)	1.000	$(300,000)
Working capital needed	Now	(75,000)	—	(75,000)	1.000	(75,000)
Net annual cash receipts (above)	1–10	80,000	1 − 0.30	56,000	5.650	316,400
Road repairs	6	(40,000)	1 − 0.30	(28,000)	0.507	(14,196)

Depreciation deductions:

Year	Cost	MACRS Percentage	Depreciation Deduction						
1 . . .	$300,000	14.3%	$42,900	1	42,900	0.30	12,870	0.893	11,493
2 . . .	300,000	24.5	73,500	2	73,500	0.30	22,050	0.797	17,574
3 . . .	300,000	17.5	52,500	3	52,500	0.30	15,750	0.712	11,214
4 . . .	300,000	12.5	37,500	4	37,500	0.30	11,250	0.636	7,155
5 . . .	300,000	8.9	26,700	5	26,700	0.30	8,010	0.567	4,542
6 . . .	300,000	8.9	26,700	6	26,700	0.30	8,010	0.507	4,061
7 . . .	300,000	8.9	26,700	7	26,700	0.30	8,010	0.452	3,621
8 . . .	300,000	4.5	13,500	8	13,500	0.30	4,050	0.404	1,636

Salvage value of equipment			10	100,000	1 − 0.30	70,000	0.322	22,540
Release of working capital			10	75,000	—	75,000	0.322	24,150
Net present value								$ 35,190

* Taxable cash receipts and tax-deductible cash expenses are multiplied by (1 − Tax rate) to get the after-tax cash flow. Depreciation deductions are multiplied by the tax rate itself to get the cash flow figure (i.e., tax savings from the depreciation tax shield).

value will be zero at the end of the life of an asset. Thus, any salvage value received is fully taxable as income to the company. The after-tax benefit is determined by multiplying the salvage value by (1 − Tax rate), as discussed earlier.

Since the net present value of the proposed mining project is positive, the equipment should be purchased and the mine opened. The reader should study Exhibit 15–7 until all of its points are thoroughly understood. *Exhibit 15–7 is a key exhibit in the chapter!*

The Total-Cost Approach and Income Taxes

As stated in the preceding chapter, the total-cost approach is used to compare two or more competing investment proposals. To provide an example of this approach when income taxes are involved, assume the following data:

The *Daily Globe* has an auxiliary press that was purchased two years ago. The newspaper is thinking about replacing this old press with a newer, faster model. The alternatives are:

Buy a new press.   A new press could be purchased for $150,000. It would have a useful life of eight years, after which time it would be salable for $10,000. The old press could be sold now for $40,000. (The book value of the old press is $63,000.) If the new press is purchased, it would be depreciated using the

MACRS tables and would be in the five-year property class. The new press would cost $60,000 each year to operate.

Keep the old press. The old press was purchased two years ago at a cost of $90,000. The press is in the MACRS five-year property class and is being depreciated by the optional straight-line method. The old press will last for eight more years, but it will need an overhaul in five years that will cost $20,000. Cash operating costs of the old press are $85,000 each year. The old press will have a salvage value of $5,000 at the end of eight more years.

The tax rate is 30 percent. The *Daily Globe* requires an after-tax return of 10 percent on all investments in equipment.

Should the *Daily Globe* keep its old press or buy the new press? The solution using the total-cost approach is presented in Exhibit 15–8. Most of the items in

EXHIBIT 15–8

Income Taxes and Capital Budgeting: Total-Cost Approach

Items and Computations				Year(s)	(1) Amount	(2) Tax Effect	After-Tax Cash Flows (1) × (2)	10 Percent Factor	Present Value of Cash Flows
Buy the new press:									
Cost of the new press				Now	$(150,000)	—	$(150,000)	1.000	$(150,000)
Annual cash operating costs.				1–8	(60,000)	1 − 0.30	(42,000)	5.335	(224,070)
Depreciation deductions:									

Year	Cost	MACRS Percentage	Depreciation Deduction						
1 ..	$150,000	20.0%	$30,000	1	30,000	0.30	9,000	0.909	8,181
2 ..	150,000	32.0	48,000	2	48,000	0.30	14,400	0.826	11,894
3 ..	150,000	19.2	28,800	3	28,800	0.30	8,640	0.751	6,489
4 ..	150,000	11.5	17,250	4	17,250	0.30	5,175	0.683	3,535
5 ..	150,000	11.5	17,250	5	17,250	0.30	5,175	0.621	3,214
6 ..	150,000	5.8	8,700	6	8,700	0.30	2,610	0.564	1,472

Cash flow from sale of the old press:									
Cash received from the sale.				Now	40,000	—	40,000	1.000	40,000
Tax savings from the loss on sale:									
Present book value		$63,000							
Sale price (above)		40,000							
Loss on the sale		$23,000		1	23,000	0.30	6,900	0.909	6,272
Salvage value of the new press				8	10,000	1 − 0.30	7,000	0.467	3,269
Present value of cash flows									$(289,744)

Keep the old press:									
Annual cash operating costs.				1–8	$(85,000)	1 − 0.30	$(59,500)	5.335	$(317,433)
Overhaul needed.				5	(20,000)	1 − 0.30	(14,000)	0.621	(8,694)
Depreciation deductions:									

Year	Cost	Depreciation Deduction							
1 ..	$90,000	$18,000*	1	18,000	0.30	5,400	0.909	4,909	
2 ..	90,000	18,000	2	18,000	0.30	5,400	0.826	4,460	
3 ..	90,000	18,000	3	18,000	0.30	5,400	0.751	4,055	
4 ..	90,000	9,000	4	9,000	0.30	2,700	0.683	1,844	
Salvage value of the old press.			8	5,000	1 − 0.30	3,500	0.467	1,635	
Present value of cash flows								$(309,224)	
Net present value in favor of purchasing the new press.								$ 19,480	

* $90,000 ÷ 5 years = $18,000 per year. Two years' depreciation has already been taken on the old press.

this exhibit have already been discussed in connection with Exhibit 15–7. Only a couple of points need elaboration:

Annual cash operating costs. Since there are no revenues identified with the project, we simply place the cash operating costs on an after-tax basis and discount them as we did in Chapter 14.

Sale of the old press. The computation of the cash inflow from sale of the old press is somewhat more involved than the other items in Exhibit 15–8. Note that *two* cash inflows are connected with this sale. The first is a $40,000 cash inflow in the form of the sale price. The second is a $6,900 cash inflow in the form of a reduction in income taxes, resulting from the tax shield provided by the loss sustained on the sale. This tax shield functions in the same way as the tax shield provided by depreciation deductions. That is, the $23,000 loss shown in the exhibit on sale of the old press (the difference between the sale price of $40,000 and the book value of $63,000) is fully deductible from income in the year the loss is sustained. This loss shields income from taxation, thereby causing a reduction in the income taxes that would otherwise be payable. The tax savings resulting from the loss tax shield are computed by multiplying the loss by the tax rate (the same procedure as for depreciation deductions): $23,000 × 0.30 = $6,900.

A second solution to this problem is presented in Exhibit 15–9, where the incremental-cost approach is used. Notice both from this exhibit and from Exhibit 15–8 that the net present value is $19,480 in favor of buying the new press.

EXHIBIT 15–9

Income Taxes and Capital Budgeting: Incremental-Cost Approach

Items and Computations	Year(s)	(1) Amount	(2) Tax Effect	After-Tax Cash Flows (1) × (2)	10 Percent Factor	Present Value of Cash Flows
Cost of the new press	Now	$(150,000)	—	$(150,000)	1.000	$(150,000)
Savings in annual cash operating costs	1–8	25,000	1 − 0.30	17,500	5.335	93,363
Overhaul avoided	5	20,000	1 − 0.30	14,000	0.621	8,694

Difference in depreciation:

Year	Depreciation Deduction New Press	Old Press	Difference						
1	$30,000	$18,000	$12,000	1	12,000	0.30	3,600	0.909	3,272
2	48,000	18,000	30,000	2	30,000	0.30	9,000	0.826	7,434
3	28,800	18,000	10,800	3	10,800	0.30	3,240	0.751	2,433
4	17,250	9,000	8,250	4	8,250	0.30	2,475	0.683	1,690
5	17,250	—	17,250	5	17,250	0.30	5,175	0.621	3,214
6	8,700	—	8,700	6	8,700	0.30	2,610	0.564	1,472

Cash flow from sale of the old press:

Cash received from the sale				Now	40,000	—	40,000	1.000	40,000
Tax savings from the loss on sale (see Exhibit 15–8)				1	23,000	0.30	6,900	0.909	6,272

Difference in salvage value in eight years:

Salvage from the new press	$10,000								
Salvage from the old press	5,000								
Difference	$ 5,000			8	5,000	1 − 0.30	3,500	0.467	1,635

Net present value in favor of purchasing the new press. . . . . $ 19,480

Note: The figures in this exhibit are derived from the *differences* between the two alternatives given in Exhibit 15–8.

PREFERENCE DECISIONS—THE RANKING OF INVESTMENT PROJECTS

In the preceding chapter, we indicated that there are two types of decisions that must be made relative to investment opportunities. These are screening decisions and preference decisions. Screening decisions have to do with whether or not some proposed investment is acceptable to a firm. We discussed ways of making screening decisions in the preceding chapter, where we studied the use of the cost of capital as a screening tool. Screening decisions are very important in that many investment proposals come to the attention of management, and those that are not worthwhile must be screened out.

Preference decisions come *after* screening decisions and attempt to answer the following question: "How do the remaining investment proposals, all of which have been screened and provide an acceptable rate of return, rank in terms of preference? That is, which one(s) would be *best* for the firm to accept?" Preference decisions are more difficult to make than screening decisions. The reason is that investment funds are usually limited, and this often requires that some (perhaps many) otherwise very profitable investment opportunities be forgone.

Preference decisions are sometimes called *ranking* decisions, or *rationing* decisions, because they attempt to ration limited investment funds among many competing investment opportunities. The choice may be simply between two competing alternatives, or many alternatives may be involved that must be ranked according to their overall desirability. Either the time-adjusted rate of return method or the net present value method can be used in making preference decisions.

Objective 5
Rank investment projects in order of preference using (1) the time-adjusted rate of return method, and (2) the net present value method with the profitability index.

Time-Adjusted Rate of Return Method

When using the time-adjusted rate of return method to rank competing investment projects, the preference rule is: *The higher the time-adjusted rate of return, the more desirable the project.* If one investment project promises a time-adjusted rate of return of 18 percent, then it is preferable over another project that promises a return of only 15 percent.

Ranking projects according to time-adjusted rate of return is a widely used means of making preference decisions. The reasons are probably twofold. First, no additional computations are needed beyond those already performed in making the initial screening decisions. The rates of return themselves are used to rank acceptable projects. Second, the ranking data are easily understood by management. Rates of return are very similar to interest rates, which the manager works with every day.

Net Present Value Method

If the net present value method is being used to rank competing investment projects, the net present value of one project cannot be compared directly to the net present value of another project unless the investments in the projects are of equal size. For example, assume that a company is considering two competing investments, as shown below:

	Investment	
	A	**B**
Investment required	$(80,000)	$(5,000)
Present value of cash inflows . . .	81,000	6,000
Net present value	$ 1,000	$ 1,000

Each project has a net present value of $1,000, but the projects are not equally desirable. A project requiring an investment of only $5,000 that produces cash inflows with a present value of $6,000 is much more desirable than a project requiring an investment of $80,000 that produces cash flows with a present value of only $81,000. In order to compare the two projects on a valid basis, it is necessary in each case to divide the present value of the cash inflows by the investment required. The ratio that this computation yields is called the **profitability index.** The formula for the profitability index is:

$$\frac{\text{Present value of cash inflows}}{\text{Investment required}} = \text{Profitability index}$$

The profitability indexes for the two investments above would be:

	Investment	
	A	B
Present value of cash inflows . . .	$81,000 (a)	$6,000 (a)
Investment required	$80,000 (b)	$5,000 (b)
Profitability index, (a) ÷ (b)	1.01	1.20

The preference rule to follow when using the profitability index to rank competing investment projects is: *The higher the profitability index, the more desirable the project.* Applying this rule to the two investments above, and considering only the financial data provided in the example, investment B should be chosen over investment A.

In computing the "Investment required" in a project, the amount of cash outlay should be reduced by any salvage recovered from the sale of old equipment. Also, the "Investment required" includes any working capital that the project may need, as explained in the preceding chapter. Finally, we should note that the "Present value of cash inflows" figure used in the profitability index formula is often a "net" amount. For example, if a project has small *out*flows (such as for repairs or for an overhaul) that occur after the project starts, then the present value of these small outflows should be deducted from the present value of the project's inflows and the resulting net figure used in the profitability index computation.

Comparing the Preference Rules

The profitability index is conceptually superior to the time-adjusted rate of return as a method of making preference decisions. This is because the profitability index will always give the correct signal as to the relative desirability of alternatives, even if the alternatives have different lives and different patterns of earnings. By contrast, if lives are unequal, the time-adjusted rate of return method can lead the manager to make incorrect decisions.

Assume the following situation:

Parker Company is considering two investment proposals, only one of which can be accepted. Project A requires an investment of $5,000 and will provide a single cash inflow of $6,000 in one year. Therefore, it promises a time-adjusted rate of return of 20 percent. Project B also requires an investment of $5,000. It will provide cash inflows of $1,360 each year for six years. Its time-adjusted rate of return is 16 percent. Which project should be accepted?

Although project A promises a time-adjusted rate of return of 20 percent, as compared to only 16 percent for project B, project A is not necessarily preferable over project B. It is preferable *only* if the funds released at the end of the year under project A can be reinvested at a high rate of return in some *other* project for the five remaining years. Otherwise, project B, which promises a return of 16 percent over the *entire* six years, is more desirable.

Let us assume that the company in the example above has a cost of capital of 12 percent. The net present value method, with the profitability index, would rank the two proposals as follows:

	Project	
	A	**B**
Present value of cash inflows:		
$6,000 received at the end of one year at 12% (factor of 0.893)	$5,358 (a)	
$1,360 received at the end of each year for six years at 12% (factor of 4.111).		$5,591 (a)
Investment required	$5,000 (b)	$5,000 (b)
Profitability index, (a) ÷ (b)	1.07	1.12

The profitability index indicates that project B is more desirable than project A. This is in fact the case if the funds released from project A at the end of one year can be reinvested at only 12 percent (the cost of capital). Although the computations will not be shown here, in order for project A to be more desirable than project B, the funds released from project A would have to be reinvested at a rate of return *greater* than 14 percent for the remaining five years.

In short, the time-adjusted rate of return method of ranking tends to favor short-term, high-yield projects, whereas the net present value method of ranking (using the profitability index) tends to favor longer-term projects.

SUMMARY

Unless a company is a tax-exempt organization, such as a school or a governmental unit, income taxes should be considered in making capital budgeting computations. When income taxes are a factor in a company, tax-deductible cash expenditures must be placed on an after-tax basis by multiplying the expenditure by (1 − Tax rate). Only the after-tax amount is used in determining the desirability of an investment proposal. Similarly, taxable cash inflows must be placed on an after-tax basis by multiplying the cash inflow by the same formula.

Although depreciation deductions do not involve a present outflow of cash, they are valid expenses for tax purposes and as such affect income tax payments. Depreciation deductions shield income from taxation, resulting in decreased taxes being paid. This shielding of income from taxation is commonly called a depreciation tax shield. The savings in income taxes arising from the depreciation tax shield are computed by multiplying the depreciation deduction by the tax rate itself. Since accelerated methods of depreciation provide the bulk of their tax shield early in the life of an asset, they are superior to the straight-line method of depreciation, from a present value of tax savings point of view.

Preference decisions relate to ranking two or more investment proposals according to their relative desirability. This ranking can be performed using either the time-adjusted rate of return or the profitability index. The profitability index, which is the ratio of the present value of a proposal's cash inflows to the investment required, is generally regarded as the best way of making preference decisions when discounted cash flow is being used.

REVIEW PROBLEM: CAPITAL BUDGETING AND TAXES

A company is considering two investment projects. Relevant cost and cash inflow information on each project is given below:

	Project	
	A	**B**
Investment in passenger buses	$70,000	
Investment in working capital		$70,000
Net annual cash inflows	13,500	13,500
Life of the project.	8 years*	8 years

* Useful life of the buses.

The buses will have a $5,000 salvage value in eight years, and they will be depreciated by the MACRS optional straight-line method. At the end of eight years, the working capital in project B will be released for use elsewhere.

The company requires an after-tax return of 10 percent on all investments. The tax rate is 30 percent.

Required 1. What MACRS property class will the buses be placed in for purposes of computing depreciation?
2. Compute the net present value of each investment project.
3. Compute the profitability index for each investment project.

Solution to Review Problem 1. Since the buses have an eight-year useful life, they will be in the MACRS five-year property class. (See Exhibit 15–4.)
2. See the table on the next page.
3. The formula for the profitability index is:

$$\frac{\text{Present value of cash inflows}}{\text{Investment required}} = \text{Profitability index}$$

Applying this formula to the data in (2) above, we get:

	Project	
	A	**B**
Present value of cash inflows:		
Net annual cash inflows.	$50,416	$50,416
Tax savings from depreciation (total).	15,193	—
Salvage value of the buses	1,635	—
Release of working capital	—	32,690
Total cash inflows (a).	$67,244	$83,106
Investment required (b).	$70,000	$70,000
Profitability index (a) ÷ (b)	0.96	1.19

Note from (2) above that project A has a negative net present value and therefore is not an acceptable investment. This also can be seen in the profitability index computation in that project A has a profitability index of less than 1.00. If a project has a profitabil-

Items and Computations		Year(s)	(1) Amount	(2) Tax Effect	(1) × (2) After-Tax Cash Flows	10 Percent Factor	Present Value of Cash Flows
Project A:							
Investment in passenger buses		Now	$(70,000)	—	$(70,000)	1.000	$(70,000)
Net annual cash inflows		1–8	13,500	1 − 0.30	9,450	5.335	50,416
Depreciation deductions:							

Year	Cost	Depreciation Deduction						
1.	$70,000	$ 7,000*	1	7,000	0.30	2,100	0.909	1,909
2.	$70,000	14,000	2	14,000	0.30	4,200	0.826	3,469
3.	$70,000	14,000	3	14,000	0.30	4,200	0.751	3,154
4.	$70,000	14,000	4	14,000	0.30	4,200	0.683	2,869
5.	$70,000	14,000	5	14,000	0.30	4,200	0.621	2,608
6.	$70,000	7,000*	6	7,000	0.30	2,100	0.564	1,184

Salvage value of the buses		8	5,000	1 − 0.30	3,500	0.467	1,635
Net present value							$ (2,756)
Project B:							
Investment in working capital		Now	$(70,000)	—	$(70,000)	1.000	($70,000)
Net annual cash inflows		1–8	13,500	1 − 0.30	9,450	5.335	50,416
Release of working capital		8	70,000	—	70,000	0.467	32,690
Net present value							$ 13,106

* $70,000 ÷ 5 years = $14,000; $14,000 × ½ = $7,000. The half-year convention must be observed when computing depreciation for the first and last years.

ity index of less than 1.00, it means that the project is returning less than a dollar of cash inflow for each dollar of investment. By contrast, project B is returning $1.19 of cash inflow for each dollar of investment.

KEY TERMS FOR REVIEW

Accelerated Cost Recovery System (ACRS)   A method of depreciation mandated by Congress in 1981 that was replaced in 1986 by the *Modified Accelerated Cost Recovery System*. (p. 717)

After-tax benefit   The amount of net cash inflow realized by an organization from a taxable cash receipt after income tax effects have been considered. The amount is determined by multiplying the cash receipt by (1 − Tax rate). (p. 715)

After-tax cost   The amount of net cash outflow resulting from a tax-deductible cash expense after income tax effects have been considered. The amount is determined by multiplying the cash expense by (1 − Tax rate). (p. 714)

Depreciation tax shield   A reduction in the amount of income subject to tax that results from the presence of depreciation deductions on the income statement. The reduction in tax is computed by multiplying the depreciation deduction by the tax rate. (p. 717)

Half-year convention   A requirement under the Modified Accelerated Cost Recovery System that permits a company to take only a half year's depreciation in the first and last years of an asset's depreciation period. (p. 719)

Investment tax credit   A credit based on the cost of equipment purchased that is a direct reduction of income taxes in the year the equipment is placed in service. The percentage rate of the credit is set by Congress and is subject to frequent change. (p. 722)

Modified Accelerated Cost Recovery System (MACRS)   A method of depreciation required for income tax purposes that places a depreciable asset into one of eight property classes according to the asset's useful life. (p. 717)

Objective 6
Define or explain the key terms listed at the end of the chapter.

Optional straight-line method   A method of computing depreciation deductions under MACRS that can be used by an organization in lieu of the MACRS tables. (p. 720)

Profitability index   The ratio of the present value of a project's cash inflows to the investment required. (p. 728)

QUESTIONS

15–1   Some organizations will always use capital budgeting techniques on a before-tax basis rather than on an after-tax basis. Name several such organizations.

15–2   What is meant by after-tax cost, and how is the concept used in capital budgeting decisions?

15–3   What is a depreciation tax shield, and how does it affect capital budgeting decisions?

15–4   The three most widely used depreciation methods are straight line, sum-of-the-years' digits, and double-declining balance, with the depreciation period based on the asset's actual useful life. Explain why a company might use one or more of these methods, instead of the Modified Accelerated Cost Recovery System (MACRS), for computing depreciation expense in its published financial statements.

15–5   Why are accelerated methods of depreciation superior to the straight-line method of depreciation from an income tax point of view?

15–6   Ludlow Company is considering the introduction of a new product line. Would an increase in the income tax rate tend to make the new investment more or less attractive? Explain.

15–7   Assume that an old piece of equipment is sold at a loss. From a capital budgeting point of view, what two cash inflows will be associated with the sale?

15–8   Assume that a new piece of equipment costs $40,000 and that the tax rate is 30 percent. Should the new piece of equipment be shown in the capital budgeting analysis as a cash outflow of $40,000, or should it be shown as a cash outflow of $28,000 [$40,000 × (1 − 0.30)]? Explain.

15–9   Assume that a company has cash operating expenses of $15,000 and a depreciation expense of $10,000. Can these two items be added together and treated as one in a capital budgeting analysis, or should they be kept separate? Explain.

15–10   Distinguish between capital budgeting screening decisions and capital budgeting preference decisions. Why are preference decisions more difficult to make than screening decisions?

15–11   Why are preference decisions sometimes called *rationing* decisions?

15–12   How is the profitability index computed, and what does it measure?

15–13   What is the preference rule for ranking investment projects under the net present value method?

15–14   Can an investment with a profitability index of less than 1.00 be an acceptable investment? Explain.

15–15   What is the preference rule for ranking investment projects under time-adjusted rate of return?

EXERCISES

E15–1   a.   Neal Company would like to initiate a management development program for its executives. The program would cost $100,000 per year to operate. What would be the after-tax cost of the program if the company's income tax rate is 30 percent?

       b.   Smerk's Department Store has rearranged the merchandise display cases on the first floor of its building, placing fast turnover items near the front door. This rearrangement has caused the company's contribution margin (and taxable income) to increase by $40,000 per month. If the company's income tax rate is 25 percent, what is the after-tax benefit from this rearrangement of facilities?

c. Perfect Press, Inc., has just purchased a new binding machine at a cost of $210,000. The machine has a 12-year useful life and a $14,000 salvage value. Using the MACRS optional straight-line method, determine the yearly tax savings from the depreciation tax shield. Assume that the income tax rate is 30 percent.

d. Repeat (c) above, this time using the MACRS tables in Exhibit 15–5.

Various assets used by organizations are listed below.

E15–2

Assets	Useful Life
a. A pickup truck used by a construction company	5 years
b. An office building used by an advertising agency	50 years
c. Power lines used in distribution of electricity.	22 years
d. Small tools used on the assembly line of an auto plant	? years
e. Petroleum distilling equipment	16 years
f. An apartment house rented to college students	180 years*
g. A computer used by an airline to schedule flights	? years
h. A desk in the office of an attorney	10 years
i. Shrubbery and trees planted around a new medical clinic . . .	? years
j. A printing press used by a newspaper	18 years
k. A frozen food display case used by a retail market	15 years
l. Lab equipment used by a pharmaceutical company in cancer research	7 years

* We're just kidding; it's really 45 years.

Indicate the MACRS property class into which each of the assets above should be placed for depreciation purposes.

Required

Morgan Industries has an opportunity to penetrate a new market by making some modifications to one of its existing products. These modifications would require the purchase of various tools and small items of equipment that would cost $80,000 and have a four-year useful life. The equipment would have a $7,500 salvage value and would be depreciated using the MACRS tables.

E15–3

The modified product would generate before-tax net cash receipts of $35,000 per year. It is estimated that the equipment would require repairs in the third year that would cost $14,000. The company's tax rate is 30 percent, and its after-tax cost of capital is 12 percent.

1. Compute the net present value of the proposed investment in tools and equipment.
2. Would you recommend that the tools and equipment be purchased? Explain.

Required

Dwyer Company is considering two investment projects. Relevant cost and cash flow information on the two projects is given below:

E15–4

	Project	
	A	**B**
Investment in heavy trucks	$130,000	
Investment in working capital		$130,000
Net annual cash inflows	25,000	25,000
Life of the project	9 years*	9 years

* Useful life of the trucks.

The trucks will have a $15,000 salvage value in nine years, and they will be depreciated using the optional straight-line method. At the end of nine years, the working capital will be released for use elsewhere. The company requires an after-tax return of 12 percent on all investments. The tax rate is 30 percent. (Be sure you place the trucks in the correct property class for depreciation purposes.)

Required Compute the net present value of each investment project. (Round all dollar amounts to the nearest whole dollar.)

E15–5 (This exercise should be assigned only if E15–4 is also assigned.) Refer to the data in E15–4.

Required
1. Compute the profitability index for each investment project.
2. Is an investment project with a profitability index of less than 1.0 an acceptable project? Explain.

E15–6 The Midtown Cafeteria employs five people to operate several items of antiquated dishwashing equipment. The cost of wages for these people and for maintenance of the equipment is $85,000 per year. Management is considering the purchase of a single, highly automated dishwashing machine that would cost $160,000 and have a useful life of 12 years. This machine would require the services of only three people to operate at a cost of $48,000 per year. A maintenance contract on the machine would cost an additional $2,000 per year. New water jets would be needed on the machine in six years at a total cost of $15,000.

 The old equipment is fully depreciated and has no resale value. The new machine will have a salvage value of $9,000 at the end of its 12-year useful life. The Midtown Cafeteria uses the MACRS tables for depreciation purposes. Management requires a 14 percent after-tax return on all equipment purchases. The company's tax rate is 30 percent.

Required
1. Determine the before-tax net annual cost savings that the new dishwashing machine will provide.
2. Using the data from (1) and other data from the exercise, compute the new dishwashing machine's net present value. (Round all dollar amounts to the nearest whole dollar.) Would you recommend that it be purchased?

E15–7 Information on four investment proposals is given below:

| | **Investment Proposal** | | | |
	A	B	C	D
Investment required	$(90,000)	$(100,000)	$(70,000)	$(120,000)
Present value of cash inflows	126,000	90,000	105,000	160,000
Net present value	$ 36,000	$ (10,000)	$ 35,000	$ 40,000
Life of the project	5 years	7 years	6 years	6 years

Required
1. Compute the profitability index for each investment proposal.
2. Rank the proposals in terms of preference.

PROBLEMS

Ethics and the Manager **P15–8** The Fore Corporation is an integrated food processing company that has operations in over two dozen countries. Fore's corporate headquarters is in Chicago, and the company's executives frequently travel to visit Fore's foreign and domestic facilities.

 Fore has a fleet of aircraft that consists of two business jets with international range and six smaller turbine aircraft that are used on shorter flights. Company policy is to assign aircraft to trips on the basis of minimizing cost, but the practice is to assign the aircraft based on the organizational rank of the traveler. Fore offers its aircraft for short-term lease or for charter by other organizations whenever Fore itself does not plan to use the aircraft. Fore surveys the market often in order to keep its lease and charter rates competitive.

 William Earle, Fore's vice president of finance, has claimed that a third business jet can be justified financially. However, some people in the controller's office have surmised that the real reason for a third business jet was to upgrade the aircraft used by Earle. Presently, the people outranking Earle keep the two business jets busy, with the result that Earle usually flies in smaller turbine aircraft.

The third business jet would cost $11 million. A capital expenditure of this magnitude requires a formal proposal with projected cash flows and net present value computations using Fore's minimum required rate of return. If Fore's president and the finance committee of the board of directors approve the proposal, it will be submitted to the full board of directors. The board has final approval on capital expenditures exceeding $5 million, and has established a firm policy of rejecting any discretionary proposal that has a negative net present value.

Earle asked Rachel Arnett, assistant corporate controller, to prepare a proposal on a third business jet. Arnett gathered the following data.

- Acquisition cost of the aircraft, including instrumentation and interior furnishing.
- Operating cost of the aircraft for company use.
- Projected avoidable commercial airfare and other avoidable costs from company use of the plane.
- Projected value of executive time saved by using the third business jet.
- Projected contribution margin from incremental lease and charter activity.
- Estimated resale value of the aircraft.
- Estimated income tax effects of the proposal.

When Earle reviewed Arnett's completed proposal and saw the large negative net present value figure, he returned the proposal to Arnett. With a glare, Earle commented, "You must have made an error. The proposal should look better than that."

Feeling some pressure, Arnett went back and checked her computations; she found no errors. However, Earle's message was clear. Arnett discarded her projections and estimates that she believed were reasonable and replaced them with figures that had a remote chance of actually occurring but were more favorable to the proposal. For example, she used first-class airfares to refigure the avoidable commercial airfare costs, even though company policy was to fly coach. She found revising the proposal to be distressing.

The revised proposal still had a negative net present value. Earle's anger was evident as he told Arnett to revise the proposal again, and to start with a $100,000 positive net present value and work backwards to compute supporting estimates and projections.

Required

1. Explain whether Rachel Arnett's revision of the proposal was in violation of the Standards of Ethical Conduct for Management Accountants.
2. Was William Earle in violation of the Standards of Ethical Conduct for Management Accountants by telling Arnett specifically how to revise the proposal? Explain your answer.
3. What elements of the projection and estimation process would be compromised in preparing an analysis for which a preconceived result is sought?
4. Identify specific internal controls that Fore Corporation could implement to prevent unethical behavior on the part of the vice president of finance.

(CMA, adapted)

Basic Net Present Value Analysis   The Diamond Freight Company has been offered a   **P15–9**
seven-year contract to haul munitions for the government. Since this contract would represent new business, the company would have to purchase several new heavy-duty trucks at a cost of $350,000 if the contract were accepted. Other data relating to the contract follow:

Net annual cash receipts (before taxes) from the contract	$105,000
Cost of replacing the motors in the trucks in four years	45,000
Salvage value of the trucks at termination of the contract	18,000

With the motors being replaced after four years, the trucks will have a useful life of seven years. In order to raise money to assist in the purchase of the new trucks, the company will sell several old, fully depreciated trucks for a total selling price of $16,000. The company uses the MACRS tables to compute depreciation and requires a 16 percent after-tax return on all equipment purchases. The tax rate is 30 percent.

Required   Compute the net present value of this investment opportunity. Round all dollar amounts to the nearest whole dollar. Would you recommend that the contract be accepted?

P15–10   **Straightforward Net Present Value Analysis**   The Four-Seasons Timber Company estimates that the following costs would be associated with the cutting and sale of timber on land to which it has cutting rights:

Investment in equipment needed for cutting and removing the timber	$400,000
Working capital investment needed	75,000
Annual cash receipts from sale of timber, net of related cash operating costs (before taxes)	88,000
Cost of reseeding the land	60,000

The timber would be exhausted after 10 years of cutting and sales; all reseeding would be done in the 10th year. The equipment would have a useful life of 15 years, but it would be sold for an estimated 20 percent of its original cost when cutting was completed. The company uses the MACRS tables in computing depreciation deductions. The tax rate is 30 percent, and Four-Seasons' after-tax cost of capital is 12 percent. The working capital would be released for use elsewhere at the completion of the project.

Since the timber is difficult to get to and of marginal quality, management is uncertain as to whether it should proceed with the project.

Required   1.   Compute the net present value of this investment project. Round all dollar amounts to the nearest whole dollar.
2.   Would you recommend that the investment project be undertaken?

P15–11   **Various Depreciation Methods; Net Present Value**   Fencik Laboratories has been offered an eight-year contract to provide materials relating to the government's space exploration program. Management has determined that the following costs and revenues would be associated with the contract:

Cost of special equipment	$600,000
Working capital needed	115,000
Annual revenues from the contract	450,000
Annual out-of-pocket costs for materials, salaries, and so forth	280,000
Salvage value of the equipment in eight years	9,000

Although the equipment would have a useful life of nine years, it would have little salvage value remaining at the end of the contract period, as shown above. Fencik's after-tax cost of capital is 14 percent; its tax rate is 30 percent. At the end of the contract period, the working capital will be released for use elsewhere.

Required   1.   Assume that Fencik Laboratories uses the MACRS optional straight-line depreciation method. Determine the net present value of the proposed contract. (Round all dollar amounts to the nearest whole dollar.)
2.   Assume that Fencik Laboratories uses the MACRS tables to compute depreciation deductions. Determine the net present value of the proposed contract. (Round all dollar amounts to the nearest whole dollar.) How do you explain the difference in rate of return between (1) and (2)?

P15–12   **Preference Ranking of Investment Projects**   The management of Revco Products is exploring five different investment opportunities. Information on the five projects under study is given below:

	Project Number				
	1	**2**	**3**	**4**	**5**
Investment required	$(270,000)	$(450,000)	$(400,000)	$(360,000)	$(480,000)
Present value of cash inflows at a 10% discount rate	336,140	522,970	379,760	433,400	567,270
Net present value . . .	$ 66,140	$ 72,970	$ (20,240)	$ 73,400	$ 87,270
Life of the project.	6 years	3 years	5 years	12 years	6 years
Time-adjusted rate of return	18%	19%	8%	14%	16%

The company's cost of capital is 10 percent; thus, a 10 percent discount rate has been used in the present value computations above. Limited funds are available for investment, so the company can't accept all of the projects available.

1. Compute the profitability index for each investment project. *Required*
2. Rank the five projects according to preference, in terms of:
   a. Net present value.
   b. Profitability index.
   c. Time-adjusted rate of return.
3. Which ranking do you prefer? Why?

Various Depreciation Methods; Profitability Index   The computer and related equipment in Tervort Industries' computer center is not adequate for the company's needs. Although the computer is fully depreciated, it is in good operating condition and will be donated to a local school system. Management is considering two other computers as a replacement, only one of which can be purchased. Cost and other data on the two computers are given below: **P15–13**

	Computer	
	A	**B**
Cost of the computer	$225,000	$300,000
Annual savings in cash operating costs	70,000	88,500
Cost of parts replacement and a major adjustment needed in four years	9,000	10,500
Salvage value	16,000	20,000
Useful life	7 years	7 years
Depreciation method to be used	SL*	MACRS tables

* Optional straight-line method, as allowed under MACRS.

Tervort Industries' after-tax cost of capital is 12 percent. The tax rate is 30 percent. Round all dollar amounts to the nearest whole dollar.

1. Compute the net present value of each investment alternative. Based on these data, which computer should be purchased? *Required*
2. Compute the profitability index for each investment alternative. Based on these data, which computer should be purchased?

Preference Ranking of Investment Projects   Oxford Company has limited funds available for investment and must ration the funds among five competing projects. Selected information on the five projects follows: **P15–14**

Project	Investment Required	Net Present Value	Life of the Project (years)	Time-Adjusted Rate of Return (percent)
A	$160,000	$44,323	7	18
B	135,000	42,000	12	16
C	100,000	35,035	7	20
D	175,000	38,136	3	22
E	150,000	(8,696)	6	8

Oxford Company's cost of capital is 10 percent. (The net present values above have been computed using a 10 percent discount rate.) The company wants your assistance in determining which project to accept first, which to accept second, and so forth.

Required

1. Compute the profitability index for each project.
2. Rank the five projects in order of preference, in terms of:
   a. Net present value.
   b. Profitability index.
   c. Time-adjusted rate of return.
3. Which ranking do you prefer? Why?

P15–15 Net Present Value Analysis The Island Travel Service (ITS) operates out of Kuna, Hawaii. ITS has an opportunity to purchase several small charter boats that were recently repossessed by a local bank. Although the boats cost $700,000 new and are only three years old, they can be purchased by ITS for the "bargain basement" price of $430,000, payable $250,000 down and $60,000 each year for three years, without interest.

After some study, ITS's manager, Biff Coletti, has determined that the boats could be operated an average of 250 days per year. Records kept by the previous owner (now in the hands of the bank) indicate that the boats carried an average of 100 tourists per day. Mr. Coletti is confident that this could be increased to at least 140 tourists per day by dropping the tour price from $18 to $10 per person. The local bank has estimated the following annual expenses associated with the boats:

Salaries for a manager and for boat operators	$160,000
Insurance	9,000
Fuel	72,000
Bank payments*	60,000
Promotion	18,000
Maintenance	4,200
Rent for docking space	10,000
Fees and maritime taxes	6,800
Depreciation	27,333†
Total expenses	$367,333

* For the first three years only.

† $430,000 cost − $20,000 estimated salvage value = $410,000 depreciable cost; $410,000 ÷ 15 years = $27,333 per year.

To cover possible damage from docking, ITS would have to make an immediate deposit of $1,800 to the harbor authorities; this deposit would be refundable at the end of the boat's 15-year remaining useful life. In nine years, the boat hulls would require major scraping and resealing at a cost of $35,000.

If the boats are purchased, ITS will use the MACRS tables to compute depreciation for tax purposes. ITS's after-tax cost of capital is 10 percent, and the tax rate is 30 percent.

Required

1. Compute the net cash receipts (before income taxes) each year from operating the boats.
2. By use of the net present value method, determine whether the boats should be purchased. (Round all dollar amounts to the nearest whole dollar.)

Various Depreciation Methods; Net Present Value   Walter Miller, manufacturing vice president of Atlantic Industries, has been anxious for some time to purchase a piece of high-pressure equipment for use in the company's coal liquefaction research project. The equipment would cost $720,000 and would have an eight-year useful life. It would have a salvage value equal to about 5 percent of its original cost. In addition to the cost of the equipment, the company would have to increase its working capital by $10,000 to handle the more rapid processing of material by the new equipment.

An analysis that Mr. Miller has just received from his staff indicates that the equipment will not provide the 16 percent after-tax return required by Atlantic Industries. In making this analysis, Mr. Miller's staff estimated that the equipment would save the company $200,000 per year in its research program as a result of speeding up several key processes. The only significant maintenance work required on the equipment would be the installation of new pressure seals in five years at a cost of $80,000. In doing the analysis, Mr. Miller had instructed his staff to depreciate the equipment by the MACRS optional straight-line method, since the company always uses straight-line depreciation for accounting purposes. The company's tax rate is 30 percent.

Upon seeing the analysis done by Mr. Miller's staff, the company's controller has suggested that the analysis be redone using the MACRS tables rather than the optional straight-line method. Somewhat irritated by this suggestion, Mr. Miller replied, "You accountants and your fancy bookkeeping methods! What difference does it make what depreciation method we use—we have the same investment, the same cost savings, and the same total depreciation either way. That equipment just doesn't measure up to our rate of return requirements. How you make the bookkeeping entries for depreciation won't change that fact."

1. Compute the net present value of the equipment, using the optional straight-line method for computing depreciation as instructed by Mr. Miller.
2. Compute the net present value of the equipment, using the MACRS tables as suggested by the controller. Round all dollar amounts to the nearest whole dollar.
3. Explain to Mr. Miller how the depreciation method used can affect the rate of return generated by an investment project.

Required

Uneven Cash Flows; Net Present Value   "All of the engineering studies say that tar sand is excellent for use in road construction," said Holly Edwards, chief engineer for Dieter Mining Company. "With road construction projected to be at peak levels over the next 10 years, now is the time for us to extract and sell the tar sand off of tract 370 in the southern part of the state."

"I'm not so sure," replied Tom Collins, the vice president. "Prices are really soft for tar sand. The best we can hope to get is $7 a ton, and the accounting people say it will cost us at least $3 a ton for utilities, supplies, and selling expenses. That doesn't leave much in the way of contribution margin."

"I know we won't get much per ton," replied Holly, "but our studies show that we have 1,735,000 tons of tar sand in the area. I figure we can extract 90,000, 145,000, and 240,000 tons the first three years, respectively, and then the remainder evenly over the next seven years. Even at only $7 a ton, that'll bring a lot of cash flow into the company."

"But you're forgetting that we have other costs, too," said Tom. "Fixed costs for salaries, insurance, and so forth directly associated with the tar sand project would be $450,000 a year. Besides that, we would have to pay out an additional $250,000 at the end of the project for filling and leveling of the land. You know how tough those environmental people can get if things don't look right. And all of this doesn't even consider the $800,000 cost of special equipment that we would need or the $75,000 we would have to put up for working capital to carry inventories and accounts receivable. I'm uneasy about the whole idea."

"You've got to look at the big picture, Tom. You'll get the working capital back in 10 years when the project is completed. In addition, we can depreciate that equipment and save a bundle in taxes at our 30 percent tax rate. Besides that, since the equipment would have a 12-year useful life it would still have some use left when the project was completed. I'm sure we could sell it to someone for at least 5 percent of its original cost."

"All of that sounds fine, Holly, but I'll still bet the project won't provide the 18 percent after-tax return we require on high-risk investments. Let's give all this to accounting and have them do a present value analysis for us."

Required
1. Compute the before-tax net cash receipts each year from the extraction and sale of the tar sand. (Do not include the cost of filling and leveling the land in this computation.)
2. Using the data from (1) above and other data from the problem as needed, prepare a net present value analysis to determine whether the company should purchase the equipment and extract the tar sand. (Round all dollar amounts to the nearest whole dollar.) You may assume that for the company *as a whole*, there will be a positive taxable income in every year, so that a tax benefit would be realized from any operating losses associated with the tar sand project.

P15–18   **Equipment Replacement; Incremental Cost Approach**   "That new RAM 8000 is the most sophisticated piece of duplicating equipment available," said Monte Salazar, purchasing agent for Blinko's Copy Service. "The copier it would replace is putting out 5,600,000 pages a year, but the RAM would increase that output by 20 percent."

"I agree it's a powerul machine," replied Angie Carlson, the operations manager. "But we can only get $110,000 out of the copier it would replace and that copier cost us $260,000 just two years ago. I don't think we can justify taking a huge loss on our old equipment every time something new hits the market. Besides, do you realize that the RAM 8000 costs $375,000?"

"Yes, and it's worth every dollar," said Monte. "To prove it, let's have accounting work up an analysis to see if the RAM 8000 meets the 14 percent after-tax rate of return that we require on new equipment."

In response to Monte's request, accounting has gathered the following information:

a.   Both the old copier and the RAM 8000 are in the MACRS five-year property class (duplicating equipment).
b.   The old copier is being depreciated by the optional straight-line method. Two years' depreciation has been taken; thus, the copier's book value is $182,000. Depreciation over the next four years will be: years 1–3, $52,000 per year; and year 4, $26,000.
c.   The RAM 8000 would be depreciated using the MACRS tables. The manufacturer estimates that it would have a $15,000 salvage value at the end of its eight-year useful life. The old copier will be worth nothing in eight years.
d.   Blinko's Copy Service pays 1.5 cents per page for paper; the company's customers pay an average of 9 cents per page for copy work.
e.   To keep the RAM 8000 operating at peak efficiency, the company would purchase a maintenance contract that would cost $4,000 more per year than its present maintenance contract.
f.   The RAM 8000 would need to have the drum and photo plates replaced in five years; the cost would be $30,000.
g.   Blinko's Copy Service has a tax rate of 30 percent.

Required
1. Compute the incremental net annual cash receipts (before taxes) expected from the RAM 8000. (Do not include the cost of the drum and photo plates in this computation.)
2. Use discounted cash flow to determine whether the RAM 8000 will provide the company's required rate of return. Use the incremental-cost approach. (Round all dollar amounts to the nearest whole dollar.)

P15–19   **A Comparison of Investment Alternatives; Total-Cost Approach**   Julia Vanfleet is professor of mathematics at a western university. She has received a $225,000 inheritance from her father's estate, and she is anxious to invest it between now and the time she retires in 12 years. Professor Vanfleet's position with the university pays a salary of $60,000 per year. Since the state in which the university is located is experiencing extreme budgetary problems, this salary is expected to remain unchanged in the foreseeable future. Professor Vanfleet is considering two alternatives for investing her inheritance.

Alternative 1. Municipal bonds can be purchased that mature in 12 years and that bear interest at 8 percent. This interest would be tax-free and paid semiannually. (In discounting a cash flow that occurs semiannually, the procedure is to halve the interest rate and double the number of periods. Use the same procedure for discounting the principal returned when the bonds reach maturity.) This alternative would permit Professor Vanfleet to stay with the university.

Alternative 2. A small retail business is available for sale that can be purchased for $225,000. The following information relates to this alternative:

a.   Of the purchase price, $80,000 would be for fixtures and other depreciable items. The remainder would be for the company's working capital (inventory, accounts receivable, and cash). The fixtures and other depreciable items would have a remaining useful life of at least 12 years and would be in the MACRS 7-year property class. At the end of 12 years these depreciable items would have a negligible salvage value; however, the working capital would be recovered (either through sale or liquidation of the business) for reinvestment elsewhere.

b.   The store building would be leased. At the end of 12 years, if Professor Vanfleet could not find someone to buy out the business it would be necessary to pay $2,000 to the owner of the building in order to break the lease.

c.   The MACRS tables would be used for depreciation purposes.

d.   Store records indicate that sales have averaged $850,000 per year and out-of-pocket costs (including rent on the building) have averaged $760,000 per year (*not* including income taxes).

e.   Since Professor Vanfleet would operate the store herself, it would be necessary for her to leave the university if this alternative were selected. Professor Vanfleet's tax rate is 20 percent, and she wants an after-tax return of at least 8 percent on her investment.

Required

Advise Professor Vanfleet as to which alternative should be selected. Use the total-cost approach to discounted cash flow in your analysis. (Round all dollar amounts to the nearest whole dollar.)

P15–20

Comparison of Total-Cost and Incremental-Cost Approaches   Reliable Waste Systems provides a solid waste collection service in a large metropolitan area. The company is considering the purchase of several new trucks to replace an equal number of old trucks now in use. The new trucks would cost $650,000, but they would require only one operator per truck (compared to two operators for the trucks now being used), as well as provide other cost savings. A comparison of total annual cash operating costs between the old trucks that would be replaced and the new trucks is provided below:

	Old Trucks	New Trucks
Salaries—operators	$170,000	$ 85,000
Fuel	14,000	9,000
Insurance	6,000	11,000
Maintenance	10,000	5,000
Total annual cash operating costs	$200,000	$110,000

If the new trucks are purchased, the old trucks will be sold to a company in a nearby city for $85,000. These trucks cost $400,000 when they were new, have a current book value of $120,000, and have been used for four years. They are in the MACRS five-year property class; the optional straight-line method is being used to depreciate these trucks for tax purposes.

If the new trucks are not purchased, the old trucks will be used for seven more years and then sold for an estimated $15,000 scrap value. However, in order to keep the old trucks operating, extensive repairs will be needed in one year that will cost $170,000. These repairs will be expensed for tax purposes in the year incurred.

The new trucks would have a useful life of seven years and would be depreciated using the MACRS tables. They would have an estimated $60,000 salvage value at the end of their useful life. The company's tax rate is 30 percent, and its after-tax cost of capital is 12 percent.

Required
1. By use of the total-cost approach to discounted cash flow, determine whether the new trucks should be purchased. (Round all dollar amounts to the nearest whole dollar.)
2. Repeat the computations in (1), this time using the incremental-cost approach to discounted cash flow.

P15–21   Net Present Value; Incremental Cost Approach; Ethics   Leland Forrest is a member of the planning and analysis staff for Instant Dinners, Inc. (IDI), an established manufacturer of microwaveable frozen foods. He has been asked by Bill Roland, chief financial officer of IDI, to prepare a net present value analysis for a proposed capital equipment expenditure that should improve profitability in the company's Western Plant. This analysis, when completed, will be given to the company's board of directors for expenditure approval.

Several years ago, as director of planning and analysis at IDI, Roland was instrumental in convincing the board of directors to open the Western Plant. However, recent competitive pressures have forced IDI to carefully evaluate all of its operations in an effort to strengthen its market position. To Roland's dismay, he has learned that the Western Plant may be sold in the near future unless significant improvements in cost control and production efficiency are achieved.

The production manager of the Western Plant, an old friend of Roland, has submitted a proposal for the acquisition of an automated materials handling system. Roland is anxious to have this proposal approved, since it will ensure the continuance of the Western Plant and preserve his friend's position. The proposal calls for the replacement of a number of forklift trucks and operators with a computer-controlled conveyor belt system that feeds directly into the Plant's refrigeration units. This automation will eliminate the need for a number of materials handlers and will increase the output capacity of the plant.

Roland has given his friend's proposal to Forrest and has instructed him to use the following information to prepare an analysis of the project:

Projected useful life of the conveyor	10 years
Purchase and installation of the conveyor	$4,500,000
Increased working capital needed*	1,000,000
Increased annual maintenance and power costs	300,000
Repairs to the conveyor needed in five years	900,000
Incremental net annual cash inflow from the increased output (sales less related cash manufacturing costs)	1,400,000
Reduction in annual labor costs (forklift operators)	100,000
Estimated salvage value of the conveyor system	850,000

* The working capital will be released for use elsewhere at the end of the life of the conveyor system.

The forklift trucks were purchased three years ago at a cost of $1,000,000. They are in the MACRS five-year property class and are being depreciated by the MACRS optional straight-line method. Thus, the trucks have a current net book value of $500,000. If the conveyor belt system is purchased, these trucks will be sold now for $100,000. At the end of their useful life the trucks will have no salvage value.

IDI has a 30 percent tax rate and a 12 percent after-tax cost of capital. If the conveyor belt system is purchased, it will be depreciated using the MACRS optional straight-line method.

When Forrest completed his initial analysis, the proposed project appeared quite healthy. However, after investigating equipment similar to that proposed (as required by the company), Forrest discovered that the estimated salvage value of $850,000 was very optimistic. Information previously provided to Roland by several vendors estimated this value to be only $200,000. Forrest also discovered that industry trade journals considered eight years to be the maximum life of computer-controlled conveyor belt systems. As a result of this new information, Forrest prepared a second analysis of the proposed project. When Roland saw the second analysis, he told Forrest to discard this revised material, warned him not to discuss the new estimates with anyone at IDI, and ordered him not to present any of the revised information to the board of directors.

1. Compute the net *annual* cash inflows promised by the conveyor system. Do not include purchase costs, repairs, or salvage values in this figure.

Required

2. Use the incremental-cost approach and the *revised* figures as determined by Leland Forrest to determine the net present value of the proposed conveyor system.

3. Refer to the Standards of Ethical Conduct for Management Accountants on page 23 and do the following:

   a. Explain how Leland Forrest, a management accountant, should evaluate Bill Roland's directives to repress the revised analysis. Take into consideration the specific standards of competence, confidentiality, integrity, and objectivity.

   b. Identify the specific steps Leland Forrest should take to resolve this situation.

(CMA, heavily adapted)

CASES

Replacement of Riding Horses; Incremental-Cost Approach; Net Present Value

C15–22

The High-Step Riding Stables, Inc., operates a number of exclusive riding stables in the western United States. The company's Northmount Stable is not doing well even though it was provided with 60 new riding horses just two years ago. Evan Black, marketing vice president, wants to sell these horses and purchase 60 Appaloosa riding horses to use in their place. He feels certain that these beautiful animals would enhance the image of the stable and greatly increase revenues. In fact, he has asked the company's accounting department to develop a projected income statement for the coming year assuming use of both the present horses and the Appaloosa horses.

	Present Horses	Appaloosa Horses
Revenue from patrons.	$275,000	$320,000
Less operating expenses:		
Salaries—manager and handlers	90,000	90,000
Feed	32,000	41,000
Insurance on the horses	8,000	12,500
Depreciation, stables and equipment	108,000	108,000
Depreciation, horses*	10,000	28,500
Total operating expenses	208,000	231,000
Income before income taxes	27,000	40,000
Less income taxes (30%)	8,100	12,000
Net income	$ 18,900	$ 28,000

* Present horses: $90,000 cost ÷ 9 years = $10,000. Appaloosa horses: $210,000 cost − (60 horses × $175 sale value = $10,500) = $199,500; $199,500 ÷ 7 years = $28,500.

Shauna Brosnan, operations vice president, is less enthused about the purchase. She stated, "I agree that the Appaloosas are beautiful, but look at what they would cost us. There are many other ways we could use that $210,000 in the company, and according to my computations all of these other ways would yield a return well over our 10 percent after-tax cost of capital."

"That's the best part of this whole deal," replied Evan. "The Appaloosas would provide a fantastic rate of return. Just look at these figures I've worked up:"

$$\frac{\text{Net income}}{\underset{\text{investment}}{\text{Initial}} - \underset{\text{old horses}}{\text{Sale of the}}} = \text{Simple rate of return}$$

$$\frac{\$28,000}{\$210,000 - \$55,000} = 18.1\%$$

"Do you have any investments that will beat 18 percent?"

"No, I'll admit I don't," replied Shauna, "and your figures are impressive; but I'm still uneasy about the whole thing. Give me time to look at these figures a little more closely, and then I'll get back with you later."

After some effort, Shauna has accumulated the following additional information:

a.   Both the horses currently owned and the Appaloosa horses are in the MACRS five-year property class. For tax purposes, the company is using the optional straight-line method to compute depreciation on the 60 horses now owned by Northmount Stable.

b.   If the Appaloosa horses are purchased, they will be depreciated by use of the MACRS tables. These horses have a remaining useful life of seven years.

c.   The 60 horses now owned by Northmount Stable will have no resale value at the end of their useful life to the stable.

d.   The Appaloosa horses would be registered; in order to maintain this registration, the company would have to pay a renewal fee of $80 per horse four years from now.

e.   To maintain a high sheen on their coats, the Appaloosa horses would have a special grain mixture added to their diets. Carrying a supply of the grain mixture on hand would require a $3,000 increase in the working capital requirements for the stable.

Required   1.   By use of net present value analysis, determine whether the Appaloosa horses should be purchased. Use the incremental-cost approach, and round all dollar amounts to the nearest whole dollar.

2.   Do you agree with the way Evan has computed the simple rate of return on the horses? Explain your answer.

C15-23   **Make or Buy Decision; Discounted Cash Flow; Incremental-Cost Approach**   Lamb Company manufactures several lines of products, including all of the component parts that go into these products. One unique part, a valve stem, requires specialized tools in its manufacture that need to be replaced. Management has decided that the only alternative to replacing these tools is to acquire the valve stem from an outside source. A supplier is willing to provide the valve stem at a unit sales price of $20 if at least 70,000 units are ordered each year.

Lamb Company's average production of valve stems over the past three years has been 80,000 units each year. Expectations are that this volume will remain constant over the next four years. Cost records indicate that unit manufacturing costs for the valve stem over the last several years have been as follows:

Direct materials	$ 3.60
Direct labor	3.90
Variable overhead	1.50
Fixed overhead*	9.00
Total unit cost	$18.00

* Depreciation of tools (that must now be replaced) accounts for one third of the fixed overhead. The balance is for other fixed overhead costs of the factory that require cash expenditures.

If the specialized tools are purchased, they will cost $2,500,000 and will have a disposal value of $100,000 at the end of their four-year useful life. Straight-line depreciation would be used for book purposes, but the MACRS tables would be used for tax purposes. Lamb

Company has a 30 percent tax rate, and management requires a 12 percent after-tax return on investment.

The sales representative for the manufacturer of the specialized tools has stated, "The new tools will allow direct labor and variable overhead to be reduced by $1.60 per unit." Data from another company using identical tools and experiencing similar operating conditions, except that annual production generally averages 100,000 units, confirms the direct labor and variable overhead cost savings. However, the other company indicates that it experienced an increase in raw material cost due to the higher quality of material that had to be used with the new tools. The other company indicates that its costs have been as follows:

Direct materials	$ 4.50
Direct labor	3.00
Variable overhead	0.80
Fixed overhead	10.80
Total unit cost	$19.10

Referring to the figures above, Eric Madsen, Lamb's production manager, stated, "These numbers look great until you consider the difference in volume. Even with the reduction in labor and variable overhead cost, I'll bet our total unit cost figure would increase to over $20 with the new tools."

Although the old tools being used by Lamb Company are now fully depreciated, they have a salvage value of $45,000. These tools will be sold if the new tools are purchased; however, if the new tools are not purchased, then the old tools will be retained as standby equipment. Lamb Company's accounting department has confirmed that total fixed overhead costs, other than depreciation, will not change regardless of the decision made concerning the valve stems. However, accounting has estimated that working capital needs will increase by $60,000 if the new tools are purchased due to the higher quality of material required in the manufacture of the valve stems.

Required

1. Prepare a discounted cash flow analysis that will help Lamb Company's management decide whether the new tools should be purchased. Use the incremental-cost approach, and round all dollar amounts to the nearest whole dollar.
2. Identify additional factors that Lamb Company's management should consider before a decision is made about whether to manufacture or buy the valve stems.

(CMA, heavily adapted)

Make or Buy Decision; Discounted Cash Flow; Total-Cost Approach   Jonfran Company manufactures three different models of paper shredders including the waste container which serves as the base. While the shredder heads are different for all three models, the waste container is the same. The number of waste containers that Jonfran will need during the next five years is estimated as follows:

C15–24

19x1	50,000	19x4	55,000
19x2	50,000	19x5	55,000
19x3	52,000		

The equipment used to manufacture the waste containers must be replaced because it has broken and can't be repaired. The new equipment would have a purchase price of $945,000 with terms of 2/10, n/30; company policy is to take all purchase discounts. The freight on the equipment would be $11,000, and installation costs would total $22,900. The equipment would be purchased and placed into service in January 19x1. It would have a five-year useful life and would be in the MACRS three-year property class. (The company uses the MACRS tables for tax purposes.) The equipment would have a salvage value of $15,000 at the end of its useful life.

The new equipment would be more efficient than the old equipment and it would slash both direct labor and variable overhead costs in half. However, the new equipment would require the use of a slightly heavier gauge of metal which would increase direct material costs by 30 percent. The company uses JIT inventory methods, but the heavier gauge metal is sometimes hard to get so the company would have to keep a small quantity on hand, which would increase working capital needs by $20,000.

The old equipment is fully depreciated and is not included in the fixed overhead. The old equipment can be sold now for $1,500; Jonfran has no alternative use for the manufacturing space at this time, so if the new equipment is not purchased the old equipment will be left in place.

Rather than replace the old equipment, one of Jonfran's production managers has suggested that the waste containers be purchased. One supplier has quoted a price of $28 per container. This price is $7 less than Jonfran's current manufacturing cost, which is presented below:

Direct materials		$10
Direct labor		8
Variable overhead		6
Fixed overhead:		
Supervision	$2	
Facilities	5	
General	4	11
Total cost per unit		$35

Jonfran employs a plantwide fixed overhead rate in its operations. If the waste containers are purchased outside, the salary and benefits of one supervisor, included in the fixed overhead at $45,000, would be eliminated. There would be no other changes in the other cash and noncash items included in fixed overhead except depreciation on the new equipment.

Jonfran is subject to a 30 percent tax rate and requires a 14 percent after-tax return on all equipment purchases.

Required Using discounted cash flow, determine whether the company should purchase the new equipment and make the waste containers or purchase the containers from the outside supplier. Use the total-cost approach and round all dollar amounts to the nearest whole dollar.

(CMA, heavily adapted)

SELECTED TOPICS FOR FURTHER STUDY

Part

IV

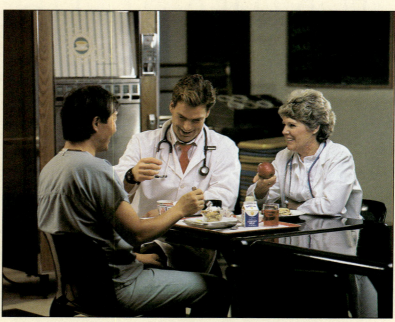

Service departments, such as this hospital cafeteria, exist to provide services to other departments. When employees eat in the cafeteria certain costs must be incurred. If these costs are not assigned back to the departments in which the employees work, the costs of running those departments will be understated. In turn, this will result in understating the costs of any products or services provided by those other departments.

Service Department Costing:

An Activity Approach

1 Explain what is meant by a service department, and explain why it is necessary to allocate service department costs to operating departments.

2 Select a first-stage allocation base (cost driver) for each service department that accurately measures consumption of services by other departments.

3 Allocate service department costs to other departments, using (a) the direct method and (b) the step method.

4 Explain why variable and fixed service department costs should be allocated separately.

5 Explain how allocated service department costs are traced to operating department flexible budgets.

6 Enumerate the guidelines that should be followed in allocating service department costs.

7 Prepare an allocation schedule involving several service departments and several operating departments.

8 Define or explain the key terms listed at the end of the chapter.

s stated in Chapter 1, most organizations have one or more service departments that carry on critical auxiliary services for the entire organization. In this chapter, we look more closely at service departments and
consider how their costs are allocated to the units they serve for planning, costing,
and other purposes.

THE NEED FOR COST ALLOCATION

Objective 1
Explain what is meant by
a service department, and
explain why it is
necessary to allocate
service department costs
to operating departments.

Departments within an organization can be divided into two broad classes: (1)
operating departments and (2) service departments. **Operating departments** include those departments or units where the central purposes of the organization
are carried out. Examples of such departments or units would include the surgery
department in a hospital; the undergraduate and graduate programs in a university; various flight groups in an airline; and producing departments such as milling,
assembly, and painting in a manufacturing company.

Service departments, by contrast, do not engage directly in operating activities.
Rather, they provide services or assistance that facilitate the activities of the
operating departments. Examples of such services include cafeteria, internal auditing, personnel, X ray, cost accounting, and purchasing. Although service departments do not engage directly in the operating activities of an organization, the
costs that they incur are generally viewed as being part of the cost of the final
product or service, the same as are materials, labor, and overhead in a manufacturing company or medications in a hospital.

The major question that we must consider in this chapter is: How does the
manager determine how much of a service department's cost is to be allocated to
each of the units that it serves? This is an important question, since the amount of
service department cost allocated to a particular unit can have a significant impact
on the cost of the goods or services that the unit is providing. As we shall see,
many factors must be considered if allocations are to be equitable between departments or other units that receive services during a period.

GUIDELINES FOR COST ALLOCATION

Several basic guidelines should be followed in allocating service department
costs. These guidelines relate to (1) selecting the proper allocation base, (2) allocating the costs of interdepartmental services, (3) allocating costs by behavior, (4)
avoiding certain allocation pitfalls, and (5) deciding whether to allocate budgeted
or actual costs. These topics are covered in order in this section.

Selecting Allocation Bases

Objective 2
Select a first-stage
allocation base (cost
driver) for each service
department that
accurately measures
consumption of services
by other departments.

In Chapter 5, we stated that many companies use a two-stage costing process. In
the first stage, costs are assigned to the operating departments; in the second
stage, costs are assigned from the operating departments to products. We focused
most of our attention in Chapter 5 on the second stage and reserved discussion of
first-stage costing procedures to this chapter. On the following pages we discuss
the assignment of costs from service departments to operating departments, *which
represents the first stage of the two-stage costing process.*

In our Chapter 5 discussion, we introduced activity-based costing and cited
advantages for its use over volume measures such as direct labor-hours in assigning costs to products. Although some persons view activity-based costing as a

new concept, only the term itself is new. Service departments have used the concept for many years as they have tried to develop equitable methods of assigning their costs to other departments. Thus, the reader should be aware that the first-stage costing procedures we discuss in this chapter contain a healthy dose of what is now termed *activity-based costing*.

How are costs assigned from service departments to operating departments? This is accomplished by identifying the activity that drives costs in a service department, and then measuring the consumption of this activity by other departments. A cost-driving activity in a service department is generally referred to as an **allocation base.** Allocation bases may include number of employees, labor-hours, square footage of space occupied, or any other measure of activity in a department. Managers try to select allocation bases that reflect as accurately as possible the benefits that are being received by the various departments from the services involved. A number of such bases may be selected according to the nature of the service department. For example, data processing may have two bases—one consisting of CPU minutes and another consisting of lines printed or units in storage. Examples of allocation bases that are frequently used by service departments are presented in Exhibit 16–1.

Once allocation bases have been chosen, they tend to remain unchanged for long periods unless it can be determined that some inequity exists that is resulting in costing errors. The criteria for selecting an allocation base may include the following:

1. Direct, traceable benefits from the service involved. Such benefits might be measured, for example, by the number of service orders handled.
2. The extent to which space or equipment is made available to a department. This availability might be measured, for example, by the square feet of space occupied in a building.

Service Department	Bases (cost drivers) Involved
Laundry	Pounds of laundry; number of items processed
Airport ground services	Number of flights
Cafeteria	Number of employees
Medical facilities	Periodic analysis of cases handled; number of employees; hours worked
Materials handling	Hours of service; volume handled
Data processing	CPU minutes; lines printed; units in storage
Custodial services (building and grounds)	Measure of square footage occupied
Engineering	Periodic analysis of services rendered; direct labor-hours
Production planning and control	Periodic analysis of services rendered; direct labor-hours
Cost accounting	Labor-hours; clients or patients serviced
Power	Measured usage (in kwh); capacity of machines
Human resources	Number of employees; turnover of labor; training hours
Receiving, shipping, and stores	Units handled; number of requisition and issue slips; square or cubic footage occupied
Factory administration	Total labor-hours
Maintenance	Machine-hours; total labor-hours (in order of preference)

EXHIBIT 16–1
Bases Used in Allocating Service Department Costs

In addition to these criteria, the manager must be sure that allocations are clear and straightforward, since complex allocation computations run the risk of being more effort than they are worth. Allocation methods should be simple and easily understood by all involved, particularly by the managers to whom the costs are being allocated.

HUGHES   FOCUS ON CURRENT PRACTICE

For many years, Hughes Aircraft allocated service department costs to operating departments using head count as the primary base because of its simplicity. Recently, the company has adopted an activity-based approach as it has taken dramatic steps to improve its costing system. Selected examples of service department allocations now made by the company are shown in the table below.

In describing the improved system, two Hughes managers stated, "For the first time operating units understand, and therefore can control, their level of cost absorption through an evaluation of their own activities. In addition, the metrics derived for each allocation serve as budgeting tools, [as] a method of communication between the providers and absorbers of an activity, and [as] a method for performance measurement in an era of continuous measurable improvement."[1]

Service Department	Allocation Bases (cost drivers)	Metrics
Human resources. . . .	Head count	$/head
	Hires	$/hire
	Union employees	$/head
	Training hours	$/training hour
Security	Square footage	$/square foot
Data processing	Lines printed	$/line
	CPU minutes	$/CPU minute
	Storage	$/storage unit

Interdepartmental Services

Objective 3
Allocate service department costs to other departments using (a) the direct method and (b) the step method.

Many service departments provide services for each other, as well as for operating departments. The cafeteria, for example, provides food for all employees, including those assigned to other service departments. In turn, the cafeteria may receive services from other service departments, such as from custodial services or from personnel. Services provided between service departments are known as **interdepartmental** or **reciprocal services.**

Three approaches are used to allocate the costs of service departments to other departments. These are known as the *direct method,* the *step method,* and the *reciprocal method.* All three methods are discussed in the following paragraphs.

Direct Method

The **direct method** is a very simple allocation approach in that it ignores the costs of services between service departments and allocates all costs directly to operating departments. Even if a service department (such as personnel) renders a large amount of service to another service department (such as the

---

[1] Jack Haedicke and David Feil, "Hughes Aircraft Sets the Standard for ABC," *Management Accounting* 72, no. 8 (February 1991), pp. 31–32.

cafeteria), no allocations are made between the two departments. Rather, all costs would go directly to the operating departments of the company. Hence the term *direct method*.

To provide a numerical example of the direct method, assume that Mountain View Hospital has two service departments and two operating departments as shown below:

| | Service Department | | Operating Department | | |
	Hospital Administration	Custodial Services	Laboratory	Daily Patient Care	Total
Departmental costs before allocation	$360,000	$90,000	$261,000	$689,000	$1,400,000
Labor-hours.	—	6,000	18,000	30,000	54,000
Proportion of labor-hours		1/9	3/9	5/9	9/9
Space occupied—square feet . . .	10,000	—	5,000	45,000	60,000
Proportion of space occupied . . .	2/12	—	1/12	9/12	12/12

Allocation of the hospital's service department costs by the direct method to the operating departments is shown in Exhibit 16–2. Note that after all allocations have been made, all of the departmental costs are contained in the two operating departments. These costs will form the basis for preparing overhead rates and for determining the overall profitability of the operating departments in the hospital.

Although the direct method is simple, it is less accurate than the other methods, since it ignores interdepartmental services. This can be a major defect in that overhead rates can be affected if the resulting errors in allocation are significant. In turn, incorrect overhead rates can lead to distorted product and service costs and to ineffective pricing. Even so, many organizations use the direct method because of its simplicity.

Step Method   Unlike the direct method, the **step method** provides for allocation of a service department's costs to other service departments, as well as to operating departments, in a sequential manner. The sequence typically begins with the department that provides the greatest amount of service to other departments. After its costs have been allocated, the process continues, step by step, ending with the department that provides the least amount of services to other service departments. This step procedure is illustrated in graphic form in Exhibit 16–3.

EXHIBIT 16–2
Direct Method of Allocation

| | Service Department | | Operating Department | | |
	Hospital Administration	Custodial Services	Laboratory	Daily Patient Care	Total
Departmental costs before allocation	$ 360,000	$ 90,000	$261,000	$689,000	$1,400,000
Allocation:					
Hospital administration costs (3/8, 5/8)*	(360,000)		135,000	225,000	
Custodial services costs (1/10, 9/10)†		(90,000)	9,000	81,000	
Total costs after allocation.	$ –0–	$ –0–	$405,000	$995,000	$1,400,000

   * Based on the labor-hours in the two operating departments, which are: 18,000 hours + 30,000 hours = 48,000 hours.

   † Based on the space occupied by the two operating departments, which is: 5,000 square feet + 45,000 square feet = 50,000 square feet.

EXHIBIT 16–3

Graphic Illustration—Step Method

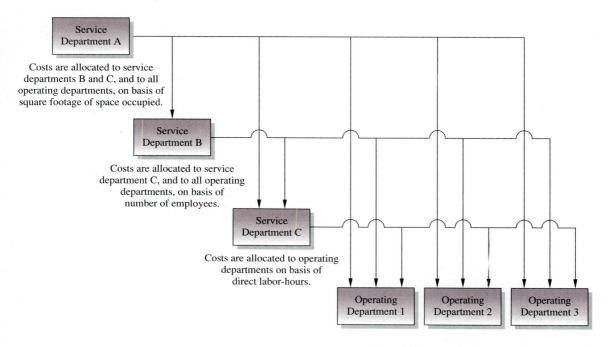

Service Department A

Costs are allocated to service departments B and C, and to all operating departments, on basis of square footage of space occupied.

Service Department B

Costs are allocated to service department C, and to all operating departments, on basis of number of employees.

Service Department C

Costs are allocated to operating departments on basis of direct labor-hours.

Operating Department 1   Operating Department 2   Operating Department 3

A numeric example of the step method is provided in Exhibit 16–4. The data in this exhibit are the same as that used earlier in connection with the direct method in Exhibit 16–2.

Since hospital administration provides the greatest amount of service to other departments, its costs are allocated first. This allocation is on the basis of labor-hours in other departments. The costs of custodial services are then allocated on the basis of square footage of space occupied.

Two things should be noted about these allocations. First, note that the costs of hospital administration are borne by another service department (custodial services) as well as by the operating departments. Second, note that those hospital administration costs that have been allocated to custodial services *are included with custodial services costs,* and that the total ($90,000 + $40,000 = $130,000) is allocated only to subsequent departments. That is, no part of custodial services' costs are reallocated back to hospital administration, even though custodial ser-

EXHIBIT 16–4

Step Method of Allocation

	Service Department		Operating Department		
	Hospital Administration	Custodial Services	Laboratory	Daily Patient Care	Total
Departmental costs before allocation	$ 360,000	$ 90,000	$261,000	$ 689,000	$1,400,000
Allocation:					
Hospital administration costs ($\frac{1}{9}$, $\frac{3}{9}$, $\frac{5}{9}$)	(360,000)	40,000	120,000	200,000	
Custodial services costs ($\frac{1}{10}$, $\frac{9}{10}$)*		(130,000)	13,000	117,000	
Total costs after allocation	$ –0–	$ –0–	$394,000	$1,006,000	$1,400,000

* As in Exhibit 16–2, this allocation is based on the space occupied by the two operating departments.

vices may have provided services to hospital administration during the period. This is a key idea associated with the step method: After the allocation of a service department's costs has been completed, costs of other service departments are not reallocated back to it.

Reciprocal Method   The **reciprocal method** is so named because it gives full recognition to interdepartmental services. Under the step method discussed above only partial recognition of interdepartmental services is possible, since the step method always allocates costs forward—never backward—as shown earlier in Exhibit 16–3. The reciprocal method, by contrast, allocates service department costs in *both* directions. Thus, if Custodial Services in the prior example provides service for Hospital Administration and the reciprocal method is being used, then part of Custodial Services' costs will be allocated *back* to Hospital Administration. At the same time, part of Hospital Administration's costs will be allocated *forward* to Custodial Services. This type of reciprocal allocation requires the construction and use of simultaneous linear equations. These equations are complex and will not be illustrated here. Examples of the reciprocal method can be found in cost accounting books if the reader wants to study the topic further.

The reciprocal method is rarely used in practice for two reasons. First, the computations are complex as we have noted; this complexity is increased if more than two service departments are involved. Although the complexity issue could be overcome by use of computers, there is no evidence to show that computers have made the reciprocal method more popular. Second, the step method usually provides results that are a reasonable approximation of the results that the reciprocal method would provide. Thus, little motivation exists for companies to use the more complex reciprocal method.

Revenue Producing Departments   To conclude our discussion of allocation methods, it is important to note that even though most service departments are cost centers and therefore generate no revenues, a few service departments such as the cafeteria may charge for the services they perform. If a service department generates revenues, these revenues should be offset against the department's costs, and only the net amount of cost remaining after this offset should be allocated to other departments within the organization. In this manner, the other departments will not be required to bear costs for which the service department has already been reimbursed.

Allocating Costs by Behavior

Whenever possible, service department costs should be separated into variable and fixed classifications and allocated separately. This approach is necessary to avoid possible inequities in allocation, as well as to provide more useful data for planning and control of departmental operations.

Objective 4
Explain why variable and fixed service department costs should be allocated separately.

Variable Costs   Variable costs represent direct costs of providing services and will generally vary in total in proportion to fluctuations in the level of service consumed. Food cost in a cafeteria would be a variable cost, for example, and one would expect this cost to vary proportionately with the number of persons using the cafeteria over a given period of time.

As a general rule, variable costs should be charged to consuming departments according to whatever activity causes the incurrence of the costs involved. If, for example, the variable costs of a service department such as maintenance are caused by the number of machine-hours worked in the producing departments, then variable maintenance costs should be allocated to the producing departments on a machine-hours basis. By this means, the departments directly responsible for the incurrence of servicing costs are required to bear them in proportion to their actual usage of the service involved.

Technically, the assigning of variable servicing costs to consuming departments can more accurately be termed *charges* than allocations, since the service department is actually charging the consuming departments at some fixed rate per unit of service provided. In effect, the service department is saying, "I'll charge you X dollars for every unit of my service that you consume. You can consume as much or as little as you desire; the total charge you bear will vary proportionately."

Fixed Costs   The fixed costs of service departments represent the costs of having long-run service capacity available. As such, these costs are most equitably allocated to consuming departments on a basis of *predetermined lump-sum amounts*. By "predetermined lump-sum amounts" we mean that the amount charged to each consuming department is determined in advance and, once determined, does not change from period to period. Typically, the lump-sum amount charged to a department is based either on the department's peak-period or long-run average servicing needs. The logic behind lump-sum allocations of this type is as follows:

When a service department is first established, its capacity will be determined by the needs of the departments that it will service. This capacity may reflect the peak-period needs of the other departments, or it may reflect their long-run average or "normal" servicing needs. Depending on how much servicing capacity is provided for, it will be necessary to make a commitment of resources to the servicing unit, which will be reflected in its fixed costs. It is generally felt that these fixed costs should be borne by the consuming departments in proportion to the individual servicing needs that have been provided for. That is, if available capacity in the service department has been provided to meet the peak-period needs of consuming departments, then the fixed costs of the service department should be allocated in predetermined lump-sum amounts to consuming departments on this basis. If available capacity has been provided only to meet "normal" or long-run average needs, then the fixed costs should be allocated on this basis.

Once set, allocations should not vary from period to period, since they represent each consuming department's "fair share" of having a certain level of service capacity available and on line. The fact that a consuming department does not need a peak level or even a "normal" level of servicing every period is immaterial; if it requires such servicing at certain times, then the capacity to deliver it must be available. It is the responsibility of the consuming departments to bear the cost of that availability.

To illustrate this idea, assume that Novak Company has just organized a maintenance department to service all machines in the cutting, assembly, and finishing departments. In determining the capacity that should be built into the newly organized maintenance department, the various producing departments estimated that they would have the following peak-period needs for maintenance:

Department	Peak-Period Maintenance Needs in Terms of Number of Hours of Maintenance Work Required	Percent of Total Hours
Cutting	900	30
Assembly	1,800	60
Finishing	300	10
	3,000	100

Therefore, in allocating the maintenance department fixed costs to the producing departments, 30 percent should be allocated to the cutting department, 60 percent to the assembly department, and 10 percent to the finishing department. These lump-sum allocations *will not change* from period to period unless there is some shift in servicing needs due to structural changes in the organization.

FOCUS ON CURRENT PRACTICE

Bellcore (Bell Communications Research) has 25 service centers that provide support to the company's operating units. Several years ago the company discovered that some service center rates had increased to intolerable levels because of an antiquated costing system that improperly accumulated costs on which the rates were set.

For example, at one point the company's word processing service center was charging $50 per typed page to the operating units. This forced engineers, researchers, and other highly paid people within the operating units to divert a considerable amount of time to typing their own documents and doing other clerical work. The exorbitant rates forced other users to go outside the company for typing, graphics, and related services. After a major restructuring of the cost allocation system, including better tracing of costs to the service centers, rates in word processing, graphics, and other service centers were brought into line with competing rates elsewhere.[2]

Pitfalls in Allocating Fixed Costs

Rather than allocate fixed costs in predetermined lump-sum amounts, some firms allocate them by use of a *variable* allocation base. What's wrong with this practice? The answer is that it can distort decisions and create serious inequities between departments. The inequities will arise from the fact that the fixed costs allocated to one department will be heavily influenced by what happens in *other* departments or segments of the organization.

To illustrate, assume that Kolby Products has an auto service center that provides maintenance work on the fleet of autos used in the company's two sales territories. The auto service center costs are all fixed. Contrary to good practice, the company allocates these fixed costs to the sales territories on the basis of miles driven (a variable base). Selected cost data for the last two years are given below:

---

[2] Edward J. Kovac and Henry P. Troy, "Getting Transfer Prices Right: What Bellcore Did," *Harvard Business Review*, 89, no. 5 (September–October 1989).

	Year 1	**Year 2**
Auto service center costs (all fixed) . . .	$120,000 (a)	$120,000 (a)
Sales territory A—miles driven	1,500,000	1,500,000
Sales territory B—miles driven	1,500,000	900,000
Total miles driven	3,000,000 (b)	2,400,000 (b)
Allocation rate per mile, (a) ÷ (b)	$0.04	$0.05

Notice that sales territory A maintained an activity level of 1,500,000 miles driven in both years. On the other hand, sales territory B allowed its activity to drop off from 1,500,000 miles in year 1 to only 900,000 miles in year 2. The auto service center costs that would have been allocated to the two sales territories over the two-year span are as follows:

Year 1:
    Sales territory A: 1,500,000 miles at $0.04 . . . . . $ 60,000
    Sales territory B: 1,500,000 miles at $0.04   60,000
    Total cost allocated $120,000
Year 2:
    Sales territory A: 1,500,000 miles at $0.05 . . . . . $ 75,000
    Sales territory B: 900,000 miles at $0.05   45,000
    Total cost allocated $120,000

In year 1, the two sales territories share the service department costs equally. In year 2, however, the bulk of the service department costs are allocated to sales territory A. This is not because of any increase in activity in sales territory A; rather, it is because of the *decrease* in effort in sales territory B, which did not maintain its activity level during year 2. Even though sales territory A maintained the same level of activity in both years, the use of a variable allocation base has caused it to be penalized with a heavier cost allocation in year 2 because of what has happened in *another* territory of the company.

This kind of inequity is almost inevitable when a variable allocation base is used to allocate fixed costs. The manager of sales territory A undoubtedly will be upset about the inequity forced on his territory, but he will feel powerless to do anything about it. The result will be a loss of confidence in the system and the accumulation of a considerable backlog of ill feeling.

Should Actual or Budgeted Costs Be Allocated?

Should a service department allocate its *actual* costs to operating departments, or should it allocate its *budgeted* costs? The answer is that budgeted costs should be allocated. What's wrong with allocating actual costs? Allocating actual costs burdens the operating departments with the inefficiencies of the service department managers. If actual costs are allocated, then any lack of cost control on the part of the service department manager is simply buried in a routine allocation to other departments.

Any variance over budgeted costs should be retained in the service department and closed out at year-end against the company's revenues or against cost of goods sold, along with other variances. Operating department managers rarely complain about being allocated a portion of service department costs, but they complain bitterly if they are forced to absorb service department inefficiencies.

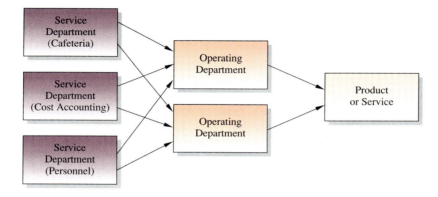

First Stage

Service department costs are allocated to operating departments.

Second Stage

Operating department overhead costs, plus allocated service department costs, are applied to products and services by means of departmental overhead rates.

EXHIBIT 16–5

Effect of Allocations on Products and Services

EFFECT OF ALLOCATIONS ON OPERATING DEPARTMENTS

Once allocations have been completed, what do the operating departments do with the allocated service department costs? Since the amounts allocated are presumed to represent each department's ''fair share'' of the cost of services provided for it, the allocations are included in performance evaluations of the operating departments and also included in determining their individual profitability.

In addition, if the operating departments are responsible for developing overhead rates for costing of products or billing of services, then the allocated costs are combined with the other costs of the operating departments, and the total is used as a basis for rate computations. This rate development process is illustrated in Exhibit 16–5.

Typically, the flexible budget serves as the means for combining allocated service department costs with operating department costs and for computing overhead rates. An example of the combining of these costs on a flexible budget is presented in Exhibit 16–6. Note from the exhibit that both variable and fixed service department costs have been allocated to Superior Company's milling department and are included on the latter's flexible budget. Since allocated service department costs become an integral part of the flexible budget, they are automatically included in overhead rate computations, as shown at the bottom of the exhibit. If this had been the flexible budget of an operating department in a service company, rather than a manufacturing company, then the overhead rate computation would have been for purposes of developing an appropriate billing rate for services.

Objective 5
Explain how allocated service department costs are traced to operating department flexible budgets.

A SUMMARY OF COST ALLOCATION GUIDELINES

To summarize the material covered in preceding sections, we can note five key points to remember about allocating service department costs:

1. If possible, the distinction between variable and fixed costs in service departments should be maintained.

Objective 6
Enumerate the guidelines that should be followed in allocating service department costs.

EXHIBIT 16–6
Flexible Budget
Containing Allocated
Service Department
Costs

SUPERIOR COMPANY
Flexible Budget—Milling Department

Budgeted direct labor-hours   50,000

Overhead Costs	Cost Formula (per hour)	Direct Labor-Hours		
		40,000	50,000	60,000
Variable costs:				
Indirect labor	$1.45	$ 58,000	$ 72,500	$ 87,000
Indirect material	0.90	36,000	45,000	54,000
Utilities	0.10	4,000	5,000	6,000
Allocation—cafeteria	0.15	6,000	7,500	9,000
Total variable costs	$2.60	104,000	130,000	156,000
Fixed costs:				
Depreciation		85,000	85,000	85,000
Supervisory salaries.		110,000	110,000	110,000
Property taxes		9,000	9,000	9,000
Allocation—cafeteria		21,000	21,000	21,000
Allocation—human resources		45,000	45,000	45,000
Total fixed costs		270,000	270,000	270,000
Total overhead costs		$374,000	$400,000	$426,000

$$\text{Predetermined overhead rate} = \frac{\$400,000}{50,000 \text{ DLH}} = \$8 \text{ per direct labor-hour}$$

2. Variable costs should be allocated at the budgeted rate, according to whatever activity (miles driven, direct labor-hours, number of employees) causes the incurrence of the cost involved.

   a. If the allocations are being made at the beginning of the year, they should be based on the budgeted activity level planned for the consuming departments. The allocation formula would be:

   Budgeted rate × Budgeted activity = Cost allocated

   b. If the allocations are being made at the end of the year, they should be based on the actual activity level that has occurred during the year. The allocation formula would be:

   Budgeted rate × Actual activity = Cost allocated

   Allocations made at the beginning of the year would be to provide data for computing overhead rates for costing of products and billing of services in the operating departments. Allocations made at the end of the year would be to provide data for comparing actual performance against planned performance.

3. Fixed costs represent the costs of having service capacity available. Where feasible, these costs should be allocated in predetermined lump-sum amounts. The lump-sum amount going to each department should be in proportion to the servicing needs that gave rise to the investment in the service department in the first place. (This might be either peak-period needs for servicing or long-run average needs.) Budgeted fixed costs, rather than actual fixed costs, should always be allocated.

4. If it is not feasible to maintain a distinction between variable and fixed costs in a service department, then the costs of the department should be allocated to

consuming departments according to the base that appears to provide the best measure of benefits received.

5. Where possible, reciprocal services between departments should be recognized.

IMPLEMENTING THE ALLOCATION GUIDELINES

We will now show the implementation of these guidelines by the use of specific examples. We will focus first on the allocation of costs for a single department, and then develop a more extended example where multiple departments are involved.

Objective 7
Prepare an allocation schedule involving several service departments and several operating departments.

Basic Allocation Techniques

For purposes of illustration, assume that Seaboard Airlines is divided into a Freight Division and a Passenger Division. The company has a single aircraft maintenance department that provides servicing to both divisions. Variable servicing costs are budgeted at $10 per flight-hour. The fixed costs of the department are budgeted at $750,000 per year. Peak-period flight-hours per year and budgeted flight-hours for the coming year are shown below:

	Flight-Hours	
	Peak Period	**Budgeted**
Freight Division	12,000	9,000
Passenger Division	18,000	15,000
Total flight-hours	30,000	24,000

Given these data, the amount of cost that would be allocated to each division from the aircraft maintenance department at the beginning of the coming year would be:

	Division	
	Freight	**Passenger**
Variable cost allocation:		
$10 × 9,000 flight-hours	$ 90,000	
$10 × 15,000 flight-hours		$150,000
Fixed cost allocation:		
40%* × $750,000	300,000	
60%* × $750,000		450,000
Total cost allocated	$390,000	$600,000

* These allocations are based on peak-period flight-hours in each division:

Freight Division: 12,000 flight-hours ÷ 30,000 flight-hours = 40%.
Passenger Division: 18,000 flight-hours ÷ 30,000 flight-hours = 60%.

As explained earlier, these allocated costs would be included in the flexible budgets of the respective divisions and included in the computation of divisional overhead rates.

At the end of the year, Seaboard Airlines' management may want to make a second allocation, this time based on actual activity, in order to compare actual performance for the year against planned performance. To illustrate, assume that year-end records show that actual costs in the aircraft maintenance department for the year were: variable costs, $260,000; and fixed costs, $780,000. We will assume that one division logged more flight-hours during the year than planned and the other one logged less flight-hours than planned.

	Flight-Hours	
	Budgeted (see above)	Actual
Freight Division	9,000	8,000
Passenger Division	15,000	17,000
Total flight-hours	24,000	25,000

The amount of actual service department cost chargeable to each division for the year would be as follows:

	Division	
	Freight	Passenger
Variable cost allocation:		
$10 × 8,000 flight-hours	$ 80,000	
$10 × 17,000 flight-hours		$170,000
Fixed cost allocation:		
40% × $750,000	300,000	
60% × $750,000		450,000
Total cost allocated	$380,000	$620,000

Notice that the variable cost is allocated according to the budgeted rate ($10 per hour) times the *actual activity* for the year, and that the fixed cost is allocated according to the original budgeted amount. As stated in the guidelines given earlier, allocations are always based on budgeted rates and amounts in order to avoid passing on inefficiency from one department to another. Thus, a portion of the actual costs of the aircraft maintenance department for the year will not be allocated, as shown below:

	Variable	Fixed
Total actual costs incurred	$260,000	$780,000
Costs allocated (above)	250,000*	750,000
Spending variance—not allocated . .	$ 10,000	$ 30,000

* $10 per flight-hour × 25,000 actual flight-hours = $250,000.

These variances will be closed out against the company's overall revenues for the year, along with any other variances that may occur.

An Extended Example

Proctor Company has three service departments—building maintenance, cafeteria, and inspection. The company also has two operating departments—shaping and assembly. The service departments provide services to each other, as well as to the operating departments. Types of costs in the service departments and bases for allocation are:

Department	Type of Cost	Base for Allocation
Building maintenance . . .	Fixed costs	Square footage occupied
Cafeteria	Variable costs Fixed costs	Number of employees 10% to inspection, 40% to shaping, and 50% to assembly
Inspection	Variable costs Fixed costs	Direct labor-hours 70% to shaping and 30% to assembly

Proctor Company allocates service department costs by the step method in the following order:

1. Building maintenance.
2. Cafeteria.
3. Inspection.

Assume the following budgeted cost and operating data for 19x1:

Department	Variable Cost	Fixed Cost
Building maintenance . . .	—	$130,000
Cafeteria	$200 per employee	250,000
Inspection	$0.06 per direct labor-hour	548,000

Department	Number of Employees	Direct Labor-Hours	Square Footage of Space Occupied (square feet)
Building maintenance . . .	6*	—	3,000
Cafeteria	9*	—	4,000
Inspection	30	—	1,000
Shaping	190	300,000	8,000
Assembly	250	500,000	13,000
Total.	485	800,000	29,000

* Although there are employees in both of these service departments, under the step method costs are only allocated *forward*—never backward. For this reason, the costs of the cafeteria will be allocated *forward* on the basis of the number of employees in the inspection, shaping, and assembly departments.

In addition to the service department costs listed above, the company's shaping department has budgeted $1,340,000 in overhead costs for 19x1, and its assembly department has budgeted $1,846,000 in overhead costs.

Cost allocations from the service departments to the operating departments are as shown in Exhibit 16–7. To save space, we have computed the operating department's predetermined overhead rates at the bottom of the exhibit.

No Distinction Made between Fixed and Variable Costs

As stated in the guidelines given earlier, in some cases it may not be feasible to maintain a distinction between fixed and variable service department costs. We noted that in such cases the costs should be allocated to operating departments according to the base that appears to provide the best measure of benefits received. An example of such an allocation was given earlier in Exhibit 16–4, where we first illustrated the step method. The reader may wish to turn back and review this example before reading on.

EXHIBIT 16–7

THE PROCTOR COMPANY
Beginning-of-Year Cost Allocations for Purposes of Preparing Predetermined Overhead Rates

	Building Maintenance	Cafeteria	Inspection	Shaping	Assembly
Variable costs to be allocated	$ –0–	$ 94,000	$ 42,000	$ —	$ —
Cafeteria allocation at $200 per employee:					
30 employees × $200	—	(6,000)	6,000	—	—
190 employees × $200	—	(38,000)	—	38,000	—
250 employees × $200	—	(50,000)	—	—	50,000
Inspection allocation at $0.06 per direct labor-hour:					
300,000 DLH × $0.06	—	—	(18,000)	18,000	—
500,000 DLH × $0.06	—	—	(30,000)	—	30,000
Total	–0–	–0–	–0–	56,000	80,000
Fixed costs to be allocated.	130,000	250,000	548,000		
Building maintenance allocation at $5 per square foot:*					
4,000 square feet × $5	(20,000)	20,000	—	—	—
1,000 square feet × $5	(5,000)	—	5,000	—	—
8,000 square feet × $5	(40,000)	—	—	40,000	—
13,000 square feet × $5	(65,000)	—	—	—	65,000
Cafeteria allocation:†					
10% × $270,000.	—	(27,000)	27,000	—	—
40% × $270,000.	—	(108,000)	—	108,000	—
50% × $270,000.	—	(135,000)	—	—	135,000
Inspection allocation:‡					
70% × $580,000.	—	—	(406,000)	406,000	—
30% × $580,000.	—	—	(174,000)	—	174,000
Total	–0–	–0–	–0–	554,000	374,000
Total allocated costs	$ –0–	$ –0–	$ –0–	610,000	454,000
Other flexible budget costs at the planned activity level				1,340,000	1,846,000
Total overhead costs				$1,950,000	$2,300,000 (a)
Budgeted direct labor-hours				300,000	500,000 (b)
Predetermined overhead rate, (a) ÷ (b)				$6.50	$4.60

*Square footage of space . . . .   29,000 square feet
Less building maintenance space . . . .   3,000 square feet
Net space for allocation . . . .   26,000 square feet

$$\frac{\text{Building maintenance fixed costs, \$130,000}}{\text{Net space for allocation, 26,000 square feet}} = \$5 \text{ per square foot}$$

†Cafeteria fixed costs. $250,000
Allocated from building maintenance   20,000
Total cost to be allocated $270,000

Allocation percentages are given in the problem.

‡Inspection fixed costs $548,000
Allocated from building maintenance   5,000
Allocated from cafeteria   27,000
Total cost to be allocated $580,000

Allocation percentages are given in the problem.

Should All Costs Be Allocated?

As a general rule, any service department costs that are incurred as a result of specific services provided to operating departments should be allocated back to these departments and used to compute overhead rates and to measure profitability. The only time when this general rule is not followed is in those situations where in the view of management, allocation would result in an undesirable behavioral response from people in the operating departments. Some servicing costs, for example, are clearly beneficial to operating departments but may not be utilized fully, particularly in times of cost economizing. Systems design is a good example of such a cost. Utilization of systems design services may be very beneficial to operating departments in terms of improving overall efficiency, reducing waste, and assuring adherence to departmental policies. But if a department knows that it will be charged for the systems design services it uses, it may be less inclined to take advantage of the benefits involved, especially if the department is feeling some pressure to trim costs. In short, the departmental manager may opt for the near-term benefit of avoiding a direct charge, in lieu of the long-term benefit of reduced waste and greater efficiency.

To avoid discouraging use of a service that is beneficial to the entire organization, some firms do not charge for the service at all. These managers feel that by making such services a "free" commodity, departments will be more inclined to take full advantage of their benefits.

Other firms take a somewhat different approach. They agree that charging according to usage may discourage utilization of such services as systems design, but they argue that such services should not be free. Instead of providing free services, these firms take what is sometimes called a **retainer fee approach.** Each department is charged a flat amount each year, regardless of how much or how little of the service it utilizes. The thought is that if a department knows that it is going to be charged a certain amount for systems design services, *regardless of usage,* then it will probably utilize the services at least to that extent.

FOCUS ON CURRENT PRACTICE

It can be unwise for a service department to offer "free" services to other departments, as shown by the following experience:

> [A hospital] established a policy of allowing its employees to eat all they wanted in the cafeteria, free of charge. The administration believed that the hospital's cost of providing this employee benefit would be low because the kitchen facilities were a fixed cost. Labor costs also would be low because of the mass production of food for the hospital's patients.

However, the hospital's food services costs shot up. An investigation revealed that the employees were wasting large amounts of food. Some were taking several entrees, tasting them, and throwing the rest away.

When the policy was changed and the employees were charged a token amount—about a third of a diner's prices—the wasting of food declined dramatically. In fact, the decrease in the food service department's costs was greater than the revenue generated by the nominal charge.[3]

---

[3] Leon B. Hoshower and Robert P. Crum, "Controlling Service Center Costs," *Management Accounting* 69, no. 5 (November 1987), p. 44. Used by permission.

Beware of Sales Dollars as an Allocation Base

Over the years, sales dollars have been a favorite allocation base for service department costs. One reason is that a sales dollars base is simple, straightforward, and easy to work with. Another reason is that people tend to view sales dollars as a measure of well-being, or "ability to pay," and, hence, as a measure of how readily costs can be absorbed from other parts of the organization.

Unfortunately, sales dollars often constitute a very poor allocation base, for the reason that sales dollars vary from period to period, whereas the costs being allocated are often largely *fixed* in nature. As discussed earlier, if a variable base is used to allocate fixed costs, inequities can result between departments since the costs being allocated to one department will depend in large part on what happens in *other* departments. For example, a letup in sales effort in one department will shift allocated costs off that department and onto other, more productive departments. In effect, the departments putting forth the best sales efforts are penalized in the form of higher allocations, simply because of inefficiencies elsewhere that are beyond their control. The result is often bitterness and resentment on the part of the managers of the better departments.

Consider the following situation encountered by one of the authors:

A large men's clothing store has one service department and three sales departments—suits, shoes, and accessories. The service department's costs total $60,000 per period and are allocated to the three sales departments according to sales dollars. A recent period showed the following allocation:

	Department			
	Suits	**Shoes**	**Accessories**	**Total**
Sales by department	$260,000	$40,000	$100,000	$400,000
Percentage of total sales.	65%	10%	25%	100%
Allocation of service department costs, based on percentage of total sales	$ 39,000	$ 6,000	$ 15,000	$ 60,000

In a following period, the manager of the suit department launched a very successful program to expand sales by $100,000 in his department. Sales in the other two departments remained unchanged. Total service department costs also remained unchanged, but the allocation of these costs changed substantially, as shown below:

	Department			
	Suits	**Shoes**	**Accessories**	**Total**
Sales by department	$360,000	$40,000	$100,000	$500,000
Percentage of total sales.	72%	8%	20%	100%
Allocation of service department costs, based on percentage of total sales	$ 43,200	$ 4,800	$ 12,000	$ 60,000
Increase (or decrease) from prior allocation	4,200	(1,200)	(3,000)	—

The manager of the suit department complained that as a result of his successful effort to expand sales in his department, he was being forced to carry a larger share of the service department costs. On the other hand, the managers of the departments that showed no improvement in sales were being relieved of a portion of the costs that they had been carrying. Yet there had been no change in the amount of services provided for any department.

The manager of the suit department viewed the increased service department cost allocation to his department as a penalty for his outstanding performance, and he wondered whether his efforts had really been worthwhile after all in the eyes of top management.

Sales dollars should be used as an allocation base only in those cases where there is a direct causal relationship between sales dollars and the service department costs being allocated. In those situations where service department costs are fixed in nature, they should be allocated according to the guidelines discussed earlier in the chapter.

SUMMARY

Service departments are organized to provide some needed service in a single, centralized place, rather than to have all units within the organization provide the service for themselves. Although service departments do not engage directly in production or other operating activities, the costs that they incur are vital to the overall success of an organization and therefore are properly included as part of the cost of its products and services.

Service department costs are charged to operating departments by an allocation process. In turn, the operating departments include the allocated costs within their flexible budgets, from which overhead rates are computed for purposes of costing of products or billing of services.

In order to avoid inequity in allocations, variable and fixed service department costs should be allocated separately. The variable costs should be allocated according to whatever activity causes their incurrence. The fixed costs should be allocated in predetermined lump-sum amounts according to either the peak-period or the long-run average servicing needs of the consuming departments. Budgeted costs, rather than actual costs, should always be allocated in order to avoid the passing on of inefficiency between departments. Any variances between budgeted and actual service department costs should be kept within the service departments for analysis purposes, then written off against revenues or against cost of goods sold, along with other variances.

REVIEW PROBLEM: DIRECT AND STEP METHODS

Kovac Printing Company has three service departments and two operating departments. Selected data for the five departments relating to the most recent period follow:

	Service Department			Operating Department		
	A	B	C	1	2	Total
Overhead costs	$360,000	$210,000	$96,000	$400,000	$534,000	$1,600,000
Number of employees . . .	120	70	280	630	420	1,520
Square feet of space occupied	10,000	20,000	40,000	80,000	200,000	350,000
Hours of press time	—	—	—	30,000	60,000	90,000

The company allocates service department costs in the following order and using the bases indicated: department A (number of employees), department B (space occupied), and department C (hours of press time). The company makes no distinction between variable and fixed service department costs.

1. Use the direct method to determine the amount of service department cost that should be allocated to each department.   *Required*

2.   Use the step method to determine the amount of service department cost that should be allocated to each department.

1.   Under the direct method, service department costs are allocated directly to the operating departments. Supporting computations for these allocations follow:

	Allocation Bases					
	Department A		**Department B**		**Department C**	
Department 1 data	630 employees	3/5	80,000 square feet	2/7	30,000 hours	1/3
Department 2 data	420 employees	2/5	200,000 square feet	5/7	60,000 hours	2/3
Totals	1,050 employees	5/5	280,000 square feet	7/7	90,000 hours	3/3

Given these allocation rates, the allocations to the operating departments would be as follows:

	Service Department			Operating Department		
	A	**B**	**C**	**1**	**2**	**Total**
Overhead costs	$ 360,000	$ 210,000	$ 96,000	$400,000	$534,000	$1,600,000
Allocation:						
Department A:						
(3/5; 2/5)	(360,000)			216,000	144,000	
Department B:						
(2/7; 5/7)		(210,000)		60,000	150,000	
Department C:						
(1/3; 2/3)			(96,000)	32,000	64,000	
Total overhead cost after allocations......	$ –0–	$ –0–	$ –0–	$708,000	$892,000	$1,600,000

2.   Under the step method, services rendered between service departments are recognized when costs are allocated to other departments. Starting with department A, supporting computations for these allocations follow:

	Allocation Bases					
	Department A		**Department B**		**Department C**	
Department B data . . .	70 employees	5%	—		—	
Department C data . . .	280 employees	20	40,000 square feet	1/8	—	
Department 1 data . . .	630 employees	45	80,000 square feet	2/8	30,000 hours	1/3
Department 2 data . . .	420 employees	30	200,000 square feet	5/8	60,000 hours	2/3
Totals	1,400 employees	100%	320,000 square feet	8/8	90,000 hours	3/3

Given these allocation rates, the allocations to the various departments would be as follows:

	Service Department			Operating Department		
	A	**B**	**C**	**1**	**2**	**Total**
Overhead costs	$ 360,000	$ 210,000	$ 96,000	$400,000	$534,000	$1,600,000
Allocation:						
Department A: (5%; 20%; 45%; 30%)*	(360,000)	18,000	72,000	162,000	108,000	
Department B: (1/8; 2/8; 5/8) . . .		(228,000)	28,500	57,000	142,500	
Department C: (1/3; 2/3)			(196,500)	65,500	131,000	
Total overhead cost after allocations	$ –0–	$ –0–	$ –0–	$684,500	$915,500	$1,600,000

* Allocation rates can be shown either in percentages, in fractions, or as a dollar rate per unit of activity. Both percentages and fractions are shown in this problem for sake of illustration. *It is better to use fractions if percentages would result in odd decimals.*

KEY TERMS FOR REVIEW

Allocation base Any measure of activity (such as labor-hours, number of employees, or square footage of space) that is used to charge service department costs to other departments. (p. 751)

Direct method The allocation of all of a service department's costs directly to operating departments without recognizing services provided to other service departments. (p. 752)

Interdepartmental services Services provided between service departments. Also see *Reciprocal services.* (p. 752)

Operating department A department or similar unit in an organization within which the central purposes of the organization are carried out. (p. 750)

Reciprocal method A method of allocating service department costs that gives full recognition to interdepartmental services. (p. 755)

Reciprocal services Services provided between service departments. Also see *Interdepartmental services.* (p. 752)

Retainer fee approach A method of allocating service department costs in which other departments are charged a flat amount each period regardless of usage of the service involved. (p. 765)

Service department A department that provides support or assistance to operating departments and that does not engage directly in production or in other operating activities of an organization. (p. 750)

Step method The allocation of a service department's costs to other service departments, as well as to operating departments, in a sequential manner. The sequence starts with the service department that provides the greatest amount of service to other departments. (p. 753)

Objective 8
Define or explain the key terms listed at the end of the chapter.

QUESTIONS

16–1 What is the difference between a service department and an operating department? Give several examples of service departments.

16–2 In what way are service department costs similar to costs such as lubricants, utilities, and factory supervision?

16–3   "Products and services can be costed equally well with or without allocations of service department costs." Do you agree? Why or why not?

16–4   How do service department costs enter into the final cost of products and services?

16–5   What criteria are relevant to the selection of allocation bases for service department costs?

16–6   What are interdepartmental service costs? How are such costs allocated to other departments under the step method?

16–7   How are service department costs allocated to other departments under the direct method?

16–8   If a service department generates revenues of some type, how do these revenues enter into the allocation of the department's costs to other departments?

16–9   What guidelines should govern the allocation of fixed service department costs to other departments? The allocation of variable service department costs?

16–10   "A variable base should never be used in allocating fixed service department costs to operating departments." Explain.

16–11   Why might it be desirable not to allocate some service department costs to operating departments?

16–12   What is the purpose of the retainer fee approach to cost allocation?

EXERCISES

E16–1   The Ferre Publishing Company has three service departments and two operating departments. Selected data from a recent period on the five departments follow:

| | Service Department | | | Operating Department | | |
	A	B	C	1	2	Total
Overhead costs	$140,000	$105,000	$48,000	$275,000	$430,000	$998,000
Number of employees	60	35	140	315	210	760
Square feet of space occupied	15,000	10,000	20,000	40,000	100,000	185,000
Hours of press time	—	—	—	30,000	60,000	90,000

The company allocates service department costs by the step method in the following order: A (number of employees), B (space occupied), and C (hours of press time). The company makes no distinction between variable and fixed service department costs.

Required   Using the step method, make the necessary allocations of service department costs.

E16–2   Refer to the data for the Ferre Publishing Company in E16–1. Assume that the company allocates service department costs by the direct method, rather than by the step method.

Required   Assuming that the company uses the direct method, how much overhead cost would be chargeable to each operating department? Show computations in good form.

E16–3   Hannibal Steel Company has a transport services department that provides trucks to haul ore from the company's mine to its two steel mills—the Northern Plant and the Southern Plant. The transport services department has sufficient capacity to handle peak-period needs of 140,000 tons per year for the Northern Plant and 60,000 tons per year for the Southern Plant. At this level of activity, budgeted costs for the transport services department total $350,000 per year, consisting of $0.25 per ton variable cost and $300,000 fixed cost.

   During 19x8, the coming year, 120,000 tons of ore are budgeted to be hauled for the Northern Plant and 60,000 tons of ore for the Southern Plant.

Compute the amount of transport services cost that should be allocated to each plant at the beginning of 19x8, for purposes of computing predetermined overhead rates. (The company allocates variable and fixed costs separately.)

Required

Refer to the data in E16–3. Assume that it is now the end of 19x8. During the year, the transport services department actually hauled the following amounts of ore for the two plants: Northern Plant, 130,000 tons; Southern Plant, 50,000 tons. The transport services department incurred $364,000 in cost during the year, of which $54,000 was variable cost and $310,000 was fixed cost.

E16–4

Management wants end-of-year service department cost allocations in order to compare actual performance against planned performance.

1. Determine how much of the $54,000 in variable cost should be allocated to each plant.
2. Determine how much of the $310,000 in fixed cost should be allocated to each plant.
3. Will any of the $364,000 in transport services cost not be allocated to the plants? Explain.

Required

Westlake Hospital has a radiology department that provides X-ray services to the hospital's three operating departments. The variable costs of the radiology department are allocated on a basis of the number of X rays provided for each department. Budgeted and actual data relating to the cost of X rays taken during 19x3 are given below:

E16–5

	Variable Costs—19x3	
	Budgeted	**Actual**
Radiology department	$18 per X ray	$20 per X ray

The budgeted and actual number of X rays provided for each operating department during 19x3 follows:

	Pediatrics	**OB Care**	**General Hospital**
Budgeted number of X rays.	7,000	4,500	12,000
Actual number of X rays taken	6,000	3,000	15,000

Determine the amount of radiology department variable cost that should be allocated to each of the three operating departments at the end of 19x3, for purposes of comparing actual performance against planned performance.

Required

Refer to Westlake Hospital in E16–5. In addition to the radiology department, the hospital also has a janitorial services department that provides services to all other departments in the hospital. The fixed costs of the two service departments are allocated on the following bases:

E16–6

Department	**Basis for Allocation**
Janitorial services	Square footage of space occupied:
	Radiology department . . . . 6,000 square feet
	Pediatrics. . . . . 30,000 square feet
	OB care . . . . 24,000 square feet
	General hospital . . . . . . 90,000 square feet
Radiology	Long-run average X-ray needs per year:
	Pediatrics. . . . . 9,000 X rays
	OB care . . . . 6,000 X rays
	General hospital . . . . . . 15,000 X rays

Budgeted and actual fixed costs in the two service departments for 19x3 follow:

	Janitorial Services	Radiology
Budgeted fixed costs	$375,000	$590,000
Actual fixed costs	381,000	600,000

Required

1. Show the allocation of the fixed costs of the two service departments at the beginning of 19x3 for purposes of computing overhead rates in the operating departments. The hospital uses the step method of allocation.

2. Show the allocation of the fixed costs of the two service departments at the end of 19x3 for purposes of comparing actual performance against planned performance.

E16–7 Konig Products allocates its fixed administrative expenses to its three divisions on a basis of sales dollars. During 19x1, the fixed administrative expenses totaled $2,000,000. These expenses were allocated as follows:

	Division			
	A	**B**	**C**	**Total**
Total sales—19x1	$16,000,000	$15,000,000	$9,000,000	$40,000,000
Percentage of total sales . . .	40%	37.5%	22.5%	100%
Allocation (based on the above percentages)	$ 800,000	$ 750,000	$ 450,000	$ 2,000,000

During 19x2, the following year, Division B increased its sales by two thirds. The sales levels in the other two divisions remained unchanged. As a result of Division B's sales increase, the company's 19x2 sales data appeared as follows:

	Division			
	A	**B**	**C**	**Total**
Total sales—19x2	$16,000,000	$25,000,000	$9,000,000	$50,000,000
Percentage of total sales	32%	50%	18%	100%

Fixed administrative expenses in the company remained unchanged at $2,000,000 during 19x2.

Required

1. Using sales dollars as an allocation base, show the allocation of the fixed administrative expenses between the three divisions for 19x2.

2. Compare your allocation from (1) above to the allocation for 19x1. As the manager of Division B, how would you feel about the allocation that has been charged to you for 19x2?

3. Comment on the usefulness of sales dollars as an allocation base.

PROBLEMS

P16–8 Various Allocation Methods Sharp Motor Company has an Auto Division and a Truck Division. The company has a cafeteria that serves the employees of both divisions. The costs of operating the cafeteria are budgeted at $40,000 per month plus $3 per meal served. The cafeteria has a capacity to serve 80,000 meals per month—based on peak needs of 52,000 meals per month in the Auto Division and 28,000 meals per month in the Truck Division. The company pays all the cost of the meals.

For June, the Auto Division has estimated that it will need 35,000 meals served, and the Truck Division has estimated that it will need 20,000 meals served.

Required

1. At the beginning of June, how much cafeteria cost should be allocated to each division for flexible budget planning purposes?

2. Assume that it is now the end of June. Cost records in the cafeteria show that actual fixed costs for the month totaled $42,000 and that actual meal costs totaled $128,000.

Due to unexpected layoffs of employees during the month, only 20,000 meals were served to the Auto Division. Another 20,000 meals were served to the Truck Division, as planned. How much of the actual cafeteria costs for the month should be allocated to each division? (Management uses these end-of-month allocations to compare actual performance with planned performance.)

3. Refer to the data in (2) above. Assume that the company follows the practice of allocating *all* cafeteria costs to the divisions in proportion to the number of meals served to each division during the month. On this basis, how much cost would be allocated to each division for June?

4. What criticisms can you make of the allocation method used in (3) above?

5. If managers of operating departments know that fixed service department costs are going to be allocated on a basis of long-run average usage of the service involved, what will be their probable strategy as they report their estimate of this usage to the company's budget committee? As a member of top management, what would you do to neutralize any such strategies?

Cost Allocation: Step Method versus Direct Method   The Ashley Company has budgeted costs in its various departments as follows for the coming year: P16-9

Factory administration	$270,000
Custodial services	68,760
Personnel	28,840
Maintenance	45,200
Machining—overhead.	376,300
Assembly—overhead	175,900
Total cost	$965,000

The company allocates service department costs to other departments, in the order listed below. Bases for allocation are to be chosen from the following:

	Number of Employees	Total Labor-Hours	Square Feet of Space Occupied	Direct Labor-Hours	Machine-Hours
Factory administration	12	—	5,000	—	—
Custodial services	4	3,000	2,000	—	—
Personnel	5	5,000	3,000	—	—
Maintenance	25	22,000	10,000	—	—
Machining	40	30,000	70,000	20,000	70,000
Assembly	60	90,000	20,000	80,000	10,000
	146	150,000	110,000	100,000	80,000

Machining and assembly are operating departments; the other departments all act in a service capacity. The company does not make a distinction between fixed and variable service department costs; allocations are made to using departments according to the base that appears to provide the best measure of benefits received (as discussed in the chapter).

1. Allocate service department costs to using departments by the step method. Then compute predetermined overhead rates in the operating departments, using a machine-hours basis in machining and a direct labor-hours basis in assembly.   *Required*

2. Repeat (1) above, this time using the direct method. Again compute predetermined overhead rates in machining and assembly.

3. Assume that the company doesn't want to bother with allocating service department costs but simply wants to compute a single plantwide overhead rate based on total overhead costs (both service department and operating department) divided by total direct labor-hours. Compute the appropriate overhead rate.

4. Suppose that the company wants to bid on a job during the year that will require machine and labor time as follows:

	Machine-Hours	Direct Labor-Hours
Machining department	190	25
Assembly department.	10	75
Total hours	200	100

Using the overhead rates computed in (1), (2), and (3) above, compute the amount of overhead cost that would be assigned to the job if the overhead rates were developed using the step method, the direct method, and the plantwide method.

P16–10 End-of-Month Cost Allocations   Reese Company has a power services department that provides electrical power for other departments within the company. The power services department's budget for June 19x2 is $40,800. Of this amount, $30,000 is considered to be a fixed cost.

Power consumption in the company is measured by kilowatt-hours (kwh) used. The monthly power requirements of the company's other four departments are as follows (in kwh):

	Service Department		Operating Department		
	A	B	X	Y	Total
Long-run average usage	28,000	60,000	120,000	192,000	400,000
Budgeted for June	24,000	48,000	120,000	168,000	360,000
Actual use during June	16,000	50,000	89,000	145,000	300,000

The power services department incurred $40,200 in costs during June 19x2, of which $8,400 was variable and $31,800 was fixed. The department allocates variable and fixed costs separately.

Required 1. Assume that management makes an allocation of power costs at the end of each month in order to compare actual performance against budgeted performance. How much of the power services department's actual costs for June 19x2 would be allocated to each department?

      2. Will any portion of the month's power costs not be allocated to the four departments? Explain.

P16–11 Beginning- and End-of-Year Allocations   Bennett Products, Inc., has a maintenance department that services the equipment in the company's forming department and assembly department. The cost of this servicing is allocated to the departments on a basis of machine-hours of activity. Cost and other data relating to the maintenance department and to the other two departments for 19x5 are presented below.

Data for the maintenance department:

	19x5	
	Budget	Actual
Variable costs for lubricants.	$ 96,000*	$110,000
Fixed costs for salaries and other	150,000	153,000

* Budgeted at $0.40 per machine-hour.

Data for the forming and assembly departments:

Machine-Hours of Activity

	Peak-Period Needs	19x5 Budget	19x5 Actual
		Budget	Actual
Forming department	210,000	160,000	190,000
Assembly department	90,000	80,000	70,000
Total machine-hours	300,000	240,000	260,000

The company allocates variable and fixed costs separately.

Required

1. Assume that it is the beginning of 19x5. An allocation of maintenance department cost must be made to the operating departments to assist in computing predetermined overhead rates. How much of the budgeted maintenance department cost above would be allocated to each department?

2. Assume that it is now the end of 19x5. Management would like data to assist in comparing actual performance against planned performance in the maintenance department and in the other departments.

    a. How much of the actual maintenance department costs above would be allocated to the forming department and to the assembly department? Show all computations.

    b. Is there any portion of the actual maintenance department costs that would not be allocated to the other departments? If all costs would be allocated, explain why; if a portion would not be allocated, compute the amount and explain why it would not be allocated.

Cost Allocation in a Hospital; Step Method Woodbury Hospital has three service **P16–12** departments and three operating departments. Estimated cost and operating data for all departments in the hospital for the forthcoming quarter are presented in the table below:

	Service Department			Operating Department			
	Housekeeping Services	Food Services	Admin. Services	Labor-atory	Radiology	General Hospital	Total
Variable costs	$ —	$193,860	$158,840	$243,600	$304,800	$ 74,500	$ 975,600
Fixed costs	87,000	107,200	90,180	162,300	215,700	401,300	1,063,680
Total costs	$87,000	$301,060	$249,020	$405,900	$520,500	$475,800	$2,039,280
Meals served	—	—	800	2,000	1,000	68,000	71,800
Peak period needs—meals	—	—	800	2,400	1,600	95,200	100,000
Square feet of space	5,000	13,000	6,500	10,000	7,500	108,000	150,000
Files processed	—	—	—	14,000	7,000	25,000	46,000
Long-run average—files processed	—	—	—	18,000	12,000	30,000	60,000

The costs of the service departments are allocated by the step method, using the bases and in the order shown in the following table:

Service Department	Costs Incurred	Bases for Allocation
Housekeeping services	Fixed	Square feet of space
Food services	Variable	Meals served
	Fixed	Peak-period needs—meals
Administrative services	Variable	Files processed
	Fixed	Long-run average—files processed

All billing in the hospital is done through the laboratory, radiology, or general hospital. The hospital's administrator wants the costs of the three service departments allocated to these three billing centers.

Required   Prepare the cost allocation desired by the hospital administrator. (Use the step method.) Include under each billing center the direct costs of the center, as well as the costs allocated from the service departments.

P16–13   **Equity in Allocations; Computer Center**   "These allocations don't make any sense at all," said Bob Cosic, manager of National Airlines' Freight Division. "We used the computer less during the second quarter than we did during the first quarter, yet we were allocated more cost. Is that fair? In fact, we picked up the lion's share of the computer's cost during the second quarter, even though we're a lot smaller than the Domestic Passenger Division."

National Airlines established a new computer center in the latter part of 19x1 to service its three operating divisions. The company allocates the cost of the center to the divisions on a basis of the number of pages of printout for invoices, tickets, and so forth, provided each quarter. Allocations for the first two quarters of 19x2, to which Mr. Cosic was referring, are given below:

			Division	
			Passenger	
	Total	**Freight**	**Domestic**	**Overseas**
First quarter actual results:				
Pages of printout	300,000	90,000	180,000	30,000
Percentage of total	100%	30%	60%	10%
Computer cost allocated.	$172,000	$51,600	$103,200	$17,200
Second quarter actual results:				
Pages of printout	200,000	80,000	70,000	50,000
Percentage of total	100%	40%	35%	25%
Computer cost allocated.	$168,000	$67,200	$58,800	$42,000

"Now don't get upset, Bob," replied Colleen Rogers, the controller. "Those allocations are fair. As you can see, your division received the largest share of the computer's output during the second quarter and therefore it has been allocated the largest share of cost. Although use of the computer center was off somewhat during the second quarter, keep in mind that most of the center's costs are fixed and therefore continue regardless of how much the computer is used. Also, remember that we built enough capacity into the computer center to handle the divisions' peak-period needs, and that cost has to be absorbed by someone. The fairest way to handle it is to charge according to usage from quarter to quarter. When you use the computer more, you get charged more; it's as simple as that."

"That's just the point," replied Cosic. "I didn't use the computer more, I used it less. So why am I charged more?"

The computer center has enough capacity to handle 400,000 pages of printout each quarter. This represents expected peak-period needs of 120,000 pages in the Freight Division, 200,000 pages in the Domestic Passenger Division, and 80,000 pages in the Overseas Passenger Division. However, management does not expect these levels of activity to be reached for two or three years, and even then they will be reached only in the third or fourth quarter when traffic is highest in the airline industry.

Required   1.   Is there any merit to Mr. Cosic's complaint? Explain.
2.   By use of the high-low method, determine the cost formula for the computer center in terms of a variable rate per page and total fixed cost each quarter.
3.   Reallocate the computer center costs for the first and second quarters in accordance with the cost allocation principles discussed in the chapter. Allocate the variable and fixed costs separately.

P16–14   **Cost Allocation in a Resort; Step Method**   The Bayview Resort has three operating units—the convention center, food services, and guest lodging—through which all billing is done. These three operating units are supported by three service units—general administration, cost accounting, and laundry. The costs of the service units are allocated by the step method, using the bases and in the order shown below:

General administration:
   Fixed costs—allocated 10% to cost accounting, 4% to the laundry, 30% to the convention center, 16% to food services, and 40% to guest lodging.

Cost accounting:
   Variable costs—allocated on a basis of the number of items processed each period.
   Fixed costs—allocated on a basis of peak-period needs for items processed.

Laundry:
   Variable costs—allocated on a basis of the number of pounds of laundry processed each period.
   Fixed costs—allocated on a basis of peak-period needs for pounds of laundry processed.

   Cost and operating data for all units in the resort for a recent quarter are given in the table following:

	Service Department			Operating Department			
	General Adminis- tration	Cost Ac- counting	Laundry	Conven- tion Center	Food Services	Guest Lodging	Total
Variable costs	$ –0–	$ 70,000	$143,000	$ –0–	$ 52,000	$ 24,000	$ 289,000
Fixed costs.	200,000	110,000	65,900	95,000	375,000	486,000	1,331,900
Total overhead costs	$200,000	$180,000	$208,900	$95,000	$427,000	$510,000	$1,620,900
Pounds of laundry processed	—	—	—	20,000	15,000	210,000	245,000
Peak-period needs—pounds of laundry processed	—	—	—	30,000	18,000	252,000	300,000
Number of items processed	1,000	—	800	1,200	3,000	9,000	15,000
Peak-period needs—number of items processed	1,500	—	1,400	2,600	4,000	12,000	21,500

Since all billing is done through the convention center, food services, and guest lodging, the resort's general manager wants the costs of the three service units allocated to these three billing centers.

Required   Prepare the cost allocation desired by the resort's general manager. Include under each billing center the direct costs of the center, as well as the costs allocated from the service units.

P16–15   **Multiple Departments; Step Method; Predetermined Overhead Rates**   Bonneville Castings, Inc., has two producing departments, department A and department B, and three service departments. The service departments and the bases on which their costs are allocated to using departments are listed below:

Department	Cost	Allocation Bases
Building and grounds	Fixed	Square footage occupied
Medical services.	Variable	Number of employees
	Fixed	Employee needs at full capacity
Equipment maintenance	Variable	Machine-hours
	Fixed	40% to department A
		60% to department B

Service department costs are allocated to using departments by the step method in the order shown above. The company has developed the cost and operating data given in the following table for purposes of preparing overhead rates in the two producing departments:

	Building and Grounds	Medical Services	Equipment Maintenance	Department A	Department B	Total
Variable costs	$ –0–	$22,200	$16,900	$146,000	$320,000	$ 505,100
Fixed costs	88,200	60,000	24,000	420,000	490,000	1,082,200
Total	$88,200	$82,200	$40,900	$566,000	$810,000	$1,587,300
Budgeted employees	6	4	30	450	630	1,120
Employee needs at capacity	8	4	45	570	885	1,512
Square footage of space occupied	600	500	1,400	12,000	15,500	30,000
Budgeted machine-hours	—	—	—	70,000	105,000	175,000

Required

1. Show the allocation of service department costs to using departments, for purposes of preparing overhead rates in departments A and B.

2. Assuming that overhead rates are set on a basis of machine-hours, compute the overhead rate for each producing department.

3. Assume the following *actual* data for the year for the medical services department:

Actual variable costs $23,800

Actual employees for the year:
Building and grounds   6
Medical services   4
Equipment maintenance   32
Department A   460
Department B   625
                                    1,127

Compute the amount of end-of-year medical services variable cost that should be allocated to each department. (Management uses these end-of-year allocations to compare actual performance against planned performance.)

CASES

C16–16   Step Method versus Direct Method   "This is really an odd situation," said Jim Carter, general manager of Highland Publishing Company. "We get most of the jobs we bid on that require a lot of press time in the printing department, yet profits on those jobs are never as high as they ought to be. On the other hand, we lose most of the jobs we bid on that require a lot of time in the binding department. I would be inclined to think that the problem is with our overhead rates, but we're already computing separate overhead rates for each department like the trade journals advise. So what else could be wrong?"

Highland Publishing Company is a large organization that offers a variety of printing and binding work. The printing and binding departments are supported by three service departments. The costs of these service departments are allocated to other departments in the order listed below. (For each service department, use the allocation base that provides the best measure of service provided, as discussed in the chapter.)

	Total Labor-Hours	Square Feet of Space Occupied	Number of Employees	Machine-Hours	Direct Labor-Hours
Personnel	20,000	4,000	10	—	—
Custodial services	30,000	6,000	15	—	—
Maintenance	50,000	20,000	25	—	—
Printing	90,000	80,000	40	150,000	60,000
Binding	260,000	40,000	120	30,000	175,000
	450,000	150,000	210	180,000	235,000

Budgeted overhead costs in each department for the current year are shown below (no distinction is made between variable and fixed costs):

Personnel	$ 360,000
Custodial services	141,000
Maintenance	201,000
Printing	525,000
Binding	373,500
Total budgeted costs	$1,600,500

Because of its simplicity, the company has always used the direct method to allocate service department costs to the two operating departments.

Required

1. By use of the step method, allocate the service department costs to the other departments. Then compute predetermined overhead rates for the current year, using a machine-hours basis in the printing department and a direct labor-hours basis in the binding department.
2. Repeat (1) above, this time using the direct method. Again compute predetermined overhead rates in the printing and binding departments.
3. Assume that during the current year the company bids on a job that requires machine and labor time as follows:

	Machine-Hours	Direct Labor-Hours
Printing department	15,400	900
Binding department	800	2,000
Total hours	16,200	2,900

   a. Determine the amount of overhead cost that would be assigned to the job if the company used the overhead rates developed in (1) above. Then determine the amount of overhead cost that would be assigned to the job if the company used the overhead rates developed in (2) above.
   b. Explain to Mr. Carter, the general manager, why the step method would provide a better basis for computing predetermined overhead rates than the direct method.

Determining Allocation Base: Legal Services   Spiral Laboratories, Inc., manufactures and distributes generic pharmaceuticals for sale to customers through retail outlets. Spiral is organized along product lines, with profit and loss responsibilities assigned to the unit manager of each product line. The unit managers receive incentive compensation based on product-line performance.

C16–17

Currently, Spiral is reviewing its policies regarding the use of legal services. Historically, the company has utilized various outside legal firms, as needed by the unit managers and members of the corporate staff. The cost of legal services to the corporation has been increasing. Recently, the decision was made to hire an in-house attorney to better coordinate and assist in the legal matters of the corporation. The goal is to lower the overall costs of legal services by reducing the use of outside legal services; however, the unit managers still have the option of using outside legal services. Legal services are anticipated to be a continuing need at the corporate level and a periodic need at the unit level.

The corporate controller has identified the following four alternatives for allocating the cost of corporate legal services provided by the in-house attorney.

a. An annual charge to each product-line unit based on the budgeted sales volume of the unit. There would also be a fixed, annual charge to corporate headquarters based on a percentage of total legal costs.
b. No charge to the product-line units with corporate headquarters absorbing all costs for in-house legal services.
c. A fixed, hourly charge for the actual services required by each product-line unit. This

hourly charge would be determined on the basis of comparative costs for services obtained from external sources.

d. A fixed, hourly charge for actual services required by product-line units that is based on full recovery of the cost of the corporate legal services. Under- or over-absorption of in-house legal costs would be charged to the product-line units at year-end.

Required   1. Describe the probable behavioral effects on the product-line unit managers of Spiral Laboratories caused by the use of each of the four cost allocation methods.

2. Describe the possible effects on the adequacy and quality of legal services to be provided and/or utilized under each of the four cost allocation methods.

3. Describe the probable effects caused by the use of each of the four cost allocation methods on the behavior of Spiral Laboratories' corporate attorney.

(CMA, adapted)

C16–18   **Direct Method; Plantwide Overhead Rates versus Departmental Overhead Rates**
Hobart Products manufactures a complete line of fiberglass attaché cases and suitcases. Hobart has three manufacturing departments—molding, component, and assembly—and two service departments—power and maintenance.

The sides of the cases are manufactured in the molding department. The frames, hinges, locks, and so forth, are manufactured in the component department. The cases are completed in the assembly department. Varying amounts of materials, time, and effort are required for each of the various cases. The power department and maintenance department provide services to the manufacturing departments.

Hobart has always used a plantwide overhead rate. Direct labor-hours are used to assign the overhead to products. The overhead rate is computed by dividing the company's total estimated overhead cost by the total estimated direct labor-hours to be worked in the three manufacturing departments.

Whit Portlock, manager of cost accounting, has recommended that the company use departmental overhead rates rather than a single, plantwide rate. Planned operating costs and expected levels of activity for the coming year have been developed by Mr. Portlock and are presented below:

	Service Department	
	Power	**Maintenance**
Departmental activity measures:		
Maximum capacity	100,000 kwh	Adjustable*
Estimated usage in the coming year . . .	80,000 kwh	12,500 hours*
Departmental costs:		
Materials and supplies	$ 500,000	$ 25,000
Variable labor	140,000	–0–
Fixed overhead	1,200,000	375,000
Total service department costs	$1,840,000	$400,000

* Hours of maintenance time.

	Manufacturing Department		
	Molding	**Component**	**Assembly**
Departmental activity measures:			
Direct labor-hours	50,000	200,000	150,000
Machine-hours	87,500	12,500	–0–
Departmental costs:			
Raw materials.	$1,630,000	$3,000,000	$ 125,000
Direct labor.	350,000	2,000,000	1,300,000
Variable overhead	210,500	1,000,000	1,650,000
Fixed overhead	1,750,000	620,000	749,500
Total departmental costs	$3,940,500	$6,620,000	$3,824,500

| | **Manufacturing Department** | | |
	Molding	Component	Assembly
Use of service departments:			
Maintenance:			
Estimated usage in hours of maintenance time for the coming year . . . . \	9,000	2,500	1,000
Long-run average usage in hours of maintenance time	10,500	3,000	1,500
Power:			
Estimated usage in kilowatt-hours for the coming year	36,000	32,000	12,000
Peak-period needs in kilowatt-hours	50,000	35,000	15,000

Required

1. Assume that the company will use a single, plantwide overhead rate for the coming year, the same as in the past. Under these conditions, compute the plantwide rate that should be used.

2. Assume that Whit Portlock has been asked to develop departmental overhead rates for the three manufacturing departments for comparison with the plantwide rate. In order to develop these rates, do the following:

   a. By use of the direct method, allocate the service department costs to the manufacturing departments. In each case, allocate the variable and fixed costs separately.

   b. Compute overhead rates for the three manufacturing departments for the coming year. In computing the rates, use a machine-hours basis in the molding department and a direct labor-hours basis in the other two departments.

3. Assume that Hobart Products has one small attaché case that has the following annual requirements for machine time and direct labor time in the various departments:

	Machine-Hours	Direct Labor-Hours
Molding department	3,000	1,000
Component department	800	2,500
Assembly department	—	4,000
Total hours.	3,800	7,500

   a. Compute the amount of overhead cost that would be allocated to this attaché case if a plantwide overhead rate is used. Repeat the computation, this time assuming that departmental overhead rates are used.

   b. Management is concerned because this attaché case is priced well below competing products of competitors. On the other hand, certain other of Hobart's products are priced well above the prices of competitors with the result that profits in the company are deteriorating because of declining sales. Looking at the computations in (a) above, what effect is the use of a plantwide rate having on the costing of products and therefore on selling prices?

4. What additional steps could Hobart Products take to improve its overhead costing?

(CMA, heavily adapted)

Allocating Computer Center Costs   Marfrank Company is a manufacturing organization that has six departments—production, finance, marketing, personnel, research and development (R&D), and information systems. Each department is administered by a vice president. The information systems department (ISD) was established in 1994 when Marfrank Company decided to acquire a new mainframe computer and develop a new information system.

During 1994, the company developed the basic systems needed by the six departments, and these systems were operational by the end of 1994. Thus, the current year, 1995, is considered to be the first year in which the ISD costs can be estimated with a high degree of

C16–19

accuracy. Marfrank Company's president wants the other five departments to be aware of the magnitude of these costs; therefore, the ISD costs for 1995 are to be allocated to the other five departments on a quarterly basis, according to their actual use of ISD services.

Jon Werner, the vice president over ISD, suggested that "actual usage" be defined as pages of computer output. This basis was suggested because all departments depend on the computer for their reports and other printed documents. The use of pages of computer output as the allocation base resulted in the allocation presented below for the first quarter, 1995:

Department	Percent of Total Pages Printed	Allocated Cost
Finance	50	$112,500
Marketing	30	67,500
Personnel	9	20,250
Production	6	13,500
R&D	5	11,250
Total	100	$225,000

After this allocation was completed and the dollar figures were communicated to the departments, both the finance and marketing departments objected to pages of computer output as the allocation base. Both departments recognized that they were responsible for most of the computer output in terms of reports, but they believed that the ISD costs associated with pages of output were among the least of all ISD costs. Thus, these departments requested that a more equitable allocation basis be developed.

Elaine Jergens, Marfrank Company's controller, was given the task of developing a more equitable allocation method. After meeting with Jon Werner, she concluded that ISD provided three distinct services to other departments. These services were systems development; computer processing, as represented by central processing unit (CPU) time; and report generation. Accordingly, she recommended that a predetermined rate be developed for each of these services from budgeted ISD costs and activity for each year. The ISD costs would then be assigned to the other five departments using the predetermined rate times the actual activity involved. Any difference between actual costs incurred and costs allocated to the other departments would be absorbed by ISD.

Jergens and Werner concluded that systems development could be charged on the basis of hours devoted to systems development and programming, computer processing based on CPU time used for operations (exclusive of database development and maintenance), and report generation based on pages of output. The only cost that should not be included in any of the predetermined rates would be purchased software; these packages were usually acquired for a specific department's use. Thus, Jergens concluded that purchased software would be charged at cost to the department for which it was purchased. In order to revise the first quarter allocation, Jergens gathered the information on ISD costs and services shown below.

INFORMATION SYSTEMS DEPARTMENT COSTS

	Estimated Annual Costs	Actual First-Quarter Costs	Percentage Devoted to		
			Systems Development	Computer Processing	Report Generation
Wages and benefits:					
Administration	$100,000	$ 25,000	60	20	20
Computer operators.	55,000	13,000		20	80
Analysts/programmers	165,000	43,500	100		
Maintenance:					
Hardware	24,000	6,000		75	25
Software.	20,000	5,000		100	
Output supplies	50,000	11,500			100
Purchased software	45,000	16,000*	—	—	—
Utilities	28,000	6,250		100	
Depreciation:					
Mainframe computer	325,000	81,250		100	
Printing equipment	60,000	15,000			100
Building improvements	10,000	2,500	100		
Total department costs	$882,000	$225,000			

* Note: All software purchased during the first quarter of 1995 was for the benefit of the production department.

INFORMATION SYSTEMS DEPARTMENT SERVICES

	Systems Development	Computer Operations (CPU)	Report Generation
Annual capacity	4,500 hours	360 CPU hours	5,000,000 pages

Actual Usage—First Quarter, 1995	Hours	CPU Time (hours)	Pages of Output
Finance	100	8	600,000
Marketing	250	12	360,000
Personnel	200	12	108,000
Production.	400	32	72,000
R & D	50	16	60,000
Total usage	1,000	80	1,200,000

Required

1. Compute a predetermined rate for each of the service categories of ISD—systems development, computer processing, and report generation.

2. Using the predetermined rates developed in (1), determine the amount each of the other five departments would be charged for services provided by ISD during the first quarter of 1995.

3. The method proposed by Elaine Jergens for charging the ISD costs to the other five departments may result in a difference between ISD's actual costs and its allocated costs.
   a. Explain the nature of this difference.
   b. Discuss whether this proposal by Jergens will improve cost control in ISD.
   c. Explain whether Jergens' proposed method of charging user departments for ISD costs will improve planning and control in the user departments.

(CMA, adapted)

The statement of cash flows is required in annual reports to shareholders along with an income statement and a balance sheet. The statement of cash flows is a required statement for good reason. In a recent survey more than half of the shareholders questioned found the statement of cash flows to be useful in investment decisions.

"How Well Am I Doing?" Statement of Cash Flows

LEARNING OBJECTIVES

After studying Chapter 17, you should be able to:

1 Describe the purpose of the statement of cash flows.

2 State the general rules for determining whether transactions should be classified as operating activities, investing activities, or financing activities.

3 Explain what is meant by a direct exchange transaction and explain how such a transaction is reported to statement users.

4 Identify items that should be presented in gross amounts and items that should be presented in net amounts on the statement of cash flows.

5 Explain the difference between the direct method and the indirect method of determining the "Net cash provided by operating activities."

6 Compute the "Net cash provided by operating activities" using the indirect method.

7 Prepare a statement of cash flows without the use of working papers.

8 Prepare working papers to gather data for a statement of cash flows.

9 Adjust the income statement to a cash basis using the direct method.

10 Define or explain the key terms listed at the end of the chapter.

Three major statements are prepared annually by most companies—an income statement, a balance sheet, and a statement of cash flows. The statement of cash flows is less well known than the income statement or the balance sheet, but many view it as being equal in importance. This importance is underscored by the fact that the Financial Accounting Standards Board (FASB) requires that a statement of cash flows be provided whenever a balance sheet and an income statement are made available to users of financial data. In this chapter, our focus is on the development of the statement of cash flows and on its use as a tool for assessing the well-being of a company.

PURPOSE AND USE OF THE STATEMENT

Objective 1
Describe the purpose of the statement of cash flows.

The purpose of the **statement of cash flows** is to highlight the major activities that have provided cash and that have used cash during a period, and to show the resulting effect on the overall cash balance. The statement is a powerful analytical tool that can be used by managers, investors, and creditors in the following ways:

1. To determine the amount of cash provided by operations during a period and to reconcile this amount with net income.
2. To assess an organization's ability to meet its obligations as they come due and to assess its ability to pay cash dividends.
3. To determine the amount of investment in new plant, equipment, and other noncurrent assets during a period.
4. To determine the type and extent of financing required to expand the investment in long-term assets or to bolster operations.
5. To assess an organization's ability to generate a positive cash flow in future periods.

For the statement of cash flows to be useful to managers and others in gathering information such as that above, it is important that companies employ a common definition of cash and organize the statement in a consistent manner. Issues relating to the definition of cash are considered in this section. The next section discusses issues relating to the organization of the statement of cash flows.

Definition of Cash

In preparing a statement of cash flows for inclusion in an annual report, the FASB has stated that the term *cash* must be broadly defined to include both cash and cash equivalents. **Cash equivalents** consist of short-term, highly liquid investments such as treasury bills, commercial paper, and money market funds. These items are termed *marketable securities* on the balance sheet. Investments of this type are considered to be "equivalent" to cash in that they are made solely for the purpose of generating a return on cash that is temporarily idle. Because short-term investments are just temporary uses of cash and therefore part of a company's overall cash management program, they are included with cash in preparing a statement of cash flows.

In the past, some companies have used the term *funds* in lieu of the term *cash* in describing the contents of a statement of cash flows. Since the term *funds* often means different things to different people, the FASB has stated that its use should be discontinued and that more descriptive terms, such as *cash,* or *cash and cash equivalents,* should be used in its place.

ORGANIZATION OF THE STATEMENT

For many years, companies have had wide latitude in organizing the content of a statement of cash flows. One popular format has been to divide the statement into two sections—one titled "Sources of cash" and the other titled "Uses of cash"—and to classify all cash flows under one of these two heads. Generally, this format has provided a separate figure for the amount of cash generated by operations, but it has provided little else in the way of organized data; as a result, investors and creditors have had difficulty in comparing one company with another.

   To provide greater comparability of data, the FASB now requires that the statement of cash flows be divided into three sections. The first section must contain all cash flows relating to *operating activities* for a period; the next section must contain all cash flows relating to *investing activities;* and the final section must contain all cash flows relating to *financing activities.* Below we discuss the guidelines to be followed in classifying a company's cash flows under these three heads.

Objective 2
State the general rules for determining whether transactions should be classified as operating activities, investing activities, or financing activities.

Operating Activities

As a general rule, any transactions that enter into the determination of net income are classified as **operating activities.** These transactions can result in either cash inflows or cash outflows.

   Cash inflows come from the sale of goods or the providing of services; interest received from *all* sources; dividends received on stock held as an investment; and cash received from miscellaneous sources, such as rental income.

   In reading this list of cash inflows, the reader may wonder why dividends received on stock held as an investment is treated as an *operating* item when the stock itself obviously represents an *investment* item. The reasons are twofold: first, the dividends enter into the determination of income; and second, investing activities are narrowly defined to include only the *principal amount* of stock purchased or sold. Thus, the income from an investment item such as stock is classified as part of operating activities even though the stock itself is classified under a different heading.

   Cash outflows that are classified as operating activities consist of payments made for items *that appear as expenses on the income statement.* These would include payments to suppliers for inventory; payments to employees for services; payments to other entities for insurance, utilities, rent, and so forth; and payments to governmental agencies for taxes. In addition, payments to banks and other lenders for interest are included as part of operating activities even though the loans themselves are part of a company's financing activities. The reasons for this apparent inconsistency are the same as those given above for dividends: interest enters into the determination of income, and financing activities are narrowly defined to include only the principal amount borrowed or repaid.

   The cash inflows and outflows discussed above are summarized in Exhibit 17–1.

Investing Activities

Generally speaking, any transactions that are involved in the acquisition or disposition of noncurrent assets are classified as **investing activities.** These transactions include acquiring or selling property, plant, and equipment; acquiring or selling securities held for long-term investment, such as bonds and stocks of other com-

EXHIBIT 17–1

A Summary of
Operating, Investing,
and Financing
Activities

Operating Activities

General rule: Any transactions that enter into the determination of net income are classified as
operating activities. These transactions include:

Cash receipts from:
Sale of goods or providing of services
Interest (from all sources)
Dividends (on stock of other companies)
Miscellaneous income, such as from rentals

Cash payments to:
Suppliers for purchases of inventory
Employees for services
Other entities for insurance, utilities, rent, and so forth
Creditors for interest on debt
Government agencies for taxes

Investing Activities

General rule: Any transactions that are involved in the acquisition or disposition of noncurrent
assets are classified as investing activities. These transactions include:

Cash provided by:
Sale of property, plant, and equipment
Sale of securities, such as bonds and stocks of other companies, that are not cash equivalents
Collection of a loan made to another company

Cash used to:
Purchase property, plant, and equipment
Purchase securities, such as bonds and stocks of other companies, that are not cash equivalents
Lend money to another company, such as to a subsidiary

Financing Activities

General rule: Any transactions involving borrowing from creditors (other than the payment of interest), and any transactions involving the owners of a company (except stock dividends
and stock splits), are classified as financing activities. These transactions include:

Cash provided by:
Borrowing from short-term or long-term creditors through notes, bonds, mortgages, and similar
forms of debt
Sale of capital stock to owners

Cash used to:
Retire notes, bonds, mortgages, and similar forms of short-term and long-term debt
Repurchase capital stock from owners
Pay cash dividends to owners

panies; and lending money to another entity (such as to a subsidiary) and the
subsequent collection of the loan. Exhibit 17–1 provides a tabular summary of the
cash inflows and cash outflows relating to investing activities.

Financing Activities

As a general rule, any transactions involving borrowing from creditors (other than
the payment of interest), and any transactions involving the owners of a company
(except stock dividends and stock splits), are classified as **financing activities.**

Cash inflows from financing activities include amounts obtained from creditors
through the issuance of notes, bonds, mortgages, and similar forms of short-term
and long-term debt. Amounts obtained from owners come from the sale of capital
stock (preferred and common).

Cash outflows from financing activities include the repayment of amounts borrowed from short-term and long-term creditors, the repurchase of stock held by
the owners of a company, and the payment of cash dividends to owners. The
payment of cash dividends is classified as a financing item, rather than as an
operating item, because dividends do not enter into the determination of income.
In repaying creditors for amounts borrowed, if a gain or a loss is involved (such as

retiring bonds for less than their carrying value), then the gain or loss should be classified as a financing item along with the debt to which it relates.

Refer to Exhibit 17–1 for a summary of the cash inflows and cash outflows relating to financing activities. Note from this exhibit that accounts payable is not included among the forms of debt representing financing activities. This is because accounts payable is used to obtain *goods and services* rather than to obtain cash. Also the goods and services obtained (such as inventory, utilities, and supplies) relate to a company's day-to-day operating activities rather than to its financing activities. The reader should also note that stock dividends and stock splits are not included as financing activities. This is because neither stock dividends nor stock splits involve the use of cash and therefore do not appear on a statement of cash flows.

DIRECT EXCHANGE TRANSACTIONS

Companies sometimes acquire assets or dispose of liabilities through **direct exchange transactions.** Examples of direct exchange transactions include the issue of capital stock in exchange for property and equipment, the conversion of long-term debt or preferred stock into common stock, and the acquisition of property and equipment under a long-term lease agreement.

Objective 3
Explain what is meant by a direct exchange transaction and explain how such a transaction is reported to statement users.

Such exchanges have a common identifying characteristic in that they affect only noncurrent balance sheet accounts and have no effect on cash. Even though direct exchange transactions have no effect on cash, they must still be considered when the statement of cash flows is prepared. This is because these exchanges involve significant financing and investing activities, the existence of which must be made known to statement users. However, rather than being reported as part of a statement of cash flows, direct exchanges are reported in a separate, accompanying schedule. To illustrate how this is done, assume the following situation:

Delsey Company acquired a tract of land to be used as a building site and paid for it in full by issuing 5,000 shares of its own common stock, which had a par value of $100 per share. Since the stock was selling for $120 per share at the time the land was acquired, the exchange was recorded as follows:

Land (5,000 shares × $120)	600,000	
Common Stock, $100 par (5,000 shares × $100).		500,000
Paid-In Capital in Excess of Par (5,000 shares × $20)		100,000

This transaction had no effect on cash, but it did involve both an investing activity (the acquisition of land) and a financing activity (the issue of common stock) through a direct exchange. To report this exchange to statement users, Delsey Company should provide the following information in a separate schedule:

Schedule of noncash investing and financing activities:
    Common stock issued to acquire land for a
      building site $600,000

OTHER FACTORS IN PREPARING THE STATEMENT OF CASH FLOWS

We must consider two other factors before we can illustrate the preparation of a statement of cash flows. These two factors are (1) whether amounts on the statement should be presented gross or net, and (2) whether operating activities should be presented by use of the direct method or the indirect method.

Cash Flows: Gross or Net?

Objective 4
Identify items that should
be presented in gross
amounts and items that
should be presented in net
amounts on the statement
of cash flows.

For both *financing* and *investing* activities, items on the statement of cash flows should be presented in gross amounts rather than in net amounts. To illustrate, assume that a company purchases $500,000 in property during a year and sells other property for $300,000. Instead of showing a $200,000 net investment in property for the year, the company must show the gross amounts of both the purchases and the sales. In like manner, if a company receives $800,000 from the issue of bonds and then pays out $600,000 to retire other bonds, the receipts and the payments should be shown in their gross amounts, rather than being netted against each other.

The gross method of reporting does not extend to *operating* activities, where it is often necessary to net items against each other. For example, if $400,000 is added to accounts receivable as a result of sales during a year, and if $300,000 of receivables is collected, then only the $100,000 net difference would be used in determining the cash flow from operating activities for the year.

Operating Activities: Direct or Indirect Reporting?

Objective 5
Explain the difference
between the direct method
and the indirect method of
determining the "Net cash
provided by operating
activities."

The net result of the cash inflows and outflows arising from day-to-day operations is known formally as the **"Net cash provided by operating activities."** It is possible to compute this figure by either the *direct method* or the *indirect method*.

Under the **direct method,** the income statement is reconstructed on a cash basis from top to bottom. In place of sales, we have cash collected from customers; in place of cost of goods sold, we have payments to suppliers for inventory; and in place of operating expenses, we have payments to employees for services, payments for insurance, and so forth. The net result between the cash receipts and the cash payments represents the "Net cash provided by operating activities" for the period.

Under the **indirect method,** the "Net cash provided by operating activities" is computed by starting with net income (as reported on the income statement) and adjusting the net income figure to a cash basis. That is, rather than making *direct* adjustments to sales, cost of goods sold, and other income statement items in order to compute the "Net cash provided by operating activities," these adjustments are made *indirectly* through the net income figure. Thus the term, *indirect method.* The indirect method has an advantage over the direct method in that it shows the reasons for any differences between net income and the "Net cash provided by operating activities." The indirect method is also known as the **reconciliation method.**

In preparing a statement of cash flows, should the manager use the direct method or the indirect method? For external reporting purposes, the FASB *recommends* and *encourages* the use of the direct method. But we must note that the indirect method is preferred by most companies, and therefore it is used most often in actual practice. The reasons why companies prefer the indirect method are discussed later in the chapter, after we have studied both methods in greater detail.

As we have noted, the direct and indirect methods are very different in their approach. We will be most effective in our study, therefore, if we discuss the two methods separately. Since many people find the indirect method to be the easier of the two methods to apply, we will discuss it first. The indirect method also lends itself readily to working papers, so we will use it as a base for illustrating the use of working papers in preparing a statement of cash flows. After laying this foundation, we will then turn our attention to the direct method and show how the income statement can be adjusted to a cash basis for external reporting purposes.

FOCUS ON CURRENT PRACTICE

The American Institute of Certified Public Accountants (AICPA) makes an annual survey of the accounting and reporting practices of 600 industrial and merchandising firms. The 1991 survey found that 585 of the 600 companies surveyed (97.5 percent) used the indirect method in preparing a statement of cash flows for their annual reports. Only 15 of the 600 companies (2.5 percent) used the direct method. Moreover, the survey showed that the number of companies using the indirect method is increasing.[1] Another survey of 100 banks conducted by a large public accounting firm found that 96 used the indirect method and only 4 used the direct method of reporting cash flows from operating activities.[2]

THE INDIRECT METHOD OF DETERMINING THE "NET CASH PROVIDED BY OPERATING ACTIVITIES"

The items for which adjustments must be made to determine the "Net cash provided by operating activities" can be grouped into five broad categories, as follows:

Objective 6
Compute the "Net cash provided by operating activities" using the indirect method.

1. Depreciation, depletion, and amortization.
2. Changes in current asset accounts affecting revenue or expense.
3. Changes in current liability accounts affecting revenue or expense.
4. Gains or losses on sales of assets.
5. Changes in the Deferred Income Taxes account.

A simple model is available that starts with net income and shows the adjustments that must be made for each of the items listed above in computing a cash flow figure under the indirect method. This model is presented in Exhibit 17–2. The various parts of the model are discussed in this section.

Depreciation, Depletion, and Amortization

As shown in Exhibit 17–2, depreciation and related items are added back to net income in computing the cash provided by operating activities. The mechanics of this process sometimes leads people to the hasty conclusion that depreciation is a source of cash to an organization. We must state emphatically that depreciation is not a source of cash. We add it back to net income for the reason that it requires no cash outlay during a period, yet it is deducted as an expense in arriving at net income. Thus, by adding it back, we are able to cancel out its effect and leave as part of net income only those items of revenue and expense that *do* affect the amount of cash provided during a period.

Besides depreciation, other deductions that reduce net income without involv-

---

[1] AICPA, *Accounting Trends and Techniques: 1991*, Section 5: Statement of Cash Flows (New York: 1991), p. 420.
[2] James Don Edwards and Cynthia D. Heagy, "Relevance Gained: FASB Modifies Cash Flow Statement Requirements for Banks," *Journal of Accountancy* 171, no. 6 (June 1991), p. 84.

EXHIBIT 17–2
General Model:
Indirect Method of
Determining the "Net
Cash Provided by
Operating Activities"

	Add (+) or Deduct (−) to Adjust Net Income
Net income.	$XXX
Adjustments needed to convert net income to a cash basis:	
Depreciation, depletion, and amortization expense	+
Add (deduct) changes in current asset accounts affecting revenue or expense:*	
Increase in the account	−
Decrease in the account	+
Add (deduct) changes in current liability accounts affecting revenue or expense:†	
Increase in the account	+
Decrease in the account	−
Add (deduct) gains or losses on sales of assets:	
Gain on sales of assets.	−
Loss on sales of assets.	+
Add (deduct) changes in the Deferred Income Taxes account:	
Increase in the account	+
Decrease in the account	−
Net cash provided by operating activities	$XXX

* Examples include accounts receivable, accrued receivables, inventory, and prepaid expenses.

† Examples include accounts payable, accrued liabilities, and deferred revenue.

ing an outflow of cash include depletion of natural resources and amortization of goodwill, patents, and similar items. Like depreciation, these items are added back to net income under the indirect method in computing the amount of cash provided by operating activities.

Changes in Current Asset and Current Liability Accounts

In adjusting the net income figure to a cash basis, the model in Exhibit 17–2 shows that certain additions and deductions must be made for changes in the current asset and current liability accounts. An explanation is provided in Exhibit 17–3 as to what the changes in these accounts mean and why the adjustments are needed. This exhibit should be studied with care, and the "Add" and "Deduct" signal in the last column should be traced back into Exhibit 17–2.

Gains and Losses on Sales of Assets

Observe from Exhibit 17–2 that gains on sales of assets are deducted from net income in computing the cash provided by operating activities. The reason is that such gains represent part of the total cash proceeds from sale of the asset involved, and these proceeds must be included in full under *investing* activities. If gains are not deducted from net income, then double counting will result since the gain will be counted once as part of net income and then counted a second time as part of the cash proceeds arising from the sale transaction.

Losses are added back to net income to adjust it to a cash basis. This is because losses are noncash deductions and, like depreciation, reduce net income but do not involve an outflow of cash.

	Change in the Account	This Change Means that . . .	Therefore, to Adjust to a Cash Basis under the Indirect Method, We Must . . .
Accounts Receivable and Accrued Receivables	Increase	Sales (revenues) have been reported for which no cash has been collected.	Deduct the amount from net income to show that cash-basis sales are less than reported sales (revenues).
	Decrease	Cash has been collected for which no sales (revenues) have been reported for the current period.	Add the amount to net income to show that cash-basis sales are greater than reported sales (revenues).
Inventory	Increase	Goods have been purchased that are not included in cost of goods sold (COGS).	Deduct the amount from net income to show that cash-basis COGS is greater than reported COGS.
	Decrease	Goods have been included in COGS that were purchased in a prior period.	Add the amount to net income to show that cash-basis COGS is less than reported COGS.
Prepaid Expenses	Increase	More cash has been paid out for services than has been reported as expense.	Deduct the amount from net income to show that cash-basis expenses are greater than reported expenses.
	Decrease	More has been reported as expense for services than has been paid out in cash.	Add the amount to net income to show that cash-basis expenses are less than reported expenses.
Accounts Payable and Accrued Liabilities	Increase	More has been reported as expense for goods and services than has been paid out in cash.	Add the amount to net income to show that cash-basis expenses for goods and services are less than reported expenses.
	Decrease	More cash has been paid out for goods and services than has been reported as expense.	Deduct the amount from net income to show that cash-basis expenses for goods and services are greater than reported expenses.
Deferred Revenue	Increase	More cash has been received than has been reported as revenue.	Add the amount to net income to show that cash-basis revenue is greater than reported revenue.
	Decrease	More has been reported as revenue than has been received in cash.	Deduct the amount from net income to show that cash-basis revenue is less than reported revenue.

EXHIBIT 17–3
Explanation of Adjustments for Changes in Current Asset and Current Liability Accounts (see Exhibit 17–2)

Changes in the Deferred Income Taxes Account

Deferred income taxes represent amounts deducted currently on the income statement as income tax expense but not remitted to the Internal Revenue Service until a later time (perhaps several years later). Such taxes are generally carried as a long-term liability on the balance sheet. In adjusting the net income figure to a cash basis, changes in the Deferred Income Taxes account follow the same rules as for current liabilities. An increase in the account means that more expense has been shown on the income statement for taxes than has been paid out in cash. Therefore, in accordance with the rules already discussed (in Exhibit 17–3), we must add the increase back to net income to show that cash-basis expenses are less than reported expenses. The opposite will be true for a decrease in the Deferred Income Taxes account—the decrease must be deducted from net income to show that the amount of cash paid out was greater than reported expenses.

AN EXAMPLE OF THE STATEMENT OF CASH FLOWS

Objective 7
Prepare a statement of cash flows without the use of working papers.

To pull together the ideas developed in preceding sections, we turn now to the financial statements of Imperial Company presented in Exhibits 17–4, 17–5, and 17–6 and prepare a statement of cash flows. The numbers in these exhibits have been simplified for ease of computation and discussion.

Four Basic Steps to the Statement of Cash Flows

There are four basic steps to follow in preparing a statement of cash flows. These steps are:

1. Find the change that took place in the Cash account during the year.
2. Determine the "Net cash provided by operating activities" by analyzing the changes in the appropriate balance sheet accounts and by following the model given in Exhibit 17–2 (or by following the model given for the direct method later in the chapter).
3. Analyze each additional balance sheet account and determine whether the change in the account was the result of an investing activity or a financing activity.
4. Summarize the cash flows obtained in steps 2 and 3 into operating, investing, and financing activities. The net result of the cash flows for these three activities will equal the change in cash obtained in step 1.

For step 1, we can determine from Imperial Company's comparative balance sheet in Exhibit 17–4 that the Cash account has decreased by $2,100 during 19x2. By following the remaining steps above, we can prepare a statement of cash flows and find the reasons for this decrease.

Cash Provided by Operating Activities

Imperial Company's income statement shows that net income was $6,500 for 19x2. Starting with this figure and using the model presented in Exhibit 17–2 as a guide, an analysis of the cash provided by operating activities for 19x2 is given below:

Operating Activities

Net income.	$ 6,500
Adjustments needed to convert net income to a cash basis:	
Depreciation expense for the year	4,000
Add (deduct) changes in current assets:	
Increase in accounts receivable.	(1,500)
Decrease in inventory	2,000
Increase in prepaid expenses	(100)
Add (deduct) changes in current liabilities:	
Decrease in accounts payable	(3,000)
Increase in accrued liabilities.	1,000
Net cash provided by operating activities	$ 8,900

"How Well Am I Doing?" Statement of Cash Flows • 17

795

EXHIBIT 17–4

IMPERIAL COMPANY
Comparative Balance Sheet
December 31, 19x2, and 19x1

	19x2	19x1
Assets		
Current assets:		
Cash	$ 900	$ 3,000
Accounts receivable, net	7,000	5,500
Inventory	8,000	10,000
Prepaid expenses	600	500
Total current assets	16,500	19,000
Long-term investments	2,000	5,000
Plant and equipment	80,000	60,000
Less accumulated depreciation	8,000	4,000
Net plant and equipment	72,000	56,000
Total assets	$90,500	$80,000
Liabilities and Stockholders' Equity		
Current liabilities:		
Accounts payable	$ 5,000	$ 8,000
Accrued liabilities	1,000	—
Total current liabilities	6,000	8,000
Bonds payable	24,000	10,000
Stockholders' equity:		
Common stock	20,000	25,000
Retained earnings	40,500	37,000
Total stockholders' equity	60,500	62,000
Total liabilities and stockholders' equity	$90,500	$80,000

EXHIBIT 17–5

IMPERIAL COMPANY
Income Statement
For the Year Ended December 31, 19x2

Sales		$70,000
Less cost of goods sold		40,000
Gross margin		30,000
Less operating expenses:		
Selling expenses	$ 9,000	
Administrative expenses	10,500	
Depreciation expense	4,000	
Total operating expenses		23,500
Net income		$ 6,500

EXHIBIT 17–6

IMPERIAL COMPANY
Statement of Retained Earnings
For the Year Ended December 31, 19x2

Retained earnings, December 31, 19x1	$37,000
Add: Net income	6,500
	43,500
Deduct: Dividends paid	3,000
Retained earnings, December 31, 19x2	$40,500

The $4,000 depreciation expense figure used above is taken from Imperial Company's income statement. Note that this amount also agrees with the change in the Accumulated Depreciation account on the company's balance sheet in Exhibit 17–4.

Looking further at the balance sheet, the company has three current asset accounts in addition to Cash—Accounts Receivable, Inventory, and Prepaid Expenses. Adjustments have been made above for changes in these accounts (and for changes in the current liabilities) according to the guidelines given in Exhibit 17–3. These adjustments are summarized as follows: Accounts Receivable has increased by $1,500; since an increase in Accounts Receivable represents sales for which no cash has been received, the $1,500 is deducted from net income above in determining the cash provided by operating activities. Inventory has decreased by $2,000; as discussed in Exhibit 17–3, this decrease means that items have been included in Cost of Goods Sold that were purchased in a prior year. Since no cash was disbursed this year for these items, the $2,000 is added back to net income. Finally, Prepaid Expenses have increased by $100; this $100 represents payments for services (such as rent) that are not included as expenses on the income statement. The $100 is therefore deducted from the net income figure above to show that cash-basis expenses are greater than reported expenses.

Imperial Company has two current liability accounts—Accounts Payable and Accrued Liabilities. Accounts Payable has decreased by $3,000; this decrease means that the company made payment for goods and services that were acquired in a preceding year. Since the cash payment was made this year, we must deduct the $3,000 from net income to show that cash basis expenses for goods and services are greater than reported expenses. Finally, the Accrued Liabilities account has increased by $1,000; this $1,000 represents items such as salaries that have been recorded as an expense but for which no cash payment has been made. Therefore, the $1,000 is added back to net income to show that cash expenses are less than reported expenses.

Changes in Other Balance Sheet Accounts

Having analyzed the current asset and current liability accounts and determined the cash provided by operating activities, we must now analyze each remaining balance sheet account and determine whether the change in the account was caused by an investing activity or a financing activity. So far as the end result is concerned, it makes no difference which of the remaining accounts we analyze first, nor does it matter in which order we proceed. This is simply a matter of choice. Since the Retained Earnings account usually contains a number of significant changes, managers often start with it.

Retained Earnings   From the comparative balance sheet in Exhibit 17–4, we can see that Retained Earnings has increased by $3,500 during 19x2. To determine the cause of this change, we need to look at another exhibit—Exhibit 17–6—that contains an analysis of the Retained Earnings account. We can see from this exhibit that the $3,500 increase in Retained Earnings is a net result of $6,500 in net income for the year and $3,000 in dividends paid during the year. The net income figure has already been used in our computation of the cash provided by operating activities; the $3,000 dividends paid would be classified as a financing activity, as discussed earlier in Exhibit 17–1.

Financing Activities

Cash was provided by:

Cash was used to:

    Pay dividends to owners $3,000

Long-Term Investments

Imperial Company's comparative balance sheet in Exhibit 17–4 shows that long-term investments decreased by $3,000 during 19x2. Long-term investments generally consist of securities (stocks and bonds) of other companies that are being held for some reason. If the amount of these investments decreases during a period, the most likely conclusion is that they were sold. From the guidelines given in Exhibit 17–1, any transaction involving the disposition of a noncurrent asset would be an investing activity. Since we have no evidence of any gain or loss on the sale, the entry on the cash flow statement would be as follows:

Investing Activities

Cash was provided by:

    Sale of long-term investments $3,000

Cash was used to:

Plant and Equipment

The Plant and Equipment account has increased by $20,000 during 19x2, as shown by the comparative balance sheet in Exhibit 17–4. Since there is nothing on Imperial Company's statements to indicate that there were any sales of plant and equipment during 19x2, we can assume that this $20,000 represents the company's gross purchases for the year. (Remember, we can't "net" sales and purchases of assets off against each other; all amounts must be shown "gross" on the statement of cash flows.) The guidelines in Exhibit 17–1 indicate that a purchase of plant and equipment would be an investing activity.

Investing Activities

Cash was provided by:

    Sale of long-term investments . . . $ 3,000

Cash was used to:

    Purchase plant and equipment . . .   20,000

Accumulated Depreciation

Imperial Company's Accumulated Depreciation account has increased by $4,000 during 19x2, as shown in Exhibit 17–4. This change was accounted for earlier in our computation of the cash provided by operating activities.

Bonds Payable

Moving down Imperial Company's 19x2 balance sheet in Exhibit 17–4, we find that Bonds Payable increased $14,000 during the year. Since we see no evidence of any bonds having been retired during the year, we can assume that the $14,000 represents the gross amount of bonds issued. The guidelines in Exhibit 17–1 show that an issue of long-term debt is a financing activity.

Financing Activities

Cash was provided by:

    Issue of bonds $14,000

Cash was used to:

    Pay dividends to owners   3,000

Common Stock

Imperial Company's Common Stock account decreased by $5,000 during 19x2. Since we see no evidence of any stock having been issued during the year, we can assume that the $5,000 represents the company's only stock transaction. The most likely explanation for a $5,000 decrease in the Common Stock account is a repurchase of stock from the owners. Such a repurchase would be a financing activity, as shown in Exhibit 17–1.

Financing Activities

Cash was provided by:
Issue of bonds $14,000

Cash was used to:
Pay dividends to owners   3,000
Repurchase common stock   5,000

The Completed Statement of Cash Flows

We can now organize the results of our analytical work into statement form. Using the data we have developed, a complete statement of cash flows for Imperial Company is presented in Exhibit 17–7.

We noted at the beginning of this example that Imperial Company's Cash account had decreased by $2,100 during the year. We have now isolated the reasons for this decrease, as shown in the company's statement of cash flows.

EXHIBIT 17–7

IMPERIAL COMPANY
Statement of Cash Flows
For the Year Ended December 31, 19x2

Operating Activities

Net income. . . . . $ 6,500

Adjustments needed to convert net income to a cash basis:
Depreciation expense for the year   4,000

Add (deduct) changes in current assets:
Increase in accounts receivable . . . .   (1,500)
Decrease in inventory   2,000
Increase in prepaid expenses . . . .   (100)

Add (deduct) changes in current liabilities:
Decrease in accounts payable . . . .   (3,000)
Increase in accrued liabilities   1,000
Net cash provided by operating activities   8,900

Investing Activities

Cash was provided by:
Sale of long-term investments . . . . $ 3,000

Cash was used to:
Purchase plant and equipment . . . .   (20,000)
Net cash used for investing activities . . . .   (17,000)

Financing Activities

Cash was provided by:
Issue of bonds   14,000

Cash was used to:
Pay dividends to owners . . . .   (3,000)
Repurchase common stock . . . .   (5,000)
Net cash provided by financing activities   6,000

Net decrease in cash . . . .   (2,100)
Cash balance, January 1, 19x2   3,000
Cash balance, December 31, 19x2 . . . . $ 900

The Statement of Cash Flows as a Planning Tool

The statement of cash flows is highly regarded as a management planning tool. Although it deals with historical costs, any lack of forward planning, coordination, or balance in working toward long-run objectives becomes quickly evident in the story it has to tell. For example, a company may have as its stated objective to double plant capacity in five years using only cash provided by operating activities. If the company at the same time is paying dividends equal to half of its earnings and is retiring large amounts of long-term debt, the discrepancy between long-run plans and current actions will be brought to light very quickly by the information contained in the statement of cash flows.

Some of the more significant ways in which managers use the statement for planning purposes include:

1. To coordinate dividend policy with other actions of the company.
2. To plan the financing of new product lines, additional plant and equipment, or acquisitions of other companies.
3. To find ways of strengthening a weak cash position and thereby strengthening credit lines.

FOCUS ON CURRENT PRACTICE

Shareholders as well as managers find the statement of cash flows to be a useful tool, as evidenced by a survey of 246 shareholders who own at least 100 shares of a single stock listed on either the New York or American Stock Exchange. Over half of these shareholders stated that they read the statement of cash flows "somewhat thoroughly" when they receive an annual report. Only about one out of four reported difficulty in understanding the content of the statement, whereas more than half stated that they found the statement of cash flows to be useful in investment decisions.[3]

A WORKING PAPER APPROACH TO THE STATEMENT OF CASH FLOWS

Objective 8
Prepare working papers to gather data for a statement of cash flows.

The procedure relied on to this point of simply developing a statement of cash flows through logic has allowed us to concentrate our efforts on learning basic concepts, with a minimum of time expended on mechanics. For some companies, this simple logic procedure is completely adequate as a means of developing a statement of cash flows.

For other companies, however, the balance sheet is so complex that working papers are needed to help organize the changes in the various accounts into statement form. A number of working paper approaches to the statement of cash flows are available. The one we have chosen to illustrate relies on the use of T-accounts to assist in the analysis and organization of data. To illustrate the T-account approach to working paper preparation, we will use the financial statements of Universal Company found in Exhibits 17–8 and 17–9.

---

[3] Marc J. Epstein and Moses L. Pava, "How Useful Is the Statement of Cash Flows?" *Management Accounting* 74, no. 1 (July 1992), pp. 52–55.

EXHIBIT 17–8

UNIVERSAL COMPANY
Comparative Balance Sheet
December 31, 19x5, and 19x4

	19x5	19x4
Assets		
Current assets:		
Cash	$ 11,000	$ 3,000
Marketable securities	5,000	7,000
Accounts receivable, net	72,000	81,000
Inventory	103,000	93,000
Prepaid expenses	2,000	6,000
Total current assets	193,000	190,000
Investment in Company Y (note 1).	79,000	85,000
Plant and equipment (note 2)	340,000	295,000
Less accumulated depreciation	110,000	180,000
Net plant and equipment	230,000	115,000
Total assets	$502,000	$390,000
Liabilities and Stockholders' Equity		
Current liabilities:		
Accounts payable	$105,000	$ 90,000
Accrued liabilities	6,000	12,000
Total current liabilities	111,000	102,000
Deferred income taxes	15,000	10,000
Long-term notes payable	78,000	28,000
Total liabilities.	204,000	140,000
Stockholders' equity:		
Common stock	175,000	140,000
Retained earnings	123,000	110,000
Total stockholders' equity	298,000	250,000
Total liabilities and stockholders' equity	$502,000	$390,000

Note 1: Part of the investment in Company Y was sold during the year at a selling price of $8,000.

Note 2: Equipment that had cost $160,000 new, and on which there was accumulated depreciation of $87,000, was sold during the year for $70,000.

EXHIBIT 17–9

UNIVERSAL COMPANY
Income Statement and
Reconciliation of Retained Earnings
For the Year Ended December 31, 19x5

Sales		$500,000
Less cost of goods sold		300,000
Gross margin		200,000
Less operating expenses (note 3)		109,000
Net operating income		91,000
Nonoperating items:		
Gain on sale of investments	$ 2,000	
Loss on sale of equipment	3,000	1,000
Income before taxes		90,000
Less income taxes (30%)		27,000
Net income		63,000
Retained earnings, January 1, 19x5		110,000
Total		173,000
Less dividends distributed:		
Cash dividends	40,000	
Stock dividends, common	10,000	50,000
Retained earnings, December 31, 19x5		$123,000

Note 3: Operating expenses contain $17,000 of depreciation expense.

The T-Account Approach

Note from Universal Company's comparative balance sheet (Exhibit 17–8) that cash and cash equivalents (marketable securities) have increased from $10,000 ($3,000 + $7,000) in 19x4 to $16,000 ($11,000 + $5,000) in 19x5—an increase of $6,000. To determine the reasons for this change we will again prepare a statement of cash flows. As before, our basic analytical approach will be to analyze the changes in the various balance sheet accounts. The only function the T-accounts will serve will be to assist us in the mechanical process of organizing our information as it develops.

In Exhibit 17–10 (page 802), we have prepared T-accounts and entered into these T-accounts the beginning and ending balances for every account on Universal Company's comparative balance sheet, except for Cash and Marketable Securities. The exhibit also contains a T-account titled "Cash," which we will use to accumulate the cash "Provided" and the cash "Used" as these amounts develop through our analysis of the other accounts.

The procedure is to make entries directly in the T-accounts to explain the actions that have caused the changes in the various account balances. To the extent that these changes have affected cash, appropriate entries are made in the T-account representing Cash.

Retained Earnings   As we stated earlier in the chapter, the Retained Earnings account is generally the most useful starting point in developing a statement of cash flows. A detail of the change in Universal Company's Retained Earnings account is presented in Exhibit 17–9. We can note from the exhibit that net income of $63,000 was added to Retained Earnings during 19x5 and that dividends of $50,000 were charged against Retained Earnings. The dividends consisted of $40,000 in cash dividends and $10,000 in stock dividends.

Exhibit 17–11 (page 803) contains a second set of T-accounts for Universal Company in which entries have been made to show the effect of the year's activities on the company's Cash account. These entries for Retained Earnings are as follows: Entry (1) shows the increase in Retained Earnings that resulted from the net income reported for 19x5 and the corresponding increase that would have taken place in the Cash account:

(1)

Cash—Provided.	63,000	
Retained Earnings		63,000

Entry (2) records the payment of cash dividends on common stock and the corresponding drain on Cash:

(2)

Retained Earnings	40,000	
Cash—Used		40,000

Entry (3) records the distribution of a stock dividend to common stockholders. A stock dividend has no effect on Cash. It simply capitalizes a portion of Retained Earnings and results in no outflow of assets:

(3)

Retained Earnings	10,000	
Common Stock		10,000

The reader should trace all three of these entries into the T-accounts in Exhibit 17–11.

EXHIBIT 17–10

T-Accounts Showing Changes in Account Balances—Universal Company

Cash

Provided	Used

Accounts Receivable

Bal.	81,000		
Bal.	72,000		

Inventory

Bal.	93,000		
Bal.	103,000		

Prepaid Expenses

Bal.	6,000		
Bal.	2,000		

Investment in Company Y

Bal.	85,000		
Bal.	79,000		

Plant and Equipment

Bal.	295,000		
Bal.	340,000		

Accumulated Depreciation

		Bal.	180,000
		Bal.	110,000

Accounts Payable

		Bal.	90,000
		Bal.	105,000

Accrued Liabilities

		Bal.	12,000
		Bal.	6,000

Deferred Income Taxes

		Bal.	10,000
		Bal.	15,000

Long-Term Notes Payable

		Bal.	28,000
		Bal.	78,000

Common Stock

		Bal.	140,000
		Bal.	175,000

Retained Earnings

		Bal.	110,000
		Bal.	123,000

EXHIBIT 17–11

T-Accounts after Posting of Account Changes—Universal Company

Cash

	Provided			Used	
(1)	63,000	Net income			
(4)	9,000	Decrease in accounts receivable			
(6)	4,000	Decrease in prepaid expenses			
(8)	3,000	Loss on sale of equipment			
(10)	17,000	Depreciation expense			
(11)	15,000	Increase in accounts payable			
(13)	5,000	Increase in deferred income taxes			
	98,000	Net cash provided by operating activities			
(7)	8,000	Sale of Company Y investment			
(8)	70,000	Sale of equipment			
(14)	50,000	Issue of long-term notes			
(15)	25,000	Sale of common stock			
(5)		Increase in inventory		10,000	
(7)		Gain on sale of investments		2,000	
(12)		Decrease in accrued liabilities		6,000	
(2)		Payment of cash dividends		40,000	
(9)		Purchase of plant and equipment		205,000	

Accounts Receivable

Bal.	81,000	(4)	9,000
Bal.	72,000		

Inventory

Bal.	93,000		
(5)	10,000		
Bal.	103,000		

Prepaid Expenses

Bal.	6,000	(6)	4,000
Bal.	2,000		

Investment in Company Y

Bal.	85,000	(7)	6,000
Bal.	79,000		

Plant and Equipment

Bal.	295,000	(8)	160,000
(9)	205,000		
Bal.	340,000		

Accumulated Depreciation

		Bal.	180,000
(8)	87,000	(10)	17,000
		Bal.	110,000

Accounts Payable

		Bal.	90,000
		(11)	15,000
		Bal.	105,000

Accrued Liabilities

		Bal.	12,000
(12)	6,000		
		Bal.	6,000

Long-Term Notes Payable

		Bal.	28,000
		(14)	50,000
		Bal.	78,000

Deferred Income Taxes

		Bal.	10,000
		(13)	5,000
		Bal.	15,000

Common Stock

		Bal.	140,000
		(3)	10,000
		(15)	25,000
		Bal.	175,000

Retained Earnings

		Bal.	110,000
(2)	40,000	(1)	63,000
(3)	10,000		
		Bal.	123,000

Observe from Exhibit 17–11 that these three entries fully explain the change that has taken place in the Retained Earnings account during 19x5. We can now proceed through the remainder of the accounts in the exhibit, analyzing the change between the beginning and ending balances in each account, and recording the appropriate entries in the T-accounts.

Current Asset Accounts   The use of T-accounts greatly simplifies the computation of the "Net cash provided by operating activities." This is because the T-accounts automatically show the correct adjustment to make for the changes in the current asset and current liability accounts in order to adjust the net income figure to a cash basis. To demonstrate, Universal Company's Accounts Receivable has decreased by $9,000; the entry to record this change would be:

(4)

Cash—Provided.	9,000	
Accounts Receivable.		9,000

The Inventory account has increased by $10,000; the entry to record this change would be:

(5)

Inventory.	10,000	
Cash—Used		10,000

Finally, the Prepaid Expenses account has decreased by $4,000; the entry to record this change would be:

(6)

Cash—Provided.	4,000	
Prepaid Expenses		4,000

As before, the reader should trace all three of these entries into the T-accounts in Exhibit 17–11. Note that by posting the change to the appropriate account (e.g., Accounts Receivable has been credited for $9,000 to show the decrease in the account), we *automatically* show the correct adjustment to cash as an offsetting entry. *Thus, the model given in Exhibit 17–2 for computing the cash provided by operating activities is not needed when working papers are prepared, since the adjustments shown in the model are made within the working papers themselves.*

Observe that in arranging the data on the working papers we have placed all operating items near the top of the Cash T-account, clustered around the net income figure. Then we have placed all investing and financing items in the lower portion of the Cash T-account. This helps us to assemble our data in an orderly manner.

Investment in Company Y   The next account on Universal Company's comparative balance sheet is its investment in Company Y. This investment has decreased by $6,000 during 19x5. Since note 1 on the comparative balance sheet indicates that this decrease represents a sale from which the company received $8,000, the entry to record the transaction would be as follows:

(7)

Cash—Provided.	8,000	
Investment in Company Y		6,000
Gain on Sale of Investments		2,000

Note from the income statement in Exhibit 17–9 that the $2,000 gain on this sale is included as part of the company's $63,000 net income for the year. Thus, the gain is entered in the working papers in Exhibit 17–11 as a deduction from the net income figure. This deduction will avoid double counting of the gain and will allow all $8,000 of the sale price to be treated as an investing item.

Plant and Equipment   The next account to be analyzed is Plant and Equipment. The T-accounts in Exhibit 17–11 show that this account has increased by $45,000 during 19x5. The increase could simply represent $45,000 in plant and equipment purchases. On the other hand, there may have been retirements or sales during the year that are concealed in this net change.

From the footnote 2 to the balance sheet, we find that certain items of equipment were, indeed, sold during 19x5 at a sale price of $70,000. The entry to record this sale and its effect on Cash would be:

(8)

Cash—Provided	70,000
Accumulated Depreciation.	87,000
Loss on Sale of Equipment	3,000
Plant and Equipment	160,000

Note that the loss recorded above appears as a deduction on the company's income statement in Exhibit 17–9. Since this deduction is similar to depreciation and does not involve an outflow of cash, the loss is added back to net income in the working papers in Exhibit 17–11.

How much did the company expend on plant and equipment purchases during the year? Overall, we know that the Plant and Equipment account increased by $45,000. Since this $45,000 increase is what remains *after* the $160,000 retirement of equipment recorded above, then purchases during the year must have amounted to $205,000 ($45,000 + $160,000 = $205,000). Entry (9) records these purchases in the T-accounts:

(9)

Plant and Equipment.	205,000
Cash—Used	205,000

Accumulated Depreciation   The note on Universal Company's income statement indicates that depreciation expense totaled $17,000 for the year. The entry to record this depreciation in the T-accounts would be:

(10)

Cash—Provided	17,000
Accumulated Depreciation	17,000

This entry, along with entry (8) above, explains the change in the Accumulated Depreciation account for the year.

Current Liabilities   The T-accounts in Exhibit 17–11 show that Universal Company has two current liability accounts—Accounts Payable and Accrued Liabilities. Accounts Payable has increased by $15,000 during 19x5. The entry in the T-accounts to show this increase would be:

(11)

Cash—Provided	15,000
Accounts Payable	15,000

The Accrued Liabilities account has decreased by $6,000; the entry to record this change would be:

(12)

Accrued Liabilities	6,000	
Cash—Used		6,000

Since both of these changes are used to adjust net income to a cash basis, their cash effect is included in the upper portion of the Cash T-account along with the other operating items.

Deferred Income Taxes   Universal Company's Deferred Income Taxes account has increased by $5,000 during 19x5. This means that the company has paid out *less* in taxes during the year than has been reported as expense on the income statement. The entry to record this $5,000 increase in deferred taxes and to adjust net income to a cash basis would be:

(13)

Cash—Provided	5,000	
Deferred Income Taxes		5,000

Long-Term Notes Payable   Universal Company's financial statements give no indication of any long-term notes having been retired during the year. Therefore, we must assume that the $50,000 increase in the Long-Term Notes Payable account represents the gross amount of borrowing for the year. The entry to record this borrowing would be:

(14)

Cash—Provided	50,000	
Long-Term Notes Payable		50,000

Common Stock   Universal's Common Stock account has increased by $35,000 during 19x5. We have already accounted for $10,000 of this increase in entry (3) above where we recorded a stock dividend paid in common stock. Since we have no information to the contrary, we must assume that the remaining $25,000 represents a sale of common stock to owners. The entry to record this sale would be:

(15)

Cash—Provided	25,000	
Common Stock		25,000

With entry (15), our analysis of changes in Universal Company's balance sheet accounts is complete.

Preparing the Statement of Cash Flows from the Completed T-Accounts

The Cash T-account in Exhibit 17–11 now contains the entries for those transactions that have affected Universal Company's cash position during the year. Our only remaining task is to organize these data into a formal statement of cash flows. This statement is easy to prepare, since the data relating to operating activities are grouped in the upper portion of the Cash T-account and the data relating to investing and financing activities are grouped in the lower portion of the account. Following the guidelines given earlier (Exhibit 17–1), these data have been organized into a formal statement of cash flows in Exhibit 17–12. As an exercise, the reader should review the contents of this statement and explain in his or her own words why cash increased by $6,000 during 19x5.

EXHIBIT 17–12

UNIVERSAL COMPANY
Statement of Cash Flows
For the Year Ended December 31, 19x5

Operating Activities

Net income.	$ 63,000
Adjustments needed to convert net income to a cash basis:	
Depreciation expense for the year	17,000
Add (deduct) changes in current assets:	
Decrease in accounts receivable	9,000
Decrease in prepaid expenses	4,000
Increase in inventory	(10,000)
Add (deduct) changes in current liabilities:	
Increase in accounts payable	15,000
Decrease in accrued liabilities	(6,000)
Add (deduct) gains and losses on sales of assets:	
Gain on sale of investments	(2,000)
Loss on sale of equipment	3,000
Add the increase in deferred income taxes	5,000
Net cash provided by operating activities	98,000

Investing Activities

Cash was provided by:		
Sale of Company Y stock	$ 8,000	
Sale of equipment.	70,000	
Cash was used to:		
Purchase plant and equipment	(205,000)	
Net cash used for investing activities		(127,000)

Financing Activities

Cash was provided by:		
Issue of long-term notes	50,000	
Sale of common stock	25,000	
Cash was used to:		
Pay dividends to owners	(40,000)	
Net cash provided by financing activities		35,000
Net increase in cash and cash equivalents		6,000
Cash and cash equivalents, January 1, 19x5		10,000
Cash and cash equivalents, December 31, 19x5.		$ 16,000

THE DIRECT METHOD OF DETERMINING THE "NET CASH PROVIDED BY OPERATING ACTIVITIES"

As stated earlier in the chapter, to compute the "Net cash provided by operating activities" under the direct method, we must reconstruct the income statement on a cash basis from top to bottom. A model is presented in Exhibit 17–13 that shows the adjustments that must be made to sales, expenses, and so forth to adjust each to a cash basis. To illustrate the computations involved, we have included in the exhibit the data just used for Universal Company.

   Note that Universal Company's "Net cash provided by operating activities" figure ($98,000) agrees with the amount computed above by the indirect method. We would expect the two amounts to agree, since the direct and indirect methods are just different roads to the same destination. The "Operating activities" section of Universal Company's statement of cash flows—prepared under the direct method—is presented in Exhibit 17–14. (The investing and financing sections of the statement will be the same as shown for the indirect method in Exhibit 17–12.)

Objective 9
Adjust the income statement to a cash basis using the direct method.

EXHIBIT 17–13

General Model: Direct
Method of Determining
the ''Net Cash
Provided by Operating
Activities''

Revenue or Expense Item	Add (+) or Deduct (−) to Adjust to a Cash Basis	Illustration— Universal Company	
Sales revenue (as reported).		$500,000	
Adjustments to a cash basis:			
1. Increase in accounts receivable.	−		
2. Decrease in accounts receivable	+	+9,000	$509,000
Cost of goods sold (as reported).		300,000	
Adjustments to a cash basis:			
3. Increase in inventory	+	+10,000	
4. Decrease in inventory	−		
5. Increase in accounts payable	−	−15,000	
6. Decrease in accounts payable	+		295,000
Operating expenses (as reported)		109,000	
Adjustments to a cash basis:			
7. Increase in prepaid expenses.	+		
8. Decrease in prepaid expenses	−	−4,000	
9. Increase in accrued liabilities.	−		
10. Decrease in accrued liabilities	+	+6,000	
11. Period's depreciation, depletion, and amortization . . .	−	−17,000	94,000
Income tax expense (as reported)		27,000	
Adjustments to a cash basis:			
12. Increase in accrued taxes payable	−		
13. Decrease in accrued taxes payable	+		
14. Increase in deferred income taxes	−	−5,000	
15. Decrease in deferred income taxes	+		22,000
Net cash provided by operating activities			$ 98,000

EXHIBIT 17–14

Direct Method of
Reporting Operating
Activities Data

Operating Activities

Cash received from customers		$509,000
Less cash disbursements for:		
Cost of merchandise purchased.	$295,000	
Operating expenses	94,000	
Income taxes	22,000	
Total cash disbursements		411,000
Net cash provided by operating activities		$ 98,000

Similarities and Differences in the Handling of Data

Although we arrive at the same destination under either the direct or the indirect
methods, not all data are handled in the same way in the adjustment process. Stop
for a moment, flip back to the general model for the indirect method on page 792,
and compare the adjustments made in that model to the adjustments made for the
direct method in Exhibit 17–13. The adjustments for accounts that affect revenue
are the same in the two models. In either case, we adjust our figures to a cash basis
by deducting increases in the accounts and adding decreases in the accounts. The
adjustments for accounts that affect expenses, however, are handled in *opposite*
ways in the two models. This is because under the indirect method we are making
our adjustments to *net income,* whereas under the direct method we are making
our adjustments to the *expense accounts* themselves.

To illustrate this difference, note the handling of prepaid expenses and depreciation in the two models. Under the indirect method (Exhibit 17–2), an increase in the Prepaid Expenses account is *deducted* from net income in computing the amount of cash provided by operations. Under the direct method (Exhibit 17–13), an increase in Prepaid Expenses is *added* to operating expenses. The reason for the difference can be explained as follows: An increase in Prepaid Expenses means that more cash has been paid out for items such as insurance than has been included as expense for the period. Therefore, to adjust net income to a cash basis we must either deduct this increase from net income (indirect method) or we must add this increase to operating expenses (direct method). Either way, we will end up with the same figure for cash provided by operations. In like manner, depreciation is added to net income under the indirect method to cancel out its effect (Exhibit 17–2), whereas it is deducted from operating expenses under the direct method to cancel out its effect (Exhibit 17–13). These same differences in the handling of data are true for all other expense items in the two models.

In the matter of gains and losses on sales of assets, no adjustments are needed at all under the direct method. These gains and losses are simply ignored, since they are not part of sales, cost of goods sold, operating expenses, or income taxes. For example, observe from Exhibit 17–13 that Universal Company's $2,000 gain on sale of investments and $3,000 loss on sale of equipment were not involved in the adjustment of the company's income statement to a cash basis. In this sense, the direct method is somewhat simpler than the indirect method.

Special Rules—Direct and Indirect Methods

When using the direct method to compute the cash provided by operating activities, companies are required, at a minimum, to present the following breakdowns of cash received and cash paid out:

Cash receipts:

1. Cash collected from customers.
2. Interest and dividends received.
3. Other operating cash receipts, if any.

Cash Payments:

1. Cash paid to employees and to suppliers for goods and services (for inventory, utilities, and so forth).
2. Interest paid.
3. Income taxes paid.
4. Other operating cash payments, if any.

Also, when the direct method is used, the FASB requires that the company provide a reconciliation between net income and the "Net cash provided by operating activities," as determined by the indirect method. Thus, *when a company elects to use the direct method, it must also present computations by the indirect method as supplementary data.* These data must be presented in a separate schedule accompanying the statement of cash flows.

On the other hand, if a company elects to use the indirect method to compute the cash provided by operating activities, then it must also provide a special breakdown of data. The company must provide a separate disclosure of the amount of interest and the amount of income taxes paid during the year. The

FASB requires this separate disclosure so that users can take the data provided by the indirect method and make estimates of what the amounts for sales, income taxes, and so forth, would have been if the direct method had been used instead.

Comparison of the Direct and Indirect Methods

Historically, *when a choice between the direct and indirect methods has been available,* few companies have chosen the direct method. We can cite three reasons why. First, it is argued that the direct method is more difficult to use than the indirect method because it involves a complete restructuring of the income statement. Moreover, this restructuring can't be integrated readily into working papers. Second, since the direct method adjusts all figures on the income statement to a cash basis, there is concern it may imply that the cash basis of reporting is a better measure of performance than the accrual basis. Third, although the direct method shows the amount of cash provided by operating activities, it does not tell statement users *why* the cash provided differs from net income. Statement users are left on their own to reconcile the two figures (which may pose an almost impossible task for some users). The indirect method, by contrast, *starts* with the net income figure and shows why the "Net cash provided by operating activities" figure is different.

On the other hand, managers who argue in favor of the direct method state that by restructuring the income statement to a cash basis, statement users can see clearly how cash is generated by operations without having the picture blurred by irrelevant, noncash items such as depreciation. These managers argue that including depreciation on the statement of cash flows confuses and may even mislead statements users. This confusion is avoided under the direct method, it is argued, since the direct method deals only with actual cash receipts and cash payments.

SUMMARY

The statement of cash flows is one of the three major statements prepared by business firms. Its purpose is analytical in that it attempts to explain how cash has been provided and used during a period. As such, the statement of cash flows is highly regarded as a tool for assessing the well-being of a firm and for assessing how well its management is performing.

The statement of cash flows is organized in terms of operating, investing, and financing activities. Operating activities encompass those transactions involved in the determination of net income, investing activities encompass those transactions involved in the acquisition or disposition of noncurrent assets, and financing activities encompass those transactions involved with owners and involved with borrowing from creditors. As this list of transactions suggests, to determine the reason for any change in the Cash account, we must analyze changes in all other balance sheet accounts.

The net result of cash flows arising from day-to-day operations is known as the "Net cash provided by operating activities." This figure can be computed by either the direct method or the indirect method. Under the direct method, the income statement is reconstructed on a cash basis. Under the indirect method, adjustments for sales, cost of goods sold, and other income statement items are made indirectly through the net income figure.

REVIEW PROBLEM: CASH PROVIDED BY OPERATING ACTIVITIES

Rockford Company's comparative balance sheet for 19x2, the current year, and the company's income statement for the year follow:

ROCKFORD COMPANY
Comparative Balance Sheet
December 31, 19x2, and 19x1

	19x2	19x1
Assets		
Cash	$ 6	$ 10
Accounts receivable, net	180	270
Inventory	205	160
Prepaid expenses	17	20
Plant and equipment	430	309
Less accumulated depreciation	(218)	(194)
Long-term investments	60	75
Total assets	$ 680	$ 650
Liabilities and Stockholders' Equity		
Accounts payable	$ 230	$ 310
Accrued liabilities	70	60
Bonds payable.	135	40
Deferred income taxes	15	8
Common stock	140	200
Retained earnings	90	32
Total liabilities and stockholders' equity . . .	$ 680	$ 650

ROCKFORD COMPANY
Income Statement
For the Year Ended December 31, 19x2

Sales		$1,000
Less cost of goods sold.		530
Gross margin		470
Less operating expenses		352*
Net operating income		118
Nonoperating items:		
Gain on sale of investments	$6	
Loss on sale of equipment	4	2
Income before taxes		120
Less income taxes		48
Net income		$ 72

* Contains $50 depreciation expense.

Required

1. By use of the indirect method, determine the cash provided by operating activities for 19x2.
2. By use of the direct method, adjust the company's income statement for 19x2 to a cash basis.

Solution to Review Problem

1. To determine the cash provided by operating activities by the indirect method, we start with net income and adjust it for depreciation expense, changes in current assets and current liabilities, any gains or losses on asset sales, and changes in deferred income taxes, as shown in Exhibit 17–2. These amounts can be obtained from Rockford Company's income statement and comparative balance sheet. The computations follow:

Operating Activities

Net income	$ 72
Adjustments needed to convert net income to a cash basis:	
Depreciation expense for the year	50
Add (deduct) changes in current assets:	
Decrease in accounts receivable	90
Increase in inventory	(45)
Decrease in prepaid expenses	3
Add (deduct) changes in current liabilities:	
Decrease in accounts payable	(80)
Increase in accrued liabilities	10
Gains and losses on sales of assets:	
Gain on sale of investments	(6)
Loss on sale of equipment	4
Increase in deferred income taxes	7
Net cash provided by operating activities	$105

2. Using the format for the direct method provided in Exhibit 17–13, Rockford Company's income statement for 19x2 is adjusted to a cash basis as follows:

Sales		$1,000
Adjustments to a cash basis:		
Plus decrease in accounts receivable	+90	$1,090
Cost of goods sold	530	
Adjustments to a cash basis:		
Plus increase in inventory	+45	
Plus decrease in accounts payable	+80	655
Operating expenses	352	
Adjustments to a cash basis:		
Less decrease in prepaid expenses	−3	
Less increase in accrued liabilities	−10	
Less depreciation expense	−50	289
Income taxes	48	
Adjustments to a cash basis:		
Less increase in deferred income taxes	−7	41
Net cash provided by operating activities		$ 105

The reader should note that the $105 "Net cash provided" figure agrees with the $105 figure computed by the indirect method in (1) above.

KEY TERMS FOR REVIEW

Objective 10
Define or explain the key terms listed at the end of the chapter.

Cash equivalents   Short-term, highly liquid investments such as treasury bills, commercial paper, and money market funds that are made solely for the purpose of generating a return on funds that are temporarily idle. (p. 786)

Direct exchange transactions   Transactions involving only noncurrent accounts, such as the issue of capital stock in exchange for property or equipment, the conversion of long-term debt into common stock, and the acquisition of property under a long-term lease agreement. (p. 789)

Direct method   A method of computing the cash provided by operating activities in which the income statement is reconstructed on a cash basis. (p. 790)

Financing activities   A section on the statement of cash flows that includes all transactions (other than payment of interest) involving borrowing from creditors and all transactions (except stock dividends and stock splits) involving the owners of a company. (p. 788)

Indirect method   A method of computing the cash provided by operating activities that starts with net income (as reported on the income statement) and adjusts the net income figure to a cash basis. It is also known as the *reconciliation method*. (p. 790)

Investing activities   A section on the statement of cash flows that includes any transactions that are involved in the acquisition or disposition of noncurrent assets. (p. 787)

Net cash provided by operating activities   The net result of the cash inflows and cash outflows that arise from day-to-day operations. (p. 790)

Operating activities   A section on the statement of cash flows that includes any transactions that enter into the determination of net income. (p. 787)

Reconciliation method   See *Indirect method*. (p. 790)

Statement of cash flows   A statement designed to highlight the major activities that have provided cash and that have used cash during a period, and that shows the resulting effect on the overall cash balance. (p. 786)

QUESTIONS

17–1   What is the purpose of a statement of cash flows?

17–2   What are *cash equivalents*, and why are they included with cash on a statement of cash flows?

17–3   What are the three major sections on a statement of cash flows, and what are the general rules that determine the transactions that should be included in each section?

17–4   Why is interest paid on amounts borrowed from banks and other lenders considered to be an operating activity when the amounts borrowed are financing activities?

17–5   If an asset is sold at a gain, why is the gain deducted from net income when computing the cash provided by operating activities figure under the indirect method?

17–6   Why aren't transactions involving accounts payable considered to be financing activities?

17–7   Give an example of a direct exchange, and explain how such exchanges are handled when preparing a statement of cash flows.

17–8   Assume that a company repays a $300,000 loan from its bank and then later in the same year borrows $500,000. What amount(s) would appear on the statement of cash flows?

17–9   How do the direct and the indirect methods differ in their approach to computing the cash provided by operating activities?

17–10   In determining the cash provided by operating activities under the indirect method, why is it necessary to add depreciation back to net income? What other income statement items are similar to depreciation and must be handled in the same way?

17–11   A business executive once stated, "Depreciation is one of our biggest sources of cash." Do you agree that depreciation is a source of cash? Explain.

17–12   If the balance in Accounts Receivable increases during a period, how will this increase be handled under the indirect method in computing the cash provided by operating activities?

17–13   If the balance in Accounts Payable decreases during a period, how will this decrease be handled under the direct method in computing the cash provided by operating activities?

17–14   During the current year, a company declared and paid a $60,000 cash dividend and a 10 percent stock dividend. How will these two items be treated on the current year's statement of cash flows?

17–15   Would a sale of equipment for cash be considered a financing activity or an investing activity? Why?

17–16 A merchandising company showed $250,000 in cost of goods sold on its income statement. The company's beginning inventory was $75,000, and its ending inventory was $60,000. Accounts payable for merchandise were $50,000 at the beginning of the year and $40,000 at the end of the year. Using the direct method, adjust the company's cost of goods sold to a cash basis.

EXERCISES

E17–1 For the year ended December 31, 19x2, Hanna Company reported a net income of $35,000. Balances in the company's current asset and current liability accounts at the beginning and end of the year were:

	December 31	
	19x2	19x1
Current assets:		
Cash	$ 30,000	$ 40,000
Accounts receivable, net	125,000	106,000
Inventory.	213,000	180,000
Prepaid expenses	6,000	7,000
Current liabilities:		
Accounts payable	210,000	195,000
Accrued liabilities	4,000	6,000

The Deferred Income Taxes account on the balance sheet increased by $4,000 during the year, and $20,000 in depreciation expense was deducted on the income statement.

Required By use of the indirect method, determine the cash provided by operating activities for the year.

E17–2 Refer to the data for Hanna Company in E17–1. Assume that the company's income statement for 19x2 was as follows:

Sales	$350,000
Less cost of goods sold.	140,000
Gross margin	210,000
Less operating expenses	160,000
Income before taxes	50,000
Less income taxes (30%)	15,000
Net income	$ 35,000

Required Using the direct method (and the data from E17–1), convert the company's income statement to a cash basis.

E17–3 Below are certain transactions that took place in Placid Company during the past year:

a. Equipment was purchased at a cost of $30,000.
b. An $8,000 cash dividend was declared and paid.
c. Sales for the year totaled $1,000,000.
d. Short-term investments were purchased at a cost of $10,000.
e. Equipment was sold during the year.
f. A gain was realized on the equipment sold in (e).
g. Preferred stock was sold to investors.
h. A $6,000 stock dividend was declared and issued.
i. Interest was paid to long-term creditors.
j. Salaries and wages were paid to employees.
k. Stock of another company was purchased.
l. Bonds were issued that will be due in 10 years.

m. Rent was received from subleasing of space.
n. Common stock was repurchased and retired.

Prepare an answer sheet with the following headings: *Required*

| | | Activity | | Not |
Transaction	Operating	Investing	Financing	Reported
a.				
b.				
Etc.				

Enter the transactions above on your answer sheet and indicate how the effects of each transaction would be reported on a statement of cash flows by placing an *X* in the appropriate column.

Comparative financial statement data for Cargill Company follow: **E17–4**

	December 31	
	19x7	**19x6**
Cash	$ 3	$ 6
Accounts receivable, net	22	24
Inventory	50	40
Plant and equipment	240	200
Less accumulated depreciation	(65)	(50)
Total assets	$250	$220
Accounts payable	$ 40	$ 36
Common stock	150	145
Retained earnings	60	39
Total liabilities and stockholders' equity . . .	$250	$220

For 19x7, the company reported net income as follows:

Sales	$275
Cost of goods sold	150
Gross margin	125
Operating expenses	90
Net income	$ 35

Dividends of $14 were declared and paid during 19x7. Depreciation expense for the year was $15.

By use of the indirect method, prepare a statement of cash flows for 19x7.   *Required*

Refer to the data for Cargill Company in E17–4.   **E17–5**

By use of the direct method, convert the company's income statement to a cash basis.   *Required*

Changes in various accounts and gains and losses on sales of assets during 19x3 for Argon   **E17–6**
Company are given below:

Item	Amount
Accounts Receivable, Net	$ 90,000 decrease
Accrued Interest Receivable	4,000 increase
Inventory	120,000 increase
Prepaid Expenses	3,000 decrease
Accounts Payable	65,000 decrease
Accrued Liabilities	8,000 increase
Deferred Income Taxes	12,000 increase
Sale of equipment	7,000 gain
Sale of long-term investments . . .	10,000 loss

Required   Prepare an answer sheet using the following column headings:

Item	Amount	Add	Deduct

On your answer sheet, enter the items and amounts shown above. For each item, place an *X* in the Add or Deduct column to indicate whether the dollar amount should be added to or deducted from net income under the indirect method in computing the cash provided by operating activities for the year.

E17–7   The income statement for Wiley Company for the current year is given below:

WILEY COMPANY

Income Statement
For the Year Ended December 31, 19x5

Sales	$150,000
Cost of goods sold	90,000
Gross margin	60,000
Operating expenses	40,000*
Income before taxes	20,000
Income taxes	8,000
Net income	$ 12,000

* Includes $7,500 depreciation.

Amounts from selected balance sheet accounts follow:

	19x5	
	January 1	**December 31**
Accounts Receivable, Net. . . .	$30,000	$40,000
Inventory	45,000	54,000
Prepaid Expenses	6,000	8,000
Accounts Payable	28,000	35,000
Accrued Liabilities	8,000	5,000
Income Taxes Payable	2,500	2,000
Deferred Income Taxes	4,000	6,000

Required   1.   Using the direct method, determine the cash provided by operating activities by converting the company's income statement to a cash basis. Show all computations.
2.   Assume that the company had a $9,000 gain on sale of investments during the year and a $3,000 loss on sale of equipment. How would these two items have affected your computations in (1) above? Explain.

E17–8   The following changes took place during 19x8 in Pavolik Company's balance sheet accounts:

Cash	$ 5 D		Accounts Payable	$ 35 I
Accounts Receivable, Net	110 I		Accrued Liabilities	4 D
Inventory	70 D		Bonds Payable	150 I
Prepaid Expenses	9 I		Deferred Income Taxes	8 I
Long-Term Investments	6 D		Common Stock	80 D
Plant and Equipment	200 I		Retained Earnings	54 I
Accumulated Depreciation	(60) I			
Land	15 D			

D = Decrease; I = Increase.

Long-term investments that had cost the company $6 were sold during the year for $16, and land that had cost $15 was sold for $9. In addition, the company declared and paid $30 in cash dividends during the year. No sales or retirements of plant and equipment took place during 19x8.

The company's income statement for the year follows:

Sales		$700
Less cost of goods sold		400
Gross margin.		300
Less operating expenses.		184
Net operating income		116
Nonoperating items:		
Gain on sale of investments . . .	$10	
Loss on sale of land.	6	4
Income before taxes.		120
Less income taxes		36
Net income		$ 84

The company's cash balance on January 1, 19x8, was $90, and its balance on December 31, 19x8, was $85.

1. Use the indirect method to determine the cash provided by operating activities for the year.   *Required*
2. Prepare a statement of cash flows for the year.

Refer to the data for Pavolik Company in E17–8.   **E17–9**

Use the direct method to convert the company's income statement for 19x8 to a cash basis.   *Required*

PROBLEMS

Indirect Method; Statement of Cash Flows without Working Papers   Comparative   **P17–10**
financial statements for Weaver Company follow:

WEAVER COMPANY
Comparative Balance Sheet
December 31, 19x5, and 19x4

	19x5	19x4
Assets		
Cash	$ 9	$ 15
Accounts receivable, net	340	240
Inventory	125	175
Prepaid expenses	10	6
Plant and equipment	610	470
Less accumulated depreciation	(93)	(85)
Long-term investments	16	19
Total assets	$1,017	$840
Liabilities and Stockholders' Equity		
Accounts payable	$ 310	$230
Accrued liabilities	60	72
Bonds payable.	290	180
Deferred income taxes	40	34
Common stock	210	250
Retained earnings	107	74
Total liabilities and stockholders' equity . . .	$1,017	$840

WEAVER COMPANY
Income Statement
For the Year Ended December 31, 19x5

Sales		$800
Less cost of goods sold		500
Gross margin		300
Less operating expenses		213*
Net operating income		87
Nonoperating items:		
Gain on sale of investments	$7	
Loss on sale of equipment	4	3
Income before taxes		90
Less income taxes		27
Net income		$ 63

* Contains $24 depreciation expense.

During 19x5, the company sold some equipment for $20 that had cost $40 and on which there was accumulated depreciation of $16. In addition, the company sold long-term investments for $10 that had cost $3 when purchased several years ago. Cash dividends totaling $30 were paid during 19x5.

Required
1. By use of the indirect method, determine the cash provided by operating activities for 19x5.
2. Use the information in (1) above, along with an analysis of the remaining balance sheet accounts, and prepare a statement of cash flows for 19x5.

P17–11   Direct Method; Statement of Cash Flows without Working Papers   Refer to the financial statement data for Weaver Company in P17–10.

Required
1. By use of the direct method, adjust the company's income statement for 19x5 to a cash basis.
2. Use the information obtained in (1) above, along with an analysis of the remaining balance sheet accounts, and prepare a statement of cash flows for 19x5.

P17–12   Indirect Method; Statement of Cash Flows without Working Papers   Balance sheet accounts for Joyner Company contained the following amounts at the end of years 1 and 2:

	Year 2	Year 1
Debits		
Cash	$ 4,000	$ 21,000
Accounts Receivable, Net	250,000	170,000
Inventory	310,000	260,000
Prepaid Expenses	7,000	14,000
Loan to Hymas Company	40,000	—
Plant and Equipment	510,000	400,000
Total debits	$1,121,000	$865,000
Credits		
Accumulated Depreciation	$ 132,000	$120,000
Accounts Payable	310,000	250,000
Accrued Liabilities	20,000	30,000
Bonds Payable	190,000	70,000
Deferred Income Taxes	45,000	42,000
Common Stock	300,000	270,000
Retained Earnings	124,000	83,000
Total credits	$1,121,000	$865,000

The company's income statement for year 2 follows:

Sales	$900,000
Less cost of goods sold	500,000
Gross margin	400,000
Less operating expenses	328,000
Net operating income	72,000
Gain on sale of equipment	8,000
Income before taxes	80,000
Less income taxes	24,000
Net income	$ 56,000

Equipment that had cost $40,000 and on which there was accumulated depreciation of $30,000 was sold during year 2 for $18,000. Cash dividends totaling $15,000 were declared and paid during year 2, and depreciation expense totaled $42,000 for the year.

Required

1. By use of the indirect method, compute the cash provided by operating activities for year 2.
2. Prepare a statement of cash flows for year 2.
3. Prepare a brief explanation as to why cash declined so sharply during the year.

Direct Method; Statement of Cash Flows without Working Papers   Refer to the financial statement data for Joyner Company in P17–12. Sam Conway, president of the company, considers $15,000 to be a minimum cash balance for operating purposes. As can be seen from the balance sheet data, only $4,000 in cash was available at the end of the current year. The sharp decline is puzzling to Mr. Conway, particularly since sales and profits are at a record high.   **P17–13**

Required

1. By use of the direct method, adjust the company's income statement to a cash basis for year 2.
2. Using the data from (1) above and other data from the problem as needed, prepare a statement of cash flows for year 2.
3. Explain to Mr. Conway why cash declined so sharply during the year.

Classifying Transactions on a Statement of Cash Flows   Below are a number of transactions that took place in Seneca Company during the past year.   **P17–14**

a. Common stock was sold for cash.
b. Interest was paid on a note that will be due in two years.
c. Bonds were retired at a loss.
d. A long-term loan was made to a subsidiary.
e. Interest was received on the loan in (d).
f. A 10 percent stock dividend was declared and issued on common stock.
g. A building was acquired by the issue of 30,000 shares of common stock.
h. Equipment was sold for cash.
i. A gain was realized on the sale of equipment in (h).
j. Because of a need to pay obligations, short-term investments were sold.
k. Cash dividends were declared and paid.
l. Preferred stock was converted into common stock.
m. Deferred income taxes were paid; the taxes had been carried as a long-term liability.
n. Dividends were received on stock of another company held as an investment.
o. Equipment was purchased by giving a long-term note to the seller.

Prepare an answer sheet with the following column headings: *Required*

Transaction	Cash Provided, Used, or Neither	Activity			Reported in a Separate Schedule	Not on the Statement
		Operating	Investing	Financing		

Enter the letter of the transaction in the left column, and indicate whether the transaction would have provided cash, used cash, or neither. Then place an *X* in the appropriate column to show the proper classification of the transaction on the statement of cash flows, or to show if it would not appear on the statement at all.

P17–15 **Indirect Method; Statement of Cash Flows without Working Papers**   Mary Walker, president of Rusco Products, considers $14,000 to be the minimum cash balance for operating purposes. As can be seen from the statements below, only $8,000 in cash was available at the end of 19x5. Since the company reported a large net income for the year, and also issued both bonds and common stock, the sharp decline in cash is puzzling to Ms. Walker.

RUSCO PRODUCTS
Comparative Balance Sheet
July 31, 19x5, and 19x4

	19x5	19x4
Assets		
Current assets:		
Cash	$ 8,000	$ 21,000
Accounts receivable, net	120,000	80,000
Inventory	140,000	90,000
Prepaid expenses	5,000	9,000
Total current assets	273,000	200,000
Long-term investments	50,000	70,000
Plant and equipment	430,000	300,000
Less accumulated depreciation	60,000	50,000
Net plant and equipment	370,000	250,000
Total assets	$693,000	$520,000
Liabilities and Stockholders' Equity		
Current liabilities:		
Accounts payable	$123,000	$ 60,000
Accrued liabilities	8,000	17,000
Total current liabilities	131,000	77,000
Bonds payable	70,000	
Deferred income taxes	20,000	12,000
Stockholders' equity:		
Preferred stock	80,000	96,000
Common stock	286,000	250,000
Retained earnings	106,000	85,000
Total stockholders' equity	472,000	431,000
Total liabilities and stockholders' equity	$693,000	$520,000

RUSCO PRODUCTS
Income Statement
For the Year Ended July 31, 19x5

Sales		$500,000
Less cost of goods sold		300,000
Gross margin		200,000
Less operating expenses		158,000
Net operating income		42,000
Nonoperating items:		
Gain on sale of investments	$10,000	
Loss on sale of equipment	2,000	8,000
Income before taxes		50,000
Less income taxes		20,000
Net income		$ 30,000

The following additional information is available for the year 19x5:

a. Dividends totaling $9,000 were declared and paid.

b. Equipment was sold during the year at a selling price of $8,000. The equipment had cost $20,000 and had accumulated depreciation of $10,000.

c. The decrease in the Preferred Stock account is the result of a conversion of preferred stock into an equal dollar amount of common stock.

d. Long-term investments that had cost $20,000 were sold during the year for $30,000.

1. By use of the indirect method, compute the cash provided by operating activities for 19x5. *Required*

2. Using the data from (1) and other data from the problem as needed, prepare a statement of cash flows for 19x5.

3. Explain to the president the major reasons for the decline in the company's cash position.

Direct Method; Statement of Cash Flows without Working Papers Refer to the financial statements for Rusco Products in P17–15. Since the Cash account decreased so dramatically during 19x5, the company's executive committee is anxious to see how the income statement would appear on a cash basis. **P17–16**

1. By use of the direct method, adjust the company's income statement for 19x5 to a cash basis. *Required*

2. Using the data from (1) and other data from the problem as needed, prepare a statement of cash flows for 19x5.

3. Prepare a brief explanation for the executive committee, setting forth the major reasons for the sharp decline in cash during the year.

Indirect Method; Working Papers; Statement of Cash Flows In early 19x7, Roberto Martens was made president of Helio Sales Company. Mr. Martens is widely regarded as a hard-hitting sales executive, but he has little patience with financial matters. **P17–17**

After many years of no sales growth, sales rose 25 percent in 19x7 under Mr. Martens' leadership. One major change made by Mr. Martens was to increase the number of distribution warehouses in the company in order to more adequately service customer needs. He plans further expansion of the company's warehouse facilities in 19x8, providing adequate funding can be obtained from the company's bank or from other sources. A comparative balance sheet for the last two years is presented below:

HELIO SALES COMPANY
Comparative Balance Sheet
May 31, 19x7, and 19x6

Assets	19x7	19x6
Current assets:		
Cash	$ (7,000)	$ 42,000
Accounts receivable, net	230,000	168,000
Inventory	490,000	380,000
Prepaid expenses	16,000	23,000
Total current assets	729,000	613,000
Plant and equipment	820,000	710,000
Less accumulated depreciation	(260,000)	(290,000)
Net plant and equipment	560,000	420,000
Goodwill	71,000	87,000
Total assets	$1,360,000	$1,120,000

Liabilities and Stockholders' Equity

Current liabilities:		
Accounts payable	$ 290,000	$ 205,000
Accrued liabilities	80,000	93,000
Total current liabilities	370,000	298,000
Long-term debt	230,000	165,000
Deferred income taxes	47,000	39,000
Stockholders' equity:		
Common stock	410,000	400,000
Retained earnings	303,000	218,000
Total stockholders' equity	713,000	618,000
Total liabilities and stockholders' equity . . .	$1,360,000	$1,120,000

The company's income statement for 19x7 follows:

HELIO SALES COMPANY

Income Statement
For the Year Ended May 31, 19x7

Sales	$1,000,000
Less cost of goods sold	530,000
Gross margin	470,000
Less operating expenses	290,000
Net operating income	180,000
Gain on sale of equipment	10,000
Income before taxes	190,000
Less income taxes	60,000
Net income	$ 130,000

The following additional information is available about operations for the year 19x7:

a. Equipment that had cost $130,000 and on which there was accumulated depreciation of $122,000 was sold for $18,000.

b. Early in the year, the company repurchased 2,000 shares of stock at $35 per share from a dissident stockholder. The shares were resold near year-end at $40 per share.

c. The company's goodwill is being amortized against earnings.

d. Cash dividends declared and paid during the year totaled $45,000.

e. There was no retirement of long-term debt during the year.

Required
1. Prepare T-account working papers for a statement of cash flows.
2. Using the indirect method and the data from your working papers, prepare a statement of cash flows for 19x7.
3. Write a brief memo to Mr. Martens explaining the reasons for the decrease in cash during the year.

P17–18 Direct Method; Adjusting the Income Statement to a Cash Basis   Refer to the data for Helio Sales Company in P17–17. The company's president, Roberto Martens, was shocked when he received the 19x7 balance sheet data showing that the company's Cash account was overdrawn. After mulling over the statements for awhile, he exclaimed: "These statements don't make any sense. We've had the most profitable year in our history, our assets have increased by nearly a quarter of a million dollars, and yet we don't have a dime in the bank. It looks like the more we make, the poorer we get."

As the company's chief financial officer, you recognize that Mr. Martens doesn't fully understand the concepts of accrual accounting. Therefore, you believe it would be helpful to him to see the company's income statement on a cash basis.

Required   By use of the direct method, adjust the company's income statement to a cash basis.

"How Well Am I Doing?" Statement of Cash Flows • 17

823

Indirect Method; Working Papers; Statement of Cash Flows "This doesn't seem **P17-19**
possible," said Julie Poduska, president of Brinker Skate Company. "Last year we lost
$40,500, we went on paying dividends anyway, and we doubled our investment in Streeter
Company. But yet our cash position is stronger than it was at the start of the year. I think a
mistake has been made somewhere. Let's do a complete analysis of cash so that we can
find the mistake before our report goes out."

The company's balance sheet accounts at the beginning and end of the year are shown
below:

	December 31	
	19x3	**19x2**
Debits		
Cash	$ 48,000	$ 33,000
Accounts Receivable, Net.	162,000	174,000
Inventory	318,000	267,000
Prepaid Expenses	12,000	6,000
Long-Term Investments.	42,000	21,000
Plant and Equipment	1,120,000	1,083,000
Goodwill	38,000	54,000
Total debits	$1,740,000	$1,638,000
Credits		
Accumulated Depreciation	$ 240,000	$ 228,000
Accounts Payable	270,000	180,000
Accrued Liabilities	30,000	37,500
Bonds Payable	435,000	360,000
Common Stock, No Par.	510,000	450,000
Retained Earnings	255,000	382,500
Total credits	$1,740,000	$1,638,000

The income statement for 19x3 is presented below:

Sales	$1,300,000
Less cost of goods sold.	810,500
Gross margin	489,500
Less operating expenses	524,000
Net operating income (loss).	(34,500)
Loss on sale of equipment	(6,000)
Net loss	$ (40,500)

The following additional information relating to 19x3 has been assembled by the company:

a. Depreciation expense for the year totaled $_____?_____ .
b. The goodwill is being amortized against earnings.
c. In order to maintain an unbroken record of dividend payments, the company declared
and paid $27,000 in cash dividends.
d. Equipment costing $48,000, on which there was accumulated depreciation of $25,000,
was sold for $17,000.
e. Equipment costing $_____?_____ was purchased during the year.
f. The company declared and distributed a stock dividend during the year. It consisted of
3,000 shares of stock, declared when the market value was $20 per share.

1. Prepare T-account working papers for a statement of cash flows.   *Required*
2. Using the indirect method, prepare a statement of cash flows for the year 19x3.
3. Prepare a brief explanation for Ms. Poduska as to why cash increased during the year.

Direct Method; Adjusting the Income Statement to a Cash Basis   Refer to the data for   **P17-20**
Brinker Skate Company in P17–19. Upon receiving a copy of the company's 19x3 financial

statements, a loan officer at the company's bank stated, "There's something odd here. Brinker Skate Company lost $40,500 last year and paid out $27,000 in cash dividends. But yet the Cash account increased by $15,000. I want the company to adjust its income statement to a cash basis so that we can see what's really happening with operations."

Required 1. Using the direct method, adjust the company's income statement for 19x3 to a cash basis.

2. Would it be of greater value to the bank to see the "Net cash provided by operating activities" figure computed by the direct method or by the indirect method? Explain your position.

P17–21 Missing Data; Indirect Method; Statement of Cash Flows Below are listed the *changes* in Yoric Company's balance sheet accounts for the past year (19x3):

	Debits	Credits
Cash	$ 17,000	
Accounts Receivable, Net	110,000	
Inventory		$ 65,000
Prepaid Expenses.		8,000
Loans to Subsidiaries		30,000
Long-Term Investments	80,000	
Plant and Equipment	220,000	
Accumulated Depreciation.		5,000
Accounts Payable.		32,000
Accrued Liabilities	9,000	
Bonds Payable		400,000
Deferred Income Taxes		16,000
Common Stock.	170,000	
Retained Earnings		50,000
	$606,000	$606,000

The following additional information is available about last year's activities:

a. Net income for the year was $____?____ .

b. The company sold equipment during the year for $15,000. The equipment had cost the company $50,000 when purchased and it had $37,000 in accumulated depreciation at the time of sale.

c. Cash dividends were declared and paid during the year, $20,000.

d. Depreciation expense for the year was $____?____ .

e. The opening and closing balances in the Plant and Equipment and Accumulated Depreciation accounts for 19x3 are given below:

	Opening	Closing
Plant and Equipment.	$1,580,000	$1,800,000
Accumulated Depreciation . . .	675,000	680,000

f. There were no stock dividends or stock splits during the year.

g. The balance in the Cash account at the beginning of 19x3 was $23,000; the balance at the end of the year was $____?____ .

h. If data are not given explaining the change in an account, make the most logical assumption as to the cause of the change.

Required Using the indirect method, prepare a statement of cash flows for the year 19x3. Show all computations for items that appear on your statement.

P17–22 **Indirect Method; Statement of Cash Flows** "See, I told you things would work out,"
Comprehensive Problem said Barry Kresmier, president of Lomax Company. "We expanded sales from $1.6 million to $2.0 million in 19x2, nearly doubled our warehouse space, and ended the year with more

cash in the bank than we started with. A few more years of expansion like this and we'll be the industry leaders."

"Yes, I'll admit our statements look pretty good," replied Sheri Colson, the company's vice president. "But we're doing business with a lot of companies we don't know much about and that worries me. I'll admit, though, that we're certainly moving a lot of merchandise; our inventory is actually down from last year."

A comparative balance sheet for Lomax Company containing data for the last two years is given below:

LOMAX COMPANY
Comparative Balance Sheet
December 31, 19x2, and 19x1

	19x2	19x1
Assets		
Current assets:		
Cash	$ 42,000	$ 27,000
Marketable securities.	19,000	13,000
Accounts receivable, net	710,000	530,000
Inventory	848,000	860,000
Prepaid expenses	10,000	5,000
Total current assets	1,629,000	1,435,000
Long-term investments	60,000	110,000
Loans to subsidiaries.	130,000	80,000
Plant and equipment	3,170,000	2,600,000
Less accumulated depreciation	810,000	755,000
Net plant and equipment	2,360,000	1,845,000
Goodwill	84,000	90,000
Total assets	$4,263,000	$3,560,000
Liabilities and Stockholders' Equity		
Current liabilities:		
Accounts payable	$ 970,000	$ 670,000
Accrued liabilities	65,000	82,000
Total current liabilities	1,035,000	752,000
Long-term notes	820,000	600,000
Deferred income taxes	95,000	80,000
Total liabilities.	1,950,000	1,432,000
Stockholders' equity:		
Common stock	1,800,000	1,650,000
Retained earnings	513,000	478,000
Total stockholders' equity	2,313,000	2,128,000
Total liabilities and stockholders' equity . . .	$4,263,000	$3,560,000

The following additional information is available about the company's activities during 19x2, the current year:

a. Equipment costing $100,000 was acquired by giving a note to the seller that will be due in two years.
b. A stock dividend totaling $60,000 was declared and issued to the common stockholders.
c. Cash dividends declared and paid to the common stockholders totaled $75,000.
d. Some $380,000 in long-term notes outstanding on January 1, 19x2, were repaid during the year.
e. Equipment was sold during the year for $70,000. The equipment had cost $130,000 and had $40,000 in accumulated depreciation on the date of sale.
f. Long-term investments were sold during the year for $110,000. These investments had cost $50,000 when purchased several years ago.

g.   The company reported sales, expenses, and net income during 19x2 as follows:

Sales		$2,000,000
Less cost of goods sold		1,300,000
Gross margin.		700,000
Less operating expenses.		490,000*
Net operating income		210,000
Nonoperating items:		
Gain on sale of investments . . .	$60,000	
Loss on sale of equipment	20,000	40,000
Income before taxes.		250,000
Less income taxes		80,000
Net income		$ 170,000

* Contains $95,000 in depreciation expense and $6,000 in amortization of goodwill.

Required   1.   Prepare T-account working papers for a statement of cash flows.
2.   Using the indirect method, prepare a statement of cash flows for the year 19x2.
3.   What problems relating to the company's activities are revealed by the statement of cash flows that you have prepared?

P17–23   **Direct Method; Adjusting the Income Statement to a Cash Basis**   Refer to the data for Lomax Company in P17–22. All of the long-term notes issued during 19x2 (other than the note issued for the purchase of equipment) are being held by Lomax's bank. The bank's management wants the income statement adjusted to a cash basis so that it can compare the cash basis statement against the accrual basis statement.

Required   Use the direct method to convert Lomax Company's 19x2 income statement to a cash basis.

P17–24   **Missing Data; Indirect Method; Statement of Cash Flows**   Oxident Products is the manufacturer of a vitamin supplement. Listed below are the *changes* that have taken place in the company's balance sheet accounts as a result of the past year's activities:

Debit Balance Accounts	Net Increase (Decrease)
Cash	$ (10,000)
Accounts Receivable, Net	(81,000)
Inventory	230,000
Prepaid Expenses	(6,000)
Loans to Subsidiaries	100,000
Long-Term Investments	(120,000)
Plant and Equipment	500,000
Net increase	$ 613,000

Credit Balance Accounts	
Accumulated Depreciation	$ 90,000
Accounts Payable	(70,000)
Accrued Liabilities.	35,000
Bonds Payable	400,000
Deferred Income Taxes.	8,000
Preferred Stock	(180,000)
Common Stock	270,000
Retained Earnings	60,000
Net increase	$ 613,000

The following additional information is available about last year's activities:

"How Well Am I Doing?" Statement of Cash Flows • 17

827

a. There were no stock dividends, stock splits, or stock conversions (i.e., one class of stock converted into another class) during the year.

b. The company sold equipment during the year for $40,000. The equipment had cost the company $100,000 when purchased and it had $70,000 in accumulated depreciation at the time of sale.

c. Net income for the year was $_____?_____ .

d. The balance in the Cash account at the beginning of the year was $52,000; the balance at the end of the year was $_____?_____ .

e. The company declared and paid $30,000 in cash dividends during the year.

f. Long-term investments that had cost $120,000 were sold during the year for $80,000.

g. Depreciation expense for the year was $_____?_____ .

h. The opening and closing balances in the Plant and Equipment and Accumulated Depreciation accounts for the past year are given below:

	Opening	Closing
Plant and Equipment.	$2,700,000	$3,200,000
Accumulated Depreciation . . .	1,410,000	1,500,000

i. If data are not given explaining the change in an account, make the most logical assumption as to the cause of the change.

Using the indirect method, prepare a statement of cash flows for the past year. Show all computations for items that appear on your statement.   *Required*

Investors and creditors rely on financial statement analysis to assess the financial condition of companies. Those who buy and sell common stock pay particularly close attention to earnings per share in assessing a company's future prospects.

"How Well Am I Doing?" Financial Statement Analysis

LEARNING OBJECTIVES

After studying Chapter 18, you should be able to:

1 Explain the need for and limitations of financial statement analysis.

2 Prepare financial statements in comparative form and explain how such statements are used.

3 Place the balance sheet and the income statement in common-size form and properly interpret the results.

4 Identify the ratios used to measure the well-being of the common stockholder, and state each ratio's formula and interpretation.

5 Explain what is meant by the term *financial leverage,* and show how financial leverage is measured.

6 Identify the ratios used to measure the well-being of the short-term creditor, and state each ratio's formula and interpretation.

7 Identify the ratios used to measure the well-being of the long-term creditor, and state each ratio's formula and interpretation.

8 Define or explain the key terms listed at the end of the chapter.

N o matter how carefully prepared, all financial statements are essentially historical documents. They tell what *has happened* during a particular year or series of years. The most valuable information to most users of financial statements, however, concerns what probably *will happen* in the future. The purpose of financial statement analysis is to assist statement users in *predicting the future* by means of comparison, evaluation, and trend analysis.

THE IMPORTANCE OF STATEMENT ANALYSIS

Objective 1
Explain the need for and limitations of financial statement analysis.

Virtually all users of financial data have concerns that can be resolved to some degree by the predictive ability of statement analysis. Stockholders are concerned, for example, about such matters as whether they should hold or sell their shares of stock, whether the present management group should remain or be replaced, and whether the company should have their approval to sell a new offering of senior debt. Creditors are concerned about such matters as whether income will be sufficient to cover the interest due on their bonds or notes, and whether prospects are good for their obligations to be paid at maturity. Managers are concerned about such matters as dividend policy, the availability of funds to finance future expansion, and the probable future success of operations under their leadership.

The thing about the future that statement users are most interested in predicting is profits. It is profits, of course, that provide the basis for an increase in the value of the stockholder's stock and that encourage the creditor to risk his or her money in an organization. And it is largely profits that make future expansion possible. The dilemma is that profits are uncertain. For this reason, one must have various analytical tools to assist in interpreting the key relationships and trends that serve as a basis for judgments of potential future success. Without financial statement analysis, the story that key relationships and trends have to tell may remain buried in a sea of statement detail.

In this chapter, we consider some of the more important ratios and other analytical tools that analysts use in attempting to predict the future course of events in business organizations.

Importance of Comparisons

Financial statements are not only historical documents but they are also essentially static documents. They speak only of the events of a single period of time. However, statement users are concerned about more than just the present; they are also concerned about the *trend of events* over time. For this reason, financial statement analysis directed toward a single period is of limited usefulness. The results of financial statement analysis for a particular period are of value only when viewed in *comparison* with the results of other periods and, in some cases, with the results of other firms. It is only through comparison that one can gain insight into trends and make intelligent judgments as to their significance.

Unfortunately, comparisons between firms within an industry are often made difficult by differences in accounting methods in use. For example, if one firm values its inventories by LIFO and another firm values its inventories by average cost, then direct dollar-for-dollar comparisons between the two firms may not be possible. In such cases, comparisons can still be made, but they must focus on data in a broader, more relative sense. Although the analytical work required here may be tougher, it is often necessary if the manager is to have any data available for comparison purposes.

The Need to Look beyond Ratios

There is a tendency for the inexperienced analyst to assume that ratios are sufficient in themselves as a basis for judgments about the future. Nothing could be further from the truth. The experienced analyst realizes that the best-prepared ratio analysis must be regarded as tentative in nature and never as conclusive in itself. Ratios should not be viewed as an end, but rather they should be viewed as a *starting point*, as indicators of what to pursue in greater depth. They raise many questions, but they rarely answer any questions by themselves.

In addition to looking at ratios, the analyst must look at other sources of data in order to make judgments about the future of an organization. The analyst must look, for example, at industry trends, at technological changes that are anticipated or that are in process, at changes in consumer tastes, at regional and national changes in economic factors, and at changes that are taking place within the firm itself. A recent change in a key management position, for example, might rightly serve as a basis for much optimism about the future, even though the past performance of the firm (as shown by its ratios) may have been very mediocre.

STATEMENTS IN COMPARATIVE AND COMMON-SIZE FORM

As stated above, few figures appearing on financial statements have much significance standing by themselves. It is the relationship of one figure to another and the amount and direction of change from one point in time to another that are important in financial statement analysis. How does the analyst key in on significant relationships? How does the analyst dig out the important trends and changes in a company? Three analytical techniques are in widespread use:

1. Dollar and percentage changes on statements.
2. Common-size statements.
3. Ratios.

All three techniques are discussed in following sections.

Dollar and Percentage Changes on Statements

A good beginning place in financial statement analysis is to put statements in comparative form. This consists of little more than putting two or more years' data side by side. Statements cast in comparative form will underscore movements and trends and may give the analyst valuable clues as to what to expect in the way of financial and operating performance in the future.

Objective 2
Prepare financial statements in comparative form and explain how such statements are used.

An example of financial statements placed in comparative form is given in Exhibits 18–1 and 18–2. These are the statements of Brickey Electronics, a hypothetical firm. The data on these statements are used as a basis for discussion throughout the remainder of the chapter.

Horizontal Analysis
Comparison of two or more years' financial data is known as **horizontal analysis.** Horizontal analysis is greatly facilitated by showing changes between years in both dollar *and* percentage form, as has been done in Exhibits 18–1 and 18–2. Showing changes in dollar form helps the analyst to zero in on key factors that have affected profitability or financial position. For example, observe in Exhibit 18–2 that sales for 19x2 were up $4 million over 19x1, but that this increase in sales was more than negated by a $4.5 million increase in cost of goods sold.

EXHIBIT 18–1

BRICKEY ELECTRONICS
Comparative Balance Sheet
December 31, 19x2, and 19x1
(dollars in thousands)

	19x2	19x1	Increase (Decrease) Amount	Increase (Decrease) Percent
Assets				
Current assets:				
Cash	$ 1,200	$ 2,350	$(1,150)	(48.9)*
Accounts receivable, net	6,000	4,000	2,000	50.0
Inventory	8,000	10,000	(2,000)	(20.0)
Prepaid expenses	300	120	180	150.0
Total current assets	15,500	16,470	(970)	(5.9)
Property and equipment:				
Land	4,000	4,000	–0–	–0–
Buildings and equipment, net	12,000	8,500	3,500	41.2
Total property and equipment	16,000	12,500	3,500	28.0
Total assets	$31,500	$28,970	$ 2,530	8.7
Liabilities and Stockholders' Equity				
Current liabilities:				
Accounts payable	$ 5,800	$ 4,000	$ 1,800	45.0
Accrued payables	900	400	500	125.0
Notes payable, short term	300	600	(300)	(50.0)
Total current liabilities	7,000	5,000	2,000	40.0
Long-term liabilities:				
Bonds payable, 8%.	7,500	8,000	(500)	(6.3)
Total liabilities.	14,500	13,000	1,500	11.5
Stockholders' equity:				
Preferred stock, $100 par, 6%, $100 liquidation value	2,000	2,000	–0–	–0–
Common stock, $12 par	6,000	6,000	–0–	–0–
Additional paid-in capital	1,000	1,000	–0–	–0–
Total paid-in capital	9,000	9,000	–0–	–0–
Retained earnings	8,000	6,970	1,030	14.8
Total stockholders' equity	17,000	15,970	1,030	6.4
Total liabilities and stockholders' equity . . .	$31,500	$28,970	$ 2,530	8.7

* Since we are measuring the amount of change between 19x1 and 19x2, the dollar amounts for 19x1 become the "base" figures for expressing these changes in percentage form. For example, Cash decreased by $1,150 between 19x1 and 19x2. This decrease expressed in percentage form is computed as follows: $1,150 ÷ $2,350 = 48.9%. Other percentage figures in this exhibit and in Exhibit 18–2 are computed in the same way.

Showing changes between years in percentage form helps the analyst to gain *perspective* and to gain a feel for the *significance* of the changes that are taking place. One would have a different perspective of a $1 million increase in sales if the prior year's sales were $2 million than if the prior year's sales were $20 million. In the first situation, the increase would be 50 percent—undoubtedly a significant increase for any firm. In the second situation, the increase would be only 5 percent—perhaps a reflection of just normal growth.

Trend Percentages   Horizontal analysis of financial statements can also be carried out by computing *trend percentages*. **Trend percentages** state several years' financial data in terms of a base year. The base year equals 100 percent, with all other years stated as some percentage of this base. To illustrate, assume that

BRICKEY ELECTRONICS

EXHIBIT 18–2

**Comparative Income Statement and Reconciliation
of Retained Earnings
For the Years Ended December 31, 19x2, and 19x1
(dollars in thousands)**

	19x2	19x1	Increase (Decrease) Amount	Percent
Sales	$52,000	$48,000	$4,000	8.3
Cost of goods sold	36,000	31,500	4,500	14.3
Gross margin.	16,000	16,500	(500)	(3.0)
Operating expenses:				
Selling expenses	7,000	6,500	500	7.7
Administrative expenses.	5,860	6,100	(240)	(3.9)
Total operating expenses	12,860	12,600	260	2.1
Net operating income	3,140	3,900	(760)	(19.5)
Interest expense	640	700	(60)	(8.6)
Net income before taxes.	2,500	3,200	(700)	(21.9)
Less income taxes (30%)	750	960	(210)	(21.9)
Net income	1,750	2,240	$ (490)	(21.9)
Dividends to preferred stockholders, $6 per share (see Exhibit 18–1). . . .	120	120		
Net income remaining for common stockholders	1,630	2,120		
Dividends to common stockholders, $1.20 per share	600	600		
Net income added to retained earnings	1,030	1,520		
Retained earnings, beginning of year . . .	6,970	5,450		
Retained earnings, end of year	$ 8,000	$ 6,970		

Martin Company has reported the following sales and income data for the past five years:

	19x5	19x4	19x3	19x2	19x1
Sales	$725,000	$700,000	$650,000	$575,000	$500,000
Net income . . .	99,000	97,500	93,750	86,250	75,000

By simply looking at these data, one can see that both sales and net income have increased over the five-year period reported. But how rapidly have sales been increasing, and have the increases in net income kept pace with the increases in sales? By looking at the raw data alone, it is difficult to answer these questions. The increases in sales and the increases in net income can be put into better perspective by stating them in terms of trend percentages, with 19x1 as the base year. These percentages are given below:

	19x5	19x4	19x3	19x2	19x1
Sales	145%	140%	130%	115%*	100%
Net income . . .	132	130	125	115	100

* For 19x2: $575,000 ÷ $500,000 = 115%; for 19x3: $650,000 ÷ $500,000 = 130%; and so forth.

Notice that the growth in sales dropped off somewhat between 19x3 and 19x4, and then dropped off even more between 19x4 and 19x5. Also notice that the growth in net income has not kept pace with the growth in sales. In 19x5, sales are 1.45 times greater than in 19x1, the base year; however, in 19x5, net income is only 1.32 times greater than in 19x1.

Common-Size Statements

Objective 3
Place the balance sheet and the income statement in common-size form and properly interpret the results.

Key changes and trends can also be highlighted by the use of *common-size statements*. A **common-size statement** is one that shows the separate items appearing on it in percentage form as well as in dollar form. Each item is stated as a percentage of some total of which that item is a part. The preparation of common-size statements is known as **vertical analysis.**

EXHIBIT 18–3

BRICKEY ELECTRONICS
Common-Size Comparative Balance Sheet
December 31, 19x2, and 19x1
(dollars in thousands)

			Common-Size Percentages	
	19x2	19x1	19x2	19x1
Assets				
Current assets:				
Cash	$ 1,200	$ 2,350	3.8*	8.1
Accounts receivable, net	6,000	4,000	19.0	13.8
Inventory	8,000	10,000	25.4	34.5
Prepaid expenses	300	120	1.0	0.4
Total current assets	15,500	16,470	49.2	56.9
Property and equipment:				
Land	4,000	4,000	12.7	13.8
Buildings and equipment, net	12,000	8,500	38.1	29.3
Total property and equipment	16,000	12,500	50.8	43.1
Total assets	$31,500	$28,970	100.0	100.0
Liabilities and Stockholders' Equity				
Current liabilities:				
Accounts payable	$ 5,800	$ 4,000	18.4	13.8
Accrued payables	900	400	2.8	1.4
Notes payable, short term	300	600	1.0	2.1
Total current liabilities	7,000	5,000	22.2	17.3
Long-term liabilities:				
Bonds payable, 8%.	7,500	8,000	23.8	27.6
Total liabilities.	14,500	13,000	46.0	44.9
Stockholders' equity:				
Preferred stock, $100 par, 6%,				
$100 liquidation value	2,000	2,000	6.4	6.9
Common stock, $12 par	6,000	6,000	19.0	20.7
Additional paid-in capital	1,000	1,000	3.2	3.5
Total paid-in capital	9,000	9,000	28.6	31.1
Retained earnings	8,000	6,970	25.4	24.0
Total stockholders' equity	17,000	15,970	54.0	55.1
Total liabilities and stockholders' equity	$31,500	$28,970	100.0	100.0

* Each asset account on a common-size statement is expressed in terms of total assets, and each liability and equity account is expressed in terms of total liabilities and stockholders' equity. For example, the percentage figure above for Cash in 19x2 is computed as follows: $1,200 ÷ $31,500 = 3.8%.

EXHIBIT 18–4

BRICKEY ELECTRONICS
Common-Size Comparative Income Statement
For the Years Ended December 31, 19x2, and 19x1
(dollars in thousands)

	19x2	19x1	Common-Size Percentages 19x2	19x1
Sales	$52,000	$48,000	100.0	100.0
Cost of goods sold	36,000	31,500	69.2*	65.7
Gross margin	16,000	16,500	30.8	34.3
Operating expenses:				
Selling expenses	7,000	6,500	13.5	13.5
Administrative expenses	5,860	6,100	11.2	12.7
Total operating expenses	12,860	12,600	24.7	26.2
Net operating income	3,140	3,900	6.0	8.1
Interest expense	640	700	1.2	1.5
Net income before taxes	2,500	3,200	4.8	6.6
Income taxes (30%).	750	960	1.4	2.0
Net income	$ 1,750	$ 2,240	3.4	4.6

* Note that the percentage figures for each year are expressed in terms of total sales for the year. For example, the percentage figure for cost of goods sold in 19x2 is computed as follows: $36,000 ÷ $52,000 = 69.2%.

The Balance Sheet   One application of the vertical analysis idea is to state the separate assets of a company as percentages of total assets. A common-size statement of this type is shown in Exhibit 18–3 for Brickey Electronics.

Notice from Exhibit 18–3 that placing all assets in common-size form clearly shows the relative importance of the current assets as compared to the noncurrent assets. It also shows that significant changes have taken place in the *composition* of the current assets over the last year. Notice, for example, that the receivables have increased in relative importance and that both cash and inventory have declined in relative importance. Judging from the sharp increase in receivables, the deterioration in the cash position may be a result of inability to collect from customers.

The Income Statement   Another application of the vertical analysis idea is to place all items on the income statement in percentage form in terms of sales. A common-size statement of this type is shown in Exhibit 18–4.

By placing all items on the income statement in common size in terms of sales, it is possible to see at a glance how each dollar of sales is distributed between the various costs, expenses, and profits. For example, notice from Exhibit 18–4 that 69.2 cents out of every dollar of sales was needed to cover cost of goods sold in 19x2, as compared to only 65.7 cents in the prior year; also notice that only 3.4 cents out of every dollar of sales remained for profits in 19x2—down from 4.6 cents in the prior year.

Common-size statements are also very helpful in pointing out efficiencies and inefficiencies that might otherwise go unnoticed. To illustrate, in 19x2, Brickey Electronics' selling expenses increased by $500,000 over 19x1. A glance at the common-size income statement shows, however, that on a relative basis selling expenses were no higher in 19x2 than in 19x1. In each year, they represented 13.5 percent of sales.

RATIO ANALYSIS—THE COMMON STOCKHOLDER

Objective 4
Identify the ratios used to
measure the well-being of
the common stockholder,
and state each ratio's
formula and
interpretation.

The common stockholder has only a residual claim on the profits and assets of a corporation. It is only after all creditor and preferred stockholder claims have been satisfied that the common stockholder can step forward and receive cash dividends or a distribution of assets in liquidation. Therefore, a measure of the common stockholder's well-being provides some perspective of the depth of protection available to others associated with a firm.

Earnings per Share

An investor buys and retains a share of stock with the expectation of realizing a return in the form of either dividends or capital gains. Since earnings form the basis for dividend payments, as well as the basis for any future increases in the value of shares, investors are always interested in a company's reported *earnings per share*. Probably no single statistic is more widely quoted or relied on in investor actions than earnings per share, although it has some inherent dangers, as discussed below.

Earnings per share is computed by dividing net income remaining for common stockholders by the number of common shares outstanding. "Net income remaining for common stockholders" is equal to the net income of a company, reduced by the dividends due to the preferred stockholders.

$$\frac{\text{Net income} - \text{Preferred dividends}}{\text{Number of common shares outstanding}} = \text{Earnings per share}$$

Using the data in Exhibits 18–1 and 18–2, we see that the earnings per share for Brickey Electronics for 19x2 would be:

$$\frac{\$1,750,000 - \$120,000}{500,000 \text{ shares*}} = \$3.26 \tag{1}$$

* \$6,000,000 ÷ \$12 = 500,000 shares.

Two problems can arise in connection with the computation of earnings per share. The first arises whenever an extraordinary gain or loss appears as part of net income. The second arises whenever a company has convertible securities on its balance sheet. These problems are discussed in the following two sections.

Extraordinary Items and Earnings per Share

If a company has extraordinary gains or losses appearing as part of net income, *two* earnings per share figures must be computed—one showing the earnings per share resulting from *normal* operations and one showing the earnings per share impact of the *extraordinary* items. This approach to computing earnings per share accomplishes three things. First, it helps statement users to recognize extraordinary items for what they are—unusual events that probably will not recur. Second, it eliminates the distorting influence of the extraordinary items from the basic earnings per share figure. And third, it helps statement users to properly assess the *trend* of *normal* earnings per share over time. Since one would not expect the extraordinary or unusual items to be repeated year after year, they should be given less weight in judging earnings performance than is given to profits resulting from normal operations.

In addition to reporting extraordinary items separately, the accountant also reports them *net of their tax effect*. By "net of their tax effect," we mean that

Incorrect Approach

EXHIBIT 18–5

Reporting Extraordinary
Items Net of Their Tax
Effects

Sales		$100,000	
Cost of goods sold		60,000	
Gross margin		40,000	
Operating expenses:			
Selling expenses	$18,000		
Administrative expenses . . .	12,000		
Fire loss	6,000	36,000	
Net income before taxes		4,000	
Income taxes (30%)		1,200	
Net income		$ 2,800	

Extraordinary gains and losses should not be included with normal items of revenue and expense. This distorts a firm's normal income-producing ability.

Correct Approach

Sales		$100,000
Cost of goods sold		60,000
Gross margin		40,000
Operating expenses:		
Selling expenses	$18,000	
Administrative expenses . . .	12,000	30,000
Net operating income		10,000
Income taxes (30%)		3,000
Net income before extra-ordinary item		7,000
Extraordinary item:		
Fire loss, net of tax		4,200
Net income		$ 2,800

Reporting the extraordinary item separately and net of its tax effect leaves the normal items of revenue and expense unaffected.

Original loss	$6,000
Less reduction in taxes at a 30% rate	1,800
Loss, net of tax	$4,200

whatever impact the unusual item has on income taxes is *deducted from* the unusual item on the income statement. Only the net, after-tax gain or loss is used in earnings per share computations.

To illustrate these ideas, let us assume that Amata Company has suffered a fire loss of $6,000 and that management is wondering how the loss should be reported on the company's income statement. The correct and incorrect approaches to reporting the loss are shown in Exhibit 18–5.

As shown under the "Correct Approach" in the exhibit, the $6,000 loss is reduced to only $4,200 after tax effects are taken into consideration. The reasoning behind this computation is as follows: The fire loss is fully deductible for tax purposes. Therefore, this deduction will reduce the firm's taxable income by $6,000. If taxable income is $6,000 lower, then income taxes will be $1,800 *less* (30% × $6,000) than they *otherwise* would have been. In other words, the fire loss of $6,000 saves the company $1,800 in taxes that otherwise would have been paid. The $1,800 savings in taxes is deducted from the loss that caused it, leaving a net loss of only $4,200. This same $4,200 figure could have been obtained by multiplying the original loss by the formula (1 − Tax rate): [$6,000 × (1 − 0.30) = $4,200]. *Any* before-tax item can be put on an after-tax basis by use of this formula.

This same procedure is used in reporting extraordinary gains. The only difference is that extraordinary gains *increase* taxes; thus, any tax resulting from a gain must be deducted from it, with only the net gain reported on the income statement.

To continue our illustration, assume that the company in Exhibit 18–5 has 2,000 shares of common stock outstanding. Earnings per share would be reported as follows:

Earnings per share on common stock:
    On net income before extraordinary item ($7,000 ÷ 2,000 shares)* . . . $ 3.50
    On extraordinary item, net of tax ($4,200 ÷ 2,000 shares) . . . . (2.10)
Net earnings per share . . . . $ 1.40

    * Sometimes called the *primary* earnings per share.

In sum, computation of earnings per share as we have done above is necessary to avoid misunderstanding of a company's normal income-producing ability. Reporting *only* the flat $1.40 per share figure would be misleading and perhaps cause investors to regard the company less favorably than they should.

Fully Diluted Earnings per Share

A problem sometimes arises in trying to determine the number of common shares to use in computing earnings per share. Until recent years, the distinction between common stock, preferred stock, and debt was quite clear. The distinction between these securities has now become somewhat diffused, however, due to a growing tendency to issue convertible securities of various types. Rather than simply issuing common stock, firms today often issue preferred stock or bonds that carry a **conversion feature** allowing the purchaser to convert holdings into common stock at some future time.

When convertible securities are present in the financial structure of a firm, the question arises as to whether these securities should be retained in their unconverted form or treated as common stock in computing earnings per share. The American Institute of Certified Public Accountants has taken the position that convertible securities should be treated *both* in their present and prospective forms. This requires the presentation of *two* earnings per share figures for firms that have convertible securities outstanding, one showing earnings per share assuming no conversion into common stock and the other showing full conversion into common stock. The latter figure is known as the **fully diluted earnings per share.**

To illustrate the computation of a company's fully diluted earnings per share, let us assume that the preferred stock of Brickey Electronics in Exhibit 18–1 is convertible into common on the basis of five shares of common for each share of preferred. Since 20,000 shares of preferred are outstanding, conversion would require issuing an additional 100,000 shares of common stock. Earnings per share on a fully diluted basis would be:

$$\frac{\text{Net income}}{(500{,}000 \text{ shares outstanding} + 100{,}000 \text{ converted shares})}$$

$$= \frac{\$1{,}750{,}000}{600{,}000 \text{ shares}} = \$2.92 \quad (2)$$

In comparing equation (2) with equation (1) on page 836, we can note that the earnings per share figure has dropped by 34 cents. Although the impact of full dilution is relatively small in this case, it can be very significant in situations where large amounts of convertible securities are present.

Price-Earnings Ratio

The relationship between the market price of a share of stock and the stock's current earnings per share is often quoted in terms of a **price-earnings ratio**. If we

Brickey Electronics has earned a return of 7.3 percent on average assets employed over the last year.

Return on Common Stockholders' Equity

One of the primary reasons for operating a corporation is to generate income for the benefit of the common stockholders. One measure of a company's success in this regard is the rate of **return on common stockholders' equity** that it is able to generate. The formula is:

$$\frac{\text{Net income} - \text{Preferred dividends}}{\substack{\text{Average common stockholders' equity (Average} \\ \text{total stockholders' equity} - \text{Preferred stock)}}}$$
$$= \text{Return on common stockholders' equity}$$

For Brickey Electronics, the return on common stockholders' equity is 11.3 percent for 19x2, as shown below:

Net income.	$ 1,750,000
Deduct preferred dividends.	120,000
Net income remaining for common stockholders . . .	$ 1,630,000 (a)
Average stockholders' equity.	$16,485,000*
Deduct preferred stock	2,000,000
Average common stockholders' equity	$14,485,000 (b)
Return on common stockholders' equity, (a) ÷ (b) . .	11.3% (7)

* $15,970,000 + $17,000,000 = $32,970,000; $32,970,000 ÷ 2 = $16,485,000.

Compare the return on common stockholders' equity above (11.3 percent) with the return on total assets computed in the preceding section (7.3 percent). Why is the return on common stockholders' equity so much higher? The answer lies in the principle of *financial leverage* (sometimes called "trading on the equity"). Financial leverage is discussed in the following paragraphs.

Financial Leverage

Financial leverage (often called *leverage* for short) involves the financing of assets in a company with funds that have been acquired from creditors or from preferred stockholders at a fixed rate of return. If the assets in which the funds are invested are able to earn a rate of return *greater* than the fixed rate of return required by the suppliers of the funds, then we have **positive financial leverage** and the common stockholders benefit.

Objective 5
Explain what is meant by the term *financial leverage*, and show how financial leverage is measured.

For example, assume that a firm is able to earn an after-tax return of 12 percent on its assets. If that firm can borrow from creditors at a 10 percent interest rate in order to expand its assets, then the common stockholders can benefit from positive leverage. The borrowed funds invested in the business will earn an after-tax return of 12 percent, but the after-tax interest cost of the borrowed funds will be only 7 percent [10% interest rate × (1 − 0.30) = 7%]. The difference will go to the common stockholders.

We can see this concept in operation in the case of Brickey Electronics. Notice from Exhibit 18–1 that the company's bonds payable bear a fixed interest rate of 8 percent. The after-tax interest cost of these bonds is only 5.6 percent [8% interest rate × (1 − 0.30) = 5.6%]. The company's assets (which would contain the proceeds from the original sale of these bonds) are generating an after-tax return of 7.3 percent, as we computed earlier. Since this return on assets is greater than the after-tax interest cost of the bonds, leverage is positive, and the difference accrues to the benefit of the common stockholders. This explains in part why the return on common stockholders' equity (11.3 percent) is greater than the return on total assets (7.3 percent).

Sources of Financial Leverage   Financial leverage can be obtained from several sources. One source is long-term debt, such as bonds payable or notes payable. Two additional sources are current liabilities and preferred stock. Current liabilities are always a source of positive leverage in that funds are provided for use in a company with no interest return required by the short-term creditors involved. For example, when a company acquires inventory from a supplier on account, the inventory is available for use in the business, yet the supplier requires no interest return on the amount owed to him.

Preferred stock can also be a source of positive leverage so long as the dividend payable to the preferred stockholders is less than the rate of return being earned on the total assets employed. In the case of Brickey Electronics, positive leverage is being realized on the preferred stock. Notice from Exhibit 18–1 that the preferred dividend rate is only 6 percent, whereas the assets in the company are earning at a rate of 7.3 percent, as computed earlier. Again, the difference goes to the common stockholders, thereby helping to bolster their return to the 11.3 percent computed above.

Unfortunately, leverage is a two-edged sword. If assets are unable to earn a high enough rate to cover the interest costs of debt, or to cover the preferred dividend due to the preferred stockholders, *then the common stockholder suffers.* The reason is that part of the earnings from the assets that the common stockholder has provided to the company will have to go to make up the deficiency to the long-term creditors or to the preferred stockholders, and the common stockholder will be left with a smaller return than would otherwise have been earned. Under these circumstances, we have **negative financial leverage.**

The Impact of Income Taxes   Long-term debt and preferred stock are not equally efficient in generating positive leverage. The reason is that interest on long-term debt is tax deductible, whereas preferred dividends are not. This makes long-term debt a much more effective source of positive leverage than preferred stock.

To illustrate this point, assume that a company is considering three ways of financing a $100,000 expansion of its assets:

1. $100,000 from an issue of common stock.
2. $50,000 from an issue of common stock, and $50,000 from an issue of preferred stock bearing a dividend rate of 8 percent.
3. $50,000 from an issue of common stock, and $50,000 from an issue of bonds bearing an interest rate of 8 percent.

Assuming that the company can earn an additional $15,000 each year before interest and taxes as a result of the expansion, the operating results under each of the three alternatives are shown in Exhibit 18–6.

If the entire $100,000 is raised from an issue of common stock, then the return to the common stockholders will be only 10.5 percent, as shown under alternative 1 in the exhibit. If half of the funds are raised from an issue of preferred stock,

EXHIBIT 18–6

Leverage from Preferred Stock and Long-Term Debt

	Alternative 1: $100,000 Common Stock	Alternatives: $100,000 Issue of Securities	
		Alternative 2: $50,000 Common Stock; $50,000 Preferred Stock	Alternative 3: $50,000 Common Stock; $50,000 Bonds
Earnings before interest and taxes.	$ 15,000	$15,000	$15,000
Deduct interest expense (8% × $50,000)	—	—	4,000
Net income before taxes	15,000	15,000	11,000
Deduct income taxes (30%).	4,500	4,500	3,300
Net income.	10,500	10,500	7,700
Deduct preferred dividends (8% × $50,000)	—	4,000	—
Net income remaining for common (a)	$ 10,500	$ 6,500	$ 7,700
Common stockholders' equity (b)	$100,000	$50,000	$50,000
Return on common stockholders' equity, (a) ÷ (b) . . .	10.5%	13.0%	15.4%

then the return to the common stockholders increases to 13 percent, due to the positive effects of leverage. However, if half of the funds are raised from an issue of bonds, then the return to the common stockholders jumps to 15.4 percent, as shown under alternative 3. Thus, long-term debt is much more efficient in generating positive leverage than is preferred stock. The reason is that the interest expense on long-term debt is tax deductible, whereas the dividends on preferred stock are not.

The Desirability of Leverage The leverage principle amply illustrates that having some debt in the capital structure can substantially benefit the common stockholder. For this reason, most companies today try to keep a certain level of debt within the organization—a level at least equal to that which is considered to be "normal" within the industry. Occasionally one comes across a company that boasts of having no debt outstanding. Although there may be good reasons for a company to have no debt, in view of the benefits that can be gained from positive leverage the possibility always exists that such a company is shortchanging its stockholders. As a practical matter, many companies, such as commercial banks and other financial institutions, rely heavily on leverage to provide an attractive return on their common shares.

Book Value per Share

Another statistic frequently used in attempting to assess the well-being of the common stockholder is book value per share. The **book value per share** measures the amount that would be distributed to holders of each share of common stock if all assets were sold at their balance sheet carrying amounts and if all creditors were paid off. Thus, book value per share is based entirely on historical costs. The formula for computing it is:

$$\frac{\text{Common stockholders' equity (Total stockholders' equity} - \text{Preferred stock)}}{\text{Number of common shares outstanding}} = \text{Book value per share}$$

The book value of Brickey Electronics' common stock is:

$$\frac{\$17,000,000 - \$2,000,000}{500,000 \text{ shares}} = \$30 \tag{8}$$

If this book value is compared with the $40 market value that we have assumed in connection with the Brickey Electronics stock, then the stock appears to be somewhat overpriced. It is not necessarily true, however, that a market value in excess of book value is an indication of overpricing. As we discussed earlier, market prices are geared toward future earnings and dividends. Book value, by contrast, purports to reflect nothing about the future earnings potential of a firm. As a practical matter, it is actually geared to the *past* in that it reflects the balance sheet carrying value of already completed transactions.

Of what use, then, is book value? Unfortunately, the answer must be that it is of limited use so far as being a dynamic tool of analysis is concerned. It probably finds its greatest application in situations where large amounts of liquid assets are being held in anticipation of liquidation. Occasionally some use is also made of book value per share in attempting to set a price on the shares of closely held corporations.

RATIO ANALYSIS—THE SHORT-TERM CREDITOR

Objective 6
Identify the ratios used to measure the well-being of the short-term creditor, and state each ratio's formula and interpretation.

Although the short-term creditor is always well advised to keep an eye on the fortunes of the common stockholder, as expressed in the ratios of the preceding section, the short-term creditor's focus of attention is normally channeled in another direction. The short-term creditor is concerned with the near-term prospects of having obligations paid on time. As such, he or she is much more interested in cash flows and in working capital management than in how much accounting net income a company is reporting.

Working Capital

The excess of current assets over current liabilities is known as **working capital.** The working capital for Brickey Electronics is given below:

	19x2	19x1
Current assets	$15,500,000	$16,470,000
Current liabilities	7,000,000	5,000,000
Working capital	$ 8,500,000	$11,470,000	(9)

The amount of working capital available to a firm is of considerable interest to short-term creditors, *since it represents assets financed from long-term capital sources that do not require near-term repayment.* Therefore, the greater the working capital, the greater is the cushion of protection available to short-term creditors and the greater is the assurance that short-term debts will be paid when due.

Although it is always comforting to short-term creditors to see a large working capital balance, a large balance standing by itself is no assurance that debts will be paid when due. Rather than being a sign of strength, a large working capital balance may simply mean that stagnant or obsolete inventory is building up. Therefore, to put the working capital figure into proper perspective, it must be supplemented with other analytical work. The following four ratios (the current ratio, the acid-test ratio, the accounts receivable turnover, and the inventory turnover) should all be used in connection with an analysis of working capital.

Current Ratio

The elements involved in the computation of working capital are frequently expressed in ratio form. A company's current assets divided by its current liabilities is known as the **current ratio:**

$$\frac{\text{Current assets}}{\text{Current liabilities}} = \text{Current ratio}$$

For Brickey Electronics, the current ratio for 19x1 and 19x2 would be:

19x2	**19x1**	
$\dfrac{\$15,500,000}{\$7,000,000} = 2.21 \text{ to } 1$	$\dfrac{\$16,470,000}{\$5,000,000} = 3.29 \text{ to } 1$	(10)

Although widely regarded as a measure of short-term debt-paying ability, the current ratio must be interpreted with a great deal of care. A *declining* ratio, as above, might be a sign of a deteriorating financial condition. On the other hand, it might be the result of a paring out of obsolete inventories or other stagnant assets. An *improving* ratio might be the result of an unwise stockpiling of inventory, or it might point up an improving financial situation. In short, the current ratio is useful, but tricky to interpret. To avoid a blunder, the analyst must take a hard look at the individual assets and liabilities involved.

The general rule of thumb calls for a current ratio of 2 to 1. This rule, of course, is subject to many exceptions, depending on the industry and the firm involved. Some industries can operate quite successfully on a current ratio of slightly over 1 to 1. The adequacy of a current ratio depends heavily on the *composition* of the assets involved. For example, although Company X and Company Y below both have current ratios of 2 to 1, one could hardly say that they are in comparable financial condition. Company Y most certainly will have difficulty in meeting its obligations as they come due.

	Company	
	X	**Y**
Current assets:		
Cash	$ 25,000	$ 2,000
Accounts receivable, net	60,000	8,000
Inventory	85,000	160,000
Prepaid expenses.	5,000	5,000
Total current assets	$175,000	$175,000
Current liabilities.	$ 87,500	$ 87,500
Current ratio	2 to 1	2 to 1

Acid-Test Ratio

A much more rigorous test of a company's ability to meet its short-term debts can be found in the **acid-test (quick) ratio.** Merchandise inventory and prepaid expenses are excluded from total current assets, leaving only the more liquid (or "quick") assets to be divided by current liabilities.

$$\frac{\text{Cash} + \text{Marketable securities} + \text{Current receivables*}}{\text{Current liabilities}} = \text{Acid-test ratio}$$

* This would include both accounts receivable and any short-term notes receivable.

The acid-test ratio is designed to measure how well a company can meet its obligations without having to liquidate or depend too heavily on its inventory. Since inventory is not an immediate source of cash and may not even be salable in times of economic stress, it is generally felt that to be properly protected each dollar of liabilities should be backed by at least $1 of quick assets. Thus, an acid-test ratio of 1 to 1 is broadly viewed as being adequate in many firms.

The acid-test ratios for Brickey Electronics for 19x1 and 19x2 are given below:

	19x2	19x1
Cash	$1,200,000	$2,350,000
Accounts receivable . . .	6,000,000	4,000,000
Total quick assets	$7,200,000	$6,350,000
Current liabilities.	$7,000,000	$5,000,000
Acid-test ratio	1.03 to 1	1.27 to 1

(11)

Although Brickey Electronics has an acid-test ratio for 19x2 that is within the acceptable range, an analyst might be concerned about several disquieting trends revealed in the company's balance sheet. Notice that short-term debts are rising, while the cash position seems to be deteriorating. Perhaps the weakened cash position is a result of the greatly expanded volume of accounts receivable. One wonders why the accounts receivable have been allowed to increase so rapidly in so brief a time.

In short, as with the current ratio, to be used intelligently the acid-test ratio must be interpreted with one eye on its basic components.

Accounts Receivable Turnover

The **accounts receivable turnover** is a measure of how many times a company's accounts receivable have been turned into cash during the year. It is frequently used in conjunction with an analysis of working capital, since a smooth flow from accounts receivable into cash is an important indicator of the "quality" of a company's working capital and is critical to its ability to operate. The accounts receivable turnover is computed by dividing sales on account by the average accounts receivable balance for the year.

$$\frac{\text{Sales on account}}{\text{Average accounts receivable balance}} = \text{Accounts receivable turnover}$$

The accounts receivable turnover for Brickey Electronics for 19x2 is:

$$\frac{\text{Sales on account}}{\text{Average accounts receivable balance}} = \frac{\$52,000,000}{\$5,000,000^*} = 10.4 \text{ times} \quad (12)$$

* $4,000,000 + $6,000,000 = $10,000,000; $10,000,000 ÷ 2 = $5,000,000 average.

The turnover figure can then be divided into 365 to determine the average number of days being taken to collect an account (known as the **average collection period**).

$$\frac{365 \text{ days}}{\text{Accounts receivable turnover}} = \frac{365}{10.4 \text{ times}} = 35 \text{ days} \quad (13)$$

Whether the average of 35 days taken to collect an account is good or bad depends on the credit terms Brickey Electronics is offering its customers. If the credit terms are 30 days, then a 35-day average collection period would be viewed as being very good. Most customers will tend to withhold payment for as long as the credit terms will allow and may even go over a few days. This factor, added to the ever-present few slow accounts, can cause the average collection period to exceed normal credit terms by a week to 10 days and should not be a matter for too much alarm.

On the other hand, if the company's credit terms are 10 days, then a 35-day average collection period may be a cause for some concern. The long collection period may be a result of the presence of many old accounts of doubtful collectibility, or it may be a result of poor day-to-day credit management. The firm may be making sales with inadequate credit checks on the companies to which the sales are being made, or perhaps no follow-ups are being made on slow accounts.

Inventory Turnover

The **inventory turnover ratio** measures how many times a company's inventory has been sold during the year. It is computed by dividing the cost of goods sold by the average level of inventory on hand:

$$\frac{\text{Cost of goods sold}}{\text{Average inventory balance}} = \text{Inventory turnover}$$

The average inventory figure is usually computed by taking the average of the beginning and ending inventory figures. Since Brickey Electronics has a beginning inventory figure of $10,000,000 and an ending inventory figure of $8,000,000, its average inventory for the year would be $9,000,000. The company's inventory turnover for 19x2 would be:

$$\frac{\text{Cost of goods sold}}{\text{Average inventory balance}} = \frac{\$36,000,000}{\$9,000,000} = 4 \text{ times} \tag{14}$$

The number of days being taken to sell the entire inventory one time (called the **average sale period**) can be computed by dividing 365 by the inventory turnover figure:

$$\frac{365 \text{ days}}{\text{Inventory turnover}} = \frac{365}{4 \text{ times}} = 91\frac{1}{4} \text{ days} \tag{15}$$

Grocery stores tend to turn their inventory over very quickly, perhaps as often as every 12 to 15 days. On the other hand, jewelry stores tend to turn their inventory over very slowly, perhaps only a couple of times each year.

If a firm has a turnover that is much slower than the average for its industry, then there may be obsolete goods on hand, or inventory stocks may be needlessly high. Excessive inventories simply tie up funds that could be used elsewhere in operations. Managers sometimes argue that they must buy in very large quantities in order to take advantage of the best discounts being offered. But these discounts must be carefully weighed against the added costs of insurance, taxes, financing, and risks of obsolescence and deterioration that result from carrying added inventories.

An inventory turnover that is substantially faster than the average is usually an indication of one of two things. First, it may be an indication that inventory levels are inadequate. Historically, this has been the key reason for a rapid turnover of goods. In more recent years, however, another factor affecting inventory turnover has come into play as companies have adopted JIT inventory methods. Under

JIT, inventories are purposely kept low for reasons discussed in prior chapters. Thus, a company utilizing JIT inventory methods may have an inventory turnover figure that is very high as compared to other companies. Indeed, one of the goals of JIT is to increase inventory turnover by systematically reducing the amount of inventory on hand.

RATIO ANALYSIS—THE LONG-TERM CREDITOR

Objective 7
Identify the ratios used to measure the well-being of the long-term creditor, and state each ratio's formula and interpretation.

The position of long-term creditors differs from that of short-term creditors in that they are concerned with both the near-term *and* the long-term ability of a firm to meet its commitments. They are concerned with the near term since whatever interest they may be entitled to is normally paid on a current basis. They are concerned with the long term from the point of view of the eventual retirement of their holdings.

Since the long-term creditor is usually faced with somewhat greater risks than the short-term creditor, firms are often required to agree to various restrictive covenants, or rules, for the long-term creditor's protection. Examples of such restrictive covenants would include the maintenance of minimum working capital levels and restrictions on payment of dividends to common stockholders. Although these restrictive covenants are in widespread use, they must be viewed as being a poor second to *prospective earnings* from the point of view of assessing protection and safety. Creditors do not want to go to court to collect their claims; they would much prefer staking the safety of their claims for interest and eventual repayment of principal on an orderly and consistent flow of funds from operations.

Times Interest Earned Ratio

The most common measure of the ability of a firm's operations to provide protection to the long-term creditor is the **times interest earned ratio.** It is computed by dividing earnings *before* interest expense and income taxes by the yearly interest charges that must be met:

$$\frac{\text{Earnings before interest expense and income taxes*}}{\text{Interest expense}} = \text{Times interest earned}$$

* This amount is the same as *net operating income* on many financial statements.

For Brickey Electronics, the times interest earned ratio for 19x2 would be:

$$\frac{\$3,140,000}{\$640,000} = 4.9 \text{ times} \tag{16}$$

Earnings before income taxes must be used in the computation since interest expense deductions come *before* income taxes are computed. Income taxes are secondary to interest payments in that the latter have first claim on earnings. Only those earnings remaining after all interest charges have been provided for are subject to income taxes.

Various rules of thumb exist to gauge the adequacy of a firm's times interest earned ratio. Generally, earnings are viewed as adequate to protect long-term creditors if the times interest earned ratio is 2 or more. Before making a final judgment, however, it would be necessary to look at a firm's long-run *trend* of earnings, then decide how vulnerable the firm is to cyclical changes in the economy.

Debt-to-Equity Ratio

Although long-term creditors look primarily to prospective earnings and budgeted cash flows in attempting to gauge the risk of their position, they cannot ignore the importance of keeping a reasonable balance between the portion of assets being provided by creditors and the portion of assets being provided by the stockholders of a firm. This balance is measured by the **debt-to-equity ratio:**

$$\frac{\text{Total liabilities}}{\text{Stockholders' equity}} = \text{Debt-to-equity ratio}$$

	19x2	19x1	
Total liabilities	$14,500,000	$13,000,000 (a)	
Stockholders' equity	17,000,000	15,970,000 (b)	
Debt-to-equity ratio, (a) ÷ (b)	0.85 to 1	0.81 to 1	(17)

The debt-to-equity ratio indicates the amount of assets being provided by creditors for each dollar of assets being provided by the owners of a company. In 19x1, creditors of Brickey Electronics were providing 81 cents of assets for each $1 of assets being provided by stockholders; the figure increased only slightly to 85 cents by 19x2.

It should come as no surprise that creditors would like the debt-to-equity ratio to be relatively low. The lower the ratio, the greater the amount of assets being provided by the owners of a company and the greater is the buffer of protection to creditors. By contrast, common stockholders would like the ratio to be relatively high, since through leverage common stockholders can benefit from the assets being provided by creditors.

In most industries, norms have developed over the years that serve as guides to firms in their decisions as to the "right" amount of debt to include in the capital structure. Different industries face different risks. For this reason, the level of debt that is appropriate for firms in one industry is not necessarily a guide to the level of debt that is appropriate for firms in a different industry.

SUMMARY OF RATIOS AND SOURCES OF COMPARATIVE RATIO DATA

As an aid to the reader, Exhibit 18–7 contains a summary of the ratios discussed in this chapter. Included in the exhibit are the formula for each ratio and a summary comment on each ratio's significance to the manager.

Exhibit 18–8 contains a listing of published sources that provide comparative ratio data organized by industry. These sources are used extensively by managers, investors, and analysts in doing comparative analyses and in attempting to assess the well-being of companies.

EXHIBIT 18–7
Summary of Ratios

Ratio	Formula	Significance
Earnings per share (of common stock)	(Net income − Preferred dividends) ÷ Number of common shares outstanding	Tends to have an effect on the market price per share, as reflected in the price-earnings ratio
Fully diluted earnings per share	Net income ÷ (Number of common shares outstanding + Common stock equivalent of convertible securities)	Shows the potential effect on earnings per share of converting convertible securities into common stock
Price-earnings ratio	Market price per share ÷ Earnings per share	An index of whether a stock is relatively cheap or relatively expensive in relation to current earnings
Dividend payout ratio	Dividends per share ÷ Earnings per share	An index showing whether a company pays out most of its earnings in dividends or reinvests the earnings internally
Dividend yield ratio	Dividends per share ÷ Market price per share	Shows the dividend return being provided by a stock, which can be compared to the return being provided by other stocks
Return on total assets	Net income + [Interest expense × (1 − Tax rate)] ÷ Average total assets	Measure of how well assets have been employed by management
Return on common stockholders' equity	(Net income − Preferred dividends) ÷ Average common stockholders' equity (Average total stockholders' equity − Preferred stock)	When compared to the return on total assets, measures the extent to which financial leverage is being employed for or against the common stockholders
Book value per share	Common stockholders' equity (Total stockholders' equity − Preferred stock) ÷ Number of common shares outstanding	Measures the amount that would be distributed to holders of each share of common stock if all assets were sold at their balance sheet carrying amounts and if all creditors were paid off
Working capital	Current assets − Current liabilities	Represents current assets financed from long-term capital sources that do not require near-term repayment
Current ratio	Current assets ÷ Current liabilities	Test of short-term debt-paying ability
Acid-test (quick) ratio	(Cash + Marketable securities + Current receivables) ÷ Current liabilities	Test of short-term debt-paying ability without having to rely on inventory
Accounts receivable turnover	Sales on account ÷ Average accounts receivable balance	Measure of how many times a company's accounts receivable have been turned into cash during the year
Average collection period (age of receivables)	365 days ÷ Accounts receivable turnover	Measure of the average number of days taken to collect an account receivable
Inventory turnover	Cost of goods sold ÷ Average inventory balance	Measure of how many times a company's inventory has been sold during the year
Average sale period (turnover in days)	365 days ÷ Inventory turnover	Measure of the average number of days taken to sell the inventory one time
Times interest earned	Earnings before interest expense and income taxes ÷ Interest expense	Measure of the likelihood that creditors will continue to receive their interest payments
Debt-to-equity ratio	Total liabilities ÷ Stockholders' equity	Measure of the amount of assets being provided by creditors for each dollar of assets being provided by the stockholders

"How Well Am I Doing?" Financial Statement Analysis • 18

851

Source	Content	
Almanac of Business and Industrial Financial Ratios. Prentice-Hall. Published annually.	An exhaustive source that contains common-size income statements and financial ratios by industry and by size of companies within each industry.	**EXHIBIT 18–8** Published Sources of Financial Ratios
Annual Statement Studies. Robert Morris Associates. Published annually.	A widely used publication that contains common-size statements and financial ratios on individual companies. The companies are arranged by industry.	
Moody's Industrial Manual and *Moody's Bank and Finance Manual*. Dun & Bradstreet. Published annually.	An exhaustive source that contains financial ratios on all companies listed on the New York Stock Exchange, the American Stock Exchange, and regional American exchanges.	
Key Business Ratios. Dun & Bradstreet. Published annually.	Fourteen commonly used financial ratios are computed for major industry groupings. This source contains data on over 800 lines of business.	
Standard & Poor's Industry Survey. Standard & Poor's. Published annually.	Various statistics, including some financial ratios, are provided by industry and on leading companies within each industry grouping.	

SUMMARY

The data contained in financial statements represent a quantitative summary of a firm's operations and activities. If a manager is skillful at analyzing these statements, he or she can learn much about a company's strengths, its weaknesses, its developing problems, its operating efficiency, its profitability, and so forth.

Many analytical techniques are available to assist managers in analyzing financial statements and in assessing the direction and importance of trends and changes. In this chapter, we have discussed three such analytical techniques—dollar and percentage changes in statements, common-size statements, and ratio analysis. The reader should refer to Exhibit 18–7 for a detailed listing of the ratios that we have discussed. This listing also contains a brief statement as to the significance of each ratio involved.

REVIEW PROBLEM: FINANCIAL LEVERAGE

Selected financial data from the September 30, 19x7, year-end statements of Kosanka Company are given below:

Total assets	$5,000,000
Current liabilities.	350,000
Long-term debt (12% interest rate).	750,000
Preferred stock, $100 par, 7%	800,000
Total stockholders' equity	3,100,000
Interest paid on long-term debt	90,000
Net income	470,000

Total assets at the beginning of the year were $4,800,000; total stockholders' equity was $2,900,000. There has been no change in the Preferred Stock account during the year. The company's tax rate is 30 percent.

1. Compute the return on total assets.
2. Compute the return on common stockholders' equity.
3. Is the company's financial leverage positive or negative? Explain.

Required

Solution to Review Problem

1. Return on total assets:

$$\frac{\text{Net income} + [\text{Interest expense} \times (1 - \text{Tax rate})]}{\text{Average total assets}} = \frac{\text{Return on}}{\text{total assets}}$$

$$\frac{\$470,000 + [\$90,000 \times (1 - 0.30)] = \$533,000}{1/2\ (\$5,000,000 + \$4,800,000) = \$4,900,000} = 10.9\% \text{ (rounded)}$$

2. Return on common stockholders' equity:

Net income as reported.	$ 470,000
Less preferred dividends: 7% × $800,000.	56,000
Net income to common.	$ 414,000 (a)
Average stockholders' equity:	
1/2 ($3,100,000 + $2,900,000)	$3,000,000
Less preferred stock	800,000
Common stockholders' equity	$2,200,000 (b)
Return on common stockholders' equity	
(a) ÷ (b)	18.8% (rounded)

3. The company has positive financial leverage, since the return on common stockholders' equity (18.8 percent) is greater than the return on total assets (10.9 percent). The positive financial leverage is obtained from the current liabilities, which bear no interest cost; from the long-term debt, which has an after-tax interest cost of only 8.4 percent [12% interest rate × (1 − 0.30) = 8.4%]; and from the preferred stock, which carries a dividend rate of only 7 percent. Both the 8.4 percent and 7 percent figures are smaller than the 10.9 percent return that the company is earning on its total assets; thus, the difference goes to the common stockholders, boosting their return to 18.8 percent.

KEY TERMS FOR REVIEW

Objective 8
Define or explain the key terms listed at the end of the chapter.

(Note: Definitions and formulas for all financial ratios are given in Exhibit 18–7. These definitions and formulas are not repeated here.)

Common-size statements   A statement that shows the items appearing on it in percentage form as well as in dollar form. On the income statement, the percentages are based on total sales; on the balance sheet, the percentages are based on total assets or total equities. (p. 834)

Conversion feature   The ability to exchange either bonds or preferred stock for common stock at some future time. (p. 838)

Financial leverage   The financing of assets in a company with funds that have been acquired from creditors or from preferred stockholders at a fixed rate of return. (p. 841)

Horizontal analysis   A side-by-side comparison of two or more years' financial statements. (p. 831)

Negative financial leverage   A situation in which the fixed return to a company's creditors and preferred stockholders is greater than the return on total assets. In this situation, the return on common stockholders' equity will be *less* than the return on total assets. (p. 842)

Positive financial leverage   A situation in which the fixed return to a company's creditors and preferred stockholders is less than the return on total assets. In this situation, the return on common stockholders' equity will be *greater* than the return on total assets. (p. 841)

Trend percentages   The expression of several years' financial data in percentage form in terms of a base year. (p. 832)

Vertical analysis   The presentation of a company's financial statements in common-size
form. (p. 834)

QUESTIONS

18-1 What three analytical techniques are used in financial statement analysis?

18-2 Distinguish between horizontal and vertical analysis of financial statement data.

18-3 What is the basic objective in looking at trends in financial ratios and other data? Rather than looking at trends, to what other standard of comparison might a statement user turn?

18-4 In financial analysis, why does the analyst compute financial ratios rather than simply studying raw financial data? What dangers are there in the use of ratios?

18-5 What pitfalls are involved in computing earnings per share? How can these pitfalls be avoided?

18-6 What is meant by reporting an extraordinary item on the income statement net of its tax effect? Give an example of both an extraordinary gain and an extraordinary loss net of its tax effect. Assume a tax rate of 30 percent.

18-7 Assume that two companies in the same industry have equal earnings. Why might these companies have different price-earnings ratios? If a company has a price-earnings ratio of 20 and reports earnings per share for the current year of $4, at what price would you expect to find the stock selling on the market?

18-8 Armcor, Inc., is in a rapidly growing technological industry. Would you expect the company to have a high or a low dividend payout ratio?

18-9 Distinguish between a manager's *financing* and *operating* responsibilities. Which of these responsibilities is the return on total assets ratio designed to measure?

18-10 What is meant by the dividend yield on a common stock investment? In computing dividend yield, why do you use current market value rather than original purchase price?

18-11 What is meant by the term *financial leverage?*

18-12 The president of a medium-sized plastics company was recently quoted in a business journal as stating, "We haven't had a dollar of interest-paying debt in over 10 years. Not many companies can say that." As a stockholder in this firm, how would you feel about its policy of not taking on interest-paying debt?

18-13 Why is it more difficult to obtain positive financial leverage from preferred stock than from long-term debt?

18-14 If a stock's market value exceeds its book value, then the stock is overpriced. Do you agree? Explain.

18-15 Weaver Company experiences a great deal of seasonal variation in its business activities. The company's high point in business activity is in June; its low point is in January. During which month would you expect the current ratio to be highest? At what point would you advise the company to end its fiscal year? Why?

18-16 A company seeking a line of credit at a bank was turned down. Among other things, the bank stated that the company's 2 to 1 current ratio was not adequate. Give reasons why a 2 to 1 current ratio might not be adequate.

18-17 If you were a long-term creditor of a firm, would you be more interested in the firm's long-term or short-term debt-paying ability? Why?

18-18 A young college student once complained to one of the authors, "The reason that corporations are such big spenders is that Uncle Sam always picks up part of the tab." What did he mean by this statement?

EXERCISES

E18–1   A comparative income statement is given below for Dearborn Sales, Ltd.:

DEARBORN SALES, LTD.
Comparative Income Statement
For the Years Ended June 30, 19x5, and 19x4

	19x5	19x4
Sales	$8,000,000	$6,000,000
Less cost of goods sold.	4,984,000	3,516,000
Gross margin	3,016,000	2,484,000
Less operating expenses:		
Selling expenses	1,480,000	1,092,000
Administrative expenses	712,000	618,000
Total expenses.	2,192,000	1,710,000
Net operating income.	824,000	774,000
Less interest expense.	96,000	84,000
Net income before taxes	$ 728,000	$ 690,000

Members of the company's board of directors are surprised to see that net income increased by only $38,000 when sales increased by two million dollars.

Required   1.   Express each year's income statement in common-size percentages. Carry computations to one decimal place.

2.   Comment briefly on the changes between the two years.

E18–2   Noble Company's current assets, current liabilities, and sales have been reported as follows over the last five years:

	19x5	19x4	19x3	19x2	19x1
Sales	$2,250,000	$2,160,000	$2,070,000	$1,980,000	$1,800,000
Cash	$ 30,000	$ 40,000	$ 48,000	$ 65,000	$ 50,000
Accounts receivable, net . . .	570,000	510,000	405,000	345,000	300,000
Inventory	750,000	720,000	690,000	660,000	600,000
Total	$1,350,000	$1,270,000	$1,143,000	$1,070,000	$ 950,000
Current liabilities.	$ 640,000	$ 580,000	$ 520,000	$ 440,000	$ 400,000

Required   1.   Express the asset, liability, and sales data in trend percentages. (Show percentages for each item.) Use 19x1 as the base year, and carry computations to one decimal place.

2.   Comment on the results of your analysis.

E18–3   The financial statements for Castile Products, Inc., are given below:

CASTILE PRODUCTS, INC.
Balance Sheet
December 31, 19x4

Assets

Current assets:	
Cash	$ 6,500
Accounts receivable, net	35,000
Merchandise inventory	70,000
Prepaid expenses	3,500
Total current assets	115,000
Property and equipment, net	185,000
Total assets	$300,000

Liabilities and Stockholders' Equity

Liabilities:

Current liabilities	$ 50,000
Bonds payable, 10%	80,000
Total liabilities	130,000

Stockholders' equity:

Common stock, $5 par value	$ 30,000	
Retained earnings	140,000	
Total stockholders' equity		170,000
Total liabilities and equity		$300,000

CASTILE PRODUCTS, INC.
Income Statement
For the Year Ended December 31, 19x4

Sales	$420,000
Less cost of goods sold	292,500
Gross margin	127,500
Less operating expenses	89,500
Net operating income	38,000
Interest expense	8,000
Net income before taxes	30,000
Income taxes (30%)	9,000
Net income	$ 21,000

Account balances on January 1, 19x4, were: accounts receivable, $25,000; and inventory, $60,000. All sales were on account.

Compute financial ratios as follows: *Required*

1. Current ratio. (Industry average: 2.5 to 1.)
2. Acid-test ratio. (Industry average: 1.3 to 1.)
3. Debt-to-equity ratio.
4. Accounts receivable turnover in days. (Terms: 2/10, n/30.)
5. Inventory turnover in days. (Industry average: 64 days.)
6. Times interest earned.
7. Book value per share. (Market price: $42.)

E18–4 Refer to the financial statements for Castile Products, Inc., in E18–3. In addition to the data in these statements, assume that Castile Products, Inc., paid dividends of $2.10 per share during the year ended December 31, 19x4. Also assume that the company's common stock had a market price of $42 on December 31.

Compute the following: *Required*

1. Earnings per share.
2. Dividend payout ratio.
3. Dividend yield ratio.
4. Price-earnings ratio. (Industry average: 10.)

E18–5 Refer to the financial statements for Castile Products, Inc., in E18–3. Assets at the beginning of the year totaled $280,000, and the stockholders' equity totaled $161,600.

Compute the following: *Required*

1. Return on total assets.
2. Return on common stockholders' equity.
3. Was financial leverage positive or negative for the year? Explain.

E18–6 Russo Products had a current ratio of 2.5 to 1 on June 30 of the current year. On that date, the company's assets were:

Cash		$ 90,000
Accounts receivable	$300,000	
Less allowance for doubtful accounts . . .	40,000	260,000
Inventory.		490,000
Prepaid expenses		10,000
Plant and equipment, net		800,000
Total assets		$1,650,000

Required   1. What was the company's working capital on June 30?
2. What was the company's acid-test ratio on June 30?
3. The company paid an account payable of $40,000 immediately after June 30.
  a. What effect did this transaction have on working capital? Show computations.
  b. What effect did this transaction have on the current ratio? Show computations.

E18–7 Austin Company reported income as follows for the past year:

AUSTIN COMPANY
Income Statement
For the Year Ended September 30, 19x6

Sales	$600,000
Less cost of goods sold	350,000
Gross margin	250,000
Less operating expenses	190,000
Net income before taxes	60,000
Less income taxes (30%)	18,000
Net income	$ 42,000

A $30,000 loss resulting from flood-damaged merchandise is included in the operating expenses above.

Required   1. Redo the company's income statement by showing the loss net of tax.
2. Assume that the company has 20,000 shares of common stock outstanding. Compute the earnings per share as it should appear in the company's annual report to its stockholders.

E18–8 Selected financial data from the June 30, 19x8, year-end statements of Safford Company are given below:

Total assets	$3,600,000
Long-term debt (12% interest rate) . . .	500,000
Preferred stock, $100 par, 8%	900,000
Total stockholders' equity	2,400,000
Interest paid on long-term debt	60,000
Net income.	280,000

Total assets at the beginning of the year were $3,000,000; total stockholders' equity was $2,200,000. There has been no change in the preferred stock during the year. The company's tax rate is 30 percent.

Required   1. Compute the return on total assets.
2. Compute the return on common stockholders' equity.
3. Is financial leverage positive or negative? Explain.

PROBLEMS

Ratio Analysis and Common-Size Statements   Paul Sabin organized Sabin Electronics about 10 years ago in order to produce and sell several electronic devices on which he had secured patents. Although the company has been fairly profitable over the years, it is now experiencing a severe cash shortage. For this reason, it is requesting a $500,000 long-term loan from Gulfport State Bank, $100,000 of which will be used to bolster the Cash account and $400,000 of which will be used to modernize certain key items of equipment. The company's financial statements for the two most recent years follow:

P18–9

SABIN ELECTRONICS
Comparative Balance Sheet

	This Year	Last Year
Assets		
Current assets:		
Cash	$ 70,000	$ 150,000
Marketable securities	—	18,000
Accounts receivable, net	480,000	300,000
Inventory	950,000	600,000
Prepaid expenses	20,000	22,000
Total current assets	1,520,000	1,090,000
Plant and equipment, net	1,480,000	1,370,000
Total assets	$3,000,000	$2,460,000
Liabilities and Stockholders' Equity		
Liabilities:		
Current liabilities	$ 800,000	$ 430,000
Bonds payable, 12%	600,000	600,000
Total liabilities	1,400,000	1,030,000
Stockholders' equity:		
Preferred stock, $25 par, 8%	250,000	250,000
Common stock, $10 par	500,000	500,000
Retained earnings	850,000	680,000
Total stockholders' equity	1,600,000	1,430,000
Total liabilities and equity	$3,000,000	$2,460,000

SABIN ELECTRONICS
Comparative Income Statement

	This Year	Last Year
Sales	$5,000,000	$4,350,000
Less cost of goods sold	3,875,000	3,450,000
Gross margin	1,125,000	900,000
Less operating expenses	653,000	548,000
Net operating income	472,000	352,000
Less interest expense	72,000	72,000
Net income before taxes	400,000	280,000
Less income taxes (30%)	120,000	84,000
Net income	280,000	196,000
Dividends paid:		
Preferred dividends	20,000	20,000
Common dividends	90,000	75,000
Total dividends paid	110,000	95,000
Net income retained	170,000	101,000
Retained earnings, beginning of year	680,000	579,000
Retained earnings, end of year	$ 850,000	$ 680,000

During the past year, the company introduced several new product lines and raised the selling prices on a number of old product lines in order to improve its profit margin. The company also hired a new sales manager, who has expanded sales into several new territories. Sales terms are 2/10, n/30. All sales are on account. Assume that the following ratios are typical of firms in the electronics industry:

Current ratio	2.5 to 1
Acid-test ratio.	1.3 to 1
Average age of receivables	18 days
Inventory turnover in days	60 days
Debt-to-equity ratio	0.90 to 1
Times interest earned	6.0 times
Return on total assets	13%
Price-earnings ratio	12

Required   1. To assist the Gulfport State Bank in making a decision about the loan, compute the following ratios for both this year and last year.
      a.   The amount of working capital.
      b.   The current ratio.
      c.   The acid-test ratio.
      d.   The average age of receivables. (The accounts receivable at the beginning of last year totaled $250,000.)
      e.   The inventory turnover in days. (The inventory at the beginning of last year totaled $500,000.)
      f.   The debt-to-equity ratio.
      g.   The number of times interest was earned.
    2. For both this year and last year:
      a.   Present the balance sheet in common-size form.
      b.   Present the income statement in common-size format down through net income.
    3. Comment on the results of your analysis in (1) and (2) above, and make a recommendation as to whether or not the loan should be approved.

P18–10   Investor Ratios; Recommendation on Stock Purchase   Refer to the financial statements and other data in P18–9. Assume that you are an account executive for a large brokerage house, and that one of your clients has asked for a recommendation about the possible purchase of Sabin Electronics' stock. You are not acquainted with the stock, and for this reason wish to do certain analytical work before making a recommendation.

Required   1. You decide first to assess the well-being of the common stockholders. For both this year and last year, compute:
      a.   The earnings per share.
      b.   The fully diluted earnings per share. The preferred stock is convertible into common stock at the rate of two shares of common for each share of preferred. The bonds are not convertible.
      c.   The dividend yield ratio for common. The company's stock is currently selling for $40 per share; last year it sold for $36 per share.
      d.   The dividend payout ratio for common.
      e.   The price-earnings ratio. How do investors regard Sabin Electronics as compared to other firms in the industry? Explain.
      f.   The book value per share of common. Does the difference between market value and book value suggest that the stock is overpriced? Explain.
    2. You decide next to assess the rate of return which the company is generating. Compute the following for both this year and last year:
      a.   The return on total assets. (Total assets at the beginning of last year were $2,300,000.)
      b.   The return on common equity. (Stockholders' equity at the beginning of last year was $1,329,000.)
      c.   Is the company's financial leverage positive or negative? Explain.

"How Well Am I Doing?" Financial Statement Analysis • 18

859

3. Would you recommend that your client purchase shares of Sabin Electronics' stock? Explain.

Effect of Leverage on the Return on Common Equity   Several investors are in the process of organizing a new company. The investors believe that $1,000,000 will be needed to finance the new company's operations, and they are considering three methods of raising this amount of money.

P18–11

Method A: All $1,000,000 can be obtained through issue of common stock.

Method B: $500,000 can be obtained through issue of common stock and the other $500,000 can be obtained through issue of $100 par value, 8 percent preferred stock.

Method C: $500,000 can be obtained through issue of common stock, and the other $500,000 can be obtained through issue of bonds carrying an interest rate of 8 percent.

The investors organizing the new company are confident that it can earn $170,000 each year before interest and taxes. The tax rate will be 30 percent.

1. Assuming that the investors are correct in their earnings estimate, compute the net income that would go to the common stockholders under each of the three financing methods listed above.

Required

2. Using the income data computed in (1) above, compute the return on common equity under each of the three methods.

3. Why do methods B and C provide a greater return on common equity than does method A? Why does method C provide a greater return on common equity than method B?

Effect of Various Transactions on Working Capital, Current Ratio, and Acid-Test Ratio   Denna Company's working capital accounts at December 31, 19x6, are given below:

P18–12

Cash	$ 50,000
Marketable Securities	30,000
Accounts Receivable, net	200,000
Inventory	210,000
Prepaid Expenses.	10,000
Accounts Payable	150,000
Notes Due within One Year	30,000
Accrued Liabilities	20,000

During 19x7, Denna Company completed the following transactions:

x. Paid a cash dividend previously declared, $12,000.
a. Issued additional shares of capital stock for cash, $100,000.
b. Sold inventory costing $50,000 for $80,000, on account.
c. Wrote off uncollectible accounts in the amount of $10,000.
d. Declared a cash dividend, $15,000.
e. Paid accounts payable, $50,000.
f. Borrowed cash on a short-term note with the bank, $35,000.
g. Sold inventory costing $15,000 for $10,000 cash.
h. Purchased inventory on account, $60,000.
i. Paid off all short-term notes due, $30,000.
j. Purchased equipment for cash, $15,000.
k. Sold marketable securities costing $18,000 for cash, $15,000.
l. Collected cash on accounts receivable, $80,000.

1. Compute the following amounts and ratios as of December 31, 19x6:
   a. Working capital.
   b. Current ratio.
   c. Acid-test ratio.

Required

2. For 19x7, indicate the effect of each of the transactions given above on working capital, the current ratio, and the acid-test ratio. Give the effect in terms of increase, decrease, or none. Item (x) is given below as an example of the format to use:

	The Effect on		
Transaction	Working Capital	Current Ratio	Acid-Test Ratio
(x) Paid a cash dividend previously declared . . .	None	Increase	Increase

P18–13   Common-Size Statements; Trend Analysis; Selected Ratios   Comparative financial statements for the last three years are shown below for Palomar Company:

PALOMAR COMPANY
Comparative Income Statement
For the Years Ended May 31, 19x5, 19x4, and 19x3
(in thousands)

	19x5	19x4	19x3
Sales	$15,000	$12,000	$10,000
Less cost of goods sold	9,600	7,260	6,000
Gross margin	5,400	4,740	4,000
Less operating expenses	4,000	3,540	3,000
Net income before taxes	1,400	1,200	1,000
Less income taxes (30%)	420	360	300
Net income	$ 980	$ 840	$ 700

PALOMAR COMPANY
Comparative Balance Sheet
May 31, 19x5, 19x4, and 19x3
(in thousands)

	19x5	19x4	19x3
Assets			
Current assets:			
Cash	$ 80	$ 100	$ 90
Accounts receivable, net	720	500	400
Inventory	1,800	900	750
Total current assets	2,600	1,500	1,240
Plant and equipment, net	3,400	3,000	2,760
Total assets	$6,000	$4,500	$4,000
Liabilities and Stockholders' Equity			
Liabilities:			
Current liabilities	$1,250	$ 700	$ 500
Long-term debt	750	300	300
Total liabilities	2,000	1,000	800
Stockholders' equity:			
Common stock	1,000	1,000	1,000
Retained earnings	3,000	2,500	2,200
Total stockholders' equity	4,000	3,500	3,200
Total liabilities and stockholders' equity	$6,000	$4,500	$4,000

At the end of 19x4, Mr. John Pushard became president of Palomar Company. Mr. Pushard had become president after serving for many years as a district sales manager and then as vice president, sales. He knew that 19x5 (his first year as president) had been the best year in the company's history as a result of a 25 percent increase in sales and an extensive cost-cutting effort that he initiated. For this reason, he was staggered when he received the statements above and noticed the sharp drop in cash and the dramatic increase in current liabilities. He muttered to himself, "With $15,000,000 coming in from sales, how could our Cash account show a balance of only $80,000? These statements must be goofy."

Required

1. Prepare the income statement and the balance sheet in common-size form for all three years. (Round computations to one decimal place.)
2. Prepare trend percentages covering the three years for both the income statements and the balance sheets. (Round computations to one decimal place, e.g., 115.6 percent.)
3. For all three years, compute the following:
   a. The working capital.
   b. The current ratio. (Industry average: 2.5 to 1.)
   c. The acid-test ratio. (Industry average: 1.0 to 1.)
   d. The accounts receivable turnover in days. (Industry average: 13.0 days.) All sales are on account. The accounts receivable balance at the beginning of 19x3 was $360,000.
   e. The inventory turnover in days. (Industry average: 40.0 days). The inventory balance at the beginning of 19x3 was $650,000.
4. Comment on the results of your analytical work above. What strengths, weaknesses, or developing problems do you see in the company?

Comprehensive Problem on Ratio Analysis   You have just been hired as a loan officer at Slippery Rock State Bank. Your supervisor has given you a file containing a request from Lydex Company for a $3,000,000, five-year loan. Financial statement data on the company for the last two years are given below:

P18–14

LYDEX COMPANY
Comparative Balance Sheet

	This Year	Last Year
Assets		
Current assets:		
Cash	$ 960,000	$ 1,260,000
Marketable securities.	–0–	300,000
Accounts receivable, net	2,700,000	1,800,000
Inventory	3,900,000	2,400,000
Prepaid expenses	240,000	180,000
Total current assets	7,800,000	5,940,000
Plant and equipment, net	9,300,000	8,940,000
Total assets	$17,100,000	$14,880,000
Liabilities and Stockholders' Equity		
Liabilities:		
Current liabilities	$ 3,900,000	$ 2,760,000
Note payable, 10%.	3,600,000	3,000,000
Total liabilities.	7,500,000	5,760,000
Stockholders' equity:		
Preferred stock, 8%, $30 par value.	1,800,000	1,800,000
Common stock, $80 par value	6,000,000	6,000,000
Retained earnings	1,800,000	1,320,000
Total stockholders' equity	9,600,000	9,120,000
Total liabilities and stockholders' equity . . .	$17,100,000	$14,880,000

LYDEX COMPANY
Comparative Income Statement

	This Year	Last Year
Sales (all on account)	$15,750,000	$12,480,000
Less cost of goods sold	12,600,000	9,900,000
Gross margin.	3,150,000	2,580,000
Less operating expenses.	1,590,000	1,560,000
Net operating income	1,560,000	1,020,000
Less interest expense	360,000	300,000
Net income before taxes.	1,200,000	720,000
Less income taxes (30%)	360,000	216,000
Net income	840,000	504,000
Dividends paid:		
Preferred dividends	144,000	144,000
Common dividends	216,000	108,000
Total dividends paid	360,000	252,000
Net income retained	480,000	252,000
Retained earnings, beginning of year . . .	1,320,000	1,068,000
Retained earnings, end of year	$ 1,800,000	$ 1,320,000

Helen McGuire, who just a year ago was appointed president of Lydex Company, argues that although the company has had a "spotty" record in the past, it has "turned the corner," as evidenced by a 25 percent jump in sales and by a greatly improved earnings picture between last year and this year. McGuire also points out that investors generally have recognized the improving situation at Lydex, as shown by the increase in market value of the company's common stock, which is currently selling for $72 per share (up from $40 per share last year). McGuire feels that with her leadership and with the modernized equipment that the $3,000,000 loan will permit the company to buy, profits will be even stronger in the future. McGuire has a reputation in the industry for being a good manager who runs a "tight" ship.

Not wanting to botch your first assignment, you decide to generate all the information that you can about the company. You determine that the following ratios are typical of firms in Lydex Company's industry:

Current ratio	2.3 to 1
Acid-test ratio	1.2 to 1
Average age of receivables . . .	30 days
Inventory turnover.	60 days
Return on assets	9.5%
Debt-to-equity ratio	0.65 to 1
Times interest earned.	5.7
Price-earnings ratio.	10

Required   1. You decide first to assess the rate of return that the company is generating. Compute the following for both this year and last year:
   a. The return on total assets. (Total assets at the beginning of last year were $12,960,000.)
   b. The return on common equity. (Stockholders' equity at the beginning of last year totaled $9,048,000.)
   c. Is the company's financial leverage positive or negative? Explain.

2. You decide next to assess the well-being of the common stockholders. For both this year and last year, compute:
   a. The earnings per share.
   b. The fully diluted earnings per share. The preferred stock is convertible into common at the rate of one share of common for each share of preferred.
   c. The dividend yield ratio for common.

d. The dividend payout ratio for common.

e. The price-earnings ratio. How do investors regard Lydex Company as compared to other firms in the industry? Explain.

f. The book value per share of common. Does the difference between market value per share and book value per share suggest that the stock at its current price is a bargain? Explain.

3. You decide, finally, to assess creditor ratios to determine both short-term and long-term debt-paying ability. For both this year and last year, compute:

a. Working capital.

b. The current ratio.

c. The acid-test ratio.

d. The average age of receivables. (The accounts receivable at the beginning of last year totaled $1,560,000.)

e. The inventory turnover. (The inventory at the beginning of last year totaled $1,920,000.) Also compute the number of days required to turn the inventory one time (use a 365-day year).

f. The debt-to-equity ratio.

g. The number of times interest was earned.

4. Evaluate the data computed in (1) to (3) above, and using any additional data provided in the problem, make a recommendation to your supervisor as to whether the loan should be approved.

Common-Size Financial Statements   Refer to the financial statement data for Lydex Company given in P18–14.   **P18–15**

Required

For both this year and last year:

1. Present the balance sheet in common-size format.
2. Present the income statement in common-size format down through net income.
3. Comment on the results of your analysis.

Determining the Effect of Transactions on Various Financial Ratios   In the right-hand column below, certain financial ratios are listed. To the left of each ratio is a business transaction or event relating to the operating activities of Delta Company.   **P18–16**

Business Transaction or Event	Ratio
1. The company declared a cash dividend.	Current ratio
2. Sold inventory on account at cost.	Acid-test ratio
3. The company issued bonds with an interest rate of 8%. The company's return on assets is 10%.	Return on common stockholders' equity
4. The company's net income decreased by 10% between last year and this year. Long-term debt remained unchanged.	Times interest earned
5. A previously declared cash dividend was paid.	Current ratio
6. The market price of the company's common stock dropped from 24½ to 20. The dividend paid per share remained unchanged.	Dividend payout ratio
7. Obsolete inventory totaling $100,000 was written off as a loss.	Inventory turnover ratio
8. Sold inventory for cash at a profit.	Debt-to-equity ratio
9. Changed customer credit terms from 2/10, n/30 to 2/15, n/30 to comply with a change in industry practice.	Accounts receivable turnover ratio
10. Issued a common stock dividend on common stock.	Book value per share
11. The market price of the company's common stock increased from 24½ to 30.	Book value per share
12. The company paid $40,000 on accounts payable.	Working capital
13. Issued a common stock dividend to common stockholders.	Earnings per share
14. Paid accounts payable.	Debt-to-equity ratio
15. Purchased inventory on open account.	Acid-test ratio

Business Transaction or Event	Ratio
16. Wrote off an uncollectible account against the Allowance for Bad Debts.	Current ratio
17. The market price of the company's common stock increased from 24½ to 30. Earnings per share remained unchanged.	Price-earnings ratio
18. The market price of the company's common stock increased from 24½ to 30. The dividend paid per share remained unchanged.	Dividend yield ratio

Required   Indicate the effect that each business transaction or event would have on the ratio listed opposite to it. State the effect in terms of increase, decrease, or no effect on the ratio involved, and give the reason for your choice of answer. In all cases, assume that the current assets exceed the current liabilities both before and after the event or transaction. Use the following format for your answers:

Effect on Ratio	Reason for Increase, Decrease, or No Effect
1.	
Etc.	

P18–17   **Extraordinary Gains and Losses; Earnings per Share**   Rusco Products, Inc., has 20,000 shares of no-par common stock outstanding. The company's income statement for 19x7 as prepared by the company's accountant is given below:

Sales		$750,000
Less cost of goods sold.		400,000
Gross margin		350,000
Less operating expenses:		
Selling expenses	$140,000	
Administrative expenses	90,000	
Loss from sale of unused plant . . .	50,000	280,000
Income before taxes		70,000
Less income taxes (30%)		21,000
Net income		$ 49,000

The earnings per share for the company's common stock over the past three years is given below:

	19x6	19x5	19x4
Earnings per share—common . . .	$3.60	$3.00	$2.40

Required   1.   Consider the income statement as prepared by the company's accountant. Why might an investor have difficulty interpreting this statement so far as determining Rusco Products, Inc.'s ability to generate normal after-tax earnings is concerned?
2.   Recast the company's income statement in better form, showing the loss from unused plant net of tax.
3.   Assume that rather than having a $50,000 loss, the company has a $50,000 gain from sale of unused plant. Redo the income statement, showing the gain net of tax.
4.   Using the income statements that you prepared in (2) and (3) above, compute the earnings per share of common stock.
5.   Explain how your computation of earnings per share would be helpful to an investor trying to evaluate the trend of Rusco Products, Inc.'s earnings over the past few years.

P18–18   **Interpretation of Completed Ratios**   Paul Ward is interested in the stock of Pecunious Products, Inc. Before purchasing the stock, Mr. Ward would like to learn as much as possible about the company. However, all he has to go on is the current year's (19x3) annual report, which contains no comparative data other than the summary of ratios given below:

	19x3	19x2	19x1
Sales trend	128.0	115.0	100.0
Current ratio	2.5:1	2.3:1	2.2:1
Acid-test ratio	0.8:1	0.9:1	1.1:1
Accounts receivable turnover	9.4 times	10.6 times	12.5 times
Inventory turnover	6.5 times	7.2 times	8.0 times
Dividend yield	7.1%	6.5%	5.8%
Dividend payout ratio	40%	50%	60%
Return on total assets	12.5%	11.0%	9.5%
Return on common equity	14.0%	10.0%	7.8%
Dividends paid per share*	$1.50	$1.50	$1.50

* There have been no issues or retirements of common stock over the three-year period.

Mr. Ward would like answers to a number of questions about the trend of events in Pecunious Products, Inc., over the last three years. His questions are:

a. Is it becoming easier for the company to pay its bills as they come due?
b. Are customers paying their accounts at least as fast now as they were in 19x1?
c. Is the total of the accounts receivable increasing, decreasing, or remaining constant?
d. Is the level of inventory increasing, decreasing, or remaining constant?
e. Is the market price of the company's stock going up or down?
f. Is the amount of the earnings per share increasing or decreasing?
g. Is the price-earnings ratio going up or down?
h. Is the company employing financial leverage to the advantage of the common stock-holders?

Answer each of Mr. Ward's questions, using the data given above. In each case, explain how you arrived at your answer.   *Required*

Part 1 Investor Ratios (P18–20 and P18–21 delve more deeply into the data presented below. Each problem is independent.) Empire Labs, Inc., was organized several years ago to produce and market several new "miracle drugs." The company is small but growing, and you are considering the purchase of some of its common stock as an investment. The following data on the company are available for the past two years:

**P18–19
Comprehensive Problem**

EMPIRE LABS, INC.
Comparative Income Statement
For the Years Ended December 31, 19x2, and 19x1

	19x2	19x1
Sales	$20,000,000	$15,000,000
Less cost of goods sold	13,000,000	9,000,000
Gross margin	7,000,000	6,000,000
Less operating expenses	5,260,000	4,560,000
Net operating income	1,740,000	1,440,000
Less interest expense	240,000	240,000
Net income before taxes	1,500,000	1,200,000
Less income taxes (30%)	450,000	360,000
Net income	$ 1,050,000	$ 840,000

EMPIRE LABS, INC.
Comparative Retained Earnings Statement
For the Years Ended December 31, 19x2, and 19x1

	19x2	19x1
Retained earnings, January 1	$2,400,000	$1,960,000
Add net income (above)	1,050,000	840,000
Total	3,450,000	2,800,000
Deduct cash dividends paid:		
Preferred dividends	120,000	120,000
Common dividends	360,000	280,000
Total dividends paid	480,000	400,000
Retained earnings, December 31	$2,970,000	$2,400,000

EMPIRE LABS, INC.
Comparative Balance Sheet
December 31, 19x2, and 19x1

	19x2	19x1
Assets		
Current assets:		
Cash	$ 200,000	$ 400,000
Accounts receivable, net	1,500,000	800,000
Inventory	3,000,000	1,200,000
Prepaid expenses	100,000	100,000
Total current assets	4,800,000	2,500,000
Plant and equipment, net	5,170,000	5,400,000
Total assets	$9,970,000	$7,900,000
Liabilities and Stockholders' Equity		
Liabilities:		
Current liabilities	$2,500,000	$1,000,000
Bonds payable, 12%	2,000,000	2,000,000
Total liabilities	4,500,000	3,000,000
Stockholders' equity:		
Preferred stock, 8%, $10 par	1,500,000	1,500,000
Common stock, $5 par	1,000,000	1,000,000
Retained earnings	2,970,000	2,400,000
Total stockholders' equity	5,470,000	4,900,000
Total liabilities and stockholders' equity	$9,970,000	$7,900,000

After some research, you have determined that the following ratios are typical of firms in the pharmaceutical industry:

Dividend yield ratio	3%
Dividend payout ratio	40%
Price-earnings ratio	16
Return on total assets	13.5%
Return on common equity	20%

The company's common stock is currently selling for $60 per share. During 19x1, the stock sold for $45 per share.

Required   1.   In analyzing the company, you decide first to compute the earnings per share and related ratios. For both 19x1 and 19x2, compute:
a.   The earnings per share.
b.   The fully diluted earnings per share. Assume that each share of the preferred stock is convertible into two shares of common stock. The bonds are not convertible.
c.   The dividend yield ratio.

d. The dividend payout ratio.
e. The price-earnings ratio.
f. The book value per share of common stock.

2. You decide next to determine the rate of return that the company is generating. For both 19x1 and 19x2, compute:
    a. The return on total assets. (Total assets were $6,500,000 on January 1, 19x1.)
    b. The return on common stockholders' equity. (Common stockholders' equity was $2,900,000 on January 1, 19x1.)
    c. Is financial leverage positive or negative? Explain.
3. Based on your work in (1) and (2), does the company's common stock seem to be an attractive investment? Explain.

Part 2 Creditor Ratios   Refer to the data in P18–19. Although Empire Labs, Inc., has been very profitable since it was organized several years ago, the company is beginning to experience some difficulty in paying its bills as they come due. Management has approached Security National Bank requesting a two-year, $500,000 loan to bolster the cash account.

P18–20
Comprehensive Problem

Security National Bank has assigned you to evaluate the loan request. You have gathered the following data relating to firms in the pharmaceutical industry:

Current ratio . . . .   2.4 to 1
Acid-test ratio . . . .   1.2 to 1
Average age of receivables . . .   16 days
Inventory turnover in days . . .   40 days
Times interest earned. . . . . .   7 times
Debt-to-equity ratio . . . . . .   0.70 to 1

The following additional information is available on Empire Labs, Inc.:

a. All sales are on account.
b. On January 1, 19x1, the accounts receivable balance was $600,000 and the inventory balance was $1,000,000.

1. Compute the following amounts and ratios for both 19x1 and 19x2:
    a. The working capital.
    b. The current ratio.
    c. The acid-test ratio.
    d. The accounts receivable turnover in days.
    e. The inventory turnover in days.
    f. The times interest earned.
    g. The debt-to-equity ratio.
2. Comment on the results of your analysis in (1) above.
3. Would you recommend that the loan be approved? Explain.

Required

Part 3 Common-Size Statements   Refer to the data in P18–19. The president of Empire Labs, Inc., is deeply concerned. Sales increased by $5 million in 19x2, yet the company's net income increased by only a small amount. Also, the company's operating expenses went up in 19x2, even though a major effort was launched during the year to cut costs.

P18–21
Comprehensive Problem

1. For both 19x1 and 19x2, prepare the income statement and the balance sheet in common-size form. (Round computations to one decimal place.)
2. From your work in (1), explain to the president why the increase in profits was so small in 19x2. Were any benefits realized from the company's cost-cutting efforts? Explain.

Required

Interpretation of Ratios   Thorpe Company is a wholesale distributor of professional equipment and supplies. The company's sales have averaged about $900,000 annually for

P18–22

the three-year period 19x3–x5. The firm's total assets at the end of 19x5 amounted to $850,000.

Ruth Harlan, the president of Thorpe Company, has asked the controller to prepare a report summarizing the financial aspects of the company's operations for the past three years. This report will be presented to the board of directors at their next meeting.

In addition to comparative financial statements, the controller has decided to present a number of relevant financial ratios that can assist in the identification and interpretation of trends. At the request of the controller, the accounting staff has calculated the following ratios for the three-year period 19x3–x5:

	19x5	19x4	19x3
Current ratio	2.18	2.13	2.00
Acid-test ratio	0.97	1.10	1.20
Accounts receivable turnover	7.13	8.57	9.72
Percent of total debt to total assets	38%	41%	44%
Ratio of sales to fixed assets (sales divided by fixed assets)	1.99	1.88	1.75
Sales as a percent of 19x3 sales (trend analysis)	106%	103%	100%
Gross margin percentage	38.5%	38.6%	40.0%
Net income to sales	8.0%	7.8%	7.8%
Return on total assets	8.7%	8.6%	8.5%
Return on common stockholders' equity	14.1%	14.6%	15.1%
Inventory turnover	3.80	4.80	5.25
Percent of long-term debt to total assets	19%	22%	25%

In the preparation of his report, the controller has decided first to examine the financial ratios independently of any other data to determine if the ratios themselves reveal any significant trends over the three-year period.

Required   Answer the following questions. Indicate in each case which ratio(s) you used in arriving at your conclusion.

1. The current ratio is increasing while the acid-test ratio is decreasing. Using the ratios provided, identify and explain the contributing factor(s) for this apparently divergent trend.

2. In terms of the ratios provided, what conclusion(s) can be drawn regarding the company's use of financial leverage during the 19x3–x5 period?

3. Using the ratios provided, what conclusion(s) can be drawn regarding the company's net investment in plant and equipment?

(CMA, adapted)

P18–23   **Incomplete Statements; Analysis of Ratios**   Incomplete financial statements for Pepper Industries are given below:

PEPPER INDUSTRIES
Balance Sheet
March 31, 19x8

Current assets:		
Cash	$	?
Accounts receivable, net		?
Inventory		?
Total current assets		?
Plant and equipment, net		?
Total assets	$	?

Liabilities:
Current liabilities.	$ 320,000
Bonds payable, 10%	?
Total liabilities.	?

Stockholders' equity:
Common stock, $5 par value	?
Retained earnings	?
Total stockholders' equity.	?
Total liabilities and stockholders' equity . . .	$?

PEPPER INDUSTRIES
Income Statement
For the Year Ended March 31, 19x8

Sales	$4,200,000
Less cost of goods sold	?
Gross margin	?
Less operating expenses	?
Net operating income.	?
Less interest expense.	80,000
Net income before taxes	?
Less income taxes (30%)	?
Net income	$?

The following additional information is available about the company:

a. All sales during the year were on account.
b. There were no issues or retirements of common stock during the year.
c. The interest expense on the income statement relates to the bonds payable; the amount of bonds outstanding did not change during the year.
d. Selected balances at the *beginning* of the current fiscal year (April 1, 19x7) were:

Accounts receivable.	$ 270,000
Inventory	360,000
Total assets	1,800,000

e. Selected financial ratios computed from the statements above for the current year are:

Earnings per share	$2.30
Debt-to-equity ratio.	0.875 to 1
Accounts receivable turnover . . .	14.0 times
Current ratio.	2.75 to 1
Return on total assets.	18.0%
Times interest earned	6.75 times
Acid-test ratio	1.25 to 1
Inventory turnover	6.5 times

Compute the missing amounts on the company's financial statements. (Hint: What's the *Required* difference between the acid-test ratio and the current ratio?)

APPENDIXES

V

We have included 12 appendixes as supplements to the topical coverage of *Managerial Accounting*. The first 10—Appendixes A through J—are placed at the end of the chapters to which they relate. The last two—Appendix K and Appendix L—contain material on quality control and on pricing that relate to several chapters. Therefore, these appendixes are presented on the following pages so that instructors can have maximum flexibility in deciding where to cover quality control and pricing issues. In the view of the authors, the quality control material is best covered with either Chapter 5 or Chapter 10, and the pricing material is best covered with either Chapter 12 or Chapter 13. Instructors can omit either appendix, however, without harming the continuity of the course. A complete listing of the appendixes to *Managerial Accounting* follows.

Appendix	Coverage
A	Further Classification of Labor Costs (Chapter 2)
B	Production Report—FIFO Method (Chapter 4)
C	Cost Flows in an Activity-Based Costing System (Chapter 5)
D	The Least-Squares Method (Chapter 6)
E	Economic Order Quantity (EOQ) and the Reorder Point (Chapter 9)
F	General Ledger Entries to Record Variances (Chapter 10)
G	Linear Programming (Chapter 13)
H	The Concept of Present Value (Chapter 14)
I	Inflation and Capital Budgeting (Chapter 14)
J	Future Value and Present Value Tables (Chapter 14)
K	Quality Costs and Reports (on the following pages)
L	Pricing Products and Services (on the following pages)

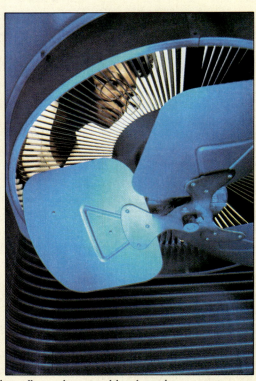

Traditionally, quality control has focused on inspections at various points in the production process. Units identified as defective by quality assurance inspectors are either scrapped or reworked. This is an expensive way to control for quality. It requires quality assurance inspectors, rework labor, and material losses from scrapped units. Companies are now finding that it is much less costly to design production processes to prevent defects from happening in the first place.

Quality Costs and Reports

I n recent years, international competition has become an increasingly important factor in many industries, with the result that some companies have seen an eroding of their market share. This eroding of market share has been most pronounced in those companies whose products are viewed by customers as being low in quality. The demand from customers for ever-higher quality in goods and services has led companies to make huge investments in automated manufacturing systems and to introduce various quality control programs. Of course, these investments and programs involve costs, and management must have methods available to measure the costs both in terms of amount and effectiveness. In this appendix, our focus is on identifying those costs associated with quality assurance and on methods of reporting such costs to management.

KEY DEFINITIONS

Objective 1
Distinguish between grade, quality of design, and quality of conformance.

The word *quality* has various meanings, but for our purposes **quality** can be defined as conformance to customer expectations in terms of features and performance of the product or service involved.[1] Thus, quality is achieved when a product or service contains all of the features that a customer would expect and when the product or service performs in such a way that the customer is satisfied. In this context, three factors underlie the overall quality of a product or service. These factors are *grade, quality of design,* and *quality of conformance*.

Grade

Grade relates to differences in degree, worth, or ranking between products or services that have the same functional use. For example, a 24-pin dot matrix printer and a laser printer have the same functional use in that both are designed to handle the output of a computer. But the laser printer is viewed as being higher in grade than the dot matrix printer because of its clearer print face and its greater speed. In like manner, a laser printer that can handle output in color is viewed as being higher in grade than one that can print only in black.

Companies provide products and services that differ in grade because of differences in needs and purchasing power between customers. As needs increase and as customers become more affluent, they purchase the higher-grade products because of the features that these products contain. The laser printer is purchased, for example, because of a need for clearer reports, a need for faster output, or a need to print in color. Since higher-grade products fill more needs and thus render greater satisfaction, they are viewed as being higher in quality than lower-grade products. Thus, grade and quality go hand in hand in the eyes of the customer. The higher the grade of a product, the greater is its expected quality.

Quality of Design

To compete in a particular product market, a company must do three things. First, it must determine customers' expectations relating to features and performance for the various grades of the product that could be offered. Second, the company must identify the grade level(s) at which it wishes to compete. And third, it must develop product specifications that are appropriate for the grade level(s) chosen.

---

[1] Wayne J. Morse, Harold P. Roth, and Kay M. Poston, *Measuring, Planning, and Controlling Quality Costs* (Montvale, N.J.: National Association of Accountants, 1987), p. 8. Much of the material in this section is based on this excellent study.

If a company wants to compete in the top-of-the-line laser printer market, for example, it must determine the features that customers would expect to find in a printer sold in that market and then proceed to develop a printer that contains these features. **Quality of design** is the degree to which a company's design specifications for a product or service meet customers' expectations *for the grade level chosen*.[2] That is, a product or service has a high quality of design if—for the grade level chosen—it contains all the features and operates in the way that customers would expect it to operate. Thus, a laser printer competing in the top-grade color market that is capable of printing in sharp, clear colors would have a high quality of design, whereas another printer competing in the same market that is capable of printing only ill-defined and blotchy colors would have a low quality of design.

The costs associated with quality of design are opportunity costs and come in the form of lost sales. Over time, customers will gravitate toward those products that consistently deliver the features they want. These features can be very subtle in nature and can include how a product looks, sounds, and feels.

  FOCUS ON CURRENT PRACTICE

Nissan Motor Company has hired anthropologists to probe into what makes people buy a car and to determine those small touches in design that can make a car more "user friendly." Honda Motor Company has designed its door locks, stereo buttons, and turn signals to require exactly the same pressure to operate, which gives its cars a more "comfortable" feel. This attention to quality of design avoids reactions such as that of one car owner who wrote to the manufacturer and complained that working his turn signal was "akin to breaking a chicken's leg."[3]

In sum, quality of design is a key consideration in measuring the overall quality of a product. If a product's design is such that its features and performance fail to meet customers' expectations for the grade level chosen, then the customers will simply turn elsewhere.

Quality of Conformance

A product can be high in grade and have a high quality of design, but it can still be low in overall quality if defects or other problems in the course of manufacture cause it to fall short of what the designers intended. **Quality of conformance** is the degree to which the actual product that is manufactured or the actual service that is rendered meets its design specifications and is free of defects or problems that might affect appearance or performance.[4] For example, a color laser printer might be well designed as shown by the clear, even output provided by design prototypes. It would have a low quality of conformance, however, if units manufactured and shipped to customers were assembled in a sloppy manner, resulting in

---

[2] Ibid., p. 10.

[3] "A New Era for Auto Quality," *Business Week*, no. 3184 (October 22, 1990), p. 85.

[4] Morse et al., "Measuring, Planning, and Controlling Quality Costs," p. 11.

EXHIBIT K–1
Relationship between Grade, Quality of Design, and Quality of Conformance

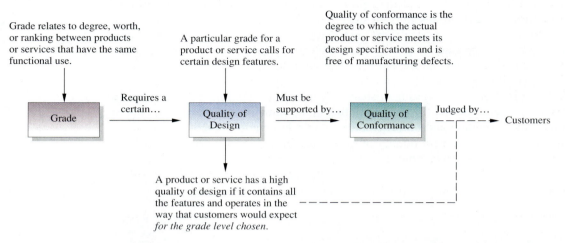

Grade relates to degree, worth, or ranking between products or services that have the same functional use.

A particular grade for a product or service calls for certain design features.

Quality of conformance is the degree to which the actual product or service meets its design specifications and is free of manufacturing defects.

Grade → Requires a certain… → Quality of Design → Must be supported by… → Quality of Conformance → Judged by… → Customers

A product or service has a high quality of design if it contains all the features and operates in the way that customers would expect *for the grade level chosen.*

frequent breakdowns or blotchy, uneven output. Thus, for a product or service to have a high quality of conformance, it must function in the way the designer intended and be free of defects, breakdowns, and related problems.

To summarize the key definitions covered in this section, the relationship between grade, quality of design, and quality of conformance is shown in graphic form in Exhibit K–1.

QUALITY OF CONFORMANCE—A CLOSER LOOK

Objective 2
Identify the four types of quality costs.

The bulk of all quality costs incurred by a company are associated with the quality of conformance. These costs can be broken down into four broad groups. Two of these groups—known as *prevention costs* and *appraisal costs*—are incurred in an effort to keep poor quality of conformance from occurring. The other two groups of costs—known as *internal failure costs* and *external failure costs*—are incurred because poor quality of conformance has occurred. Examples of the kinds of costs involved in each of these four groups are given in Exhibit K–2.

Several things should be noted about the quality costs shown in the exhibit. First, note that quality costs don't relate to just manufacturing; rather, they relate to all activities in a company from initial research and development (R&D) through customer servicing. Second, note that the number of costs associated with quality is very large; therefore, total quality cost is likely to be quite high unless management gives this area special attention. Finally, note how different the costs are in the four groupings. We will now look at each of these groupings more closely.

Prevention Costs

The most effective way to minimize quality costs while maintaining a high quality of output is to avoid having quality problems arise in the first place. This is the purpose of **prevention costs;** such costs relate to any activity that will reduce or eliminate the manufacture of defective products or the providing of substandard service in a company. Companies have learned that it is much less costly to prevent a problem from ever happening than it is to find and correct the problem after it has occurred.

Prevention Costs

Systems development
Quality engineering
Quality training
Quality circles
Statistical process control activities
Supervision of prevention activities
Quality data gathering, analysis, and reporting
Quality improvement projects
Technical support provided to suppliers
Audits of the effectiveness of the quality
  system

Appraisal Costs

Test and inspection of incoming materials
Test and inspection of in-process goods
Final product testing and inspection
Supplies used in testing and inspection
Supervision of testing and inspection activities
Depreciation of test equipment
Maintenance of test equipment
Setups for testing
Plant utilities in the inspection area
Field testing and appraisal at customer site

Internal Failure Costs

Net cost of scrap
Net cost of spoilage
Rework labor and overhead
Reinspection of reworked products
Retesting of reworked products
Downtime caused by defects and other quality
  problems
Disposal of defective products
Analysis of the cause of defects in production
Re-entering of data because of keypunch
  errors
Rewriting of computer programs because of
  software errors

External Failure Costs

Cost of field servicing, and handling
  complaints
Warranty repairs
Warranty replacements
Repairs and replacements beyond the
  warranty period
Product recalls
Liability arising from defective products
Returns and allowances arising from quality
  problems
Lost sales arising from a reputation for poor
  quality

EXHIBIT K–2
Typical Quality Costs

HEWLETT PACKARD   FOCUS ON CURRENT PRACTICE

A member of top management from Hewlett-Packard has stated that "the earlier you detect and prevent a defect, the more you can save. If you throw away a defective 2-cent resistor before you use it, you lose 2 cents. If you don't find it until it has been soldered into a computer component, it may cost $10 to repair the part. If you don't catch the defect until it is in the computer user's hands, the repair will cost hundreds of dollars. Indeed, if a $5,000 computer must be repaired in the field, the expense may exceed the manufacturing cost."[5]

Note from Exhibit K–2 that prevention costs include those activities relating to quality circles and statistical process control. **Quality circles** consist of small groups of employees that meet on a regular basis to discuss ways to improve the quality of output. Both management and workers are included in these circles. Quality circles are widely used and can be found in the utility, telecommunications, health, and finance industries as well as in manufacturing. **Statistical process control (SPC)** is a technique whereby workers use charts to monitor the quality of the parts or components that pass through their workstations. By using SPC, companies are able to involve workers directly in quality control, and to take a piece-by-piece and step-by-step approach to maintaining the overall quality of

[5] David A. Garvin, "Product Quality: Profitable at Any Cost," *The New York Times* 134 (March 3, 1985), p. F3. Copyright © 1985 by The New York Times Company. Reprinted by permission.

their products. Note also from the list of prevention costs in Exhibit K–2 that companies provide technical support to their suppliers as a method of preventing defects. In our discussion of JIT systems in Chapter 5, we learned that such support to suppliers is vital and that suppliers in turn must certify that they will deliver materials that are free of defects.

Appraisal Costs

If defective parts and products can't be prevented, then the next best thing is to catch them as early as possible. **Appraisal costs,** which are sometimes called *inspection costs,* are incurred to identify defective products *before* the products are shipped to customers. Unfortunately, performing appraisal activities doesn't keep defects from happening again in a company, and managers are beginning to realize that maintaining an army of inspectors is a costly (and ineffective) approach to quality control.

FOCUS ON CURRENT PRACTICE

Professor John K. Shank of Dartmouth College has aptly stated, "The old-style approach was to say, 'We've got great quality. We have 40 quality control inspectors in the factory.' Then somebody realized that if you need 40 inspectors, it must be a lousy factory. So now the trick is to run a factory without any quality control inspectors; each employee is his or her own quality control person."[6]

In our discussion of JIT in Chapter 5, we found that employees in modern factories are, indeed, responsible for their own quality control. This approach to appraisal, along with high quality of design, allows quality to be *manufactured* into products rather than *inspected* into products.

Internal Failure Costs

If a product fails to conform to its design specifications, then failure costs are incurred. Failure costs can be either internal or external. **Internal failure costs** result from identification of defects during the appraisal process. Such costs include scrap, rejected products, reworking of defective units, and downtime caused by quality problems. It is crucial that any failure in product conformance be discovered during production or before a product is shipped, or else defective items will be placed in the hands of customers. Of course, the more effective a company's appraisal activities, the greater the chance of catching defects internally and the greater the level of internal failure costs (as compared to external failure costs). Unfortunately, appraisal activities focus on symptoms rather than on causes and they do nothing to reduce the number of defective items. Appraisal activities do bring defects to the attention of management, however, so that steps can be taken to improve the quality of conformance.

---

[6] Robert W. Casey, "The Changing World of the CEO," *PPM World* 24, no. 2 (1990), p. 31.

An executive from a large U.S. company, after returning from a trip to Japan, asked the manager of one of the company's plants what percentage of the plant's output made it all the way through the manufacturing process without defects being noted. The plant had never kept this information, and when it was finally compiled, the executive was stunned to find that less than 10 percent of all products made it through the plant without rework of some type. The company initiated an immediate review of its quality program, and a year after implementing extensive changes, the number of products going through this plant without defects was increased to 60 percent. By means of the JIT concept of continuous improvement, the company's goal over time is to increase this figure to 100 percent.[7]

External Failure Costs

When a product that is defective in some way is delivered to a customer, then **external failure costs** result. As shown in Exhibit K–2, external failure costs include warranty repairs and replacements, product recalls, liability arising from legal action against a company, and lost sales arising from a reputation for poor quality. Such costs can be devastating to a company and, if left unchecked, can decimate profits.

In a product recall some years ago, a large manufacturer of tires and other rubber products found it necessary to recall and replace 7.5 million steel-belted radial tires because of numerous failures in use that allegedly led to many deaths and injuries. The cost of this recall was nearly $135 million after taxes, which was more than the company's net income in the year that the recall took place.[8]

In the past, some companies have taken the attitude, "Let's go ahead and ship everything to customers, and we'll take care of any problems under the warranty." This attitude generally results in high external failure costs, increasing customer ill will, and declining market share.

Distribution of Quality Costs

We stated earlier that a company's total quality cost is likely to be very high unless management gives this area special attention. Indeed, studies show that

---

[7] Robert S. Kaplan, "Measuring Manufacturing Performance," *The Accounting Review* 63, no. 4 (October 1983), p. 690.

[8] Harold P. Roth and Wayne J. Morse, "Let's Help Measure and Report Quality Costs," *Management Accounting* 55, no. 2 (August 1983), p. 51.

EXHIBIT K–3
Effect of Quality Costs
on Quality of
Conformance

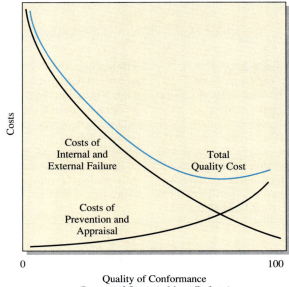

Costs

Costs of
Internal and
External Failure

Total
Quality Cost

Costs of
Prevention and
Appraisal

0   100

Quality of Conformance
(Percent of Output without Defects)

quality costs for U.S. companies range between 10 and 20 percent of total sales, whereas experts say that these costs should be more in the 2 to 4 percent range. How does a company reduce its total quality cost but yet maintain a high quality of conformance? The answer lies in a *redistribution* of the quality costs that the company incurs. Refer to the graph in Exhibit K–3.

The graph shows that when the quality of conformance is low, total quality cost is high and that most of this cost consists of costs of internal and external failure. However, as a company spends more and more on costs of prevention and appraisal, total quality cost drops rapidly; the graph shows that this drop is due to a sharp reduction in the costs of internal and external failure. Thus, a company can reduce its total quality cost by focusing its efforts on prevention and appraisal so that failures are minimized and any defects are detected before delivery of products to customers.

As a company's quality program becomes more refined and as its failure costs begin to fall, efforts toward further reduction of these costs should focus more on prevention activities and less on appraisal activities. Appraisal can only *find* defects whereas prevention can *eliminate* them. We stated earlier that quality should be manufactured into products; the way to manufacture quality into products is to take those steps needed to *prevent* defects from occurring.

QUALITY COST REPORTS

Objective 3
Describe the content of a
quality cost report.

We noted earlier that quality costs don't relate to just manufacturing; rather, they relate to all activities in a company from initial R&D through customer servicing. Therefore, as part of the quality cost system, companies must extract the quality costs from each activity and accumulate these costs on a **quality cost report.** Such a report then becomes the backbone of the quality cost system in that it will show management the type of quality costs being incurred, as well as the amount and trend of these costs. A typical quality cost report is shown in Exhibit K–4.

VENTURA COMPANY
Quality Cost Report
For Years 1 and 2

	Year 2		Year 1	
	Amount	Percent*	Amount	Percent*
Prevention costs:				
Systems development	$ 400,000	0.80	$ 270,000	0.54
Quality training.	210,000	0.42	130,000	0.26
Supervision of prevention activities.	70,000	0.14	40,000	0.08
Quality improvement projects	320,000	0.64	210,000	0.42
Total	1,000,000	2.00	650,000	1.30
Appraisal costs:				
Inspection	600,000	1.20	560,000	1.12
Reliability testing.	580,000	1.16	420,000	0.84
Supervision of testing and inspection	120,000	0.24	80,000	0.16
Depreciation of test equipment.	200,000	0.40	140,000	0.28
Total	1,500,000	3.00	1,200,000	2.40
Internal failure costs:				
Net cost of scrap	900,000	1.80	750,000	1.50
Rework labor and overhead	1,430,000	2.86	810,000	1.62
Downtime due to defects in quality	170,000	0.34	100,000	0.20
Disposal of defective products	500,000	1.00	340,000	0.68
Total	3,000,000	6.00	2,000,000	4.00
External failure costs:				
Warranty repairs	400,000	0.80	900,000	1.80
Warranty replacements	870,000	1.74	2,300,000	4.60
Allowances	130,000	0.26	630,000	1.26
Cost of field servicing	600,000	1.20	1,320,000	2.64
Total	2,000,000	4.00	5,150,000	10.30
Total quality cost	$7,500,000	15.00	$9,000,000	18.00

* As a percentage of total sales. We assume that in each year sales totaled $50,000,000.

Several things should be noted from the data in the exhibit. First, note that Ventura Company's quality costs are poorly distributed in both years, with most of the costs being traceable to either internal failure or external failure. The external failure costs are particularly high in year 1 in comparison to other costs. Second, note that the company increased its spending on prevention and appraisal activities in year 2. As a result, internal failure costs go up in that year (from $2 million in year 1 to $3 million in year 2), but external failure costs drop sharply (from $5.15 million in year 1 to only $2 million in year 2). The reason internal failure costs go up is that, through increased appraisal activity, defects are being caught and corrected before products are shipped to customers. Thus, the company is incurring more cost for scrap, rework, and so forth, but it is saving huge amounts in warranty repairs, warranty replacements, and other external failure costs.

Third, note that as a result of greater emphasis on prevention and appraisal, *total* quality cost has decreased in year 2. As continued emphasis is placed on prevention and appraisal in future years, total quality cost should continue to decrease in the same manner that we see in the exhibit. That is, future increases in prevention and appraisal costs should be more than offset by net decreases in failure costs. Thus, total quality cost should continue to fall. Finally, note that total quality cost equals 18 percent of sales in year 1 and 15 percent of sales in year 2. Through the JIT concept of continuous improvement, the company should strive to reduce this figure to the range of 2 to 4 percent of sales. Experience shows that such a reduction is possible through a concerted effort toward *prevention* of defects.

Quality Cost Reports in Graphic Form

As a supplement to the quality cost report shown in Exhibit K–4, companies frequently prepare quality cost information in graphic form. Graphic presentations include pie charts, bar graphs, trend lines, and so forth. The data for Ventura Company from Exhibit K–4 is presented in bar graph form in Exhibit K–5.

The first bar graph in Exhibit K–5 is scaled in terms of dollars of quality cost, and the second is scaled in terms of quality cost as a percentage of sales. The reader should note that in both graphs the data are "stacked" upward. That is, appraisal costs are stacked on top of prevention costs, internal failure costs are stacked on top of the sum of prevention costs plus appraisal costs, and so forth, until total quality costs are represented in the graphs. The percentage figures in the second graph show that total quality cost equals 18 percent of sales in year 1 and 15 percent of sales in year 2, the same as reported earlier in Exhibit K–4.

Data in graphic form help managers to see trends more clearly and to see the magnitude of the various costs in relation to each other. Such graphs are easily prepared using computer graphics packages.

Uses of Quality Cost Information

The information provided by a quality cost system is used by managers in several ways. First, quality cost information helps managers see the financial significance of quality. Studies have shown that managers usually are not aware of the magnitude of their quality costs because, as we have noted, these costs cut across departmental lines and are not normally tracked and accumulated by the cost

EXHIBIT K–5

Quality Cost Reports in Graphic Form

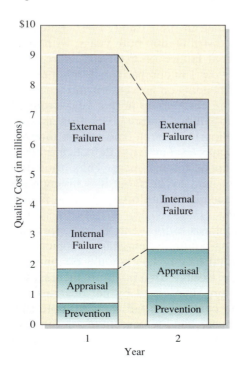
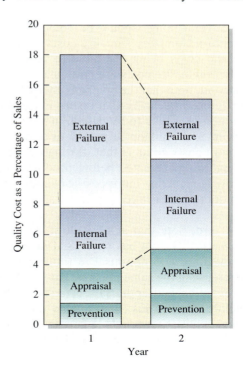

system. Thus, when first presented with a quality cost report, managers often are surprised when they see the amount of cost involved.

Second, quality cost information helps managers to identify the relative importance of the quality problems faced by the firm. For example, the quality cost report may show that scrap is a major quality problem or that the company is incurring huge warranty costs. With this information, management can see where to focus its efforts.

Third, quality cost information helps managers to see whether their quality costs are poorly distributed and, when needed, it helps them to work toward a better distribution of costs. We learned earlier that quality costs should be distributed more toward prevention and appraisal activities and less toward failures of various types.

Fourth, quality cost information provides a basis for establishing budgets for quality costs as management seeks to reduce the total cost involved. The budgets, in turn, provide a basis for performance evaluation from year to year.

Counterbalancing these uses, we must recognize three limitations of quality cost information. First, simply measuring and reporting quality costs does not solve quality problems. Problems can be solved only by action on the part of management. Second, a lag will usually exist between when quality improvement programs are put into effect and when the results are seen. Initially, total quality cost may even increase as quality control systems are designed and installed. Decreases in these costs may not begin to occur until the quality program has been in effect for a year or more. And third, some important quality costs are typically omitted from the quality cost report. These costs include the opportunity cost of lost sales arising from poor product design or customer ill will, and the cost of top management time in designing and administering the quality program. The reason these costs are omitted from cost reports is that they are difficult to quantify.

INTERNATIONAL ASPECTS OF QUALITY

A realization that quality must be manufactured (rather than inspected) into products came many years earlier in European and Japanese companies than in U.S. companies. In the 1950s, Japanese companies started developing methods of quality control that focused on prevention activities and in which quality was the responsibility of *every* employee—not just those in the quality control department. Quality circles had their origin in Japan in 1962, and this control tool still has its widest use in that country. Also, heavy responsibility has been placed on suppliers in Japan for many years to deliver ''zero defects'' material to manufacturers, whereas this idea is just beginning to gain widespread acceptance in the United States.

In the 1960s, both European and Japanese companies began to make large investments in quality training programs, and in the 1970s, they began to make investments in automated facilities. The training programs consisted of on-going, *companywide* training—not just one day quality control seminars for selected managers that have been so popular in this country. As a result of their early start and huge investment in quality control techniques, by the 1980s the European and Japanese companies were setting the world standard for quality products. This emphasis on quality has not diminished, and managers can expect to find well developed quality control programs in most European companies and in virtually any Japanese company with which they may do business.

The ISO 9000 Standards

The level of quality in products sold to companies in Europe is now monitored by a set of quality control guidelines issued in 1987 by the International Standards Organization (ISO), which is based in Geneva, Switzerland. These quality guidelines, known as the **ISO 9000 standards,** provide a way for companies to certify to their customers that:

1. They have a quality control system in use, and the system clearly defines an expected level of quality.
2. The system is fully operational and is backed up with detailed documentation of quality control procedures.
3. The intended level of quality is being achieved on a sustained, consistent basis.

The ISO 9000 standards form a series, which consists of five separate standards. The first standard—which gives the series its name—is ISO 9000. This standard provides basic definitions and acts as a road map for using the other standards. With ISO 9000 available as a map on how to proceed, a company can choose to be certified under either ISO 9001, ISO 9002, ISO 9003, or ISO 9004.

ISO 9001 provides the broadest certification and is used by companies involved in the whole range of activities from design and development through production, installation, and servicing. This would include engineering, construction, and manufacturing firms that design, produce, install, and service their products. The next standard, ISO 9002, covers companies whose products must adhere to already existing requirements and specifications. Such companies would include those in the chemical, food, and pharmaceutical industries. The third standard, ISO 9003, relates only to final inspection and testing of products that have been manufactured by someone else. Companies receiving certification under this standard would include equipment distributors who inspect and test the products they receive from a supplier before delivering the products to their own customers. The final standard, ISO 9004, provides specific guidelines for developing and implementing a quality system.

The Need for Documentation   The key to receiving certification under the ISO 9000 standards is documentation. It's one thing for a company to say that it has a quality control system in operation, but it's quite a different thing to be able to document the steps in that system. This documentation must be so detailed and precise under ISO 9000 that if all the employees in a company were suddenly replaced, the new employees could use the documentation to manufacture the product exactly as the old employees had been doing. Even companies with good quality control systems find that it takes up to two years of painstaking work to develop documentation of this type. But these companies often find that in addition to providing the data needed to pass an ISO 9000 certification audit, the documentation results in improvements to their quality systems.

An International Standard   The ISO 9000 standards have become an international measure of quality. Although these standards were developed to control the quality of goods sold in European countries, they have become so widely accepted that no company can ignore them—even if it isn't selling directly in Europe. NATO, for example, has adopted the ISO 9000 standards, and the U.S. Department of Defense will soon require adherence by all of its suppliers. Moreover, large companies such as Du Pont and IBM are likely to put pressure on their

   FOCUS ON CURRENT PRACTICE

Over the years, E.I. du Pont de Nemours & Company has been a leader in
quality control systems. Despite this emphasis on quality, for many years the engineers at one of Du Pont's plants were
unable to control a high defect rate in the
output from a molding press that makes
plastic connectors for computers. As
part of the documentation needed for
certification under the ISO 9000 standards, workers on the press were required to detail in writing how they do
their jobs. When engineers compared the
workers' notes, they found that the
workers were inconsistent in the way
they calibrated probes that measured
press temperature. As a result, the press
temperature was often set incorrectly.
When this problem was corrected, the
defect rate for the press fell from 30 percent to only 8 percent of output.[9]

own suppliers to comply with the ISO 9000 standards, since these large companies
must document the quality of the materials going into their products as part of
their own ISO 9000 certification. In short, the ISO 9000 standards are here to stay,
and any company—regardless of where it may be doing business—can ignore
them only at its own peril.[10]

KEY TERMS FOR REVIEW

Appraisal costs   Costs that are incurred to identify defective products before the products
are shipped to customers. (p. 878)

External failure costs   Costs that are incurred when a product or service that is defective
in some way is delivered to a customer. (p. 879)

Grade   Differences in degree, worth, or ranking between products or services that have
the same functional use. (p. 874)

Internal failure costs   Costs that are incurred as a result of identification of defective
products during the appraisal process. (p. 878)

ISO 9000 standards   Quality control requirements issued by the International Standards
Organization that relate to products sold in European countries. (p. 884)

Prevention costs   Costs that are incurred to prevent quality problems from arising in the
first place. (p. 876)

Quality   The conformance of a product or service to customer expectations in terms of
features and performance. (p. 874)

Quality circles   Small groups of employees that meet on a regular basis to discuss ways to
improve the quality of output. (p. 877)

Quality cost report   A report that extracts the quality costs from each activity along the
value chain and accumulates the cost in such a way that management can see the kinds
of quality costs being incurred, as well as their magnitude and trend. (p. 880)

Quality of conformance   The degree to which the actual product manufactured or the
actual service rendered meets its design specifications and is free of defects or other
problems that might affect appearance or performance. (p. 875)

Objective 4
Define or explain the key terms
listed at the end of the appendix.

[9] "Want EC Business? You Have Two Choices," *Business Week*, no. 3288 (October 19, 1992), p. 58.
[10] For further discussion, see A. Faye Borthick and Harold P. Roth, "Will Europeans Buy Your Company's
Products?" *Management Accounting* 74, no. 1 (July 1992), pp. 28–32.

Quality of design   The degree to which a company's design specifications for a product or service meets customers' expectations for the grade level chosen. (p. 875)

Statistical process control (SPC)   A technique whereby workers use charts to monitor the quality of the parts or components that pass through their workstations. (p. 877)

QUESTIONS

K–1 Distinguish between grade, quality of design, and quality of conformance.

K–2 Costs associated with the quality of conformance can be broken down into what four broad groups? How do these groups differ?

K–3 What is meant when a company is said to have a poor distribution of quality costs?

K–4 What is the most effective way to reduce total quality cost in a company?

EXERCISE

EK–1 Listed below are a number of costs that are incurred in connection with a company's quality control system.

a.	Product testing.	l.	Depreciation of test equipment.
b.	Product recalls.	m.	Returns and allowances arising from poor quality.
c.	Rework labor and overhead.		
d.	Quality circles.	n.	Disposal of defective products.
e.	Downtime caused by defects.	o.	Technical support to suppliers.
f.	Cost of field servicing.	p.	Setups for testing.
g.	Inspection of goods.	q.	Systems development.
h.	Quality engineering.	r.	Warranty replacements.
i.	Warranty repairs.	s.	Field testing at customer site.
j.	Statistical process control.	t.	Product design.
k.	Net cost of scrap.		

Required
1. Classify each of the costs above into one of the following categories: prevention cost, appraisal cost, internal failure cost, or external failure cost.
2. Which of the costs in (1) are incurred in an effort to keep poor quality of conformance from occurring? Which of the costs in (1) are incurred because poor quality of conformance has occurred?

PROBLEMS

PK–2 Quality Cost Report   In response to intensive foreign competition, the management of Florex Company has attempted over the past year to improve the quality of its products. A statistical process control system has been installed and other steps have been taken to decrease the amount of warranty and other field costs, which have been trending upward over the past several years. Costs relating to quality and quality control over the last two years are given below:

	This Year	Last Year
Inspection	$ 900,000	$ 750,000
Quality engineering	570,000	420,000
Depreciation of test equipment	240,000	210,000
Rework labor	1,500,000	1,050,000
Statistical process control	180,000	—
Cost of field servicing	900,000	1,200,000
Supplies used in testing	60,000	30,000
Systems development	750,000	480,000
Warranty repairs	1,050,000	3,600,000
Net cost of scrap	1,125,000	630,000
Product testing	1,200,000	810,000
Product recalls	750,000	2,100,000
Disposal of defective products	975,000	720,000

Sales have been flat over the past few years, at $75,000,000 per year. A great deal of money has been spent in the effort to upgrade quality, and management is anxious to see whether or not the effort has been effective.

Required

1. Prepare a quality cost report that contains data for both this year and last year. Prepare the report in the format illustrated in Exhibit K–4. Carry percentage computations to two decimal places.
2. Prepare a bar graph showing the distribution of the various quality costs by category.
3. Prepare a written evaluation to accompany the reports you have prepared in (1) and (2). This evaluation should discuss the distribution of quality costs in the company, changes in this distribution that you see taking place, the reasons for changes in costs in the various categories, and any other information that would be of value to management.

Quality Cost Report   "Maybe the emphasis we've placed on upgrading our quality control system will pay off in the long run, but it doesn't seem to be helping us much right now," said Renee Penretti, president of Halogen Products. "I thought improved quality would give a real boost to sales, but sales have remained flat at $50,000,000 for the last two years."

PK–3

Halogen Products has seen its market share decline in recent years due to increased foreign competition. An intensive effort to strengthen the quality control system was initiated a year ago (on January 1, 19x2) in the hope that better quality would strengthen the company's competitive position and also reduce warranty and servicing costs. Costs relating to quality and quality control over the last two years are given below:

	For the Year	
	19x2	**19x1**
Product testing	$ 800,000	$ 490,000
Rework labor	1,000,000	700,000
Systems development	530,000	320,000
Warranty repairs	700,000	2,100,000
Net cost of scrap	620,000	430,000
Supplies used in testing	30,000	20,000
Field servicing	600,000	900,000
Quality engineering	400,000	280,000
Warranty replacements	90,000	300,000
Inspection	600,000	380,000
Product recalls	410,000	1,700,000
Statistical process control	370,000	—
Disposal of defective products	380,000	270,000
Depreciation of testing equipment	170,000	110,000

Required

1. Prepare a quality cost report that contains data for both 19x1 and 19x2. Prepare the report in the format illustrated in Exhibit K–4. Carry percentage computations to two decimal places.
2. Prepare a bar graph showing the distribution of the various quality costs by category.
3. Prepare a written evaluation to accompany the reports you have prepared in (1) and (2). This evaluation should discuss the distribution of quality costs in the company, changes in this distribution that you detect have taken place over the last year, and any other information you believe would be useful to management.

Japanese automobile companies use target costing to control the costs of new models. The projected characteristics of the new model determine how much it can be sold for—the projected selling price. The desired profit is subtracted from this projected selling price to arrive at the target cost for the new model. The target cost for the entire car is then decomposed into target costs for each element of the car—down to a target cost for each individual part. Relentless pressure is maintained to ensure that the target costs will be met within three months of a new model's market launch.

Pricing Products and Services

1 Compute the target selling price of a product by use of cost-plus pricing under either the absorption or the contribution approach.

2 Derive the markup percentage needed to achieve a target ROI for a product under either the absorption or the contribution approach.

3 Explain how target costing is used in developing new products.

4 Compute and use the billing rates used in time and material pricing in service organizations.

5 Define or explain the key terms listed at the end of the appendix.

Some businesses have no pricing problems at all. They make a product that is in competition with other, identical products for which a market price already exists. Customers will not pay more than this price, and there is no reason for any firm to charge less. Under these circumstances, no price calculations are necessary. Every firm charges the prevailing market price. Markets for basic raw materials such as farm products and minerals follow this pattern.

In this appendix, we are concerned with the more common situation in which the firm is faced with the problem of setting its own prices. The pricing decision in such situations can be critical. Since the prices charged for a firm's products largely determine the quantities customers are willing to purchase, the setting of prices dictates the inflows of revenues into the firm. If these revenues consistently fail to cover all the costs of the firm, then in the long run the firm cannot survive. This is true regardless of how carefully costs may be controlled or how innovative managers and employees are in carrying out their responsibilities.

COST-PLUS PRICING

Objective 1
Compute the target selling price of a product by use of cost-plus pricing under either the absorption or the contribution approach.

At the most basic level, the price of a product or service should cover all of the costs that are *traceable* to the product or service. When we say traceable, we mean the traceable fixed costs as well as the traceable variable costs. If revenues are not sufficient to cover these costs, then the firm would be better off without the product or service.[1] In addition to the traceable costs, all products and services must assist in covering the common costs of the organization. These common costs include such items as general factory, advertising, and top management salaries.

In practice, the most common approach to the pricing of products is to employ some type of cost-plus pricing formula. Typically, **cost-plus pricing** involves the determination of a cost base and then adding to this base a predetermined **markup** to arrive at a target selling price.

In Chapters 3 and 8, we found that products can be costed in at least two different ways—by the absorption approach or by the contribution approach (with variable costing). The most common method followed in cost-plus pricing is to add a percentage markup to product cost computed using the absorption method, but we consider both costing methods below.[2]

The Absorption Approach

Under the absorption approach to cost-plus pricing, the cost base is defined as the cost to manufacture one unit. Selling, general, and administrative (SG&A) expenses are not included in this cost base, but rather are provided for through the markup. Thus, the markup must be high enough to cover SG&A expenses as well as to provide the company with a "satisfactory" profit margin.

To illustrate, let us assume that Ritter Company is in the process of setting a selling price on a product that has just undergone some modifications in design.

---

[1] There are exceptions. These exceptions most often occur when there are interdependencies among products—sales of one product affect sales of another or making one product affects the costs of making another.

[2] One study found that 83 percent of the 504 companies surveyed used some form of full cost (either absorption cost or absorption cost plus selling, general, and administrative expenses) as a basis for pricing. The remaining 17 percent used only variable costs as a basis for pricing decisions. See V. Govindarajan and Robert N. Anthony, "How Firms Use Cost Data in Pricing Decisions," *Management Accounting* 65, no. 1 (July 1983), pp. 30–36.

The accounting department has provided cost estimates for the redesigned product as shown below.

	Per Unit	Total
Direct materials.	$6	
Direct labor.	4	
Variable manufacturing overhead	3	
Fixed manufacturing overhead	—	$70,000
Variable selling, general, and administrative expenses	2	
Fixed selling, general, and administrative expenses	—	60,000

The first step in the absorption costing approach to cost-plus pricing is to compute the cost to manufacture one unit. For Ritter Company, this amounts to $20 per unit at a volume of 10,000 units, as computed in Exhibit L–1.

Let us assume that to obtain its target price, Ritter Company has a general policy of marking up the cost to manufacture by 50 percent. A price quotation sheet for the company prepared using the absorption approach is presented in Exhibit L–2. Note that even though this pricing approach is termed cost-plus, SG&A costs are not included in the cost base. Instead, the markup is made big enough to hopefully cover the SG&A expenses. Later in this chapter we will see how some companies compute these markup percentages.

If Ritter Company produces and sells 10,000 units of the product at a price of $30 per unit, net income will be $20,000 as illustrated in Exhibit L–3.

	Per Unit	Total
Direct materials	$ 6.00	$ 60,000
Direct labor	4.00	40,000
Variable manufacturing overhead	3.00	30,000
Fixed manufacturing overhead	7.00*	70,000
Total manufacturing cost	$20.00	$200,000

* $70,000 ÷ 10,000 units = $7.

EXHIBIT L–1

Ritter Company: Cost to Manufacture 10,000 Units

Direct materials	$ 6
Direct labor	4
Variable manufacturing overhead.	3
Fixed manufacturing overhead (based on 10,000 units)	7
Cost to manufacture	20
Markup to cover selling, general, and administrative expenses and desired profit—50% of cost to manufacture	10
Target selling price	$30

EXHIBIT L–2

Price Quotation Sheet—Absorption Basis (10,000 Units)

RITTER COMPANY

Income Statement
Absorption Basis

Sales (10,000 units at $30)	$300,000
Cost of goods sold (10,000 units at $20)	200,000
Gross margin	100,000
Selling, general, and administrative expenses (10,000 units at $2 variable plus $60,000 fixed)	80,000
Net income	$ 20,000

EXHIBIT L–3

The Contribution Approach

The contribution approach to cost-plus pricing differs from the absorption approach in that it emphasizes costs by behavior rather than by function. Thus, under the contribution approach, the cost base consists of all of the variable costs associated with a product including variable SG&A expenses. Since fixed costs are not included in the base, the markup must be adequate to cover those costs.

To illustrate, refer again to the cost data for Ritter Company on page 891. We will assume, as before, that direct labor is a variable expense. The base to use in cost-plus pricing under the contribution approach would be $15, as computed below:

Direct materials	$ 6
Direct labor	4
Variable manufacturing overhead	3
Variable selling, general, and administrative expenses	2
Total variable expenses	$15

Let us assume Ritter Company uses a markup of 100 percent of variable expenses to arrive at its target prices. A price quotation sheet prepared using this method is shown in Exhibit L–4.

Notice again that even though this pricing method is termed cost-plus pricing, some of the costs are left out of the cost base. In this case, the cost base does not include fixed costs, so it is hoped that the markup is sufficient to cover those costs.

To conclude the Ritter Company example, let us again assume the company produces and sells 10,000 units at a selling price of $30 per unit. The company's income statement as it would appear under a contribution format is shown in Exhibit L–5.

The contribution approach is essentially the approach favored by economists. The rule advocated by economists—"set marginal revenue equal to marginal cost"—can be interpreted as "mark up variable cost by a factor reflecting how

EXHIBIT L–4

Price Quotation Sheet—Contribution Basis

Direct materials	$ 6
Direct labor	4
Variable manufacturing overhead	3
Variable selling, general, and administrative expenses	2
Total variable expenses	15
Markup to cover fixed expenses and desired profit— 100% of variable expenses	15
Target selling price	$30

EXHIBIT L–5

RITTER COMPANY

Income Statement
Contribution Basis

Sales (10,000 units at $30)		$300,000
Less variable expenses (10,000 units at $15)		150,000
Contribution margin		150,000
Less fixed expenses:		
Manufacturing	$70,000	
Selling, general, and administrative	60,000	130,000
Net income		$ 20,000

sensitive customers are to price changes." However, computing the *ideal* markup on variable cost using this rule would involve estimating demand schedules, which is beyond the scope of this book.

DETERMINING THE MARKUP PERCENTAGE

How did Ritter Company arrive at its markup percentage of 50 percent of per unit manufacturing cost under the absorption approach? This figure could be a widely used rule of thumb in the industry or just a tradition in the firm that seems to work. The markup percentage may also be the result of an explicit computation by a manager. As we have discussed, the markup over cost should be largely determined by market conditions. However, a popular approach is to at least start with a markup based on cost and desired profit. The reasoning goes like this. The markup must be large enough to cover SG&A expenses and to provide at least an adequate return on investment (ROI). The firm should therefore set a target ROI figure and then structure the markup so that this target figure is achieved.

Objective 2
Derive the markup percentage needed to achieve a target ROI for a product under either the absorption or the contribution approach.

Markup on an Absorption Basis

Formulas can be used to determine the appropriate markup percentage, given the ROI figure that management wishes to obtain for the organization and assumed volume. Under the absorption approach to cost-plus pricing, the formula is:

$$\text{Markup percentage on absorption cost} = \frac{\text{Desired return on assets employed} + \text{SG\&A expenses}}{\text{Volume in units} \times \text{Unit cost to manufacture}}$$

To show how the basic formula above is applied, assume Hart Company has determined that an investment of $2,000,000 is necessary to produce and market 50,000 units of a product each year. The $2,000,000 investment would cover purchase of equipment and provide funds needed to carry inventories and accounts receivable. The company's accounting department estimates that the following costs would be associated with the manufacture and sale of the product:

Number of units sold annually	50,000
Required investment in assets	$2,000,000
Unit cost to manufacture	30
Selling, general, and administative expenses.	700,000

If Hart Company desires a 25 percent ROI, then the required markup for the product would be:

$$\text{Markup percentage on absorption cost} = \frac{\text{Desired return on assets employed} + \text{SG\&A expenses}}{\text{Volume in units} \times \text{Unit cost to manufacture}}$$

$$= \frac{(25\% \times \$2,000,000) + \$700,000}{50,000 \text{ units} \times \$30}$$

$$= \frac{\$1,200,000}{\$1,500,000} = 80\%$$

Using this markup percentage and the absorption cost approach to setting target prices, the selling price would be set at $54 (as shown in the table below Exhibit L–6).

EXHIBIT L–6

Income Statement and
ROI Analysis—Hart
Company

HART COMPANY

Budgeted Absorption Cost Income Statement

Sales (50,000 units × $54)	$2,700,000
Less cost of goods sold (50,000 units × $30)	1,500,000
Gross margin	1,200,000
Less selling and administration expenses	700,000
Net operating income	$ 500,000

Projected ROI

$$\text{ROI} = \frac{\text{Net operating income}}{\text{Average operating assets}}$$

$$= \frac{\$500,000}{\$2,000,000}$$

$$= 25\%$$

Unit cost to manufacture	$30
Add 80% markup: 0.80 × $30	24
Target selling price	$54

Exhibit L–6 demonstrates that the $54 selling price would permit Hart Company to achieve a 25 percent ROI, *providing that 50,000 units are sold*. If it turns out that more than 50,000 units are sold, the ROI will be greater than 25 percent; if less than 50,000 units are sold, the ROI will be less than 25 percent. The target ROI will be attained only if the budgeted sales volume is attained.

Markup on a Contribution Basis

A similar approach can be taken to establishing a markup percentage if the contribution approach to cost-plus pricing is used. In that case, the formula becomes:

$$\begin{array}{c}\text{Markup percentage} \\ \text{on variable costs}\end{array} = \frac{\begin{array}{c}\text{Desired return on} \\ \text{assets employed}\end{array} + \begin{array}{c}\text{Fixed} \\ \text{costs}\end{array}}{\begin{array}{c}\text{Volume} \\ \text{in units}\end{array} \times \begin{array}{c}\text{Unit variable} \\ \text{expenses}\end{array}}$$

Like the absorption cost basis however, the target ROI will be attained only if the budgeted sales volume is attained. In reality, neither of these methods guarantees a certain level of profits or a certain return on assets. A manager should only feel secure when market conditions make it reasonably certain that the budgeted sales volume will be reached at the target selling price.

TARGET COSTING

Objective 3
Explain how target costing is used in developing new products.

Our discussion thus far has presumed that a product has already been developed, has been costed, and is ready to be marketed as soon as a price is set. In many cases, the sequence of events is just the reverse. That is, the company will already *know* what price should be charged, and the problem will be to *develop* a product that can be marketed profitably at the desired price. Even in this situation, where the normal sequence of events is reversed, cost is still a crucial factor. The company's approach will be to employ *target costing*. **Target costing** is the process of determining the maximum allowable cost for a new product and then developing a prototype that can be profitably manufactured and distributed for that maximum target cost figure. The target cost for a product is computed by starting with the product's anticipated selling price and deducting the desired profit, as follows:

$$\text{Anticipated selling price} - \text{Desired profit} = \text{Target cost}$$

The product development team is directed to design the product so that it can be made for no more than the target cost.

FOCUS ON CURRENT PRACTICE

Target costing is widely used in Japan. In the automobile industry, the target cost for a new model is decomposed into target costs for each of the elements of the car—down to a target cost for each of the individual parts. The designers draft a trial blueprint, and a check is made to see if the estimated cost of the car is within reasonable distance of the target cost. If not, design changes are made, and a new trial blueprint is drawn up. This process continues until there is sufficient confidence in the design to make a prototype car according to the trial blueprint. If there is still a gap between the target cost and estimated cost,

the design of the car will be further modified.

After repeating this process a number of times, the final blueprint is drawn up and turned over to the production department. In the first three months of production, the target costs will ordinarily not be achieved due to problems in getting a new model into production. However, after that three-month period, target costs are compared to actual costs and discrepancies between the two are investigated with the aim of eliminating the discrepancies and achieving target costs.[3]

Reasons for Using Target Costing

The target costing approach was developed in recognition of two important characteristics of markets and costs. The first is that many firms really have less control over price than they would like to think. The market (that is, supply and demand) really determines prices, and a firm that attempts to ignore this does so at its peril. Therefore, the anticipated market price is taken as a given in target costing. The second observation is that most of the cost of a product is determined in the design stage. Once a product has been designed and has gone into production, there is not much that can be done to significantly reduce its cost. Most of the opportunities to reduce cost come from designing the product so that it is simple to make, uses inexpensive parts, and is robust and reliable. If the firm has little control over market price and little control over cost once the product has gone into production, then it follows that the major opportunities for affecting profit come in the design stage where valuable features that customers are willing to pay for can be added and where most of the costs are really determined. So that is where the effort is concentrated—in designing and developing the product. The difference between target costing and other approaches to product development is profound. Instead of designing the product and then finding out how much it costs,

---

[3] Yasuhiro Monden and Kazuki Hamada, "Target Costing and Kaizen Costing in Japanese Automobile Companies," *Journal of Management Accounting Research* 3 (Fall 1991), pp. 16–34.

the target cost is first set and then the product is designed so that the target cost is attained.

An Example of Target Costing

To provide a simple numerical example of target costing, assume the following situation: Handy Appliance Company feels that there is a market niche for a hand mixer with certain new features. Surveying the features and prices of hand mixers already on the market, the marketing department believes that a price of $30 would be about right for the new mixer. At that price, marketing estimates that 40,000 of the new mixers could be sold annually. In order to design, develop, and produce these new mixers, an investment of $2,000,000 would be required. The company desires a 15 percent ROI. Given these data, the target cost to manufacture, sell, distribute, and service one mixer is $22.50 as shown below.

Projected sales (40,000 mixers × $30)	$1,200,000
Less desired profit (15% × $2,000,000)	300,000
Target cost for 40,000 mixers	$ 900,000
Average target cost per mixer	
($900,000 ÷ 40,000 mixers)	$22.50

This $22.50 target cost would be broken down into target costs for the various functions: manufacturing, marketing, distribution, after-sales service, and so on. Each functional area would be responsible for keeping its actual costs within target.

SERVICE COMPANIES—TIME AND MATERIAL PRICING

Objective 4
Compute and use the billing rates used in time and material pricing in service organizations.

Some companies—particularly in service industries—use a variation on cost-plus pricing called **time and material pricing.** Under this method, two pricing rates are established—one based on direct labor time and the other based on the cost of direct material used. The rates include allowances for selling, general, and administrative expenses; for other direct costs; and for a desired profit. This pricing method is widely used in repair shops, in printing shops, and by many professionals such as accountants, attorneys, physicians, and consultants.

Time Component

The time component is typically expressed as a rate per hour of labor. The rate is computed by adding together three elements: (1) the direct costs of the employee, including salary and fringe benefits; (2) a pro rata allowance for selling, general, and administrative expenses of the organization; and (3) an allowance for a desired profit per hour of employee time. In some organizations (such as a repair shop), the same hourly rate will be charged regardless of which employee actually works on the job; in other organizations, the rate may vary by employee. For example, in a public accounting firm, the rate charged for a new assistant accountant's time will generally be less than the rate charged for an experienced senior accountant or for a partner.

Material Component

The material component is determined by adding a **material loading charge** to the invoice price of any materials used on the job. The material loading charge is designed to cover the costs of ordering, handling, and carrying materials in stock, plus a profit margin on the materials themselves. Typically, a material loading charge will fall somewhere between 30 percent and 50 percent of the invoice cost of the materials.

An Example of Time and Material Pricing

To provide a numerical example of time and material pricing, assume the following data:

> The Quality Auto Shop uses time and material pricing for all of its repair work. The following costs have been budgeted for the coming year:

	Repairs	Parts
Mechanics' wages	$300,000	$ —
Service manager—salary	40,000	—
Parts manager—salary	—	36,000
Clerical assistant—salary	18,000	15,000
Retirement and insurance—		
16% of salaries and wages	57,280	8,160
Supplies	720	540
Utilities	36,000	20,800
Property taxes	8,400	1,900
Depreciation	91,600	37,600
Invoice cost of parts used	—	400,000
Total budgeted cost	$552,000	$520,000

EXHIBIT L–7
Time and Material Pricing

	Time Component: Repairs		Parts: Material Loading Charge	
	Total	Per Hour*	Total	Percent†
Cost of mechanics' time:				
Mechanics' wages	$300,000			
Retirement and insurance (16% of wages)	48,000			
Total costs	348,000	$14.50		
For repairs—other cost of repair service. For parts—costs of ordering, handling, and storing parts:				
Repairs service manager—salary	40,000		$ —	
Parts manager—salary	—		36,000	
Clerical assistant—salary	18,000		15,000	
Retirement and insurance (16% of salaries)	9,280		8,160	
Supplies	720		540	
Utilities	36,000		20,800	
Property taxes	8,400		1,900	
Depreciation	91,600		37,600	
Total costs	204,000	8.50	120,000	30
Desired profit:				
24,000 hours × $7	168,000	7.00	—	
15% × $400,000	—		60,000	15
Total amount to be billed	$720,000	$30.00	$180,000	45

* Based on 24,000 hours.

† Based on $400,000 invoice cost of parts. The charge for ordering, handling, and storing parts, for example, is computed as follows: $120,000 cost ÷ $400,000 invoice cost = 30%.

The company expects to bill customers for 24,000 hours of repair time. A profit of $7 per hour of repair time is considered to be a reasonable return to the company. For parts, the company wants to earn a profit equal to 15 percent of the invoice cost of parts used.

Computations showing the billing rate and the material loading charge to be used over the next year are presented in Exhibit L–7. Note that the billing rate, or time component, is $30 per hour of repair time and the material loading charge is 45 percent of the invoice cost of parts used. Using these rates, a repair job that requires 4.5 hours of mechanic's time and $200 in parts would be billed as follows:

Labor time: 4.5 hours × $30		$135
Parts used:		
Invoice cost	$200	
Material loading charge: 45% × $200	90	290
Total price of the job		$425

Rather than using labor-hours as a basis for computing the time rate, a machine shop, a printing shop, or a similar organization might use machine-hours. Some organizations also charge different machine-hour rates depending on the type of machine used.

KEY TERMS FOR REVIEW

Objective 5
Define or explain the key terms listed at the end of the appendix.

Cost-plus pricing A pricing method in which a predetermined markup is applied to a cost base to determine a target selling price. (p. 890)

Markup The difference between the selling price of a product or service and its cost. The markup is usually expressed as a percentage of cost. (p. 890)

Material loading charge A markup applied to the cost of materials that is designed to cover the costs of ordering, handling, and carrying materials in stock and to provide for some profit. (p. 896)

Target costing The process of determining the maximum allowable cost for a new product and then developing a prototype that can be profitably manufactured and distributed for that maximum target cost figure. (p. 894)

Time and material pricing A pricing method, often used in service firms, in which two pricing rates are established—one based on direct labor time and the other based on direct materials used. (p. 896)

QUESTIONS

L–1 What is meant by *cost-plus pricing?* What is the difference between the absorption and contribution approaches to cost-plus pricing?

L–2 In what sense is the term *cost-plus pricing* a misnomer?

L–3 Discuss the following statement: "Full cost can be viewed as a floor of protection. If a firm always sets its prices above full cost, it will never have to worry about operating at a loss."

L–4 In cost-plus pricing, what elements must be covered by the markup when the cost base consists of the cost to manufacture a product? What elements must be covered when the cost base consists of a product's variable costs?

L–5 What is *target costing?* How do target costs enter into the pricing decision?

L–6 What is time and material pricing? What type of organization would be most likely to use time and material pricing?

L–7 What is a material loading charge in time and material pricing?

EXERCISES

EL-1

Ortega Company must determine a target selling price for one of its products. Cost data relating to the product are given below:

	Per Unit	Total
Direct materials	$ 8	
Direct labor	12	
Variable overhead	3	
Fixed overhead	—	$350,000
Variable selling and administrative expense . .	2	
Fixed selling and administrative expense . . .	—	200,000

The costs above are based on an anticipated volume of 50,000 units produced and sold each period. The company uses cost-plus pricing, and it has a policy of obtaining target selling prices by adding a markup of 50 percent of cost to manufacture or by adding a markup of 80 percent of variable costs.

1. Assuming that the company uses absorption costing, compute the target selling price for one unit of product. *Required*
2. Assuming that the company uses the contribution approach to costing, compute the target selling price for one unit of product.

EL-2

Martin Company is considering the introduction of a new product. In order to determine a target selling price, the company has gathered the following information:

Number of units to be produced and sold each year	14,000
Unit cost to manufacture	$ 25
Projected annual selling, general, and administrative expenses . . .	50,000
Estimated investment required by the company	750,000
Desired ROI	12%

The company uses cost-plus pricing and the absorption costing method.

1. Compute the markup the company will have to use to achieve the desired ROI. *Required*
2. Compute the target selling price per unit.

EL-3

Martice, Ltd., is ready to introduce a new product on the market and is trying to determine what price to charge. The new product has required a $2,000,000 investment in equipment and working capital. The company wants a 15 percent ROI on all products. The following cost information is available on the new product:

	Per Unit	Annual Total
Variable production costs (direct materials, direct labor, and variable overhead)	$32	
Fixed manufacturing overhead costs	—	$400,000
Variable selling and administrative expenses	8	
Fixed selling and administrative expenses	—	200,000

The company uses cost-plus pricing and the contribution approach to costing.

1. Assume that the company expects to sell 75,000 units each year. What percentage markup on variable costs would be required to achieve the target ROI? Using this markup, what would be the selling price per unit? *Required*
2. Repeat the computations in (1) above, assuming that the company expects to sell 45,000 units each year.

EL–4 The Reliable TV Repair Shop incurs the following annual costs in its repair operations:

Repair technicians:
    Wages $120,000
    Fringe benefits   30,000
Selling, administrative, and other costs of the repairs operation per year. . .   90,000
Materials:
    Costs of ordering, handling, and storing parts. . . . .   20% of invoice cost

The shop has 10,000 hours of repair time per year it can bill to customers. The company desires a profit of $6 per hour of repair time and a profit on materials equal to 40 percent of invoice cost. The company uses time and material pricing.

Required 1. Compute the time rate and the material loading charge that would be used to bill jobs.
2. One of the company's repair technicians has just completed a repair job that required 2.5 hours of time and $80 in parts (invoice cost). Compute the amount that would be billed for the job.

EL–5 Shimada Products is anxious to enter the electronic calculator market. Management believes that in order to be competitive, the electronic calculator that the company is developing can't be priced at more than $15. Shimada requires a minimum return of 12 percent on all investments. An investment of $500,000 would be required in order to acquire the equipment needed to produce 30,000 calculators each year.

Required Compute the target cost of one calculator.

PROBLEMS

PL–6 **Pricing Potpourri** Unless otherwise indicated, each of the following parts is independent. In all cases, show computations to support your answer.

1. Jordan Company incurs the following unit costs in producing and selling 20,000 units of one of its products each year:

Production costs:
    Direct materials. $32
    Direct labor   28
    Variable manufacturing overhead   4
    Fixed manufacturing overhead   56
Selling and administrative costs:
    Variable   16
    Fixed   23

Assume that the company uses the absorption approach to cost-plus pricing and desires a markup of 40 percent. Compute the target selling price per unit.
2. Refer to the data in (1) above. Assume that the company uses the contribution approach to cost-plus pricing and desires a markup of 110 percent. Compute the target selling price per unit.
3. Refer to the data in (1) above. What is the absolute minimum price below which the Jordan Company should not price its product, even in special situations involving the use of idle capacity?
4. Baker, Inc., estimates that the following costs and activity would be associated with the manufacture and sale of a product:

Number of units sold annually   20,000
Required investment in assets. $600,000
Cost to manufacture one unit   45
Selling and administrative expenses (annual)   72,000

The company uses the absorption approach to cost-plus pricing and desires an 18 percent ROI. What is the required markup in percentage terms?

5. Stempel Company desires a 20 percent ROI. The company estimates that an investment of $1,000,000 would be needed to produce and sell 20,000 units of a product each year. Other costs associated with the product would be:

	Variable (per unit)	Fixed (total)
Production (materials, labor, and overhead).	$60	$500,000
Selling and administrative.	20	100,000

The company uses the contribution approach to cost-plus pricing. Given these data, what markup would be required for the company to achieve its target ROI?

6. You have just received a bill for $116 for materials used in doing some electrical repair work on your home. You feel that this charge is unreasonable, and at your insistence the company has given you the following breakdown:

Invoice cost of materials	$ 80
Charge for ordering, handling, and storing materials	24
Profit margin on the materials	12
Total charge for materials	$116

Compute the material loading charge (in percentage terms) being used by the company.

7. Styron Company uses time and material pricing. The time rate is $42 per hour. The material loading charge is 15 percent for ordering, handling, and storing material and 20 percent for a desired profit on materials. Given these data, what is the total charge on a job that requires 4.5 hours of labor time and $280 in materials?

8. Mercred Company, a manufacturer of consumer products, wants to introduce a new toaster. To compete effectively, the toaster should not be priced at more than $35. The company requires a 20 percent ROI on all new products. In order to produce and sell 100,000 toasters each year, the company would need to make an investment of $3,000,000. Compute the target cost per toaster.

Time and Material Pricing   City Appliance, Inc., operates an appliance service business with a fleet of trucks dispatched by radio in response to calls from customers. The company's profit margin has dropped steadily over the last two years, and management is concerned that pricing rates for time and material may be out of date. According to industry trade magazines, the company should be earning $8.50 per hour of repair service time, and a profit of 10 percent of the invoice cost of parts used. The company maintains a large parts inventory in order to give prompt repair service to customers.

PL-7

Costs associated with repair work and with the parts inventory over the past year are provided below:

	Repairs	Parts
Repair service manager—salary	$ 25,000	$ —
Parts manager—salary	—	20,000
Repair technicians—wages.	180,000	—
Office assistant—salary	9,000	3,000
Depreciation—trucks and equipment	15,400	—
Depreciation—buildings and fixtures	6,000	17,500
Retirement benefits (15% of salaries and wages)	32,100	3,450
Health insurance (5% of salaries and wages)	10,700	1,150
Utilities	2,600	12,000
Truck operating costs	36,000	—
Property taxes	900	3,400
Liability and fire insurance.	1,500	1,900
Supplies	800	600
Invoice cost of parts used	—	210,000
Total costs.	$320,000	$273,000

During the past year, customers were billed for 20,000 hours of repair time.

Required   1. Using the data above, compute the following:
   a. The rate that would be charged per hour of repair service time using time and material pricing.
   b. The material loading charge that would be used in billing jobs. The material loading charge should be expressed as a percentage of the invoice cost of parts.
   2. During the past year, the company billed repair service time at $20 per hour and added a material loading charge of 35 percent to parts. Are these rates adequate? Explain. (No computations are necessary.)
   3. Assume that the company adopts the rates that you have computed in (1) above. What would be the total price charged on a repair job that requires 1½ hours of service time and $108 in parts?

Integrative Problem **PL–8** **Standard Costs; Markup Computations; Pricing Decisions**   Wilderness Products, Inc., has designed a self-inflating sleeping pad for use by backpackers and campers. The following information is available on the new product:

   a. An investment of $1,350,000 will be necessary to carry inventories and accounts receivable and to purchase some new equipment needed in the manufacturing process. The company requires a 24 percent return on investment for new product lines.
   b. A standard cost card has been prepared for the sleeping pad, as shown below:

	Standard Quantity or Hours	Standard Price or Rate	Standard Cost
Direct materials.	4.0 yards	$ 2.70 per yard	$10.80
Direct labor	2.4 hours	8.00 per hour	19.20
Overhead (⅕ variable).	2.4 hours	12.50 per hour	30.00
Total standard cost per pad			$60.00

   c. The only variable selling or administrative expenses on the pads will be $9 per pad sales commission. Fixed selling and administrative expenses will be (per year):

Salaries	$ 82,000
Warehouse rent	50,000
Advertising and other	600,000
Total.	$732,000

   d. Since the company manufactures many products, it is felt that no more than 38,400 hours of direct labor time per year can be devoted to production of the new sleeping pads.
   e. Overhead costs are allocated to products on a basis of direct labor-hours.

Required   1. Assume that the company uses absorption costing.
   a. Compute the markup that the company needs on the pads in order to achieve a 24 percent ROI.
   b. Using the markup you have computed, prepare a price quotation sheet for a single sleeping pad.
   c. Assume that the company is able to sell all of the pads that it can produce. Prepare an income statement for the first year of activity, and compute the company's ROI for the year on the pads, using the ROI formula from Chapter 12.
   2. Assume that the company uses the contribution approach.
   a. Compute the markup that the company needs on the pads in order to achieve a 24 percent ROI.
   b. Using the markup you have computed, prepare a price quotation sheet for a single sleeping pad.
   c. Prepare an income statement for the first year of activity.

3. After marketing the sleeping pads for several years, the company is experiencing a falloff in demand due to an economic recession. A large retail outlet will make a bulk purchase of pads if its label is sewn in and if an acceptable price can be worked out. What is the absolute minimum price that would be acceptable for this special order?

Missing Data; Markup Computations: ROI; Pricing South Seas Products, Inc., has designed a new surfboard to replace its old surfboard line. Because of the unique design of the new surfboard, the company anticipates that it will be able to sell all the boards that it can produce. On this basis, the following incomplete budgeted income statement for the first year of activity is available:

PL-9 Integrative Problem

Sales (? boards at ? per board)	$?
Less cost of goods sold (? boards at ? per board)	1,600,000
Gross margin	?
Less selling and administrative expenses	1,130,000
Net income	$?

Additional information on the new surfboard is given below:

a. An investment of $1,500,000 will be necessary to carry inventories and accounts receivable and to purchase some new equipment needed in the manufacturing process. The company requires an 18 percent return on investment for all products.

b. A partially completed standard cost card for the new surfboard follows:

	Standard Quantity or Hours	Standard Price or Rate	Standard Cost
Direct materials	6 feet	$4.50 per foot	$27
Direct labor	2 hours	? per hour	?
Manufacturing overhead	?	? per hour	?
Total standard cost per surfboard			$?

c. The company will employ 20 workers in the manufacture of the new surfboards. Each will work a 40-hour week, 50 weeks a year.

d. Other information relating to production and costs follows:

Variable manufacturing overhead cost (per board)	$ 5
Variable selling cost (per board)	10
Fixed manufacturing overhead cost (total)	600,000
Fixed selling and administrative cost (total)	?
Number of boards produced and sold (per year)	?

e. Overhead costs are allocated to production on a basis of direct labor-hours.

Required

1. Complete the standard cost card for a single surfboard.
2. Assume that the company uses absorption costing.
   a. Compute the markup that the company needs on the surfboards in order to achieve an 18 percent ROI.
   b. Using the markup you have computed, prepare a price quotation sheet for a single surfboard.
   c. Assume, as stated, that the company is able to sell all of the surfboards that it can produce. Complete the income statement for the first year of activity, and then compute the company's ROI for the year, using the ROI formula from Chapter 12.
3. Assume that the company uses the contribution approach.
   a. Compute the markup that the company needs on the surfboards in order to achieve an 18 percent ROI.
   b. Using the markup you have computed, prepare a price quotation sheet for a single surfboard.
   c. Prepare an income statement for the first year of activity.

Author Index

905

Subject Index